Pages
Pension fund planning	326-27
Portfolio selection	358-64
Equitable tax burdens in Peoria, IL	407, 435-36
Oil drilling decision	498-99
Capital budgeting with uncertain demands	518-24, 524-32, 558
Bid for offshore oil tract	558
Lab robotics investment decision	559-63
Natural gas well-drilling decision	564-71
Forecasting earnings per share for new startup airline	632-34
Managing the development of a financial analysis software package	679-83
Controlling the budget for a large credit card project	683-89

Marketing

Copier service pricing	38-45
Advertising and pricing	62-64
Sales management	220-21
Salesforce allocation	237-38
Media selection under certainty	254-58
Sales territory assignment	322-23
Optimizing marketing expenditures	336-37
Media selection under uncertainty	411-20
Marketing campaign for home and garden tractors	463-67, 468-70
Conducting market research study	470-76
Test market decision	476-83
Magazine advertising rate base	499-501
Omelet pans promotion-how many pans to order	533-38, 539-42
Brand-switching model	555
Optimal promotion of a discontinued TV model	558
Using traffic flow to forecast sales in gas station expansion decision	608-17
Forecasting demand for coal	635-39
Forecasting automobile sales	650
Forecasting magazine circulation	652-54

Public Sector

	Pages
Personnel scheduling	101-102, 108-109
Cash management	126-29
Determining optimal diets	171-72
Transportation planning	239-44
Personnel assignments	232-39
Travel routing	244-46
Equipment replacement	246-48
Traffic management	248-49
Municipal bond underwriting	324-25
Pension fund planning	326-27
Tax compliance and tax revenue planning	389-96
Educational program design	408-10
Selecting which software system to implement	422-27
Equitable tax burdens in Peoria, IL	407, 435-36
Managing a large project	659-70
Probability of completing the project on time	675-77
Controlling the budget for a project	683-89

Human Resources

Personnel scheduling	101-102, 108-109
Personnel assignments	232-39
Personnel and production planning	266-68
Hiring a secretary	581-83
Number of repair persons to hire to maintain technical equipment	592-93
How many telephone operators to hire at L.L. Bean	603-604
Scheduling part-time hours at a local bank	650-51

Other

Selecting a job out of college	435
Selecting which graduate school to attend	435
Choosing which automobile to buy	435
Deciding whether to take an umbrella to work	444
Derrick failure analysis	555
Convenience store milk-ordering decision	556
Annual solicitation campaign	557
Forecasting number of guests at a Marriott hotel	654-56

DECISIONEERING

ADVANCED MODELING TOOLS

Changing the Future of Modeling

The world of quantitative analysis and decision-making has changed. The art and science of developing accurate, manageable and auditable models can determine an organization's survival. By enhancing an organization's ability to easily conduct quantitative analysis with fully integrated risk and sensitivity analysis, the structure of business activities, projects, relationships and deals can be fine-tuned for increased performance and decreased risk.

Spreadsheet users build quantitative models to help make decisions based on numerical assumptions. But they have always lacked the ability to go beyond "what-if" analysis to pinpoint causal relationships. And most organizations now work within slimmer margins and tighter budgets, and rely on technology to replace the work of staff.

Given these conditions, there exists a need to turn today's spreadsheets into more powerful model-building tools. Decisioneering, Inc. meets this need by providing advanced modeling tools to make better-informed strategic decisions and avoid the consequences of inadequate analyses.

This textbook discusses various ways in which Decisioneering, Inc.'s Crystal Ball software application can be used to increase the efficiency and accuracy of simulation, risk analysis and forecasting. Through the examples and models described in this book, you will see why over seventy of the leading *Fortune 100* companies rely on Crystal Ball to manage risk and ensure validity of their planning models.

The compact disc provided with this textbook offers readers a firsthand look at the power of Crystal Ball. The student version of Crystal Ball provides users with a working version of the software and access to many of the key features of this powerful tool. For information about an upgrade to the fully functional commercial version of Crystal Ball, call Decisioneering at 800.289.2550 or 303.534.1515.

In addition to Crystal Ball, Decisioneering offers Analytica, the world's first general purpose, object-oriented, visual modeling tool. Analytica's graphical interface and quantitative analysis revolutionizes the way your organizations analyze opportunities and make decisions. Find out more about Analytica by downloading a FREE Analytica evaluation copy at www.decisioneering.com.

► **Crystal Ball Software Included with this Book!**

CRYSTAL BALL

ANALYTICA

DECISIONEERING, INC. • (303) 534-1515 • 1515 Arapahoe, Suite 1311 • Denver, Colorado, 80202 • www.decisioneering.com

WHERE DO YOU WANT TO GO TOMORROW?

CRYSTAL BALL®

Wherever you want to go tomorrow, Crystal Ball will take you there.

Easy-to-use and fully integrated with Microsoft Excel and Lotus 1-2-3, Crystal Ball helps you understand and quantify the uncertainties and risks in your spreadsheet models. Crystal Ball automates the what-if process by applying a range of values or a probability distribution to each uncertain variable. The software generates random scenarios for these variables by recalculating the model hundreds, even thousands, of times. Crystal Ball then graphically displays the results, showing all possible outcomes. The user can determine the probability of meeting or exceeding any target, which in the past was determined with little more than a series of guesses.

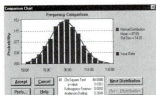

Distribution Fitting analyzes your historical data and recommends an appropriate input distribution.

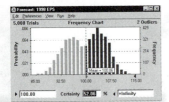

Forecast Charts show both the range and likelihood of results for your model.

Overlay Charts allow you to either compare alternatives with each other, or view forecasts against historical results.

Automate the What-If Process.

Each time you perform a what-if analysis, you get a glimpse of your risk landscape. But trying to forecast with spreadsheet scenarios is like painting a mural with a ball-point pen. Crystal Ball uses Monte Carlo simulation to quickly perform thousands of what-if analyses.

Stop Guessing.

Everyone must take risks to succeed. However, blind risks too often lead to costly errors. Crystal Ball puts the odds in your favor by helping you choose the most promising calculated risks.

End Analysis Paralysis.

With what-if analyses, there are always more scenarios you can run and more data you can consider -- but you never know when you're done. Crystal Ball lets you see through the clutter, summarizing all the possible scenarios in a single chart.

Know What Matters.

With Crystal Ball's Sensitivity Analysis you will know which factors really drive results. You can focus your talents on the right problem and complete analysis sooner and with less effort.

Look Sharp.

Smart decisions alone aren't enough. You need to communicate your decisions. Crystal Ball's graphics and reports are the professional way to show your clients, investors and management that you thought through all the angles and made informed choices.

Crystal Ball can help you answer questions like:

"What's the likelihood that this investment will yield a $1-million-dollar return?"
"How much does the inflation rate influence my economic evaluation?"
"What are the odds of being over budget on this project?"

Management Science

INTRODUCTORY

Management Science

FIFTH EDITION

Decision Modeling
with
Spreadsheets

G.D. Eppen   University of Chicago

F.J. Gould

C.P. Schmidt   University of Alabama

Jeffrey H. Moore   Stanford University

Larry R. Weatherford   University of Wyoming

Prentice Hall

Upper Saddle River, New Jersey 07458

Library of Congress Cataloging-in-Publication Data

Weatherford, Lawrence R.
   Introductory management science : decision modeling with
spreadsheets.—5th ed. / Lawrence R. Weatherford, Jeffrey H.
Moore.
     p.   cm.
   Rev. ed. of: Introductory management science / F.J. Gould. 4th ed.
c.1993
   Includes bibliographical references and Index
   ISBN 0-13-889395-0
   1. Management—Mathematical models.   2. Management science.
I. Moore, Jeffrey H. (Jeffrey Hillsman) II. Gould, F.J. (Floyd
Jerome).   Introductory management science. III. Title.
HD30.25.368 1998
658.4'033—DC21

                                          97–18316
                                           CIP

Senior Acquisitions Editor: Tom Tucker
Editorial Assistant: Melissa Back
Marketing Manager: Debbie Clare
Production Editor: Susan Rifkin
Production Coordinator: Cindy Spreder
Managing Editor: Katherine Evancie
Senior Manufacturing Supervisor: Paul Smolenski
Manufacturing Manager: Vincent Scelta
Design Director: Pat Smythe
Interior Design: Ox and Company, Inc.
Cover Design: John Romer
Interior Art/Cover Art: Marjory Dressler
Composition: Carlisle Communications, Inc.

 ©1998, 1993, 1991, 1987, 1984 by Prentice Hall, Inc.
A Simon & Schuster Company
Upper Saddle River, NJ 07458

Microsoft Excel, Solver, and Windows are registered trademarks of the
Microsoft Corporation in the U.S.A. and other countries. Screen shots and
icons reprinted with permission from Microsoft Corporation. This book is
not sponsored or endorsed by or affiliated with the Microsoft Corporation.

Crystal Ball, @Risk, and TreePlan are registered trademarks of
Decisioneering, Palisade, and Decision Support Services respectively.

Printed in the United States of America

10 9 8 7 6 5 4 3 2 1

ISBN 0-13-889395-0

Prentice-Hall International (UK) Limited, *London*
Prentice-Hall of Australia Pty. Limited, *Sydney*
Prentice-Hall Canada, Inc., *Toronto*
Prentice-Hall Hispanoamericana, S. A., *Mexico*
Prentice-Hall of India Private Limited, *New Delhi*
Prentice-Hall of Japan, Inc., *Tokyo*
Simon & Schuster Asia Pte. Ltd., *Singapore*
Editora Prentice-Hall do Brasil, Ltda., *Rio de Janeiro*

About the Authors

spreadsheets should play in management education. Currently, he is the Director of TELL, the Stanford Business School's Technology Educational Learning Laboratory, a new facility devoted to understanding the use of technology in management and in management education.

In 1996, he received Stanford's Sloan Teaching Excellence Award for his core course in Decision Support Modeling.

Dr. Moore holds a BSEE with specialty in digital circuit design from the University of Cincinnati, a joint MBA/CS degree from Texas A&M University, and a Ph.D. in Business from the University of California at Berkeley. He also holds a Professional Engineer certification (E.E., Ohio).

Jeffrey H. Moore

Jeffrey Moore joined the faculty at Stanford's Graduate School of Business in 1972 after more than 10 years work as a Communications Engineer, Computer Systems Analyst, and Management Analyst. Since joining Stanford, he has designed and taught courses in the Operations and Information Technology area at the Executive, MBA and Ph.D. levels. In addition to his administrative responsibilities, he teaches the core course in modeling and is a popular lecturer in four of Stanford's Senior Executive programs. In his research, he concentrates on decision support systems and computer use by senior executives. He has written more than 40 papers in these and other areas, and has done extensive consulting for private industry both nationally and internationally in the application of information technology and modeling for decision support.

He has worked on several courseware projects to introduce Excel for modeling and decision support to graduate level MBA's and executives. This has included work under several grants from Microsoft, IBM, and Hewlett Packard, and early work with Frontline Systems in the testing and development of Excel's Solver, particularly the linear optimization options. In 1978–79 he pioneered one of the first courses to use spreadsheet modeling in a business school, and soon thereafter, orchestrated Stanford's conversion of its Decision Science core course to spreadsheets, the first major business school to do so. Since that time, he has been involved in the development of modeling and statistical applications of spreadsheets, and has developed GLP, Stanford's Graphical LP Optimizer, and Regress, an Excel-based regression package now used at Stanford and elsewhere.

In 1995–96 he served on the INFORMS Business School Educational Task Force which surveyed more than 300 university instructors in the teaching of management science and has made presentations at its conferences on the important role

Larry R. Weatherford

Larry Weatherford is an Associate Professor in the College of Business at the University of Wyoming. He received his BA from Brigham Young University in 1982, and his MBA and Ph.D. from the Darden Graduate School of Business at the University of Virginia in 1991. He received the Outstanding Teaching Award for the College of Business in his first year as a professor. In the ensuing years he has also earned the "Outstanding Faculty Member" award by Alpha Kappa Psi, the Outstanding Junior Research Award for the College of Business, and most recently the University-wide Ellbogen Meritorious Classroom Teaching Award. He has published several scholarly articles in such journals as *Operations Research, Decision Sciences, Transportation Science, Naval Research Logistics, Cornell Hotel and Restaurant Administration Quarterly, International Journal of Technology Management, Journal of Combinatorial Optimization* and *Omega.*

On the practitioner side, he was featured in the "Questions and Answers" section of *Scorecard* (the Revenue Management Quarterly) in the second quarter of 1994. He also wrote the technical brief section of *Scorecard* for the same issue. Larry has made presentations of his research to the Yield Management study group of AGIFORS and the IATA International Revenue Management conference the past several years. He has worked on revenue management projects with several major airline and hotel corporations.

On the personal side, Larry is married to the lovely Jenny and they have 6 children (yes, they are all from the same union)! Most of his outside interests are centered in his family and church. Any other spare time is spent playing racquetball or golf or reading a fun book.

Brief Contents

Preface   xxi

Part 1   Models and Modeling   1

Chapter 1   Introduction to Modeling   2
       2   Spreadsheet Modeling   28

Part 2   Optimization   65

Chapter 3   Linear Optimization   66
       4   Linear Programming: Graphical Analysis   136
       5   LP Models: Interpreting Solver
           Sensitivity Report   173
       6   Linear Programming: Applications   225
       7   Integer Optimization   288
       8   Nonlinear Optimization   328
       9   Multi-Objective Decision Making and Heuristics   397

Part 3   Probabilistic Models   441

Chapter 10   Decision Analysis   442
      11   Monte Carlo Simulation   506
      12   Queuing   573
      13   Forecasting   605
      14   Project Management: PERT and CPM   657

Appendix   A   Basic Concepts in Probability   A-1
Appendix   B   Excel Features Useful for Modeling   B-1
Appendix   C   Solver Tips and Messages   C-1
Index   I-1

Contents

Preface   xxi

Part 1   Models and Modeling   1

CHAPTER 1   Introduction to Modeling   2

Application Capsule:
Credit and Collections Decisions at AT&T
Capital Corporation   2

1.1   **Introduction**   3
1.2   **The Modeling Process**   3
    Models in the Firm   5
    Models and Managers   6
1.3   **A Word on Philosophy**   6
    Realism   6
    Intuition   7
1.4   **Types of Models**   9
    Symbolic (Quantitative) Models   10
    Decision Models   11
1.5   **Building Models**   12
    Studying the Environment   12
    Formulation   12
    Symbolic Construction   14
1.6   **Modeling with Data**   15
1.7   **Data-Related Issues**   17
    Forms and Sources of Data   17
    Aggregation of Data   17
    Refinement of Data   18
1.8   **Deterministic and Probabilistic Models**   18
    Deterministic Models   18
    Probabilistic Models   19
1.9   **Model Building Cycles**   19
1.10   **Modeling and Decision-Making**   22
    Model Validation   22
    A Final Perspective   23
1.11   **Modeling Terminology**   23

1.12   **Summary**   23
    Key Terms   24
    Self-Review Exercises   24
    Discussion Questions   26
    References   27

CHAPTER 2   Spreadsheet Modeling   28

Application Capsule:
Modeling Coast Guard Tender Operations   28

2.1   **Introduction**   29
2.2   **Example One–Simon Pie**   29
    "What if?" Projection   36
2.3   **Example Two–XerTech Copy, Inc.**   38
2.4   **Example Three–Rosa Raisins**   45
2.5   **Example Four–Production at**
    Oak Products, Inc.   52
    Optimization Models   55
2.6   **Constraints and Constrained**
    Optimization   56
2.7   **Summary**   57
    Key Terms   57
    Self-Review Exercises   57
    Problems   59

    Case: Kayo Computer   60
    Case: The Watson Truck Rental Company   61
    Case: Personal Financial Plan 61
    Case: Benson Appliance Corporation   62
        Reference 64

Part 2   Optimization   65

CHAPTER 3   Linear Optimization   66

Application Capsule:
Fleet Assignment at Delta Air Lines   66
3.1   **Introduction to Linear Programming**   67

xiii

3.2	**Formulating LP Models**	**68**
	Constraints	68
	The Objective Function	69
	PROTRAC, Inc.	69
	PROTRAC Data	70
	Evaluating Various Decisions	72
	Observations on the PROTRAC Model	74
3.3	**Guidelines and Comments on Model Formulation**	**75**
3.4	**Sunk Versus Variable Cost**	**76**
3.5	**The PROTRAC Spreadsheet Model**	**78**
	Creating the PROTRAC Spreadsheet	78
	Optimizing the Spreadsheet	80
3.6	**The LP Model and Spreadsheet Modeling**	**80**
	Spreadsheet LP Modeling Rules	82
3.7	**Overview of Solver**	**84**
	Using Solver	85
	Solver Terminology	86
3.8	**Optimizing the PROTRAC Model with Solver**	**87**
3.9	**Recommendations for Solver LP Models**	**95**
3.10	**Crawler Tread: A Blending Example**	**97**
	Creating the LP Model	99
	The Crawler Tread LP Model	100
3.11	**Learning to Formulate LP Models**	**100**
3.12	**Example 1: Astro and Cosmo (A Product Mix Problem)**	**100**
3.13	**Example 2: Blending Gruel (A Blending Problem)**	**101**
3.14	**Example 3: Security Force Scheduling (A Scheduling Problem)**	**101**
3.15	**Example 4: Longer Boats Yacht Company—A Vignette in Constrained Break-Even Analysis**	**103**
3.16	**Further Hints for Developing LP Models**	**104**
3.17	**Summary**	**106**
3.18	**Solutions to Example Problems**	**107**
	Solution to Crawler Tread	107
	Solution to Example 1: Astro and Cosmo	107
	Solution to Example 2: Blending Gruel	108
	Solution to Example 3: Security Force Scheduling	108
	Solution to Example 4: Longer Boats Yacht Company	109
	Key Terms	111
	Self-Review Exercises	111
	Problems	114
	Case: Red Brand Canners	123
	Case: An Application of Modeling to Foreign Exchange Markets	126
	References	127

CHAPTER 4	**Linear Programming: Graphical Analysis**	**130**
	Application Capsule: *More Bang for the Buck: LP Helps the USAF Stock Its Arsenal*	130
4.1	**Introduction**	**131**
4.2	**Plotting Inequalities and Contours**	**131**
	Plotting Inequalities	131
	Contour Lines	132
4.3	**The Graphical Solution Method Applied to PROTRAC, Inc.**	**133**
	PROTRAC Model	134
	Plotting the Constraints	134
	Effect of Adding Constraints	135
	The Feasible Region	137
	Plotting the Objective Function	138
	Finding the Optimal Solution	140
4.4	**Active and Inactive Constraints**	**141**
	Graphical Interpretations of Active and Inactive Constraints	143
4.5	**Extreme Points and Optimal Solutions**	**144**
	A New Objective Function	144
	A New Optimal Corner	145
4.6	**Summary of the Graphical Solution Method for a Max Model**	**146**
4.7	**The Graphical Method Applied to a Min Model**	**146**
	The "Downhill" Direction	146
	Finding the Optimal Solution	147
4.8	**Unbounded and Infeasible Models**	**149**
	Unbounded Models	149
	Infeasible Models	150
4.9	**Graphical Sensitivity Analysis**	**151**
	Application Capsule: *The Diet Model*	152
4.10	**Changes in the Objective Function Coefficients**	**153**
4.11	**Changes in the Right-Hand Sides**	**155**
4.12	**Tightening and Loosening an Inequality Constraint**	**157**
4.13	**Redundant Constraints**	**158**
4.14	**What is an Important Constraint?**	**159**
	Redundant Constraints	159
	Active and Inactive Constraints	159
4.15	**Adding or Deleting Constraints**	**161**
4.16	**Summary**	**163**
	Key Terms	164
	Self-Review Exercises	165
	Problems	167
	Case: The Simplex Method	171
	References	172

CHAPTER 5   LP Models: Interpreting Solver Sensitivity Report   173

Application Capsule: *Product Planning at a Chinese Chemical Plant*   173

5.1   Introduction   174

5.2   Equality Constraint Form   174
Optimal Values of Slack and Surplus Variables   175
Positive Variables and Corner Solutions   177
Degeneracy and Nondegeneracy   178

5.3   Sensitivity Analysis of the PROTRAC LP Model   179
The Solution   179
RHS Sensitivity and the Shadow Price   181
Objective Function Coefficient Sensitivity and Alternative Optima   186
Reduced Cost   188

5.4   The Crawler Tread Output: A Dialogue with Management (Sensitivity Analysis in Action)   189

Application Capsule: *Against the Grain: LP Modeling Helps a Cabinet Company Save on Its Raw Materials*   190

5.5   A Synopsis of the Solution Output   198

5.6   Sensitivity Report Interpretation for Alternative Spreadsheet Models   198
Simple Upper and Lower Bounds   201
Shadow Price Interpretation   204

5.7   Summary   204
Key Terms   205
Self-Review Exercises   205
Problems   206

Case: Questions Based on the Red Brand Canners Case   215
Case: Crawler Tread and a New Angle   216
Case: Saw Mill River Feed and Grain Company   220
Case: Kiwi Computer   221
References   224

CHAPTER 6   Linear Programming: Applications   225

Application Capsule: *Ici on parle HASTUS: Montréal Streamlines Its Transportation Scheduling with LP*   225

6.1   Introduction   226

6.2   The Transportation Model   226
PROTRAC's Distribution Problem: Sending Diesel Engines from Harbors to Plants   226
The LP Formulation and Solution   228
Degeneracy in Transportation Models   230

6.3   Variations on the Transportation Model   230
Solving Max Transportation Models   231
When Supply and Demand Differ   231
Eliminating Unacceptable Routes   231
Integer-Valued Solutions   231

Application Capsule: *Play Ball! The American League Uses an LP Assignment Model to Schedule Umpiring Crews*   232

6.4   The Assignment Model   232
PROTRAC-Europe's Auditing Problem   232
Solving by Complete Enumeration   233
The LP Formulation and Solution   234
Relation to the Transportation Model   234
The Assignment Model: Other Considerations   235

6.5   Network Models   239

6.6   Capacitated Transshipment Model   239

Application Capsule: *New Merchandise Arriving Daily: Network Models Help a Discount Chain Keep Shipping Costs at Bargain-Basement Levels*   239
Network Terminology   240
LP Formulation of the Model   240
Properties of the LP   241

6.7   General Formulation of the Capacitated Transshipment Model   242
Integer Optimal Solutions   244
Efficient Solution Procedures   244

6.8   The Shortest-Route Model   244
An Application of Shortest Route: Equipment Replacement   246

Application Capsule: *Japan's Hanshin Expressway*   246

6.9   The Maximal-Flow Model   248
An Application of Maximal-Flow: The Urban Development Planning Commission   248

6.10   Notes on Implementation of Network Models   249

6.11   Financial and Production Planning   251
Financial Considerations   251
The Combined Model   252
Effect of Financial Considerations   254

6.12   The Media Selection Model   254
Promoting PROTRAC's New Product   255

6.13   Dynamic Models   258
Dynamic Inventory Models   259
A Multiperiod Inventory Model   261

6.14   Examples of Dynamic Models   266
Bumles, Inc. (Production and Inventory Control)   266

Winston-Salem Development Corporation
(Financial Planning) 268

6.15 Summary **270**
Key Terms 271
Self-Review Exercises 272
Problems 273

Case: Trans World Oil Company 281
Case: Production Planning at Bumles 283
Case: Biglow Toy Company 285
References 287

CHAPTER 7   Integer Optimization **288**

Application Capsule: *American Airlines
Uses Integer Program for Crew-Pairing
Optimization* 288
7.1   Introduction to Integer Optimization **289**
When Integer Solutions Matter 289
LP Versus ILP 290
**7.2   Types of Integer Linear Programming
Models** **290**
7.3   Graphical Interpretations of ILP Models 291
Optimizing the ILP Model: A Modification
of PROTRAC, Inc. 291
The LP Relaxation 292
Rounded Solutions 294
Enumeration 295
7.4   Applications of Binary Variables **295**
Capital Budgeting: An Expansion Decision 296
Logical Conditions 298
**7.5   An ILP Vignette: Steco's Warehouse
Location—A Fixed Charge Model** **300**
Modeling Considerations 300
The MILP Model 301

Application Capsule: *How Can I Help You?
AT&T Woos Customers by Saving Them
Money With the Aid of a Mixed
Integer Program* 302
7.6   The Branch-and-Bound ILP Algorithm **304**
An ILP Example 304
MILPs 310
Summary of Branch and Bound 310
Sensitivity 312
Heuristic Algorithms 313
**7.7   Notes on Implementation of Integer
Optimization Models** **313**
Kelly-Springfield 313
Flying Tiger Line 313
Hunt-Wesson Foods 313
**7.8   Summary of Integer Optimization
Models** **314**
Key Terms 315
Self-Review Exercises 315

Problems 318
Case: Assigning Sales Representatives 322
Case: Municipal Bond Underwriting 324
Case: Cash Flow Matching 326
References 327

CHAPTER 8   Nonlinear Optimization **328**

Application Capsule: *Asset and Liability
Management at Pacific Financial Asset
Management Company* 328
**8.1   Introduction to Nonlinear
Optimization Models** **329**
**8.2   Unconstrained Optimization in Two
or More Decision Variables** **330**
**8.3   Nonlinear Optimization with
Constraints: A Descriptive Geometric
Introduction** **331**
Graphical Analysis 331
Comparisons between LP and NLP 332
Equality-Constrained NLPs 334
8.4   Using Solver for NLP Models **335**
**8.5   Example Nonlinear Models with
Inequality Constraints** **336**
Economic Interpretation of Lagrange
Multiples and Reduced Gradients 337
Optimality in NLPs 339
Use of an Initial Guess 344
8.6   Solvability of NLP Models **346**
Nonlinear Programs That Can Be Solved:
Concave and Convex Programs 347
Nonlinear Programs That We Try to Solve 350
8.7   Introduction to Quadratic Programming **352**
8.8   Solver Solution of QP Problems **353**
**8.9   Geometric Interpretation of QP
Sensitivity Analysis** **354**
Tracing the Optimal Solution 355
The Optimal Value of the Objective
Function (OV) 356
8.10   Portfolio Selection **357**
The Portfolio Model 357
Application Capsule: *Portfolio
Structuring at Prudential Securities* **358**
Formulating the Portfolio Model 358
8.11   A Portfolio Example with Data **360**
Formulating the Model 361
Spreadsheet Solution 362
8.12   Inventory Control **364**
STECO Wholesaling: The Current Policy 365
Developing the EOQ Model 367
The EOQ Formula: Q^* 369
Sensitivity Analysis 370

8.13 Examples of Inventory Models 371
Quantity Discounts and STECO's
Overall Optimum 371
Production Lot Size: STECO's Heat-
Treatment Model 375

8.14 Notes on NLP Implementation 378
Key Terms 379
Self-Review Exercises Nonlinear Models 380
*Self-Review Exercises Quadratic
Programming* 381
Self-Review Exercises Inventory Modeling 383
Nonlinear Programming Problems 383
Quadratic Programming Problems 385
Inventory Problems 386
Case: Just-in-Time 388
Case: Internal Revenue Service
(1994–1995) 389
References 396

**CHAPTER 9   Multi-Objective Decision
Making and Heuristics** 397

Application Capsule: *Facilities Planning
at the University of Missouri* 397

9.1 Introduction 398
**9.2 Facility Scheduling (Sequencing
Computer Jobs)** 399
Sequence-Dependent Setup Time 399
Heuristic Solutions 400

**9.3 Scheduling with Limited Resources
(Workload Smoothing)** 401
A Simple Example 401
Workload Smoothing Heuristic 403

9.4 Multiple Objectives 407

Application Capsule: *The Taxman Cometh:
Peoria Fine-Tunes Its Tax System with the
Help of Goal Programming* 407
Goal Programming 408
Absolute Priorities 411
Combining Weights and Absolute Priorities 419

9.5 Analytic Hierarchy Process 421
9.6 Notes on Implementation 427
Key Terms 428
Self-Review Exercises 429
Problems 430
Case: Sleepmore Mattress Manufacturing:
Plant Consolidation 437
References 439

Part III   Probabilistic Models 441

CHAPTER 10   Decision Analysis 442

Application Capsule: *Testing Student
Athletes for Drug Use* 442

10.1 Introduction 443
10.2 Three Classes of Decision Models 444
Decisions Under Certainty 444
Decisions Under Risk 445
Decisions Under Uncertainty (Optional) 451

**10.3 The Expected Value of Perfect Information:
Newsboy Model Under Risk** 454

10.4 Utilities and Decisions Under Risk 455
The Rationale for Utility 456
Creating and Using a Utility Function 458

10.5 A Mid-Chapter Summary 462

**10.6 Decision Trees: Marketing Home and
Garden Tractors** 463
Alternate Marketing and
Production Strategies 463
Creating a Decision Tree 464
Appending the Probabilities and
Terminal Values 466
Folding Back 467

Application Capsule: *Oglethorpe Power:
Invest in a Major Transmission System?* 468

10.7 Sensitivity Analysis 468
Expected Return as a Function of the
Probability for a Strong Market 468

**10.8 Decision Trees: Incorporating New
Information** 470
A Market Research Study for Home
and Garden Tractors 470
Obtaining Revised Probabilities Based
on New Information 471
Incorporating Posterior Probabilities
in the Decision Tree 473
The Expected Value of Sample Information 476

**10.9 Sequential Decisions: To Test or
Not to Test** 476
Analyzing Sequential Decisions 477
The Impact of Utilities 479
Other Features of TreePlan 480
Sensitivity of the Optimal Decision to
Prior Probabilities 482

10.10 Management and Decision Theory 483
Assessing Subjective Probabilities 484

10.11 Notes on Implementation 485
Role of Personal Judgment 485

10.12 Summary 486
Key Terms 486
Self-Review Exercises 487
Problems 488

Case 1: Johnson's Metal 497
Case 2: To Drill or Not to Drill 498
Case 3: Shumway, Horch, and Sager (A) 499

Appendix 10.1 Conditional Probability
and Bayes' Theorem 501
References 505

CHAPTER 11 Monte Carlo Simulation 506

Application Capsule: AT&T's Call
Processing Simulator 506

11.1 Introduction 507
When Should Simulation Be Used? 508
Simulation and Random Variables 508

11.2 Generating Random Variables 510

Application Capsule: Robot Riddle:
Simulation Helps GM of Canada to
Automate Its Auto Assembly 511

Using a Random Number Generator
in a Spreadsheet 511
A Generalized Method 512
The General Method Applied to
Continuous Distributions 515
Generating Random Variables
Using Add-ins 516

11.3 Simulating with a Spreadsheet 518
A Capital Budgeting Example: Adding a
New Product to PROTRAC's Line 518
The Model with Random Demand 518
Evaluating the Proposal 520

11.4 Simulating with Spreadsheet Add-ins 524
A Capital Budgeting Example: Adding
a New Product to PROTRAC's Line 524
The Model with Random Demand 525
Evaluating the Proposal 526
Other Distributions of Demand 530

11.5 An Inventory Control Example:
Foslins Housewares 532
The Omelet Pan Promotion: How
Many Pans to Order? 533
Profit Versus Order Quantity 534
Recapitulation 538

11.6 Simulation of Foslins' Model With a
More Realistic Demand Assumption 539
The Foslins' Spreadsheet: Simulating
Demand More Realistically 539
The Effect of Order Quantity 540

11.7 Midwest Express: Airline
Overbooking Model 542

Application Capsule: Checks and Balances:
An Ohio Bank Uses Simulation to
Streamline Its Operations 545

11.8 Capacity Balancing 546
Modeling a Work Cell 546
Simulating Balanced Capacity 546
Simulating Unbalanced Capacity 549

11.9 Notes on Implementation 550

11.10 Summary 551
Key Terms 552
Self-Review Exercises 553
Problems 554

Case: CyberLab (A) 559
Case: Sprigg Lane (A) 564
References 572

CHAPTER 12 Queuing 573

Application Capsule: Shortening the
New York City Police Department's
Arrest-to-Arraignment Time 573

12.1 Introduction 574

12.2 The Basic Model 575
Assumptions of the Basic Model 575
Characteristics of the Basic Model 577

12.3 A Taxonomy of Queuing Models 579

Application Capsule: Merging Traffic:
A Queuing Simulation Helps Eliminate
a Costly Bottleneck 579

12.4 Little's Flow Equation and
Related Results 580

12.5 The M/G/1 Queue 581

12.6 Model 1: An M/M/s Queue
(Hematology Lab) 583

12.7 Economic Analysis of Queuing Systems 586

12.8 Model 2: A Finite Queue (WATS Lines) 589

12.9 Model 3: The Repairperson Model 592

12.10 Transient Versus Steady-State Results:
Order Promising 593

12.11 The Role of the Exponential Distribution 596

12.12 Queue Discipline 597

12.13 Notes on Implementation 597

12.14 Summary 598
Key Terms 598
Self-Review Exercises 599
Problems 600

Case: How Many Operators? 603
References 604

CHAPTER 13   Forecasting   605

Application Capsule: *Forecasting Improvement at L.L. Bean*   605

13.1   Introduction   606

13.2   Quantitative Forecasting   607

13.3   Casual Forecasting Models   607
Curve Fitting: An Oil Company Expansion   608
Which Curve To Fit?   617
Summary   619

13.4   Time-Series Forecasting Models   620
Extrapolating Historical Behavior   620
Curve Fitting   621
Moving Averages: Forecasting
STECO's Strut Sales   621
Exponential Smoothing: The Basic Model   626
Holt's Model (Exponential Smoothing
with Trend)   632
Seasonality   634
The Random Walk   639

**13.5   The Role of Historical Data:
Divide and Conquer   641**

13.6   Qualitative Forecasting   642
Expert Judgment   642
The Delphi Method and Consensus Panel   643
Grass Roots Forecasting and
Market Research   643

13.7   Notes on Implementation   644

Application Capsule: *Yes Virginia...:
An Economic Forecasting Model Helps
Keep an Unemployment Insurance Trust
Fund in the Black*   645
Key Terms   646
Self-Review Exercises   647
Problems   648
Case: The Bank of Laramie   650
Case: Shumway, Horch, and Sager (B)   652
Case: Marriott Room Forecasting   654
References   656

**CHAPTER 14   Project Management:
PERT and CPM   657**

Application Capsule: *When Is the
Synchronized Swimming, por favor?
Management Science Goes to the
Barcelona Olympics*   657

14.1   Introduction   658

**14.2   A Typical Project: The Global Oil
Credit Card Operation   659**
The Activity List   659
The Gantt Chart   660
The Network Diagram   661

**14.3   The Critical Path—Meeting the
Board's Deadline   664**
The Critical Path Calculation   664
Ways of Reducing Project Duration   670

14.4   Variability in Activity Times   673
Estimating the Expected Activity Time   673
Probability of Completing the Project
on Time   675
Testing the Assumptions with
Spreadsheet Simulation   676

14.5   A Mid-Chapter Summary: PERT   678

14.6   CPM and Time-Cost Trade-Offs   678
A Financial Analysis Project for
Retail Marketing   679
Crashing the Project   680
A Linear Programming Model   681

14.7   Project Cost Management: PERT/COST   683
Planning Costs for the Credit Card
Project: the PERT/COST System   683
Application Capsule: *Project
Management in the Persian Gulf War*   684
Controlling Project Costs   685

14.8   Notes on Implementation   690

14.9   Summary   691
Key Terms   692
Self-Review Exercises   693
Problems   694
References   702

Appendix A   Basic Concepts in Probability   A-1
I.   Introduction   A-1
Random Variables   A-1
Types of Probabilities   A-1

II.   Discrete Probabilities   A-2
A. The Probability Mass Function (PMF)   A-2
B. The Cumulative Distribution
Function (CDF)   A-3

III.   Continuous Probabilities   A-3
A. The Probability Density Function   A-3
B. The Cumulative Distribution Function   A-4
C. Important Examples   A-4
D. Using the Normal Table   A-5

IV.   Expected Values   A-7
A. Expected Value of a Random Variable   A-7
B. Expected Value of a Function of
a Random Variable   A-8
C. Expected Return   A-9

V.   Multivariate Distributions   A-10
A. Joint Distributions   A-10
B. Independent Random Variables   A-11
C. Expectation and Variance of Sums   A-11

**Appendix B Excel Features Useful
for Modeling**   **B-1**
  Configuring the Worksheet   B-1
  Manipulating Windows on Worksheets   B-5
  Selecting Cells   B-6
  Editing Cells   B-8
  Filling Cells   B-10
  Formatting Cells   B-12
  Arrays of Cells   B-16
  Naming Cells   B-19
  Wizards   B-21
  Other Useful Commands   B-24

Appendix C Solver Tips and Messages   **C-1**
Common Solver Modeling Problems   **C-2**
Useful Tips to Remember   **C-3**
Solver Options   **C-4**
Interpreting Solver Messages   **C-5**
  Successful Completion Messages   C-5
  Unsuccessful Completion Messages   C-7
Index   **I-1**

Preface — To the Student of Management

Congratulations! By learning Microsoft Excel you have joined the 35 million users who have made spreadsheets the *lingua franca* of management, a revolution in management that is barely a decade old. This book is not about Excel; it is about how you can use Excel for the analysis of management situations. Our approach will consist of developing and then analyzing an Excel model of the situation. From this analysis, recommended decisions to improve the situation will be considered. A wide range of models will be developed along with the appropriate concepts to allow you to generalize these examples to the variety of situations that you will encounter in your career as a manager.

The building of explicit models for analysis and managerial decision making has traditionally been called *management science.*

Webster's New World Dictionary defines *oxymoron* as "a figure of speech in which opposite or contradictory ideas or terms are combined." Common examples include sweet sorrow, thunderous silence, jumbo shrimp, sport sedan, bureaucratic efficiency, proprietary standard . . . you can probably think of many more. And management science?

The same dictionary says that *management* is "the act, art, or manner of managing, or handling, controlling, directing, and so on." If management is an art, is management science then an oxymoron—a contradiction in terms?

Not to us!

Science is the process of using observation and testing to establish principles and then using these principles to answer questions. Much of business is based on the same approach. Actuaries use statistical models to set insurance rates. Organizations use discounted cash flow models to make decisions on capital expenditures. Sales executives use models based on demand elasticity to determine prices, and pension fund managers use investment models to control their investment portfolios.

This book is devoted to models that may appear in many different management situations. Indeed, many of the models we will study are *generic* models. Just as the model for discounting cash flows can be used for problems with different time periods, different interest rates, and different cash flows, so can the models studied in this text be used in widely different situations.

We believe that you will find this book interesting (to say nothing of useful) to the extent that you (1) focus upon *real-world situations* and the role of spreadsheet models in addressing such situations, and (2) engage in the hands on building and analysis of these models. For our part, we have tried to keep the focus on *the relationship between management and model.* Much of the responsibility for maintaining this focus, however, rests with you. As you work your way through this text, you will find that it is full of specific models. It is easy to become so immersed in the technical details of the models and their Excel representation that you lose track of the general skills that you must develop to be either a good manager or a good modeler. Here are four ideas that are fundamental to effective decision making. It will be useful to keep them in mind and to see how the specific models you will work with contribute to your understanding of them.

Framing. To model a situation, you first have to "frame" it. That is, you must develop an organized way of thinking about the situation. Remember, most management problems come to us in the form of symptoms, not as clear problem statements. Your sales representative in Spokane tells you that your chief competitor is beating you by offering direct sales transaction processing over the Internet. In the everyday sense of the word, that's a management problem. In our language, that's a symptom. A problem involves possible decisions and a method for measuring their effectiveness. The art of moving from a symptom to a crisp problem statement is called framing. It is an essential skill of an effective manager.

Constrained optimization and *decisions under risk* are two important and useful frames we will cover that apply to a wide variety of management situations. Unfortunately, it does not seem possible merely to describe the frames and assume that you can then use them correctly. You have to understand how the models are created and the relationships between decisions and results before you can advance to using the frames in an intuitive way. You have to learn about the models and how they are used in various situations before you can make the ideas your own. This requires taking the time to critically review the works of others and practice on your own. Thus the book is full of examples and their spreadsheet representation, and cases and problems for you to sharpen your own spreadsheet modeling skills.

Optimality and Sensitivity. In this text you will encounter many business models, and you will see that analysis of these models produces "optimal" decisions. That sounds great—what could be better than an "optimal" decision? But language can be deceptive if you do not have a thorough understanding of the concepts behind it. In this context, an *optimal decision* is one that gives the best answer to the abstract problem formulated in the model—for example, an answer that maximizes profits. But is it the best answer to the real-world situation that prompted you to make the model in the first place? This is what you must decide—preferably, *before* implementing the recommendations of the model. Whether or not to implement a particular recommendation is always a judgment call, but the quality of this judgment will depend heavily on how well you understand the relationship between the model and the real situation it is designed to mirror.

It is also important to assess the *sensitivity* of the answer—that is, how much the answer given by a model depends on the particular numerical values used for the model's inputs. Managers are usually most comfortable with decisions that hold for a wide range of input values, so that a good decision cannot suddenly be transformed into a bad one by a small change in one model input. Sensitivity analysis is thus an important topic throughout this text.

Cost Concepts. This text deals with individual business decisions, such as how many items to order or where to build a new factory. One of the basic building blocks for the models you will construct is costs. You will have the opportunity to work with the concepts of fixed, marginal, and opportunity costs. Determining the proper cost relationships in a model is crucial to arriving at good decisions. It is a skill that will stand you in good stead in your career.

Healthy Skepticism. It is important to be skeptical. Learn to beware of experts, of solutions provided by computer models—yours and especially another's—and certainly of your own intuition. Our most valuable associates are those who say, "You can't be right! If you were right, then we would know that the following condition must be true, and it obviously isn't and thus you are wrong." Working directly with models—hands on—enhances your ability to analyze and dissect the route from assumptions to conclusions. The end-chapter cases are specifically designed to illustrate this concept. Asking the right question is the first step in reaching a good decision. You will have the opportunity to work on developing this skill.

The key ingredient in successfully modeling management situations is you. Remember, you are in "competition" with the 35 million others who preceded you in this revolution by mastering spreadsheet mechanics. But how many of them can use a spreadsheet to successfully model a challenging management situation and defend their analysis on sound conceptual grounds? It is clearly possible to do the work assignments in this text, get a passing grade in the course, and still have the material make no impact on you or your career. To avoid this tragic result, you have to *own* these modeling ideas, which means you must make them a part of your intuition. The text can help, your teacher can help, but ultimately you have to do it on the basis of your own "hands on" work with Excel modeling. Learning something is, after all, a personal experience, and you can achieve it only with personal effort.

To the Instructor

As evident in our message above, spreadsheet based management science has a lot to offer your students. We believe a good textbook coupled with your teaching and enthusiasm can play a critical role in helping to shape the attitudes of tomorrow's managers towards the proper use of quantitative modeling in business. Certainly, spreadsheets have become the near-exclusive tool used by millions of managers in analyzing business problems. They now contain many powerful tools that can be used to analyze more sophisticated models and make better decisions. Given the pervasive use of spreadsheets in management, our task is to focus students upon developing their modeling skills—how to "paint" onto the blank canvas of the worksheet to develop helpful, practical business models—and not upon algorithms or mathematical puzzles.

With this in mind, the fifth edition was revised entirely by the new authors, Jeff Moore and Larry Weatherford, top to bottom, to make it state-of-the-art in the spreadsheet tools that it teaches and to help you make it more relevant to the management careers your students face. With this in mind, content has shifted away from solution procedures and other mathematical details toward additional case material. For example, new cases from the Stanford and Darden Graduate Schools of Business have been added in almost all chapters. We also think that it is very important for the student to be aware of the continuing successful use of these quantitative methods by actual businesses and thus have included updated chapter-opening vignettes and application capsules that demonstrate payoffs, often on the order of millions of dollars, by well-known businesses who have applied these modeling techniques.

This textbook is designed for introductory courses in applying the Microsoft Excel spreadsheet to management decision modeling at the undergraduate or MBA level. It introduces students to the key ideas of modeling and management decision making that will be important to them throughout their careers. Addressing the needs of readers interested in either general management or more specialized decision science careers, the book emphasizes

- the importance of strong conceptual foundations for all topics, as opposed to "cookbook" spreadsheet prescriptions
- role of spreadsheet modeling in the larger context of management decision-making, as opposed to algorithmic techniques.

We have adopted a very "hands on" approach to modeling many different challenges a business may face in the areas of operations, finance, human resources, marketing, and the public sector, to name a few. Students strongly prefer this approach because (1) they learn marketable skills they will use immediately in their careers, and more importantly, (2) they develop valuable modeling habits and insights of longer term benefit. Many students have called us to say that this was one of the most valuable courses they took in college.

The revised book has a strong focus on models—what they are, how they are created, how they are used, what kinds of insights they provide—and on the critical importance of managerial judgment in utilizing those insights. At the same time, for readers interested in the more technical aspects of the subject, there is an unparalleled treatment of optimization and decision analysis techniques.

Spreadsheet applications and examples in Microsoft Excel, including the use of popular spreadsheet add-ins (Solver, Crystal Ball, @Risk, and TreePlan), are integrated throughout as the modeling paradigm.

Considerable attention has been paid to the procedural (almost tutorial) steps to build and analyze decision-making models in Excel. The emphasis again is "hands on" use of Excel and its add-ins. The book provides many screen "shots" of Excel models and includes four software application packages students will use long after the course is completed:

- A new graphic visualization program, GLP, for interactive optimization of linear programming models—software included with the textbook.
- *Exclusive* student version of the Monte Carlo simulation add-in, Crystal Ball—software included with the textbook.
- Decision analysis add-in software, TreePlan—software included with the textbook.
- Excel templates for queuing models—software included with textbook.

We have also expanded the introductory coverage of modeling philosophy and added a new chapter on general spreadsheet modeling techniques that introduces students to the application of spreadsheets to managerial modeling. We have also significantly revised two chapters—the chapter on Multi-objective Decision Making has added a new section on analytic hierarchy process (AHP), and the chapter on Forecasting has expanded the coverage of time-series forecasting models, and added the treatment of seasonality in data, as well as a case on forecasting at Marriott hotels.

This edition features new material on applying models in the service sector of the economy, in addition to the traditional manufacturing examples in previous editions. Continuing the fine tradition of previous editions, the text offers unequaled coverage of optimization.

The text is divided into three parts; the first deals with general modeling issues; the second with optimization models; and the third with probabilistic (stochastic) models. This provides a logical organizational framework for the material while allowing for greater emphasis on and enhanced coverage of currently "hot" areas such as AHP, Monte Carlo simulation, multi-objective decision making, and the general use of spreadsheets in modeling. There is more material than can be covered in a typical first course. We believe our organization of topics allows each instructor the flexibility to tailor their course to different audiences and needs.

Appendices on the Solver and the special features of Excel for modeling not normally covered in mechanics-of-spreadsheets courses have been added to enable the student to improve their spreadsheet skills and gain a greater appreciation for the modeling capability of Excel.

ACCOMPANYING MATERIALS

New copies of the book include a CD-ROM containing the following software and courseware at no extra charge:

- New graphic visualization program, GLP, for interactive optimization of linear programming models for the material in Chapters 4 and 7.
- *Exclusive* student version of the Monte Carlo simulation add-in, Crystal Ball, for the material in Chapter 11. Compatible with Excel 97 (version 8.0).
- Decision analysis add-in software, TreePlan, for the material in Chapter 10. Compatible with Excel 97 (version 8.0).
- Excel templates for queuing models for the material in Chapter 12. Compatible with Excel 97 (version 8.0).

- Voice annotated "playback" demonstrations on use of the major Excel add-ins.
- Excel spreadsheet files for all in-text examples and any relevant data for end-of-chapter problems and cases.

SUPPLEMENTARY ITEMS FOR TEXT ADOPTERS

- Excel Solutions (for the Instructor) to every example, problem and case in the book. Instructors may use these as is, take out some of the detail, or modify them as desired.
- Presentation slides for each chapter in PowerPoint with the appropriate Excel spreadsheets (013-904780-8).
- Access to protected Web Page for more timely supplementary materials (www.prenhall.com/eppen)
- Instructor's Solutions Manual (013-904756-5)
- Test Item File (013-904764-6)
- Custom Test for Windows (013-904772-7)

ACKNOWLEDGMENTS

As the authors responsible for this edition, we would like to thank the original authors of the first four editions, Gary Eppen and F.J. Gould, joined in later editions by Charles Schmidt, for their arduous efforts in creating a classic textbook that was worthy of being revised.

We would like to thank our editor, Tom Tucker, for his patience in bringing this revision to pass. We believe if it wasn't for his guidance, and direction, the book would not be nearly the product that it is.

We would like to thank our many reviewers of this edition (see the list below) for their insightful comments and ideas. This is a much better book because of them. We also thank the contributors to the expanded case studies of this edition, C.P. Bonini, Evan Porteus, Robert Wilson, Haim Mendelson, Krishnan Anand, and Sam Bodily.

We thank the more than 300 instructors who participated in the extensive INFORMS Management Science Teaching Survey. Their comments and suggestions have validated many of the changes made in this edition.

We would also like to thank our secretaries, Heather Harper, Vonda Barnes and Marge Holford, for the long hours of dedicated service in scanning in the old edition of the book and editing. We are also indebted to Kevin Lewis' eagle eyes for spotting any mistakes that had slipped through the cracks to that point, as well as to the University of Wyoming MBA Decision Modeling class of the Fall 1997 for class-testing the book.

We are grateful to Professor David Ashley for the queuing templates and to Professor Mike Middleton for the TreePlan software.

Finally, we would like to thank Daniel Fylstra and John Watson of Frontline Systems and Software Engines for making Solver a reality. They have been a joy to work with. Also, at Microsoft, Lewis Lewin, and former Stanford business students, Steve Ballmer and Pete Higgins, deserve thanks for their instrumental roles in creating the Excel tools that have made it the preferred choice for modeling and analysis by managers. Their cooperation with and receptivity to suggestions from academics in determining Excel's and Solver's product design and feature set is a model that we wish more software developers would follow.

We hope you find that this text and its supporting materials enhance your teaching efforts. We always like to hear from you—especially when it's to pass along your ideas for how the text can be improved—so, please feel free to send along your reactions.

Jeffrey Moore, Palo Alto, CA

Email: moore_jeffrey@gsb.stanford.edu

Phone: (650) 723-4058

FAX: (650) 725-7979

Lawrence R. Weatherford, Laramie, WY

Email: lrw@uwyo.edu

Phone: (307) 766-3639

FAX: (307) 766-3488

REVIEWERS FOR THE FIFTH EDITION

Kenneth H. Brown, University of Northern Iowa; Mitale De, Wilfrid Laurier University; Greg DeCroix, University of Washington; Abe Feinberg, California State University; Phillip C. Fry, Boise State University; Thomas A. Grossman, Jr., University of Calgary; Anne D. Henriksen, University of New Mexico; Steven Nahmias, Santa Clara University; Robert Nau, Duke University; Gary Reeves, University of South Carolina; David A. Schilling, The Ohio State University; Rick L. Wilson, Oklahoma State University

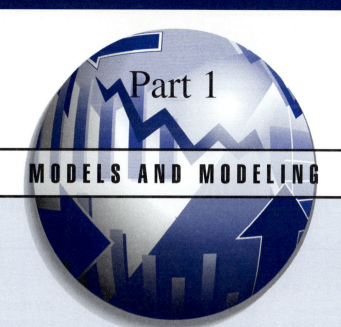

Part 1

MODELS AND MODELING

In this part we initiate the modeling approach to applying Excel for managerial decision support. Our approach consists of developing an Excel model of a management situation, analyzing the model with the tools of Excel, and decision making based upon that analysis. The early chapters are devoted to a class of models, called deterministic models. So it makes sense to ask, "What do we mean by *deterministic?*"

The word *deterministic* means that all aspects of the model are *known with certainty*. For example, in a production planning model we will assume that we know *exactly* how long it takes to produce a particular part, say, 20 minutes each, or equivalently, three parts per hour. We thus know that in eight hours of work we can produce: 8 hours * 3 parts per hour = 24 parts.

All of us have used deterministic models. From the first time we deduced that five nickel-pieces of candy cost a quarter, we always knew the exact value of all the factors in our analysis. Indeed, we naturally tend to assume that the world around us is deterministic. On reflection, however, we realize that it is

not. In the example above, we know that some of those part production times are going to be 19 minutes and others 23. Perhaps it will take only 7 hours and 41 minutes to produce our 24 parts.

Why, then, do we use deterministic models when we know that they do not perfectly describe reality? The answer is simple—the models are useful. Deterministic models may not be perfect, but they are often a reasonably good approximation of reality, almost always better than no model at all. The results they yield make it well worth the time and effort required to construct and analyze such models. For this reason, deterministic models are the workhorses in applying spreadsheets to analyzing management situations, and we devote both Parts 1 and 2 of the book to their study. Later, in Part 3 of the book we will relax this deterministic assumption for models that require us to consider uncertainty explicitly.

Chapter 1 Introduction to Modeling
Chapter 2 Spreadsheet Modeling

Introduction to Modeling

CHAPTER OUTLINE

1.1 Introduction

1.2 The Modeling Process

1.3 A Word on Philosophy

1.4 Types of Models

1.5 Building Models

1.6 Modeling with Data

1.7 Data-Related Issues

1.8 Deterministic and Probabilistic Models

1.9 Model Building Cycles

1.10 Modeling and Decision Making

1.11 Modeling Terminology

1.12 Summary

KEY TERMS

SELF-REVIEW EXERCISES

DISCUSSION QUESTIONS

REFERENCES

APPLICATION CAPSULE — Credit and Collections Decisions at AT&T Capital Corporation

Owning and managing over $12 billion in assets, AT&T Capital Corporation (AT&T CC) is the largest publicly held leasing and financing company in the United States. Small-ticket commercial leasing, involving capital equipment valued at $50,000 or less, is a multibillion dollar strategic segment of AT&T CC's business. In this highly competitive market, AT&T CC must make credit approval decisions quickly (or risk losing customers to another lessor), accurately (or risk bad-debt losses), and cost-effectively (or risk decisioning costs that erode profits). In addition, management of collections activities on delinquent accounts must be cost-effective to control bad-debt losses, reduce financial servicing costs, and improve cash flow.

Taking a life cycle approach, AT&T CC developed a computer-based decision support system to manage each customer's credit risk throughout the course of the relationship. Models and systems were developed to support three phases of the relationship: (1) making initial credit decisions, (2) managing the credit line and subsequent credit decisions, and (3) collecting accounts. For each phase risk-prediction and decision-making models determine what decision to make. Benefits included quicker response times to the customer, gains in AT&T CC business volume, and increases in profitability.

For initial credit decisions, credit profile information and credit reports are used to predict a customer's future payment performance. An optimization model is used to determine the sourcing of credit information from different credit bureaus. Another optimization model determines approval decisions and assigned credit lines. The approval decision making uses the dollar exposure and credit score prediction to determine decisions of Approve, Reject, or Refer for Review. This process now automates about 68% of initial credit decisions, permitting an increase of $40 million in annual business volume while cutting costs of decision making by $550,000 annually. Another division at AT&T CC used the model to decrease its costs by over $600,000 annually, including a 40% reduction in the cost of obtaining credit reports.

Managing the customer credit line involves continuous evaluation of the customer's creditworthiness to reclassify his/her credit line into credit "buckets." Customers are ratcheted up to the next level or down to a lower level of credit when the credit-scoring model predicts a new threshold. The credit-line management model has resulted in an annual savings of $300,000 per year while supporting a $6 million increase in business volume.

The collections from customers in arrears is managed by a suite of statistical models that recommend one of up to five treatment scenarios for collection activity. A portfolio management model automatically selects and queues customers in arrears for a service representative's work list. This has resulted in a productivity gain of 15%, yielding a sustained reduction in delinquent receivables of $16 million and corresponding cash flow increase of $1 million per month. With the model, AT&T CC's provision for doubtful accounts declined by 15% while the business volume grew by 23%.

Overall, applications of these risk analysis, statistical, optimization, and portfolio management models have reduced credit management decision costs by $3.5 million annually while supporting business volume gains of $86 million annually and reducing bad-debt losses by $1.1 million annually. According to AT&T CC, these investments in "decision automation and optimization are now viewed as a significant source of competitive advantage and profitability improvement." (See Curnow et al.)

1.1 INTRODUCTION

At the heart of AT&T's success is a collection of management models for supporting credit decision making, and management models are what we are going to study. This book is about building managerial decision-making models using spreadsheets—what they are, how they are constructed, how they are used, and what they can tell us.

Managers have long regarded quantitative modeling for decision making with mixed emotions. While acknowledging the benefits of quantitative models, general managers have often viewed the modeling process itself as a "black art" to be practiced only by mathematicians, high-paid consultants, or computer specialists. Unfortunately, this delegation of modeling to specialists removes the manager from the process, a step that often leads to misapplication or nonapplication of the results. This, in turn, leads to increased skepticism by managers as to the real value of modeling, except to provide boilerplate appendices of model results—that frequently age like fine wine—in unread reports. Money and effort are thus wasted in ceremonial modeling activities that ultimately have little or no impact upon the client manager, nor the organization that commissioned the model, because neither learns from nor is changed by the modeling process.

Two recent technologies have revolutionized modeling by allowing managers to construct and analyze models for themselves. The two technologies are powerful personal computers and sophisticated, user-friendly spreadsheet software. These technologies have caused, paraphrasing Professor Sam Savage, "the analytical curtain to fall . . ." as an impediment to the direct application of modeling by general managers for decision making. In other words, the previously required analytical skills of advanced mathematics, computer programming, algorithmic thinking, and other technical training have nearly vanished as a prerequisite. This direct **decision support** use of models not only leads to better decisions, but in addition, managers gain important insights that previously were lost. This learning-from-modeling approach allows the manager to address the *most* important issue of any decision-making situation: determining what fundamental questions to ask, what alternatives to investigate, and where to focus attention.

> **By modeling various alternatives for future system design, Federal Express has, in effect, made its mistakes on paper. Computer modeling works; it allows us to examine many different alternatives and it forces the examination of the entire problem.**
>
> **Frederick W. Smith**
> **Chairman and CEO of Federal Express Corporation**

1.2 THE MODELING PROCESS

Figure 1.1 presents the steps of managerial decision making. When faced with a situation involving conflicting or competing alternatives, the situation is analyzed by the manager; decisions are reached to resolve the conflicts; the decisions are implemented;

FIGURE 1.1

Managerial Approach to
Decision Making

and the organization receives the consequences in the form of payoffs, not all of which are monetary. In this book we focus upon applying spreadsheet modeling to decision support; that is, the first two stages of analyzing the situation and reaching decisions about it.

Figure 1.2 defines the modeling process applied to the first two stages that we will use throughout this book. Note that the diagram is divided into a top and bottom half separated by a dashed line. Below the dashed line is the real, chaotic, everyday world faced by managers who must decide how to deal with a challenging situation, such as the allocation of resources to competing tasks, the scheduling of activities, or designing a marketing strategy. The process starts in the lower left corner with the challenging management situation.

Historically, managers relied almost exclusively on their own intuition as the primary vehicle for making decisions. Although of great value, especially for experienced managers, intuition is by definition devoid of a rational analytic process. A manager practicing intuition alone for decision making learns only from the feedback of final outcomes, an expensive and unforgiving teacher.

The modeling process, as represented by the "symbolic world" half of the figure above the dashed line, recommends a course of action to supplement (not replace) the use of intuition in making decisions. This indirect route involves abstracting the problematic aspects of the management situation into a quantitative model that represents the essence of the situation.

After building the (quantitative) model, it is analyzed to generate some results or conclusions that emanate from the model alone; that is, without regard to the abstractions previously made. Next, interpretation of the model-based results back to the real-world situation occurs, taking into account what was left out during the earlier abstraction phase. When augmented by the manager's intuition and experience, this modeling process leads to better decisions and insights that affect learning.

As illustrated in Figure 1.3, the modeling process itself is not a scientific method endeavor that can be left entirely to specialists. Managerial judgment pervades all aspects of the process. Hence, intimate involvement by the manager throughout the modeling process is critical for success back in the real world.

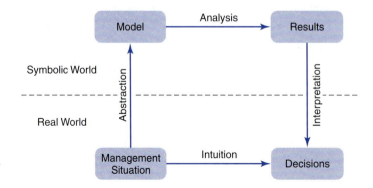

FIGURE 1.2

The Modeling Process

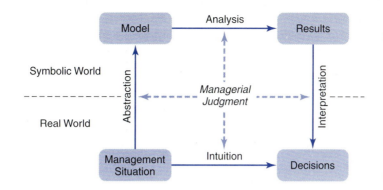

FIGURE 1.3

The Role of Judgment in the Modeling Process

The crucial role of managers occurs during the abstraction, model formulation, interpretation, and later, the implementation of decisions. Therefore, it is essential that you understand

1. What sorts of management situations are amenable to modeling,

2. What the prospects are for gathering or retrieving data and analyzing the model to obtain recommendations or results (within an affordable amount of time and money), and

3. What you can do to get the greatest possible value out of the model in terms of model interpretation and decision implementation.

MODELS IN THE FIRM

Models often play different roles at different levels of the firm. At the top levels, models more typically provide information in the form of results and insights, not necessarily recommended decisions. They are useful as strategic planning tools: to help forecast the future, explore alternatives, develop multiple-contingency plans, increase flexibility, and decrease reaction time. At lower levels, models are more frequently used to provide recommended decisions. In many plants, for example, assembly-line operations are completely automated. In some cases, such as the AT&T example, decisions are produced by a model of the operation and immediately implemented with only exceptional managerial involvement. More commonly, however, automation's contribution to modeling is the ready collection of operational data. These data are then used by managers to update their spreadsheet model periodically. The revised model is then reanalyzed to produce new recommended decisions, followed by managerial reinterpretation and implementation of new decisions.

Models have different uses at different levels of the firm for a number of reasons. At progressively lower levels of an organization, alternatives and objectives are apt to become clearer. Interactions are easier to specify quantitatively, accurate data are often more available and the future environment more certain. Also, the frequency of repeated decision making is high, affording the opportunity to amortize the cost of model development and data collection over many decision-making opportunities. For example, at the bottom of the hierarchy a decision may concern the scheduling of a particular machine. We know the products that will be run on it and the costs of changing the machine from the production of one product to any other product. The goal of the model may be to find a schedule that produces the necessary amounts by the due dates and minimizes changeover and storage costs.

Contrast the clarity and explicitness of that problem with a multibillion-dollar top-management decision between "invest and grow" and "produce to generate current earnings." Models can certainly be applied to such broad and fuzzy problems, but the models themselves are loaded with questionable assumptions and uncertainties. In such cases, the validity of the model and agreement on objectives may be as difficult to determine as the appropriate decision.

MODELS AND MANAGERS

Models are used in as many ways as there are people who build them. They can be used to sell an idea or a design, to order optimal quantities of nylon hosiery, or to better organize a giant multinational corporation. In spite of these differences, a few generalities apply to all decision support models. All such models provide a framework for logical and consistent analysis and are used for at least seven reasons:

1. Models force you to be explicit about your objectives.

2. Models force you to identify and record the types of decisions that influence those objectives.

3. Models force you to identify and record interactions and trade-offs among those decisions.

4. Models force you to think carefully about variables to include and their definitions in terms that are quantifiable.

5. Models force you to consider what data are pertinent for quantification of those variables and determining their interactions.

6. Models force you to recognize constraints (limitations) on the values that those quantified variables may assume.

7. Models allow communication of your ideas and understanding to facilitate teamwork.

It follows from these features that a model can be used as a consistent tool for evaluating and communicating different policies. That is, each policy or set of decisions is evaluated by the same objective according to the same formulas for describing interactions and constraints. Moreover, models can be explicitly adjusted and improved with historical experience, a form of adaptive learning.

A final point: Spreadsheet models provide the opportunity for the systematic use of powerful analytical methods never before available to general managers. They can handle a large number of variables and interactions. The mind alone is capable of storing and communicating only so much information.

> Models allow us to use the analytical power of spreadsheets hand in hand with the data storage and computational speed of computers.

1.3   A WORD ON PHILOSOPHY

"Philosophy" represents our effort to bridge the gap between the classroom experience with models and your experiences as a manager in the real world. In the classroom all the problems are clearly stated (at least we intend them to be so), all the data are neatly given, and the solution may be a single number in the back of the book. Of course, absolutely none of this is true "below the line" of Figure 1.2 in the real world. It thus pays to take a moment to comment further about the role of models in the real world.

REALISM

We start with a theme sounded earlier. No model captures all of reality. Each model is an abstraction. That is, it includes only some of the possible interactions and only approximately represents the relationships among them. This provides us with a very simple and pragmatic explanation of why and when models are used.

> A model is valuable if you make better decisions when you use it than when you don't.

The approach is much like that of science or engineering. The models may not exactly describe the lift on an airplane wing, but we design better planes with the models than without them. The same concept holds for managerial decision models.

INTUITION

Some managers continue to think that quantitative models and management intuition stand in opposition to each other: "Either we will be creative in addressing this situation or we will use a computer." Nothing could be further from the truth. The effective (and creative) use of models depends crucially on good management judgment and intuition.

Intuition plays a major role in problem recognition and model formulation. You have to "see" the potential for using a quantitative model to get the process started; that is, you must have an intuitive feeling that a model will capture the essence of the situation and yield a useful result before you are willing to invest in the modeling process.

Intuition is also crucial during interpretation and implementation. Although analysis of many of the models in this book produces "optimal" decisions, it is important to understand that such decisions are the optimal solution to the symbolic abstraction "above the line" in Figure 1.2. They may or may not be a good response to the real-world situation.

> The term *optimality* is a model-related rather than a real-world concept. One optimizes models, but rarely, if ever, real-world situations.

Only rarely is it meaningful to talk about "optimal solutions" for the real-life situations of business (much less of government) management. That is why it is crucial that you as a manager make sure that the decisions suggested by a model make sense by satisfying your intuition. If the recommendations do not appeal to your managerial intuition, then it is necessary to decide whether the model is wrong. Indeed, a crucial aspect of your managerial role is to evaluate the model itself and to determine just how much weight should be accorded to its recommendations. The situation, or even the formulation of the model, may need to be rethought. The point is that modeling does not provide an opportunity for a manager to put intuition on hold. In fact, one of the worst mistakes a manager can make is to blindly allow a model to make his or her decisions because the "spreadsheet says so." The environment might change, and a model that was producing perfectly good results could start producing bad advice. You must always be alert to the possibility that something has changed and that the old answers just won't work anymore. Indeed, there is much evidence that the modeling process works best when the environment surrounding a business situation changes enough to render standard policies or rules of thumb inadequate.

Of course, there is no guarantee that using a "good" model will always give a good outcome; but without perfect clairvoyance it is the most rational approach that can be taken. Moreover, like the modeling process itself, management situations are really circular not strictly sequential. This means that they keep coming up and have to be revised and reworked. This fact provides one of the major motivations for studying quantitative models. Your chances for anticipating when a model will and will not yield good real-world results are dramatically improved by understanding the concepts that are used in the model.

To better understand what we have covered on the modeling process, assume you are the manager below and follow the manager-modeler dialog.

Manager Let me make sure I understand. Essentially, you are saying that because managers have not been actively involved in the modeling process, many modeling efforts have been wasted, at least in terms of their impact upon the real world of final decision making and upon the managers themselves.

Right.

Manager And that the development of powerful personal computers and spreadsheets now makes it possible for managers like me to do their own modeling in a fast and easy way without relying upon a technical specialist.

Yes, in many situations.

Manager   And that the indirect route—building a model, analyzing it, and interpreting it—should augment but not replace my own intuition.

> *Correct, particularly where some aspects of the situation can be quantified into a model that will supplement your intuitive treatment of the nonquantifiable aspects of the situation.*

Manager   I see. So, in conclusion, adopting this modeling process will give me the answers I need to my problem.

> *Surprisingly . . . , no.*

Manager   What? Are you teasing me with that answer? You and I both know that working with computers is never as fast nor as easy to use as claimed, spreadsheets included. And now you are telling me that using computers and spreadsheet modeling is *not* going to provide the answer to my management problem?

> *In a sense, yes, that is what I am saying.*

Manager   Well, congratulations! You have just unsold me on using modeling by saying it is irrelevant to answering my problem.

> *Hold on! You have just touched upon a central misunderstanding about the modeling process for decision support. Look at the first two figures again. It is not an accident that neither the word* problem *nor the word* answer *appears in either. Our ultimate goal is to address overall improvement in decision making for managerial situations and not just give "answers."*

Manager   Look, I am not interested in a meaningless academic debate about semantic distinctions.

> *That is not my point. Of course, we will devote considerable attention in this book to providing "an" answer, if not "the" answer, to a given problem. My point is that the very articulation of your real-world situation into a problem statement has already launched you up the abstraction ladder into the modeling process. That is, problems, as such, do exist above the dashed line in the figure, and hence, answers to those problems exist, but only above the dashed line—outside of the real world that you face. However, "answers" to your abstracted "problem" are rarely, if ever, solutions to your management situation by themselves. The answers must be carefully interpreted in the real-world context that you face before making a final decision. And, as a result, that final implemented decision may be quite different from the answer produced by analyzing the model.*

Manager   OK, I see what you are saying. In other words, I must understand what specific abstract problem the model's answers are addressing, and how those answers were arrived at, before I can properly interpret them as decision aids to help me resolve my more chaotic real-world situation.

> *Precisely. Think of the answers not as results in and of themselves but, coupled with the problem statements they address, as important ways to update your intuition about the managerial situation that motivated you in the first place. This "intuition updating" has benefits that transcend the immediate payoff from better decision making in the current situation because enhancing one's intuition is at the core of learning. Moreover, the benefits of learning are cumulative across situations, culminating in the wisdom we all seek. So, the commitment to modeling should be driven by your desire to understand the situation at a deeper level, not only for the immediate benefit of better decision making but also as an important step in refining your management intuition. Refined intuition—wisdom, if you will—about management situations is the hallmark of a successful manager. Never forget the modeler's creed: "The goal of modeling is insight, not just answers."*

Manager Well, it sounds to me that you just built a "verbal model" to help me get "insight" into the proper role my involvement should play in modeling in order to "refine my intuition" about the modeling process.

> *Touché!*

Manager Earlier you said that the modeling process was not scientific. I thought the whole purpose of quantitative modeling was to be more scientific.

> *On the contrary, I said that the modeling process was not an application of the scientific method. The purpose of the classic scientific method is to eliminate human judgment as a polluting or biasing influence upon knowledge and understanding. As a result, verification of theories or results through repeated, controlled experimentation is at the core of knowledge acquisition in the sciences. Unfortunately, managerial situations almost never permit the luxury of replicated, controlled experiments because of cost or time constraints. So, we must substitute management judgment as an imperfect control or guide at every step in the modeling process. The analysis-of-the-model phase of the modeling process will be scientific in the sense that logic and computation to yield rational deductions will be employed, but otherwise judgmental influences are pervasive.*

Manager In other words, modeling and analysis alone cannot protect me from the consequences of "garbage in–garbage out" in decision making.

> *Correct. And you, the manager, must be completely involved in the process, because only you can be the arbitrator of the GIGO content of the abstraction, the resulting model, the analysis of it, the relevance of the results, and their interpretation. After all, you are the one who ultimately will be held responsible for the final decision, right?*

Manager You bet I am! OK, this has been very helpful in clearing up the role I need to play and the benefits I can expect from modeling.

> *Actually, there is another extremely important benefit to the modeling process we haven't discussed, the usefulness of a model as a communication aid. Important decisions are rarely made in isolation, but involve the cooperation and concurrence of others, especially those charged with implementing the final decision. Properly done, the model building process, resulting model, and the decision-making rationale it provides can be a powerful teamwork building tool for explaining and communicating ideas and conclusions to others, and getting their feedback and cooperation.*

Manager OK, OK, you've got me involved! Now can we get on with spreadsheet modeling? I have decisions to make . . .

> *Not yet. There are some more considerations to address first: some of the different kinds of quantitative models available, the steps in building a model, and the important role played by data in spreadsheet modeling.*

1.4   TYPES OF MODELS

There are three types of models. Engineers build model airplanes, and urban planners build model cities. Both of these are **physical models.** We use a second type of model so frequently, that we often fail to recognize it, an **analog model.** Analog models represent a set of relationships through a different, but analogous, medium. A highway road map is an analog model of the terrain, a car's speedometer represents speed by analogous displacement of a needle on a gauge, and a pie chart represents the magnitude of several cost components by wedge-shaped areas.

The most abstract is the **symbolic model,** in which all concepts are represented by quantitatively defined variables and all relationships are represented mathematically, instead of physically or by analog. For example, physicists construct quantitative models of

TABLE 1.1 Types of Models		
MODEL TYPE	**CHARACTERISTICS**	**EXAMPLES**
Physical Model	Tangible Comprehension: Easy Duplicate and Share: Difficult Modification and Manipulation: Difficult Scope of Use: Lowest	Model Airplane, Model House, Model City
Analog Model	Intangible Comprehension: Harder Duplicate and Share: Easier Modification and Manipulation: Easier Scope of Use: Wider	Road Map, Speedometer, Pie Chart
Symbolic Model	Intangible Comprehension: Hardest Duplicate and Share: Easiest Modification and Manipulation: Easiest Scope of Use: Widest	Simulation Model, Algebraic Model, Spreadsheet Model

the universe, and economists build quantitative models of the economy. Because they use quantitatively defined variables interrelated by equations, symbolic models are often called mathematical models, quantitative models, or, in our case, spreadsheet models.

Managers work with all three types of models, most commonly with analog models in the form of charts and graphs and with symbolic models in the form of spreadsheet output and MIS reports. Table 1.1 summarizes the characteristics of the three types of models.

Despite these models' diversity, they all have one common aspect:

A model is a carefully selected abstraction of reality.

We will concentrate on building symbolic models (particularly as represented in spreadsheets) and analyzing them to produce tabular (symbolic) and chart (analog) results.

SYMBOLIC (QUANTITATIVE) MODELS

As defined earlier, a symbolic model uses mathematics to represent the relationships among the data of interest. A symbolic model requires these data to be quantifiable, that is, expressible in numerical form. Consider the following common examples. A model to evaluate the alternatives of buying a house versus renting an apartment considers the down payments required, mortgage rates, cash flow, appreciation and depreciation, in brief, numerical data. A model to help you decide whether to work for an MBA degree would consider length of time required, the tuition and other expenses, salary potential, and the like; that is, numerical data. In short, numerical data are the guts of symbolic models.

Let us examine more closely a very simple example of a symbolic model. If you are currently in Chicago, Illinois, and plan to be in Cleveland, Ohio, for dinner, you might want to estimate the time it will take you to drive from Chicago to Cleveland. To do so you might look up the mileage in an atlas or on the Internet and divide it by your typical average speed. Your model is therefore

$$T = \frac{D}{S}$$ where T = time, D = distance, and S = speed.

This model is certainly useful. Note, however, that it is a simplification of reality, for you have ignored many factors that could influence your travel time. You have made no effort to include construction delays, weather conditions, stops to buy gas or to visit the restroom, and so on. Nevertheless, if you are planning to leave at 9 A.M. and $T = 6$ hours, then the model is clearly good enough for your purposes. That is, you can be pretty confident that you will arrive in Cleveland in time for dinner.

Suppose, however, that you cannot leave until noon and have a reservation to meet a very important person at a fancy restaurant at 6:30 P.M. You might then feel that the model is too simple for comfort, and would want to refine it to incorporate more detail to bring it closer to reality. You could, for example, add an expression to represent your stops along the way. The model would then be

$$T = \frac{D}{S} + (R*N)$$ where R is the average time spent at a rest stop, and N is the number of times you expect to stop.

You could go on improving your model by incorporating more factors. Some of those factors might have to be estimates or approximations. The two points that you need to keep in mind are:

1. A model always simplifies reality.
2. You incorporate enough detail into your model so that
   - The result meets your needs,
   - It is consistent with the data you have available, and
   - It can be analyzed in the time you have to devote to the process.

DECISION MODELS

In this book we emphasize decision models: symbolic models in which some of the variables represent decisions that must (or at least could) be made. You obviously cannot change the distance between Chicago and Cleveland. You can, however, choose your speed, the number of times you stop, and the time you take at each stop. These are therefore decision variables. (There may be some limits on these variables—you obviously cannot drive at 300 mph, your gas tank can hold only a certain amount of gasoline, the tank takes a certain amount of time to fill, and so on. We will discuss such limits in Chapter 2, because they are central to the construction of realistic models.)

Objectives Decisions are usually made to achieve a particular objective. Thus, in addition to decision variables, decision models typically include an explicit performance measure that gauges the attainment of that objective. A crucial role in model building is to specify how the decision variables will affect the performance measure. Consider the following examples:

1. *Sales force allocation model:* The decision variables might be how many salespeople to assign to each territory. A typical performance measure would be sales revenue, and the objective might be to maximize sales revenue.
2. *Job-shop scheduling model:* The decision variables might be how many hours to schedule given parts on given machines, and in what sequence. Possible objectives might be to minimize costs, the total completion time, or tardiness on deliveries.
3. *Cash-management model:* The decision variables might be the amount of funds to be held in each of several categories (cash, Treasury bills, bonds, stocks) each month. A typical objective might be to minimize the foregone interest income from holding liquid assets; that is, cash or cash equivalents.

To summarize:

1. Decision models selectively describe the managerial situation.
2. Decision models designate decision variables.
3. Decision models designate performance measure(s) that reflect objective(s).

1.5   BUILDING MODELS

Whether simple or complex, a model must be constructed by people. Unfortunately, there are no automatic "expert systems" for model building except in narrow, highly specialized applications. The computer revolution and accompanying software developments may someday lead to automated model building packages for general managers. Currently, however, model building involves a great deal of art and imagination as well as a bit of technical know-how.

In a business environment, quantitative modeling involves specifying the interactions among many variables. To accomplish this quantification, the problem must be stated mathematically. We shall see many examples of model building in the chapters that follow. Do not be misled by the specific examples in the text, for in the real world there is usually no single "correct way" to build a model. Different models may give a different perspective on the same situation in much the same way that paintings by Picasso and van Gogh would make the same view look different. Although model building is an art, like art the fundamentals can be taught. As an overall guide, you can break down the process of building a model into three steps:

1.   Study the environment of the managerial situation.
2.   Formulate a selective representation of the situation.
3.   Construct and analyze a symbolic (quantitative) model.

STUDYING THE ENVIRONMENT

Those new to modeling often undervalue the first of the steps, a study of the environment. The stated problem is often not a proper abstraction of the real situation. Often, the stated problem is really a description of a symptom. A variety of factors, including organizational conflicts, differences between personal and organizational goals, and the overall complexity of the situation, may stand between the manager and a clear understanding of the situation. Many times it is assumed that the facts are known when they really aren't. Prior experience is the most essential ingredient for success—both experience in building models and working experience in the environment to be studied.

FORMULATION

The second step, formulation of the model, involves basic conceptual analysis, in which assumptions and simplifications have to be made. Formulation requires the model builder to select or isolate from the total environment those aspects of reality relevant to the situation at hand. Because the management situations we are concerned with involve decisions and objectives, these must be explicitly identified and defined. There may be various ways to define the decision variables, and the most appropriate definition may not be apparent initially. The objectives, too, may be unclear. Even the most capable managers may not know precisely what results they want to achieve. Equally problematic, there may be too many objectives to be satisfied, and it may be necessary to choose one out of many. (It will become evident that it is usually impossible to optimize two different objectives at the same time. Thus, generally speaking, it is nonsensical to seek to obtain "the most return for the least investment" or the "greatest good for the most people.")

Figure 1.4 presents the first (and often most crucial) step in formulating a decision model, the identification of the model's major conceptual ingredients. In this first step, we postpone creating the working details of the model. Instead, we focus on identifying (1) the model's **inputs,** the things to be worked on by the model, and (2) the model's **outputs,** the things to be produced by the model. For this reason, the model at this point is called a "black box" because we do not know (yet) what logic will be put inside the box.

Once we have identified the model's inputs and outputs, we must refine them into two subdivisions. Inputs, called **exogenous variables,** are divided into (1) **decisions,**

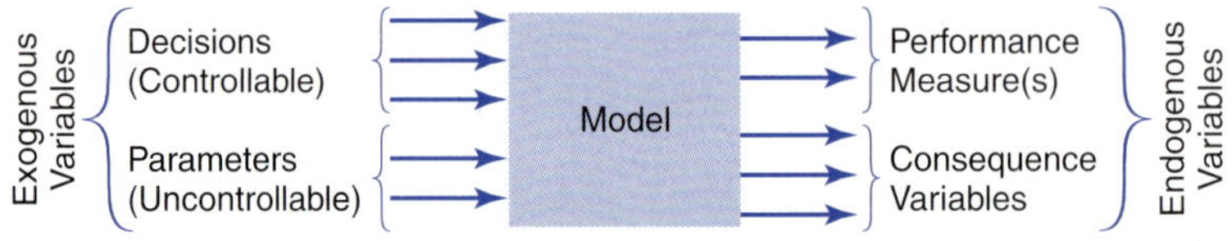

FIGURE 1.4

The "Black Box" View of a Model

variables that you, the manager, control, that is, the decision variables; and (2) **parameters,** variables that others, including "Mother Nature," control.[1] Examples of decision variables would be the prices to charge for your product, the location of a proposed facility, or the decision to sell a subsidiary or not. Examples of parameters are the prices charged by competitors for a similar product, a physical capacity constraint on a warehouse, the unit cost of raw materials, or next month's rainfall. Many uncontrolled input values may not be known in advance. Treating these inputs as parameters allows the model to be built as if they were known. Later, numeric values for these quantities can be specified after analyzing data to estimate their values, or simply given assumed values during analysis of the model.

Outputs, called **endogenous variables,** are divided into (1) **performance measures,** variables that measure the degree of goal attainment, and (2) **consequence variables,** variables that display other consequences that aid in understanding and interpreting the model's results. Performance measures are especially important because they are the criteria used to gauge how well you are meeting your ultimate objectives. For this reason performance measures are often called **objective functions.** Examples are revenue, market share, total cost, worker morale, customer satisfaction, and return on investment. Examples of consequence variables are revenue breakdown, number of items shipped, or other "want to know" quantities.

As simple as the black box conceptual ingredients framework is, it forces you to consider early in the modeling process what to include and what to exclude from the model, and how to classify the relevant factors. Here are some questions that illustrate how thought-provoking the simple ideas of Figure 1.4 are:

- For my private-sector company, is profit a decision or is it a performance measure?
- What exactly are the relevant sets of decision variables, as opposed to the ones of secondary or tertiary importance? For example, is the price of my product the single significant decision to consider, assuming, say, my promotion budget is fixed (by someone else?) at some given amount? Or should both product price and size of the promotion budget be considered as decisions to be made by me simultaneously?
- Do I, the manager, really control the price of my product, in which case price is a decision variable? Or is my product's price determined by competitive market forces, in which case price is a parameter?
- Is quantity of the product to sell a decision variable, and therefore, a controllable input to the model? Or is product quantity sold an output of the model (consequence variable), given its price as an input?
- Is worker morale a performance measure, and thus something I can influence managerially via human resource decisions? Or is it a parameter that I must accept as given? Either way, how do I measure morale? If morale is too slippery a concept to define into a variable precisely, then should I leave it out of the model and consider it later as part of the model interpretation phase? Or should I use, say, worker absenteeism as a surrogate or proxy measure for morale? In that case, what factors might affect absenteeism? And which subset of them are my decision variables?
- If market share is to be a performance measure, then what exactly is the definition of the market whose share my decisions will affect? Do I mean regional, national, or international market share? Or all three? Do I mean market share this year, next year, or five years hence? Should I measure market share in units sold or in revenue?

---

[1] We use *parameter* here in its broadest managerial sense: "exogenous factors, such as market price or tax rate, that help define a model and determine its behavior." Some modelers prefer to substitute *uncontrolled exogenous variable* or *random variable* instead of *parameter*. This permits a more restrictive definition for *parameter* to characterize the underlying uncertainty in an uncontrolled exogenous variable.

- Should I include competitor sales as input parameters in the model? But, if competitor sales are exogenous inputs, that implies I cannot affect them and must accept them as given. But, surely, I can affect my competitors' sales volumes by aggressive price discounting or expanded advertising, both of which could be my decision variables. In that case, competitor market share should be an endogenous output (consequence variable) instead of an exogenous input to my model. But, if it is an output, then should competitor market share be considered a performance measure—to be minimized?

- Should I use my own performance measures, time scale, and worldview in my model or the ones preferred by my boss?

- Should the model focus on day-to-day operational decisions, longer-run strategic planning decisions, or both?

- What should I include in the way of performance measures or parameters from external stakeholder constituencies, such as government regulators, consumer groups, and shareholders?

The techniques we will develop for modeling are applicable no matter how the model inputs and outputs are defined. However, the questions illustrate the importance of management judgment in clearly defining the elements of the black box.

A suggested approach to the formulation step is to define the objective and its performance measure(s) first, that is, the critical model outputs. Then consider what model inputs (decision variables and parameters) are related to achieving that objective by influencing the performance measure(s). From that base the critical step of defining the decision variables and parameters that influence goal attainment follow more naturally. This backward reasoning ultimately produces the same black box formulation of the model. However, this working backward approach is often easier because managers naturally think about situations in terms of objectives and performance measures.

SYMBOLIC CONSTRUCTION

Once a formulation is accomplished (and this may be a verbal or written process), a symbolic model must be constructed.

Experience has shown that generalist managers founder in model building at the point that the mathematical equations within the black box relating the variables must be developed. Indeed, this step requires care because, along with data, these equations become the "guts" of the whole modeling process. This topic is important enough that we will devote considerable attention to it throughout the book. Indeed, the central theme of this book is that many practical models can be built and analyzed by a single manager using modern spreadsheet techniques. Even in more complex situations requiring an interdisciplinary team, preliminary modeling can be initiated by a generalist manager.

One reason for this belief is that most equations within a symbolic model are simple accounting relationships (Profit = Revenue − TotalCost) or physical definitions (NumberMonths = 12 ∗ NumberYears) and, therefore, are well within the easy grasp of any manager. The remaining relationships in the model are more difficult to develop. However, most managerial models have only a few complicated equations. In theses cases, some practice is required to develop the correct mathematics for interrelating two or more variables as part of the model's logic. A useful technique is to exploit your ability to sketch a graph giving a picture of the desired relationship(s). That is, you start, not with the final mathematical equation, but with a graph of it, and then you (or a talented colleague) deduce an acceptable equation from that graph.[2] The technique for accomplishing this also works for analyzing raw data, such as might be necessary for estimating the values of parameters. We call this technique "modeling with data," a topic important enough to warrant its own development in the next section.

---

[2]As we will see in Chapter 2, Excel provides a tool to assist equation development from such graphs.

Managerial decisions are based to a large extent on the evaluation and interpretation of data. However, data can be interpreted only through the lens of some conceptual framework. It is difficult to say which comes first, the framework or the gathering of data. Certainly, data are required for effective modeling. Efforts toward better modeling often lead to the acquisition and storage of more or new types of data. The existence of data increases the potential for the use of models. C. West Churchman, an early advocate of management modeling, has claimed that there exist in reality no truly "raw" data in the sense that the act of collecting and tabulating the numbers always reflects the biases of some framework's worldview, that is, a (mental) model. Nevertheless, one of the characteristics of advanced civilization, at least in terms of technology, seems to be the simultaneous acquisition and use of both data and models.

Symbolic models provide a way to evaluate and interpret data consistently and with greater attention to detail than afforded by mental models. Symbolic models can also be used to generate data, and data are usually required to build a model, for example, to estimate model parameters. In fact, it is not uncommon for the success or failure of a modeling effort to be related to issues of data availability, accuracy, and relevance. A great deal of attention should center on the subject of data in the practical building and use of management models. For example, a model requiring detailed data could be rendered useless if the data are not available or are costly and time-consuming to collect.

In this section, we introduce some of the considerations pertinent to the use of data in model building. The scenario for this discussion, and others in this book, is a hypothetical firm called PROTRAC.

A midwestern company, PROTRAC produces over 200 items distributed among farm machinery, industrial and construction machinery, chemical products, and lawn and garden equipment. Its main source of revenue is the sale of machine tools for agriculture, construction, forestry, landscaping, earth moving, and materials handling. These products are made in 14 factories, most of which are located in the United States, and are sold worldwide.

Decisions at PROTRAC are based to a large extent on available information, that is, on the evaluation and interpretation of data. Previously, we stated that from the modeling point of view, a recommended decision by a model is defined to be a number, such as a price or a quantity to sell. Keep this very precise definition in mind. We also want you to be very clear on what we mean by **data.** For our purposes, the word *data* also means numbers.

To see how numbers and models become intimately connected, consider a PROTRAC management decision on how much money to allocate to European marketing. Before making such a decision, management may want to have some idea of the effect of this allocation on total European sales. Therefore, an executive has queried data on European marketing expenditures and total European sales revenue for a 12-year period from the corporate database and has imported the data into her Excel spreadsheet, as presented in Figure 1.5.

This spreadsheet is simply one means of conveying the requested data. The format of the table is purely a matter of convenience; importantly, it is not intended to connote any special relationship among the various numbers. However, suppose that after studying the data in Figure 1.5, the executive assumes or hypothesizes some relationship between marketing expenditures and sales. She may feel, for example, that for her product total sales revenue in a given year depend directly only on the marketing expenditure in that year and not the sales revenue nor marketing expenditures in prior years. Put another way, she believes that total sales revenue is independent of time. (The words *depend directly* imply that a higher expenditure on marketing leads to higher sales.) Thus, the executive may feel that sales of $1.8 million in 1992 were significantly related only to the marketing expenditures of $400,000 in 1992. Alternatively, she may feel that the 1992 sales are more truly related to the marketing expenditure in 1989. Or, she may hypothesize that 1992 sales depend equally on the 1989, 1990, and 1991 marketing expenditures.

	A	B	C
		Mktg.	Sales
1	Year	Exp.	Rev.
2	1986	$ 0	$ 0
3	1987	$ 50	$ 450
4	1988	$100	$ 650
5	1989	$200	$1,150
6	1990	$150	$1,000
7	1991	$250	$1,390
8	1992	$400	$1,800
9	1993	$300	$1,565
10	1994	$350	$1,715
11	1995	$445	$2,080
12	1996	$500	$2,140
13	1997	$550	$2,200

FIGURE 1.5

PROTRAC European Marketing
Expenditures and Sales
Revenue, 1986–1997
(thousands of dollars)

Numerous possible relationships could be hypothesized. The appropriate relationships would obviously depend on many factors associated with the actual PROTRAC environment. Also, we have phrased the hypothesized relationships in vague, semi-quantitative language. That is, we hypothesized that 1992 sales depended directly on 1992 marketing expenditures, but we did not hypothesize a specific quantitative relationship. We could make a specific quantitative statement: Actual sales in 1992 are 4.5 times the marketing expenditure in the same year. This means that in 1992 there were, *on the average,* 4.5 dollars of sales for each dollar of marketing. However, this fact by itself certainly does not permit us to conclude that a $600,000 marketing expenditure in 1992 would have led to a $2.7 million level of sales. Furthermore, does the 1992 factor of proportionality have any bearing on the current decision? In 1997, for example, the factor of proportionality was 4.0, not 4.5. How do the 1997 data relate to the 1992 data? Are current PROTRAC marketing techniques more like they were in 1997 than in 1992? Or has the operation basically remained unchanged between 1992 and 1997?

And what about other relevant factors, such as general economic conditions? If we hypothesize some causal relationship between marketing and sales in each year, then the data reveal that *on the average* each dollar expended on marketing in 1992 was more effective than in 1997. What real-world factors might lie behind these different degrees of effectiveness in the different years? That is, what real-world interactions do the data reflect? There could be differences in advertising techniques, or differences in market softness and demand which, in turn, could be due to different economic conditions, weather, or government policies.

As a manager, you must consider these kinds of questions as soon as you begin to interpret the data in the table. But the point of the present discussion is this: As soon as you begin to hypothesize *any* relationship among your data, you are beginning to formulate the equation(s) of a model. That is, you are beginning to interpret the data as reflecting important underlying relationships. Therefore, Figure 1.5 takes on a special significance: It becomes a selective representation of reality. As such, a simple table of the data fits our earlier definition of a model. It is important to emphasize that the data by themselves do not represent a model. The numbers by themselves do not mean anything aside from records of fact (e.g., in 1992, total European sales revenue was $1.8 million). It is only when some relationship is ascribed to the numbers that a model, at least in embryonic form, exists.

FORMS AND SOURCES OF DATA

These data may already be recorded in a computer database—ready for import into a spreadsheet—or be recorded on paper, or, quite commonly, not systematically recorded at all, thereby requiring a separate data collection effort. The data may be measured in pounds or tons, francs or dollars. Questions of units are often important in working with data. For example, in what currency should PROTRAC management measure European sales? If the answer is dollars, what exchange rates should be used to convert foreign currencies into dollars? These rates vary from time to time, and the effect of these variances could be insignificant wrinkles in our calculations, or they could cause the world to look significantly different. A decision of how to collect, store, and interpret the data is governed by the uses to which the data will be put. Unfortunately, data often found in business databases have been collected for other purposes, such as financial reporting, and great care must be paid to understanding the sources and definitions of the data, if data are to be redeployed for managerial modeling and decision-making purposes.

Data may come from records of the past. Data may be generated by making direct observations or estimates in the present. In particular, the data may be produced by a model that requires certain decisions as inputs. Or, finally, data can be produced by making forecasts of the future.

AGGREGATION OF DATA

One of the key considerations in using data is the degree of aggregation desired. For example, does a model require data on total yearly sales over the past five years, or on total yearly sales per country over the past five years, or on total yearly sales per plant over the past five years, or on total yearly sales per plant per product over the past five years? This list of requirements describes data in increasingly disaggregated form. Disaggregated data are more detailed and are generally more difficult and costly to obtain. However, they are also more valuable because they contain more information. Furthermore, it is possible to aggregate disaggregated data, but it is not always possible to go the other way. Thus, if total yearly sales per plant per product are known, it is possible to obtain total sales per product per country, or total sales per country, or total sales per product, or total sales per plant. However, it is clearly not possible in this case to go from the aggregated down to the disaggregated numbers. The benefits of summarization of data that aggregation provides come at a cost; aggregation throws away information.

Although disaggregated data are desirable because they contain more information, it is also true that data may be too disaggregated for incorporation into a spreadsheet[3] or for an individual manager's convenience of use. In terms of a decision on whether or not to build new plants in Europe, PROTRAC executives may want to compare a small select collection of aggregated data. That is, their decision may be based on a simplified model in which they selectively represent reality with only a few chosen numbers written on the "back of an envelope."

It should be obvious that, ignoring processing costs, more data can only lead to better decisions. (If this is not obvious, at least it should be clear that more data cannot lead to worse decisions.) However, it is also true that the degree of disaggregation an individual decision maker can digest is limited. Fortunately, spreadsheet models can work with much more detail than an individual; this is a major reason for their use. Remember, as managerial situations become more complex and sophisticated, *details* become increasingly important. However, the sword is double-edged. Though models typically like

---

[3]Modern spreadsheets, such as Excel, have options to submit database queries over a network to large external database servers. These external data are then aggregated by the server database software, according to the dictates of the query, and appear in the spreadsheet cells, ready for modeling use.

to have disaggregated data, sometimes the disaggregation itself creates insurmountable problems. For example, disaggregation may create too many variables, thus making the model too large and unwieldy to use, or it may require costly and time-consuming effort in data collection. In this respect, the balance is between the ideal of using the most data available (highly detailed and disaggregated) and the practical matter of maintaining model simplicity.

REFINEMENT OF DATA

The term *refinement* is often used synonymously with disaggregation, but this is not quite correct. Highly refined data (often called highly structured) refers to highly disaggregated data, but the converse is not always true. A considerable amount of data may be readily accessible from the networked corporate "data warehouse" database. This data may be relevant to the situation under study but often the data are not in the correct form. We may have yearly data on total sales volume and yearly data on total number of plants operating, but for our model we may require average sales per plant in each year. The average sales per plant can be created by performing some simple spreadsheet manipulations on the existing data. This process of manipulating, or "massaging," or "crunching" data is more appropriately termed refining the data. Such refinements can involve extensive spreadsheet manipulations, depending on what is available and what is needed for modeling purposes.

1.8 DETERMINISTIC AND PROBABILISTIC MODELS

We know that this book is devoted to decision models. There is, however, a large and diverse body of knowledge that falls under this general heading. It is thus useful to have a taxonomy, or way of organizing the material, so that you can see the forest before getting enmeshed in the trees. For example, models for decision making are often classified by the business function they address (finance, marketing, cost accounting, operations, etc.) or by applications discipline or industry involved (science, engineering, economics, military, nonprofit, transportation, venture capital, etc.). They can also be classified by organizational level where they are used (strategic versus tactical), by time frame employed (long run versus short run), by type of mathematics employed (linear equations versus nonlinear equations), and by modeling technology used (spreadsheet, custom software package, paper and pencil, etc.). Each such typology provides added insight to the uses and applicability of modeling. We will use another one to organize our approach to modeling in this book, deterministic versus probabilistic models.

DETERMINISTIC MODELS

Deterministic models are those models in which all of the relevant data are assumed to be known with certainty. That is, deterministic models presume that when the model is analyzed all the needed information for decision making will be available. An example of a deterministic model would be the assignment of airline crews to each of an airline's daily flights over the next month, given flight schedules, staff available, legal constraints on work hours, union work rules, and so forth. As we will see in the chapters on deterministic modeling, such models can handle complex situations with many decisions and constraints. Deterministic models tend to have highest utility when there are few uncontrolled model inputs that are uncertain. As a result, deterministic models are often, but not always, used for decision making internal to an organization, such as the airline crew scheduling example.

Deterministic models are covered in Parts 1 and 2 of this book. The rest of Part 1 is devoted to general Excel spreadsheet modeling while most of Part 2 is devoted to constrained optimization models. In Part 2 you will be introduced to **linear programming** (LP), which is the workhorse of constrained optimization models.[4] In Part 2 you will learn to formulate LP models, optimize them, and interpret the solution. A variety of other models also appear in Part 2. These include integer, nonlinear, and multi-objective programming, which are first cousins of LP.

Deterministic models are important for five reasons:

1. An amazing variety of important management problems can be formulated as deterministic models.

2. Many spreadsheets have the technology to optimize deterministic models, that is, find optimal decisions. For large LP models in particular this can be done very quickly and reliably.

3. The techniques for analysis produce as a by-product a great deal of information that is useful for managerial interpretation of results.

4. Constrained optimization in particular is an extremely useful way to think about situations even when you are not going to build a model and optimize it.

5. Practice with deterministic models helps to develop your ability to formulate models in general.

PROBABILISTIC MODELS

In **probabilistic,** or stochastic, models some element of the model is not known with certainty. That is, probabilistic models presume that some important variables, called random variables, will not have their values known before decisions are made, and this ignorance must be incorporated into the model. An example of a probabilistic model would be the decision to take a start-up Internet company public by offering shares of stock for sale before it is known whether the market for such offerings will be favorable (bull market), yielding a high stock price, or unfavorable (bear market), yielding a low stock price. As we will see in Part 3 of the book, such models incorporate uncertainty via probabilities on the random variables, in this case the future condition of the stock market. These models tend to have highest utility when there are many uncertain model inputs and fewer constraints. As a result, uncertainty models are often used for strategic decision making involving an organization's relationship to its (uncertain) environment, such as the public stock offering example.

In Part 3 of the book you will learn what kinds of criteria you can use when there is uncertainty concerning part of the model and how to find an optimal decision in view of those criteria. Here again we have quantitative decision problems in which we are trying to optimize some function of the decision variables. Topics in this part of the book include decision analysis, queuing, simulation, project management, and forecasting. Because uncertainty plays a central role in these models, this part of the book requires some knowledge of probability and statistics. Appendix A to this book provides a brief overview of probability concepts. Although it certainly will not make you an expert, it does provide an introduction to (or a review of) the key concepts required for an understanding of these chapters.

1.9   MODEL BUILDING CYCLES

To further understand how models fit into the modeling process it will be convenient for us to classify symbolic models along the dimensions illustrated by the diamond in Figure 1.6. The right versus the left of the diamond refers to the polar extremes of building deterministic models versus building probabilistic models.

Of course, no model is either completely deterministic (no uncertainty in any variables) nor completely probabilistic (uncertainty attached to all variables' values). Returning to the previous airline crew scheduling example, weather or sickness could disrupt flights

---

[4] The "linear" in LP refers to the requirement that every relationship in the model be specified as a linear equation. The "programming" in LP has nothing to do with computer programming or software development. Rather, its origin is related to "finding a schedule or *program* of activities to accomplish a task efficiently."

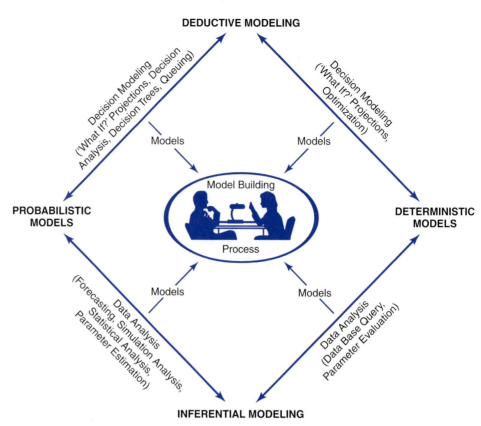

FIGURE 1.6

Types of Models

or the availability of crew members in unexpected ways, thereby compromising the model's proposed crew assignments. Similarly, market conditions for the Internet stock offering example might be foreseeable with adequate certainty or the stock offering model could include a decision to postpone the offering at the last minute if conditions become unfavorable, thereby mitigating the effects of the uncertainty.

The top versus the bottom of the diamond refers to the polar extremes of deductive modeling versus inferential modeling. Deductive modeling presumes that the model can be initially developed by focusing upon the variables themselves, interrelating them in the model by making assumptions about the algebraic relationships and the values of any parameters. As a result, deductive modeling tends to be "top down" in development, placing a premium upon the modeler's prior knowledge and judgments of both mathematical relationships and data values, and of the future applicability of such prior knowledge. The resulting models tend to be "data poor" initially, involving only 10s or 100s of data items, often expressed as assumed parameters of the model.

Instead of starting with assumptions, inferential modeling presumes that the model can be developed by focusing upon variables themselves as reflected in existing data collections, interrelating them in the model by analyzing the data to determine the relationships and to estimate the values of any parameters. As a result, inferential modeling tends to be "bottom up" in development, placing a premium upon accurate, readily available data and judgments about the future applicability of the data. The resulting models tend to be "data rich" initially, involving 100s or many 1000s of data items, often ultimately refined to estimate parameters of the model.

The diamond also illustrates that *all* four of the faceted dimensions of the diamond are addressed by managers in the model building process, particularly in the early formative stages. That is, model building is rarely done by using only one dimension or by following a simple "cookbook" recipe for combining the dimensions. Instead, model elements are

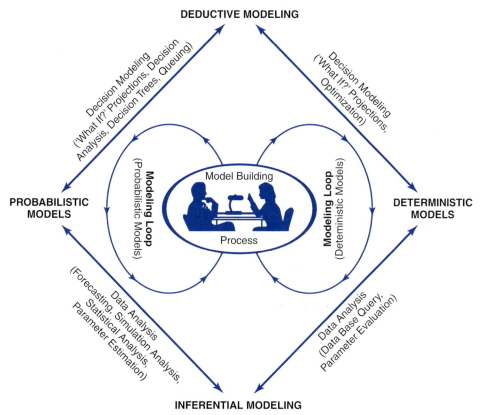

FIGURE 1.7

Model Building Cycles

tried, tested, evaluated (often subjectively at first), revised, retested, and so on in an iterative fashion by jumping from one "facet" of the diamond to another in a creative or brainstorming manner. For example, a manager at PROTRAC might start to build a product costing model via decision modeling by assuming or by (deductive) reasoning that total cost of goods sold is 60% of total revenue, where the 60% "cost of goods" percentage is known (deterministic). This sends her from the top of the diagram to the right facet of a deterministic model. Later in the modeling process, she might elect to "have a look at some historical data on revenues and costs," thereby moving down to the right-hand data analysis facet of the diamond in the diagram. After analyzing the historical data (inference), she might elect to revise the percentage to, say, 63%. Next, she might decide to examine the effect that revision has upon overall costs or profitability for the PROTRAC model as a whole. This would send her back to the right-hand decision modeling facet ("What if?" projections of total costs and profitability) to subjectively evaluate the model's veracity. This iterative approach is illustrated by the modeling loop in the right half of Figure 1.7.

Still later in the model building process, her colleagues might convince her that the cost-of-goods percentage is not fixed at the 63%, but varies somewhat randomly because of variability in the commodity prices PROTRAC pays for raw materials. This would send the modeling process over to the left half in the diagram for her to iteratively develop cost-of-goods percentages and commodity price relationships (deduction) and analyze data to test them (inference) concerning the parameters of the probability distribution governing the values for the cost-of-goods percentage, that is, the modeling loop on the diagram's left half. Still later, she might elect to simplify her model by ignoring the acknowledged uncertainty for the cost-of-goods percentage (because further "What if?" projections suggest that the variability in commodity prices doesn't materially affect decision making, for example). This would shift the cost-of-goods relationship portion of the model back to the right half of the diamond in the diagram. This last shift illustrates that horizontal loops exist in the modeling process in addition to the vertical ones diagrammed in Figure 1.7.

The trial-and-error, iterative approach to model building illustrated in Figure 1.7 is highly creative. It is what makes managerial model building more of an art than a science. And, like art, you learn by looking critically at examples done by others and by practice, practice, practice.

1.10 MODELING AND DECISION MAKING

Generally speaking, the successful application of modeling to real-world decision making can be broken down into four stages that closely parallel the items in the modeling process of Figure 1.1:

1. Model formulation and model building, the process of taking real-world managerial situations, abstracting them into a formulation, and then developing the mathematical terms of a symbolic model;

2. Analysis of the model to generate results;

3. Interpretation and validation of model results, making sure that the available information obtained from the analysis is understood in the context of the original real-world situation; and

4. Implementation, putting the validated knowledge gained from the interpretation of model results to work in real-world decision making.

As with model building itself, the four stages above are almost never performed sequentially. Instead, managers execute the stages iteratively. A model is built cyclically as described in the previous section. It is then analyzed to produce results, which are interpreted critically to produce recommendations that often fail to pass the simplest of validation tests: Do the interpreted results and recommendations violate common sense?

Common sense is the most obvious litmus test for validating a model. Barring easily identified logic errors in the model, if the results or recommendations violate common sense, there is no choice but to return to stage 1 to diagnose whether the managerial situation was inadequately defined, too much realism was lost in formulation, the model itself is deficient, or the like. More than a few iterations are commonly made before an acceptable model is produced, or on occasion, before a manager realizes that his or her common sense was inadequate originally. Either way, it is wrong to conclude that the iterations were wasted: Substantial learning occurs during the process itself as both models and managerial understanding are improved.

MODEL VALIDATION

Common sense alone is hardly a scientific way to validate a modeling effort. Unfortunately, other techniques for validation have their shortcomings, as well. For example, a frequent validation claim is that an organization saved $X in costs or made $Y in profit after using a model for decision making. This begs the question of whether that much performance improvement (or more!) would have happened without the model.

Because controlled experimentation is typically infeasible, one imperfect way to validate a model is to use it to "predict history." That is, historical data on decisions, parameters, and outcomes for a similar situation are taken from a known decision-making epoch and input into the model. Next, the two sets of outcomes, from the model and from history, are compared for similarity as validation. Finally, the model is analyzed and any additional payoff from an improved decision-making recommendation becomes evidence for the worth of the model, assuming, of course, that historical validity implies future validity.

In the final analysis, it must be remembered that managerial performance is subjectively evaluated every day under ill-defined decision-making conditions. As a decision support technology for those same managers, it is unreasonable to hold modeling to a higher, nearly unreachable scientific standard. In the final analysis, the validation of a model, like the worth of modeling, is a value judgment. Experience has shown that managers who commit to active involvement in the process have very little difficulty making these value judgments.

TABLE 1.2 Modeling Terminology

MODELING TERM	MANAGEMENT LINGO	FORMAL DEFINITION	EXAMPLE
Decision Variable	Lever	Controllable Exogenous Input Quantity	Investment Amount
Parameter	Gauge	Uncontrollable Exogenous Input Quantity	Interest Rate
Consequence Variable	Outcome	Endogenous Output Variable	Commissions Paid
Performance Measure	Yardstick	Endogenous Variable Used for Evaluation (Objective Function Value)	Return on Investment

A FINAL PERSPECTIVE

While different classes may choose to emphasize different parts of the material, depending on the perspective of the instructor and the needs of the students, remember this book emphasizes throughout the managerial approach shown in Figure 1.1. This managerial approach to modeling is more concerned with identifying situations, formulating models, analyzing them, interpreting the results, and implementing decisions. The central thrust behind our coverage of model building is an interest in applying these approaches to the real world. Without that, you, the spreadsheet user, would be a pure mathematician/programmer, and you, the manager, would be without a job.

1.11   MODELING TERMINOLOGY

With this introduction we think that you are just about ready to turn to Chapter 2, which begins the examination of building spreadsheet models. However, let us close this chapter with one important caveat. While most of the terms we have used in describing modeling are straightforward, a given model's terminology necessarily becomes increasingly precise as model building evolves. This is caused by the need to carefully define the model's variables and relationships. Unfortunately, this requirement comes at a price: The use of model building jargon (e.g., *decision variable, parameter, exogenous,* etc.) is viewed as discordant by other managers, who are often key players during implementation. Table 1.2 presents a few modeling terms, their definitions, and examples, along with suggested management phrases for colloquial use. The more colorful management lingo is often very useful in communicating black box modeling ideas to others.

1.12   SUMMARY

This chapter has provided an overview of the use of quantitative decision-making models, with special emphasis on their role as tools for the manager. The interaction between manager and model has been stressed, with attention given to the manager's role as ultimate decision maker and as a builder, user, and evaluator of models. We have explored the relationship between modeling and managerial intuition in the decision-making process.

Models are a limited representation of reality, and for this reason the results from analyzing a model are not necessarily the solution for the original management situation. In particular, we have emphasized that the notion of "optimal" is a mathematical, as opposed to real-world, concept. If a model is properly formulated and its output carefully interpreted, however, it can provide a wealth of valuable information to a decision maker.

We have introduced the concepts of decision variables, parameters, constraints, objectives, and performance measures, all of which are important components of models. We have introduced different types of models and the critical role played by data in modeling. We have discussed the iterative process by which models are created, the role played by different kinds of models in business organizations, and issues surrounding model validation. Importantly, we have emphasized the role models play in increasing managerial understanding, in the communication of ideas to others, and in facilitating teamwork.

Key Terms

Decision Support.   The use of data, models and analysis to give insights that aid decision making.

Modeling Process.   The iterative application of abstraction, model building, analysis, and interpretation, coupled with intuition and judgment, to help make decisions.

Management Science.   The systematic application of the modeling process to managerial situations.

Physical Model.   A model, such as a model airplane, whose components are physical artifacts of an entity's actual properties.

Analog Model.   A model using different media to represent actual properties, such as displacement of a clock's hands to represent time.

Symbolic Model (Quantitative Model).   A model using data, variables, and mathematical relationships to represent abstracted properties, such as a model of a country's economy.

Black Box Model.   An incomplete symbolic model in which only its input and output variables are defined, but without defined mathematical relationships.

Exogenous Variables.   Quantitative variables whose values are determined external to a symbolic model, that is, inputs to a symbolic model.

Endogenous Variables.   Quantitative variables whose values are determined by the relationships of a symbolic model, that is, outputs of a symbolic model.

Decision (Decision Variable).   An exogenous variable whose value is under the control of and determined by a decision maker.

Parameter.   A variable whose value is not determined by a decision maker, but is set exogenously.

Performance Measure (Objective Function).   An endogenous variable that gauges the degree of goal attainment for a model.

Decision Model.   A symbolic model with decision variables and at least one performance measure.

Consequence Variable.   An endogenous variable providing additional information to assist managerial interpretation of model results.

Deterministic Model.   A model in which all data are known with certainty.

Probabilistic Model.   A model in which some data are not known with certainty, but whose uncertainty is captured by known probabilities.

Linear Program (LP).   A deterministic model consisting of linear equations and a single performance measure (objective function) to be optimized subject to satisfaction of given set of constraints.

Symbolic LP Model.   The algebraic representation of an LP.

Deductive Modeling.   Symbolic model building in which the values of variables, parameters, and the mathematical relationships among them are assumed from prior knowledge.

Inferential Modeling.   Symbolic model building in which varibles, parameters and the mathematical relationships among them are estimated by analysis of data.

Self-Review Exercises

True-False

1. **T F** The more complicated the model, the more useful it generally is.

2. **T F** Models usually ignore much of the world.

3. **T F** Decision models require numerical values for decision variables.

4. **T F** A decision model often captures interactions and trade-offs between certain variables or quantities of interest.

5. **T   F** There is usually no single correct way to build a model of a management situation.

6. **T   F** One advantage of the modeling process is that it often eliminates the need to be very familiar with the environment being studied.

7. **T   F** In practice, models are sometimes built by teams of individuals drawn from different disciplines.

8. **T   F** By definition, optimization models always provide the best decision for the real-world situation.

9. **T   F** A model is a good substitute for executive judgment and experience.

10. **T   F** An important role of management can be the evaluation of a model (determining whether a model should be used and its results implemented).

11. **T   F** Although spreadsheets make calculations easy, they have no real impact on decision making.

12. **T   F** "What if?" models are useful only for examining changes in the values of decision variables.

13. **T   F** Data are needed only after the model is built.

14. **T   F** As soon as you begin to hypothesize *any* relationship among your data, you are beginning to formulate the equation(s) of a model.

15. **T   F** Data are used in building models.

16. **T   F** A model provides a consistent means to interpret and evaluate data.

17. **T   F** Aggregated data contain more information than do disaggregated data.

18. **T   F** "Highly structured data" means the opposite of "highly refined data."

Multiple Choice

19. A model is
    a. a selective representation of reality
    b. an abstraction
    c. an approximation
    d. an idealization
    e. all of the above

20. Decisions are often based on
    a. an evaluation of numerical data
    b. numbers produced by models
    c. the use of intuitive models that are never written down
    d. all of the above

21. A model
    a. cannot be useful unless it mirrors a real situation in great detail
    b. is a tool for the decision maker
    c. is rarely revised once it has been constructed
    d. all of the above

22. A model
    a. forces a manager to be explicit about objectives
    b. forces a manager to identify explicitly the types of decisions that influence objectives
    c. forces a manager to recognize explicitly constraints placed on the values that variables can assume
    d. all of the above

23. Models
    a. play different roles at different levels of the firm
    b. are rarely used in the strategic planning process
    c. are a costly way of making routine daily decisions
    d. all of the above

24. Constrained optimization means
    a. that the underlying model is a very precise representation of reality
    b. achieving the best possible (mathematical) result considering the restrictions
    c. both of the above

25. Consider a prospective manager with interests and abilities that lie far from the quantitative techniques field. The point of studying a spreadsheet modeling course might be
    a. to be able to knowledgeably accept or reject the use of quantitative tools
    b. to acquire new ways of looking at the environment
    c. to become more familiar with the kind of assistance a spreadsheet might provide
    d. all of the above

26. With "What if?" analysis, we are sure to find
    a. an optimal solution
    b. a good solution
    c. a feasible solution (if one exists)
    d. none of the above

27. In a probabilistic model, some element of the problem
    a. is a random variable with known distribution
    b. is a random variable about which nothing is known
    c. takes on various values that must be precisely calculated before the model can be solved
    d. will not be known until the model has been clearly formulated

28. A manager who wishes to maximize profit and minimize cost
    a. needs two objectives in her model
    b. can get the desired result by maximizing (profit minus cost)
    c. has an impossible goal and must choose one objective
    d. must make use of a probabilistic model

29. Linear programming models in general
    a. can be optimized even if they are large
    b. are more useful for analyzing problems than for solving them
    c. are probabilistic in nature
    d. are rarely solved by a computer

30. Every quantitative model
   a. represents data of interest in numerical form
   b. requires the use of a computer for a full solution
   c. must be deterministic
   d. all of the above

31. The use of decision models
   a. is possible only when all variables are known with certainty
   b. reduces the role of judgment and intuition in managerial decision making
   c. requires managers to have a high degree of proficiency with computers
   d. none of the above

Answers

1.	F	**9.**	F	**17.**	F	**25.**	d
2.	T	**10.**	T	**18.**	F	**26.**	d
3.	T	**11.**	F	**19.**	e	**27.**	a
4.	T	**12.**	F	**20.**	d	**28.**	c
5.	T	**13.**	F	**21.**	b	**29.**	a
6.	F	**14.**	T	**22.**	d	**30.**	a
7.	T	**15.**	T	**23.**	a	**31.**	d
8.	F	**16.**	T	**24.**	b		

Discussion Questions

1-1. "The difficult managerial situations are those for which models do not exist." Interpret this statement. Give some examples.

1-2. What is the relationship between data and models?

1-3. At what point do the spreadsheet entries comprising a table of given data begin to take on the role of a model?

1-4. What is the advantage of having disaggregated data? What is the advantage of aggregated data?

1-5. Suppose that you want to become a managerial decision maker but your special abilities and interests are far from the quantitative field. What is the point to your studying an introductory spreadsheet-modeling text?

1-6. What reasons can you think of to explain the fact that many models are built and never implemented? Does the absence of implementation mean that the entire model development activity was a waste of time and resources?

1-7. What is your interpretation of the phrase "a successful application of a model"?

1-8. Profit maximization is commonly taken as the performance measure for the (private-sector) firm. Is this necessarily the case? Can you think of other objectives that might be appropriate? (Do not worry about whether they are readily quantifiable.)

1-9. It is often said that there are no optimal decisions for the complex problems of business. Yet optimization models produce "optimal decisions." In what sense, then, are such decisions optimal?

1-10. Consider the following statement: "Our production policy should be to achieve maximum output at minimum cost." Comment on this statement.

1-11. What is the meaning of a mathematical equation when the data (parameter values) are not known with precision? What kinds of assumptions would tend to justify the use of models in such situations?

1-12. "Quantifying the elements of a decision problem is the easy part; the really difficult part is analyzing the model." Do you agree? Why or why not?

1-13. You are in the middle of a presentation to your company's chief executive officer in which you are justifying your request for approval of a multimillion-dollar project to market a new invention. He interrupts you in mid sentence, "Let's just cut to the chase. What levers do you want and what yardstick should I use if I approve this project?" Interpret his request in the context of modeling.

1-14. ABC Consulting specializes in building and analyzing decision models for a fee paid by its manager clients. "It's a very profitable business," says Rick James, ABC's president. "We go into the organization, get briefed by the client manager on the problem at hand. Then we assess the problem and gather the necessary data. Next, we build a model on our ABC computers, or adapt one in our growing library of models, analyze it, and return to the client and make a presentation to management with our recommendations." He continues, "Do we ever go over the equations of the model itself with the client manager or give a copy of the spreadsheet model to the client? Of course not!" Why does ABC not give the model to the manager? Why might its clients not demand such delivery? What are the advantages and disadvantages of this approach to modeling? Answer this last question first from the viewpoint of Rick James and then from the viewpoint of a client manager.

1-15. Under what organizational circumstances do you believe that the modeling process would be more or less successful in supporting business decision making? To help you structure your discussion, consider the following:

   a. A collegial organization involving decision making by consensus versus an internally competitive organization in which decisions are made by adversarial arguments.

   b. A large centralized organization in which all decisions are made by a committee at the top versus a large decentralized organization in which most decision making is made by local managers.

   c. A small organization run by a single entrepreneur versus a larger organization run by functional managers in finance, accounting, marketing, manufacturing, and the like.

   d. A line manager versus a staff manager.

   e. A company introducing a new product into a new market versus a company marketing a mature product into a traditional market.

   f. An organization in which all the managers are spreadsheet literate versus one in which they are not.

   g. An organization that has a central planning department of experts who do all business model development for the company versus one with no such department.

   h. An organization with high levels of management job turnover versus one with little job turnover.

   i. An organization experiencing rapid growth in revenues versus one with slowly growing revenues.

   j. A highly profitable organization versus one that is experiencing losses.

   k. A service organization versus a manufacturing organization.

   l. An organization in a "first world" economy, such as France, versus one in a "newly emerging" economy, such as Vietnam.

   m. An organization in which the managers have engineering or science college degrees versus an organization in which the managers have college degrees in liberal arts.

1-16. "As managerial situations become more complex and sophisticated, *details* become increasingly important." Why would this be true? What relevance does this statement have to modeling?

1-17. What does C. West Churchman mean when he says that raw data don't exist?

1-18. Your new boss, the VP of International Sales, has called you into her office and informs you, "I have decided to open a new sales office in Singapore. But, I need to convince our boss, the Senior VP of Marketing, to go along with this decision in a meeting next Friday. I will ask you to join us, and I want you to build me a spreadsheet model with lots of equations, charts, and other stuff that will help me convince him. Remember, I want that Singapore office approved!" Is this tactic an appropriate use of modeling? What would you do in response to this request by your boss and why?

1-19. It has been said that no data ever cause a model to be rejected, no matter how disconfirming are the data. The only thing that causes one model to be rejected is another model. Do you agree or disagree? Why or why not? Assuming the statement were true, what role do data play in model validation?

References

George Curnow, Gary Kochman, Steven Meester, Debashish Sarkar, and Keith Wilton, "Automating Credit and Collections at AT&T Capital Corporation," *Interfaces,* 27, no. 1 (1997), 29–52.

Peter Horner, "Eyes on the Prize," *OR/MS Today*, August 1991, pp. 34–35.

Spreadsheet Modeling

CHAPTER OUTLINE

2.1 Introduction

2.2 Example One—Simon Pie

2.3 Example Two—XerTech Copy, Inc.

2.4 Example Three—Rosa Raisins

2.5 Example Four—Production at Oak Products, Inc.

2.6 Constraints and Constrained Optimization

2.7 Summary

KEY TERMS

SELF-REVIEW EXERCISES

PROBLEMS

CASE STUDY: Kayo Computer

CASE STUDY: Watson Truck Rental Company

CASE STUDY: Personal Financial Plan

CASE STUDY: Benson Appliance Corporation

REFERENCES

APPLICATION CAPSULE   **Modeling Coast Guard Tender Operations**

One function of the United States Coast Guard is to maintain the 50,000 aids to navigation, or navaids, used by mariners to navigate United States (U.S.) waterways around the continental United States, Alaska, Hawaii, and U.S. territories, such as those in the Caribbean and the western Pacific. These navaids include lighthouses, lighted and unlighted buoys, lights, and day beacons. A navaid or aid to navigation (ATON) is either a floating buoy secured by a chain to sinkers or a fixed structure on land or pilings. Navaids mark underwater hazards and vessel traffic lanes. Large open-ocean buoys can be as large as 9 feet in diameter, 38 feet tall, and can weigh over 10 tons. Each navaid is serviced once a year to keep it operational. For a permanent buoy this involves verifying the buoy's latitude and longitude, replacing missing letters or numbers, and repainting. The average time to service a buoy ranges from 25 to 260 minutes, depending on the nature of the servicing, as well as the weather and environment in which it is done.

The Coast Guard employs a variety of buoy tender classes to (1) deploy federal navaids, (2) perform routine servicing, and (3) respond to random outages. The Coast Guard needed to replace the two largest vessel classes in its buoy tender fleet (i.e., the seagoing buoy tender and the coastal buoy tender). They had 26 seagoing and 11 coastal tenders that serviced 7500 navaids. The estimated replacement cost was $50 million for each seagoing tender and $20 million for a coastal tender. A model was created on a desktop computer to help support the Coast Guard's planned replacement of this 37-vessel fleet. The model analyzed the scheduling of the fleet in order to most efficiently service the navaids. The model had to consider many things, including the maintenance that would be expected, how far the tenders would have to travel to service each buoy, and the associated cost.

Complicating factors included the fact that the buoy tenders performed other missions as well, like search and rescue, enforcement of laws/treaties, and oil-spill cleanup. Each type of vessel had different capabilities. For example, the seagoing tender could lift up to 20 tons of weight, could work in seas of up to 6 feet, and could stay at sea for up to 45 days; while the coastal tender primarily works closer to the coast in shallower waters that the seagoing tender could not transit. They also have less lift capacity and endurance.

Another complication to the model was trying to estimate the effects of bad weather. The total number of hours lost in a year depended on whether the buoys were fully exposed to the weather, partially exposed, or completely protected.

The resulting decision support model recommended that the optimal vessel mix would be a fleet of 16 seagoing and 14 coastal tenders. As long as the tenders were efficiently scheduled, the new fleet would provide sufficient coverage. This represented a decrease of 7 tenders in the fleet for a savings of $350 million in capital acquisition costs, as well as a reduction of 500 personnel billets (positions) and its associated savings. (See Bucciarelli et al.)

2.1 INTRODUCTION

Chapter 1 introduced some basic ideas and rationale for symbolic modeling and reviewed the art of model building as being an iterative process. This chapter will focus upon building Excel spreadsheets for some deterministic models by means of several extended examples. In the process you will be exposed to several ideas:

1. Suggested ways to translate a black box representation into a spreadsheet model,
2. Recommendations for good spreadsheet model design and layout,
3. Suggestions for documenting your models, and
4. Useful features of Excel for modeling and analysis.

Importantly, you will also see several examples of models. Recall, modeling is an art form, learned in part by critical review of examples and, ultimately, by practice.

A final comment before we begin. The spreadsheet models we will review are small, primarily for pedagogical convenience. Modern spreadsheets, like Excel, are capable of supporting much larger, even gargantuan, models. Indeed, there are many instances of successful use of enormous models. However, neither size of the model nor its mathematical sophistication alone necessarily implies usefulness. Simple, small models can also have great utility if they assist decision making. Moreover, successful large sophisticated models almost always evolve from successful management experience with a rudimentary precursor.

No manager will take seriously a model he or she does not understand or that is cumbersome to use and maintain. The biggest mistake a manager can make initially is to build a spreadsheet model with too much detail in a vain attempt to avoid losing any realism. Simplicity should be kept in mind, especially in the early stages of modeling. Remember, at least initially, a spreadsheet model must compete successfully against its popular predecessor, the "back of the envelope."

2.2 EXAMPLE ONE—SIMON PIE

Simon Pie Company generates profit from combining two purchased ingredients (fruit and frozen dough) into apple pies, processing the pies (cooking, packaging, delivering, etc.), and selling them to local grocery stores. The company's founder, Samuel Simon, intends to build an Excel model to explore his options. Before jumping to Excel, however, he applies the ideas in Chapter 1 by defining a black box diagram, working backward from a performance measure to define its conceptual elements. (Recall, model formulation is defining the model's input and output variables comprising the black box picture of the model.)

Simon's need for immediate profits makes the performance measure choice of weekly profit easy. In thinking through the situation, Simon concludes that, all else considered, setting the wholesale pie price is his most critical decision. Simon's marketing plan precludes altering the size or the quality of its pies, and the grocery stores merely mark up their pie cost (Simon's wholesale price). Thus, quantities, and hence costs, of pies sold are determined by Simon's (wholesale) pie price. From this Simon concludes that price of the apple pies is the decision variable and that, plus the cost parameters, will determine Simon's profit, as shown in Figure 2.1. The cost parameters consist of Simon's

FIGURE 2.1

Black Box View of
Simon Pie Model

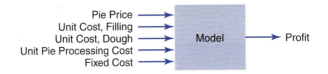

monthly fixed cost for rent, interest expense on a commercial loan, and so on; the unit cost per pie of fruit and dough; and the unit cost of pie processing, which includes pie baking, packaging, and delivering.

The second step in modeling is model building, the logic inside the black box. Many managers experience "modeler's block" at this point, a curse in every way similar to writer's block. The cure to each is the same: Start writing. Because model building is iterative, first attempts will be revised many times before a satisfactory model is developed; the trick is to start.

Some managers new to modeling find influence diagrams useful to help structure their thinking, and coincidentally break through modeler's block. **Influence diagrams** provide a good way to organize an approach to modeling and have the side benefit of beginning model documentation. An influence diagram pictures the connections between the model's exogenous variables and a performance measure, but postpones defining the model's mathematical logic. An influence diagram is created by starting with a performance measure variable. (If there are multiple performance measures, pick one of them.) Then decompose the performance measure variable into two or more intermediate variables, which combine mathematically in the model to define the value of that performance measure. These intermediate variables will eventually reside inside the black box logic of the model. Next, further decompose each of the intermediate variables into still more related intermediate variables. This decomposition process continues until an exogenous variable is defined; that is, until you pop out of the black box by defining an input decision variable or a parameter. Let us illustrate this process for Simon Pie.

Starting with the performance measure, Profit, Simon defines its two components, Revenue and Total Cost. In turn, Simon decomposes each of these two intermediate variables into constituent parts, and in turn, each of them into parts, and so forth, as shown in Figure 2.2. Simon's diagramming stops when all the model's input variables are defined.

There are no hard and fast rules for how much detail to include in an influence diagram; its purpose is to aid the start of model building, not to completely identify every intermediate variable in the final model. Later, during model development, appropriate details will emerge as more of the logic is formalized.

Inspection of Figure 2.1 and Figure 2.2 reveals a lot about Simon's thinking. Not only does it include the factors he considers relevant for turning pies into profits, but by excluding other factors, the diagram represents his business worldview. For example, the diagram makes clear that neither competitor reactions nor the general economy are relevant to his payoff, at least in the short run. Also, there are no inventories, presumably because pies are baked and sold fresh. Working capital and other cash flow variables are missing, and so must not materially affect his profits. The details of procurement, baking schedules, deliveries, spoilage, and human resources are all missing. Of course, he may be planning to add these and other factors later in the modeling process in order to simplify the initial model, a wise tactic.

The next step, building the model, requires the equations relating the variables to be specified. If written out, most of the equations would be straightforward:

$$\text{Profit} = \text{Revenue} - \text{Total Cost}$$
$$\text{Revenue} = \text{Pie Price} * \text{Pies Demanded}$$
$$\text{Total Cost} = \text{Processing Cost} + \text{Ingredients Cost} + \text{Fixed Cost}$$
$$\text{Ingredients Cost} = \text{Quantity Filling} * \text{Unit Cost Filling} + \text{Quantity Dough} * \text{Unit Cost Dough}$$
$$\text{Processing Cost} = \text{Pies Demanded} * \text{Unit Pie Processing Cost}$$

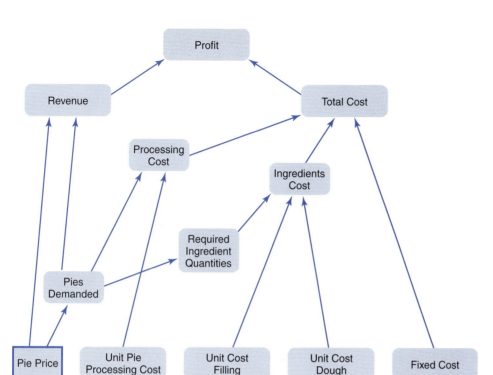

TIP: *Diagrams are easily constructed in Excel by switching to a new worksheet, turning "grid lines" off, and displaying Excel's Drawing Toolbar. Selecting its tools, modifiers, and options allows a surprisingly rich array of drawings to be built. For example, in Figure 2.2 the decision variable, Pie Price, is indicated by a square box, while all the other variables use a rounded box. You are free to adopt whatever conventions aid you in modeling and documentation.*

FIGURE 2.2

Simon Pie Model
Influence Diagram

The Pies Demanded equation requires more thought. Simon considers the demand for pies to be a function of pie price with higher prices producing lower demand (sales). He believes that at a price of $12 there would be no demand for his pies and that below a $12 price he would gain about 4000 pies sold per week for each $1 reduction in price. Assuming for simplicity that the demand relationship is expressed by a linear equation, this produces the following equation for Simon's weekly pie demand in thousands of pies, valid for Pie Price between $0 and $12.

$$\text{Pies Demanded} = 48 - 4 * \text{Pie Price}$$

Figure 2.3 presents the Excel worksheet of Simon's weekly profit model. The results are computed for Simon's current parameter values and its current pie price of $8. Notice how the model is represented in Excel. It is systematically organized and presented to make model interpretation easy. In general, spreadsheet models should adhere to the following recommendations:

1. Input variables are presented together and labeled.
2. Model results are clearly labeled.
3. The units of measure are given where appropriate.
4. The physical results are separated from the financial or economic results.
5. Numbers are stored in separate cells as data and referred to in formulas by cell references. Placing numbers outside of formulas that use them and at the top of the worksheet aids model modification and documentation.
6. Bold fonts, cell indentations, and cell underlines are optionally used to facilitate label interpretation.

In reviewing the model's behavior for lower pie prices, Simon notes that the model's Processing Cost formula produces the correct historical cost for Pies Demanded of 16,000, but not for other values of Pies Demanded. To explore this further, Simon examines his actual Processing Cost data for different levels of pie production. This data plus the projected

FIGURE 2.3

Initial Simon Pie Weekly
Profit Model

	A	B
1	**Simon Pie Co. -- Weekly Profit Model**	
2	**Decision Variable:**	
3	Pie Price	$8.00
4	**Parameters:**	
5	Unit Processing Pie Cost ($ per pie)	$2.05
6	Unit Cost, Fruit Filling ($ per pie)	$3.48
7	Unit Cost, Dough ($ per pie)	$0.30
8	Fixed Cost ($000's)	$12
9	Pie Demand Equation	
10	Intercept	48
11	Slope (Linear Coefficient)	-4
12		
13		
14		
15		
16	**Physical Results (000's)**	
17	Pies Demanded and Sold	16.0
18	**Financial Results ($000's)**	
19	Revenue	$128
20	Processing Cost	$33
21	Ingredients Cost	$60
22	Overhead Cost	$12
23	Total Cost	$105
24	Profit (before tax)	$23

	A	B
1	**Simon Pie Co. -- Weekly Prof**	
2	**Decision Variable:**	
3	Pie Price	8
4	**Parameters:**	
5	Unit Processing P	2.05
6	Unit Cost, Fruit Fi	3.48
7	Unit Cost, Dough	0.3
8	Fixed Cost ($000'	12
9	Pie Demand Equa	
10	Intercept	48
11	Slope (Linear C	-4
12		
13		
14		
15		
16	**Physical Results ((**	
17	Pies Demanded and	=B10+B11*B3
18	**Financial Results (**	
19	Revenue	=B17*B3
20	Processing Cost	=B5*B17
21	Ingredients Cost	=(B6+B7)*B17
22	Overhead Cost	=B8
23	Total Cost	=SUM(B20:B22)
24	Profit (before tax)	=B19-B23

FIGURE 2.4

Simon Pie Actual Versus
Projected Processing Cost

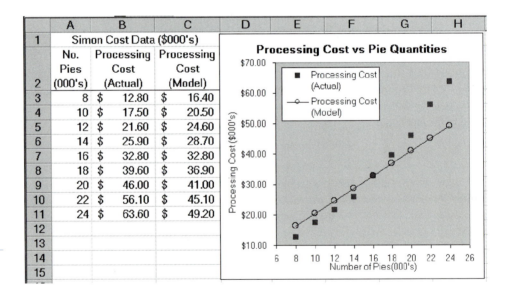

	A	B	C
1	Simon Cost Data ($000's)		
2	No. Pies (000's)	Processing Cost (Actual)	Processing Cost (Model)
3	8	$ 12.80	$ 16.40
4	10	$ 17.50	$ 20.50
5	12	$ 21.60	$ 24.60
6	14	$ 25.90	$ 28.70
7	16	$ 32.80	$ 32.80
8	18	$ 39.60	$ 36.90
9	20	$ 46.00	$ 41.00
10	22	$ 56.10	$ 45.10
11	24	$ 63.60	$ 49.20

Processing Cost from the model (= 2.05 ∗ Pies Demanded) are tabulated and charted in Figure 2.4. Not only does the model's Processing Cost formula provide a poor fit to the data, but the chart of Processing Cost data suggests a nonlinear equation is more appropriate for Simon to use.

While mathematical deduction can be used to develop the logic of a better Processing Cost equation, another way to develop an equation representing the Processing Cost is to use Excel's Trendline capability to fit an equation to the data. To do this Simon selects the data points on the chart, presses the right mouse button, and chooses the Trendline menu item from the pop-up menu as shown in Figure 2.5.

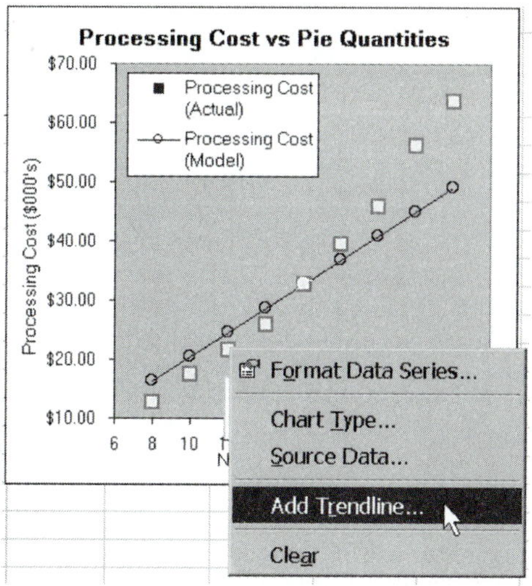

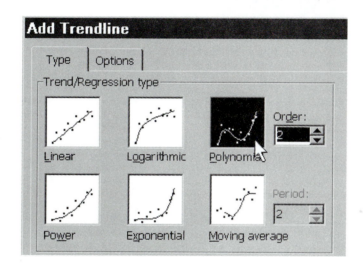

FIGURE 2.5

Trendline to Revise
Processing Cost Formula

FIGURE 2.6

Second Order
Polynomial Equation

Simon chooses a quadratic relationship, that is, a second order polynomial, to see if a simple polynomial equation is a better representation for the data, as shown in Figure 2.6.

Simon elects to have the equation intercept the origin and clicks OK, as shown in Figure 2.7. The final equation is presented in Figure 2.8 and by inspection is a better fit to the Processing Cost data.[1]

Figure 2.9 presents the revised Simon Pie model incorporating the new Processing Cost equation.

The steps outlined above are an example of the model building loop discussed in Chapter 1. Starting with a simple deductive model, you examine the behavior of each important equation against actual data or against hypothetical data that reflect your judgments. Each equation is then revised in the original model, as appropriate. In the Simon Pie example, similar iterative procedures would govern Simon's review of other hypothesized relationships in the model, such as for determining ingredients cost equations or the pie demand equation.

---

[1]This modeling with data approach for reckoning an equation is appropriate for determining hypothetical relationships or for curves that closely fit the data. In the case of real data, if the fitted curve is not close to all data points, subtle issues of dealing with "noise" in data require use of a probabilistic model for interpreting the fit. This case is postponed until Chapter 13 on forecasting.

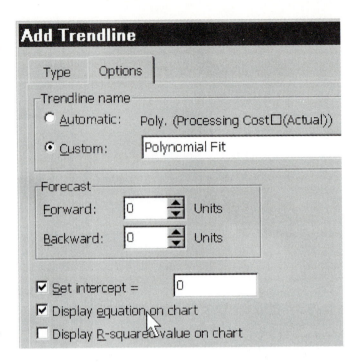

FIGURE 2.7

Trendline Options

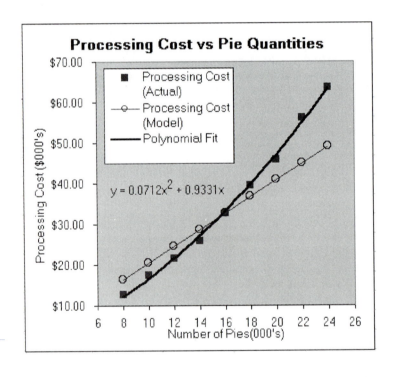

FIGURE 2.8

Cost Equation

One consequence of refining a model to include revised equations is the appearance of more technically oriented coefficients in the spreadsheet. That is, data begin to appear in the model that have no counterpart in typical management reports. Many modelers elect to "bury" these technical coefficients into the spreadsheet formulas, a violation of recommendation 5 above. A suggested remedy is use of Excel's Group and Outline options. Group and Outline can be used to suppress technical details when printing the model for reporting while preserving them in the Excel worksheet. In the Simon Pie model, the technical coefficients of the two equations, Pies Demanded and Processing

	A	B
1	**Simon Pie Co. -- Weekly Profit Model**	
2	**Decision Variable:**	
3	Pie Price	$8.00
4		
5	**Parameters:**	
6	Unit Cost, Fruit Filling ($ per pie)	$3.48
7	Unit Cost, Dough ($ per pie)	$0.30
8	Fixed Cost ($000's)	$12
9	Equation Coefficients	
10	Pie Demand Equation	
11	Intercept	48
12	Slope (Linear Coefficient)	-4
13	Processing Cost Equation	
14	Linear Coefficient	0.9331
15	Quadratic Coefficient	0.0712
16	**Physical Results (000's)**	
17	Pies Demanded and Sold	16.0
18	**Financial Results ($000's)**	
19	Revenue	$128
20	Processing Cost	$33
21	Ingredients Cost	$60
22	Overhead Cost	$12
23	Total Cost	$106
24	Profit (before tax)	$22

	A	B
1	**Simon Pie Co. —**	
2	**Decision Variable:**	
3	Pie Price	8
4		
5	**Parameters:**	
6	Unit Cost, Fruit Fillir	3.48
7	Unit Cost, Dough ($	0.3
8	Fixed Cost ($000's)	12
9	Equation Coefficier	
10	Pie Demand Equati	
11	Intercept	48
12	Slope (Linear Co	-4
13	Processing Cost Ec	
14	Linear Coefficien	0.9331
15	Quadratic Coeffic	0.0712
16	**Physical Results (0**	
17	Pies Demanded and S	=B11+B12*B3
18	**Financial Results (**	
19	Revenue	=B17*B3
20	Processing Cost	=(B14+B15*B17)*B
21	Ingredients Cost	=(B6+B7)*B17
22	Overhead Cost	=B8
23	Total Cost	=SUM(B20:B22)
24	Profit (before tax)	=B19-B23

FIGURE 2.9

Revised Simon Pie Model

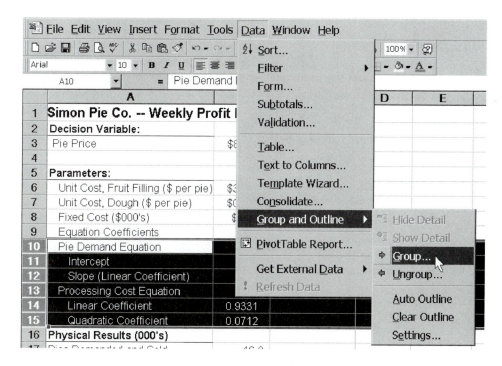

FIGURE 2.10

Grouping Rows for Outlining in the Simon Pie Model

Cost, can be suppressed for printing reports by selecting their rows and choosing the Group menu item, as shown in Figure 2.10.

Clicking the − button in the outline in Figure 2.11 will collapse those rows for printing and display.

Clicking the + button will reveal the rows again for modeling and analysis, as shown in Figure 2.12.

1 2		A	B
	1	**Simon Pie Co. -- Weekly Profit Model**	
	2	Decision Variable:	
	3	Pie Price	$8.00
	4		
	5	Parameters:	
	6	Unit Cost, Fruit Filling ($ per pie)	$3.48
	7	Unit Cost, Dough ($ per pie)	$0.30
	8	Fixed Cost ($000's)	$12
	9	Equation Coefficients	
	10	Pie Demand Equation	
	11	Intercept	48
	12	Slope (Linear Coefficient)	-4
	13	Processing Cost Equation	
	14	Linear Coefficient	0.9331
	15	Quadratic Coefficient	0.0712
	16	**Physical Results (000's)**	
	17	Pies Demanded and Sold	16.0

FIGURE 2.11

Outlining in Simon Pie Model

1 2		A	B
	1	**Simon Pie Co. -- Weekly Profit Model**	
	2	Decision Variable:	
	3	Pie Price	$8.00
	4		
	5	Parameters:	
	6	Unit Cost, Fruit Filling ($ per pie)	$3.48
	7	Unit Cost, Dough ($ per pie)	$0.30
	8	Fixed Cost ($000's)	$12
	9	Equation Coefficients	
	16	**Physical Results (000's)**	
	17	Pies Demanded and Sold	16.0

FIGURE 2.12

Collapsed Outline in
Simon Pie Model

"WHAT IF?" PROJECTION

Once the behavior of the individual relationships are validated, systematic analysis of the model can begin. The simplest analysis applied to spreadsheet models is to project the consequences of alternative inputs, called a **"What if?" projection.**[2] A "What if?" projection is exactly what the name suggests. Simon wants to know what happens to some endogenous variable of interest if some characteristic of his operating environment (a parameter) or his decision variable changes in a specified way. Obviously, such questions are fundamental to any management task, and hence, "What if?" projection is by far the most popular use made of spreadsheet models. Using his final model, Simon may examine the Profit consequences of changes in his assumptions and/or decisions. Figure 2.13 shows different snapshot results of two of Simon's "What if?" questions, the Profit for Pie Price amounts of $7 and $9, respectively.

Although straightforward, "What if?" projection in Excel suffers from three shortcomings:

1. Unless separate snapshot printouts are made, the results of a new "What if?" projection overwrites the results of any previous one when the worksheet recalculates for the new input, thereby making comparisons difficult;

2. It is hard to "see" or "get a feel" for the relationships while reviewing only one "What if?" result at a time; and

3. Analysis of the model by repeated "What if?" projections is somewhat haphazard.

Fortunately, Excel has built in commands to address each of these shortcomings. In the case that the model is contained in a single column, the most general way to tabulate multiple "What if?" projections is by copying the model into adjacent columns, one column for each "What If?" scenario.[3] In effect, each column becomes a copy of the original model,

---

[2] Some modelers call this "forecasting," but we prefer to preserve that term for use with probabilistic models.
[3] If the model already occupies several columns, then Excel's report generator, the Scenario Manager, is an alternative way to generate multiple scenarios.

	A	B
1	**Simon Pie Co. -- Weekly Profit Model**	
2	**Decision Variable:**	
3	Pie Price	$7.00
4		
5	**Parameters:**	
6	Unit Cost, Fruit Filling ($ per pie)	$3.48
7	Unit Cost, Dough ($ per pie)	$0.30
8	Fixed Cost ($000's)	$12
9	Equation Coefficients	
16	**Physical Results (000's)**	
17	Pies Demanded and Sold	20.0
18	**Financial Results ($000's)**	
19	Revenue	$140
20	Processing Cost	$47
21	Ingredients Cost	$76
22	Overhead Cost	$12
23	Total Cost	$135
24	Profit (before tax)	$5

	A	B
1	**Simon Pie Co. -- Weekly Profit Model**	
2	**Decision Variable:**	
3	Pie Price	$9.00
4		
5	**Parameters:**	
6	Unit Cost, Fruit Filling ($ per pie)	$3.48
7	Unit Cost, Dough ($ per pie)	$0.30
8	Fixed Cost ($000's)	$12
9	Equation Coefficients	
16	**Physical Results (000's)**	
17	Pies Demanded and Sold	12.0
18	**Financial Results ($000's)**	
19	Revenue	$108
20	Processing Cost	$21
21	Ingredients Cost	$45
22	Overhead Cost	$12
23	Total Cost	$79
24	Profit (before tax)	$29

FIGURE 2.13

Two "What if?" Projections for Simon Pie Model

	A	B	C	D	E	F	G	H
1	**Simon Pie Co. -- Weekly Profit Model**							
2	**Decision Variable:**							
3	Pie Price	$6.00	$7.00	$8.00	$9.00	$9.50	$10.00	$11.00
4								
5	**Parameters:**							
6	Unit Cost, Fruit Filling ($ per pie)	$3.48	$3.48	$3.48	$3.48	$3.48	$3.48	$3.48
7	Unit Cost, Dough ($ per pie)	$0.30	$0.30	$0.30	$0.30	$0.30	$0.30	$0.30
8	Fixed Cost ($000's)	$12	$12	$12	$12	$12	$12	$12
9	Equation Coefficients							
16	**Physical Results (000's)**							
17	Pies Demanded and Sold	24.0	20.0	16.0	12.0	10.0	8.0	4.0
18	**Financial Results ($000's)**							
19	Revenue	$144	$140	$128	$108	$95	$80	$44
20	Processing Cost	$63	$47	$33	$21	$16	$12	$5
21	Ingredients Cost	$91	$76	$60	$45	$38	$30	$15
22	Overhead Cost	$12	$12	$12	$12	$12	$12	$12
23	Total Cost	$166	$135	$106	$79	$66	$54	$32
24	Profit (before tax)	($22)	$5	$22	$29	$29	$26	$12

FIGURE 2.14

Simon Pie Model—Alternative Decisions

allowing the consequences of multiple changes in data values to be compared and contrasted, as illustrated in Figure 2.14.

Also, in the case of a systematic change in a single variable, this layout of the model is suited for using the Chart Wizard to produce graphs of model results, as shown in Figure 2.15. In this example, from the graph it is easy to verify that the performance measure, Profit, is largest at a Pie Price of about $9.25 and that the break-even point of zero Profit occurs at a Pie Price of about $6.75.

The Simon Pie model in Figure 2.14 uses columns for replicating the model to allow multiple "What if?" projections to be tabulated together, in this case for several candidate weekly pie prices. In other versions of the model, columns may be designated as time intervals, as shown in Figure 2.16 in which four weekly models have been aggregated to produce a consolidated monthly model. For Simon Pie the monthly model is created by summation of variables from the four weekly models. In other settings, consolidation is more complicated than simple summations. For example, quantities of inventories might have to be tracked over time.

TIP: *If the X-axis data are not evenly spaced—that is, no common interval between points—be sure to use Excel's XY Scatter plot chart type. Other chart types will distort the chart's true appearance if X-axis data are not evenly spaced. See the Excel Appendix for additional information.*

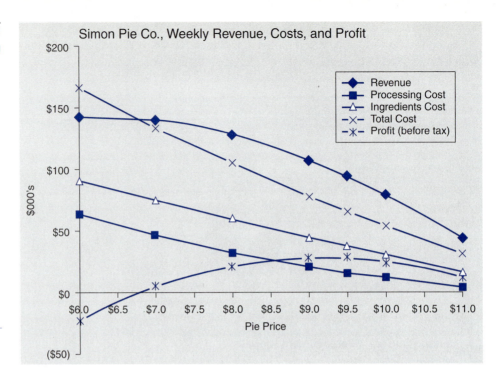

FIGURE 2.15

Revenue, Cost, and Profit Graph, Simon Pie

	A	B	C	D	E	F
1	**Simon Pie Co. -- Monthly Profit Model**					
2		Week 1	Week 2	Week 3	Week 4	Total
3	**Decision Variable:**					
4	Pie Price	$9.00	$9.40	$8.90	$9.20	
5	**Parameters:**					
6	Unit Cost, Fruit Filling ($ per pie)	$3.48	$3.43	$3.52	$3.47	
7	Unit Cost, Dough ($ per pie)	$0.30	$0.28	$0.31	$0.30	
8	Fixed Cost ($000's)	$12	$12	$12	$12	
9	Equation Coefficients					
16	**Physical Results (000's)**					
17	Pies Demanded and Sold	12.0	10.4	12.4	11.2	46.0
18	**Financial Results ($000's)**					
19	Revenue	$108.00	$97.76	$110.36	$103.04	$419.16
20	Processing Cost	$ 21.45	$17.41	$ 22.52	$ 19.38	$ 80.76
21	Ingredients Cost	$ 45.36	$38.58	$ 47.49	$ 42.22	$173.66
22	Overhead Cost	$ 12.00	$12.00	$ 12.00	$ 12.00	$ 48.00
23	Total Cost	$ 78.81	$67.99	$ 82.01	$ 73.61	$302.42
24	Profit (before tax)	$ 29.19	$29.77	$ 28.35	$ 29.43	$116.74

FIGURE 2.16

Simon Pie Monthly Model

2.3   EXAMPLE TWO—XERTECH COPY, INC.

Many spreadsheet models have only a few model inputs (parameters and decision variables), and logic and performance measures defined almost exclusively by definitions from financial accounting. Analysis consists of examining alternative outcomes for various model inputs, as illustrated by the XerTech example.

Emily and Bill Peterson have decided to start a company, XerTech Copy, that will place self-service copy machines onto customer premises in libraries, universities, high schools, shopping malls, and so on. They plan to keep capital costs to a minimum by leasing heavy-duty copiers that have a self-service coin device attached. In addition to the lease cost and other expenses of the copier, XerTech would pay a fee to the customer organization providing the space for the copier. This fee would consist of a fixed monthly space rent. As part of their business plan for XerTech, Emily and Bill have made the following assumptions:

Number of Copiers Leased (decision variable)	40
Price Charged per Copy (decision variable)	$.05
Variable Cost per Copy (supplies, repairs, etc.)	$.03
Monthly Copier Space Rental Rate (decision variable)	$150
Other Monthly Expenses:	
Lease Cost of Each Copier	$250
Coin Collection Labor per Copier	$35
Miscellaneous Fixed Costs per Copier	$50

They developed the spreadsheet model in Figure 2.17 for analyzing the profitability of their new venture. Similar to the Simon Pie example, the layout of the Petersons' Excel worksheet is in a form we recommend for ease of building, debugging, and interpretation of models. They have (1) placed text labels in many of the rows and columns and (2) included the units of measure for each quantity. These labels assist in understanding the meaning of the numbers in the spreadsheet. Also, the first seven rows present (3) the important exogenous inputs (parameters) to the model. All the formulas use cell references to these parameter cells instead of using the parameter data directly as

	A	B	C	D	E	F
1	**XerTech Copy Inc.**					
2	Average Monthly Expense per Copier			No. of Copiers Leased		40
3	Monthly Lease Cost	$250.00				
4	Copier Service Cost	$35.00		Price Charged per Copy		$0.05
5	Other Fixed Costs	$50.00		Variable Cost per Copy		$0.03
6	Fixed Expense per Copier	$335.00		Margin per Copy		$0.02
7	Space Rental Rate	$150.00				
8						
9	Monthly					
10	Copies/Month/Copier	30,000				
11	Revenue	$60,000				
12	Cost of Goods Sold	$36,000				
13	Contribution Margin	$24,000				
14	General & Admin. Costs	$19,400				
15	Net Income	$4,600				

	A	B	C	D	E	F
1	**XerTech Copy Inc.**					
2	Average Monthly Expe				No. of Copiers Leased	40
3	Monthly Lease Cost	250				
4	Copier Service Cost	35			Price Charged per Copy	0.05
5	Other Fixed Costs	50			Variable Cost per Copy	0.03
6	Fixed Expense per Copier	=SUM(B3:B5)			Margin per Copy	=F4-F5
7	Space Rental Rate	150				
8						
9	Monthly					
10	Copies/Month/Copier	30000				
11	Revenue	=$F$2*B10*$F$4				
12	Cost of Goods Sold	=$F$2*B10*$F$5				
13	Contribution Margin	=B11-B12				
14	General & Admin. Costs	=$F$2*($B$6+$B$7)				
15	Net Income	=B13-B14				

FIGURE 2.17

The First XerTech Spreadsheet

numbers in the formula equations. The remaining rows constitute (4) the input variable of interest (Copies per Month per Copier), and (5) the main logic of the model, in this case an income statement that produces the output performance measure calculation, Monthly Net Income.

The Petersons are considering several alternative arrangements for copier space rental payments. In addition to offering the fixed monthly space rent of $150 per copier per month, they might prefer to offer their customers a lower space rent plus a per-copy commission payment for each copy made. For example, the customer organization might prefer to receive a space rent of only $50 per month per copier but receive a commission of one-half cent per copy made. A third option being considered is a fixed monthly rent of $75 plus a per-copy commission payment of one cent, paid only for that portion of the monthly volume that exceeds a predetermined cutoff, such as 20,000 copies per month. Before announcing these alternative rental schemes, the Petersons are interested in knowing how the break-even volumes for their new venture compare among the three alternatives.

Rather than writing and analyzing each alternative as a separate model in different worksheets, presenting three models, one alternative per column, in a single worksheet is the preferred formulation. This allows immediate managerial comparisons across the major alternatives, as shown in Figure 2.18.

	A	B	C	D
1	**XerTech Copy Inc.**			
2	Average Monthly Expense per Copier		No. of Copiers Rented	40
3	Monthly Lease Cost	$250.00		
4	Copier Service Cost	$35.00	Price Charged per Copy	$0.05
5	Other Fixed Costs	$50.00	Variable Cost per Copy	$0.03
6	xed Expense per Copier	$335.00	Margin per Copy	$0.02
7				
8		Alternative 1	Alternative 2	Alternative 3
9		Fixed Rental Fee	Rental Fee + Commission	Rental Fee + Commission above Cutoff
10	Copies/Month/Copier	30,000	30,000	30,000
11	Space Rental Rate	$150.00	$50.00	$75.00
12	Commission Rate		$0.005	$0.01
13	Commission cuts in at			20,000
14	Monthly Income	With No Commission	With Commission	With Commission on Sales>Cut Off
15	Revenue	$60,000	$60,000	$60,000
16	Cost of Goods Sold	$36,000	$42,000	$40,000
17	Contribution Margin	$24,000	$18,000	$20,000
18	General & Admin. Costs	$19,400	$15,400	$16,400
19	Net Income	$4,600	$2,600	$3,600

	A	B	C	D
1	**XerTech C**			
2	Average Month		No. of Copiers Rented	40
3	Monthly Lease	250		
4	Copier Service	35	Price Charged per Copy	0.05
5	Other Fixed Co	50	Variable Cost per Copy	0.03
6	Fixed Expense	=SUM(B3:B5)	Margin per Copy	=D4-D5
7				
8			Scenario	
9		Fixed Rental Fee	Rental Fee + Commission	Rental Fee + Commission above Cutoff
10	Copies/Month/	30000	30000	30000
11	Space Rental F	150	50	75
12	Commission Re		0.005	0.01
13	Commission cu			20000
14	Monthly Income	With No Commission	With Commission	With Commission on Sales>Cut Off
15	Revenue	=$D$2*B10*$D$4	=$D$2*C10*$D$4	=$D$2*D10*$D$4
16	Cost of Goods S	=$D$2*B10*$D$5	=$D$2*C10*($D$5+C12)	=$D$2*(D10*$D$5+IF(D10<=D13,0,D12*(D10-D13)))
17	Contribution Ma	=B15-B16	=C15-C16	=D15-D16
18	General & Adm	=$D$2*($B$6+B11)	=$D$2*($B$6+C11)	=$D$2*($B$6+D11)
19	Net Income	=B17-B18	=C17-C18	=D17-D18

FIGURE 2.18

The Second XerTech Spreadsheet: Three Rental Payment Alternatives

Since columns are devoted to major alternatives in the XerTech model, recording "What if?" projections for an alternative by copying formulas across columns as in Simon Pie is not possible. However, if only one exogenous variable is to be systematically varied, Excel's Data Table 1 command can be used to record the "What if?" projections for any one of the alternatives. That is, Data Table 1 allows a single exogenous variable to be varied over a specified range and tabulates the results for each of multiple endogenous variables (consequential and performance measure variables).

Before evoking **Data Table,** the values of the one exogenous variable must be defined in an empty area on a worksheet. The values may be given in a column or in a row; this example, shown in Figure 2.19, will present the values in a row. Next, each of the endogenous variables of interest is presented in a separate row below the first one. There is no limit to the number of these rows. The column to the left of the exogenous variable row (column G in Figure 2.19) is special. It must contain an empty cell (G2 in this case) for the row containing the values of the exogenous variable, and for the remaining rows (G3:G7), a cell reference to the model's cell that computes that row's endogenous quantity. Optionally, the next column to the left (column F in Figure 2.19) may contain labels. (These labels are for documentation and are not a part of the Data Table command.) The final layout of the Data Table (called a Data Table 1 because only one exogenous variable is allowed to vary) and its formulas for the first alternative XerTech model is given in Figure 2.19.

Next, select the cells of all the table's rows, including the left column cell references to the model, but not the labels, if present, and select the Table command as shown in Figure 2.20.

Since the exogenous variable's values are given in the first row (row 2 in this case), the cell reference in the model into which those values are to be placed is indicated in the Table

	F	G	H	I	J	K	L	M	N
1	Data Table — Alternative 1								
2	Copies/Month/Copier		10000	15000	20000	25000	30000	35000	40000
3	Revenue	$60,000							
4	Cost of Goods Sold	$36,000							
5	Contribution Margin	$24,000							
6	General & Admin. Costs	$19,400							
7	Net Income	$4,600							

	F	G	H	I	J	K	L	M	N
1	Data Table — Alternative 1								
2	Copies/Month/Copier		10000	15000	20000	25000	30000	35000	40000
3	Revenue	=B15							
4	Cost of Goods Sold	=B16							
5	Contribution Margin	=B17							
6	General & Admin. Costs	=B18							
7	Net Income	=B19							

FIGURE 2.19

Data Table 1 Layout

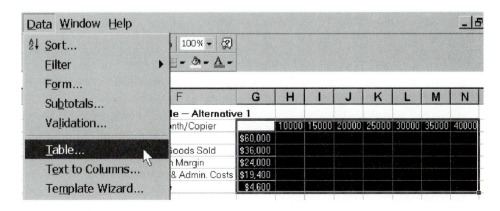

FIGURE 2.20

Evoking Data Table

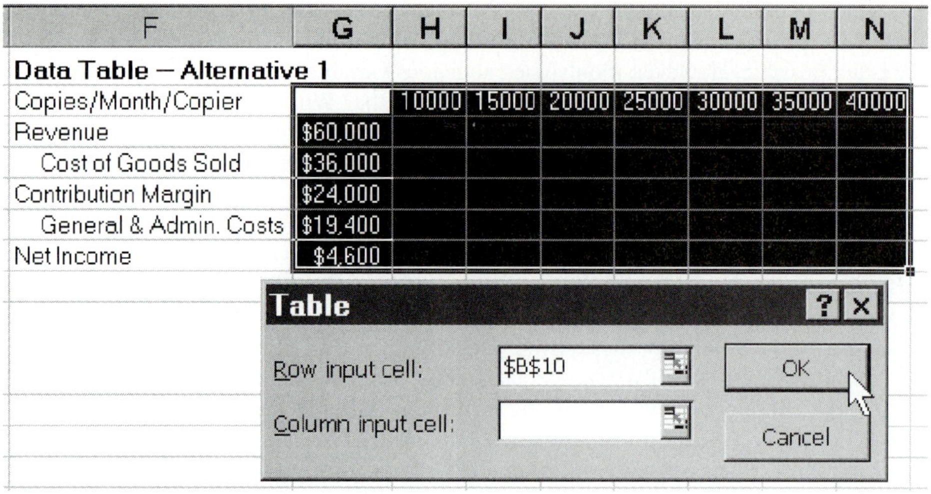

F	G	H	I	J	K	L	M	N
Data Table — Alternative 1								
Copies/Month/Copier		10000	15000	20000	25000	30000	35000	40000
Revenue	$60,000							
Cost of Goods Sold	$36,000							
Contribution Margin	$24,000							
General & Admin. Costs	$19,400							
Net Income	$4,600							

Table ? ×

Row input cell: $B$10   OK

Column input cell: Cancel

FIGURE 2.21

Completing the Table Dialog

F	G	H	I	J	K	L	M	N
Data Table — Alternative 1								
Copies/Month/Copier		10000	15000	20000	25000	30000	35000	40000
Revenue	$60,000	$20,000	$30,000	$40,000	$50,000	$60,000	$70,000	$80,000
Cost of Goods Sold	$36,000	$12,000	$18,000	$24,000	$30,000	$36,000	$42,000	$48,000
Contribution Margin	$24,000	$8,000	$12,000	$16,000	$20,000	$24,000	$28,000	$32,000
General & Admin. Costs	$19,400	$19,400	$19,400	$19,400	$19,400	$19,400	$19,400	$19,400
Net Income	$4,600	($11,400)	($7,400)	($3,400)	$600	$4,600	$8,600	$12,600

FIGURE 2.22

Completed Data Table 1

dialog in the "Row input cell" field, as shown in Figure 2.21. (Conversely, had they been listed in a column, the "Column input cell" field would have been used.) The other input cell dialog box is left empty.

Clicking OK causes the model to be evaluated for each input value of the exogenous variable, tabulating the listed endogenous variable values from the model for that input value, as shown in Figure 2.22.

As with the Simon Pie example, this information can be used create a chart, as shown in Figure 2.23. Note: Because of the blank cell in the upper left corner of the table, the Chart Wizard automatically ignores the unnecessary information in column G.

From the graph it is easy to verify that the performance measure, Net Income, is linear in copier volume and that the break-even point (zero Net Income) occurs at a copier volume of about 24,000 per month per copier.

More precise estimates of interesting model outputs can be found by use of Excel's **Goal Seek** command. Goal Seek automatically searches for a value of a single model input variable that yields a given desired value of a single endogenous output variable, typically a performance measure. For example, Goal Seek can be used to find the break-even value for Copies per Month per Copier. First, select the "Goal Seek . . ." item from Excel's Tools menu, as shown in Figure 2.24.

By typing the cell references or by clicking the worksheet cell, specify the endogenous output variable cell ("Set cell") as being Net Income, specify the "To value" cell as the break-even value of zero, select the "By changing cell" as being monthly copier volume, and click OK, as shown in Figure 2.25.

Excel will systematically iterate the model of Alternative 1 for different Changing Cell input values to achieve the desired output Set cell result, if possible, as shown in Figure 2.26.[4] In this case the break-even volume is found to be 24,250 copies per month per copier.

---

[4]A systematic search is performed, starting from the cell's initial value. If more than one changing cell value produces the desired target value of the output cell, the first one found will stop the Goal Seek search. Discontinuities in a model caused by, for example, IF() statements, may cause Goal Seek to fail.

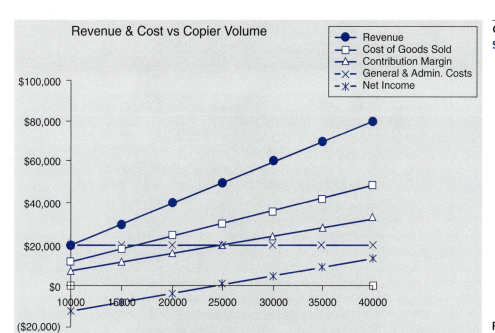

FIGURE 2.23

Chart of Data Table 1 Results

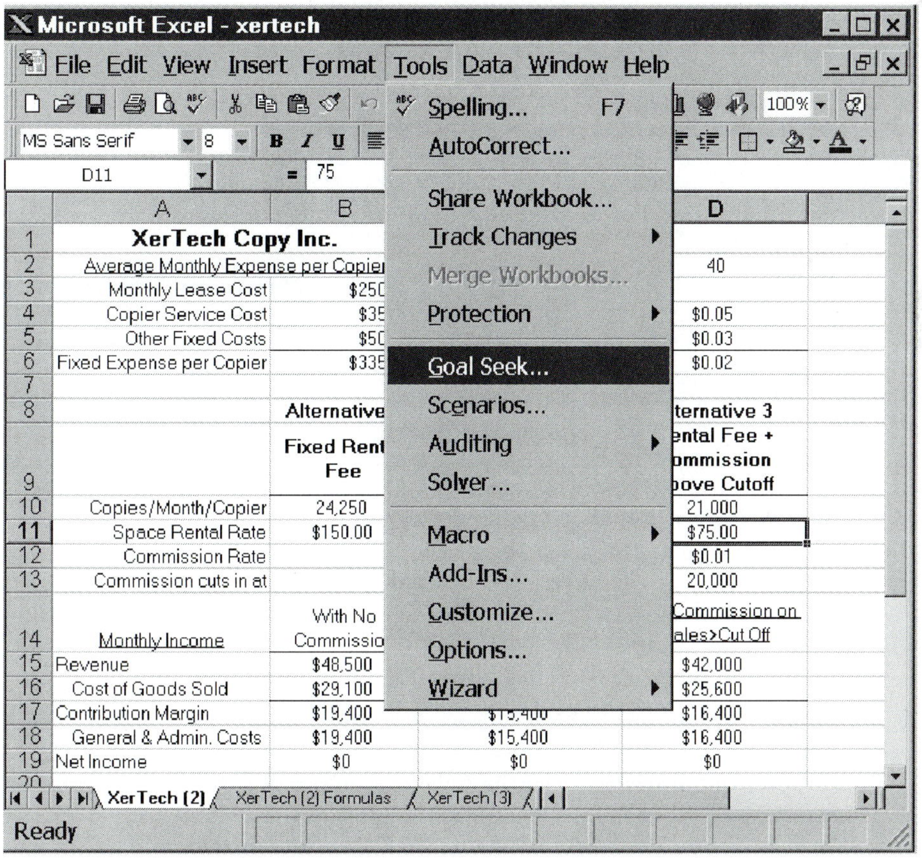

FIGURE 2.24

Goal Seek

TIP: *Specifying cell references in Excel dialogs by clicking the worksheet cells produces absolute cell reference addresses in the dialog box. In all cases the use of either absolute or relative cell references in dialogs produces the same results.*

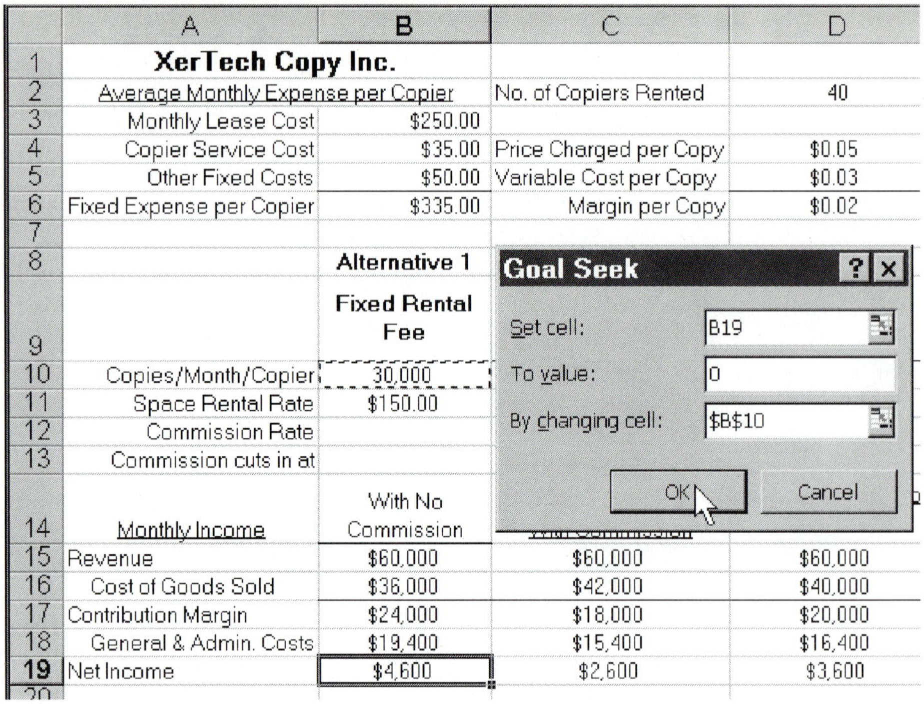

	A	B	C	D
1	**XerTech Copy Inc.**			
2	Average Monthly Expense per Copier		No. of Copiers Rented	40
3	Monthly Lease Cost	$250.00		
4	Copier Service Cost	$35.00	Price Charged per Copy	$0.05
5	Other Fixed Costs	$50.00	Variable Cost per Copy	$0.03
6	Fixed Expense per Copier	$335.00	Margin per Copy	$0.02
7				
8		Alternative 1		
9		Fixed Rental Fee		
10	Copies/Month/Copier	30,000		
11	Space Rental Rate	$150.00		
12	Commission Rate			
13	Commission cuts in at			
14	Monthly Income	With No Commission		
15	Revenue	$60,000	$60,000	$60,000
16	Cost of Goods Sold	$36,000	$42,000	$40,000
17	Contribution Margin	$24,000	$18,000	$20,000
18	General & Admin. Costs	$19,400	$15,400	$16,400
19	Net Income	$4,600	$2,600	$3,600

Goal Seek dialog box:
- Set cell: B19
- To value: 0
- By changing cell: $B$10
- [OK] [Cancel]

FIGURE 2.25

Goal Seek Dialog

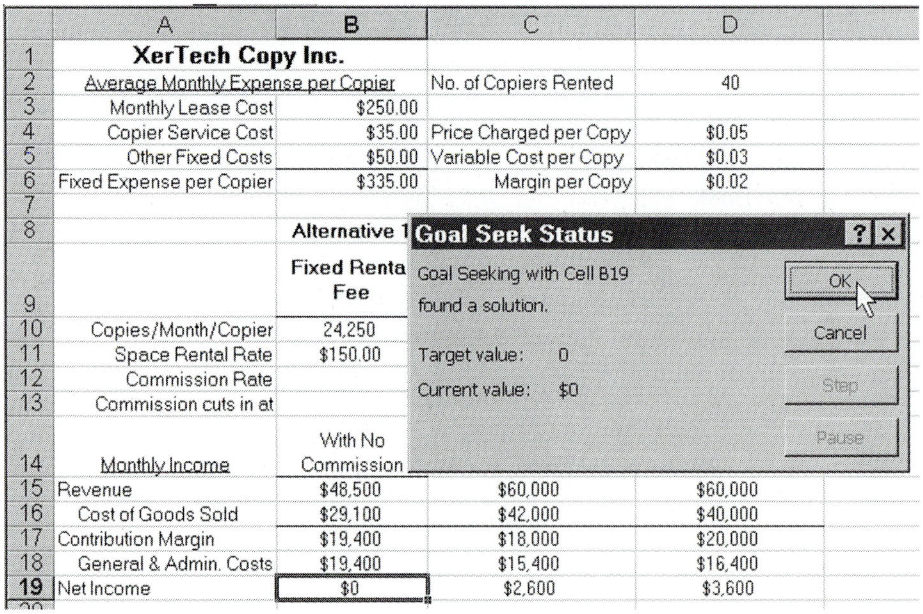

	A	B	C	D
1	**XerTech Copy Inc.**			
2	Average Monthly Expense per Copier		No. of Copiers Rented	40
3	Monthly Lease Cost	$250.00		
4	Copier Service Cost	$35.00	Price Charged per Copy	$0.05
5	Other Fixed Costs	$50.00	Variable Cost per Copy	$0.03
6	Fixed Expense per Copier	$335.00	Margin per Copy	$0.02
7				
8		Alternative 1		
9		Fixed Rental Fee		
10	Copies/Month/Copier	24,250		
11	Space Rental Rate	$150.00		
12	Commission Rate			
13	Commission cuts in at			
14	Monthly Income	With No Commission		
15	Revenue	$48,500	$60,000	$60,000
16	Cost of Goods Sold	$29,100	$42,000	$40,000
17	Contribution Margin	$19,400	$18,000	$20,000
18	General & Admin. Costs	$19,400	$15,400	$16,400
19	Net Income	$0	$2,600	$3,600

Goal Seek Status dialog box:
- Goal Seeking with Cell B19 found a solution.
- Target value: 0
- Current value: $0
- [OK] [Cancel] [Step] [Pause]

FIGURE 2.26

Monthly Break-Even Volume, Alternative 1

Repeated application of Goal Seek to each of the three Net Income cells produces the required break-even comparisons, as shown in Figure 2.27.

The Petersons are also interested in the points of indifference in Net Income across the three alternatives. For example, assuming 30,000 copies per month per copier, the original alternative of fixed rental payment of $150 per month per copier and the alternative commission rates and cutoff shown in Figure 2.27, what fixed rental rates for each of the two new alternatives produce indifference in terms of Net Income in comparison to the original alternative? To answer this question, add formulas to the worksheet of Figure 2.18 to subtract the Net Income of Alternative 2 and the Net Income of Alternative 3 from that of Alternative 1, respectively, as shown in Figure 2.28.

	Alternative 1	Alternative 2	Alternative 3
	Fixed Rental Fee	Rental Fee + Commission	Rental Fee + Commission above Cutoff
Copies/Month/Copier	24,250	25,667	21,000
Space Rental Rate	$150.00	$50.00	$75.00
Commission Rate		$0.005	$0.01
Commission cuts in at			20,000
Monthly Income	With No Commission	With Commission	With Commission on Sales>Cut Off
Revenue	$48,500	$51,334	$42,000
Cost of Goods Sold	$29,100	$35,934	$25,600
Contribution Margin	$19,400	$15,400	$16,400
General & Admin. Costs	$19,400	$15,400	$16,400
Net Income	$0	$0	$0

FIGURE 2.27

Break-Even Comparisons

	A	B	C	D
				With Commission on Sales>Cut Off
14	Monthly Income	With No Commission	With Commission	
15	Revenue	=$D$2*B10*$D$4	=$D$2*C10*$D$4	=$D$2*D10*$D$4
16	Cost of Goods S	=$D$2*B10*$D$5	=$D$2*C10*($D$5+C12)	=$D$2*(D10*$D$5+IF(D10<=D13,0,D12*(D10-D13)))
17	Contribution Ma	=B15-B16	=C15-C16	=D15-D16
18	General & Adm	=$D$2*($B$6+B11)	=$D$2*($B$6+C11)	=$D$2*($B$6+D11)
19	Net Income	=B17-B18	=C17-C18	=D17-D18
20		Net Inc., Alternative 1 - 2	=B19-C19	
21			Net Inc., Alternative 1 - 3	=B19-D19

FIGURE 2.28

Calculating Alternatives' Net Income Differences

This allows reapplication of Goal Seek to find the points of indifference; that is, the points where the difference in Net Income compared to Alternative 1 are zero, as shown in Figure 2.29 and Figure 2.30.

While the results in Figure 2.30 are easy to deduce algebraically for this case, the Goal Seek approach works for more complicated models where the algebra would be prohibitively difficult to work out.

If only two model inputs are of "What if?" interest, then a compact analysis is available by directly expanding the model or using Excel's Data Table 2 command. This will be illustrated in the next example.

2.4   EXAMPLE THREE—ROSA RAISINS

Located in California's Napa Wine Country, Rosa Raisins (RR) is a food processing company that purchases surplus grapes in the autumn from grape growers, dries them into raisins, applies a layer of sugar, and sells the sugar-coated raisins to cereal and candy companies. In the spring, at the beginning of the grape growing season, RR has several interrelated decisions to make. The first involves how many grapes to buy under an existing grower supply contract, and the second relates to the price to charge for the sugar-coated raisins RR sells.

RR has an option contract with a grower who, if asked in the spring, must supply a given amount of grapes in the autumn at a fixed cost of $.25 per pound. The balance between RR's grape requirements and any supplied by the grower must be purchased by RR in the autumn from the open market at a price that could vary from an historical low of $.15 per pound to a high of $.35 per pound.

The other major decision facing RR is the price to charge for sugar-coated raisins. RR has several customers—large breakfast cereal and candy processors—who, together, buy all RR's output of sugar-coated raisins. RR negotiates with these processors as a group to

	A	B	C	D	E
8		Alternative 1	Alternative 2	Alternative 3	
9		Fixed Rental Fee	Rental Fee + Commission	Rental Fee + Commission above Cutoff	
10	Copies/Month/Copier	30,000	30,000	30,000	
11	Space Rental Rate	$150.00	$50.00	$75.00	
12	Commission Rate		$0.005	$0.01	
13	Commission cuts in at			20,000	
14	Monthly Income	With No Commission	With Commission	**Goal Seek**	
15	Revenue	$60,000	$60,000	Set cell: $C$20	
16	Cost of Goods Sold	$36,000	$42,000		
17	Contribution Margin	$24,000	$18,000	To value: 0	
18	General & Admin. Costs	$19,400	$15,400		
19	Net Income	$4,600	$2,600	By changing cell: $C$11	
20	Net Inc., Alternative 1 - 2		$2,000		
21			Net Inc., Alternative 1 - 3		

FIGURE 2.29

Finding Space Rent Indifference, Alternative 2

	A	B	C	D
8		Alternative 1	Alternative 2	Alternative 3
9		Fixed Rental Fee	Rental Fee + Commission	Rental Fee + Commission above Cutoff
10	Copies/Month/Copier	30,000	30,000	30,000
11	Space Rental Rate	$150.00	$0.00	$50.00
12	Commission Rate		$0.005	$0.01
13	Commission cuts in at			20,000
14	Monthly Income	With No Commission	With Commission	With Commission on Sales>Cut Off
15	Revenue	$60,000	$60,000	$60,000
16	Cost of Goods Sold	$36,000	$42,000	$40,000
17	Contribution Margin	$24,000	$18,000	$20,000
18	General & Admin. Costs	$19,400	$13,400	$15,400
19	Net Income	$4,600	$4,600	$4,600
20	Net Inc., Alternative 1 - 2		$0	
21			Net Inc., Alternative 1 - 3	$0

FIGURE 2.30

Indifference Points, Alternatives 2 and 3

arrive at a price for the sugar-coated raisins and the quantity of sugar-coated raisins the processors will buy at that negotiated price. The negotiations with these processors takes place in the spring (before the autumn open market price of grapes is known) and RR's management is considering its alternatives.

RR's management concludes that the following represents its best judgment about the raisin price-quantity negotiations with the processors. Based upon prior years' experience, RR's management believes that (1) if it prices the sugar-coated raisins at $2.15 per pound, the processors as a group will demand, that is, order, 700,000 pounds of sugar-coated raisins, and (2) the total demand for sugar-coated raisins will increase by 15,000 pounds for each penny reduction in sugar-coated raisin price below $2.15.

Sugar-coated raisins are made by washing and drying grapes into raisins, followed by spraying the raisins with a sugar coating that RR buys for $.30 per pound. It takes 2.5 pounds of grapes plus .05 pound of sugar coating to make one pound of sugar-coated raisins, the balance being water that evaporates during grape drying. In addition to the raw materials cost of the grapes and sugar coating, RR's processing plant incurs a variable cost of $.20 to process one pound of grapes into raisins up to its capacity of 3,500,000 pounds of grapes. Processing more than 3,500,000 pounds of grapes requires RR to outsource the processing of those grapes to a competitor, who charges RR $.60 to process a pound of grapes into raisins. RR also incurs other fixed (overhead) costs in the grape processing plant of $200,000 per year.

Jan Thurston, RR's chief negotiator, has built the Excel model in Figure 2.31 to analyze the situation in order to guide her in the upcoming raisin price-quantity negotiations. Her goal is to examine the effect of various scenarios upon RR's profits. Figure 2.32 shows two "What if?" projections for alternative raisin prices, grapes purchased on contract, and open market price parameter values. Although many different projections could be examined using the techniques developed in the Simon Pie example, Thurston is interested in varying only two model inputs. If model analysis is restricted to at most only two input variables, then tabular or graphical representation is preferable for displaying results. In contrast to Data Table 1, Data Table 2 allows two exogenous variables to be varied over specified ranges but tabulates the results only for a single endogenous variable, usually a performance measure.

Thurston is primarily interested in annual Pre-Tax Profit as her performance measure, and so, opts for Data Table 2 analysis, varying one decision variable, sugar-coated raisin price, and one parameter, open market grape price, assuming for now the other decision variable, contract grapes purchased, is fixed at 1,000,000 pounds. Before evoking Data Table, the ranges of values for the two exogenous variables must be defined in some empty area on the Excel worksheet, as shown in Figure 2.33. Thurston has selected sugar-coated raisin prices ranging from $1.20 to $2.00 in increments of $.05 and open market grape prices ranging from $.15 to $.35 also in increments of $.05. One set of prices is entered as a row of values and the other as a column of values. As documentation, Thurston labeled each series with Text Box objects (from Excel's Drawing Toolbar) for future reference.

In the upper-left corner cell, at the intersection of each series, a reference to the single performance measure cell is entered, in this case B33, Pre-Tax Profit. Next, selecting all the

TIP: *To save typing, use Excel's Fill Series item from the Edit menu or Autofill to enter each range of values. See the Excel Appendix for details.*

	A	B
1	Rosa Raisins Model	
2	**Decision Variables:**	
3	Sugar-Coated Raisin Price per pound	$2.10
4	Contract Grapes to Buy (000's of pounds)	1,000
5	**Exogenous Market Parameters:**	
6	Contract Grape Price per pound	$0.25
7	Open Market Grape Price per pound	$0.25
8	Cost of Sugar per pound	$0.30
9	**Processing Parameters:**	
10	Internal Grape Processing Cost per Pound	$0.20
11	Internal Grape Processing Capacity (Pounds)	3,500
12	Outsourced Grape Processing Cost	$0.60
13	Pounds of Grapes per Pound of Raisins	2.5
14	Pounds of Sugar per Pound of Raisins	0.05
15	Annual Fixed Cost ($000's)	$200
16	**Raison Demand Equation Coefficients:**	
17	Base Price Parameter	$2.15
18	Base Demand (Intercept Coefficient)	700
19	Linear (Slope) Coefficient	15
20	**Physical Requirements:** (000's of pounds)	
21	Sugar-Coated Raisins Demand	775
22	Grapes Required to Meet Demand	1,841
23	Grapes Purchased under Contract	1,000
24	Grapes Purchased in Open Market	841
25	**Financial Results ($ 000's):**	
26	Revenue	$1,628
27	Internal Processing Cost	$368
28	Outsourced Processing Cost	$0
29	Raw Material, Contract Grapes	$250
30	Raw Material Cost, Open Market Grapes	$210
31	Raw Material Cost, Sugar	$12
32	Other Fixed Costs	$200
33	Profit (before tax)	$588

	A	B
1	Rosa Raisins M	
2	**Decision Variable**	
3	Sugar-Coated Raisi	2.1
4	to Buy (000's of	1000
5	**Exogenous Mark**	
6	Contract Grape Pri	0.25
7	Open Market Grape	0.25
8	Cost of Sugar per p	0.3
9	**Processing Param**	
10	Internal Grape Proc	0.2
11	Internal Grape Proc	3500
12	Outsourced Grape	0.6
13	Pounds of Grapes p	2.5
14	Pounds of Sugar pe	0.05
15	Annual Fixed Cost	200
16	**Raison Demand E**	
17	Base Price Para	2.15
18	Base Demand (Ir	700
19	Linear (Slope) C	15
20	**Physical Require**	
21	Sugar-Coated Raisi	=B18+B19*(B17-B3)*100
22	Grapes Required to	=B13*B21*(1-B14)
23	Grapes Purchased	=B4
24	Grapes Purchased	=MAX(0,B22-B23)
25	**Financial Results**	
26	Revenue	=B21*B3
27	Internal Processi	=MIN(B22,B11)*B10
28	Outsourced Proc	=IF(B22>B11,B22-B11,0)*B12
29	Raw Material, C	=B6*B23
30	Raw Material Co	=B7*B24
31	Raw Material Co	=B8*B14*B21
32	Other Fixed Cos	=B15
33	Profit (before tax)	=B26-SUM(B27:B32)

FIGURE 2.31

The Rosa Raisins Model

cells in the rectangular range, F16:W21, Thurston chooses the Table item in the Data menu. The Table dialog is then displayed, as shown in Figure 2.34.

At this point Thurston must connect each of the table's two data series to its respective exogenous input variable cells in the RR model. Since the Raisin Price series is the "row" series in the table, it is linked to cell B3 in the RR model via the "Row input cell" in the dialog. Similarly, Open Market Grape Price, the "column" series, is linked to that variable in the RR model, cell B7. Clicking OK causes Excel to take each pair of inputs, input those values into the specified input cells in the RR model, recalculate the worksheet, and place the resulting Pre-Tax Profit value into the corresponding cell in the table, as shown in Figure 2.35.

The compact representation of the table allows (1) convenient inspection of the results for finding high profit cells. However, the Data Table 2 representation allows for two other important analyses: (2) examining for possible independence between the two model input variables, and (3) sensitivity analysis. Because of their importance to model analysis in general, each of the three will be discussed separately.

As with the previous example, the obvious utility of a Data Table is the ease of inspecting the results in Figure 2.35 looking for high profit combinations of the two input series; that is, for a given row, Open Market Grape Price, examining cells in the data table reveals the profit-maximizing Raisin Price. Inspection also reveals that for any given Open Market Grape Price, there is a single Raisin Price that maximizes Pre-Tax Profit.

A less obvious, but important, second analysis focuses upon what, if any, pattern exists in the set of maximal Pre-Tax Profits for the given Open Market Grape Prices. That is, Thurston is interested to see if the profit-maximizing Raisin Price is dependent on or independent of Open Market Grape Price. The relationship is shown in the partial table in Figure 2.36 in which the maximum Pre-Tax Profit for each Open Market Grape Price has been shaded. The table in Figure 2.36 is often called a "payoff table" because it lists Thurston's Raisin Price alternatives, the values of the Open Market Grape Prices (one of which will eventually obtain), and the Pre-Tax Profit performance measure "payoff" that attaches to each combination. Note that Thurston would lower her profit-maximizing Raisin Price, if

	A	B
1	**Rosa Raisins Model**	
2	**Decision Variables:**	
3	Sugar-Coated Raisin Price per pound	$1.95
4	Contract Grapes to Buy (000's of pounds)	2,000
5	**Exogenous Market Parameters:**	
6	Contract Grape Price per pound	$0.25
7	Open Market Grape Price per pound	$0.20
8	Cost of Sugar per pound	$0.30
9	**Processing Parameters:**	
10	Internal Grape Processing Cost per Pound	$0.20
11	Internal Grape Processing Capacity (Pounds)	3,500
12	Outsourced Grape Processing Cost	$0.60
13	Pounds of Grapes per Pound of Raisins	2.5
14	Pounds of Sugar per Pound of Raisins	0.05
15	Annual Fixed Cost ($000's)	$200
16	**Raison Demand Equation Coefficients:**	
17	Base Price Parameter	$2.15
18	Base Demand (Intercept Coefficient)	700
19	Linear (Slope) Coefficient	15
20	**Physical Requirements:** (000's of pounds)	
21	Sugar-Coated Raisins Demand	1,000
22	Grapes Required to Meet Demand	2,375
23	Grapes Purchased under Contract	2,000
24	Grapes Purchased in Open Market	375
25	**Financial Results ($ 000's):**	
26	Revenue	$1,950
27	Internal Processing Cost	$475
28	Outsourced Processing Cost	$0
29	Raw Material, Contract Grapes	$500
30	Raw Material Cost, Open Market Grapes	$75
31	Raw Material Cost, Sugar	$15
32	Other Fixed Costs	$200
33	Profit (before tax)	$685

	A	B
1	**Rosa Raisins Model**	
2	**Decision Variables:**	
3	Sugar-Coated Raisin Price per pound	$2.10
4	Contract Grapes to Buy (000's of pounds)	500
5	**Exogenous Market Parameters:**	
6	Contract Grape Price per pound	$0.25
7	Open Market Grape Price per pound	$0.20
8	Cost of Sugar per pound	$0.30
9	**Processing Parameters:**	
10	Internal Grape Processing Cost per Pound	$0.20
11	Internal Grape Processing Capacity (Pounds)	3,500
12	Outsourced Grape Processing Cost	$0.60
13	Pounds of Grapes per Pound of Raisins	2.5
14	Pounds of Sugar per Pound of Raisins	0.05
15	Annual Fixed Cost ($000's)	$200
16	**Raison Demand Equation Coefficients:**	
17	Base Price Parameter	$2.15
18	Base Demand (Intercept Coefficient)	700
19	Linear (Slope) Coefficient	15
20	**Physical Requirements:** (000's of pounds)	
21	Sugar-Coated Raisins Demand	775
22	Grapes Required to Meet Demand	1,841
23	Grapes Purchased under Contract	500
24	Grapes Purchased in Open Market	1,341
25	**Financial Results ($ 000's):**	
26	Revenue	$1,628
27	Internal Processing Cost	$368
28	Outsourced Processing Cost	$0
29	Raw Material, Contract Grapes	$125
30	Raw Material Cost, Open Market Grapes	$268
31	Raw Material Cost, Sugar	$12
32	Other Fixed Costs	$200
33	Profit (before tax)	$655

FIGURE 2.32

Two Rosa Raisins
"What if?" Scenarios

	E	F	G	H	I	J	K	L	M	N	O	P	Q	R	S	T	U	V	W
14																			
15																Raisin Price			
16		=$B$33	$1.20	$1.25	$1.30	$1.35	$1.40	$1.45	$1.50	$1.55	$1.60	$1.65	$1.70	$1.75	$1.80	$1.85	$1.90	$1.95	$2.00
17	Open Mkt Grape Price	$0.15																	
18		$0.20																	
19		$0.25																	
20		$0.30																	
21		$0.35																	

FIGURE 2.33

Layout for RR's Data Table 2 Command

	E	F	G	H	I	J	K	L	M	N	O	P	Q	R	S	T	U	V	W
14																			
15				Raisin Price															
16		$588	$1.20	$1.25	$1.30	$1.35	$1.40	$1.45	$1.50	$1.55	$1.60	$1.65	$1.70	$1.75	$1.80	$1.85	$1.90	$1.95	$2.00
17	Open Mkt Grape Price	$0.15																	
18		$0.20		Table								? X							
19		$0.25																	
20		$0.30		Row Input Cell:		$B$3				OK									
21		$0.35																	
22				Column Input Cell:		$B$7				Cancel									
23																			
24																			
25																			

FIGURE 2.34

Relating Table Row and Column Inputs to RR's Model

	E	F	G	H	I	J	K	L	M	N	O	P	Q	R	S	T	U	V	W
14																			
15				Raisin Price															
16		$588	$1.20	$1.25	$1.30	$1.35	$1.40	$1.45	$1.50	$1.55	$1.60	$1.65	$1.70	$1.75	$1.80	$1.85	$1.90	$1.95	$2.00
17	Open Mkt Grape Price	$0.15	($167)	($20)	$120	$252	$377	$494	$604	$706	$801	$865	$874	$875	$868	$854	$833	$804	$767
18		$0.20	($369)	($213)	($65)	$77	$210	$336	$455	$566	$670	$743	$761	$771	$773	$768	$755	$735	$707
19		$0.25	($572)	($407)	($249)	($99)	$43	$178	$306	$426	$539	$621	$647	$666	$677	$681	$677	$666	$648
20		$0.30	($774)	($600)	($434)	($275)	($123)	$21	$157	$286	$407	$499	$534	$562	$582	$595	$600	$598	$588
21		$0.35	($976)	($794)	($618)	($450)	($290)	($137)	$8	$146	$276	$377	$421	$457	$486	$508	$522	$529	$528

FIGURE 2.35

Pre-Tax Profit Data Table for RR Model (Contract Grape Quantity = 1000)

	E	F	Q	R	S	T	U	V	W
14									
15					Raisin Price				
16		$588	$1.70	$1.75	$1.80	$1.85	$1.90	$1.95	$2.00
17	Open Mkt Grape Price	$0.15	$874	$875	$868	$854	$833	$804	$767
18		$0.20	$761	$771	$773	$768	$755	$735	$707
19		$0.25	$647	$666	$677	$681	$677	$666	$648
20		$0.30	$534	$562	$582	$595	$600	$598	$588
21		$0.35	$421	$457	$486	$508	$522	$529	$528

FIGURE 2.36

Checking Table for Independence of the Two Factors

she knew in advance that the Open Market Grape Price were to fall, thereby confirming a dependent relationship between the two sets of prices and profit. If the profit-maximizing Raisin Price had remained the same no matter the value of Open Market Grape Price, then that independence would allow Thurston to ignore the uncertainty in the future Open Market Grape Price in her Raisin Price negotiations.

In general, if a decision variable is independent of some other input parameter, then variations in that parameter can be ignored, an important modeling insight. In this case, however, the optimal Raisin Price is not independent of the Open Market Grape Price; lower Open Market Grape Prices imply lower Raisin Prices to maximize profit. Since the Open Market Grape Price is not known at the time Thurston must negotiate the Raisin Price, she must, therefore, make a forecast of the Open Market Grape Price in order to proceed. For now, we assume Thurston will use her best guess of the eventual Open Market Grape Price. (Later in Chapter 10 on Decision Analysis, we will examine more rational ways to model uncertain situations like this than just guessing.)

The payoff table in Figure 2.36 affords the third analysis technique to assist Thurston in her negotiations, **sensitivity analysis.** In general, sensitivity analysis refers to assessing how the changes in some model input variable affect the changes in some other variable,

	O	P	Q	R	S	T	U	V	W
16	$1.60	$1.65	$1.70	$1.75	$1.80	$1.85	$1.90	$1.95	$2.00
17	$801	$865	$874	$875	$868	$854	$833	$804	$767
18	$670	$743	$761	$771	$773	$768	$755	$735	$707
19	$539	$621	$647	$666	$677	$681	$677	$666	$648
20	$407	$499	$534	$562	$582	$595	$600	$598	$588
21	$276	$377	$421	$457	$486	$508	$522	$529	$528
22									
23					Raisin Price Change				
24				-5%	-3%	0%	3%	5%	
25				$1.75	$1.80	$1.85	$1.90	$1.95	
26	Open Mkt Grape Price Change	-40%	$0.15	28%	27%	25%	22%	18%	
27		-20%	$0.20	13%	13%	13%	11%	8%	
28		0%	$0.25	-2%	-1%	$681	-1%	-2%	
29		20%	$0.30	-18%	-15%	-13%	-12%	-12%	
30		40%	$0.35	-33%	-29%	-25%	-23%	-22%	

	O	P	Q	R	S	T	U	V
16	1.6	1.65	1.7	1.75	1.8	1.85	1.9	1.95
17	800.718	865.4375	873.9	874.875	868.3437	854.3125	832.7812	803.75
18	669.625	743.25	760.6	770.5	772.875	767.75	755.125	735
19	538.531	621.0625	647.3	666.125	677.4062	681.1875	677.4687	666.25
20	407.437	498.875	534.0	561.75	581.9375	594.625	599.8125	597.5
21	276.343	376.6875	420.7	457.375	486.4687	508.0625	522.1562	528.75
22								
23						Raisin Price Change		
24				=(R25-$T$25)/$T$25	=(S25-$T	=(T25-$T$25)/$T$25	=(U25-$T	=(V25-$T
25				1.75	1.8	1.85	1.9	1.95
26	Open Mkt Grape Price Change	=(Q26-$Q$28)/$Q$28	0.15	=(R17-$T$28)/$T$28	=(S17-$T	=(T17-$T$28)/$T$28	=(U17-$T	=(V17-$T
27		=(Q27-$Q$28)/$Q$28	0.2	=(R18-$T$28)/$T$28	=(S18-$T	=(T18-$T$28)/$T$28	=(U18-$T	=(V18-$T
28		=(Q28-$Q$28)/$Q$28	0.25	=(R19-$T$28)/$T$28	=(S19-$T	=T19	=(U19-$T	=(V19-$T
29		=(Q29-$Q$28)/$Q$28	0.3	=(R20-$T$28)/$T$28	=(S20-$T	=(T20-$T$28)/$T$28	=(U20-$T	=(V20-$T
30		=(Q30-$Q$28)/$Q$28	0.35	=(R21-$T$28)/$T$28	=(S21-$T	=(T21-$T$28)/$T$28	=(U21-$T	=(V21-$T

FIGURE 2.37

Sensitivity of Pre-Tax Profit to Grape Price

such as a performance measure variable or a decision variable. For example, does a 10% change in some parameter produce a 1% change in the profit or a 10% change or a 100% change? Loosely speaking, if an X% change in some input variable produces a much less than X% change in the other variable, then that other variable is said to be "insensitive" to the input variable. If an X% change in the input variable produces much more than X% change in the other variable, then that output variable is said to be "sensitive" to that input variable. Like independence, insensitivity is often a desirable property relating the two variables. In contrast, it is the relatively sensitive relationships that should attract managerial interest. For example, if profit were shown to be insensitive to the value of some parameter, then that parameter's value need not be determined with great accuracy. In this example, Thurston must commit to a Raisin Price before learning the Open Market Grape Price, and moreover, we just observed that the optimal Raisin Price is not independent of that Open Market Grape Price. Put another way, Thurston's decision would be easy if the Open Market Grape Price were known in advance. As it is, Thurston must choose a column (Raisin Price) in Figure 2.35 and then in the autumn "Mother Nature" chooses the row (Open Market Grape Price).

Sensitivity analysis allows Thurston to see in profit percentage change terms how different Open Market Grape Prices would affect Pre-Tax Profit once she commits to a particular Raisin Price. To illustrate, assume Thurston is convinced beyond a doubt that the Open Market Grape Price will be $.25. From Figure 2.36, her best Raisin Price is thus $1.85, yielding a Pre-Tax Profit of $681,000. Figure 2.37 re-expresses the payoff table of Figure 2.36 into percentage terms to allow examination of the sensitivity of Pre-Tax Profit to changes in Open Market Grape Price in the neighborhood of Thurston's "base case" of Open Market Grape Price = $.25 and Raisin Price = $1.85. Clearly, Pre-Tax Profit is not insensitive to changes in Open Market Grape Price, if Thurston's belief that it will be $.25 is wrong. But it is not highly sensitive either; a ± 40% change in Open Market Grape Price induces a ± 25% change in Pre-Tax Profit, given Thurston's Raisin Price = $1.85 decision.

	O	P	Q	R	S	T	U	V
31								
32					Raisin Price Change			
33				-5%	-3%	0%	3%	5%
34				$1.75	$1.80	$1.85	$1.90	$1.95
35	Open Mkt Grape Price Change	-40%	$0.15	2.4%	1.6%	$854	-2.5%	-5.9%
36		-20%	$0.20	0.4%	0.7%	$768	-1.6%	-4.3%
37		0%	$0.25	-2.2%	-0.6%	$681	-0.5%	-2.2%
38		20%	$0.30	-5.5%	-2.1%	$595	0.9%	0.5%
39		40%	$0.35	-10%	-4.3%	$508	2.8%	4.1%

	O	P	Q	R	S	T	U	V
31								
32					Raisin Price Change			
33				=(R34-$T$34)/$T$34	=(S34-$T$34)/$T$34	=(T34-$	=(U34-$T	=(V34-$T$34)/$T$34
34				1.75	1.8	1.85	1.9	1.95
35	Open Mkt Grape Price Change	=(Q35-$C	0.15	=(R17-$T17)/$T17	=(S17-$T17)/$T17	=T17	=(U17-$T	=(V17-$T17)/$T17
36		=(Q36-$C	0.2	=(R18-$T18)/$T18	=(S18-$T18)/$T18	=T18	=(U18-$T	=(V18-$T18)/$T18
37		=(Q37-$C	0.25	=(R19-$T19)/$T19	=(S19-$T19)/$T19	=T19	=(U19-$T	=(V19-$T19)/$T19
38		=(Q38-$C	0.3	=(R20-$T20)/$T20	=(S20-$T20)/$T20	=T20	=(U20-$T	=(V20-$T20)/$T20
39		=(Q39-$C	0.35	=(R21-$T21)/$T21	=(S21-$T21)/$T21	=T21	=(U21-$T	=(V21-$T21)/$T21

FIGURE 2.38

Sensitivity of Pre-Tax Profit for Raisin Price = $1.85

From a decision-making standpoint, however, it is *not* the sensitivity of Pre-Tax Profit to the Open Market Grape Price parameter that should concern Thurston at this point. Instead, it should be the sensitivity of her Raisin Price *decision* to changes in Open Market Grape Prices. Careful study of Figure 2.37 reveals that Pre-Tax Profit is relatively *insensitive* to Open Market Grape Price, even though that may not appear to be the case at first glance. For example, let us assume that Thurston has committed to Raisin Price = $1.85 and the worst possible outcome occurs: Open Market Grape Price = $.35 instead of the $.25 Thurston expected, yielding the outcome in cell T30, a 25% drop in Pre-Tax Profit over the base case. Since grapes are a raw material to RR, the higher grape price is going to hurt profit no matter what Raisin Price Thurston had chosen. So, it is not the 25% drop in profit that is relevant, but rather how much Thurston could have mitigated the damage to profit *had she known* the Open Market Grape Price would equal $.35 in advance. From Figure 2.37 we see that had Thurston received perfect information in advance that the Open Market Grape Price would be $.35, she would have chosen Raisin Price = $1.95, yielding a Pre-Tax Profit 22% lower (cell V30 in Figure 2.37) than her base case. As it is, she had no prior information and chose Raisin Price = $1.85, resulting in a lowered profit of 25%, only a three percentage point difference from the perfect information case. Similar analysis can be applied to the more happy occurrence of Open Market Grape Price lower than the base case. Again, the relevant comparison is not the absolute change in Pre-Tax Profit from the base case cell, but the relative difference in Pre-Tax Profit that would occur between Thurston's base case Raisin Price of $1.85 and the Raisin Price she would have chosen instead, given perfect information in advance on Open Market Grape Price. For example, if the Open Market Grape Price = $.15 actually occurs, then the relevant comparison should be between cell R17 and cell T17 in Figure 2.37 and not between cell R17 and cell T19.

This insensitivity is better illustrated by the table in Figure 2.38. In this table the comparisons are not to the base case cell, T17, but to the Pre-Tax Profit that would occur given Thurston's decision to set Raisin Price = $1.85 compared to the improved Pre-Tax Profit decision she would have made had she known the actual Open Market Grape Price in advance. From Figure 2.38 this Pre-Tax Profit foregone difference is between .7% and 4.1%, occurring for Open Market Grape Price changes ranging ± 40%.

As this example illustrates, sensitivity analysis can be a bit confusing at first, but it is at the core of many managerial insights afforded by modeling. Fortunately, a graph can "speak a thousand words" regarding such insights by use of a well-designed Excel chart.

Profit versus Raisin Price and Open Market Grape Price

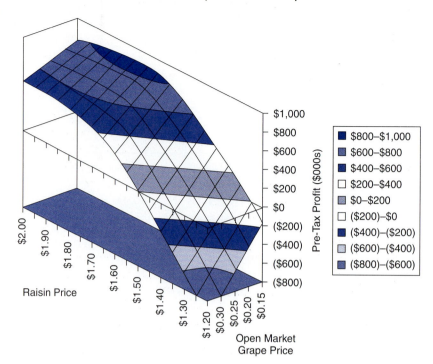

FIGURE 2.39

3-D Surface Chart of RR's
Pre-Tax Profit

The Data Table 2 tabulation of Figure 2.35 is complemented by Excel's Chart Wizard for presenting the sensitivity information visually. Selecting the range F16:W21 in Figure 2.35 and choosing Chart Wizard's 3-D Surface chart type produces, after some additional formatting, the plot in Figure 2.39.[5]

Although Figure 2.39 is visually appealing, sensitivity analysis is difficult to see from 3-D chart contours, and the more prosaic XY Scatter chart is often more valuable for seeing relationships. Figure 2.40 presents an XY Scatter chart of the same data, using one series for each Open Market Grape Price. For any given Open Market Grape Price, Pre-Tax Profit is relatively insensitive to Raisin Price for prices above about $1.65, as is obvious from inspecting Figure 2.40.

None of the three examples we have studied explicitly models any constraints upon variables in the model. Constraints acting to limit the range of acceptable values of variables are common in modeling, as illustrated by the Oak Products example.

2.5   EXAMPLE FOUR—PRODUCTION AT OAK PRODUCTS, INC.

Oak Products, Inc. (OP) produces a line of high-quality solid oak chairs. There are six chairs in the product line: Captain, Mate, American High, American Low, Spanish King, and Spanish Queen. These chairs have been designed to use a number of interchangeable component parts—long and short dowels, heavy and light seats, and heavy and light rungs. In addition, each type of chair has a distinguishing rail that caps the back. The interchangeable parts help protect OP against sudden shifts in demand. It is November 15, and Tom Burr, the plant manager, is set to meet James White from production control to finalize the production plan for the next week. At OP, the finishing activity (i.e., sanding, spraying, and drying of the component parts) requires one week. For this reason, only

---

[5]As with 2-D charts, 3-D charts treat as categorical, the data values for the independent variable axes in all non-XY Scatter plot charts. Thus, each input series must have evenly spaced intervals to avoid distortion in the dependent variable plot.

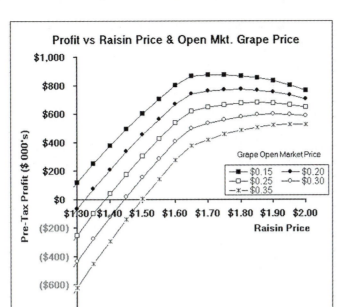

FIGURE 2.40

XY Scatter Chart of RR's Pre-Tax Profit

components that are already on hand and finished can be used in chairs that will be produced in the next week.

Jim White has developed a production model and the result is the spreadsheet model shown in Figure 2.41.

As in the other examples, Jim's spreadsheet is used to represent his model in a layout we recommend for ease of building, debugging, and interpretation. In Jim's spreadsheet, columns are devoted to representing decision "activities"; that is, the act of producing a given chair type, including production level and consumption of chair parts. To make this clear Jim has placed text labels in the rows and columns to assist in understanding the meaning of the numbers. For example, the datum 4 in B6 indicates that 4 short dowels are used in producing one Captain chair. Also, Jim has placed his suggested production plan in the cells B3:G3. Thus, Jim's proposal is to produce 40 chairs of each type, yielding a total profit of $8760. The entries in the cells H6:J6 indicate that

1. Jim's production plan will use a total of 1600 short dowels;
2. The starting inventory of short dowels, a parameter, is at 1900; and
3. Jim's plan will leave a final inventory of 300 short dowels.

Figure 2.42 illustrates the use of Excel's Naming capability to create names for ranges of cells in Jim's model. This improves readability of worksheet formulas in comparison to the formulas shown in Figure 2.41. Names can be used in any spreadsheet model to improve documentation but are particularly helpful when referring to collections of adjacent cells, as in the Oak Production model.

Using Jim's model, the production planning session proceeds as follows:

Jim: I've used the usual procedure to determine production—that is, to make the same quantity of each product and maximize the total amount produced. This time we run out of long dowels first, but we do pretty well. We produce 40 of each chair and make $8760.

Tom: I know that we've always produced equal quantities of each chair, but this time things are different. The president tells me that solid wood products are a hot item now, and we will sell out no matter what we produce. He says to make as much profit as possible. What should we do?

Jim: I don't know the complete answer, but I do have an idea. American Highs are clearly our most profitable item, but notice that they also use the most long dowels and we're

TIP: Named variables are global within an Excel workbook. That is, they are available to all worksheets within it. This allows a cell in one worksheet model to reference a variable in any other worksheet by its name. For details of creating range names, see the Excel Appendix.

	A	B	C	D	E	F	G	H	I	J
1	Chair Style	Capt.	Mate	AmerHi	AmerLo	SpainK	SpainQ			
2	Profit / Chair	$36	$40	$45	$38	$35	$25	TOTAL PROFIT		
3	Qty.Produced	40	40	40	40	40	40	$8,760		
4		Chair Component Requirements						Total Usage	Starting Inventory	End. Inv.
5	Long Dowels	8	0	12	0	8	4	1280	1280	0
6	Short Dowels	4	12	0	12	4	8	1600	1900	300
7	Legs	4	4	4	4	4	4	960	1090	130
8	Heavy Seats	1	0	0	0	1	1	120	190	70
9	Light Seats	0	1	1	1	0	0	120	170	50
10	Heavy Rungs	6	0	4	0	5	0	600	1000	400
11	Light Rungs	0	4	0	5	0	6	600	1000	400
12	Capt. Rails	1	0	0	0	0	0	40	110	70
13	Mate Rails	0	1	0	0	0	0	40	72	32
14	Amer. Rails	0	0	1	1	0	0	80	93	13
15	Span. Rails	0	0	0	0	1	1	80	85	5

TIP: *Figure 2.41 uses the SUMPRODUCT() function. This function multiplies each pair of the corresponding cells in its arguments and then adds up all the resulting products. This function is used frequently in spreadsheet models. If it is unfamiliar to you, review its operation in the Excel Appendix.*

	A	B	C	D	E	F	G	H	I	J
1	Chair Style	Cap	Ma	Am	Ame	Sp	Sp			
2	Profit / Chair	36	40	45	38	35	25	TOTAL PROFIT		
3	Qty.Produced	40	40	40	40	40	40	=SUMPRODUCT($B$3:$G$3,B2:G2)		
4		Cha						Total Usage	Starti	End. Inv.
5	Long Dowels	8	0	12	0	8	4	=SUMPRODUCT($B$3:$G$3,B5:G5)	1280	=I5-H5
6	Short Dowels	4	12	0	12	4	8	=SUMPRODUCT($B$3:$G$3,B6:G6)	1900	=I6-H6
7	Legs	4	4	4	4	4	4	=SUMPRODUCT($B$3:$G$3,B7:G7)	1090	=I7-H7
8	Heavy Seats	1	0	0	0	1	1	=SUMPRODUCT($B$3:$G$3,B8:G8)	190	=I8-H8
9	Light Seats	0	1	1	1	0	0	=SUMPRODUCT($B$3:$G$3,B9:G9)	170	=I9-H9
10	Heavy Rungs	6	0	4	0	5	0	=SUMPRODUCT($B$3:$G$3,B10:G10)	1000	=I10-H10
11	Light Rungs	0	4	0	5	0	6	=SUMPRODUCT($B$3:$G$3,B11:G11)	1000	=I11-H11
12	Capt. Rails	1	0	0	0	0	0	=SUMPRODUCT($B$3:$G$3,B12:G12)	110	=I12-H12
13	Mate Rails	0	1	0	0	0	0	=SUMPRODUCT($B$3:$G$3,B13:G13)	72	=I13-H13
14	Amer. Rails	0	0	1	1	0	0	=SUMPRODUCT($B$3:$G$3,B14:G14)	93	=I14-H14
15	Span. Rails	0	0	0	0	1	1	=SUMPRODUCT($B$3:$G$3,B15:G15)	85	=I15-H15

FIGURE 2.41

The First OP Spreadsheet

	H	I	J
1			
2	TOTAL PROFIT		
3	=SUMPRODUCT(Qty.Produced,Profit___Chair)		
4	Total Usage	Starting Inventory	End. Inv.
5	=SUMPRODUCT(Qty.Produced,Long_Dowels)	1280	=Starting_Inventory-Total_Usage
6	=SUMPRODUCT(Qty.Produced,Short_Dowels)	1900	=Starting_Inventory-Total_Usage
7	=SUMPRODUCT(Qty.Produced,Legs)	1090	=Starting_Inventory-Total_Usage
8	=SUMPRODUCT(Qty.Produced,Heavy_Seats)	190	=Starting_Inventory-Total_Usage
9	=SUMPRODUCT(Qty.Produced,Light_Seats)	170	=Starting_Inventory-Total_Usage
10	=SUMPRODUCT(Qty.Produced,Heavy_Rungs)	1000	=Starting_Inventory-Total_Usage
11	=SUMPRODUCT(Qty.Produced,Light_Rungs)	1000	=Starting_Inventory-Total_Usage
12	=SUMPRODUCT(Qty.Produced,Capt.__Rails)	110	=Starting_Inventory-Total_Usage
13	=SUMPRODUCT(Qty.Produced,Mate__Rails)	72	=Starting_Inventory-Total_Usage
14	=SUMPRODUCT(Qty.Produced,Amer.__Rails)	93	=Starting_Inventory-Total_Usage
15	=SUMPRODUCT(Qty.Produced,Span.__Rails)	85	=Starting_Inventory-Total_Usage

FIGURE 2.42

Use of Range Names to Improve Formula Documentation

short of long dowels. If I give up 2 American Highs, I lose $90 of profit, but I gain 24 long dowels. I can use those dowels to make 3 Captains, in which case, I'll gain $108. So what if we make 100 Captains and no American Highs?

(Jim enters this new proposal into the cells B3:G3. The Excel spreadsheet of this result is shown in Figure 2.43.)

Tom: Jim, that's great! You've increased weekly profits by $360. I wonder if we can do better? I'm sure we can. In fact, I think we can use your idea again. Spanish Kings require 8 long dowels, while Spanish Queens require only 4. I should be able to give up a King and lose $35, but make 2 Queens and gain $50. So, what if we make no Kings and a total of 120 Queens? [The result is shown in Figure 2.44.]

	A	B	C	D	E	F	G	H	I	J
1	Chair Style	Capt.	Mate	AmerHi	AmerLo	SpainK	SpainQ			
2	Profit / Chair	$ 36	$ 40	$ 45	$ 38	$ 35	$ 25	TOTAL PROFIT		
3	Qty.Produced	100	40	0	40	40	40	$ 9,120		
4				Chair Component Requirements				Total Usage	Starting Inventory	End. Inv.
5	Long Dowels	8	0	12	0	8	4	1280	1280	0
6	Short Dowels	4	12	0	12	4	8	1840	1900	60
7	Legs	4	4	4	4	4	4	1040	1090	50
8	Heavy Seats	1	0	0	0	1	1	180	190	10
9	Light Seats	0	1	1	1	0	0	80	170	90
10	Heavy Rungs	6	0	4	0	5	0	800	1000	200
11	Light Rungs	0	4	0	5	0	6	600	1000	400
12	Capt. Rails	1	0	0	0	0	0	100	110	10
13	Mate Rails	0	1	0	0	0	0	40	72	32
14	Amer. Rails	0	0	1	1	0	0	40	93	53
15	Span. Rails	0	0	0	0	1	1	80	85	5

FIGURE 2.43

Jim's Revised Spreadsheet

	A	B	C	D	E	F	G	H	I	J
1	Chair Style	Capt.	Mate	AmerHi	AmerLo	SpainK	SpainQ			
2	Profit / Chair	$ 36	$ 40	$ 45	$ 38	$ 35	$ 25	TOTAL PROFIT		
3	Qty.Produced	100	40	0	40	0	120	$ 9,720		
4				Chair Component Requirements				Total Usage	Starting Inventory	End. Inv.
5	Long Dowels	8	0	12	0	8	4	1280	1280	0
6	Short Dowels	4	12	0	12	4	8	2320	1900	-420
7	Legs	4	4	4	4	4	4	1200	1090	-110
8	Heavy Seats	1	0	0	0	1	1	220	190	-30
9	Light Seats	0	1	1	1	0	0	80	170	90
10	Heavy Rungs	6	0	4	0	5	0	600	1000	400
11	Light Rungs	0	4	0	5	0	6	1080	1000	-80
12	Capt. Rails	1	0	0	0	0	0	100	110	10
13	Mate Rails	0	1	0	0	0	0	40	72	32
14	Amer. Rails	0	0	1	1	0	0	40	93	53
15	Span. Rails	0	0	0	0	1	1	120	85	-35

FIGURE 2.44

Tom's Revised Spreadsheet

Jim: There's some good news and some bad news. The good news is that your economics was right. Weekly profits increased by $600. The bad news is that we don't have the inventory to support this plan. The model shows negative ending inventory for short dowels and a bunch of other things. This means that we have to use more short dowels than we have. It's just not possible.

Tom: I see what you mean. Clearly I overshot the mark. I understand that we could decrease the production of Spanish Kings and increase the production of Spanish Queens somewhat and increase profits. With enough effort, I guess we could figure out how much we can push this trade-off before running out of inventory. But even so, how do we know it's a good solution? I really wonder what's best.

OPTIMIZATION MODELS

Like the other examples, the Oak Products model is certainly a quantitative decision model. It specifies the relationship between the decision variables (the quantity of each chair to produce) and the parameters (the number of parts used in each chair and the supplies of parts) and computes a performance measure (the total profit) and other consequence variables (ending inventories). It does not, however, tell us how many chairs to produce. When you think about it, that is a funny question. How many chairs to produce to do what? We might want to know how many chairs to produce to use up as much of our parts inventory as possible. Or how many chairs to produce to satisfy normal customer demand for each model. As with the previous examples, it is more likely that we would want to know how many chairs to produce in order to maximize OP's weekly profit. The point is that before we can decide what we want to do, we have to know what we want to accomplish; that is, we have to specify our objective.

Unfortunately, none of the analytical techniques we have covered in the examples of this chapter permit "What if?" projections, including Data Tables and charts, while simultaneously adhering to specified constraints. You might, for example, want to make sales or profits large in one problem and costs or delivery times small in another while honoring constraints on capacities, resources, and time.

2.6 CONSTRAINTS AND CONSTRAINED OPTIMIZATION

If Tom and Jim decide that they want to make their weekly profit as large as possible, then the Oak Products model becomes an **optimization model.** The Oak Products model is an example of a constrained optimization problem: a problem in which we wish to maximize (or minimize) some performance measure function of the decision variables subject to a set of constraints. A constraint is a limitation on the range of allowable decisions. In this particular case the constraints are the quantities of various parts available to produce chairs, but there are many different types of constraints. Indeed, managers make most of their personal and professional decisions in situations where the allowable decisions have been restricted in some way. In our private lives we are nearly always dealing with limitations of some sort—of time, of money, of space, of energy. In business, the kinds of constraints encountered are even more numerous. A manager must often take into account capital requirements, personnel availability, delivery schedules, import quotas, union work rules, factory capacities, environmental regulations, inventory costs, legal requirements, and a host of other factors. It is perhaps not surprising, therefore, that constrained optimization—achieving the best possible result given the restrictions that apply—is one of the most active areas of management research.

The Oak Products formulation is a standard type of managerial planning linear programming (LP) model, and the best, or **optimal solution** is easily obtained. One of the most commonly employed analytical tools, linear programming, is a special procedure for carrying out constrained optimization. There are several spreadsheet "add-in" application packages that take a model and then **optimize** it. Two such packages are Solver and What's Best. The optimized result for the Oak Products model is shown in Figure 2.45. It is interesting to note that the model projects that weekly profit would be increased by $1174 over Jim's revised plan and that no Spanish style chairs are part of the optimal solution; that is, the **optimal decision** is to produce zero Spanish style chairs.

Solver is included with Excel and will be covered extensively in Part 2's chapters.

FIGURE 2.45

The Optimal Solution to OP's Model

	A	B	C	D	E	F	G	H	I	J
1	Chair Style	Capt.	Mate	AmerHi	AmerLo	SpainK	SpainQ			
2	Profit / Chair	$ 36	$ 40	$ 45	$ 38	$ 35	$ 25	TOTAL PROFIT		
3	Qty.Produced	100	72	40	53	0	0	$ 10,294		
4				Chair Component Requirements				Total Usage	Starting Inventory	End. Inv.
5	Long Dowels	8	0	12	0	8	4	1280	1280	-0
6	Short Dowels	4	12	0	12	4	8	1900	1900	0
7	Legs	4	4	4	4	4	4	1060	1090	30
8	Heavy Seats	1	0	0	0	1	1	100	190	90
9	Light Seats	0	1	1	1	0	0	165	170	5
10	Heavy Rungs	6	0	4	0	5	0	760	1000	240
11	Light Rungs	0	4	0	5	0	6	553	1000	447
12	Capt. Rails	1	0	0	0	0	0	100	110	10
13	Mate Rails	0	1	0	0	0	0	72	72	-0
14	Amer. Rails	0	0	1	1	0	0	93	93	-0
15	Span. Rails	0	0	0	0	1	1	0	85	85

2.7   SUMMARY

This chapter has introduced you to spreadsheet modeling, primarily by a series of short examples. We have suggested ways to translate a black box representation into a spreadsheet model, given recommendations for good spreadsheet model design and layout, offered suggestions for documenting your models, and introduced you to useful features of Excel for modeling and analysis.

Influence diagrams facilitate the building of models and provide model documentation. Model equations are built iteratively by revising relationships to conform to hypothesized relationships contained in data. "What if?" projections are the primary analysis tools for exercising spreadsheet models. Replicating the model, Goal Seek, Data Table, and charting are all useful in evaluating collections of "What if?" projections.

The layout of the model in the spreadsheet is critically important in developing models that are understandable, free of logic bugs, easy to maintain and document, and easy to communicate to others. Making the logic clear, avoiding numbers in formulas, labeling variables, and use of variable names all contribute to good spreadsheet modeling practice.

Key Terms

Influence Diagram. A hierarchical flow-chart drawing beginning with a performance measure and using arrows to clarify the relationships of it to the variables and parameters of a model.

"What if?" Projection. Substituting decision and/or parameter values into a symbolic model to calculate their effect upon performance measure(s) and consequence variables.

Data Table. The systematic tabulation of a performance measure and/or consequence variable values for a range of values of one or two exogenous variables.

Goal Seek. Finding the value of a single exogenous variable that produces a given value of a single endogenous variable.

Sensitivity Analysis. Calculating in percentage terms the effect a given percentage change in an exogenous variable has upon another variable.

Production Model. A decision model in which decision variable(s) specify the quantities of one or more items to manufacture.

Product Mix Model. A production model with more than one item to manufacture.

Optimization Model. A deterministic decision model consisting of a single performance measure (objective function) to be optimized subject to satisfaction of a given set of constraints.

Optimize. To maximize or minimize an objective function.

Optimal Decision. A feasible set of values for the decision that optimizes the objective function of an optimization model.

Optimal Solution. Alternative term for optimal decision.

Self-Review Exercises

True-False

1. **T F** It doesn't make much difference how a model is presented on a spreadsheet, as long as the calculations are correct.

2. **T F** Putting numbers into formulas improves spreadsheet documentation.

3. **T F** Units of measure are important to include in spreadsheet models.

4. **T F** Given hypothetical data on two variables, Excel's Trendline is useful for investigating alternative algebraic formulas that relate them.

5. **T F** There is usually no single correct way to draw an influence diagram.

6. **T F** Columns in a spreadsheet model are always used to represent time.

7. **T F** The analysis of spreadsheet models requires that profit be the performance measure.

8. **T F** Goal Seek is a procedure for optimizing spreadsheet models.

9. **T F** Managers have no need to concern themselves with the formulas in a spreadsheet model, only the results of the model.

10. **T F** Groups and Outlines can be used to conceal important details of the model in Excel spreadsheet printouts.

11. **T F** It is a good idea to separate calculations of intermediate variables for physical quantities from those related to accounting for their costs.

12. **T F** "What if?" projections are useful only for examining changes in the values of decision variables.

13. **T F** Data Tables are useful for creating tabulations of "What if?" projections.

14. **T F** Data Tables have no use other than for calculating numbers to be input to the Excel Chart Wizard.

15. **T F** Goal Seek is useful for finding values of an exogenous variable that produce the same performance measure value as that of another alternative model.

Multiple Choice

16. A good spreadsheet model will
    a. have model results clearly labeled
    b. give units of measure for its variables
    c. separate input variables from endogenous variables
    d. make it clear how endogenous variables are calculated from input variables
    e. all of the above

17. Optimization models contain
    a. decision variables
    b. an objective function
    c. both of the above

18. An optimization model
    a. provides the best decision in a mathematical sense
    b. provides the best decision within the limited context of the model
    c. can provide a consistent tool for evaluating different policies
    d. all of the above

19. With "What if?" projections, we are sure to find
    a. an optimal solution
    b. a good solution
    c. a feasible solution (if one exists)
    d. none of the above

20. An optimal decision in the Oak Products model is one that
    a. uses all available component parts
    b. uses as many as possible of the least expensive parts
    c. maximizes contribution margin (revenue minus costs)
    d. maximizes weekly profit
    e. maximizes the total number of chairs produced

21. A Data Table 1 command
    a. requires a range of values for one exogenous variable
    b. allows specification of multiple endogenous variables
    c. both of the above
    d. none of the above

22. A Data Table 2 command
    a. requires a range of values for two exogenous variables
    b. allows specification of multiple endogenous variables
    c. both of the above
    d. none of the above

23. Sensitivity analysis
    a. compares the changes in an endogenous variable to changes in an exogenous variable
    b. cannot be applied to decision variables
    c. cannot be applied to comparing two parameter values
    d. both a and b above
    e. both a and c above
    f. all of the above

24. Named cells and named ranges
    a. make spreadsheet formulas easier to interpret
    b. assist documenting the spreadsheet model
    c. hide the underlying structure of formulas
    d. both a and b above
    e. both a and c above
    f. all of the above

25. Excel features that can be used to aid model interpretation and documentation are
    a. use of bold fonts
    b. cell indentations for labels and results
    c. underlining and shading cells
    d. borders on cells
    e. all of the above

Answers

1.	F	8.	F	14.	F	20.	d
2.	F	9.	F	15.	T	21.	c
3.	T	10.	T	16.	e	22.	a
4.	T	11.	T	17.	c	23.	a
5.	T	12.	F	18.	d	24.	d
6.	F	13.	T	19.	d	25.	e
7.	F						

2-1. Simon does not consider his Simon Pie model to be valid for Pie Price outside of the range $6 to $11. Use IF() statements and/or Excel's conditional formatting to modify the model to produce warnings if a price outside of this range is input to the model.

2-2. The Petersons decide that the Variable Cost per Copy is more complicated than in the current XerTech model in which supplies cost $.02 per copy and the average repair cost per copy is $.01. They now believe that the average repair cost per copy is more than proportional to the monthly number of copies made per copier. They estimate the relationship as below. Modify the XerTech model to incorporate this new information and prepare a report for the Petersons with these new results.

MONTHLY DATA

# of Copies/Copier (000's)	Repair Cost/Copier
20	$ 50
30	150
40	400
50	1000

2-3. Use Data Table to examine the profit sensitivity of the Simon Pie model to changes in the following parameters: unit cost of pie filling, unit cost of dough, fixed cost, slope of the pie demand equation, intercept of the pie demand equation.

2-4. Bartel Job Shop Co. has received an offer to assemble approximately 15,000 electronic "portasols" for $26.50 each. Using its existing manufacturing facility, Bartel estimates its variable cost of assembling each portasol is $21. Alternatively, Bartel can subcontract some of the assembly steps to Wizard Fabrication Co., thereby reducing Bartel's assembly cost to $18 each. Wizard will charge Bartel a fixed fee of $42,000 for their contract. Another option for Bartel is to lease a parts insertion robot for $150,000. If leased, the robot will reduce Bartel's variable assembly cost to $11. Prepare a model to project the total profit from accepting this offer for each of the three alternative production options. At what level of portasol production would Bartel be indifferent between using its existing facility and subcontracting or between subcontracting and leasing the robot? Prepare a managerial report summarizing your recommendations for different possible quantities of portasols.

2-5. You have founded a company to sell thin client computers to the food processing industry for Internet transaction processing. Before investing in your new company, a venture capitalist has asked for a five year pro-forma income statement showing unit sales, revenue, total variable cost, marketing expense, fixed cost, and profit before tax. You expect to sell 1600 units of the thin client computers in the first year for a price of $1800 each. Swept along by Internet growth, you expect to double unit sales each year for the next five years. However, competition will force a 15% decline in price each year. Fortunately, technical progress allows initial variable manufacturing costs of $1000 for each unit to decline by 6% per year. Fixed costs are estimated to be $1,000,000 per year. Marketing expense is projected to be 14% of annual revenue. When it becomes profitable to do so, you will lease an automated assembly machine that reduces variable manufacturing costs by 20% but doubles the annual fixed cost; the new variable manufacturing cost will also decline by 6% per year. Net Present Value (NPV) will be used to aggregate the stream of annual profits, discounted at 15% per year. Ignoring tax considerations, build a spreadsheet model for the venture capitalist. How many units will you need to sell in the first year (1) to break even in the first year or (2) to break even in the second year? To what parameters is NPV most sensitive? Prepare a managerial report summarizing your findings.

2-6. Simon has decided that his model (Simon Pie example) needs to be modified for the slow winter selling season. During this season, he can achieve the weekly quantity of pies demanded given in the model only if he advertises his pies very heavily. With less advertising, pies demanded will be a percentage of the pie quantity given by the model. He estimates the relationship by the following data, where a 100% Market Potential means that the quantity of pies projected by the original model will be sold and a 50% Market Potential means that only one half of that projected quantity will be sold. He will pick a weekly advertising amount between $5000 and $12,000. Modify the Simon Pie model to incorporate this new information and recommend pricing and advertising decisions to Simon. Examine the sensitivity of weekly profit to advertising amount.

Advertising ($000's per Week)	% of Market Potential
$ 5	40%
7	65
10	80
12	88

Case Study — Kayo Computer[1]

Kayo Computer assembles and sells personal computers. Each computer needs one custom-designed printed circuit board (PCB). Kayo has contracted to buy the PCBs from an outside PCB manufacturer, Apex Manufacturing. The one-year contract stipulates that Kayo pays $200 per board to Apex for up to 2000 PCBs. If the annual order quantity exceeds 2000 PCBs, then Apex is obligated to give a discount of $40 per board for the portion beyond 2000, thus selling them at $160.

Kayo can also buy the same PCBs from another manufacturer, TCI Electronics, that offers a lower price of $120 per PCB but asks a one-time payment of $100,000 as a nonrefundable design and engineering fee. Kayo's engineers have determined that Kayo may use PCBs from either of the two manufacturers, or from both in any mixture without any manufacturing cost or compatibility problems.

The PCB along with other components are assembled by Kayo into its personal computer. The variable assembly cost of the Kayo personal computer is $450 each with an annual fixed cost of $1,500,000. Kayo sells the assembled computer for $1000 each. At the moment no one is sure how many Kayo computers the company can sell for the next year. Jenny Silk, VP of Finance at Kayo Computer, informs you that this model of Kayo computer will be discontinued after next year and so any one-time fee that might be paid to TCI must be justified based on next year's sales alone. She has asked you to help her evaluate certain economic and legal issues as part of her financial plan for the next year.

Questions

1. Build a spreadsheet model that captures the profitability of the Kayo personal computer for next year. As a start, assume that 5000 computers can be sold next year and only 1000 of the PCBs are purchased from Apex (the balance being supplied by TCI).

2. If total sales were 5000 units, how many PCBs would you recommend Kayo buy from Apex and how many from TCI to maximize next year's profits? (Use a Data Table to help you search for your preferred recommendation.)

3. In reviewing the Apex contract, you note that it requires Kayo to purchase at least 20% of the PCBs used in the Kayo computers sold (and not less than 1000 PCBs) from Apex. The contract also contains a liquidated damages clause in the event of Kayo's default in the amount of $100,000. What would be the economic effect if unforeseen changes caused Kayo to default on the 20%/1000 minimum contracted purchase provision (by substituting more TCI boards) in the event that 5000 Kayo computers can be sold next year? Assuming that Apex would be open to renegotiating the contract, what new terms and/or maximum settlement amount would you recommend to Silk for her consideration in the discussions with Apex? Justify your recommendation with relevant spreadsheet exhibits.

4. A market analysis reveals that unit sales will depend on the price of the computer. At the price of $1000, about 5000 units will be sold, but for every increase (or decrease) of $100, sales will decrease (or increase, respectively) by 1000 units. Use Data Table 2 to maximize Kayo's profit next year, by finding (a) the optimal price and (b) the optimal number of boards to buy from Apex while still honoring the original contract.

The Watson Truck Rental Company[1]

Consisting of 50 large trucks rented by industrial contractors, the Watson Truck Rental Company is for sale for $1,000,000. Eric Watson, the seller, wants you to develop a three-year economic analysis to assist buyers in evaluating the company.

Watson pays property taxes of $35,000 per year, and it costs $4800 per truck per year to administer and maintain the fleet. The property taxes are expected to grow at a rate of 4% per year, and the maintenance costs are estimated to grow 7% per year.

Truck rental rate is currently $1000 per month each. At this rental rate on average 60% of the trucks are rented each month. Watson believes that if he lowered the rent by $100 per truck per month, he would increase the average rental percentage by seven percentage points and that this increment would apply to each additional reduction in rent rate of $100. For example, at a $600 truck rental rate 88% of the trucks would be rented each month. Whatever truck rental rate is set for the first year will be increased by 9% per year for years 2 and 3. Average percent of trucks rented in years 2 and 3 will be the same as determined in the first year, regardless of the increased rental rate in those years.

At the end of three years, Watson assumes the buyer will resell the truck business for cash at a profit. The selling price at that time is assumed to be three times the revenue in year 3.

Cash flow in each year is assumed to be the same as the net income (revenue minus expenses) for that year. Effects of depreciation and other factors relating to income taxes can be ignored. Cash flow in year 3 includes in addition the cash from the resale of the business. Overall investment profit is defined to be the Net Present Value of the annual cash flows (discount rate = 10%) including the purchase price at the *beginning* of year 1. Assume no trucks are bought or sold during the three years.

Questions

1. Identify the decision variables, the exogenous variables, the performance measure, the intermediate variables, and any constraints in this problem and use these to build an Excel model.
2. Use a Data Table to find the initial truck rental rate that achieves the highest overall investment profit after the property is sold in three years.
3. Investigate the sensitivity of overall investment profit to the following variables: purchase price, maintenance cost per truck, annual property taxes, and sales multiplication factor. (Use the rental rate found from question 2 above for this analysis.) To which factor is profit most sensitive?
4. Prepare a managerial report for Eric Watson summarizing your findings and recommendations.

Personal Financial Plan[1]

You recently received a $100,000 inheritance from your great uncle Wilberforce. You and your spouse are concerned with what to do with the money.

Salary

You and your spouse's salaries amount to $80,000, and you confidently expect that total to grow at 15 percent per year. You have decided to keep a tight budget and peg your family expenditures to a fixed percent, tentatively set at 75%, of your salaries. Of course, since your salaries will grow, so will these expenditures. Note that these are based on gross salaries (not net after taxes).

Taxes

The Congress has just passed a new tax bill—one with a flat-tax rate. Under this law, a couple (such as you and your spouse) have a deduction of $15,000, and the combined state and federal tax rate is 35 percent for all income above this base of $15,000. Also a capital gains tax has been instituted: Forty percent of all capital gains are taxed as regular income.

Tax Shelter Investment

You have the option of investing any amount of your funds in a real estate venture. One advantage of this investment is that it will incur accounting losses (tax losses due to depreciation) in each of the next five years while simultaneously returning a small (nontaxable) cash payment. At the end of the five years the property will be sold, you will share in the profits, and you will pay capital gain taxes on these profits. For each $1000 invested in the project, the following are the various factors:

Annual Tax Loss	$ 200
Annual Cash Payment to You	$ 40 (not taxable)
Amount Returned at End of Year 5	$1800
Capital Gain Tax Liability in Year 5	$2300

Mutual Fund Investment

The only other investment you are considering is a money market fund. This fund pays interest at a rate of 14% per year and this interest income is taxable. You can invest any amount in this fund at any time.

For convenience, assume the interest is paid in any year on the balance at the beginning of that year (the end of the prior year). The $100,000 inheritance has been tentatively placed in the money market fund but can be withdrawn immediately if needed.

You and your spouse wish to build a personal financial model that will allow you to see how your wealth (market fund balance) will grow by the end of five years. You wish to use this model to decide how much to invest in the tax shelter investment, and to examine how sensitive your plan is to some of the assumptions made.

Questions

Use your model to answer the following questions:

1. How much should you invest in the tax shelter plan?
2. Suppose your salary growth rate is only 10%. How does this affect your wealth at the end of five years? Explain this result.
3. Increase each of the tax shelter investment parameters by 10%. (Do each separately.) Which has the greatest impact on your five-year wealth?
4. What is the maximum percentage of your salaries that you can consume (spend) without running into debt (so that your money market fund balance is never negative)?
5. What would the yield on the money market fund have to be for you to be indifferent between investing fully in the real estate investment and investing nothing in it?

Case Study   Benson Appliance Corporation[1]

The Benson Appliance Corporation manufactures two kinds of small appliances at its single plant in Aurora, Illinois. Both of the company's products, electric knives and electric can openers, are marketed exclusively through manufacturing representatives, who service retail appliance dealers. Representatives are paid a fixed salary, plus a commission on each unit sold. Most retailers add a standard markup to Benson's wholesale price.

Throughout the 1970s and 1980s industry sales grew steadily at about 10% annually, and everybody followed the price leadership of the large appliance manufacturers. However, this cozy situation eventually attracted numerous small competitors. Total industry sales continued to expand, but no individual manufacturer could expect his sales to expand after 1990. During 1991 and early 1992, many of Benson's competitors engaged actively in price cutting. Benson had established an image of quality for both products, so it elected to maintain prices and to initiate a modest advertising campaign, instead. This occurred in 1992, along with some experimental price manipulations to determine the sales sensitivity of each product to price. By the end of 1992, prices had stabilized throughout the industry, leaving Benson's products with both a price and a quality image somewhat above average. Benson's 1992 income statement appears in Exhibit 1.

The manufacture of small appliances is such that Benson can expand production of either product to almost any reasonable level on short notice. However, the unit variable manufacturing cost of either product increases by 25% if the total annual production volume of that product exceeds 400,000 units. Thus, if knife production were 450,000 units, the first 400,000 units would cost $8 each in variable manufacturing cost, and the remaining 50,000 units would cost $10 each. Similarly, the first 400,000 openers would cost $16 each, and any excess over 400,000 units would cost $20 each. Variable manufacturing costs are mostly direct materials and relatively unskilled direct labor. Fixed manufacturing costs are allocated equally to the two products regardless of production volumes, since their facilities take up about the same plant space. Variable marketing costs are mostly sales commissions and freight expenses. Further details of Benson's costs appear in Exhibit 2.

Maximilian Benson, president, founder, and sole stockholder of the Benson Appliance Corporation, is in the process of formulating his 1993 budget and operating plan. This had been an easy task throughout the late 1970s and 1980s, when he simply charged the market price and projected a 10% annual sales growth. Now, however, Mr. Benson was not sure what to do. He asked his marketing manager, Clare Voyance, to report whatever conclusions she had drawn from the price and advertising experiments conducted during 1992 and to recommend prices and advertising budgets for 1993.

Ms. Voyance reported that sales of each product were influenced by both price and advertising, although in somewhat different ways. As long as both prices and advertising expenditures remained within certain reasonable operating limits, Ms. Voyance believed that she could project 1993 sales results fairly accurately.

"At every level of advertising expenditure, our unit knife sales appear to vary approximately linearly with knife price, so long as we keep the price between $12 and $23," Ms. Voyance reported. "I chose these limits because we would fail to recover even our variable costs at a price below $12, and our sales would vanish at prices much above $23. Within this range, an extra 100,000 units are sold every time we cut the knife price by an extra dollar. This is true regardless of whether or not we advertise. To see the effect of advertising on sales, I plotted unit knife sales (on the vertical axis) against price charged per knife (on the horizontal axis). Then, if we advertise, the effect of advertising is to shift the unit sales line upward at every price by an amount directly proportional to how much we spend. We sell an extra 4000 knives for every extra $10,000 we spend on knife advertising, at least up to the $300,000 you authorized last year, Max. Actually, we only spent $100,000 on knife advertising in 1992, and we charged an average price of $20 per unit. This resulted in sales of 400,000 knives. Had we done no advertising at all, as in all years before 1992, we still would have sold 360,000 knives.

"At every level of advertising expenditure, our unit opener sales also vary approximately linearly with opener price, so long as we keep the price between $20 and $30," Ms. Voyance continued. "I chose these limits for the same reasons as before. However, the effect of advertising openers depends on the price we charge, which is different from advertising's effect on knife sales. As with knives, unit sales are increased in direct proportion to advertising expenditures, but the proportionality factor is different at different opener prices. In fact, the proportionality factor appears to be a linear function of the opener price. At the 1992 average price of $25 per unit, we could sell an extra 1500 openers for every extra $10,000 spent on advertising, at least up to your maximum authorization of $200,000. As it was, we spent $100,000 advertising openers, and we sold 400,000 units. Had we increased the price to $30, advertising would have had no impact on opener sales, no matter how heavily we advertised. Sales would have remained steady at 100,000 openers. Once again, I plotted unit opener sales (on the vertical axis) against price charged per opener (on the horizontal axis), and the effect of advertising openers is to rotate the unit sales line in a clockwise direction around the pivot price of $30, with the effect always being proportional to advertising expenditures, but increasingly so as the opener price falls."

"Clare," Mr. Benson asked, "why did you choose to spend $100,000 each last year advertising knives and openers? I authorized up to $300,000 for knives and up to $200,000 for openers, and I am willing to spend up to the same amounts (for each product, separately) in 1993. Furthermore, it's OK with me if you charge any price within your reasonable operating limits for each product next year."

"Well, Max," Ms. Voyance replied, "we sort of fell into it by accident. Truman Hardy, the production manager, was very anxious to keep average unit manufacturing costs down. After all, the annual bonus you pay him depends on his suc-

cess in doing just that. Since the average unit manufacturing cost of each product is half of the fixed manufacturing cost plus variable manufacturing cost for that product, all divided by the number of units produced, and since you had already decided not to alter the 1992 price on either product by more than one dollar compared to the previous year's price, Truman reasoned that we should stick with exactly the same prices we charged in the previous year and advertise just enough to drive the sales of each product up to 400,000 units. That would minimize average costs, according to Truman. It also suggested an equal division of the advertising budget between the two products, which seemed fine, because we had no basis for doing otherwise. Last year was our first experience with advertising."

"One other thing, Clare," Mr. Benson continued. "Do last year's results suggest any cross-impact between the two products?"

"Fortunately not," Ms. Voyance replied. "The two products have different brand names. As far as we can tell, changing the price or the advertising on either one has negligible impact on the other product's sales."

"OK, Clare, what do you recommend for 1993?" asked Mr. Benson.

"I suggest we push for increased sales volume, greater revenue, and more market share," she replied. "We can do this by cutting both prices and by advertising both products more heavily than last year. Since the market has stabilized and there is very little inflation, I believe that 1993 will be virtually a repeat of 1992. Hence, all of my conclusions about last year apply equally to next year. I feel that now is just the time to build market share, since we have higher than average prices, and we have slack in the advertising budget. Reducing our prices to the industry average will not be seen as an aggressive move. Building market share will not be difficult, if we act now, and this will contribute to long-term profitability. On the other hand, we can certainly maintain last year's somewhat high prices without any damage, if that is what you want, Max."

"That sounds fine for you, Clare," retorted Mr. Benson. "Your bonus depends on Benson's sales revenue. But what does it do to 1993 profits? I care about company profits, and I don't want to wait forever to receive them."

Questions

1. Create a spreadsheet model for 1993 that projects for both knives and openers: average unit manufacturing cost, unit sales, dollar sales revenues, and overall dollar profit.
2. Use Data Table(s) to find the optimal value of the dollar profit for 1993 (within the operating limits specified in the case) and the optimal value of average unit manufacturing cost for 1993.
3. Truman Hardy did not use a computer for his analysis, but he did succeed in minimizing the average unit manufacturing

cost for 1992. His argument was: *"To minimize average unit manufacturing cost: 400,000 units should be produced so as to spread the fixed manufacturing costs over as large a production volume as possible, without incurring the increased variable manufacturing costs that apply to higher volumes."* Do you accept Mr. Hardy's argument in general? Why or why not?

4. For 1993, recommend a pair of prices and a pair of advertising expenditures to Mr. Benson. Explain why you are making these recommendations. Tell Mr. Benson whether your recommendations are apt to be resisted by any of his employees. If such resistance is likely, explain to Mr. Benson how he might go about soliciting their approval and obtaining their cooperation.

EXHIBIT 1 **1992 Income Statement for Benson Appliance Corporation (All figures in thousands of dollars)**

Total Sales	$18,000
Total Manufacturing Costs	11,100
Gross Margin	6,900
Total Marketing Costs	3,600
Total General and Administrative Costs	860
Total Advertising Costs	200
Profit Before Taxes	2,240

Note: A total of 400,000 electric knives were sold during 1992 at an average unit price of $20, and 400,000 electric can openers were sold at an average unit price of $25.

EXHIBIT 2 **Cost Analysis for Benson Appliance Corporation (All figures in dollars based on 1992 results)**

	PRODUCT TYPE	
	Electric Knives	Electric Can Openers
Variable Costs:		
Unit Variable Manufacturing Cost		
Volume =< 400,000 Units	$8	$16
Volume > 400,000 Units	10	20
Unit Variable Marketing Cost	2	2
Fixed Costs:[*]		
Fixed Manufacturing cost	$1,500,000	
Fixed Marketing Cost	2,000,000	
Fixed General and Administrative Cost	500,000	
Budgeted Costs[†]		
Advertising	$200,000	

[*]*Note:* In addition, 2% of total dollar sales revenue is required to cover partially variable general and administrative costs.
[†]The 1993 advertising budget has yet to be set.

Reference

Mark Bucciarelli and Kip Brown," A Desktop-OR Success: Modeling Coast Guard Buoy Tender Operations," *Interfaces*, 25, no. 4 (1995), 1–11.

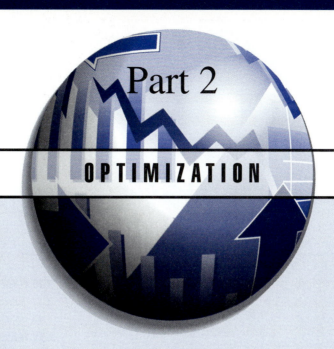

Part 2

OPTIMIZATION

As evident in the discussion at the end of Chapter 2, finding an optimal solution to a model is of great interest. Excel's Goal Seek command is highly suggestive as an efficient search technique for finding decision values that produce desirable results. However, Goal Seek has shortcomings:

1. Goal Seek cannot honor any constraints on variables in its search.
2. Goal Seek allows adjustment of only a single exogenous variable.
3. Goal Seek must have the desired performance measure value specified in advance, that is, you must know the optimal payoff value before Goal Seek can search for the decision that produces that payoff.

Chapters 3, 4, and 5 will introduce Solver, an Excel tool that generalizes Goal Seek to remove the three shortcomings above. Solver is almost as easy to apply to a given model as Goal Seek. However, Solver is a powerful tool and its use requires care to avoid the pitfalls that can entrap the unwary modeler. For example, using Solver on some models may produce a solution that is in fact not optimal, while for others it is easy to misinterpret

Solver's results. Avoiding these pitfalls requires us to understand some concepts for optimizing models. Initially, our approach will be to restrict attention to models having linear relationships among all the variables. Linear models are much easier to understand, work with, and to optimize with Solver. Chapters 6 and 7 will present applications to illustrate the wide applicability of linear optimization to management situations. In addition, the theory we develop for understanding how linear models are optimized provides the basis for the nonlinear models developed in Chapter 8. Chapter 9 concludes this Part by considering optimization given multiple performance measures.

Chapter 3 Linear Optimization

Chapter 4 Linear Programming: Graphical Analysis

Chapter 5 Linear Programming: Interpreting the Solver Sensitivity Report

Chapter 6 Linear Programming: Applications

Chapter 7 Integer Optimization

Chapter 8 Nonlinear Optimization

Chapter 9 Multi-Objective Decision Making and Heuristics

CHAPTER

3

Linear Optimization

CHAPTER OUTLINE

3.1 Introduction

3.2 Formulating LP Models

3.3 Guidelines and Comments on Model Formulation

3.4 Sunk Versus Variable Cost

3.5 The PROTRAC Spreadsheet Model

3.6 The LP Model and Spreadsheet Modeling

3.7 Overview of Solver

3.8 Optimizing the PROTRAC Model with Solver

3.9 Recommendations for Solver LP Models

3.10 Crawler Tread: A Blending Example

3.11 Learning to Formulate LP Models

3.12 Example 1: Astro and Cosmo (A Product Mix Problem)

3.13 Example 2: Blending Gruel (A Blending Problem)

3.14 Example 3: Security Force Scheduling

3.15 Example 4: Longer Boats Yacht Company

3.16 Further Hints for Developing LP Models

3.17 Summary

3.18 Solutions to Example Problems

KEY TERMS

SELF-REVIEW EXERCISES

PROBLEMS

CASE STUDY: Red Brand Canners

CASE STUDY: Application of Modeling to Foreign Exchange Markets

REFERENCES

APPLICATION CAPSULE   Fleet Assignment at Delta Air Lines

Delta Air Lines flies over 2500 domestic flight legs every day, using about 450 aircraft from 10 different fleets that vary by speed, capacity, amount of noise generated, and the like. A flight leg might consist of a Boeing 757 flying from Atlanta (leaving at 6:21 A.M.) to Boston (arriving at 8:45 A.M.). The fleet assignment problem is to match aircraft (e.g., Boeing 747, 757, DC-10, or MD80) to flight legs so that seats are filled with paying passengers. The pattern that the aircraft fly along the route system is called the schedule. The schedule is the heartbeat of an airline. Delta is one of the first airlines to solve to completion this fleet assignment problem—one of the largest and most difficult problems in the airline industry.

An airline seat is the most perishable commodity in the world. Each time an aircraft takes off with an empty seat, a revenue opportunity is lost forever. So the schedule must be designed to capture as much business as possible, maximizing revenues with as little direct operating cost as possible. The airline industry combines the worst of two worlds—it has the capital-intensive quality of the manufacturing sector and the low profit margin quality of the retail sector. Airlines are capital, fuel, and labor intensive. Survival and success depend on the ability to operate flights along the schedule as efficiently as possible.

Both the size of the fleet and the number of different types of aircraft have a significant impact on schedule planning. The basic trade-off is that if the airline assigns too small a plane to a particular market, it will leave potential passengers behind, while if it assigns too large a plane, it will suffer the expense of the larger plane transporting empty seats. The goal is to have the right plane at the right place at the right time, but the many constraints on the way that planes can actually be operated make this difficult to accomplish.

Delta implemented a large scale linear program (LP) to assign fleet types to flight legs so as to minimize a combination of operating and passenger "spill" costs, subject to a variety of operational constraints. The most important operational constraint is the number of aircraft available in each fleet. Some of the complicating factors include planning for scheduled maintenance (e.g., which is the best city to do the maintenance?), matching which pilots have the skills to fly which aircraft, providing sufficient opportunity for pilot rest time, as well as other factors such as the range and speed capability of the aircraft and airport restrictions (e.g., noise levels).

The typical size of the LP model that Delta has to optimize daily is 40,000 constraints and 60,000 decision variables. Use of this LP model is expected to save Delta $300 million over the next three years. American Airlines has also reported using such LP models to help it save millions of dollars. (See Subramanian et al.)

3.1   INTRODUCTION TO LINEAR PROGRAMMING

As we saw in the Oak Products example at the end of Chapter 2, constrained optimization models are important because they capture the essence of many important management situations. Recall from the Oak Products example, a constrained optimization model takes the form of a performance measure to be optimized over a range of feasible values of the decision variables. The feasible values of the decision variables are determined by a set of inequality constraints. That is, we must choose the values of the decision variables in such a way as to satisfy the inequality constraints while making the performance measure as large (maximization model) or as small (minimization model) as possible. For Oak Products, this was the task of finding the values of six quantity-to-produce decision variables, one for each chair type, while satisfying eleven constraints on the resources available.

Of course, "What if?" projections with the Oak Products model is one way to investigate the consequences of alternative product mixes; that is, the values of each of the six chair production quantities. Our goal is now more ambitious. In this chapter, we want to move beyond "What if?" projections to address the question of "What's best?" by finding optimal decisions. In so doing, we must avoid random or unsystematic search over a range of decision alternatives for fear of missing the optimal decision. However, a systematic "What if?" search over the range of decision alternatives for a typical constrained optimization model would quickly become tedious even if you were the most obsessive spreadsheet user. Moreover, you cannot appeal to the Data Table command to help automate the search, as it handles at most two decision variables at a time.

Even if you could utilize an extended (more than two variable) Data Table, consider the time it would take you to do a "What if?" investigation for the Oak Products production model assuming each of the six decision variables could take on, say, 100 different candidate production quantity values. Exhaustive "What if?" investigation of all the combinations of the first decision variable (quantity of Captain chairs to produce) for each of its 100 candidate values with each of the other 5 decision variables over each of their 100 values in order to tally the profit implications of each combination is practically impossible—no matter how extended the Data Table command becomes or how fast your computer.

Each of the 100 values of the first decision variable would need to be paired with the 100 values of the second decision variable (quantity of Mate chairs to produce). This yields 10,000 "What if?" inputs to give to the spreadsheet model, which in turn would compute the model's profit numbers and constraints for these 10,000 input values. But for each of these 10,000 input values there are 100 values of the third decision variable to examine, yielding 1,000,000 "What if?" inputs into the spreadsheet for tabulation for the first three decision variables. Do you see the pattern developing? Each added decision variable *multiplies* the previous number of "What if?" input combinations by 100. Since there are altogether 6 decision variables for the Oak Products model, the total number of "What if?" inputs for the spreadsheet model to tally is 100 times itself 6 times, yielding 100^6 or 10^{12} possible alternatives to investigate. That is a million million "What if?" alternatives to examine for feasibility (no constraints violated) and profitability!

(For fun, consider a slightly larger version of the Oak Products model having 20 chair types to produce instead of 6. Again, assume each chair-type decision variable could take on 100 candidate production quantities. As before, the task is to completely enumerate all possible combinations of the 100 input values for each of the 20 chair types to ascertain the profit-maximizing combination. To make it interesting, assume you were given simultaneous use of the computing capacity of all the 40 million or so computers connected to the Internet and each of them would be dedicated to running the Oak Products spreadsheet model at the rate of, say, 100,000 or even 1,000,000 "What if?" projections per second. Use Excel to compute how many days tallying all the alternative "What if?" projections would occupy all the computers connected to the Internet for this 20 decision variable example. The answer might surprise you.)

Of course, the vast majority of chair production combinations in the Oak Products example are uninteresting because they would violate one or more constraints in the model or have low profitability. But which combinations of alternatives are those? It is difficult to know in advance without first "What if?" testing of each of them in Excel—a "Catch-22" situation. In short, constrained optimization models are a breed apart from the more simple "What if?" models we developed earlier. We must find a faster and more efficient way to "What if?" search over the set of decision alternatives. To do this we must, in effect, "turn the table around" by taking the spreadsheet model *inputs* normally used for "What if?" analysis—the decision variables in this case—and make them into model *outputs*. This allows us to bypass exhaustive enumeration of many thousands of "What if?" input alternatives in favor of more efficient search procedures.

The Oak Products example involved six decisions (the quantity of chairs of each of six types to manufacture) and eleven constraints. Like the Delta Air Lines model described earlier, some optimization models involve thousands or even tens of thousands of decision variables and constraints requiring special software and large scale computers. However, many interesting management-oriented optimization models involve tens or hundreds of decision variables and constraints. For models in this latter range of size, a spreadsheet package provides a near-perfect combination of flexibility, convenience of modeling, ease of use, and computational power for optimization.

Very efficient search techniques exist to optimize constrained linear models. For historical reasons a constrained linear model is called a linear program (LP). However, the flexibility of a spreadsheet requires some attention to LP model representation in it before we can proceed with the details of the optimization process itself. Our goals in this chapter are (1) to develop some techniques for formulating LP models; (2) to give some recommended rules for expressing LP models in a spreadsheet that facilitates application of Solver, the optimizer package built into Excel (and several other spreadsheet packages); and (3) to use Solver to optimize spreadsheet LP models far more efficiently than exhaustive search.

3.2   **FORMULATING LP MODELS**

CONSTRAINTS

For our purposes, a first step in model formulation will be the recognition of **constraints.** In Chapter 2's Oak Products model we saw numerous causes for the appearance of constraints. Constraints can be thought of as *restrictions* on the set of allowable decisions. Specific illustrations of such restrictions are particularly evident when dealing with the problems of management. For example:

1. A portfolio manager has a certain amount of capital at his or her discretion. Investment decisions are restricted by the amount of that capital and government regulations, such as those of the Securities and Exchange Commission.

2. The decisions of a plant manager are restricted by the capacity of the plant and the availability of resources.

3. The staffing and flight plans of an airline are restricted by the maintenance needs of the planes and the number of employees on hand.

4. An oil company's decision to use a certain type of crude oil in producing gasoline is restricted by the characteristics of the gasoline (e.g., the octane rating and the anti-knock capabilities).

In the context of modeling, a restriction, or constraint, on the allowable decisions is a concept of special importance. Constraints are often in one of two forms: *limitations* or *requirements*. The constraints may be further classified to reflect physical limitations or requirements, economic limitations or requirements, or policy limitations or requirements. In the examples listed above:

1. The portfolio manager is constrained by limitations of capital (economic limitation) and the stipulations of the Securities and Exchange Commission (policy limitations or requirements).

2. Production decisions are constrained by limitations on capacity (physical limitations) and resource availability (physical and economic limitations).

E-9 produced will use 10 hours of machining in department A. Each F-9 produced will use 15 hours in department A. Hence, for any particular production plan

10(no. E-9s produced) + 15(no. F-9s produced) = total hours used in dept. A.

This can be expressed more easily if we introduce some simple notation. Let

$$E = \text{number of E-9s to be produced}$$
$$F = \text{number of F-9s to be produced}$$

Then the expression for the total hours used in department A becomes

$$10E + 15F = \text{total hours used in dept. A}$$

But, as already stated, that at most 150 hours is available in department A, it follows that the decision variables E and F must satisfy the condition (i.e., the restriction)

$$10E + 15F \leq 150 \tag{3.1}$$

This is the constraint on hours used in department A. The symbol $\leq$ means *less than or equal to* and condition (3.1) is called an **inequality constraint.** The number 150 is called the **right-hand side** (RHS) of the inequality. The left-hand side (LHS) of the inequality clearly depends on the unknowns E and F, and is called a **constraint function.** The inequality (3.1) is a concise symbolic way of stating the constraint that the total number of hours used in department A to produce E units of E-9 and F units of F-9 must not exceed the 150 hours available.

We also see that each E-9 produced will use 20 hours of machining in department B and each F-9 produced will use 10 hours of machining in department B. Since there are at most 160 hours available in department B, it follows that the values of E and F must also satisfy

$$20E + 10F \leq 160 \tag{3.2}$$

Inequalities (3.1) and (3.2) represent two of the constraints in the current problem. Are there any others? The foregoing discussion of major considerations indicates that there is also a union agreement to be honored (i.e., major consideration 4). Each E-9 produced will use 30 hours of testing, and each F-9 produced will use 10 hours of testing. Thus

$$30E + 10F = \text{total hours used for testing}$$

The total labor hours used in testing cannot fall below 135 hours. Hence, we obtain the constraint

$$30E + 10F \geq 135 \tag{3.3}$$

The symbol $\geq$ means *greater than or equal to,* and condition (3.3) is also called an inequality constraint. Note that condition (3.3) is an inequality of the $\geq$ type (a requirement), as opposed to conditions (3.1) and (3.2), which are inequalities of the $\leq$ type (limitations).

Another constraint is that at least one F-9 must be produced for every three E-9s produced. This is stated in symbols as

$$\frac{E}{3} \leq F$$

Since both sides of an inequality can be multiplied by the same positive number without changing the direction of the inequality, we can multiply both sides of this latter constraint by 3 to obtain

$$E \leq 3F$$

Later in Chapter 5, we will see that proper interpretation of spreadsheet optimization reports is facilitated if such an inequality is expressed with all of the decision variables on the left side (thereby forming the constraint function). Thus, in this case we subtract $3F$ from both sides to obtain the convenient expression

$$E - 3F \leq 0 \tag{3.4}$$

You may often write the coefficients for this kind of constraint incorrectly. For example, you might write $3E \leq F$. Begin by first writing something, and then check that the constraint does in algebra what it says in English.

The sixth major consideration states that at least five units must be produced next month, in any combination whatever. This constraint is simply stated as

$$E + F \geq 5 \tag{3.5}$$

We have now specified in concise symbolic form five inequality constraints associated with PROTRAC's production problem. Since it does not make physical sense to produce a negative number of E-9s or F-9s, we must include the two additional conditions

$$E \geq 0, F \geq 0 \tag{3.6}$$

Conditions such as (3.6), which require E and F to be nonnegative, are called **nonnegativity conditions.** It is important to bear in mind that the term *nonnegative* is not the same as the term *positive*. The difference is that *nonnegative* allows for the possibility of the value zero, whereas the term *positive* forbids this value.

In summary, here are the constraints and the nonnegativity conditions for the PRO-TRAC, Inc. model:

$10E + 15F$	≤ 150	**(3.1)**
$20E + 10F$	≤ 160	**(3.2)**
$30E + 10F$	≥ 135	**(3.3)**
$E - 3F$	≤ 0	**(3.4)**
$E + F$	≥ 5	**(3.5)**
$E \geq 0, F \geq 0$		**(3.6)**

EVALUATING VARIOUS DECISIONS

In the model above, the choice of values for the pair of variables (E, F) is called a decision; E and F are called **decision variables** because these are quantities that management controls. Clearly, in this problem a decision is a production mix. For example, $E = 6, F = 5$ is a decision to make six E-9s and five F-9s. Some nonnegative decisions will satisfy all of the constraints (3.1) through (3.5) of our model and some will not. For example, the decision $E = 6, F = 5$ can be seen to satisfy constraints (3.1), (3.3), (3.4), and (3.5) and to violate constraint (3.2). To see this, we substitute $E = 6, F = 5$ into constraints (3.1) through (3.5) and evaluate the results. Doing this, we obtain

Constraint 1.

$$10E + 15F \leq 150$$
$$10(6) + 15(5) \leq 150$$
$$60 + 75 \leq 150$$
$$135 \leq 150 \text{ true}$$

Hence, this constraint is satisfied when $E = 6, F = 5$.

Constraint 2.

$$20E + 10F \leq 160$$
$$20(6) + 10(5) \leq 160$$
$$120 + 50 \leq 160$$
$$170 \leq 160 \text{ false}$$

Hence, this constraint is violated when $E = 6, F = 5$.

In the same fashion, the decision $E = 6$, $F = 5$ satisfies constraints (3.3), (3.4), and (3.5). Similarly, the production mix $E = 5$, $F = 4$ satisfies all the constraints.

The mix, or decision, $E = 6$, $F = 5$ is not allowable because, as we have just seen, there are not enough hours available in department B (constraint 3.2) to support this decision. Another way of saying the same thing is that this decision is not allowable because it has violated one of the constraints. Of the infinitely many nonnegative pairs of numbers (E, F), some pairs, or decisions, will violate at least one of the constraints, and some will satisfy all the constraints. In our model, only decisions that satisfy *all* the constraints are allowable. Such decisions are called **feasible decisions.**

The Objective Function. Of all the allowable, or feasible, decisions, which one should be made? As we have noted earlier, every linear programming model has a specific objective as well as constraints. The management of PROTRAC, Inc. would like to maximize next month's profit, so this is the objective. PROTRAC's profit clearly comes from two sources.

1. There is profit contribution from the sale of E-9s.
2. There is profit contribution from the sale of F-9s.

In our earlier discussion of major factors to be considered it was stated that the unit contribution margin is $5000 for each E-9 and $4000 for each F-9. Since PROTRAC makes $5000 for each E-9 produced, and since E denotes the number of E-9s to be produced, we see that

$$5000E = \text{profit contribution from producing } E \text{ units of E-9}$$

Similarly,

$$4000F = \text{profit contribution from producing } F \text{ units of F-9}$$

Thus, the decision to produce E units of E-9 and F units of F-9 results in a total profit contribution given by

$$\text{total profit contribution} = 5000E + 4000F \qquad (3.7)$$

Note, in general, that when only revenue data are given (or available) the only thing that can be done is to maximize revenue subject to the constraints. If only variable cost data are available, then all that can be done is to minimize the cost of having to produce a certain product mix. However, if variable cost and revenue data are available, it is usually more advantageous to maximize profit contribution rather than revenue.

An Optimal Solution. Of all the infinitely many decisions that satisfy all the constraints (i.e., of all feasible decisions), one that gives the largest total profit contribution will be called a *solution* to PROTRAC's problem, or, as often referred to, an **optimal solution.** Thus, we seek a decision that will *maximize* total profit contribution relative to the set of all possible feasible decisions. Such a decision is called an **optimal decision.** Since total profit contribution is *a function* of the variables E, F, we refer to the expression $5000E + 4000F$ as the *objective function,* and we want to find feasible values of E and F that **optimize** (which in this case means maximize) the objective function. Our objective, then, in symbolic terms, is stated concisely as

$$\text{maximize } 5000E + 4000F$$

or, even more simply, this is usually written as

$$\text{Max } 5000E + 4000F \qquad (3.8)$$

The objective function is to be maximized *only* over the set of feasible decisions.

For instance, it was seen earlier that the decision $E = 5$, $F = 4$ is feasible because it satisfies all the constraints. Corresponding to this decision, the *objective value* would be

$$\text{total profit} = 5000E + 4000F$$
$$= 5000(5) + 4000(4) = 41{,}000$$

Associated with the decision E 5 6, F 5 5 the objective value would be

$$\text{total profit contribution} = 5000E + 4000F$$
$$= 5000(6) + 4000(5) = 50{,}000$$

Improving the Objective Value. Although this objective value is larger than the previous one, and thereby more attractive, we recall that $E = 6$, $F = 5$ is not a feasible decision because it violates one of the constraints. Hence, PROTRAC is not able to consider this decision. It must be discarded. Is there a preferred *feasible* decision; that is, one for which the objective value exceeds 41,000? For example, the decision $E = 6$, $F = 3.5$ satisfies all the constraints and yields an objective value of 44,000, which is clearly an improvement over 41,000. Is this production plan ($E = 6$, $F = 3.5$) an optimal decision (i.e., a solution to our model) or is it possible to do even better? Remember that only feasible decisions can be considered—that is, the production alternatives that satisfy *all* the constraints.

OBSERVATIONS ON THE PROTRAC MODEL

In the following section we shall see how to rigorously (i.e., without guesswork) optimize this model and many others like it from their spreadsheet representation. Also, we shall see how Solver is used to do much of the work for us. Let us first, however, take a moment to review the complete symbolic formulation of the PROTRAC, Inc. model and to make several observations on the form of this model.

In the preceding discussion we translated a verbal description of a real-world situation into a complete symbolic model with an objective function and constraints. This model, which we call the **symbolic LP model,** is

$$\text{Max } 5000E + 4000F \text{ (objective function)}$$
$$\text{subject to (s.t.)}$$
$$10E + 15F \leq 150 \text{ (hours in department A)}$$
$$20E + 10F \leq 160 \text{ (hours in department B)}$$
$$30E + 10F \geq 135 \text{ (testing hours)}$$
$$E - 3F \quad \leq 0 \quad \text{(mix constraint)}$$
$$E + F \quad \geq 5 \quad \text{(total units requirement)}$$
$$E, F \quad \geq 0 \quad \text{(nonnegativity conditions)}$$

Linear Functions. Notice that in the LP model above, all the constraint functions (recall that the constraint functions are the left-hand sides of the inequality constraints) and the objective function are **linear functions** of the decision variables. As you may recall, the graph of a linear function of two variables is a straight line. In general, a linear function is one where each variable appears in a separate term together with its coefficient (i.e., there are no products or quotients of variables; no exponents other than 1; no logarithmic, exponential, IF() statements, or trigonometric terms). As you can see, this is true of each function in the model above. By contrast, $14E + 12EF$ is a nonlinear function because of the term $12EF$ involving a product of the variables. Also, $9E^2 + 8F$ is nonlinear because the variable E is raised to the power 2. Other examples of nonlinear functions are $6\sqrt{E} + F$ and $19 \, Log \, E + 12E^2F$. Examples of Excel functions that frequently introduce nonlinearity into models are IF(), MAX(), MIN(), LN(), and ABS().

As you might imagine, from the mathematical point of view, nonlinear functions are more difficult to deal with. The power of linear programming, in applications, stems from the power of linear relationships (equalities and inequalities) and from the fact that linear models can be readily used in real situations by managers with little training in the underlying mathematics. For our purposes at this time the important facts to be remembered are

1. A linear program always has an objective function (to be either maximized or minimized) and constraints.
2. All functions in the problem (objective and constraints) are *linear functions.*

Integrality Considerations. In making a final observation, let us take another look at the complete formulation of the PROTRAC, Inc. model. It should be pointed out that unless we put in specific additional constraints, which force the decision variables to be integers, we must be prepared to accept fractional solutions. In many LP models, such as in the PROTRAC, Inc. model, it will be true that fractional values for the decision variables do not have meaningful physical interpretations. For example, a solution that says "produce 3.12 E-9s and 6.88 F-9s" may not be directly implementable. On the other hand, there are many problems for which fractions obviously have meaning (e.g., "produce 98.65 gallons of crude oil"). In those cases where fractional answers are not meaningful, there are four possible recourses:

1. Add a so-called **integrality condition** to the LP model, which forces one or more decision variables to take on only integer values. This changes the model to what is called an integer optimization model or **integer program.** Integer programming models involve many additional considerations beyond the usual linear program. Integer programs are discussed at length in Chapter 7.
2. Solve the model as an ordinary LP and then round (e.g., to the nearest integer) any decision variable for which a fractional answer cannot be implemented. In many cases this simple and plausible tactic produces solutions that may not be feasible or may not be optimal. The advantages and disadvantages of this approach are also discussed in Chapter 7.
3. Consider the one-month PROTRAC model results to be an *average* month's production for a multiple month model. For example, a solution that says "produce 3.5 E-9s and 6.25 F-9s" can be implemented as "follow a production plan that produces 3.5 E-9s every month but (a) sells 3 E-9s in one month leaving one half an E-9 as 'work-in-process' inventory that is carried over to be finished the next month, and (b) sells 4 E-9s every other month. Similarly, produce 6.25 F-9s every month but (a) sell only 6 F-9s each month carrying any fractional F-9 as work-in-process inventory into the next month, except (b) sell 7 F-9s in every fourth month." Clearly, such a rule results in production and sales averaged over each four-month interval of 3.5 E-9s and 6.25 F-9s per month, as stipulated by the LP solution. The advantages and disadvantages of using an average month model as a surrogate for production decisions across several months are discussed in Chapter 6 on formulating "dynamic models," that is, multi-time-period models.
4. Consider the one-month PROTRAC model results to be for planning purposes only and not operational decisions to be implemented *per se.* That is, the model results will serve only as a guide for final decision making, which necessarily will involve many other real-world considerations not captured by the more abstract LP model. Such considerations may very likely force the final management decisions to deviate from the fractional-valued LP decisions anyway. In this case, the LP model solution provides a starting point for such considerations or the basis for managerial insight which you recall was the original rationale for modeling developed in Chapter 1.

In practice, all of these approaches are adopted. For the present it will suffice to assume that either fractional solutions are meaningful for the purpose of implementation or that the model is the basis for planning and insight—option 4 above.

3.3   GUIDELINES AND COMMENTS ON MODEL FORMULATION

In translating a managerial situation into a symbolic model, you may find it helpful first to create a verbal model. That is, you might proceed as follows:

1. Express each constraint in words; in doing this, pay careful attention to whether the constraint is a requirement of the form ≥ (at least as large as), a limitation of the form ≤ (no larger than), or = (exactly equal to).

2. Then express the objective and its performance measure objective function in words.

Steps 1 and 2 should then allow you to

3. Verbally identify the decision variables.

It is usually of great importance that your decision variables be correctly defined. Sometimes you may feel that there are several possible choices. For example, should they represent pounds of finished product or pounds of raw material? One guideline that is often useful is to ask yourself the question, *What decisions must be made in order to optimize the objective function?* The answer to this question will help lead you to identify the decision variables correctly.

Having accomplished steps 1 through 3, invent symbolic notation for the decision variables. Then

4. Express each constraint in symbols (i.e., in terms of the decision variables).

5. Express the objective function in symbols (in terms of the decision variables).

At this stage it is advisable to check your work for consistency of units of measurement. For example, if the coefficients in the objective function are in dollars per *pound,* the decision variables that appear in the objective function should be in pounds, not tons or ounces. Similarly, check that for each constraint the units on the right-hand side and the units on the left-hand side are the same. For example, if one of the constraints is a limitation of ≤ form on labor hours, the right-hand side will be labor hours. Then if, as above, the decision variables are pounds, the data for this constraint function (i.e., the numerical coefficients for each decision variable on the left-hand side of the constraint) should be in labor hours per pound. To put it quite simply, you do not want to end up with hours on one side of any equality or inequality and minutes or seconds or pounds or tons on the other.

At this point it would be a good idea to comment on one other aspect of model formulation. We have seen that inequality constraints may be of the form ≤ or ≥. Students often ask whether a linear programming model can have a *strict inequality* constraint, such as < or >. The answer is *no.* The reason for this is to assure that a well-formulated model will have a solution. The mathematical details required to justify this assertion lie outside our scope of interest. However, this is not a costly prohibition, for in just about any situation you can imagine involving inequality constraints, it is true that the ≤ or ≥ representation entirely captures the real-world meaning. For example, if a variable X must be < 15, then using $X \leq 14.9999999999$ in the model will likely be adequate for management purposes.

Let us now discuss one final aspect of model formulation. This deals with the nature of the cost data to be employed.

3.4   SUNK VERSUS VARIABLE COST

In many real-world situations there are often two types of costs: **sunk costs,** also referred to as **fixed costs,** and **variable costs.** Contrary to the first impressions that students sometimes have, sunk costs play no part in optimization.

> Only the variable costs are relevant in optimization models.

The sunk, or fixed, costs have already been paid, which means that no future decisions can affect these expenditures. For example, suppose that 800 pounds and 500 pounds of two grades of aluminum (grade 1 and grade 2) have been purchased for future delivery, at specified prices, $5 and $10 per pound, respectively, and that the contract has been signed. Management's problem is, in part, to determine the optimal use of these 1300 pounds of aluminum so as, perhaps, to maximize profit obtained from producing aluminum knuckles and conduits. Associated with these two products there will be revenues and variable costs incurred in their production (costs of machining, stamping, and so on). In formulations of this type of model, the sunk costs of $9000 associated with the contracted purchase are irrelevant. This amount has already been spent and hence the *quantities to be purchased* are no longer decision variables. The variables will be how much product should be produced, and the relevant cost in this determination is only the variable cost. More specifically, the formulation corresponding to the description above might be as follows. Let

K = number of knuckles to be produced (decision variable)

C = number of conduits to be produced (decision variable)

$10 = revenue per knuckle

$30 = revenue per conduit

$4 = cost of producing a knuckle (variable cost)

$12 = cost of producing a conduit (variable cost)

For each product we must calculate what accountants call the *unit contribution margin;* that is, the difference between per unit revenue and per unit variable cost. The unit contribution margins are

for knuckles: $10 − $4 = $6

for conduits: $30 − $12 = $18

Suppose that each knuckle uses 1 unit of grade 1 aluminum and 2 units of grade 2 aluminum. Each conduit uses 3 units of grade 1 and 5 units of grade 2. Then we obtain the following symbolic linear programming model:

$$\text{Max } 6K + 18C$$
$$\text{s.t. } K + 3C \leq 800 \text{ (grade 1 limitation)}$$
$$2K + 5C \leq 500 \text{ (grade 2 limitation)}$$
$$K \geq 0, \quad C \geq 0$$

One way to see the irrelevance of the sunk cost is to note that the objective function in the formulation is the total profit contribution. The income, or net profit, would be

$$\text{net profit} = \text{profit contribution} - \text{sunk cost}$$
$$= 6K + 18C - 9000$$

However, finding feasible values of K and C that maximize $6K + 18C - 9000$ is the same as finding feasible values that maximize $6K + 18C$. The constant term of 9000 can therefore be ignored. The bottom line here is that maximizing a function plus a constant, or even a positive constant times a function, gives in either case the same result, in terms of optimal values of decision variables, that you would obtain without the constant. However, adding (or subtracting) the same constant to (or from) each decision variable *coefficient* in the objective function may change the result.

To summarize, sunk costs affect only the accounting report of income or net profit in financial statements. Sunk costs play no part in decision making because by definition they are unrelated to future decisions, the subject of the modeling activity. Of course, there is no harm in subtracting the sunk cost from the objective function in the model—the same optimal decisions will be found when the model is optimized. However, there is great harm in attempting to allocate the sunk costs to the production activities if that allocation involves adjusting the variable cost coefficients in the model instead of just subtracting the total allocated costs from total contribution.

A common mistake made by managers is to confuse an organization's accounting policies for allocating fixed costs to activities with the proper (short-run) decision making involving those activities. For example, suppose the company above has a policy to split the $9000 sunk cost, say, in half, charging the Knuckle Department $4500 and the Conduit Department $4500. This would have no effect upon departmental decision making—reported profit from each department would be reduced by $4500 and reported overall corporate profit would reflect the same $9000 cost. But if the Knuckle Department revises the knuckle production cost coefficient in its LP production model from the variable cost of $4 used originally to $4 + $4500/K, where the $4500/K term is the average of the apportioned sunk cost per knuckle produced, then nonoptimal decisions will occur when the model is optimized. Why is this? Because the actual incremental cost of producing an additional knuckle is $4—no more and no less. Adding the additional term to the knuckle variable cost to reflect an averaging of the sunk costs, therefore, misstates the incremental (marginal) cost of knuckle production, and it is the behavior of the incremental costs that is important in optimizing decisions.

To see this, assume that $K = 1000$ knuckles were being produced when the allocation of the sunk costs occurred. Under the "averaging-of-sunk-costs" scheme, the Knuckle Department will record that its average cost of knuckle production was $4 + $4500/1000 = $8.50 per knuckle. We know that producing the $K+1$st knuckle will cost the department an additional $4, its variable cost of production. However, substituting $8.50 as the knuckle production cost coefficient in the LP model misstates the cost dynamics by forcing the model to use $8.50 as the incremental cost of that knuckle. This, in turn, will lead to much smaller than optimal quantities of knuckle production when the model is optimized. In short, calculating an average cost quantity from an apportioned sunk or fixed cost and then treating it as if it were a marginal or variable cost is a common management mistake to avoid in formulating an LP (or any other) model.

Treatment of sunk and variable costs is nicely illustrated in the Red Brand Canners case at chapter's end. This case is a good illustration of how both sunk and variable costs arise in real-world situations.

3.5 THE PROTRAC SPREADSHEET MODEL

CREATING THE PROTRAC SPREADSHEET

The LP model for PROTRAC production in terms of the decision variables E (= the number of E-9s to produce) and F (= the number of F-9s to produce) is given by:

$$\text{Max } 5000E + 4000F \qquad \text{(maximize profit contribution)}$$

Subject to

$10E + 15F$	≤ 150	(capacity in department A)
$20E + 10F$	≤ 160	(capacity in department B)
$E - 3F$	≤ 0	(market position balance)
$30E + 10F$	≥ 135	(hours used in testing)
$E + F$	≥ 5	(minimum production requirement)
$E \geq 0$ and $F \geq 0$		(nonnegativity conditions)

Note that the constraints have been regrouped to put all constraints of a like-type of inequality together. The reason for grouping constraints will become clear when Solver is introduced. A spreadsheet version of the PROTRAC model, available as PROTRAC.XLS, is shown in Figure 3.1. The figure shows the model results for the E-9 production of 6 and F-9 production of 5 illustrated in the previous section. Notice that, as before, these production quantities violate the department B capacity constraint, requiring more hours than available in that department next month.

Although most of the entries in the spreadsheet are self-explanatory, you should consult the formulas for the spreadsheet to verify that the spreadsheet has faithfully captured the symbolic model for PROTRAC production. (As usual, consult the Excel Appendix for additional information on any spreadsheet items you do not understand.)

Also, pay close attention in Figure 3.1 to the layout of the spreadsheet model and how labels, coefficients, and decision variables are used, and how "slack" is computed.

Labels In particular, some cells contain labels. The labels are used in the same way that you would use labels to help read a table of data. Their purpose is to clarify the meaning of other entries in the spreadsheet.

	A	B	C	D	E	F	G
1		**Protrac Production Plan**					
2	Product:	E-9	F-9				
3	Production Qty.	6	5	Profit			
4	Unit Contri. Mar.	$5,000	$4,000	$50,000			
5	Constraints	Resource Usage		Total LHS		RHS	Slack
6	Dept. A	10	15	135	≤	150	15
7	Dept B	20	10	170	≤	160	-10
8	Mix Requirement	1	-3	-9	≤	0	9
9	Test Hours	30	10	230	≥	135	95
10	Total Units	1	1	11	≥	5	6

	A	B	C	D	E	F	G
1	Protrac Proc						
2	Product:	E-9	F-9				
3	Production Qt	6	5	Profit			
4	Unit Contri. M	5000	4000	=SUMPRODUCT($B$3:$C$3,B4:C4)			
5	Constraints	Res		Total LHS		RHS	Slack
6	Dept. A	10	15	=SUMPRODUCT($B$3:$C$3,B6:C6)	≤	150	=F6-D6
7	Dept B	20	10	=SUMPRODUCT($B$3:$C$3,B7:C7)	≤	160	=F7-D7
8	Mix Requirem	1	-3	=SUMPRODUCT($B$3:$C$3,B8:C8)	≤	0	=F8-D8
9	Test Hours	30	10	=SUMPRODUCT($B$3:$C$3,B9:C9)	≥	135	=D9-F9
10	Total Units	1	1	=SUMPRODUCT($B$3:$C$3,B10:C10)	≥	5	=D10-F10

TIP: *The easiest way to produce inequality symbols, such as the ≤ in cell E6, is to type the < character into the cell and then underline it using Excel's underline tool.*

FIGURE 3.1

The PROTRAC Production LP Model

Coefficients and Decision Variables Other cells contain numbers. Generally these numbers will represent

1. The numeric value of coefficients which are the *data* for the given LP model.
2. Numeric values called **decision values** or just **decisions** for short.

Formulas Still other cells contain *formulas*. In the spreadsheet representation of an LP model, formulas are required to represent the objective function and the constraint functions. In some instances, there may be underlying formulas that determine the numeric value of various coefficients in the model. For some coefficients, numeric values will be entered directly. Other coefficients might be computed from formulas.

With the exception of column G the entries in the spreadsheet should be self-explanatory. You can see that the data in columns B and C rows 6 through 10 come directly from the symbolic LP model for PROTRAC. Although these data have been labeled as "Resource Usage," the only "resources" in this problem are labor hours in departments A and B, respectively, and the label is appropriate only for rows 6 and 7. There is no need to be pedantic. In creating the spreadsheet representation, you can choose any labeling text that suits your purpose. Our purpose here is simply to illustrate the process.

Computing Slack The entries that appear in G6:G10 are often termed *slack*.

In spreadsheet LP models, *slack* is the difference between the constraint function and the right-hand side, computed so that it is nonnegative.

Slack calculations in the spreadsheet LP model are optional. They give an indication of how close the constraint is to **binding,** that is, evaluated as an equality; zero slack indicates a binding constraint. For example, look at the slack formula in cell G6. This slack value corresponds to the department A capacity constraint, which is $10E + 15F \le 150$. The spreadsheet shows the formula F6 − D6 for the slack value. If we substitute the contents of F6 and D6, we see that F6 − D6 is

$$150 - 135$$

	A	B	C	D	E	F	G
1		Protrac Production Plan					
2	Product:	E-9	F-9				
3	Production Qty.	2	8	Profit			
4	Unit Contri. Mar.	$5,000	$4,000	$42,000			
5	Constraints	Resource Usage		Total LHS		RHS	Slack
6	Dept. A	10	15	140	≤	150	10
7	Dept B	20	10	120	≤	160	40
8	Mix Requirement	1	-3	-22	≤	0	22
9	Test Hours	30	10	140	≥	135	5
10	Total Units	1	1	10	≥	5	5

FIGURE 3.2

The PROTRAC Production LP Model for $E = 2$ and $F = 8$

which is the "right-hand side of the first constraint minus the left-hand side." Thus, the slack value for this constraint is unused capacity. Now consider the test hours constraint, $30E + 10F \geq 135$. The entry in cell G9 of the spreadsheet shows that the slack formula for the test hour constraint is the "left-hand side minus the right-hand side," which is the order of subtraction required to make this slack value nonnegative. What we have just illustrated is the following rule:

> For a ≤ constraint, slack is the right-hand side minus the left-hand side.
>
> For a ≥ constraint, slack is the left-hand side minus the right-hand side.

Often more descriptive labels are used in place of *Slack*. For ≤ constraints, a label such as *Unused, Remainder, Residue,* or *Balance* may be preferable. For ≥ constraints, a label such as *Surplus, Oversupply, Excess,* or *Overage* may be preferable.

The obvious use of the PROTRAC spreadsheet model is to perform "What if?" projections for different production decisions—that is, values of E-9 and F-9—by typing values into cells B3 and C3, respectively, and observing cell D4, the resulting profit contribution, while keeping the slack cells, G6 through G10, nonnegative. If, for example, we enter the value 2 into cell B3 and 8 into cell C3 (meaning $E = 2$ and $F = 8$), then the spreadsheet will display the result shown in Figure 3.2.

For example, cell D6 now contains the number 140, which is the number of labor hours in department A when PROTRAC produces the mix ($E = 2$, $F = 8$). Corresponding to this constraint we see, from cell G6, that the slack value is 10, which is $150 - 140$. Hence there are 10 hours of unused labor in department A. See if you can find a high profit by iteratively trying out different decision values for E and F in a "What if?" fashion. You'll quickly see that finding a high profit while not violating any constraints (avoiding negative slack) is not so easy, even for a simple LP model like PROTRAC.

OPTIMIZING THE SPREADSHEET

With Solver you can transform any spreadsheet LP model into an optimized model with a few clicks of the mouse. Figure 3.3 shows the optimized spreadsheet for the PROTRAC LP model. This optimized spreadsheet has computed optimal values for the decision variables E and F. Thus, reading cells B3 and C3, the optimal decision values, which we denote as E^*, F^*, are ($E^* = 4.5$, $F^* = 7$). The spreadsheet also shows optimal numeric values in the LHS constraint function and slack columns.

3.6   THE LP MODEL AND SPREADSHEET MODELING

You have now seen how to capture the PROTRAC production model in two forms, the symbolic LP model and the spreadsheet representation of the LP model.

You may well be wondering, "Do I need to write both the symbolic LP model and the spreadsheet model for every managerial situation I wish to model? Also, why did you lay out the spreadsheet model of PROTRAC as you did? Finally, how did you get Solver to produce the optimal solution in Figure 3.3?"

	A	B	C	D	E	F	G
1	Protrac Production Plan						
2	Product:	E-9	F-9				
3	Production Qty.	4.5	7	Profit			
4	Unit Contri. Mar.	$5,000	$4,000	$50,500			
5	Constraints	Resource Usage		Total LHS		RHS	Slack
6	Dept. A	10	15	150	≤	150	0
7	Dept B	20	10	160	≤	160	0
8	Mix Requirement	1	-3	-16.5	≤	0	16.5
9	Test Hours	30	10	205	≥	135	70
10	Total Units	1	1	11.5	≥	5	6.5

FIGURE 3.3

Profit-Maximizing Values of *E* and *F*

The best answer to your first question is "Yes, until you become more proficient, you should write both the symbolic (algebraic) LP model and the spreadsheet version of it." A spreadsheet is very useful for representing managerial LP models, and is especially useful for subsequent "What if?" manipulations. However, for novices a spreadsheet is not always the best approach to the initial LP model formulation. Experience has shown that until you become more proficient with LP modeling directly in Excel, the preferred approach to quickly producing a bug-free LP model is to break down the process into two steps:

1. **Writing and debugging the symbolic LP model:** Write out the model on paper as a symbolic LP. Proceed to debug it, which means examine your written formulation and look for errors in the logic of the formulation.

2. **Translating and debugging the spreadsheet representation of the symbolic LP model:** Use the symbolic LP model as a guide in creating the spreadsheet representation. Then further debug the spreadsheet representation of the model by trying out several candidate sets of values for the decision variables to see if any obvious errors occur (constraint violations for decisions known to be feasible, nonsense values for LHS or performance measure cells, etc.).

Next, try to optimize it with Solver. An incorrectly formulated model will often trigger a Solver error message. Again, you must now debug your work, possibly by returning to step 1 above.

The symbolic model in step 1 is useful for documentation and allows you to "see" the entire model before delving into the details of its spreadsheet representation. Spreadsheet formulas are often a poor substitute for this global perspective of the LP model and how it relates to the original real-world situation. For a rather complicated model it is easier to examine and mentally analyze the structure of the symbolic LP model first. In fact, elucidating the structure of the underlying LP model will occupy much of our attention for the next few chapters after we address your last two questions.

In answer to your second question ("Why did you lay out the spreadsheet model of PROTRAC as you did?"), the layout of the PROTRAC production model reflects a style of spreadsheet model formulation that we recommend you follow in the beginning for spreadsheet representations of LP models. Haphazard construction of the spreadsheet version of the LP model is by far the most frequent reason for student frustration and lack of results in the optimization phase with Solver that we cover next. Detecting subtle errors in the interrelationships among cells in formulas and avoiding certain interpretation problems for Solver-generated reports is greatly facilitated if initially you follow the style evident in the PROTRAC production model. Later, in Chapter 6, as you become more proficient with LP formulations, we will introduce you to more compact and elegant spreadsheet layouts of LP models. Until then, if you are new to LP modeling, the recommendations for laying out an LP spreadsheet model are as follows:

- Each decision variable is allocated to a separate column and each constraint is allocated to a separate row in the spreadsheet.

- Except for optional labels, the decision variables are grouped into a contiguous block of columns and, except for optional labels, the constraints are grouped into a contiguous block of rows.

- Each decision variable cell and the objective function cell has a label at the top of its column, and each constraint has a label in the leftmost cell of its row. (Do not break a label by putting pieces of it into multiple cells. If a label cannot fit into a single cell, widen the cell width or use the "Wrap Text" option under the Alignment tab in the Format Cells menu to vertically expand the size of the cell.)

- The unit payoff (e.g., contribution margin or cost) coefficients are contained in a separate row of cells immediately above or below their respective decision variables, and the objective function formula appears in a cell in the same row.

- The decision variable cells and the objective function cell (payoff) are formatted with cell borders and/or cell shading—to facilitate readability.

- For each constraint the coefficient involving a given decision variable is placed as a datum in the cell at the intersection of that decision variable's column and that constraint's row.

- Following the coefficients in each constraint row is a cell computing the constraint function value (left-hand-side totals), followed by a cell indicating the direction of the inequality, followed by the right-hand-side proviso cell. Optionally a "slack" cell formula may be included giving the difference between the LHS and RHS quantities computed so that the cell's value is always nonnegative when the constraint is satisfied:

  Slack cell is = RHS − LHS for ≤ (limitation) constraints, and

  Slack cell is = LHS − RHS for ≥ (requirement) constraints

- For the constraint rows the right-hand-side cells should contain constants or formulas not involving the decision variables. To avoid Solver Report interpretation problems later, any constraint right-hand-side formula related directly or indirectly to the decision variables should be algebraically moved to the left-hand side of that constraint.

- Use *no* IF(), ABS(), MAX(), MIN(), and so on functions or other nonlinear functions within the cells of your LP model formulation. Such functions are acceptable in cells elsewhere in the spreadsheet, but *only* if their evaluation cannot affect the objective function cell's calculation directly or indirectly during the Solver optimization process in which alternative decision values are tested.

- Including any nonnegativity constraints on the decision variables into the spreadsheet itself is optional, and typically, they are omitted in favor of specifying them directly in Solver's dialog box.

SPREADSHEET LP MODELING RULES

One consequence of this recommended method of laying out the spreadsheet model is that all the important coefficients in the model are contained in cells that can be easily changed without editing any spreadsheet formulas. Also, the grouping of decision variables and constraints allows convenient use of the spreadsheet Copy command to replicate formulas across cells, such as for the LHS constraint function totals. The layout that results from application of these rules is illustrated visually by Figure 3.4. For now, we recommend you follow this layout scheme for your LP models.

An example of a poorly laid out spreadsheet version of the PROTRAC LP model is given in Figure 3.5.

Notice that, although logically equivalent to the PROTRAC symbolic LP model, this spreadsheet version of the model has all the model's relationships completely buried into the (normally unseen) cell formulas. As discussed in Chapter 2, this "hard-wiring" of the

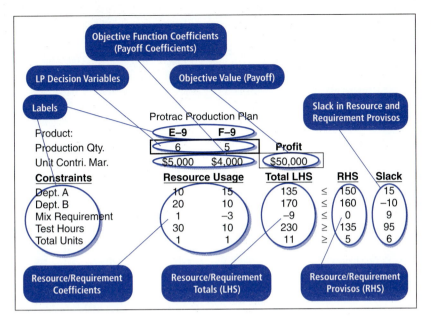

FIGURE 3.4

Recommended Layout for the PROTRAC LP Model

	A	B	C	D
1		**Protrac Production Plan**		
2	Product:	E-9	F-9	Profit
3	Production Qty.	6	5	$50,000
4		Resource Demands		
5	Dept. A	OK		
6	Dept B	Not OK		
7		Requirements		
8	Mix Requirement	Met		
9	Test Hours	Met		
10	Total Units	Met		

	A	B	C	D
1	**Protrac Pr**			
2	Product:	E-9	F-9	Profit
3	Production	6	5	=5000*B3+4000*C3
4		Resource Demands		
5	Dept. A	=IF(10*$B$3+15*$C$3<=150,"OK","Not OK")		
6	Dept B	=IF(20*$B$3+10*$C$3<=160,"OK","Not OK")		
7		Requirements		
8	Mix Require	=IF($B$3-3*$C$3<=0,"Met","Not Met")		
9	Test Hours	=IF(30*$B$3+10*$C$3>=135,"Met","Not Met")		
10	Total Units	=IF($B$3+$C$3>=5,"Met","Not Met")		

FIGURE 3.5

Alternative PROTRAC Production Spreadsheet Model

symbolic relationships into formulas is considered poor modeling practice. This is especially true for models to be optimized. Debugging a failed Solver run is very difficult for a model layout such as in Figure 3.5.

Figure 3.5 points to an important distinction when using a spreadsheet for optimization. Hiding the LP model's coefficients into formulas may produce a clean-looking spreadsheet for external managerial reporting purposes, but it creates one that is cumbersome for purposes of decision support modeling. Generally, thought must be given in advance to the purpose of the spreadsheet model before it is constructed in order to avoid a model layout that is difficult to maintain, modify, or interpret.

Protrac Production Plan

	A	B	C	D	E	F	G	H	I
3		Product:	E-9	F-9					
4		Production Qty.	6	5	Profit				
5		Unit Contri. Mar.	$5,000	$4,000	$50,000				
6		Constraints	Resource Usage		Total Hours		Hrs Avail.	Slack	
7		Dept. A	10	15	135	≤	150	15	
8		Dept. B	20	10	170	≤	160	-10	
9					Total Hours		Hrs Req.		
10		Testing	30	10	230	≥	135	95	
11					Total Quantity		Prod. Req.		
12		Production	1	1	11	≥	5	6	
13		Mix Requirement	1	-3	-9	≤	0	9	
15		Resource Demands			Totals		E-9	F-9	
16		Dept. A	OK		Profit		$30,000	$20,000	
17		Dept B	Not OK		Production Qty		6	5	
18		Requirements			Dept. A Hours		60	90	
19		Test Hours	Met		Dept. B Hours		120	60	
20		Total Production	Met		Testing Hours		180	60	
21		Mix Requirement	Met						

	A	B	C	D	E	F	G	H	I
2		Pr							
3		Product:	E-9	F-9					
4		Production Q	6	5	Profit				
5		Unit Contri. M	5000	4000	=SUMPRODUCT($C$4:$D$4,C5:D5)				
6		Constraints	Resource Usage		Total Hours		Hrs Avail.	Slack	
7		Dept. A	10	15	=SUMPRODUCT($C$4:$D$4,C7:D7)	≤	150	=G7-E7	
8		Dept. B	20	10	=SUMPRODUCT($C$4:$D$4,C8:D8)	≤	160	=G8-E8	
9					Total Hours		Hrs Req.		
10		Testing	30	10	=SUMPRODUCT($C$4:$D$4,C10:D10)	≥	135	=E10-G10	
11					Total Quantity		Prod. Req.		
12		Production	1	1	=SUMPRODUCT($C$4:$D$4,C12:D12)	≥	5	=E12-G12	
13		Mix Requi	1	-3	=SUMPRODUCT($C$4:$D$4,C13:D13)	≤	0	=G13-E13	
15		Resource D			Totals		E-9	F-9	
16		Dept. A	=IF(H7>=0,"OK","Not OK")		Profit		=$C$4*C5	=$D$4*D5	
17		Dept B	=IF(H8>=0,"OK","Not OK")		Production Qty		=C4	=D4	
18		Requirements			Dept. A Hours		=$C$4*C7	=$C$4*D7	
19		Test Hours	=IF(H10>=0,"Met","Not Met")		Dept. B Hours		=$C$4*C8	=$C$4*D8	
20		Total Produc	=IF(H12>=0,"Met","Not Met")		Testing Hours		=$C$4*C10	=$C$4*D10	
21		Mix Requirer	=IF(H13>=0,"Met","Not Met")						

FIGURE 3.6

Combined Modeling and Reporting PROTRAC Model

While remaining consistent with the recommendations, improvements to the previous LP model layouts are possible to (1) add shading of unused cells, (2) add labels where appropriate to the LP model, and (3) include separate informational modules, as exemplified in Figure 3.6.[2] Separate report modules, either within the spreadsheet as shown in rows 15 through 21, or in a separate managerial report sheet within the workbook (using appropriate cell linking formulas), can further aid in debugging your LP models, and also communicating the model results to others. Often a bit of creativity is required to find the best way to represent the LP model while staying within the recommendations for LP model layout.

3.7   OVERVIEW OF SOLVER

Solver is an add-in package to Excel that numerically optimizes constrained models, such as an LP model. In doing this, Solver uses a technique called a mathematical programming algorithm to efficiently find the optimal decisions for a given spreadsheet model. An algo-

---

[2] The IF statements in this spreadsheet are acceptable because the objective function formula in cell D4 is independent of them. Thus the linearity requirements are not violated for the LP model.

rithm is simply a computer code that follows an iterative recipe for finding the optimal decisions. For LPs Solver uses a very efficient optimization algorithm—that works only on LP models—called the "Simplex Method." Not surprisingly, to benefit from this powerful capability there are some prices to pay. As discussed previously, you must set up the spreadsheet model in the appropriate form so that Solver can optimize it; you must adhere to certain technical restrictions imposed on your spreadsheet model by Solver; and most importantly, you must understand the limitations of optimization models to properly interpret Solver's results.

Solver can optimize both linear and nonlinear models. For now, we will focus only upon linear models because they are far less prone to technical difficulties. Remember: For LP optimization *every* formula in your model that includes the decision variables directly (or indirectly via a chain of cell references) and that directly or indirectly affects the objective function cell *must* be linear. The restriction (linearity) is imposed by Solver's Simplex linear programming method that works correctly only for spreadsheet formulas involving linear relationships. Do not forget that many built-in Excel functions—those operations preceded by *function-name*()—involve nonlinear relationships and are not usable in your spreadsheet LP model if you intend to use the linear optimization option of Solver. In particular,

- The occurrence of exponentiation in Excel equations,
- The use of Excel's IF(), ABS(), and LOG() functions, to name three, and
- Forming ratios (X/Y) or products ($X*Y$) of (decision) variables

directly or indirectly, will very likely cause your model to violate linearity if these affect values of your objective function directly or indirectly via the constraints.

> All Excel formulas used in your spreadsheet LP model must involve strictly linear relationships among the (decision) variables, either directly or indirectly, as they pertain to calculation of the objective function cell and the specification of any constraints.

As mentioned previously, it is OK to have nonlinear formulas in your spreadsheet, even if they employ use of decision variable cells, if those formulas do not relate to determining the value of the objective function cell directly, or indirectly through any constraints. An example of this is the calculation of a nonlinear statistic used only for management reporting purposes and not used elsewhere in your spreadsheet's LP formulas.

USING SOLVER

The Solver add-in package consists essentially of two programs. The first is an Excel Visual Basic program that translates your spreadsheet model to an internal representation used by the second program. The second program, residing in memory outside of Excel as a separate software module, carries out the actual optimization and returns the solution to the first program for updating of the spreadsheet. The two communicate by means of Microsoft's application programming interface, the details of which need not concern us. Upon choosing the "Solver. . ." item from Excel's Tools menu, you evoke the first Solver program that prepares your spreadsheet for optimization and calls the second optimizer program.

Your use of Solver, therefore, consists of several steps:

1. Start Excel and perform spreadsheet modeling operations normally. You can develop your Excel model, perform "What if?" and debugging analyses, and print the results in the usual way.

2. Once the model is developed and debugged (and saved to disk!), you optimize it by choosing the "Solver. . ." item from Excel's Tools menu.

3. The Solver add-in and its optimization module will be loaded into memory.[3] When the loading is finished, Solver brings up a dialog box to collect information for the optimization process.

4. After specifying certain housekeeping details, such as which cell contains the objective function formula to be optimized and which cells contain decision variables, you click the dialog's "Solve" button.

5. Solver will then translate your model and begin the optimization process. For small LP models this takes several seconds, or for big models, several minutes or longer.

6. Assuming there are no errors in your spreadsheet LP model, Solver will bring up a Solver Results dialog box in which you can request reports and have Solver update your original model with the optimal decision cell values. Solver creates each requested report on a separate worksheet in your workbook that you can save or print.

7. At this point, you are now in a position to continue "What If" projections to, for example, perform sensitivity analyses in the neighborhood of the optimum decisions.

A diagrammatic view of the steps in using Solver is given in Figure 3.7.

SOLVER TERMINOLOGY

Now that you have the "big picture" of how Solver works, we turn to details of how to instruct Solver to optimize your LP model. First, we need to clarify the terminology Solver uses to view your LP model. This change in terminology is necessary because Solver views the world only through the cells of a spreadsheet and not as the symbolic representation we use in LP models. Otherwise, the differences are nominal. Table 3.3 summarizes the differences in nomenclature between that used for our LP models and Solver.

One additional consideration is important to remember for LP models. Typically, negative decisions have no meaning, and so, often there should be a nonnegativity constraint on the LP's decision variables. Because they are so obvious, these nonnegativity constraints are rarely listed explicitly on the Excel spreadsheet version of the LP model. Overlooking this nonnegativity specification on the decision variables is by far the most common oversight when using Solver for optimizing LP models:

> If negative decisions have no meaning, remember to specify the nonnegativity constraints on your LP model's decision variables before optimizing it with Solver.

TABLE 3.3 Solver Terminology

LP MODELING TERMINOLOGY	SOLVER TERMINOLOGY
Objective Function	Target Cell
Decision Variables	Changing Cells
Constraints	Constraints
Constraint Function (LHS)	Constraint Cell Reference
RHS	Constraint
LP Model	Assume Linear Model

---

[3]Macintosh users of Solver should increase Excel's default memory allocation by about 1 Mbyte to accommodate Solver (and other add-ins). Otherwise, inadequate memory will slow Excel drastically.

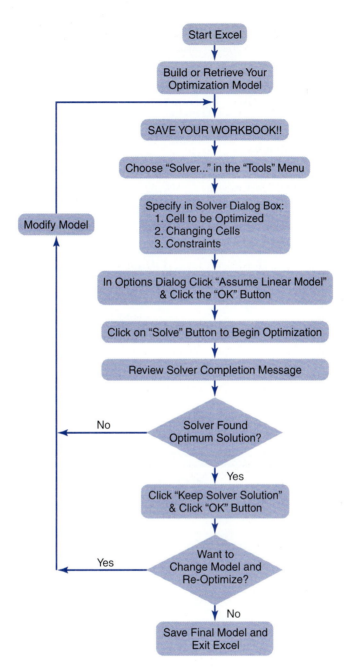

FIGURE 3.7

Solver Flowchart

3.8 OPTIMIZING THE PROTRAC MODEL WITH SOLVER

Learning to use Solver is best if you follow along the steps in this section while sitting at your computer. (If in the process, you run into technical difficulties with Solver, consult the Solver Appendix.) As outlined in the steps of the flowchart in Figure 3.7, if you haven't done so already, launch Excel and open the PROTRAC.XLS workbook containing the PROTRAC spreadsheet model we built previously. Invoke the Solver add-in by selecting "Solver..." from the Tools menu, as shown in Figure 3.8.[4]

---

[4]Usually, the Solver add-in is not automatically installed for Excel during Microsoft's Setup procedure. If Solver is missing from the Tools menu, rerun Setup from your Microsoft Office CD-ROM or Excel floppy disks and use the Custom option in Setup to install Solver. See the Add-In topic in the Excel Appendix for details.

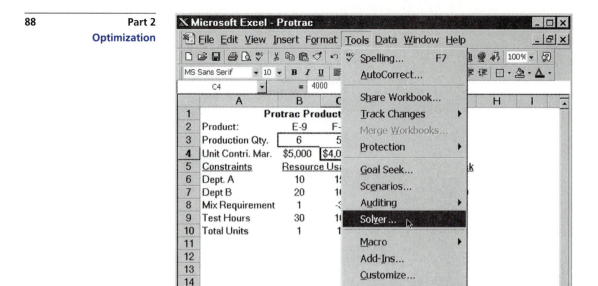

FIGURE 3.8

Invoking Solver

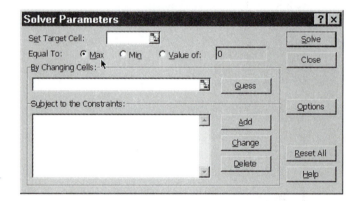

FIGURE 3.9

Solver Parameters Dialog

After the Solver add-in loads into memory, which may take several seconds, the Solver Parameters dialog box should appear, as shown in Figure 3.9. Note that Solver defaults to a "Max"-imization model and the dialog cursor is in the first field: "Set Target Cell."

You can move the Solver Parameters dialog box around on the screen by click-dragging its title bar so that you can see all parts of your PROTRAC spreadsheet. This is very useful because the easiest way to specify cells in the dialog box is to click the cell directly on your underlying spreadsheet model. Clicking on the desired cell(s) eliminates the chance of typographical errors and is usually faster, as well.

The first field, labeled "Set Target Cell," is asking for the cell to be optimized, that is, your model's performance measure. In the PROTRAC model, you could type D4 directly into the "Set Target Cell" box, or better yet, click on cell D4 in the spreadsheet to enter it automatically. This latter approach was used in Figure 3.10. Notice the marquee around cell

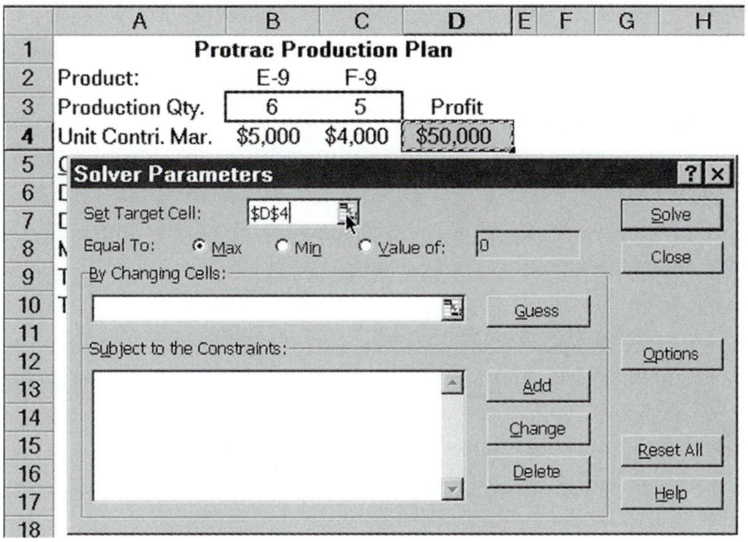

FIGURE 3.10

Specifying Solver's Target Cell

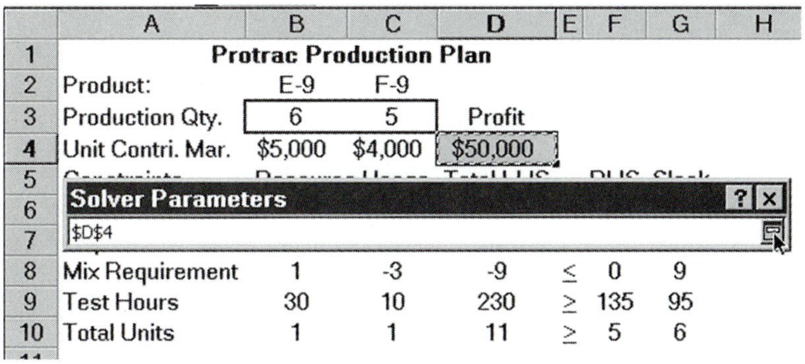

TIP: *If you click on the icon at the right of any Solver Parameters field (under the cursor arrow in Figure 3.10), the dialog will minimize to show only that field, as shown in Figure 3.11. This reveals more of the worksheet to facilitate cell selection. To maximize the dialog back to its full size after cell clicking, press the Enter key or click the icon at the right of the field in Figure 3.11.*

FIGURE 3.11

Minimizing the Solver Parameters Dialog

D4 as confirmation. (When you click on the spreadsheet to enter cell references, Solver inserts $s that signify absolute references. You may use either absolute references—from cell clicking—or relative references—from direct typing of cell references. Either will produce the same result.)

The next field in the dialog box, labeled "Equal To," allows you to define the type of optimization. In this case, you want to maximize the PROTRAC's Profit performance measure cell. To select this option, click on the radio button next to "Max." Alternatively, you could click another radio button to "Min"imize the cell value (for example, if a model's performance measure were Total Cost) or click "Value of" to cause the Target Cell to become equal to a value of your choosing. (This last option allows Solver to perform goal seeking for constrained models with multiple decision variables, an option that cannot be handled by the "unconstrained, single decision variable" Goal Seek command we covered in Chapter 2.)

The next field, labeled "By Changing Cells," allows you to specify the PROTRAC model's decision variables, consisting in this case of cells B3 and C3. So, click in the "By Changing Cells" box, and then on the PROTRAC spreadsheet click-drag over the two cells B3:C3. That will copy the correct range of decision variable cells into the dialog box, as shown in Figure 3.12—again note the marquee around the PROTRAC decision variable cells as confirmation. (You can try Solver Parameters' "Guess" button as a shortcut, but that option frequently guesses the wrong decision variable cell references.)

Next you must define the PROTRAC model's constraints for Solver. Clicking on the button labeled "Add," which is to the right of the box labeled "Subject to the Constraints," will bring up the Add Constraint dialog that allows you to enter a constraint, as shown in Figure 3.13. Note that Add Constraint defaults to a less than or equal to constraint.

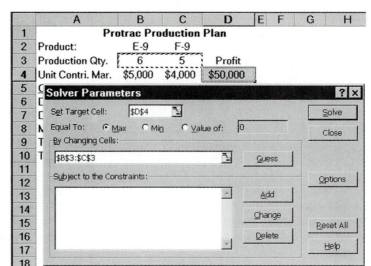

FIGURE 3.12

Specifying Solver's Changing Cells

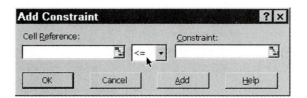

FIGURE 3.13

Specifying Solver's Constraint Cells

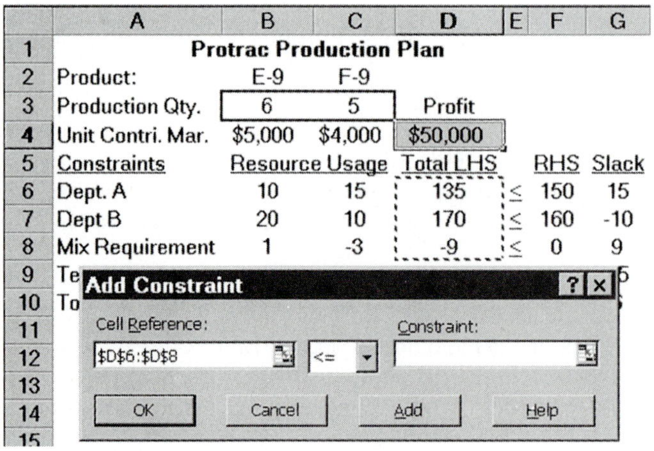

FIGURE 3.14

Specifying the LHS of PROTRAC's "≤" Constraints

TIP: *Sometimes Solver's Add Constraint dialog complains by beeping when you attempt click-dragging and refuses to respond. You can "unlock" this condition by repeatedly pressing the "Tab" key to cycle through all of the options in the Add Constraint dialog until you return to the original field in the dialog. Then, you can click-drag to complete your cell range specification.*

If groups of contiguous constraint rows in your spreadsheet model are reordered to cluster together those of the same type of inequality, that is, all are "<=" or ">=", you can specify them all at once by using cell ranges. Otherwise, you must enter each constraint individually, by repeatedly clicking the "Add" button in the Add Constraint dialog.

With the cursor in the left "Cell Reference" field of the Add Constraint dialog, click-drag on the PROTRAC spreadsheet the cells comprising the Total LHS for the three "≤" constraints, that is, D6:D8, as shown in Figure 3.14. *Note:* Solver will not accept formulas in the "Cell Reference" field; all entries must be references to spreadsheet cells—which, of course, commonly do contain formulas.

Next, place the cursor in the right-hand box of the Add Constraint dialog and click-drag over the corresponding three RHS cells: F6:F8. Your three resource limitations or "upper-bound" constraints should look as in Figure 3.15.

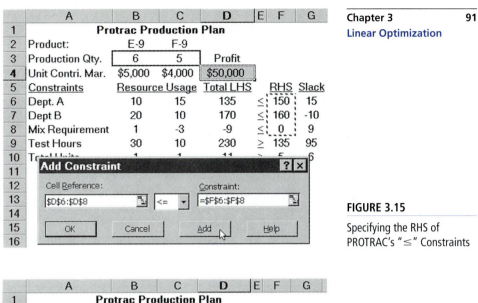

FIGURE 3.15

Specifying the RHS of
PROTRAC's "≤" Constraints

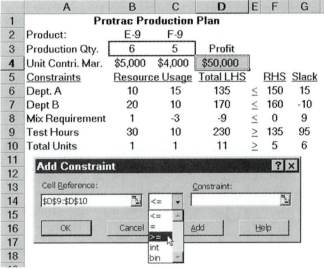

FIGURE 3.16

Specifying the LHS of
PROTRAC's "≥" Constraints

Finally, click the Add Constraint dialog's "Add" button to add these three constraints to Solver's specification, and clear the Add Constraint dialog box for more constraints.

Next, we are ready to specify PROTRAC's "≥" constraints. The procedure is the same as above. With the cursor in the left "Cell Reference" field, click-drag on the PROTRAC spreadsheet the cells comprising the Total LHS for the two "≥" constraints, that is, D9:D10. In the center of the Add Constraint dialog, choose the "greater than or equal to" (">=") sign, as shown in Figure 3.16. Note that all three inequality options ("<=", "=", and ">=") are available in the center constraint drop down list. (Ignore the fourth and fifth options in the list labeled "int" and "bin"; they are used for models that require some of the decision cells to have integer values, a topic we will cover in Chapter 7.)

Next, place the cursor in the right-hand box of the Add Constraint dialog and click-drag over the corresponding two RHS cells: F9:F10. Your two requirements or "lower-bound" constraints should look as in Figure 3.17.

This completes the specification of the five constraints on the PROTRAC model. However, you're *not* done with specifying the PROTRAC model's constraints: You must remember to specify the nonnegativity constraints on cells B3 and C3. We do that in a later step under Solver Options.

Now you can click on the Add Constraint dialog's "OK" button to finish the adding of constraints and return to the Solver Parameters dialog box. (If you ever inadvertently

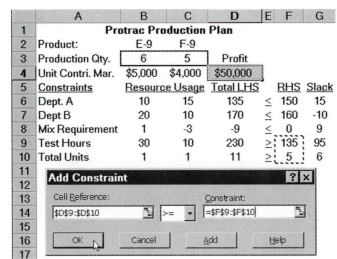

FIGURE 3.17

Specifying the RHS of
PROTRAC's "≥" Constraints

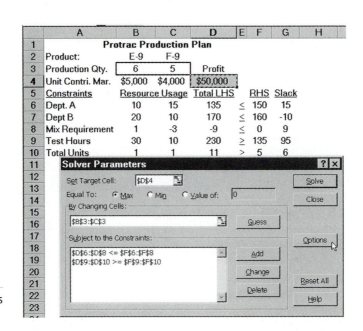

FIGURE 3.18

PROTRAC's Solver Parameters
Specification

click "Add," simply click "Cancel" and you will be returned to the Solver Parameters dialog box.)

Your Solver specification for the PROTRAC model should look as in Figure 3.18. (Although we did not need to use them, the "Change" and "Delete" constraint buttons, listed below the "Add" button in the Solver Parameters dialog, work in a manner similar to "Add." First, highlight the constraint you wish to change or delete and then click on either of these buttons. Then follow a procedure similar to the steps for "Add." *Note:* the "Reset All" button clears all entries in the Solver Parameters dialog in case you wish to start your Solver specification process all over again.)

Finally, since we are working with an LP model that has strictly linear relationships, you *must* click the "Options" button in the Solver Parameters dialog box, as shown under the cursor arrow in Figure 3.18. The Solver Options dialog box will then appear, as shown in Figure 3.19.

Click the check boxes next to "Assume Linear Model" and "Assume Non-Negative." The first specifies to Solver that the model is an LP and the second applies the nonnegativity constraints to the decision variables. (Ignore the other options for now; they relate to optimizing integer and nonlinear models, to displaying of intermediate results, to saving/loading

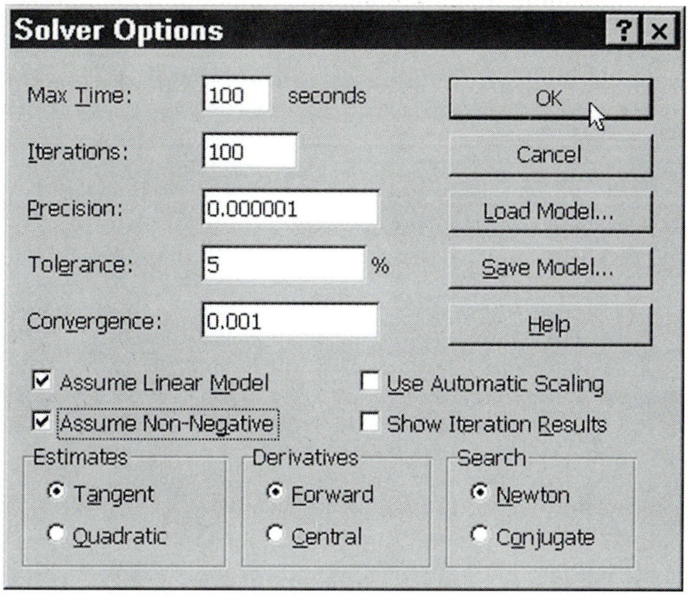

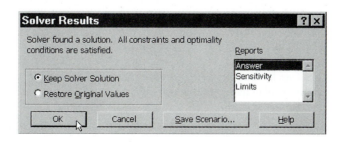

FIGURE 3.19

Specifying Model Linearity and Nonnegativity Constraints

more than one Solver model formulation per worksheet, etc.) Click "OK" to return to the Solver Parameters dialog.

You have specified the model completely by telling Solver about:

- The constraints,
- The range of cells that Solver is to change (the decision variables),
- The cell containing the objective function to optimize (the cell to be maximized in this case), and
- That your model is an LP.

Lastly, click the "Solve" button. You can follow the progress of Solver's iterative search Simplex algorithm in Excel's Message Box in the Status Bar at the lower left-hand corner of the Excel window. Optimization will happen very fast for so small a model as PROTRAC. So, you might not see the messages from Solver this time.

In general, Solver will display "Setting up problem . . ." while the Solver Visual Basic program translates your spreadsheet model. Then Solver passes control to the optimizer module. The optimizer module displays the number of "iterations" and the value of the objective function cell as it explores PROTRAC's set of feasible decisions during the optimization process. This information is useful to monitor Solver's progress for large models that might take many seconds or minutes to solve.

If you have made no mistakes to this point, after a second or two, the Solver Results dialog should display a completion message, as shown in Figure 3.20. *Be sure to read the top sentences in this dialog.* Solver may stop short of optimality. Unfortunately, the Solver Results dialog always looks exactly the same except for the top sentence(s). If, in your haste to click the "OK" button to dismiss the Solver Results dialog, you don't read the message,

FIGURE 3.20

The Solver Results Dialog Box

Microsoft Excel 8.0 Answer Report

Target Cell (Max)

Cell	Name	Original Value	Final Value
$D$4	Unit Contri. Mar. Profit	$50,500	$50,500

Adjustable Cells

Cell	Name	Original Value	Final Value
$B$3	Production Qty. E-9	4.5	4.5
$C$3	Production Qty. F-9	7	7

Constraints

Cell	Name	Cell Value	Formula	Status	Slack
$D$6	Dept. A Total LHS	150	$D$6<=$F$6	Binding	0
$D$7	Dept B Total LHS	160	$D$7<=$F$7	Binding	0
$D$8	Mix Requirement Total LHS	-16.5	$D$8<=$F$8	Not Binding	16.5
$D$9	Test Hours Total LHS	205	$D$9>=$F$9	Not Binding	70
$D$10	Total Units Total LHS	11.5	$D$10>=$F$10	Not Binding	6.5

FIGURE 3.21

The Solver Answer Report for PROTRAC

you may miss important information about your solution. For example, just because Solver finished, that doesn't mean it found the optimum solution. So, read the message—each and every time. The two key sentences to look for in the Solver Results dialog are:

- Solver found a solution, and
- All constraints and optimality conditions are satisfied.

If you do not see *both* of these two sentences, Solver has failed to optimize your LP model. In that eventuality, (1) click the "Help" button for additional—but usually inadequate—information about the Solver Results dialog, or (2) consult the Solver Appendix for additional Tips and Hints on how to proceed.

If you got the successful completion message, as shown in Figure 3.20, you have the option to "Keep Solver Solution" or throw it away by "Restore(-ing the) Original Values" for the PROTRAC decision variable cells before Solver started. You also have the option of receiving up to three reports on the solution, each formatted as a new worksheet added to your PROTRAC.XLS workbook.

Select the Answer report, accept the default of "Keep Solver Solution," and click OK. Ignore the Sensitivity Report and the Limits Report for now. We will address them later.[5]

Figure 3.21 shows the Answer Report for the PROTRAC model. The Answer Report should appear in your PROTRAC.XLS workbook under the worksheet tab named "Answer Report 1" if that name isn't already used for another worksheet in the workbook. Remember: The Answer Report (and either of the other reports) is just another Excel worksheet that happens to have its row and column designators and grid lines turned off. You may turn them back on by setting the proper check marks in the "View" tab dialog evoked from the "Options. . ." item in Excel's Tools menu. As a result, you may freely reformat, print, or copy the cells of any Solver report in the normal way for any worksheet. For example, superfluous rows were deleted and several columns had their contents centered in the Answer Report shown in Figure 3.21.

Your original PROTRAC spreadsheet should now appear as in Figure 3.22, in which Solver has recorded the optimal decision values for E-9 and F-9 production, 4.5 and 7, respectively. The spreadsheet then recalculates one last time to produce the profit-maximizing payoff of $50,500.

Note that the cells in the Slack column have changed to reflect the optimal production decisions. If the slack cell for a constraint shows 0 slack, then that constraint is said to be "binding at optimality." Binding constraints prevent Solver from producing more profit. That is, increasing profit by additional E-9 and/or F-9 production would drive one or more slack cells below 0, violating one or more constraints. Constraints having nonzero (and, therefore by design, having positive) slack are not binding at optimality. Nonbinding constraints cannot hamper Solver's ability to produce additional payoff. This is true regardless

TIP: *If you forget to select a report and dismiss the Solver Results dialog, there is no way to recreate the report without re-optimizing the model to get back to the Solver Results dialog.*

[5]For future reference: In versions prior to Excel 97, more than one report can be selected by holding down the Control key (Windows Excel) or the Command key (Macintosh Excel) and then clicking on each of the desired reports.

	A	B	C	D	E	F	G
1	Protrac Production Plan						
2	Product:	E-9	F-9				
3	Production Qty.	4.5	7	Profit			
4	Unit Contri. Mar.	$5,000	$4,000	$50,500			
5	Constraints	Resource Usage		Total LHS		RHS	Slack
6	Dept. A	10	15	150	≤	150	0
7	Dept B	20	10	160	≤	160	0
8	Mix Requirement	1	-3	-16.5	≤	0	16.5
9	Test Hours	30	10	205	≥	135	70
10	Total Units	1	1	11.5	≥	5	6.5

FIGURE 3.22

The Profit-Maximizing Values of E and F

of whether you optimize a maximization model or a minimization model. As a result, it is the binding constraints that are of interest to you in any LP model. The occurrence of zero Slack in the Dept. A and Dept. B resource constraints means that these are the two binding constraints; that is, "bottlenecks" that prevent further improvement in PROTRAC payoff.

If you compare Figure 3.22 to the Answer Report in Figure 3.21, you will see that the layout we have chosen for the PROTRAC spreadsheet presents directly all the information contained in the Answer Report. That is, except for formatting differences, the Answer Report information is completely duplicated on the original PROTRAC spreadsheet. As a result, the Answer Report is largely redundant, and we will omit it in future Solver optimizations.

You are free at this point to explore alternatives in the neighborhood of optimality by doing additional "What if?" projections for PROTRAC's E-9 and/or F-9 production quantities around their optimum values. For example, what is the consequence on profit and constraint slacks of rounding the E-9 production decision up to 5 or down to 4?

Alternatively, you can see the immediate effect on profit of adding additional hours of capacity in department A and/or B by changing the proper right-hand side cell, and then running Solver again to re-optimize the model with the new right-hand-side value(s). In this way, you can explore how much profit is helped or hurt by such a change. For example, a proposal to increase departmental capacities by adding the additional hours of a second shift's operation could be evaluated by examining the new profit, net of any added-capacity costs, after re-optimizing the revised higher-capacity model. Of course, you can change the contribution margin coefficients and/or the technical coefficients in the constraints to examine their effect on profit, as well. Remember, for each change you must evoke the Solver dialog again and click the Solve button to get a new optimum.

3.9   RECOMMENDATIONS FOR SOLVER LP MODELS

To facilitate your use of Solver, you should develop three LP modeling habits.

First, make sure your LP model's numbers are scaled so that the difference between the smallest and largest numbers in the spreadsheet to be optimized is no more than 6 or 7 orders of magnitude. For example, a model with one of its decision variables defined as a "Utilization Percent" (having a value of, say, 5%) along with a payoff measure in dollars may produce incorrect Solver solutions, if the dollar performance measure cell grows to, say, 8 digits (tens of millions of dollars). This causes a span in your spreadsheet model of 10 orders of magnitude between the smallest valued cell (.05) and the largest ($10,000,000, for example). The resulting internal round-off and truncation errors, which get compounded during Solver optimization, may cause so great a loss of internal precision that Solver will not be able to finish the process reliably. This situation may result in nonoptimal solutions and/or bogus Solver Results completion messages ("The conditions for Assume Linear are not satisfied"—when, in fact, they are).

In this case, and in similar cases, the remedy is simple: Change the scale of measure of the very large or very small numbers in your spreadsheet model. In this example, we could re-scale money in the LP model to be defined as millions of dollars instead of dollars. This causes no loss of the model's generality and will keep the range of its numbers small—in this revised example the difference between the smallest number (.05) and the largest number ($10) is now only 4 orders of magnitude.

TIP: *Beginning with Excel 97, checking the "Use Automatic Scaling" item in the Solver Options dialog (see Figure 3.19) helps with most scaling problems, but this cannot be guaranteed to successfully eliminate all problems with scaling. (This option does not work for LP models in Solver versions prior to Excel 97.)*

Other than forgetting any nonnegativity constraints, poorly scaled models cause the most trouble in optimizing LP models with Solver.

The less insidious causes of Solver failures are usually easier to track down, such as an overconstrained model ("Solver could not find a feasible solution" completion message).

Second, Solver accepts RHS entries in the Solver Parameters dialog showing numeric constants or cell references or formulas, and doing this in your modeling does not harm the optimization process. Nevertheless, good Solver modeling practice should avoid their use. That is, you should never place any constants or the cell address of variables whose values could change during optimization into the RHS of a constraint in the Solver Parameters dialog itself. In other words, all RHSs in the Constraints section of the Solver Parameters dialog should contain cell references pointing to constraint RHS cells in your spreadsheet that contain either (1) constants or (2) formulas whose evaluation will never change during Solver optimization, i.e., formulas that are *not* related to the values of the decision variables directly or indirectly.

If it is acceptable to Solver, why avoid such practices? Let us illustrate this recommendation with an example—in this case a modification to the original PROTRAC model. Suppose PROTRAC's management decides that no more than 4 E-9s and no more than 6 F-9s should be produced next month. Clearly the optimal decisions from the PROTRAC LP model just optimized by Solver violate these new policy constraints, and so, the PROTRAC model must be revised to include two new constraints and then re-optimized. One way to do this is shown in Figure 3.23. Note the two new upper-bound constraints in the Solver Parameters dialog.

When the "Solve" button is clicked, Solver correctly optimizes this revised model, with a new solution as shown in Figure 3.24.

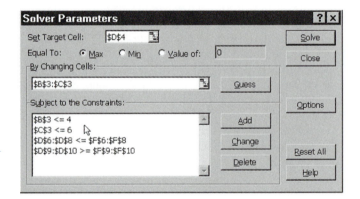

FIGURE 3.23

Revised PROTRAC Model's Solver Parameters Specification

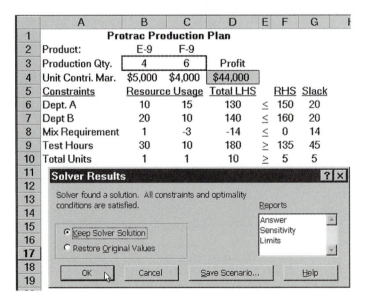

FIGURE 3.24

Optimal Solution to the Revised PROTRAC Model

Note the disadvantage of this revised PROTRAC model formulation: There is no clue on the spreadsheet regarding two of the revised model's constraints; from the spreadsheet in Figure 3.24, it appears no constraints are binding. As a result, you would have to (1) generate and consult the Answer Report after every optimization and (2) translate that report's information back to the spreadsheet model for interpretation, a cumbersome procedure. In addition, this style of modeling with Solver is another form of "hard-wiring" of data, in this case into the Solver Parameters dialog instead of into a formula, but with the same effect: The complete structure of the model is not obvious, and any model changes require "editing," in this case, of the Solver Parameters dialog. The recommended approach is to add the two new constraints to the PROTRAC model on the worksheet itself as two additional constraint rows, and then modify the Solver Parameters dialog to include their specification along with the original PROTRAC constraints.

Since there is no loss of generality in laying out the spreadsheet this way, we recommend, therefore, that

1. RHSs in the constraints specified in the Solver Parameters dialog should always contain cell references (to the RHS cells in the spreadsheet model itself), and

2. The RHS cells on the spreadsheet model itself should contain constants and not formulas (or, more precisely, no formulas that involve decision variables directly or indirectly).

TIP: All the Solver Parameters dialog settings for each worksheet are preserved when you save your workbook to disk.

Third, for larger LP models you can facilitate documentation by using Excel's Range Naming commands, illustrated earlier in Chapter 2, to range name the model's performance measure cell, its decision cells, its constraint function (Total LHS) cells, and its RHS cells. If you do this, Solver will automatically substitute the range names for the corresponding cell ranges in the Solver Parameters dialog.

This completes our detailed overview of Solver. At this point you should save your PROTRAC workbook to disk to preserve the LP's optimal decisions and the Answer Report.

TIP: Pressing the PrintScreen key will copy a picture of your display screen including any Solver dialog boxes onto the Clipboard. Pressing Alt-PrintScreen will copy a picture of the frontmost window or a Solver dialog onto the Clipboard. From the Clipboard, you can paste the picture into an Excel worksheet or Word document for model documentation.

3.10   CRAWLER TREAD: A BLENDING EXAMPLE

Although the PROTRAC, Inc. formulation turned out to be a maximization model, many real-world models occur in a minimization context. When profit is the objective, then clearly maximization is called for; but if, for example, cost is the objective, then minimization is called for. As an example of a minimization model, we consider the following Crawler Tread model.

Iron ore from four different mines will be blended to make treads for a new product at PROTRAC, a medium-size crawler tractor, the E-6, designed especially to compete in the European market. Analysis has shown that in order to produce a blend with suitable tensile qualities, minimum requirements must be met on three basic elements, denoted for simplicity as A, B, and C. In particular, each ton of ore must contain at least 5 pounds of basic element A, at least 100 pounds of basic element B, and at least 30 pounds of basic element C. These data are summarized in Table 3.4.

TABLE 3.4 Requirements of Basic Elements	
BASIC ELEMENT	MINIMUM REQUIREMENT PER TON OF BLEND (pounds of each element)
A	5
B	100
C	30

The ore from each of the four different mines possesses each of the three basic elements, but in different amounts. These compositions, in pounds per ton, are given in Table 3.5.

Notice that a ton of ore from the first mine contains 10 pounds of basic element A and hence satisfies the minimum requirement on this element of 5 pounds per ton. Similarly, this same ton of ore contains 90 pounds of basic element B and 45 pounds of basic element C, hence satisfying the requirement on basic element C but not on basic element B. Similarly, you can verify that a single ton of ore from the second mine will not satisfy the requirement on A or C. A single ton of ore from mine 3 will not satisfy requirements on B and C, and a single ton from mine 4 will not satisfy the requirement on A. However, many different blends can easily be found that will indeed satisfy the minimal requirements on all three basic elements. An example of such a blend would be a mixture composed of one-half ton from mine 1 and one-half ton from mine 4. The amount of basic element A in this blended ton is computed as follows:

$$\text{pounds of A} = (\text{pounds of A in 1 ton from mine 1})(1/2)$$
$$+ (\text{pounds of A in 1 ton from mine 4})(1/2)$$

Hence

$$\text{pounds of A} = 10(1/2) + 2(1/2) = 5 + 1 = 6$$

Since $6 \geq 5$, the minimal requirement on basic element A is satisfied by this blend. Similarly, for the same blended ton, we can compute

$$\text{pounds of B} = (\text{pounds of B in 1 ton from mine 1})(1/2)$$
$$+ (\text{pounds of B in 1 ton from mine 4})(1/2)$$

Hence

$$\text{pounds of B} = 90(1/2) + 175(1/2) = 132.5$$

In a similar fashion

$$\text{pounds of C} = 45(1/2) + 37(1/2) = 41$$

Comparing 132.5 with the requirement of 100 pounds of B, and 41 with the requirement of 30 pounds of C, it is seen that this blend of one-half ton from mine 1 and one-half ton from mine 4 easily satisfies all the minimal requirements, and hence this is said to be a *feasible blend*. There are many other possible blends of 1 ton that satisfy all the minimal requirements and hence which are also feasible. However, since the ore from each mine has a different cost, different blends will also have different costs. The cost data are given in Table 3.6.

TABLE 3.5 Compositions from Each Mine

BASIC ELEMENT	MINE (pounds per ton of each element)			
	1	2	3	4
A	10	3	8	2
B	90	150	75	175
C	45	25	20	37

TABLE 3.6 Cost of Ore from Each Mine

MINE	DOLLAR COST PER TON OF ORE
1	800
2	400
3	600
4	500

For example, the cost of the feasible blend one-half ton from mine 1 and one-half ton from mine 4 is

$$\text{(cost per ton from mine 1)}(1/2) + \text{(cost per ton from mine 4)}(1/2) =$$
$$800(1/2) \qquad + \qquad 500(1/2) \qquad = \$650$$

Compare this cost with the cost of some of the other feasible blends that you may have discovered. The objective of management in the Crawler Tread problem is to discover a *least-cost feasible blend.* Let us see how this problem can be formulated as an LP model.

CREATING THE LP MODEL

Since we are interested in finding an *optimal* 1-ton blend, we set up the *decision variables* as follows:

$$T_1 = \text{fraction of a ton to be chosen from mine 1}$$
$$T_2 = \text{fraction of a ton to be chosen from mine 2}$$
$$T_3 = \text{fraction of a ton to be chosen from mine 3}$$
$$T_4 = \text{fraction of a ton to be chosen from mine 4}$$

Then, using the data from Table 3.5, the amounts of the basic elements in 1 ton of blend are calculated as follows:

$$\text{pounds of basic element A in 1 ton of blend}$$
$$= 10T_1 + 3T_2 + 8T_3 + 2T_4 \qquad \qquad \textbf{(3.9)}$$
$$\text{pounds of basic element B in 1 ton of blend}$$
$$= 90T_1 + 150T_2 + 75T_3 + 175T_4 \qquad \qquad \textbf{(3.10)}$$
$$\text{pounds of basic element C in 1 ton of blend}$$
$$= 45T_1 + 25T_2 + 20T_3 + 37T_4 \qquad \qquad \textbf{(3.11)}$$

We can now combine expressions (3.9), (3.10), and (3.11) with the minimal requirements designated in Table 3.4 to obtain the three (requirement) constraints:

$$10T_1 + 3T_2 + 8T_3 + 2T_4 \geq 5 \qquad \qquad \textbf{(3.12)}$$
$$90T_1 + 150T_2 + 75T_3 + 175T_4 \geq 100 \qquad \qquad \textbf{(3.13)}$$
$$45T_1 + 25T_2 + 20T_3 + 37T_4 \geq 30 \qquad \qquad \textbf{(3.14)}$$

Are there any other constraints in this model? Of course, we must include the usual non-negativity conditions $T_1, T_2, T_3, T_4 \geq 0$, but there is still another important constraint that must be included. Since there are no other contributions to the 1 ton aside from the four mines, the fractional contributions from each mine must add up to 1. That is, we must include the constraint

$$T_1 + T_2 + T_3 + T_4 = 1 \qquad \qquad \textbf{(3.15)}$$

The latter constraint, sometimes called a *material balance condition,* is an **equality constraint,** and it restricts the values of the decision variables in such a way that the left-hand side *exactly* equals the right-hand side. This illustrates an important principle:

> The constraints in a linear programming model can be equalities as well as inequalities.

Using the data in Table 3.6, it is easy to see that the cost of any blend is given as follows:

$$\text{cost of 1 ton of blend} = 800T_1 + 400T_2 + 600T_3 + 500T_4$$

Noting that the objective is to minimize cost, we can now write the complete symbolic model for Crawler Tread:

THE CRAWLER TREAD LP MODEL

$$\text{Min } 800T_1 + 400T_2 + 600T_3 + 500T_4$$
$$\text{s.t.} \quad 10T_1 + 3T_2 + 8T_3 + 2T_4 \quad \geq 5$$
$$90T_1 + 150T_2 + 75T_3 + 175T_4 \quad \geq 100$$
$$45T_1 + 25T_2 + 20T_3 + 37T_4 \quad \geq 30$$
$$T_1 + T_2 + T_3 + T_4 \quad = 1$$
$$T_1, T_2, T_3, T_4 \quad \geq 0$$

You should verify that all functions in this model are linear and consequently it is a LP model.

This completes our introduction to LP formulations with Solver. Next, we return to the major theme of this book, formulating useful models to aid decision making. Before starting the next section, however, test your abilities with spreadsheet modeling and Solver: Take the symbolic LP model for Crawler Tread and implement it as a spreadsheet model using the spreadsheet formulation style of this chapter. Then, optimize it with Solver. Our version of Crawler Tread appears at the end of this chapter, but don't ruin the opportunity to test your understanding by peeking at it. Build the spreadsheet LP model and try to solve it first. After doing Crawler and a few of the more structured problems in the next section, adhering to the long list of spreadsheet formulation rules we recommend will begin to come naturally.

3.11   LEARNING TO FORMULATE LP MODELS

The remainder of this chapter contains examples of some formulations that you can use to cement your ability to make the transition between the real-world managerial situation and the symbolic LP model and thence to the Solver-ready spreadsheet model. This transition—the way in which the model has been set up, the way the constraints and the objectives have been formulated—is of prime importance.

To get formulation experience, try to model the following problems on your own. Develop the symbolic LP model as quickly as possible and *do not read more into a problem than precisely what is given.* At this stage do not introduce additional constraints or logical nuances or flights of imagination of your own that might, in your opinion, make the model more realistic. Do not, for example, worry about "what happens next week" if the problem never refers to "next week." The problems that we pose are chosen to help you develop a facility for model formulation assuming the abstraction step from the real-world situation is completed. In order to do this, and so that you may check your work and gauge your progress, it must be true that within the described context the correct formulation should be unambiguous. In other words, contrary to real-world situations, for this restricted set of example problems there is a "right answer." Later, when you have more experience, the latitude for shades of interpretation and real-world subtleties will be broader. Because the topic of formulation is so important, and because practice is the only way to master this topic, a long list of problems appears at the end of this chapter.

Again, we repeat our advice: Do not simply read the problem and then immediately read the formulation given at the end of the chapter. That would be the best way to deceive yourself about what you understand. Do not read the solution until either (1) you are certain you have correctly modeled the problem on your own or (2) you are absolutely convinced that you have hit an impasse. Peeking ahead at the solution before you have struggled with model formulation robs you of learning how to formulate LP models.

3.12   EXAMPLE 1: ASTRO AND COSMO (A PRODUCT MIX PROBLEM)

A TV company produces two types of TV sets, the Astro and the Cosmo. There are two production lines, one for each set, and there are two departments, both of which are used in the production of each set. The capacity of the Astro production line is 70 TV sets per day. The

TABLE 3.7 Astro and Cosmo Data

	DAILY CAPACITY	LABOR UTILIZATION PER SET (HR)		PROFIT PER SET ($)
		Dept. A	Dept. B	
Astro	70	1	1	20
Cosmo	50	2	1	10
Total Availability		120	90	

TABLE 3.8 Gruel Blending Data

	CONTENTS AND PRICE PER 16 OZ OF GRUEL			
Gruel	Protein Content (oz)	Carbohydrate Content (oz)	Fat Content (oz)	Price ($)
1	3	7	5	4
2	5	4	6	6
3	2	2	6	3
4	3	8	2	2

capacity of the Cosmo line is 50 TV sets per day. In department A picture tubes are produced. In this department the Astro set requires 1 labor hour and the Cosmo set requires 2 labor hours. Presently in department A a maximum of 120 labor hours per day can be assigned to production of the two types of sets. In department B the chassis is constructed. In this department the Astro set requires 1 labor hour and the Cosmo also requires 1 labor hour. Presently, in department B a maximum of 90 labor hours per day can be assigned to production of the two types of sets. The profit contributions are 20 and 10 dollars, respectively, for each Astro and Cosmo set. These data are summarized in Table 3.7.

If the company can sell as many Astro and Cosmo sets as it produces, what should be the daily production plan (i.e., the daily production) for each set? Review the PROTRAC, Inc. E and F model and then try to formulate Astro and Cosmo as a LP model. Write the symbolic LP model, develop the spreadsheet LP model, and optimize it with Solver.

3.13   EXAMPLE 2: BLENDING GRUEL (A BLENDING PROBLEM)

A 16-ounce can of dog food must contain protein, carbohydrate, and fat in at least the following amounts: protein, 3 ounces; carbohydrate, 5 ounces; fat, 4 ounces. Four types of gruel are to be blended together in various proportions to produce a least-cost can of dog food satisfying these requirements. The contents and prices for 16 ounces of each gruel are given in Table 3.8.

Review the Crawler Tread blending model and then formulate this gruel blending problem as a linear program. Write the symbolic LP model, develop the spreadsheet LP model, and optimize it with Solver. HINT: Let X_i denote the proportion of gruel i in a 16-ounce can of dog food, $i = 1, 2, 3, 4$.

3.14   EXAMPLE 3: SECURITY FORCE SCHEDULING (A SCHEDULING PROBLEM)

A personnel manager must schedule the security force in such a way as to satisfy the staffing requirements shown in Table 3.9.

TABLE 3.9 Security Staffing Requirements

TIME	MINIMUM NUMBER OF OFFICERS REQUIRED
Midnight–4 A.M.	5
4 A.M.–8A.M.	7
8 A.M.–Noon	15
Noon–4 P.M.	7
4 P.M.–8 P.M.	12
8 P.M.–Midnight	9

TABLE 3.10 Shift Schedule

SHIFT	STARTING TIME	ENDING TIME
1	Midnight	8:00 A.M.
2	4:00 A.M.	Noon
3	8:00 A.M.	4:00 P.M.
4	Noon	8:00 P.M.
5	4:00 P.M.	Midnight
6	8:00 P.M.	4:00 A.M.

Officers work 8-hour shifts. There are 6 such shifts each day. The starting and ending times for each shift are given in Table 3.10.

The personnel manager wants to determine how many officers should work each shift in order to minimize the total number of officers employed, while still satisfying the staffing requirements. We can define the decision variables as follows:

$$X_1 = \text{number of officers working shift 1}$$
$$X_2 = \text{number of officers working shift 2}$$

$$.$$
$$.$$
$$.$$

$$X_6 = \text{number of officers working shift 6}$$

In formulating the objective function, note that the total number of officers is the sum of the number of officers assigned to each shift. Now write out the objective function, noting that the personnel manager wants to minimize this sum. The objective function is

$$X_1 + X_2 + X_3 + X_4 + X_5 + X_6$$

In formulating the constraints, you want to be sure that a particular set of values for $X_1, \ldots, X_6$ satisfies the staffing requirements. Some device is needed to see which officers are on duty during each of the 4-hour intervals in Table 3.9. A tabular arrangement, such as the one shown in Table 3.11, is helpful in making this determination. Here we see that the officers who work shift 1 are on duty during each of the first two time intervals, and so on. The table also shows (adding down columns) how many officers work in each time interval (e.g., in the first time interval $X_1 + X_6$ officers are on duty; thus we write the first constraint $X_1 + X_6 \geq 5$).

Now try to write out the remaining constraints for this model. Write the symbolic LP model, develop the spreadsheet LP model, and optimize it with Solver.

TABLE 3.11 Officers on Duty in Each Interval

	TIME INTERVAL					
SHIFT	Midnight to 4:00 A.M.	4:00 A.M. to 8:00 A.M.	8:00 A.M. to Noon	Noon to 4:00 P.M.	4:00 P.M. to 8:00 P.M.	8:00 P.M. to Midnight
1	X_1	X_1				
2		X_2	X_2			
3			X_3	X_3		
4				X_4	X_4	
5					X_5	X_5
6	X_6					X_6
Requirements	5	7	15	7	12	9

The examples thus far have shown a product mix model (Astro and Cosmo), a blending model (gruel), and a scheduling model (security force). These are all illustrations of *types* of LPs that you encounter in real-world modeling. Here is another important type of LP, called a *break-even model*.

3.15   EXAMPLE 4: LONGER BOATS YACHT COMPANY— A VIGNETTE IN CONSTRAINED BREAK-EVEN ANALYSIS

The Longer Boats Yacht Company produces three high-performance racing sloops. These three boats are called the Sting, the Ray, and the Breaker. Pertinent revenue and cost data for the next planning period are given in Table 3.12.

As you can see from these data, the *fixed cost* of each of these activities is considerable. A fixed cost is a lump cost that is paid regardless of the quantity to be produced. Thus, the same fixed cost of $3,000,000 for Rays will occur whether the production run consists of 0 boats, 1 boat, or 40 boats. The high fixed costs include the costs of design modification, mold reconstruction, and yacht basin testing.

Figure 3.25 shows a break-even analysis of the production of Stings. We see that if Longer Boats were to produce only Stings, it would have to produce at least 1000 boats to break even.

Longer Boats' problem is more complicated, however. First, for the next planning period management has already contracted to produce 700 Stings. Another customer has requested 400 Breakers, a request that management would like to honor. Longer Boats' marketing surveys have convinced management that at most 300 Rays should be produced. Management is still interested in how much it must sell to break even, but now there are three products as well as previous commitments or restrictions to take into consideration. Starting from basic principles, management notes that at break-even

$$\text{total revenue} = \text{total cost}$$

TABLE 3.12 Longer Boats' Data

SLOOP	SELLING PRICE PER UNIT ($)	VARIABLE COST PER UNIT ($)	FIXED COST ($)
Sting	10,000	5,000	5,000,000
Ray	7,500	3,600	3,000,000
Breaker	15,000	8,000	10,000,000

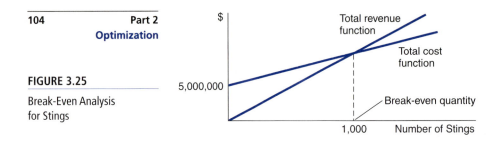

Break-Even Analysis
for Stings

Since Longer Boats is a relatively new company and is experiencing the cash flow problems associated with rapid growth, management would like to minimize the capital outflow. The fixed costs are, of necessity, incurred in their totality, and thus the goal becomes one of minimizing total variable costs. Management's goal is to find the production plan with the lowest total variable cost that honors the constraints and yields total revenue equal to total cost. Write the symbolic LP model, develop the spreadsheet LP model, and optimize it with Solver.

3.16   FURTHER HINTS FOR DEVELOPING LP MODELS

As you can see from the models formulated thus far in this chapter, LP modeling is simply the reasoned and careful specification of the model ingredients (decision variables, constraints, objective function, etc.) appropriate to a linear optimization model. However, like the "sunk costs" issue discussed previously, there are other pitfalls to avoid in formulating LP models. Let us identify a few of the common ones, followed by a brief discussion of each.

- Like all else in modeling, avoid putting too much detail into your model or you will never get the model completely and consistently formulated. Later, your spreadsheet formulation of the (overcomplicated) model will carry over these inconsistencies, which will appear as difficult-to-detect "bugs" in the spreadsheet. It is better to formulate a minimally sufficient set of decision variables and constraints, just to get started. It is much, much easier to add complexity in the form of more variables and constraints later to a simple model that you have come to understand thoroughly.

- Avoid nonlinear relationships, at least initially, in your modeling. Instead, use linear equations, possibly with bounds on the values of its variables via added constraints, as approximations in the region of interest for the more realistic, but complex nonlinear relationships. Although we will cover nonlinear models in Chapter 8, nonlinear optimization is much more difficult to achieve and is fraught with pitfalls of its own. Even if you need to include some nonlinear relationships in your model, it is best to develop a simpler linear model first and then add the nonlinear relationships later.

    Be aware that just like P2 (5 P*P) produces a nonlinearity in a model if P is a decision variable, so does P*Q produce a nonlinearity, if P and Q are both decision variables. In other words, you cannot multiply (or divide) two decision variables without introducing nonlinearity into the model.

    Note that some nonlinear relationships can be converted to linear ones easily without any loss of generality in the model. For example, the "Product Mix" constraint in the PROTRAC model required at least 1 F-9 be produced for every 3 E-9s. Expressing this constraint as $E/F \leq 3$ is algebraically correct, but is a nonlinear function of one of the decision variables, F, in the denominator of the ratio. However, standard manipulations of the equation produces the equivalent constraint, $E - 3F \leq 0$, which is linear in both of the decision variables. (Aside: All the standard algebraic manipulations applied to both sides of an equation also work identically if applied to both sides of an inequality with one exception: Multiplying or dividing both sides of an inequality by a negative number *reverses* the direction of the inequality. For example, if $E - 3F \leq 0$, then multiplying both sides by -1 produces the equivalent inequality $-E + 3F \geq 0$.)

- Don't become concerned too early with the real-world consequences of noninteger values of decision variables that might occur when the model is optimized. We will also cover models that require the decision variables to be integer-valued later in Chapter 7. However, like nonlinear relationships, the requirement of integer values for decision variables introduces additional complexity in optimization that is best ignored at first.

- Many interesting LP models involve decision making over multiple time periods, such as choosing monthly production quantities for each of several months in cases where the months are not independent of each other. Although of great managerial interest, it is best to model the situation for a single time period (one month in this case) first and then modify it later to add the more complicated multi-month formulation. We will examine these models in detail in Chapter 6.

- Be sure the LP model has some "tension" built into it that forces nonobvious trade-offs to be made when it is optimized. For example, a cost-minimization model without any $\geq$ (requirements) constraints will very likely produce the real-world nonsense result of setting all decision variables to zero when it is optimized; that is, costs are minimized by going out of business. Similarly, a profit-maximization model without any $\leq$ (resource) constraints will very likely produce the pleasant, but impractical result of infinite profit, as one or more decision variables is increased toward infinity during the model optimization process. This latter outcome is called an "unbounded solution" in LP parlance.

- Be very suspicious of equality constraints—limit them in your LP modeling, if possible, to those cases where a definitional relationship must be maintained. For example, it is acceptable to include a constraint that Profit = Sales Revenue − Total Cost, an accounting identity, or a constraint that Ending Inventory = Beginning Inventory + Production − Shipments, a material balance constraint. However, even these equations bear managerial scrutiny. Inventories may "shrink" because of spoilage or theft, and Revenues booked may not be collected, and so forth. Hence the proper formulation may be given by inequality constraints, "Profit $\leq$ ..." and "Ending Inventory $\leq$ ...," respectively. In general, try to write relationships as inequalities, even if you believe they should be equalities at optimality. Later, when the model is optimized you can check to see if the inequality constraint is binding, that is, satisfied as an equality, as you expected. If not, then you can search for the reason why, thereby learning in the process.

  The major difficulty with including equality constraints is the risk of overconstraining your model, producing low payoff decisions when it is optimized, or in the worst case, no feasible decisions at all. Be especially sensitive to the inclusion of implied "organizational" policy constraints that manifest themselves as equalities in your model. For example, an unwritten policy in a company might be stated as "We have always followed the practice of assigning one supervisor (S) to every 10 workers (W) here at XYZ Corporation. Therefore, we must impose the constraint $W = 10S$." If there is no compelling reason for including this policy, payoff may be improved by leaving such constraints out of the model. On the other hand, if policy constraints are important to include in the model, then consider including them as inequalities instead of equalities. For example, the above constraint might be relaxed to "... no more than 10 workers are to be assigned to a supervisor," which produces $W \leq 10S$ as a constraint. This lowers the chance of the "no-feasible-decisions" result when the model is optimized, and moreover, allows for the possibility that the best strategy is to abandon the exact "10-to-1" historical policy.

- Do *not* add constraints unless they are actually required by the situation being modeled. This commonly occurs when you allow your (often wrong) intuition about the nature of the optimal solution to force stipulations onto the LP model from the beginning. That is, you create a self-fulfilling prophecy by predetermining the model's solution before the model is optimized! As a result, you will never learn whether your intuition was correct, and worse, if your intuition is wrong, you risk the "no-feasible-decisions" result when the model is optimized. For example, a manager states, "It is obvious to me that in this situation it would never be cost-effective to have Ending Inventory be other than zero. So, I'll add Ending Inventory = 0 as a constraint to the model just to be sure." Not only does this risk overconstraining the model, as above, but the manager loses the opportunity to gain insight if the optimal solution of his/her model without that constraint would result in a positive ending inventory.

Subsequent chapters contain additional examples of formulations that you can use to cement your ability to make the transition between the real-world situation and the LP model of it. This transition—the way in which the LP model has been set up, the way the constraints and the objectives have been formulated—is of prime importance. As you develop your skills in LP model formulation, you will add your own "tips" to the list above.

3.17   SUMMARY

Constraints were defined to be mathematical conditions that rule out certain combinations of values for the decision variables, and feasible or allowable decisions were defined to be values of the variables that satisfy *all* the constraints. Linear programming was seen to involve a search for a feasible decision that optimizes an objective function. More specifically, linear programming was defined to be a mathematical model with the following properties:

1. There is a linear objective function that is to be maximized or minimized.
2. There are linear constraints, each a mathematical inequality (either $\leq$ or $\geq$) or an equality.

The flexibility of spreadsheet modeling requires some discipline be followed to facilitate building a spreadsheet representation that (1) is faithful to the LP model, (2) is self-documenting, (3) is suitable for optimization by Solver, and (4) does not cause problems later with interpretation of Solver's reports. There are four things to keep in mind to avoid pitfalls in using Solver.

1. Any formula affecting the objective function cell or the constraints must be linear if it involves the decision variables either directly or indirectly via other cell formulas.
2. Algebraically, a linear model is just a special case of a nonlinear model. However, this is not true for Solver's optimization software; it uses different software for optimizing the two classes of models. If you mistakenly forget to set the "Assume Linear" option and optimize an LP model via Solver's nonlinear optimizer, you may not get the optimal solution; and even if you do, Solver's reports, covered later, are different for the two types of procedures.
3. The right-hand-side field of each constraint in the Solver Parameters dialog box should reference spreadsheet cells that are constants or evaluate to constants that will not change during optimization. Moreover, you may not put any formula into the *left*-hand-side field of a constraint in the Solver Constraint dialog box. Therefore, it is best to avoid confusion by not putting formulas or constants explicitly into either the LHS or RHS field in the Solver Add Constraint dialog. It is recommended that you put formulas or constants in spreadsheet cells and specify the corresponding worksheet cell references in the Add Constraint dialog box fields.
4. Range naming of the decision variable cells, the performance measure cell, groups of like-type-inequality constraint LHS cells, and groups of like-type-inequality RHS cells, is a useful documentation step for larger LP models.

Completing the Solver Parameters dialog entails specifying the Target cell, the Changing Cells, the constraints, and setting the Assume Linear option, before solving the model. After optimization completes, Solver displays the Solver Results dialog containing important completion messages and allowing one or more Solver reports to be generated. Upon completion the spreadsheet displays the optimal solution generated by Solver.

Several examples were given to show how a real-world situation can be translated into a symbolic LP model. The examples illustrated that a profit objective leads to a maximization (Max) model, whereas a cost objective gives a minimization (Min) model. We also saw that a constraint of the "limitation" type is usually translated into a mathematical inequality of the $\leq$ form, and a constraint of the "requirement" type is usually translated into a $\geq$ inequality. In some situations, such as in blending problems, logical considerations will require the presence of equality constraints. Guidelines were also given on how to proceed with developing the LP model and its spreadsheet formulation.

SOLUTION TO CRAWLER TREAD

The spreadsheet model, showing the optimal solution, is given in Figure 3.26 along with the Solver Parameters, and relevant portions of Solver Options, and formulas.

SOLUTION TO EXAMPLE 1: ASTRO AND COSMO

The symbolic LP model for Astro and Cosmo is given by:

$$A = \text{daily production of Astros} \quad \text{(TV sets/day)}$$
$$C = \text{daily production of Cosmos} \quad \text{(TV sets/day)}$$

$$\text{Max } 20A + 10C$$

$$\begin{array}{rrl}
\text{s.t.} & A & \leq 70 \\
& C & \leq 50 \\
& A + 2C & \leq 120 \\
& A + C & \leq 90 \\
& A, C & \geq 0
\end{array}$$

In this model not all the decision variables appear in all the constraints. The variable C does not appear in the constraint $A \leq 70$. Not all the decision variables have to appear explicitly in every constraint.[6] The spreadsheet model is given in Figure 3.27 along with the Solver Parameters and the optimal solution. The SUMPRODUCT() formulas for Profit and Total LHS cells are similar to those of the Crawler Tread example above and are omitted for this and later examples. The binding constraints for "Labor Dept. B" and "Prod. Capacity, Astro" do not show a zero Slack. Small negative or positive numbers occur in many Solver solutions because of Excel's finite arithmetic precision. In this and similar cases, the values represent extremely small numbers at the limit of Excel's computational precision and can be assumed to be zero for practical purposes.

	A	B	C	D	E	F	G	H	I
1		**Crawler Tread Production Plan**							
2	Mine	T1	T2	T3	T4				
3	Ton Fractions	0.259	0.704	0.037	0	Total			
4	Cost/Ton	$800	$400	$600	$500	$511.11			
5	Constraints	Composition per Ton				Total Elements	Requirements	Surplus	
6	A	10	3	8	2	5.00	$\geq$	5	0
7	B	90	150	75	175	131.67	$\geq$	100	31.67
8	C	45	25	20	37	30.00	$\geq$	30	0
9	Balance	1	1	1	1	1.00	$=$	1	0

	F	G	H	I
3	Total			
4	=SUMPRODUCT($B$3:$E$3,B4:E4)			
5	Total Elements		Requirements	Surplus
6	=SUMPRODUCT($B$3:$E$3,B6:E6)	$\geq$	5	=F6-H6
7	=SUMPRODUCT($B$3:$E$3,B7:E7)	$\geq$	100	=F7-H7
8	=SUMPRODUCT($B$3:$E$3,B8:E8)	$\geq$	30	=F8-H8
9	=SUMPRODUCT($B$3:$E$3,B9:E9)	$=$	1	=F9-H9

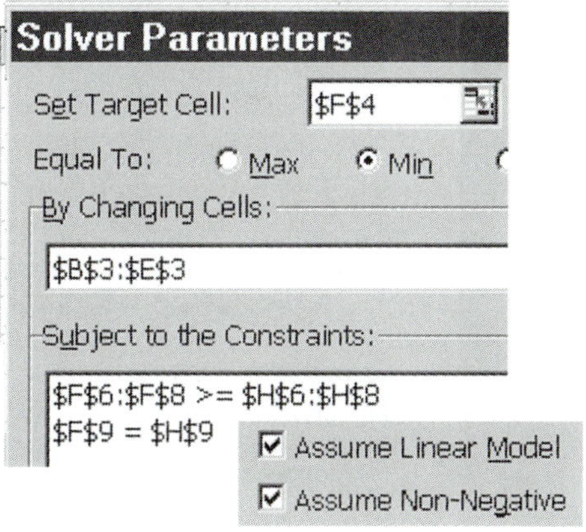

Solver Parameters

Set Target Cell: $F$4

Equal To: ○ Max ● Min

By Changing Cells:

$B$3:$E$3

Subject to the Constraints:

$F$6:$F$8 >= $H$6:$H$8
$F$9 = $H$9

☑ Assume Linear Model
☑ Assume Non-Negative

FIGURE 3.26

Crawler Tread Model

---

[6]You may think of all decision variables being included, but with zero coefficients in places. Thus, the constraint $A \leq 70$ is the same as $A + 0*C \leq 70$.

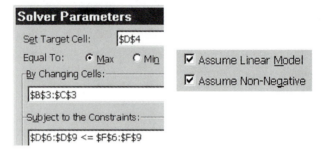

	A	B	C	D	E	F	G
1	Astro and Cosmo						
2		Astro	Cosmo				
3	Production Quantities	70.0	20.0	Profit			
4	Contribution Margins	$ 20	$ 10	$ 1,600			
5	Constraints	Resource Usage		Total		Avail.	Slack
6	Labor Dept. A	1	2	110	≤	120	10
7	Labor Dept. B	1	1	90	≤	90	-1.6E-10
8	Prod. Capacity, Astro	1		70	≤	70	-7.6E-12
9	Prod. Capacity, Cosmo		1	20	≤	50	30

Solver Parameters

Set Target Cell: $D$4

Equal To: ⊙ Max   ○ Min

☑ Assume Linear Model

By Changing Cells:

☑ Assume Non-Negative

$B$3:$C$3

Subject to the Constraints:

$D$6:$D$9 <= $F$6:$F$9

FIGURE 3.27

Astro and Cosmo Model

SOLUTION TO EXAMPLE 2: BLENDING GRUEL

The LP model for blending gruel is given by:

$$\text{Min } 4x_1 + 6x_2 + 3x_3 + 2x_4$$
$$\text{s.t. } 3x_1 + 5x_2 + 2x_3 + 3x_4 \geq 3$$
$$7x_1 + 4x_2 + 2x_3 + 8x_4 \geq 5$$
$$5x_1 + 6x_2 + 6x_3 + 2x_4 \geq 4$$
$$x_1 + x_2 + x_3 + x_4 = 1$$
$$x_1, x_2, x_3, x_4 \geq 0$$

The spreadsheet model is shown in Figure 3.28, along with the Solver Parameters and the optimal solution.

Note that in Example 1, from the point of view of implementation, fractional values for the decision variables would probably be unacceptable. In Example 2, however, fractional values would be expected and acceptable.

SOLUTION TO EXAMPLE 3: SECURITY FORCE SCHEDULING

The security force scheduling model is given by:

$$\text{Min } x_1 + x_2 + x_3 + x_4 + x_5 + x_6$$
$$\text{s.t. } x_1 + x_6 \geq 5$$
$$x_1 + x_2 \geq 7$$
$$x_2 + x_3 \geq 15$$
$$x_3 + x_4 \geq 7$$
$$x_4 + x_5 \geq 12$$
$$x_5 + x_6 \geq 9$$
$$x_i \geq 0, \qquad i = 1, 2, \ldots, 6$$

Example 3 illustrates another setting where integer values would be needed.

The spreadsheet model is shown in Figure 3.29, along with the Solver Parameters and the optimal solution. (You may get a different schedule from Solver, but it will have the same minimum Total #. This is because this model has several alternative optimal schedules.)

This type of problem has been used to schedule operators for several telephone companies, as well as for companies that have "800" numbers. Typically, each hour is broken into 15-minute segments; thus each 24-hour day has 96 constraints. The number of variables is determined by the different possible shifts allowed.

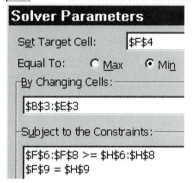

	A	B	C	D	E	F	G	H	I
1	Blending Gruel								
2	Gruel	#1	#2	#3	#4				
3	Proportion of Gruel	0	0.167	0.333	0.5	Cost			
4	Cost/16 oz.	$4	$6	$ 3	$2	$3.00			
5	Constraints	Resource Provided				Total			Excess
6	Protein	3	5	2	3	3	≥	3	1.3E-15
7	Carbohydrate	7	4	2	8	5.333	≥	5	0.333
8	Fat	5	6	6	2	4	≥	4	1.8E-15
9	Total Proportion	1	1	1	1	1	=	1	2.2E-16

(Column H header, vertical: Requirements)

Solver Parameters

Set Target Cell: $F$4

Equal To: ○ Max   ● Min

☑ Assume Linear Model
☑ Assume Non-Negative

By Changing Cells:

$B$3:$E$3

Subject to the Constraints:

$F$6:$F$8 >= $H$6:$H$8
$F$9 = $H$9

FIGURE 3.28

Blending Gruel Model

	A	B	C	D	E	F	G	H	I	J	K
1	Security Force Scheduling										
2	Shift	#1	#2	#3	#4	#5	#6	Total #			
3	# on Shift	0	7	8	0	12	5	32			
4	Constraints	Resource Available						Total			Excess
5	Mid. - 4am	1					1	5	≥	5	0
6	4am - 8 am	1	1					7	≥	7	0
7	8am - Noon		1	1				15	≥	15	-7E-13
8	Noon - 4pm			1	1			8	≥	7	1
9	4pm - 8pm				1	1		12	≥	12	1E-12
10	8pm - Mid.					1	1	17	≥	9	8

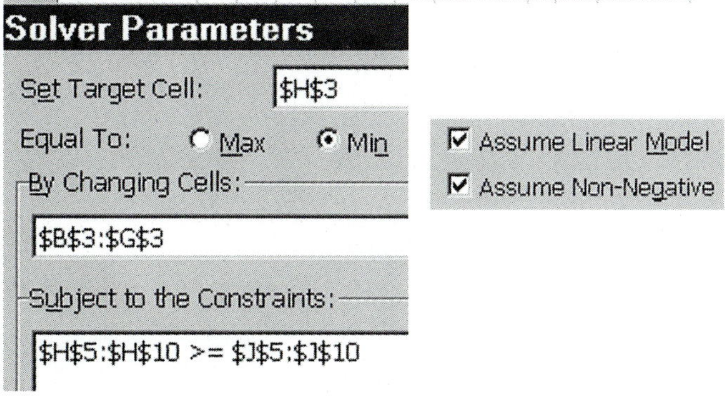

(Column J header, vertical: Requirements)

Solver Parameters

Set Target Cell: $H$3

Equal To: ○ Max   ● Min

☑ Assume Linear Model
☑ Assume Non-Negative

By Changing Cells:

$B$3:$G$3

Subject to the Constraints:

$H$5:$H$10 >= $J$5:$J$10

FIGURE 3.29

Security Force
Scheduling Model

SOLUTION TO EXAMPLE 4: LONGER BOATS YACHT COMPANY

To obtain an expression of the break-even in terms of the production quantities, the following decision variables are defined:

S = number of Stings to produce

R = number of Rays to produce

B = number of Breakers to produce

The break-even constraint, then, is

$$10,000S + 7500R + 15,000B = 5000S + 3600R + 8000B + 18,000,000$$

or

$$5000S + 3900R + 7000B = 18,000,000$$

We note that there is an infinite number of sets of values for S, R, and B that satisfy this constraint. Thus, in the multiproduct case, there are many break-even points, whereas in the single-product case, there is only one. In the multiproduct case, then, management must specify an additional restriction in order to identify a particular break-even point of interest. The fixed costs are of necessity incurred in their totality, and thus the goal of minimizing capital outlay becomes one of minimizing total variable costs. The total variable cost (the objective function) is

$$5000S + 3600R + 8000B$$

The complete model reflecting the break-even constraint, as well as the preestablished requirements and limits on demand, is as follows:

$$\text{Min } 5000S + 3600R + 8000B$$
$$5000S + 3900R + 7000B = 18,000,000$$
$$S \geq 700$$
$$B \geq 400$$
$$R \leq 300$$
$$S \geq 0, \qquad R \geq 0, \qquad B \geq 0$$

The spreadsheet model is shown in Figure 3.30, along with the Solver Parameters and the optimal solution. Note that the original data disaggregations are preserved with formulas performing the aggregations to allow flexibility in data editing for "What if?" projections.

	A	B	C	D	E	F	G	H
1	($ 000s)	Stings	Breakers	Rays				
2	Selling Price	$ 10.0	$ 15.0	$ 7.5				
3	Variable Cost	$ 5.0	$ 8.0	$ 3.6			Total	
4	Fixed Cost	$ 5,000	$ 3,000	$10,000			$18,000	
5								
6	Break Even Model ($ in 000's)							
7		Stings	Breakers	Rays				
8	# to Produce	2806	400	300	Cost			
9	Unit Cost	$ 5.0	$ 8.0	$ 3.6	$ 18,000			
10	Constraints		Resource Usage		Total			Slack
11	Break Even	$ 5.0	$ 7.0	$ 3.9	$ 18,000	=	$18,000	-4E-05
12	Min Prod. Stings	1			2806	≥	700	2106
13	Min Prod. Breakers		1		400	≥	400	3E-10
14	Max Prod. Rays			1	300	≤	300	0

(Requirements — vertical label in column G)

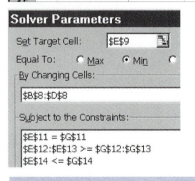

Solver Parameters

Set Target Cell: $E$9

Equal To: ○ Max ⦿ Min ○

By Changing Cells:

$B$8:$D$8

Subject to the Constraints:

$E$11 = $G$11
$E$12:$E$13 >= $G$12:$G$13
$E$14 <= $G$14

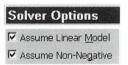

Solver Options

☑ Assume Linear Model

☑ Assume Non-Negative

Cell	Formula	Copy To
B9	= B3	C9:D9
B11	= B2 − B3	C11:D11
G4	= SUM(B4:D4)	
G11	= G4	

FIGURE 3.30

Longer Boats Constrained Break-Even Model

Constraint.   A mathematical inequality (an inequality constraint) or equality (an equality constraint) that must be satisfied by the variables in the model.

Objective Function.   Every linear program has a linear objective function that represents the performance measure to be either maximized or minimized.

Constrained Optimization Model.   A model whose objective is to find values of decision variables that optimize an objective function subject to constraints.

Optimal Product Mix.   Alternative term for optimal production plan.

Optimal Production Plan.   The optimal decision for a production model; that is, the optimal quantities of each product to be produced.

Inequality Constraint.   A constraint requiring some function of the decision variables in a model to be ≥ (greater than or equal to) or ≤ (less than or equal to) a constant.

Right-Hand Side.   The number on the right-hand side (RHS) of a constraint.

Constraint Function.   The left-hand side (LHS) of a constraint. It depends on the decision variables.

Nonnegativity Conditions.   Conditions in a model that stipulate that the decision variables can have only nonnegative *(positive or zero)* values.

Decision Variables.   The variables under the decision maker's control. These are the variables that appear in the models that we have formulated in this chapter.

Feasible Decision.   A decision that satisfies all the constraints of a model, including the nonnegativity conditions. Feasible means allowable.

Optimal Decision.   A feasible decision that optimizes the objective function.

Optimal Solution.   Alternative term for optimal decision.

Optimize.   To maximize or minimize.

Symbolic LP Model.   The algebraic representation of an LP problem.

Linear Function.   A function in which each variable appears in a separate term. There are no powers other than 1, and for example, there are no logarithmic, exponential, IF() statements or trigonometric terms.

Integrality Condition.   A requirement that one or more variables in a model have only integer values.

Integer Program.   A model in which one or more variables can have only integer values.

Sunk Costs.   Costs whose values have already been determined, and therefore cannot be affected by subsequent decisions.

Fixed Costs.   Alternative term for sunk costs.

Variable Costs.   Costs whose values will be determined by decisions yet to be made, and which can therefore serve as variables in an optimization model.

Decision Values.   A set of numerical values for the decision variables.

Decision.   Alternative term for decision value.

Binding Constraint.   A constraint whose constraint function evaluation equals its right-hand-side value.

Solver.   A spreadsheet add-in program that can optimize the spreadsheet representation of an LP model.

Equality Constraint.   A constraint requiring some function of the decision variables in a model to be exactly equal to a constant.

Self-Review Exercises

True-False

1. **T   F** In the context of modeling, restrictions on the allowable decisions are called constraints.

2. **T   F** Not every LP has to have constraints.

3. **T   F** Any model with an objective function, constraints, and decision variables is an LP.

4. **T   F** A limitation is expressed as a ≥ constraint.

5. **T   F** The nonnegativity conditions mean that all decision variables must be positive.

6. **T   F** Since fractional values for decision variables may not be physically meaningful, in practice (for the purpose

of implementation) we sometimes round the optimal LP solution to integer values.

7. **T   F** All the constraints in an LP are inequalities.

8. **T   F** Properly defining the decision variables is an important step in model formulation.

Multiple Choice

11. A constraint limits the values
    a. that the objective function can assume
    b. that the decision variables can assume
    c. neither of the above
    d. both a and b

12. Constraints may represent
    a. limitations
    b. requirements
    c. balance conditions
    d. all of the above

13. Linear programming is
    a. a constrained optimization model
    b. a constrained decision-making model
    c. a mathematical programming model
    d. all of the above

14. In an LP Max model
    a. the objective function is maximized
    b. the objective function is maximized and then it is determined whether this occurs at an allowable decision
    c. the objective function is maximized over the allowable set of decisions
    d. all of the above

15. The *distinguishing* feature of an LP (as opposed to more general mathematical programming models) is
    a. the model has an objective function and constraints
    b. all functions in the problem are linear
    c. optimal values for the decision variables are produced

16. In translating a word problem into a symbolic model, it is often helpful to
    a. express each constraint in words
    b. express the objective in words
    c. verbally identify the decision variables
    d. all of the above

17. Model formulation is important because
    a. it enables us to use algebraic techniques
    b. in a business context, most managers prefer to work with symbolic models
    c. it forces management to address a clearly defined problem
    d. it allows the manager to postpone decision making while appearing to be busy

18. The nonnegativity requirement is often included in an LP because
    a. it makes the model easier to solve
    b. it makes the model correspond more closely to the real-world situation
    c. neither of the above
    d. both a and b

9. **T   F** The objective function of a cost-minimization model need only consider variable, as opposed to sunk, costs.

10. **T   F** The way in which a problem has been formulated as a model is of considerable interest to the manager, who may one day have to pass judgment on the validity of the model.

Questions 19 through 26 refer to the following problem:
Three itinerant industrialists, Lotta Anderson, Claire Mosley, and Finny Jones, are en route to Hollywood to seek their fortunes. The flight time is 40 hours at a fuel cost of $100 per gallon. In a Hollywood deli they strike up a quick friendship with the notorious Peter Rehnberg. Peter's net income per year is $40,000—his alimony payments are $60,000. Knowing almost everyone in town, Peter is able to spin out a stairway to the stars for our three fortune seekers. They are now inspecting capsule medicine products by passing the capsules over a special lighting table where they visually check for cracked, partially filled, or improperly tainted capsules. Currently, any of our three moguls can be assigned to the visual inspection task. However, they differ in height, accuracy, and speed abilities. Consequently, their employer (Flora Sager) pays them at slightly different wage rates. The significant differences are summed up in the following table.

INSPECTOR	SPEED (UNITS/HR)	ACCURACY (%)	HOURLY WAGE ($)	HEIGHT
Lotta	300	98	11.80	5 ft 10 in.
Claire	200	99	10.40	4 ft 3 in.
Finny	350	96	11.00	5 ft 2 in.

Operating on a full 8-hour shift, Flora needs to have at least 2000 capsules inspected with no more than 2% of these capsules having inspection errors. In addition, because of the devastating carpal tunnel syndrome, no one inspector can be assigned this task for more than 4 hours per day. Let

$$X_1 = \text{number of hours worked by Lotta}$$
$$X_2 = \text{number of hours worked by Claire}$$
$$X_3 = \text{number of hours worked by Finny}$$

The objective is to minimize the cost of 8 hours of inspection. Assume that the inspection process must be in operation for all 8 hours. In other words, continuous production must occur during the 8-hour period. In addition, Lotta, Claire, and Finny are the only inspectors, no more than one inspector can work at a time, and the plumber works at most 4 hours per day.

19. A correct accuracy constraint is
    a. $(0.98)(300)X_1 + (0.99)(200) X_2 + (0.96)(350) X_3 \geq 2000$
    b. $(0.02)(300)X_1 + (0.01)(200) X_2 + (0.04)(350) X_3 \leq (0.02)(2000)$
    c. $-2X_2 + 7X_3 \leq 0$
    d. none of the above

20. The production requirement constraint is correctly written as $300X_1 + 200X_2 + 350X_3 = 2000$.
    a. T
    b. F

21. Excluding the nonnegativity constraints, a proper formulation for this problem will contain six constraints.
   a. T
   b. F

22. It is possible that the correct formulation for this problem will have no feasible decisions. (Answer this question for the given data.)
   a. T
   b. F

23. If it were not for the accuracy requirement and the 4-hour limitation, the optimal solution would have only Finny working.
   a. T
   b. F

24. The optimal solution will require that at least two of the three employees inspect.
   a. T
   b. F

25. A feasible policy is provided by
   a. 4 hours Claire, 4 hours Finny
   b. 4 hours Lotta, 4 hours Claire
   c. both a and b

26. Let policy A be $X_1 = 4$, $X_2 = 4$, $X_3 = 0$. Let policy B be $X_1 = 3$, $X_2 = 4$, $X_3 = 1$. Note that each policy is feasible. Since A produces 2000 capsules and B produces 2050, A is preferred.
   a. T
   b. F

27. A parameter in a model can be a number or a symbol.
   a. T
   b. F

28. Consider the constraint $10E + 15F \leq R$, where R is a parameter for hours in department A. Now suppose values of R are given by $(1 - e^{-(.05MA)})$ where MA is a new decision variable. If we substitute this into the original constraint, it becomes $10E + 15F \leq 200 (1 - e^{-(.05MA)})$. This new constraint is linear in E, F, and the new parameter MA.
   a. T
   b. F

29. In the spreadsheet representation of an LP, a constraint function is represented as a formula in a cell.
   a. T
   b. F

30. For feasible decisions, the slack cells if present in the spreadsheet will contain nonnegative numbers.
   a. T
   b. F

31. Excel can be used to create a spreadsheet representation of an LP but it will *not* optimize the spreadsheet.
   a. T
   b. F

32. A parameter
   a. is a number in a model or a symbol that is exogenous to the model (i.e., a symbol whose numerical value must be supplied to the model)
   b. may be represented by a symbol (such as R) whose value must be determined by the model
   c. both of the above

33. A suggested way to create a spreadsheet representation of an LP is to first write out the symbolic LP model and then use this as a guideline to create a spreadsheet model.
   a. T
   b. F

34. A spreadsheet representation of an LP can be useful because
   a. parameters representing raw data may enter into the model nonlinearly
   b. it makes the model easy to debug
   c. both of the above

Answers

1. T	10. T	19. c	28. b
2. F	11. d	20. b	29. a
3. F	12. d	21. a	30. a
4. F	13. d	22. b	31. a
5. F	14. c	23. b	32. a
6. T	15. b	24. a	33. a
7. F	16. d	25. b	34. a
8. T	17. c	26. b	
9. T	18. b	27. a	

Problems

All end-of-chapter Problems in this text have been graded by level of difficulty: no • [default] = introductory, •• = intermediate, ••• = challenging.

•3-1. Match each of the following terms with the most appropriate description below.

(a) Linear program   1. The unknowns in an LP that represent decisions to be made.
(b) Requirement   2. Usually, a constraint of $\geq$ form.
(c) Variable cost   3. A concept that is proper to include in the model.
(d) Sunk cost   4. Usually, not relevant to the model (break-even analysis would be an exception).
(e) Decision variables   5. Usually, a constraint of $\leq$ form.
(f) Constraint function   6. The left-hand side of the constraint.
(g) Restriction   7. Synonymous with constraint.
(h) Limitation   8. A special type of constrained optimization model.

•3-2. Which of the following mathematical relationships could be found in a linear programming model? For those relationships that could not be found in an LP, state the reasons.

(a) $3x_1 + x_2 \leq \sqrt{5}$
(b) $\sqrt{x_1} + x_2 \leq 10$
(c) $\sqrt{2}x_1 - \pi x_3 \leq e$
(d) $x_1^2 + 2x_2 = 0$
(e) $x_1 + x_1 x_2 + x_3 = 5$
(f) $x_1 + \log(x_2) = 5$
(g) $\log(10) x_1 + e^2 x_2 = 6$
(h) $e_1^x + x_2 = 23$
(i) the Excel formula for the RHS of a constraint in which F6 is a decision variable:
=IF($F$6>=2,SUM(G1:G10),SUM(G1:G5))

•3-3. *A Production Problem.* The Swelte Glove Company manufactures and sells two products. The company makes a profit of $12 for each unit of product 1 sold and a profit of $4 for each unit of product 2. The labor-hour requirements for the products in each of the three production departments are summarized in the following table. The supervisors of these departments have estimated that the following numbers of labor hours will be available during the next month: 800 hours in department 1, 600 hours in department 2, and 2000 hours in department 3. Assuming that the company is interested in maximizing profits, develop the linear programming model.

DEPARTMENT	LABOR-HOUR REQUIREMENT Product 1	Product 2
1	1	2
2	1	3
3	2	3

•3-4. *A Production Problem.* Wood Walker owns a small furniture shop. He makes three different styles of tables: A, B, C. Each table requires a certain amount of time for cutting component parts, for assembling, and for painting. Wood can sell all the units he makes. Furthermore, model C may be sold without painting. Wood employs several individuals who work on a part-time basis, so the time available for each of these activities varies from month to month. Use the data that follows to formulate an LP model that will help Wood determine the product mix that will maximize his profit next month.

MODEL	CUTTING (HR)	ASSEMBLING (HR)	PAINTING (HR)	PROFIT PER TABLE ($)
A	3	4	5	25
B	1	2	5	20
C	4	5	4	50
Unpainted C	4	5	0	30
Capacity	150	200	300	

•3-5.   *Financial Planning.* Willie Hanes is president of a one-person investment firm that manages stock portfolios for a number of clients. A new client has just requested the firm to manage a $100,000 portfolio. The client would like to restrict the portfolio to a mix of the three stocks shown in the following table. Formulate an LP to show how many shares of each stock Willie should purchase to maximize the estimated total annual return.

STOCK	PRICE PER SHARE ($)	ESTIMATED ANNUAL RETURN PER SHARE ($)	MAXIMUM POSSIBLE INVESTMENT ($)
Gofer Crude	60	7	60,000
Can Oil	25	3	25,000
Sloth Petroleum	20	3	30,000

•3-6.   *A Blending Problem.* Douglas E. Starr, the manager of Heavenly Hound Kennels, Inc., provides lodging for pets. The kennels' dog food is made by mixing three grain products to obtain a well-balanced dog diet. The data for the three products are shown in the following table. If Douglas wants to make sure that each of his dogs consumes at least 8 ounces of protein, 1 ounce of carbohydrate, and no more than 0.5 ounces of fat each day, how much of each grain product should each dog be fed in order to minimize Douglas's cost? (*Note:* 16 ounces = 1 pound.)

GRAIN PRODUCT	COST PER POUND ($)	PROTEIN (%)	CARBOHYDRATE (%)	FAT (%)
A	0.45	62	5	3
B	0.38	55	10	2
C	0.27	36	20	1

•3-7.   *A Blending Problem.* McNaughton, Inc. produces two steak sauces, Spicy Diablo and mild Red Baron. These sauces are both made by blending two ingredients, A and B. A certain level of flexibility is permitted in the formulas for these products. The allowable percentages, along with revenue and cost data, are given in the following table. Up to 40 quarts of A and 30 quarts of B could be purchased. McNaughton can sell as much of these sauces as it produces. Formulate an LP whose objective is to maximize the net profit from the sale of the sauces.

	INGREDIENT		SALES PRICE PER QUART
SAUCE	A	B	($)
Spicy Diablo	at least 25%	at least 50%	3.35
Red Baron	at most 75%	*	2.85
Cost per Quart	$1.60	$2.59	

*No explicit maximum or minimum percentage.

•3-8.   *A Blending Problem.* Corey Ander's Spice Company has a limited amount of three ingredients that are used in the production of seasonings. Corey uses the three ingredients—HB01, HB02, and HB03—to produce either turmeric or paprika. The marketing department reports that the firm can sell as much paprika as it can produce, but it can sell up to a maximum of 1700 bottles of turmeric. Unused ingredients can be sold on the open market. Prices are quoted in $/ounce. The current prices are: HB01— $0.60, HB02— $0.70, HB03— $0.55. In addition, Corey has signed a contract to supply 600 bottles of paprika to Wal-Mart. Additional data are shown in the following table. Formulate Corey's problem as a revenue-maximizing LP.

	INGREDIENTS (OZ/BOTTLE)			DEMAND (BOTTLES)	SALES PRICE PER BOTTLE ($)
	HB01	HB02	HB03		
Turmeric	4	2	1	1700	3.25
Paprika	3	2	3	Unlimited	2.75
Availability (ounces)	8000	9000	7000		

••3-9. *A Blending Problem.* Guy Chung, superintendent of buildings and grounds at Gotham University, is planning to put fertilizer on the grass in the quadrangle area early in the spring. The grass needs nitrogen, phosphorus, and potash in at least the amounts given in the following table.

MINERAL	MINIMUM WEIGHT (LB)
Nitrogen	10
Phosphorus	7
Potash	5

Three kinds of commercial fertilizer are available; analysis and prices per 1000 pounds are given in the following table. Guy can buy as much of each of these fertilizers as he wishes and mix them together before applying them to the grass. Formulate an LP model to determine how much of each fertilizer he should buy to satisfy the requirements at minimum cost.

FERTILIZER	NITROGEN CONTENT (LB)	PHOSPHORUS CONTENT (LB)	POTASH CONTENT (LB)	PRICE ($)
I	25	10	5	10
II	10	5	10	8
III	5	10	5	7

Fertilizer Characteristics (per 1000 lb)

••3-10. *A Production Problem.* Ebel Mining Company owns two different mines that produce a given kind of ore. The mines are located in different parts of the country and hence have different production capacities and ore quality. After crushing, the ore is graded into three classes: high grade, medium grade, and low grade. Ebel has contracted to provide its parent company's smelting plant with 12 tons of high-grade, 8 tons of medium-grade, and 24 tons of low-grade ore per week. It costs Ebel $20,000 per day to run the first mine and $16,000 per day to run the second. However, in a day's operation the first mine produces 6 tons of high-grade, 2 tons of medium-grade, and 4 tons of low-grade ore, while the second mine produces daily 2 tons of high-grade, 2 tons of medium-grade, and 12 tons of low-grade ore. How many days a week should each mine be operated in order to fulfill Ebel's commitments most economically? (It is acceptable to schedule a mine for a fraction of a day.)

••3-11. *A Production Problem.* Two products are manufactured on each of three machines. A pound of each product requires a specified number of hours on each machine, as presented in the following table. Total hours available on machines 1, 2, and 3 are 10, 16, and 12, respectively. The profit contributions per pound of products 1 and 2 are $4 and $3, respectively. Define the decision variables and formulate this problem as a profit-maximizing linear program and solve it.

MACHINE	MACHINE-HOUR REQUIREMENT	
	Product 1	Product 2
1	3	2
2	1	4
3	5	3

••3-12. Sally's Solar Car Co. has a plant that can manufacture family sedans, station wagons, and sports coupes. The selling price, variable cost, and fixed cost for manufacturing these cars are given in the following table.

MODEL	PROFIT CONTRIBUTION ($)	VARIABLE PRODUCTION TIME (HR)	FIXED COST ($)
Sedan	6,000	12	2,000,000
Station Wagon	8,000	15	3,000,000
Coupe	11,000	24	7,000,000

Sally currently has orders for 100 sedans, 200 station wagons, and 300 coupes. She must satisfy these orders. She wants to plan production so she will break even as quickly as possible—that is, she wants to make sure that the total contribution margin will equal total fixed costs and that total variable production cost is minimized. Formulate this problem as an LP and solve it.

••3-13. *Break-Even Analysis.* Reese Eichler, a manufacturer of superfluous air filtration equipment, produces two units, the Umidaire and the Depollinator. Data pertaining to sales price and costs are shown in the following table. Reese's firm has already contracted to provide 500 Umidaires and would like to calculate the break-even quantities for both types of units. Formulate the cost-minimizing LP model and solve it.

PRODUCT	SELLING PRICE PER UNIT ($)	VARIABLE COST PER UNIT ($)	FIXED COST ($)
Umidaire	450	240	150,000
Depollinator	700	360	240,000

••3-14. *Portfolio Planning.* An investment company currently has $10 million to invest. The goal is to maximize expected return earned over the next year. Its four investment possibilities are summarized in the following table. In addition, the company has specified that at least 30% of the funds must be placed in common stock and Treasury bonds, and no more than 40% in money market funds and municipal bonds. All of the $10 million currently on hand will be invested. Formulate an LP model that tells how much money to invest in each instrument and solve it.

INVESTMENT POSSIBILITY	EXPECTED EARNED RETURN (%)	MAXIMUM ALLOWABLE INVESTMENT (MILLIONS $)
Treasury Bonds	8	5
Common Stock	6	7
Money Market	12	2
Municipal Bonds	9	4

•••3-15. *Farm Management.* A firm operates four farms of comparable productivity. Each farm has a certain amount of usable acreage and a supply of labor hours to plant and tend the crops. The data for the upcoming season are shown in the following table.

FARM	USABLE ACREAGE	LABOR HOURS AVAILABLE PER MONTH
1	500	1700
2	900	3000
3	300	900
4	700	2200

The organization is considering three crops for planting. These crops differ primarily in their expected profit per acre and in the amount of labor they require, as shown in the following table.

CROP	MAXIMUM ACREAGE	MONTHLY LABOR HOURS REQUIRED PER ACRE	EXPECTED PROFIT PER ACRE ($)
A	700	2	500
B	800	4	200
C	300	3	300

Furthermore, the total acreage that can be devoted to any particular crop is limited by the associated requirements for harvesting equipment. In order to maintain a roughly uniform workload among the farms, management's policy is that the percentage of usable acreage planted must be the same at each farm. However, any combination of the crops may be grown at any of the farms as long as all constraints are satisfied (including the uniform-workload requirement). Management wishes to know how many acres of each crop should be planted at the respective farms in order to maximize expected profit. Formulate this as a linear programming model and solve it.

•••3-16. *A Blending Problem.* A vineyard wishes to blend four different vintages to make three types of blended wine. The supply of the vintages and the sales prices of the blended wines are shown in the following table together with certain restrictions on the percentage composition of the three blends. In particular, vintages 2 and 3 together must make up at least 75% of Blend A and at least 35% of Blend C. In addition, Blend A must contain at least 8% of vintage 4, while Blend B must contain at least 10% of vintage 2 and at most 35% of vintage 4. Any amounts of Blends A, B, and C can be sold. Formulate an LP model that will make the best use of the vintages on hand and solve it.

BLEND	VINTAGE				SALES PRICE PER GALLON
	1	2	3	4	
A	*	at least 75% 2 & 3 in any proportion		at least 8%	80
B	*	at least 10%	*	at most 35%	50
C	*	at least 35% 2 & 3 in any proportion		*	35
SUPPLY (gallons)	130	200	150	350	
*Indicates no restriction.					

•••3-17. *A Scheduling Problem.* A certain restaurant operates 7 days a week. Waiters are hired to work 6 hours per day. The union contract specifies that each must work 5 consecutive days and then have 2 consecutive days off. All waiters receive the same weekly salary. Staffing requirements are shown in the following table. Assume that this cycle of requirements repeats indefinitely, and ignore the fact that the number of waiters hired must be an integer. The manager wishes to find an employment schedule that satisfies these requirements at a minimum cost. Formulate this problem as a linear program and solve it.

DAY	MINIMUM NUMBER OF WAITER HOURS REQUIRED
Monday	150
Tuesday	200
Wednesday	400
Thursday	300
Friday	700
Saturday	800
Sunday	300

•••3-18. *A Production Problem.* A plant can manufacture four different products (A, B, C, D) in any combination. Each product requires time on each of four machines in minutes per pound of product, as shown in the following table. Each machine is available 60 hours per week. Products A, B, C, and D may be sold at prices of $9, $7, $6, and $5 per pound, respectively. Variable labor costs are $2 per hour for machines 1 and 2 and $3 per hour for machines 3 and 4. Material cost for each pound of product A is $4. The material cost is $1 for each pound of products B, C, and D. Formulate a profit-maximizing LP model for this problem, given the maximum demands for each product below, and then solve it.

PRODUCT	MACHINE 1	2	3	4	MAXIMUM DEMAND
A	5	10	6	3	400
B	3	6	4	8	100
C	4	5	3	3	150
D	4	2	1	2	500

•••3-19. *A Production Problem.* A manufacturer has four jobs, A, B, C, and D, that must be produced this month. Each job may be handled in any of three shops. The time required for each job in each shop, the cost per hour in each shop, and the number of hours available this month in each shop are given in the following table. It is also possible to split each job among the shops in any proportion. For example, one fourth of job A can be done in 8 hours in shop 1, and one third of job C can be done in 19 hours in shop 3. The manufacturer wishes to determine how many hours of each job should be handled by each shop in order to minimize the total cost of completing all four jobs. Identify the decision variables, and formulate an LP model for this problem and solve it.

SHOP	TIME REQUIRED (HR) A	B	C	D	COST PER HOUR OF SHOP TIME ($)	SHOP TIME AVAILABLE (HR)
1	32	151	72	118	89	160
2	39	147	61	126	81	160
3	46	155	57	121	84	160

•••3-20. *A Scheduling Problem.* While it is operating out of Stockholm, the aircraft carrier *Mighty* is on maneuvers from Monday through Friday and in port over the weekend. Next week the captain would like to give shore leave for Monday through Friday to as many of the 2500-sailor crew as possible. However, he must carry out the maneuvers for the week and satisfy navy regulations. The regulations are

(a) Sailors work either the A.M. shift (midnight to noon) or the P.M. shift (noon to midnight) any day they work, and during a week they must remain on the same shift every day they work.

(b) Each sailor who works must be on duty exactly four days, even if there is not enough "real work" on some days.

The number of sailors required each shift of each day is shown in the following table. Formulate and solve this problem as a linear programming problem so that one would know how many sailors work on each day.

	M	TU	W	TH	F
A.M.	900	1000	450	800	700
P.M.	800	500	1000	300	750

•••3-21. *A Process Mix Problem.* A small firm has two processes for blending each of two products, charcoal starter fluid and lighter fluid for cigarette lighters. The firm is attempting to decide how many hours to run each process. The inputs and outputs for running the processes for one hour are given in the following table. Let x_1 and x_2 be the number of hours the company decides to use process 1 and process 2, respectively. Because of a federal allocation program, the maximum amounts of kerosene and benzene available are 300 units and 450 units, respectively. Sales commitments require that at least 600 units of starter fluid and 225 units of lighter fluid be produced. The per hour profits that accrue from process 1 and process 2 are $450 and $390, respectively. Formulate this as a profit-maximizing linear programming model and solve it.

PROCESS	INPUTS		OUTPUTS	
	Kerosene	Benzene	Starter Fluid	Lighter Fluid
1	3	9	15	6
2	12	6	9	24

•••**3-22.** *Portfolio Planning with the CAPM Model.* (*Note:* This problem will be especially interesting to students with a background in investments. Others should be cautioned that it includes terms not defined in this text.) An investment company currently has $10 million to invest. Its goal is to maximize expected return over the next year. The company wants to use the capital asset pricing model (CAPM) to determine each investment's expected return. The CAPM formula is:

$$ER = Rf + b\,(Rm - Rf), \text{ where}$$
$$ER = \text{expected return}$$
$$Rf = \text{risk-free rate}$$
$$b \quad = \text{investment beta (market risk)}$$
$$Rm = \text{market return}$$

The market return and risk-free rate fluctuate, and the company wants to be able to reevaluate its decision on a weekly basis. Its four investment possibilities are summarized in the following table. In addition, the company has specified that at least 30% of the funds must be placed in Treasury bonds and money markets, and no more than 40% in common stock and municipal bonds. All of the $10 million currently on hand will be invested.

(a) Formulate this problem as an LP model.

(b) Optimize the model if the market return is 12% and the risk-free rate is 6%.

INVESTMENT POSSIBILITY	BETA	MAXIMUM ALLOWABLE INVESTMENT (MILLIONS $)
Treasury Bonds	0	7
Common Stock	1	2
Money Market	$\frac{1}{3}$	5
Municipal Bonds	$\frac{1}{2}$	4

•••**3-23.** In the human diet, 16 essential nutrients have been identified. Suppose that there are 116 foods. A pound of food j contains a_{ij} pounds of nutrient i. Suppose that a human being must have N_j pounds of each nutrient i in the daily diet and that a pound of food j costs C_j cents. What is the least-cost daily diet satisfying all nutritional requirements? Use summation notation to write the symbolic formulation of this model. Aside from the question of palatability, can you think of an important constraint that this problem omits?

•••**3-24.** *Waiter Scheduling.* For this problem, you will need to use Excel's VLOOKUP command. See the Excel Appendix for details of VLOOKUP. A certain restaurant operates 7 days a week. Waiters are hired to work 6 effective hours per day. The restaurant attracts individuals and small groups, which we will call regular demand. In addition, the restaurant attracts a number of larger groups (Rotary, Lions, Quarterback Club, etc.) that schedule weekly meetings. The union contract specifies that each waiter must work 5 consecutive days and then have 2 consecutive days off. All waiters receive the same weekly salary. The minimum required waiter hours is a function of the regular daily demand plus the waiter hours needed to staff the scheduled group meetings for the day. The regular daily demands (in waiter hours) and the number of group meetings currently scheduled each day are given in the following table.

DAY	REGULAR DAILY DEMAND (WAITER HOURS)	SCHEDULED LARGER GROUP MEETINGS
Monday	125	1
Tuesday	200	0
Wednesday	350	1
Thursday	300	0
Friday	650	3
Saturday	725	4
Sunday	250	2

The manager uses the following table to determine the waiter hours required for the larger group meetings. The manager would like to find an employment schedule that satisfies required waiter hours at a minimum cost. Assume that this cycle repeats indefinitely, and ignore the fact that the number of waiters hired must be an integer. Because demand may change from time to time, the spreadsheet model should be constructed in such a way that all the data are entered directly into their own cells. The spreadsheet should represent the appropriate LP for any set of these data. Optimize the spreadsheet for the data presented.

NUMBER OF GROUP MEETINGS PER DAY	WAITER HOURS NEEDED
0	0
1	24
2	36
3	52
4	64
5	80

•••**3-25.** *Farm Management.* A firm operates four farms of comparable productivity. Each farm has a certain amount of usable acreage and a supply of labor hours to plant and tend the crops. The data for the upcoming season are shown in the following table.

FARM	USABLE ACREAGE	LABOR HOURS AVAILABLE PER MONTH
1	500	1700
2	900	3000
3	300	900
4	700	2200

The organization is considering three crops for planting. These crops differ in their expected profit per acre and in the amount of labor required, as shown below. Also shown is the fact that each crop requires a different type of harvester, with a different cost. The total acreage that can be devoted to any particular crop is limited by the firm's decision as to how many hours of harvesting equipment to rent. The firm has made a fixed investment of $19,000 in a harvesting equipment cooperative. For this investment, it can use any of the three types of harvesters at the costs given below, up to the fixed $19,000. A harvester typically works at a slower rate when it is first put into operation on a farm. Each season, as the crew once again becomes familiar with the machine and any small problems are worked out the rate of production increases. This phenomenon is generally referred to as learning. In this case, the harvesting rate after t hours is given by the equation

$$\text{rate} = n\,(1 - e^{\lambda t}) \text{ acres per hour where}$$

$n =$ long-run rate of harvesting, in acres per hour

$\lambda =$ short-run adjustment factor

The total acreage harvestable in a certain time period, say T hours, can then be found by integrating the rate with respect to time:

$$\text{total acreage harvestable in } T \text{ hours} = \int_0^T n(1 - e^{-\lambda t})dt$$

$$= n[T - (1/\lambda)(1 - e^{-\lambda T})]$$

The long-run rates and short-run adjustment factors for each type of equipment can be found in the following table. Management has decided to use 400, 315, and 335 harvesting machine hours for crops A, B, and C, respectively. In order to maintain a roughly uniform workload among the farms, management's policy is that the percentage of usable acreage planted must be the same at all farms. However, any combination of the crops may be grown at any of the farms as long as all constraints are satisfied (including the uniform-workload requirements). Management wishes to know how many acres of each crop should be planted at the respective farms in order to maximize expected profit.

CROP	MONTHLY LABOR HOURS REQUIRED PER ACRE	EXPECTED PROFIT PER ACRE ($)	λ	n	HARV. MACHINE COST/HR ($)
A	2	500	.02	2	15
B	4	200	.02	3	20
C	3	300	.03	1	20

(a) Create a spreadsheet model of this LP. The spreadsheet should be constructed in such a way that the rental hours for each of the harvesting machines are entered as parameters.

(b) Optimize this model.

(c) Suggest another choice of harvesting machine hours that the farm could select. Does your choice yield a higher profit? Can you find a choice that does?

•••**3-26.** *Producing Forestry and Earthmoving Equipment.* Suppose that forestry equipment produces a net revenue of $802 per unit and requires 700 pounds of iron, 50 hours of labor, 30 hours of heat treatment, and 1 transmission per unit. Earthmoving equipment yields a net revenue of $660 per unit and requires 4200 pounds of iron, 110 hours of labor, 12 hours of heat treatment, and 1 transmission per unit. The company's capacity during this period is 680,000 pounds of iron, 21,000 hours of labor, and 6000 hours of heat treatment. Transmissions are supplied by a wholly owned subsidiary that produces transmissions for the entire product line. The capacity for transmissions for forestry and earthmoving equipment is then determined by the number of production hours dedicated to their production at the subsidiary plant. Production of transmissions involves three phases: setup, start-up, and regular production. The duration and production rates for these phases are given in the following table.

PHASES	DURATION (HR)	TRANSMISSION (UNITS/HR)
Setup	8	0
Start-up	120	.5
Regular Production	—	1

(a) For example, if 10 hours are available at the subsidiary, 8 of these are required for setup, during which there is no production, and 2 are in the start-up phase, during which $2(.5) = 1$ transmission would be produced. If $H \geq 128$ hours are used, 120 of the hours will produce .5 transmission/hr, while $H - 128$ hours will produce one transmission/hr. Hence, the total transmissions produced would be $60 + H - 128 = H - 68$. Show the equations that determine the limit on transmissions capacity if T hours are available at the subsidiary for $T = 6$, $T = 108$, and $T = 308$.

(b) Evaluate the equations you created in (a). Your answers should be 0, 50, and 240.

(c) Define the decision variables and formulate this as a revenue-maximizing LP model. The spreadsheet should be constructed in such a way that the number of labor hours in the subsidiary plant can be entered as parameters, and the appropriate constraint will be created in the LP. HINT: In this problem, you can use nested IF()s to determine which phase the scheduled hours will reach. Why can you use these IF()s within the LP?

(d) Find the optimal solution if 358 hours of production time are available at the subsidiary plant.

•••3-27. *Workforce and Production Planning.* Review the PROTRAC E and F model. Now assume that the available production hours in departments A and B depend on the number of workers assigned to each department. Management decides that it is reasonable to approximate the capacity in these departments with the functions shown below:

$$\text{Capacity Dept. A} = 200(1-e^{-.05(MA)})$$
$$\text{Capacity Dept. B} = 250(1-e^{-.08(MB)})$$

where *MA* and *MB* are the number of workers assigned to departments A and B, respectively. In the original version of this problem, it was assumed that 28 workers were assigned to department A (i.e., *MA* = 28) and 13 were assigned to department B (i.e., *MB* = 13). Thus

$$\text{Capacity Dept. A} = 200(1-e^{-1.4}) = 150.68$$
$$\text{Capacity Dept. B} = 250(1-e^{-1.04}) = 161.64$$

(The capacities were rounded to 150 and 160, respectively, for the earlier PROTRAC model.)

(a) Modify the PROTRAC.XLS worksheet so that number of workers in departments A and B can be entered directly as parameters and modify the departmental capacity formulas, as appropriate.

(b) Assume that 36 workers are assigned to department A and 17 workers are assigned to department B. Use the spreadsheet to determine if the plan E = 6 and F = 9 is feasible and what profit it would yield. Find the best solution you can in three attempts.

(c) Use Solver to find the optimal production policy when *MA* = 36 and *MB*= 17. Can Solver optimize this model as an LP? Why or why not?

(d) Assume *MA* = 28. Plot the optimal profit as a function of *MB* for *MB* ranging from 10 to 30 in intervals of 2. To do this, Solver will have to be run 11 times, and you must copy the optimal profit and *MA* value into a table of cells. After the 11 runs of data have been obtained, use the Chart Wizard to plot the data. What phenomenon does the graph of this optimal profit function illustrate?

Case Study — Red Brand Canners[1]

Here is a simple but interesting case that captures several points that are important in real-world model formulation. In any real problem it is important for the manager to distinguish between those facts and data that are relevant and those that are not. Distinguishing the two may be especially difficult because on occasion confused or incorrect concepts will be strongly held by members of the management team. This case is designed to reproduce such a situation. The present task will simply involve model formulation. You will deal with this case again, however, in Chapter 5, where you will be asked to produce solutions, analyses, critiques, and interpretations.

On Monday, September 13, 1996, Mitchell Gordon, vice-president of operations, asked the controller, the sales manager, and the production manager to meet with him to discuss the amount of tomato products to pack that season. The tomato crop, which had been purchased at planting, was beginning to arrive at the cannery, and packing operations would have to be started by the following Monday. Red Brand Canners was a medium-sized company that canned and distributed a variety of fruit and vegetable products under private brands in the western states.

William Cooper, the controller, and Charles Myers, the sales manager, were the first to arrive in Mr. Gordon's office. Dan Tucker, the production manager, came in a few minutes later and said that he had picked up Produce Inspection's latest estimate of the quality of the incoming tomatoes. According to the report, about 20 percent of the crop was grade "A" quality and the remaining portion of the 3,000,000-pound crop was grade "B."

[1] © 1996 by the Board of Trustees of the Leland Stanford Junior University. All rights reserved.

Chapter 3 — Linear Optimization — 123

Gordon asked Myers about the demand for tomato products for the coming year. Myers replied that for all practical purposes they could sell all the whole canned tomatoes they could produce. The expected demand for tomato juice and tomato paste, on the other hand, was limited. The sales manager then passed around the latest demand forecast, which is shown in Exhibit 1. He reminded the group that the selling prices had been set in light of the long-term marketing strategy of the company, and potential sales had been forecast at those prices.

Bill Cooper, after looking at Myers' estimates of demand, said that it looked like the company "should do quite well (on the tomato crop) this year." With the new accounting system that had been set up, he had been able to compute the contribution for each product, and according to this analysis the incremental profit on the whole tomatoes was greater than for any other tomato product. In May, after Red Brand had signed contracts agreeing to purchase the grower's production at an average delivered price of 18 cents per pound, Cooper had computed the tomato products' contributions (see Exhibit 2).

Dan Tucker brought to Cooper's attention that, although there was ample production capacity, it was impossible to produce all whole tomatoes, because too small a portion of the tomato crop was A quality. Red Brand used a numerical scale to record the quality of both raw produce and prepared products. This scale ran from zero to ten, the higher number representing better quality. Rating tomatoes according to this scale, A tomatoes averaged nine points per pound and B tomatoes averaged five points per pound. Tucker noted that the minimum average input quality for canned whole tomatoes was eight points per pound, and for juice it was six. Paste could be made entirely from B grade tomatoes. This meant that whole tomato production was limited to 800,000 pounds.

Gordon stated that this was not a real limitation. He had recently been solicited to purchase any amount up to 80,000 pounds of grade A tomatoes at 25½ cents per pound and at that time had turned down the offer. He felt, however, that the tomatoes were still available.

Myers, who had been doing some calculations, said that although he agreed that the company "should do quite well this year," it would not be by canning whole tomatoes. It seemed to him that the tomato cost should be allocated on the basis of quality and quantity rather than by quantity only, as Cooper had done. Therefore, he had recomputed the marginal profit on this basis (see Exhibit 3), and from his results, Red Brand should use 2,000,000 pounds of the B tomatoes for paste, and the remaining 400,000 pounds of B tomatoes and all the A tomatoes for juice. If the demand expectations were realized, a contribution of $144,000 would be made on this year's tomato crop.

Questions

1. Why does Tucker state that the whole tomato production is limited to 800,000 pounds (i.e., where does the number 800,000 come from)?

2. What is wrong with Cooper's suggestion to use the entire crop for whole tomatoes?

3. How does Myers compute his tomato costs in Exhibit 3? How does he reach his conclusion that the company should use 2,000,000 pounds of B tomatoes for paste, the remaining 400,000 pounds of B tomatoes, and all of the A in juice? What is wrong with Myers' reasoning?

4. Without including the possibility of the additional purchases suggested by Gordon, formulate as an LP the problem of determining the optimal canning policy for this season's crop. Define your decision variables in terms of pounds of tomatoes. Express the objective function coefficients in cents per pound.

5. How should your model be modified to include the possibility of the additional purchases suggested by Gordon?

Alternate Questions for Red Brand Canners

Suppose Produce Inspection could use three grades to estimate the quality of the tomato crop.

A tomatoes average nine points per pound, B tomatoes average six points per pound, and C tomatoes average three points per pound. Using this system the report would indicate that 600,000 pounds are grade A quality, 1,600,000 pounds are grade B, and the remaining 800,000 pounds are grade C. Paste has no minimum average quality requirement.

6. What is the maximum production in pounds of canned whole tomatoes? Can Cooper's suggestion be implemented?

Myers extends his analysis to three grades in Exhibit 4. On the basis of Exhibit 4 Myers recommends using all grade C tomatoes and 1,200,000 pounds of grade B tomatoes for paste, and all grade A tomatoes and all remaining grade B tomatoes for juice.

7. How does Myers compute his tomato costs in Exhibit 4? How does he reach his conclusion to use 800,000 pounds of grade C and 1,200,000 pounds of grade B for paste, and the rest of the tomatoes for juice? What is wrong with Myers' reasoning?

8. Without including the possibility of the additional purchases suggested by Gordon, formulate as an LP the

EXHIBIT 1 Demand Forecasts

PRODUCT	SELLING PRICE PER CASE	DEMAND FORECAST (CASES)
24-2 ¹/₂ whole tomatoes	$12.00	800,000
24-2 ¹/₂ choice peach halves	$16.20	10,000
24-2 ¹/₂ peach nectar	$13.80	5,000
24-2 ¹/₂ tomato juice	$13.50	50,000
24-2 ¹/₂ cooking apples	$14.70	15,000
24-2 ¹/₂ tomato paste	$11.40	80,000

problem of determining the optimal canning policy for this season's crop. Define your decision variables in terms of pounds of tomatoes. Express the objective function in cents.

9. How should your model be modified to include the possibility of the additional purchases suggested by Gordon?

EXHIBIT 2 Product Item Profitability

PRODUCT	24-2$\frac{1}{2}$ WHOLE TOMATOES	24-2$\frac{1}{2}$ CHOICE PEACH HALVES	24-2$\frac{1}{2}$ PEACH NECTAR	24-2$\frac{1}{2}$ TOMATO JUICE	24-2$\frac{1}{2}$ COOKING APPLES	24-2$\frac{1}{2}$ TOMATO PASTE
Selling Price	$12.00	$16.20	$13.80	$13.50	$14.70	$11.40
Variable Costs:						
Direct Labor	3.54	4.20	3.81	3.96	2.10	1.62
Variable OHD	.72	.96	.69	1.08	.66	.78
Variable Selling	1.20	.90	1.20	2.55	.84	1.14
Packaging Mat'l.	2.10	1.68	1.80	1.95	2.10	2.31
Fruit[1]	3.24	5.40	5.10	3.60	2.70	4.50
Total Variable Costs	10.80	13.14	12.60	13.14	8.40	10.35
Contribution	1.20	3.06	1.20	.36	6.30	1.05
Less Allocated OHD	.84	2.10	1.56	.63	2.25	.69
Net Profit	.36	.96	(.36)	(.27)	4.05	.36

[1]Product usage is as given below.

PRODUCT	POUNDS PER CASE
Whole Tomatoes	18
Peach Halves	18
Peach Nectar	17
Tomato Juice	20
Cooking Apples	27
Tomato Paste	25

EXHIBIT 3 Marginal Analysis of Tomato Products

Z = Cost per pound of A tomatoes in cents
Y = Cost per pound of B tomatoes in cents

(1) $(600{,}000 \text{ lb} \times Z) + (2{,}400{,}000 \text{ lb} \times Y) = (3{,}000{,}000 \text{ lb} \times 18¢)$
(2) $Z/9 = Y/5$

  Z = 27.96 cents per pound
  Y = 15.54 cents per pound

PRODUCT	CANNED WHOLE TOMATOES	TOMATO JUICE	TOMATO PASTE
Selling Price	$12.00	$13.50	$11.40
Variable Cost (Excl. Tomato Costs)	7.56	9.54	5.85
	$4.44	$3.96	$5.55
Tomato Cost	4.47	3.72	3.90
Marginal Profit	($.03)	$0.24	$1.65

EXHIBIT 4 Myers' Marginal Analysis of Tomato Products

Z = Cost per pound of A tomatoes in cents
Y = Cost per pound of B tomatoes in cents
X = Cost per pound of C tomatoes in cents

(1) $(800{,}000 \text{ lb} \times Z) + (1{,}600{,}000 \text{ lb} \times Y) +$
    $(800{,}000 \text{ lb} \times X) = (3{,}000{,}000 \text{ lb} \times 18¢)$
(2) $Z/9 = Y/6$
(2) $Y/6 = X/3$

  Z = 27.93 cents per pound
  Y = 18.61 cents per pound
  X = 9.30 cents per pound

PRODUCT	CANNED WHOLE TOMATOES	TOMATO JUICE	TOMATO PASTE
Selling Price	$12.00	$13.50	$11.40
Variable Cost (Excl. Tomato Costs)	7.56	9.54	5.85
	$4.44	$3.96	$5.55
Tomato Cost	4.47	3.72	2.33
Marginal Profit	($.03)	$0.24	$3.22

The following case shows a more realistic and, as you might expect, more difficult, illustration of spreadsheet modeling. The major purposes of this case are to show what the model can do and to gain a more complete understanding of the logic captured by the spreadsheet through the LP model for this problem.

PROTRAC has manufacturing and sales operations in five major trading countries: United States, United Kingdom, France, Germany, and Japan. Due to the different cash needs in the various countries at various times, it is often necessary to move available funds from one country and denomination to another. In general, there will be numerous ways to rearrange funds to satisfy cash requirements out of availabilities. On this particular morning the divisions in France and Japan are short of cash. Specifically, the requirements are, respectively, 7 million francs and 1040 million yen. The divisions in the United States, Britain, and Germany are long on cash. They have surpluses of 2 million dollars, 5 million pounds, and 3 million marks. Since there are many possible ways of redistributing the cash to satisfy the shortages out of the surpluses, the issue to be addressed is how one compares the possible conversion strategies. Because of high short-term U.S. interest rates, the firm has decided to evaluate its final cash position by this measure: the equivalent total dollar value of its final cash holdings.

On this morning, as usual, at 7:00 A.M. Jack Walker, the corporate treasurer, and Ezra Brooks, VP for overseas operations, meet at corporate headquarters to determine what funds, if any, should be moved. Refer to Exhibits 1 and 2 as you go through the dialogue. The conversation proceeds as follows:

Ezra: Good morning, Jack. I have something to show you. I've asked Fred to set this exchange model up on a spreadsheet. I think it will make our lives considerably easier.

Jack: I like the idea, but you'll have to explain the model to me.

Ezra: Sure, Jack. It contains all the usual information, but let's go through it step by step. The figures in the rectangle defined by C3 through G7 are the exchange rates. If we let a_{ij} be the rate in row i and column j, then one unit of currency i will exchange for a_{ij} units of currency j. In fact, these data reflect the bid-ask prices. For example, if we sell one British pound we get $1.665. That is, 1.665 is the bid price, in dollars, for a pound. On the other hand, if we sell one dollar we will receive 0.591 pounds. This means we can buy a pound for 1/0.591 = $ 1.692 (the asking price, in dollars, for a pound is 1.692). Hence the bid-ask spread is (1.665, 1.692). You can see that if we start with $1 and buy as many pounds as possible and then use those pounds to buy dollars we end up with 0.591 × 1.665 = $0.9810 dollars—we lose money.

Jack: That's the transaction cost. So obviously we want to minimize these transaction costs by not moving more money around than we have to. But where does this model say something about our cash needs today?

Ezra: Our current cash holdings are shown in column C rows 17 to 21. All figures are in millions; we have 2 million dollars,

5 million pounds, and 3 million marks. Our requirements appear in column G in the same rows. You can see that we need 7 million French francs and 1040 million yen. As you know, our policy is to satisfy requirements in such a way that the dollar value of final holdings is maximized.

Jack: Great! So let's figure out what to do.

Ezra: That's the good part. We simply put our decisions in the appropriate cells in the currency transactions section labeled "Sell\Buy." I've already entered what I think would be our typical decisions in this set of circumstances. Cells C10 through C14 show that I've sold 2 million marks and 4.3 million pounds in return for 8.389 million dollars. I've then taken 1.3 million of those dollars and purchased 7 million francs, and with the remaining 9 million dollars I bought 1047 million yen. All of these numbers appear in cells C11, C13, E10, and G10 of the currency transactions section. For example, you see in E10 that we used 1.3 million dollars to buy francs, and E15 shows that this purchase yielded 7 million francs. You can see by comparing C17 through C21 with F17 through F21 that we have satisfied our goals. Indeed, H17 through H21 show how much additional cash we have in each denomination. As you can see, the policy I've entered gives final holdings worth 12.106 million dollars.

Jack: I see that we've met our cash requirements, but you know how I am, Ez. I'd feel that I understood better if I could see all of the formulas used to do the calculations.

Ezra: That's easy. I'll simply print out the spreadsheet formulas and you can look through it at your leisure!

Jack (some time later that morning): All of this seems clear, Ez, but why did we follow such a complicated strategy?

Ezra: As you know, we have always run our exchange operation through Country Bank in New York, and this is its recommended strategy.

Jack: I guess that seeing the problem in the spreadsheet model makes it easier to think about the trading strategy. I sure would like to know if this really is a good approach.

Ezra: I worried about that for a while, too, but the foreign exchange market is very efficient for these major currencies, so it probably doesn't make much difference what strategy we follow.

Jack: I can't say that banal invocations of efficiency make me any more confident. As you know, I've made millions exploiting market inefficiencies. Anyway, I don't have more time this morning to look for a better approach. Let's go with what we have.

As you are already aware, the foreign exchange model presented in Exhibits 1 and 2 is a linear programming model, and the optimal solution can be easily found with Solver. The spreadsheet for the optimal solution is shown in Exhibit 3. The optimal dollar value of the final cash positions is 12.184 million, as compared with the 12.106 million that was obtained with Ezra's solution. We note that in some sense Ezra is right.

The difference is about .6%: $(12.184 - 12.106)/12.184 = .0064$. On the other hand, when large sums are being transferred, even a small percentage can be a lot of money. In this example, the difference is $78,000, a handsome quantity that can be captured with almost no effort.

Questions

1. Write out the LP model for the foreign exchange problem. In your model use the following notation for the data given in the problem description:

   a_{ij} = exchange rate from currency i into currency j (i.e., 1 unit of currency i will exchange for a_{ij} units of currency j)

   $c_i = \frac{1}{2}(a_{ij} + 1/a_{ji})$ = "average dollar value" of currency i

   b_i = initial holding in currency i

   L_i = minimum amount of currency i required as final holding

   Denote the decision variables, as follows:

   X_{ij} = amount of currency i changed into currency j, $j \neq i$

   Y_i = final holding in currency i

2. In the dialogue, Jack says, "We want to minimize these transaction costs by not moving more money around than we have to." Suppose we define OV_1 = maximum "average dollar value" that can be generated from initial holdings

   Note that finding the value of OV_1 requires more than simply evaluating each initial position in terms of average dollar value. For example, converting 1 pound to average dollar value gives $1.665; converting 1 pound to 9.12 francs to average dollar value gives $(9.12)(.1840) = \$1.67808$. Thus, it is preferable to convert initial holdings of pounds into francs rather than to leave the pound position intact. In fact, in order to find OV_1 one must solve a linear program. The solution is shown in Exhibit 4, which was created by setting the final cash requirement to zero and then optimizing the value of final holdings. We see that $OV_1 = 12.261$. Now let OV_2 = maximum "average dollar value" of final holdings subject to the cash requirements constraints. That is, OV_2 is the optimized objective value shown in Exhibit 3 ($OV_2 = 12.184$).

In a case like this, a more highly constrained LP cannot have a better OV than a less highly constrained LP, so it must always be true that $OV_2 \leq OV_1$. Let us define, for the problem,

$$\text{Transactions Costs} = OV_1 - OV_2$$

Using this definition, is the statement by Jack correct? That is, does the optimized solution in Exhibit 3 minimize transaction costs?

3. Recall the spreadsheet presented in Exhibit 1. Use this spreadsheet to answer the following questions:

   (a) Suppose that the exchange rates for two currencies (say the franc and the mark) are such that if we start with 1 franc and execute the trade 1 franc → marks → francs we end up with more than 1 franc. What would the optimal value of the objective function be under these circumstances? What economic term is used to describe this condition?

   (b) Comment on the following statement: If PROTRAC has no specific cash requirements, the optimal solution would be to stand pat (i.e., in order to maximize "average dollar value" of final holdings, one should do no trading).

   (c) Comment on the following statement: Because the foreign exchange market is efficient, we have seen that the best solution isn't much better (in percentage terms) than Ezra's solution. It is also true, for the same reason, that the worst solution isn't much worse (again in percentage terms) than Ezra's. HINT: Find the solution that minimizes "average dollar value" of final holdings.

   (d) Comment on the following statement: Consider a general problem like the PROTRAC problem. Such a problem might include hundreds of currencies. However, those currencies for which PROTRAC has no initial holding or no required cash position can be dropped from the formulation without affecting the optimal value of the objective function.

References

J. Abara, "Applying Integer Linear Programming to the Fleet Assignment Problem," *Interfaces,* 19, no. 4 (1989), 20–28

Radhka Subramanian, Richard Scheff, John Quillinan, Steve Wiper, Roy Marsten, "Coldstart: Fleet Assignment at Delta Air Lines," *Interfaces,* 24, no.1 (1994), 104–120.

EXHIBIT 1 Spreadsheet Model For Currency Trading

	A	B	C	D	E	F	G	H	I
1		Currency Trading Model							
2			Dollar	Pound	FFranc	DMark	Yen	Avg. Dollar Value	
3		Dollar	1	0.591	5.385	1.594	116.3	1.0000	
4		Pound	1.665	1	9.12	2.607	193.1	1.6785	
5		FFranc	0.1823	0.1095	1	0.2965	21.11	0.1840	
6		DMark	0.6149	0.3694	3.351	1	72.14	0.6211	
7		Yen	0.00847	0.005093	0.0465	0.01379	1	0.0085	
8									
9		Sell \ Buy	Dollar	Pound	FFranc	DMark	Yen	Total Sold	
10		Dollar	0	0	1.3	0	9	10.3	
11		Pound	4.3	0	0	0	0	4.3	
12		FFranc	0	0	0	0	0	0	
13		DMark	2	0	0	0	0	2.000	
14		Yen	0	0	0	0	0	0	
15		Total Purchased	8.389	0	7.0	0	1047		
16			Initial Holding (millions)	Amount Purchased (millions)	Amount Sold (millions)	Final Holding (millions)	Cash Required (millions)	Excess Held (Slack)	$ Value of Final Holding
17		Dollar	2	8.389	10.3	0	>=0	0.089	$ 0.089
18		Pound	5	-	4.3	0.700	>=0	0.700	$ 1.175
19		FFranc	0	7.001	-	7.001	>=7	0.000	$ 1.288
20		DMark	3	-	2	1	>=0	1.000	$ 0.621
21		Yen	0	1,047	-	1,047	>=1040	6.700	$ 8.933
22								Total	$ 12.106

EXHIBIT 2 Spreadsheet Formulas For Currency Trading Model

	A	B	C	D	E	F	G	H	I
1		Currenc							
2			Dollar	Pound	FFranc	DMark	Yen	Avg. Dollar Val	
3		Dollar	1	0.591	5.385	1.594	116.3	=(C3+1/C3)/2	
4		Pound	1.665	1	8.933	2.507	193.1	=(C4+1/D3)/2	
5		FFranc	0.1823	0.1095	1	0.2965	21.11	=(C5+1/E3)/2	
6		DMark	0.6149	0.3694	3.351	1	72.14	=(C6+1/F3)/2	
7		Yen	0.00847	0.005093	0.0465	0.01379	1	=(C7+1/G3)/2	
8									
9		Sell \ Bu	Dollar	Pound	FFranc	DMark	Yen	Total Sold	
10		Dollar	0	0	1.3	0	9	=SUM(C10:G10)	
11		Pound	4.3	0	0	0	0		
12		FFranc	0	0	0	0	0	Copy	
13		DMark	2	0	0	0	0		
14		Yen	0	0	0	0	0		
15		Total P	=SUMPRODUCT(C3:C7,C10:C14)	Copy					
16			Initial Holding (millions)	Amount Pu	Amount	Final Holding	Cash F	Excess Held (S	$ Value of Fin
17		Dollar	2	=C15	=H10	=C17-E17+D17	0	=F17-G17	=H3*F17
18		Pound	5	=D15			0		
19		FFranc	0	=E15	Copy		7	Copy	
20		DMark	3	=F15			0		
21		Yen	0	=G15			1040		
22								Total	=SUM(I17:I21)

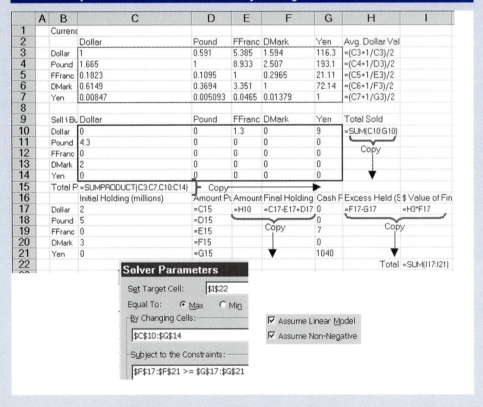

Solver Parameters

Set Target Cell: $I$22

Equal To: ⦿ Max   ○ Min

By Changing Cells:

$C$10:$G$14

Subject to the Constraints:

$F$17:$F$21 >= $G$17:$G$21

☑ Assume Linear Model
☑ Assume Non-Negative

EXHIBIT 3 Optimized Spreadsheet For Currency Trading

	A	B	C	D	E	F	G	H	I
1		Currency Trading Model							
2			Dollar	Pound	FFranc	DMark	Yen	Avg. Dollar Value	
3		Dollar	1	0.591	5.385	1.594	116.3	1.0000	
4		Pound	1.665	1	9.12	2.607	193.1	1.6785	
5		FFranc	0.1823	0.1095	1	0.2965	21.11	0.1840	
6		DMark	0.6149	0.3694	3.351	1	72.14	0.6211	
7		Yen	0.00847	0.005093	0.0465	0.01379	1	0.0085	
8									
9		Sell \ Buy	Dollar	Pound	FFranc	DMark	Yen	Total Sold	
10		Dollar	0	0	0	0	2.000	2	
11		Pound	0	0	5.000	0	0	5	
12		FFranc	0	0	0	38.600	0	38.600	
13		DMark	0	0	0	0	11.192	11.192	
14		Yen	0	0	0	0	0	0	
15		Total Purchased	0	0	45.60	11.445	1040		
16			Initial Holding (millions)	Amount Purchased (millions)	Amount Sold (millions)	Final Holding (millions)	Cash Required (millions)	Excess Held (Slack)	$ Value of Final Holding
17		Dollar	2	-	2.0	0.0	>=0	0.000	$ 0
18		Pound	5	-	5.0	0.0	>=0	0.000	$ 0
19		FFranc	0	45.600	38.600	7.0	>=7	0.000	$ 1.288
20		DMark	3	11.445	11.192	3.253	>=0	3.253	$ 2
21		Yen	0	1,040	-	1040	>=1040	0.000	$ 8.876
22								Total	$ 12.184

EXHIBIT 4 Optimized Model with Final Cash Requirements Equal Zero

	A	B	C	D	E	F	G	H	I
1		Currency Trading Model							
2			Dollar	Pound	FFranc	DMark	Yen	Avg. Dollar Value	
3		Dollar	1	0.591	5.385	1.594	116.3	1.0000	
4		Pound	1.665	1	9.12	2.607	193.1	1.6785	
5		FFranc	0.1823	0.1095	1	0.2965	21.11	0.1840	
6		DMark	0.6149	0.3694	3.351	1	72.14	0.6211	
7		Yen	0.00847	0.005093	0.0465	0.01379	1	0.0085	
8									
9		Sell \ Buy	Dollar	Pound	FFranc	DMark	Yen	Total Sold	
10		Dollar	0	0	0	0	0.000	0	
11		Pound	0	0	5.000	0	0	5	
12		FFranc	0	0	0	45.600	0	45.600	
13		DMark	0	0	0	0	0.000	0.000	
14		Yen	0	0	0	0	0	0	
15		Total Purchased	0	0	45.60	13.520	0		
16			Initial Holding (millions)	Amount Purchased (millions)	Amount Sold (millions)	Final Holding (millions)	Cash Required (millions)	Excess Held (Slack)	$ Value of Final Holding
17		Dollar	2	-	0.0	2.0	>=0	2.000	$ 2
18		Pound	5	-	5.0	0.0	>=0	0.000	$ -
19		FFranc	0	45.600	45.600	0.0	>=0	0.000	$ 0.000
20		DMark	3	13.520	-	16.520	>=0	16.520	$ 10
21		Yen	0	0	-	0	>=0	0.000	$ 0.000
22								Total	$ 12.261

CHAPTER OUTLINE

4.1 Introduction

4.2 Plotting Inequalities and Contours

4.3 The Graphical Solution Method Applied to PROTRAC

4.4 Active and Inactive Constraints

4.5 Extreme Points and Optimal Solutions

4.6 Summary of the Graphical Solution Method for a Max Model

4.7 The Graphical Method Applied to a Min Model

4.8 Unbounded and Infeasible Models

4.9 Graphical Sensitivity Analysis

4.10 Changes in the Objective Function Coefficients

4.11 Changes in the Right-Hand Sides

4.12 Tightening and Loosening an Inequality Constraint

4.13 Redundant Constraints

4.14 What Is an Important Constraint?

4.15 Adding or Deleting Constraints

4.16 Summary

KEY TERMS

SELF-REVIEW EXERCISES

PROBLEMS

CASE STUDY: The Simplex Method

REFERENCES

APPLICATION CAPSULE	More Bang for the Buck: LP Helps the USAF Stock Its Arsenal

The United States Air Force has a distinguished record of winning important battles. Americans recall with pride the success of our pilots in the skies over Germany during World War II, and more recently in the Persian Gulf. This success results in part from a relentless search for new tactics and technology. Thus it is no surprise that in recent years the Air Force has turned to a modern approach—using LP—in the evaluation and procurement of weapon systems and in the annual battle of the budget.

Each year the Air Force must present a weapons development plan to Congress. To prepare this plan, it is necessary to decide (1) what new projects to start, (2) what current projects to continue, and (3) what projects to discontinue. The final recommendation is highly dependent on the level of funding available.

A key consideration is the effectiveness of each weapon system and its possible contribution, in a mix of weapons, to achieving a desired increase in target value destroyed. Effectiveness estimates must be made for a great many combinations of aircraft, munitions, and targets (tanks, command and communication facilities, bridges, and the like). These factors interact in complex ways. Different munitions require aircraft to fly at different altitudes for different durations, and their vulnerability to enemy antiaircraft fire will vary accordingly. Even a small change in the rate at which air-

craft are lost can have a major effect on the cost-effectiveness of a system, to say nothing of the loss of human life.

The Air Force must also assess annually the consequences of a possible increase or decrease in the budget—that is, how sensitive a given proposal might be to a change in the level of funding. Budget changes can affect the mix of weapon systems purchased as well as the number of any particular weapon acquired. The number of items purchased, in turn, can drastically affect the purchase price per unit.

For analyses of this kind, the Air Force has developed a linear program that can evaluate trade-offs among both aircraft types and munitions. It can not only specify the optimal mix of weapons needed to destroy a particular target set but also display graphically such relationships as

- The ratio of funds expended on aircraft versus munitions
- Target value destroyed as a function of expenditure on individual weapons, or on a mixture of weapons
- Target value destroyed versus expenditure as a function of conflict duration

This information is plotted out in the form of two-dimensional graphs, with axes properly scaled, so that managers and analysts can study possible trade-offs and perform "What if?" analyses. (See Might.)

4.1   INTRODUCTION

Two-dimensional geometry can be used as a picture to illustrate many of the important elements of LP models and how they are optimized with Solver. Although two-dimensional geometry is a very special case, it is easy to work with, and many general concepts that apply to higher-dimensional models can be communicated with two-dimensional pictures. In particular, two-dimensional geometry is useful in providing the basis for the graphical solution approach. This is a simple way to solve an LP model having only two decision variables. Although most real-world models have more than two decision variables, and hence the graphical solution method will not be applicable, it nevertheless provides a good intuitive basis for much that follows. In other words, the purpose of this chapter is to provide graphical insights into the general LP model. This will provide a good foundation for the use of LP in a variety of real-world applications. Moreover, in our later discussions of Solver results, we shall make frequent use of geometric illustrations.

At the outset we briefly recall the technique for plotting inequalities, which provides the basis for the graphical analysis that follows.

4.2   PLOTTING INEQUALITIES AND CONTOURS

Let us begin by plotting the set of points (x_1, x_2) that satisfies the *inequality*

$$2x_2 - x_1 \leq -2 \qquad\qquad (4.1)$$

PLOTTING INEQUALITIES

To accomplish this we will use the following general procedure for plotting inequalities:

- **Step 1: Plot equality.** Convert the inequality to an equality and plot the straight line that represents this equation. In our example the equality is $2x_2 - x_1 = -2$. The plot of this equation is shown in Figure 4.1. One way to do this is: (a) Set $x_1 = 0$ and solve for x_2 ($x_2 = -2/2 = -1$) and find that point on the x_2 axis. (b) Set $x_2 = 0$ and solve for x_1 ($-x_1 = -2$; $x_1 = 2$) and find that point on the x_1 axis. (c) Connect the two points.

- **Step 2: Choose trial point.** Choose any trial point that is not on the line. If the point $x_1 = 0, x_2 = 0$ is not on the straight line, then it is a convenient point. In our example, we select $x_1 = 0, x_2 = 0$ as the trial point. See Figure 4.1.

- **Step 3: Evaluate left-hand-side expression.** Substitute the trial point into the expression on the left-hand side of the inequality. In the example, the expression is $2x_2 - x_1$. Substituting in the values $x_1 = 0, x_2 = 0$ yields a numerical value of 0.

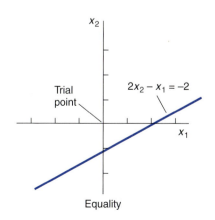

Equality

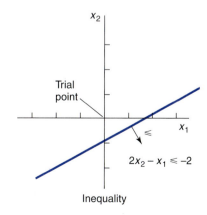

Inequality

FIGURE 4.1

Plotting $2x_2 - x_1 \leq -2$

• *Step 4: Determine if the trial point satisfies the inequality.*

   a. If the trial point *satisfies* the original inequality, then the straight line plotted in step 1 and all points on the *same* side of the line as the trial point satisfy the inequality.

   b. If the trial point does not satisfy the original inequality, then the straight line and all points not on the same side as the trial point satisfy the inequality.

In our example, since 0 *is not* ≤ -2, the trial point does *not* satisfy the inequality. Condition b above holds, and the straight line and all points on the opposite side of the line from (0, 0) satisfy the inequality. This set is shown in Figure 4.1. Note the convention of denoting the relevant side of the equality line with an arrow and $\leq$ or $\geq$, as appropriate.

Students often acquire the incorrect impression that the $<$ side of an inequality plot is always below the equality line. Hence, to plot the points satisfying a $\leq$ relation, they change the $\leq$ to $=$, graph the equality, and then hastily include all points that lie below the equality line. This may be incorrect, since the $<$ side can be above and not below. For example, let us graph the inequality $2x_1 - x_2 \leq 2$. Following the procedure outlined above, we first plot the equation $2x_1 - x_2 = 2$ as shown in Figure 4.2. Now consider the trial point ($x_1 = 0, x_2 = 0$), which is *above* the line. At this point $2x_1 - x_2 = 2(0) - 0 = 0$ and, since 0 is less than 2, we have identified the $<$ side of the line in Figure 4.2. Hence, in this case, the points satisfying the $\leq$ inequality are the points on the line along with all the points on the same side as the point ($x_1 = 0, x_2 = 0$), that is, points *on* and *above* the line. This is also shown in Figure 4.2. A comparison of Figure 4.1 and Figure 4.2 should convince you that there is no general relationship between the sense of the inequality (i.e., $\geq$ or $\leq$) and the *above* or the *below* side of the equality plot. The appropriate side can always be found using a trial point, as we have demonstrated.

The technique described above provides the basic tool for plotting the constraints in an LP, for such constraints are always mathematical equalities or inequalities. In summary, to plot an inequality constraint of either the $\leq$ or the $\geq$ type:

1. Change the inequality to an equality, to obtain an equation, and then plot the straight line that represents this equation.

2. Choose any trial point that is not on this line. (If the point [$x_1 = 0, x_2 = 0$] is not on the straight line, it is the easiest trial point.)

3. Substitute this trial point into the left side of the inequality constraint. Since the trial point is not on the line, the result is either less than the right-hand side or greater than the right-hand side. If the result is less than the right-hand side, the line and all points on the side containing the trial point satisfy the $\leq$ inequality, and the line and all points on the other side satisfy the $\geq$ inequality. If the result is greater than the right-hand side, the conclusion is reversed.

CONTOUR LINES

Contours, also called **isoquants,** play an important role in the geometric representation of LP models. A *contour* of a function f of two variables is the set of all pairs (x_1, x_2) for which $f(x_1, x_2)$ takes on some specified *constant value*. When f is a profit function, the contours are often referred to as **isoprofit lines,** and when f is a cost function the contours represent **isocost lines.**

FIGURE 4.2

Plotting $2x_2 - x_1 \leq 2$

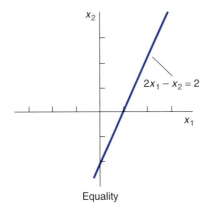

Equality

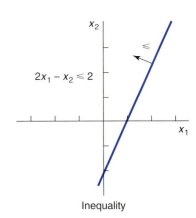

Inequality

As an example of a contour, suppose that we are selling two products. The profit per unit of product 1 is $2, and the profit per unit of product 2 is $4. Then the total profit obtained from selling x_1 units of product 1 and x_2 units of product 2 is given by a function f of two variables defined by

$$\text{profit} = f(x_1, x_2) = 2x_1 + 4x_2$$

Let us now plot all possible sales combinations of x_1 and x_2 for which we obtain $4 of profit. To do this we plot the equation

$$2x_1 + 4x_2 = 4 \qquad\qquad\qquad\qquad \textbf{(4.2)}$$

The plot is shown by the lowest of the three lines in Figure 4.3. This line is called the 4-contour of the function f.

In reality, since negative sales do not make sense, we would be interested in only that part of the 4-contour in Figure 4.3 that lies between the two distinguished points on the axes. Do not worry about this now. It will be dealt with in the next section.

Clearly, we can replace the value 4 in the right-hand side of expression (4.2) with any other constant and then plot the result to obtain a different contour of f. Figure 4.3 also shows two other contours of f, those corresponding to right-hand sides, in expression (4.2), with values 6 and 8. You can readily see that these contours are parallel lines, and you can deduce that in fact there are infinitely many such contours, one for each possible numerical value of the right-hand side in (4.2).

The two concepts reviewed in this section, plotting equalities and plotting contours, will be employed to obtain graphical solutions of LP models with two decision variables.

In summary:

> Plotting contours reduces to plotting equalities. The contours of a linear function are a family of parallel lines. Plotting inequalities also reduces to plotting equalities, or contours, and then identifying the correct side.

4.3 THE GRAPHICAL SOLUTION METHOD APPLIED TO PROTRAC

The **graphical solution method** provides an easy way of solving LP models with two decision variables. Since the PROTRAC model from Chapter 3 has only two decision variables, E and F, we can employ that model to illustrate the graphical approach. The complete model for this LP is

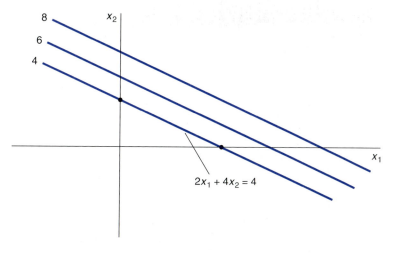

$2x_1 + 4x_2 = 4$

FIGURE 4.3

4-, 6-, and 8-Contours of $2x_1 + 4x_2$

PROTRAC MODEL

$$\text{Max } 5000E + 4000F \qquad \text{(max profit contribution)} \qquad \textbf{(4.3)}$$

$$\text{s.t. } E + F \geq 5 \qquad \text{(minimum production requirement)} \qquad \textbf{(4.4)}$$

$$E - 3F \leq 0 \qquad \text{(market position balance)} \qquad \textbf{(4.5)}$$

$$10E + 15F \leq 150 \qquad \text{(capacity in department A)} \qquad \textbf{(4.6)}$$

$$20E + 10F \leq 160 \qquad \text{(capacity in department B)} \qquad \textbf{(4.7)}$$

$$30E + 10F \geq 135 \qquad \text{(labor hours used in testing)} \qquad \textbf{(4.8)}$$

$$E, F \geq 0 \qquad \text{(nonnegativity conditions)} \qquad \textbf{(4.9)}$$

where we recall that the decision variables are defined as

$$E = \text{number of E-9s to be produced, and}$$

$$F = \text{number of F-9s to be produced}$$

The labels (4.3) through (4.9) are used in the following discussion to distinguish the objective function and the constraints. We will use the Stanford Graphic LP Optimizer, GLP.EXE, to graph and analyze the LP model. GLP is a separate Windows program; it does not require Excel.[1] Graphical LP optimization is best understood by following along the steps below by running GLP on your PC.[2]

PLOTTING THE CONSTRAINTS

Our first goal is to show how all the feasible decisions for this model can be graphically portrayed. After starting GLP, configure the scale options (X Min = 0, X Max = 8, Y Min = 0, Y Max = 10, X Zoom = 120, Y Zoom = 78, and Decimal Number = 0) as shown in Figure 4.4. Next, let us first construct a coordinate system with values of E on the horizontal axis and values of F on the vertical axis by typing the axis labels in the "X" and "Y" boxes as shown in Figure 4.4. (We could just as easily assign F to the horizontal and E to the vertical—the results are the same.) Thus, every point in the two-dimensional space in Figure 4.4 is associated with a specific production alternative. For example, the cursor in Figure 4.4 is pointing to the production alternative $E = 3$, $F = 4$. We now wish to see which of the possible combinations of (E, F) are feasible; that is, satisfy the restrictions (4.4) through (4.9). To do this, we will begin to eliminate possible areas of the graph. With each added constraint, the feasible area will get smaller.

Since the nonnegativity conditions (4.9) require $E \geq 0$ and $F \geq 0$, we need only consider the so-called **nonnegative quadrant** in looking for feasible production combinations, that is, feasible combinations of the decision variables (E, F). GLP always assumes the nonnegativity conditions, and so, displays only the nonnegative quadrant, as indicated in Figure 4.4.

Not every point in the nonnegative quadrant is feasible. For example, consider the first constraint, (4.4):

$$E + F \geq 5 \qquad \textbf{(4.4)}$$

Clearly, the combination $E = 1$, $F = 1$, although corresponding to a point in the nonnegative quadrant, violates this constraint. Obviously, we must further limit our graphic representation of the candidates for feasibility.

In order to depict accurately the feasible combinations, we must proceed by taking one constraint at a time. We begin with the first constraint,

$$E + F \geq 5 \qquad \textbf{(4.4)}$$

---

[1]Being a Windows program, GLP is not available for the Macintosh. Macintosh users may execute GLP by means of a Windows emulator package, such as SoftWindows by Insignia Solutions or Virtual PC by Connectix Corporation.

[2]Copy the GLP.EXE program from the CD-ROM accompanying this book to your PC's hard disk. From the Windows **Start** menu, select the **Run** item and **Browse** to locate the GLP.EXE program on your hard disk; when found, highlight it, click Open, and then click OK to run GLP. GLP works best if your display is set to a resolution of 800 by 600 (Super VGA) or higher.

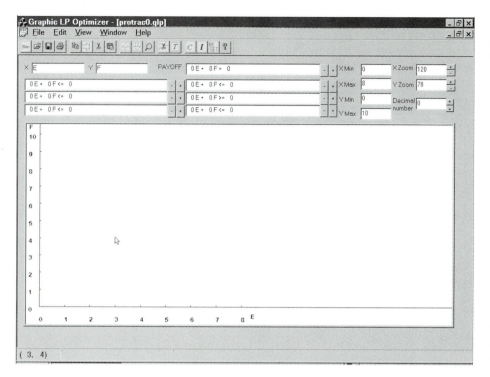

FIGURE 4.4

Nonnegative Quadrant for
Graphic LP Optimizer

The discussion in Section 4.2 indicated that to plot this constraint you should first plot the line $E + F = 5$ and then find the $>$ side, which in this case is all points above the diagonal line. To plot the constraint, type an optional label followed by a colon, followed by the (4.4) inequality constraint in the upper-left equation box, as shown in Figure 4.5; GLP will then plot the constraint line for you. (When finished typing, you can click on the constraint's label on the graph and drag it to position it near the constraint line, as shown in Figure 4.5.) Following this procedure you should verify that all points in the nonnegative quadrant that satisfy the first constraint are precisely those shown above the line in Figure 4.4. This region represents nonnegative production plans that satisfy the one single constraint, (4.4), but not necessarily the others. For example, you can quickly verify that the plan $E = 10$, $F = 10$ violates constraint (4.6). Clearly, we must restrict the candidate decisions still further by reapplying the prescription just followed.

Thus, we now consider the second constraint,

$$E - 3F \leq 0 \tag{4.5}$$

In Figure 4.6 the plot of this condition appears together with constraint (4.4). The production alternatives above the lines (4.4) and (4.5) of Figure 4.6 satisfy

$$E + F \geq 5 \tag{4.4}$$
$$E - 3F \leq 0 \tag{4.5}$$
$$E \geq 0, F \geq 0 \tag{4.9}$$

EFFECT OF ADDING CONSTRAINTS

However, the region above the two constraints will still contain some points that will violate some of the remaining constraints (4.6), (4.7), and (4.8). Thus, we must continue to superimpose one by one the remaining constraints. First, however, let us note that superimposing the second constraint (4.5) on the picture in Figure 4.6 has further restricted the decision variables and, graphically, has "trimmed down" the set of candidates for feasible

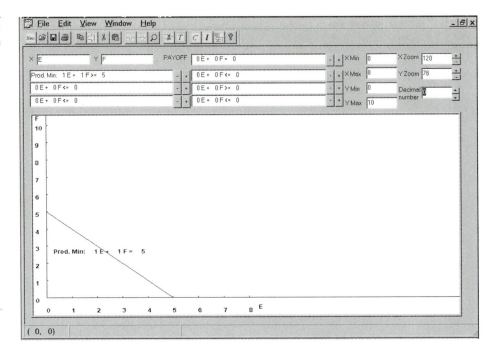

FIGURE 4.5

First PROTRAC LP
Model Constraint

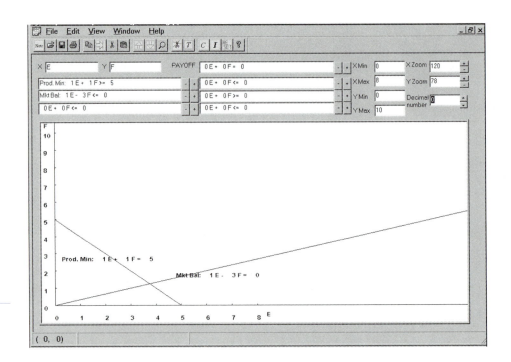

FIGURE 4.6

First Two Constraints of
PROTRAC LP Model, (4.4)
and (4.5)

decisions. As we continue to superimpose "tighter and tighter" conditions (i.e., more and more restrictions) on the decision variables, it should be clear that from the geometric point of view these restrictions will tend to trim down the constraint set even further. This phenomenon, the successive trimming down of the constraint set, illustrates the following important general principle. *(General* in this context means "also valid for models with more than two decision variables.")

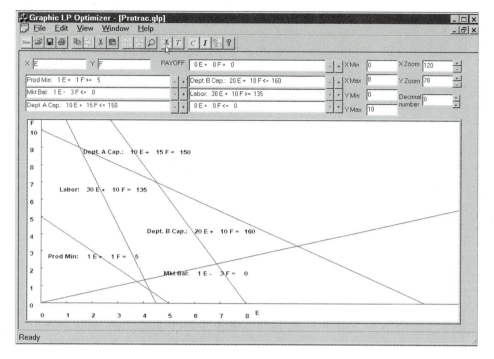

TIP: *Once you have completed the drawing of all constraints, clicking the Auto
Zoom tool (to the left of the
Trim Lines tool in Figure 4.7)
will adjust the scaling numbers for X and Y to values that
will fill the window. Otherwise,
you can click one of the +/−
boxes for either of the X or Y
Zoom numbers and then hold
down the Enter key to have
GLP adjust the value incre-
mentally.*

FIGURE 4.7

Constraint Set for PROTRAC
LP Model

Adding more constraints will always either trim down the set of allowable decisions or leave the set unaffected. Adding additional constraints can never enlarge the set of allowable decisions.

THE FEASIBLE REGION

You may type the other constraints for the PROTRAC LP model or just open the PRO-TRAC.GLP file to see the rest of the constraints. The culmination of superimposing constraints (4.6), (4.7), and (4.8) on Figure 4.6 yields Figure 4.7, which is a graphic portrayal of all feasible values of the decision variables.

This figure, with all five constraints plotted in the nonnegative quadrant, shows the set of production plans that *simultaneously* satisfies *all five* of the constraints, as well as the nonnegativity conditions. In LP terminology, this set is called the **constraint set,** *feasible set,* or **feasible region.** Clicking the Toggle Trim Lines tool, under the cursor in Figure 4.7, removes line segments outside of the feasible region; clicking the "C" tool to the right will shade the feasible region, as shown in Figure 4.8. That is, the shaded area in Figure 4.8 is the feasible region for the PROTRAC LP model.

The set of all nonnegative values of the decision variables that satisfies all the constraints simultaneously is called the constraint set, or the feasible region.

In keeping with our definition of feasible region, any production plan (i.e., any pair of values for *[E, F]*) that satisfies all the constraints, including the nonnegativity conditions, is known as a **feasible solution** or *feasible decision.* These feasible plans, or decisions, are the allowable production alternatives according to our model. Note that it is *incorrect* to speak of a feasible value of *E* separately, or a feasible value of *F* separately. Think carefully about this statement, for it is important to understand that *the term* feasible, *in this two-dimensional illustration, always applies to a pair of numbers, not to a single number.* We want to reemphasize that a "solution" is more than just two values. It is a point on the graph. If there were three variables, it would be a point in three-dimensional space, and for four variables, it couldn't be "pictured."

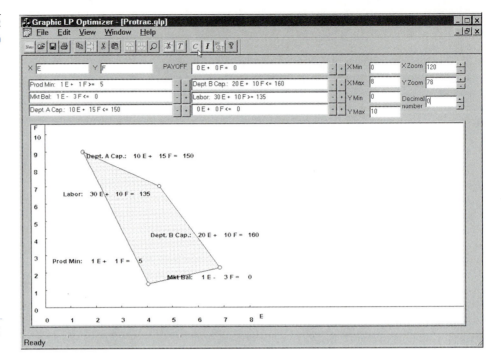

FIGURE 4.8

Feasible Region for PROTRAC
LP Model

To illustrate these feasible pairs geometrically, we have seen that you merely plot the constraint set. We used several pictures to lead up to our graph of the entire constraint set simply for illustrative purposes. In practice you would use GLP or graph paper to plot everything on the same coordinate systems, superimposing one constraint at a time. To accomplish this, for each constraint

1. Change the inequality to an equality.
2. Plot the equality.
3. Identify the correct side for the original inequality.

Having performed steps 1, 2, and 3 for each constraint, the feasible set is the region that, simultaneously, is on the correct side of all the lines.

PLOTTING THE OBJECTIVE FUNCTION

Obtaining a graphical portrayal of the constraint set is the first step in the graphical solution procedure. Now we want to use the graphical portrayal to find the *optimal* solution to the model. Since we are dealing with a profit-maximization model, we must find a feasible production alternative that gives the highest possible value to the objective function

$$\text{profit contribution} = 5000E + 4000F \qquad \textbf{(4.10)}$$

If we begin to arbitrarily select feasible plans from Figure 4.8 and evaluate the objective function at each such point, trying to find the largest possible profit, we would soon realize that this process could be endless. There are infinitely many feasible pairs *(E, F)*. How would this trial-and-error process ever terminate? We must find, systematically and quickly, a way to discover a profit-maximizing feasible plan.

Now recall that, since in this case the objective function is a profit function, the contours of the objective function are called isoprofit lines, or, more simply, *profit lines.* Our next task is to superimpose on Figure 4.8 several arbitrary profit lines. For example, let us begin by setting expression (4.10) equal to 20,000 by typing (4.10) and 20000 as the RHS in GLP's "PAYOFF" box, thereby superimposing on Figure 4.8 the corresponding profit line,

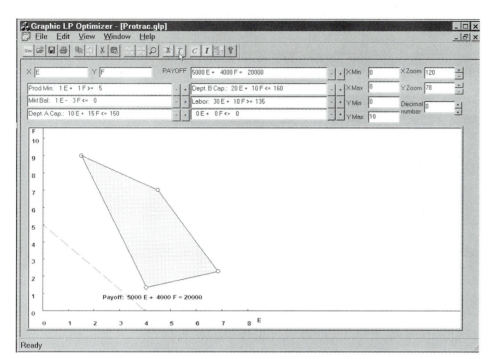

FIGURE 4.9

20,000-Contour of the
PROTRAC LP Profit Function

as shown in Figure 4.9. (The Toggle Text tool, "T," has been clicked to suppress display of the constraint labels, and the "Payoff" label on the graph has been clicked-dragged to be positioned next to the 20,000-contour in Figure 4.9 for improved readability.)

GLP restricts this Payoff line to the nonnegative quadrant because we are interested only in nonnegative values for E and F. Thus, any point on the line in Figure 4.9 corresponds to a production plan that will yield a profit contribution of $20,000. You can see from this figure that there are an infinite number of nonnegative production plans that will yield a profit of $20,000. However, the fact that the profit line in Figure 4.9 does not intersect the shaded feasible region means that none of the production plans on this line are feasible.

Let us therefore experiment by selecting a different profit line to superimpose on Figure 4.9. For example, let us set expression (4.10) equal to 32,000 and plot the profit contribution line

$$\text{profit contribution} = 5000E + 4000F = 32,000$$

To plot the new contour, type 32000 as the RHS of the equation in the "PAYOFF" box, as shown in Figure 4.10. You can see from Figure 4.10 that the 32,000-contour intersects the feasible region. Every production plan that lies on the intersection of this line with the feasible region is feasible, and yields a profit of $32,000. There are, as you can see, infinitely many such plans.

Our objective is to find a point in the feasible region that yields the highest profit. Are there any feasible plans that yield a higher profit than $32,000? Look at Figure 4.10 and see if you can answer this question.

The key to correct identification of feasible plans with a profit greater than $32,000 lies in noting that the 32,000 profit line is parallel to the 20,000 profit line of Figure 4.9 and lies above it (i.e., to the northeast). In general, as we increase profit, we increase the value of C in the profit equation

$$\text{profit contribution} = 5000E + 4000F = C$$

and the profit line moves parallel to the 20,000 and the 32,000 profit lines. The direction of the motion is northeasterly because this is, in this particular example, the direction in which profit increases. The direction of increasing contour values is called the **optimizing direction.** In this case we will call it the **uphill direction.**

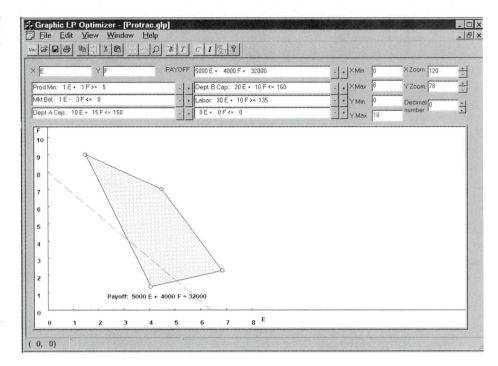

FIGURE 4.10

32,000-Contour of the
PROTRAC LP Profit Function

FINDING THE OPTIMAL SOLUTION

Now that we have seen how to plot the feasible region and the objective function contours, we are armed with enough information to find the solution to the PROTRAC model. As in our mind's eye, we move, or "slide," the profit lines out to the northeast, without changing the tilt, we can identify feasible plans that yield higher and higher values for the objective function. At some point we will discover that any further movement in this direction will take the profit line beyond the feasible region, at which point all production plans on the line will be unacceptable. Can you now identify the position of the highest-valued contour that touches the feasible region in at least one point? Any feasible plan on this line will be an **optimal solution** to the PROTRAC model.

To make the parallel outward displacement of the profit line in Figure 4.10, click the Payoff line and drag it to the "northeast"; GLP will keep each contour parallel to the others and update the Payoff RHS amount as you drag the line outward. You will see that the highest-valued contour is the one shown in Figure 4.11. This is called the maximum profit line. If you can click the "Auto Max" tool, shown under the cursor in Figure 4.11, GLP will maximize the Payoff for you and display the optimal values of E and F. (The Toggle Text tool has been clicked in Figure 4.11 to redisplay the constraint labels, and the Decimal Number field has been increased to 1 to display the fractional optimal value of E.)

In this model only one point in the feasible region lies on the maximum profit line, so this point is called a **unique optimal solution** to our model. From Figure 4.11 we see the value of the **maximum profit line** (i.e., the maximum attainable profit contribution) is $50,500, the same optimal profit contribution produced by Solver for the PROTRAC LP model in Chapter 3. Resorting to some algebra it is easy to see where this value comes from, as follows.

Figure 4.11 indicates that the optimal value of E is 4.5, and the optimal value of F is 7. You can see in Figure 4.11 that the optimal solution occurs at *the intersection* of the two constraint lines.

$$10E + 15F = 150 \qquad \textbf{(4.11)}$$
$$20E + 10F = 160 \qquad \textbf{(4.12)}$$

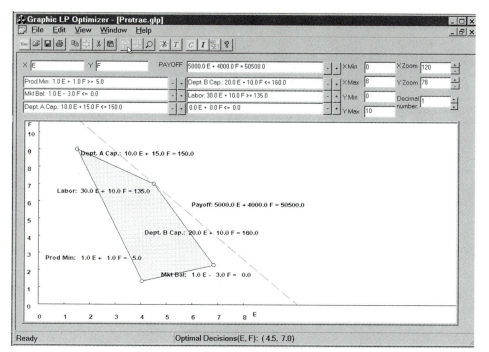

FIGURE 4.11

Optimality in the PROTRAC LP Model

We thus have two linear equations, which can be solved for the two unknowns, E and F, by either elimination or substitution methods. For example, using substitution, equation (4.12) can be rearranged to give

$$10F = 160 - 20E \qquad \text{or} \qquad F = 16 - 2E$$

Substituting this expression into equation (4.11) gives $E = 4.5$. This value for E can in turn be inserted into either of the original equations, yielding $F = 7$. The solution of the two binding constraints (4.11) and (4.12) for the two unknowns, E and F, is what GLP (and Solver) does to evaluate the optimal values of the two decision variables.

Let us use the notations E^* and F^* to distinguish the optimal values of the decision variables, E and F, respectively. We have found the optimal production plan $E^* = 4.5$ and $F^* = 7$. This is the *optimal solution,* or, more simply, *the solution* to the PROTRAC model. Using these optimal values $(E^* = 4.5, F^* = 7)$, we can now see how the value of the maximum profit is computed by GLP (and Solver) as follows:

$$\text{maximum profit contribution} = 5000E^* + 4000F^*$$
$$= 5000(4.5) + 4000(7) = 22{,}500 + 28{,}000 = 50{,}500$$

This is the value of the maximum profit contour in Figure 4.11 and is called the **optimal objective value,** or, sometimes, merely the **optimal value.** The term *solution,* or *optimal solution,* always refers to the optimal values of the decision variables. The term *optimal value* (singular), which we often call the OV, refers to the objective function evaluated at the solution. In the PROTRAC model, the optimal production plan $(E^* = 4.5, F^* = 7)$ is the solution; the optimal profit of \$50,500 is the OV.

4.4   ACTIVE AND INACTIVE CONSTRAINTS

In addition to the optimal production plan and the optimal profit, the other consequence variables we saw from Solver in Chapter 3 for the PROTRAC LP model can also be determined by answering these questions:

1. How many hours will the optimal solution use in department A?
2. How many hours will the optimal solution use in department B?
3. How many labor hours will the optimal solution use in testing?

Recall that the hours used in department A are given by the left-hand side of the inequality (4.6). That is, referring back to the model, we see that

$$\text{hours used in department A} = 10E + 15F$$

Since we are going to assign the optimal values $E = E^* = 4.5$, and $F = F^* = 7$, the expression is evaluated as follows:

$$\text{hours used (at optimality) in department A} = 10E^* + 15F^*$$
$$= 10(4.5) + 15(7) = 150$$

We say that "at optimality, 150 hours are used in department A." In order to answer question 2, we recall that the hours in department B are given by the left-hand side of inequality (4.7). Hence, at optimality

$$\text{hours used in department B} = 20E^* + 10F^*$$
$$= 20(4.5) + 10(7) = 160$$

Finally, to answer question 3 we employ the left-hand side of inequality (4.8) to discover that, at optimality

$$\text{labor hours used in testing} = 30E^* + 10F^*$$
$$= 30(4.5) + 10(7) = 205$$

Let us now pursue these elaborations a bit further to introduce some important new terminology. We have just seen that the optimal production plan will consume 150 hours in department A. But we also recall from the model that 150 hours is the total amount of labor *available* in department A. Hence, for the optimal policy we see that

$$\text{hours of labor used} = \text{hours of labor available}$$

and the constraint is satisfied with *equality*. But how can that be, for the constraint on labor hours in department A is an *inequality* constraint, not an equality constraint? The answer is simple if you interpret the $\leq$ symbol correctly. Our $\leq$ constraint on labor in department A allows the use of labor to be either $<$ the amount *or* $=$ the amount available. Hence, equality is permissible. What is *not* permissible is for the labor usage to *exceed* the availability.

For this constraint, since there is no labor left unused, the constraint is said to be **active,** or equivalently, **binding.** Note that from the manager's point of view an active constraint plays a role of considerable importance. For example, if there were any further production of E-9s or F-9s, this active constraint would be violated. In this sense the active constraint prevents the earning of additional profits.

By applying analogous reasoning to the constraint on labor hours in department B, you can easily verify that this constraint is also active.

In Chapter 3 we saw that the constraints in an LP model are always of the form $=$, $\leq$, or $\geq$. *An equality constraint is always active. An inequality constraint, of either the $\leq$ or $\geq$ type, is active only if, when evaluated at optimality, equality holds between the left-hand side and the right-hand side.*

Let us now consider the constraint on testing. Recall that this constraint requires, by a union agreement, that *at least* 135 labor hours (the right-hand side of the constraint) be used, whereas the answer to question 3 has shown that 205 hours (the left-hand side) will actually be used. Since we are using 70 hours in *excess* of what is required, there is said to be, at optimality, a *surplus* of 70 hours in this constraint. Here we have an example of an inequality constraint that is *not* active at optimality. As you might guess, such a constraint is said to be **inactive.**

The terms *active* and *inactive* are applicable to each constraint in the model. For example, if we evaluate, at optimality, the left-hand side of the market balance constraint labeled (4.5), we see that

$$E - 3F = 4.5 - 3(7) = 4.5 - 21 = -16.5$$

Since constraint (4.5) stipulates that $E - 3F \leq 0$, and since the actual value of the left-hand side is -16.5, we see that the left-hand side falls 16.5 units *below* the right-hand side. This constraint is said to have a *slack* of 16.5 units, and is also *inactive*.

Summarizing this terminology, we see that

1. If, at optimality (i.e., when evaluated at the optimal solution), the left-hand side of a constraint equals the right-hand side, that constraint is said to be *active*, or *binding*. Thus, an *equality* constraint is always active. An inequality constraint may or may not be active.

2. If a constraint is not active, it is said to be *inactive*. For a constraint of the $\geq$ type, the difference between the left-hand side and the right-hand side (the excess) is often called **surplus.** For a constraint of the $\leq$ type, the difference between the right-hand side and the left-hand side (the amount unused) is often called **slack.**

3. At optimality, each *inequality* constraint in a model has a slack or surplus value, and for feasible decisions this value is always nonnegative. For a given constraint the slack or surplus value is zero if and only if that constraint is active.

GRAPHICAL INTERPRETATIONS OF ACTIVE AND INACTIVE CONSTRAINTS

We have seen how to identify algebraically those constraints that are active and those that are inactive, and hence have positive surplus or slack. We obtained this information by "plugging" the optimal values of the decision variables into the constraints. We have just seen that the third and fourth constraints, which represent labor capacity in departments A and B, are active in this model. From Figure 4.11 you can see that these constraints "pass through" the optimal solution. In other words, the optimal solution "lies" on these constraints. Although we did not use the term *active*, we indeed solved for the values of E^* and F^* by implicitly recognizing that constraints for department A hours and department B hours are active.

> Geometrically, an active constraint is one that passes through the optimal solution.

We have seen that constraints for testing hours and market balance are inactive. A quick check also shows that the production minimum constraint (4.4) is inactive. That is,

$$E^* + F^* = 4.5 + 7 = 11.5 > 5$$

Thus, we can see that

> Geometrically, an inactive constraint is one that does not pass through the optimal solution.

The active and inactive constraints are easy to spot in the process of applying the graphical solution method. Indeed, that is the very goal of the graphical method, for once the active constraints are identified, as you have seen, then simultaneous equations can be solved to obtain the optimal solution. Each inactive constraint will have surplus or slack, depending upon whether the corresponding inequality is $\geq$ or $\leq$. However, the numerical value of the surplus or slack cannot be read from the picture. It must be determined algebraically, as in the foregoing illustrations.

4.5   **EXTREME POINTS AND OPTIMAL SOLUTIONS**

As you have seen, the solution to the PROTRAC model occurs at a corner of the feasible region—namely, at the corner where (what we have called) the department A hours and department B hours constraints intersect. In LP jargon the corners of the feasible region are called **extreme points.** The two terms, *extreme points* and *corners,* will be used interchangeably in our discussion.

A NEW OBJECTIVE FUNCTION

To understand the importance of the extreme points, let us take a different linear objective function, with the same constraint set, and solve the model again. For example, suppose that we change the price of F-9s in such a way that the contribution margin is raised from $4000 to $10,000 per unit. Let us see how this change in the objective function affects the solution to the problem. First, since we have changed only the objective function, leaving the constraints as they were, the feasible region remains unchanged. All that is new is that the contours of the objective function will assume a new tilt. A profit line of this new objective function (the 50,500-contour) is shown after typing 10000 as the new coefficient for F in the "PAYOFF" box in Figure 4.12.

Sliding the new profit line uphill, or clicking the Auto Max tool, gives the new optimal solution shown in Figure 4.13.

Note from Figure 4.13 that at the new optimal point the *active* constraints have changed. Now the department A hours and labor for testing hours constraints are active, whereas previously the department A and department B hours were active. Thus, you can see that the change in the slope of the objective function has moved the optimal solution away from the previous corner, but it has moved to another *corner,* or extreme point. As previously, we can verify the optimal decisions of the new optimal solution by simultaneously solving the two new binding constraint equations. Thus we have

$$10E^* + 15F^* = 150 \text{ (department A hours constraint)}$$
$$30E^* + 10F^* = 135 \text{ (labor hours in testing constraint)}$$

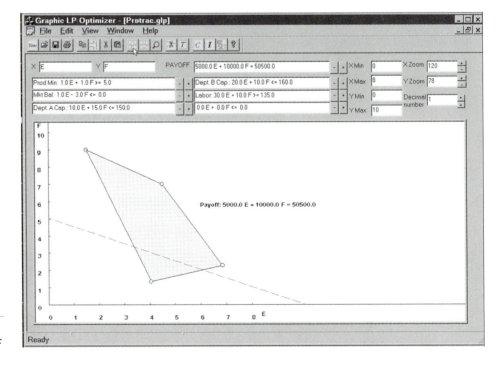

FIGURE 4.12

PROTRAC LP when Objective Function Is $5000E + 10,000F$

A NEW OPTIMAL CORNER

Solving these equations yields $E^* = 1.5$ and $F^* = 9$, as computed by GLP in Figure 4.13. This is the new optimal production plan. As you might have predicted, the new price structure, which has increased the relative profitability of F-9s, leads to an optimal production plan that specifies a cutback in E-9s and an increase in F-9s. You can also note from Figure 4.13 that at the new optimal solution there is now positive slack in labor in department B.

What we have seen is that with each of two different objective functions for PROTRAC's LP model, we obtained an optimal corner solution. In fact, you can experiment for yourself to see that no matter how much you change the objective function, as long as it remains linear, there will always be an optimal corner solution. You can even change the constraint set and there will still always be an optimal corner solution, as long as everything is kept linear.

In Figure 4.14 you see an arbitrary six-sided constraint set and contours of three *different* objective functions, denoted *f, g,* and *h.* For each objective function the arrow indicates the direction in which we want to slide the plotted contour to optimize the objective function. Note that in each case there is an optimal solution at a corner. The objective function *g* in Figure 4.14 illustrates the interesting case in which *the optimal objective contour coincides with one of the constraint lines on the boundary of the feasible region. In this case there will be many optimal solutions, namely the corners B and C and all the boundary points in between.* This is called a case of **multiple optima,** or **alternative optima.** However, even in this case, when there is not a *unique* optimal solution, it is still true that there is a corner solution that is optimal (in fact, there are two). Thus, the geometry illustrates an important fact about any LP model with any number of decision variables:

> In an LP model, if there is an optimal solution, there is always at least one optimal corner solution.

In future chapters we will see other important implications of the fact that if there is an optimal solution, there will always be at least one at a corner.

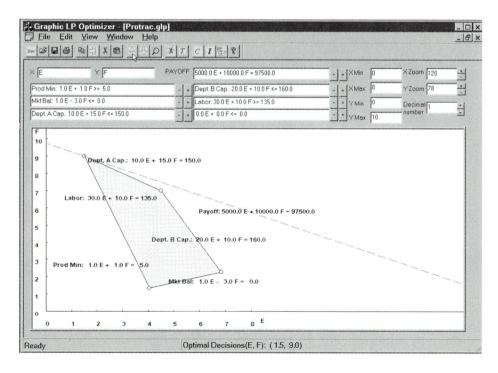

TIP: If you click on the Payoff line with the right mouse button near where it intersects one axis and then drag, GLP will rotate the Payoff line around the other axis intercept.

FIGURE 4.13

New PROTRAC LP Optimal Solution when the Objective Function Is $5000E + 10,000F$

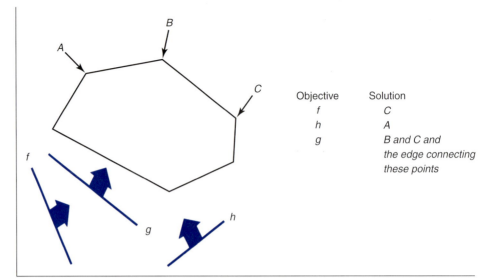

FIGURE 4.14

You Always Get a
Corner Solution

4.6   SUMMARY OF THE GRAPHICAL SOLUTION METHOD FOR A MAX MODEL

Our discussion thus far has presented the following procedure for solving an LP model in two decision variables:

1. Superimpose the graph of each constraint on the same nonnegative quadrant. The non-negative values of the decision variables that simultaneously satisfy (lie on the correct side of) all the constraints form the feasible *region,* also called the *constraint set.*

2. Draw an arbitrary profit *line,* also called a *contour,* of the objective function to obtain the slopes of the objective function contours.

3. Determine the uphill direction by, for example, evaluating the objective function at any trial point that is not on the profit line you have just constructed.

4. Now, given the slope of the profit line from step 2, and the uphill direction from step 3, determine visually the corner of the constraint set that lies on the highest possible profit line that still intersects this set.

5. The values of the decision variables at this corner (i.e., the coordinates of the corner) give the solution to the model. These values are found by identifying the active con-straints and then simultaneously solving two linear equations in two unknowns.

6. The optimal value of the objective function (i.e., the maximum profit) is obtained by "plugging in" the optimal values for the decision variables and evaluating the objec-tive function.

7. You have already identified the active constraints. The inactive constraints can also be read from your graph. They are those that do not pass through the solution.

4.7   THE GRAPHICAL METHOD APPLIED TO A MIN MODEL

THE "DOWNHILL" DIRECTION

As we noted in Section 3.10, many real-world models occur in a minimization context, and this was illustrated with the Crawler Tread model. Thus far we have dealt only with the graphical representation of a Max model. The method applied to a Min model is quite sim-ilar, the only difference being that *the optimizing direction of the objective function* is now

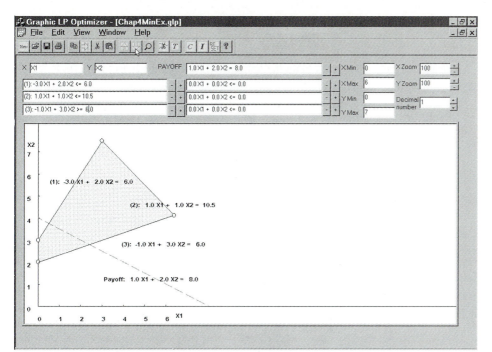

FIGURE 4.15

Feasible Region with
8-Contour Payoff for the
Min Model

"downhill" rather than "uphill." Recall that in a Max model the objective function contours are often isoprofit lines or, more simply, profit lines. In a Min model, the objective function contours are often isocost lines or, more simply, cost lines. Our goal, in a Min model, is to determine a corner of the feasible region that lies on the *lowest-valued* objective function contour that still intersects the feasible region. As an example, let us apply the graphical method to the following simple minimization model in two decision variables, which we denote as x_1 and x_2.

$$\text{Min } x_1 + 2x_2$$
$$\text{s.t. } -3x_1 + 2x_2 \leq 6 \quad (1)$$
$$x_1 + x_2 \leq 10.5 \quad (2)$$
$$-x_1 + 3x_2 \geq 6 \quad (3)$$
$$x_1, x_2 \geq 0$$

The feasible region and 8-contour Payoff line for this model is shown in Figure 4.15.

FINDING THE OPTIMAL SOLUTION

In order to find an optimal corner solution, we must

1. Plot a typical objective function contour to obtain the slope of such contours.
2. Determine the optimizing direction, which, since we are dealing with a Min model, is in this case the downhill direction.
3. With a parallel displacement of the objective function contour (from step 1), in the downhill direction (from step 2), determine which corner of the feasible region is optimal.
4. Solve the appropriate equations to obtain the exact optimal values of the decision variables. Then obtain the OV.

   Let us now carry out these steps.

1. In Figure 4.15 we superimpose the contour, objective value $x_1 + 2x_2 = 8$, by typing the equation in GLP's "PAYOFF" box.

2. To determine the downhill direction, we click-drag the Payoff line from which we see that the southwest direction is downhill.

3. By dragging the Payoff line to the southwest (or clicking the Auto Min tool under the cursor in Figure 4.15), we obtain the optimal solution shown in Figure 4.16.

4. Note that the optimal solution lies on the intersection of the third constraint and the x_2 axis. The equation of the x_2 axis is $x_1 = 0$. Hence, the optimal solution is given by the two equations $x_1^* = 0$ and $-x_1^* + 3x_2^* = 6$. Thus, $x_1^* = 0$, and $x_2^* = 2$, as indicated in Figure 4.16. The OV (optimal objective value) of 4 in Figure 4.16 is confirmed by evaluating the objective function at the optimal values for the decision variables.

$$OV = \text{optimal objective value} = x_2^* + 2x_2^* = 0 + 2(2) = 4$$

The example above shows that the graphical analysis for a Min model is exactly the same as that for a Max model, as long as the objective contours are always moved in the *optimizing direction*.

One caveat here always deserves emphasis. Students on occasion fall into the trap of thinking that in a Max model the solution will always be the corner "farthest away" from the origin. And for a Min model, they instinctively feel that if the origin is feasible, it must be optimal, and if the origin is not feasible, then the corner "closest to" the origin will be optimal. *Such reasoning may be false.* The incorrect logic has to do with the false impression that the uphill direction is always outward from the origin (the northeast), and the downhill direction is always inward toward the origin. In fact, there is no general relationship between uphill or downhill and the origin, just as there is no general relationship between the sense of an inequality ($\leq$ or $\geq$) and the above or below side of the equality plot in our graphical representation (see Section 4.2).

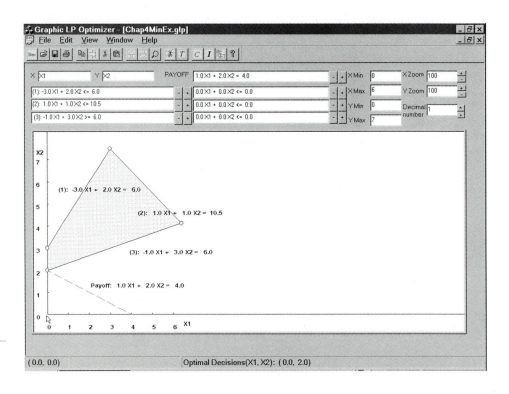

FIGURE 4.16

Optimal Solution for the Min Model

4.8   UNBOUNDED AND INFEASIBLE MODELS

Thus far we have developed a geometric portrayal of LP models in two decision variables. This portrayal has provided the basis for solving such models and has also illustrated the important conclusion that "*if* there is an optimal solution, there will always be at least one at a corner." But how can an LP fail to have an optimal solution? In this section we use the geometric representation to see how that can occur.

UNBOUNDED MODELS

Recall the graphical display of the PROTRAC LP model as shown in Figure 4.11, but let us now change the model by supposing that the constraints labeled (4.6) and (4.7) have been inadvertently omitted. Thus, we obtain the model

$$\text{Max } 5000E + 4000F$$

$$
\begin{array}{lrcl}
\text{s.t.} & E + F & \geq 5 & (1) \\
 & E - 3F & \leq 0 & (2) \\
 & 30E + 10F & \geq 135 & (5) \\
 & E, F & \geq 0 &
\end{array}
$$

The graphical analysis for this new model is shown in Figure 4.17. You can see that the constraint set now extends indefinitely to the northeast, and it is possible to slide the profit line arbitrarily far in this direction. Clicking the Auto Max tool will produce the message given in Figure 4.17.

Since for this particular model the northeast is the optimizing direction, we can find allowable decisions that give arbitrarily large values to the objective function. In other words, we can obtain profits approaching infinity. Such a model has no solution, because the objective function is **unbounded.** That is, for any set of allowable values for the decision variables we can always find other allowable values that improve the objective value. Models of this type are termed **unbounded models.** Unbounded models are "pathological." They can arise, as in Figure 4.17, when one or more important constraints have been left out of the model, or possibly because of typing errors when entering a model into GLP or the spreadsheet for Solver optimization. In the real world no one has yet discovered how to

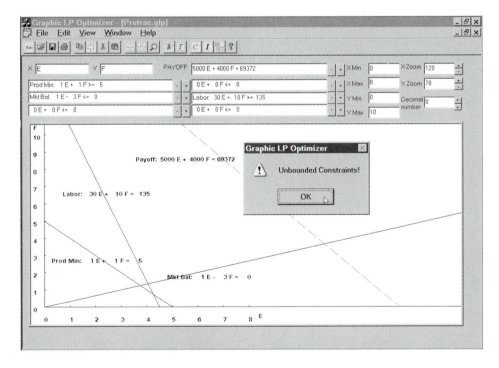

FIGURE 4.17

Unbounded PROTRAC
LP Model

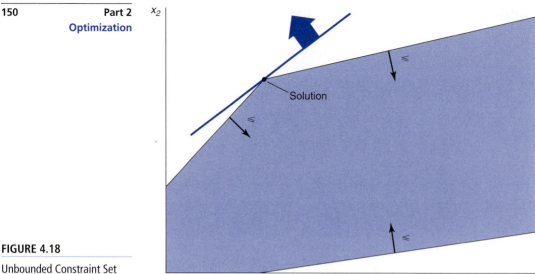

FIGURE 4.18

Unbounded Constraint Set
but an LP Solution

obtain an infinite profit, and you can be assured that when a model is correctly formulated and correctly entered into the spreadsheet it will not be unbounded.

Students sometimes confuse the term *unbounded model* with the concept of an **unbounded constraint set.** The latter terminology refers to a feasible region in which at least one decision variable can be made arbitrarily large in value. If an LP is unbounded, the constraint set must also be unbounded, as illustrated by Figure 4.17. However, it is possible to have an unbounded constraint set without having an unbounded model. This is illustrated graphically in Figure 4.18, which shows a hypothetical LP model in two decision variables, x_1 and x_2. The model has three constraints and an unbounded constraint set, but there is an optimal solution.

INFEASIBLE MODELS

As introduced in Chapter 3, there is another type of pathology to be aware of in LP. It is called **infeasibility** or, alternatively, **inconsistency.** This term refers to a model with an empty constraint set; that is, there is no combination of values for the decision variables that simultaneously satisfies all the constraints. A graphical illustration of an **infeasible model** is obtained by changing the first constraint in the PROTRAC model to $E + F \leq 5$ instead of $E + F \geq 5$. This gives us the new model

$$\text{Max } 5000E + 4000F$$

$$\text{s.t. } E + F \leq 5 \qquad ①$$
$$E - 3F \leq 0 \qquad ②$$
$$10E + 15F \leq 150 \qquad ③$$
$$20E + 10F \leq 160 \qquad ④$$
$$30E + 10F \geq 135 \qquad ⑤$$
$$E, F \geq 0$$

The constraint set for this LP is graphically represented in Figure 4.19. You can see that there is no pair of values (E, F) that satisfies *all* the constraints.

As Figure 4.19 illustrates, *infeasibility depends solely on the constraints and has nothing to do with the objective function.* Obviously, an infeasible LP has no solution, but this pathology will not appear if the model has been formulated correctly. In other words, in well-posed real models, infeasibility always means that the model has been incorrectly specified, either because of logical errors or because of typing errors when entering the

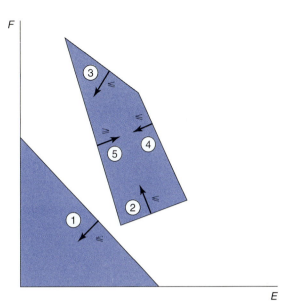

FIGURE 4.19

Infeasible PROTRAC LP Model

model into GLP or the spreadsheet. Logical errors may mean that either too many constraints, or the wrong constraints, have been included.

In summary:

Every linear program will fall into one of the following three nonoverlapping categories:

1. The model has an optimal solution.
2. There is no optimal solution, because the model is unbounded.
3. There is no optimal solution, because the model is infeasible.

In practice, a correctly formulated real-world LP will always have a solution. States 2 and 3 can arise only from (1) errors in model formulation or (2) errors in entering the model into GLP or the spreadsheet.

4.9   GRAPHICAL SENSITIVITY ANALYSIS

The PROTRAC LP model was formulated and optimized by Solver in Chapter 3. In this chapter we have introduced a graphical perspective to help you visualize the important role that extreme points of the feasible region play when Solver optimizes a constrained linear model. You may well feel that you now have a good solution to PROTRAC and thus are free to turn attention to other matters. In many, if not most, cases this simply is not true. Often the solution to a model is only a starting point and is, in itself, the least interesting part of the analysis. Remember that the model is an abstraction of the real-world situation. If you were the responsible manager at PROTRAC you would need to ask numerous additional questions before you would be confident enough about the Solver results to implement them. For example, there may be rather significant considerations that because of their complexity have not been built into the model. To the extent that a model is a simplification of reality, there will always be factors that are left out. These factors may, for example, be of a political or ethical nature. Such considerations are usually difficult to quantify. Having optimized the simplified model, you must now turn to address how well the optimal solution "fits in" with other considerations, which may not have been included. There may, as another example, be inexactitudes and uncertainty in some of the data that

Preparing the best possible meals at the least possible cost is the objective of food-systems management for most feeding programs (e.g., hospitals, nursing homes, schools, and prisons). Menu planning is the key component since the menu determines food, equipment, and personnel requirements. Menu planning, however, deceives both nutrition experts and the public by appearing to be a simple procedure. The model must consider numerous constraints. For example, the Food and Nutrition Board identified minimum intake levels for 29 nutrients (often called recommended daily allowances). Other health-care agencies have recommended upper limits for intakes of fat, cholesterol, and sodium. All in all, it can get quite complex to plan menus that meet all the nutritional constraints.

Nutrition cannot be the only goal, however. Simple spreadsheet diet models can easily be developed that meet the nutritional constraints at a minimum cost, but nobody in his or her right mind would eat the recommended diet. The diet is generally the equivalent of the human dog biscuit. One particularly humorous story comes from the father of linear programming, George Dantzig. When George first created a personal diet model in the early 1950s to help him lose weight by controlling his diet, it recommended a bunch of weird stuff AND 500 gallons of vinegar. He eliminated vinegar as a possibility and the next "optimal" diet included 200

bouillon cubes/day. When he tried to drink 4 cubes dissolved in hot water for breakfast the next day, he had to spit the briny mixture out! After several more iterations of adding constraints and getting ridiculous recommendations, his wife finally took over the diet herself.

Obviously, this example, although true, is a little extreme on what can go wrong with spreadsheet formulation of a diet based on nutrition alone, but the fact is that the consumer's food preferences must be considered. Good diet models will include these additional constraints. Generally they are included in one of two ways—a separation rating or a frequency constraint. The first approach looks at how much time should pass before the item is eaten again (e.g., no more mashed potatoes for three more days). In the latter approach, you simply indicate how many times/week you'd be willing to eat the particular food item.

Institutions that have implemented these spreadsheet-generated menus have: (1) realized 10 to 30% cost savings; (2) always met the nutrient constraints, which wasn't always the case before; and (3) actually had the same acceptance by the customers in terms of taste as those meals planned with traditional methods.

The case at the end of this chapter discusses the diet problem and summarizes Dantzig's contributions to the development of the simplex method used by Solver to optimize LP models. (See Lancaster and Dantzig.)

were used in the model. In real-world situations this is the norm rather than the exception. The motto is: "Do the best with what you have."

In most cases, you will want to know: How *sensitive* is the optimal solution to the inexact data? We may have an estimate of the absentee rate for next month's labor force, and the model has been run using this estimate. What happens to the optimal solution if we change the estimate by 5%, 10%, or even 15%? Will the optimal objective function value (OV) vary wildly, or will it remain more or less unchanged? Obviously, as was the case for the sensitivity analysis example in Chapter 2, the answer to such questions will help to determine the credibility of the model's recommendations. For example, if the OV changes very little with large changes in the value of a particular parameter, you would not be concerned about uncertainty in that value. If, on the other hand, the OV varies wildly with small changes in that parameter, you cannot tolerate much uncertainty in its value. In this case more resources might be worth committing to establish or forecast a more precise value for the parameter in question.

Although some of the foregoing considerations can be dealt with only informally, we fortunately do have some rigorous and precise tools at our disposal. These tools are in the realm of **sensitivity analysis** or **postoptimality analysis.** Both of these terms mean essentially the same thing, and the topic is of such significance that the entire next chapter is devoted to understanding the sensitivity information contained in the Solver solution to an LP model. Making good use of spreadsheet analysis is, of course, a problem faced by all managers in the real world. In the remainder of this chapter we lay further groundwork for being able to understand clearly the meaning of Solver results. Extending the graphical approach will make it relatively easy to do this. The ability to *see*, geometrically, how changes in the model affect the solution in this special two-decision-variable case makes it much easier to understand the changes that will occur in larger, more realistic models.

In order to introduce sensitivity analysis in a very specific way, let us again refer to the original PROTRAC LP model from Section 4.3, repeated below with the constraints labeled for reference. Recall that the purpose of this model is to recommend a production target *for next month.* Therefore, all the numerical data in the model are supposed to be pertinent to this period of interest, namely one month in the future.

$$\text{Max } 5000E + 4000F$$

$$\text{s.t. } E + F \geq 5 \qquad ①$$
$$E - 3F \leq 0 \qquad ②$$
$$10E + 15F \leq 150 \qquad ③$$
$$20E + 10F \leq 160 \qquad ④$$
$$30E + 10F \geq 135 \qquad ⑤$$
$$E, F \geq 0 \qquad ⑥$$

A major application of LP involves planning models such as this, where future plans and policies are to be determined, and in such models future data are naturally required. Obviously in many real-world situations such data may not be known with complete certainty. Suppose, for example, that the stated unit contribution margins of $5000 per E-9 and $4000 per F-9 are only estimates based on revenues and projected variable costs for next month and that some of the costs of raw materials to be purchased next month are subject to change. Unfortunately, in order to achieve the lead time required in the planning process, the model must be run now, before the exact data are known. Thus, we must use the numbers above, which are our best current estimates, knowing full well that the actual unit contribution margins next month could differ. We might have some fairly solid ideas about the possible ranges in which the true values will lie, and the unit contribution margins of $5000 and $4000 might be our best estimates with such ranges. But how do we deal with the fact that the data are not known with complete certainty? That is one important topic covered in sensitivity analysis.

Another possible concern may involve uncertainty in some of the constraint data. In LP, this type of uncertainty usually focuses on the right-hand sides of the constraints. For example, consider the number 135, which is the right-hand side of the contractual labor hour agreement constraint. It represents the minimal number of hours that must be spent on product testing next month. In a real-life application it is possible that such a number could also be uncertain. The actual minimal requirement that will be in force next month could be arrived at in a rather complicated way depending, for example, on the results of quality tests of this month's production, results that can be *estimated* only at the time the planning process occurs. Thus, the value of 135 is only a "best estimate." Again, PROTRAC management must cope with the uncertainty in such data.

These two examples reflect the major focus of sensitivity analysis and the topics discussed in the following two sections. The first example, in which unit contribution margins are uncertain, illustrates what we call *changes in the objective function coefficients.* The second example illustrates *changes in the right-hand sides.* In an LP model, the objective function coefficients and the right-hand sides are often called **parameters,** and for this reason the term **parametric analysis** is sometimes also used for the investigation of the effects of changing the values of these parameters. However, to be consistent with nomenclature from Chapter 1 and with Solver's reports, we will refer to these investigations as sensitivity analysis. Let us see how graphical analysis can provide insight into the effects of such changes.

4.10 CHANGES IN THE OBJECTIVE FUNCTION COEFFICIENTS

Suppose that the constraint data remain unchanged and only the objective coefficients are changed. Then the only effect on the model, from the geometric viewpoint, is that the slope of the profit lines is changed. We have, in fact, already seen an illustration of this phenomenon in Section 4.5. In Figure 4.13 all data in the PROTRAC model remained unchanged except for the fact that the contribution margin of F-9s was raised from $4000 to $10,000 per unit. We saw that the effect of this change was to change the tilt of the profit lines to such an extent that a new corner solution was obtained.

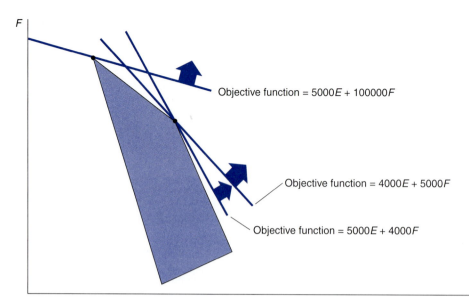

Objective function = 5000*E* + 100000*F*

Objective function = 4000*E* + 5000*F*

Objective function = 5000*E* + 4000*F*

FIGURE 4.20

PROTRAC Model with Contours of Three Different Profit Functions and the Corresponding Solutions

You can also quickly see that some changes in the objective function coefficients will *not* change the optimal solution, even though the profit lines will have a different slope. For example, let us replace the old objective function $5000E + 4000F$ with a new objective function $4000E + 5000F$. As we saw in Figure 4.11, the solution with the old objective function is $E^* = 4.5$, $F^* = 7.0$. The new objective function $4000E + 5000F$ assigns a lower contribution margin to E-9s and a higher contribution margin to F-9s. You might therefore expect to obtain an optimal solution calling for production of fewer than 4.5 E-9s and more than 7.0 of the more profitable F-9s. However, Figure 4.20 presents a graphical analysis that shows that this is not the case. In this figure there are three different objective functions:

$$(1)\ 5000E + 4000F,\ (2)\ 4000E + 5000F,\ \text{and}\ (3)\ 5000E + 10,000F$$

It is evident that the negative slopes of the contours associated with each of the three functions become progressively less steep (i.e., the contours become flatter) as the profitability of

F-9s increases relative to E-9s (i.e., as the ratio $\dfrac{\text{coefficient of } F}{\text{coefficient of } E}$ increases). However, although

the objectives $5000E + 4000F$ and $4000E + 5000F$ have contours with different slopes, *the slopes are not sufficiently different to give us a new corner solution.* For each of these two objectives the optimal solution is the same, namely $E^* = 4.5$ and $F^* = 7.0$.

On the other hand, it is important to note that in this case the optimal profits (i.e., the optimal objective values) will differ. In the former case we have

$$\text{optimal profit} = 5000E^* + 4000F^* = 5000(4.5) + 4000(7) = 50{,}500$$

whereas in the latter case

$$\text{optimal profit} = 4000E^* + 5000F^* = 4000(4.5) + 5000(7) = 53{,}000$$

You can verify these outcomes by typing the two objective functions into GLP's "PAYOFF" box and optimizing the LP. In conclusion, what we have just seen can be summarized thus:

> Changing the objective function coefficients changes the slopes of the objective function contours. This may or may not affect the optimal solution.

4.11 CHANGES IN THE RIGHT-HAND SIDES

Let us now ignore the objective function and focus on the right-hand sides of the constraint functions. Again, graphical analysis will nicely explain the effects of changes in these parameters. As a specific example, let us suppose that the fifth constraint of the PROTRAC LP model

$$30E + 10F \geq 135 \quad \text{(labor hours used in testing)} \tag{4.13}$$

is changed to

$$30E + 10F \geq 210 \tag{4.14}$$

and suppose that all other constraint data remain as they are given. Since 135 is a smaller number than 210, expression (4.13) is easier to satisfy than (4.14). For example, the pair $E = 3$, $F = 5$ satisfies (4.13) for

$$30E + 10F = 30(3) + 10(5) = 90 + 50 = 140$$

Since 140 is $\geq$ 135, (4.13) is satisfied. But 140 is less than 210 and hence the pair $E = 3$, $F = 5$ does *not* satisfy condition (4.14). Another way of saying this is that fewer *combinations of values for E and F will satisfy (4.14)*.

Because of this fact, it would be reasonable to expect that the change from (4.13) to (4.17) might, in some sense, "shrink" the feasible region. From the geometric point of view, you can see that changing the right-hand side of a constraint creates a parallel shift in the constraint line. In this case, then, the reasoning above suggests that, in changing the RHS from 135 to 210, the fifth constraint line—corresponding to (4.13)—will shift in such a way as to eliminate some of the feasible region. Figure 4.21 shows the original constraint set with the constraints labeled ① through ⑤.

Figure 4.22 shows the new constraint set with the fifth constraint (4.13) replaced by (4.14). Although, geometrically speaking, the constraint set in Figure 4.22 looks quite different from the one in Figure 4.21, all that has been done is to slide the constraint labeled ⑤ farther outward from the origin to its new position.

You should experiment by assigning different values to this right-hand side with the GLP formulation from Section 4.3, and to the other right-hand sides, to see the variety of different-looking feasible regions that can arise from such simple perturbations. You can do this in GLP by typing different RHS values for the constraints, by click-dragging the

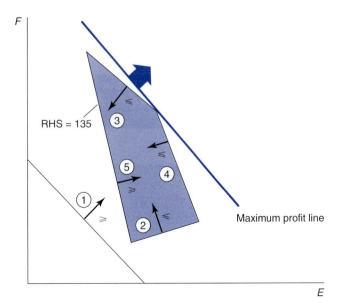

FIGURE 4.21

Graphical Analysis of the
Original PROTRAC LP Model

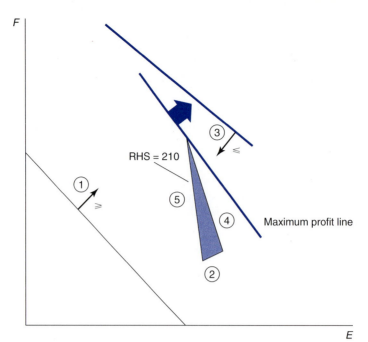

FIGURE 4.22

Graphical Analysis of the
PROTRAC LP Model with New
RHS for the Fifth Constraint

constraint lines,[3] or by clicking the $+/-$ buttons at the right of each GLP equation box. One particularly interesting case arises if you further increase the right-hand side of the fifth constraint to 270, leaving all the other constraint data unchanged. You are asked in Problem 4-27 to show that in this case you will have created an inconsistent set of constraints. That is, the model becomes infeasible.

Return now to Figure 4.22. The optimal solution is shown for the objective function $5000E + 4000F$. Comparing this with the graphical analysis for the original model, Figure 4.21, you can see that the solution to the new model is entirely different from the old. We have

Old model:

Active constraints: ③ and ④

Inactive constraints: ①, ②, and ⑤

Solution (by solving active constraints): $E^* = 4.5$, $F^* = 7$

Optimal profit = OV = 50,500

New model:

Active constraints: ④ and ⑤

Inactive constraints: ①, ②, and ③

Solution computed by GLP or by hand would be as follows:

$$\text{Constraint ④: } 20E + 10F = 160$$
$$\text{Constraint ⑤: } \underline{30E + 10F = 210}$$
$$\text{Subtracting: } -10E \qquad\quad = -50$$
$$E \quad = \quad 5$$
$$\text{Substituting: } 20(5) + 10F = 160$$
$$F = 6$$

Hence, $E^* = 5$, $F^* = 6$, and optimal profit = OV = $5000E^* + 4000F^*$
$$= 5000(5) + 4000(6) = 49,000$$

---

[3]You must be in "un-trim" mode to directly click-drag constraints.

It should be clear from this analysis that changing even one right-hand-side value can have a profound effect on the solution. In Chapter 5 it will be shown that Solver can be used to provide sensitivity information on the effects of such changes. For now, we summarize what we have graphically seen in this section for two-dimensional models. These results, as with the previous results for changing an objective function coefficient, are also valid for models with more than two decision variables.

> Changing a right-hand-side value results in a parallel shift of the changed constraint. This *may* affect both the optimal solution and the OV (the optimal objective value). The effect will depend on exactly which right-hand-side values are changed, and by how much.

4.12   TIGHTENING AND LOOSENING AN INEQUALITY CONSTRAINT

We conclude this discussion on sensitivity analysis by making some general observations on the effects of right-hand-side changes for *inequality constraints.* This will lead us to several useful new terms. In the discussion above we compared the two constraints

$$30E + 10F \geq 135 \qquad \textbf{(4.13)}$$

and

$$30E + 10F \geq 210 \qquad \textbf{(4.14)}$$

and noted that since each constraint is of the $\geq$ form, and since the right-hand side of (4.14) is larger than the right-hand side of (4.13), the constraint (4.14) is more difficult to satisfy. This process of increasing the RHS of a $\geq$ constraint is called **tightening the constraints.** The constraint (4.14) is *tighter* than (4.13). Similarly, if the RHS of a $\leq$ constraint is decreased, the constraint becomes more difficult to satisfy and hence is tighter.

> Tightening an inequality constraint means making it more difficult to satisfy. For a $\geq$ constraint this means increasing the RHS. For a $\leq$ constraint this means decreasing the RHS.

Suppose that instead of increasing the RHS of (4.13) we decrease it so that, for example, the constraint becomes

$$30E + 10F \geq 100 \qquad \textbf{(4.15)}$$

You should be able to see that since the right-hand side has become smaller, and since (4.15) is a $\geq$ constraint, there are now *more* combinations of values for E and F that will satisfy the constraint. Thus, the constraint has become easier to satisfy. This process of decreasing the RHS of a $\geq$ constraint is called **loosening the constraint.** The constraint (4.15) is *looser* than (4.13). Similarly, if the RHS of a $\leq$ constraint is increased, the constraint becomes easier to satisfy and hence is looser.

> Loosening an inequality constraint means making it easier to satisfy. For a $\geq$ constraint this means decreasing the RHS. For a $\leq$ constraint this means increasing the RHS.

The geometric effects of tightening and loosening are easily illustrated. We see that in moving from Figure 4.21 to Figure 4.22, constraint ⑤ has been tightened and the feasible region contracted. Moving from Figure 4.22 to Figure 4.21 loosens constraint ⑤ and the feasible region expands. These geometric results, that tightening contracts and loosening expands, are what you probably would have predicted, but another possibility must be considered.

Consider constraint ①, $E + F \geq 5$. Note in Figure 4.21 that it currently plays no role in determining the shape of the feasible set. Also, with a suitably small change in its right-hand side, say from 5 to 5.1 or 4.9, the line will incur a small parallel displacement and still not intersect the original feasible set. Thus, in this case we see that a suitably small amount of tightening or loosening of constraint ① has no effect on the feasible set. We now summarize our observation on the geometric effects of tightening and loosening inequality constraints.

> Tightening an inequality constraint either contracts the constraint set or leaves it unaffected. Loosening an inequality constraint either expands the constraint set or leaves it unaffected.

These results are generally true for inequality constraints and do not depend on the dimension of the model (the number of decision variables) or on whether the constraint is of $\leq$ or $\geq$ form. It should be emphasized that in this analysis we have assumed that one constraint is manipulated while all the others remain fixed. The effects of tightening (loosening) several at a time are also to contract (expand) or, possibly, to leave the feasible region unchanged. However, if some constraints are tightened and others simultaneously loosened, there is little that can be categorically stated about the result. We conclude this section with the observation that tightening a constraint too much can produce infeasibility, as occurred when the RHS of constraint ⑤ was increased to 270.

4.13   REDUNDANT CONSTRAINTS

A constraint such as constraint ① in Figure 4.21 is termed **redundant.** Although five constraints are plotted in this figure, only four of them are required to define the feasible region. This is because, as the figure clearly indicates, any combination of E and F values that satisfies the constraints labeled ②, ③, ④, and ⑤ will automatically satisfy the constraint labeled ① as well. In this sense the first constraint is superfluous. Here is a precise definition.

> A redundant constraint is one whose removal does not change the feasible region.

Since a redundant constraint could, by definition, be discarded without changing the feasible region, its elimination will also have no effect on the optimal solution to the model. Why bother, then, to include such a constraint in the model? There are two important reasons:

1. Redundant constraints are generally not very easy to recognize. Even in the simple case of models with two decision variables, if you are looking only at the algebraic form of the mathematical model, the redundant constraints are not immediately spotted. For example, it is not obvious from the symbolic LP formulation that the constraint $E + F \geq 5$ is redundant in the PROTRAC model. The graphical representation, of course, makes it clear for this two-dimensional model. However, since graphical analysis is limited to two-dimensional models, it is not useful for detecting redundancy in larger models.

2. A constraint that is redundant today may not be redundant tomorrow. For example, suppose that the management of PROTRAC decides to explore the effects of a new policy decision to produce at least seven, rather than five, units of E and F in total. Then the RHS of the first constraint changes to 7 instead of 5. The modified first constraint is plotted as a dashed line in Figure 4.23, and it is seen that the new constraint is no longer redundant. In other words, *tightening* the requirement from 5 to 7 forces us to cut off some previously allowable decisions.

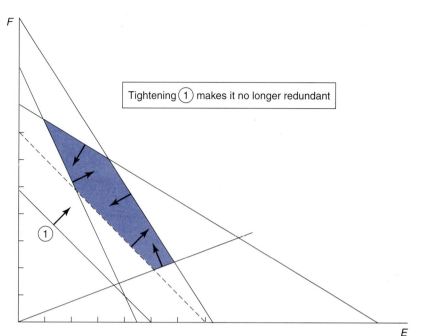

Tightening ① makes it no longer redundant

FIGURE 4.23

Tightening the PROTRAC LP's
First Constraint

It is quite possible that a constraint that is redundant for a given set of data may no longer be redundant when some of the data are changed.

It is often for this reason that a redundant constraint is kept in a model. It is common practice to solve planning models many times with different sets of data in order to gain insight into possible future scenarios. Since there are conditions of interest (values of the data) for which this constraint may become *important,* it is best to include it in the LP model.

4.14   WHAT IS AN IMPORTANT CONSTRAINT?

As suggested previously, there may be a distinction between "important" and "unimportant" constraints. Indeed, we have seen that, in general, an LP model may have numerous constraints. It would be of interest to know whether some of the many constraints may have special importance in the model. The management of PROTRAC certainly has an interest in knowing which constraints are most restrictive in the sense of limiting the possibilities for greater profit.

REDUNDANT CONSTRAINTS

The discussion in the previous section suggests that, *for a given set of data, the redundant constraints (if there are any) are the least important.* That is, we have already observed that constraint ① is redundant, which means that it can be ignored without changing the constraint set and hence without changing the optimal solution. Since it does not affect the solution, it is, *for the given set of data,* of little importance. But can we say more? Just in terms of what we have so far learned, can you identify other constraints in the model that seem to be "more important" than the others?

ACTIVE AND INACTIVE CONSTRAINTS

In Figure 4.24 the graphical analysis of the original PROTRAC LP model is reproduced. This figure shows that there are indeed other constraints in the model that can be ignored without affecting the solution, namely, constraints ② and ⑤.

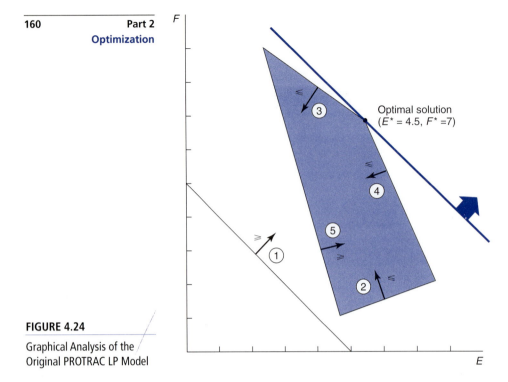

FIGURE 4.24

Graphical Analysis of the
Original PROTRAC LP Model

The graphical analysis of the model with constraints ①, ②, and ⑤ deleted is given in Figure 4.25.

Although the feasible region has become greatly enlarged, the optimal solution remains unchanged. Recall that in this model constraints ①, ②, and ⑤ are the **inactive constraints.** The phenomenon we have just observed is generally true, even in higher-dimensional models.

> In any LP model, *for a fixed set of data,* the inactive constraints can be removed without affecting the optimal solution. The optimal solution is determined entirely by the active constraints.

Thus, for a given set of data the **active constraints** are the important ones, in the sense that they completely determine the solution. If we could only know in advance which constraints are active, the task of solving an LP would reduce to the relatively easy problem of solving a system of simultaneous linear equations, such as the equations for the lines labeled ③ and ④ in Figure 4.24. Although we may agree that the active constraints are most important, this information becomes available only *after* the model is solved, for unfortunately the modeler has no way of knowing, in advance, which of the inequality constraints will be active.[4] Consequently, a more complicated simplex algorithm is used by Solver to solve general LP models.

In concluding this section, we wish to emphasize that when the data in a model change, the set of active and inactive inequality constraints can also change. *In other words, the unimportant (inactive) constraints for one set of data may become important (active) when the model is re-solved with different data.* You can think of a model as being "a logical framework or structure" that underlies the assigned numerical values of the parameters. This logical framework captures interactions among variables as well as requirements and limitations. The logical framework in a sense is independent of the actual values assigned

---

[4]Recall that an equality constraint, by definition, is always active.

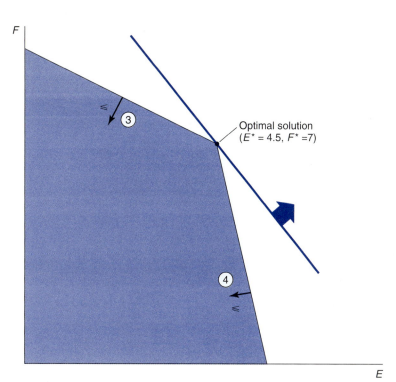

Optimal solution
($E^* = 4.5$, $F^* = 7$)

FIGURE 4.25

Graphical Analysis of
PROTRAC with Constraints
①, ②, and ⑤ Deleted

to the parameters (i.e., the data). Different data values will give different realizations to the model. In this larger context it is not really meaningful to label some constraints as being more important than others. *The importance of the constraints is a relative question whose answer will depend on the values assigned to the data.*

4.15 ADDING OR DELETING CONSTRAINTS

The graphical analysis immediately demonstrates one final general observation concerning the effects of adding or deleting constraints. Comparing Figure 4.24 and Figure 4.25 shows immediately what can happen when constraints are deleted. Deleting the constraint labeled ① (the redundant constraint) had no effect on the model. Deleting ② allowed the feasible region to enlarge. Deleting ⑤ allowed it to further enlarge, as represented in Figure 4.25. Thus for any LP model we can make this general statement:

Deleting constraints leaves the feasible region either unchanged or larger.

We previously observed the impact of adding constraints to a model. This impact was demonstrated during the course of plotting the constraint set for the PROTRAC model with GLP. You will recall that superimposing successive constraints had the effect of "trimming down" the constraint set. This too is true in general.

Adding constraints leaves the feasible region either unchanged or smaller.

Since adding constraints may have the effect of trimming down the feasible region, adding a new constraint to a model may happen to "trim off" a piece of the constraint set that contains the previous optimal solution. If this happens, the result may be a reduced OV (optimal objective value) for the new model. This effect is shown in Figure 4.26, where a

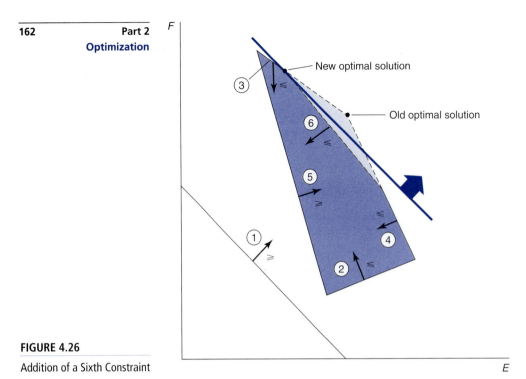

FIGURE 4.26

Addition of a Sixth Constraint

sixth inequality constraint has been added to the PROTRAC model. The crosshatched region in Figure 4.26 portrays the part of the constraint set that is eliminated by the addition of the constraint labeled ⑥.

The uphill direction in this diagram is to the northeast, and the new maximum profit line is not as far uphill as the former maximum profit line. Hence, the imposition of a new constraint has led to a reduction in the optimal profit. Of course, this is why managers prefer to operate with as few constraints as possible. *The larger the number of constraints, the greater the chance that the optimal objective value is less desirable.* The general result can be formulated thus:

> Adding constraints to a model will either impair the OV or leave it unchanged. Deleting constraints will either improve the OV or leave it unchanged.

The results of adding and deleting constraints are analogous to the results of tightening and loosening inequality constraints, both in terms of effects on the feasible region and on the optimal objective value. Thus, in the above displayed result, the phrase *Tightening inequality constraints* could be substituted for *Adding constraints to a model.* The phrase *Loosening inequality constraints* could be substituted for *deleting constraints.*

Note that a similar reasoning yields the following general result for adding or deleting decision variables:

> Adding variables will either improve the OV or leave it unchanged, while deleting variables will either impair the OV or leave it unchanged.

The powerful role of two-dimensional geometry in illustrating certain important concepts has been explained in this chapter. In particular, we used the geometric approach to solve LP models in two decision variables, to illustrate the meaning of active and inactive constraints, to show the important connection between optimal solutions and corners to the feasible region, and finally, to illustrate pathological properties.

We saw that the graphical solution method involves two main steps: determining the set of feasible decisions and then selecting the best of these decisions. The underlying prerequisite for these steps is the ability to plot linear equalities and linear inequalities. The techniques needed were briefly reviewed in Section 4.2.

The task of determining the set of feasible decisions typically reduces to portraying the values of the decision variables that satisfy a collection of linear inequalities. (There could also be equalities in the system, but this merely means that the feasible decisions must also lie on each equality line.) In Section 4.3 we saw that this set is determined by successively superimposing the plots of the constraints and then identifying the points that lie on the correct side of *all* the inequalities.

To find the best feasible decision, plot a single objective function contour, identifying the optimizing direction (uphill for a Max model, downhill for a Min model), and then displacing the contour parallel to itself in the optimizing direction, identify a corner solution. We demonstrated how to apply the GLP graphic optimizer for this purpose. We saw in Section 4.5 that if an LP has an optimal solution, there will always be at least one optimal corner solution, also called an extreme point solution.

The graphical procedure illustrates that it is only necessary to identify the active constraints. Then, the optimal values of the decision variables are obtained by simultaneously solving these equations. From the geometric point of view, active constraints were defined as those that pass through the optimal corner of the feasible region. Algebraically, an active constraint is one for which the left-hand side, when evaluated at optimality, is equal to the right-hand side. *Surplus* and *slack* are terms used to denote the nonnegative difference between the two sides of an inequality constraint. The term *surplus* is often used for a $\geq$ constraint, and *slack* for a $\leq$ constraint.

Section 4.6 is devoted to a summary of the graphical solution method for a Max model, and in Section 4.7 we saw that the technique was easily extended to Min models. The only necessary modification for a Min model is to make sure that the contours of the objective contour are displaced in a downhill direction in the process of finding the best feasible decision.

Section 4.8 considered two pathological cases in which an LP model does not have an optimal solution. In an unbounded Max model the objective function can assume arbitrarily large values (arbitrarily negative values in an unbounded Min model). This typically implies that one or more important constraints have been omitted in formulating the model. An infeasible model is one in which there are no feasible solutions: That is, the set of decision variable values that satisfy all the constraints is empty. Such a result may occur because of incorrect formulation, such as insisting that two or more contradictory conditions must hold. Unbounded and infeasible models can also occur as a result of transcription errors made when entering the model into GLP, or in general, into the spreadsheet LP model.

This chapter also used graphical analysis to introduce the topic of sensitivity analysis, which is also called postoptimality analysis. The general approach in sensitivity analysis is to assume that an LP model has been solved and then to investigate the effect of making various changes in the model. Typically, one is interested in the effect of the changes on the optimal solution and on the optimal value of the objective function.

In Section 4.10 we saw that changing the objective function coefficients changes the slope of the objective function contours. This may or may not affect the optimal solution.

Sections 4.11 and 4.12 dealt with changes in the right-hand side of the constraints. We first observed that changing a right-hand-side value results in a parallel shift of the changed constraint. This may affect both the optimal solution and the optimal objective value. The effect will depend on exactly which right-hand-side values are changed. Changes in the right-hand side of an inequality constraint can be thought of as tightening or loosening the constraint. Tightening a constraint means making it more difficult to satisfy. For a $\geq$ constraint this means increasing the RHS. For a $\leq$ constraint this means decreasing the RHS. Similarly, loosening a constraint means making it easier to satisfy. For a $\geq$ constraint this means decreasing the RHS. For a $\leq$ constraint this means increasing the RHS. From a geometric point of view, tightening an inequality constraint either contracts the constraint set or leaves it unaffected. Loosening an inequality constraint either expands the constraint set or leaves it unaffected. From a practical point of view, these operations can further limit, further augment, or leave unchanged the options available to the manager.

Another way in which a model could be modified after its original formulation and solution is by adding or deleting constraints. The effect of these changes was investigated in Section 4.15. En route to this analysis it was noted that a redundant constraint is one whose removal does not change the feasible region. Also, as discussed in Section 4.14, an inactive constraint can be removed from the model without changing the optimal solution. One might therefore be tempted to remove redundant or inactive constraints from a model before solving it, if it were possible to identify such constraints. In fact, however, redundant constraints are usually not recognizable, and the inactive constraints are revealed only after the model has been solved. Moreover, the concepts of redundant and inactive are data-dependent. If you change the data, the redundant constraints and the inactive constraints may change. It is productive to think of the model as being the "logical framework or structure" that describes the operation of the system under consideration, independently of the numerical values assigned to the parameters. Since constraints that are redundant or inactive for one set of parameter values may not remain in that status when the parameter values are changed, the notion of searching for redundant or inactive constraints seems as inappropriate as it is difficult. Deleting constraints leaves the feasible region either unchanged or enlarged, whereas adding constraints leaves the feasible region either unchanged or smaller, and hence the effects of deleting and adding are analogous to the effects of loosening and tightening.

Key Terms

Contour. A contour of the function $f(x_1, x_2)$ is the set of all combinations of values for the variables (x_1, x_2) such that the function f takes on a specified constant value.

Isoquant. A synonym for *contour.*

Isoprofit Line. A contour of a profit function.

Isocost Line. A contour of a cost function.

Graphical Solution Method. A two-dimensional geometric analysis of LP models with two decision variables.

Nonnegative Quadrant. The northeast sector of the two-dimensional coordinate system in which both variables have nonnegative values.

Feasible Region. The set of combinations of values for the decision variables that satisfies the nonnegativity conditions and *all* the constraints simultaneously, that is, the allowable decisions.

Constraint Set. A synonym for *feasible region.*

Feasible Solution. One that satisfies the nonnegativity conditions and all the constraints. Graphically, the feasible solutions are in one-to-one correspondence with the points in the feasible region.

Optimizing Direction. The direction in which decisions with better objective function values lie.

Uphill Direction. The optimizing direction for a Max model.

Optimal Solution. A point in the feasible region that maximizes the objective function.

Unique Optimal Solution. Refers to the case in which an LP has one and only one optimal solution.

Maximum Profit Line. The optimal contour of the objective function in a two-dimensional graphical analysis.

Optimal Objective Value (Optimal Value). The optimal value of the objective function: that is, the value of the objective function when evaluated at the optimal solution. Abbreviated as OV.

Active Constraint. A constraint for which, when evaluated at optimality, the left-hand side equals the right-hand side. Geometrically, this corresponds to a constraint line on which the optimal solution lies.

Binding Constraint. A synonym for *active constraint.*

Inactive Constraint. An inequality constraint that does not pass through the optimal solution. Hence, for a given set of data, the removal of an inactive constraint will not change the optimal solution.

Surplus. The amount by which the left-hand side of a $\geq$ constraint, when evaluated at optimality, exceeds the right-hand side. Surplus is always nonnegative.

Slack. The amount by which the left-hand side of a $\leq$ constraint, when evaluated at optimality, is less than the right-hand side. Slack is always nonnegative.

Extreme Point. Corner of the feasible region. If an LP has a solution, there is always at least one extreme point solution.

Alternative Optima. Refers to the case in which an LP has more than one optimal solution.

Multiple Optima. A synonym for *alternative optima.*

Downhill Direction. The optimizing direction for a Min model.

Unbounded Objective Function. An objective function that, over the feasible region, can be made arbitrarily large (positive) for a Max model, or arbitrarily negative for a Min model.

Unbounded Model. An LP model for which the optimal value can be increased without limit. Such a model has no solution.

Unbounded Constraint Set. Constraint set in which at least one decision variable can be made arbitrarily large in value.

Infeasibility. A term referring to an infeasible model.

Inconsistency. A synonym for *infeasibility.*

Infeasible Model. An LP model with an empty feasible region. Such a model has no solution.

Sensitivity Analysis. Analyzing the effect on the model, in particular the effect on the optimal solution and the optimal value of the objective function, of changes in various parameters.

Postoptimality Analysis. A synonym for *sensitivity analysis.*

Parameters. Refers to the numerical data in an LP model. The values of the parameters may change, and the model may be re-solved with these changed values.

Parametric Analysis. A synonym for *sensitivity analysis.*

Tightening a Constraint. Refers to changes in the RHS of an inequality constraint that make the constraint more difficult to satisfy. This is accomplished by increasing the RHS of a $\geq$ constraint and decreasing the RHS of a $\leq$ constraint.

Loosening a Constraint. Refers to changes in the RHS of an inequality constraint that make the constraint easier to satisfy. This is accomplished by decreasing the RHS of a $\geq$ constraint and increasing the RHS of a $\leq$ constraint.

Redundant Constraint. A constraint whose removal does not change the feasible region.

Self-Review Exercises

True-False

1. **T F** The feasible region is the set of all points that satisfies at least one constraint.

2. **T F** In two-dimensional models, the intersection of any two constraints gives an extreme point of the feasible region.

3. **T F** An optimal solution uses up all of the limited resources available.

4. **T F** A well-formulated model will be neither unbounded nor infeasible.

5. **T F** Infeasibility, as opposed to unboundedness, has nothing to do with the objective function.

6. **T F** If an LP is not infeasible, it will have an optimal solution.

7. **T F** Consider any point on the boundary of the feasible region. Such a point satisfies all the constraints.

8. **T F** An active inequality constraint has zero slack or surplus, which means that the optimal solution satisfies the constraint with equality.

9. **T F** Sensitivity analysis greatly increases the possibility that a model can be useful to management.

10. **T F** Consider a model in which, for some of the data, we know there is an error. For example, some of the data represent estimates of future values for certain parameters. Suppose sensitivity analysis reveals that the OV is highly sensitive to these parameters. Such information provides more confidence in the recommendations of the model.

11. **T F** Sensitivity analysis is a precise tool.

12. **T F** Changing the RHS of a constraint changes its slope.

13. **T   F** Changing an RHS cannot affect the set of inactive constraints.

14. **T   F** Loosening an inequality constraint means changing the RHS to make it easier to satisfy.

15. **T   F** A ≥ constraint is tightened by increasing the RHS.

16. **T   F** Tightening a redundant inequality constraint cannot affect the feasible region.

17. **T   F** For a given set of data, the inactive constraints are less important than the active ones.

18. **T   F** Adding constraints to a model may help (i.e., improve) the OV.

Multiple Choice

19. The graphical method is useful because
    a. it provides a general way to solve LP models
    b. it gives geometric insight into the model and the meaning of optimality
    c. both a and b

20. The phrase *unbounded LP* means that
    a. all decision variables can be made arbitrarily large without leaving the feasible region
    b. the objective contours can be moved as far as desired in the optimizing direction and still touch at least one point in the constraint set
    c. not all of the constraints can be satisfied

21. Consider an optimal solution to an LP. Which of the following must be true?
    a. At least one constraint (not including nonnegativity conditions) is active at the point.
    b. Exactly one constraint (not including nonnegativity conditions) is active at the point.
    c. Neither of the above.

22. Active constraints
    a. are those on which the optimal solution lies
    b. are those which, at optimality, do not use up all the available resources
    c. both a and b

23. An isoprofit contour represents
    a. an infinite number of feasible points, all of which yield the same profit
    b. an infinite number of optimal solutions
    c. an infinite number of decisions, all of which yield the same profit

24. Which of the following assertions is true of an optimal solution to an LP?
    a. Every LP has an optimal solution.
    b. The optimal solution always occurs at an extreme point.
    c. The optimal solution uses up all resources.
    d. If an optimal solution exists, there will always be at least one at a corner.
    e. All of the above.

25. Every corner of the feasible region is defined by
    a. the intersection of two constraint lines
    b. some subset of constraint lines and nonnegativity conditions
    c. neither of the above

26. An unbounded feasible region
    a. arises from an incorrect formulation

    b. means the objective function is unbounded
    c. neither of the above
    d. both a and b

27. Sensitivity analysis
    a. allows us to more meaningfully interpret the spreadsheet solution
    b. is done after the optimal solution is obtained, and is therefore called postoptimality analysis
    c. is sometimes called parametric analysis
    d. all of the above

28. Sensitivity analysis
    a. can be done graphically in two dimensions
    b. can increase our confidence in a model
    c. can weaken our confidence in the recommendations of a model
    d. all of the above
    e. both a and b

29. The value of the geometric approach, in two dimensions, is
    a. to solve the model quickly
    b. to understand what is happening in higher dimensions
    c. to better understand two-dimensional algebra

30. In LP, sensitivity analysis
    a. can deal with changes in the objective function coefficients
    b. can deal with changes in RHS
    c. both of the above

31. Changing an objective function coefficient
    a. produces a new optimal solution
    b. changes the tilt of the objective function contours
    c. gives a new OV
    d. all of the above

32. Tightening an inequality constraint
    a. improves the OV
    b. cannot improve the OV
    c. hurts the OV

33. A redundant constraint
    a. may not be easy to recognize
    b. should always be dropped from the model
    c. may not be redundant if the data are changed
    d. all of the above
    e. both a and c
    f. both a and b
    g. both b and c

Answers

1.	F	10.	F	18.	F	26.	c
2.	F	11.	T	19.	b	27.	d
3.	F	12.	F	20.	b	28.	d
4.	T	13.	F	21.	c	29.	b
5.	T	14.	T	22.	a	30.	c
6.	F	15.	T	23.	c	31.	b
7.	T	16.	F	24.	d	32.	b
8.	T	17.	T	25.	b	33.	e
9.	T						

Problems

4-1. Plot the set of points (x_1, x_2) that satisfies each of the following conditions:
  (a) $2x_1 + 6x_2 = 12$
  (b) $2x_1 + 6x_2 > 12$
  (c) $2x_1 + 6x_2 \geq 12$
  (d) $2x_1 + 6x_2 < 12$
  (e) $2x_1 + 6x_2 \leq 12$

4-2. Plot the set of points (x_1, x_2) that satisfies each of the following conditions:
  (a) $4x_1 + 3x_2 = 12$
  (b) $4x_1 + 3x_2 > 12$
  (c) $4x_1 + 3x_2 \geq 12$
  (d) $4x_1 + 3x_2 < 12$
  (e) $4x_1 + 3x_2 \leq 12$

4-3. **(a)** Plot the set of points that satisfies $-2x_1 - 6x_2 > -12$.
  (b) Is this plot above or below the line $-2x_1 - 6x_2 = -12$?
  (c) This plot is the same as which of the sets plotted in Problem 4-1?

4-4. **(a)** Plot the set of points that satisfies $-4x_1 - 3x_2 < -12$.
  (b) Is this plot above or below the line $-4x_1 - 3x_2 = -12$?
  (c) This plot is the same as which of the sets plotted in Problem 4-2?

4-5. Claire Archer, a colorful dealer in stereo equipment, puts together amps and preamps. An amp takes 12 hours to assemble and 4 hours for a high-performance check. A preamp takes 4 hours to assemble and 8 hours for a high-performance check. In the next month Claire will have 60 hours of assembly time available and 40 hours of high-performance check time available. Use GLP to plot the combinations of amps and preamps that will satisfy:
  (a) The constraint on assembly time.
  (b) The constraint on performance check time.
  (c) Both constraints simultaneously.

4-6. One can of grade A dog food contains 12 mg of protein and 4 mg of fat, while one can of grade B dog food contains 3 mg of protein and 8 mg of fat. Del Matthews manages a small kennel that boards dogs. To feed his boarders tomorrow he would like to obtain a blend of dog foods that contains at least 30 mg of protein and 24 mg of fat. Use GLP to plot the combination of cans of grade A and grade B that Del can buy to satisfy:
  (a) The constraint on the amount of protein.
  (b) The constraint on the amount of fat.
  (c) Both constraints simultaneously.

4-7. In Problem 4-5, suppose that Claire makes a profit of $10 on each amp and $5 on each preamp. Plot the $10, $20, and $60 profit contours.

4-8. In Problem 4-6, assume that one can of grade A food costs $0.80 and one can of grade B food costs $0.60. Plot the combinations of the two grades that Del can buy for
  (a) $4.80
  (b) $2.40

4-9. Consider Claire's activity as described in Problems 4-5 and 4-7. Suppose that because of limitations on transistor availability she has determined that there are two additional constraints in her model. Namely, she can produce a maximum of 4 preamps and 6 amps in the next month. Taking all constraints into account,

    (a) Find Claire's optimal (profit-maximizing) production plan using GLP's graphical analysis.

    (b) What is the OV?

    (c) Which constraints are active?

    (d) Which constraints are inactive and what are their slack values?

4-10. Assuming the costs presented in Problem 4-8, use GLP to find how many cans of each grade of dog food Del should buy to satisfy the requirements from Problem 4-6 at minimum total cost.

••4-11. Could the omission of any two constraints make Claire's model (Problem 4-9) unbounded?

4-12. Suppose that when Del arrives at the store there is only one can of grade A dog food available and that he cannot buy the dog food anywhere else. Does this change the minimum cost solution you found in Problem 4-10? If so, how?

4-13. Suppose that Claire's constraint on amps, $A \le 6$, is replaced by $A \ge 6$. How does this affect the model?

4-14. If Del must buy at least three cans of grade B dog food, does this affect the minimum cost solution you found in Problem 4-10? If so, how? (*Note:* For the purposes of this problem it is assumed that Del can buy fractional cans of dog food.)

4-15. Consider the following LP:

$$\text{Max } x_1 + x_2$$
$$\text{s.t. } x_1 + 2x_2 \le 6$$
$$3x_1 + 2x_2 \le 12$$
$$x_1, x_2 \ge 0$$

    (a) Use the GLP to find the optimal solution and the OV.

    (b) Change the objective function to $2x_1 + 6x_2$ and find the optimal solution.

    (c) How many extreme points does the feasible region have? Find the values of (x_1, x_2) at each extreme point.

4-16. Consider the following LP:

$$\text{Max } 2x_1 + 3x_2$$
$$\text{s.t. } 3x_1 + x_2 \ge 6$$
$$x_1 + 7x_2 \ge 7$$
$$x_1 + x_2 \le 4$$
$$x_1, x_2 \ge 0$$

    (a) Use GLP to find the optimal solution and the OV.

    (b) Change the objective function to $3x_1 + 2x_2$ and find the optimal solution.

    (c) How many extreme points does the feasible region have? Find (x_1, x_2) at each extreme point.

4-17. Consider the following LP:

$$\text{Max } 3x_1 + 4x_2$$
$$\text{s.t. } -2x_1 + 4x_2 \le 16$$
$$2x_1 + 4x_2 \le 24$$
$$-6x_1 - 3x_2 \ge -48$$
$$x_1, x_2 \ge 0$$

    (a) Use GLP to find the optimal solution and the OV.

    (b) Find the slack and surplus values for each constraint.

4-18. Consider the following LP:

$$\text{Max } 6x_1 + 2x_2$$
$$\text{s.t. } 2x_1 + 4x_2 \le 20$$

$$3x_1 + 5x_2 \geq 15$$
$$x_1 \geq 3$$
$$x_2 \geq 0$$

(a) Use GLP to find the optimal solution and the OV.
(b) Find the slack and surplus values for each constraint.

•• **4-19.** Consider the following LP:

$$\text{Min } 5x_1 + 2x_2$$
$$\text{s.t. } 3x_1 + 6x_2 \geq 18$$
$$5x_1 + 4x_2 \geq 20$$
$$8x_1 + 2x_2 \geq 16$$
$$7x_1 + 6x_2 \leq 42$$
$$x_1, x_2 \geq 0$$

(a) Use GLP to find the optimal solution and the OV.
(b) Which constraints are active? Which are inactive?
(c) What are the slack and surplus values associated with each constraint?
(d) How many extreme points does the feasible region have?
(e) Change the objective function to $15x_1 + 12x_2$. What are the alternative optimal corner solutions?

4-20. In Problem 4-18 change the objective function to $x_1 + 3x_2$. Answer parts (a) and (b) for the new model.

••• **4-21.** Consider the following LP:

$$\text{Max } 600E + 1000F$$
$$\text{s.t. } 100E + 60F \leq 21{,}000$$
$$4000E + 800F \leq 680{,}000$$
$$E + F \leq 290$$
$$12E + 30F \leq 6000$$
$$E, F \geq 0$$

(a) Let E be the horizontal axis and F the vertical axis, and use GLP to find the optimal solution to this model and the OV.
(b) One of the constraints is redundant in the sense that it plays no role in determining the constraint set. Which one is it?
(c) What is the minimum change in the RHS of this constraint that would cause the constraint to become active?
(d) The coefficient of E in the third constraint is currently 1. What is the minimum increase in this coefficient that would cause the constraint to become active?
(e) Suppose that the coefficient of E, say C_E, in the objective function is increased, whereas the coefficient of F, say C_F, remains fixed. At what value for the coefficient of E would alternative optima first become encountered?

••• **4-22.** Consider the following model:

$$\text{Max } 3x_1 + x_2$$
$$\text{s.t. } 6x_1 + 3x_2 \geq 12$$
$$4x_1 + 8x_2 \geq 16$$
$$6x_1 + 5x_2 \leq 30$$
$$6x_1 + 7x_2 \leq 36$$
$$x_1, x_2 \geq 0$$

(a) Use GLP to find the optimal solution and the OV.
(b) Consider a Min model with the constraint set above. Assume that the objective function is $x_1 + Bx_2$. What is the largest value of B so that the optimal solution lies at the intersection of the lines $6x_1 + 3x_2 = 12$ and $4x_1 + 8x_2 = 16$? Find the optimal solution and the OV.

(c) In a Max model, assume that the objective function is $Ax_1 + Bx_2$. Determine the set of values for A and B for which the optimal solution lies at the intersection of $6x_1 + 5x_2 = 30$ and $6x_1 + 7x_2 = 36$. Use a graph to show the set of values.

4-23. In the PROTRAC model, suppose that the objective function is changed to $5000E + 2000F$.
   (a) Use GLP to determine the effect on the optimal solution.
   (b) What is the effect on the OV?

4-24. In the PROTRAC model, suppose that the objective function is changed to $2500E + 5000F$.
   (a) Use GLP to determine the effect on the optimal solution.
   (b) What is the effect on the OV?

4-25. Notice in Figure 4.20 the two objective functions

$$5000E + 4000F$$

$$5000E + 10{,}000F$$

The figure indicates that when the per unit contribution margin of F is increased from 4000 to 10,000, without changing the per unit contribution margin of E, the optimal value of E decreases. Why should the optimal value of E depend on the coefficient of F? Try to answer this question in words.

4-26. In the PROTRAC model, suppose that the objective function is changed to $1000E + 1500F$.
   (a) Use GLP to decide whether there will be a new optimal solution.
   (b) What is the effect on the OV?

4-27. In the PROTRAC GLP model, replace the RHS of the fifth constraint (labor hours for testing), which is currently 135, with the value 270. State the effect on the constraint set.

••**4-28.** In the PROTRAC GLP model, how much can you increase the RHS of constraint 2 before it becomes redundant? How small can the RHS be made without destroying feasibility?

••**4-29.** Consider the LP

$$\text{Max } 30x_1 + 10x_2$$
$$\text{s.t.} \quad 2x_1 + x_2 \quad \leq 4$$
$$2x_1 + 2x_2 \quad \leq 6$$
$$x_1, x_2 \quad \geq 0$$

   (a) Solve with GLP and state the optimal solution.
   (b) Keeping all other data as is, what per unit contribution margin should the product, whose current optimal value is zero, have in order that this product enter the optimal solution at a positive level?
   (c) How many optimal corner solutions exist after making the change described in part (b)? What are they?
   (d) In the original model, how much can the RHS of the second constraint be increased (decreased) before the optimal solution is changed?
   (e) Answer part (d) for the RHS of the first constraint.
   (f) How do you explain the difference between parts (d) and (e)?
   (g) What will be the impact of adding the constraint $4x_1 + x_2 = 4$ to the original model?
   (h) What is the impact (on the optimal solution) of adding the constraint $3x_1 + 3x_2 \leq 15$ to the original model?
   (i) Fill in the blanks: The difference between parts (g) and (h) is that the original optimal solution already _____ the constraint in (h) but does not _____ the constraint in (g).

••**4-30.** Consider the LP

$$\text{Max } 2x_1 + x_2$$
$$\text{s.t.} \quad 3x_1 + 3x_2 \quad \leq 12$$
$$x_1 + 3x_2 \quad \leq 6$$
$$x_1, x_2 \quad \geq 0$$

In terms of this model, answer parts (a–g) in Problem 4-29.
   (h) What will be the impact of adding the constraint $x_1 + x_2 \leq 1$ to the original model?

4-31. Of the two constraints

$$-3x_1 + 2x_2 \geq -6$$
$$-3x_1 + 2x_2 \geq -10$$

(a) Which is tighter?
(b) Which of the constraints, if either, does the point $(x_1 = 2, x_2 = 1)$ satisfy?
(c) What about the point $(x_1 = 3, x_2 = 0)$?

4-32. Of the two constraints

$$4x_1 - 3x_2 \le 12$$
$$4x_1 - 3x_2 \le -12$$

(a) Which is tighter?
(b) Which of the constraints, if either, does the point $(x_1 = -2, x_2 = 3)$ satisfy?
(c) What about the point $(x_1 = 2, x_2 = 3)$?

4-33. Which of the two constraints in Problem 4-31 is looser?
4-34. Which of the two constraints in Problem 4-32 is looser?
4-35. Fill in the blanks: Increasing the RHS of a $\le$ constraint means that there will be _____ combinations of decision-variable values that satisfy the constraint. This means that one is _____ the constraint.
4-36. Fill in the blanks: Increasing the RHS of a $\ge$ constraint means that there will be _____ combinations of decision-variable values that satisfy the constraint. This means that one is _____ the constraint.
4-37. Choosing from the words *enlarge, diminish, smaller, larger, unchanged,* fill in the blanks: Tightening a constraint cannot _____ the constraint set and may leave it _____ or _____.
4-38. Choosing from the words supplied in Problem 4-37, fill in the blanks: Loosening a constraint cannot _____ the constraint set and may leave it _____ or _____.
••4-39. In the PROTRAC GLP model, which constraint is redundant? Will this constraint remain redundant if its RHS value is increased by 10%, all other data held fixed?
••4-40. In the PROTRAC GLP model, for what values of the RHS will constraint 5 become redundant, assuming all other data are held fixed?
••4-41. Suppose that you have created a model and that by some means you are able to identify a redundant constraint. Would you say it is generally true that such a constraint should be dropped from the model? Why (or why not)?
••4-42. How would your answer to Problem 4-41 differ if the model were to be run one and only one time?
•••4-43. Suppose you know that in a given run of a model a particular constraint will be redundant. Does it follow that this constraint will also be inactive?
4-44. Discuss briefly the notion of "important" versus "unimportant" constraints.
4-45. Match up the phrases in the two columns. (*Note:* Some phrases may have more than one match.)
(a) Adding constraints   1. May enlarge the feasible region
(b) Deleting constraints   2. May make the feasible region smaller
(c) Important constraints   3. Depend on the data set
(d) Tightening constraints   4. May improve the OV
(e) Loosening constraints   5. May hurt the OV

Case Study   The Simplex Method

Today we take for granted the ability to solve linear programming models. You have seen how quickly an LP model can be entered into a spreadsheet, and with a few clicks of the mouse, how to optimize the model by using Solver. But it hasn't always been this way.

In 1982 George Stigler won the Nobel Prize in economics for his "seminal studies of industrial structures, functioning of markets, and causes and effects of public regulation." You may be surprised to learn that earlier in his career he was working on what we now call the diet problem. He had set out to find the least expensive diet that would satisfy the nine nutritional requirements determined by the National Research Council in 1943. Stigler had 77 foods, ranging from wheat flour to strawberry jam, to choose from. His formulation of the model was the same as the one we saw for the Gruel example in Chapter 3.

In a 1945 paper reporting his results, titled "The Cost of Subsistence," Stigler wrote that "there does not appear to be any direct method of finding the minimum of a linear function subject to linear conditions." George Dantzig changed all that when he developed the simplex method in the late 1940s.

Chapter 4   171
Linear Programming:
Graphical Analysis

Without the simplex method to help him, Stigler "solved" his diet model by a combination of clever insights and brute force. At the time, he could not prove that he had a good—to say nothing of optimal—solution. Later, when the problem was solved with the simplex algorithm, it turned out that his methods had produced a solution that was very close to (though not quite) optimal.

The cost-minimizing diet suggested in Stigler's paper and its annual cost (based on 1939 prices) are shown below. (Obviously, there was not a constraint for taste in this model.)

COMMODITY	QUANTITY	ANNUAL COST ($)
Wheat Flour	370 lbs	13.33
Evaporated Milk	57 cans	3.84
Cabbage	111 lbs	4.11
Spinach	23 lbs	1.85
Dried Navy Beans	285 lbs	16.80
Total Annual Cost		$39.93

It is interesting to think that in approximately 50 years the diet model has gone from a puzzle that challenged one of the finest economic scholars of all time to a simple exercise for beginning students.

Questions

The simplex method is essentially a hill-climbing method. Once it has found a corner solution, it looks at all of its immediate neighboring corners and asks, "If I move to one of these corners, will the value of the objective function be improved?" If the answer is yes, the algorithm moves to one such corner and then again asks whether or not a move to a neighbor will improve things further. If the answer is no, the algorithm proclaims victory and quits.

1. Consider Figure 4.21 and assume that the simplex algorithm started at the corner created by the intersection of constraints 2 and 5. Show how a hill-climbing algorithm is guaranteed to arrive at the optimal solution.
2. On paper, create a diagram like Figure 4.21 with a different feasible region for which a hill-climbing algorithm is *not* guaranteed to yield an optimal or even a good solution. Can a feasible region like the one you have created occur in a linear programming model; that is, could you create such a region in GLP?
3. On paper, create a diagram like Figure 4.21 to show a situation in which a hill-climbing algorithm might take many or just a few steps in its route to find an optimal solution.
4. Consider a new diagram for a general (i.e., nonlinear) model with only one decision variable. With the value of the decision variable on the *x* axis and the value of the objective function on the *y* axis, use such a diagram to illustrate the fact that in general a hill-climbing algorithm as described above will not always lead to an optimal solution.

References

George Dantzig, "The Diet Problem," *Interfaces*, 20, no. 4 (1990), 43–47.

Lilly Lancaster, "The Evolution of the Diet Model in Managing Food Systems," *Interfaces*, 22, no. 5 (1992), 59–68.

Robert J. Might, "Decision Support for Aircraft and Munitions Procurement," *Interfaces*, 17, no. 5 (1987), 55–63.

LP Models: Interpreting Solver Sensitivity Report

CHAPTER OUTLINE

5.1 Introduction

5.2 Equality Constraint Form

5.3 Sensitivity Analysis of the PROTRAC LP Model

5.4 The Crawler Tread Output: A Dialogue with Management (Sensitivity Analysis in Action)

5.5 A Synopsis of the Solution Output

5.6 Sensitivity Report Interpretation for Alternative Spreadsheet Models

5.7 Summary

KEY TERMS

SELF-REVIEW EXERCISES

PROBLEMS

CASE STUDY: Questions Based on the Red Brand Canners Case

CASE STUDY: Crawler Tread and a New Angle

CASE STUDY: Saw Mill River Feed and Grain Company

CASE STUDY: Kiwi Computer

REFERENCES

APPLICATION CAPSULE　　**Product Planning at a Chinese Chemical Plant**

The Dalian Dyestuff Plant, one of the largest chemical dye plants in China, includes 11 workshops that produce about 100 different kinds of dyes and other chemical products. The products are sold in both domestic and foreign markets. Some products are end products while others are semifinished. For example, soda is one product that is made by an electrolytic reaction technology that generates chlorine as a by-product. To prevent air pollution, chlorine should either be disposed of properly or used as a raw material in producing other products.

With economic reform taking place in China, the government, which used to control 100% of the products that Dalian could produce, now controls only about 20% of the products

made. This change means that the plant managers now have to decide which products and how much of each to produce. This is particularly challenging because the economy is growing and changing so rapidly.

An LP-based optimization model was implemented at the Dalian Dyestuff Plant. The objective is to maximize the company's profit over a one-year period. The system contains subsystems for production planning, accounting and finances, inventory, and information services. Operational results indicate that the system increased annual profits by at least 4 million RMB (about .5 million US$), or an increase in profits of 10%. (See Yang.)

5.1   INTRODUCTION

In Chapter 4 we stated that you should be interested in much more than simply the solution to an LP model. We stated that the process of analyzing an optimization model for different parameter values is termed *sensitivity analysis,* and we then dealt with some of the geometry that underlies LP sensitivity analysis. In this chapter we look in detail at how, in practice, you can use the wealth of information contained in Solver analysis of an LP model. This can be an important, even daily, problem faced by managers in the real world—the problem of making good use of spreadsheet analysis. This discussion culminates in Section 5.4, in a realistic scenario involving a manager and the modeler.

5.2   EQUALITY CONSTRAINT FORM

In optimizing linear programs, Solver uses the simplex method, which is designed to attack models with only equality constraints. To convert an LP model with inequality constraints to one with equality constraints, Solver internally adds new variables, called slack and surplus variables, to its representation of the LP model. As an illustration, recall the PRO-TRAC LP model

$$\text{Max } 5000E + 4000F$$

$$
\begin{aligned}
\text{s.t.} \quad & E + F & \geq 5 \\
& E - 3F & \leq 0 \\
& 10E + 15F & \leq 150 \\
& 20E + 10F & \leq 160 \\
& 30E + 10F & \geq 135 \\
& E, F & \geq 0
\end{aligned}
$$

(5.1)

This LP model has two decision variables and five constraints, two of them $\geq$ and (ignoring the nonnegativity constraints) three of them $\leq$. To convert this model into an equivalent model in *equality constraint form,* Solver will add slack variables to the second, third, and fourth constraints (the $\leq$ constraints) and subtract surplus variables from the first and fifth constraints (the $\geq$ constraints). Letting $s_1, s_2, s_3, s_4,$ and s_5 denote the five new variables, we obtain the model actually optimized by Solver.

$$\text{Max } 5000E + 4000F$$

$$
\begin{aligned}
\text{s.t.} \quad & E + F - s_1 & = 5 \\
& E - 3F + s_2 & = 0 \\
& 10E + 15F + s_3 & = 150 \\
& 20E + 10F + s_4 & = 160 \\
& 30E + 10F - s_5 & = 135 \\
& E, F, s_1, s_2, s_3, s_4, s_5 & \geq 0
\end{aligned}
$$

(5.2)

Note that the added nonnegativity constraints on the new variables forces them to be zero or positive. Thus, the slack/surplus variables represent the extra amount that must be added/subtracted from the left-hand side to turn the inequalities into equalities.

The foregoing discussion demonstrates two important points:

- Any $\leq$ constraint can be converted to an equality by adding a new nonnegative slack variable to the left-hand side.
- Any $\geq$ constraint can be converted to an equality by subtracting a new nonnegative surplus variable from the left-hand side.

This internal form of the model still has five constraints, but the addition of slack and surplus has increased the number of decision variables used by Solver internally to seven instead of two. Notice that slack and surplus variables do not explicitly appear in Solver's objective function. However, since

$$5000E + 4000F = 5000E + 4000F + 0s_1 + 0s_2 + 0s_3 + 0s_4 + 0s_5$$

it is acceptable to think of the surplus and slack variables as being included in the objective function, but with zero coefficients.

OPTIMAL VALUES OF SLACK AND SURPLUS VARIABLES

In Chapter 4 we used the graphical solution method to show that $E^* = 4.5$ and $F^* = 7$ is the solution to the PROTRAC LP model (5.1). This means that the optimal values of the other variables (the slacks and surpluses) in the equality constraint model (5.2) are given by

$$s^*_1 = (E^* + F^*) - 5 = 11.5 - 5 = 6.5$$
$$s^*_2 = 0 - (E^* - 3F^*) = 0 - (4.5 - 21) = 16.5$$
$$s^*_3 = 150 - (10E^* + 15F^*) = 150 - (45 + 105) = 0$$
$$s^*_4 = 160 - (20E^* + 10F^*) = 160 - (90 + 70) = 0$$
$$s^*_5 = (30E^* + 10F^*) - 135 = (135 + 70) - 135 = 70$$

It would be useful at this point for you to review the material on active and inactive constraints in Chapter 4. We recall from that material: An *active* or *binding* constraint is one for which, *at optimality,* the left-hand side equals the right-hand side. From the geometric point of view, an active constraint is one on which the optimal solution lies. We saw that in the PROTRAC LP model the active constraints are the third and fourth. The calculation above shows that their slack variables (s^*_3 and s^*_4) are zero. On the other hand, the first, second, and fifth constraints are inactive, and their slack/surplus variables are positive. Thus, we can make these generalizations:

- Active constraints are those for which the optimal values of the slack or surplus variables are zero.
- Inactive constraints are those for which the optimal values of the slack or surplus variables are positive.

In particular, when at optimality a constraint has a zero value for the slack or surplus variable,[1] it means, geometrically speaking, that the solution to the model lies on that constraint. A brief look at the geometry of our new model will also reveal a property that is important to correctly interpreting the information contained in Solver's Sensitivity Report. This property has to do with the number of positive variables at any corner (and in particular at an optimal corner) of the constraint set.

We have seen that all variables (decision variables, slack and surplus variables) are required to be nonnegative (positive or zero). We illustrate that at any corner of the constraint set (and in particular at an optimal corner), the maximum number of positive *(greater than zero)* variables, counting decision variables, slacks, and surpluses, is at most equal to the number of constraints in the model (not counting the nonnegativity constraints).

To illustrate this "count" property, consider the model shown in (5.3).

---

[1] In the language of Chapter 4, we simply said that such a constraint has zero slack or surplus, without introducing the concept of a slack or surplus variable.

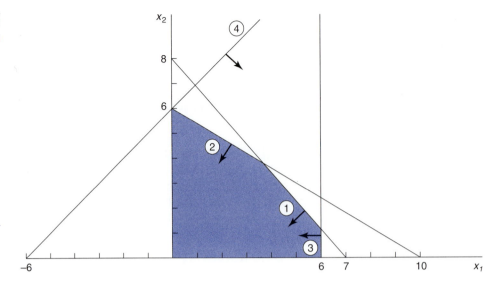

FIGURE 5.1

Constraint Set for the
Inequality Constrained
Model (5.3)

$$\text{Max } x_1 + x_2$$

$$
\begin{aligned}
\text{s.t.} \quad 8x_1 + 7x_2 \quad &\leq 56 && \text{①} \\
-6x_1 - 10x_2 \quad &\geq -60 && \text{②} \\
x_1 \quad &\leq 6 && \text{③} \\
-x_1 + x_2 \quad &\leq 6 && \text{④} \\
x_1, x_2 \quad &\geq 0
\end{aligned}
$$

$$(5.3)$$

The constraint set for this model is plotted in Figure 5.1, where the appropriate constraints are labeled ① through ④.

Now consider the equality constraint form of the same model. It is

$$\text{Max } x_1 + x_2$$

$$
\begin{aligned}
\text{s.t.} \quad 8x_1 + 7x_2 + s_1 \quad &= 56 && \text{①} \\
-6x_1 - 10x_2 - s_2 \quad &= -60 && \text{②} \\
x_1 + s_3 \quad &= 6 && \text{③} \\
-x_1 + x_2 + s_4 \quad &= 6 && \text{④} \\
x_1, x_2, s_1, s_2, s_3, s_4 \quad &\text{all nonnegative}
\end{aligned}
$$

$$(5.4)$$

The original model had four constraints and two variables. The equality constraint form has the same number of constraints, but six variables. It is important to note that, when referring to the number of variables in the equality constraint model, *we count slack and surplus as well as decision variables.* Since (5.4) has two decision variables and four slack/surplus variables, there are six variables in this form of the model. Also, in referring to the number of constraints, *we do not count the nonnegativity conditions.*

Our geometric representation of (5.4) is nearly the same as that of (5.3), the only difference being that each constraint will be labeled with its slack or surplus variable. This is shown in Figure 5.2, where for convenience we have labeled the five corners (with Roman numerals) and also identified several points that will be of interest.

Labeling the constraints with the slack and surplus variables allows you to make the following "visual" observations:

1. At any point interior to the feasible region, all variables are positive. This is illustrated by point P_0 in Figure 5.2. At this point you can directly read $x_1 = 1$ and $x_2 = 1$. Using the values and the constraints in (5.4) you could explicitly calculate the values for s_1, s_2, s_3, and

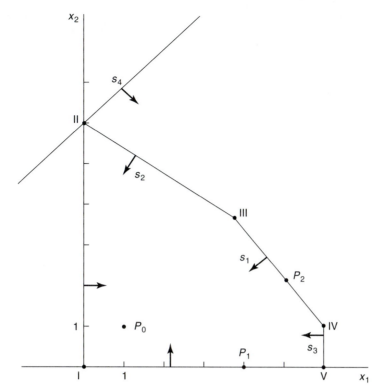

FIGURE 5.2

Constraint Set for Equality
Constraint Form of the LP
Model (5.4)

s_4 at P_0 and you would see that these values are also positive. However, you need not perform this algebra, for the figure immediately shows us that all slacks and surpluses are positive at P_0.

2. At any point on the boundary, at least one variable will be zero. This is illustrated at points P_1 and P_2. At P_1 you can see that $x_2 = 0$; all other variables are positive. Similarly, at P_2, which lies on the first constraint line, only s_1 is zero. Special boundary points of interest are the corners of the feasible region. For example, since the corner labeled III lies on the first and second constraint lines, the two variables s_1 and s_2 are zero at this corner, with all other variables positive. These examples show that the zero variables on the boundary could be decision variables as well as slack or surplus variables. Corner V, for example, shows that a decision variable (x_2) and a slack variable (s_3) can both be zero on the boundary.

POSITIVE VARIABLES AND CORNER SOLUTIONS

On the basis of such observations, we can now illustrate the main result of this section by counting the positive variables at each of the five corners of the constraint set. The result is shown in Table 5.1.

What this table shows, quite simply, is *which* variables are positive at each corner, and, in addition, *how many* variables are positive at each corner. Remember that there are four constraints in the model (5.4). The table thus illustrates an important general fact:

> For any LP model in equality constraint form, the number of positive variables at any corner is less than or equal to the number of constraints.

This result has an important implication for Solver's solution of an LP. You may recall from Chapter 4 that in an LP model, if there is an optimal solution, there is always an optimal corner solution (there may be noncorner optima as well). The simplex method used by

TABLE 5.1	Counting Positive Variables at Corners		
CORNER	**ZERO VARIABLES**	**POSITIVE VARIABLES**	**POSITIVE COUNT**
I	x_1, x_2	s_1, s_2, s_3, s_4	4
II	x_1, s_2, s_4	x_2, s_1, s_3	3
III	s_1, s_2	x_1, x_2, s_3, s_4	4
IV	s_1, s_3	x_1, x_2, s_2, s_4	4
V	x_2, s_3	x_1, s_1, s_2, s_4	4

Solver always produces an optimal corner (assuming, of course, that the model is neither infeasible nor unbounded). Moreover, the simplex method solves a model in equality constraint form and, for such a model, in accord with the conclusion displayed above: The number of positive variables at *any* corner (hence at an optimal corner) is less than or equal to the number of constraints. Thus, we can now see one reason why the above count property is of interest:

> The Solver solution to an LP model always has at most m positive variables, where m is the number of constraints.

We have a practical need for this last conclusion for the following reason:

> When the Solver solution has less than m positive variables, the solution is called *degenerate,* and in this case special care must be taken in interpreting Solver's Sensitivity Report.

DEGENERACY AND NONDEGENERACY

Since the ramifications of degeneracy are noteworthy, let us briefly pause to define the concept formally. A corner such as II in Figure 5.2, where the number of positive variables is *less than* the number of constraints, is termed a degenerate corner.[2] The remaining corners, I, III, IV, and V, where the number of positive variables is exactly equal to the number of constraints, are termed nondegenerate corners. If the optimal solution to an LP has less than m positive variables, it is termed a **degenerate solution** since it occurs at a degenerate corner. Analogously, a solution with exactly m positive variables is called a **nondegenerate solution.**

We have now become acquainted with the LP model that Solver optimizes, namely the equality constraint model. We have seen an important property of this model, namely that any optimal solution produced by Solver will have at most m positive variables (exactly m meaning nondegenerate), where m is the number of constraints in the model; and we have learned that the correct interpretation of Solver's Sensitivity Report will require the awareness of whether or not the optimal solution is nondegenerate. Let us now look at Solver's Sensitivity Report.

---

[2]The origin of the phrase *degenerate corner* arises from technicalities of the simplex method. Its occurrence does not imply anything unusual or bad about the model itself. On the other hand, the emotive connotation provides a useful way to remember degeneracy's meaning: At a corner, degeneracy is what happens when too many constraints lie on top of one another!

5.3   SENSITIVITY ANALYSIS OF THE PROTRAC LP MODEL

In this section we further analyze the PROTRAC LP model. For ease of reference let us reproduce the model here together with the graphical analysis displayed originally in Figure 4.11.

$$
\begin{array}{lllll}
\text{Max} & 5000E + 4000F & & & \text{(max profit contribution)} \\
\text{s.t.} & E + F & \geq & 5 & \text{(minimum production requirement)} & ① \\
& E - 3F & \leq & 0 & \text{(market position balance)} & ② \\
& 10E + 15F & \leq & 150 & \text{(capacity in department A)} & ③ \quad \textbf{(5.5)} \\
& 20E + 10F & \leq & 160 & \text{(capacity in department B)} & ④ \\
& 30E + 10F & \geq & 135 & \text{(labor hours used in testing)} & ⑤ \\
& E, F & \geq & 0 &
\end{array}
$$

As we have already observed, the optimal solution is $E^* = 4.5$, $F^* = 7$. In Chapter 4 we used the term OV to denote the optimal value of the objective function. Recall, for the LP model (5.5) we have

$$
\begin{aligned}
OV = \text{maximum profit} \quad &= \ 5000E^* + 4000F^* \\
&= \ 5000(4.5) + 4000(7) = 50{,}500
\end{aligned}
$$

as shown in Figure 5.3. We have also seen (see Chapter 4) that the two capacity constraints on labor hours available in departments A and B are active at optimality.

The three remaining constraints are inactive. Also, recall that at optimality the number of positive variables will always be less than or equal to the number of binding or active constraints. If it is less than the number of active constraints, the solution is degenerate.

THE SOLUTION

The Solver optimized PROTRAC LP model from Chapter 3 is given in Figure 5.4 along with Solver's Sensitivity Report for the solution.

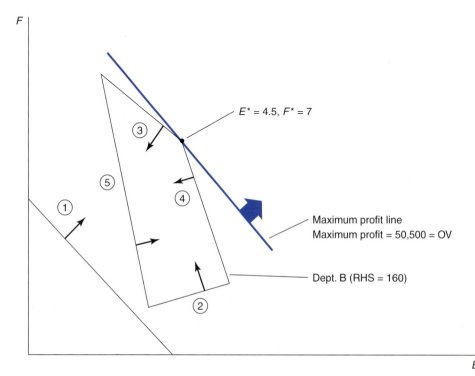

FIGURE 5.3

PROTRAC LP Model Revisited

	A	B	C	D	E	F	G
1		**Protrac Production Plan**					
2	Product:	E-9	F-9				
3	Production Qty.	4.5	7	Profit			
4	Unit Contri. Mar.	$5,000	$4,000	$50,500			
5	Constraints	Resource Usage		Total LHS		RHS	Slack
6	Dept. A	10	15	150	≤	150	0
7	Dept B	20	10	160	≤	160	0
8	Mix Requirement	1	-3	-16.5	≤	0	16.5
9	Test Hours	30	10	205	≥	135	70
10	Total Units	1	1	11.5	≥	5	6.5

Microsoft Excel 8.0 Sensitivity Report

Adjustable Cells

Cell	Name	Final Value	Reduced Cost	Objective Coefficient	Allowable Increase	Allowable Decrease
$B$3	Production Qty. E-9	4.5	0	5000	3000	2333.33
$C$3	Production Qty. F-9	7	0	4000	3500	1500

Allowable increase and decrease in profitability of F without changing E* or F*

Constraints

Cell	Name	Final Value	Shadow Price	Constraint R.H. Side	Allowable Increase	Allowable Decrease
$D$6	Dept. A Total LHS	150	150	150	90	47.14
$D$7	Dept B Total LHS	160	175	160	73.33	40
$D$8	Mix Requirement Total LHS	-16.5	0	0	1E+30	16.5
$D$9	Test Hours Total LHS	205	0	135	70	1E+30
$D$10	Total Units Total LHS	11.5	0	5	6.5	1E+30

Reflects valid range for shadow price of 175

Additional profit obtained if an additional hour of labor is available in department B

FIGURE 5.4

The Solver Solution and Sensitivity Report for PROTRAC LP Model

---

TIP: *For each LHS cell in a constraint, Solver scans to the left on the model's worksheet until it encounters a label, if any. Then it scans above the LHS cell on the model's worksheet until it encounters a label, if any. The two labels, if present, are concatenated by Solver to form the label for that constraint in the Sensitivity Report. The same process is done for labeling the decision variable cells in the Sensitivity Report. Wise choice of labels in the model's worksheet can produce a self-documenting set of labels in the Sensitivity Report.*

We make the following observations:

1. The optimal profit contribution is $50,500.

2. The optimal values of the decision variables are $E^* = 4.5$, $F^* = 7$.

3. The "Slack" column gives the values of the slack and/or surplus variables. In the geometric analysis (Figure 5.3), we saw that the constraints on departments A and B are active. All others are inactive. In the model's worksheet, you can see that this shows up as zero slack values in cells G6 and G7 and positive slack or surplus on the remaining three constraints (cells G8:G10).

4. The solution is nondegenerate. In Figure 5.3 only two constraint lines intersect at the optimal corner, and there are two positive values for the decision variables at that intersection. That is the geometric interpretation. In the Solver optimized spreadsheet model, nondegeneracy is revealed by the fact that there are five positive variables (E^*, F^*, and the slacks in cells G8:G10), which equals the number of constraints.

Let us now move on to discuss the analysis in the Solver Sensitivity Report. It is important to note that *sensitivity analysis is based on the proposition that all data except for one number in the model are held fixed,* and we ask for information about the effect upon the optimal solution of changing the one piece of data that is allowed to vary. The information we might be interested in could include (1) the effect on the OV (i.e., the maximum possible profit) and (2) the effect on the optimal policy (i.e., the decision values, E^*, F^*). In Section 5.4 you will see a realistic scenario in which sensitivity analy-

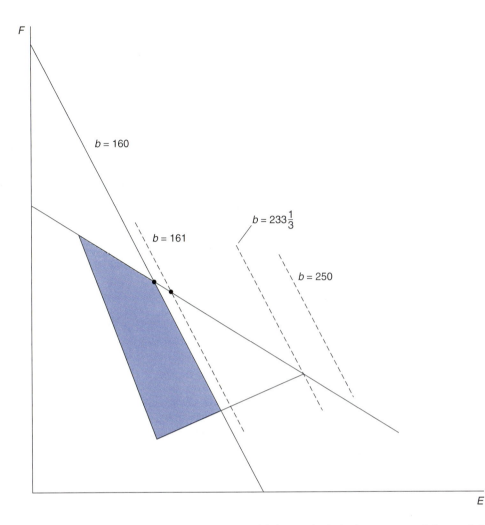

F

b = 160

$b = 233\frac{1}{3}$

b = 161

b = 250

FIGURE 5.5

E   Three New Values for *b*

sis is employed. In mathematical terms, sensitivity analysis is the concept of the partial derivative, where all variables are held constant except for one. This is also known in economics as *marginal analysis.*

RHS SENSITIVITY AND THE SHADOW PRICE

First consider a situation in which we hold all numbers fixed except for the availability of labor hours in department B. What if, instead of having 160 hours available, we were to have 161 hours available? What would be the effect on the OV? Since this constraint on labor-hour availability is the ≤ form, we can say, using the language of Section 4.12, that increasing the RHS amounts to "loosening" the constraint, which means making it easier to satisfy. Hence, you would certainly expect that the change from 160 to 161 will not decrease the OV. Will it, though, improve the OV; and if so, by how much?

First, let us use the tools we have already acquired, namely geometric analysis, to answer our questions. Then we shall relate this analysis to the Solver Sensitivity Report. Let the symbol *b* denote the value of the RHS on the department B constraint. Thus, in Figure 5.3, *b* = 160. In Figure 5.5 we superimpose the department B constraint for the values *b* = 161, *b* = 233⅓, and *b* = 250. We know from the discussion in Section 4.11 that these three new values for *b* correspond, geometrically, to parallel displacements (away from the origin) of the constraint line.

Also since an increase in *b* means that we are loosening this constraint, the geometric interpretation is that the constraint set, if it changes at all, will expand. The new constraint sets, together with the optimal solutions corresponding to the labor-hour availabilities in

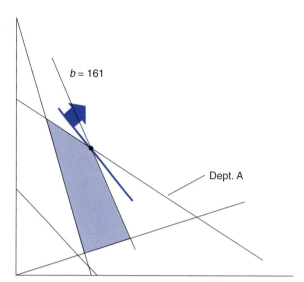

FIGURE 5.6

$b = 161$

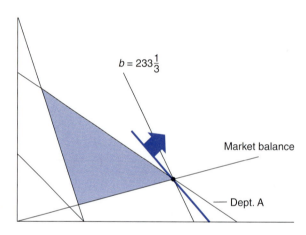

FIGURE 5.7

$b = 233\ 1/3$

department B of 161, 233⅓, and 250, are shown in Figures 5.6, 5.7, and 5.9, respectively. These figures reveal some interesting facts that you can verify directly by altering the PROTRAC model of Chapter 4 with GLP:

$b = 161$ When $b = 161$ (Figure 5.6) the constraints on departments A and B continue to be active. This means that the new solution is given by the two equations:

$$10E + 15F = 150 \quad \text{and} \quad 20E + 10F = 161$$

Solving, we obtain $E^* = 4.575$, $F^* = 6.95$.[3] The new maximum profit becomes

$$OV = 5000E^* + 4000F^* = 5000(4.575) + 4000(6.95) = 50{,}675$$

Notice that

$$\Delta OV = \text{increase in profit} = (\text{profit when } b = 161) - (\text{profit when } b = 160) =$$
$$50{,}675 - 50{,}500 = 175$$

---

[3]Here is an interesting point. You might have intuitively supposed that adding another hour of labor to department B should lead to producing a little more E and a little more F in some appropriate mix, but we see that this is not what happens. Our new solution shows that the optimal policy gives 0.075 more E but 0.05 less F. The geometry (Figure 5.5) shows you why this happens.

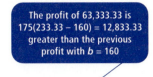

The profit of 63,333.33 is 175(233.33 − 160) = 12,833.33 greater than the previous profit with *b* = 160

	A	B	C	D	E	F	G
1	**Protrac Production Plan**						
2	Product:	E-9	F-9				
3	Production Qty.	10	3.3333	Profit			
4	Unit Contri. Mar.	$5,000	$4,000	$63,333			
5	Constraints	Resource Usage		Total LHS		RHS	Slack
6	Dept. A	10	15	150	≤	150	0
7	Dept B	20	10	233.33333	≤	233.333	0
8	Mix Requirement	1	-3	-7.64E-14	≤	0	8E-14
9	Test Hours	30	10	333.33333	≥	135	198.33
10	Total Units	1	1	13.333333	≥	5	8.3333

New value of *b*

Three active constraints instead of two, hence a degenerate optimal solution

Microsoft Excel 8.0 Sensitivity Report

Adjustable Cells

Cell	Name	Final Value	Reduced Cost	Objective Coefficient	Allowable Increase	Allowable Decrease
$B$3	Production Qty. E-9	10	0	5000	3000	2333.333
$C$3	Production Qty. F-9	3.333	0	4000	3500	1500

Constraints

Cell	Name	Final Value	Shadow Price	Constraint R.H. Side	Allowable Increase	Allowable Decrease
$D$6	Dept. A Total LHS	150	150	150	200	0
$D$7	Dept B Total LHS	233.333	175	233.333	0	113.333
$D$8	Mix Requirement Total LHS	-7.6E-14	0	0	1E+30	0
$D$9	Test Hours Total LHS	333.333	0	135	198.333	1E+30
$D$10	Total Units Total LHS	13.333	0	5	8.333	1E+30

Allowable increase is now zero

Same shadow price as for b = 160

FIGURE 5.8

Solver Solution and Sensitivity Report for $b = 233.333$

This value of 175 is also, as shown in Figure 5.4, the **shadow price** corresponding to the constraint on department B. What we have just illustrated is that on the Sensitivity Report, the shadow price[4] for the department B constraint shows the amount of change in the optimal objective value as the RHS of that constraint is increased a unit, with all other data held fixed.

> In general, the shadow price on a given constraint can be interpreted as the rate of change in OV as the RHS of that constraint increases with all other data held fixed.

***b* = 233 1/3** Figure 5.7 shows that when $b = 233\frac{1}{3}$ the three constraints, department A, department B, and market balance, are all active.

The Solver solution and Sensitivity Report for this revised model are shown in Figure 5.8. Figure 5.8 shows zero slack values on the three active constraints. There are only four positive variables. Since this model has five constraints and since the optimal

TIP: *The Sensitivity Report is just a worksheet with its grid-lines turned off. You can alter the formatting of its contents for improved appearance. Important: The decimal formatting for each shadow price defaults to the format of the LHS cell for its constraint. If the LHS cell is formatted to zero or a small number of decimal places, this may produce the appearance of a 0 shadow price when in fact it is a small fraction, such as 0.023. Get into the habit of cursoring over the 0 entries in the Sensitivity Report to verify whether the entry is actually a 0 or a small number requiring an increased decimal format specification.*

---

[4]It is called a "price" because it reflects the maximum price you would be willing to pay for an additional hour of capacity. It is called a "shadow" price because its value is masked or shadowed until the model is optimized and sensitivity analysis is done by Solver.

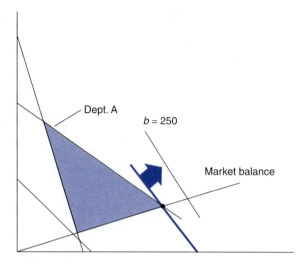

FIGURE 5.9

$b = 250$

solution has only four positive variables, the solution is, according to the definition given in Section 5.2, *degenerate*. Note on the output that the current solution is $E^* = 10$, $F^* = 3\frac{1}{3}$. Also,

$$OV = 5000E^* + 4000F^* = 5000(10) + 4000\,(3\frac{1}{3}) = 63{,}333\frac{1}{3}$$

When $b = 233\frac{1}{3}$, the RHS on department B's labor constraint has been increased $73\frac{1}{3}$ units beyond the original value of 160. Consistent with the interpretation above of the shadow price, which was given as 175, we see that the OV has increased by

$$\Delta OV = 63{,}333\frac{1}{3} - 50{,}500 = 12{,}833\frac{1}{3} = (175)(73\frac{1}{3})$$

***b* > 233⅓**   When b increases up to and beyond the value $233\frac{1}{3}$, Figure 5.7 and Figure 5.9 show that the labor constraint on department B becomes redundant. The values of E^* and F^* and the OV remain as in Figures 5.7 and 5.8. For example, the Solver solution and Sensitivity Report corresponding to $b = 250$ appear in Figure 5.10.

Note that the solution is once again nondegenerate, with the active constraints (meaning ones with 0 slack) now being those on department A and market balance (compare with Figure 5.9). Also note that the shadow price on the department B constraint has dropped from 175 to zero. This change in the shadow price shows that the interpretation of its meaning given above must be restricted to a specific range in RHS values. The range of RHS values for which the shadow price remains constant is the **allowable RHS range.** The appropriate range appears on the Sensitivity Report in the "Constraints" section under the "Allowable Increase" and "Allowable Decrease" columns.

Thus, the Solver Sensitivity Reports shown in Figures 5.4, 5.8, and 5.10 tell us that

1. When $b = 160$ (Figure 5.4) the shadow price of 175 is valid for an allowable increase (in b) of $73\frac{1}{3}$ hours and an allowable decrease of 40 hours. Since $160 - 40 = 120$, and $160 + 73\frac{1}{3} = 233\frac{1}{3}$, we see that *for b values between 120 and 233⅓ hours, the change in the OV for each unit of RHS increase, with all other data held fixed, is 175.*

2. When $b = 233\frac{1}{3}$ (Figure 5.8) the shadow price remains at 175, but the allowable increase is 0, which means that the value 175 does not apply to RHS values any larger than $233\frac{1}{3}$. Indeed, the geometric analysis shows that the constraint becomes inactive and redundant when $b > 233\frac{1}{3}$. *Small changes in the RHS of an inactive constraint cannot affect the OV, and hence for an inactive constraint the shadow price will always be zero.*

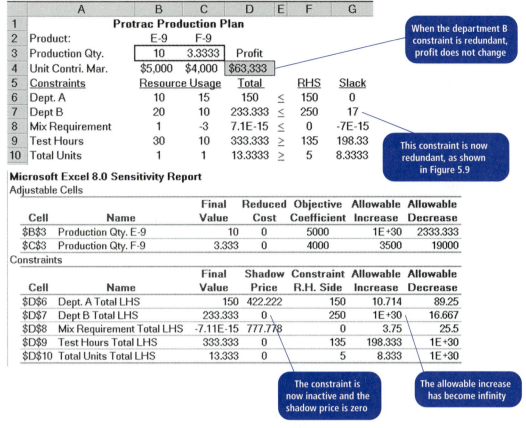

The following callouts appear around the figure:

When the department B constraint is redundant, profit does not change

This constraint is now redundant, as shown in Figure 5.9

The constraint is now inactive and the shadow price is zero

The allowable increase has become infinity

	A	B	C	D	E	F	G
1	**Protrac Production Plan**						
2	Product:	E-9	F-9				
3	Production Qty.	10	3.3333	Profit			
4	Unit Contri. Mar.	$5,000	$4,000	$63,333			
5	Constraints	Resource Usage		Total		RHS	Slack
6	Dept. A	10	15	150	≤	150	0
7	Dept B	20	10	233.333	≤	250	17
8	Mix Requirement	1	-3	7.1E-15	≤	0	-7E-15
9	Test Hours	30	10	333.333	≥	135	198.33
10	Total Units	1	1	13.3333	≥	5	8.3333

Microsoft Excel 8.0 Sensitivity Report

Adjustable Cells

Cell	Name	Final Value	Reduced Cost	Objective Coefficient	Allowable Increase	Allowable Decrease
$B$3	Production Qty. E-9	10	0	5000	1E+30	2333.333
$C$3	Production Qty. F-9	3.333	0	4000	3500	19000

Constraints

Cell	Name	Final Value	Shadow Price	Constraint R.H. Side	Allowable Increase	Allowable Decrease
$D$6	Dept. A Total LHS	150	422.222	150	10.714	89.25
$D$7	Dept B Total LHS	233.333	0	250	1E+30	16.667
$D$8	Mix Requirement Total LHS	-7.11E-15	777.778	0	3.75	25.5
$D$9	Test Hours Total LHS	333.333	0	135	198.333	1E+30
$D$10	Total Units Total LHS	13.333	0	5	8.333	1E+30

FIGURE 5.10

Solver Solution and Sensitivity Report for $b = 250$

3. When $b = 250$ (Figure 5.10) we see that now, with the relevant constraint inactive, the shadow price is indeed zero and the allowable increase is infinite.[5] That is, for any further increase in b the constraint will remain inactive and the shadow price will remain at the value 0. In Figure 5.10 the allowable decrease of 16.66 will take the RHS back to 233⅓. For values of b less than 233⅓ we have seen in Figure 5.8 that the shadow price is 175, not zero.

In summary,

1. The shadow price on a given constraint can be interpreted as the rate of change in OV as the RHS of that constraint increases (i.e., the change per unit increase in RHS) with all other data held fixed.[6] The interpretation of the shadow price is valid only within a range for the given RHS. This range is specified by the Allowable Increase and Allowable Decrease columns in the Constraints section of the Sensitivity Report. It is a range in which the shadow price is constant. Outside this allowable range the shadow price may change to a different value.

2. According to the interpretation above, the shadow price of an inactive constraint will always be zero. An inactive constraint means that the constraint has slack or surplus (i.e., not binding).

3. Note that the RHS sensitivity information that the Sensitivity Report provides does *not* tell us how the optimal decision E^*, F^* changes. It merely explains the way in which the OV will change as the RHS changes.

---

[5]The largest number Excel can represent is 1E+30, i.e., a 1 followed by 30 zeros. For practical purposes this is considered infinitely big by the scale of numbers used in the original PROTRAC LP model.

[6]The Sensitivity Report will not apply when more than one parameter is being changed.

4. When we have a degenerate solution some of the shadow prices will have either a zero allowable increase or zero allowable decrease. In this case we obtain in the Sensitivity Report only a limited amount of information. Namely, we know only about the effect on the OV of one-sided changes in the RHS.

OBJECTIVE FUNCTION COEFFICIENT SENSITIVITY AND ALTERNATIVE OPTIMA

Consider increasing the coefficient of F in the objective function; that is, increasing its per unit profitability, while holding the coefficient of E fixed. We have seen (in Figure 4.20) that the contours of the objective function become flatter (have a less negative slope) as this coefficient increases. Figure 5.3 shows that the optimal solution remains at the corner $E^* = 4.5$, $F^* = 7$ until the coefficient of F increases enough that contours of the objective function are parallel to constraint ③. When the contours of the objective function are parallel to constraint ③, there are *two* optimal corner solutions: the current corner *(E* = 4.5, F* = 7)*, and the corner determined by the intersection of constraints ③ and ⑤. In general, the term **alternative optimal solutions** is used for situations such as this one, in which there is more than one set of decision variables that yield the same optimal value of the objective function.

If the coefficient of F continues to increase, the current solution ($E^* = 4.5$, $F^* = 7$) will no longer be optimal, and the point determined by the intersection of constraints ③ and ⑤ will be the unique optimum. The allowable increase for the coefficient of F is thus determined by the increase in the coefficient that makes the contours of the objective function parallel to constraint ③. When, we may ask, does this occur?

The contours of the objective function are parallel to constraint ③ when the two lines have the same slope, which means that the coefficients satisfy the equality:

$$\frac{\text{coefficient of } E \text{ in } ③}{\text{coefficient of } F \text{ in } ③} = \frac{\text{coefficient of } E \text{ in objective}}{\text{coefficient of } F \text{ in objective}}$$

Thus

$$\frac{10}{15} = \frac{5000}{\text{coefficient of } F \text{ in objective}}$$

and therefore

$$\text{coefficient of } F \text{ in objective} = (5000)(15/10) = 7500$$

The current coefficient of F in the objective function is 4000. It becomes parallel to ③; that is, alternative optima occur if this value increases to 7500. Thus, the current optimal solution remains valid as long as the increase in F's coefficient is ≤ 3500. *This is termed the allowable increase in the coefficient of F.* It is the value shown in Figure 5.4 under Allowable Increase for F. This combination of algebra and geometry explains both the meaning and the value of this entry on the report.

In general, the **objective coefficient ranges** give the ranges of objective function coefficients over which no change in the optimal solution will occur. Further, by observing how the change in coefficients affects the slope of the objective function, we can make the following important generalizations:

> Changing the objective function coefficients changes the slope of the objective function contours. This change in slope may or may not affect the optimal solution and the optimal value of the objective function.

Now recall that as the coefficient of F increased (holding the coefficient of E fixed) we eventually obtained a new solution in which the optimal value of F increased. This result agrees with your intuition since increasing the profitability of F would not cause you to produce F at a lower level! This case illustrates a general concept:

In a Max model, increasing the profitability of an activity and keeping all other data un-changed cannot reduce the optimal level of that activity.

Chapter 5   187
LP Models: Interpreting
Solver Sensitivity Report

The situation for a cost-minimization model is just reversed. Since we want to mini-mize total cost, we certainly would not expect that increasing the cost of an activity, while keeping all other data unchanged, could lead to a higher optimal level of that activity. This case illustrates another general concept:

In a Min model, increasing the cost of an activity and keeping all other data unchanged cannot increase the optimal level of that activity.

Meaning of Objective Coefficient Ranges We can now summarize the significant points concerning the objective coefficient ranges of the Sensitivity Report. In interpreting this portion of the report you must be careful to distinguish between the cases of a nonde-generate and a degenerate solution.

For a nondegenerate solution:

1. The columns Allowable Increase and Allowable Decrease in the Changing Cells part of the report tell you how much the coefficient of a given variable in the objective func-tion may be increased or decreased without changing the optimal solution, where all other data are assumed to be fixed. Of course, as the profitability varies in this range, the OV values are given by

$$OV = 5000E^* + [(\text{profitability of } F) \cdot F^*]$$

As an illustration, imagine that the coefficient of F is assigned the value 6000, which is within the allowable range shown in Figure 5.4. Then the solution remains at ($E^* = 4.5$, $F^* = 7$) and

$$OV = 5000E^* + 6000F^* = 5000(4.5) + 6000(7) = 64,500$$

2. When a coefficient is changed by less than the allowable amounts, the current optimal solution remains the unique optimal solution to the model.

3. When a particular coefficient is increased by its allowable amount, there will be an al-ternative optimal corner solution with, for a Max model, a larger optimal value for the distinguished variable. (For a Min model, increasing a coefficient the allowable amount will produce an alternative optimum corner with a lower optimal value for the distinguished variable.)

4. When a variable's coefficient is decreased by its allowable amount, there will be an-other alternative optimal corner solution with the distinguished variable having a lower (higher) optimal value for a Max (Min) model.

One other fact of interest applies to a *nondegenerate* solution. *When you see, for some Objective Coefficient in the Sensitivity Report, a zero entry under either of the columns Allowable Increase or Allowable Decrease, you know that there is at least one alternative optimal corner point solution to the model at hand.* Moreover, whenever there are alternative optima such a signal will appear. This principle is illustrated in

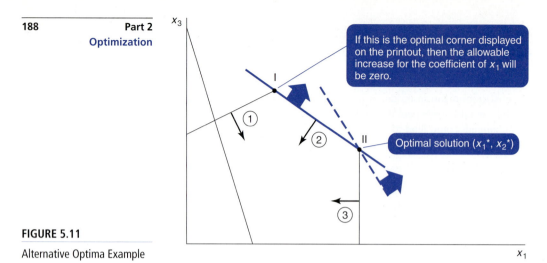

FIGURE 5.11

Alternative Optima Example

Figure 5.11, a hypothetical maximization LP example in two decision variables and three inequality constraints. The objective function contour is parallel to the second constraint (labeled ②), and in employing the graphical solution technique you can see that the corners labeled I and II are alternative optima for this model. Solver, because of the simplex method it employs to optimize the LP model, will find only one of these two corners as an optimal solution and the Sensitivity Report applies only to that corner.[7] Let us suppose that corner I is the solution found by Solver. The geometry in Figure 5.11 shows that any increase in the coefficient of x_1 will change the objective function contour to a tilt like that of the dashed line, and corner II becomes the unique optimal solution. The Solver Sensitivity Report for the solution at corner I would have, as a signal for this phenomenon, a zero value under the Allowable Increase column for changes in the objective coefficient for x_1.

Let us now consider the case of a Sensitivity Report showing a *degenerate optimal solution.* In this case two caveats must be observed.

For a degenerate solution

1. The signals described above for alternative optima should be ignored.

2. As long as an objective function coefficient is varied in the indicated range, the optimal solution will not change. This fact was also true in the nondegenerate case. In the latter case, however, alternative optima were obtained when the coefficient was changed to the limit of its range, and then, as this direction of change continued, the original optimal solution dropped out. In the degenerate case this result can no longer be guaranteed. All we can say is that any objective function coefficient must be changed by *at least, and possibly more than,* the indicated allowable amounts in order to produce a new optimal solution.

REDUCED COST

We have explained everything in the Sensitivity Report except for the entries under the column "Reduced Cost." The following facts pertain to these entries. This is another instance where, in order to give a correct interpretation, you must first observe whether the solution is nondegenerate.

---

[7]When alternative optima exist for an LP model, imperceptible differences in CPU arithmetic precision will often cause Solver on one computer model to find one alternative optimal corner solution; while the same worksheet will Solve to another alternative optimal corner solution on another computer model. For example, Excel-Solver on a Macintosh and Excel-Solver on a Windows PC may converge to different alternative optimal corner solutions for the same worksheet.

1. In a *nondegenerate* solution, the reduced cost of any particular decision variable is defined to be *the amount the coefficient of that variable in the objective function would have to change in order to have a positive optimal value for that variable.* Thus, if a variable is already positive at optimality, its reduced cost is zero (as is the case for both decision variables in Figures 5.4, 5.8, and 5.10). If the optimal value of a variable is zero, then from the definition of reduced cost you can see that the reduced cost is either the Allowable Increase or Allowable Decrease that corresponds to the given variable (one of these values will be infinite; the other will be the reduced cost). For example, suppose that we change the data in the PROTRAC E and F model in such a way that the optimal value $E^* = 0$. Then the reduced cost of E is the amount its contribution margin (the coefficient of E in the objective function) would have to be *increased* in order to have an optimal solution with $E^* > 0$. This is precisely the entry that you would find corresponding to E in the Allowable Increase column. In this case, for any decrease in the coefficient of E (making E less profitable), the value E^* will remain at zero. Hence, the corresponding Allowable Decrease entry would be infinite.

2. Another equivalent interpretation of reduced cost for a nondegenerate solution, can be given. In a nondegenerate solution, the reduced cost of a decision variable (whose optimal value is currently zero) is the rate (per unit amount) at which the objective value is hurt as that variable is "forced into" (i.e., is forced to assume positive values in) an optimal solution. In the example above, with $E^* = 0$, the OV would decrease if we forced ourselves to find an optimal solution with the *additional* constraint that $E = 1$. (To see that the OV would *decrease* you need merely recognize that in the current model the optimal value of E is zero. Forcing E to be 1, then, can only yield us lower payoff.) This *rate of decrease* as E^* is initially forced to be positive would be given by the reduced cost of E.

Recall that a constraint's shadow price gives the rate of change in the OV as that constraint's RHS is increased. Since in this example $E^* = 0$, the nonnegativity constraint on E is therefore active. If E is then forced to be positive, that is the same as raising the RHS on its nonnegativity constraint. Thus this equivalent interpretation is easily articulated: For models having nonnegativity constraints, the reduced cost is simply the shadow price on a given decision variable's nonnegativity constraint. Additional examples of the two interpretations above will appear in Section 5.4.

3. Now consider a *degenerate solution* with a decision variable whose optimal value is zero. The coefficient of that variable in the objective function must be changed by *at least, and possibly more than,* the reduced cost in order for there to be an optimal solution with that variable appearing at a positive level.

This completes our exploration of the meaning of each entry in Solver's Sensitivity Report. Although our discussion has been introductory, if you have mastered the material presented from Chapter 3 up to this point, you are now able to use LP in practical situations; to formulate models, optimize them with Solver, and correctly interpret Solver's Sensitivity Report.[8] Section 5.4 is intended to increase your familiarity with model interpretation by showing you how the Sensitivity Report might be employed in a realistic scenario. The orientation is managerial, with an emphasis on the sensitivity information and its use. In Section 5.5, we give a synopsis of how to interpret the Sensitivity Report. Finally, in Section 5.6 we give a cautionary tale on the pitfalls of sensitivity analysis.

 5.4   **THE CRAWLER TREAD OUTPUT: A DIALOGUE WITH
MANAGEMENT (SENSITIVITY ANALYSIS IN ACTION)**

This model was introduced in Section 3.10. Recall that the ore from four different locations is blended to make crawler tractor treads. Each ore contains three essential elements, denoted for simplicity as A, B, and C, that must appear in the final blend at minimum threshold levels. PROTRAC pays a different price per ton for the ore from each location. The cost-minimizing blend is obtained by solving the following LP model, where $T_i =$ the fraction of a ton of ore from location i in one ton of the blend.

---

[8]The Solver Limits Report is of limited practical importance and will not be covered.

Wellborn Cabinet, Inc. owns a cabinet manufacturing facility in Alabama. The operation consists of a sawmill, four dry kilns, and a wood cabinet assembly plant with a rough mill for making blanks (cabinet components). Wellborn obtains the lumber used for manufacturing the cabinets in two ways: (1) buying logs that are processed by its sawmill to make lumber, which is then used in the assembly plant; (2) buying lumber that has been sawed elsewhere. Currently, about 73% of the input comes from the company's own sawmill.

Both logs and lumber are graded #1 or #2; #1 is of better quality and more expensive. About two thirds of the total volume of logs that Wellborn had been buying were #1. Purchased lumber, accounting for about 27% of the lumber used, was of two types: green (18%), which had to be dried in the company's kilns, and dry (9%). Nearly all of the dry lumber was also grade #1.

The cost of wood makes up about 45% of the total material cost of making cabinets. Management thus wanted to know if its approach to buying wood for the cabinet assembly plant was the most economical. To help answer this question, Auburn University's Technical Assistance Center, in cooperation with the School of Forestry, analyzed the company's operation. An LP model of blank production was created, with constraints that included the capacities of the sawmill and kilns, the required output of blanks, and the available supply of raw materials.

Optimizing the model revealed that the company could minimize the cost of producing blanks by purchasing only two kinds of wood: #2 grade logs with small-end diameters of 9 to 15 inches (88% by volume) and #2 common green lumber (12%). This purchasing policy would reduce Wellborn's raw materials costs by nearly one third, an annual saving of about $412,000.

The model provided managers with much additional useful information:

- Shadow prices associated with the purchase of logs of various sizes enabled management to make the most cost-effective selection from among the logs available at any given time.
- Sensitivity analysis revealed the price ranges for which the solution prescribed by the model would remain optimal. In particular, it indicated that reductions of up to 20% in the price of dry lumber or #1 grade logs would not affect the optimal purchase policy.
- A slack value of zero for the operation of the dry kilns indicated that this operation represented a bottleneck—kiln capacity was the only factor limiting increased production. A 22% increase in kiln capacity would permit an increase of 29% in blank output without any additional changes. (See Carino et. al.)

$$\text{Min } 800T_1 + 400T_2 + 600T_3 + 500T_4 \qquad \text{(total cost)}$$
$$\text{s.t.} \quad 10T_1 + 3T_2 + 8T_3 + 2T_4 \geq 5 \qquad \text{(requirement on A)}$$
$$90T_1 + 150T_2 + 75T_3 + 175T_4 \geq 100 \qquad \text{(requirement on B)}$$
$$45T_1 + 25T_2 + 20T_3 + 37T_4 \geq 30 \qquad \text{(requirement on C)}$$
$$T_1 + T_2 + T_3 + T_4 = 1 \qquad \text{(blend condition)}$$
$$T_i \geq 0, i = 1, 2, 3, 4$$

Let us now discuss and analyze the spreadsheet reports for the solution to this model. Place yourself in the position of the manager who is responsible for planning future production. A number of questions are on your mind. The modeler responds.

Manager First of all, what is the solution to our LP model?
I have optimized the model with Solver, and here's the output (see Figure 5.12). *By "solution" I take it you mean the optimal values of the decision variables. You can see that the optimal values (cells B3:E3) are approximately T_1 5 0.26, T_2 5 0.70, T_3 5 0.04, T_4 5 0.00. (For convenience, T_1 is labeled T1 in the worksheet, T_2 is labeled T2, etc., and we should use those labels hereafter.)*

Manager Okay. How much does a ton of this blend cost?
The OV, which is the optimal value of the objective function, is also identified. You can see that the minimum cost is $511.11 (cell F4).

	A	B	C	D	E	F	G	H	I
1	Crawler Tread Production Plan								
2	Mine	T1	T2	T3	T4				
3	Ton Fractions	0.259	0.704	0.037	0.000	Total Cost			
4	Cost/Ton	$800	$400	$600	$500	$511.11			
5	Constraints	Composition per Ton				Total		RHS	Slack
6	A	10	3	8	2	5.00	≥	5	0.00
7	B	90	150	75	175	131.67	≥	100	31.67
8	C	45	25	20	37	30.00	≥	30	0.00
9	Balance	1	1	1	1	1	=	1	0

Microsoft Excel 8.0 Sensitivity Report

Adjustable Cells

Cell	Name	Final Value	Reduced Cost	Objective Coefficient	Allowable Increase	Allowable Decrease
$B$3	Ton Fractions T1	0.259	0.00	800	223.636	120
$C$3	Ton Fractions T2	0.7037	0.00	400	66.848	300
$D$3	Ton Fractions T3	0.037	0.00	600	85.714	118.269
$E$3	Ton Fractions T4	0.000	91.11	500	1E+30	91.11

Constraints

Cell	Name	Final Value	Shadow Price	Constraint R.H. Side	Allowable Increase	Allowable Decrease
$F$6	A Total	5.00	44.44	5	2.375	0.25
$F$7	B Total	131.67	0.00	100	31.667	1E+30
$F$8	C Total	30.00	4.44	30	0.714	7
$F$9	Balance Total	1	155.56	1	0.25	0.043

FIGURE 5.12

Solver Solution and
Sensitivity Report for Crawler
Tread Model

Manager   I'd like to keep my costs under $500 per ton. Isn't there any way I can do this?

It is impossible to find a lower-cost mixture that satisfies the constraints you have imposed.

Manager   You mean the requirements on essential elements?

Exactly.

Manager   Well, maybe I can modify those requirements. I really do want to keep my costs under $500 per ton.

Then you certainly will have to loosen your requirements. We can discuss how to do that.

Manager   All right. But first, I recall that the requirements were expressed as minimum threshold levels. Is there any way I can tell exactly how much of each essential element gets into the optimal mix?

That information is obtained from columns F and I of the spreadsheet. The first three constraints of the model are the requirements on essential elements.

Manager   I see a column labeled "Slack."

For convenience the column is labeled "Slack," but in general it means "slack or surplus," whichever is appropriate.

Manager   Okay, the surplus for constraint A is zero (cell I6) and the requirement on A was 5 pounds. This means that exactly 5 pounds of A is produced per ton.

Exactly.

Manager   Okay, and I understand what happens for constraints B and C. But the last constraint in the original model was an equality constraint. That means that it has neither a slack nor a surplus variable. Right?

Correct.

Manager   Then why is there a slack value of zero printed in cell I9? Doesn't that suggest there is a slack or surplus variable for that constraint?

You may be right, but the suggestion is unintended. For a constraint that was originally an equality the entry in this cell is always zero. As you have correctly observed, the actual surplus amounts in this model are associated only with the first three constraints of the original model.

Manager Fine. Now let's return to the surplus variable in cell I6. I see that its optimal value is zero. What does that have to do with the amount of essential element A in the final mix? I thought I saw the answer before, but now I'm confused.

It's easy. Since the optimal surplus value is zero, the optimal mix contains exactly 5 pounds of A.

Manager I see. And since the surplus in cell I8 is zero, the optimal mix must contain exactly 30 pounds of C. Is that right?

Precisely, and you can also figure out how much B there is.

Manager Okay. For B, I have to look at cell I7. Since the surplus is 31.67, it must be true that the constraint is not active. But where do I go from here?

Well, this means that in the optimal mix the minimum requirement of 100 pounds is actually exceeded by 31.67. That is, there are 131.67 pounds of B actually included, as shown in cell F7.

Manager Isn't that odd? You'd think I could make a cheaper blend by using less B. Why should I use more than 100 pounds if I need only 100?

That is a very good question. You see, the combination of ores that satisfies the requirements on A and C at a minimum cost just happens to contain more than 100 pounds of B. Any combination of ores that includes less B will either not have enough of A and/or C, or, if it does have enough, it will cost more than $511.11 per ton. In other words, forcing yourself to include less of the excess amount of B while still satisfying the requirements on A and C will end up costing you more. You may have to think about that assertion, but it is exactly what the solution to the model is telling us.

Manager Okay. I guess I can see your point. So how can I get my total cost down to $500 or less?

You will have to loosen your constraints. This means loosening the requirements on A or C.

Manager Why not on B?

Because, in order to satisfy the requirements on A and C at minimum cost, you're already including over 100 pounds of B, which is more than your minimal threshold. In other words, the requirement on B is not active. You could loosen this requirement to a smaller number, such as 98, and the optimal mix would still contain the same composition and cost. Thus, loosening the requirement on B to a smaller number won't get us anywhere. You have to loosen one of the active requirements.

Manager You mean one where there's zero surplus.

Precisely.

Manager Okay. So I have to relax the requirement on A or C. But which one? And how much?

We can use the information under the "Shadow Price" heading of the Sensitivity Report to analyze these questions.

Manager Remind me what that column means.

It means rate of change in the OV as we increase the right-hand side. Since we are interested in loosening a ≥ constraint, we will be decreasing the right-hand side. Now let's look at the shadow price on constraint A. It is +44.44. The positive sign means that as the right-hand side is increased, the OV cost is increased or hurt. Thus, as the right-hand side is loosened, or decreased, the OV is improved. What all of this boils down to is the common-sense idea that, as your requirement for A is loosened, your minimum cost will go down. The shadow *price tells us it goes down at the rate of $44.44 per decreased pound of A and up at the rate of $44.44 per increased pound of A.*

Manager Loosening the requirement for A must mean reducing it from 5 pounds to something less. Right?
Right.

Manager And the shadow price of +44.44 says that for each pound of reduction that total cost goes down $44.44?
Right.

Manager Great. This means if I require only 4 pounds per ton of A, instead of 5, the cost goes down to about $466.67 and I'm under $500. Right?
Well, not quite. But you're right in spirit. You have the correct rate of change, but this rate applies only to some interval of values around the original value of 5. The appropriate interval may not allow you to analyze the decrease of a whole unit—maybe only half a unit, for example.

Manager Even so, if I cut the requirement to 4.5 pounds, I'd save (1/2)(44.44), which is over $22. My final cost would still be under $500!
True enough, but the allowable interval may not even include 4.5.

Manager Obviously, we need to know that interval.
Right.

Manager I see. In the Allowable Decrease column for constraint A we have 0.25. That must mean I can analyze a change from 5 down to 4.75. Right?
Right.

Manager So my saving would be 0.25(44.44), which is $11.11, and this gets me down to exactly $500. But what if I relaxed the requirement a little more, like to 4.50. Wouldn't that reduce the cost further?
Probably, but I can't tell you exactly how much because the rate of change may be different after a decrease of 0.25.

Manager In other words, that must mean the shadow price may change.
Exactly.

Manager Okay. Now just to see if I have it all straight, let me analyze the potential savings if I relax the requirement on C.
Go ahead.

Manager The original right-hand side is 30. The Sensitivity Report shows an allowable decrease of 7, so I can go down to 23. The corresponding shadow price is +4.44. This is my rate of savings as I decrease the right-hand side from 30. Hence, if I decrease the requirement to 23, I save 7(4.44) = $31.08. This also gets me well under $500. In fact, if I cut down the requirement only 2.5 pounds, I can apply the same rate of change, and consequently I should save (2.5)(4.44) = $11.10 and this just about gets me down to a cost of $500. How am I doing?
Very well.

Manager Okay. I see that I can get the cost per ton down to $500 if I relax the requirement on A to 4.75 pounds per ton *or* the requirement on C to 27.5 pounds per ton. But what if I relax both requirements on A and C, perhaps a little less but both at the same time? Then what?
Sorry, but again we don't have precise information on the Sensitivity Report to answer that. The only way to tackle that question would be to re-solve the model numerous times with different right-hand sides for A and C.

Manager So when I use the shadow price on one of the right-hand-side values, it's important to keep the others unchanged.
Correct.

Manager So let me review this. I know that I can get my cost per ton down to $500 if I re-lax the requirement on A to 4.75 pounds per ton *or* the requirement on C to 27.5 pounds per ton. Which should I do?

The model cannot give you a guideline on that. You might note that the required relaxation on A would be 0.25/5, or 5%, and on C it would be 2.5/30 = 8 1/3%. But I don't know whether that is helpful. The point is that you, as the manager, have to decide on which change would do more harm to the properties of the blend. I think it probably boils down to an engineering question.

Manager Yes, I think you are right, and I know who to talk with about that.

Good.

Manager By the way, I've also been noticing the column that says Allowable Increase. I would guess that pertains to increases in the right-hand side.

Right again.

Manager Would you just run through the analysis on the increase side to make sure that I'm with you?

Let's take the requirement on A. Suppose that you want to tighten this require-ment.

Manager Since we are dealing with a $\geq$ constraint, tightening would mean an increase in the right-hand side, which is the required amount of A.

Correct. Tightening a requirement can never help the OV and may hurt. In this case the shadow price of +44.44 tells us that increasing the right-hand side will hurt. This means that the cost will go up. The Allowable Increase of 2.375 tells us that if we increase the original amount, 5, by any amount up to 2.375, the in-crease in minimum cost is given by 44.44 times that amount.

Manager In other words, the same shadow price pertains to both increases and decreases in the right-hand side. So, the shadow price is the rate of change in the objective value as the right-hand side varies over that entire allowable range.

Right. And loosening a constraint will always mean that the OV cannot be hurt and may be improved. Tightening means that the OV cannot be improved and may be hurt.

Manager I even notice that the shadow price on B is zero, which means that the changes in the value of 100 don't have any effect. I guess that means we don't even need a constraint on B. Why is that?

Because, as I mentioned earlier, if you satisfy the requirements for A and C at a minimum cost, the requirement for B will be satisfied automatically.

Manager So am I correct? Could the constraint on B be discarded?

I would think not. If you would ever want to change some of the data and then re-solve the model, the constraint on B could become important. In particular, we can see from the Allowable Increase of 31.667 that if the RHS were to exceed 131.667, this constraint would become binding. So I don't really want to say that it can be removed from the model.

Manager Could you be a little more explicit, without getting into a lot of terminology?

All right. Just as an example, last week I heard from Mr. Shmootz that the cost of ore from location 2 might increase.

Manager Mr. Shmootz?

Yes.

Manager Well, I must admit that such a possibility is something I'm concerned about. But I don't see how we can take that kind of uncertainty into account.

This relates to your question. The cost of ore from location 2 is the coefficient of T2 in the objective function, namely the 400 in cell C4. If this cost is increased, we would expect our OV to increase. If the cost of ore from location 2 goes up enough, we might even expect that less of it, or maybe even none of it, would be used in the optimal blend. This means more of the others must be used because the total amount used has to sum up to 1 ton. This means that the relative importance of the constraints could change. Previous constraints that had been tight might not be, and vice versa. A lot of things can happen when you start playing with the data.

Manager Tell me again what you mean by a tight constraint.
It means a constraint with an optimal slack or surplus value of zero. Such a constraint is also called active, or binding, or effective.

Manager Okay. What about an equality constraint? Is it considered active or binding?
Yes. Always. In this terminology, although the constraint on B is currently inactive, it could become active if the data in the model are changed.

Manager Fine. But I'm still confused. What does all this have to do with the cost of ore from location 2?
Let's look at the cost of ore from location 2. We can actually determine the range over which this cost can vary without influencing the optimal blend. In particular, look at the portion of the Sensitivity Report labeled Adjustable Cells. In the row corresponding to T2 there are items called Allowable Increase and Allowable Decrease. This gives the range in which the cost of T2 can vary.

Manager You mean without changing the optimal production mix?
Yes.

Manager Okay. In other words, the cost of T2 is now $400 in our model. You mean that the report says it could be anywhere between $100 and about $466.85 and the optimal production mix stays the same?
Exactly.

Manager I don't see how we can know that.
It's all in the computations done for you by Solver.

Manager Okay. So if the cost increases from $400 to $450, we have nothing to worry about.
Well, I don't know about that. We know that the optimal production mix will stay the same. This means that the optimal values of all the variables, including the slacks, stay the same. But our total cost will increase by $50 times the amount of T2 being used in the current solution.

Manager I see. The OV will go from the old value, $511.11, to the new value, $511.11 + 50(0.70370) = 546.30. Yes, I see what you mean. Everything stays the same except the total cost. Did you say that even the slack/surplus values stay the same?
Yes. If all the decision variables stay the same, you can see from the spreadsheet formulas that the slack/surplus variables would have to also.

Manager That must mean the constraints that are active also stay the same.
Yes.

Manager I see. By the way, what happens if the cost of T2 increases by more than the allowable amount?
Well, since we have a Min model I know that increasing the cost of an input cannot increase its use. Therefore, as the cost of T2 increases I know that the optimal value of T2 can never increase. In fact, since the current solution is nondegenerate, I know that when the cost of T2 increases by more than the allowable amount, the optimal value of T2 will in fact surely decrease.

Manager Wait a minute. Slow down. You said nondegenerate. Remind me again about degeneracy.
Yes. This simply means that in the optimized spreadsheet the number of variables with a positive optimal value, including both decision and slack or surplus variables, is equal to the number of constraints. Figure 5.12 shows that at optimality three decision variables and one surplus variable are positive. Since there are four constraints in the model, we have a nondegenerate solution. This is a technicality but it is important in interpreting some of the Sensitivity Report.

Manager All right. Fine. So if the per unit cost of ore from mine 2 increases by more than its allowable amount, we will get an optimal solution with a smaller value of T2.
Yes. And not only that. The optimal values of some of the other variables may also change, but it isn't possible to say exactly which ones or how much. This means that a surplus that was positive could become zero, and hence a constraint that was inactive could become active. And it could also mean that a constraint that previously had zero surplus could now become inactive in the sense that its surplus becomes positive. In other words, once the cost coefficient change exceeds the limit of the indicated range, all sorts of things can happen.

Manager You're talking about a cost coefficient change that *exceeds* the allowable limit. What if it actually hits the limit?
Then, again since the current solution is nondegenerate, we know that there will be alternative optimal solutions, the current solution together with a new one that has less T2 in it.

Manager Well, it seems to me that we have considerable information about the influence of uncertainty. That strikes me as remarkable.
I agree.

Manager Okay. Thank you very much. I think I can do pretty well now on my own with the Sensitivity Report analysis. We should really call it model sensitivity analysis, shouldn't we?
Yes.

Manager Okay. Thanks again. I'm amazed at how much we can learn about the actual model, above and beyond the optimal solution.
Right. That is because of the ease of computing sensitivity information for LP models. By the way, do you mind if I ask you just one question to more or less check you out?

Manager Okay. Shoot.
You have already noticed on the spreadsheet that the optimal value of T4 is zero.

Manager True.
I happen to know that ore from location 4 has some desirable tensile properties that haven't really been built into the model.

Manager That is true.
Also, I understand from Mr. Shmootz that it isn't unreasonable to renegotiate the cost of T4 periodically.

Manager Are you referring to the fact that PROTRAC has some family connections in the location 4 enterprise?
Something like that. But my point is this. How much would the cost of T4 have to decrease before you'd be willing to buy some?

Manager Let's see. The current cost of T4 is $500 per ton. I think what you're trying to ask me is this: How much must this cost decrease before we obtain an optimal policy that uses some T4? Is that your question?
Yes.

Manager Okay. To find the answer, I look at the Sensitivity Report, where I see that if the cost of T4 decreases by less than $91.11 per ton, then, according to what you just said, the optimal value of this variable remains unchanged. That means it remains at zero. Consequently, taking into account what you just said about nondegeneracy, I know that if its cost is negotiated down to $408.89 or less, there will be an optimal solution with T4 positive. Right?
Correct. Now can you tell me what happens to the optimal objective value?

Manager I guess I can figure that out. If the cost decreases by no more than $91.11, no change occurs in the optimal values of any of the variables. In the objective func-

tion only the cost of T4 is changing. But since the value of T4 stays at zero, the OV won't change either. I guess it stays at $511.11 as long as the reduction in cost is less than $91.11.
Correct.

Manager But what happens if the reduction exactly equals $91.11? You've told me that in this case the optimal value of T4 will become positive. Is that right?
Not quite. There will be two optimal extreme point or corner solutions: the current one, and another one that has a positive optimal value of T4 and some new values for some of the other variables. But I don't know exactly how the others will change.

Manager Okay, but does this mean that when the cost of T4 is reduced by exactly $91.11, the total cost suddenly drops down from $511.11?
No, since these are alternative optima the OV equals $511.11 at each.

Manager Can we tell how much of T4 will be used in the alternative optimum?
I'm afraid not from the Sensitivity Report. All we know is that there will be some positive value for this variable. To find out its precise value we would have to resolve the model for a reduction in the cost of T4 just barely more than $91.11.

Manager And how do you know all that?
From the mathematics of optimizing LP models. And remember that these statements about alternative optimal solutions depend on the nondegeneracy of the current solution.

Manager What if the nondegeneracy weren't satisfied?
Then we would have what is termed a degenerate solution. All we could say then is that the optimal solution will not change if the cost of T4 stays within the allowable range. Conceivably, the cost would decrease by more than $91.11 and we would still not get a new optimal solution. Thus you can see that in the degenerate case the output gives us somewhat less information.

Manager Well, by now I think I know all that I need to about what's going on. Do you agree?
Yes. Shall we stop?

Manager Really, since I'm doing so well, I have to ask one final question. What about that column under the heading Reduced Cost?
It is really meaningful only for a decision variable whose optimal value is zero. For this model it tells how much the per unit cost of that variable can be reduced before the optimal value of the variable will become positive.

Manager We just answered that question about T4.
I know.

Manager But we didn't use this column. We used the Allowable Decrease part of the report. In fact, I see that the same value, 91.11, appears in both places.
Right.

Manager So why bother with this Reduced Cost column if the same value appears under the Allowable Decrease column?
Simply for convenience. The reduced cost pertains to variables whose optimal value is zero. You can easily spot these variables in the Sensitivity Report. In the next column you can immediately read the reduced cost, which is a little easier than interpreting the allowable increase or decrease amounts. For convenience, you can think of these Reduced Cost entries as the shadow prices on the model's nonnegativity constraints for mine production. That's all there is to it.

Manager Thank you. It's been very instructive!
My pleasure.

When an LP model is optimized, the Solver optimized worksheet and Sensitivity Report contains the following information:

1. Optimal values are given for the decision variables, the slack and surplus variables, and the objective function. From the total LHS amounts you can quickly deduce the value of the constraint functions (the amount of resources used, the levels of requirements satisfied, and so on) at an optimal solution. The constraints with zero slack or surplus are called *active, effective,* or *binding.* Those with positive slack or surplus are called *inactive,* or *nonbinding.*

2. The shadow price tells you the rate of change in the OV (optimal value of the objective function) as the right-hand side (RHS) of a constraint increases. If the shadow price is positive, then the OV and RHS move in the same direction: Increases in the RHS increase the OV and *vice versa.* If the shadow price is negative, then the OV and RHS move in opposite directions: Increases in the RHS decrease the OV and *vice versa.* Allowable Increase and Decrease give you an allowable range of RHS changes over which the shadow price is valid.

3. The Allowable Increase and Decrease of Objective Coefficients tell you the allowable changes that can be made in the objective function coefficients without changing the optimal solution (the optimal values of the variables). For a *nondegenerate* solution, if an objective function coefficient is changed by an amount that *equals* an allowable change, there will be an alternative optimal corner point solution with new values for the variables. If the coefficient is changed by an amount that *exceeds* the allowable change, there will be a new (assuming nondegeneracy) optimal solution.

4. Reduced Cost output applies to decision variables whose optimal value is zero. It can be interpreted as the shadow prices on the nonnegativity constraints, if they are present, and provides the same information as deduced from the Allowable Increase or Decrease information for these variables.

5.6   SENSITIVITY REPORT INTERPRETATION FOR ALTERNATIVE SPREADSHEET MODELS

The recommendations for laying out the spreadsheet LP models that we have been using since Chapter 3 are quite restrictive. In particular, they result in a layout that leads to a "wide" model consuming many columns for larger models with many decision variables. Also, the resulting model layout is often not as managerially appealing as other layouts that take better advantage of the row-and-column orientation of a spreadsheet. Beginning with the next chapter on applications of LP modeling, we want to expose you to these more appealing model layouts. As you might guess, there are some prices to pay for using an appealing model representation: You must exercise a bit more care in model building, and especially, in interpreting the Sensitivity Report provided by Solver to avoid some nasty pitfalls. However, by now you should be somewhat comfortable with the steps for LP spreadsheet model formulation and Sensitivity Report interpretation and can accommodate to these added demands. The new modeling and interpretation pitfalls are best illustrated by a simple example.

Wayne Foley, recently promoted to manager of the newest branch of the Friendly Loan Company, is eager to please his new boss by loaning his annual $15 million budget profitably. Each local branch office at Friendly generates profit by the interest income from three types of loans: First Mortgage loans on real estate at 7% annual interest, Furniture loans collateralized by liens on home furnishings at 12% annual interest, and Signature loans with no collateral at 15% annual interest. Having the highest risk, Signature loans carry the highest loan interest rate.

Friendly's home office has set loan limits to guide branch managers and to protect the company from excessive amounts of high-risk loans. Friendly requires each branch manager to place at least 60% of its budget into First Mortgages and no more than 10% of its budget in risky Signature loans. Using these loan interest rates, loan policy limitations, and the $15 million loan budget allocated to him for the upcoming year, Wayne has built the LP model in Figure 5.13, which displays his model, its formulas, the Solver dialog, and the optimal allocation of his loan budget.

Notice several features of Wayne's model. First, its spreadsheet formulation is compact; there are no unnecessary calculations for LHS values, and for readability, the constraints are immediately adjacent to the quantities they affect. Also, Wayne is cleverly making some cells do double duty, both as a RHS value and as an inequality symbol. For example, cell G5 actually contains the $15 million budget datum, as is clear from the formulas printout in Figure 5.13. The "<=" appearing in G5 is part of that cell's formatting specification, called a "format dressing." Similar formatting was applied to the formula cells, C6 and E6. (See the Excel Appendix for details on cell formatting.) He has also included a side calculation for the average return of his loan portfolio in cell G7 (=F4/G5). Before proceeding, verify for yourself that Wayne's model correctly captures the three mandated constraint limits on Budget, Signature, and First Mortgage loan amounts.

Not surprisingly, the Solver solution to Wayne's LP model loans out all $15 million, placing $9 million into First Mortgages, $1.5 million into Signature loans, and the balance into Furniture loans to yield annual Total interest income of $1,395,000. Wayne's side calculation in cell G7 shows an average return of 9.3% for his loan portfolio. Wayne also notes that all three constraints in the model are binding (two policy constraints on loan types and one budget constraint).

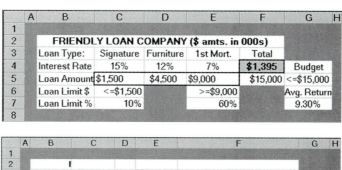

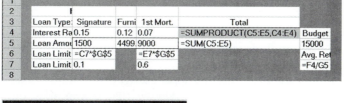

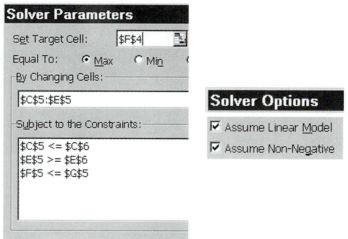

FIGURE 5.13

Wayne's Loan Portfolio Model

Eager to apply his newfound LP modeling knowledge, Wayne reviews the model's Solver Sensitivity Report in Figure 5.14 and, seeing the shadow price on his $15 million budget constraint, immediately reaches for the phone to call his boss to ask for a bigger loan budget. Surprised by Wayne's claim that he can produce a 12% return on any additional budget allocation, Wayne's boss comments that no other branch manager can produce more than about 9 1/3 percent overall return. "That's because they don't understand optimization, marginal analysis, and the power of shadow prices," Wayne retorts. Not wanting to dampen the enthusiasm of his new strange-talking branch manager, the boss asks if Wayne can generate this 12% return for another $5,000,000. Quickly checking the report's Allowable Increase amount for the budget constraint, Wayne confidently tells his boss to "send all $5,000,000 and more" to the branch.

As he hangs up the phone, however, Wayne begins to feel a bit uneasy. "There certainly are three constraints listed in my model's Solver dialog box in addition to the required non-negativity condition. What happened to the two binding loan type constraints in the Sensitivity Report? Instead of one, shouldn't there be three constraints listed along with their shadow prices in the Sensitivity Report?" he asks himself. As his uneasiness turns to fear, he elects to verify Solver's Sensitivity Report information by typing his new budget limit, $20,000, into cell G5. He runs Solver again for this new RHS limit, producing the results in Figure 5.15. Fear turns to shock as Wayne notices that the Average Return in cell G7 for the re-optimized model is unchanged at 9.3%. Since the marginal return on the extra $5 million is 12%, he reasons that the average return for his new loan portfolio should have gone up.

Microsoft Excel 8.0 Sensitivity Report

Adjustable Cells

Cell	Name	Final Value	Reduced Cost	Objective Coefficient	Allowable Increase	Allowable Decrease
$C$5	Loan Amount Signature	$1,500	0.030	15%	1E+30	0.03
$D$5	Loan Amount Furniture	$4,500	0.000	12%	0.03	0.05
$E$5	Loan Amount 1st Mort.	$9,000	-0.050	7%	0.05	1E+30

Constraints

Cell	Name	Final Value	Shadow Price	Constraint R.H. Side	Allowable Increase	Allowable Decrease
$F$5	Loan Amount Total	$15,000	0.120	$15,000	1E+30	4500

FIGURE 5.14

Sensitivity Report for Wayne's Loan Model

	A	B	C	D	E	F	G	H
1								
2		**FRIENDLY LOAN COMPANY ($ amts. in 000s)**						
3		Loan Type:	Signature	Furniture	1st Mort.	Total		
4		Interest Rate	15%	12%	7%	$1,860	Budget	
5		Loan Amount	$2,000	$6,000	$12,000	$20,000	<=$20,000	
6		Loan Limit $	<=$2,000		>=$12,000		Avg. Return	
7		Loan Limit %	10%		60%		9.30%	
8								

Microsoft Excel 8.0 Sensitivity Report

Adjustable Cells

Cell	Name	Final Value	Reduced Cost	Objective Coefficient	Allowable Increase	Allowable Decrease
$C$5	Loan Amount Signature	$2,000	0.03	15%	1E+30	0.03
$D$5	Loan Amount Furniture	$6,000	0.00	12%	0.03	0.05
$E$5	Loan Amount 1st Mort.	$12,000	-0.05	7%	0.05	1E+30

Constraints

Cell	Name	Final Value	Shadow Price	Constraint R.H. Side	Allowable Increase	Allowable Decrease
$F$5	Loan Amount Total	$20,000	0.120	$20,000	1E+30	6000

FIGURE 5.15

Wayne's Loan Portfolio Model for $20 Million Budget

No longer trusting either Solver or Excel, Wayne grabs his calculator and taps out $(1860 - 1395)/5000$, the difference in Total interest income from the two Solver solutions divided by the incremental budget amount, verifying what he already suspects—that the marginal return for the extra \$5 million is actually 9.3% and not 12%. Looking skeptically at the budget constraint's shadow price and range information in the new model's Sensitivity Report in Figure 5.15, Wayne concludes that, unbelievably, Solver has lied to him twice. Sheepishly, Wayne reaches for the phone to offer his boss a mea culpa.

What happened? Are the data poorly scaled, producing erroneous Solver reports? If not, does Solver indeed lie or mislead for some models? If it doesn't, how do you explain the .120 budgetary shadow prices in Figures 5.14 and 5.15, given the results Wayne produced by re-solving? Could the solution be degenerate, causing Wayne to misinterpret a range of allowable increase? How do you tell if the solution is degenerate or not by looking at Wayne's model? And what did happen to the shadow price information for the other two loan type constraints missing from Wayne's Solver Sensitivity Report?

Although always worthy of suspicion, in this case the range of data in Wayne's model is not wide enough to cause numerical problems within Solver, as checking the Use Automatic Scaling box in Solver Options dialog and re-solving will verify. To understand more clearly what happened to poor Wayne, let us re-formulate the model using the recommended formulation rules from Chapter 3, as shown in Figure 5.16, which displays the optimal solution and its Sensitivity Report.

Clearly the two LP formulations produce the same optimal loan decisions and Total interest income as shown in Figures 5.13 and 5.16. The differences pertain to the models' Sensitivity Report and its interpretation. To answer the other questions above, note the following for the results of the LP model built by the rules of Chapter 3. First, immediately apparent in Figure 5.16 is the presence of all three constraints in the Sensitivity Report and their associated shadow prices and ranges of RHS changes. Second, the shadow price for Wayne's budget constraint in Figure 5.16 is the correct marginal value (9.3%). Third, the solution to either formulation is not degenerate, as easily verified by counting the total nonzero decision variables and slacks ($= 3$) in Figure 5.16 and comparing that to the number of constraints ($= 3$). And fourth, in contrast to the Sensitivity Report of Wayne's model, the Reduced Cost column in Figure 5.16 correctly lists zeros for all three decision variables, because none of the decision variables is zero; that is, none of their nonnegativity constraints is binding.

Of course, all this implies that Wayne's original Sensitivity Report in Figure 5.14 is misleadingly bad—with its missing shadow prices and ranges, incorrect reduced cost numbers, and an erroneous budgetary shadow price—and that the recommended LP formulation of Figure 5.16 is good. On the other hand, Wayne's spreadsheet model layout in Figure 5.13 is certainly managerially easier to understand and interpret than the recommended spreadsheet formulation of Figure 5.16. It would seem that you must make a Hobson's choice: a pleasing and compact managerial layout of the LP model coupled with confusing or erroneous sensitivity results, or a rigid layout of the model coupled with correct sensitivity results. Paradoxically, this is not the case; both models are completely correct, and *neither* Sensitivity Report contains any errors whatsoever. That is, you can have the benefits of a more managerially appealing model layout in the spreadsheet without producing any Solver-related errors in the Sensitivity Report. But this requires a bit more understanding of Solver that, unfortunately, Wayne lacked. So, to resolve the paradox let us delve a little more into Solver's workings.

SIMPLE UPPER AND LOWER BOUNDS

The time and memory requirements for Solver to optimize a model are determined primarily by the size of the coefficient matrix of cells making up the LHS of the set of constraints, for example, C7:E9 in Figure 5.16. The size of this constraint coefficient matrix is proportional to the product of the number of variables (columns) and the number

	A	B	C	D	E	F	G	H	I	J
1										
2		**FRIENDLY LOAN COMPANY ($ amts. in 000's)**								
3		Loan Type:	Signature	Furniture	1st Mort.	Budget	Total			
4		Interest Rate	15%	12%	7%		$1,395			
5		Loan Amount	$1,500	$4,500	$9,000	$15,000				
6		Constraints					Total	RHS	Slack	
7		Budget				1	$15,000	<=$15,000	0.0	
8		Sign. Limit	1			-10%	0.0	<=0	0.0	
9		Mortg. Min.			1	-60%	0.0	>=0	0.0	
10										

	A	B	C	D	E	F	G	H	I	J
1										
2		FRIEN								
3		Loan T	Signatu	Furniture	1st Mo	Budget	Total			
4		Interes	0.15	0.12	0.07		=SUMPRODUCT($C$5:$E$5,C4:E4)			
5		Loan A	1500	4500	9000	=SUM(C5:E5)				
6		Constr					Total	RHS	Slack	
7		Budge				1	=SUMPRODUCT($C$5:$F$5,C7:F7)	15000	=H7-G7	
8		Sign. L	1			-0.1	=SUMPRODUCT($C$5:$F$5,C8:F8)	0	=H8-G8	
9		Mortg.			1	-0.6	=SUMPRODUCT($C$5:$F$5,C9:F9)	0	=G9-H9	
10										

Microsoft Excel 8.0 Sensitivity Report
Adjustable Cells

Cell	Name	Final Value	Reduced Cost	Objective Coefficient	Allowable Increase	Allowable Decrease
$C$5	Loan Amount Signature	$1,500	0.00	15%	1E+30	0.03
$D$5	Loan Amount Furniture	$4,500	0.00	12%	0.03	0.05
$E$5	Loan Amount 1st Mort.	$9,000	0.00	7%	0.05	0.155

Constraints

Cell	Name	Final Value	Shadow Price	Constraint R.H. Side	Allowable Increase	Allowable Decrease
$G$7	Budget Total	$15,000	0.093	$15,000	1E+30	15000
$G$8	Sign. Limit Total	0	0.030	0	4500	1500
$G$9	Mortg. Min. Total	0	-0.050	0	4500	9000

FIGURE 5.16

Wayne's Loan Portfolio Model
Using Rules from Chapter 3

of constraints (rows). Anything that can be done to reduce either of these numbers will have a multiplicitive effect in reducing the overall matrix size, and hence, the speed of optimization. Solver incorporates an advanced procedure that allows any upper or lower constraint bounds directly on the decision variables (in addition to the nonnegativity bounds) to be honored without actually considering them as constraints. This treatment of decision variable bounds, called "simple upper and lower bounds," keeps the coefficient matrix smaller, producing faster Solver optimization times while consuming less random access memory on the PC, or equivalently, allowing larger LP models to be optimized on a given PC. The price paid for the use of this simple upper and lower bounds feature is the loss of some Sensitivity Report information produced after optimization. The only sensitivity information available for any simple upper- and lower-bound constraints are their shadow prices, but without the associated range-of-applicability information produced for shadow prices on a normal constraint.

Since, at most, only one upper- or lower-bound constraint can be binding on a given decision variable at optimality, and no range information is available, a compact Sensitivity Report results if the relevant nonzero shadow price on a simple upper- or lower-bound constraint, if any, is listed next to its associated decision variable. The Reduced Cost column in the Sensitivity Report always has one cell per decision variable, and so, Solver places any nonzero shadow price on an upper- or lower-bound constraint into the Reduced Cost column next to the relevant decision variable. For example, the shadow prices on the two loan type constraints are given in the conventional way in Figure 5.16 as 3% and −5% on the Signature and First Mortgage constraints, respectively. Those values are presented in Figure 5.14 for Wayne's model in the Reduced Cost column next to the Signature and First Mortgage decision variables, respectively. Since each of these two decision variables has two constraints given in the LP model, it is not immediately clear which bound is the binding one producing that variable's nonzero shadow price entry in the Reduced Cost column for Wayne's model.

The Signature loan amount has both a simple lower-bound constraint (the "≥ 0" nonnegativity constraint) and a simple upper-bound constraint ("≤ $1500"). However, both bounds on the Signature decision cannot be binding simultaneously. Inspection reveals that the upper bound is binding; and so, the 0.03 number in the Reduced Cost column of Wayne's model must be the shadow price on the "Signature ≤ $1500" constraint. Because it is not binding, the "Signature ≥ 0" constraint, therefore, must have a shadow price of zero.

Similarly, there are two lower bound constraints on the First Mortgage decision ("1st Mortgage ≥ 0" and "1st Mortgage ≥ 9000"), both of which cannot be binding. Since the First Mortgage decision is $9000, the shadow price entry in the Reduced Cost column of Wayne's model must be for the binding "1st Mortgage ≥ 9000" simple lower-bound constraint. Because it is not binding, the "1st Mortgage ≥ 0" constraint, therefore, must have a shadow price of zero.

Thus, there is no loss of shadow price information from utilizing simple upper and lower bounds in LP formulations once you know where to look for them and how to deduce the bound to which any nonzero shadow price refers. Since simple lower and upper bounds on decisions lead to a more appealing spreadsheet layout and faster solution times (noticeable for large models), their use is common in spreadsheet LP model formulations. Be aware, however, that their use produces Sensitivity Reports that violate the standard definition for Reduced Cost given in Section 5.3.

Recall one interpretation for the reduced cost on a decision variable represents it as the shadow price on that variable's nonnegativity constraint. Instead, the reduced cost numbers for Solver LP models containing simple upper and lower bounds are the shadow prices for whichever bound, if any, is binding on that decision variable. Table 5.2 gives a more complete picture of the values the Reduced Cost shadow price entry may have in Solver models containing simple upper and lower bounds.

Is there a way to deduce the RHS range information present in the Sensitivity Report of Figure 5.16 under the Allowable Increase and Decrease columns, but missing when simple upper and lower bounds are used? Unfortunately, the answer is no. If that were possible, Solver would always present a Sensitivity Report like Figure 5.16. If the RHS range information for simple upper and lower bounds is important, then you must reformulate the spreadsheet representation of the LP model in Figure 5.13 to avoid Solver's detecting the presence of simple upper and lower bounds and re-optimize the model. Solver will not evoke its simple upper and lower bounding procedure if the upper or lower bound on any decision variable is specified indirectly on the worksheet. This "indirect reference" can be achieved by use of some intervening formula, such as the SUMPRODUCT formulas in Figure 5.16, which relate each decision variable to its bound via a third LHS cell. Otherwise, if Solver sees any

TABLE 5.2 Reduced Cost Values		
VALUE OF DECISION VARIABLE AT OPTIMALITY	REDUCED COST ENTRY, MAXIMIZATION MODEL	REDUCED COST ENTRY, MINIMIZATION MODEL
Lower-Bound (≥) Binding	Zero or Negative Shadow Price	Zero or Positive Shadow Price
Upper-Bound (≤) Binding	Zero or Positive Shadow Price	Zero or Negative Shadow Price
Neither Bound Binding	Zero Shadow Price	Zero Shadow Price

Changing Cells cell references in the "Subject to the Constraints" box of the Solver Parameters dialog (other than any nonnegativity ones), then it will evoke its special bounding procedure. For example, Wayne's model in Figure 5.13 references the Changing Cells, C5 and E5, in the first two constraints listed in the "Subject to the Constraints" box of the Solver Parameters dialog, and that triggered Solver's upper- and lower-bounding procedure.

SHADOW PRICE INTERPRETATION

As mentioned earlier, the Solver shadow price on Wayne's budget constraint of .120 is *not* incorrect; rather, it was Wayne's interpretation of that shadow price that got him into trouble. Note that Wayne's model in Figure 5.13 has formulas on the right-hand side of the Loan Limit constraints for Signature and First Mortgage loans in cells C6 and D6, respectively, a violation of one of the recommended spreadsheet formulation rules in Chapter 3. Recall the definition of a shadow price is the change in the LP's OV per unit of change in a given constraint's RHS value *holding all other data, including the other RHSs, constant.* Therefore, the shadow price of .120 reported in Wayne's Figure 5.14 Sensitivity Report should be interpreted as follows: Holding the Loan Limit RHSs for Signature and First Mortgage loans at their original dollar amount bounds of $1500 and $9000, respectively, the improvement in the objective function value is .12 for each additional budget dollar.

Holding Signature and First Mortgage loans at their original RHS dollar values allows the incremental budget dollar only one option in Wayne's model, to be allocated as a Furniture loan returning 12%. Thus, Solver is correctly reporting the shadow price for Wayne's model. Of course, holding the Signature and First Mortgage loans at their original RHS dollar values is inconsistent with the results of a re-optimized solution in which all *three* RHSs will be adjusted to reflect the revised RHS limits implied by an additional budget dollar. Wayne's mistake was assuming that Friendly's percentage policy constraints on total budget would be maintained in his model's Sensitivity Report, but that is not true in his model because of the formulas appearing on two of his RHSs.

The LP formulation in Figure 5.16 avoids this mistaken interpretation by referencing the total loan amounts instead of total budget amount in the constraints and by placing all formulas on the LHS of constraints leaving constants for all RHSs. Having the loan-related formulas on the LHS of constraints forces Solver to make the necessary adjustments in all three LHSs when evaluating an incremental budget dollar's contribution. This adjustment of the LHSs produces a Sensitivity Report yielding the correct .093 shadow price in Figure 5.16. Clearly, the formulation of Figure 5.16 reflects Wayne's intended model for Friendly's policy constraints.[9]

The conclusion from this example is that the use of simple upper and lower bounds and the use of formulas on RHSs of formulations can lead to more compact and managerially appealing spreadsheet models. For these reasons, we will use such model formulations extensively in the applications of Solver in the next three chapters. Keep in mind, however, that such formulations may require additional care in interpreting the managerially valuable information in Solver's Sensitivity Report.

5.7   SUMMARY

The emphasis in this chapter was on the interpretation of the Solver Sensitivity Report for an LP model, as presented in Sections 5.3, 5.4, 5.5, and 5.6. We stressed the wealth of information available through sensitivity analysis on the right-hand sides and on the objective function coefficients. The role of degeneracy and signals for alternative optima were also discussed.

---

[9]Note that in Wayne's original model if he had interpreted his loan requirements as being applied to the total amount loaned (LHS) instead of the budget amount (RHS), then his model would also have produced the .093 shadow price.

In the first part of this chapter (Section 5.2) we explored the role of slack and surplus variables and studied the construction and the geometry of an LP model. In Section 5.6 we explored the confusing Sensitivity Report results generated by Solver when upper or lower bounds are placed directly upon decision variables and the pitfalls in shadow price interpretation that may occur when placing formulas on the RHS of constraints or otherwise basing some of a model's formulas upon the LHS versus the RHS of binding constraints.

Key Terms

Slack or Surplus Variable. Used to convert an inequality constraint to an equality constraint.

Degenerate Solution. A solution for which the number of positive-valued variables is less than the number of active constraints.

Nondegenerate Solution. A solution for which the number of variables with positive optimal values is equal to the number of active constraints.

Shadow Price. The ith shadow price on the Solver Sensitivity Report is the rate of change in OV as the ith RHS is increased.

Allowable RHS Range. Range of RHS values for which the shadow price remains constant.

Alternative Optimal Solutions. The existence of more than one optimal solution.

Objective Coefficient Ranges. Gives ranges of objective function coefficients over which no change in the optimal solution will occur.

Self-Review Exercises

True-False

1. **T F** If a point does not satisfy the $\leq$ constraint, the associated slack value is negative.

2. **T F** Degeneracy is important because we must give more restrictive interpretations to the Solver output when the optimal solution is degenerate.

3. **T F** Shadow price, for a given constraint, is the rate of change in OV as the RHS increases.

4. **T F** The shadow price on the ith constraint is a nonconstant linear function of b_i over the range given by allowable decrease and allowable increase.

5. **T F** Positive slack variables at optimality indicate redundant constraints.

6. **T F** A $\leq$ constraint with positive optimal slack will always have an infinite allowable increase for the RHS.

The following questions (7–8) refer to the spreadsheet output shown in Figure 5.12:

7. **T F** If the requirements on A and C are each increased by 0.5 pound, sensitivity analysis tells us that the optimal cost will increase by \$24.44.

8. **T F** The fact that the shadow prices are all ≥ 0 is exclusively explained by the fact that we are dealing with a Min model.

Multiple Choice

9. A degenerate optimal solution
   a. has fewer than m positive variables (where m is the number of constraints)
   b. provides no information on alternative optima
   c. may not provide information on the full range of allowable increase and allowable decrease in objective coefficients
   d. all of the above

10. "Improvement" in an LP model means
    a. the OV is increased for a Max model
    b. the OV is decreased for a Min model
    c. both a and b

11. For a nondegenerate optimal solution to a Max model, if the objective function coefficient c_1 increases by (exactly) the allowable increase

a. the OV may change
b. the previous optimal solution remains optimal
c. there will be a new optimal solution with a larger optimal value of x_1
d. all of the above

12. We have just solved a cost Min model and $x_1^* = 0$. Management wants to know: "How much does the cost of x_1 have to be reduced before we will begin to use it at a positive level in an optimal solution?" The answer appears in which portion of the worksheet or Solver Sensitivity Report?
a. values of variables
b. allowable changes in RHS of first constraint
c. allowable increase in the coefficient of x_1
d. reduced cost

13. Suppose that the first constraint of an LP, evaluated at a given point P_0, has a zero value for the slack variable. Then
a. P_0 lies on the boundary of the feasible region
b. P_0 lies on the first constraint line
c. both a and b

14. A correct relationship is
a. a constraint with zero shadow price must be inactive
b. a constraint with positive shadow price must be active
c. both a and b

The following questions (15–18) refer to the spreadsheet output shown in Figure 5.12:

15. If the requirement on A is changed from 5 to 6.5
a. the OV will decrease by $66.66
b. the OV will improve by $66.66
c. the OV will increase by $66.66
d. the OV will not change

16. If the requirement on C is reduced from 30 to 20
a. the OV will decrease by $44.44
b. the OV will increase by $44.44
c. the OV will improve by at least $31.00

17. If the cost of ore from location 2 is decreased to $300 per ton
a. the OV will not change
b. the optimal solution will not change
c. neither a nor b
d. both a and b

18. If the cost of ore from location 1 is reduced to $680 per ton
a. there will be a new optimal solution with $T1^* > 0.259$
b. there will be alternative optima
c. the optimal solution above remains optimal
d. all of the above

Answers

1.	T	6.	T	11.	d	15.	c
2.	T	7.	F	12.	d	16.	c
3.	T	8.	F	13.	b	17.	b
4.	F	9.	d	14.	b	18.	d
5.	F	10.	c				

Problems

5-1. Consider an LP in 3 variables and 14 constraints. An optimal Solver solution will have at most how many positive variables?

5-2. For the following model:

$$\text{Max } x_1 + x_2$$
$$\text{s.t. } x_1 + x_2 \geq 3$$
$$2x_1 + x_2 \leq 12$$
$$x_1 + x_2 \leq 12$$
$$x_1 \geq 0, x_2 \geq 0$$

(a) Use GLP to plot a geometric representation of the model. Are there any degenerate corners?
(b) Add the constraint $x_1 + x_2 \leq 8$. Now are there any degenerate corners?

5-3. Consider an LP in 80 variables and 30 constraints.
(a) An optimal nondegenerate Solver solution will have how many positive variables?
(b) An optimal degenerate Solver solution will have how many positive variables?

··5-4. Karma Computers produces two computer models, Standard and Deluxe. A Standard model is produced by assembling a single disk drive with a Standard Chassis. A Deluxe model is produced by assembling two disk drives with a Deluxe Chassis. The Standard model has a net profit per unit of $300 while the Deluxe model has a net profit per unit of $400. The current inventory of Karma consists of 60 Standard Chassis, 50 Deluxe Chassis, and 120 Disk Drives.

(a) Formulate the Karma LP model and use GLP to plot a geometric representation of it.

(b) Optimize the Karma model with GLP and use that result to fill in the missing values in the blank cells of the worksheet in Figure 5.17.

	A	B	C	D	E	F	G
1	KARMA COMPUTER						
2	Decision Variables	S	D				
3	Quantity			PROFIT			
4	Contrib. Margin	$300	$400				
5	Subject To:			LHS		RHS	Slack
6	Schas Constr	1			≤	60	
7	Dchas Constr		1		≤	50	
8	Ddrive Constr				≤		

FIGURE 5.17

(c) Use the results from the worksheet above to fill in the missing values for Final Value and Constraint R.H. Side in the blank cells of the Karma model Sensitivity Report below. Next, use the GLP Karma model to determine the values of the remaining missing cells in the Sensitivity Report in Figure 5.18.

Microsoft Excel 8.0 Sensitivity Report

Adjustable Cells

Cell	Name	Final Value	Reduced Cost	Objective Coefficient	Allowable Increase	Allowable Decrease
$B$3	Quantity S			300		
$C$3	Quantity D			400	200	400

Constraints

Cell	Name		Final Value	Shadow Price	Constraint R.H. Side	Allowable Increase	Allowable Decrease
$D$6	Schas Constr	LHS			60	60	
$D$7	Dchas Constr	LHS			50		20
$D$8	Ddrive Constr	LHS					60

FIGURE 5.18

5-5. Refer to Figure 5.4.

(a) Suppose that 5 more hours of labor are made available in department A. What will be the change in the OV?

(b) Suppose that 20 fewer hours of labor are available in department A. What will be the change in the OV?

(c) The shadow price on department A is valid for what range of values of the RHS?

5-6. The shadow price on an inactive constraint always has what value? What can you say about the shadow price on an active constraint?

5-7. Consider a constraint with a positive optimal slack value. What must the shadow price be?

5-8. Refer to the Solver output shown in Figure 5.4.

(a) Suppose that the right-hand side of the Total Units constraint in row 10 is changed to 6. What is the effect on the OV?

(b) By how much can the total unit requirements constraint be tightened before the shadow price could possibly change?

(c) Suppose that 50 more hours of labor are available in department B. By how much will the OV change?

··5-9. Note that in Figure 5.8 there is an allowable increase of zero for the capacity of department B. What anomaly is responsible for this?

5-10. Refer to Figure 5.8. Is the exhibited solution degenerate or nondegenerate? Support your answer.

5-11. Refer to Figure 5.4. Suppose that the contribution margin of E is reduced to $4000 per unit.

(a) What is the resulting optimal solution?

(b) What is the *change* in the OV?

5-12. Refer to Figure 5.4. Suppose that the contribution margin of F is increased to $5000 per unit.

(a) What is the resulting optimal solution?

(b) What is the *change* in the OV?

5-13. Refer to Figure 5.12.

(a) How much would the price per ton of ore from location 4 have to decrease in order for it to become attractive to purchase it?

(b) Suppose that the price of ore from location 1 decreases by $80 per ton. Is there any change in the optimal solution or in the OV?

(c) Suppose that the price of ore from location 1 increases by $100 per ton. Is there any change in the optimal solution? What, if any, is the associated change in the cost of an optimally blended ton?

5-14. Refer to Figure 5.12.

(a) Suppose that the price of ore from location 3 increases by $50 per ton. Is there any change in the optimal solution? What, if any, is the associated change in the OV?

(b) Analyze the effect on the optimal solution of decreasing the cost of ore from location 3 by exactly $118.269 per ton. (For example, does the present solution remain optimal? Is there an additional optimal solution, and if so how can it be characterized?)

(c) For the change described above in part (b), what is the new OV?

5-15. You have just solved an LP model. You observe that you have a nondegenerate solution and for some objective function coefficient you see a zero entry under the Allowable Increase column. What does this tell you?

··5-16. Explain how to use the reduced costs to know if there are alternative optimal solutions.

5-17. Employing the terms *rate* and *OV*, give the correct interpretation of shadow price in the Solver Sensitivity Report.

··5-18. Consider the Buster Sod model: Buster Sod operates an 800-acre irrigated farm in the Red River Valley of Arizona. Sod's principal activities are raising wheat, alfalfa, and beef. The Red River Valley Water Authority has just given its water allotments for next year (Sod was allotted 1000 acre-feet), and Sod is busy preparing his production plan for next year. He figures that beef prices will hold at around $500 per ton and that wheat will sell at $2 per bushel. Best guesses are that he will be able to sell alfalfa at $22 per ton, but if he needs more alfalfa to feed his beef than he can raise, he will have to pay $28 per ton to get the alfalfa to his feedlot.

Some technological features of Sod's operation are wheat yield, 70 bushels per acre; alfalfa yield, 4 tons per acre. Other features are given in the accompanying table. Define the variables:

ACTIVITY	LABOR, MACHINERY, AND OTHER COSTS ($)	WATER REQUIREMENTS (ACRE-FT)	LAND REQUIREMENTS (ACRES)	ALFALFA REQUIREMENTS (TONS)
1 acre of wheat	20	2	1	
1 acre of alfalfa	28	3	1	
1 ton of beef	50	0.05	0.1	5

$Wheat$ = wheat raised and sold (acres)

$Alfalfa\ Acres$ = alfalfa raised (tons)

$Beef$ = beef raised and sold (tons)

$Alfalfa\ Bought$ = alfalfa bought (tons)

$Alfalfa\ Sold$ = alfalfa sold (tons)

An LP formulation and solution to Buster Sod's model are shown in Figure 5.19. Using the information in Figure 5.19, answer the following questions.

(a) Show calculations that explain the values of the coefficient of *Wheat* in the objective function and the coefficients of *Alfalfa Acres* in the first and second constraints.

(b) How much water is being used?

(c) How much beef is being produced?

(d) Does Sod buy or sell alfalfa?

(e) How much should Sod pay to acquire another acre-ft of water?

(f) Interpret the shadow price on "Acres Limit" of 800.

	A	B	C	D	E	F	G	H	I	J
1		Wheat	Alfalfa	Beef	Alfalfa Bought	Alfalfa Sold				
2	Yield	70 Bu/Ac	4 Tons/Ac							
3	Price	$2 /Bu		$500 /T	$28 /Ton	$22 /Ton				
4	Costs	$20 /Ac	$28 /Ac	$50 /T						
5		Wheat Acres	Alfalfa Acres	Beef Tons	Alfalfa Bought Tons	Alfalfa Sold Tons				
6		0	0	8,000	40,000	0	Profit			
7		$120 /Ac	$(7)/Ac	$450 /T	$(28)/Ac	$22 /Ac	$2,480,000			
8							Total		Available	Slack
9	Acres Limit	1	0.25	0.1			800 ≤		800	-0
10	Water Limit	2	0.75	0.05			400 ≤		1000	600
11	Balance		-1	5	-1	1	-7.276E-12 =		0	0

Microsoft Excel 8.0 Sensitivity Report

Adjustable Cells

Cell	Name	Final Value	Reduced Cost	Objective Coefficient	Allowable Increase	Allowable Decrease
$B$6	Wheat Ac	0	-2980	120	2980	1E+30
$C$6	Alfalfa Ac	0	-754	-7	754	1E+30
$D$6	Beef Tons	8000	0	450	1E+30	298
$E$6	Alfalfa Bought Tons	40000	0	-28	6	55.85
$F$6	Alfalfa Sold Tons	0	-6	22	6	1E+30

Constraints

Cell	Name	Final Value	Shadow Price	Constraint R.H. Side	Allowable Increase	Allowable Decrease
$G$9	Acres Limit Total	800	3100	800	1200	800
$G$10	Water Limit Total	400	0	1000	1E+30	600
$G$11	Balance Total	0	28	0	40000	1E+30

FIGURE 5.19

Buster Sod Model LP Solution and Sensitivity Report

(g) What happens to the optimal planting policy if the price of wheat triples? What happens to the OV?

(h) How much profit will Sod receive from the optimal operation of his farm?

(i) What happens to the optimal value of the objective function if the cost of alfalfa purchased increases from $28 to $29?

Note: The coefficient of *Alfalfa Bought* is currently −$28 and it will become −$29. Thus the coefficient will *decrease* by $1.

(j) How much can the cost of buying alfalfa decrease before the current optimal planting policy will change?

5-19. A plant can manufacture five different products in any combination. Each product requires time on each of three machines, as shown in the following table. All figures are in minutes per pound of product.

PRODUCT	MACHINE-TIME (MIN/LB)		
	1	2	3
A	12	8	5
B	7	9	10
C	8	4	7
D	10	0	3
E	7	11	2

Each machine is available 128 hours per week. Products A, B, C, D, and E are purely competitive, and any amounts made may be sold at per pound prices of $5, $4, $5, $4, and $4, respectively. Variable labor costs are $4 per hour for machines 1 and 2, and $3 per hour for machine 3. Material costs are $2 for each pound of products A and C, and $1 for each pound of products B, D, and E. You wish to maximize profit to the firm. The LP solution and Sensitivity Report are shown in Figure 5.20.

(a) How many hours are spent on each of the three machines?

(b) What are the units of the shadow prices on the constraints that control machine capacity?

(c) How much should the firm be willing to spend to obtain another hour of time on machine 2?

(d) How much can the sales price of product A increase before the optimal production plan changes? State your answer in the proper units.

	A	B	C	D	E	F	G	H	I	J
1 Product	A	B	C	D	E					
2 Price/Lb.	$5	$4	$5	$4	$4					
3 Cost/Hr Mach. 1	$4	$4	$4	$4	$4					
4 Cost/Hr Mach. 2	$4	$4	$4	$4	$4					
5 Cost/Hr Mach. 3	$3	$3	$3	$3	$3					
6 Matrl.Costs/Lb	$2	$1	$2	$1	$1					
7 Product	A	B	C	D	E			Mach. Hours Avail/Week	
8 Pounds Prod.	0	0	512	0	512	Profit		128	
9 Contr. Mar./Lb	$1.417	$1.433	$1.850	$2.183	$1.700	$ 1,817.60			
10							Total	Min.Avail./Wk.	Slack
11 Mach. 1 Min.	12	7	8	10	7		7680 ≤	7680	7E-07
12 Mach. 2 Min.	8	9	4	0	11		7680 ≤	7680	2E-08
13 Mach. 3 Min.	5	10	7	3	2		4608 ≤	7680	3072
14	=B2-SUMPRODUCT(B3:B5,B11:B13)/60-B6; Copied to C9:F9								
15									

Microsoft Excel 8.0 Sensitivity Report

Adjustable Cells

Cell	Name	Final Value	Reduced Cost	Objective Coefficient	Allowable Increase	Allowable Decrease
$B$8	Pounds Prod. A	0	-1.380	1.417	1.380	1E+30
$C$8	Pounds Prod. B	0	-0.245	1.433	0.245	1E+30
$D$8	Pounds Prod. C	512	0	1.85	0.093	0.041
$E$8	Pounds Prod. D	0	-0.075	2.183	0.075	1E+30
$F$8	Pounds Prod. E	512	0	1.700	0.1125	0.081

Constraints

Cell	Name	Final Value	Shadow Price	Constraint R.H. Side	Allowable Increase	Allowable Decrease
$G$11	Mach. 1 Min. Total	7680	0.2258	7680	2671.304	2792.727
$G$12	Mach. 2 Min. Total	7680	0.0108	7680	4388.571	3840
$G$13	Mach. 3 Min. Total	4608	0	7680	1E+30	3072

FIGURE 5.20

Solution for Five-Product, Three-Machine Model

··5-20. *A Product Mix/Process Selection Model.* Two products, A and B, are processed on three machines. Both products have two possible routings. Routing 1 processes the product on machines 1 and 2 while routing 2 processes the product on machines 1 and 3. Processing times in hours per unit are given in following table.

PRODUCT	ROUTING	MACHINE-TIME (HR/UNIT)		
		1	2	3
A	1	2	1	
A	2	2		1.5
B	1	1	2	
B	2	1		3

The costs per hour on machines 1, 2, and 3 are $20, $30, and $18, respectively. Each machine is available for 40 hours per week. Any amount of products A and B may be sold at $110 and $150 per unit, respectively. The LP solution and Sensitivity Report are shown in Figure 5.21 where

$$A_i = \text{units of A produced by routing } i \ (i = 1, 2)$$
$$B_i = \text{units of B produced by routing } i \ (i = 1, 2)$$

(a) Show calculations that explain the values of the coefficients in the objective function.

(b) How much product B is being produced? How much by the first routing? (Interpret the numbers as production rates. Thus 4.44 would represent 4.44 units per week. This could be accomplished by producing 4 units and starting the 5th in the first week, finishing the 5th through the 8th units and starting the 9th in the second week, etc.)

(c) How many hours are used on each of the three machines?

(d) What are the units of the shadow prices on the machine capacity constraints?

(e) Suppose that there is an opportunity to work up to 8 hours of overtime on machine 2 at a cost of $45 per hour (50% more than the regular time cost of $30 per hour). Should machine 2 be scheduled for 8 hours of overtime?

	A	B	C	D	E	F	G	H	I
1	Product	A1	A2	B1	B2				
2	Price	$110	$110	$150	$150				
3	Cost/Hr Mach. 1	$ 20	$ 20	$ 20	$ 20				
4	Cost/Hr Mach. 2	$ 30	$ 30	$ 30	$ 30				
5	Cost/Hr Mach. 3	$ 18	$ 18	$ 18	$ 18				
6	Product	A1	A2	B1	B2				
7	Qty. Prod.	4.444	0.000	17.778	13.333	Profit			
8	Contr. Margin	$ 40	$ 43	$ 70	$ 76	$2,435.56			
9						Total		Hrs.Avail.	Slack
10	Mach. 1 Hrs.	2	2	1	1	40 ≤		40	-0
11	Mach. 2 Hrs.	1		2		40 ≤		40	-0
12	Mach. 3 Hrs.		1.5		3	40 ≤		40	0

Microsoft Excel 8.0 Sensitivity Report

Adjustable Cells

Cell	Name	Final Value	Reduced Cost	Objective Coefficient	Allowable Increase	Allowable Decrease
$B$7	Qty. Prod. A1	4.444	0	40	100	0
$C$7	Qty. Prod. A2	0	0	43	0	1E+30
$D$7	Qty. Prod. B1	17.78	0	70	0	50
$E$7	Qty. Prod. B2	13.33	0	76	1E+30	0

Constraints

Cell	Name	Final Value	Shadow Price	Constraint R.H. Side	Allowable Increase	Allowable Decrease
$F$10	Mach. 1 Hrs. Total	40	3.333	40	53.333	6.667
$F$11	Mach. 2 Hrs. Total	40	33.333	40	13.333	26.667
$F$12	Mach. 3 Hrs. Total	40	24.222	40	20.000	40

FIGURE 5.21

LP Formulation for Problem 5-20

··5-21. *A Blending Model.* A vineyard wishes to blend four different vintages to make three types of blended wine. Restrictions are placed on the percentage composition of the blends (see accompanying table).

BLEND	VINTAGE				SALES PRICE PER GALLON ($)
	1	2	3	4	
A	at least 75% 1 & 2		*	at most 5%	70
B	*	at least 35% 2 & 3		*	40
C		at least 50% 1 & 3, no restriction on 2		at most 40%	30
Supply (gallons)	180	250	200	400	
*Indicates no restriction.					

	A	B	C	D	E	F	G
1	Decisions	Blend A	Blend B	Blend C	Total	Supply
2	Vintage 1	180.00	0	0	180	<=180
3	Vintage 2	246.71	3.29	0	250	<=250
4	Vintage 3	0	200.00	6.46E-26	200	<=200
5	Vintage 4	22.46	377.54	0	400	<=400
6	Total Produced	449.17>=	580.83>=	0.00>=		
7	Total Sold	449.17	580.83	0.00	Profit	
8	Sales Price	$70	$40	$30	$54,675	
9	Min Blend %	Blend A	Blend B	Blend C		
10	Vintage 1	180.00		0		
11	Vintage 2	246.71	3.29			
12	Vintage 3		200.00	6.46E-26		
13	Vintage 4					
14	Less % of Total	75%	35%	50%		
15	Balance	89.83	0.00	0.00		
16	Must Be	>=0	>=0	>=0		
17						
18	Max Blend %	Blend A	Blend B	Blend C		
19	Vintage 1					
20	Vintage 2					
21	Vintage 3					
22	Vintage 4	22.46		0		
23	Less % of Total	5%	0%	40%		
24	Balance	0.00	0.00	0.00		
25	Must Be	<=0	<=0	<=0		

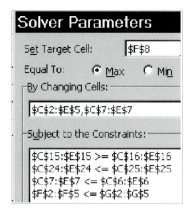

Solver Parameters

Set Target Cell: $F$8

Equal To: ⦿ Max   ◯ Min

By Changing Cells:

$C$2:$E$5,$C$7:$E$7

Subject to the Constraints:

$C$15:$E$15 >= $C$16:$E$16
$C$24:$E$24 <= $C$25:$E$25
$C$7:$E$7 <= $C$6:$E$6
$F$2:$F$5 <= $G$2:$G$5

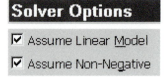

Solver Options

☑ Assume Linear Model
☑ Assume Non-Negative

Cell	Formula	Copy To
C6	= SUM(C2:C5)	D6:E6
C10	= C2	C11, D11:D12, E10, E12
C15	= SUM(C10:C13) – C$6*C14	D15:E15, C24:E24

FIGURE 5.22

LP Model and Solution for
Problem 5-21

The LP solution is shown in Figure 5.22 and the Sensitivity Report is shown in Figure 5.23.

(a) What is the purpose of the constraints in F2:G5?

(b) What is the purpose of the constraints in C15:E16 and C24:E25?

(c) Explain why the LHS and RHS of the constraint C15:C16 have the values they do. What restriction does the constraint represent?

(d) What is the maximum revenue that can be achieved by blending the four vintages?

(e) How much of each blend should be produced? What is the composition of each blend?

(f) Is the current solution degenerate or nondegenerate? How can you tell?

A	B	C	D	E	F	G	H
1	Microsoft Excel 8.0 Sensitivity Report						
2	Adjustable Cells						
3			Final	Reduced	Objective	Allowable	Allowable
4	Cell	Name	Value	Cost	Coefficient	Increase	Decrease
5	$C$2	Vintage 1 Blend A	180.00	0.00	0	1E+30	0
6	$D$2	Vintage 1 Blend B	0.00	-50.000	0	50.000	1E+30
7	$E$2	Vintage 1 Blend C	0.00	0.00	0	0	1E+30
8	$C$3	Vintage 2 Blend A	246.71	0.00	0	0	0
9	$D$3	Vintage 2 Blend B	3.29	0.00	0	0	0.000
10	$E$3	Vintage 2 Blend C	0.00	0.00	0	0.000	1E+30
11	$C$4	Vintage 3 Blend A	0.00	0.00	0	0	1E+30
12	$D$4	Vintage 3 Blend B	200.00	0.00	0	0	0
13	$E$4	Vintage 3 Blend C	0.00	0.00	0	37.5	0
14	$C$5	Vintage 4 Blend A	22.46	0.00	0	771.429	46.154
15	$D$5	Vintage 4 Blend B	377.54	0.00	0	46.154	21.862
16	$E$5	Vintage 4 Blend C	0.00	-56.250	0	56.250	1E+30
17	$C$7	Total Sold Blend A	449.17	0.00	70	38.571	30.000
18	$D$7	Total Sold Blend B	580.83	0.00	40	30.000	14.211
19	$E$7	Total Sold Blend C	0.00	0.00	30	22.500	30
20	Constraints						
21			Final	Shadow	Constraint	Allowable	Allowable
22	Cell	Name	Value	Price	R.H. Side	Increase	Decrease
23	$C$15 Balance	Blend A	89.83	0.00	0	89.833	1E+30
24	$D$15 Balance	Blend B	0.00	-50.00	0	155.816	2.079
25	$E$15 Balance	Blend C	0.00	0.00	0	0	1E+30
26	$C$24 Balance	Blend A	0.00	50.00	0	5.643	20.731
27	$D$24 Balance	Blend B	0.00	0.00	0	1E+30	0
28	$E$24 Balance	Blend C	0.00	106.25	0	0	80.000
29	$F$2	Vintage 1 Total	180	72.5	180	112.857	180
30	$F$3	Vintage 2 Total	250	72.5	250	112.857	239.717
31	$F$4	Vintage 3 Total	200	72.5	200	3.198	200
32	$F$5	Vintage 4 Total	400	22.5	400	445.188	5.940
33	$C$7	Total Sold Blend A	449.17	70.00	0	1E+30	449.167
34	$D$7	Total Sold Blend B	580.83	40.00	0	1E+30	580.833
35	$E$7	Total Sold Blend C	0.00	30.00	0	1E+30	0

FIGURE 5.23

Sensitivity Report for Problem 5-21

(g) What is the minimum amount by which the selling price of blend C would have to change, and in what direction, before it would become optimal to produce blend C?

(h) What are the shadow prices of the four vintages? What are the units of these shadow prices?

(i) Suppose an earthquake destroys half of the available vintage 3. What can you say about the impact on the optimal solution and the optimal revenue?

··5-22. The Party Nut Company has on hand 550 pounds of peanuts, 150 pounds of cashews, 90 pounds of Brazil nuts, and 70 pounds of hazelnuts. It packages and sells four varieties of mixed nuts in standard 8-ounce (half-pound) cans. The mix requirements and the contribution margin per can are shown in the accompanying table. The firm can sell all that it can produce. What mixes of products should it produce to maximize profit contribution?

MIX	CONTENTS	CONTR. MARGIN PER CAN
1 (peanuts)	Peanuts only	$0.26
2 (party mix)	No more than 50% peanuts; at least 15% cashews; at least 10% Brazil nuts	0.40
3 (cashews)	Cashews only	0.51
4 (luxury mix)	At least 30% cashews; at least 20% Brazil nuts; at least 30% hazelnuts	0.52

The model can be formulated as the linear program shown in Figure 5.24. Note that in the model given in Figure 5.24 the coefficient for Peanut Mix in the objective function is $.52 rather than $.26 because there are two 8-ounce cans for each pound of peanuts sold as peanuts only.

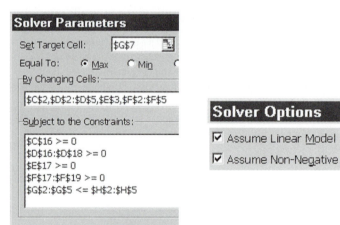

	A	B	C	D	E	F	G	H
1		Decisions	Peanut Mix	Party Mix	Cashew Mix	Luxury Mix	Total	Supply
2		Peanuts	380.00	123.333		46.667	550	<=550
3		Cashews		80.00	0.00	70	150	<=150
4		Brazils		43.33		46.667	90	<=90
5		Hazelnuts		0.00		70	70	<=70
6		Total	380.00	246.667	0.00	233.333	Profit	
7		Contr. Margin	$0.52	$0.80	$1.02	$1.04	$637.60	
8								
9		Blend %	Peanut Mix	Party Mix	Cashew Mix	Luxury Mix		
10		Peanuts	=100% of Total	<=50% of Total				
11		Cashews		>=15% of Total	=100% of Total	>=30% of Total		
12		Brazils		>=10% of Total		>=20% of Total		
13		Hazelnuts				>=30% of Total		
14								
15		Balance >= 0	Peanut Mix	Party Mix	Cashew Mix	Luxury Mix		
16		Peanuts	0	0				
17		Cashews		43.000	0	0		
18		Brazils		18.667		0		
19		Hazelnuts				0		

	B	C	D	E	F	G
6	Total	=SUM(C2:C5)	=SUM(D2:D5)	=SUM(E2:E5)	=SUM(F2:F5)	Profit
7	Contr. Margin	0.52	0.8	1.02	1.04	=SUMPRODUCT($C$6:$F$6,C7:F7)
8						
9	Blend %	Peanut Mix	Party Mix	Cashew Mix	Luxury Mix	
10	Peanuts	1	0.5			
11	Cashews		0.15	1	0.3	
12	Brazils		0.1		0.2	
13	Hazelnuts				0.3	
14						
15	Balance >= 0	Peanut Mix	Party Mix	Cashew Mix	Luxury Mix	
16	Peanuts	=C2-C10*C$6	=-(D2-D10*D$6)			
17	Cashews		=D3-D11*D$6	=E3-E11*E$6	=F3-F11*F$6	
18	Brazils		=D4-D12*D$6		=F4-F12*F$6	
19	Hazelnuts				=F5-F13*F$6	

Solver Parameters

Set Target Cell: $G$7

Equal To: ⦿ Max ○ Min

By Changing Cells:

$C$2,$D$2:$D$5,$E$3,$F$2:$F$5

Subject to the Constraints:

$C$16 >= 0
$D$16:$D$18 >= 0
$E$17 >= 0
$F$17:$F$19 >= 0
$G$2:$G$5 <= $H$2:$H$5

Solver Options

☑ Assume Linear Model
☑ Assume Non-Negative

FIGURE 5.24

LP Model and Solution for the Party Nut Model

In the Sensitivity Report in Figure 5.25 we have purposely deleted several of the shadow prices and reduced costs. Use this output to answer the questions. If it is impossible to answer the question, state why.

(a) Explain the calculation that justifies $1.02 as the coefficient of Cashew Mix in the objective function.

(b) How many cans of Party Mix are produced in the optimal solution?

(c) Is the shadow price on the G3:H3 constraint ≥ 0 or ≤ 0? Explain why.

(d) What is the value of the shadow price on the constraint D18 ≥ 0? How do you know?

(e) What is the meaning of the fact that the content of cell D17 is positive? Explain (not using LP jargon).

(f) What is the effect on the optimal solution and the OV if the sales price of the Peanut Mix increases to $0.27 per 8-ounce can?

(g) What is the numerical value of the shadow price on the G2:H2 constraint? (*Hint:* What would you do with another pound of peanuts if you had them?)

(h) Why is the allowable increase for the RHS of the G2:H2 constraint infinity? (*Hint:* The answer to part (g) provides the basis for the rationale.)

(i) Provide an explanation as to why it is possible to have an optimal solution even though there is a positive surplus on the D11 constraint.

(j) What are the numerical values for the reduced costs for Peanuts in the Party Mix and Cashews in the Cashew Mix?

··5-23. Why is the allowable decrease on the objective coefficient of *F* equal to 1500 in Figure 5.8 and 19,000 in Figure 5.10?

··5-24. Note that the RHS of the market balance mix constraint in Row 8 has an allowable increase of 1E+30 in Figure 5.8 and 3.75 in Figure 5.10. Yet, as you can see by comparing Figures 5.7 and 5.9, the optimal corner is the same in both cases. Use the geometry to explain this difference in the values of allowable increase.

Microsoft Excel 8.0 Sensitivity Report
Adjustable Cells

Cell	Name	Final Value	Reduced Cost	Objective Coefficient	Allowable Increase	Allowable Decrease
$C$2	Peanuts Peanut Mix	380.00	0	0.52	0.06	0.12
$D$2	Peanuts Party Mix	123.33		0.8	0.09	0.06
$D$3	Cashews Party Mix	80.00	0	0.8	0.24	0.06
$D$4	Brazils Party Mix	43.33	0	0.8	0.36	0.56
$D$5	Hazelnuts Party Mix	0	-0.24	0.80	0.24	1E+30
$E$3	Cashews Cashew Mix	0		1.02	0.06	1E+30
$F$2	Peanuts Luxury Mix	46.67	0	1.04	1E+30	0.36
$F$3	Cashews Luxury Mix	70	0	1.04	0.56	0.24
$F$4	Brazils Luxury Mix	46.67	0	1.04	0.56	0.36
$F$5	Hazelnuts Luxury Mix	70	0	1.04	1E+30	0.24

Constraints

Cell	Name	Final Value	Shadow Price	Constraint R.H. Side	Allowable Increase	Allowable Decrease
$G$2	Peanuts Total	550		550	1E+30	380
$G$3	Cashews Total	150		150	93.33	61.43
$G$4	Brazils Total	90	1.08	90	143.33	23.33
$G$5	Hazelnuts Total	70	1.32	70	56	70
$C$16	Peanuts Peanut Mix	0	0	0	0	1E+30
$D$16	Peanuts Party Mix	0	-0.56	0	61.67	93.33
$D$17	Cashews Party Mix	43.00	0	0	43	1E+30
$D$18	Brazils Party Mix	18.67		0	18.67	1E+30
$E$17	Cashews Cashew Mix	0	0	0	0	1E+30
$F$17	Cashews Luxury Mix	0	-0.56	0	46.67	70
$F$18	Brazils Luxury Mix	0	-0.56	0	23.33	46.67
$F$19	Hazelnuts Luxury Mix	0	-0.80	0	28	56

FIGURE 5.25

Sensitivity Report for the Party Nut Model

Case Study   Questions Based on the Red Brand Canners Case

We first saw the Red Brand Canners (RBC) case in Chapter 3, where the model was formulated and assumptions were discussed. In the following questions, the analysis continues. You are asked to solve several formulations in Excel and then analyze the Solver Sensitivity Reports.

1. Use Solver to optimize your LP formulation of the Red Brand Canners production model. Do not include the option of purchasing up to 80,000 additional pounds of grade A tomatoes.

2. What is the net profit obtained after netting out the cost of the crop?

3. Myers has proposed that the net profit obtained from his policy would be $144,000. Is this true? If not, what is his net profit (taking into account, as in Question 2, the cost of the crop)?

4. Suppose Cooper suggests that, in keeping with his accounting scheme as advanced in Exhibit 2 of the original case, the crop cost of 18 cents per pound should be subtracted from each coefficient in the objective function. Change your formulation accordingly, and again solve the model. You should obtain an optimal objective value that is greater than that obtained in Question 2. Explain this apparent discrepancy (assume that unused tomatoes will spoil).

5. Suppose that unused tomatoes could be resold at 18 cents per pound. Which solution would be preferred under these conditions? How much can the resale price be lowered without affecting this preference?

6. Use the Sensitivity Report from Question 1 to determine whether the additional purchase of up to 80,000 pounds of grade A tomatoes should be undertaken. Can you tell how much should be purchased?

7. Use a reformulated model to obtain an optimal product mix using the additional purchase option. The solution to your reformulated model should explicitly show how the additional purchase should be used.

8. Suppose that in Question 1 the Market Research Department feels it could increase the demand for juice by 25,000 cases by means of an advertising campaign. How much should Red Brand be willing to pay for such a campaign?

9. Suppose in Question 1 that the price of juice increased 30 cents per case. Does your Solver Sensitivity Report tell you whether the optimal production plan will change?

10. Suppose that RBC is forced to reduce the size of the product line in tomato-based products to 2. Would you need to rerun the Solver to tell which product should be dropped from the line?

11. Suppose that in Question 1 an additional lot of 50,000 pounds of grade B tomatoes is available. How much should RBC be willing to pay for this lot of grade B tomatoes?

Alternate Questions for Red Brand Canners

For the following questions assume three grades of tomatoes, as in the alternate questions in Chapter 3.

12. Use Solver to optimize your LP formulation of Question 8 of the Alternate Questions for Red Brand Canners from Chapter 3.

13. What is the net profit obtained after netting out the cost of the crop?

14. Myers claims the net profit from his policy of producing 2,000,000 lb paste and 1,000,000 lb juice is $268,800. Is this correct? If not, what is his net profit (taking into account, as in Question 13, the cost of the crop)?

15. Suppose Cooper suggests that, in keeping with his accounting scheme as advanced in Exhibit 2 of the original case, the crop cost per pound should be subtracted from each coefficient in the objective function. Change your formulation accordingly, and again solve the model, assuming a crop cost of 21 cents per pound. You should obtain a solution that is different from that obtained in Question 12. Which solution has a higher net profit (assume unused tomatoes will spoil)? Is it correct to include tomato costs in the objective function?

16. If in Question 15 unused tomatoes could be resold for 21 cents a pound, which solution would be preferred? How much can the resale price be lowered without affecting this preference?

17. Use the Sensitivity Report from Question 12 to determine whether the additional purchase of up to 80,000 pounds of grade A tomatoes should be undertaken. Can you tell how much should be purchased?

18. Use a reformulated model to obtain an optimal product mix using the additional purchase option. The solution to your reformulated model should explicitly show how the additional purchase should be used.

19. Suppose that in Question 12 the Market Research Department feels it could increase the demand for paste by 3000 cases by means of an advertising campaign. How much should Red Brand be willing to pay for such a campaign?

20. Suppose in Question 12 that the price of canned whole tomatoes decreased by 48 cents per case. Does your Solver Sensitivity Report tell you whether the optimal production plan will change?

21. Suppose that the Market Research Department suggests that if the average quality of paste is below 4 the product will not be acceptable to customers. Would you need to rerun Solver to determine the optimal production plan if this constraint were added to the model?

22. Suppose that in Question 12 an additional lot of 200,000 pounds of grade C tomatoes is available. How much would RBC be willing to pay for this lot of grade C tomatoes?

| Case Study | Crawler Tread and a New Angle |

In important respects, part of a manager's task invokes analysis and evaluation of the work of others as opposed to producing "from rock bottom" his or her own formulation and analysis. In this diagnostic role the manager will judge someone else's model. Have the correct questions been asked? Has a correct analysis been performed? The following vignette captures the spirit of such a situation. You are asked to comment on the analysis of a new opportunity.

Ralph Hanson has been the chief metallurgist at PROTRAC's cast-iron foundry for the last five years. He brings several important qualities to this position. First, he has an excellent background. He graduated from Case Western with an MMS (master of material science) and had five years' experience with U.S. Steel before joining PROTRAC. He has used this training and experience to implement several changes that have contributed to product quality and process efficiency. In addition, he has become an effective manager. Through a combination of formal course work and self-education, he has become familiar with many modern management techniques and approaches and has worked to see that these new methods are exploited whenever it is appropriate. Indeed, Ralph is responsible for introducing the use of LP models into the ore-blending and scrap-recycling activities at PROTRAC.

Ralph was the chief metallurgist when Crawler Tread, the first ore-blending application, was completed. By now both Ralph and Sam Togas, the plant manager, are comfortable with the use of LP models in the ore-blending area. Ralph typically formulates, solves, and interprets the output himself. Currently, he is facing a new problem. The recession has seriously affected the demand for heavy equipment, and PROTRAC has excess capacity in most departments, including the foundry. However, the defense industries are booming. A manufacturer of tanks requires a high-grade ore for producing tank treads. Indeed, the requirements are exactly the same as PROTRAC used in the Crawler Tread model (see Section 5.4). The tank manufacturer is willing to pay PROTRAC $850 per ton of ore for up to 150,000 tons to be delivered within the next month. Ralph learns that he can have up to 98,000 tons of ore available. This is made up of 21,000 tons from mine 1; 40,000 from mine 2; 15,000 from mine 3; and 22,000 from mine 4.

On the basis of these data, Ralph formulates a new LP model. In this model, T_i is the thousands of tons of ore from mine i (for $i = 1, 2, 3, 4$) that are used in the blend, and B is the thousands of tons of blended ore. He carefully annotates the formulation so that he can easily explain his analysis to Sam, the plant manager. The formulation and solution that Ralph used in his presentation are shown in Exhibit 1.

Sam was delighted with the project. It yielded a contribution margin of $30,500,000 and occupied resources (labor and machinery) that otherwise would have been idle. He immediately had the legal department draw up a contract for the sale of 98,000 tons of ore.

When Ralph arrived the next morning, Sam was waiting for him. The following discussion took place:

Sam: The contract is ready and I was about to call and confirm the arrangement, but there is a new development. We've just received a telex from mine 1. Due to the cancellation of another order, we can have up to another 3000 tons of ore at the standard price of $800 per ton if we want it. What should we do? Why don't you go back and re-solve your model including the possibility of the additional 3000 tons from mine 1 and draw up a new contract if the new solution is better. Obviously, we can't do worse than we are doing now, and that's not bad.

Ralph: Actually, we don't have to do that. One of the great things about LP is that we can answer many questions involving changes from the original model. In particular, the shadow price on the amount of T_1 available provides an upper bound on how much more we should pay to have the opportunity of buying an additional ton of ore from mine 1. If the shadow price is positive, say $10, we should be willing to pay up to $10 more for the opportunity to buy another ton of ore (i.e., up to $810 for a ton of ore from mine 1). If it is zero, increasing the amount of ore that is available from mine 1 will not enable us to increase profit.

A quick inspection of the solution reveals that the shadow price on this constraint is zero.

Ralph: Since we can't increase our contribution margin, let's just leave the contract as it is and get back to work.

Sam: Darn it, Ralph, I don't understand this. We can buy the ore for $800 a ton and sell it for $850 a ton and you tell me we shouldn't do it.

Ralph: I know it's hard to see, but I know that if the right-hand side of the constraint (cell I7) is increased, the optimal value of the objective function will remain the same. This implies that additional tons of ore from mine 1 won't help us. I suppose it's because we can't add this additional ore to our blend and still satisfy the minimum elements requirements. Remember that the ore from mine 1 has only 90 pounds of element B per ton, and the blend must have at least 100.

Sam: Look, Ralph, I have to meet with the grievance committee now. I just can't spend any more time on this project. I can't say I understand your answer, but you're the expert. Let's go with the current contract.

Questions

1. Is Ralph's interpretation of the numbers on the report correct?
2. Is Ralph's response to the additional purchase opportunity correct? If you believe he has erred, where is the flaw?
3. Suppose row 11 (Total Ore Avail. constraint) were dropped from the model. What would be the shadow price on the Ore Limit Mine 1 constraint? The Ore Limit Mine 2 constraint?
4. Can you figure out what will happen to the OV if the RHS of the Mine 2 constraint (cell I8) is changed to 39.999?
5. Suppose the RHS of the Mine 2 constraint (cell I8) is increased to 40.001. What are the new optimal values of T_1, T_2, T_3, and T_4?
6. Figure out why the Allowable Increase on this constraint (cell I8) is 0.5714.
7. Is the solution to Ralph's model degenerate? If so, can you tell which constraint(s) causes the degeneracy in his model?
8. Exhibit 2 presents an attempt by Ralph to reformulate the LP into a more compact form similar to Wayne Foley's model in Section 5.6. Its optimal solution is the same, but the Sensitivity Report looks different from the one in Exhibit 1. How do you explain the Objective Coefficients and Reduced Costs listed in Exhibit 2. Sensitivity Report as compared to the same in Exhibit 1's Sensitivity Report? Can you answer Questions 4 and 5 above using Exhibit 2?

EXHIBIT 1 Ralph's LP Model

	A	B	C	D	E	F	G	H	I	J
1	Product	Blend	T1	T2	T3	T4				
2	Qty. Prod. (000s)	98.0	21.0	40.0	15.0	22.0	Profit			
3	Contr. Mar.	$850	$(800)	$(400)	$(600)	$(500)	$30,500			
4							Total		RHS	Slack
5	Blended Ore	1	-1	-1	-1	-1	0	=	0	0
6	Blended Limit	1					98	≤	150	52
7	Ore Limit Mine 1		1				21	≤	21	1E-04
8	Ore Limit Mine 2			1			40	≤	40	0
9	Ore Limit Mine 3				1		15	≤	15	0
10	Ore Limit Mine 4					1	22	≤	22	0
11	Total Ore Avail.		1	1	1	1	98	≤	98	0
12	Minimum A		5	-2	3	-3	4	≥	0	4
13	Minimum B		-10	50	-25	75	3065	≥	0	3065
14	Minimum C		15	-5	-10	7	119	≥	0	119

Microsoft Excel 8.0 Sensitivity Report

Adjustable Cells

Cell	Name	Final Value	Reduced Cost	Objective Coefficient	Allowable Increase	Allowable Decrease
$B$2	Qty. Prod. (000s) Blend	98.0	0.0	850	1E+30	50
$C$2	Qty. Prod. (000s) T1	21.0	0.0	-800	200	50
$D$2	Qty. Prod. (000s) T2	40.0	0.0	-400	1E+30	400
$E$2	Qty. Prod. (000s) T3	15.0	0.0	-600	1E+30	200
$F$2	Qty. Prod. (000s) T4	22.0	0.0	-500	1E+30	300

Constraints

Cell	Name	Final Value	Shadow Price	Constraint R.H. Side	Allowable Increase	Allowable Decrease
$G$1:	Minimum A Total	4	0	0	4	1E+30
$G$1:	Minimum B Total	3065	0	0	3065	1E+30
$G$1:	Minimum C Total	119	0	0	119	1E+30
$G$5	Blended Ore Total	0	850	0	52	98
$G$6	Blended Limit Total	98	0	150	1E+30	52
$G$7	Ore Limit Mine 1 Total	21	0	21	1E+30	0
$G$8	Ore Limit Mine 2 Total	40	400	40	0.5714	0
$G$9	Ore Limit Mine 3 Total	15	200	15	2	0
$G$1:	Ore Limit Mine 4 Total	22	300	22	0.5	0
$G$1	Total Ore Avail. Total	98	50	98	0	0.8

EXHIBIT 2 Ralph's Second LP Model

	A	B	C	D	E	F	G	H
1	Product	T1	T2	T3	T4	Blend	Profit	
2	Contr. Mar.	$ (800)	$ (400)	$ (600)	$ (500)	$850	$ 30,500	
3	Qty. Prod. (000s)	21.0	40.0	15.0	22.0	98.0	<=98	
4	Supply or Demand Limit	<=21	<=40	<=15	<=22	<=150		
5	Element Constraints					Total	RHS	Slack
6	Minimum A	5	-2	3	-3	4	>=0	4
7	Minimum B	-10	50	-25	75	3065	>=0	3065
8	Minimum C	15	-5	-10	7	119	>=0	119

	A	B	C	D	E	F	G	H
1	Product	T1	T2	T3	T4	Blend	Profit	
2	Contr. Mar.	-800	-400	-600	-500	850	=SUMPRODUCT($B$3:$F$3,B2:F2)	
3	Qty. Prod. (000s)	21	40	15	22	=SUM(B3:E3)	98	
4	ly or Demand Limit	21	40	15	22	150		
5	Element Constrain					Total	RHS	Slack
6	Minimum A	5	-2	3	-3	=SUMPRODUCT($B$3:$E$3,B6:E6)	0	=F6-G6
7	Minimum B	-10	50	-25	75	=SUMPRODUCT($B$3:$E$3,B7:E7)	0	=F7-G7
8	Minimum C	15	-5	-10	7	=SUMPRODUCT($B$3:$E$3,B8:E8)	0	=F8-G8

Microsoft Excel 8.0 Sensitivity Report

Adjustable Cells

Cell	Name	Final Value	Reduced Cost	Objective Coefficient	Allowable Increase	Allowable Decrease
$B$3	Qty. Prod. (000s) T1	21	50	50	1E+30	50
$C$3	Qty. Prod. (000s) T2	40	450	450	1E+30	450
$D$3	Qty. Prod. (000s) T3	15	250	250	1E+30	250
$E$3	Qty. Prod. (000s) T4	22	350	350	1E+30	350

Constraints

Cell	Name	Final Value	Shadow Price	Constraint R.H. Side	Allowable Increase	Allowable Decrease
$F$6	Minimum A Total	4	0	0	4	1E+30
$F$7	Minimum B Total	3065	0	0	3065	1E+30
$F$8	Minimum C Total	119	0	0	119	1E+30
$F$3	Qty. Prod. (000s) Blend	98	0	150	1E+30	52
$F$3	Qty. Prod. (000s) Blend	98	0	98	1E+30	0

The purpose of this case is to exercise both judgmental and technical skills. You will have to decide, on the basis of Mr. Overton's objectives, just what information you should provide him. You will then have to formulate an LP model (or models), optimize it (or them), and present, in a summary report, the relevant results.

On Monday, August 28, 1996, Mr. Overton called in his sales manager and purchasing manager to discuss the company's policy for the coming month. Saw Mill had accepted orders from Turnbull Co. and McClean Bros. and had the option of accepting an order from Blue River, Inc. It also had the option of buying some additional grain from Cochrane Farm. Mr. Overton,

managing director of Saw Mill, had to decide by the end of the week what action to take.

Usually all purchases of grain are completed by the end of August. However, Saw Mill still has the possibility of an extra purchase of grain from Cochrane Farm. This commitment has to be made by September 1. The grain would be delivered to the Midwest Grain Elevator by the 15th of the month. This elevator acts simply as a storage facility for Saw Mill.

It is immutable company policy to charge a markup of 15% on the cost of the grain supplied to customers. Payments to the Midwest Grain Elevator are treated as an overhead, and this policy is not to be challenged. Turnbull,

ORDERING COMPANY	QUANTITY (BUSHELS)	MAXIMUM PERCENT MOISTURE (PER LB)	MINIMUM WEIGHT PER BUSHEL (LB)	MAXIMUM PERCENT DAMAGE (PER LB)	MAXIMUM PERCENT FOREIGN MATERIAL (PER LB)	DELIVERY DATE
Turnbull	40,000–45,000	13	56	2	2	9/20
McClean	32,000–36,000	15.5	54	5	3	9/22
Blue River	50,000–54,000	15	56	2	4	9/26

TYPE OF CORN	QUANTITY (BUSHELS)	COST PER BUSHEL ($)	PERCENT MOISTURE CONTENT	WEIGHT PER BUSHEL (LB)	PERCENT TOTAL DAMAGE (PER LB)	PERCENT FOREIGN MATERIAL (PER LB)
1	30,000	1.45	12	57	2	1.5
2	45,000	1.44	15	57	2	1
3	25,000	1.45	12	58	3	3
4	40,000	1.42	13	56	4	2
5	20,000	1.38	15	54	4	2
6	30,000	1.37	15	55	5	3
7	75,000	1.37	18	57	5	1
8	15,000	1.39	14	58	2	4
9	16,000	1.27	17	53	7	5
10	20,000	1.28	15	55	8	3
11	10,000	1.17	22	56	9	5

McClean, and Blue River have agreed to pay, for their current orders, whatever price Saw Mill charges. However, Saw Mill realizes that if its price becomes too high, future business will be lost.

The details of the Turnbull, McClean, and Blue River orders are presented in the first table above. The quantity, as well as the maximum moisture content, minimum weight per bushel, maximum percentage damaged, and maximum percentage foreign material are presented.

The company has the option to supply any amount of grain that it wishes, within the specified range. It must, of

course, satisfy the requirements. By September 4, Saw Mill must inform Turnbull and McClean how much grain they will receive. By the same date it must inform Blue River if it will accept its order and how much grain will be delivered if it accepts.

Saw Mill blends the grains that it owns to satisfy customer orders. On August 28, the company had 326,000 bushels of corn stored in the elevator. Obviously, it would be impossible to identify the exact composition of each kernel of corn that the Saw Mill River Feed and Grain Company delivered to the elevator. Hence, the second table above represents aggregated amounts of characteristics of different types of corn credited to Saw Mill River's account with the elevator. The 326,000 bushels are segregated into 11 types of corn, which differ according to (1) quantity available, (2) cost per

[1]From an idea by Jonathan Kornbluth, based upon data originally published in Thomas H. Naylor, Eugene T. Byrne, and John M. Vernon *Introduction of Linear Programming: Methods & Cases* (Belmont, CA: Wadsworth Publishing, 1971).

bushel, (3) percentage moisture content, (4) weight per bushel, (5) percentage damaged, and (6) percentage foreign material.

The grain on offer from Cochrane Farm is one load of up to 50,000 bushels, with an average of 15% moisture, 3% damage, and 2% foreign material. The load has a density of 57 pounds per bushel, and Straddle (the purchasing manager) is convinced that the order can be obtained at a cost of $1.41 per bushel.

Develop an LP model to help analyze Mr. Overton's model. (Use notation T_i = bushels of corn type i to be sent to Turnbull. Similarly for M_i and B_i. Also let corn type 12 denote the corn from Cochrane Farm.) In no more than one page, labeled "Executive Summary," plus relevant exhibits from your model provide as concisely as possible information that will help Overton answer his questions. His main objectives are to maximize profit and to keep prices to the customers sufficiently low to attract future business. He can be expected to use his judgment to make the eventual decision; your job is to provide information that will enable him to look at the important trade-offs. You should also make your own recommendations.

Your presentation will be judged on the economy of your formulation (i.e., formulate your model, or models, *for the given set of data* as efficiently as possible) as well as on your recommendations concerning
(a) to buy or not buy from Cochrane;
(b) to accept or not to accept the Blue River option;
(c) how much corn to supply to Blue River, Turnbull, and McClean.

Case Study   Kiwi Computer

Kiwi Computer of New Zealand manufactures two types of personal computers: a portable model and a desktop model. Kiwi assembles the cases and printed circuit boards at its only plant, which also manufactures the cases and stuffs the circuit boards with components. Monthly production is limited by the capacities in the following table.

OPERATION	PORTABLE	DESKTOP
Case Production	4000	2000
Board Stuffing	2500	3000
Portable Assembly	2000	—
Desktop Assembly	—	1800

For example, 4000 portable cases can be produced in a month and no desktop cases, or no portable cases and 2000 desktop cases, or if equal time is devoted to both, 2000 portable and 1000 desktop cases can be produced. In order to be feasible, production of portable and desktop computers for a month must satisfy all the constraints simultaneously. The set of feasible production plans is shown in Exhibit 1.

The wholesale prices charged by Kiwi to retail computer stores are $1500 for the desktop and $1400 for the portable. In order to be competitive, Kiwi has to price its computers several hundred dollars below those of a very large and well-known computer manufacturer.

The entry of this manufacturer has caused a boom in the industry as the market has shifted from one aimed primarily at business professionals alone to business and home computer users. Because of this shift, the market was now a "seller's market," and currently, Kiwi sells as many computers of either model as it produces. During the first quarter of the year Kiwi produced 2000 portables a month and 600 desktops. Both board stuffing and portable assembly were operating at capacity, but there was slack in case production and desktop assembly. Kiwi's

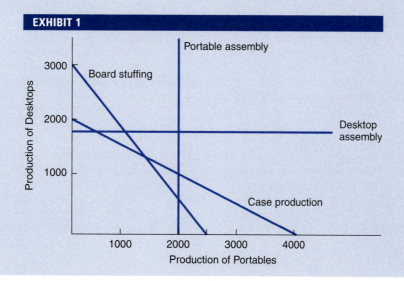

EXHIBIT 1

EXHIBIT 2

	TOTAL FIXED OVERHEAD ($000)*	FIXED OVERHEAD PER UNIT ($)
Case Production	247	95
Board Stuffing	533	205
Desktop Assembly	249	415
Portable Assembly	230	115
Total	1259	

*Based on production of 600 desktop and 2000 portable computers per month.

cost accountants determined fixed overhead and standard costs as shown in Exhibits 2 and 3. The fixed overhead data in Exhibit 3 are derived from the fixed overhead totals in Exhibit 2.

EXHIBIT 3

	DESKTOPS		PORTABLES	
Direct Materials		$800		$ 690
Direct Labor				
Case Production	$20		$15	
Board Stuffing	100		90	
Final Assembly	5	125	10	115
Fixed Overhead				
Case Production	$ 95		$ 95	
Board Stuffing	205		205	
Final Assembly	415	715	115	415
Total		$1640		$1220

At a quarterly meeting of the company's executives, great dissatisfaction was expressed at Kiwi's recent profit performance. The president expected much better profits as a result of the seller's market. In response, the sales manager pointed out that it was impossible to sell the desktop computer at a profit. Therefore, to improve profitibility, he suggested that it be dropped from the company's product line.

The controller objected to this suggestion. He maintained that the real problem faced by desktop computers was that they had to absorb the entire fixed overhead of the desktop assembly department with only a small number of units being produced. He claimed that the production and sale of desktop computers were in fact making a positive contribution to overhead and profits. This contribution was just insufficient to cover the fixed costs. He concluded, "If we produce more desktop computers, we can lower the fixed final assembly cost of $415. It's high now because we are producing so few units."

The sales manager was appalled to hear this. It was the controller's job to provide all Kiwi executives with accounting information that would help them make appropriate business decisions. If the controller's surmise were really correct, then cost figures in Exhibit 3 were quite misleading—and had been for some time.

Following up on the controller's surmise, the production manager suggested a way to increase production, "We can in-

crease production if we outsourced some of the board stuffing to a subcontractor. We could supply the boards and components and pay the subcontractor some negotiated price to stuff each desktop board and a (probably different) negotiated price to stuff each portable board."

At this point, the president entered the discussion. He concluded the meeting by asking the sales manager, the controller, and the production manager to get together and come up with a recommendation concerning the company's product mix and subcontracting. He told them to assume that demand would remain high and current capacity would remain fixed. Specifically, he asked them to consider jointly two questions raised by their comments. His questions were as follows:

A. Assuming no change in capacity, prices charged for computers, and assuming no outsourcing of board stuffing, what would be Kiwi's most profitable mix of desktop and portable computers and would that mix involve fewer desktop computers as suggested by the sales manager?

B. What would be the maximum price per stuffed board that Kiwi should be willing to pay the subcontractor to stuff desktop boards, and what would be the maximum price per stuffed board that Kiwi should be willing to pay the subcontractor to stuff portable boards and still make as much profit as could be made by stuffing all boards of both model computers entirely within Kiwi's plant?

Questions

Part A. Subcontracting not allowed.

1. In Exhibit 3 the standard overhead cost assigned to desktop computers for final assembly is $415. Clearly indicate how this figure was derived.
2. (a) Do the desktop units make a contribution to profit? In other words, given that the overhead costs are fixed in the short run, is the company's profit higher than it would be if no desktop units were produced?
   (b) A correct computation of per unit profitabilities will show that the portable is more profitable than the desktop. Does this mean that more (or only) portables should be produced? Why?
3. In answering this question assume that boards cannot be stuffed by a subcontractor. Formulate an LP model for determining the optimal product mix.
4. Answer the president's first question by optimizing your model using Solver and indicate the optimal mix of desktop and portable computers. Noninteger answers are acceptable.
5. Find the best feasible integer answer that can be achieved by rounding to adjacent integers your answers from Question 4.
6. (a) Go back and recalculate the company's "standard costs" using your integer answers from Question 5 and compare with those in Exhibit 3.

(b) How much larger is the profit using the new mix (using the integer answers from Question 5) than the old (i.e., 600 desktops, 2000 portables)?

Part B. Subcontracting allowed.

We now allow some boards to be stuffed by a subcontractor. Assume that production of a computer with a board stuffed by the subcontractor requires the same amount of time in case production and final assembly as production of a computer with a board stuffed at the factory.

7. Assume that the subcontractor is going to charge $110 for each desktop board stuffed and $100 for each portable board stuffed. Kiwi provides the subcontractor with the necessary materials. Should Kiwi employ the subcontractor to stuff boards? Argue why or why not without formulating and solving a new LP model.

8. Now formulate an LP model that includes subcontracting. In your formulation, distinguish between computers produced with internally and externally stuffed boards.

9. Assume that in addition to the per board charge the subcontractor is now going to include a fixed charge for stuffing a batch of boards (same charge regardless of the number of boards or their type). For what fixed charge will Kiwi be indifferent between subcontracting and stuffing all boards internally?

Part C. Sensitivity analysis.

10. Refer to the linear programming formulation in Question 8. Is the optimal solution degenerate? Explain.

11. Refer to the linear programming formulation in Question 8. Do alternative optima exist? Explain.

12. Refer to the linear programming formulation in Question 8. The subcontractor currently charges $110 for each desktop board stuffed. By how much would this charge have to decrease so that it would be optimal for Kiwi to have the subcontractor stuff desktop boards? Why?

13. Refer to the linear programming formulation in Question 3. Assume Kiwi can increase the board-stuffing capacity so that either 600 additional desktop boards or 500 additional portable boards or any equivalent combination can be stuffed. Should Kiwi increase the capacity if the cost would be $175,000 per month? Answer *without* re-solving the LP model.

14. Refer to the LP formulation in Question 3. Suppose a redesign of the desktop unit to use fewer chips reduces the cost of direct materials by $200. Does your Sensitivity Report tell you whether the optimal production plan will change? Explain.

15. Answer the president's second question.

Alternative Questions on Kiwi Computer

Kiwi is considering consolidating desktop assembly and portable assembly into one department. The new department would be capable of assembling 3000 portables in a month and no desktops, or no portables and 2200 desktops, or if equal time were devoted to both, 1500 portables and 1100 desktops could be assembled. It estimates that the monthly fixed overhead for this department would be less than $479,000, the current combined overhead for the desktop and portable assembly departments. In answering the following questions, assume the departments will be combined.

Part A. Subcontracting not allowed.

1. Let D, P equal the monthly production rate of desktops and portables, respectively, and F the fixed overhead of the new unified assembly department. Express total profit as a function of D, P, and F.

2. Must the value of F be known in order to determine the optimal product mix? Assume that fixed overhead is not affected by the values of D and P.

3. In answering this question assume that boards cannot be stuffed by a subcontractor. Formulate an LP model for determining the optimal product mix.

4. Optimize your model using Solver and indicate the optimal mix of desktop and portable computers. Noninteger answers are acceptable.

5. Find the best feasible integer answer that can be achieved by rounding to adjacent integers your answers from Question 4.

6. Suppose that the optimal profit (revenue minus *all* costs) is $330,286 if the two assembly departments are not combined. What is the largest that the fixed overhead of a combined assembly department could be and Kiwi still prefer to combine the departments?

Part B. Subcontracting allowed.

7. Assume that the subcontractor is going to charge $150 for each desktop board stuffed and $135 for each portable board stuffed. Kiwi provides the subcontractor with the necessary materials. Should Kiwi employ the subcontractor to stuff boards? Argue why or why not without formulating and solving a new LP model.

8. Now formulate an LP model that includes subcontracting. In your formulation, distinguish between computers produced with internally and externally stuffed boards.

9. Assume that in addition to the per board charge the subcontractor is now going to include a fixed charge for stuffing a batch of boards (same charge regardless of the num-

ber of boards or their type). For what fixed charge will Kiwi be indifferent between subcontracting and stuffing all boards internally?

Part C. Sensitivity analysis.

10. Refer to the LP formulation in Question 8. Is the optimal solution degenerate? Explain.
11. Refer to the LP formulation in Question 8. Do alternative optima exist? Explain.
12. Refer to the LP formulation in Question 8. The subcontractor currently charges $150 for each desktop board stuffed. Could the subcontractor lower his price enough so that it would be optimal for Kiwi to have him stuff desktop boards? Explain.

13. Refer to the LP formulation in Question 3. Assume Kiwi can increase the board-stuffing capacity so that either 600 additional desktop boards or 500 portable boards or any equivalent combination can be stuffed. Should Kiwi increase the capacity if the cost would be $175,000 per month? Answer *without* resolving the LP model.
14. Refer to the LP formulation in Question 3. Suppose a redesign of the desktop unit to use fewer chips reduces the cost of direct materials by $200. Does your spreadsheet report tell you whether the optimal production plan will change? Explain.

References

De-Li Yang and Weiqin Mou, "An Integrated Decision Support System in a Chinese Chemical Plant," *Interfaces,* 23, no. 6 (1993), 93–100.

Honorio Carino and Clinton LeNoir, "Optimizing Wood Procurement in Cabinet Manufacturing," *Interfaces,* 18, no. 2 (1988), 10–19.

CHAPTER 6

Linear Programming: Applications

CHAPTER OUTLINE

6.1 Introduction

6.2 The Transportation Model

6.3 Variations on the Transportation Model

6.4 The Assignment Model

6.5 Network Models

6.6 Capacitated Transshipment Model

6.7 General Formulation of the Capacitated Transshipment Model

6.8 The Shortest-Route Model

6.9 The Maximal-Flow Model

6.10 Notes on Implementation of Network Models

6.11 Financial and Production Planning

6.12 The Media Selection Model

6.13 Dynamic Models

6.14 Examples of Dynamic Models

6.15 Summary

KEY TERMS

SELF-REVIEW EXERCISES

PROBLEMS

CASE STUDY: Trans World Oil Company

CASE STUDY: Production Planning at Bumles

CASE STUDY: Biglow Toy Company

REFERENCES

APPLICATION CAPSULE Ici On Parle HASTUS: Montréal Streamlines Its Transportation Scheduling with LP

Controlling the costs of public transportation is a problem that knows no national boundaries. One highly successful approach was developed by Société de la Communauté Urbaine de Montréal (S.T.C.U.M.) in Canada. This organization, with a staff of 8000 and an annual budget of more than $575 million, provides close to 400 million passenger trips per year. To do so, it runs 1700 buses and 750 subway cars, for which it must schedule 3000 drivers and other personnel daily.

Efficient scheduling is extremely important—it improves service and working conditions and can have a dramatic impact on operating costs. Such scheduling is difficult because of the large variation in service levels required during the course of the day. During peak demand hours, nearly 1500 vehicles may be needed, compared to a fifth that number during slack periods. Scheduling must take into account vehicle frequencies on each route during the day, as well as the effect on average vehicle speed of traffic conditions (such as rush-hour congestion) at different times.

Transit-system scheduling is done in two successive operations. Vehicle scheduling is done first. The aim is to provide the number of buses and subway trains required to maintain desired service frequencies on each route. Crew scheduling then assigns drivers to the vehicles. To facilitate these tasks S.T.C.U.M., in cooperation with the Center for Research on Transportation of the University of Montréal, developed the HASTUS system. The program consists of three main software modules:

- One module is used to provide optimum vehicle scheduling, using network optimization models described in this chapter.
- A second module uses LP models to obtain a "good" initial solution for crew scheduling. Carefully chosen simplifications reduce the enormous number of variables to 3000, so that the model can be solved very rapidly.
- The final module refines the solution to produce detailed driver scheduling assignments, using assignment and shortest-route optimization models also described in this chapter.

The scheduling department has carefully compared the costs of parallel manual and computer-generated solutions. HASTUS was found to reduce manual scheduling errors, saving at least $100,000 per year in unnecessary wages. The system thus paid for itself in less than three months. In addition, HASTUS has been shown to reduce unproductive paid time of drivers and other employees by

20%, compared to existing manual solutions. The total annual savings amount to some $4 million: $3 million in manpower scheduling and an additional $1 million in vehicle scheduling.

The system also permits managers to perform sensitivity and "What if?" analysis. Simulations that would have required weeks using manual techniques can now be done in minutes. Such analyses have helped management to tailor the most cost-effective proposals in negotiations with its labor unions.

HASTUS is easy to learn and use, and has proved popular with schedulers because it makes their jobs more interesting and challenging. The success of the program has been so great that today versions of HASTUS in several languages are helping planners in 40 cities around the world.

6.1 INTRODUCTION

Linear programming is a workhorse in the world of quantitative models. The ability to handle hundreds to thousands of decision variables and constraints, and the incredible number of interactions that these numbers imply, makes LP an important tool in a wide variety of problems.

In this chapter we concentrate on some applications of linear programming. In particular, we consider ten specific models. Section 6.2 is devoted to the *transportation model.* In this model, management must determine how to allocate products from its various warehouses to its customers in order to satisfy demand at the lowest possible transportation cost. This model is important because of its many successful applications and because it can be solved quickly and efficiently. In Section 6.3 we investigate several variations on the transportation model, such as when supply and demand differ.

Section 6.4 is devoted to the *assignment model.* This model enables management to determine the optimal assignment of salespeople to districts, jobs to machines, or editors to manuscripts. The model itself is a special type of transportation model. Both are special cases of a more general class of models called *network models* that we examine in Sections 6.5 through 6.10. Network models are often applied to logistics situations involving the movement or assignment of physical entities.

A financial and production planning model is presented in Section 6.11. Although it is small and relatively simple by the standards of actual applications, it illustrates how more complicated planning models can be constructed and solved. Section 6.12 considers an important marketing model. Called the *media selection model,* it is concerned with designing an effective advertising campaign. More precisely, management must decide how many ads to place in each of several possible advertising media. The decision is constrained by an overall budget allocation, the number of openings for ads in the various media, and rules of thumb insisted on by management. The media selection model is a specific example of an important class of management models. These are profit-maximization models in which a decision variable yields declining marginal profits for increased values of the variable. Next, in Sections 6.13 and 6.14 we investigate dynamic models in which decision making occurs over time. We illustrate dynamic models with several examples in which physical inventory of products plays a role, including one for cash management over time.

6.2 THE TRANSPORTATION MODEL

PROTRAC'S DISTRIBUTION PROBLEM: SENDING DIESEL ENGINES FROM HARBORS TO PLANTS

PROTRAC has four assembly plants in Europe. They are located in Leipzig, Germany (1); Nancy, France (2); Liege, Belgium (3); and Tilburg, the Netherlands (4). The engines used by these plants are produced in the United States, shipped to harbors in Amsterdam (A), Antwerp (B), and Le Havre (C) and are then sent to the plants for assembly.

Production plans for the third quarter, July through September, have been set. The *requirements* (the *demand* at **destinations**) for E-4 diesel engines are in Table 6.1.

The *available* number of E-4 engines at harbors (the *supply* at **origins**) in time to be used in the third quarter are shown in Table 6.2. Note that this is a balanced model in the sense that the total supply of engines available equals the total number required. Figure 6.1 illustrates the model. In this figure the numbers above the harbors indicates the supply available; and the numbers above the plants indicate the quantity demanded. The lines indicate the possible delivery routes.

PROTRAC must decide how many engines to send from each harbor to each plant. The engines are transported by common carrier, and charges are on a per engine basis.

TABLE 6.1 Demand for Diesel Engines

PLANT	NUMBER OF ENGINES REQUIRED
(1) Leipzig	400
(2) Nancy	900
(3) Liege	200
(4) Tilburg	500
	2000

TABLE 6.2 Supply of Diesel Engines

HARBOR	NUMBER OF ENGINES AVAILABLE
(A) Amsterdam	500
(B) Antwerp	700
(C) Le Havre	800
	2000

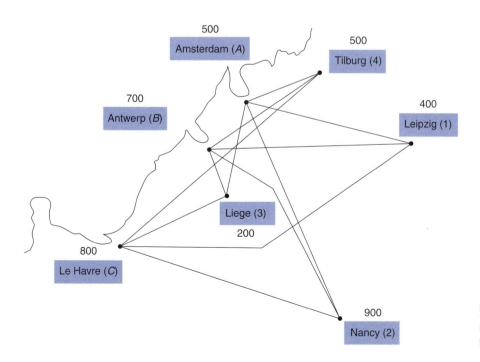

FIGURE 6.1

PROTRAC's Transportation Problem

TABLE 6.3 Cost to Transport an Engine from an Origin to a Destination ($)

FROM ORIGIN	TO DESTINATION			
	(1) Leipzig	(2) Nancy	(3) Liege	(4) Tilburg
(A) Amsterdam	120	130	41	62
(B) Antwerp	61	40	100	110
(C) Le Havre	102.50	90	122	42

The relevant costs are given in Table 6.3. For ease of presentation, we will refer to the harbors with letters and the plants with numbers, as indicated in the supply and demand information above.

THE LP FORMULATION AND SOLUTION

PROTRAC's goal is to minimize the total cost of transporting the E-4 engines from the harbors to the plants. Since the transportation cost for any specific harbor-plant combination (e.g., Antwerp-Nancy) is directly proportional to the number of engines sent from the harbor to the plant ($40 per engine in the Antwerp-Nancy example), we can formulate this situation as an LP model. To do so, we let

$$x_{ij} = \text{number of engines sent from harbor } i \text{ to plant } j$$
$$i = \text{A, B, C}$$
$$j = 1, 2, 3, 4$$

Thus, x_{C4} is the number of engines sent from C, Le Havre, to 4, Tilburg. With this definition, the total transportation cost, which is our objective function, becomes

$$120x_{A1} + 130x_{A2} + \cdots + 42x_{C4}$$

The model has two general types of constraints:

1. The number of items shipped from a harbor cannot exceed the number that are available. For example,

$$x_{A1} + x_{A2} + x_{A3} + x_{A4}$$

is the total number of engines shipped from A. Since only 500 engines are available at A, the constraint is

$$x_{A1} + x_{A2} + x_{A3} + x_{A4} \leq 500$$

A similar constraint is required for each origin.[1]

2. Demand at each plant must be satisfied. For example,

$$x_{A1} + x_{B1} + x_{C1}$$

is the total number of engines sent to plant 1. Since at least 400 engines are required at plant 1, the constraint is

$$x_{A1} + x_{B1} + x_{C1} \geq 400$$

A similar constraint is required for each plant. As with the supply constraints, equalities could be used for the demand constraints because supply and demand are balanced.

---

[1] Since the supply and demand are balanced for this model, equality constraints could be used instead of inequalities in expressing the supply restrictions.

PROTRAC Transportation Model

Unit Cost From\To	Leipzig	Nancy	Liege	Tilburg
Amsterdam	$ 120.0	$ 130.0	$ 41.0	$ 62.0
Antwerp	$ 61.0	$ 40.0	$100.0	$ 110.0
Le Havre	$ 102.5	$ 90.0	$122.0	$ 42.0

Shipments From\To	Leipzig	Nancy	Liege	Tilburg	Total
Amsterdam	300	0	200	0	500
Antwerp	0	700	0	0	700
Le Havre	100	200	0	500	800
Total	400	900	200	500	
Required	>=400	>=900	>=200	>=500	

Total Cost From\To	Leipzig	Nancy	Liege	Tilburg	Total
Amsterdam	$36,000	$ -	$8,200	$ -	$ 44,200
Antwerp	$ -	$28,000	$ -	$ -	$ 28,000
Le Havre	$10,250	$18,000	$ -	$21,000	$ 49,250
Total	$46,250	$46,000	$8,200	$21,000	$121,450

Solver Parameters

Set Target Cell: $G$19

Equal To: ○ Max ● Min

By Changing Cells:

$C$9:$F$11

Subject to the Constraints:

$C$12:$F$12 >= $C$13:$F$13
$G$9:$G$11 <= $H$9:$H$11

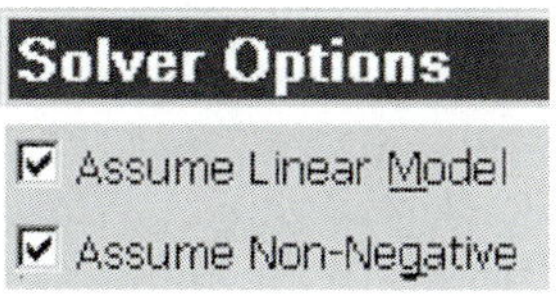

Solver Options

☑ Assume Linear Model
☑ Assume Non-Negative

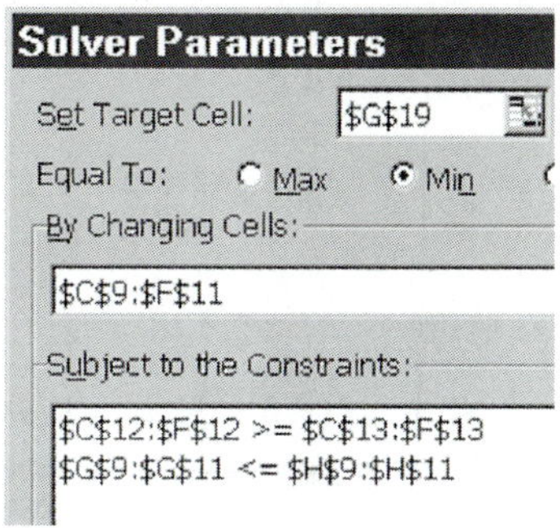

Cell	Formula	Copy To
C16	= C4*C9	C16:F18
G9	= SUM(C9:F9)	G10:G11
C12	= SUM(C9:C11)	D12:F12

FIGURE 6.2

The Optimal Solution for PROTRAC's Transportation Model

The Excel formulation, solution, and Sensitivity Report for PROTRAC's transportation model are presented in Figure 6.2 and Figure 6.3, respectively. Note how the model's layout takes advantage of the "from-to" organization of a transportation model and the use of three blocks of cells: cost parameters, decision variables, and total costs.[2] In Figure 6.2 we see that 6 of the 12 possible routes are used, and that the minimum possible transportation cost is $121,450. Moreover, Sensitivity Report analysis indicates that, for example, total costs would fall at the rate of $107.50 per engine for up to 200 engines if Nancy's requirements were reduced, and total costs would fall at the rate of $17.50 per engine for up to 300 engines if Le Havre's supply of engines were increased. (Movement in the opposite direction—increased demand or reduced supply—is not "Allowable" because it would cause infeasibility.) To test your understanding of the model's Sensitivity Report try answering the following question. By how much would the cost of shipping an engine from Antwerp to Liege have to fall before PROTRAC would find that route attractive?

---

[2] As described in Chapter 5, format "dressing" is used to display RHS data along with the model's constraint symbols.

Microsoft Excel 8.0 Sensitivity Report
Adjustable Cells

Cell	Name	Final Value	Reduced Cost	Objective Coefficient	Allowable Increase	Allowable Decrease
$C$9	Amsterdam Leipzig	300	0	120	2.5	17.5
$D$9	Amsterdam Nancy	0	22.5	130	1E+30	22.5
$E$9	Amsterdam Liege	200	0	41	98.5	41
$F$9	Amsterdam Tilburg	0	2.5	62.0	1E+30	2.5
$C$10	Antwerp Leipzig	0	8.5	61	1E+30	8.5
$D$10	Antwerp Nancy	700	0	40	8.5	1E+30
$E$10	Antwerp Liege	0	126.5	100	1E+30	126.5
$F$10	Antwerp Tilburg	0	118	110	1E+30	118
$C$11	Le Havre Leipzig	100	0	102.5	8.5	2.5
$D$11	Le Havre Nancy	200	0	90	22.5	8.5
$E$11	Le Havre Liege	0	98.5	122	1E+30	98.5
$F$11	Le Havre Tilburg	500	0	42	2.5	59.5

Constraints

Cell	Name	Final Value	Shadow Price	Constraint R.H. Side	Allowable Increase	Allowable Decrease
$G$9	Amsterdam Total	500	0	500	1E+30	0
$G$10	Antwerp Total	700	-67.5	700	200	0
$G$11	Le Havre Total	800	-17.5	800	300	0
$C$12	Total Leipzig	400	120	400	0	300
$D$12	Total Nancy	900	107.5	900	0	200
$E$12	Total Liege	200	41	200	0	200
$F$12	Total Tilburg	500	59.5	500	0	300

FIGURE 6.3

The Sensitivity Report for PROTRAC's Transportation Model

DEGENERACY IN TRANSPORTATION MODELS

Balanced transportation models—that is, models for which total supply equals total demand—always have one redundant constraint. Why is this? Suppose you were told the optimal shipment quantities from Antwerp and Le Havre to each of the four plants in the PROTRAC model above (i.e., you were told the optimal values in the cells of rows 10 and 11 of Figure 6.2). Knowing that total supply must equal total demand, a bit of deduction would quickly yield the shipments from Amsterdam to each of the four plants in row 9. A similar argument would allow you to find the quantities of shipments to a fourth plant if you were told the optimal quantities of shipments to each of the other three plants. Thus, a balanced transportation model could have one of its constraints dropped without affecting the optimal solution.

Since at least one constraint is redundant in a balanced transportation model, the shadow price on at least one constraint will be zero in the Solver Sensitivity Report, as is the case for the PROTRAC model in Figure 6.3. This implies that the solution to a balanced transportation model with m sources and n destinations will have *at most* $m + n - 1$ positive decision variables. If less than $(m + n - 1)$ decision variables are positive, then the solution is degenerate. That is, in a balanced transportation model, the solution must have exactly $(m + n - 1)$ positive decision variables at optimality in order to be nondegenerate. Performing the count for the decision variables of the PROTRAC model in Figure 6.2 shows that it is nondegenerate. However, **degeneracy** in transportation models is a common occurrence in practice. Its presence is more of a technicality and causes no particular concern except regarding the interpretation of the model's Sensitivity Report, as discussed for degenerate solutions of LP models in Chapter 5.

6.3 VARIATIONS ON THE TRANSPORTATION MODEL

In general, the term **transportation model** refers to an LP model that finds the least expensive way of satisfying demands at n destinations with supplies from m origins.

SOLVING MAX TRANSPORTATION MODELS

Suppose that in the example your goal was to maximize the value of the objective function rather than minimize it. You could use the same model with one small, but fundamental, change. Define the objective function coefficients as contribution margins, that is, unit returns, rather than unit costs. The Solver formulation is then modified to be a Maximization instead of a Minimization model.

WHEN SUPPLY AND DEMAND DIFFER

Suppose that in the example model the supply at Amsterdam was 600 engines rather than 500. Then, when all demand is satisfied, the sum, over the three origins, of the engines left over will be l00. Because inequalities were used in the Solver model in Figure 6.2, this causes no special problems. The supply that was not allocated at each origin would appear as slack in the supply constraint for that origin.

If demand exceeds supply, the LP model has no feasible solution. PROTRAC management might, however, be interested in supplying as much demand as possible at minimum cost. There are two approaches to model this situation. We can rewrite the harbor supply constraints to be equalities, thereby forcing all available supply of engines to be shipped to some plant, and rewrite the demand constraint to be a ≤ inequality for each destination plant's demand; that is, shipments of engines to a plant will not exceed its demand. Unfilled demand will appear as slack on each of these demand constraints upon Solver optimization. Alternatively, we can revise the model to append a **dummy origin** with supply equal to the difference between total actual demand and total actual supply. This dummy origin is an imaginary source that is added to a transportation model so that total supply equals total demand. The cost of supplying any destination from this origin is zero. Any supply allocated by Solver from the dummy origin to a destination is interpreted as unfilled demand. An advantage of this second approach is that you can assign unit costs to each of the dummy-origin-to-destination decision variable links. If these costs accurately reflect the opportunity costs of unmet demand at that destination, Solver will then account for these costs in concert with the transportation costs in its optimization and Sensitivity Report information.

ELIMINATING UNACCEPTABLE ROUTES

Assume that certain routes in a transportation model are unacceptable. Organizational constraints such as regional restrictions or delivery time could indicate that certain origins could not serve certain destinations. (For example, assume that the Amsterdam-to-Liege route could not be used.) This fact is handled in formulating transportation models by assigning an arbitrarily large cost identified as M to that route. M is chosen so large that M plus or minus a finite number is still larger than any other cost number in the formulation. This would then automatically eliminate the use of that route since the cost of doing so would be very much larger than that of any other feasible alternative. In the case of this example, assigning a unit cost coefficient to cell E4 in Figure 6.2 of, say, $10,000,000 would effectively eliminate that route from consideration by Solver.

INTEGER-VALUED SOLUTIONS

This observation is concerned with the fact that the transportation model has integer solutions under quite general conditions. From earlier chapters we know that, in general, LP models do *not* produce integer solutions. Even general LP models in which all of the parameters are integer (e.g., the original PROTRAC LP model) do not necessarily produce integer solutions. The transportation model is an exception.

If all of the supplies and demands in a transportation model have integer values, the optimal values of the decision variables will also have integer values.

APPLICATION CAPSULE

Play Ball! The American League Uses an LP Assignment Model to Schedule Umpiring Crews

Each year, the American League, after the difficult task of scheduling 162 games for its 14 teams, must assign the umpiring crews that will work each game. Typically, teams play one another in series consisting of 2, 3, or 4 games, with each team playing a total of 52 series in the course of the 26-week season. One of the league's seven umpiring crews must be assigned to each series.

Not surprisingly, with teams in cities across the entire North American continent, from Baltimore to Seattle and from Texas to Toronto, minimizing total travel costs is one of the principal goals of the schedulers. However, it is not the only factor that must be taken into consideration. To guarantee fairness, there are limits to the number of times each crew is exposed to each team, for both its home and its away games. Moreover, every effort is made to avoid a crew being assigned to the same team for more than two consecutive series.

Travel restrictions impose additional constraints on the schedule. Some of the more important examples include:

- A crew cannot work a night game in one city and an afternoon game in another city the next day.
- Because of time changes, a crew cannot travel from a West Coast city to Chicago or any eastern city without a day off between series.

- Because of limited airline flight schedules, a crew traveling into or out of Toronto must have a day off if it is coming from or going to any city other than New York, Boston, Detroit, or Cleveland.

While the total number of possible crew assignments is far too large for each one to be evaluated individually, the scheduling of umpires can be formulated as a relatively simple assignment model. The league now uses a PC-based decision support system, developed by Dr. Jim Evans of the University of Cincinnati, that produces a better schedule in less than half the time previously required.

The program color-codes each crew in the screen display of schedule assignments. This makes it easy for the user to follow a particular crew and examine the flow of its assignments. In addition to the assignment scheduling model, the system includes a statistical computation and database program that makes it easy to keep track of crew/team combinations. As a result, the balance of crew exposures has improved since the system came into use. In its first year of use, the system saved the American League some $30,000 in travel costs. (See Blaise et. al.)

Let us now turn to an important special case of the transportation model, called the *assignment model*.

6.4 THE ASSIGNMENT MODEL

The **assignment model** occurs in many management contexts. In general, it is the problem of determining the optimal assignment of n "indivisible" agents or objects to n tasks. For example, management might have to assign salespeople to sales territories or service representatives to service calls or editors to manuscripts or commercial artists to advertising copy. The agents or objects to be assigned are indivisible in the sense that no agent can be divided among several tasks. The important constraint, for each agent, is that *he or she be assigned to one and only one task.*

PROTRAC-EUROPE'S AUDITING PROBLEM

Let us illustrate the assignment model with a particular problem facing the president of PROTRAC-Europe. PROTRAC's European headquarters is in Brussels. This year, as part of his annual audit, the president has decided to have each of the four corporate vice-presidents visit and audit one of the assembly plants during the first two weeks in June. As you recall, the assembly plants are located in Leipzig, Germany; Nancy, France; Liege, Belgium; and Tilburg, the Netherlands.

There are a number of advantages and disadvantages to various assignments of the vice-presidents to the plants. Among the issues to consider are:

1. Matching the vice-presidents' areas of expertise with the importance of specific problem areas in a plant.

2. The time the audit will require and the other demands on each vice-president during the two-week interval.

TABLE 6.4 Assignment Costs in $000s for Every Vice-President–Plant Combination

V.-P.	PLANT			
	Leipzig (1)	Nancy (2)	Liege (3)	Tilburg (4)
Finance (F)	24	10	21	11
Marketing (M)	14	22	10	15
Operations (O)	15	17	20	19
Personnel (P)	11	19	14	13

TABLE 6.5 One Assignment Alternative

V.-P.	ASSIGNMENT	COST
	Plant	
F	1	24
M	2	22
O	3	20
P	4	13
	Total Cost ($000s)	79

3. Matching the language ability of a vice-president with the dominant language used in the plant.

Attempting to keep all these factors in mind and arrive at a good assignment of vice-presidents to plants is a challenging problem. The president decides to start by estimating the cost to PROTRAC of sending each vice-president to each plant. The data are shown in Table 6.4.

With these costs, the president can evaluate any particular assignment of vice-presidents to plants. For example, if he chooses the assignment in Table 6.5, he incurs a total cost of $79,000.

SOLVING BY COMPLETE ENUMERATION

Since there are only a finite number of ways to make the vice-president assignments, one might try *complete enumeration,* that is, calculate the cost of each feasible assignment pattern, and pick the lowest. However, similar to the Oak Products example of Chapter 3, complete enumeration of all alternatives quickly becomes burdensome. Let us see how many solutions there are to this vice-president assignment model. Consider assigning the vice-presidents in the order F, M, O, P. We have the following steps:

1. F can be assigned to any of four plants.
2. Once F is assigned, M can be assigned to any of the three remaining plants.
3. Similarly, O can be assigned to any of the two remaining plants.
4. P must be assigned to the only available plant.

There are, thus, $4 \times 3 \times 2 \times 1 = 24$ possible solutions. In general, if there were n vice-presidents and n plants, there would be $n(n-1)(n-2)(n-3) \cdots (2)(1)$ solutions, which is n factorial, $n!$. As n increases, $n!$ increases extremely rapidly. Here is the relation between n and $n!$ for (integral) values of n between 1 and 10:

n	1	2	3	4	5	6	7	8	9	10
$n!$	1	2	6	24	120	720	5040	40,320	362,880	3,628,800

Thus, if the president were currently worrying about which of his 10 salespeople to assign to each of the 10 sales districts, it is clear that complete enumeration would not be an easy approach to model in Excel. (For 20 salespeople assigned to 20 sales districts, there are $20! \approx 2.4 \times 10^{18}$ possible assignments.) This shows how quickly combinatorial problems can grow. While it may be easy to solve smaller models by inspection, insight, or intuition, when they grow even moderately larger, a sure and efficient optimization method is needed.

THE LP FORMULATION AND SOLUTION

To create the model we use the same definition of variables as we used for the transportation model. In particular, we let

$$x_{ij} = \text{number of vice-presidents of type } i \text{ assigned to plant } j$$
$$i = \text{F, M, O, P}$$
$$j = 1, 2, 3, 4$$

PROTRAC's assignment model is shown in Figure 6.4, which also displays the cost-minimizing assignment. In this figure we note that there is only one of each type of vice-president available (the supply), and one vice-president is required at each plant (the demand). Also, it is a balanced model in the sense that the total number of vice-presidents available equals the total number required. Hence, equality constraints could have been used instead of the inequality ones. Each of the numbers in cells C18:F21 is PROTRAC's cost for that assignment.

In this formulation the first constraint in Figure 6.4 states that the number of vice-presidents "sent" from Finance, F, must be no more than 1. Similar restrictions are placed on vice-presidents M, O, and P, respectively. Thus, each decision variable cell in C10:F13 is constrained to be between 0 and 1 by these upper-bound constraints and the nonnegativity specification in the Solver Options dialog. The "Required" constraint on Leipzig stipulates that at least 1 vice-president be assigned to plant 1. The remaining constraints place a similar requirement on plants 2, 3, and 4, respectively.

Since Figure 6.4 also gives the optimal solution, we see that all decision variables are 0 or 1, and the optimal assignment is in Table 6.6.

RELATION TO THE TRANSPORTATION MODEL

This hauntingly familiar representation is, of course, reminiscent of the transportation model introduced in Section 6.2. There is only one difference. In the assignment model, we must respect the additional feature that supply cannot be distributed to more than one destination. That is, as previously mentioned, each unit of supply (each vice-president) must go to one and only one destination. An answer that sent three fourths of a vice-president to Leipzig and the remaining one fourth to Liege would not be meaningful and is, therefore, prohibited. Recall for transportation models that, if all the supplies and demands are integers, the optimal allocations will also be integers. In the assignment model, all supplies and demands are one; and hence integer. Thus, we can be assured that we will not obtain fractional allocations. We conclude that:

> The assignment model can be formulated as a transportation model in which the supply at each origin and the demand at each destination is equal to 1.

	A	B	C	D	E	F	G	H	I
1									
2		Assignment Model							
3		Unit Cost VP\To	Leipzig	Nancy	Liege	Tilburg			
4		Finance	$ 24	$ 10	$ 21	$ 11			
5		Marketing	$ 14	$ 22	$ 10	$ 15			
6		Operations	$ 15	$ 17	$ 20	$ 19			
7		Personnel	$ 11	$ 19	$ 14	$ 13			
8									
9		Assignment VP\To	Leipzig	Nancy	Liege	Tilburg	Total	Available	
10		Finance	0	1	0	0	1	<=1	
11		Marketing	0	0	1	0	1	<=1	
12		Operations	1	0	0	0	1	<=1	
13		Personnel	0	0	0	1	1	<=1	
14		Total	1	1	1	1			
15		Required	>=1	>=1	>=1	>=1			
16									
17		Total Cost VP\To	Leipzig	Nancy	Liege	Tilburg	Total		
18		Finance	-	$ 10	-	-	$10		
19		Marketing	-	-	$ 10	-	$10		
20		Operations	$ 15	-	-	-	$15		
21		Personnel	-	-	-	$ 13	$13		
22		Total	$ 15	$ 10	$ 10	$ 13	$48		
23									

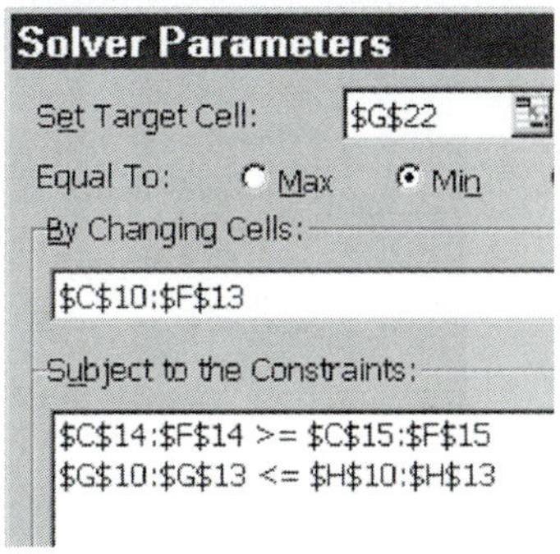
Solver Parameters
Set Target Cell: $G$22
Equal To: Max Min
By Changing Cells:
$C$10:$F$13
Subject to the Constraints:
$C$14:$F$14 >= $C$15:$F$15
$G$10:$G$13 <= $H$10:$H$13

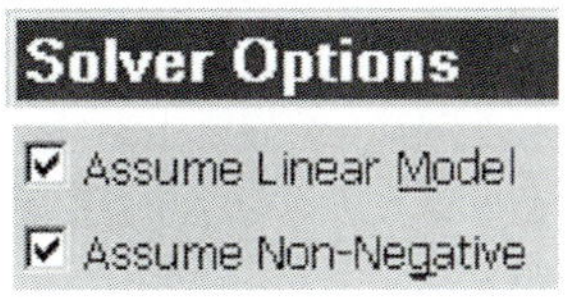
Solver Options
Assume Linear Model
Assume Non-Negative

Cell	Formula	Copy To
C18	= C4*C10	C18:F21
G10	= SUM(C10:F10)	G11:G13
C14	= SUM(C10:C13)	D14:F14

FIGURE 6.4

The Optimal Solution for the PROTRAC Assignment Model

As a result, in the solution of PROTRAC's assignment model, each decision variable cell in C10:F13 will contain either a 0 or a 1 where a 1 represents the assignment of a specific vice-president to a specific plant.[3]

THE ASSIGNMENT MODEL: OTHER CONSIDERATIONS

PROTRAC's assignment model is a minimization model in which the number of vice-presidents equals the number of plants, and every possible assignment is acceptable. Next

[3]Decision variables constrained by a model to be either a 0 or a 1 value, as in this example, are often called "indicator" or "binary" variables.

TABLE 6.6 The Optimal Assignment

ASSIGNMENT		COST
V.-P.	Plant	
F	2	10
M	3	10
O	1	15
P	4	13
	Total Cost ($000s)	48

TABLE 6.7 Assignment Costs in $000s, Supply Exceeds Demand

V.-P.	PLANT			NUMBER OF V.-P.s AVAILABLE
	Leipzig (1)	Nancy (2)	Liege (3)	
F	24	10	21	1
M	14	22	10	1
O	15	17	20	1
P	11	19	14	1
Number of V.-P.s Required	1	1	1	4 / 3

we consider assignment-like models in which all these conditions do not hold. In particular, we consider situations where

1. There are an unequal number of "persons" to assign and "destinations" needing assignees.
2. There is a maximization model.
3. There are unacceptable assignments.

Unequal Supply and Demand: The Auditing Problem Reconsidered   We wish to consider two cases. First, assume that supply exceeds demand. In particular, assume that the president himself decides to audit the plant in Tilburg. He must then decide which of the four vice-presidents to assign to each of the three remaining plants, as given in the cost matrix in Table 6.7.

To formulate this revised model we would simply drop the constraint that required a vice-president at Tilburg for the model in Figure 6.4. The result of this change is that the slack in one of the four vice-president supply constraints would be 1 in the new optimal solution; that is, one vice-president would not be assigned to a plant.

We now consider the case where demand exceeds supply. For example, assume that the vice-president of personnel has to visit PROTRAC's International Headquarters in Illinois during the first two weeks in June and is thus unable to participate in the European audit. The president's problem is then represented by the cost matrix in Table 6.8.

Demand > Supply: Adding a Dummy Vice-President   In this form the model is infeasible. It is clearly impossible to satisfy the demand for four vice-presidents with a supply of three. If the president wanted to find which three plants to audit in order to min-

TABLE 6.8 Assignment Costs in $000s, Demand Exceeds Supply

| V.-P. | PLANT | | | | NUMBER OF V.-P.s AVAILABLE |
	1	2	3	4	
F	24	10	21	11	1
M	14	22	10	15	1
O	15	17	20	19	1
Number of V.-P.s Required	1	1	1	1	3 / 4

TABLE 6.9 Adding a Dummy Vice-President

| V.-P. | PLANT | | | | NUMBER OF V.-P.s AVAILABLE |
	1	2	3	4	
F	24	10	21	11	1
M	14	22	10	15	1
O	15	17	20	19	1
Dummy	0	0	0	0	1
Number of V.-P.s Required	1	1	1	1	4

Dummy supply; now supply = demand

Zero cost to assign the dummy

imize his cost, he could (1) modify the inequalities in the constraints in a way similar to that done in the transportation example earlier when demand exceeded supply or (2) add a dummy vice-president to the cost matrix as shown in Table 6.9. In the solution, the dummy vice-president would be assigned to a plant. In reality, this plant would not be audited. Like the earlier transportation example, an advantage of the second approach, however, is that it might make more sense to think that PROTRAC would incur some cost if a plant was not audited by a vice-president and that this cost could vary from plant to plant. Under these assumptions the new row of the model could be labeled "not audited" and the appropriate cost should be entered in each cell.

The optimal solution is the solution that minimizes the cost of the audits undertaken by F, M, and O. At any rate, when demand exceeds supply, one or more new rows of supply, with costs if appropriate, can be appended to the model to allow a feasible solution to be found.

Maximization Models Consider an assignment model in which the response from each assignment is a profit rather than a cost. For example, suppose that PROTRAC must assign new salespeople to sales territories. Four trainees are ready to be assigned and three territories require a new salesperson. One of the salespeople will have to wait until another territory becomes available before he or she can be assigned.

The effect of assigning any salesperson to a territory is measured by the anticipated marginal increase in profit contribution due to the assignment. Naturally, PROTRAC is interested in maximizing total profit contribution. The *profit* matrix for this model is presented in Table 6.10. The only new feature of this figure is that the number in each cell represents a profit contribution rather than a cost. The spreadsheet formulation and optimal solution for this model are shown in Figure 6.5.

TABLE 6.10 Maximization Assignment Problem

SALESPERSON	TERRITORY			NUMBER OF SALESPEOPLE AVAILABLE
	1	2	3	
A	40	30	20	1
B	18	28	22	1
C	12	16	20	1
D	25	24	27	1
Number of Salespeople Required	1	1	1	4 / 3

Profit if A is assigned to 3

	A	B	C	D	E	F	G	H
1								
2		**Assignment Model**						
3		Contribution Salesperson\To	Territory 1	Territory 2	Territory 3			
4		A	$ 40	$ 30	$ 20			
5		B	$ 18	$ 28	$ 22			
6		C	$ 12	$ 16	$ 20			
7		D	$ 25	$ 24	$ 27			
8								
9		Assignment Salesperson\To	Territory 1	Territory 2	Territory 3	Total	Available	
10		A	1	0	0	1	<=1	
11		B	0	1	0	1	<=1	
12		C	0	0	0	0	<=1	
13		D	0	0	1	1	<=1	
14		Total	1	1	1			
15		Required	<=1	<=1	<=1			
16								
17		Total Contribution Salesperson\To	Territory 1	Territory 2	Territory 3	Total		
18		A	$ 40	-	-	$40		
19		B	-	$ 28	-	$28		
20		C	-	-	-	$ 0		
21		D	-	-	$ 27	$27		
22		Total	$ 40	$ 28	$ 27	$95		
23								

Solver Parameters

Set Target Cell: $F$22

Equal To: ● Max ○ Min

By Changing Cells:

$C$10:$E$13

Subject to the Constraints:

$C$14:$E$14 <= $C$15:$E$15
$F$10:$F$13 <= $G$10:$G$13

Solver Options

☑ Assume Linear Model
☑ Assume Non-Negative

FIGURE 6.5

The LP for the Maximization Assignment Model

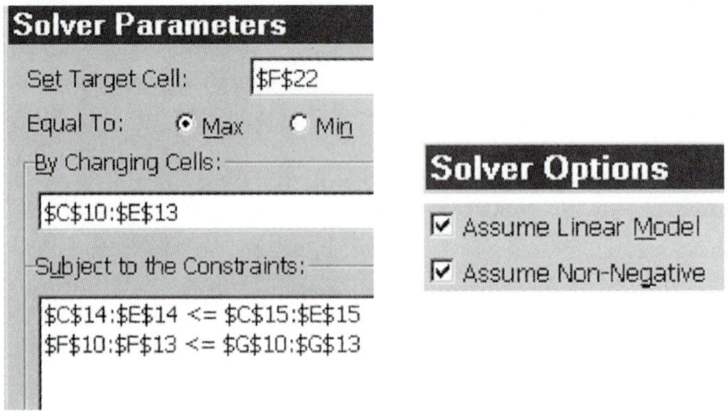

Cell	Formula	Copy To
C18	= C4*C10	C18:E21

238

Situations with Unacceptable Assignments Suppose that you are building an assignment model and you know that certain assignments are simply unacceptable. For example, assume that because of a strong personality conflict the president of PROTRAC-Europe is sure that he does not want to have the vice-president of operations (O) audit the assembly plant at Nancy (2). To achieve this goal, simply assign an arbitrarily *large cost* to cell D6 in Figure 6.4. Choose such a large number that subtracting any finite number from it still leaves a value that is larger than other relevant numbers. Such an assignment will automatically eliminate the assignment of vice-president O to Nancy. This is, of course, the same general approach used to ensure that unacceptable routes are not part of the optimal solution in a transportation model.

6.5   NETWORK MODELS

The transportation and assignment models covered in the previous sections are members of a more general class of models involving sources and destinations, called *network models*. We begin by illustrating a more general form of the transportation model, called a *transshipment* model. With this example in hand we will be in a position to consider the *network model* and its importance in both theory and practice, as well as several special forms of the model.

6.6   CAPACITATED TRANSSHIPMENT MODEL

Seymour Miles is the distribution manager for Zigwell Inc., PROTRAC's largest midwestern distributor. Zigwell distributes its crawler tractors in five midwestern states. Currently, Seymour has ten E-9s at what we shall designate as site ①. These crawlers must be delivered to two major construction sites denoted as sites ③ and ④. Three E-9s are required at

---

APPLICATION CAPSULE   **New Merchandise Arriving Daily: Network Models Help a Discount Chain Keep Shipping Costs at Bargain-Basement Levels**

Finding the most economical way of routing merchandise from suppliers to warehouses and from warehouses to retail stores is a complex problem for many retailing chains. The problem is particularly difficult when the company is growing at a rate of 30% per year. This was the case with Marshall's, the off-price clothing retailer. Adding new stores at a rapid rate, Marshall's needed to be able to alter shipping patterns quickly to accommodate its expansion, as well as decide where new distribution centers should be located. To help accomplish these objectives, Marshall's adopted a computerized logistics planning system.

One part of this system, Network Optimization, consists of three software modules designed to minimize shipping costs.

- An "inbound" module deals with the flow of merchandise from suppliers to warehouses and processing centers.
- An "outbound" module deals with shipments from warehouses and processing centers to retail outlets.
- A third module analyzes the placement of new warehouses, a decision which strongly affects the first two modules.
  Each module has four components:
1. A network generator, which builds network links and nodes
2. A network editor that allows users to modify the network by directly changing costs, demands, and constraints

3. An optimization program
4. A post-processor for displaying the optimization results in a readable format for use by management.

Each of the three modules required a separate modeling approach to capture important economic trade-offs of the particular situation and still ensure computational feasibility. Size was a real challenge with both the inbound and outbound models, each of which initially required the solution of a network with 350,000 links. Use of a heuristic method and other ingenious simplifications reduced that number to around 20,000. Thus streamlined, the models could be run on a PC rather than a mainframe, allowing them to incorporate such user-friendly features as interactive graphics. Now the workhorses of the entire system, they have enabled managers to examine a variety of scenarios, changing such factors as the number of trucks used and their capacities, costs, and warehouse locations, and then quickly reoptimizing. The speed of the process allows interactive feedback for sensitivity analysis.

Use of these models enabled Marshall's to evaluate both costs and service levels of its delivery network, producing estimated savings of $250,000 per year. In addition, the model helped determine the site for a new distribution center, expected to save the company $1.4 million in shipping costs. (See Carlisle et. al.)

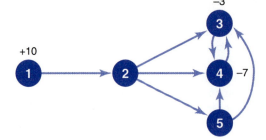

FIGURE 6.6

Network Diagram for
Seymour's Model

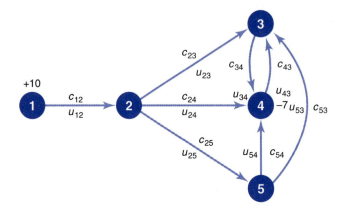

FIGURE 6.7

Capacities and Costs
Appended

site ③, and seven are required at site ④. Because of prearranged schedules concerning driver availability, these crawlers may be distributed only according to any of the alternative routes shown in Figure 6.6.

NETWORK TERMINOLOGY

Figure 6.6 is an example of a **network diagram.** Each of the arrows between sites is termed an **arc,** or **branch,** of the network. The arc from ② to ④ is sometimes denoted symbolically by the pair (2,4). Each site is termed a **node** of the network.

The figure shows a $+10$ identified with site ①. This means that ten E-9s (items of *supply*) are available at this site. The identifiers -3 and -7 attached to sites ③ and ④, respectively, denote the *requirements,* or *demands,* at these two sites. The figure also indicates that E-9s may be delivered to site ③ via any of the alternative routings ①→②→③, ①→②→④→③, ①→②→⑤→④→③, or ①→②→⑤→③.

Which of the allowable routes is ultimately selected will be determined by the associated *costs* of traversing the routes and *capacities* along the routes. These additional data are shown in Figure 6.7. For convenience the costs and capacities are represented in symbolic (i.e., parametric) notation. The costs c_{ij} are *per unit costs.* For example, the cost of traversing arc (5,3) is c_{53} per crawler. These costs are primarily due to fuel, tolls, and the cost of the driver for the average time it takes to traverse the arc. Because of preestablished agreements with the teamsters, Zigwell must change drivers at each site it encounters on a route. Because of limitations on the current availability of drivers, there is an upper bound on the number of crawlers that may traverse any given arc. Thus, as an example, u_{53} is the upper bound or capacity on arc (5,3).

LP FORMULATION OF THE MODEL

Seymour's problem is to find a shipment plan that satisfies the demands at minimum cost, subject to the capacity constraints. You can now appreciate the trade-offs facing Seymour. For example, if $(c_{25} + c_{53})$ is less than c_{23}, the route ①→②→⑤→③ will have a total cost that is less than the total cost of route ①→②→③, and hence ①→②→⑤→③ is preferred to ①→②→③. However, the maximum number of E-9s that can be sent across the preferred route is $\text{MIN}(u_{12}, u_{25}, u_{53})$. If this number is less than 3, the number of E-9s required at 3, all of the shipment cannot be accomplished via ①→②→⑤→③. This is a model in only five nodes and eight arcs, and even in a simplified example such as this the optimal solution may not be obvious. Imagine such a model with 30 or 40 nodes and many more arcs.

Seymour's model is called a **capacitated transshipment model.** This model is basically identical to the transportation model covered earlier except that:

1. Any plant or warehouse can ship to any other plant or warehouse, and

2. There can be upper and/or lower bounds (capacities) on each shipment (branch).

Because these capacities can be added to the model, and shipments can cross (trans) from warehouse to warehouse (or plant to plant), it is called the capacitated transshipment model. We now show that this model can easily be expressed as an LP. First, define the decision variables

$$x_{ij} = \text{total number of E-9s sent on arc } (i,j)$$
$$= \text{flow from node } i \text{ to node } j$$

Then the model is

$$\text{Min } c_{12}x_{12} + c_{23}x_{23} + c_{24}x_{24} + c_{25}x_{25} + c_{34}x_{34} + c_{43}x_{43} + c_{53}x_{53} + c_{54}x_{54}$$

$$
\begin{array}{rl}
\text{s.t.} & +x_{12} = 10 \\
& -x_{12} + x_{23} + x_{24} + x_{25} = 0 \\
& -x_{23} - x_{43} - x_{53} + x_{34} = -3 \\
& -x_{24} + x_{43} - x_{34} - x_{54} = -7 \\
& -x_{25} + x_{53} + x_{54} = 0
\end{array}
$$

$$0 \leq x_{ij} \leq u_{ij}, \text{ all arcs } (i,j) \text{ in the network}$$

PROPERTIES OF THE LP

There are now a number of observations to be made about this model.

1. The model is indeed an LP. There is one variable x_{ij} associated with each arc in the network (Figure 6.7). There are eight arcs in this network and thus eight corresponding variables, $x_{12}, x_{23}, x_{24}, x_{25}, x_{43}, x_{53}, x_{34}$, and x_{54}. The objective is to minimize total cost.

2. There is one material **flow balance equation** associated with each node in the network. The first equation says that the total flow *out* of node ① is ten units. Recall that this is the total supply at node ①. The second equation says that the total flow *out of* node ② (namely, x_{23} $+ x_{24} + x_{25}$) minus the total flow *into* node ② (namely, x_{12}) is zero. In other words, the total flow out of node ② must equal the total flow into node ②. The third equation says that the total flow *out of* node ③ (namely x_{34}) must be 3 units less than the total flow *into* node ③ (namely, $x_{23} + x_{43} + x_{53}$). This is the mathematical way of expressing the requirement for a *net delivery* of 3 units to node ③. The equations for nodes ④ and ⑤, respectively, have similar interpretations. Thus, the equation for each node expresses a flow balance and takes into account the fact that the node may be either a supply point or a demand point or neither. Intermediate nodes (such as ② and ⑤ in Figure 6.6) that are neither supply points nor demand points are often termed *transshipment nodes.*

3. The positive right-hand sides correspond to nodes that are net suppliers (origins). The negative right-hand sides correspond to nodes that are net destinations. The zero right-hand sides correspond to nodes that have neither supply nor demand. The sum of all right-hand-side terms is zero, which means that the total supply in the network equals the total demand.

4. The *special structure* of this network model is revealed by placing the data of the constraints in the format shown in Table 6.11, called a **node-arc incidence matrix.** Each row of the table corresponds to a node and contains the data of the corresponding constraint in the LP. Each column of the table corresponds to an arc (or a variable). Since there are eight arcs in the model, there are eight corresponding columns in the table. The key to the *special structure* of this network model is the fact that in each column of the node-arc incidence matrix there is a $+1$ and a -1, and the remaining terms are zero. The $+1$ is in the row corresponding to the node

TABLE 6.11 Node-Arc Incidence Matrix

NODE	ARC								RHS
	(1,2)	(2,3)	(2,4)	(2,5)	(4,3)	(5,3)	(3,4)	(5,4)	
1	+1	0	0	0	0	0	0	0	10
2	−1	+1	+1	+1	0	0	0	0	0
3	0	−1	0	0	−1	−1	+1	0	−3
4	0	0	−1	0	+1	0	−1	−1	−7
5	0	0	0	−1	0	+1	0	+1	0

at which the arc originates. The -1 is in the row corresponding to the node at which the arc terminates. Consider the column under arc (2,5) in Table 6.11. Since this arc originates at node ②, there is a $+1$ in row 2. Since the arc terminates at node ⑤, there is a -1 in row 5. All other entries in this column are zero. It should be noted that the node-arc incidence matrix can be created directly from Figure 6.6 without first writing down the LP. Similarly, Figure 6.6 could be constructed from the data in the table (or from the LP). In other words, Figure 6.6 and the node-arc incidence table are equivalent ways of communicating the network structure of Seymour's model.

5. Since Seymour's model is an LP, it can be optimized with Solver like any other LP.

6.7 GENERAL FORMULATION OF THE CAPACITATED TRANSSHIPMENT MODEL

Seymour's model is a special case of the following general symbolic LP form of a network model. Again, the decision variables x_{ij} will denote the "flow" from node i to node j across the arc connecting these two nodes, and L_j represents the supply at node j.

$$\text{Minimize} \sum_{ij} c_{ij} x_{ij}$$
$$\text{s.t.} \sum_{k} x_{jk} - \sum_{k} x_{kj} = L_j \quad j = 1, 2, \ldots, n$$
$$0 \le x_{ij} \le u_{ij}, \text{ all } (i,j) \text{ in the network}$$

Let us observe that

1. The sum $\sum_{ij} c_{ij} x_{ij}$ in the objective function is understood to be over all arcs in the network. Thus, the objective is to minimize the total cost of the flow.

2. Consider the jth constraint, for some fixed value of j. The sum $\sum_{k} x_{jk}$ is understood to be over all k for which arc (j,k), with j fixed, is in the network. Thus, $\sum_{k} x_{jk}$ is the total flow *out* of the specified node j. Similarly, $\sum_{k} x_{kj}$ is over all k for which arc (k,j), with j fixed, is in the network. Thus, $\sum_{k} x_{kj}$ is the total flow *into* node j. Therefore, the jth constraint is a flow balance equation that says

total flow out of node j − total flow into node j = supply at node j

where negative supply (i.e., $L_j < 0$) represents a requirement. Nodes with negative supply are called **destinations,** *sinks,* or *demand points.* Nodes with positive supply (i.e., $L_j > 0$) are called **origins,** *sources,* or *supply points.* Nodes with zero supply are called *transshipment points.*

3. For simplicity it is assumed that $\sum_{j} L_j = 0$ (i.e., total supply = total demand) and all $c_{ij} \ge 0$.

Capacited Transshipment Model

Capacity From\To	Site 1	Site 2	Site 3	Site 4	Site 5
Site 1		10			
Site 2			4	3	3
Site 3				2	
Site 4			4		
Site 5			3	5	

Unit Cost From\To	Site 1	Site 2	Site 3	Site 4	Site 5
Site 1		$100			
Site 2			$45	$50	$20
Site 3				$60	
Site 4			$85		
Site 5			$10	$55	

Shipments From\To	Site 1	Site 2	Site 3	Site 4	Site 5	Total Shipped
Site 1		10				10
Site 2			4	3	3	10
Site 3				1		1
Site 4						0
Site 5				3		3
Total Received	0	10	4	7	3	
Shipped − Received	10	0	-3	-7	0	
Required Net	=10	=0	=-3	=-7	=0	

Total Cost From\To	Site 1	Site 2	Site 3	Site 4	Site 5	Total
Site 1		$1,000				$1,000
Site 2			$180	$150	$60	$390
Site 3				$60		$60
Site 4						
Site 5				$165		$165
Total		$1,000	$180	$375	$60	$1,615

Cell	Formula	Copy To
J10	= C10*J3	J10:N14
H10	= SUM(C10:G10)	H11:H14
C15	= SUM(C10:C14)	D15:G15

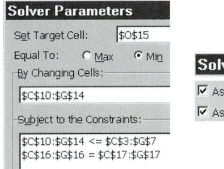

Solver Parameters

Set Target Cell: $O$15

Equal To: ○ Max   ● Min

By Changing Cells:

$C$10:$G$14

Subject to the Constraints:

$C$10:$G$14 <= $C$3:$G$7
$C$16:$G$16 = $C$17:$G$17

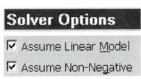

Solver Options

☑ Assume Linear Model

☑ Assume Non-Negative

FIGURE 6.8

Seymour's Transshipment Model

4. The last set of constraints places *capacities* on the flows x_{ij}. As a special case some of the u_{ij} could be infinitely large, meaning that these are arcs with no capacity constraints. Setting a zero value for a u_{ij} would be equivalent to eliminating arc (i,j) from the network.

5. The given data for the model are the c_{ij}'s, the L_j's, and the u_{ij}'s.

Figure 6.8 gives a spreadsheet formulation for Seymour's transshipment model. Example u_{ij} capacities and c_{ij} unit costs are specified as parameters in rows 3 to 7. The RHS specification of the requirements constraint is given in row 17.

The "Shipped − Received" quantities in row 16 are computed by subtracting the Total Received quantities in C15:G15 from the Total Shipped quantities in H10:H14.[4] For these example parameter values, the optimal solution for the decision variables and total costs are given in rows 10 to 14.

The capacitated transshipment model (often called the **network** model) is important because several important management decision models are special cases. In particular the

---

[4] The only way to do this in Excel by a single formula requires array operations using the TRANSPOSE function. Highlight C16:G16 and enter the array formula {=TRANSPOSE(H10:H14)-C15:G15} into C16. See the Excel Appendix for details on array operations. Otherwise, separate formulas must be entered for each cell: C16 contains "=H10-C15", D16 contains "H11-D15", and so on.

transportation model, assignment model, and shortest-route model, described next, are special cases of the capacitated transshipment model, and the maximal flow model, described in Section 6.9, is closely related.

INTEGER OPTIMAL SOLUTIONS

There are two advantages in being able to identify a model as a special case of the network (or capacitated transshipment) model. First, theoretical results that are established for the general model apply automatically to the specific cases. The outstanding example of this phenomenon is the integer property of the network model. The integer property can be stated thus:

> If all terms L_j and u_{ij} are integers in the capacitated transshipment model, there will always be an integer-valued optimal solution to this model.

From earlier chapters you know that LP models do not in general yield optimal solutions that have integer-valued variables. The network model with integer values for all L_j and u_{ij} does. This has an important implication on the usefulness of the various special versions of the network model.

EFFICIENT SOLUTION PROCEDURES

The second reason it is useful to identify a model as a special case of the capacitated transshipment model is that the *structure* of this model typically makes it possible to apply special solution methods that optimize the model more quickly than the simplex method used by Solver. This makes it possible to optimize extremely large network models quickly using special purpose network optimization software.

The impact of some of the superefficient solution methods derived from the special structure of the network model is rather amazing. For example, the Internal Revenue Service constructed a network model with 50,000 constraints and 600 million variables. Only one hour of a mainframe computer's time was required to optimize this model.

The next two sections are devoted to the shortest-route model and the maximal-flow model, respectively. In each case the model is represented with a network diagram, and a special spreadsheet formulation for solving the model is presented. The shortest-route model is another special case of the capacitated transshipment model.

6.8 THE SHORTEST-ROUTE MODEL

The **shortest-route model** refers to a network for which each arc (i,j) has an associated number, c_{ij}, which is interpreted as the distance (or possibly the cost, or time) from node i to node j. A *route,* or a *path,* between two nodes is any sequence of arcs connecting the two nodes. The objective is to find the shortest (or least-cost or least-time) routes from a specific node to each of the other nodes in the network.

As an illustration, Aaron Drunner makes frequent wine deliveries to seven different sites. Figure 6.9 shows the seven sites together with the possible travel routes between sites. Note that here, unlike in the transshipment model, the arcs are *nondirected.* That is, on each arc, flow is permitted in either direction. It is certainly possible to have directed arcs between the nodes, with the cost from node 1 to 2 different than from 2 to 1. This might be the case when there is rush-hour traffic in one direction but not in the other, or when traffic is able to go from 1 to 2 but not from 2 to 1 (one-way street). Each arc in Figure 6.9 has been labeled with the distance between the nodes the arc connects. The home base is denoted H. Aaron feels that his overall costs will be minimized by making sure that any future delivery to any given site is made along the shortest route to that site. Thus, his objective is to specify the shortest routes from node H to any of the other seven nodes. Note that in this model, as stated, the task is not to find optimal x_{ij}'s. The task is to find an optimal route.

Figure 6.10 gives Aaron's model for finding the shortest path between any two nodes, in this case from Home to Site 5. The starting node, Home, and the ending node,

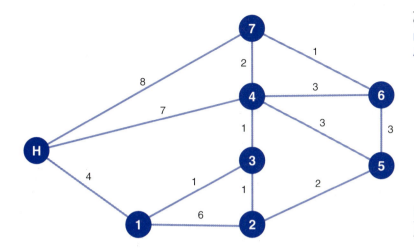

FIGURE 6.9

Aaron's Network of Sites

Shortest Route Model

Connectivity From\To	Home	Site 1	Site 2	Site 3	Site 4	Site 5	Site 6	Site 7
Home		1			1			1
Site 1	1		1	1				
Site 2		1		1		1		
Site 3		1	1		1			
Site 4	1			1		1	1	1
Site 5			1		1		1	
Site 6				1	1			1
Site 7	1			1		1		

Distance From\To	Home	Site 1	Site 2	Site 3	Site 4	Site 5	Site 6	Site 7
Home		4			7			8
Site 1	4		6	1				
Site 2		6		1		2		
Site 3		1	1		1			
Site 4	7			1		3	3	2
Site 5			2		3		3	
Site 6				3	3			1
Site 7	8				2		1	

Route From\To	Home	Site 1	Site 2	Site 3	Site 4	Site 5	Site 6	Site 7	Total From
Home		1							1
Site 1				1					1
Site 2						1			1
Site 3			1						1
Site 4									0
Site 5									0
Site 6									0
Site 7									0
Total To	0	1	1	1	0	1	0	0	
Total From - Total To	1	0	0	0	0	-1	-0	0	
Required Net	=1	=0	=0	=0	=0	=-1	=0	=0	

Total Distance	Home	Site 1	Site 2	Site 3	Site 4	Site 5	Site 6	Site 7	Total
Home		4						0	4
Site 1				1					1
Site 2						2			2
Site 3			1						1
Site 4									0
Site 5									0
Site 6									0
Site 7							0		0
Total		4	1	1		2	0	0	8

Cell	Formula	Copy To
M13	= C13*M3	M13:T20

Solver Parameters

Set Target Cell: $U$21

Equal To: ○ Max   ● Min

By Changing Cells:

$C$13:$J$20

Subject to the Constraints:

$C$13:$J$20 <= $C$3:$J$10
$C$22:$J$22 = $C$23:$J$23

Solver Options

☑ Assume Linear Model

☑ Assume Non-Negative

FIGURE 6.10

Aaron's Model for Shortest
Path from H to Node 5

Site 5, are specified in row 23 by a 1 and −1, respectively. Cells M3:T10 specify the arc distances as parameters. Other than the use of indicator variables to signify the node-arc connectivity in cells C3:J10, the model is the same form as the general transshipment model. The decision variables are constrained to be between 0 and 1, as in the assignment model and the objective function in U21 to be minimized is the total distance.

AN APPLICATION OF SHORTEST ROUTE: EQUIPMENT REPLACEMENT

Lisa Carr is responsible for obtaining reproduction equipment (photocopier machines) for PROTRAC's secretarial service. She must choose between leasing newer equipment at high rental cost but low maintenance cost, or used equipment with lower rental costs but higher maintenance costs. Lisa has a four-year time horizon to consider. Let c_{ij} denote the cost of *leasing* new equipment at the beginning of year i, $i = 1, 2, 3, 4$, and maintaining it to the beginning of year j, where j can take on the values 2, 3, 4, 5. If the equipment is maintained only to the beginning of year j, for $j < 5$, new equipment must again be leased at the beginning of j. For example, three alternative feasible policies are:

1. Lease new equipment at the beginning of each year. Presumably, such a policy would involve the highest leasing charges and the minimum maintenance charges. The total (leasing + maintenance) cost of this policy would be $c_{12} + c_{23} + c_{34} + c_{45}$.

2. Lease new equipment only at the beginning of year 1 and maintain it through all successive years. This would undoubtedly be a policy of minimum lease cost but maximum maintenance. The total (leasing + maintenance) cost of this policy would be c_{15}.

3. Lease new equipment at the beginning of years 1 and 3. The total cost would be $c_{13} + c_{35}$.

Of all feasible policies, Lisa desires one with a minimum cost. The solution to this model is obtained by finding the shortest (i.e., in this case, minimum-cost) route from node

---

APPLICATION CAPSULE   **Japan's Hanshin Expressway**

The Hanshin Expressway started with only a 2.3 kilometer (km) stretch in 1964. This was the first urban toll expressway in Osaka. Two years later, an expressway was opened in Kobe that connected that city to Osaka. About 5000 cars per day used the expressway in the mid-1960s. This area of Japan, on the main island of Honshu, is the second most populated area of Japan (Tokyo is first). In 1992, the expressway operated a network of 200 km with an average of 828,000 cars flowing onto the expressway each day.

The average number of cars per unit of arable land in Japan is much more than that in the United States. Almost all cities and towns in Japan suffer from severe traffic congestion. Because land is scarce, it is estimated that the capacity of the road networks will never catch up with demand. Thus, the importance of finding ways to maximize utilization of the road networks will continue into the foreseeable future.

In 1970, the expressway started operating an automated traffic-control system to maximize the total traffic flowing into its expressway network. The maximum flow idea is somewhat tricky. One might think that in order to maximize flow you would let all the cars enter that wanted to and may even lower the toll to stimulate demand. But, if too many cars are allowed to enter, major congestion can occur, thus greatly decreasing the total flow on the system.

One of the controls used by the Hanshin Expressway is to limit the cars coming onto the expressway at each entrance ramp to avoid congestion. This is done by calculating maximum allowable inflows by solving a linear programming (LP) model once every five minutes using data from detectors installed every 500 meters along the expressway and at all ramps. The linear program has the objective of maximizing the flow on the expressway, which will automatically maximize the income. From the LP solution, the expressway management decide how many new cars to allow onto the expressway at each on-ramp. Management can also use the LP model if there is an accident to determine how many cars should be forced to exit upstream from the accident. In order to reduce congestion and bottlenecks, the expressway authority also analyzed the number of accidents, disabled cars, and road maintenance that could be expected. A second method of control that is used is to give drivers the most recent and accurate traffic information about the expressway and its vicinity, including expected travel times and accidents.

Management has been able to keep the cost of this traffic-control system to about 1% of the total toll revenue. The greatest benefit has been the travel time saved by the drivers. The total time saved over the decade of the 1970s was estimated at 17,850,000 hours. Based on the average hourly benefit of the citizens of Osaka, this is worth some 27,300,000,000 yen (US$260 million at 1994 exchange rates)! Hanshin's LP model has also been a prototype to the rest of Japan and Taiwan as they have tried to implement automatic traffic control to gain the same benefits. (See Yoshino et. al.)

1 to node 5 of the network shown in Figure 6.11. Each node on the shortest route denotes a replacement; that is, a year at which new equipment should be leased.

Figure 6.12 gives Lisa's equipment replacement model assuming a cost of $1600 plus maintenance of $500 in the year the equipment is leased and annual maintenance costs of $1000, $1500, and $2200 for each additional year the equipment is kept thereafter. Using the parameters in cells I3:I8, cells K3:O7 compute the cost consequences of leasing and maintaining a machine beginning in one year and continuing to a terminal year. For example, the formula in cell N3 is "$=I3+I5+I6+I7$." The beginning year and the ending year for Lisa's equipment needs are specified in row 17 by a 1 and -1, respectively. As before with the shortest-path model, indicator variables are used to signify the

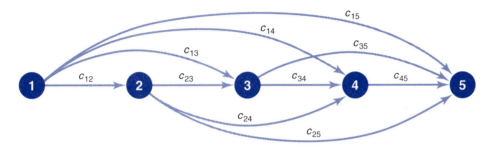

FIGURE 6.11

Network for Lisa's Equipment Replacement Decision

	A	B	C	D	E	F	G	H	I	J	K	L	M	N	O	P	Q
1		**Equipment Leasing Model**															
2		Capacity From\To	Year 1	Year 2	Year 3	Year 4	Year 5		Lease	Unit Cost From\To	Year 1	Year 2	Year 3	Year 4	Year 5		
									$1.6								
3		Year 1		1	1	1	1			Year 1		$2.1	$3.1	$4.6	$6.8		
4		Year 2			1	1	1		Maint.	Year 2			$2.1	$3.1	$4.6		
5		Year 3				1	1		$0.5	Year 3				$2.1	$3.1		
6		Year 4					1		$1.0	Year 4					$2.1		
7		Year 5							$1.5	Year 5							
8									$2.2								
9		Acquire From\To	Year 1	Year 2	Year 3	Year 4	Year 5	Total From		Total Cost From\To	Year 1	Year 2	Year 3	Year 4	Year 5	Total	
10		Year 1			1			1		Year 1			$3.1			$ 3.1	
11		Year 2						0		Year 2							
12		Year 3					1	1		Year 3					$ 3.1	$ 3.1	
13		Year 4						0		Year 4							
14		Year 5						0		Year 5							
15		Total To	0	0	1	0	1			Total			$3.1		$ 3.1	$6.2	
16		Total From – Total To	1	0	0	0	-1										
17		Required Net	=1	=0	=0	=0	=-1										
18																	

Cell	Formula	Copy To
K10	= C10*K3	K10:O14

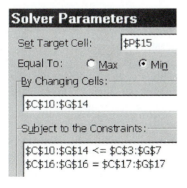

Solver Parameters

Set Target Cell: $P$15

Equal To: ○ Max   ● Min

By Changing Cells:

$C$10:$G$14

Subject to the Constraints:

$C$10:$G$14 <= $C$3:$G$7
$C$16:$G$16 = $C$17:$G$17

Solver Options

☑ Assume Linear Model

☑ Assume Non-Negative

FIGURE 6.12

Lisa's Equipment Replacement Model

node-arc connectivity in cells C3:G7 and cells K10:O14 compute the costs of the decisions in cells C10:G14.

6.9   THE MAXIMAL-FLOW MODEL

In the **maximal-flow model** there is a single *source* node (the input node) and a single *sink* node (the output node). The goal is to find the maximum amount of total flow (petroleum, cash, Internet packets, traffic) that can be routed through the network (from source to sink) in a unit of time. The amount of flow per unit time on *each arc* is limited by *capacity restrictions*. For example, pipeline diameters limit the flow of crude oil on the links of a distribution system. Flow capacities for nodes are not specified. The only requirement here is that for each node (other than the source or the sink) the flow balance equation

$$\text{flow out of the node} = \text{flow into the node}$$

must be satisfied.

Formally, letting node 1 be the source, and node n be the sink. The model is

$$\text{Max } f$$

$$\text{s.t.} \quad \sum_{j} x_{ij} - \sum_{j} x_{ji} = \begin{cases} f, \text{ if } i=1 \\ -f, \text{ if } i=n \\ 0, \text{ otherwise} \end{cases}$$

$$0 \le x_{ij} \le u_{ij}, \text{ all } (i,j) \text{ in the network}$$

We observe that:

1. The variables x_{ij} denote the flow per unit time across the arc (i,j) connecting node i and node j.

2. Consider the ith constraint, for some fixed value of i. The sum $\sum_{j} x_{ij}$ is over all j for which arc (i,j), with i fixed, is in the network. Thus, $\sum_{j} x_{ij}$ is the total flow *out of* node i. Similarly, the sum $\sum_{j} x_{ji}$ is over all j for which there is an arc (j,i) in the network (where i is fixed). Thus, $\sum_{j} x_{ji}$ is the total flow *into* node i.

3. The symbol f is a variable denoting the total flow through the network per unit time. By definition this is equal to the flow per unit time leaving the source, node 1 (the first constraint). This is also equal to the flow per unit time entering the sink, node n (the second constraint). The objective is to maximize this quantity.

4. The u_{ij}'s denote the capacities on the flows per unit time across the various arcs.

This model, together with the shortest-path model, is of interest in its own right. It also appears as a submodel in solving other, more complicated, models. For such reasons, as well as because of some of the theoretic underpinnings (which go beyond our present scope of interest), it is sometimes stated that these two models (shortest path and maximal flow) are of central importance in network theory.

AN APPLICATION OF MAXIMAL FLOW:
THE URBAN DEVELOPMENT PLANNING COMMISSION

Gloria Stime is in charge of the UDPC (Urban Development Planning Commission) *ad hoc* special-interest study group. This group's current responsibility is to coordinate the construction of the new subway system with the highway maintenance department. Because the new subway system is being built near the city's beltway, the eastbound traffic on the beltway must be detoured. The planned detour actually involves a network of alternative routes that have been proposed by the highway maintenance department. Different speed limits and traffic patterns produce different flow capacities on the various arcs of the proposed network, as shown in Figure 6.13.

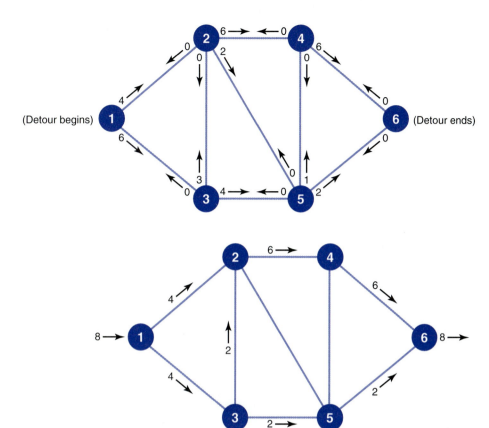

FIGURE 6.13

Proposed Network and Flow
Capacities (000s of
Vehicles/Hour)

FIGURE 6.14

A Maximal-Flow Pattern for
Gloria's Network

Node ① denotes the beginning of the detour; that is, the point at which the east-bound traffic leaves the beltway. Node ⑥ is the point at which the detoured traffic reenters the beltway. Also, in Figure 6.13, the flow capacities depend on the direction of the flow. The symbol 6 on arc (1,3) denotes a capacity of 6000 vehicles per hour in the 1 → 3 direction. The symbol 0 on the same arc means that a zero capacity exists in the 3 → 1 direction. This is because the indicated arc (1,3) denotes a one-way street from ① to ③. In this example it is seen that each of the other arcs denotes one-way travel. (The spreadsheet model to be presented will also apply to models with arcs permitting positive levels of flow in each direction.) The maximal flow is 8000 vehicles per hour, as shown in Figure 6.14. This answer was found by optimizing the spreadsheet model given in Figure 6.15.

Except for the absence of cost data, the model in Figure 6.15 is similar in form to the other network models we have seen. The (nonnegative) decision variables in cells C10:H14 are the flows from node to node constrained to be no greater than the given arc capacity parameters in cells C3:H7. This model maximizes flow out of Node 1 as its objective function in cell I10. (Equivalently, we could have maximized the flow into Node 6, cell H15, as the objective function.) The constraints in cells C17:G17 specify that the net flow at each intermediate node must sum to zero; that is, total flow into each intermediate node equals total flow out of the node.

As is common in network models, there are alternative optimal solutions to Gloria's model, as shown in Figure 6.16.

6.10   NOTES ON IMPLEMENTATION OF NETWORK MODELS

Network models are among the most important applications of management logistics and distribution, and also have wide applicability in engineering and computer science. Along this line, in recent years we have seen the appearance of a number of consulting firms that

	A	B	C	D	E	F	G	H	I	J
1				**Max Flow Model**						
2		Capacity From\To	Node 1	Node 2	Node 3	Node 4	Node 5	Node 6		
3		Node 1		4	6					
4		Node 2				6	2			
5		Node 3		3			4			
6		Node 4						6		
7		Node 5						2		
8										
9		Flow From\To	Node 1	Node 2	Node 3	Node 4	Node 5	Node 6	Total From	
10		Node 1		4	4				8	
11		Node 2				6			6	
12		Node 3		2			2		4	
13		Node 4						6	6	
14		Node 5						2	2	
15		Total To		6	4	6	2	8		
16		Total From - Total To		-0	0	0	0			
17		Required Net		=0	=0	=0	=0			
18										

Solver Parameters

Set Target Cell: $I$10

Equal To: ⊙ Max   ○ Min

By Changing Cells:

$D$10:$H$14

Subject to the Constraints:

$D$10:$H$14 <= $D$3:$H$7
$D$16:$G$16 = $D$17:$G$17

Solver Options

☑ Assume Linear Model

☑ Assume Non-Negative

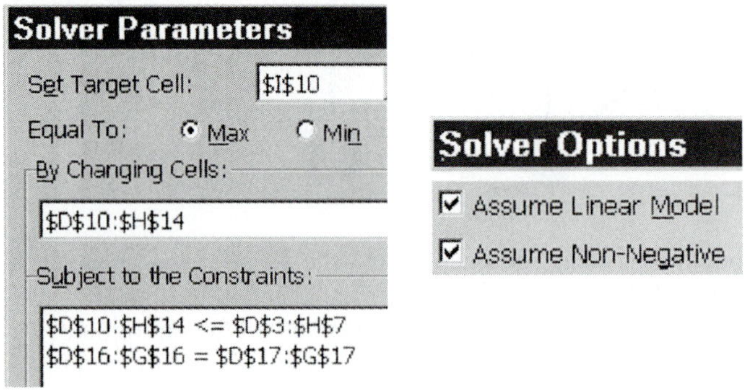

FIGURE 6.15

Maximal-Flow Spreadsheet
Model for Gloria's Network

	A	B	C	D	E	F	G	H	I	J
1				**Max Flow Model**						
2		Capacity From\To	Node 1	Node 2	Node 3	Node 4	Node 5	Node 6		
3		Node 1		4	6					
4		Node 2				6	2			
5		Node 3		3			4			
6		Node 4						6		
7		Node 5						2		
8										
9		Flow From\To	Node 1	Node 2	Node 3	Node 4	Node 5	Node 6	Total From	
10		Node 1		4	4				8	
11		Node 2				6	1		7	
12		Node 3		3			1		4	
13		Node 4						6	6	
14		Node 5						2	2	
15		Total To		7	4	6	2	8		
16		Total From - Total To		0	0	0	0			
17		Required Net		=0	=0	=0	=0			
18										

FIGURE 6.16

Alternative Optimal Solution
for Gloria's Network Model

deal exclusively with network applications. The main emphasis of such firms is often on strategic planning models from the point of view of distribution studies, where the term *distribution* is taken in a quite general sense: flow of physical product, data packets, vehicles, cash, and so on. Some of the state-of-the-art software for efficiently optimizing very large scale network applications—models too large for Solver—can be purchased from these and other software vendors.

The application of network models to real situations involves considerable skill and experience in casting models, which initially may not appear to be network models, into a network representation. To capitalize on the advantages of the network structure, it is often worth the price of "straining" the initial formulation to cast it into a network representation. As a final note, it is worth emphasizing that many real modeling situations contain submodels that may have a network form.

6.11   FINANCIAL AND PRODUCTION PLANNING

The PROTRAC, Inc. production model was introduced in Chapter 2. It is a product-mix model; that is, a model in which PROTRAC is deciding how many E-9s and F-9s to make in the coming month, in view of a number of constraints. Recall that E is the number of E-9s to produce and F is the number of F-9s. The complete model is

$$\text{Max } 5000E + 4000F$$

$$\begin{aligned}
\text{s.t.} \quad E + F &\geq 5 && \text{(total unit requirements)} \\
E - 3F &\leq 0 && \text{(mix requirements)} \\
10E + 15F &\leq 150 && \text{(hours in department A)} \\
20E + 10F &\leq 160 && \text{(hours in department B)} \\
30E + 10F &\geq 135 && \text{(testing hours)} \\
E, F &\geq 0
\end{aligned}$$

The production manager is satisfied that from his perspective this model captures the essence of the situation. He sends to the management committee a proposal that the recommendations of the model be considered for implementation.

FINANCIAL CONSIDERATIONS

When the management committee reviews the activities that are proposed for the coming month, it soon becomes clear that the PROTRAC production model captures only a part of PROTRAC's real situation. In particular, certain important financial considerations have been ignored. Specifically, PROTRAC must incur material and direct labor costs in the next month, whereas payments from the eventual customers will not be forthcoming for another three months. The current formulation ignores the fact that PROTRAC will have to borrow funds to cover at least part of the current expenditures.

The data in Table 6.12 are relevant to the financial considerations. PROTRAC has budgeted $100,000 of cash on hand to cover the current material and labor costs and plans to borrow any additional funds for these material and labor costs. PROTRAC can borrow money at an annual interest rate of 16%, but in order to hedge against downside risks, the bank has limited the total due to the bank (principal plus interest) to be no more than two

TABLE 6.12 Financial Data			
PRODUCT	PER UNIT MATERIAL AND LABOR COSTS ($)	PROFIT CONTRIBUTION ($)	SALES PRICE ($)
E	75,000	5000	80,000
F	20,000	4000	24,000

thirds of the sum of PROTRAC's cash on hand and accounts receivable. The management committee is concerned that the time value of money has been ignored in calculating the profit contributions. It feels that if present value of net cash flow is maximized fewer E-9s and more F-9s will be produced, because of the relatively high material and labor costs of the E-9s. The committee cannot agree, however, on what the proper discount rate should be. Some members argue for a 12% annual discount rate, others for a 16% rate, and a few for a 20% rate.

THE COMBINED MODEL

PROTRAC's problem is to formulate a new objective function, determine how much to borrow (if any), and devise a production plan incorporating this new information. To model this situation, it is convenient to introduce a variable. Let

$$D = \text{debt (i.e., total dollars borrowed), in thousands of dollars}$$

The net cash flow next month in dollars will be $1000D - 75,000E - 20,000F$, while (since payments will not be forthcoming for another three months) the net cash flow three months later will be $80,000E + 24,000F - 1040D$. The coefficient 1040 is derived from the above statement that PROTRAC can borrow at 16% per annum, and hence at 4% for three months. Define the discount factor, α, based on the annual discount rate, R, as $\alpha = 1/(1 + R/4)$. The objective is to maximize present value of net cash flow, so the objective function becomes in dollars

$$\text{Max } 1000D - 75,000E - 20,000F + \alpha(80,000E + 24,000F - 1040D)$$

For example, if $R = 20\%$ and $\alpha = 0.952381$, the objective function becomes

$$\text{Max } 1190.48E + 2857.14F + 9.52381D$$

Note that D actually has a positive coefficient here, because PROTRAC is assuming it can earn 20% on its investments, but has to pay back only 16% interest on borrowed funds. If $R = 16\%$ or $R < 16\%$, then the coefficient of D would be zero or negative, respectively.

Additional constraints are also required:

1. PROTRAC must borrow enough so that it is able to cover the material and labor costs associated with production. In general terms, the appropriate inequality is

$$\text{debt} + \text{cash on hand} \geq \text{material and labor costs}$$

   To expand this expression, we note that PROTRAC has $100,000 of cash on hand. In addition, from Table 6.12, total material and labor costs are $75,000 for each E and $20,000 for each F. Thus, our equation becomes, expressing everything in thousands of dollars,

$$D + 100 \geq 75E + 20F$$

2. The bank requires that the total amount due the bank (i.e., debt plus interest) must be no greater than two thirds of PROTRAC's cash on hand plus the accounts receivable. In other words

$$\frac{2}{3}(\text{cash on hand} + \text{accounts receivable}) \geq \text{debt} + \text{interest}$$

   From Table 6.12 we see that each E sells for $80,000 and each F sells for $24,000. Thus, in thousands of dollars, the total accounts receivable is $80E + 24F$ and the constraint becomes

$$100 + 80E + 24F \geq 1.5(1.04D)$$

Note that the lower bound on the value of D (implicit in the first of the above constraints) depends upon the cost of labor and materials, whereas the upper limit of D (implicit in the last of the above constraints) is based on the sales prices.

The complete formulation with selected formulas and solution of the revised PRO-TRAC model for the case $R = 20\%$ is shown in the spreadsheet of Figure 6.17. In the solution we see that PROTRAC should borrow approximately \$279,490. The surplus variables for the cash constraints in rows 20 and 21 indicate that (since the Receivables Balance constraint is active) PROTRAC will borrow as much as possible, which (since the Cash Balance has positive surplus) is more than is required to finance material and

FIGURE 6.17

PROTRAC Financial and
Production Planning Model

	A	B	C	D	E	F	G	H	I
1		Protrac Financial &Production Plan							
2					Months of Paymt. Delay		3		
3		Annual Discount Rate, R	20%		Annual Interest Rate		16%		
4		Discount Factor	0.952381		Bank Receivables Limit		2/3		
5			E-9	F-9	Debt ($000s)				
6		Price	$80,000	$24,000	$1,000				
7		Unit Var. Costs	$75,000	$20,000	$1,040				
8		P.V. Unit Cont. Mar.	$1,190.48	$2,857.14	$9.5238	Profit			
9		Decisions	1.5	9	$279.49	$30,162			
10									
11		Constraints		Resource Usage		Total Hours	Hrs Avail.	Slack	
12		Dept. A	10	15		150	<=150	0	
13		Dept. B	20	10		120	<=160	40	
14						Total Hours	Hrs Req.		
15		Testing	30	10		135	>=135	0	
16						Total Quantity	Prod. Req.		
17		Production	1	1		10.5	>=5	5.5	
18		Mix Requirement	1	-3		-25.5	<=0	25.5	
19						Total	Cash on Hand	Surplus	
20		Cash Balance($000s)	$75	$20	-1	$13.01	<=$100	$86.99	
21		Receivable Bal.($000s)	-$80	-$24	1.56	$100.00	<=$100	$0.00	
22									

Solver Parameters

Set Target Cell: $F$9

Equal To: ● Max   ○ Min

By Changing Cells:

$C$9:$E$9

Subject to the Constraints:

$F$12:$F$13 <= $G$12:$G$13
$F$15 >= $G$15
$F$17 >= $G$17
$F$18 <= $G$18
$F$20:$F$21 <= $G$20:$G$21

Solver Options

☑ Assume Linear Model
☑ Assume Non-Negative

1 2		B	C	D	E	F	G
	1	Protrac Financial &Production Plan					
	2					Months of Paymt. Delay	3
	3	Annual Discount Rate	0.2			Annual Interest Rate	0.16
	4	Discount Factor	=1/(1+C3/(12/G2))			Bank Receivables Limit	=2/3
	5		E-9	F-9	Debt ($000s)		
	6	Price	80000	24000	1000		
	7	Unit Var. Costs	75000	20000	=(1+G3/(12/G2))*1000		
	8	P.V. Unit Cont. Mar.	=-C7+$C$4*C6	=-D7+$C$4*D6	=E6-$C$4*E7	Profit	
	9	Decisions	1.5	9	279.487179487179	=SUMPRODUCT($C$9:$E$9,C8:E8)	
	10						
+	20	Cash Balance($000s)	=C7/1000	=D7/1000	-1	=SUMPRODUCT($C$9:$E$9,C20:E20)	100
	21	Receivable Bal.($000	=-C6/1000	=-D6/1000	=E7/G4/1000	=SUMPRODUCT($C$9:$E$9,C21:E21)	100
	22						

TABLE 6.13 Summary of Results

	PURE PRODUCTION	PRODUCTION AND FINANCE		
		$R = 12\%$	$R = 16\%$	$R = 20\%$
E	4.5	1.5	1.5	1.5
F	7.0	9.0	9.0	9.0
D	—	$192.50	$192.50	$279.49
OV	$50,500	$31,845	$30,577	$30,162

labor costs. This occurs because the model assumes that excess funds can be invested to earn 20% interest, while the cost of those funds is only 16%.

EFFECT OF FINANCIAL CONSIDERATIONS

We note that inserting the financial considerations in the original production mix model leads to quite a different plan from the one determined on the basis of only the production constraints. Table 6.13 summarizes the results for the original PROTRAC pure production model and this model with financial constraints for three different values of the discount rate, R. The optimal value of the objective function is less in the production and finance models because future cash flows are discounted and interest costs are included. In the production and finance model, the optimal production plan does not depend on the value of the discount rate within the observed range of 12% to 20%. The optimal debt does, but in a simple manner. If $R < 16\%$, borrow as little as possible, namely $192,500. If $R > 16\%$, borrow as much as possible, namely $279,490. If $R = 16\%$ there are alternative optimal solutions where D lies between $192,500 and $279,490.

6.12 THE MEDIA SELECTION MODEL

The media selection model is faced by a firm or advertising agency as it tries to develop an effective promotional campaign. Basically, the question is how many "insertions" (ads) the firm should purchase in each of several possible media (e.g., radio, TV, newspapers, and magazines). The goal, in a not very specific sense, is to have the advertising campaign be as effective as possible. As we shall see, the explicit objective we will adopt is subjective. Constraints on the decision maker are typically provided by the total advertising budget and the number of opportunities to place an ad that are available in each of the media. Management may further constrain the decision by insisting on various rules of thumb. For example, it might be insisted that at least a certain dollar amount be spent on a specific medium (e.g., at least $10,000 must be spent on newspaper advertising). Alternatively, it might be stipulated that no more than a certain percentage of the budget (say 50%) be spent on any one medium.

Finally, the decision may be influenced by "the law of diminishing returns"; that is, management may believe that the effectiveness of an ad decreases as the number of exposures in a medium increases during a specified period of time. For example, the tenth exposure of a TV ad in a given week would typically not have the same impact on the audience as the first or second exposure.

We will present a media selection example in detail. It is at first, however, interesting to point out that the model has an unusual objective function. Clearly, management would like to select its advertising campaign to maximize demand. Conceptually, then, the model should find the advertising campaign that maximizes demand and satisfies the budget and other constraints. Unfortunately, the link between demand and the advertising campaign is sufficiently vague so that it is difficult to construct a useful model based on this approach. The approach used is to measure the response to a particular ad in a particular medium in terms of what are

TABLE 6.14 Media Data		
ADVERTISING MEDIUM	NUMBER OF PURCHASING UNITS REACHED PER AD	COST PER AD ($)
Daytime Radio	30,000	1700
Evening TV	60,000	2800
Daily Newspaper	45,000	1200

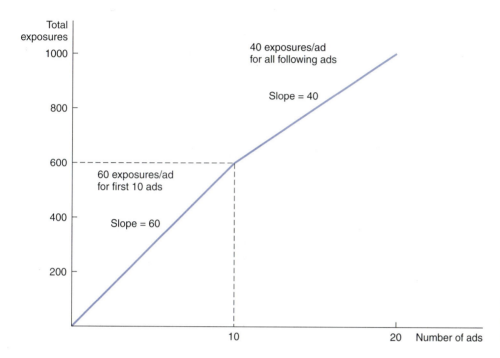

FIGURE 6.18

Total Exposures Versus Number of Radio Ads

called **exposure units.** This is a subjective measure based on management's assessment of the quality of the particular ad, the desirability of the potential market, and so on. In other words, it is an arbitrary measure of the "goodness" of a particular ad. An exposure unit can be thought of as a kind of utility function. Management's goal then becomes one of maximizing total exposure units, taking into account other properties of the model (e.g., cost per number of potential customers reached, and so on). A specific example follows.

PROMOTING PROTRAC'S NEW PRODUCT

PROTRAC has decided to enter the recreational vehicle market with the Rover, a motorcycle-like machine with three oversized tires. Since this is a new product line, an advertising campaign is planned during the introductory month, and a budget of $72,000 is set up to fund the campaign.

PROTRAC decides to use daytime radio, evening TV, and daily newspaper ads in its advertising campaign. Data concerning the cost per ad in each of these media and the number of purchasing units reached by each ad are provided by PROTRAC's advertising agency. The data are summarized in Table 6.14.

We have already mentioned that the effectiveness of an ad is measured in exposures. Management arbitrarily selects a scale from 0 to 100 for each offering of an ad. In particular, it is assumed that each of the first 10 radio ads has a value of 60 exposure units, and each radio ad after the first 10 is rated as having 40 exposures. Figure 6.18 shows a plot of total exposures as a function of the number of daytime radio ads during the month.

Note that in this figure, since each of the first 10 radio ads is rated as having 60 exposures, the slope of the first line segment is 60. After the first 10 ads, since each radio ad is rated as having 40 exposures, the slope of the second line segment is 40. Radio ads, then, suffer from diminishing returns. It is management's subjective evaluation that the first ads are more effective than later ones. This evaluation is based primarily on the assumption that a large proportion of those who see/hear the later ads in a given medium will also have seen/heard the earlier ones.

PROTRAC's analysts feel that the same situation will occur with TV and newspaper ads; that is, they, too, will suffer from diminishing returns. Indeed, they assume that in all three cases the slope (i.e., the exposures per ad) will change at the tenth ad. The exposures per ad (i.e., the slope of the two line segments), however, vary with the particular medium. These data are summarized in Table 6.15. The total exposures as a function of the number of ads in each medium are plotted in Figure 6.19.

Management wants to ensure that the advertising campaign will satisfy certain criteria that it feels are important. In particular: (1) No more than 25 ads should appear in a single medium, (2) a total number of 1,800,000 purchasing units must be reached across all media, and (3) at least one fourth of the ads must appear on evening TV. To model PROTRAC's media selection model as an LP model, we let

TABLE 6.15 Exposures per Ad		
ADVERTISING MEDIUM	**FIRST TEN ADS**	**ALL FOLLOWING ADS**
Daytime Radio	60	40
Evening TV	80	55
Daily Newspaper	70	35

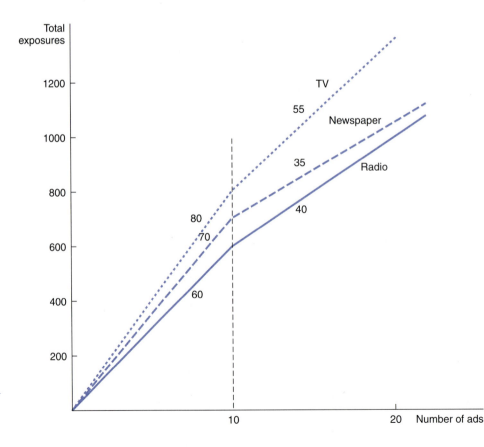

FIGURE 6.19

Total Exposures Versus Number of Ads

x_1 = number of daytime radio ads up to the first 10
y_1 = number of daytime radio ads after the first 10
x_2 = number of evening TV ads up to the first 10
y_2 = number of evening TV ads after the first 10
x_3 = number of newspaper ads up to the first 10
y_3 = number of newspaper ads after the first 10

With this notation we note that $60x_1$ is the total exposures from the number of "first 10" radio ads and $40y_1$ is the total exposures from the remaining radio ads. Thus, the objective function is

$$\text{Max } 60x_1 + 40y_1 + 80x_2 + 55y_2 + 70x_3 + 35y_3$$

Turning to the constraints, we note that

$$x_1 + y_1 = \text{total radio ads}$$
$$x_2 + y_2 = \text{total TV ads}$$
$$x_3 + y_3 = \text{total newspaper ads}$$

Referring to Table 6.14, we see that each radio ad costs $1700. The expression for the total spent on radio ads is $1700(x_1 + y_1)$. Since TV ads cost $2800 each and newspaper ads cost $1200 each, the total advertising expenditure is $1700(x_1 + y_1) + 2800(x_2 + y_2) + 1200(x_3 + y_3)$. PROTRAC has allocated $72,000 for the promotional campaign. This constraint is enforced by the following inequality:

$$1700x_1 + 1700y_1 + 2800x_2 + 2800y_2 + 1200x_3 + 1200y_3 \leq 72,000$$

The constraint that no more than 25 ads appear on daytime radio is imposed by the inequality $x_1 + y_1 \leq 25$. A similar constraint is required for each other medium.

Referring again to Table 6.14, we see that each radio ad reaches 30,000 purchasing units. Thus, the total number of purchasing units reached by radio ads is $30,000(x_1 + y_1)$. The requirement that the entire campaign reach at least 1,800,000 purchasing units is imposed by the inequality

$$30,000x_1 + 30,000y_1 + 60,000x_2 + 60,000y_2 + 45,000x_3 + 45,000y_3 \geq 1,800,000$$

Finally, the constraint that at least one fourth of the ads must appear on evening TV is guaranteed by the constraint

$$\frac{x_2 + y_2}{x_1 + y_1 + x_2 + y_2 + x_3 + y_3} \geq \frac{1}{4}$$

or

$$x_2 + y_2 \geq .25(x_1 + y_1 + x_2 + y_2 + x_3 + y_3)$$

The complete formulation is presented in the spreadsheet model of Figure 6.20. Note that the three constraints in cells H3:J3 enforce the 10-ad upper bound on the variables x_1, x_2, and x_3, while the three constraints in cells H4:J4 impose a large 1000 upper bound on the variables y_1, y_2, and y_3. There is, however, one additional point to be noted. According to the definitions, x_1 is the number of radio ads up to the first 10 and y_1 is the number of radio ads after the first 10. Let x_1^* and y_1^* be the optimal values of these variables. Clearly it would not make sense to have an optimal solution with $x_1^* < 10$ and $y_1^* > 0$; that is, it does not make sense to have placed ads after the first 10 when not all of the first 10 have been placed. Nothing in the constraints prevents this. However, it will not occur. The reason is that the marginal contribution of x_1, in the objective function, is larger than that of y_1. If $x_1 < 10$ and $y_1 > 0$ is feasible, you can see from the constraints that the values $x_1 + \epsilon$ and $y_1 - \epsilon$ will also be feasible, where ϵ is a very small positive number. Moreover, in the objective function, since the coefficient of x_1 is larger than the coefficient of y_1, this substitution will give an improved objective value. In prosaic terms, the maximization will push x_1 to its limit (10 ads) before making y_1 greater than zero. Analogous comments apply to x_2, y_2 and x_3, y_3.

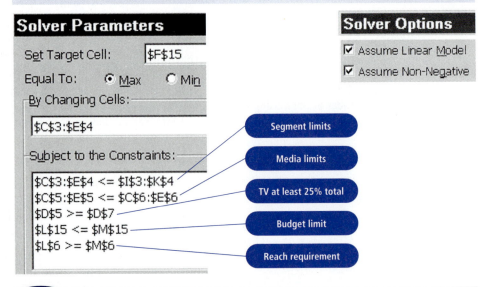

No. Ads	Radio Ads	TV Ads	Newsp. Ads	Total
Segmt. 1	10	10	10	30
Segmt. 2	0	0.47	11.41	11.87
Total	10	10.47	21.41	41.87
Media Limit	<=25	<=25	<=25	
TV % Limit		>=10.47		

Media Selection Model

	Segment Limits	Radio Ads	TV Ads	Newsp. Ads			TV % Limit
	Segmt. 1	<=10	<=10	<=10			25%
	Segmt. 2	<=1000	<=1000	<=1000			
	Purch. Units/Ad	30	60	45	Tot.Units	Required	
	Tot. Purch. Units	300	628.13	963.28	1891.41	>=1800	

Exposures Per Ad	Radio Ads	TV Ads	Newsp. Ads
Segmt. 1	60	80	70
Segmt. 2	40	55	35

Unit Cost/Ad	Radio Ads	TV Ads	Newsp. Ads
Segmt. 1	$ 1.70	$ 2.80	$ 1.20
Segmt. 2	$ 1.70	$ 2.80	$ 1.20

Total Exposures	Radio Ads	TV Ads	Newsp. Ads	Total
Segmt. 1	600	800.0	700	2,100
Segmt. 2	0	25.78	399.2	425
Total	600	825.78	1099.2	2,525

Total Cost	Radio Ads	TV Ads	Newsp. Ads	Total	
Segmt. 1	$17.00	$28.00	$12.00	$57.00	
Segmt. 2	$0.00	$1.31	$13.69	$15.00	Budget
Total	$17.00	$29.31	$25.69	$72.00	<=$72

Cell	Formula	Copy To
D7	= M3*F5	—
I6	= C5*I5	J6:K6
C13	= C3*C9	C13:E14
I13	= C3*I9	I13:K14

Solver Parameters

Set Target Cell: $F$15

Equal To: ⊙ Max   ○ Min

By Changing Cells:

$C$3:$E$4

Subject to the Constraints:

$C$3:$E$4 <= $I$3:$K$4   → Segment limits
$C$5:$E$5 <= $C$6:$E$6   → Media limits
$D$5 >= $D$7   → TV at least 25% total
$L$15 <= $M$15   → Budget limit
$L$6 >= $M$6   → Reach requirement

Solver Options

☑ Assume Linear Model
☑ Assume Non-Negative

FIGURE 6.20

Spreadsheet for the Media Selection Model

6.13   DYNAMIC MODELS

Most of the models we have covered thus far in the book have been limited to a single time period, such as a week, a month, or a year. Single-time-period models are called **static models** because time does not enter into the model other than to define the units of measure for some of the variables. In contrast, **dynamic models** are defined for multiple time periods, and obviously, are a more realistic abstraction of reality. Many managerial decision models involve decision making over time in which future decision-making possibilities are influenced by decisions made in earlier time periods. This dependence of decision making across time periods makes dynamic modeling coupled with Solver a particularly attractive method of analysis; human intuition tends to bog down when faced with many interrelated decisions. Of course, the added realism of dynamic modeling comes at a price; you must pay attention to more details in constructing a dynamic model. For example, typically each time period will have its own performance measure, but optimization requires that these individual performance measures be unified into a single measure that captures performance over all the time periods. Also, the timing of events must be precisely defined so that the sequencing of intermediate outcomes and decisions are in the proper order. These and other ideas are best illustrated by studying a simple example of inventory management over time.

DYNAMIC INVENTORY MODELS

Dynamic inventory models, often called **multiperiod inventory models,** constitute an important class of models that applies to inventories of materials, cash, and employees carried from one time period to the next. This example is a classical, so-called deterministic, single-product inventory model. It is called *deterministic* because we assume that the demand (i.e., number of orders to be satisfied) in each future period is known at the beginning of period 1. For example, a producer of polyurethane has a stock of orders for the next 6 weeks. Let d_i be a parameter that denotes this known demand (say, in terms of number of gallons that must be delivered to customers during week i), and assume that $d_i > 0$ for all i. Let C_i denote the cost of producing a gallon during week i, and let K_i denote the maximum amount that can be produced (because of capacity limitations) in week i. Finally, let h_i denote the per unit cost of inventory in stock at the end of week i. (Thus, the inventory is measured as the number of gallons carried from week i into week $i + 1$.) Suppose that the initial inventory (at the beginning of period 1 and for which no carrying charge is assessed) is known to be I_0 gallons. Find a production and inventory-holding plan that satisfies the known delivery schedule over the next 6 weeks at minimum total cost.

Before we formulate the constrained optimization model, it will be useful to develop an expression for the inventory on hand at the end of each period. Since there is an inventory carrying charge, this quantity will clearly play a role in the objective function.

Let I_i be the inventory on hand at the end of week i. Define the decision variable x_i to be the gallons of polyurethane produced in week i. The flow balance equation for week 1 is

$$I_1 = I_0 + x_1 - d_1$$

That is, the inventory on hand at the end of week 1 is equal to the inventory on hand at the end of week 0 (the beginning of week 1) plus the production in week 1 minus the deliveries in week 1. (We are assuming that all demand must be satisfied. Hence, the known demand in week i, d_i, is by definition the amount delivered in week i.) Similarly

$$I_2 = I_1 + x_2 - d_2$$

and, in general, the same reasoning yields, for any week t

$$I_t = I_{t-1} + x_t - d_t$$

This important inventory flow balance equation says that

$$\text{inventory at end of } t = \text{inventory at beginning of } t$$

$$+ \text{ production in } t - \text{demand in } t$$

in which we assume that the inventory at the end of week $t - 1$ is equal to the inventory at the beginning of week t. If we substitute the known expression for I_1 into the equation for I_2, we obtain

$$I_2 = \underbrace{I_0 + x_1 - d_1}_{I_1} + x_2 - d_2 = I_0 + \sum_{i=1}^{2} x_i - \sum_{i=1}^{2} d_i$$

In words this indicates that Production + Old Inventory − Demand = New Inventory. We could then substitute the foregoing expression for I_2 into the equation for I_3 to obtain

$$I_3 = I_0 + \sum_{i=1}^{3} x_i - \sum_{i=1}^{3} d_i$$

Repeating this procedure leads to an equivalent inventory equation

$$I_t = I_0 + \sum_{i=1}^{t} (x_i - d_i)$$

for any week t.

Note that this last expression relates the inventory at the end of week t to all previous production (the x_i values). The equation simply says that the inventory at the end of week t is equal to the initial inventory, plus the total production through week t, minus the total deliveries through week t. The variable I_t is sometimes referred to as a *consequential* or *definitional variable* because it is defined in terms of other decision variables (the x_i values) in the model. The use of definitional variables sometimes makes it easier to see the proper formulation. Before writing the verbal model for this situation, we must figure out a way of saying that production in each period must *be at least* great enough so that demand (i.e., the delivery schedule) can be satisfied. In week 1 this means that $I_0 + x_1 \geq d_1$, or $I_0 + x_1 - d_1 \geq 0$. Since $I_0 + x_1 - d_1$ is the same as I_1, this is the same as saying that the inventory at the end of week 1 is nonnegative. Satisfying week 2 demand means that inventory at the beginning of week 2 (the end of week 1) plus week 2 production $\geq d_2$. That is

$$I_1 + x_2 \geq d_2 \text{ or } I_1 + x_2 - d_2 \geq 0$$

which is the same as saying that the inventory at the end of week 2 is nonnegative. It should now be possible to see the pattern.

> The condition that demand in a time period t must be satisfied is equivalent to the condition that inventory I_t at the end of the time period t must be nonnegative.

This is illustrated in Figure 6.21.

Verbal Model

Minimize production cost + inventory cost

subject to

inventory at the end of week $t \geq 0$	$t = 1, 2, \ldots, 6$
production in week $t \leq K_t$	$t = 1, 2, \ldots, 6$

Decision Variables

$$x_t = \text{production in week } t$$

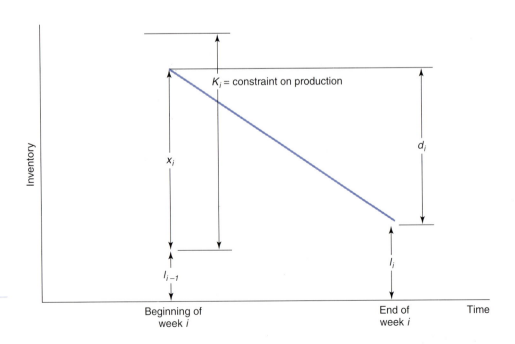

FIGURE 6.21

Diagram of Inventory Relationships

$$Min \sum_{t=1}^{6} C_t x_t + \sum_{t=1}^{6} h_t I_t$$

$$\text{s.t.} \quad \left. \begin{array}{l} I_t = I_{t-1} + x_t - d_t \\ x_t \le K_t \\ x_t \ge 0, \quad I_t \ge 0 \end{array} \right\} \quad t = 1, 2, \ldots, 6$$

In general, the structure of such models is fairly complex. That is, interactions are occurring between large numbers of variables. For example, inventory at the end of a given time period t is determined by all production decisions in time periods 1 through t. This is seen from the inventory equation.

$$I_t = I_0 + \sum_{i=1}^{t} (x_i - d_i)$$

Therefore, the cost in time period t is also determined by all production decisions in time periods 1 through t. Finally, it is noted that the formulation above can be written in an equivalent form without the I_t variables appearing.

Next, we present a practical example of a multiperiod inventory model, the situation faced by Andrew Tan.

A MULTIPERIOD INVENTOR

Andrew Tan is responsible for the final assembly and delivery of PROTRAC's large diesel-powered industrial electric generators in Singapore. The generators are assembled from imported parts, tested in Singapore, and exported to PROTRAC's Asian customers. Table 6.16 gives the number of generators that must be delivered in each of the next four months along with Andrew's estimates of monthly production capacity and variable costs of generator production. These capacities and costs differ because of the logistics of inbound shipping of parts and variability in the cost of commodity materials, particularly copper wire. Also listed in Table 6.16 are the carrying costs of storing a completed generator in a commercial warehouse from one month to the next. Commercial storage costs for large generators are a significant factor for Andrew because of Singapore's extremely limited land area. Note that it is the possibility of carrying inventory from one month to the next that makes Andrew's model a multiperiod inventory model as opposed to a collection of four static models if there were no inventory options.

Andrew's task is to produce and deliver the required number of generators over the four-month interval at the lowest total four-month cost, given that he begins January with 15 generators in inventory. The spreadsheet in Figure 6.22 presents Andrew's model along with the optimal solution. It follows a common convention for dynamic models in spreadsheets in which one column is devoted to each time period. In this model, the Ending Inventory values in cells C10:F10 are consequential (definitional) variables, in this case, calculated for each month as

= Production + Beginning Inventory − Delivery Requirements

TABLE 6.16 Monthly Data for Generator Production				
	JAN.	FEB.	MAR.	APR.
Delivery Requirements	58	36	34	59
Production Capacity	60	62	64	66
Unit Production Costs (000s)	$28	$27	$27.8	$29
Unit Inventory Carrying Cost	$300	$300	$300	$300

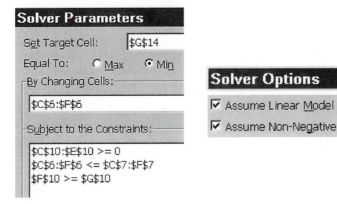

A	B	C	D	E	F	G	H
1	Singapore Electric Generator Production						
2	Unit Costs	Jan.	Feb.	Mar.	Apr.	May	
3	Production	$28.0	$27.0	$27.8	$29.0		
4	Inventory	$0.3	$0.3	$0.3	$0.3		
5							
6	Production Qty.	53	62	64	0		
7	Production Limits	<=60	<=62	<=64	<=66		
8	Begining Inventory	15	10	36	66		
9	Delivery Reqmts.	58	36	34	59		
10	Ending Inventory	10	36	66	7	>=7	
11							
12	Production Cost	$1,484.00	$1,674.00	$1,779.20	$ -		
13	Inventory Cost	$ 3.75	$ 6.90	$ 15.30	$ 10.95	Total (000s)	
14	Total	$1,487.75	$1,680.90	$1,794.50	$ 10.95	$ 4,974.10	
15							

Solver Parameters

Set Target Cell: $G$14

Equal To: ○ Max   ● Min

By Changing Cells:

$C$6:$F$6

Subject to the Constraints:

$C$10:$E$10 >= 0
$C$6:$F$6 <= $C$7:$F$7
$F$10 >= $G$10

Solver Options

☑ Assume Linear Model
☑ Assume Non-Negative

FIGURE 6.22

Andrew's Generator
Production and
Inventory Model

Each month's Beginning Inventory (cells D8:F8) is set equal to the previous month's Ending Inventory (cells C10:E10). As developed previously, a nonnegative ending inventory constraint must be added in the Solver Parameters dialog. This will prevent Solver from artificially lowering costs by shipping more generators in a month than are on hand.

Implicit in Andrew's model are two fundamental decisions that must be addressed in every dynamic model: the overall time interval covered by the model, called the model's *planning horizon,* and the number of discrete time epochs to include within that interval. For Andrew's model the planning horizon is four months, and time is divided into four month-long epochs. Both of these decisions can have profound effects upon the relevance of the model for Andrew's situation. For example, by definition, the four-month planning horizon means the model cannot take account of production and delivery requirements beyond April; that is, the world of generator production comes to an end after April, as far as the model is concerned.

Also, the discrete monthly time scale requires that Andrew approximate activities within a month by a single set of numbers applied to the whole month. For example, January's ending inventory is the difference between January production plus beginning inventory and January deliveries, a single number, even though the actual inventory amount will vary each day within the month as generators are produced and delivered. To make this clear, consider the extreme case where all production occurs on the first working day of January and all deliveries occur on the last working day of January. In that extreme case the January carrying cost of inventory is determined by the production amount plus beginning inventory and not their sum less deliveries. At the other extreme, if all production and deliveries occurred on the last working day of January, then inventory carrying costs for completed generators would be applied only to the January beginning inventory. Assuming that production and deliveries occur uniformly over the month, Andrew elected to approximate inventory costs based upon the average inventory for each month—(beginning inventory + ending inventory)/2. This is equivalent to assuming that all production and deliveries occur at mid-month. Obviously, capturing the movement of generators more accurately within a month would require breaking up the model into more time epochs, such as weekly or daily or even hourly. A finer time grid allows more precise measurements of actual movements of generators in and out of inventory, producing more accurate inventory cost tracking within the model.

In addition to using a finer time grid for more accurate within-month cost tracking, Andrew's costs associated with activities for the missing months beyond April can be accommodated by extending the model's planning horizon. Unfortunately, long planning horizons and fine time grids produce an exponential growth in the size of the dynamic model. For example, a daily model with a one-year planning horizon would have hundreds of columns, quickly exceeding Excel's 256-column limit and Solver's limit of 200 decision variables. Moreover, even if these technical barriers could be relaxed, Andrew would be faced with the need to estimate many more hundreds of parameter values, such as the daily shipping requirements for generators, the daily cost of materials, and the daily production capacity for generators. The temptation to add realism by finer time grids and longer planning horizons in dynamic models is often called the "curse of dimensionality," because adding each new column adds a new dimension to the model in terms of new decision variables, decision and consequential variable linkages across time, and parameters to be considered.

Finally, every dynamic model must also pay attention to what are called its "edge conditions." These refer to the set of parameters that must be specified at the beginning and the end of time in the model. In Andrew's model this becomes the values of initial inventory in January and ending inventory in April. As in Andrew's case of January's initial inventory of 15 generators, the beginning parameter values are usually given or easily estimated. However, the ending edge condition is more troublesome because it must stand as a reasonable starting condition for all of time beyond the planning horizon. In his model, Andrew has decided that 7 generators for the ending inventory in April would constitute a "good" initial inventory condition for subsequent months.

Figure 6.23 shows the result of optimizing Andrew's model four times, separately for each of the four months. That is, Solver was run for January alone using January production as the decision variable and January total cost as the objective function. Then the same was done for February and so on through April, a total of four Solver runs. Note that no inventories are maintained to carry over from one month to the next because each month is treated as a separate static model[5]; producing in excess of required shipments in a month raises total cost and in a static model there are no offsetting savings. It is for

	A	B	C	D	E	F	G	H
1		Singapore Electric Generator Production						
2		Unit Costs	Jan.	Feb.	Mar.	Apr.	May	
3		Production	$28.0	$27.0	$27.8	$29.0		
4		Inventory	$0.3	$0.3	$0.3	$0.3		
5								
6		Production Qty.	43	36	34	66		
7		Production Limits	<=60	<=62	<=64	<=66		
8		Begining Inventory	15	0	0	0		
9		Delivery Reqmts.	58	36	34	59		
10		Ending Inventory	0	0	0	7	>=7	
11								
12		Production Cost	$1,204.00	$ 972.00	$ 945.20	$1,914.00		
13		Inventory Cost	$ 2.25	$ -	$ -	$ 1.05	Total (000s)	
14		Total	$1,206.25	$ 972.00	$ 945.20	$1,915.05	$ 5,038.50	
15								

FIGURE 6.23

Andrew's Model Optimized as Four Static Models

[5]The two Inventory Cost numbers appearing in January and April in Figure 6.23 represent the half-month cost of carrying the beginning inventory for January and the required ending inventory for April.

Microsoft Excel 8.0 Sensitivity Report

Adjustable Cells

Cell	Name	Final Value	Reduced Cost	Objective Coefficient	Allowable Increase	Allowable Decrease
$C$6	Production Qty. Jan.	53	0	29.05	0.10	0.8
$D$6	Production Qty. Feb.	62	-1.3	27.75	1.3	1E+30
$E$6	Production Qty. Mar.	64	-0.8	28.25	0.8	1E+30
$F$6	Production Qty. Apr.	0	0.1	29.15	1E+30	0.10

Constraints

Cell	Name	Final Value	Shadow Price	Constraint R.H. Side	Allowable Increase	Allowable Decrease
$F$10	Ending Inventory Apr.	7	29.05	7	7	10
$C$10	Ending Inventory Jan.	10	0	0	10	1E+30
$D$10	Ending Inventory Feb.	36	0	0	36	1E+30
$E$10	Ending Inventory Mar.	66	0	0	66	1E+30

FIGURE 6.24

Sensitivity Report for
Andrew's Four-Month
Inventory Model

this reason that static models are often referred to as "myopic" because they ignore any consequences of current decisions upon future payoff. The advantages of a four-month dynamic model in contrast to four static monthly models is illustrated by comparing the total four-month cost difference between Figure 6.22 and Figure 6.23, a savings of more than $64,000 in this case. A little thought should convince you that the dynamic model of Andrew's four-month decision-making situation could never do worse than running four static models for the same situation.

Figure 6.24 shows the Sensitivity Report for the four-month dynamic model of Figure 6.22. Note that it is because the four production limits were specified as simple upper bounds on the production decision variables that those constraints' shadow prices appear in the Reduced Cost column of the Sensitivity Report, and hence, no range information is given for those shadow prices. Also, at first glance the objective coefficients for the model in the Sensitivity Report appear to be incorrect. For example, the objective function coefficient for January production is shown as $29,050 while the variable production cost of a generator in January is specified as $28,000 in Figure 6.22.

Many users of Solver presume that Solver somehow "reads" each objective coefficient from the appropriate cell within the active spreadsheet. In fact, Solver does not do this because the calculation of that coefficient might be spread among formulas in several cells within the original spreadsheet model. Instead, Solver "exercises" the spreadsheet for each of the decision variables individually, substituting trial values, and tabulating the effect that each such change has upon the objective function value after the spreadsheet recalculates. From that information Solver estimates the objective coefficients.[6] Of course, this does not answer the question as to why there is a discrepancy between the variable cost of production in January and the objective coefficient for January production estimated by Solver and tabulated in the Sensitivity Report.

It should be easy to see that the $29,050 represents the cost of producing a generator in January plus the $1050 inventory carrying cost for $3\frac{1}{2}$ months to carry that generator to May. (Recall, Andrew's use of average inventory levels is equivalent to assuming that production occurs in the middle of a month.) You can convince yourself that $29.05 is in fact the correct objective coefficient by opening the worksheet of Figure 6.22 in Excel, typing in a candidate production decision for January, noting the total four-month cost number, and then adding 1 to that January candidate production decision. You will observe that the incremental generator produced in January will be added to all the future months' inventory levels and will increase the ending inventory in April by one, thereby producing a $29.05 increase in four-month total cost.

---

[6]This coefficient estimation process is what is happening during Solver's "Setting up problem . . ." activity, displayed as a message after you click the Solve button. (For those of you with a mathematical inclination, Solver is developing a Taylor Series for the objective function from this information and uses that series in its optimization process. For LP models the Taylor Series estimate is exact.)

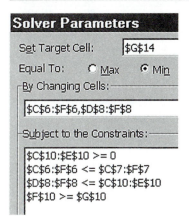

	A	B	C	D	E	F	G	H
1		Singapore Electric Generator Production						
2		Unit Costs	Jan.	Feb.	Mar.	Apr.	May	
3		Production	$28.0	$27.0	$27.8	$29.0		
4		Inventory	$0.3	$0.3	$0.3	$0.3		
5								
6		Production Qty.	53	62	64	0		
7		Production Limits	<=60	<=62	<=64	<=66		
8		Begining Inventory	15	10	36	66		
9		Delivery Reqmts.	58	36	34	59		
10		Ending Inventory	10	36	66	7	>=7	
11								
12		Production Cost	$1,484.00	$1,674.00	$1,779.20	$ -		
13		Inventory Cost	$ 3.75	$ 6.90	$ 15.30	$ 10.95	Total (000s)	
14		Total	$1,487.75	$1,680.90	$1,794.50	$ 10.95	$ 4,974.10	
15								

Solver Parameters

Set Target Cell: $G$14

Equal To: ○ Max   ● Min

By Changing Cells:

$C$6:$F$6,$D$8:$F$8

Subject to the Constraints:

$C$10:$E$10 >= 0
$C$6:$F$6 <= $C$7:$F$7
$D$8:$F$8 <= $C$10:$E$10
$F$10 >= $G$10

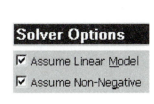

Solver Options

☑ Assume Linear Model

☑ Assume Non-Negative

FIGURE 6.25

Andrew's Production Model
with Beginning Inventory
as Decisions

To understand why $29.05 is the correct coefficient for January, recall that everything else (generators produced and delivered in other months) is being held constant, and so, there is no place for that incremental January generator to go except into ending April inventory. However, during Solver optimization of the model, that incremental January generator creates an opportunity for Solver to reduce another month's production decision. For example, if the incremental generator in January allowed Solver to reduce February's production by one, then the net effect would be the difference between the two objective coefficients for January and February, $29,050 − $27,750 = $1300. This difference is the correct incremental cost impact of these two simultaneous changes; that is, shifting production of a generator from February to January incurs the $28,000 − $27,000 = $1000 higher January production cost plus the $300 cost to carry the January-produced generator into mid-February. Thus, the confusing objective coefficients listed in the Sensitivity Report are correct and are a result of the more complex interactions among the decision variables of a dynamic model.

A second version of Andrew's model appears in Figure 6.25. This model differs from Andrew's original model in Figure 6.22 in that each month's Beginning Inventory (cells D8:F8) is not modeled as a consequential variable but as a decision variable.[7] Of course, for this approach to make sense, constraints must be added to prevent Solver from treating Beginning Inventory as a decision independent of the production decisions. In this case Beginning Inventory in D8:F8 is constrained to be no more than the previous month's Ending Inventory C10:E10. Other than this additional complication, the model of Figure 6.25 is

---

[7]Note that discontiguous ranges of decision variables can be entered into Solver's Changing Cells box separated by a comma.

Microsoft Excel 8.0 Sensitivity Report

Adjustable Cells

Cell	Name	Final Value	Reduced Cost	Objective Coefficient	Allowable Increase	Allowable Decrease
$C$6	Production Qty. Jan.	53	0	28.15	0.1	0.8
$D$6	Production Qty. Feb.	62	-1.3	27.15	1.3	1E+30
$E$6	Production Qty. Mar.	64	-0.8	27.95	0.8	1E+30
$F$6	Production Qty. Apr.	0	0.1	29.15	1E+30	0.1
$D$8	Begining Inventory Feb.	10	0	0.3	0.1	0.8
$E$8	Begining Inventory Mar.	36	0	0.3	0.1	0.8
$F$8	Begining Inventory Apr.	66	0	0.3	0.1	29

Constraints

Cell	Name	Final Value	Shadow Price	Constraint R.H. Side	Allowable Increase	Allowable Decrease
$F$10	Ending Inventory Apr.	7	29	7	7	10
$C$10	Ending Inventory Jan.	10	0	0	10	1E+30
$D$10	Ending Inventory Feb.	36	0	0	36	1E+30
$E$10	Ending Inventory Mar.	66	0	0	66	1E+30
$D$8	Begining Inventory Feb.	10	-28.15	0	10	7
$E$8	Begining Inventory Mar.	36	-28.45	0	10	7
$F$8	Begining Inventory Apr.	66	-28.75	0	10	7

FIGURE 6.26

Sensitivity Report for Andrew's Revised Model

logically equivalent to Andrew's original model in Figure 6.22. However, the benefit of this formulation is apparent in looking at its Sensitivity Report in Figure 6.26.

Note that additional information of managerial interest is displayed in this model's Sensitivity Report. For example, the sensitivity of total cost to changes in inventory carrying cost is now immediately apparent because the structure of the model in Figure 6.25 introduces additional inventory decision variables and constraints, and hence, their shadow prices and coefficient ranging, missing when inventory was modeled simply as a consequential variable. In general, thought should be given in advance when creating a dynamic model as to what should be a consequential variable and what should be a decision variable. Often, valuable additional managerial information can be created by a well-designed formulation. Note also in Figure 6.26, a side benefit of the new model: Modeling inventory as a decision variable isolates the unit costs into separate production coefficients (unit cost plus half-month carrying cost) and inventory coefficients, thereby making the objective function coefficients to appear as originally specified in the spreadsheet model.

The next section will present two more examples of dynamic models to illustrate the range of situations that can be modeled. The first, Bumles, presents a more complicated multiperiod inventory model.

6.14   EXAMPLES OF DYNAMIC MODELS

BUMLES, INC. (PRODUCTION AND INVENTORY CONTROL)

Bumles, Inc. uses part of its capacity in its South American plant to make hand-painted teapots. One teapot takes 0.5 hour of a painter's time. Bumles has 30 painters available. The plant is used for the teapots on Thursday, Friday, and Saturday each week. During the remainder of the week the productive capacity is devoted to another product line. Not all of the 30 painters will necessarily be engaged, but each painter who is engaged is available to work any part of an 8-hour day, 2 days a week. A painter can be assigned to any 2-day schedule and is paid for 16 hours of regular-time work, no matter what part of that time he or she actually spends producing teapots. If there is not enough production to keep all the workers assigned to a particular day busy for the entire day, the slack time is spent on cleaning the plant and similar activities.

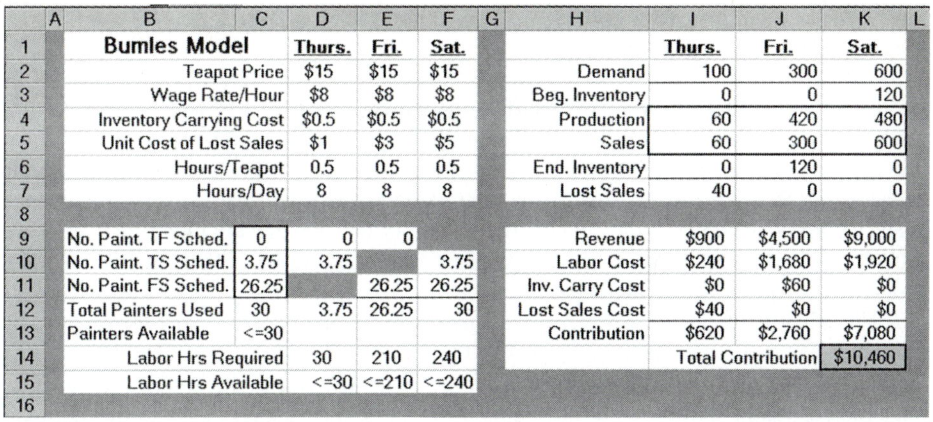

	A	B	C	D	E	F	G	H	I	J	K	L
1		**Bumles Model**		Thurs.	Fri.	Sat.			Thurs.	Fri.	Sat.	
2		Teapot Price		$15	$15	$15		Demand	100	300	600	
3		Wage Rate/Hour		$8	$8	$8		Beg. Inventory	0	0	120	
4		Inventory Carrying Cost		$0.5	$0.5	$0.5		Production	60	420	480	
5		Unit Cost of Lost Sales		$1	$3	$5		Sales	60	300	600	
6		Hours/Teapot		0.5	0.5	0.5		End. Inventory	0	120	0	
7		Hours/Day		8	8	8		Lost Sales	40	0	0	
8												
9		No. Paint. TF Sched.	0	0	0			Revenue	$900	$4,500	$9,000	
10		No. Paint. TS Sched.	3.75	3.75		3.75		Labor Cost	$240	$1,680	$1,920	
11		No. Paint. FS Sched.	26.25		26.25	26.25		Inv. Carry Cost	$0	$60	$0	
12		Total Painters Used	30	3.75	26.25	30		Lost Sales Cost	$40	$0	$0	
13		Painters Available	<=30					Contribution	$620	$2,760	$7,080	
14		Labor Hrs Required	30	210	240			Total Contribution			$10,460	
15		Labor Hrs Available	<=30	<=210	<=240							
16												

Cell	Formula	Copy To
D14	= I4*D6	E14:F14
D15	= D12*D7	E15:F15
I6	= I3−I5+I4	J6:K6
I7	= I2−I5	J7:K7
I10	= D12*D3*D7	J10:K10

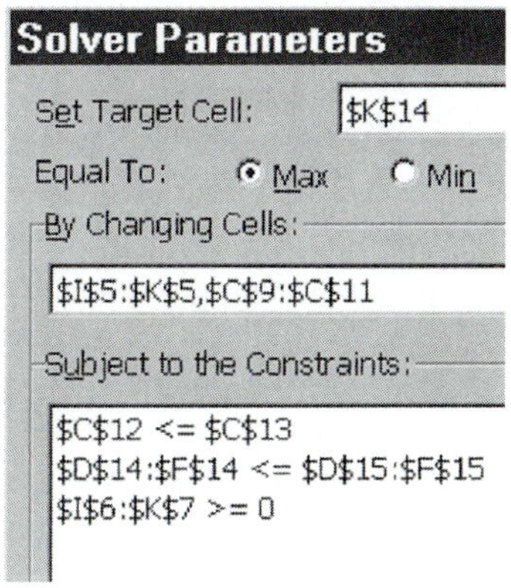

Solver Parameters

Set Target Cell: $K$14

Equal To: ⦿ Max   ○ Min

By Changing Cells:

$I$5:$K$5,$C$9:$C$11

Subject to the Constraints:

$C$12 <= $C$13
$D$14:$F$14 <= $D$15:$F$15
$I$6:$K$7 >= 0

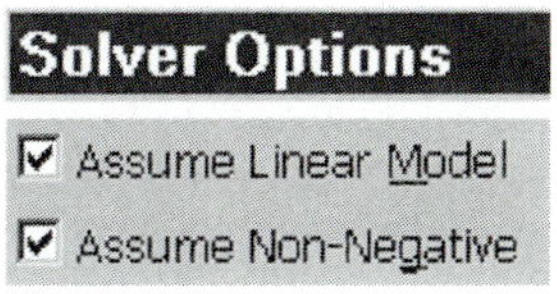

Solver Options

☑ Assume Linear Model
☑ Assume Non-Negative

FIGURE 6.27

The Bumles
Production Model

If labor costs are not taken into account, the revenue, net of other costs, from selling a teapot is $15. Demand must be satisfied on the day on which it occurs or it is lost. Production on a given day can be used to satisfy demand that day or demand later in the week (i.e., teapots produced on Thursday can be used to satisfy demand on Friday or Saturday). However, because of the change of operations to hand-painted statues on Monday, Tuesday, and Wednesday, all teapots produced in a week must be shipped that week (i.e., there is never inventory on Thursday morning). Because of increased handling costs, it costs $0.50 to carry a teapot in ending inventory from one day to the next. A unit of lost demand results in an all-inclusive penalty cost of $1 for a unit on Thursday, $3 on Friday, and $5 on Saturday. Painters are paid $8 per hour. Weekly demand for the teapots is 100 on Thursday, 300 on Friday, and 600 on Saturday.

Figure 6.27 presents the Bumles model that schedules painters and production in such a way as to maximize revenue minus cost, where cost equals labor plus penalty plus inventory-carrying costs. Since sales may be less than demand, the model relates sales, demand, and lost sales any particular day by:

$$\text{lost sales on day } x = \text{demand on day } x - \text{sales on day } x$$

In addition to the above relation between demand, sales, and lost sales, the model also includes the following material balance relationship between production, inventory, and sales:

$$\text{inventory at end of day } x = \text{inventory at beginning of day } x +$$
$$\text{production on day } x - \text{sales on day } x$$

Finally, as with Andrew's model earlier, the material balance across time periods is included by requiring beginning inventory on each day to be equal to ending inventory of the previous day. These relationships are captured in the formulas of cells I3:K7 in which the decision variables for each day are the number of teapots to produce and the number to sell. Thus, the lost sales on each day and ending inventory on each day are interpreted as definitional, that is, consequential, variables. Another way of saying this is that the inventory and lost sales are interpreted as dependent variables.

The other decisions for Bumles are the number of painters to schedule for each of the three two-day shifts in cells C9:C11. Cells D9:F11 contain references to C9:C11 to assign the painters for each schedule to the appropriate days. The Solver Parameters dialog contains the constraint I6:K7 >= 0. This stipulates that neither negative inventories nor negative lost sales occur on any day. The latter is required to assure that sales cannot exceed demand on any day.

WINSTON-SALEM DEVELOPMENT CORPORATION (FINANCIAL PLANNING)

Here is an interesting application of dynamic LP models to financial planning. Winston-Salem Development Corporation (WSDC) is trying to complete its investment plans for the next two years. Currently, WSDC has $2,000,000 on hand and available for investment. In 6 months, 12 months, and 18 months, WSDC expects to receive an income stream from previous investments. The data are presented in Table 6.17. There are two development projects in which WSDC is considering participation along with other non-WSDC investors.

1. The Foster City Development would, if WSDC participated at a 100% level, have the projected cash flow shown in Table 6.18 (negative numbers are investment, positive numbers are income). Thus, in order to participate in Foster City at the 100% level, WSDC would immediately have to lay out $1,000,000. In 6 months there would be another outlay of $700,000, and so on.

2. A second project involves taking over the operation of some old Middle-Income Housing on the condition that certain initial repairs be made. The cash flow stream for this project, at a 100% level of participation, would be as shown in Table 6.19.

TABLE 6.17 Income from Previous Investments			
	6 MONTHS	**12 MONTHS**	**18 MONTHS**
Income	$500,000	$400,000	$380,000

TABLE 6.18 Foster City Cash Flow					
	INITIAL	**6 MONTHS**	**12 MONTHS**	**18 MONTHS**	**24 MONTHS**
Income	$-1,000,000	$-700,000	$1,800,000	$400,000	$600,000

TABLE 6.19 Middle-Income Housing Cash Flow					
	INITIAL	**6 MONTHS**	**12 MONTHS**	**18 MONTHS**	**24 MONTHS**
Income	$-800,000	$500,000	$-200,000	$-700,000	$2,000,000

Because of company policy, WSDC is not permitted to borrow money. However, at the beginning of each 6-month period all surplus funds (those not allocated to either Foster City or Middle-Income Housing) are invested into a certificate of deposit (CD) for a return of 7% for that 6-month period. WSDC can participate in any project at a level less than 100%, in which case other investors make up the difference, and all of the cash flows of that project are reduced proportionally for WSDC. For example, if WSDC were to opt for participation in Foster City at the 30% level, the cash flows associated with this decision would be 0.3 times the data given in the Foster City table. The task currently facing WSDC is to decide how much of the $2,000,000 on hand should be invested in each of the projects and how much should simply be invested for the 7% semiannual return. Management's goal is to *maximize the cash on hand at the end of 24 months.*

The constraints in this model must say that at the beginning of each of the four 6-month periods: money invested $\leq$ money on hand. Therefore, define the decision variables

F = fractional participation in the Foster City project
M = fractional participation in the Middle-Income Housing project
S_1 = surplus initial funds (not invested in F or M initially) to be invested in a CD at 7%
S_2 = surplus funds after 6 months to be invested in a CD at 7%
S_3 = surplus funds after 12 months to be invested in a CD at 7%
S_4 = surplus funds after 18 months to be invested in a CD at 7%

Then the first constraint must say

$$\text{initial investment} \leq \text{initial funds on hand} \quad \text{or}$$
$$1,000,000F + 800,000M + S_1 \leq 2,000,000$$

Because of the interest paid, S_1 becomes $1.07S_1$ after 6 months, and similarly for S_2, S_3, and S_4, the remaining three constraints are

$$700,000F + S_2 \leq 500,000M + 1.07S_1 + 500,000$$
$$200,000M + S_3 \leq 1,800,000F + 1.07S_2 + 400,000$$
$$700,000M + S_4 \leq 400,000F + 1.07S_3 + 380,000$$

The constraints above balance the flows (of cash in this case) from one time period to another. Note that equalities could have been used in the constraints instead of inequalities, because uninvested cash earns no return. However, good modeling practice suggests avoiding equalities unless necessary. Formulating models like this as inequalities allows Solver to confirm this belief about idle cash for you when it makes the inequality constraints binding during optimization.

The objective function is to maximize the (undiscounted) cash on hand at the end of 24 months, which is

$$600,000F + 2,000,000M + 1.07S_4$$

We have thus derived the following model:

$$
\begin{aligned}
\text{Max} \quad & 600,000F + 2,000,000M + 1.07S_4 \\
\text{s.t.} \quad & 1,000,000F + 800,000M + S_1 && \leq 2,000,000 \\
& 700,000F - 500,000M - 1.07S_1 + S_2 && \leq 500,000 \\
& -1,800,000F + 200,000M - 1.07S_2 + S_3 && \leq 400,000 \\
& -400,000F + 700,000M - 1.07S_3 + S_4 && \leq 380,000 \\
& F \leq 1, \text{ and } M \leq 1 \\
& F \geq 0, M \geq 0, S_i \geq 0, i = 1, 2, 3, 4
\end{aligned}
$$

The spreadsheet model is given in Figure 6.28. The decision variables are the amount of surplus cash to invest in CDs (cells D12:G12) and the percentage participation in the two projects (cells C7:C8). The investment amounts in cells D7:G8 are given by multiplying the Project Participation percentage by the project cash flow requirements in cells D3:I4. For convenience and to conform with the constraints above, the sign convention on investments is reversed in the Cash Outlays portion of the model.

	Winston Salem Development Project							
CD Int. Rate	7%	**Initial**	**6 Mo.**	**12 Mo.**	**18 Mo.**		**24 Mo.**	
Foster City Cash Flow		$ (1,000)	$ (700)	$ 1,800	$ 400		$ 600	
Middle Income Cash Flow		$ (800)	$ 500	$ (200)	$ (700)		$ 2,000	
			Cash Outlays					
Funds Invested	**Project Participation**	**Initial Investment**	**6 Months**	**12 Months**	**18 Months**		**Cash Returned (24 Months)**	
Foster City	100%	$ 1,000	$ 700	$(1,800)	$ (400)		$ 600	
Middle Income	100%	$ 800	$ (500)	$ 200	$ 700		$ 2,000	
Maturing CD's			$ (200)	$ (514)	$ (2,550)		$ 2,808	
CD Interest Income			$ (14)	$ (36)	$ (178)		197	
Total Cash Requirements		$ 1,800	$ (14)	$(2,150)	$ (2,428)		$ 5,605	
Surplus Cash into CD's		$ 200	$ 514	$ 2,550	$ 2,808			
Invested New Cash		$ 2,000	$ 500	$ 400	$ 380			
Available New Cash		<=$2000	<=$500	<=$400	<=$380			

Cell	Formula	Copy To
E9	= −D12	F9:G9
E10	= −D12*$C$2	F10:G10
D13	= D11+D12	E13:G13

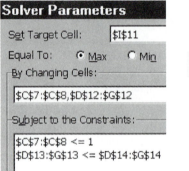

Solver Parameters

Set Target Cell: $I$11

Equal To: ⦿ Max   ○ Min

By Changing Cells:

$C$7:$C$8,$D$12:$G$12

Subject to the Constraints:

$C$7:$C$8 <= 1
$D$13:$G$13 <= $D$14:$G$14

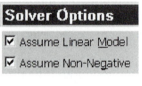

Solver Options

☑ Assume Linear Model

☑ Assume Non-Negative

FIGURE 6.28

Winston-Salem
Development Model

6.15 SUMMARY

This chapter was devoted to applications of linear programming. Section 6.2 covered the transportation model. The generic model is one of determining the least-cost method of satisfying demands at a number of destinations by shipping materials from supplies available at several origins. This model is motivated by a specific problem faced by PROTRAC-Europe. Section 6.3 discussed the adaptations that are necessary in order to solve the transportation model when the models differ from the original model. Finally, we saw that the transportation model has a special property. If all supplies and demands are integer quantities, there is an optimal integer solution.

Section 6.4 treated the assignment model following the pattern of the transportation model. The generic assignment model is one of assigning *n* persons to *n* tasks in order to minimize the total cost of the assignments. This model was again motivated by a specific problem faced by PROTRAC-Europe. In this process we noted that the assignment model is a special type of transportation model in which all supplies and demands equal 1.

Sections 6.5 through 6.10 covered network models. Network models are important for several reasons. First, a wide variety of real-world models can be cast as network models. The flows may represent physical quantities, Internet data packets, cash, vehicles, and so on. The type of model amenable to the network approach is often very large in scale. One can imagine, for example, a network model of an international enterprise involved in paper production. The network might depict the overall multiperiod distribution system from the forest through lumber storage, a variety of paper mills, widely distributed warehouses, and even wholesalers in numerous marketing districts. A model for such a vast operation offers the potential of creating considerable efficiency gains in the firm's global operations. Also, under mild restrictions on the data it will always be true that integral-valued optimal solutions exist.

Often the crucial element in network modeling is the modeler's ingenuity in being able to cast the original complex model into the network format. Usually, this is far from a trivial exercise in model formulation, and considerable on-site experience inside the operation being modeled is often a prerequisite.

Section 6.11 discussed and formulated an example of an LP model used for financial and production planning while media selection in the marketing context was discussed in Section 6.12.

Dynamic models were covered in some detail in Section 6.13. The distinction was made between static (one time period) models and dynamic models. The observation was made that in terms of payoff, a dynamic model for a given planning horizon can always do as well as a collection of static models covering the same time horizon and may do much better. Correctly formulating dynamic models requires attention to definitions of variables within a time period and timing of activities and material flow balances across time periods. Edge conditions must be determined for the starting and ending time periods. Two additional illustrative examples of dynamic models were developed in Section 6.14.

Key Terms

Transportation Model. An LP model to find the least expensive way of satisfying demands at n destinations with supplies from m origins.

Degeneracy. A condition indicated in a transportation model by the fact that fewer than $(m + n - 1)$ routes are being used.

Dummy Origin. An imaginary source that is added to a transportation model so that total supply equals total demand.

Assignment Model. The model of determining the optimal assignment of n "indivisible" agents or objects to n tasks.

Network Diagram. A schematic representation consisting of nodes and arcs over which flows may occur.

Arc. A connection between two nodes in a network.

Branch. A synonym for *arc*.

Node. An element in a network.

Capacitated Transshipment Model. A network model with supplies at specified origins, demands at specified destinations, and shipment alternatives through intermediate nodes on capacitated routes from origins to destinations.

Node-Arc Incidence Matrix. A tableau format for the constraint data in a network model. Corresponding to each arc of the network is a column of the tableau. Corresponding to each node is a row of the tableau. Each column has only two nonzero entries, +1 and −1. The +1 (−1) is in the row corresponding to the node at which the arc originates (terminates).

Destination. A node in a network with positive demand.

Origin. A node in a network with positive supply.

Network Model. Generally refers to the capacitated transshipment model or one of its special forms.

Flow Balance Equation. A material balance constraint in a network model that stipulates the supply plus total flow into a node must equal demand plus flow out of the node.

Shortest-Route Model. The model of finding shortest route from a specified node (the origin) to another node in a network.

Maximal-Flow Model. The model of routing the maximal amount of flow through a network.

Exposure Units. An arbitrary measure of the "goodness" of an ad used in solving media selection models.

Dynamic Model. A model of interrelated decision making across multiple time periods in which the possibility set of decisions in later time periods is affected by decisions in earlier periods.

Static Model. A model in which decisions are made in a single time period without regard to their effects in future periods.

Dynamic Inventory Model. A dynamic model of decision making affecting inventories of things across multiple time periods.

Multiperiod Inventory Model. Same as dynamic inventory model.

Self-Review Exercises

True-False

1. **T F** The coefficient of x_{ij} in the objective function of a transportation model is the cost of sending a unit from i to j.

2. **T F** If total demand exceeds total supply in a transportation model, to find a solution one option is to add a dummy origin with a transportation cost of zero to every destination.

3. **T F** A transportation model cannot have an optimal integer solution unless all of the supplies, demands, and transportation costs are integers.

4. **T F** A capacitated transshipment model has one variable for each node.

5. **T F** A node-arc incidence matrix for the network model has a $+1$, a -1, and all other entries 0 in each column.

6. **T F** If the right-hand side of any arc capacity inequality in a capacitated transshipment model is zero, the model is infeasible.

7. **T F** A collection of static models for each of the time periods over a planning horizon will always do at least as well as a single dynamic model defined over the same planning horizon.

Multiple Choice

8. Degeneracy occurs in a transportation model when
   a. demand exceeds supply
   b. supply exceeds demand
   c. fewer than $(m + n - 1)$ cells are used
   d. none of the above

9. The assignment model
   a. is a special case of the transportation model
   b. can be solved with the simplex algorithm
   c. always has an optimal integer solution
   d. all of the above

10. A positive right-hand side in a flow balance equation of a capacitated transshipment model indicates that
    a. the node is an origin
    b. the node is a destination
    c. the node is a transshipment node
    d. none of the above

11. Which of the following is a condition that assures that there is an optimal integer solution to a capacitated transshipment model?
    a. the right-hand side of all flow equations (the L_j's) be integer
    b. the arc capacities (the u_{ij}'s) be integer
    c. either a or b
    d. both a and b

12. The shortest-path
    a. connects every pair of nodes
    b. is the set of arcs used in tracing the shortest path from a base node H to a given destination node
    c. both a and b

Questions 13 through 17 refer to the following model: A company has two plants and three warehouses. The first plant can supply at most 500 pounds of a particular product, and the second plant at most 200 pounds. The demand at the first warehouse is 150, at the second warehouse 200, and at the third warehouse 350. The cost of manufacturing one pound at plant i and shipping it to warehouse j follows.

From Plant	TO WAREHOUSE		
	1	2	3
1	8	10.2	12.6
2	7	9	11.8

Suppose the model is to determine a shipping schedule that satisfies demand at minimum cost.

13. This model is
    a. a network model
    b. a transportation model
    c. a dynamic model
    d. all of the above
    e. a and b

14. Let x_{ij} denote the amount sent from plant i to warehouse j. The demand constraint for the first warehouse is properly written as
    a. $x_{11} + x_{21} = 150$
    b. $x_{11} + x_{21} \geq 150$

c. both a and b are correct (i.e., it does not matter whether $=$ or $\geq$ is used)

15. Let x_{ij} denote the amount sent from plant i to warehouse j. In symbols, the supply constraints can be written as

a. $\displaystyle\sum_{i=1}^{3} x_{ij} \leq s_j, j = 1, 2$

b. $\displaystyle\sum_{i=1}^{3} x_{ij} = s_j, i = 1, 2$

c. $\displaystyle\sum_{j=1}^{3} x_{ij} = s_j, i = 1, 2$

d. none of the above

e. both a and b are correct (i.e., it does not matter whether $=$ or $\leq$ is used)

16. Solver will always find an integer solution to this model.
a. T
b. F

17. Since total supply $=$ total demand, all constraints (supply and demand) must be written as equalities.
a. T
b. F

Answers

1. T	**6.** F	**10.** a	**14.** c
2. T	**7.** F	**11.** d	**15.** d
3. F	**8.** c	**12.** b	**16.** a
4. F	**9.** d	**13.** e	**17.** b
5. T			

Problems

6-1. Consider the following linear constraints of a transshipment model. Construct the corresponding incidence matrix and the associated network diagram, labeling each node with its supply or demand.

$$
\begin{aligned}
x_{13} + x_{12} + x_{14} &= 2 \\
-x_{12} + x_{24} &= 1 \\
-x_{13} + x_{35} &= 0 \\
-x_{24} - x_{14} + x_{46} + x_{45} &= 0 \\
-x_{35} + x_{56} - x_{45} &= 0 \\
-x_{46} - x_{56} &= -3 \\
x_{ij} \geq 0, \text{ all } (i,j)
\end{aligned}
$$

6-2. Consider the following constraints:

$$
\begin{aligned}
x_{12} + x_{13} &= 2 \\
-x_{12} + x_{24} + x_{25} &= 0 \\
-x_{13} + x_{34} &= 0 \\
-x_{24} - x_{34} + x_{45} &= -1 \\
-x_{25} - x_{45} &= -1
\end{aligned}
$$

Construct the corresponding incidence matrix and network diagram.

6-3. Write the linear constraints corresponding to the transshipment network of Figure 6.29.

6-4. Write the linear constraints corresponding to the transshipment network of Figure 6.30.

6-5. Construct the incidence matrix for the network shown in Problem 6-4.

6-6. Consider the distribution network shown in Figure 6.31. Find the shortest route from node ① to node ⑧ in the network.

6-7. Consider the distribution network shown in Figure 6.32. Find the shortest path from node ① to node ⑦.

6-8. In Figure 6.31, by how much does the distance on the arc from ④ to ⑦ have to decrease before it can become part of the shortest-path tree from node ① to node ⑧?

6-9. *Crude Distribution.* Lindsay Doyle is responsible for the transport of crude oil to several storage tanks. A portion of the pipeline network is shown in Figure 6.33. What is the maximal flow from node ① to node ⑦?

••6-10. Mr. Crimmage is operating the Chicago Health Club with leased equipment and space. Recently, his landlord suggested long-term leasing. Based on the long-term lease plan,

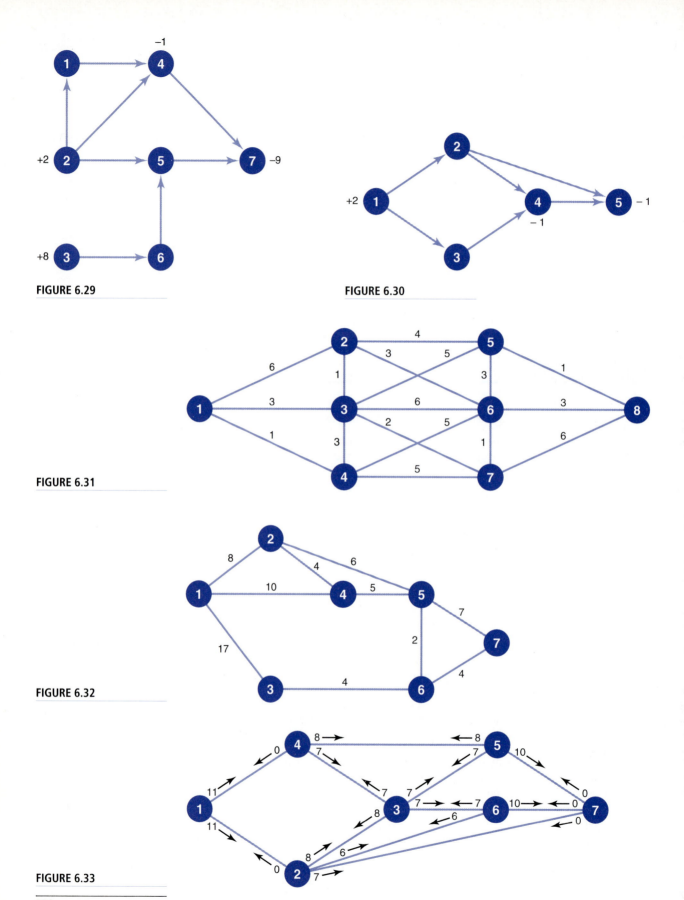

FIGURE 6.29

FIGURE 6.30

FIGURE 6.31

FIGURE 6.32

FIGURE 6.33

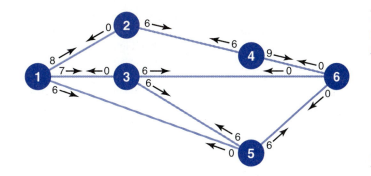

FIGURE 6.34

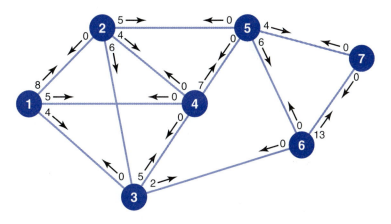

FIGURE 6.35

Mr. Crimmage obtained the accompanying table, which displays the expected net cost if he leases from the beginning of year i to the beginning of year j (in thousands of dollars).

i	j			
	2	3	4	5
1	13	25	37	45
2		12	21	30
3			10	20
4				9

Mr. Crimmage wishes to know when and how long to lease so as to minimize the cost over the next 4 years. Formulate his model and solve it. Are there alternative optimal solutions?

6-11. Determine the maximal flow from node ① to node ⑥ across the highway network shown in Figure 6.34.

6-12. Consider the network shown in Figure 6.35. Find the maximal flow. Assume ① is the source and ⑦ is the sink.

••• **6-13.** Demonstrate that the transportation model with S origins and D destinations is a special case of the capacitated transshipment model.

•• **6-14.** Demonstrate that the assignment model is a special case of the capacitated transshipment model.

••• **6-15.** Demonstrate that the model of determining the minimum-cost route from one node to another specific node can be expressed as a special case of the capacitated transshipment model.

••• **6-16.** Moebius Products, Inc. faces the following situation. It has to deliver 1000 Klein bottles per month for the next four months. The production cost per bottle is $5 during month 1, $9 during month 2, $10 during month 3, and $14 during month 4. The inventory carrying cost is $3 per bottle per month. The manager of the company would like to determine the most cost-efficient production schedule; that is, how many bottles to make at one time, and when. Assume that production is in multiples of 1000 bottles. That is, production in month i

covers demand for months i through j, for some $j \geq i$. Formulate this model as a network representation and solve it.

•••**6-17.** Consider the transshipment network of Figure 6.36. Nodes ① and ⑤ are the plant sites. The plants produce 200 and 150 truckloads, respectively. Nodes ③, ⑥, and ⑨ are the outlet sites. The outlets demand 50, 250, and 50 truckloads, respectively. The number on arc (i,j) indicates costs of transporting one truckload from i to j. Assume the cost from i to j is the same as the cost from j to i.

(a) Find the least costs of moving one truckload from ① to ③, ⑥, and ⑨.

(b) Find the least costs of moving one truckload from ⑤ to ③, ⑥, and ⑨.

(c) Formulate and solve the transportation model. What is the minimum total cost?

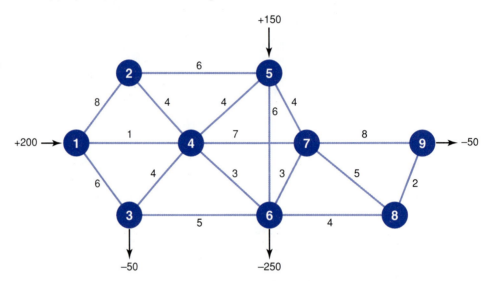

FIGURE 6.36

6-18. Slick Oil Company has three warehouses from which it can ship products to any of three retail outlets. The demand in cans for the product Gunkout is 100 at retail outlet 1; 250 at outlet 2; and 150 at outlet 3. The inventory of Gunkout at warehouse 1 is 50; at warehouse 2 is 275; and at warehouse 3 is 175. The cost of transporting one unit of Gunkout from each warehouse to each retail outlet follows. Formulate an LP to determine how many units should be shipped from each warehouse to each retailer so the demand at each retailer is met at minimum cost.

	RETAILER		
WAREHOUSE	1	2	3
1	5	7	6
2	8	9	10
3	4	3	11

6-19. Bob Frapes packages holiday gift-wrapped exotic fruits. His packages are wrapped at two locations from which they are sent to five wholesalers. The costs of packaging at locations 1 and 2 are $5.25 and $5.70, respectively. Bob's forecasts indicate demand for shipments as in the following table.

WHOLESALER	1	2	3	4	5
Shipment Required	4000	6000	2000	10,000	8000

Wrapping capacity at location 1 is 20,000 packages and at location 2 is 12,000 packages. The unit distribution costs in dollars from the two locations to the five wholesalers are given in the accompanying table. Formulate an LP model to determine how many packages Bob should send from each location to each wholesaler.

	WHOLESALER				
FROM LOCATION	1	2	3	4	5
1	.60	.40	1.20	.90	.50
2	1.50	.90	.50	.80	.80

6-20. Wonka Widget, Inc. faces the following three-period inventory model. The manufacturing cost per widget varies from period to period. These costs are $2, $4, and $3 for periods l, 2, and 3, respectively. A cost of $1 is incurred for each unit of inventory that is carried from one period to the next. Demand is 10,000, 20,000, and 30,000 units in periods 1, 2, and 3, respectively. Formulate an LP to determine how much the manufacturer should produce during each period to satisfy demand at minimum cost.

•• **6-21.** *Purchasing.* Jack Biensaulk is responsible for purchasing canned goods for GAGA food service at a large university. He knows what the demand will be over the course of the school year, and he has estimated purchase prices as well. These data are shown in the following table. He may purchase ahead of demand to avoid price increases, but there is a cost of carrying inventory of $0.20 per case per month applied to inventory on hand at the end of a month. Formulate and solve a cost-minimizing LP that will help Jack determine the timing of his purchases. HINT: Let P_t be the number of cases purchased in month t and I_t be the number of cases in inventory at the end of month t.

	SEP.	OCT.	NOV.	DEC.	JAN.	FEB.	MAR.	APR.	MAY
Demand (cases)	1000	900	850	500	600	1000	1000	1000	500
Cost per Case $	20	20	20	21	21	21	22	22	22

6-22. A manufacturer faces a three-period inventory situation for an item sale priced at $4. The manufacturing cost is $4 during the first period and $3 during the other two periods. The demand and inventory costs are the same as in Problem 6-20. The manufacturer does not have to meet the demand. However, each unit of lost sales costs the company $1.50. The production is restricted to 40,000 units during the first period and to 10,000 units during the other two periods. Formulate an LP to determine the production schedule that maximizes the manufacturer's profit.

6-23. Johnson Electric produces small electric motors for four appliance manufacturers in each of its three plants. The unit production costs vary with the locations because of differences in the production equipment and labor productivity. The customer orders that must be produced next month are shown in the accompanying table.

CUSTOMER	DEMAND
1	300
2	500
3	400
4	600

The unit production costs and monthly capacities (supplies) are shown in the following table.

PLANT	UNIT PRODUCTION COST ($)	MONTHLY PRODUCTION CAPACITY
A	17	800
B	20	600
C	24	700

The cost of supplying these customers varies from plant to plant. The unit transportation costs in dollars are given in the following table.

	TO			
FROM	1	2	3	4
A	3	2	5	7
B	6	4	8	3
C	9	1	5	4

Johnson must decide how many units to produce in each plant and how much of each customer's demand to supply from each plant. It wishes to minimize total production and transportation costs. Formulate Johnson's problem as a transportation model and solve for the optimal solution.

•• 6-24. *A Scheduling Model.* In a calculated financial maneuver, PROTRAC has acquired a new blast furnace facility for producing foundry iron. You have been asked to provide an answer to the following question: How many new slag-pit personnel should be hired and trained over the next six months? The requirements for trained employees in the pits and monthly wage rates for the next six months are given in the accompanying table.

	MONTH					
	Jan.	Feb.	Mar.	Apr.	May	June
Labor Requirements (hr)	7800	7500	7500	9200	10000	9000
Monthly Wage Rates ($)	3600	3600	3900	3900	4200	4200

Trainees are hired at the beginning of each month. One consideration to take into account is the union rule that workers must have one month of classroom instruction before they can work in the pits. Therefore, a trainee must be hired at least a month before a worker is actually needed. Each classroom student uses 80 hours of a trained slag-pit employee's time, so the employee has 80 less hours for work in the pit. Also, by contractual agreement, each trained employee can work up to 165 hours a month (total time, instructing plus in the pit). If the maximum total time available from trained employees exceeds a month's requirements, management may lay off at most 15% of the trained employees at the beginning of the month. All employees are paid a full month's salary even if they are laid off. A trainee costs $1800 a month in salary and other benefits. There are 40 trained employees available at the beginning of January. Formulate the hiring-and-training model as a linear programming model. HINT: Let x_t denote the number of trained employees on hand at the beginning of month t before any layoffs, let y_t denote the number of trainees hired in month t, and let z_t denote the number of trained employees laid off at the beginning of month t.

6-25. A partner at Foot, Thompson and McGrath, an advertising agency, is trying to decide which of four account executives to assign to each of four major clients. The estimated costs in $000s of each assignment for each executive are presented in the following table. Formulate a model and solve for the optimal solution.

	ACCOUNT			
EXEC.	1	2	3	4
A	15	19	20	18
B	14	15	17	14
C	11	15	15	14
D	21	24	26	24

•• 6-26. *Financial Planning.* An investor has two money-making activities, coded Alpha and Beta, available at the beginning of each of the next four years. Each dollar invested in Alpha at the beginning of a year yields a return two years later (in time for immediate reinvestment). Each dollar invested in Beta at the beginning of a year yields a return three years later. A third investment possibility, construction projects, will become available at the beginning of the second year. Each dollar invested in construction yields a return one year later. (This option will be available at the beginning of the third and fourth years also.) The investor starts with $50,000 at the beginning of the first year and wants to maximize the total amount of money available at the end of the fourth year. The returns on investments are given in the accompanying table.

ACTIVITY	RETURN PER DOLLAR INVESTED ($)
Alpha	1.50
Beta	1.80
Construction	1.20

   (a) Identify the decision variables and formulate an LP model. HINT: Let M_i be the money available at the beginning of year i and maximize M_5 subject to the appropriate constraints.

   (b) Can you determine the solution by direct analysis without Solver?

6-27. PROTRAC is deciding which of four salespeople to assign to each of four midwestern sales districts. Each salesperson is apt to achieve a different sales volume in $000s in each district. The estimates are given in the following table. PROTRAC would like to maximize total sales volume. However, it is impossible to assign salesperson B to district 1 or salesperson A to district 2 since these assignments would violate personnel rotation policies. Model this problem and find the optimal solution.

	DISTRICT			
SALESPERSON	**1**	**2**	**3**	**4**
A	65	73	55	58
B	90	67	87	75
C	106	86	96	89
D	84	69	79	77

•• 6-28. *An Arbitrage Model.* A speculator operates a silo with a capacity of 6000 bushels for storing corn. At the beginning of month 1, the silo contains 5000 bushels. Estimates of the selling and purchase prices of corn during the next four months are given in the following table.

MONTH	PURCHASE PRICE PER 1000 BUSHELS ($)	SELLING PRICE PER 1000 BUSHELS ($)
1	45	40
2	50	45
3	60	56
4	70	65

Corn sold during any given month is removed from the silo at the beginning of that month. Thus 5000 bushels are available for sale in month 1. Corn bought during any given month is put into the silo during the middle of that month, but it cannot be sold until the following month. Assume that the cost of storing the corn is based on average inventory and that it costs $0.01 to store one bushel for one month. The storage cost for a month must be paid at the end of the month. All purchases must be paid for with cash by the delivery time. The speculator has $100 to invest and has no intention of borrowing to buy corn or pay storage costs. Therefore, if he has no cash at the beginning of a month, he must sell some of his stock to pay the storage charge at the end of the month and to pay for the corn if he purchases any. Given the sales and purchase prices and the storage cost, the speculator wishes to know how much corn to buy and sell each month so as to maximize total profits shortly after the beginning of the fourth month (which means after any sale that may occur in that month). Formulate and solve the LP model. HINT: Let A_t denote bushels in the silo immediately after delivering the quantity sold in month t (x_t), and B_t bushels in the silo immediately after receiving the quantity purchased in month t (y_t), and P_t the cash position at the end of month t.

6-29. Sam has four repair bays in the maintenance shop and three jobs to assign to them. Because of differences in the equipment available, the people assigned to each bay, and the characteristics of the job, each job requires a different amount of time in each bay. The estimated times in minutes for each job in each bay are given in the accompanying table. Sam would like to minimize the total time required. Formulate the model and obtain the optimal solution. Are there alternative optimal solutions?

	JOB		
BAY	1	2	3
A	27	48	30
B	38	51	28
C	27	55	23
D	35	59	24

••• 6-30. Fernwood Lumber produces plywood. The cost to produce 1000 board feet of plywood varies from month to month because of the variation in handling costs, energy consumption, and raw materials costs. The production cost per 1000 board feet in each of the next 6 months is shown in the following table.

	MONTH					
	1	2	3	4	5	6
Production Cost ($)	900	950	1250	1050	900	850

Demand for the next 6 months is as follows:

	MONTH						
	1	2	3	4	5	6	TOTAL
Demand	60	70	110	80	70	60	450

Fernwood can produce up to 90,000 board feet per month. It also has the option of carrying inventory from one month to the next for a carrying cost of $25 per 1000 board feet per month. For example, 1000 board feet produced in month 1 for demand in month 2 incurs a carrying charge of $25. Furthermore, unsatisfied demand in one month can be filled in later periods at the cost of $40 per 1000 board feet per month-delay. Fernwood would like to know how much to produce each month and how much inventory to carry in order to satisfy demand at minimum cost. Formulate Fernwood's problem as a transportation model and solve for the optimal solution.

6-31. A realtor plans to sell four plots of land and has received individual bids from each of five developers. Because of the amount of capital required, these bids were made with the understanding that no developer would purchase more than one plot. The bids in $000s are shown in the accompanying table. The realtor wants to maximize total income from these bids. Formulate the model and optimize it.

	DEVELOPER				
PLOT	1	2	3	4	5
A	19	19	29	23	24
B	23	21	27	19	25
C	19	19	22	0	20
D	23	0	19	21	18

The Trans World Oil Company is an international producer, refiner, transporter, and distributor of oil, gasoline, and petrochemicals. Trans World is a holding company with subsidiary operating companies that are wholly or partially owned. A major problem for Trans World is to coordinate the actions of these various subsidiaries into an overall corporate plan, while at the same time maintaining a reasonable amount of operating autonomy for the subsidiary companies.

To deal with this dilemma, an annual corporate-wide plan which detailed the pattern of shipments among the various subsidiaries was developed. This plan was not rigid but provided general guidelines and the plan was revised periodically to reflect changing conditions. Within the framework of this plan, the operating companies could make their own decisions and plans.

This corporate plan was originally done on a trial and error basis. There were two problems with this approach. First, the management of the subsidiaries complained that the planners did not take into account the operating conditions under which the subsidiary had to operate. The plan might call for operations or distribution plans that were impossible to accomplish. And secondly, the corporate management was concerned that the plan did not optimize for the total company.

The technique of linear programming seemed a possible approach to aid in the annual planning process, that would be able to answer at least in part, the two objections above. In addition the building of such a model would make it possible to make changes in plans quickly when the need arose.

Far Eastern Operations

The details of the 1996 planning model for the Far Eastern Operations are now described.

There are two sources of crude oil, Iran and Borneo. The Iranian crude is relatively heavier (24° API), and the Far Eastern sector could obtain as much as 60,000 barrels per day (b/d) at a cost of $18.50 per barrel at Abadan during 1996. A second source of crude is from the Brunei fields in Borneo. This is a lighter crude oil (36° API). Under the terms of an agreement with the Netherlands Petroleum Company in Borneo, a fixed quantity of 40,000 b/d of Brunei crude, at a cost of $20.50 per barrel is to be supplied during 1996.

There are two subsidiaries that have refining operations. The first is in Australia, operating a refinery in Sydney with a capacity of 50,000 b/d throughout. The company also marketed its products throughout Australia, as well as having a surplus of refined products available for shipment to other subsidiaries.

The second subsidiary is in Japan, which operates a 30,000 b/d capacity refinery. Marketing operations are conducted in Japan, and excess production is available for shipment to their Far Eastern subsidiaries.

In addition, there are two marketing subsidiaries without refining capacity of their own. One of these is in New Zealand and the other in the Philippines. Their needs can be supplied by shipments from Australia, Japan, or the Trans World Oil subsidiary in the United States. The latter is not a regular part of the Far Eastern Operations, but may be used as a source of refined products.

Finally, the company has a fleet of tankers that move the crude oil and products among the subsidiaries.

Refinery Operations

The operation of a refinery is a complex process. The characteristics of the crudes available, the desired output, the specific technology of the refinery, etc. make it difficult to use a simple model to describe the process. In fact, management at both Australia and Japan have complex linear programming models involving approximately 300 variables and 100 constraints for making detailed decisions on a daily or weekly basis.

For annual planning purposes the refinery model is greatly simplified. The two crudes (Iranian and Brunei) are input. Two general products are output—(a) gasoline products; and (b) other products known collectively as distillate. In addition, although the refinery had processing flexibility that permitted a wide range of yields, for planning purposes it was decided to include only the use of the values at highest and lowest conversion rates (process intensity). Each refinery could use any combination of the two extreme intensities. These yields are shown in Table 1.

The incremental costs of operating the refinery depended somewhat upon the type of crude and process intensity. These costs are shown in Table 1. Also shown are the incremental transportation costs from either Borneo or Iran.

Marketing Operations

Marketing is conducted in two home areas (Australia and Japan) as well as in the Philippines and New Zealand. Demand for gasoline and distillate in all areas has been estimated for 1996 and is shown in the following table.

	1996 DEMAND (THOUSANDS OF B/D)	
Area	Gasoline	Distillate
Australia	9.0	21.0
Japan	3.0	12.0
Philippines	5.0	8.0
New Zealand	5.4	8.7
Total	22.4	49.7

Variable costs of supplying gasoline or distillate to New Zealand and the Philippines are shown in the following table.

	VARIABLE COSTS OF SHIPMENT OF GASOLINE/DISTILLATE IN $/BBL.	
From\To:	New Zealand	Philippines
Australia	.30	.45
Japan	.30	.60

TABLE 1 Refinery Costs and Yields

LOCATION, CRUDE, PROCESS INTENSITY	Incremental Cost of Crude/bbl.	Incremental Shipping Costs/bbl.	Incremental Refining Costs/bbl.	Total Costs	YIELDS (BBL. OUTPUT PER BBL. CRUDE INPUT)	
					Gasoline	Distillate
Australia:						
Brunei Crude, Low (BLA)	$20.50	$.78	$.36	$21.64	.259	.688
Brunei Crude, High (BHA)	20.50	.78	.84	22.12	.365	.573
Iran Crude, Low (ILA)	18.50	1.86	.45	20.81	.186	.732
Iran Crude, High (IHA)	18.50	1.86	.90	21.26	.312	.608
Japan:						
Brunei Crude, Low (BLJ)	20.50	.72	.48	21.70	.259	.688
Brunei Crude, High (BHJ)	20.50	.72	1.02	22.24	.350	.588
Iran Crude, Low (ILJ)	18.50	1.77	.60	20.87	.186	.732
Iran Crude, High (IHJ)	18.50	1.77	1.17	21.44	.300	.620

Tanker Operations

Tankers are used to bring crude from Iran and Borneo to Australia and Japan and to transport refined products from Australia and Japan to the Philippines and New Zealand. The variable costs of these operations are included in the previous shipment table. However, there is a limited capacity of tankers available. The fleet had a capacity of 6.9 equivalent (standard sized) tankers.

The amount of capacity needed to deliver one barrel from one destination to another depends upon the distance traveled, port time, and other factors. The table below lists the fraction of one standard sized tanker needed to deliver 1,000 b/d over the indicated routes. It is also possible to charter independent tankers. The rate for this was $8,600 per day for a standard sized tanker.

Tanker Usage Factors (Fraction of Standard Sized Tanker Needed to Deliver 1000 b/d)

BETWEEN	AUSTRALIA	JAPAN
Iran	.12	.11
Borneo	.05	.045
Philippines	.02	.01
New Zealand	.01	.06

United States Supply

United States operations on the West Coast expected a surplus of 12,000 b/d of distillate during 1996. The cost of distillate at the loading port of Los Angeles is $19.80 per barrel. There is no excess gasoline capacity. The estimated variable shipping costs and tanker requirements of distillate shipments from the United States are:

	VARIABLE COST OF SHIPMENTS ($ PER BBL.)	TANKER REQUIREMENTS (FRACTION OF STANDARD SIZED TANKER NEEDED TO DELIVER 1000 B/D)
New Zealand	2.10	.18
Philippines	1.65	.15

Required

1. Formulate a linear program which could be used to generate a comprehensive plan for the whole Far Eastern operations.

2. Use the model to respond to the following four new requests.

Memo To: Trans World Oil Headquarters

From: Australian Affiliate

Re: Supplements to Annual Plan

Since submitting data for annual planning purposes, two additional opportunities have arisen. We would like to include them in the plans.

A. *Bid on Gasoline Contract with Australian Government*

The government of Australia will submit to bid a contract for 1.5 thousand b/d of gasoline for 1996. We expect we could win this contract and still make a profit at a bid price of $29.20 per barrel. We would like permission to submit this bid for the contract.

B. *Expansion of Australian Refinery*

For the past two years, the Australian refinery has been operating at full capacity. We request authorization for capital expenditures to increase the refinery capacity to 65 thousand b/d. There are several reasons for the need for this expansion:

1. Australia can supply the current requirements in New Zealand and the Philippines more cheaply than can Japan.
2. The proposed bid on Australian government gasoline contract (above).
3. We understand the New Zealand affiliate is considering increasing its requirements by 4.8 thousand b/d. [See next memo.]

The cost of this expansion is $6,000,000. To recover this investment, we need an annual savings of $1,228,000.

(This assumes a cost of capital rate of 20%. Depreciation tax effects are included. With these considerations, the $1,228,000 savings per year is equivalent to the $6 million investment.)

Case Study   Production Planning at Bumles

(Before attacking this case you will want to review the solution to the Bumles example in this chapter, for the correct formulation of this model will be similar.) Bumles, Inc. uses part of its capacity to make two types of hand-painted statues. The finished products can reasonably be grouped into two categories, A and B. A requires 0.5 hours of a painter's time and B requires 0.75 hours. Bumles has 45 painters available, but not all of these painters need to be used. The plant is used for hand-painted statues on Monday, Tuesday, and Wednesday each week. During the remainder of the week the productive capacity is devoted to another product line. Each painter who is engaged is available to work painting statues any part of an eight-hour day, two days a week. A painter can be assigned to any two-day schedule and is paid for 16 hours of regular-time work, no matter what part of that time he actually spends producing statues. If there is not enough production to keep all the workers assigned to a particular day busy for the entire day, the slack time is spent on cleaning the plant and similar activities. In addition, on any day, Bumles can request each working painter to work up to 4 hours of overtime (i.e., if Ed Jones normally works on Tuesday, Bumles can have him work 2, 3, or any other number between 0 and 4, hours of overtime on that day).

Revenue from selling an A is $21 and a B is $30. Demand must either be satisfied on the day on which it occurs or it is lost. Production on a given day can be used to satisfy demand that day or demand later in the week, that is, statues produced on Monday can be used to satisfy demand on Monday, Tuesday, or Wednesday, and statues produced on Tuesday can be used to satisfy demand on Tuesday or Wednesday. However, because of the change of operations in production, all statues produced in a week must be shipped that week, that is, there is never inventory on hand Monday morning. Because of increased handling costs, it costs $0.25 to carry an A and $0.30 to carry a B in inventory from one day to the next. A unit of lost demand results in an all-inclusive penalty cost of $2 for a unit of A on Monday, $4 on Tuesday, and $5 on Wednesday. The per unit penalty costs for B are $5 on Monday, $10 on Tuesday, and $11 on Wednesday. Painters are paid $10 per hour of regular time and $15 per hour of overtime.

Demand varies significantly at Bumles. Management is considering two generic demand patterns, Pre-Christmas

Rush and After-Christmas Slump, shown in the accompanying tables.

Pre-Christmas Rush

	M	T	W
A	1500	1000	150
B	240	90	1100

After-Christmas Slump

	M	T	W
A	240	48	64
B	160	32	64

Bill Bumle, the executive vice-president, notes that A's yield a contribution of $21/0.5 = \$42$ per labor hour, whereas B's yield a contribution of $30/0.75 = \$40$ per labor hour. He also notes that the penalty for lost sales increases as the week goes on. He concludes that Bumles should first satisfy all demand for A's starting with Wednesday, then Tuesday, then Monday, and then use any leftover capacity to produce B's.

Specific Questions

1. Comment on the approach suggested by Bill Bumle.
2. Ignoring integrality conditions (i.e., allowing the possibility of fractional values of all decision variables), create an Excel LP model that will schedule painters and production in such a way as to maximize revenue minus cost, where cost equals labor plus penalty and inventory-carrying costs. The model should be correct for any set of demands. In your formulation the first six constraints should reflect the demand for A on Mondays, Tuesdays, and Wednesdays, and the demand for B on Mondays, Tuesdays, and Wednesdays. Thus, to solve the model for any set of demands one must provide only the RHSs for these constraints. In your formulation of the model, pay attention to relationships between production, sales, lost sales, demand, and inventory on any particular day. For example,

   demand on day t = sales on t + lost sales on t

3. What are the decision variables? Define them carefully.
4. For each of the above two specific demand patterns, optimize the model.

Then, for both demand patterns summarize the following into a report for a general manager:

5. How many items of what to produce each day.
6. How to schedule as many of the painters as you use, for example, schedule 14.3 painters to work a Monday/Tuesday schedule, and so on.
7. How many hours of overtime to use each day.
8. How much inventory of each product to carry each day.
9. How many units of lost sales to have each day.
10. Use your model to answer the following question: Assume that a year consists of 32 weeks of pre-Christmas

rush demand and 18 weeks of after-Christmas slump demand. If Bumles wants each of the 45 painters to work an equal number of weeks, how many weeks will each painter work?

Additional Considerations

[The questions in this section should be answered by using the model created in Question 2 above, with new parameters and performing additional analysis as needed.]

The painters' union has suggested a contract with a guaranteed annual wage (GAW) provision. In particular, this agreement specifies that a painter must be paid at least $11,500 per year for work on hand-painted statues. If, at the end of the year, the amount earned is less than $11,500, the firm simply gives the painter a check to make up the difference. Bumles plans to use all 45 painters even if the GAW provision is not accepted, but if it is all 45 painters will earn at least $11,500 per year.

To estimate the effect of this proposal on the Bumles operation, Bill assumes that 30 weeks of the 50-week year will have pre-Christmas rush demands, and the other 20 weeks will have the demand schedule shown in the following table.

	M	T	W
A	240	48	300
B	160	32	200

He also assumes that a detailed schedule can be worked out so that each painter earns the same pay during a year. Based on your LP model and Bill's assumptions

11. What is Bumles' total annual profit without the GAW provision?
12. Does your solution to Question 11 satisfy the GAW provision? What effect will accepting the GAW provision have on Bumles' profitability (increase, decrease, or no effect)? Show the spreadsheet calculations to support your answers.
13. How much would average wages have to be in the low-demand weeks for the annual wage to be $11,500? For the low-demand weeks, formulate an LP model that Bumles could use to find a production plan that would meet the GAW provision. Present a justification for your model and optimize it.
14. Suppose the GAW provision is accepted. How much would Bumles save per year by using the plan found in Question 13 compared with the plan of Question 11 where additional payments would have to be made to the painters at the end of the year?

Sensitivity Questions

[These questions refer to the Sensitivity Reports for the models you created to answer Questions 1–10.]

15. In the current solution to the pre-Christmas version of the model, if we combine regular and overtime pay then each painter is paid $280/week. If another painter should become available, what is the maximum weekly amount that Bumles should pay him or her?

16. Suppose that, in the pre-Christmas model, the demand for A on Monday increases by 10 units. What happens to the OV?
17. Answer Question 16 for the after-Christmas model.
18. What is responsible for the major difference in the answers to Questions 16 and 17?
19. Suppose that, in the pre-Christmas model, management's recent experience calls for an adjustment in the penalty cost for unsatisfied demand for A on Monday. The new value is set at $3. What happens to the optimal solution and the OV?
20. In Question 19, suppose the new value is reset to $4. What is the effect on the optimal solution and the OV? (Give the best answer you can based on the Sensitivity Report.)
21. Suppose that, in the pre-Christmas problem, the selling price of A is reduced to $15 and B is reduced to $20. Can you give a bound on the new OV?

Case Study — Biglow Toy Company

In late August 1997, Jean Biglow, treasurer of Biglow Toy Company, was concerned with financing its sales operations during the upcoming Christmas selling season. To cope with the Christmas sales peak, Jean planned to build up Biglow's toy inventory throughout the fall. This would generate substantial cash deficits in October, November, and December. Some means of short-term financing had to be found to cover these deficits. On the other hand, Jean anticipated a cash surplus in January and February, when Biglow's retailers paid their Christmas invoices. A small cash surplus was also anticipated in September as a result of over-the-summer toy purchases.

Jean tried to maintain a minimum balance in Biglow's cash account throughout the year. This was to protect against errors in estimating both the size and timing of future cash flows. The planned minimum balance was normally set as a fixed percentage of each month's anticipated dollar sales volume. This procedure had proven adequate in the past against virtually all contingencies.

Except for deciding how to finance the fall buildup in inventory, Jean had already completed a six-month financial plan. This covered the period September 1997 through February 1998. Selected portions of the plan are shown in the table below.

The accounts receivable balances shown in the table refer to the beginning of each month. Thus Jean anticipates $700,000 in accounts receivable at the beginning of September, $500,000 at the beginning of October, and so forth.

On the average, Biglow receives a 3% discount from its toy suppliers for prompt payment of purchases. Jean normally takes advantage of such discounts, whenever possible, and so, the planned payments shown in the table assume prompt payment and realization of the 3% average discount. If Biglow's payments are delayed, the discount will be lost, and actual payments will exceed planned payments, accordingly.

The cash surplus and deficit figures shown in the table are net of all other operations, including anticipated sales receipts, planned payments for purchases, and all other planned receipts and payments. These figures are also net of the standard provision for each month's minimum cash balance. Thus, Jean expects a surplus of $200,000 from operations during September, a deficit of $300,000 from operations during October, and so forth. Each of the surplus and deficit figures shown in the table represents the incremental (not cumulative) surplus or deficit anticipated during that month.

As indicated in Exhibit 1, Jean has three sources of short-term borrowing to meet Biglow's monthly cash needs. These are:

1. Pledging accounts receivable balances; that is, factoring;
2. Delaying payments of purchases; and
3. Obtaining a six-month bank loan.

A local bank has agreed to loan Biglow funds at the beginning of any month against a pledge of its accounts receivable balance. The maximum loan that Biglow can obtain from this source is 75% of the accounts receivable balance outstanding at the beginning of that month. Whatever is borrowed, if anything, must be returned to the bank at the beginning of the next month, plus an interest payment of 1.5% of the amount actually borrowed.

Payments to suppliers for purchases may be delayed for a maximum of one month. Thus, up to $1,000,000 in payments currently scheduled for November may be delayed until December. Whatever portion, if any, of these planned payments is delayed would become available to finance the anticipated deficit from operations during November. However, Jean's own policy strictly forbids delaying payments more than one month beyond the month when they are supposed to be paid. Also, the average 3% discount is lost on all payments that are actually delayed. For example, if Jean delays the planned

Six-Month Financial Plan (All figures in thousands of dollars)

	SEP	OCT	NOV	DEC	JAN	FEB
Accounts Receivable Balance	$700	$500	$700	$1200	$1000	$500
Planned Payments for Purchases	$800	$900	$1000	$600	$400	$500
Cash Surplus from Operations	$200	-	-	-	$300	$1500
Cash Deficit from Operations	-	$300	$600	$900	-	-

payment of $1,000,000 for November then the payment in December for this delayed amount will be $1,000,000/.97 = 1,000,000*1.031 = $1,031,000$ approximately.

The local bank is also willing to make a one-time loan to Biglow of any amount from a minimum of $400,000 to a maximum of $1,000,000 for six months. If such a loan is taken, the entire loan will be received by Biglow at the beginning of September and repaid at the end of February. In addition, Biglow must pay the bank a 1% monthly interest charge at the end of each month. Once taken, it is not possible to increase the loan nor to repay any portion of it during the six-month period. The 1% monthly interest charge therefore applies to the entire amount, if any, actually borrowed.

At the end of every month, Jean inspects the current balance in Biglow's cash account. Whatever excess funds remain over and above the minimum balance planned for the next month are invested immediately in 30-day government securities. Securities are purchased at the beginning of the next month and sold at the end of that month. Upon selling the se-

curities, Biglow receives one-half percent interest on the excess funds, if any, actually invested. No excess funds are anticipated for the month of August, but Jean plans to continue this investment procedure between September and February.

The sources and uses of funds are diagrammed for the first two months in Exhibit 2 in which **AS** is the amount borrowed by pledging **A**ccounts Receivable in **S**eptember, **AO** is the amount borrowed by pledging **A**ccounts Receivable in **O**ctober, **PS** is the amount made available by postponing **P**ayments in **S**eptember, **PO** is the amount made available by postponing **P**ayments in **O**ctober, and **L** is the amount of the (one-time) six month **L**oan in September, if any.

Jean must decide how to cover the operating deficits indicated in Table 1 by utilizing some combination of the three sources of short-term borrowing. Jean expects to maintain at least the planned minimum balances in Biglow's cash account at the end of each month as a reserve for contingencies while minimizing the net dollar cost of whatever six-month financing plan is adopted.

EXHIBIT 1 Sources and Uses of Funds for Biglow Toy Company

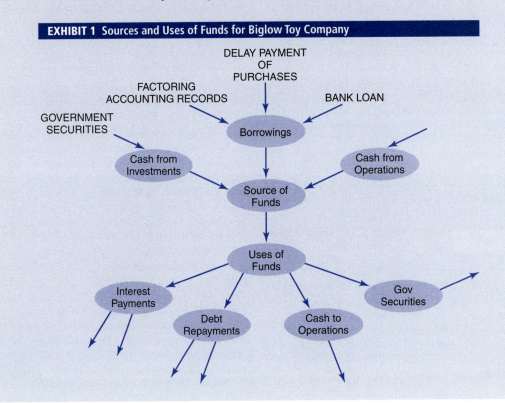

EXHIBIT 2 Sources and Uses of Funds for September and October

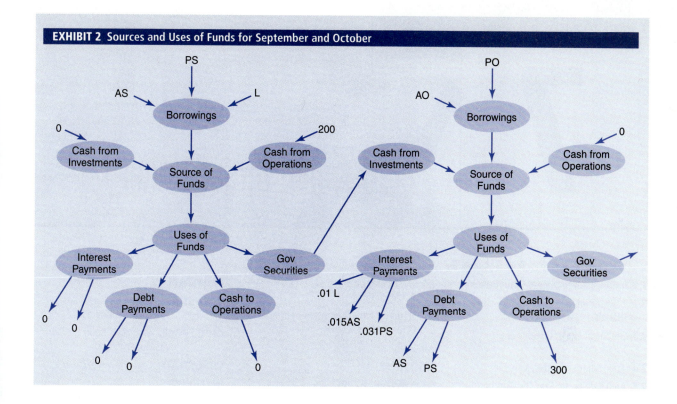

References

Jean-Yves Blais, Jacques Lamont, and Jean-Marc Rousseau, "The HASTUS Vehicle and Manpower Scheduling System at the Société de la Communauté Urbaine de Montréal," *Interfaces,* 20, no. 1 (January–February 1990).

James Evans, "A Microcomputer-Based Decision Support System Scheduling Umpires in the American Baseball League," *Interfaces,* 18, no. 6 (November–December 1988).

David Carlisle, Kenneth Nickerson, Stephen Porbst, Denise Rudolph, Yosef Sheffi, and Warren Powell, "A Turnkey Microcomputer-Based Logistics Planning System," *Interfaces,* 17, no. 4 (July–August 1987).

Tsuyoshi Yoshino, Tsuna Sasaki, and Toshiharu Hasegawa, "The Traffic-Control System on the Hanshin Expressway," *Interfaces,* 25, no. 1 (1995), 94–108.

Integer Optimization

CHAPTER OUTLINE

7.1 Introduction to Integer Optimization

7.2 Types of Integer Linear Programming Models

7.3 Graphical Interpretations of ILP Models

7.4 Applications of Binary Variables

7.5 An ILP Vignette: STECO's Warehouse Location—A Fixed Charge Model

7.6 The Branch-and-Bound ILP Algorithm

7.7 Notes on Implementation of Integer Optimization Models

7.8 Summary

KEY TERMS

SELF-REVIEW EXERCISES

PROBLEMS

CASE STUDY: Assigning Sales Representatives

CASE STUDY: Municipal Bond Underwriting

CASE STUDY: Cash Flow Matching

REFERENCES

APPLICATION CAPSULE   **American Airlines Uses Integer Program for Crew-Pairing Optimization**

American Airlines (AA) employs more than 8,300 pilots and 16,200 flight attendants to fly one of the largest fleets in the United States, with over 510 aircraft. Total crew cost, which includes salaries, benefits, and expenses, exceeds $1.3 billion per year and is second only to fuel cost. But unlike fuel costs, a large part of crew costs are controllable. Therefore, a priority of the crew resources department at AA is to develop crew assignment plans that achieve high levels of crew utilization. To meet this goal, the crew resources department has come to rely heavily on an integer program.

AA schedules its flights once every month. Each flight must be assigned a crew (pilots and flight attendants). Crews reside in 12 different cities called crew bases; therefore, the assignment of a crew to flights must be such that the crew works a sequence of flights that starts and ends at the same crew base. This sequence of flights is called a pairing and typically lasts three days. A crew works four to five pairings each month.

The construction of crew pairings is complicated by a complex array of union and Federal Aviation Authority (FAA) work rules. These rules vary by crew type (pilot or flight attendant), crew size, aircraft type, and type of operation (domestic or international). Work rules concern duty periods and rests. A stringent union rule specifies maximum duty length of between 14 and 16 hours during the day. In the actual model, a shorter duty length is imposed at the planning stage in anticipation of delays during actual operations. The FAA imposes rules to minimize crew fatigue and ensure passenger safety.

The cost of a pairing includes a complex formula for pay involving the guaranteed hours of pay and the actual hours flown, as well as more straightforward items like hotel, per-diem, and ground transportation costs. Of course, the goal is to come up with an assignment of crews to all flights for the next month that minimizes this total cost. The model can also be used on a more strategic basis to recommend whether an existing crew base should be closed or a new base should be opened.

Crew pairing optimization is an enormously complex combinatorial problem. It has been the subject of intense research since the 1950s because small improvements leverage into large dollar savings. In fact, a 1% increase in AA's crew utilization translates into $13 million worth of savings each year. AA estimates that the model generates annual savings in excess of $20 million. The model has been so successful that it has also been sold to 11 other major airlines and one railroad company. (See Ranga et. al)

7.1   INTRODUCTION TO INTEGER OPTIMIZATION

This chapter is devoted to models that could be formulated and solved as linear programming models except for the complication that some or all of the variables are required to assume integer values. Such models are called **integer linear programming (ILP)** models.[1] Integer linear programming has become an important specialized area of management modeling. In this introductory chapter, it will be possible only to scratch the surface—to illustrate the importance of the topic, as well as one of the most useful solution methods.

At the outset, let us recall from previous chapters that in a linear programming model the variables are permitted to take on fractional values, such as 6.394, and in keeping with the principle that "whatever is allowed will occur," fractional answers must be expected.[2] In spite of this, actual (real-world) decision variables often must be integers. For example, a firm produces bags of cattle feed. A solution that requires it to make 3000.472 bags does not make sense. In such situations a noninteger solution is often adapted to the integer requirement by simply rounding or truncating the results to a neighboring integer. This method produces what we call a **rounded solution.** Using such a solution is acceptable to management in situations where, in a significant practical sense, the rounding does not matter. For example, there is no significant difference either in the objective function or in the constraints between producing 19,283.64 and 19,283 bags of Big Bull cattle feed. Indeed, there are probably enough approximations used in assembling the data for the model that management would be content with any production figure near the 19,000-bag level. Generally, the larger the LP solution decision variable values, the more likely that a rounded integer answer will be acceptable in practice.

WHEN INTEGER SOLUTIONS MATTER

There are, however, a number of important models where this rather cavalier attitude toward the integer requirements of the real model does not work. This complication can be caused by the scale of the variables under consideration. For example, if the solution to an LP model suggested that Boeing should build 3.6 747s and 4.8 777s, management probably would not be comfortable just going ahead and deciding to build four 747s and five 777s, or, for that matter any other rounded combination. The magnitude of the financial return and the commitment of resources associated with each unit of aircraft make it advisable to determine the best possible *integer solution.*

As another example, it will be seen that many models use integer variables to indicate logical decisions. For example, we will see models where we want X_7 to equal 1 if we should build a warehouse in Kansas City and X_7 to equal 0 if we should not. Suppose that the solution to an LP version of this model yielded a noninteger value (e.g., $X_7 = 0.38$). We shall see that this value contains no useful information about the solution to the real model. Clearly, we cannot build 0.38 of a warehouse. We certainly could select warehouses of different sizes, but nevertheless, either we have a warehouse in Kansas City or we do not. You might guess that, in a case such as this, rounding to the nearest integer (0 in this case) would be a way to approach this difficulty. Unfortunately, that is not guaranteed to give a good (to say nothing of optimal) solution. Indeed, we shall see that rounding may not even lead to a feasible solution in cases such as these.

There are many important management models that would be LPs except for the requirement of integer values for some of the decision variables, where you *cannot* find a good solution by using straight LP optimization in Solver and then rounding off the resulting optimal values of the decision variables. These models must be solved with methods designed especially to solve large integer programming models.

---

[1] Not all integer programming problems are necessarily linear, and many of the things we say in this chapter about ILPs apply to integer programs in general. However, since we deal only with linear models in this chapter, we will use the abbreviation ILP throughout to avoid the need for additional terminology and minimize the possibility of confusion.
[2] An exception to this is described in Chapter 6. Transportation models with integral supplies and demands will always produce integer-valued optimal solutions. In fact, this remarkable property is true of the more general class of network models.

Integer linear programming models have been important for years, and a great deal of time and effort have been devoted to research on the optimization of these models. These efforts are returning dividends, and marked progress has been made in this area. Of course, the great strides in computer technology have also made a crucial contribution to the increased ability to solve large integer linear programming models that would have been impossible to optimize a decade ago.

LP VERSUS ILP

In spite of the impressive improvement in our ability to solve integer programming models, the technology is still quite different from what we have available to attack models in which the decision variables need not be integer. Many models that can be solved easily as LP formulations become unsolvable for practical purposes if the decision variables are required to be integers (i.e., the time and cost needed to compute a solution are too large). In practice, integer programming models often take ten times longer and frequently hundreds or thousands of times longer to optimize than when not using integer restrictions.

In the following sections we first describe two general classes of integer linear programming models and use graphical analysis to illustrate the relationship between linear programming, integer linear programming, and the process of rounding LP solutions to obtain a possible solution to the ILP. This graphical approach will provide an intuitive feeling for the nature of the integer model we are confronting. We then turn our attention to a special variety of integer models in which the integer variables are restricted to the binary values of 0 or 1. Using such "indicator" or "Boolean" variables allows us to *formulate* a variety of logical conditions that are not otherwise easily captured. A number of important practical models involve such conditions, and several of these formulations are discussed. We then turn to the topic of how Solver optimizes integer linear models, via the "branch-and-bound" method, in order to give you better understanding of the problems of utilizing integer formulations for decision making. Then our attention turns to the topic of integer linear programming in practice, emphasizing strategic considerations as well as discussing possibilities for sensitivity analysis.

7.2   **TYPES OF INTEGER LINEAR PROGRAMMING MODELS**

Integer programming is a general term for mathematical programming models with *integrality conditions* (conditions stipulating that some or all of the decision variables must have integer values). We have already pointed out that integer linear programming (ILP) models are linear programming models with the additional characteristic that some or all of the decision variables are required to take on integer values. There are several classifications within this category of models.

An **all-integer linear program** is, as the name suggests, a model in which *all* of the decision variables are required to be integers. For example

$$\text{Min} \quad 6x_1 + 5x_2 + 4x_3$$
$$\text{s.t.} \quad 108x_1 + 92x_2 + 58x_3 \geq 576$$
$$7x_1 + 18x_2 + 22x_3 \geq 83$$
$$x_1, x_2, x_3 \geq 0 \text{ and } integer \qquad \textbf{(7.1)}$$

is an all-integer model. Without the additional constraints x_1, x_2, x_3 integer (i.e., the integrality conditions), this model is an LP model.

A model in which *only some* of the variables are restricted to integer values and others can assume any nonnegative number (i.e., *any continuous value*) is referred to as a **mixed integer linear program (MILP).** For example, suppose that in the previous model only x_1 and x_2 were required to be integer and x_3 was not. In some models the integer variables are restricted to the value 0 or 1. Such models are called **binary, or 0–1, integer linear programs.** These models are particularly important because the 0–1 variables may be used to represent dichotomous decisions (yes/no decisions).[3] A variety of scheduling, plant location, production planning, and portfolio construction models are 0–1 integer linear programming models. They are discussed in some detail in Section 7.4. As we shall see, 0–1 variables can be found in all-integer models and in MILPs.

We will often consider the LP model that results if we start with an ILP and ignore the integer restrictions. This LP model is referred to as the **LP relaxation** of the ILP. For example, if we remove the phrase "and *integer*" from the ILP presented in model (7.1), the resulting LP is the LP relaxation of the original integer program.

7.3   GRAPHICAL INTERPRETATIONS OF ILP MODELS

In Chapter 4 we saw that it is possible to gain substantial insight into the nature and the solution of LP models by examining the graphical analysis of a problem with two decision variables. The same approach is useful for an ILP model, and we now turn our attention to that topic.

OPTIMIZING THE ILP MODEL: A MODIFICATION OF PROTRAC, INC.

Consider a modified version of the PROTRAC E and F model discussed in Chapters 3 through 5. In particular, consider the modified model

$$
\begin{aligned}
\text{Max} \quad & 18E + 6F \\
\text{s.t.} \quad & E + F && \geq 5 && (1) \\
& 42.8E + 100F && \leq 800 && (2) \\
& 20E + 6F && \leq 142 && (3) \\
& 30E + 10F && \geq 135 && (4) \\
& E - 3F && \leq 0 && (5) \\
& E, F \geq 0 \text{ and integer} &&&& \textbf{(7.2)}
\end{aligned}
$$

For a detailed description of the original model, see Chapter 3. In brief, E is the number of E-9s and F is the number of F-9s that PROTRAC decides to produce. The objective function is the profit as a function of the production decision. Constraint (1) reflects a need to meet previous commitments. Constraints (2) and (3) are production time restrictions in departments A and B, respectively. Constraint (4) represents part of a union agreement, and constraint (5) is imposed because of management's attitude about the appropriate product mix. Other than the parameter changes the only important change between (7.2) and the LP model in Chapter 3 is the word *integer*. As we shall see shortly, the impact of this single word is profound.

To solve this model with a graphical approach, we prescribe three steps:

1. Find the feasible set for the LP relaxation of the ILP model.

2. Identify the integer points inside the set determined in step 1.

3. Find, among those points determined in step 2, one that optimizes the objective function.

The first two steps have been accomplished by the GLP program in Figure 7.1. The shaded region is the feasible set for the LP relaxation, and the dark dots, enabled by clicking the "I" tool shown under the cursor, are the integer points contained in this set. This set of integer points is the set of feasible solutions to the ILP. In other words, there are only 13 feasible

---

[3]Creative use of binary variables permits many conditional statements to be successfully incorporated into an optimization model, thereby avoiding the need to use Excel's IF() function. Recall, if the objective function or constraints are related to the decision variables directly or indirectly by means of an IF() function, then Solver may fail to converge to an optimum.

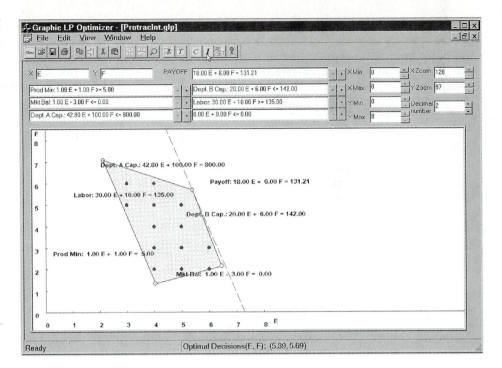

FIGURE 7.1

Feasible Set for Revised
PROTRAC ILP

solutions to the ILP model. They are the points (3, 6), (4, 6), (3, 5), (4, 5), (5, 5), (4, 4), (5, 4), (4, 3), (5, 3), (6, 3), (4, 2), (5, 2), and (6, 2).

To optimize the model, we must now determine which of the feasible points yields the largest value of the objective function. We proceed as in an LP model; that is, by moving a contour of the objective function in an *uphill direction* (since we are dealing with a Max model) until it is not possible to move it farther and still intersect a feasible point.

The result of this process is shown in Figure 7.2 in which the "Auto Max" tool, under the cursor, has been clicked. We see that the optimal solution to the ILP is the point $E = 6$ and $F = 3$. Since the objective function is $18E + 6F$, this solution yields an optimal value of the objective function of $18(6) + 6(3) = 126$, as shown in Figure 7.2.

THE LP RELAXATION

Figure 7.3 sketches the solution and labels several nearby points. We can use Figure 7.3 to illustrate some important facts about the LP relaxation. We first note that the optimal solution to the LP relaxation occurs at the intersection of the two lines $42.8E + 100F = 800$ and $20E + 6F = 142$, as shown in Figure 7.1. This result is obtained by pushing, uphill, the contour of the objective function as far as possible and still have it intersect the feasible set for the LP relaxation. Since the intersection of the two constraints does not occur at an integer point, the optimal solution to the LP relaxation is not feasible for the ILP. As shown in Figure 7.1, the optimal values of the decision variables for the LP relaxation yields $E^* = 5.39, F^* = 5.69$. Also shown, the **optimal value** of the objective function, termed the **OV,** for the LP relaxation is 131.21.

Comparing these two optimal values (126 for the ILP and 131.21 for the LP relaxation), we see that the OV for the LP relaxation is larger than for the original ILP. This fact is a special case of a phenomenon that we observed in our earlier discussions of linear programming. Think of creating an ILP or an MILP by starting with the LP relaxation and adding the integer restrictions. We know that *in any optimization model, adding constraints cannot help and may hurt the optimal value of the objective function.* Thus, we make the following comments:

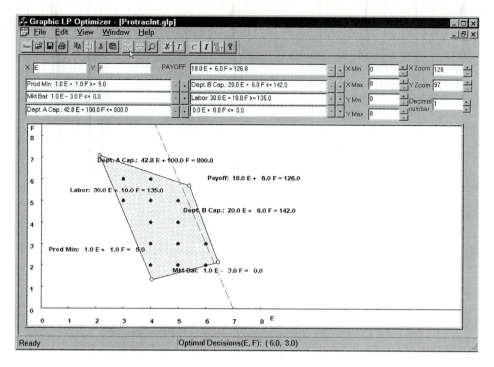

FIGURE 7.2

Optimal Integer Solution
to Revised PROTRAC Model

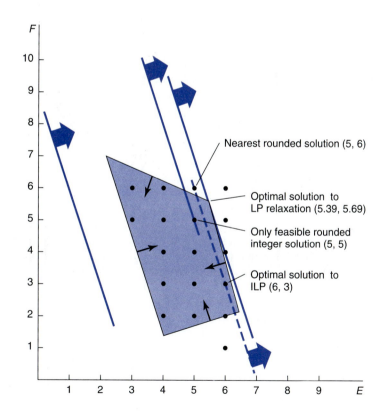

FIGURE 7.3

Graphical Solution
to PROTRAC ILP

1. In a *Max* model the OV of the LP relaxation always provides an *upper bound* on the OV of the original ILP. Adding the integer constraints either hurts or leaves unchanged the OV for the LP. In a Max model, hurting the OV means making it smaller.

2. In a *Min* model the OV of the LP relaxation always provides a *lower bound* on the OV of the original ILP. Again, adding the integer constraints either hurts or leaves unchanged the OV for the LP. In a Min model, hurting the OV means making it larger.

ROUNDED SOLUTIONS

We have observed that the optimal solution to the LP relaxation is $E^* = 5.39$, $F^* = 5.69$. Each of these variables could be rounded up or down and hence there are four rounded solutions ([5, 5], [5, 6], [6, 5], [6, 6]) near the optimal solution to the LP relaxation. In general, with two decision variables there are four rounded neighbor solutions; with n decision variables there could be 2^n such points.

Let us now examine in more detail some of the potential problems that can arise when using a rounded solution. Refer to Figure 7.3. If we solve the LP relaxation and round each variable to the nearest integer, we obtain (5, 6), which is infeasible. In this case the point (5, 5) is the only feasible point that can be obtained by rounding (5.39, 5.69). The other candidates, (5, 6), (6, 6), and (6, 5), are all infeasible.

This model illustrates two important facts about rounded solutions:

1. *A rounded solution need not be optimal.* In this case the value of the objective function at the only feasible rounded solution is

$$18(5) + 6(5) = 120$$

This compares with a value of 126 for the optimal value of the ILP. We see, then, that a proportional loss of $6/126$, or almost 5%, is incurred by using this rounded solution rather than the optimal solution.

2. *A rounded solution need not be near the optimal ILP solution.* Students often have an intuitive idea that even though a rounded solution may not be optimal, it should be "near" the optimal ILP solution. Referring again to Figure 7.3, we see that the rounded solution is not one of the immediate integer neighbors of the optimal ILP solution. Indeed, only four points in the feasible set ([3, 6], [4, 6], [3, 5], and [4, 5]) are farther from the optimal solution than the rounded solution. It seems hard to claim that in this example the rounded solution is near the optimal ILP solution.

In Figure 7.4 we introduce another ILP that illustrates an additional and even more drastic problem associated with rounded solutions. In this figure the shaded area is the feasible set for the LP relaxation, the dots are integer points, and the circled dot is the only feasible solution to the ILP. The optimal solution to the LP relaxation is indicated at the tip of the wedge-shaped feasible set. Notice that if we start with the optimal solution to the LP (roughly [3.3, 4.7]) and then round this to any of the four neighboring integer points, we obtain an infeasible point. That is, for this example, *no manner of rounding can produce feasibility.*

In summary, we have noted that an intuitively appealing way of attacking an ILP is to solve the LP relaxation of the original model and then round the solution to a neighboring integer point. We have seen that this approach can have certain problems.

1. None of the neighboring integer points may be feasible.
2. Even if one or more of the neighboring integer points is feasible
   a. Such a point need not be optimal for the ILP.
   b. Such a point need not even be near the optimal ILP solution.

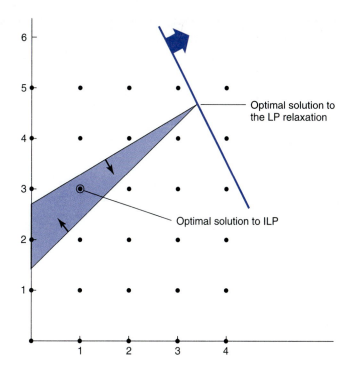

FIGURE 7.4

All Rounded Solutions
Are Infeasible

ENUMERATION

The graphical approach was used to illustrate some important ideas about ILPs. However, since there are only 13 feasible points in Figure 7.1 for the PROTRAC ILP, you may get the mistaken impression that you can reasonably list all the feasible points, evaluate the objective function at each of them, and select the best one; that is, solve the model by **complete enumeration.** In this case, one could do that. Unfortunately, however, as with LPs, complete enumeration is not a reasonable procedure for most ILPs. Suppose, for example, that we had an ILP with 100 0–1 variables. In this case there could be up to 2^{100}, which is 1.27×10^{30}, feasible points. Even with the fastest supercomputer, it would take many lifetimes to enumerate all of these points.

It is interesting to compare the enumeration method for ILPs with the simplex method used by Solver for LPs. As we have seen, the simplex method can be viewed as a way of visiting corners of the constraint set and evaluating the objective function at the corners visited. It is also true that there can be billions of corners on the constraint set of a large LP. The important point, however, is that *not all corners are visited.* Indeed, the simplex method is very efficient. It proceeds in such a way as to improve the value of the objective function at each successive corner. Once no improvement is possible, the procedure stops and indicates that an optimal solution has been reached. At this time there is no comparable method for ILPs. There are methods (to be discussed later) that are better than complete enumeration, but they are not able to eliminate large numbers of alternative solutions as quickly and efficiently as the simplex method does for LPs.

7.4   APPLICATIONS OF BINARY VARIABLES

Binary, or 0–1, variables play an especially important role in the applications of ILPs. These variables make it possible to incorporate yes-or-no decisions, sometimes called dichotomous decisions, into an optimization format. Two quick examples will illustrate what we mean:

1. In a plant location model we let $x_j = 1$ if we choose to have a plant at location j and $x_j = 0$ if we do not.

2. In a routing model we let $x_{ijk} = 1$ if truck k goes from city i to city j and $x_{ijk} = 0$ if it does not.

TABLE 7.1 PROTRAC's Capital Budgeting Alternatives

ALTERNATIVE	PRESENT VALUE OF NET RETURN ($000s)	CAPITAL REQUIRED IN YEAR BY ALTERNATIVE ($000s)				
		1	2	3	4	5
Expand Belgian Plant	400	100	50	200	100	0
Expand Small Machine Capacity in U.S.	700	300	200	100	100	100
Establish New Plant in Chile	800	100	200	270	200	100
Expand Large Machine Capacity in U.S.	1000	200	100	400	200	200
Capital Available in Each Year		500	450	700	400	300

Thus, you can see from these examples that the use of 0–1 variables provides us with a new formulational tool. In this section we will see some examples of how 0–1 variables are used to make dichotomous decisions in several applications. We will also see how they can be manipulated to enforce various types of logical conditions.

CAPITAL BUDGETING: AN EXPANSION DECISION

Many firms make decisions on capital investments on an annual basis. In large firms the decisions are often the culmination of a long process that starts with recommendations from individual departments and continues through various firmwide and divisionwide competitions. It is not unusual for the final selection to rest with the board of directors. In smaller firms the process is not so elaborate, but the capital budgeting decision is still a fundamental part of an annual evaluation of the firm's future.

In its simplest form, the capital budgeting decision is a matter of choosing among n alternatives in order to maximize the return subject to constraints on the amount of capital invested over time. As a particular example, suppose that PROTRAC's board of directors faces the data summarized in Table 7.1. The dollar amounts in this table are in thousands. The board must select one or more of the alternatives. If the board decides to expand the Belgian plant, the present value of the net return to the firm is $400,000. This project requires $100,000 of capital in the first year, $50,000 in the second, and so on. The board has previously budgeted up to $500,000 for all capital investments in year 1, up to $450,000 in year 2, and so on.

An ILP Model for Capital Budgeting at PROTRAC This model can be modeled as an ILP in which all the variables are 0–1 variables. This is called a 0–1 ILP. In particular, let $x_i = 1$ if project i is accepted and $x_i = 0$ if project i is not accepted. The model then becomes

$$\text{Max} \quad 400x_1 + 700x_2 + 800x_3 + 1000x_4 \quad \text{(Present value from accepted projects)}$$

$$\text{s.t.} \quad 100x_1 + 300x_2 + 100x_3 + 200x_4 \leq 500 \quad \text{(Capital required in year 1 / Capital available in year 1)}$$

$$50x_1 + 200x_2 + 200x_3 + 100x_4 \leq 450$$

$$200x_1 + 100x_2 + 270x_3 + 400x_4 \leq 700$$

$$100x_1 + 100x_2 + 200x_3 + 200x_4 \leq 400$$

$$100x_2 + 100x_3 + 200x_4 \leq 300$$

$$x_i = 0 \text{ or } 1; i = 1, \dots, 4$$

Here the objective function is the total present value of the net returns and each constraint controls the amount of capital used in each of the five periods.

The LP Relaxation Let us approach this model by first solving the LP relaxation. The formulation and solution are shown in Figure 7.5 . Note that in working with the LP relaxation

Alternative Investment	Expand Belgian Plant	Expand Small Machine Cap. In US	Estab. New Plant in Chile	Expand Large Machine Cap. In US			
		PROTRAC Capital Budget Model ($000s)					
Symbol	X1	X2	X3	X4			
Decision	0.67	0.67	0.33	1.00	Total PV		
PV, Net Return	$400	$700	$800	$1000	$ 2,000.00		
Capital Constraints					Capital Req.	Capital Avail.	Slack
Capital Req. Yr. 1	$100	$300	$100	$200	500.00	<=$500	0
Capital Req. Yr. 2	$50	$200	$200	$100	333.33	<=$450	116.67
Capital Req. Yr. 3	$200	$100	$270	$400	690.00	<=$700	10
Capital Req. Yr. 4	$100	$100	$200	$200	400.00	<=$400	0
Capital Req. Yr. 5		$100	$100	$200	300.00	<=$300	0

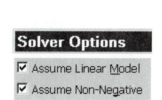

Solver Parameters

Set Target Cell: | Total_PV |

Equal To: ⦿ Max   ○ Min

By Changing Cells:

Decision

Subject to the Constraints:

Capital_Req. <= Capital_Avail.
Decision <= 1

Solver Options

☑ Assume Linear Model

☑ Assume Non-Negative

FIGURE 7.5

LP Relaxation of PROTRAC's Capital Budgeting Model

to a 0–1 ILP, we ignore the constraints $x_i = 0$ or 1. Instead, we add the constraints $x_i \leq 1$, $i = 1, 2, 3, 4$ in addition to the nonnegativity constraints (as shown in Figure 7.5). Thus, in the relaxation, instead of $x_i = 0$ or 1, we have x_i constrained to an interval (i.e., $0 \leq x_i \leq 1$). It would be nice if in the optimal solution each x_i were, fortuitously, to take one extreme or the other of these allowable values (either 0 or 1), for then the original ILP would be solved. Unfortunately, as Figure 7.5 shows, this happened only with x_4; the values of x_1, x_2, and x_3 are fractional.[4] Since x_3 should equal 1 if PROTRAC establishes a plant in Chile and 0 if it does not, the result $x_3 = 0.33$ is not meaningful. We also note that attempting to find a solution to the ILP model by solving the LP relaxation and then rounding does not work very well. Standard nearest-integer rounding rules (i.e., round numbers ≤ 0.499 to 0 and numbers ≥ 0.500 to 1) yield the solution $x_1 = 1, x_2 = 1, x_3 = 0, x_4 = 1$. A quick spreadsheet check for these values reveals that this solution is infeasible since it grossly violates the first constraint.

The Optimal ILP Solution   To obtain the optimal ILP solution for the PROTRAC capital budgeting model, we must use Solver's *integer programming* option. The formulation and solution of the ILP are shown in Figure 7.6. Note that the four constraints that require the x_i's to be ≤ 1 have been dropped. In Solver, the constraint "Decision = binary", that is, "C5:F5 = binary," indicates that all four of the decision variables are 0–1 variables.[5]

The solution shows that PROTRAC management should accept the first three alternatives; x_4 is now zero, whereas in the LP relaxation it was 1. Note also that the objective function value (OV) is now 1900. This is a reduction of 100 (5%) from the optimal value of the objective function for the LP relaxation. In practice, one may well be interested in solving integer programs with hundreds of 0–1 variables. After seeing the analysis of this small

---

[4]Your solution may differ; the model has alternative optimal solutions.
[5]The designation "binary" or "integer" in the Solver dialog can be applied only to decision variables, that is, Solver's "Changing Cells."

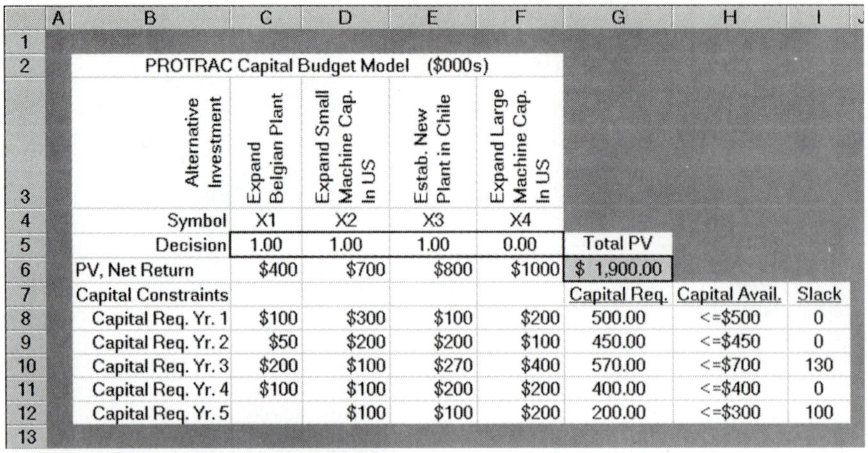

A	B	C	D	E	F	G	H	I	J
1									
2	PROTRAC Capital Budget Model ($000s)								
3		Alternative Investment	Expand Belgian Plant	Expand Small Machine Cap. In US	Estab. New Plant in Chile	Expand Large Machine Cap. In US				
4		Symbol	X1	X2	X3	X4				
5		Decision	1.00	1.00	1.00	0.00	Total PV			
6		PV, Net Return	$400	$700	$800	$1000	$ 1,900.00			
7		Capital Constraints					Capital Req.	Capital Avail.	Slack	
8		Capital Req. Yr. 1	$100	$300	$100	$200	500.00	<=$500	0	
9		Capital Req. Yr. 2	$50	$200	$200	$100	450.00	<=$450	0	
10		Capital Req. Yr. 3	$200	$100	$270	$400	570.00	<=$700	130	
11		Capital Req. Yr. 4	$100	$100	$200	$200	400.00	<=$400	0	
12		Capital Req. Yr. 5		$100	$100	$200	200.00	<=$300	100	
13										

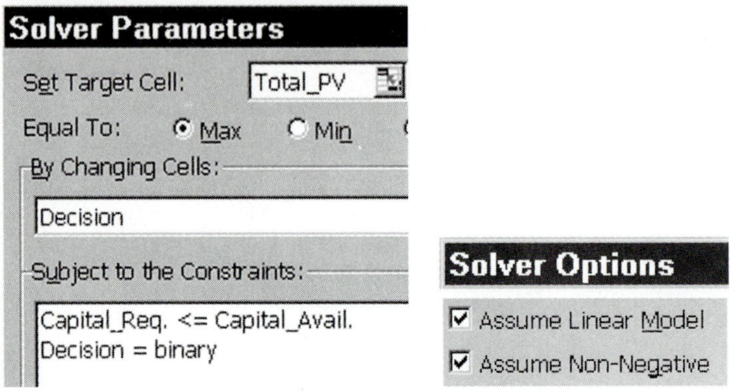

Solver Parameters

Set Target Cell: Total_PV

Equal To: ⊙ Max   ○ Min

By Changing Cells:

Decision

Subject to the Constraints:

Capital_Req. <= Capital_Avail.
Decision = binary

Solver Options

☑ Assume Linear Model
☑ Assume Non-Negative

FIGURE 7.6

ILP Model of PROTRAC's
Capital Budgeting Model

example and the problems associated with the relaxation approach, you can well appreciate the even greater importance, in larger and more complex applications, of using Solver's special methods to solve the ILP model.

LOGICAL CONDITIONS

An important use of 0–1 variables is to impose constraints that arise from logical conditions. Several examples are cited below.

No More Than *k* of *n* Alternatives   Suppose $x_i = 0$ or 1, for $i = 1, \ldots, n$. The constraint

$$x_1 + x_2 + \cdots + x_n \leq k$$

implies that, at most, k alternatives of n possibilities can be selected. That is, since each x_i can be only 0 or 1, the above constraint says that not more than k of them can equal 1. For the data given in the previous table, assume that PROTRAC feels that no more than one foreign project can be accepted. For this reason, the board wants to rule out an alternative that includes both the Belgian expansion and a new plant in Chile. Adding the constraint

$$x_1 + x_3 \leq 1$$

to the ILP in Figure 7.6 implies that the solution can contain at most one of the overseas alternatives.

Dependent Decisions   You can use 0–1 variables to force a dependent relationship on two or more decisions. Suppose, for example, that PROTRAC's management does not want to select alternative k unless it first selects alternative m. The constraint

$$x_k \leq x_m$$ **(7.3)**

or, equivalently,

$$x_k - x_m \leq 0$$

enforces this condition. Note that if m is not selected, then $x_m = 0$. Condition (7.3) then forces x_k to be 0 (i.e., alternative k is not selected). Alternatively, if m is selected, $x_m = 1$; then (7.3) becomes $x_k \leq 1$. This leaves the program free to select $x_k = 1$ or $x_k = 0$.

As an example, again consider Figure 7.4, and suppose that PROTRAC's management feels that, if they are going to expand within the United States, their competitive position implies that they must definitely expand the large machine capacity. Adding the constraint

$$x_2 \leq x_4$$

to the ILP in Figure 7.6 assures that the model cannot select "Expand Small Machine Capacity" unless "Expand Large Machine Capacity" is also selected.

Similarly, suppose the board decided, "If we're going to expand our domestic capacity, we're going to expand both lines." Adding the constraint

$$x_2 = x_4$$

to the ILP in Figure 7.6 would enforce this condition since it requires that x_4 and x_2 take the same values.

Lot Size Constraints Consider a portfolio manager with the following constraints: (1) If he purchases security j, he must purchase at least 200 shares; and (2) he may not purchase more than 1000 shares of security j. Let x_j be the number of shares of security j purchased. The constraint that if j is purchased, then at least 200 shares must be purchased, is called a "minimum lot size" or "batch size" constraint. Note that we cannot create such a constraint in an LP model. The constraints

$$200 \leq x_j \leq 1000$$

do not do the job since they insist that x_j always be at least 200. We want the condition either $x_j = 0$ or $200 \leq x_j \leq 1000$. To achieve this we will make use of a 0–1 variable, say y_j, for security j. The variable y_j has the following interpretation:

- If $y_j = 1$, then purchase security j.
- If $y_j = 0$, do not purchase security j.

Now consider the two constraints

$$x_j \leq 1000y_j \tag{7.4}$$
$$x_j \geq 200y_j \tag{7.5}$$

We see that if $y_j = 1$, then (7.4) and (7.5) imply that $200 \leq x_j \leq 1000$. On the other hand, if $y_j = 0$, then (7.4) implies that $x_j \leq 0$. Similarly, (7.5) implies that $x_j \geq 0$. These two inequalities together imply that $x_j = 0$. Thus, if $y_j = 1$ when we purchase j, and 0 when we do not, we have the proper conditions on x_j.

How can we be sure that $y_j = 1$ if we purchase security j? The inequality (7.4) ($x_j \leq 1000y_j$) guarantees it. We see that in this inequality you cannot have both $x_j > 0$ and $y_j = 0$. Thus, if $x_j > 0$, y_j must equal 1. We see then that inequalities (7.4) and (7.5) together guarantee the "minimum lot size" constraint.

k of m Constraints Mischa Gaas, an exchange student from the Middle East, came to the university for graduate work. He was told by his adviser that anyone intending to earn a Ph.D. degree in history had to satisfy at least two of the following criteria: "You must be single, rich, or crazy." Unfortunately Mischa was destitute and married. In fact, before entering into matrimony, he spent years looking for a bride who was tall, dark, beautiful, and rich. Finally in frustration he said to himself, "Three out of four ain't bad"; and the woman he chose (who chose him) was not rich. These are examples of models in which k of m constraints must be satisfied. In general notation, let the "superset" of m constraints be

$$g_i(x_1, \ldots, x_n) \leq b_i, \qquad i = 1, \ldots, m$$

Now introduce m new 0–1 variables y_i and let U be chosen a very large number, so large that, for each i, $g_i(x_i, \ldots, x_n) \leq U$ for every x satisfying any set of k inequalities taken from the above m. Then the following $m + 1$ constraints express the desired condition:

$$\sum_{i=1}^{m} y_i = k$$

$$g_i(x_1, \ldots, x_n) \leq b_i y_i + (1 - y_i)U, \qquad i = 1, \ldots, m$$

Note that $\sum_{i=1}^{m} y_i = k$ forces k of the y_i variables to have the value 1. This means that exactly k of the above inequalities are equivalent to

$$g_i(x_1, \ldots, x_n) \leq b_i$$

The remaining inequalities are equivalent to

$$g_i(x_1, \ldots, x_n) \leq U$$

and by the assumption of the very large number choice for U, each such constraint is redundant.

 7.5   **AN ILP VIGNETTE: STECO'S WAREHOUSE LOCATION— A FIXED CHARGE MODEL**

In order to conserve capital, STECO, a steel wholesaler, leases its regional warehouses. It currently has a candidate list of three warehouses it can lease. The cost per month to lease warehouse i is F_i. Also, warehouse i can load a maximum of T_i trucks per month.

There are four sales districts, and the typical monthly demand in district j is d_j truckloads. The average cost of sending a truck from warehouse i to district j is c_{ij}. STECO wants to know which warehouses to lease and how many trucks to send from each warehouse to each district. Note that STECO pays no lease cost for a given warehouse unless it plans to dispatch at least one truck from it. If any trucks are sent from a warehouse, then the entire monthly lease amount must be paid. Lot size models incorporating this cost behavior are common and are called *fixed charge models*. A flow-diagram representation of STECO's fixed charge model is illustrated in Figure 7.7.

The data for this model are presented in Table 7.2. We see, for example, that it costs $7750 to lease warehouse A for a month and that up to 200 trucks can be loaded and dispatched from this warehouse. Also, the monthly demand in sales district 1 is 100 truckloads. The numbers in the body of the table are the variable costs of sending a truck from warehouse i to sales district j (e.g., the variable cost of sending a truck from B to 3 is $100).

MODELING CONSIDERATIONS

If you want to attack this model with a mixed integer linear programming (MILP) model, you must first decide which variables (if any) you will treat as integers and which (if any) you will treat as continuous variables.

The decision to lease a particular warehouse or not seems to require a 0–1 variable since the cost of leasing warehouse i does not vary with the level of activity (i.e., with the number of trucks sent from it). We will thus let

$$y_i = 1 \text{ if we lease warehouse } i, \text{ and } y_i = 0 \text{ if we do not}$$

At first glance it also seems appropriate to treat the number of trucks sent from a warehouse to a district as an integer variable. Trucks are, after all, integer entities, and it does not make sense to talk about sending one third of a truck from here to there. However, several factors could persuade us to treat the number of trucks as a continuous variable.

1. This is a planning model, not a detailed operating model. In actual operation the demands in the districts will vary. STECO management will have to devise methods of handling this

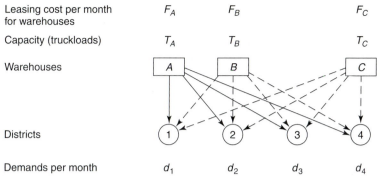

| Leasing cost per month for warehouses | F_A | F_B | F_C |

| Capacity (truckloads) | T_A | T_B | T_C |

Warehouses

Districts

| Demands per month | d_1 | d_2 | d_3 | d_4 |

FIGURE 7.7

Warehouse Location Model

	COST PER TRUCK SALES DISTRICT ($)				MONTHLY CAPACITY (NUMBER OF TRUCKS)	MONTHLY LEASING COSTS ($)
TABLE 7.2 Warehouse Location Data						
WAREHOUSE	1	2	3	4		
A	170	40	70	160	200	7750
B	150	195	100	10	250	4000
C	100	240	140	60	300	5500
Monthly Demand (truckloads)	100	90	110	60		

uncertainty. Trucks assigned to a specific warehouse might be allocated among adjacent districts on a daily as-needed basis, or STECO might use common carriers to satisfy excess demand. At any rate, the number of trucks that the solution to our mathematical programming model says should go from warehouse i to district j is only an *approximation* of what will actually happen on any given day. Thus, treating these entities as continuous variables and rounding to the nearest integer to determine how many trucks to assign to each warehouse should provide a useful answer and a good approximation of the *average* monthly operating cost.

2. Treating the number of trucks as integer variables may make the model much more difficult to solve. This is simply a reflection of the general fact that the greater the number of integer variables and the greater the number of integer values each can take on, the more difficult it is to solve an ILP.

3. It certainly costs much more to lease one of the warehouses than to send a truck from a warehouse to a sales district. The relative magnitude of these costs again implies that it is relatively more important to treat the "lease or not lease" decision as an integer variable, as opposed to the trucks. To illustrate this point, note that it costs $5500 per month to lease warehouse C and $60 to send a truck from warehouse C to sales district 4. Suppose that we modeled the problem as an LP. If $y_C = 0.4$ in the optimal solution, rounding to 0 causes a $2200 change in the OV (optimal value of the objective function), whereas if $x_{C4} = 57.8$, rounding either up or down has less than a $60 effect.

In summary, there are, in this example, arguments that suggest little advantage to treating the number of trucks as integers. We thus proceed to formulate STECO's warehouse location model as an MILP, and we will have a pleasant surprise.

THE MILP MODEL
To model STECO's model as an MILP, we will let

$$y_i = 1 \text{ if lease warehouse } i, \quad y_i = 0 \text{ if not;} \quad i = A, B, C$$
$$x_{ij} = \text{the number of trucks sent from warehouse } i \text{ to district } j;$$
$$i = A, B, C; \quad j = 1, \ldots, 4$$

We shall now construct the model by developing each of its component parts. First consider the objective function. The expression

$$170x_{A1} + 40x_{A2} + 70x_{A3} + \cdots + 60x_{C4}$$

is the total cost associated with the trucks, and

$$7750y_A + 4000y_B + 5500y_C$$

is the total leasing cost. Thus, the total cost-minimizing objective function is

$$\text{Min } 7750y_A + 4000y_B + 5500y_C + 170x_{A1} + \cdots + 60x_{C4}$$

Now consider the constraints. We must consider both demand and capacity. The following constraint guarantees that demand will be satisfied at sales district 1:

$$x_{A1} + x_{B1} + x_{C1} \geq 100$$

Four constraints like this (one for each district) are required to guarantee that demand is satisfied.

The constraint

$$x_{A1} + x_{A2} + x_{A3} + x_{A4} \leq 200y_A \quad \text{or} \quad x_{A1} + x_{A2} + x_{A3} + x_{A4} - 200y_A \leq 0$$

serves two purposes. It guarantees that capacity at warehouse A is not exceeded, and it forces us to lease warehouse A if we want to send anything out of this warehouse. To see this, recall that y_i, or in this case y_A, must equal 0 or 1. First, assume that $y_A = 1$. The inequality above then becomes

$$x_{A1} + x_{A2} + x_{A3} + x_{A4} \leq 200$$

APPLICATION CAPSULE   **How Can I Help You? AT&T Woos Customers by Saving Them Money with the Aid of a Mixed Integer Program**

AT&T, a major supplier of services to the telemarketing industry, is always looking for ways of helping its customers expand their operations. One of the models facing companies that do a large volume of telemarketing (using toll-free 800 numbers to take customer orders) is deciding on the number and location of sites for telemarketing offices. It was therefore in AT&T's best interests to develop a set of programs that would aid its customers in this process.

AT&T's researchers soon found that, contrary to the general perception, the location of telemarketing offices was not always dictated primarily by real estate or communications costs. Rather, political or psychological considerations often played a major role. Thus, an office might be located in the same city as the regional headquarters or in a city where upper management wanted to have a presence, even though these might not be cost-efficient choices.

AT&T developed a model that analyzes the costs of plausible candidate sites and allows users to evaluate various site configurations on the basis of both quantitative and qualitative factors. The model, a mixed integer program similar to a facility-location planning model, is solved by means of a branch-and-bound code. It answers four questions:

1. How many telemarketing centers should be opened?
2. Where should centers be located?
3. What geographic regions should be served by each center?
4. How many attendant positions are required at each location?

Originally developed on a mainframe, the model was adapted for use on a PC, with more graphic display and user interaction added. It provides not only an optimal solution that minimizes the three operational cost factors (communications, labor, and real estate) but alternative solutions as well, so that the user can take factors other than costs into account. To this end, an analytical hierarchy process, described in Chapter 9, has been added to the model, allowing users to include qualitative or subjective factors in the decision process.

The AT&T model has greatly accelerated the siting of telemarketing offices while saving customers many hours of research and consulting costs—savings that some customers estimated at up to $240,000. Moreover, a number of customers have reported savings averaging $1 million per year from use of the locations identified by the model rather than ones they had previously considered.

From AT&T's point of view, the model has proven its worth in terms of enhanced customer relations and sales of services. At least 46 AT&T customers have made decisions on site locations with the aid of the model, in the process committing themselves to $375 million per year in network services and $31 million in new equipment purchases. As a result of business generated by the model, AT&T's share of this market has risen from 30% to 40%. (See Spencer et. al.)

STECO Warehouse Location Model

Unit Costs	Whse. Mo. Lease Cost	Unit Cost per Truck From/To	District 1	District 2	District 3	District 4		Mo. No. Trucks Capacity
Whse A	$7750	A	$170	$40	$70	$160		200
Whse B	$4000	B	$150	$195	$100	$10		250
Whse C	$5500	C	$100	$240	$140	$60		300

Decisions	Yes/No	No. Trucks From/To	District 1	District 2	District 3	District 4	Total Trucks	Capacity
Lease Whse A	1	A	0	90	110	0	200	<=200
Lease Whse B	0	B	0	0	0	0	-	<=0
Lease Whse C	1	C	100	0	0	60	160	<=300
		Total	100	90	110	60		
		Mo. Demand	>=100	>=90	>=110	>=60		

Total Cost	Whse. Mo. Lease Cost	Total Truck Cost From/To	District 1	District 2	District 3	District 4	Total Truck Cost	Total Mo. Cost
Lease Whse A	$7,750	A	$0	$3,600	$7,700	$0	$11,300	$19,050
Lease Whse B	$0	B	$0	$0	$0	$0	$0	$0
Lease Whse C	$5,500	C	$10,000	$0	$0	$3,600	$13,600	$19,100
Total	$13,250	Total	$10,000	$3,600	$7,700	$3,600	$24,900	$38,150

Cell	Formula	Copy To
J9	= J4*C9	J10:J11
C16	= C9*C4	C17:C18
E16	= E4*E9	E16:H18
J16	= C16+I16	J17:J19

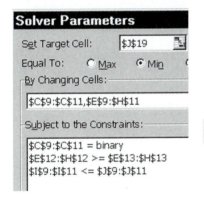

Solver Parameters

Set Target Cell: $J$19
Equal To: ○ Max   ● Min
By Changing Cells:
$C$9:$C$11,$E$9:$H$11
Subject to the Constraints:
$C$9:$C$11 = binary
$E$12:$H$12 >= $E$13:$H$13
$I$9:$I$11 <= $J$9:$J$11

Solver Options
☑ Assume Linear Model
☑ Assume Non-Negative

FIGURE 7.8
STECO's Warehouse Location Model

that is, no more than a total of 200 trucks can be sent out of warehouse A. You have previously seen this type of capacity constraint in transportation models. Now consider the case when y_A is 0. Then the inequality becomes

$$x_{A1} + x_{A2} + x_{A3} + x_{A4} \le 0$$

that is, no items can be sent out of warehouse A. This constraint then guarantees that nothing can be sent out of warehouse A unless $y_A = 1$. Note that when $y_A = 1$, the term $7750y_A$ in the objective function equals 7750. Thus, we see that nothing is sent out of warehouse A unless we incur the monthly (fixed charge) leasing cost for that particular warehouse. Three such constraints, one for each warehouse, are needed in the model.

The complete spreadsheet model and its solution are shown in Figure 7.8.

Output Analysis   A quick glance at the output shows that the optimal values of all truck allocations are integer, even though we decided in the formulation to allow these variables to be continuous. Was this just fortuitous? The answer is no. Here is the reason. We started with a warehouse location model. Note that once we have decided which warehouses to lease, the problem of finding the optimal allocation of trucks is an LP transportation model. In Chapter 6 we saw that if the supply available at each warehouse and the demand at each district are integers, then the optimal solution to the transportation model will be all integers.

We now have enough information to conclude that the optimal solution to the above warehouse location model with integer supplies and demands will always include an integer allocation of trucks. The argument involves two steps: (1) The optimal solution must lease some set of warehouses, and (2) every possible set of leased warehouses yields an integer allocation of trucks.

For this model, then, we now see that it would have been naive and costly to require as additional constraints that the x_{ij}'s be integer. The word is "Never pay for a free good."

7.6   THE BRANCH-AND-BOUND ILP ALGORITHM

The **branch-and-bound** procedure used by Solver is currently the most efficient general-purpose method for optimizing ILPs. The general idea is to partition the set of all feasible solutions to a given model into smaller and nonoverlapping subsets. Bounds on the value of the best solution in each subset are then computed. Then the branch-and-bound procedure eliminates certain subsets from consideration, thereby *partially* (as opposed to completely) *enumerating* all of the possible feasible solutions. The following example illustrates how Solver uses branch and bound to optimize ILPs.

AN ILP EXAMPLE
Let us begin with a specific model, which for convenience we refer to as (P1):

$$\text{Max } x_1 + 5x_2$$
$$\text{s.t. } 11x_1 + 6x_2 \leq 66$$
$$5x_1 + 50x_2 \leq 225$$
$$x_1, x_2 \geq 0 \text{ and integer} \qquad \textbf{(P1)}$$

In the following discussion, it will be helpful to use the graphical method discussed in Section 7.3.

Step 1: Solving the LP Relaxation   The first step is to solve the LP relaxation of (P1). If luck is with us, we may have an optimal solution right away, since it is always true that if the solution to the LP relaxation satisfies the integer restriction, it is the optimal solution. We will now use the graphical solution technique to solve the LP relaxation of (P1) and test our luck. Figure 7.9 shows (by shading) the feasible set for the LP relaxation of (P1). The dots in the shaded region are the feasible points that also satisfy the integrality conditions. Note that there are 27 such points, including the points on the axes such as $(0, 4)$ and $(4, 0)$, which are feasible. Figure 7.9 also shows the optimal corner for the LP. To find the optimal numerical values for the decision variables, we solve for the point where the two active constraints intersect; that is, we solve

$$11x_1 + 6x_2 = 66 \qquad \text{and} \qquad 5x_1 + 50x_2 = 225$$

for x_1 and x_2. This yields $x_1^* = 3.75, x_2^* = 4.125$. Since these values are not integers, we have *not* solved (P1). We have obtained some information about the problem, however.

1. Recall that OV stands for optimal value of the objective function. When we find the OV for the LP relaxation, we establish an upper bound for the OV of (P1). Let us call this upper bound U. Thus, since the objective function is $x_1 + 5x_2$, we know that

$$\text{OV for (P1)} \leq 3.75 + 5(4.125) = 24.375 = U$$

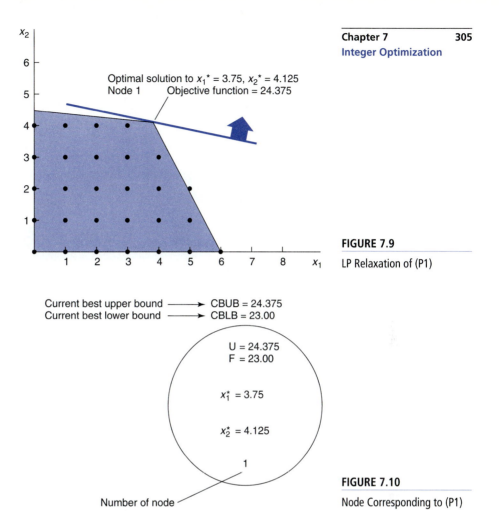

FIGURE 7.9

LP Relaxation of (P1)

FIGURE 7.10

Node Corresponding to (P1)

2. As you can see in Figure 7.9, if we take the optimal solution to the relaxed model and round it down to $x_1 = 3, x_2 = 4$ (truncate the fractional portion), we obtain a feasible solution to (P1). Now evaluating the objective function at this point (or at any other *feasible* point), we establish a *lower bound* for the OV of (P1). Let us call this value F. Hence,

$$\text{OV for (P1)} \geq 3 + 5(4) = 23 = F$$

The value of F (i.e., 23) may or may not be the OV for (P1). At present, we cannot tell. All we now know is that $23 \leq \text{OV} \leq 24.375$. We must find out whether a better solution can be found. To do this, we *branch*.

The information about a branch-and-bound solution is typically summarized in a tree-like diagram. The first node in such a diagram is shown in Figure 7.10. This node will look somewhat different from the other nodes in our tree, since we place the values for our *current* best upper bound (CBUB) on the OV and our current best lower bound (CBLB) on the OV above this node.

Step 2: Branching We proceed by dividing (P1) into two smaller models. In this example, we will branch on x_1. This is an arbitrary choice. We could just as well have branched on x_2. The branching process makes use of the fact that in the optimal solution to (P1), either $x_1 \leq 3$ or $x_1 \geq 4$. Why is this true? Because there are no integer values for x_1 in the region eliminated by forcing x_1 to be ≤ 3 or x_1 to be ≥ 4. The values of x_1 that are eliminated are $3 < x_1 < 4$. Since x_1 must be an integer, we have not eliminated any feasible points from the feasible set for (P1). We have, however, eliminated points (i.e., noninteger values) from

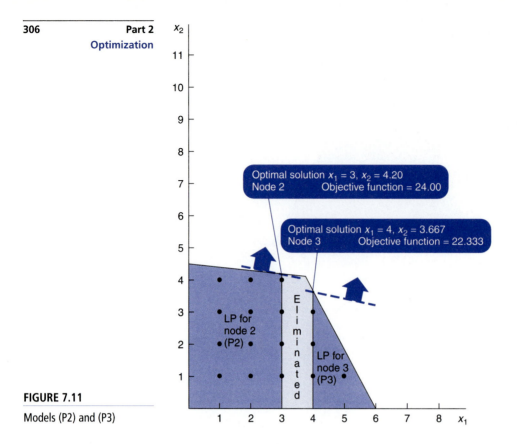

FIGURE 7.11

Models (P2) and (P3)

the feasible set of the LP relaxation of (P1). Indeed, we see that the optimal value of x_1, in the LP relaxation of (P1), is neither ≤ 3 nor ≥ 4, and hence the current optimal point (intentionally) has been eliminated by the branching process. This process creates one of its two new models by appending the constraint $x_1 \leq 3$ to (P1). The other new model is created by appending the constraint $x_1 \geq 4$ to (P1). We thus have

$$
\begin{aligned}
\text{Max} \quad & x_1 + 5x_2 \\
\text{s.t.} \quad & 11x_1 + 6x_2 \leq 66 \\
& 5x_1 + 50x_2 \leq 225 \\
& x_1 \leq 3 \\
& x_1, x_2 \geq 0 \text{ and integer} \quad \text{(P2)}
\end{aligned}
$$

and

$$
\begin{aligned}
\text{Max} \quad & x_1 + 5x_2 \\
\text{s.t.} \quad & 11x_1 + 6x_2 \leq 66 \\
& 5x_1 + 50x_2 \leq 225 \\
& x_1 \geq 4 \\
& x_1, x_2 \geq 0 \text{ and integer} \quad \text{(P3)}
\end{aligned}
$$

These two models are shown in Figure 7.11. Figure 7.11 reveals two interesting facts:

1. We have split the (P1) feasible set into two pieces and eliminated from consideration a region containing no integer points. The eliminated region is shaded light blue. The boundary lines are *not* in the region eliminated.

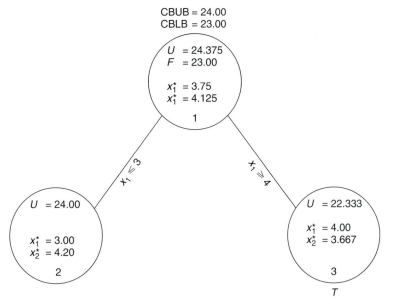

CBUB = 24.00
CBLB = 23.00

U = 24.375
F = 23.00

x_1^* = 3.75
x_1^* = 4.125

1

$x_1 \leqslant 3$

$x_1 \geqslant 4$

U = 24.00

x_1^* = 3.00
x_2^* = 4.20

2

U = 22.333

x_1^* = 4.00
x_2^* = 3.667

3

T

FIGURE 7.12

Tree with Three Nodes
Corresponding to (P1), (P2),
and (P3)

2. All of the feasible *integer* solutions to (P1) are now contained in either (P2) or (P3). Since the objective functions for (P1), (P2), and (P3) are identical, it follows that *either the optimal solution to (P2) or the optimal solution to (P3) must be the optimal solution to (P1),* the original ILP. Thus, we may forget (P1) and consider only (P2) and (P3).

Creating a Tree The branch-and-bound approach proceeds by a process that can be illustrated with a tree. The first step in this process is to solve the LP relaxations for models (P2) and (P3). The optimal solutions are shown in Figure 7.11. In model (P2) the value of U is provided by the optimal value of the objective function for the LP relaxation (namely 24.00). For (P3), we obtain $U = 22.333$. We have already observed that the optimal solution to (P1) is either in (P2) or (P3); thus the OV for (P1) must be $\leq$ the Max of the values of U provided by these two nodes. Since node 2 yields a U of 24.00 and node 3 yields a U of 22.333, our *current* best upper bound is 24.00. We thus change the value of CBUB above node 1. To change the value of CBLB, we would have to have obtained a point that is feasible in (P1) and yields a value of the objective function > 23.00, our CBLB. Since neither node 2 nor node 3 has an all-integer solution, we have not obtained a new feasible solution. (Although in this problem we could round down at nodes 2 and 3 to obtain new feasible solutions to [P1], in general the search for feasible points may be difficult, and therefore we wish to present a procedure that does not include a new feasible solution at each node.) Thus the value of CBLB remains as it was.

Figure 7.12 incorporates the information from (P2) and (P3) into a decision diagram called a *tree.* To determine what to do next we consider the nodes at the bottom of our tree, nodes 2 and 3 in this case. We note that the upper bound on node 3 is 22.333, and the current value of CBLB is 23.00. We have thus *already found a better solution than we could possibly obtain in the feasible set for (P3).* Therefore, *we can ignore (P3) and concentrate our efforts on (P2).* To indicate that (P3) has now been eliminated from consideration, we place in Figure 7.12 a T below (P3), which means that *that particular branch of the tree is now terminated.* In general, if, after calculating the value of U for a node, we find that $U \leq$ CBLB, then this node can be eliminated from further consideration by writing a T below the node, indicating that this branch of the tree has been terminated.

Let us now continue by considering (P2). We still do not know the optimal solution to (P2), for we still have a noninteger value for x_2^*. Since (P2) is an ILP, we attack it with branch and bound, and to do this we must branch again. The variable x_1 is integer in the optimal solution to (P2). Hence we must branch on x_2, which we do by using the constraints $x_2 \leq 4$ or $x_2 \geq 5$. Doing this, we replace (P2) with the models

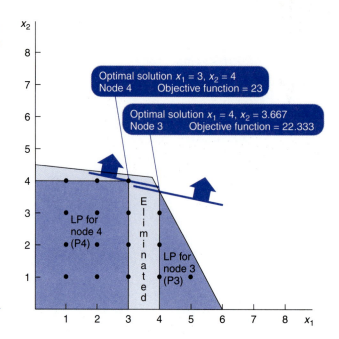

FIGURE 7.13

Models (P3), (P4), and (P5)

$$\text{Max} \quad x_1 + 5x_2$$
$$\text{s.t.} \quad 11x_1 + 6x_2 \;\; \leq 66$$
$$5x_1 + 50x_2 \;\; \leq 225$$
$$x_1 \;\; \leq 3$$
$$x_2 \;\; \leq 4$$
$$x_1, x_2 \geq 0 \text{ and integer} \qquad \text{(P4)}$$

$$\text{Max} \quad x_1 + 5x_2$$
$$\text{s.t.} \quad 11x_1 + 6x_2 \;\; \leq 66$$
$$5x_1 + 50x_2 \;\; \leq 225$$
$$x_1 \;\; \leq 3$$
$$x_2 \;\; \geq 5$$
$$x_1, x_2 \geq 0 \text{ and integer} \qquad \text{(P5)}$$

Note that the constraints for (P4) are the constraints for (P1); that is,

$$11x_1 + 6x_2 \;\; \leq 66$$
$$5x_1 + 50x_2 \leq 225$$

plus the constraint that was appended to define (P2) (i.e., $x_1 \leq 3$), plus the new constraint that is appended to define (P4) (i.e., $x_2 \leq 4$). A similar interpretation can be given to (P5). The result of this branch is shown in Figure 7.13, and the new tree is shown in Figure 7.14.

The Final Tree In comparing Figures 7.13 and 7.11, there are several important features to be noted:

1. Model (P3) remains unchanged (exactly as it was in Figure 7.11).

2. An additional set of noninteger points, including the optimal solution to the LP relaxation of (P2), has been eliminated from consideration. All of the newly eliminated area that was in the feasible set of the LP relaxation of (P1) is shaded light blue.

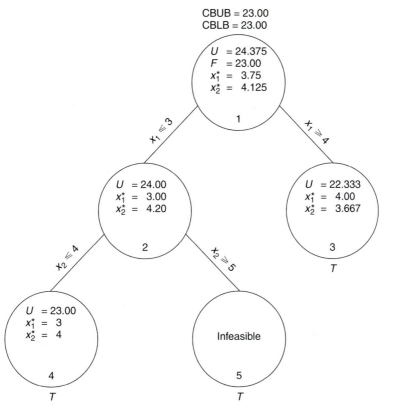

CBUB = 23.00
CBLB = 23.00

FIGURE 7.14

The Completed Tree

3. The constraint set for the LP relaxation of (P5) is empty. There are no points that satisfy the constraints $5x_1 + 50x_2 \le 225$, $x_1 \ge 0$, $x_2 \ge 5$. This also means that (P5) has no feasible solution, which means that we may now forget about (P5). This is indicated by placing, in Figure 7.14, a T below node 5, which terminates another branch of the tree. We now see that there are two causes for termination: Terminate a node when

1. Its U is $\le$ CBLB or

2. It represents an infeasible model.

Thus, we need only concentrate on (P4), and solving the LP relaxation of that model, as shown in Figure 7.13, reveals that the optimal solution to the relaxation of (P4), namely $(x_1^* = 3, x_2^* = 4)$, is all-integer. This means $(x_1^* = 3, \ x_2^* = 4)$ is the optimal solution to (P4). For this reason, (P4) is another terminal node on our tree and, in Figure 7.14, we have accordingly placed a T under that node. Thus, we have an illustration of the third cause for termination. In summary, terminate a node when

1. Its U is $\le$ CBLB,

2. It represents an infeasible model, or

3. The LP relaxation provides a solution to the integer model represented by that node.

Referring again to Figure 7.14, we note that the value of CBUB has changed from the value it held in Figure 7.12. The branch on node 2 yielded an infeasible model (node 5) and a model (node 4) with a U of 23.00. Thus the current best upper bound (CBUB) is reduced from 24.00 to 23.00. In node 4, we also have an all-integer solution. This point is thus a feasible solution to (P1). It yields a value of 23.00 for the objective function. Since our current best lower bound is 23.00, we do not change the CBLB.

In general, *when all nodes have been terminated, the branch-and-bound method is complete.* The optimal solution to the original model (P1) is the solution that established the CBLB. In this case CBLB is 23.00, and $(x_1^* = 3, x_2^* = 4)$ is the optimal solution to (Pl). Upon termination, as in Figure 7.14, it will always be the case that CBLB = CBUB.

MILPs

The branch-and-bound procedure described above can be easily modified to work on MILPs. Consider a small modification of the ILP analyzed above. In particular, assume that the model is

$$\text{Max } x_1 \ + 5x_2$$
$$\text{s.t.} \quad 11x_1 + 6x_2 \quad\ \leq 66$$
$$5x_1 \ + 50x_2 \ \leq 225$$
$$x_1 \geq 0 \text{ and integer, } x_2 \geq 0$$

The only change from the previous model is that x_2 is no longer required to be an integer (i.e., x_2 can be any nonnegative number). To solve this model, we start as before with the LP relaxation in Figure 7.9. Since x_1^* is not integer (it assumes the value 3.75), we obtain the initial value of F by rounding x_1^* down to 3. The value of x_2^* is permitted to remain fractional at 4.125. Thus, we obtain $F = 3 + 5(4.125) = 23.625$. As before, CBUB = 24.375, but now CBLB = 23.625. Now we branch, as previously, on x_1 by introducing the constraints $x_1 \leq 3$ or $x_1 \geq 4$. This yields Figure 7.11. The following information can be read from this figure:

1. Node 2 yields a U of 24.00, and node 3 yields a U of 22.333; thus the CBUB becomes 24.00.

2. The optimal solution to node 2 has an integer value for x_1; thus this is a feasible solution to (Pl). It follows that

    a. We achieve a new current best lower bound of 24.00.
    b. Node 2 can be terminated.

3. At node 3 $U \leq$ CBLB; thus node 3 can be terminated.

Since both nodes have been terminated, the optimal solution is the solution that yielded the CBLB. Thus, $x_1^* = 3.00$ and $x_2^* = 4.20$ is the optimal solution.

SUMMARY OF BRANCH AND BOUND

We summarize Solver's application of branch and bound to ILP. The adaptation for MILP should be obvious. In what follows, the phrase "solve a node" means "use Solver's simplex method to optimize the LP relaxation of the ILP corresponding to the node." A "solved node" is one for which this has been done. Otherwise, the node is "unsolved."

1. Solve the original ILP formulation. The OV for the relaxation is the value of U. If the optimal solution is all-integer, it is optimal for the ILP. Otherwise, find a feasible point for the ILP, and let F denote the OV at this point. Set the current best upper bound (CBUB) equal to U and the current best lower bound (CBLB) equal to F.

2. Commence with any solved node that has not been terminated. From this node (the parent), *branch* so as to create two new unsolved nodes (the successors) with the property that the optimal solution to one of the successor ILPs will be the optimal solution to the parent ILP. The branching may be accomplished by taking any fractional component, say x_i^*, of the optimal solution to the parent's relaxation. Let $[x_i^*]$ be the truncation of x_i^* to its integer part. Then $[x_i^*] + 1$ is the next integer larger than x_i^*. One successor will be the parent's model augmented by the constraint $x_i \leq [x_i^*]$. The other successor is formed by augmenting the parent's model with $x_i \geq [x_i^*] + 1$. Then either pick another solved node and repeat or go to step 3.

3. Commence with any unsolved node and attempt to solve. The OV for the relaxation is the value of U at the node. Terminate this branch if the LP relaxation is infeasible or if $U \leq$ CBLB or if the optimal solution is all-integer. If the optimal solution is all-integer, evaluate the objective function at this point; call the value F. Compare CBLB with F. If $F >$ CBLB, set CBLB = F. If the branch is not terminated, either repeat step 3 or go to step 2. If the node is terminated, go to step 4.

4. If all nodes are terminated, the optimal solution to the original ILP is the all-integer solution that produced the value CBLB.

From the above summary, the original ILP is decomposed into a sequence of LP models, each augmented with additional constraints on the decision variables and optimized, as part of the branch-and-bound algorithm. Hence, the branch-and-bound method used by Solver uses *numerous* optimizations of LP formulations to solve an integer program. Thus it is, in general, much more time-consuming to solve ILPs than LPs.

The operation of the branch-and-bound procedure can be observed during optimization of an ILP model by Solver as illustrated in Figure 7.15. Solver displays the progress of the branching sequence by showing a "Branch" iteration count that reflects the number of separate LP optimizations carried out thus far during the branch-and-bound procedure. The "Trial Solution" is the count of the number of corner points visited during the current LP's simplex optimization and the "Set Cell" is the value of the objective function cell during the current LP optimization. In the example of Figure 7.15, 1421 relaxed LPs have been optimized thus far; Solver is evaluating the eleventh corner point of the 1422nd LP being optimized; and that LP's objective function value is currently \$39,366.

Since for some ILPs the number of branches, and hence the number of LPs to solve, can become very large, the Solver Options dialog, shown in Figure 7.16, includes a Tolerance option—relevant only for IP models. The default Tolerance value of 5% means that the branch-and-bound procedure is continued only until the ratio (CBUB − CBLB)/CBLB is less than or equal to 5%. Because these bounds bracket the OV of the optimum ILP solution, this guarantees that the CBLB solution is within 5% of the optimum. A higher Tolerance value speeds up Solver at the risk of a reported solution potentially further from the true ILP optimum. Setting Tolerance to 0% forces Solver to find the true ILP optimum at the potential cost of much longer solution times caused by solving additional relaxed LP models in the branch-and-bound procedure.

Although Solver's branch-and-bound procedure does not support it, for very large models the branch-and-bound method can be stopped before all nodes have been terminated. The node producing the CBLB will provide an *approximate solution* to the original ILP. In this case CBLB will be less than the value CBUB, and the difference CBUB − CBLB indicates the closeness of the approximation.

Finally, let us comment on the application of the branch-and-bound technique to special ILPs with 0–l variables. In this case, suppose that one is branching on the 0–l variable y_1. Then one successor will have $y_1 = 0$. The other will have $y_1 = 1$. For the ILP in 0–l

FIGURE 7.15

Solver Messages During IP Optimization

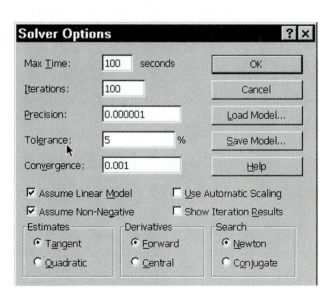

FIGURE 7.16

Solver Options for ILP

variables, another type of branch-and-bound procedure, sometimes called *partial enumeration,* has enjoyed considerable success. Also, for the general ILP other optimization methods have been applied. These include *cutting-plane methods* and *Lagrangian relaxation.* As stated at the outset of this chapter, our introductory discussion covers only the ILP technique used by Solver and merely touches the surface of this intricate topic.

SENSITIVITY

We have seen that the branch-and-bound method used by Solver is, in general, much more time-consuming to solve ILPs than LPs. Unfortunately, it is also true that the solution to an ILP contains much less information than the solution to an LP. As shown in Figure 7.17 in which the Sensitivity Report was requested following optimization of an ILP, *the solution to an ILP does not contain sensitivity information.* No information concerning the sensitivity of the OV (i.e., the optimal value of the objective function) to changes in the RHS of a constraint or to a change in the value of an objective function coefficient is produced. In other words, *an ILP solution does not include information that is equivalent to the shadow price, reduced cost, and objective coefficient sensitivity information in an LP.* This does not imply that changes in the RHS or in an objective coefficient do not affect the solution to an ILP. They do. Indeed, the solutions to ILPs can be extremely sensitive to changes in parameter values.

The following somewhat unrealistic, but for the present purpose illustrative, capital budgeting example will illustrate these points:

$$\text{Max} \quad 10x_1 + 100x_2 + 1000x_3$$
$$\text{s.t.} \quad 29x_1 + 30x_2 + 31x_3 \leq b_1$$
$$x_1, x_2, x_3 \text{ are 0 or 1}$$

The model is easily solved by inspection. Table 7.3 shows the optimal solution and the optimal value of the objective function (OV) for various values of the RHS parameter b_1. From this data we note that a change in 1 unit in the right-hand side of the constraint (say from 29 to 30) increases the OV by a factor of 10 (from 10 to 100). Clearly, if you were aware of such an opportunity, you would be anxious to make such a change.

Unfortunately, no such sensitivity information is produced when you solve an ILP with Solver. You receive from Solver only the optimal solution and the OV. Sensitivity information, such as that shown above, can be determined only by repeatedly optimizing the ILP model with new parameter values and manually tabulating the results. When the model has a number of constraints, using this approach to generate useful sensitivity data for an ILP

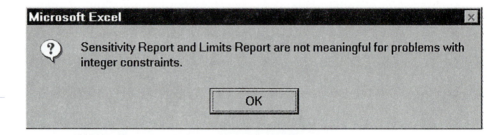

FIGURE 7.17

No Solver Sensitivity Report for ILP Models

TABLE 7.3 ILP Sensitivity Data				
	OPTIMAL SOLUTION			
b_1	x_1	x_2	x_3	OV
29	1	0	0	10
30	0	1	0	100
31	0	0	1	1000

can require you to run a large number of alternative Solver formulations. This can be an expensive and time-consuming activity.

HEURISTIC ALGORITHMS

Because of the importance of the applications, integer programming is currently an active area of research. Much of this research is in the area of heuristic algorithms. These are algorithms designed to efficiently produce "good," although not necessarily optimal, solutions.

> From the viewpoint of the manager, a heuristic procedure may certainly be as acceptable as, and possibly even preferable to, a "more exact" ILP algorithm that produces an optimal solution. The dominant considerations should be the amount of insight and guidance the model can provide and the cost of obtaining these.

7.7 NOTES ON IMPLEMENTATION OF INTEGER OPTIMIZATION MODELS

Integer solutions are an important, indeed essential, condition for the application of optimization models to many important real-world models. Recent advances in research and computer technology have made it possible to make real progress on models that involve variables that must be treated as integers. Two examples appear in the Application Capsules in this chapter. Other examples follow.

KELLY-SPRINGFIELD

The Kelly-Springfield Tire Company has a model-based system to coordinate sales forecasting, inventory control, production planning, and distribution decisions. One crucial link in this system is the production planning model. Central to this model is the effect of setup time. In the manufacture of each particular line of tires, a machine is set up by installing a piece of equipment (called a die) particular to that line. It takes a fixed amount of time (and thus a fixed cost) to remove one die from a machine and insert another. In other words, there is a fixed changeover or setup cost of moving from the production of one line of tires to another, no matter how many tires you decide to produce after the machine is set up. The decision to set up (i.e., to produce a particular line in a given production period) or not, is treated as a 0–1 variable in the MILP used to attack this model. The total integrated system (including the production planning system) is credited with impressive results. The system is estimated to have yielded savings of $500,000 a year. After an improved system was installed, average unit inventory decreased by 19%, customer service improved, productivity increased, and additional savings totaling $7.9 million annually resulted.

FLYING TIGER LINE

Another interesting application concerns the use of integer programming by the Flying Tiger Line (an all-cargo airline now owned by Federal Express) in approaching two strategic questions: the design of its service network and the selection and deployment of its aircraft fleet. The size of the MILP used to attack this model and the cost of solving it are staggering when your primary exposure has been to classroom models. One model for 33 cities, eight hubs (locations where cargo can be interchanged), and ten aircraft types included 843 constraints, 3807 continuous variables, and 156 integer (aircraft selector) variables. No explicit cost savings are included in the presentation of this application. Management's satisfaction with the project, however, is obvious from the ongoing nature of the investigation.

HUNT-WESSON FOODS

A third application is a major distribution-system study for Hunt-Wesson Foods, Inc. The model is to select sites for regional distribution centers and to determine what customer zones each distribution center should serve, as well as which of several plants should supply the distribution centers. The model is an MILP with two types of integer variables:

$y_k = 1$ if site k is used for a distribution center, and $y_k = 0$ if it is not

$y_{kl} = 1$ if customer district l is served by the warehouse at site k,

and $y_{kl} = 0$ if it is not

The quantities of material shipped are continuous variables.

The model involves 17 commodity classes, 14 plants, 45 possible distribution center sites, and 121 customer zones. The MILP model used to attack it had 11,854 constraints, 727 0–1 integer variables, and 23,513 continuous variables. A special algorithm was constructed to solve the model. In the article describing this model the authors stated that the realizable annual cost savings produced by the study were estimated to be in the low-seven figures.

The three studies cited here have a number of features in common:

1. Each attacked a major model of strategic importance to a firm.
2. Each made a significant contribution to successfully dealing with the model.
3. Each included a large scale MILP.
4. Clever modeling and/or special algorithms were required in each application.
5. Each project required a major commitment of funds and managerial talent.

The examples illustrate that a good model may enable management to achieve a level of analysis and performance that might otherwise be impossible, but such models are costly to develop and often require an ongoing and time-consuming input from management. In all of the examples the authors (of the articles) stressed a close working relationship between the analysts (modelers) and management. In the case of Kelly-Springfield, the current model has evolved over a 15-year interval with two major efforts. We see, then, that the use of models to address important management problems may well entail a serious commitment to a long process. Small tactical models may be successfully subdued with a quick "off-the-shelf" treatment. Fundamental strategic models are seldom that obliging.

7.8   SUMMARY

The introduction pointed out that integer linear programming (ILP) is an important and developing area of constrained optimization. Section 7.2 identified all-integer models (ILP) and mixed integer models (MILP) as the two main types of integer linear programs. In MILPs only some of the decision variables are restricted to integer values. Further, the importance of models involving integer variables that are restricted to the value 0 or 1 was discussed. Finally, the LP relaxation was defined. Section 7.3 used a graphical approach to solve an ILP with two decision variables. This approach was then used to investigate the conceptual relationships between an ILP and its LP relaxation. We saw that:

1. In a Max model the OV of the LP relaxation always provides an upper bound on the OV of the original ILP.
2. In a *Min* model the OV of the LP relaxation always provides a *lower bound* on the OV of the original ILP.

In Section 7.3 we also discussed *rounded solutions.* These are any rounding of the optimal solution to the LP relaxation. Thus, there are many rounded solutions. For n variables that have fractional answers, there are 2^n possible rounded solutions. For example, in the Flying Tiger model there could be $2^{156} = 9.1344 \times 10^{46}$ rounded solutions. If only 50 of these variables had fractional answers in the relaxed LP, there would still be 1.1259×10^{15} (over a quadrillion) solutions to investigate just to find the best rounded feasible solution. In some applications, as discussed in Section 7.1, any rounded solution may be an acceptable substitute for the true ILP solution. In other cases, no rounded solution will be acceptable. We saw in Section 7.3 that, in general:

3. It may be that no rounded solution is near the ILP optimum, or
4. It may be that no rounded solution is feasible (i.e., satisfies the constraints of the LP relaxation).

Section 7.4 considered the use of 0–1 variables in a variety of applications. In particular, models for a capital budgeting model and a warehouse location model were considered in some detail. Section 7.5 contained an application of the fact that certain LPs always have all-integer solutions. Section 7.6 explained the branch-and-bound approach used to solve ILPs. The graphical approach was used to show that branching is a matter of dividing the feasible set for a model into disjoint subsets. Bounding uses the optimum value of the LP relaxation to eliminate submodels from consideration. Section 7.6 dealt with two important topics concerning the real-world use of ILPs. First, we pointed out the importance of Solver's tree-pruning strategies in implementing the branch-and-bound approach. Second, we saw that sensitivity data are not produced as a natural by-product of the solution to an ILP. Further, it was illustrated that ILPs may be inconsistent and erratic in their sensitivity to changes in parameter values. These two facts combine to establish the necessity of using multiple optimization runs with different parameters to manually tabulate sensitivity information in the ILP setting. This process is often an important part of attacking a real model with an ILP model. In Section 7.7 several major applications of integer programming were cited.

Key Terms

Integer Linear Program (ILP).   A model that satisfies all the conditions of a linear program except that some or all of the variables are required to be integers.

Rounded Solution.   A feasible solution to an ILP found by solving the LP relaxation and rounding each of the integer variables either up or down.

All-integer Linear Program.   An integer linear program in which all the decision variables are required to be integers.

Mixed Integer Linear Program (MILP).   An integer linear program in which only some of the variables are required to be integers.

Binary (0–1) Integer Linear Program.   An integer linear program in which all the decision variables are required to be either 0 or 1.

LP Relaxation.   An LP model that is derived from an ILP by ignoring the integrality constraints.

Optimal Value (OV).   Short for the optimal value of the objective function.

Complete Enumeration.   Solving an ILP by listing all the feasible points, evaluating the objective function at each of them, and selecting the best solution.

Branch and Bound.   A solution technique used on ILPs based on dividing the original model into mutually exclusive parts and employing the OV from the LP relaxations to obtain bounds.

Self-Review Exercises

True-False

1. **T   F** Rounding LP solutions to meet the real-world requirement for integer decision variables is a common practice.

2. **T   F** In general, it is no more difficult to solve an IP than an LP.

3. **T   F** The binary variable in an IP may be used to represent dichotomous decisions.

4. **T   F** In a *Max* model, the OV of the LP relaxation always provides a *lower bound* on the OV of the original ILP or MILP.

5. **T   F** The first step in obtaining a rounded solution to an MILP is to solve its LP relaxation.

6. **T   F** Solving an ILP by complete enumeration involves evaluating the objective function at all corners of the feasible set of the LP relaxation.

7. **T   F** In the LP relaxation of the ILP capital budgeting model, there are as many constraints as there are time periods.

8. **T   F** In an ILP with n binary decision variables, each of which indicates the selection (or not) of an alternative, the condition that no more than k alternatives be selected can be imposed with the constraint $x_1 + x_2 + \cdots + x_n \leq k$.

9. **T F** In STECO's warehouse location model, the optimal number of trucks to send from each warehouse to each plant was an integer because after the warehouses are selected the model is a transportation model with integer supplies and demands.

10. **T F** Suppose x_1 and x_2 are both binary variables where $x_i = 1$ has the interpretation of building a plant in location i. The condition "a plant can be built in location 2 only if the plant in location 1 is also built" is captured with the constraint $x_1 \leq x_2$.

11. **T F** Consider a transportation model with integer supplies and demands and where in addition, integrality conditions are imposed on the x_{ij}'s. Since this makes the model an integer program, it must be solved by specifying Solver's changing cells to be integer.

Multiple Choice

12. In an ILP
    a. ignoring integrality restrictions, all constraint functions are linear
    b. all decision variables must be integers
    c. all decision variables must be nonnegative
    d. both a and b

13. In an MILP
    a. the objective function is linear
    b. all decision variables must be integers
    c. some coefficients are restricted to be integers, others are not
    d. all of the above

14. The LP relaxation of an ILP
    a. permits a nonlinear objective function
    b. ignores the integrality restrictions on the decision variables
    c. relaxes any nonnegativity restrictions on the decision variables
    d. all of the above

15. A rounded solution to a *Max* ILP may not be feasible because
    a. it violates the integrality constraints
    b. it violates any nonnegativity constraints
    c. its OV is smaller than the OV of the LP relaxation
    d. none of the above

16. If x_k and x_m are 0–1 variables (the value 1 meaning select) for projects k and m, respectively, the constraint, $x_k + x_m \leq 0$ implies that
    a. k cannot be selected unless m is selected
    b. k must be selected if m is selected
    c. m cannot be selected unless k is selected
    d. none of the above

17. Suppose a product can be manufactured either not at all or else in lot sizes $\geq L$, and let x be the quantity of the product produced. The following two constraints are appropriate:
    a. $x + Uy \leq 0; x - Ly \geq 0$
    b. $x - Uy \geq 0; x - Ly \geq 0$
    c. $x - Uy \leq 0; x - Ly \geq 0$
    d. $x - Uy \leq 0; x - Ly \leq 0$

    where U is an arbitrarily large number and y is a 0–1 variable.

18. In solving a *Max* ILP a lower bound for the OV of the original model can always be found by
    a. solving the LP relaxation of the ILP and using the OV of the LP

    b. finding a feasible solution to the ILP by any available means and evaluating the objective function
    c. solving the LP relaxation and then rounding fractions < 0.5 down, those ≥ 0.5 up, and evaluating the objective function at this point
    d. none of the above

19. In the branch-and-bound approach to a *Max* ILP, a node is terminated when
    a. its $U <$ CBLB
    b. the LP relaxation is infeasible
    c. the LP relaxation provides a solution to the integer model represented by that node
    d. any of the above

20. The computer solution to an MILP
    a. contains no sensitivity information
    b. contains sensitivity information on only the noninteger variables
    c. contains sensitivity information on only right-hand sides
    d. contains sensitivity information on only the objective function

More-Challenging Questions: The next ten questions are based on the following model:

A firm has ten outlets that must be supplied with a certain product. The demands (all positive) at the outlets are $d_1, d_2, \cdots, d_{10}$, and these demands must be *exactly* satisfied (i.e., d_i units must be distributed to outlet i). The firm may supply these demands by having a supplier deliver directly to each outlet. The supplier charges \$50 for each unit delivered, independent of the outlet location. The supplier would charge only \$35 per unit for any location if the location would order at least D units. Since each of the $d_j < D$, the firm can make no use of the discount. The firm is considering leasing a centrally located warehouse for $K > 0$ dollars and using this warehouse as an intermediary depot. The depot could order any quantity and could distribute to any number of outlets. It has been agreed that the depot would pay the same as the outlets (\$50 per unit if $< D$ units are ordered; \$35 per unit if the total order is at least D units).

The cost of sending a unit from the warehouse to outlet i is $C_i > 0$, $i = 1, 2, \ldots, 10$. Assume that $D < \sum_{i=1}^{n} d_i$. Management would like to know

1. Should the warehouse be leased?

2. If so, which outlets should be served by the warehouse and which should be supplied directly by the supplier?

In formulating a model to answer these questions, let

x_i = quantity sent directly from supplier to location i

y_i = quantity sent from warehouse to location i

z = quantity sent from supplier to warehouse

A correct set of constraints for this model is

$x_i + y_i = d_i, \qquad i = 1, 2, \dots, 10$

$\sum_{i=1}^{10} y_i \leq z$

$z \geq tD$

$z \leq t \sum_{i=1}^{10} d_i$

$x_i, y_i \geq 0 \quad (i = 1, 2, \dots, 10); \quad z \geq 0; \quad t = 0 \; or \; 1$

21. The correct objective function is

   a. Min $\sum_{i=1}^{10} 50x_i + \sum_{i=1}^{10} C_i y_i$

   b. Min $\sum_{i=1}^{10} 50x_i + \sum_{i=1}^{10} (C_i + 35)y_i + tK$

   c. Min $\sum_{i=1}^{10} 50x_i + 35z + \sum_{i=1}^{10} C_i y_i + tK$

   d. Min $\sum_{i=1}^{10} (50x_i + C_i y_i) + 35D$

   e. none of the above

22. For the model as stated, there will never be an optimal solution in which the depot orders a positive amount that is less than D units.
   a. T
   b. F

23. Management should lease the warehouse if
   a. the optimal value of D is positive
   b. the optimal value of t is positive
   c. the optimal value of z is positive
   d. all of the above
   e. both b and c

24. Consider location k such that $35 + C_k > 50$. Since the marginal cost of shipping directly to k from the supplier is less than the marginal cost of going through the warehouse, there will be no optimal solution in which this outlet (the kth) receives products both from the warehouse and directly from the supplier.
   a. T
   b. F

25. There always will exist an optimal solution in which no outlet receives deliveries from both the supplier (directly) and the warehouse.
   a. T
   b. F

26. Suppose $35 + C_i = 50, i = 1, \dots, 10$. Then $t^* = 0$ in any optimal solution.
   a. T
   b. F

27. This model may have an optimal solution in which the total quantity ordered from the supplier exceeds $\sum_{i=1}^{10} d_i$.
   a. T
   b. F

28. If the optimal value $z^* = \sum_{i=1}^{10} d_i$, then it is certain that the optimal solution will be $x_i^* = 0$,

$(i = 1, 2, \dots, 10), y_i^* = d_i, (i = 1, 2, \dots, 10)$, and $t^* = 1$.
   a. T
   b. F

29. This model will allow the possibility of having inventory left at the warehouse after all demands are satisfied.
   a. T
   b. F

30. Suppose each $C_i \geq 15$.
   a. Then the optimal solution to the model is obviously $x_i^* = d_i, (i = 1, 2, \dots, 10), y_i^* = 0, (i = 1, 2, \dots, 10)$, and $z^* = t^* = 0$.
   b. For some values of the parameters d_i the solution may differ, and hence it is wisest to optimize the model with Solver.

Answers

1. T	**9.** T	**17.** c	**24.** b
2. F	**10.** F	**18.** b	**25.** b
3. T	**11.** F	**19.** d	**26.** a
4. F	**12.** d	**20.** a	**27.** a
5. T	**13.** a	**21.** c	**28.** a
6. F	**14.** b	**22.** a	**29.** a
7. F	**15.** d	**23.** e	**30.** a
8. T	**16.** d		

Problems

7-1. A firm produces two products, A and C. Capacity on the A line is 7 units per day. Each unit of C requires 4 hours of drying time, and a total of 22 drying hours per day is available. Also, each unit of A requires 2 hours of polishing, and each unit of C requires 3 hours of polishing. A total of 19 hours of polishing time is available each day. Each unit of A yields a profit of $1, whereas each unit of C yields a profit of $3. The firm wants to determine a daily production schedule to maximize profits. A and C can be produced only in integer amounts.

    (a) Formulate this model as an ILP.
    (b) Use GLP to find the optimal solution to the LP relaxation.
    (c) Use GLP to find the optimal solution to the ILP.
    (d) Find an integer solution by rounding each value in the answer to part (b) to its integer part. Is this solution feasible?
    (e) How much profit would the firm lose by adopting the latter rounded solution?

7-2. Consider the following ILP:

$$Max \quad x_1 + 2x_2$$
$$s.t. \quad 3x_1 + x_2 \leq 15$$
$$3x_1 + 7x_2 \leq 42$$
$$x_1, x_2 \geq 0 \text{ and integer}$$

    (a) Use GLP to find the optimal solution to the LP relaxation.
    (b) How many feasible points are there?
    (c) Using GLP find the optimal solution to the ILP.
    (d) Find an integer feasible solution by rounding the answer to part (a). Is the rounded solution optimal?

7-3. Consider a minimization ILP. Does the optimal value for the LP relaxation provide an upper or a lower bound for the optimal value of the ILP? Explain your answer.

7-4. Consider a minimization ILP. Does the value of the objective function at a feasible rounded solution provide an upper or a lower bound for the optimal value of the ILP? Explain your answer.

7-5. Consider a maximization ILP. Does the optimal value of the LP relaxation of this model provide an upper or a lower bound for the optimal value of the ILP? Explain your answer.

7-6. Consider a maximization ILP. Does the value of the objective function at a feasible rounded solution provide an upper or a lower bound for the optimal value of the ILP? Explain your answer.

7-7. *Investment Problem.* A portfolio manager has just been given $100,000 to invest. She will choose her investments from a list of 20 stocks. She knows that the net return from investing one dollar in stock i is r_i. Thus, if she invests x_i dollars in stock i she will end up with $(1 + r_i)x_i$ dollars. In order to maintain a balanced portfolio, she adopts the following two rules of thumb:

    1. She will not invest more than $20,000 in a single stock.
    2. *If* she invests anything in a stock, she will invest at least $5000 in it.

The manager would like to maximize her return subject to these rules of thumb. Formulate this model as an MILP. Define your decision variables carefully.

•• **7-8.** *Airline Scheduling.* Alpha Airline wishes to schedule no more than one flight out of Chicago to each of the following cities: Columbus, Denver, Los Angeles, and New York. The available departure slots are 8 A.M., 10 A.M., and 12 noon. Alpha leases the airplanes at the cost of $5000 before and including 10 A.M. and $3000 after 10 A.M., and is able to lease at most two per departure slot. Also, if a flight leaves for New York in a time slot, there must be a flight leaving for Los Angeles in the same time slot. The expected profit contribution before rental costs per flight is shown in the following table. Formulate and solve a model for a profit-maximizing schedule. Define your decision variables carefully.

	TIME SLOT		
	8	10	12
Columbus	10	6	6
Denver	9	10	9
Los Angeles	14	11	10
New York	18	15	10

•• 7-9. A *Start-up Problem.* A model faced by an electrical utility each day is that of deciding which generators to start up. The utility in question has three generators with the characteristics shown in the accompanying table. There are two periods in a day, and the number of megawatts needed in the first period is 2900. The second period requires 3900 megawatts. A generator started in the first period may be used in the second period without incurring an additional start-up cost. All major generators (e.g., A, B, and C) are turned off at the end of each day. Formulate and solve this model as an MILP. Define your decision variables carefully.

GENERATOR	FIXED START-UP COST ($)	COST PER PERIOD PER MEGAWATT USED ($)	MAXIMUM CAPACITY IN EACH PERIOD (MW)
A	3000	5	2100
B	2000	4	1800
C	1000	7	3000

••7-10. *Production Planning.* A certain production line makes two products. Relevant data are given in Table 7.4 below. Total time available (for production and setup) each week is 80 hours. The firm has no inventory of either product at the start of week 1 and no inventory is allowed at the end of week 4. The cost of carrying a unit of inventory from one week to the next is $4 for each product. One unit of unsatisfied demand costs $10 for product A and $15 for product B. Demand data are given in Table 7.5. The line is shut down and cleaned each weekend. As a result, if a product is produced in a week the appropriate setup time cost is incurred. Only one product can be produced during a week. No production can take place during the time that the line is being set up. Formulate and solve this 4-week planning model as an MILP. The objective is to maximize the profit over a 4-week period.

TABLE 7.4 Product Data

	PRODUCT	
	A	B
Setup Time	5 hours	10 hours
Per Unit Production Time	0.5 hour	0.75 hour
Setup Cost	$200	$400
Per Unit Production Cost	$10	$15
Selling Price	$20	$30

TABLE 7.5 Demand Data

PRODUCT	WEEK			
	1	2	3	4
A	80	100	75	80
B	15	20	50	30

••7-11. The board of directors of a large manufacturing firm is considering the set of investments shown in the following table. Let R_i be the total revenue from investment i and C_i be the cost to make investment i. The board wishes to maximize total revenue and invest no more than a total of M dollars. Formulate this model as an ILP. Define your decision variables and write the equation symbolically.

INVESTMENT	CONDITION
1	None
2	Only if 1
3	Only if 2
4	Must if 1 *and* 2
5	Not if 1 *or* 2
6	Not if 2 *and* 3
7	Only if 2 *and not* 3

•• **7-12.** A distribution company wants to minimize the cost of transporting goods from its warehouses A, B, and C to the retail outlets 1, 2, and 3. The costs for transporting one unit from warehouse to retailer is given by the following table.

	RETAILER		
WAREHOUSE	1	2	3
A	15	32	21
B	9	7	6
C	11	18	5
Demand	200	150	175

The fixed cost of operating a warehouse is $5000 for A, $750 for B, and $600 for C, and at least two of them have to be open. The warehouses can be assumed to have unlimited storage capacity. Formulate and solve an ILP to decide which warehouses should be opened and the amount to be shipped from each warehouse to each retailer.

•• **7-13.** Use a graphical approach and the branch-and-bound algorithm to solve the ILP presented in Problem 7-1. Branch first on A, present each new model in the process together with its solution, and express the analysis in a decision diagram.

•• **7-14.** Use a graphical approach and the branch-and-bound algorithm to solve the ILP presented in Problem 7-2. Branch first on x_1. For each new model state what constraint you would add to what model to create the new model; for example, a phrase like "Add constraint $x_1 \geq 2$ to Model 1." Express the analysis in a decision diagram like those in the text.

•• **7-15.** Consider the following formulation of Problem 7-1:

$$\text{Max } A + 3C$$
$$\text{s.t.} \quad A \qquad\qquad \leq 7$$
$$4C \leq 22$$
$$2A + 3C \leq 19$$
$$A \geq 0 \text{ and integer}, \qquad C \geq 0 \text{ and integer}$$

Plot the optimal objective value as a function of the RHS of the second constraint as the value of the RHS ranges between 0 and 24. Use GLP to create the data for this plot.

•• **7-16.** Consider the ILP presented in Problem 7-2. Plot the optimal objective value as a function of the RHS of the constraint

$$3x_1 + x_2 \leq \text{RHS} \qquad \text{for } 0 \leq \text{RHS} \leq 24$$

Use GLP to create the data for this plot.

7-17. Consider the following ILP:

$$\text{Min. } 4x_1 + 5x_2$$
$$\text{s.t.} \quad 3x_1 + 6x_2 \geq 18$$
$$5x_1 + 4x_2 \geq 20$$
$$8x_1 + 2x_2 \geq 16$$
$$7x_1 + 6x_2 \leq 42$$
$$x_1 \geq 0 \text{ and integer}, \qquad x_2 \geq 0 \text{ and integer}$$

(a) Use GLP to find the optimal solution to the LP relaxation.

(b) List all the feasible points.

(c) Use GLP to find the optimal solution to the ILP.

(d) Use GLP to find a feasible rounded solution.

(e) Is (d) optimal?

(f) How large is the cost of using the rounded solution identified above relative to the optimal solution?

••**7-18.** *Line Balancing.* A job requires five operations, A, B, C, D, and E, each of which can be done on either machine 1 or machine 2. The time taken for each operation on each of the given machines is given in the following table.

Formulate and solve an ILP to assign the jobs to the machines so that if T1 is the total time taken on machine 1 and T2 the time taken on machine 2, then Max (T1, T2) is minimized.

	A	B	C	D	E
Machine 1	5	9	2	3	4
Machine 2	3	4	7	5	4

••**7-19.** Consider the STECO Warehouse Location Model in Figure 7.8. Given the optimal decisions for leasing warehouses A, B, and C, write out the transportation model that the optimal truck allocations solve.

••**7-20.** *Site Location.* The city council found that to service the city, fire stations have to be opened at either locations A, B, and C or locations A, C, and D or locations B, C, and D. The cost of opening a fire station (in millions of $) at location A is $1.5, at B is $2.3, at C is $1.8, and at D is $2.1. Formulate and solve an ILP that will allow the city council to decide which fire stations should be opened so as to service the city at minimum cost.

••**7-21.** *Capacity Expansion.* An electric utility is planning the expansion of its generating capacity for the next five years. Its current capacity is 800 megawatts (MW), but based on its forecast of demand it will require additional capacity as shown in the following table.

YEAR	MINIMUM CAPACITY (MW)
1	880
2	960
3	1050
4	1160
5	1280

The utility can increase its generating capacity by installing 10-, 50-, or 100-MW generators. The cost of installing a generator depends on its size and the year it is brought on line. See the accompanying table.

GENERATOR SIZE MW	YEAR 1	2	3	4	5
10	300	250	208	173	145
50	670	558	465	387	322
100	950	791	659	549	458

Once a generator is brought on line, its capacity is available to meet demand in succeeding years. Formulate and solve an ILP that minimizes the cost of bringing generators on line while satisfying the minimum capacity requirements.

HINT: Let x_t, y_t, and z_t be the number of 10-, 50-, and 100-MW generators brought on line in year t and c_t the total capacity in year t after these generators have been brought on line.

•••**7-22.** Norco Home Cosmetics Sales is just moving into a six-county region of southern Utah. The map below shows the location of the counties and their populations, P_i. Norco plans to assign two salespersons to this region. The company assigns two counties to each salesperson, a base county and an adjacent county. Counties are adjacent if they share a common *side;* a common corner is *not* sufficient.

For example, in the map below, counties 1 and 2 are adjacent, but 1 and 5 are not. Norco's objective is to maximize the total population of the assigned counties. A feasible solution is

P_1	P_2	P_3
1	2	3
P_4	P_5	P_6
4	5	6

to make 4 a base with 1 as the assigned adjacent and also make 3 a base with 2 as the assigned adjacent. The value of the objective function for this solution is $P_1 + P_2 + P_3 + P_4$. Define

$$B_j = \begin{cases} 1 \text{ if county } j \text{ is used as a base} \\ 0 \text{ if not} \end{cases} \quad j = 1, \ldots, 6$$

$$A_{ij} = \begin{cases} 1 \text{ if county } i \text{ is used as a county adjacent to base } j \\ 0 \text{ if not} \end{cases} \quad \begin{array}{l} j = 1, \ldots, 6; \\ i \text{ adjacent to } j \end{array}$$

Thus the variables are $B_1, B_2, B_3, B_4, B_5, B_6, A_{21}, A_{41}, A_{12}, A_{52}, A_{32}, A_{23}, A_{63}$, and so on.

(a) Double counting in the model must not occur (i.e., a county must not be used as both a base and an assigned adjacent). Write a constraint that assures no double counting for county 1.

(b) Write a constraint that says "if any salesperson is assigned to county 2 as a base then a salesperson must also be assigned to an appropriate adjacent county."

(c) Write a constraint that says "if either county adjacent to 1 is scheduled (as an adjacent to 1) then 1 must be used as a base."

(d) This model can be written with 12 inequality constraints and 1 equality constraint. True or False.

(e) This model can be written with 7 equality constraints and 6 inequality constraints. True or False.

7-23. •••Refer to the description that precedes exercise 21 in the Self-Review Exercises. Assume in addition to the conditions described there, that there is a fixed cost of $R > 0$ dollars assigned to each shipment that leaves the supplier. This implies, for example, that if the supplier makes direct shipments to locations 3, 5, and 8 and to the warehouse then an additional cost of $4R$ dollars is incurred.

Formulate this model as an MILP, using the notation introduced earlier and whatever additional notation is required.

Case Study   **Assigning Sales Representatives**

One of the main themes in the text is that you, the manager, play the role of the intermediary between the real world and the model. You must decide if the assumptions are appropriate and if the solution produced by the model makes sense in the context of the real model.

Sally Erickson is midwest sales director for Lady Lynn Cosmetics. Lady Lynn is a rapidly expanding company that sells cosmetics through representatives. These representatives originally contact most of their customers through house parties. At these parties, the representative demonstrates the products and takes orders. The guests have an opportunity to win some samples of the products and to order products.

Sally is in the process of assigning representatives to the seven eastern Iowa counties shown in Exhibit 1.

Actually, she has only two trained representatives to assign at this time. The policy at Lady Lynn is to assign a representative to a base county and one adjacent county. Actual practice is based on a heuristic model that assigns representatives sequentially. The county with the largest population is selected as the base for the first representative, and the adjacent county with the largest population is also assigned to her. The unassigned county with the largest population is assigned as the next base and so on. The populations of the counties are shown below.

1.	Buchanan	16,000
2.	Delaware	15,000
3.	Dubuque	98,000
4.	Linn	109,000

5. Jones	4,000
6. Jackson	6,000
7. Clinton	100,000

Using this scheme, the first representative would be assigned to Linn County as a base. As the map shows, Buchanan, Delaware, and Jones are the adjacent counties. Since Buchanan has the largest population of these three counties, it would be the assigned adjacent county. The second representative would be based in Clinton with Jackson as the assigned adjacent county. Sally realizes that the goal is to maximize the total population assigned to representatives. She is concerned that, since Dubuque County is nearly as large as Clinton, the proposed solution may not be optimal, and after a moment's thought she can see that it clearly is not: The pair Dubuque and Delaware beat Clinton and Jackson. She decides to abandon the traditional heuristic approach and to model the model as an IP. Although this particular model is quite simple, she believes that if she can create a successful model it could then be appropriately modified to assign the company's 60 midwest representatives to well over 300 counties. In formulating the model, she lets

$Y_i = 1$ if county i is a base, $i = 1, 2, ..., 7$
   $= 0$ if not

$X_{ij} = 1$ if adjacent county j is assigned to base, $i = 1, 2,$
   $..., 7; j = 1, 2, ..., 7$
   $= 0$ if not

The symbolic model is shown below. Sally developed a spreadsheet version of it and used Solver to optimize the model.

Max $16Y_1 + 15Y_2 + 98Y_3 + 109Y_4 + 4Y_5 + 6Y_6 + 100Y_7 +$
   $15X_{21} + 109X_{41} +$
   $16X_{12} + 98X_{32} + 109X_{42} + 4X_{52} +$
   $15X_{23} + 4X_{53} + 6X_{63} +$

$16X_{14} + 15X_{24} + 4X_{54} +$
$15X_{25} + 98X_{35} + 109X_{45} + 6X_{65} + 100X_{75} +$
$4X_{56} + 98X_{36} + 100X_{76} +$
$4X_{57} + 6X_{67}$

s.t. $X_{21} + X_{41} = Y_1$
   $X_{12} + X_{32} + X_{42} + X_{52} = Y_2$
   $X_{23} + X_{53} + X_{63} = Y_3$
   $X_{14} + X_{24} + X_{54} = Y_4$
   $X_{25} + X_{35} + X_{45} + X_{65} + X_{75} = Y_5$
   $X_{56} + X_{36} + X_{76} = Y_6$
   $X_{57} + X_{67} = Y_7$
   $Y_1 + Y_2 + Y_3 + Y_4 + Y_5 + Y_6 + Y_7 = 2$

Her solution showed that Y_4 and $Y_1 = 1$; thus, Linn and Buchanan counties were selected as the base counties. It also gave the optimal value of the objective function as 250, which implies that 250,000 people will be served by the two representatives. Sally thus is pleased to have discovered that the solution suggested by the standard heuristic approach was incorrect before she implemented that solution. She is a bit surprised that the optimal solution does not involve either Dubuque or Clinton county, but she feels sure that Solver provides the optimal solution to her model and thus she is determined to implement it.

Questions

1. Sally's solution is obviously wrong. Find, by inspection of the data, a correct optimal solution. How many alternative optima are there?

2. What is wrong with Sally's model? Write out the additional constraints that will give a correct formulation.

3. Develop a spreadsheet version of the reformulated model and optimize it with Solver to determine the optimal solution.

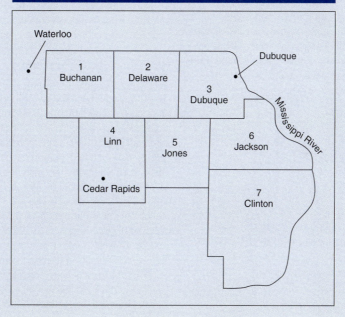

EXHIBIT 1 Seven Eastern Iowa Counties

The municipal bond market is tough and aggressive, which means that a successful underwriter must be on the cutting edge in terms of competitive bidding. Bond markets often change from hour to hour. An active underwriter may bid on several issues each day with as little as 15 to 20 minutes to prepare a bid. This case has two objectives: (1) to familiarize you with some of the mechanics of an important financial market; and (2) to develop an IP model with real-world importance. A variant of this model is actually used by several banks and investment bankers. In practice, bids are routinely prepared for models involving as many as 100 maturities and 35 coupon rates.

Basic Scenario

Each year billions of dollars of tax-exempt debt securities are offered for sale to the public. This is usually done through an underwriter acting as a broker between the issuer of the security and the public. The issuing of the securities to the underwriter is usually done through a competitive bid process. The issuer will notify prospective underwriters in advance of the proposed sale and invite bids that meet constraints set forth by the issuer. In constructing a proposed sale, the issuer divides the total amount to be raised (say $10,000) into bonds of various maturities. For example, to raise $10,000, the issuer might offer a one-year bond with face value of $2000, a two-year bond with face value of $3000, and a three-year bond with face value of $5000. At maturity, the face value of these bonds would be paid to the buyer. Thus in this example, the issuers would pay the buyers $2000 in principal at the end of year 1, and so on. A bid by an underwriter (to the issuer) has three components:

1. An agreement to pay the issuer the face value of all the bonds at the issue date ($10,000 in our example).
2. A premium paid to the issuer at the issue date (more on this later).
3. An annual interest rate for each of the bonds cited in the proposal. These rates are called the coupon rates and determine the amount of interest the issuer must pay the buyers each year. Suppose that the underwriter proposed the following coupon rates for our example.

MATURITY DATE	RATE(%)
1 year	3
2 years	4
3 years	5

The interest to be paid by the issuer would then be calculated as follows:

$$\text{Year 1} = 2000(.03) + 3000(.04) + 5000(.05) = 430$$
$$\text{Year 2} = \qquad\quad\ 3000(.04) + 5000(.05) = 370$$
$$\text{Year 3} = \qquad\qquad\qquad\quad 5000(.05) = 250$$

---

[1]This case was initially formulated by Professor R. Kipp Martin, Graduate School of Business, University of Chicago.

Historically, the net interest cost (NIC) is the criterion most often employed by the issuer in evaluating bids. The NIC is the sum of interest payments over all years for all maturities minus any premium offered by the underwriter. The winning bid is the one with the minimum NIC. The time value of money is ignored in calculating the NIC. Even though the bid with the lowest NIC may not be best for the issuer when present values are considered, this is immaterial to the underwriter since the bid is evaluated according to the NIC.

The profit of the underwriter is the difference between what the buyer pays him and what he (the underwriter) pays the issuer. That is,

$$\text{Profit} = \text{(total selling price to public)}$$
$$- \text{(total face value} + \text{premium)}$$

Thus, in preparing a bid the underwriter must

1. Determine the coupon (interest) amounts the issuer will pay on each maturity, and
2. For each maturity, estimate the selling price (i.e., the underwriter's selling price to the public) for bonds of each coupon rate. (The selling price for bonds need not be the same as the face value of the bond.)

The underwriter has two conflicting objectives. Higher coupon rates imply the bonds have a higher selling price to the public and hence more money to the underwriter, which can be used both as premium and profit. Thus the coupon rates must be set large enough so that if the bid is accepted the underwriter makes a reasonable profit. But higher coupon rates affect the interest the issuer will have to pay (higher coupon rates imply more interest) as well as the premium that the underwriter can offer the issuer. This trade-off between premium and interest may imply that lower coupon rates will decrease the cost to the issuer and hence increase the chances of winning the bid.

The approach we take is to incorporate the underwriter's profit as a constraint and then minimize NIC (the cost to the issuer) in order to maximize the chances of winning the bid.

Data for a Specific Scenario

The city of Dogpatch is going to issue municipal bonds in order to raise revenue for civic improvements. Sealed bids will be received until 5:00 P.M. on February 7, 1998, for $5,000,000 in bonds dated March 1, 1998. The bid represents an offer from the underwriter to (1) pay $5,000,000 to Dogpatch, (2) pay an additional (specified) premium to Dogpatch, and (3) include an interest schedule that Dogpatch will pay to the bondholders. The interest is payable on March 1, 1999, and annually thereafter. The bonds become due (i.e., Dogpatch must pay off the face value, without option for prior payment) on March 1 in each of the maturity years in Table 1 and in the amounts indicated. That is, Table 1 indicates Dogpatch's obligation (in terms of principal) to the bondholders.

The bonds will be awarded to the bidder on the basis of the minimum NIC. No bid will be considered with an interest rate greater than 5% or less than 3% per annum. Bidders must spec-

TABLE 1 Bond Face Amounts	
YEAR (MATURITY)	AMOUNT ($000s)
2000	250
2001	425
2002	1025
2003	1050
2004	1100
2005	1150

TABLE 3 Example Coupon Rates		
MATURITY	COUPON RATE (%)	TOTAL INTEREST ($000s)
2000	3	15.00
2001	4½	57.375
2002	4¾	194.75
2003	4½	236.25
2004	4½	297.00
2005	4½	362.25

TABLE 2 Estimating Selling Price ($000s)						
FACE VALUE	250	425	1025	1050	1100	1150
Percent	2000	2001	2002	2003	2004	2005
3	245	418	1015	1040	1080	1130
3¼	248	422	1016	1042	1084	1135
3½	250	423	1017	1044	1085	1140
3¾	251	424	1025	1046	1090	1150
4	253	430	1029	1050	1095	1155
4¼	255	435	1035	1055	1096	1160
4½	256	437	1037	1060	1105	1165
4¾	257	440	1038	1062	1110	1170
5	258	441	1040	1065	1115	1175

ify interest rates in multiples of one quarter of one percent per annum. Not more than three different interest rates will be considered (a repeated rate will not be considered a different rate). The same rate must apply to all bonds of the same maturity.

Estimating selling prices of various maturities as a function of coupon rates is a complicated process depending upon available markets and various parameters. For the sake of this example, take the data in Table 2 as given. Note that the underwriter may sell bonds to the public at more or less than the face value.

Example (A Sample Bid)

Assume an underwriter establishes the coupon rates for each maturity as in Table 3. Given these coupon rates, the bonds would be sold to the public (see estimates in Table 2) for $5,050,000. Assume the underwriter's spread or profit requirement is $8 per $1000 of face value of bonds. For a $5,000,000 issue this will be $40,000. Thus the premium paid to Dogpatch by the underwriter for this bid is

premium = $5,050,000 − $5,000,000 − $40,000
= $10,000

Questions

1. Calculate Dogpatch's NIC from the example above.
2. Suppose, as in Table 2, the underwriter has a choice between selling a 2000 bond at 4 1/4% for $255,000 or a 2000 bond at 4 1/2% for $256,000. Just in terms of minimizing NIC (ignoring other possible constraints), which would the underwriter prefer to offer? Suppose that the underwriter's profit is the same in both cases.
3. In Table 2, consider the 2000 maturity at 5%. Suppose that you as an investor can with certainty receive 5% interest on money invested on March 1, 1999. What compounded yearly rate of interest would you be receiving if you pay $258,000 for the 2000 bond and use the above investment opportunity with your first receipt of interest?
4. Formulate a constrained optimization symbolic model for solving the underwriter's model. This formulation should minimize the NIC of the underwriter's bid subject to the underwriter receiving an $8 margin per $1000 of face amount and the other constraints given. Be very clear and concise in defining any notation you use, and indicate the purpose of each constraint in your formulation.
5. Develop a constrained optimization spreadsheet model and optimize it using Solver.
6. Bid requests often include additional constraints. Assume that one such additional restriction is that coupon rates must be nondecreasing with maturity. Add the necessary constraint(s) to the symbolic model to enforce this condition. You do not need to resolve with Solver.
7. Next assume that the maximum allowed difference between the highest and lowest coupon rates is 1%. Add the necessary constraint(s) to the symbolic model to enforce this condition. You do not need to resolve with Solver.
8. Refer to your formulation in Question 4. If the bonds (regardless of maturity and coupon value) could never be sold in excess of face value, will your formulation have a feasible solution? Why or why not?
9. Assume your formulation in Question 4 has a feasible solution. Is it possible that the addition of the constraint(s) from Question 6 or the constraint(s) from Question 7 (or both taken together) make the formulation infeasible?

A Word of Advice: One danger of misformulating a rather large integer programming model, and then attempting to optimize it, is that you may waste a great deal of computer time (this of course could be true of any large model). Your solution to Question 5 above, using a correctly formulated model, should take no more than a few minutes on a Pentium-level PC.

In some applications, a stream of cash flows must be generated over a planning horizon. For example, in a personal injury lawsuit, the plaintiff must be compensated for future medical expenses or lost wages or both. Both parties often agree on an initial lump sum that is "equivalent in value" to the cash flows over time. What is an equivalent lump sum? The plaintiff, who wants to maximize the size of the payment, argues that future interest will be low so that a large lump sum is needed. The defendant argues that interest rates will be high and thus a smaller lump sum is required.

One resolution is to purchase a portfolio of bonds so that the return from the bonds satisfies the required cash flow. A bond offers a guaranteed annual payment (determined by the coupon rate) and its face value at maturity. Thus, it is clear how much each bond will contribute to meeting the cash flow. The current price of the bonds is also known and thus the "lump payment model" becomes one of finding the lowest-cost bond portfolio that will satisfy the agreed-upon cash flow.

It is reasonable to think of many pension fund planning models as cash flow matching models. In this model a corporation or a union has an obligation to meet the cash requirements of a pension fund over some planning horizon. The goal is to purchase a minimum-cost, low-risk portfolio that generates an income stream to match the cash outflow requirements of the pension plan.

Consider the following small but conceptually realistic cash flow model. The cash requirements (in millions) for the next five years are shown in Table 1.

The investment committee is considering five types of low-risk investments: an insured money market fund paying an annual rate of 5% and the four types of AAA bonds described in Table 2.

Assume that all cash transactions associated with investments occur on January 1 of each year. Table 3 shows the cash flows for each bond.

Note that in the year the bond matures the return is equal to the sum of the coupon plus the face value of the bond. Also note that bond 3 is a zero coupon bond; that is, it does not pay any interest until maturity.

There is also an opportunity for borrowing in most cash flow matching models. In this model assume that the pension fund managers have the opportunity to borrow as much cash as they want at an annual rate of 13%. Loans are made for one year only; that is, a loan made in 2000 must be paid off in 2001. However, another one-year loan could be taken out immediately.

TABLE 1   Cash Requirements

YEAR	2000	2001	2002	2003	2004
Cash Requirement	10	11	12	14	15

TABLE 2   (Values in $000,000s)

BOND	CURRENT COST	COUPON (YEARLY)	YEARS TO MATURITY	FACE VALUE
1	.97	.04	1	1.00
2	.947	.05	2	1.00
3	.79	.00	3	1.00
4	.829	.03	4	1.00

TABLE 3   (Values in $000,000s)

BOND	2000	2001	2002	2003	2004
1	−.970	1.040			
2	−.947	.050	1.050		
3	−.790	.000	.000	1.000	
4	−.829	.030	.030	.030	1.030

In the real world, cash flows (both in and out) occur at various times during the year. In the model it is assumed that:

A. All inflows (returns from the bonds, money invested in the money market fund as well as interest earned on these funds, funds borrowed during the year under consideration, and the original lump sum) are available on the morning of January 1.
B. All cash outflows (the cash required by the pension fund, payment of debt and interest from the previous year, deposits in the money market account) occur in the afternoon of January 1.

These assumptions make it possible to keep the proper relationship between the various cash flows. For example:

A. In 2000 the cash outflow needed by the pension fund, as well as any purchases of bonds or money to deposit in the money market account, must come from the original lump sum payment or from funds borrowed in 2000.
B. Debt and interest that arise from borrowing in 2000 can be paid for by borrowing funds in 2001.

Questions

1. Plot the yield curve for the four bonds listed in Table 2. To do this you must first determine for each bond the interest rate that makes the present value of the cash flows for that bond equal to zero. This is accomplished with a financial calculator or the Excel IRR() function. Now plot the interest rate as a function of the maturity of the bond for the four bonds.

2. Comment on the general shape of the function you plotted in Question 1. What does this shape suggest about the preferences and expectations of lenders? About borrowers? Does the yield curve have to have this shape? What preferences and expectations of borrowers and lenders might cause it to look otherwise?

3. Assume your goal is to minimize the original lump-sum payment. Formulate an MILP to solve this model. Assume that only an integral number of bonds may be purchased and that these purchases are made in January 2000. In the formal model define the decision variables as follows:

L = initial lump sum required
B_i = amount borrowed in year i
M_i = amount invested in money market fund in year i
X_i = number of bonds of type i purchased in 2000
C_i = cash not utilized in year i

Assume that it is not possible to borrow funds in 2004, the fifth year. In your formulation, there should be a balance constraint in each year that sources of funds must equal uses of funds.

4. In the real world, the data in Table 1 would in fact be estimates of future requirements since these would not generally be known with certainty. What other significant assumptions were made in creating this model?

5. Will there always be a feasible answer for general models of the type constructed in Question 3? That is, consider the model in Question 3 with any set of cash demands and rates of return. Will there always be a feasible solution? Explain.

6. Use Solver to optimize the model you formulated in Question 3.

7. Solve the model using the following heuristic procedure:
   (a) Solve the model from Question 3 as an LP.
   (b) Round the number of bonds to the next largest integer.
   (c) Fix the integer variables at the levels in (b) and optimize the model as an LP.

8. Calculate the value of the following ratio:

   OV Question 7(c)/OV Question 6

   Do you expect this ratio to be greater or less than 1? Why? What does the value of this ratio suggest about solving real (i.e., much bigger) cash flow matching models?

9. What interpretation do you give to the shadow prices produced by the LP solution in Question 7(a)?

10. Comment on the following statement: "The way to minimize the initial lump sum is to limit your purchase of bonds to only the bond with the highest rate of return."

11. Comment on the following statement: "If the rate of return on the money market fund exceeds the rate of return on all the bonds, then there is an optimal solution in which the money market fund is the only investment used."

References

Ranga Anbil, Eric Gelman, Bruce Patty, and Rajan Tanga, "Recent Advances in Crew-Pairing Optimization at American Airlines," *Interfaces,* 21, no. 1 (1991), 62–74.

Thomas Spencer III, Anthony Brigandi, Dennis Dargon, and Michael Sheehan, "AT&T's Telemarketing Site Selection System Offers Customer Support," *Interfaces,* 20, no. 1 (January–February 1990).

8

Nonlinear Optimization

CHAPTER OUTLINE

8.1 Introduction to Nonlinear Optimization Models

8.2 Unconstrained Optimization in Two or More Decision Variables

8.3 Nonlinear Optimization with Constraints: A Descriptive Geometric Introduction

8.4 Using Solver for NLP Models

8.5 Example Nonlinear Models with Inequality Constraints

8.6 Solvability of NLP Models

8.7 Introduction to Quadratic Programming

8.8 Solver Solution of QP Problems

8.9 Geometric Interpretation of QP Sensitivity Analysis

8.10 Portfolio Selection

8.11 A Portfolio Example with Data

8.12 Inventory Control

8.13 Examples of Inventory Models

8.14 Notes on NLP Implementation

KEY TERMS

SELF-REVIEW EXERCISES

PROBLEMS

CASE STUDY: Just-in-Time

CASE STUDY: Internal Revenue Service (1994–1995)

REFERENCES

APPLICATION CAPSULE

Asset and Liability Management at Pacific Financial Asset Management Company

Trying to decide what investments are desirable depends upon the particular situation of the investor. A person who is close to retirement should accept less risk than a young person who is setting aside money for her retirement in 40 years. Another difference is that investors who must pay taxes on their gains should be distinguished from institutional investors like insurance companies or pension funds who are generally tax exempt. Measuring the risks and rewards of various alternative investment strategies depends on individual circumstances.

In order to build a more customized investment portfolio model, Pacific Financial Asset Management Company (PFAMC) developed a new model that extended the traditional financial model for assets by Markowitz and Sharpe to include both assets and liabilities. The critical issue is to balance the risk and rewards of the strategic investment decisions in concert with the move-ments of the projected liabilities. The model developed by PFAMC is a nonlinear optimization system. The aim of the integrative asset-liability system is the preservation of the firm's wealth as measured by the market value of the assets minus the present value of the liabilities. The model has been implemented on a personal computer so that it can be interactive with the investor and thus account for the individual circumstances and risk preference. For example, large institutional investors must decide how much money to invest in each of several broad asset categories—stocks, bonds, real estate, and so on. This decision is their most important strategic planning decision.

Although this new approach requires greater information, its recommendations are more closely tailored to the investor's needs and circumstances. Both PFAMC and its clients have been very pleased with its results. (See Mulvey.)

In many business and economics problems, the functions or mathematical relationships involved are not all linear. In fact, it is probably true that the real-world problems that fit the strict mold of linearity are the exception rather than the rule. As a simple illustration:

In a linear model, price is usually assumed to be a given constant, say p, and sales, the quantity to be sold, is a variable x that is assumed to be independent of price. Hence, revenue is given by px, and we say that revenue is proportional to price. In reality, however, price may be a variable, and quantity of sales (demand) might be dependent on price. This dependency is expressed by writing sales $= f(p)$, where f is some specified (nonconstant) function of p. Thus, revenue would be given by

$$\text{revenue} = \text{price} \times \text{sales} = p \times f(p)$$

which is nonlinear in the variable p. In this case a model to find the price level that maximizes revenue would be a nonlinear model.

In general, some of the prominent (and not necessarily distinct) reasons for nonlinearity are (1) nonproportional relationships (in the example above, revenue is not proportional to price, for, depending on the specific form of $f(p)$, price may increase and revenue decrease); (2) nonadditive relationships (e.g., when two chemicals are added together the resulting volume need not be the sum of the two added volumes); and (3) efficiencies or inefficiencies of scale (e.g., when too many workers try to plant beans on the same acre of ground they begin to get into each other's way and the yield per worker will decrease, rather than remain constant[1]). In short, any number of physical, structural, biological, economic, and logical relationships may be responsible for the appearance of nonlinearity in a model.

It must be repeated at the outset that, although nonlinear phenomena are common, nonlinear models are considerably more difficult to optimize than linear models. For example, in contrast to LP, you cannot assume that Solver's nonlinear optimization procedure will always find the optimal solution for all nonlinear models. Combine this difficulty with the fact that linear models, in many contexts, provide *good approximations* to nonlinear models, and you can understand the popularity of linear models, such as LP.

As we know, a model is not the real world. It is an abstract representation of reality. The important point for the modeler is to know when a linearized version provides an *adequate* representation of the nonlinear world. The answer to such a judgmental question comes with experimentation and much experience, and even then only imperfectly and often without consensus. In this chapter we want to address those situations where nonlinear programming models are deemed to be required. Our objective is to provide some understanding of the tools and concepts necessary to deal with nonlinear programming models, and as will become apparent, some knowledge of calculus is required for complete understanding.

This part of the chapter is organized as follows. Section 8.2 reviews the facts concerning *unconstrained* optimization in several decision variables. Then we give a descriptive and geometric introduction to constrained nonlinear optimization. Section 8.3 deals with NLP (nonlinear programming) formulation and solution using Solver. Following this, we loosely define the concept of concave and convex programs and discuss in a qualitative way the kinds of nonlinear problems that can be routinely solved. Next, in Section 8.7 we focus upon a particular class of NLP called *quadratic* models. These models have wide application in financial decision making, and in Sections 8.10 and 8.11 we give two examples of quadratic models to portfolio optimization. In Section 8.12 we turn to inventory theory, another popular use of NLP. We develop the classic economic order quantity model (EOQ) and then extend it with two examples. In Section 8.14 we conclude with some notes on implementation of NLP.

---

[1]Note that this diseconomy of scale situation leads to a nonproportional relationship between total yield and number of workers.

8.2   **UNCONSTRAINED OPTIMIZATION IN TWO OR MORE DECISION VARIABLES**

Let us first consider the case of two decision variables, x_1 and x_2. Thus, we consider a function $f(x_1, x_2)$. For the case of two decision variables (i.e., two independent variables) partial derivatives from calculus are used to describe local or global optima. We shall use the notation f_{x_i} for first partial derivative, $f_{x_i x_i}$ for second partial derivative, and so on. Any point (e.g., values for x_1 and x_2) at which all first partial derivatives vanish is called a **stationary point.** We have the following *necessary condition* for optimality.

> At a local max or min both partial derivatives must equal zero (i.e., $f_{x_1} = f_{x_2} = 0$). That is, a local maximizer or a local minimizer is always a stationary point.

However, not all stationary points provide maxima and minima. We can employ the so-called second-order (meaning that second derivatives are involved) sufficient condition for optimality, which is somewhat more complicated than the necessary condition. Thus, just as for functions of a single variable, there is a first-order (first derivative) and second-order (involving second derivatives) test that can be applied to locate unconstrained local optima for functions of more than one variable. These tests are called **first-order optimality conditions** and **second-order optimality conditions.** Note that the first-order conditions are necessary; the second-order conditions are sufficient. Also note that the second-order conditions subsume the first-order ones (i.e., the second-order conditions assume that x_1^*, x_2^* is a stationary point).

In the absence of some additional properties of the function, such as convexity or concavity, a local (as opposed to global) optimizer is the most that one can generally hope to find. The first-derivative test (the necessary condition) says that the local optima are contained among the stationary points of the function. The second-derivative test (the sufficient condition) allows us to distinguish between local maximizers and minimizers, and points that are neither.

For a differentiable function of n variables, each local optimizer is a stationary point. In order to guarantee that a stationary point is, for example, a local maximizer, second-order sufficiency conditions must be invoked. Although these two types of optimality conditions have theoretic interest, they have, for many nonlinear problems in more than two variables, limited *practical relevance.* The reasons are:

1. Setting the first partial derivatives equal to zero gives a system of n equations in n unknowns. Unless this system is linear (i.e., the original function was quadratic), it is not easy to find solutions. It may well be impossible to do by hand.

2. The second-order sufficiency conditions are quite complicated, requiring the evaluation of determinants of certain entries in the matrix of second partial derivatives. Indeed, even in the case of one or two decision variables, if the function f is sufficiently complicated, it may not be possible to hand-solve the optimality conditions, and hence, this approach is not generally viable.

For these reasons, specialized optimization software packages, such as Solver, have been developed to find local optima of nonlinear functions of n variables (where n is any integer ≥ 1). Often such packages are based on hill-climbing (or hill-descent) behavior.[2] That is, for a maximization problem, an initial point is chosen, that is, a set of values for the n decision variables, and then an uphill direction is determined by approximating numerically the first derivative to the objective function at that initial point. Intuitively, for unconstrained optimization, the method moves from the initial point, along a line in an uphill direction, to the

---

[2]The hill-climbing method Solver uses for optimizing nonlinear models is completely different from the simplex method it uses to optimize an LP model.

highest point that can be attained on that line. Then a new uphill direction is defined, and the procedure is continued. The method terminates when the approximated first partial derivatives are sufficiently close to zero. Such a point, then, will always be a "local peak." Other local maxima are searched for by initiating the optimizer package to start at a different point.

The description above reveals the main role of the first-order necessary conditions in nonlinear optimizers. They are used indirectly, in the sense that they serve as a *termination criterion* for the hill-climbing computer methods that search for local optima. The second-order sufficiency conditions, for the general problem in n variables, are mainly of theoretic interest, and go beyond the introductory nature of this chapter.

In concluding this section we mention one other important result when maximizing a *concave function*. For a concave function, any stationary point is a global maximizer (for a convex function, any stationary point is a global minimizer). Whereas in the general case an optimized solution could be a local maximizer or minimizer or neither, in the concave case we are guaranteed that any solution is a global maximizer. This fact is important in optimizing quadratic nonlinear models, a topic covered in Section 8.8.

8.3 NONLINEAR OPTIMIZATION WITH CONSTRAINTS: A DESCRIPTIVE GEOMETRIC INTRODUCTION

Nonlinear optimization, up to this point, has focused on *unconstrained* optimization. More typically, in a management-oriented decision-making setting, we are interested in optimizing an objective function subject to constraints. These constraints are in the form of mathematical equalities and/or inequalities, just as in the case of linear programming, except linearity is not assumed in this case. Thus, the *general mathematical programming model,* in symbolic terms, can be written in the form illustrated below.

$$\text{Max } f(x_1, x_2, \ldots, x_n) \qquad \text{(objective function)}$$
$$\text{s.t. } g_1(x_1, \ldots, x_n) = b_1$$
$$g_2(x_1, \ldots, x_n) = b_2$$
$$\vdots \qquad\qquad\qquad \text{(m equality constraints)}$$
$$g_m(x_1, \ldots, x_n) = b_m$$
$$h_1(x_1, \ldots, x_n) \leq r_1$$
$$h_2(x_1, \ldots, x_n) \leq r_2$$
$$\vdots \qquad\qquad\qquad \text{(k inequality constraints)}$$
$$h_k(x_1, \ldots, x_n) \leq r_k$$

GRAPHICAL ANALYSIS
Just as with LP, we can use two-dimensional geometry to gain insight into this problem. For example, let us use graphical analysis to solve the specific problem

$$\text{Max} \quad x_1 - x_2$$
$$\text{s.t.} \quad -x_1^2 + x_2 \geq 1$$
$$x_1 + x_2 \leq 3$$
$$-x_1 + x_2 \leq 2$$
$$x_1 \geq 0, x_2 \geq 0$$

Note that everything in this model is linear except for the first constraint. A model is called nonlinear if at least one of the constraint functions or the objective function or both are nonlinear. Therefore, the model above is properly termed a **nonlinear program (NLP).**

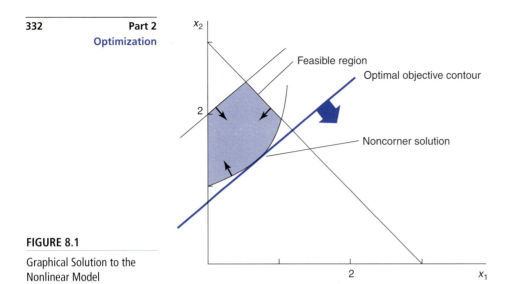

FIGURE 8.1

Graphical Solution to the
Nonlinear Model

The Feasible Region In order to use the graphical approach to solve this problem, we proceed just as we did in LP. First we plot the set of points that simultaneously satisfy *all* the constraints. This set of points is called, just as in LP, the *constraint set,* or the *feasible region.* This set represents the allowable decisions. In order to find an allowable decision that maximizes the objective function, we find the "most uphill" (i.e., highest-valued) *contour* of the objective function that still touches the constraint set. The point at which it touches will be an optimal solution (often more simply referred to as a solution) to the problem. Figure 8.1 shows the graphical solution to the problem presented above.

You can see in Figure 8.1 that the nonlinear constraint puts curvature into the boundary of the constraint set. The feasible set is no longer a polyhedron (i.e., a flat-sided figure defined by linear inequalities) as is the case with LP, and the optimal solution does not lie on a corner. Recall that in the LP case, the graphical analysis allowed us to identify the active constraints at an optimal corner, and then the *exact solution* was obtained by solving two equations in two unknowns. In general this method does not work in the nonlinear case. As shown in Figure 8.1, there is only one active constraint.

Noncorner Optima Another example of an NLP is shown in Figure 8.2, which shows a *hypothetical* nonlinear inequality constrained maximization model. In this figure the constraints are all linear, and hence the constraint set is a polyhedron. The objective function, however, is nonlinear, and again it is seen that the solution does not occur at a corner. In fact, for some nonlinear objective functions the optimal solution may not even lie on the boundary of the feasible region. Of course, a solution *could* appear at a corner, but the important point is that this property is not guaranteed, as it is in the linear model.

This fact has significant algorithmic implications. It means that in the nonlinear case, we cannot use a "corner-searching" method such as the simplex method used by Solver for finding a solution to LP models. This restriction enormously complicates the solution procedure. The topic of solution procedures will be taken up in the next three sections.

COMPARISONS BETWEEN LP AND NLP

There are several instructive parallels between LP and NLP. For example, the following four statements hold *in either type of model.*

1. Increasing (decreasing) the RHS on a $\leq$ ($\geq$) constraint loosens the constraint. This cannot contract and may expand the constraint set.

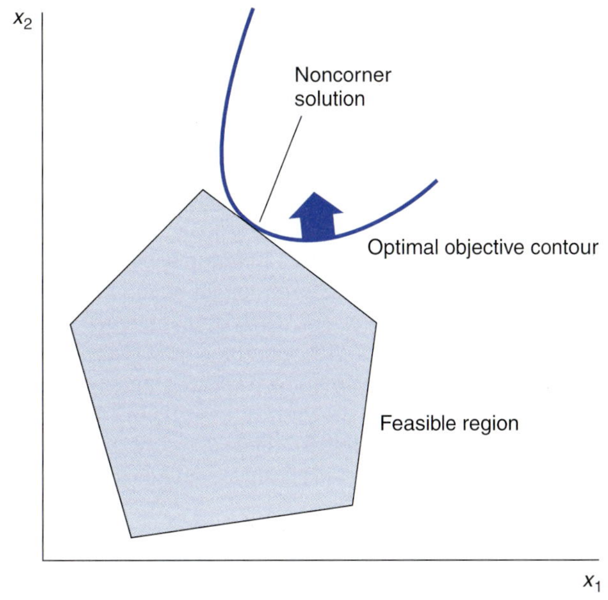

FIGURE 8.2

Noncorner Solution to NLP

2. Increasing (decreasing) the RHS on a $\geq$ ($\leq$) constraint tightens the constraint. This cannot expand and may contract the constraint set.

3. Loosening a constraint cannot hurt and may help the optimal objective value.

4. Tightening a constraint cannot help and may hurt the optimal objective value.

Another concept that is common to both LP and NLP is the notion of changes in the objective function value (OV) as a right-hand side changes, with all other data held fixed. In LP we defined (see Chapter 5) the *shadow price* on a specified constraint to be *the rate of change in OV as the RHS of that constraint increases,* with all other data unchanged. In the NLP context this rate of change is often called the **Lagrange multiplier** as opposed to the shadow price, but the meaning is the same.

The Lagrange Multiplier There is, however, one important property of shadow price associated with LP that Lagrange multipliers in the NLP context will not generally share. Recall that in an LP the shadow price is constant for a range of value for the RHS of interest. It can be easily illustrated that in the NLP context this property does not generally hold true. As an illustration, consider the following simple NLP:

$$\text{Max} \quad x^2$$
$$\text{s.t.} \quad x \leq b$$
$$x \geq 0$$

In order to maximize x^2, we want to make x as large as possible. Thus, the optimal solution is $x^* = b$, and the optimal value of the objective function, OV, is $(x^*)^2 = b^2$. Thus, you can see that the OV is a function of b. That is,

$$\text{OV}(b) = b^2$$

From basic calculus we know that the rate of change of this function as b increases is the derivative of $\text{OV}(b)$, namely $2b$. In other words, the Lagrange multiplier is *not* constant for a range of values of the RHS, b. It varies continuously with b, as might be expected.[3]

---

[3]It may be briefly noted that this same example also serves to illustrate that the optimal value for an NLP max problem can exhibit increasing marginal returns. This can never happen in LP (i.e., the OV for an LP max model is *always* concave and hence exhibits nonincreasing marginal returns).

Local Versus Global Solutions Another important difference between LP and NLP has to do with *global* versus *local solutions*. In an LP, it is always true that there cannot be a local solution that is not also global. This is not usually true for general nonlinear programming problems. In other words, such problems may have local as well as global solutions. This is illustrated by the hypothetical Max model in Figure 8.3. In this figure, the point identified as "Local max" is termed a *local constrained maximizer* because the value of the objective function at this point is no smaller than at its neighboring feasible points.

The point identified as "Global max" is termed a *global constrained maximizer* because the value of the objective function at this point is no smaller than at *all other* feasible points. As was the case with unconstrained optimization, certain convexity and concavity conditions must be satisfied to guarantee that a local constrained optimizer is also global. These properties will be defined in Section 8.6. In the absence of these properties it is generally *not* possible to know whether a given solution is a local or a global maximizer.

EQUALITY-CONSTRAINED NLPs

Many nonlinear problems in business and economics are of the following form:

$$\textbf{Maximize (or Minimize) } f(x_1, \ldots, x_n)$$
$$\text{s.t. } g_i(x_1, \ldots, x_n) = b_i, i = 1, \ldots, m(m < n)$$

That is, the goal is to maximize or minimize an objective function in n variables subject to a set of m ($m < n$) *equality* constraints. Here are three examples.

Example 1 A manufacturer can make a product on either of two machines. Let x_1 denote the quantity made on machine 1, and x_2 the amount on machine 2. Let

$$a_1 x_1 + b_1 x_1^2 = \text{cost of producing on machine 1}$$
$$a_2 x_2 + b_2 x_2^2 = \text{cost of producing on machine 2}$$

Determine the values of x_1 and x_2 that minimize total cost subject to the requirement that total production is some specified value, say R. The formulation of this problem is

$$\text{Min } a_1 x_1 + b_1 x_1^2 + a_2 x_2 + b_2 x_2^2$$
$$\text{s.t. } x_1 + x_2 = R$$

Example 2 Let $p_1, p_2,$ and p_3 denote given prices of three goods, and let B denote the available budget (i.e., B is a specified constant). Let $s_1, s_2,$ and s_3 be given constants, and let $x_1^{s_1} + x_2^{s_2} + x_3^{s_3}$ denote the "utility derived" from consuming x_1 units of good 1, x_2 units

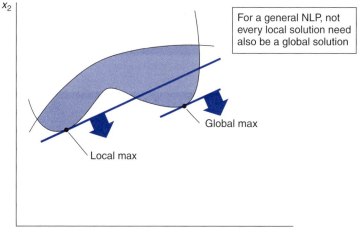

FIGURE 8.3

Local and Global Solutions

of good 2, and x_3 units of good 3. Determine the consumption mix that maximizes utility subject to the budget constraint. The formulation of this problem is

$$\text{Max } x_1^{s_1} + x_2^{s_2} + x_3^{s_3}$$
$$\text{s.t. } p_1 x_1 + p_2 x_2 + p_3 x_3 = B$$

Example 3 Consider the problem

$$\text{Max } x_1 - x_2$$
$$\text{s.t. } -x_1^2 + x_2 = 1$$

The geometric analysis is shown in Figure 8.4. This analysis shows that at the optimal solution the contour of the objective function is tangent to the equality constraint. It also suggests that the optimal solution is approximately $x_1^* = 0.5$ and $x_2^* = 1.25$. This is confirmed by the spreadsheet version of this model shown in Figure 8.5, which gives the optimal solution.

8.4   USING SOLVER FOR NLP MODELS

We have seen from our study of linear programming that it is very natural to construct linear models with linear inequality constraints, and optimize them with Solver. Solver also allows us to easily enter and optimize a model that could contain

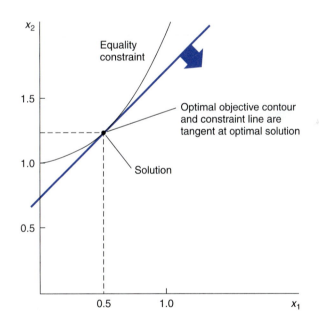

FIGURE 8.4

Graphical Solution of Example 3

	A	B	C	D	E	F	G
1		Example 3	X1	X2	Payoff		
2		Decisions:	0.50001	1.25001	-0.75		
3		Constraint:	-0.25001	1.25001	1	=1	
4							

	A	B	C	D	E	F	G
1		Example 3	X1	X2	Payoff		
2		Decisions:	0.500007	1.250	=C2-D2		
3		Constraint:	=-C2*C2	=D2	=SUM(C3:D3)	1	
4							

FIGURE 8.5

Solver Solution of Example 3

a nonlinear objective or nonlinear constraint functions or both. Remember, however, that Solver uses completely different solution methods for LP and NLP formulations. For LP optimization, Solver uses the simplex method to move from corner to corner in the feasible region. For NLP optimization Solver uses a hill-climbing method based upon a "gradient search" procedure. Summarized, the steps of the procedure are as follows. First, the procedure finds a feasible solution; that is, a set of decision variable values that satisfies the constraints. Then, from that initial starting point, a direction is computed that most rapidly improves the OV. Movement by means of changes in values of decision variables is made in that direction until a constraint boundary is encountered or until the OV no longer improves. Next, a new direction is computed from that new point, and the process is repeated. This continues until no further improvement in any direction occurs, terminating the procedure.

As discussed in the Solver Appendix, an objective function is not even necessary; if one is not given, Solver will try to identify a feasible solution. So Solver can be used to test for feasibility of the constraint set or to solve systems of linear or nonlinear equations. It is also not necessary to include any constraints, so that Solver can be used to do unconstrained optimization of NLP models.[4]

As we admonished for LP optimization, Solver is susceptible to numerical analysis errors caused by the finite precision of computer arithmetic. This is especially a problem for optimizing highly nonlinear models involving numbers spanning a wide range of values. If your model's smallest numbers and largest numbers differ by more than about seven orders of magnitude, then the Solver solution procedure is susceptible to these errors. Checking Solver Option's "Use Automatic Scaling" box will assist in preventing these errors in many instances. However, that option is *not* guaranteed to prevent this problem in all cases. It is better to manually rescale very large or very small numbers to avoid this problem in the first place. See the Solver Appendix for further discussion and examples of rescaling.

8.5 EXAMPLE NONLINEAR MODELS WITH INEQUALITY CONSTRAINTS

To illustrate NLP concepts, the balance of this section will present several more examples. These examples will involve the more general case of inequality constraints.

Optimal Marketing Expenditures A restaurant's average daily budget for advertising is $100, all of which is to be allocated to newspaper ads and radio commercials. Suppose that we let

x_1 = average number of dollars per day spent on newspaper ads

x_2 = average number of dollars per day spent on radio commercials

In terms of these quantities, the restaurant's total annual cost of running the advertising department has been estimated to be

$$\text{cost} = C(x_1, x_2) = 20{,}000 - 440x_1 - 300x_2 + 20x_1^2 + 12x_2^2 + x_1x_2$$

Find the budget allocation that will minimize this total annual cost.

The model to be solved is

$$\text{Min } 20{,}000 - 440x_1 - 300x_2 + 20x_1^2 + 12x_2^2 + x_1x_2$$

$$\text{s.t. } x_1 + x_2 = 100 \text{ and } x_1 \geq 0, x_2 \geq 0$$

The Solver optimized version of this model is given in Figure 8.6, along with its Sensitivity Report. The Lagrange multiplier indicates that the initial rate of increase in the

---

[4]Unconstrained optimization is meaningful only for nonlinear models.

	B	C	D	E	F	G	H
1	Marketing Expenditure Example						
2		NewsAds	RadioAds	(NewsAds)^2	(RadioAds)^2	NewsAds·RadioAds	
3	Decisions:	$39.355	$60.645	1548.8	3677.8	2386.7	Annual Cost
4	20,000	-440	-300	20	12	1	$61,987.10
5				Daily Total	Budget		
6	Expenditures	$39.355	$60.645	$100.00	=100		
7							

Cell	Formula
H4	= B4+SUMPRODUCT(C3:G3,C4:G4)
E6	= SUM(C6:D6)

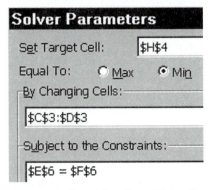

Solver Parameters

Set Target Cell: $H$4

Equal To: ○ Max   ⦿ Min

By Changing Cells:

$C$3:$D$3

Subject to the Constraints:

$E$6 = $F$6

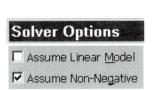

Solver Options

☐ Assume Linear Model

☑ Assume Non-Negative

Microsoft Excel 8.0 Sensitivity Report
Adjustable Cells

Cell	Name	Final Value	Reduced Gradient
$C$3	Decisions: NewsAds	$39.355	0.00
$D$3	Decisions: RadioAds	$60.645	0.00

Constraints

Cell	Name	Final Value	Lagrange Multiplier
$E$6	Expenditures Daily Total	$100.00	1,194.8

FIGURE 8.6

Optimal Marketing
Expenditures

total annual cost of the advertising department would be about $1195 for each additional budget dollar spent on advertisements.

ECONOMIC INTERPRETATION OF LAGRANGE MULTIPLIERS AND REDUCED GRADIENTS

Lagrange multipliers have an interesting and important economic interpretation. As mentioned previously, the Lagrange multipliers in NLP have almost the same interpretation as the shadow prices in LP. In other words, at optimality the value of the Lagrange multiplier is the instantaneous *rate of change* in the OV, the optimal value of the objective function, as the ith RHS, b_i, is increased, with all other data unchanged. Another way of saying this, in economic terminology, is that the ith Lagrange multiplier reflects the marginal value of the ith resource. Thus, its units are

$$\frac{\text{units of the objective function}}{\text{units of RHS of constraint } i}$$

Recall Example 1, where a manufacturer wished to minimize total product cost, the objective in dollars, subject to the restriction that the total production, say in tons, of two products had to equal R. The Lagrange multiplier for this restriction then has units of dollars per ton, and its value is the instantaneous marginal cost of producing the Rth unit.

From our earlier discussion, however, the sensitivity numbers have a somewhat more restricted meaning in the NLP Sensitivity Report. For NLP models the Lagrange multiplier of a constraint is the *initial* (i.e., instantaneous) rate of change in the optimal value of the objective function as the RHS of the constraint is increased. Like LP shadow prices, a positive Lagrange multiplier would indicate that increasing the RHS would initially "help" the objective function value in a Max model and would initially "hurt" the objective function value in a Min model. A negative Lagrange multiplier would indicate that increasing the RHS would initially "hurt" the objective function value in a Max model and would initially "help" the objective function value in a Min model. *Help* means an increase in the objective in a Max model and a decrease in the objective in a Min model. Similarly, *hurt* means a decrease in the objective in a Max model and an increase in the objective in a Min model. However, in contrast to what we've learned about linear programming, it is not possible to say over what range of increase or decrease of the RHS the stated Lagrange multiplier is valid. In fact, the usual case is for the Lagrange multiplier itself to change as soon as the RHS changes, so that the allowable increase and decrease are zero. However, this does not prevent us from using the Lagrange multiplier to *estimate* what will happen to the optimal value if the RHS is changed.

Similarly, the Reduced Gradient values in Solver's NLP Sensitivity Report have an analogous interpretation as the Reduced Cost values for the LP Sensitivity Report covered in Chapter 5. The **reduced gradient** of a variable relates to the upper- or lower-bound constraints on decision variables. A negative reduced gradient for a decision variable indicates that *increasing* the variable will initially "hurt" the objective function value in a Max model while a positive reduced gradient for a variable indicates that *increasing* the variable will initially "hurt" the objective function value in a Min model. If a decision variable is at its upper bound, the reduced gradient should be nonnegative for the solution to be optimal in a Max model; otherwise, decreasing the variable would improve the objective function value. If a decision variable is at its lower bound, the reduced gradient should be nonpositive in a Max model; otherwise, increasing the variable would improve the objective function. (The opposite conclusions are the case for Min models.) If a decision variable is between its upper and lower bounds, the reduced gradient should be zero for the solution to be optimal, as is the case for the model in Figure 8.6.

Astro and Cosmo Revisited When the Astro and Cosmo problem was formulated in Chapter 3, it was assumed that the unit profit per TV set was constant over all feasible product mixes. Suppose that in fact more TV sets can be sold only if the selling price is reduced; that is, the company faces downward sloping demand curves for its products. Suppose further that (for relevant daily production values, A and C) these demand curves are quantified by the following equations:

$$PA = .01A^2 - 1.9A + 314$$
$$PC = -.14C + 243$$

where

$$A = \text{daily production of Astros}$$
$$PA = \text{selling price of Astros}$$
$$C = \text{daily production of Cosmos}$$
$$PC = \text{selling price of Cosmos}$$

In the preceding expression, PA is the price that the company must set for Astros in order to sell all of the Astros it produces. A similar interpretation applies to PC and Cosmos. It follows that the profit per unit now depends on the total production. If the unit variable cost of an Astro is $210 and the unit variable cost of a Cosmo is $230, then the total profit is

$$\text{profit} = (PA - 210)A + (PC - 230)C$$

which gives us a nonlinear objective function. The complete NLP is given below. Note that it contains two equality constraints defining the selling price of each product in terms of its production. One of these constraints is nonlinear. Since PA is a function of A and PC is a function of C, the objective function is also nonlinear.

Max	$(PA - 210)A + (PC - 230)C$		
s.t.	PA	$= .01A^2 - 1.9A + 314$	(selling price of Astros)
	PC	$= -.14C + 243$	(selling price of Cosmos)
	A	≤ 70	(capacity of Astro line)
	C	≤ 50	(capacity of Cosmo line)
	$A + 2C$	≤ 120	(department A labor hours)
	$A + C$	≤ 90	(department B labor hours)
	$A, PA, C, PC \geq 0$		

Figure 8.7 shows how this model would appear for Solver.

Figure 8.8 gives the Sensitivity Report for the Astro and Cosmo model. The constraint on labor hours in department A is binding. The Lagrange multiplier (i.e., shadow price) on that constraint indicates that initially the OV increases at the rate of about $0.86 per unit of additional labor hours in department A. If we had 10 more hours available in department A, we might estimate that the objective function would increase by 10 × 0.858, or $8.58. However, such an estimate would be quite inaccurate, for actually increasing the RHS by 10 and reoptimizing the model gives a new objective function value of $2061.51 (not shown), an increase of only $5.24. This illustrates the previously stated fact that in NLP models Lagrange multipliers reflect only the *initial* rate of improvement in OV, and this rate may change considerably as the RHS is changed. This is true even when the RHS change is small. The initial, or marginal, information may be useful, but the bottom line is that caution should be used in extrapolating that information.

We have learned that, in linear programming, if an optimal solution exists, some corner of the feasible region must be optimal. Figure 8.9 shows that for the Astro and Cosmo nonlinear model the optimal solution does not occur at a corner of the feasible region, though it is on the boundary. In fact, for different demand curves, the optimal solution may not even be on the boundary of the feasible region.

OPTIMALITY IN NLPs

In LP models we have become accustomed to looking at the solution produced by Solver and being confident that we do indeed have the optimal solution. Life is not so simple with NLPs. Solver might stop at a solution that is not optimal, or it might stop at an optimal solution that is a local rather than a global optimum. You must be aware of these possibilities and be prepared to take appropriate action. These ideas are illustrated by the following example.

Gulf Coast Oil Model Chapter 3 presented an example of a blending problem that can be formulated as a linear program. Some blending problems, however, require a nonlinear formulation. Consider the case of Gulf Coast Oil that blends gasoline from three components: Domestic Blend, Foreign Blend, and an octane Additive used only in Premium gasoline. Foreign Blend is itself a blending of two sources. Foreign Blend is transported monthly to Gulf Coast Oil in a single 8,000,000-gallon storage compartment of a large tanker. Because the oil purchased from the two sources loses its separate identities when "pooled" in the storage compartment of the tanker, the model is called a *pooling model*. As we shall see, this "pooling" process is responsible for introducing nonlinearities into the model. Octane numbers, cost per gallon, and availability information for each component are given in Table 8.1.

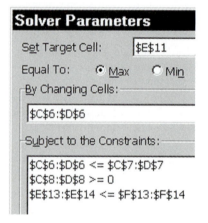

	A	B	C	D	E	F	G
1		Astro Cosmo Model					
2		Demand	Astro	Cosmo			
3		Sqrd. Term	0.01	0	Demand Coefs.		
4		Linear Term	-1.9	-0.14			
5		Constant	314	243			
6		Production	39.40	40.30			
7		Prod. Limit	<=70	<=50			
8		Price	$254.67	$237.36			
9		Unit Cost	$210.00	$230.00			
10		Cont. Marg.	$44.67	$7.36	Total		
11		Profit	$1,759.74	$296.53	$2,056		
12		Constraints			Total	Avail.	
13		Dept. A Hrs.	1	2	120	<=120	
14		Dept. B Hrs.	1	1	79.70	<=90	
15							

Cell	Formula	Copy To
C8	= C3*C6^2+C4*C6+C5	D8
C11	= C6*C10	D11
E13	= SUMPRODUCT($C$6:$D$6,C13:D13)	E14

Solver Parameters

Set Target Cell: $E$11

Equal To: ● Max   ○ Min

By Changing Cells:

$C$6:$D$6

Subject to the Constraints:

$C$6:$D$6 <= $C$7:$D$7
$C$8:$D$8 >= 0
$E$13:$E$14 <= $F$13:$F$14

Solver Options

☐ Assume Linear Model
☑ Assume Non-Negative

FIGURE 8.7

Solver Solution to Astro and Cosmo Model

Microsoft Excel 8.0 Sensitivity Report
Adjustable Cells

Cell	Name	Final Value	Reduced Gradient
$C$6	Production Astro	39.40	0.00
$D$6	Production Cosmo	40.30	0.00

Constraints

Cell	Name	Final Value	Lagrange Multiplier
$E$13	Dept. A Hrs. Total	120	0.858
$E$14	Dept. B Hrs. Total	79.70	0.00
$C$8	Price Astro	$254.67	0.00
$D$8	Price Cosmo	$237.36	0.00

FIGURE 8.8

Sensitivity Report for Astro and Cosmo Model

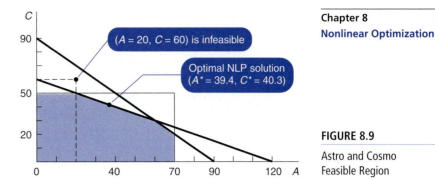

FIGURE 8.9

Astro and Cosmo
Feasible Region

TABLE 8.1 Component Characteristics

COMPONENT	OCTANE NO.	COST PER GALLON	AVAILABILITY (000s GAL/MONTH)
Domestic Blend	85	$ 0.65	10,000
Foreign Blend			
Source 1	93	$ 0.80	*
Source 2	97	$ 0.90	*
Premium Additive	900	$30	50

*Because of the way Gulf Coast Oil obtains Source 1 and Source 2, no more than 8,000,000 gallons of Source 1 *plus* Source 2 may be obtained per month.

TABLE 8.2 Product Characteristics

	MINIMUM OCTANE NO.	SALES PRICE PER GALLON
Regular Unleaded	87	$1.18
Midgrade Unleaded	89	$1.25
Premium Unleaded	94	$1.40

The problem Gulf Coast Oil faces is to decide how many gallons of Regular Unleaded, Midgrade Unleaded, and Premium Unleaded gasoline to blend each month, given that it must honor minimum supply contracts of 100,000 gallons of each type of gasoline. Each gasoline is subject to a minimum octane requirement. The octane number of a blend is the weighted average of the octane numbers of its components where the weights are the fraction of each component in the blend. Data on minimum octane numbers and (wholesale) selling prices are given in Table 8.2.

The following decision variables are used in the formulation:

$$R = \text{thousand gallons of Regular Unleaded gas produced}$$
$$M = \text{thousand gallons of Midgrade Unleaded gas produced}$$
$$P = \text{thousand gallons of Premium Unleaded gas produced}$$
$$D = \text{thousand gallons of Domestic Blend purchased}$$
$$A = \text{thousand gallons of Premium Additive purchased}$$
$$RD = \text{thousand gallons of Domestic Blend in regular unleaded}$$

RF = thousand gallons of Foreign Blend in Regular Unleaded

MD = thousand gallons of Domestic Blend in Midgrade Unleaded

MF = thousand gallons of Foreign Blend in Midgrade Unleaded

PD = thousand gallons of Domestic Blend in Premium Unleaded

PF = thousand gallons of Foreign Blend in Premium Unleaded

Taking account of the pooling nature of the model requires three additional decision variables:

$S1$ = thousand gallons purchased from Foreign Source 1

$S2$ = thousand gallons purchased from Foreign Source 2

OCT = octane number of pooled Foreign Blend

The octane number is a weighted average of the octanes from the two foreign sources determined by the following nonlinear equation:

$$OCT = \frac{93S1 + 97S2}{S1 + S2}$$

The trick of multiplying both sides by the denominator to obtain a linear equation no longer works.

$$OCT(S1 + S2) = 93S1 + 97S2$$

This expression is nonlinear because OCT is now a variable, and hence the left side contains a product of variables.

The symbolic model is given below (in thousands of gallons). Note that the minimum octane constraints are also nonlinear. Also note that the true decision variables are RD, RF, MD, MF, PD, PF, A, $S1$, and $S2$. All other variables can be interpreted as intermediate variables.

Max $1.18R + 1.25M + 1.40P - .65D - .8S1 - .9S2 - 30A$

s.t. $R =$	$RD + RF$	(composition of Regular Unleaded gasoline)
$M =$	$MD + MF$	(composition of Midgrade Unleaded gasoline)
$P =$	$PD + PF + A$	(composition of Premium Unleaded gasoline)
$D =$	$RD + MD + PD$	(total Domestic Blend used)
$RF + MF + PF =$	$S1 + S2$	(uses must equal supply of Foreign Blend)

The following four constraints are the nonlinear aspects of the model.

$85RD + OCT*RF \geq$	$87R$	(min octane number for Regular Unleaded)
$85MD + OCT*MF \geq$	$89M$	(min octane number for Midgrade Unleaded)
$85PD + OCT*PF + 900A \geq$	$94P$	(min octane number for Premium Unleaded)
$OCT(S1 + S2) =$	$93S1 + 97S2$	(pooling constraint for foreign sources)
$S1 + S2 \leq$	$8,000$	(tanker capacity for foreign sources)
$D \leq$	$10,000$	(supply limit for Domestic Blend)
$A \leq$	50	(supply limit for Premium Additive)
R, M, and Peach $\geq$	100	(contract delivery minimums)

All variables are nonnegative.

The spreadsheet model with example decision values is shown in Figure 8.10. The nine decision cells are F2:F3, C6:E7, and E8; i.e., amount of foreign purchases, amount of foreign and domestic purchases into each of the three gasolines, and amount of additive used, respectively. Note that the pooling of foreign purchased oil does not allow specific assignment of Source 1 nor Source 2 gallons to any of the three gasoline types, only the assignment of the pooled Foreign Blend. Also, the additive is used only in the Premium gasoline. These are the reasons for the grayed-out cells in the middle of the spreadsheet.

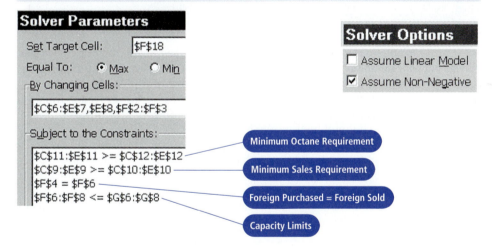

FIGURE 8.10

Gulf Coast Oil Model

	Gulf Coast Oil Model	Regular	Midgrade	Premium	Foreign Purchases		Octane	Unit Cost
2			Foreign Source 1		1.0		93	$0.80
3			Foreign Source 2		2.0		97	$0.90
4	Gasoline Sold	Regular	Midgrade	Premium	3.0 =Pooled Foreign Purchased			
5	Price Per Gallon	$1.18	$1.25	$1.40	Total	Capacity	Octane	Unit Cost
6	Foreign Blend Gal.	1.0	1.0	1.0	3	<=8000	95.67	$0.87
7	Domestic Gal.	0.0	0.0	0.0	0	<=10,000	85	$0.65
8	Prem. Additive Gal.			0	0	<=50	900	$30.00
9	Total Gallons Sold	1.0	1.0	1.0	3			
10	Minimum Sales	>=100	>=100	>=100				
11	Octane of Gas. Sold	95.67	95.67	95.67				
12	Min Octane	>=87	>=89	>=94	Total			
13	Gasoline Revenue	$1.18	$1.25	$1.40	$3.83			
14	Foreign Blend Cost	$0.87	$0.87	$0.87	$2.60			
15	Domestic Cost	$0.00	$0.00	$0.00	$0.00			
16	Prem. Additive Cost			$0.00	$0.00			
17	Total Cost	$0.87	$0.87	$0.87	$2.60			
18	Profit	$0.31	$0.38	$0.53	$1.23			

Cell	Formula	Copy To
H6	= ($F$2*H2+$F$3*H3)/($F$4+1E-30)	I6
C11	= SUMPRODUCT(C6:C8,$H$6:$H$8)/(C9+1E-30)	D11:E11
C13	= C9*C5	D13:E13
C14	= C6*$I6	C14:E15, E16
F6	= SUM(C6:E6)	F7:F9, F13:F18

Solver Parameters

Set Target Cell: $F$18

Equal To: ● Max ○ Min

By Changing Cells:

$C$6:$E$7,$E$8,$F$2:$F$3

Subject to the Constraints:

$C$11:$E$11 >= $C$12:$E$12 — Minimum Octane Requirement
$C$9:$E$9 >= $C$10:$E$10 — Minimum Sales Requirement
$F$4 = $F$6 — Foreign Purchased = Foreign Sold
$F$6:$F$8 <= $G$6:$G$8 — Capacity Limits

Solver Options

☐ Assume Linear Model
☑ Assume Non-Negative

The first two constraints of the Solver Parameters dialog refer to the gasoline minimum requirements for octane and quantity produced, respectively. The third constraint forces total Foreign Blend sold in all three gasolines to be equal to Foreign Blend purchased, and the last constraint limits the gasoline components to be less than available capacities. The values for the nine decision variables in Figure 8.10 are not feasible, but, nevertheless, Solver will find an initial starting point from them for Solver's NLP algorithm.

The solution found by Solver is given in Figure 8.11. Note that upon stopping, Solver reports that it has "converged to the solution."[5] This message might suggest that an optimum has been found; in fact, it has not. Solver must state that "all optimality conditions are satisfied" in its completion message for this to be true; that is, that the first-order conditions for an optimum have been satisfied.[6]

TIP: *Recall that during NLP optimization, Solver determines a direction, takes a "hill-climbing or descent" step in that direction, and then evaluates the constraints (for feasibility) and the first-order conditions for that new point (to determine a new direction or to terminate). Since the "step" is taken before the constraints are reevaluated, it is possible that Solver will "overstep," thereby violating one or more constraints. Normally, Solver will detect this new point's infeasibility and will correct, for example, by backing up and taking a smaller step. However, if the infeasible point triggers an Excel error message, then Solver is forced to abort optimization before it can determine that the point is infeasible and back away. Tricks are sometimes needed to avoid this problem during Solver optimization. One solution is to choose starting points far away from regions that cause Solver to overstep into an error-creating point. Another is to creatively modify cell formulas to avoid producing Excel errors while not altering the model's logic significantly. For example, the original formula for cell E11 in the Gulf Coast Oil model calculated the octane number for Premium gasoline:*

=SUMPRODUCT(E6:E8, $H$6:$H$8)/E9

During optimization Solver may overstep and force the Premium gasoline sold in cell E9 temporarily to be zero. This will trigger a "#DIV/0!" error in cell E11, stopping the NLP algorithm before Solver determines that the minimum Premium gasoline quantity constraint in cells E9:E10 is violated. The trick of adding a very small constant to the divisor in the cell E11 formula, as below, avoids the error, thereby allowing Solver to continue its NLP optimization.

=SUMPRODUCT(E6:E8, $H$6:$H$8)/(E9+1E-30)

---

[5]Your results may vary, depending on your starting point, the version of Excel you use, and your computer's CPU type.
[6]Consult the Solver Appendix for details on Solver completion messages.

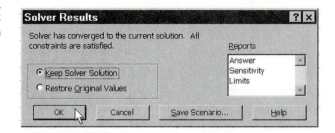

FIGURE 8.11

Solver's First Solution to Gulf
Coast Oil Model

The completion message actually means that Solver has stopped its search because the rate of change in the OV was below the Solver Convergence value, described in more detail below, for five iterations; that is, the rate of improvement in the OV was too low to continue the gradient search method. Since for NLPs, Solver always starts from the given initial set of decisions, if feasible, you can restart Solver to force it to begin optimization again to see if it will improve upon its solution. Evoking Solver a second time and simply clicking the Solve button will cause this to happen, producing the results in Figure 8.12, after only a small additional change in the decisions. Solver now reports the desirable completion message, ". . . All constraints and optimality conditions are satisfied," which means that the necessary first-order conditions for an optimum are satisfied. And the Solver solution looks reasonable. However, it would be prudent to explore different initial guesses, because this solution may be a local optimum, and not the global optimum.

USE OF AN INITIAL GUESS

When Solver optimizes an NLP, it requires an initial guess of the optimal solution. As mentioned, this initial guess, which need not be feasible (Solver will correct for that), is the starting point for the NLP method. Because of the form of the nonlinear constraints, this particular Gulf Coast Oil model is called a *nonconcave model*. As we will see in the next section, the starting point for the method can be quite important for this class of model, and several different starting points may be required to find a "good" solution. Guessing all zeros for the decisions is often a very poor choice of an initial point for nonconcave models. Much better is to guess an initial starting point near the global optimal solution to the model. Of course, this is a bit of a "Catch-22" situation: You must know the model's optimal solution to produce a good initial guess for finding the optimal solution. Nevertheless, this is an unfortunate consequence of NLP models. Particularly for nonconcave models, there is no guarantee that the Solver solution is the global optimal one. In fact, after two attempts to optimize the Gulf Coast Oil model above, Solver has converged

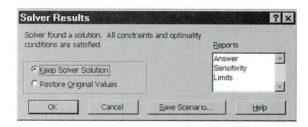

FIGURE 8.12

Solver's Optimal Solution to
Gulf Coast Oil Model

to a local optimum in Figure 8.12 and not the global optimum. The global optimum for this model is believed to be the one displayed in Figure 8.13, which also displays the Sensitivity Report.

We emphasize the solution of Figure 8.13 "is believed to be" optimal because there exists no test that guarantees this solution is the global optimum for the Gulf Coast Oil model. It was found by re-optimizing the model many times, each time using a different initial set of decision values. As we will see, there is a "nice" class of NLPs, called *concave* or *convex* programs, where we do not need to worry about a starting point. For this class of models, Solver's gradient search method finds the desired global optimum solution, no matter where it starts.

It is a useful exercise to interpret the sensitivity information in Figure 8.13. For example, forcing purchase of Foreign Source 1 gallons would reduce profits at an initial rate of $.02 per gallon, and forcing the addition of the additive to Premium gasoline would hurt profit at the rate of $4.42 per gallon, initially (Reduced Gradient values). Also, expanding tanker capacity would help profit by $.59 per gallon initially while increasing the octane requirement for Premium gasoline would hurt profit at the rate of $145.20 per octane point initially (Lagrange Multiplier values).

Before leaving this model, it is worth mentioning that some of the Solver Options for NLPs, as shown in Figure 8.14, should be investigated experimentally, especially when optimizing nonconcave or highly nonlinear models. The Convergence value is used to terminate Solver's search when the OV is improving very slowly. If the improvement is less than or equal to the default value of .001 for five iterations, Solver stops with the completion message of Figure 8.11. Setting Convergence smaller than its default value forces Solver to continue the optimization method even if the rate of change in OV is small.

Setting the Estimates option to "Quadratic" forces Solver to approximate its estimates of the variable equations in its one-dimensional searches by a quadratic (parabolic) function instead of a linear (tangent) one. Also, selecting "Central" instead of "Forward" for computing partial derivatives for the OV and constraints forces Solver to produce a more accurate approximation by estimating each directional derivative using two adjacent points to each iterative solution point instead of just one. Both of these changes improve Solver's numerical estimates of the functions for nonlinear models, but at a cost of longer solution times because of the additional calculations required at each iteration.

Gulf Coast Oil Model | Foreign Purchases | Octane | Unit Cost

				Foreign Purchases			Octane	Unit Cost
			Foreign Source 1	0.0			93	$0.80
			Foreign Source 2	8,000.0			97	$0.90
Gasoline Sold	Regular	Midgrade	Premium	8,000.0	=Pooled Foreign Purchased			
Price Per Gallon	$1.18	$1.25	$1.40	Total	Capacity	Octane	Unit Cost	
Foreign Blend Gal.	16.7	4,353.3	3,630.0	8,000	<=8000	97.00	$0.90	
Domestic Gal.	83.3	8,706.7	1,210.0	10,000	<=10,000	85	$0.65	
Prem. Additive Gal.			0	0	<=50	900	$30.00	
Total Gallons Sold	100.0	13,060.0	4,840.0	18,000				
Minimum Sales	>=100	>=100	>=100					
Octane of Gas. Sold	87.00	89.00	94.00					
Min Octane	>=87	>=89	>=94	Total				
Gasoline Revenue	$118.00	$16,325.00	$6,776.00	$23,219.00				
Foreign Blend Cost	$15.00	$3,918.00	$3,267.00	$7,200.00				
Domestic Cost	$54.17	$5,659.33	$786.50	$6,500.00				
Prem. Additive Cost			$0.00	$0.00				
Total Cost	$69.17	$9,577.33	$4,053.50	$13,700.00				
Profit	$48.83	$6,747.67	$2,722.50	$9,519.00				

Microsoft Excel 8.0 Sensitivity Report
Adjustable Cells

Cell	Name	Final Value	Reduced Gradient
$C$6	Foreign Blend Gal. Regular	16.67	0.0
$D$6	Foreign Blend Gal. Midgrade	4,353.3	0.0
$E$6	Foreign Blend Gal. Premium	3,630.0	0.0
$C$7	Domestic Gal. Regular	83.33	0.0
$D$7	Domestic Gal. Midgrade	8,706.7	0.0
$E$7	Domestic Gal. Premium	1,210.0	0.0
$E$8	Prem. Additive Gal. Premium	0.00	-4.42
$F$2	Foreign Source 1 Foreign Purchases	0.0	-0.02
$F$3	Foreign Source 2 Foreign Purchases	8,000.0	0.0

Constraints

Cell	Name	Final Value	Lagrange Multiplier
$C$11	Octane of Gas. Sold Regular	87.00	-3.00
$D$11	Octane of Gas. Sold Midgrade	89.00	-391.80
$E$11	Octane of Gas. Sold Premium	94.00	-145.20
$F$4	Premium Foreign Purchases	8,000.0	0.0
$C$9	Total Gallons Sold Regular	100.0	-0.01
$D$9	Total Gallons Sold Midgrade	13,060.0	0.0
$E$9	Total Gallons Sold Premium	4,840.0	0.0
$F$6	Foreign Blend Gal. Total	8,000	0.59
$F$7	Domestic Gal. Total	10,000	0.48
$F$8	Prem. Additive Gal. Total	0	0.0

FIGURE 8.13

Optimal Solution to the Gulf Coast Oil Model

Finally, selecting the Conjugate Search option uses less memory during optimization but requires more Solver calculations for a given level of accuracy. However, especially for large nonlinear models, the lower random access memory demands with this option may on balance improve Solver solution speed by reducing memory management overhead.

8.6   SOLVABILITY OF NLP MODELS

The methods for solving general NLP problems are markedly different from the simplex used by Solver for LPs. In LP we saw that for a problem that has an optimal solution, we could always be assured that there would in fact be at least one optimal corner solution. This

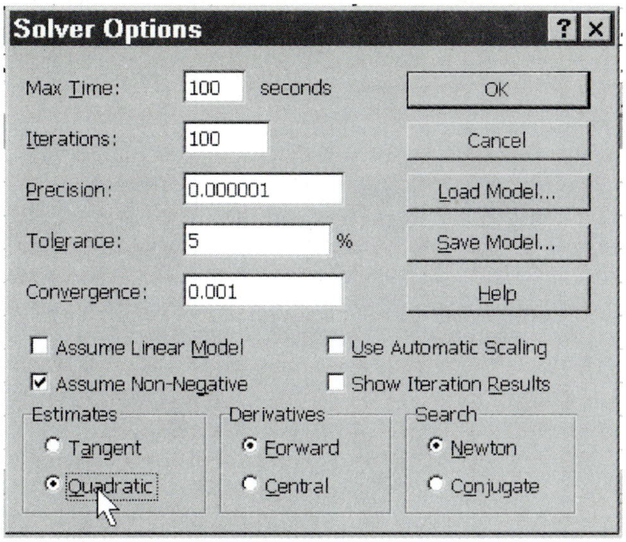

FIGURE 8.14

Solver Options Dialog

is a critically important characteristic of LP models, for the corners of the feasible region can be defined by linear equations in such a way that a simple algebraic operation allows Solver to move from one corner to any adjacent corner at which the objective value either improves or remains at the same value. Using this technique, Solver's simplex method provides a fail-safe method for attacking LP problems. None of these comments apply to the general NLP problem.

Moreover, there is no single preferred optimization method for optimizing NLPs. Without difficulty one can easily find 10 to 15 NLP optimization methods developed in the literature. However, three classes of procedures currently seem to be most useful in solving general nonlinear programs: GRG (generalized reduced gradient), SLP (successive linear programming), and SQP (successive quadratic programming). Solver uses an NLP method in the GRG class. But nonlinear programming is a very broad topic, and many interesting special types of NLP models are identified in the literature. Indeed, many of the solution methods found in the literature are designed to solve special types of NLP models. For example, some methods are designed exclusively for quadratic programming models, covered in the next section, others for models that are "mostly" linear with the nonlinear terms entering the objective function or constraints in special ways.

Rather than confronting you with a compendium of the numerous types of methods for solving NLP models, we shall give a brief description of a few major classes of nonlinear programs that one might encounter in practical applications. That is, we can break down this very general class of models into more special cases, defined by the nature of the objective function and the constraint functions, and then discuss how easily solvable these special cases are. Indeed, from the managerial perspective these are important issues: to know what type of NLP one may be facing, and the prospects for finding a solution. It will be seen that these prospects are heavily dependent on the type of nonlinear model one faces.

We might begin this overview with the observation that nonlinear models are divided into two classes: (1) those that can be solved and (2) those that one can try to solve. The models that can be solved must typically conform to certain qualifications of structure and size. The hierarchy of increasing computational difficulty is shown in Figure 8.15. In this figure, the increasing Roman numerals reflect increasing computational difficulty. Let us now consider these several classes of nonlinear programs in somewhat more detail.

NONLINEAR PROGRAMS THAT CAN BE SOLVED: CONCAVE AND CONVEX PROGRAMS

To define these problems it is necessary to introduce a new technical term, a **convex set of points.** Loosely speaking, this is a set of points without any "holes" or "indentations." More formally, a convex set is any set that has the following property:

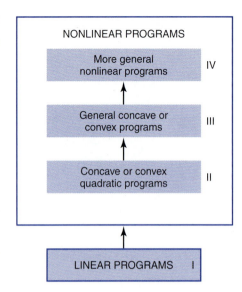

NONLINEAR PROGRAMS

More general
nonlinear programs   IV

General concave or
convex programs   III

Concave or convex
quadratic programs   II

LINEAR PROGRAMS   I

FIGURE 8.15

Increasing Computational
Difficulty

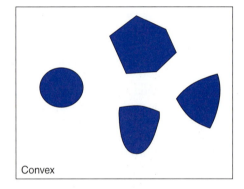 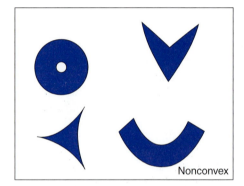

Convex

Nonconvex

FIGURE 8.16

Convex and Nonconvex
Sets of Points

Consider all possible pairs of points in the set, and consider the line segment connecting any such pair. All such line segments must lie entirely within the set.

Figure 8.16 shows two-dimensional sets of points that do not satisfy this property and hence are *not* convex sets, together with sets that are convex. The polygon in the first of these two figures may remind you of the constraint sets that occur in LP problems. This is appropriate since any constraint set for a linear program is a convex set. *The nonlinear programs that we can be reasonably sure of solving must also have convex constraint sets.*

Concave and Convex Functions   The next question to be asked then is: What kinds of nonlinear programs have convex constraint sets? It is useful to be able to use the notion of concave and convex functions in answering this question. If the function has two independent variables, a *concave function* is shaped like an upside-down bowl. In general, a concave function, by definition, has the property that the line segment connecting any two points on the graph of the function never enters the space above the graph (if it always lies strictly under the graph then the function is *strictly concave*). Similarly, if the function has two variables, a *convex function* is shaped like a bowl. In general, a convex function, by definition, has the property that the line segment connecting any two points on the graph of the function never enters the space below the graph (if it always lies strictly above the graph

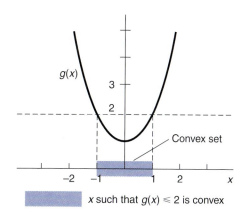

FIGURE 8.17

Constraint Sets $g(x) \leq 2$ and $g(x) \geq 2$

then the function is *strictly convex*). The same ideas hold for functions that have a single variable, or more than two variables. It should also be remarked that a linear function is considered to be both concave and convex (the above mentioned line segments always lie in the graph).

Now suppose that we have a nonlinear program with only inequality constraints.

> If the constraint function associated with each $\leq$ constraint is convex and the constraint function associated with each $\geq$ constraint is concave, the constraint set will be a convex set.

These facts are illustrated in Figure 8.17, which shows a convex function g of a single variable, given by $g(x) = x^2 + 1$. You can see that the set of x values for which $g(x) \leq 2$ is convex (i.e., this is the set $-1 \leq x \leq 1$), whereas the set of x values for which $g(x) \geq 2$ is not convex (i.e., this is the set $x \leq -1, x \geq 1$). This set is not convex because it is possible to find two points in the set (say, $x = +2$ and $x = -2$) such that the straight line that connects them passes through points (e.g., the point $x = 0$) that are not in the set.

Thus, we see that in this example the function $g(x)$ is convex and the set defined by the inequality $g(x) \leq 2$ is convex, whereas the set defined by the inequality $g(x) \geq 2$ is not convex. A similar demonstration could be constructed to show that if the function $g(x)$ is concave, then the set defined by the inequality $g(x) \geq 2$ is convex, whereas the set defined by the inequality $g(x) \leq 2$ is not convex (this is related to the fact that the negative of a concave function is convex and vice versa). We thus have a test at our disposal that will enable us to verify that certain NLPs have a convex constraint set. This test certainly will not enable us to determine if the constraint set for *any* NLP is convex or not. In particular, in the case of models involving one or more *nonlinear equality* constraints, there is great difficulty in characterizing whether or not the constraint set is convex. Concerning the discussion in this subsection, it is worth noting that the term *concave* applies only to functions, whereas the term *convex* can apply either to a function or to a set of points, depending on the context.

Now that you understand the meaning of a convex set, it is easy, at least formally, to define a concave or convex program.

> - A **concave program** is a Max model with a concave objective function and a convex constraint set.
> - A **convex program** is a Min model with a convex objective function and a convex constraint set.

The rationale for this characterization has to do with the fact that in the maximization context, just as in elementary calculus with one variable, concave objective functions are very convenient to work with in terms of the mathematical properties associated with the upside-down bowl shape. Convex objective functions (bowl-shaped) are convenient in the minimization context. Finally, the convexity of the constraint set endows the model with other attractive mathematical properties that can be exploited both theoretically and computationally. A most important characteristic of concave (or convex) programming models is that for such problems *any local constrained optimizer is a global constrained optimizer.* This fact has obvious implications for nonlinear applications of Solver.

Solution Procedures Figure 8.15 indicates that the easiest nonlinear programs are concave or convex quadratic programs. These NLPs, by definition, have linear (equality or inequality) constraints. The objective function must be quadratic and concave if it is a Max model and quadratic and convex if it is a Min model. It turns out that a variation of the simplex method can be used to solve such models, and in practice this is reasonably efficient. It is not uncommon to solve quadratic programs with hundreds of constraints and several thousand variables. As we will see in the next section, financial models such as those used in portfolio analysis are often quadratic programs, so this class of models is of considerable applied importance.

In Figure 8.15 the next level of difficulty involves general (nonquadratic) concave or convex programs. There are numerous mathematical approaches and corresponding algorithms for solving such models. For example, suppose that the problem to be solved is a Max model. Similar to the algorithm used by Solver, many NLP procedures operate as follows:

1. Find an initial feasible point "inside" the constraint set (not on the boundary).

2. Find an uphill direction (or downhill for Min models) and move along this straight line until either reaching a maximum (or minimum) along the line or hitting some boundary of the constraint set.

3. Modify the direction of motion so as to continue uphill (downhill) while remaining in the feasible region.

4. Terminate the algorithm when a point satisfying the necessary optimality conditions is found.

In this type of algorithm, as well as most others that apply to nonlinear programs that are not quadratic, there is considerable use of advanced calculus, and hence it is not possible in this development to go into much detail. Suffice it to say that *for general concave or convex programs, as opposed to linear programs, the number of nonlinear variables (i.e., those that enter into the problem nonlinearly) seems to be more significant than the number of constraints as an indicator of problem difficulty.*

NONLINEAR PROGRAMS THAT WE TRY TO SOLVE

Finally, we consider the highest level of difficulty in Figure 8.15, general nonlinear programs. These models are often called *highly nonlinear,* which usually means that the convexity and concavity properties discussed above are absent. To attack such NLPs, it is common practice to use the same optimizer, such as Solver, one would use for general concave and convex programs. The results are different, however. Any NLP optimizer will generally terminate at a point at which the necessary (i.e., first-order) optimality conditions are satisfied. For a concave or convex program, such a point is guaranteed to be a global optimizer (indeed, if the objective function is *strictly* concave, or *strictly* convex, we are guaranteed that such a point is a *unique* global optimizer). But for general nonlinear programs this need not be true, as illustrated for a problem in one variable in Figure 8.18. The objective function f, which is to be maximized, is neither concave nor convex. The solution to the problem is given by x^*, but the optimizer may terminate at any of the points x_1, x_2, x_3, or x^* (for they will satisfy the necessary conditions). To date, no one has been smart enough to invent algorithms that guarantee complete immunity from this possibility.

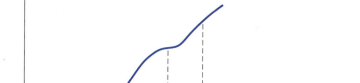

FIGURE 8.18

Nonconcave Constrained
Max Model

In practice, this difficulty is usually overcome by starting the optimizer at several different initial points, as was done in the Gulf Coast Oil model. For example, if the initial guess is somewhat larger than x_3 in Figure 8.18, any reasonable optimizer would converge to x^*. If x_1 had also been obtained by some other initial guess, it would now be rejected, because although we may not know with certainty that x^* is optimal, we would see that the objective value at x_1 is lower than that at x^*.

While the procedure of starting at different points does not guarantee that the global optimum will be found, it has a very practical justification. If the Solver optimization of the NLP can produce a *better* solution than is currently being used in practice, then the use of the NLP model might well be justified. This is consistent with the overall theme that in practice there is nothing so pure as a truly optimal solution. *As we have said, the goal in modeling is always to assist in the search for better decisions. The general considerations are the cost of improvement (the cost of the modeling effort and obtaining the solution) versus the benefit rendered by the solution.*

In concluding, let us address one additional practical aspect. How can we tell whether a nonlinear program in many variables is concave, convex, or neither? In other words, how do we know whether the objective function and the constraints have the right mathematical form? There are several answers to this question:

1. Sometimes, there are mathematical tests that can be applied to the model's functions to determine whether they are concave, convex, or neither.

2. Sometimes, economic intuition is used to assert that such-and-such a phenomenon reflects diminishing marginal returns or increasing marginal costs, and hence the associated function is concave or convex.

3. In many real situations nothing is done to address the question. One simply attempts to solve the model and then inquires as to the practical usefulness of the terminal point (the purported "solution" produced by Solver). As stated above, for a model that is thought or known to be nonconvex or nonconcave, one frequently restarts Solver from many different initial points, to explore the possibility of producing a better terminal point.

Finally, we now have the concepts to state explicitly why we have long advised you to avoid using certain Excel functions that typically produce extreme nonlinear behavior. Examples of these functions are IF(), ABS(), MIN(), and MAX(). Clearly, in most cases, these functions void the use of an LP model by destroying linearity. But they also cause problems in NLPs. These and similar functions can cause either "kinks" or discontinuities in the objective function or constraint values for some values of the decision variables. A kink occurs when the "slope," that is, the set of first partial derivatives, of a smoothly changing function value changes abruptly for some threshold value(s) of decision variable(s), because, for example, an IF() statement triggers a different relationship. Similarly, a discontinuity occurs when the threshold value(s) trigger a completely different relationship by shifting the entire objective or constraint function to a new set of values. Although not discontinuous for the function itself, a kink causes a discontinuity in the partial derivatives to the function that are used for direction finding by Solver's hill-climbing/hill-descent procedure. The result is often lack of convergence as Solver oscillates around the point where the discontinuity occurs in the function or its derivative, ultimately causing Solver to give up and quit, displaying one of its nonoptimal completion messages. Note that this problem is in addition to any difficulty with lack of concavity or convexity in the underlying NLP formulation that can lead to convergence to a local optimum instead of the global optimum.

8.7 INTRODUCTION TO QUADRATIC PROGRAMMING

As indicated in the previous section, a quadratic programming model has the important concavity (convexity) property that avoids the optimization difficulties inherent with more generalized NLPs. In fact, quadratic programming (QP), like linear integer programming, is a first cousin of linear programming, possessing many of LP's desirable properties. Compare the following:

- **Linear Programming.** Maximize or minimize the value of *linear* objective function subject to a set of linear equality and inequality constraints as well as possible nonnegativity conditions on the values of the decision variables.

- **Quadratic Programming.** Maximize or minimize the value of a *quadratic* objective function subject to a set of linear equality and inequality constraints as well as possible nonnegativity conditions on the values of the decision variables.

Obviously, the only difference in these two models is in the functional form of the objective function.

Quadratic Functions We know about linear functions. Here are some examples of quadratic functions:

$$9x_1^2 + 4x_1 + 7$$
$$3x_1^2 - 4x_1x_2 + 15x_2^2 + 20x_1 - 13x_2 - 14$$

These functions are the sum of terms involving the squares of variables (e.g., $3x_1^2$), cross products (e.g., $4x_1x_2$), linear functions (e.g., $20x_1$), and constants (e.g., 14). In general, a quadratic function in N variables can be written in the form

$$\sum_{i=1}^{N} A_i x_i^2 + \sum_{i=1}^{N-1} \sum_{j=i+1}^{N} B_{ij} x_i x_j + \sum_{i=1}^{N} C_i x_i + D$$

Note that when all of the coefficients A_i and B_{ij} are zero then the function is linear. Hence, a linear function is a special case of a quadratic function.

Of course, changing from a linear to a quadratic objective function requires an NLP algorithm to solve the model. This change also implies that many of the facts we have learned about linear programming models no longer hold. The following example illustrates some of the differences between quadratic programming models and linear programming models. The symbolic QP example is

$$
\begin{aligned}
\text{Min} \quad & (x_1 - 6)^2 + (x_2 - 8)^2 \\
\text{s.t.} \quad & x_1 && \leq 7 \\
& x_2 && \leq 5 \\
& x_1 + 2x_2 && \leq 12 \\
& x_1 + x_2 && \leq 9 \\
& x_1, x_2 && \geq 0
\end{aligned}
$$

Geometric Representation A geometric representation of this model appears in Figure 8.19. The constraint set, of course, is the same as for an LP and thus needs no new explanation. In order to see that the objective function is a special case of our previous quadratic function,

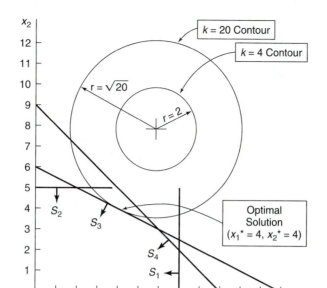

FIGURE 8.19

Graphical Solution for the QP Example

it can be rewritten in the form $x_1^2 - 12x_1 + 36 + x_2^2 - 16x_2 + 64$. You may also recognize the expression

$$(x_1 - 6)^2 + (x_2 - 8)^2 = k$$

as the equation of a circle with radius $\sqrt{k}$ and center at the point (6, 8). Thus, as shown in Figure 8.19, the contours of the objective function are concentric circles around the point (6, 8). Since these contours increase in value as the radius k increases, and since the above model is a minimization model, the optimal solution in Figure 8.19 occurs at the point (4, 4). This can be roughly described as the point where the contour "first touches" the feasible set. In this example that "touch" is a point of tangency, though in other cases a solution could occur at a corner, just as in LP. The value of the objective function at the optimal solution point (4, 4) is $(4 - 6)^2 + (4 - 8)^2 = 20$).

Comparison with LP This example clearly indicates that, in contrast to linear programming:

1. Like NLP models in general, there need not be an optimal corner solution. A method like Solver's simplex, which searches for the best corner, thus cannot be used to solve this model.
2. As a direct result of 1, there may be more positive variables in the optimal solution than there are binding constraints. As we saw with more general NLPs, what makes solving a nonlinear model difficult is that the optimal solution does not necessarily occur at an extreme point of the feasible region. In this example it occurs on the edge of the feasible region, but it is possible for it to occur in the interior. In either case, there are an infinite number of possible solutions (versus IP which has a large finite number).

8.8 SOLVER SOLUTION OF QP PROBLEMS

There are two approaches to optimizing real-world QP models: One is to use a general nonlinear programming optimizer, such as Solver, and the other is to use a specially written quadratic programming optimizer.[7] We will restrict our attention to the use of Excel's Solver.

---

[7]The commercially available version of Solver, Solver Premium Edition, contains both an NLP optimizer and a specialized quadratic optimizer.

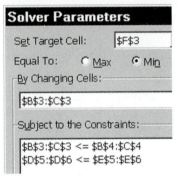

	A	B	C	D	E	F	G
1		QP Example					
2		X1	X2	(X1-6)^2	(X2-8)^2	Total	
3		4.0	4.0	4	16	=20	
4		<=7	<=5	LHS	RHS	Slack	
5		1	2	12	<=12	0	
6		1	1	8	<=9	1	
7							

Solver Parameters

Set Target Cell: $F$3

Equal To: ○ Max   ● Min

By Changing Cells:

$B$3:$C$3

Subject to the Constraints:

$B$3:$C$3 <= $B$4:$C$4
$D$5:$D$6 <= $E$5:$E$6

Solver Options

☐ Assume Linear Model

☑ Assume Non-Negative

Microsoft Excel 8.0 Sensitivity Report

Adjustable Cells

Cell	Name	Final Value	Reduced Gradient
$B$3	X1	4.0	0.0
$C$3	X2	4.0	0.0

Constraints

Cell	Name	Final Value	Lagrange Multiplier
$D$5	LHS	12	-4.0
$D$6	LHS	8	0

FIGURE 8.20

Solver Solution of the
QP Example

For the previous example, Figure 8.20 shows the model, Solver Parameters dialog, optimal solution, and the Sensitivity Report. In the next section the Lagrange Multiplier column of the Sensitivity Report is interpreted through a geometric analysis. For the present, concerning the Sensitivity Report in Figure 8.20, we simply restate the following definitions given earlier:

- Consider the number in the Lagrange Multiplier column corresponding to the ith constraint. Just as in LP this represents the rate of change in OV as the ith RHS is increased, with all other data unchanged.

- In the absence of direct upper- or lower-bound constraints, the Reduced Gradient column applies to a nonnegative variable whose optimal value is zero. For such a variable, the reduced gradient is the rate at which the objective value is "hurt" as that variable is forced to assume positive values in an optimal solution.

8.9 GEOMETRIC INTERPRETATION OF QP SENSITIVITY ANALYSIS

Using the approach we applied to NLP models, let us now consider in detail what happens to the optimal solution and the optimal value of the QP objective function as the RHS of the third constraint, i.e., the binding constraint, changes. We will refer to the value of the RHS of the third constraint as R. In the current model $R = 12$. The analysis is geometric and is tied to Figure 8.21. For convenience of exposition let

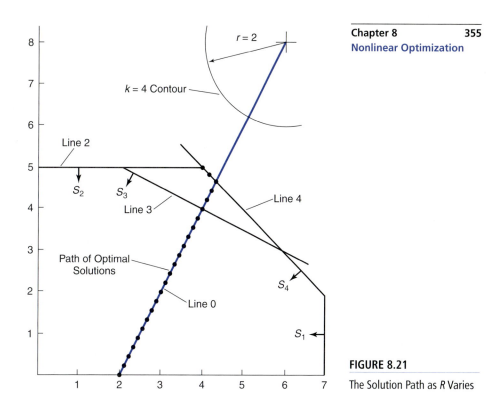

FIGURE 8.21

The Solution Path as R Varies

line 2 be the line $\qquad x_2 = 5$

line 3 be the line $\qquad x_1 + 2x_2 = 12$

line 4 be the line $\qquad x_1 + x_2 = 9$

Each of these lines is identified in Figure 8.21.

TRACING THE OPTIMAL SOLUTION

We first note that as R decreases the third constraint will move to the southwest parallel to line 3. Similarly, as R increases the third constraint moves to the northeast parallel to line 3. From geometry we recall the fact that any tangent to a circle is perpendicular to a line connecting the point of tangency and the center. Hence, as R is increased or decreased (within limits), the optimal solution to the model lies on the line joining the points ($x_1 = 4, x_2 = 4$) and ($x_1 = 6, x_2 = 8$). The equation of this line is $2x_1 - x_2 = 4$, and it is identified as line 0 in Figure 8.21.

From Figure 8.21 we now see that as R decreases the optimal solution moves down line 0 until it reaches the axis (the nonnegativity constraint on x_2). At this point $x_1 = 2$ and $x_2 = 0$ and thus $x_1 + 2x_2 = 2$. Similarly, as R increases the optimal solution moves up along line 0 until R assumes a value such that the third constraint passes through the intersection of line 4 and line 0. This value is determined by solving the equations $x_1 + x_2 = 9$ and $2x_1 - x_2 = 4$ for x_1 and x_2 to obtain the point ($x_1 = 4\frac{1}{3}, x_2 = 4\frac{2}{3}$). Substituting these values in the equation $x_1 + 2x_2 = R$, yields $R = 13\frac{2}{3}$.

As R assumes values greater than $13\frac{2}{3}$, the optimal solution moves along line 4 until R assumes a value such that the third constraint passes through the intersection of line 2 and line 4. This intersection occurs at the point ($x_1 = 4, x_2 = 5$) and since $x_1 + 2x_2 = R$, the third constraint intersects this point when $R = 14$. As R becomes larger than 14, the third constraint becomes redundant and the optimal solution remains at the point ($x_1 = 4, x_2 = 5$). We have now traced the path of the optimal solutions for all possible values of $R \geq 2$. To find the optimal solution for a specific value of R, it is only necessary to solve the appropriate two simultaneous linear equations.

THE OPTIMAL VALUE OF THE OBJECTIVE FUNCTION (OV)

Once you have the optimal solution, say (x_1^*, x_2^*), the optimal value of the objective function (OV) is obtained by evaluating the expression $(x_1^* - 6)^2 + (x_2^* - 8)^2 = OV$. We now wish to develop an expression for the OV as a function of R. This function will be identified by the notation OV(R). In particular we will restrict our attention to values of R between 2 and 13⅔; that is, to those values of R for which the optimal solution lies on line 0.

When the optimal solution lies on line 0, it lies at the intersection of the lines

$$2x_1 - x_2 = 4 \quad \text{line 0}$$
$$x_1 + 2x_2 = R \quad \text{third constraint}$$

Solving for x_1 and x_2 in terms of R we obtain

$$x_1 + 2(2x_1 - 4) = R$$

or

$$x_1^* \frac{R + 8}{5} \text{ and } x_2^* = 2\left(\frac{R + 8}{5}\right) - 4 = \frac{2R - 4}{5}$$

Note when $R = 12$, $x_1^* = 4$ and $x_2^* = 4$, which is our original result. Since the objective function is $(x_1 - 6)^2 + (x_2 - 8)^2$ its value at (x_1^*, x_2^*) is

$$\left(\frac{R+8}{5} - 6\right)^2 + \left(\frac{2R-4}{5} - 8\right)^2$$

or

$$OV(R) = \frac{R^2 - 44R + 484}{5}$$

The function OV(R), over the range $8 \leq R \leq 13⅔$, is plotted in Figure 8.22. Note that over this range the OV function is quadratic. Also note that when $R = 12$ the objective function value is 20, the same as the value produced by Solver in Figure 8.20.

Recall that the definition of the Lagrange multiplier on the third constraint is the rate of change of the OV as the RHS of the third constraint (i.e., R) is increased. In geometric terms the rate of change in the function OV(R) at some point, say $R = \hat{R}$, is the slope of the tan-

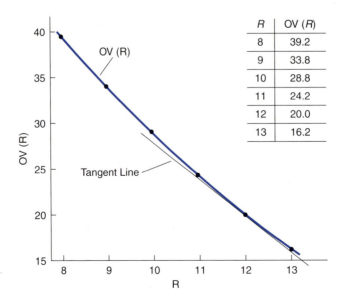

R	OV (R)
8	39.2
9	33.8
10	28.8
11	24.2
12	20.0
13	16.2

FIGURE 8.22

OV(R) versus R

gent to the graph of the function at the point $(\hat{R}, OV(\hat{R}))$. In the language of calculus, the rate of change at $\hat{R}$ is the first derivative of $OV(R)$ evaluated at $\hat{R}$. This entity is denoted $OV'(\hat{R})$. Figure 8.22 shows the tangent to the graph at the point $(R = 12, OV = 20)$. To deduce the slope, one can take the first derivative to obtain $OV'(R) = \dfrac{2R - 44}{5}$ and thus $OV'(12) = -4$.

We have already noted that since the rate of change is -4, the Lagrange multiplier in this model must be -4. This result is exactly what we see in the Sensitivity Report for this model in Figure 8.20.

Note that in Figure 8.22 the slope of the tangent is *different* for every value of R. Thus, comparing QP with LP, we find the following major difference:

- In general for a QP model, there is no allowable increase and decrease in the RHS of a constraint for which the Lagrange multiplier (i.e., shadow price) remains the same. Of course, we saw that this was true for *some* NLP models earlier. However, it is always true for a QP model.

Now let us consider what happens as we change a coefficient of a term in the objective function.

1. If we change the coefficient on some x_j variable, we relocate the center of the concentric circles. For example, in the previous objective function let us change the coefficient of x_1 from the value -12 to -18, to obtain the new objective

$$x_1^2 - 18x_1 + 36 + x_2^2 - 16x_2 + 64$$

This can be rewritten as

$$(x_1 - 9)^2 + (x_2 - 8)^2 - 45$$

which shows that the center of the concentric circles is relocated from the point $(x_1 = 6, x_2 = 8)$ to the point $(x_1 = 9, x_2 = 8)$. This relocation also produces a new optimal solution.

2. Changing a coefficient on one of the x_j^2 terms in the previous objective function will change the shapes of the contours from circles to ellipses.

Rather than dwelling on this more complicated geometry, it should already be apparent that, in contrast to LP:

- In general, for a QP model, for a coefficient in the objective function, it is not possible to give a range of values such that the optimal solution does not change.

This completes the general discussion of quadratic programming. In the next section we turn to a specific and important application.

8.10   PORTFOLIO SELECTION

Portfolio selection is a fundamental model in modern finance. In reality there are enough aspects to portfolio analysis to fill up a book, and indeed volumes have been written on the topic. Our discussion will provide only a brief glimpse into this fascinating practice.

THE PORTFOLIO MODEL

The model of **portfolio analysis** can be stated as follows: An investor has P dollars to invest in a set of n stocks and would like to know how much to invest in each stock. The chosen collection is called the investor's portfolio. The investor has conflicting goals: He or she would like a portfolio with both a large expected return and a small risk. These goals are conflicting because most often, in the real world, portfolios with high expected return also have high risk.

Few financial markets in recent years have experienced the rapid growth and innovations of the secondary mortgage market. The growth has been spurred by federal agencies created to facilitate home ownership by increasing the flow of funds available for mortgage loans. These agencies include Government National Mortgage Association (GNMA), Federal National Mortgage Association (FNMA) and Federal Home Loan Mortgage Association (FHLMC). Each of these purchase mortgage loans from mortgage originators and pool them to create mortgage-backed securities (MBSs).

These securities along with those from private issuers trade in the capital markets along with other fixed-income securities such as Treasury bills/bonds and their corporate equivalents. Issuance of these MBSs has reached over $1 trillion recently, with secondary market trading exceeding $5 billion per week. This secondary mortgage market is now comparable in size to the corporate bond market and has potential for considerable growth, given that only 40% of the mortgage debt has been converted into securities.

During recent years, Prudential has built a premier MBS department. Due to the complexity of these securities, standard fixed-income valuation tools are inadequate for MBSs. Prudential has used a variety of quantitative models, including LP and NLP, to allow the firm to quickly and accurately value and, therefore, trade these complex MBSs.

These tools are also used to properly hedge the MBSs in their inventory, as well as to help structure their clients' portfolios to achieve given objectives (e.g., maximize expected return, minimize investment risk) while staying within specified constraints. Typical constraints include minimum and maximum percentage of the portfolio to invest in any one security, the duration of the MBSs, and the total amount to be invested. The models are used hundreds of times each day by traders, salespeople, and clients. The impact of the models is that Prudential has moved from not even being ranked in the top 10 issuers of such collateralized mortgage obligations to being consistently ranked in the top 3. (See Ben-Dov et al)

Here is an example of what we mean by the term *return*. Suppose an investment of D_i dollars is put into asset i and suppose that over some specified time period this D_i dollars grows to $1.3D_i$. Then we would say that the *return* over that period is $(1.3D_i - D_i)/D_i = 0.3$. The concept of risk is more subtle and more difficult to elaborate on. For the purpose of this discussion we will assume that *risk is measured by the variance of the return on the portfolio*. Actually, this is consistent with the way that most portfolio analysts would measure risk.

Now, since the portfolio manager seeks low risk and high expected return, one way to frame the model is to minimize the variance of the return (i.e., minimize risk) subject to a given lower bound on expected return. There may also be some policy constraints on the proportion of the portfolio devoted to particular individual stocks.

FORMULATING THE PORTFOLIO MODEL

This model turns out to be a quadratic programming model. In formulating this model, one can let x_i be the proportion of the portfolio invested in stock i. For example, in a two-stock model if we had P dollars to invest, and if the optimal solution were $x_1 = 0.7$ and $x_2 = 0.3$, we would then invest a total of $0.7P$ dollars in stock 1, and the remaining $0.3P$ dollars would go to stock 2.

Let us now write out the general model for a two-asset model. We shall use the following notation:

$$\sigma_1^2 = \text{variance of yearly returns from stock } i, i = 1, 2$$

$$\sigma_{12} = \text{covariance of yearly returns from stocks 1 and 2}$$

$$R_i = \text{expected yearly return from stock } i, i = 1, 2$$

$$b = \text{lower bound on expected yearly return from the portfolio}$$

$$S_i = \text{upper bound on investment in stock } i, i = 1, 2$$

For the present purposes we simply accept the following facts:

1. The **variance** *of the yearly returns from stock i* is a number describing the "variability" of these returns from year to year. This will be made more precise in the next section.

2. The **covariance** *of the yearly returns from stocks 1 and 2* is a number that describes the extent to which the returns of the two stocks move up or down together. This also will be made more precise in the next section.

3. The *expected return of the portfolio* is defined as the number $x_1R_1 + x_2R_2$.

4. The *variance of the return of the portfolio* is defined as the number $\sigma_1^2 x_1^2 + 2\sigma_{12}x_1x_2 + \sigma_2^2 x_2^2$.

5. The **standard deviation** of the return of the portfolio is defined as the square root of the variance.

From these definitions it follows that, for the two-stock example, the portfolio model takes the form

$$\text{Min} \quad \sigma_1^2 x_1^2 + 2\sigma_{12}x_1x_2 + \sigma_2^2 x_2^2 \qquad \text{(variance of return)}$$

$$\begin{aligned}
\text{s.t.} \quad & x_1 + x_2 && = 1 && \text{(all funds must be invested)} \\
& x_1R_1 + x_2R_2 && \geq b && \text{(lower bound on the expected return of the portfolio)} \\
& x_1 && \leq S_1 \Big\} && \text{(upper bounds on investments in individual stocks)} \\
& x_2 && \leq S_2 \\
& x_1, x_2 && \geq 0 && \text{(nonnegativity implies that "short selling" of a stock} \\
& && && \text{is not allowed)}
\end{aligned}$$

To create a specific numerical example let

$$\sigma_1^2 = 0.09 \qquad R_1 = 0.06 \qquad S_1 = 0.75 \qquad b = 0.03$$
$$\sigma_2^2 = 0.06 \qquad R_2 = 0.02 \qquad S_2 = 0.9 \qquad \sigma_{12} = 0.02$$

The feasible set for this model is shown in Figure 8.23, where for convenience the objective function and both sides of the expected return constraint have been multiplied by 100. Because of the equality constraint ($x_1 + x_2 = 1$), the feasible set is the heavy line segment connecting the points (0.25, 0.75) and (0.75, 0.25). Each contour of the objective function is an ellipse with its center at the origin and its minor axis lying on a line that forms a 26.55° angle with the x_1 axis. The 2 and 4.54 contours are shown in Figure 8.23.

Note that as the value of the contour increases, the general shape of the ellipse remains the same, but it increases in size. The model is to select the smallest value for the contour so that the ellipse just touches the feasible set. As indicated in Figure 8.23, the 4.54 contour touches the feasible set at the point ($x_1^* = 0.36$, $x_2^* = 0.64$), which is the optimal solution.

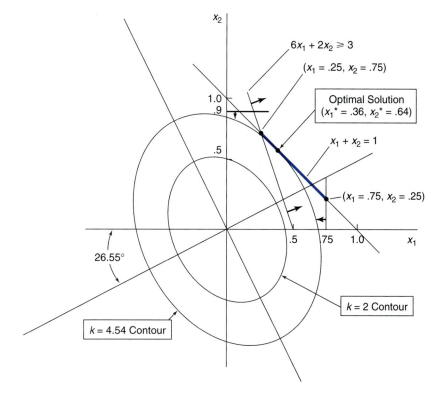

FIGURE 8.23

Graphical Solution for the Portfolio Selection Model

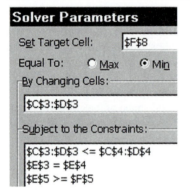

	A	B	C	D	E	F	G
1							
2		Portfolio Model	Stock 1	Stock 2	Total		
3		Decision: % in Stock	36.36%	63.64%	100%		
4		Requirements	<=75%	<=90%	=100%		
5		Expected Portfolio Return	6%	2%	3.455%	>=3%	
6		Risk Measures	Stock 1	Stock 2	Covariance		
7		Stock Variance/Covariance	0.09	0.06	0.02	Total	
8		Port. Variance/Covariance	0.0119	0.0243	0.0093	0.04545	
9							

Cell	Formula	Copy To
E5	= SUMPRODUCT(C3:D3,C5:D5)	—
C8	= C7*C3^2	D8
E8	= 2*E7*C3*D3	—

Solver Parameters

Set Target Cell: | $F$8

Equal To: ◯ Max   ◉ Min

By Changing Cells:

| $C$3:$D$3

Subject to the Constraints:

| $C$3:$D$3 <= $C$4:$D$4
| $E$3 = $E$4
| $E$5 >= $F$5

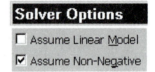

Solver Options

☐ Assume Linear Model

☑ Assume Non-Negative

FIGURE 8.24

Solver Solution for the
Portfolio Selection Model

It is not important for you to know how to construct these contours. Real portfolio models are, after all, optimized on the computer, not graphically. The geometric representation, however, is a useful way to understand the model and is helpful in interpreting properties of the solution.

The Solver solution to the above example is shown in Figure 8.24. Note that only the invest-all-funds constraint is binding. This, of course, was seen in the geometric representation in Figure 8.23. We can see from the LHS of the minimum-return constraint, that the expected return from this portfolio is 3.455%. Comparing the optimal values of x_1^* and x_2^* we see that the optimal portfolio contains more of the security with the lower expected yearly return (i.e., security 2). The reason is that the variance of security 2 is lower than that of security 1. The optimal mix is one that minimizes the portfolio variance while guaranteeing an expected portfolio return of at least 3%.

Note that Solver could equally as well been used to solve this model to maximize the portfolio return subject to a constraint that the portfolio variance not exceed a given upper bound. Since this formulation places the model's quadratic relationship as a constraint instead of as the objective function, it is not strictly speaking a quadratic model. However, such a formulation causes no difficulty with Solver's generalized gradient search procedure and many modelers prefer this latter formulation for portfolio optimization.

8.11   A PORTFOLIO EXAMPLE WITH DATA

In this section we turn to a three-asset example. In contrast to the previous example in which all the parameters were given, data will be used to estimate the parameters in this model. The model will then be optimized with Solver, and we will discuss the solution.

FORMULATING THE MODEL

In this section the three financial assets will be designated, at the outset, as x, y, and z. Let

$$X = \text{fraction of asset } x \text{ in the portfolio}$$
$$Y = \text{fraction of asset } y \text{ in the portfolio}$$
$$Z = \text{fraction of asset } z \text{ in the portfolio}$$

The terminology "asset i" will be used to refer to asset x or asset y or asset z. In the previous sections the portfolio model was presented as if the parameters that describe the distribution of future returns were known; that is, it was assumed that the expected returns, variances, and covariances were known. In the real world these parameters must be estimated from historical data. In general if n periods (years) of data are available, there will be, for each asset i, an actual historical return R_i^t associated with each period t where t ranges from 1 to n. In other words, each asset will have n historical returns. The expected periodic return from asset i is estimated with $\overline{R}_i = \dfrac{1}{n} \sum_{t=1}^{n} R_i^t$, which is the average of the asset's historical returns. The periodic historical returns R_i^t, are also used to estimate variances and covariances. The appropriate formulas are:[8]

$$\text{estimate of the variance of return for asset } i = \frac{1}{n} \sum_{t=1}^{n} (R_i^t - \overline{R}_i)^2$$

$$\text{estimate of the covariance of returns for assets } i \text{ and } j = \frac{1}{n} \sum_{t=1}^{n} (R_i^t - \overline{R}_i)(R_j^t - \overline{R}_j)$$

As before, we also define

$$b = \text{lower bound on expected return of the portfolio}$$
$$S_i = \text{upper bound on the fraction of asset } i \text{ that can be in the portfolio}$$

In terms of the parameters, the quadratic programming formulation of the three-asset model is

$$
\begin{array}{lll}
\text{Min} & \sigma_x^2 X^2 + \sigma_y^2 Y^2 + \sigma_z^2 Z^2 + 2\sigma_{xy}XY + 2\sigma_{xz}XZ + 2\sigma_{yz}YZ & \\
\text{s.t.} & R_x X + R_y Y + R_z Z \geq b & \\
& X + Y + Z = 1 & \\
& X \leq S_x & \\
& \quad Y \leq S_y & \left. \begin{array}{l} \\ \\ \\ \end{array} \right\} \text{Feasible region is same as in LP} \\
& \quad\quad Z \leq S_z & \\
& X, Y, Z \geq 0 &
\end{array}
$$

The objective function is the variance of the portfolio return, which, as stated in the previous section, is commonly considered to be the risk of the portfolio. (The rationale for this definition of risk, as well as the derivation of the objective function, is in the domain of statistics and is beyond our scope.) The first constraint expresses the lower bound on the expected return of the portfolio. The second constraint says that the investment fractions must add to one, and the remaining constraints are upper bounds.

When a portfolio is allowed to be constructed from more than three assets, the expected return is defined to be $\sum_{i=1}^{n} X_i R_i$. As before, R_i is the expected return from asset i, and X_i is

---

[8]Readers with a statistical background will note that these estimation formulas do not account for degrees of freedom loss. We use these formulas in order to agree with Excel's COVAR() function despite the slight estimation bias they introduce.

TABLE 8.3 Historical Stock Returns

YEAR	AT&T	GM	USS
1	30.0%	22.5%	14.9%
2	10.3%	29.0%	26.0%
3	21.6%	21.6%	41.9%
4	−4.6%	−27.2%	−7.8%
5	−7.1%	14.4%	16.9%
6	5.6%	10.7%	−3.5%
7	3.8%	32.1%	13.3%
8	8.9%	30.5%	73.2%
9	9.0%	19.5%	2.1%
10	8.3%	39.0%	13.1%
11	3.5%	−7.2%	0.6%
12	17.6%	71.5%	90.8%

the fraction of asset i in the portfolio. In this general case of N assets, the variance of the return of the portfolio is defined as[9]

$$\sum_{i=1}^{n} X_i^2 \sigma_i^2 + 2\sum_{i=1}^{N-1} \sum_{j=i+1}^{N} X_i X_j \sigma_{ij}$$

SPREADSHEET SOLUTION

After numerical estimates are substituted for the parameters, this quadratic programming model can be optimized with Solver. As a specific example, let us now consider three stocks and historical returns for 12 years. The three stocks chosen were AT&T, General Motors, and USX-U.S. Steel. The historical returns for the stocks are given in Table 8.3. In Table 8.3 the return in year n is defined by

$$\frac{(\text{closing price}, n) - (\text{closing price}, n-1) + (\text{dividends, n})}{(\text{closing price}, n-1)}$$

where closing prices and dividends are expressed in dollars per share.[10]

Now suppose that you wish to minimize the variance of the return of the portfolio, subject to a 15% expected return and a restriction that no more than 75% of the portfolio can be in any individual stock. The spreadsheet model, Solver solution, and Sensitivity Report are given in Figure 8.25.

Note that if "short sales" of a stock were permitted, then the nonnegativity constraints could be removed. The solution to the above model specifies a portfolio of about 53% AT&T, 35.64% GM, and 11.35% US Steel. The expected yearly return is exactly 15%. The optimal objective value indicates that the variance of yearly return is about 0.0205, which means the standard deviation is $\sqrt{.0205} = 14.33\%$. If you had believed in the validity of this model, and if you had further assumed (in addition to the validity of the model) that the portfolio returns are normally distributed with mean 15% and standard deviation of 14.33%, then according to statistical theory you might reasonably have expected that such a portfolio, in ensuing years, would have produced returns roughly between −13.7% and +43.7%. In fact, the returns over

---

[9]In matrix notation the variance of the portfolio return is written as $X^T YX$, where X is a column vector $(X_1, \ldots, X_N)$ and Y denotes the symmetric covariance matrix whose (i,j)th entry is σ_{ij} (and where $= \sigma_{ii} = \sigma_i^2$). If X is a row vector, then the portfolio return is given by XYX^T.

[10]Note the following unsatisfactory implication of this definition of averaging. Suppose there are no dividends, that in year 1 the stock goes from 1.0 to 1.5 (with a return of 0.5) and in year 2 the stock goes from 1.5 to 1 (with a return of −0.33). The average 2-year return is 0.17/2. Would you agree? This shows that estimating expected returns (and covariances) can be a delicate issue. It should be emphasized that this illustration is very introductory in nature.

	A	B	C	D	E	F	G	H
1	Portfolio Model		AT&T	GM	USS	Year		
2			30.0%	22.5%	14.9%	1		
3			10.3%	29.0%	26.0%	2		
4			21.6%	21.6%	41.9%	3		
5			-4.6%	-27.2%	-7.8%	4		
6			-7.1%	14.4%	16.9%	5		
7			5.6%	10.7%	-3.5%	6		
8			3.8%	32.1%	13.3%	7		
9			8.9%	30.5%	73.2%	8		
10			9.0%	19.5%	2.1%	9		
11			8.3%	39.0%	13.1%	10		
12			3.5%	-7.2%	0.6%	11		
13			17.6%	71.5%	90.8%	12		
14	Average Return		8.91%	21.37%	23.46%			
15	Covariance Matrix		AT&T	GM	USS		Portfolio Variance	
16		AT&T	0.0099	0.0114	0.0120			
17		GM	0.0114	0.0535	0.0508			
18		USS	0.0120	0.0508	0.0864	Total		
19	Decision: Stock %		53.01%	35.64%	11.35%	100%	0.0205	
20	Requirements		<=75%	<=75%	<=75%	=100%		
21	Expected Return		4.72%	7.62%	2.66%	15.0%	>=15%	
22								

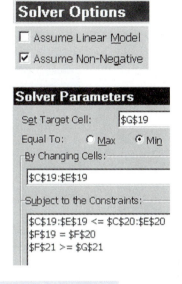

Solver Options

☐ Assume Linear Model

☑ Assume Non-Negative

Solver Parameters

Set Target Cell: $G$19

Equal To: ○ Max ● Min

By Changing Cells:

$C$19:$E$19

Subject to the Constraints:

$C$19:$E$19 <= $C$20:$E$20
$F$19 = $F$20
$F$21 >= $G$21

Cell	Formula	Copy To
C14	= AVERAGE(C2:C13)	D14:E14
C16	= COVAR(C2:C13,$C$2:$C$13)	D16:E16
C17	= COVAR(C2:C13,$D$2:$D$13)	D17:E17
C18	= COVAR(C2:C13,$E$2:$E$13)	D18:E18
G19	= SUMPRODUCT(MMULT(C19:E19,C16:E18),C19:E19)	—
C21	= C19*C14	D21:E21

Microsoft Excel 8.0 Sensitivity Report

Adjustable Cells

Cell	Name	Final Value	Reduced Gradient
$C$19	Decision: Stock % AT&T	53.01%	0
$D$19	Decision: Stock % GM	35.64%	0
$E$19	Decision: Stock % USS	11.35%	0

Constraints

Cell	Name	Final Value	Lagrange Multiplier
$F$21	Expected Return Total	15%	0.3244
$F$19	Decision: Stock % Total	100%	-0.0076

FIGURE 8.25

Solver Solution to the Portfolio Example with Data

the ensuing three years for the three assets were as shown in Table 8.4. Hence, using the model's optimal fractions, the actual portfolio returns would have been as shown in Table 8.4.

In concluding this section, we observe that the Lagrangian multiplier indicates that a 1% increase in expected return (an increase of 0.01 in cell G21) would lead to *roughly* an *increase* of 0.00324 in variance. Hence, the new variance would be about 0.0238 with the standard deviation equal to $\sqrt{.0238} = 15.4\%$. These numbers are approximate because for a QP the slopes of $OV(b)$ are instantaneous (rather than constant in intervals as is the case with LP). This fact was discussed in terms of a general quadratic program in the previous section. For the portfolio model, it is reflected by the general shape for $OV(b)$ as shown in Figure 8.26. (Note that the graph shows that tightening the expected return constraint—that is, increasing the expected return, b—hurts the OV more and more.)

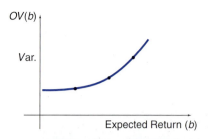

FIGURE 8.26

The Efficient Frontier

TABLE 8.4 Actual Stock Returns			
STOCK	**YEAR 1**	**YEAR 2**	**YEAR 3**
AT&T	10.3%	3.9%	3.0%
GM	51.2%	−5.0%	−20.0%
USS	64.7%	32.2%	−26.6%
Portfolio Returns	31.1%	3.9%	−8.6%

In the language of finance, this graph is called the **efficient frontier,** and its properties are studied in finance courses. For our purposes we merely observe that it is a piecewise quadratic convex function. To find any point on the graph of this function, one simply selects a value for the RHS of the constraint that sets a lower bound on the expected return, b, and reoptimizes the model with Solver.

8.12   INVENTORY CONTROL

Inventories are defined as *idle goods in storage,* waiting to be used. There are many types of inventories; for example, inventories of raw materials, inventories of in-process materials, inventories of finished goods, inventories of cash, and even inventories of individuals. Inventories are held for many reasons. Some distributors hold inventory in order to fill quickly an order placed by a customer. Otherwise, in many cases, the customer would order from a competitor. This, however, is only one reason why inventories are held. They are, in fact, held for any of the following reasons:

1. Inventories smooth out the time gap between supply and demand. For example, the corn crop is harvested in September and October, but user demand for corn is steady throughout the year. Thus, the harvest must be stored in inventory for later use.

2. The possibility of holding inventory often contributes to lower production costs, for it is more economical to produce some items in large batches even though immediate orders for the items may not exist.

3. Inventories provide a way of storing labor. For example, the availability of labor for production may be a binding constraint in some later time period but slack in the earlier periods. The possibility of producing excess output in these earlier periods and carrying the product forward in inventory frees labor in the later periods for alternative uses.

4. Finally, inventory is a way of providing quick customer service at the time an item is needed, and customers are willing to pay for this convenience.

There are generally three types of costs associated with the inventory activity: *holding costs, ordering costs,* and *stockout costs.* These inventory costs are best explained by an example. Among other products offered for sale, STECO stocks a specialized optical fiber network cable (NC) used to connect personal computers to a high-speed local area network.

Holding Costs   Currently there are 3000 NCs in STECO's stock. Each NC costs STECO $8. Thus, STECO currently has (8) × (3000) = $24,000 tied up with the inventory of this item. Suppose that STECO were to reduce this inventory to only 1000 items. Instead of

$24,000, the investment would be reduced to $8000. It would then be possible to invest some of the $16,000 that is released. In other words, by holding inventory STECO forgoes the opportunity to make other investments. This so-called **opportunity cost** is perhaps the most important contribution to inventory holding cost. The magnitude of this cost is closely tied to the interest rate. There are other holding costs, such as breakage, pilferage, insurance, warehousing, and special handling requirements. *The larger the inventories, the larger the inventory holding costs.*

Ordering Costs Each time STECO places an order to replenish its inventories an ordering cost is incurred. *This cost is independent of the quantity ordered.* It is related to the amount of time required for paperwork and accounting when an order is placed and is a direct function of the cost of involved personnel.

Stockout Costs A **stockout** means that the firm runs out of inventory. In most technical uses, the term *stockout* refers to the more specific phenomenon that orders arrive after inventory has been depleted. There are, at least in the context of a model, two ways to treat such orders. One way is to save up the orders and fill them later after the inventory has been replenished. This is called **backlogging.** The study of inventory includes models that deal with the possibility of stocking out, and in such a case some models assume backlogging; others assume no backlogging. In either case there is a cost of stocking out. This cost could include the lost profit from not making the sale (in the no-backlogging case) or from late delivery (the backlogging case), as well as discounts for a number of more intangible factors, such as the cost of possibly losing the customer, of losing goodwill, and of establishing a poor record of service. In the case of stockouts with no backlogging, we generally use the term **penalty cost,** which means the per unit cost of unsatisfied demand. In the case of stockouts with backlogging we speak of a **backlogging cost,** which means the per unit cost of backlogging demand.

For a company such as STECO, with hundreds of thousands of dollars tied up in inventory, there must be a right way and a wrong way to manage the inventory function. The main trade-offs are clear: On one hand, it is good to have inventory on hand to make sure that customers' orders can be satisfied (i.e., to avoid *stockout costs*). On the other hand, carrying inventory implies a *holding cost*. This cost can be reduced by ordering smaller quantities more often, but that approach involves increased *ordering costs*. These three cost factors must be balanced against each other.

Once the fundamental question of what items to order has been determined, the questions to be answered are the same for all inventory control systems. For every type of item held in inventory, someone must answer the two key questions of inventories: (1) *when* should a replenishment order be placed and (2) what should be the **order quantity,** or *how much* should be ordered? A multitude of factors combine to make this a difficult problem. Some of the most important considerations are

1. The extent to which future demand is known
2. The cost of stocking out and management's policy (backlogging or not)
3. The inventory holding and ordering costs
4. The possibility of long *lead times*—the period of time between when an order is placed and when the material actually arrives
5. The possibility of quantity discount purchasing plans

STECO WHOLESALING: THE CURRENT POLICY
The monthly demand for NCs during the preceding year is given in Table 8.5. The term **demand** means "orders received." It is not necessarily the same as *sales*. For example, in January of last year 5300 items were demanded. If *at least* 5300 items were in inventory, then sales equaled demand (i.e., sales were 5300). If fewer than 5300 items were in inventory, say only 5000, then sales were 5000, which is less than the demand of 5300, and consequently a stockout occurred.

TABLE 8.5 Monthly NC Demand

MONTH	DEMAND (UNITS)
January	5300
February	5100
March	4800
April	4700
May	5000
June	5200
July	5300
August	4900
September	4800
October	5000
November	4800
December	5100
Total Annual Demand	60,000
Average Monthly Demand	5000

Over a period of several years the demand has remained at a steady rate of about 5000 NCs per month. Based on this fact, STECO's policy last year was to add 5000 NCs to inventory each month. Since demand is expected to hold at about the same level in the future, this is the current policy as well. However, given this data, is this a good policy?

One way to attempt to answer this question would be to see what the policy of ordering 5000 NCs each month *would* cost in a simplified model, assuming, for example, that

1. Shipments always arrive on the first day of the month.
2. Demand is known and occurs at a constant rate of 5000 units per month.
3. All demand will be satisfied with no backlogging. In other words, stockouts are forbidden.

With these assumptions a plot of the inventory on hand at any time can be drawn, as in Figure 8.27. Notice how the inventory jumps up by 5000 units at the beginning of each month when a shipment arrives and decreases continuously at a constant rate of 5000 items per month (the constant monthly rate of demand). Also notice that a replenishment shipment from the producer arrives at the instant the inventory on hand hits zero. Thus, no stockouts occur. Given assumptions 1, 2, and 3, the cost of operating the system shown in Figure 8.27 depends only on *how much new stock is ordered* and on the *holding and ordering costs*. Let us see how the operating cost arises. First, note that a policy of ordering 5000 NCs each month combined with constant demand of 5000 per month, produces an average inventory of 2500 NCs, as shown in Figure 8.27.

Figure 8.28 shows the effect of ordering 10,000 NCs every other month. Assuming demand remains constant at 5000 per month, average inventory is doubled, but the annual number of replenishment orders is halved. Thus, a policy of increasing the order quantity increases the holding costs, because average inventory is higher, and decreases the annual ordering cost, because fewer replenishments are required.

To answer the two questions posed above, a simple model will be used, called the **economic order quantity (EOQ) model.** The EOQ model attempts to balance the cost of placing orders with the cost of holding inventory.

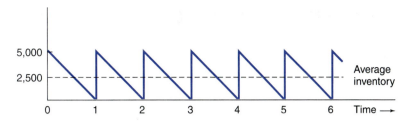

FIGURE 8.27

Inventory on Hand,
5000 Order Quantity

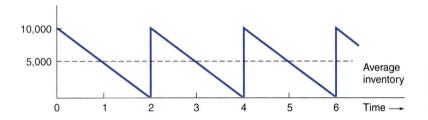

FIGURE 8.28

Inventory on Hand,
10,000 Order Quantity

DEVELOPING THE EOQ MODEL

The EOQ model in its simplest form assumes that

1. No stockouts are allowed. That is, each new order arrives (in totality) as soon as the inventory level hits zero.
2. There is a constant rate of demand.
3. The relevant costs are ordering and holding costs.

The EOQ model finds the **optimal order quantity,** which is defined to be the quantity that under the three assumptions above *minimizes the total cost per year of ordering NCs and holding them in inventory.* It is based on

1. *Ordering cost* $= C_O$. Every time an order is placed, the purchasing department must contact the supplier to determine the current price and delivery time, complete and e-mail the order form, enter the order into the inventory control system, and initiate the receiving and stockkeeping records. When the order arrives, the receiver must complete the receiving and stockkeeping records and update the order status database. All of this costs money. STECO estimates the cost of placing an order for NCs, *regardless of the number of units ordered,* to be $25. This includes two thirds of an hour of clerk-category labor at $18 per hour, one third of an hour of an assistant purchasing agent's time at $24 per hour, plus $5 in material, phone, and other telecommunications costs.
2. *Inventory holding cost* $= C_h$. Every dollar invested in inventory could be put to use elsewhere by STECO. For example, it could be put in a bank or invested in Treasury bills and earn interest for STECO. When a dollar is tied up in inventory, STECO loses the opportunity to invest it elsewhere. This lost opportunity is called the opportunity cost. Typically, the opportunity cost accounts for a large part of the cost of holding inventory. In addition, there are overhead costs such as rent, utilities, and insurance that must be allocated to the items in inventory.

The cost of holding inventory is typically expressed as the cost of holding one unit for one year and is calculated as a percentage of the cost of the item. STECO estimates that the cost of holding an NC in inventory for one year is 24% of its purchase price. The 24% figure can be subdivided into an opportunity cost of 20% plus a variable cost per item of 4%. Since each NC costs $8, the cost of holding each item in inventory for one year is

$$C_h = 0.24 \times \$8.00 = \$1.92$$

The Annual Holding and Ordering Cost The first step in calculating the optimal (i.e., cost-minimizing) order quantity is to derive an expression for the *annual holding and ordering cost* (AHO) as a function of the order quantity. It consists of two parts, annual ordering cost and annual holding cost.

$$\text{annual ordering cost} = C_O \times (\text{number of orders per year}) \tag{8.1}$$

If the order quantity is 5000 units, STECO will place 12 orders a year, since the model assumes a total demand of 60,000, and 60,000/5000 = 12. The general formula is

$$N = \frac{D}{Q} \tag{8.2}$$

where
N = number of orders per year
D = annual demand
Q = order quantity

Thus, in general

$$\text{annual ordering cost} = C_O N = C_O \left(\frac{D}{Q}\right) \tag{8.3}$$

To compute the annual holding cost STECO makes use of two facts: (1) The annual holding cost is equal to C_h times the average inventory, and (2) the average inventory is equal to one half of the maximum inventory when demand occurs at a constant rate. Since the order quantity is also the maximum amount of inventory on hand (see Figures 8.27 and 8.28), it follows that

$$\text{annual holding cost} = C_h \left(\frac{Q}{2}\right) \tag{8.4}$$

If we add together expressions (8.3) and (8.4), we see that the assumptions of the EOQ model give the following expression for the annual holding and ordering cost as a function of the order quantity Q:

$$\text{AHO}(Q) = C_O \left(\frac{D}{Q}\right) + C_h \left(\frac{Q}{2}\right) \tag{8.5}$$

Since demand occurs at the rate of D units per year, we know that these Q units will be depleted in Q/D years, which is precisely when the inventory level hits the value zero. For example, when Q = 5000 and D = 60,000, the order of 5000 units is depleted in 5000/60,000 = 1/12 year = 1 month, as we have already seen (Figure 8.27). For NCs, the relevant values of C_O, D, and C_h can be plugged into expression (8.5) to give:

$$\text{AHO}(Q) = \$25 \left(\frac{60,000}{Q}\right) + \$1.92 \left(\frac{Q}{2}\right) = \left(\frac{1,500,000}{Q}\right) + 0.96Q \tag{8.6}$$

When Q = 5000 it is seen that

$$\text{AHO}(5000) = \$300 + \$4800 = \$5100$$

Now, however, using expression (8.6), the annual holding and ordering cost for NCs can be plotted as a function of the order quantity Q, as shown in Figure 8.29. From this graph it is clear that the optimal order quantity (the one that minimizes AHO[Q]) is somewhat larger than 1000 items.

Figure 8.30 presents the spreadsheet version of STECO's inventory model. The model is nonlinear because of the Q in the denominator of the ordering cost formula. The cost formulas in cells C16:C17 are those of the ordering and holding costs, as given above. Because it is not a function of Q, Purchasing cost (= Purchase Price × Annual Demand) is a constant and is unnecessary for the calculation of the optimal Q. It is included for completeness of the total annual costs. The constraint that there be at least one order per year is included to prevent Solver from testing an (unreasonable) candidate Q = 0, thereby producing a "#DIV/0!" error in the ordering cost formula, which will abort Solver optimization. The optimal solution is displayed, confirming the graphical representation in Figure 8.29.

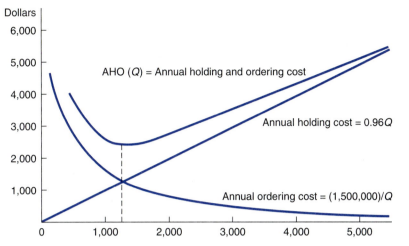

FIGURE 8.29

STECO Annual Holding and Ordering Costs as a Function of Order Quantity

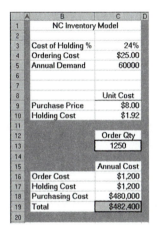

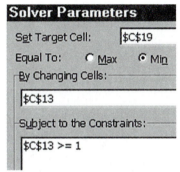

Cell	Formula
C10	= C3*C9
C16	= C4*C5/C13
C17	= C10*C13/2
C18	= C9*C5

FIGURE 8.30

STECO EOQ Model

THE EOQ FORMULA: Q*

It would obviously be useful to have an expression for $Q*$, the optimal order quantity. (The asterisk indicates the value of Q that is the optimal solution to the model.) Because of its simple form, a formula can be derived to calculate its value as a function of the parameters in the problem by using calculus to minimize the function $AHO(Q)$ presented in (8.5). A consequence of this approach is that at the optimum, the annual holding cost is equal to the annual ordering cost[11]

---

[11]That the cost-minimizing quantity occurs at the point where the two terms, annual holding cost and annual ordering cost, are equal is true for these functions. It is not true in general.

$$C_h = \left(\frac{Q*}{2}\right) = C_O\left(\frac{D}{Q*}\right) \tag{8.7}$$

or

$$(Q*)^2 = \frac{2C_OD}{C_h} \tag{8.8}$$

or

$$Q* = \sqrt{\frac{2C_OD}{C_h}} \tag{8.9}$$

It is sometimes convenient to estimate C_h by assuming that it is some percentage (say, i) of the purchase price (P); that is, $C_h = iP$. Equation 8.9 can then be rewritten

$$Q* = \sqrt{\frac{2C_OD}{iP}} \tag{8.10}$$

In our example, P, the purchase price for NCs, is $8 and i, the fraction of P that is used to calculate C_h, is 0.24.

The quantity $Q*$ is often termed the **economic order quantity** (EOQ), and it should be noted that it is expressed in terms of the input parameters C_O, C_h, and D. By substituting the NC values for D, C_O, and C_h into (8.9), the optimal order quantity for NCs is:

$$Q* = \sqrt{\frac{2 \times 60,000 \times 25}{1.92}} = 1250$$

Plugging this value into the expression for the annual holding and ordering cost for NCs (equation [8.6]) yields

$$\text{AHO}(Q*) = \text{AHO}(1250) = \frac{(1,500,000)}{1250} + (0.96)(1250)$$

$$= \$1200 + \$1200 = \$2400$$

These values are the same as found by Solver in Figure 8.30.

SENSITIVITY ANALYSIS

Whether the optimal EOQ policy should be used in the future depends on the realism of the assumptions. After all, the EOQ model, like any other model, is idealized. It is no more than a selective representation of reality: an abstraction and an approximation. In this case, as with all models, the main question is: "How sensitive are the results of the model to the assumptions and the data?"

Since the model is fairly realistic, it seems reasonable that the inventory costs obtained within the model are fairly good estimates of the costs that STECO is actually incurring. Therefore, using a policy that is optimal in the model (order quantity of 1250) seems preferable to the traditional policy of ordering 5000. However, STECO should be concerned about how sensitive the optimal order quantity and, more important, the optimal annual cost are to the data. After all, each of the parameters C_O and C_h is in itself an estimate. If STECO errs in estimating these parameters, how much effect will that error have on the difference between the calculated $Q*$ and AHO* and the true $Q*$ and AHO*? If the results are highly sensitive to the values of the estimates, it is not clear whether the optimal policy for the model should actually be implemented by STECO.

Let us therefore consider how the EOQ results might vary with changes in our estimated holding and ordering costs. Recall that STECO assumed that $C_h = \$1.92$ and $C_O = \$25$. We will consider four cases in which the true parameters are different from the values selected by STECO. These "true values" are shown in the first two columns in Table 8.6.

In case (i) STECO has overestimated both cost parameters by about 10% each. Had STECO estimated the parameters correctly, it would have ordered 1267 items and in-

TABLE 8.6 Sensitivity to $C_h + C_O$						
(1) TRUE PARAMETERS		(2)	(3)	(4)	(5)	(6)
C_h	C_O	Optimal Q	Minimum Cost ($)	STECO's Decision*	STECO's Cost ($)	Loss (%)
(i) 1.72	23	1267	2179	Q = 1250	2179	0
(ii) 1.72	27	1372	2361	Q = 1250	2371	0.42
(iii) 2.12	23	1141	2419	Q = 1250	2429	0.41
(iv) 2.12	27	1236	2621	Q = 1250	2621	0

*Based on C_h = $1.92, C_O = $25.

curred an annual holding and ordering cost of $2179. Because of STECO's parameter estimation errors, 1250 are ordered. In order to find out what costs STECO will actually incur, the AHO equation must be evaluated with its true parameter values (C_h = $1.72 and C_O = $23 in case [i]) and the value of Q determined by STECO estimates (1250). This calculation follows:

$$\text{AHO}(Q) = C_O\left(\frac{D}{Q}\right) + C_h\left(\frac{Q}{2}\right)$$

$$= 23\left(\frac{60{,}000}{1250}\right) + \$1.72\left(\frac{1250}{2}\right)$$

$$= \$2179$$

This number is shown as STECO's Cost in column (5). We thus see that if STECO underestimates the two cost parameters as shown, it has no effect on the annual ordering and holding cost (to the nearest dollar). The other three cases show that the effect on the annual ordering and holding cost of any combination of 10% errors in the estimates of C_O and C_h is negligible.

Our analysis suggests that in STECO's case the EOQ model is insensitive even to approximately 10% variations or errors in the cost estimates. It turns out that this is a property enjoyed by EOQ models in general.

8.13   EXAMPLES OF INVENTORY MODELS

The inventory model that STECO used above is the "classic" EOQ model that minimizes the annual holding and ordering cost. However, in practice there are many variations on this classic EOQ formula, each of which requires reformulation of the inventory relationships and recomputation of the EOQ quantity. We give two examples as illustrations.

QUANTITY DISCOUNTS AND STECO'S OVERALL OPTIMUM

Although included in the spreadsheet of Figure 8.30, there was previously no need to take into account the cost of purchasing the product, for the per item cost to STECO was assumed to be a constant independent of Q. However, STECO's NC supplier will offer a **quantity discount** as an incentive for more business. The supplier has agreed to offer a $0.10 discount on every NC purchased if STECO orders in lots of at least 5000 items. Of course, higher-order quantities will also reduce the number of orders placed, and hence the annual ordering cost. As already discussed (compare Figures 8.27 and 8.28), a high order quantity leads to a higher average inventory level and hence higher holding costs. Whether the discount will, on balance, be advantageous to STECO is not obvious.

Let us proceed as before; that is, to develop an annual cost curve and then find the order quantity that minimizes it. STECO's annual total cost (ATC[Q]) is the sum of the annual holding and ordering cost (AHO[Q]) and the annual purchase cost (APC), that is,

$$ATC(Q) = AHO(Q) + APC$$

From equation (8.5) and the fact that $C_h = iP$,

$$AHO(Q) = C_O\left(\frac{D}{Q}\right) + iP\left(\frac{Q}{2}\right)$$

Note that since C_h depends on the unit purchase price P, the expression for AHO also involves P. The annual purchase cost is simply the unit purchase price times annual demand. Thus,

$$APC = PD$$

It follows that

$$ATC(Q) = C_O(Q) + iP\left(\frac{Q}{2}\right) + PD$$

To see the effect of discounting, evaluate this function for two different prices, the regular price of $8.00 per unit and the potential discounted price of $7.90 per unit.

Regular price equation:

$$ATC(Q) = \frac{25 \times 60,000}{Q} + (0.24)(8.00)\left(\frac{Q}{2}\right) + (8.00)(60,000)$$

Discount price equation:

$$ATC(Q)\ \frac{25 \times 60,000}{Q} + (0.24)(7.90)\left(\frac{Q}{2}\right) + (7.90)(60,000)$$

The general shape of these curves is shown in Figure 8.31. There are several facts to notice.

1. The discount curve lies below the regular cost curve. This is so because each term in the regular price ATC(Q) is greater than or equal to the corresponding term in the discount price ATC(Q).

2. The value of Q, say Q_D^*, that minimizes the discount price ATC(Q) is larger than the value of Q, say Q_R^*, that minimizes the regular price = ATC(Q). This is true because, using equation (8.10),

$$Q_D^* = \sqrt{\frac{2 \times 25 \times 60,000}{(0.24) \times (7.90)}} > \sqrt{\frac{2 \times 25 \times 60,000}{(0.24) \times (8.00)}} = Q_R^*$$

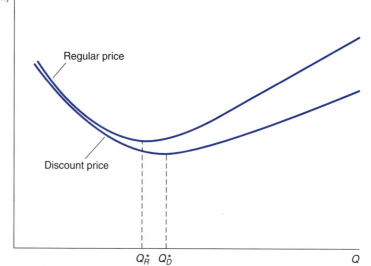

FIGURE 8.31

Annual Total Cost for
Regular and Discount Prices

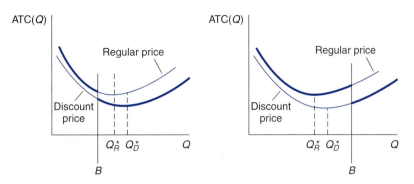

FIGURE 8.32

Effect of Minimum Order Size, B, on Order Quantity

Obviously, STECO would like to minimize its annual total cost, ATC(Q). If STECO could get the discount price regardless of the order quantity, it would of course order Q_D^*. However, assume that the discount price holds only if STECO orders at least B items at a time. Two situations could arise. These are illustrated in Figure 8.32.

The dark-line portions of the curves in these figures indicate the actual cost function that STECO faces. They illustrate that the regular price curve must be used for order quantities of B or less and that the discount price curve can be used for order quantities greater than B.

We see that if $B \leq Q_D^*$, STECO will achieve the minimum cost by ordering Q_D^*. If, however, $B > Q_R^*$, the optimal decision, in general, is not immediately obvious. The best STECO can do on the regular price curve is to order Q_R^*. The best STECO can do on the discount price curve is to order B. (STECO cannot order less than B and get the discount price, and ordering more than B increases ATC.) To determine which of these is optimal, STECO must calculate the ATC(Q) at these two points and compare them. The general rule then is

> If $B \leq Q_D^*$,   order Q_D^*.
>
> If $B > Q_D^*$, order $\begin{cases} Q_R^* \text{ if regular price} \leq \text{discount price} \\ \quad\quad \text{ATC } (Q_R^*) \quad\quad \leq \text{ATC } (B) \\ \\ B \text{ if not} \end{cases}$

To apply this rule, STECO must order at least 5000 items to get the discount. Thus $B = 5000$.

Figure 8.33 presents the spreadsheet version of the inventory model with quantity discounts. In contrast to the approach taken above, the spreadsheet model has been formulated to portray the annual cost as being an undiscounted Annual Cost in cells C16:C19 less a cost adjustment for the quantity discount, if any. That is, if the discount is taken, then an adjustment is made to the affected annual costs, Holding Cost and Purchasing Cost, to reflect the discount amounts. These costs are aggregated into the Total Net Cost, cells E16:E19. This approach permits treating the discount as a binary (integer) decision variable in cell D13. The formula in E13 is =D7*D13. Thus, if D13 is set by Solver to 0 (no discount), then the constraint becomes Order Quantity $\geq$ 0. Otherwise, if D13 is set by Solver to 1 (discount taken), then the adjustments to costs become nonzero and the constraint becomes Order Quantity $\geq$ 5000.

In this way Solver optimizes a mixed integer nonlinear program (MINLP) to evaluate the two EOQ functions, one with and one without the discount. Extending the model to multiple discounts (i.e., several quantity discount thresholds, each with an associated "adjustment" to total costs) requires straightforward addition of other binary variables, appropriate constraints to reflect the minimum quantities, and modifications to the Discount Adjustment formulas.

	NC Inventory Model			
		No Discount	With Discount	
Cost of Holding %		24%	24%	
Ordering Cost		$25.00	$25.00	
Ann. Demand		60000	60000	
Discount Amount			$0.10	
Min Order Size			5000	
		Unit Cost	Disc. Adjustment	Net Unit Cost
Purchase Price		$8.00	-$0.10	$7.90
Holding Cost		$1.92	-$0.024	$1.896
		Order Qty	Discount Taken	Min Order Qty
		5000	1	>=5000
		Annual Cost	Disc. Adjustment	Net Cost
Order Cost		$300		$300
Holding Cost		$4,800	-$60	$4,740
Purchasing Cost		$480,000	-$6,000	$474,000
Total Cost		$485,100	-$6,060	$479,040

		Unit Cost	Disc. Adjustment	Net Unit Cost
9	Purchase P 8		=-D6	=SUM(C9:D9)
10	Holding Co:	=C3*C9	=D3*D9	=SUM(C10:D10)
11				
12		Order Qty	Discount Taken	Min Order Qty
13		5000	1	=D7*D13
14				
15		Annual Cost	Disc. Adjustment	Net Cost
16	Order Cost	=C4*C5/C13		=SUM(C16:D16)
17	Holding Co:	=C10*C13/2	=D13*D10*C13/2	=SUM(C17:D17)
18	Purchasing	=C9*C5	=D13*D9*D5	=SUM(C18:D18)
19	Total Cost	=SUM(C16:C18)	=SUM(D16:D18)	=SUM(E16:E18)

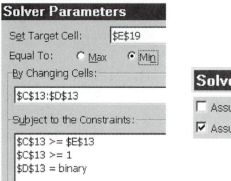

Solver Parameters

Set Target Cell: $E$19

Equal To: ○ Max   ● Min

By Changing Cells:

$C$13:$D$13

Subject to the Constraints:

$C$13 >= $E$13
$C$13 >= 1
$D$13 = binary

Solver Options

☐ Assume Linear Model
☑ Assume Non-Negative

FIGURE 8.33

STECO EOQ Model with Quantity Discounts

For the STECO case, Figure 8.33 indicates that STECO should order 5000 items to take advantage of the quantity discount. This decision saves

$$\$482,400 - \$479,040 = \$3360$$

per year over the next best decision (ordering Q_R^*). Clearly, quantity discounts can play an important role in determining an optimal inventory policy.

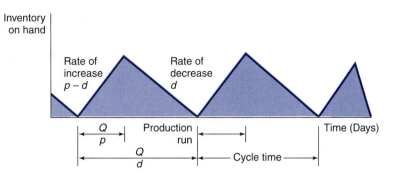

FIGURE 8.34

Inventory on Hand for the Production Lot Size Model

PRODUCTION LOT SIZE: STECO'S HEAT-TREATMENT MODEL

Although STECO is primarily a wholesaler, it does have some productive capacity. In particular, it has an extensive and modern heat-treatment fiber cable "jacketing" facility that it uses to produce a number of specialty cable items that it then holds in inventory. The heat-treatment facility has two important characteristics: There is a large setup cost associated with producing each cable product, and once the setup is complete, production is at a steady and known rate.

The setup cost, which is analogous to the ordering cost in the EOQ model, is incurred because it is necessary to change the plastic fiber molds and the operating temperature in the heat-treatment facility to meet the specifications set forth by the cable standards specification. Also, each cable must have connectors attached and undergo testing for light transmission. Thus, an order quantity of network cables does not arrive from production into inventory all at once. Rather, it arrives steadily over a period of several days. This change requires a modification in the EOQ formula, even if the assumptions of a constant rate of demand and the inventory carrying cost being equal to C_h times the average inventory are maintained.

It is usually more convenient to work with this model in terms of daily production and demand rates. Thus, consider a product in which

d = number of units demanded each day

p = number of units produced each day during a production run

C_O = setup cost that is independent of the quantity produced

c_h = cost per *day* of holding inventory
(note the change in notation to emphasize holding cost per day)

It is obvious that p must be greater than d for the model to be interesting. (If $p < d$, demand is greater than STECO's ability to produce, and holding inventory is the least of its problems.) Figure 8.34 presents a plot of what the inventory on hand would look like if STECO decided to produce in lots of Q items each.

There are several aspects of this graph that must be noted in order to calculate the average holding and setup and cost per day.

1. During a production run items are added to inventory at a rate of p units per day and removed at the rate of d per day. The net effect is an increase at the rate of $p - d$ units per day.

2. At other times, items are removed from inventory at a rate of d items per day.

3. Since Q items are produced in a run, at the rate of p items per day, each production run is Q/p days long.

4. Since Q items are produced in a run, and d is the daily demand rate, each **cycle time**— that is, the interval between the start of arrivals of replenishments—is Q/d days long.

Facts 1 and 3 can be used to find the maximum amount of inventory on hand (see Figure 8.34).

$$\text{maximum inventory} = (p - d)\frac{Q}{p}$$

Since the average inventory equals one half of the maximum inventory, it follows

$$\text{average inventory} = \frac{1}{2}(p - d)\frac{Q}{p}$$

Rearranging the terms in the expression above, we obtain

$$\text{average inventory} = = \frac{Q}{2}\left(1 - \frac{d}{p}\right)$$

$$\text{holding cost per day} = c_h\frac{Q}{2}\left(1 - \frac{d}{p}\right)$$

Similarly, since there is one setup every cycle and a cycle lasts Q/d days,

$$\text{setup cost per day} = \frac{C_O}{Q/d} = C_O\frac{d}{Q}$$

Thus, the daily holding and setup cost, denoted DHS(Q), is given by the expression

$$\text{DHS}(Q) = C_o\frac{d}{Q} + c_h\frac{Q}{2}\left(1 - \frac{d}{p}\right)$$

If you think of $c_h(1 - d/p)$ as a constant, this expression takes the same form as given by (8.5), the expression for the annual holding and ordering cost in the EOQ model.

It follows, then, that the value of Q that minimizes DHS(Q) will be given by the EOQ equation (8.9) with C_h appropriately modified. Thus, for the **production lot size model,**

$$Q^* = \sqrt{\frac{2C_od}{c_h\left(1 - \frac{d}{p}\right)}} \tag{8.11}$$

(The result could also be derived with calculus.) Substituting Q^* for Q in the expression for DHS(Q) and simplifying gives us an expression for the minimum daily holding and setup cost:

$$DHS(Q^*) = \sqrt{2C_odc_h\left(1 - \frac{d}{p}\right)}$$

Note that this expression does not depend on Q; it is valid only when the lot size is equal to the value of the expression in equation (8.11).

To apply this analysis to any particular product, STECO must estimate the various parameters for that product and then evaluate (8.11) to obtain Q^*. Thus, once the parameters are estimated, finding Q^* is reduced to a matter of evaluating the formulas.

To illustrate this model, assume the demand for this product averages 200 NCs per day. It costs $100 to set up to jacket, heat treat, and test the cables, and they can be produced at a rate of 400 NCs per day. STECO estimates the holding cost per day as ($1)(0.24)/240 = $0.001, where $1 is the production cost of the NC and 0.24 is the annual interest rate used by STECO for all products. The figure 240 is the assumed number of working days per year.

The optimal production lot size for this product, then, is

$$Q^* = \sqrt{\frac{2 \times 200 \times 100}{0.001\left(1 - \frac{200}{400}\right)}} = 8944$$

and the minimum daily holding and setup cost is

$$\sqrt{2 \times 200 \times 100 \times 0.001 \left(1 - \frac{200}{400}\right)} = \$4.47$$

A production run of this size yields a supply of NCs large enough to satisfy demand for

$$\frac{8944}{200} = 44.72 \text{ days}$$

Alternatively, Solver can be used to perform the optimization that otherwise requires the application of calculus to determine the formulas, as above, and which may not be applicable if some of the assumptions are altered. The spreadsheet NLP model for the production lot size problem is shown in Figure 8.35. In practice, STECO might adjust this quantity to take into account the fact that a number of other products also have to make use of the cable heat-treatment facility. In addition, STECO would perhaps perform a sensitivity analysis of this model in a way similar to that done for the EOQ model in Section 8.12.

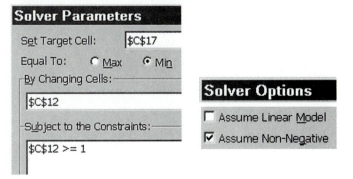

	A	B	C	D
1		Production & Inventory Model		
2		Working Days Annually	240	
3		Annual Cost of Holding %	24%	
4		Production Setup Cost	$100	
5		Annual Demand	48000	
6		Daily Demand	200	
7		Production Rate/Day	400	
8			Unit Cost	
9		Variable Production Cost	$1.00	
10		Daily Holding Cost	$0.001	
11				
12		Production Lot Size	8944	
13			Daily Cost	
14		Order Cost	$2.24	
15		Holding Cost	$2.2361	
16		Production Cost	$400.00	
17		Total	$404.47	
18				

	A	B	C	D
8			Unit Cost	
9		Variable Production Cost	1	
10		Daily Holding Cost	=C3*C9/C2	
11				
12		Production Lot Size	8944.28	
13			Daily Cost	
14		Order Cost	=C4*C6/C12	
15		Holding Cost	=C10*C12/2*(1-C6/C7)	
16		Production Cost	=C9*C7	
17		Total	=SUM(C14:C16)	
18				

Solver Parameters

Set Target Cell: $C$17

Equal To: ○ Max ● Min

By Changing Cells:

$C$12

Subject to the Constraints:

$C$12 >= 1

Solver Options

☐ Assume Linear Model

☑ Assume Non-Negative

FIGURE 8.35

Production Lot Size Model for STECO

Other variations of this or the EOQ model would consider adding a safety stock to allow for the possibility that demand might run ahead of production at the beginning of a production run. Another variation would be to incorporate the concept of backlogging inventory in which the penalty costs of unavailable inventory are traded off against the savings of lowered average inventory levels.

8.14 NOTES ON NLP IMPLEMENTATION

The practice of nonlinear optimization is in some ways even more of an art than the practice of LP. Almost all LP optimizers are, in major respects, the same, since they are variants of the simplex method.[12] However, it would not be difficult to identify as many as 10 or 15 quite different procedures for solving NLP models of which Solver uses only one. To find the best method for a given model, indeed even to understand the differences between various approaches, you, at least in this respect, must be more of an expert with mathematics. Another delicate aspect of NLP practice is the existence, from a mathematical viewpoint, of so many different types of nonlinear models with different theoretical properties (whereas there is only one type of LP). Associated with this fact is the need to reckon with the issue of local versus global solutions to the model. You must know enough about the mathematical structure of the model to have at least a feeling for the quality of the solution (e.g., local versus global) produced by Solver, and often you must experiment in order to locate improved solutions.

Although most NLP optimizers, like Solver, will compute the Lagrange multipliers (i.e., the shadow prices) and reduced gradients along with the solution, additional sensitivity analysis is generally not available. Thus, from the managerial point of view, the NLP output contains less information than an LP output provides.

Although NLP applies to a wide spectrum of models, the most common applications probably occur in situations where the model has special structure, such as for QP. For example, there may be linear constraints but a nonlinear objective function, and so on. In such cases there is hope of solving reasonably large scale models.

What do we mean by "large scale" in NLP? Again, this is much less clearly defined than it is for LP. For a concave or convex quadratic program, we can aspire to several thousand constraints and variables. This power derives from the fact that for such a model a variant of the simplex method is often employed.[13] However, for more general nonlinear models, without special structure that is used to advantage, one would consider a model with more than 500 variables to be large even for a workstation-sized computer.[14]

The last three sections of the chapter were devoted to applications of NLP in portfolio optimization in finance and the basic EOQ (economic order quantity) model and its various modifications in inventory management. The latter example, modifications of the basic EOQ model, showed how the optimal order quantity must be modified in the face of a quantity discount and for the case in which items are not ordered from an outside source, but are produced internally.

These two classes of examples of NLP in Sections 8.10 through 8.13 satisfy the requirements of concavity and convexity that make the application of NLP models attractive. As a result, NLP is widely applied in finance and inventory management applications. Other NLP applications are probably clustered in such areas as engineering design, nonlinear statistical estimation, product distribution, physical applications such as oil drilling, and finally, optimal scheduling and equipment utilization when nonlinear costs are involved.

---

[12]Recent years have seen the development of new LP optimization methods based upon approaches different from the simplex procedure used by Solver. Early evidence suggests these new methods are more efficient only for very large LP models involving thousands of variables.

[13]For example, a commercial upgrade to Excel's Solver, called Premium Edition Solver, optimizes larger NLP models (up to 400 decision variables) and includes a special-purpose optimizer for QP models, allowing up to 800 decision variables.

[14]Limitations for Excel's Solver for NLPs are no more than 200 decision variables and no more than 100 constraints, ignoring any simple lower- or upper-bound constraints on the decision variables.

Stationary Point.   A point at which all first partial derivatives vanish.

First-Order Optimality Conditions.   Necessary conditions for the existence of an optimum; all partial derivatives must equal zero.

Second-Order Optimality Conditions.   Sufficient conditions for the existence of an optimum.

Nonlinear Program (NLP).   A mathematical programming model in which at least one of the constraint functions or the objective function or both are nonlinear.

Lagrange Multiplier.   Associated with a constraint, it is the rate of change in the optimal value of the objective function as the RHS of that constraint increases. Called *shadow price* in LP models (see Chapter 5).

Reduced Gradient.   Associated with a decision variable, it is the initial rate of change in the optimal value of the objective function as that variable is moved away from any binding upper or lower bound on its value. If a nonnegative decision variable is at zero after optimization, the reduced gradient is the rate of hurt in the objective function value as the variable is forced away from its zero value. Called a *reduced cost* in LP models (see Chapter 5).

Convex Set of Points.   A set of points such that for all possible pairs of points in the set, the line segment connecting any such pair must lie entirely within the set.

Concave Program.   A Max model with a concave objective function and a convex constraint set.

Convex Program.   A Min model with a convex objective function and a convex constraint set.

Quadratic Programs (QP).   Nonlinear models that maximize or minimize the value of a quadratic objective function subject to linear constraints and possible nonnegativity conditions.

Portfolio Analysis.   The model of minimizing the variance of return subject to a requirement on expected return.

Variance.   A statistical measure of risk.

Covariance.   A statistical measure of the extent to which random quantities are correlated.

Standard Deviation.   The square root of variance.

Efficient Frontier.   The OV function of a portfolio analysis QP.

Inventory.   Units of goods, money, or individuals held in anticipation of future needs.

Holding Cost.   The cost of holding inventory; it includes opportunity cost plus direct costs such as pilferage, insurance, and obsolescence.

Opportunity Cost.   If taking one action (say, A) implies that another action (say, B) cannot be taken, the net return associated with action B is an opportunity cost of taking action A.

Ordering Cost.   One of the cost parameters in the EOQ model. The marginal cost of placing an order.

Stockout Cost.   Stated in terms of either penalty cost or backlogging cost.

Stockout.   Not having enough inventory on hand to satisfy demand.

Backlogging.   The practice of delivering goods to customers some time after the order has been received rather than immediately upon receipt of the order.

Penalty Cost.   The loss in a no-backlogging model when it is not possible to satisfy demand; usually stated as a per unit cost of unsatisfied demand.

Backlogging Cost.   One of the cost parameters in the EOQ model expanded to allow for backlogging. The cost of backlogging an item for a specified time.

Order Quantity.   Part of an inventory control system. The number of items that are ordered when an order is placed.

Demand.   The number of items ordered. Because of stockouts, this may be different from the number of items sold.

Economic Order Quantity (EOQ) Model. An inventory control model with constant rate of demand and in which relevant costs are those of ordering and holding, and possibly those of backlogging demand.

Optimal Order Quantity. The quantity that minimizes the total annual cost of ordering and holding a particular item.

Inventory Holding Cost. One of the cost parameters in the EOQ model. The cost of holding an item in inventory for a specified time.

Economic Order Quantity. The optimal order quantity derived from the EOQ model.

Quantity Discount. A purchase plan under which the seller offers a special price to the buyer if he or she purchases a specified quantity or more.

Cycle Time. The interval between the arrival of the two consecutive orders.

Production Lot Size Model. A modification of the EOQ model that allows for a finite rate of receiving materials.

Self-Review Exercises Nonlinear Models

True-False

1. **T F** Economy of scale is a nonlinear relationship.

2. **T F** An applied problem involving a nonlinear relationship cannot be modeled as an LP.

3. **T F** If the necessary conditions for a local max occur, a local max occurs.

4. **T F** If a local min occurs, the necessary conditions for a local min occur.

5. **T F** If a local min is a global min, it is the only point where the sufficient conditions for a local min hold.

6. **T F** A straight line is neither a concave nor a convex function.

7. **T F** In an NLP or an LP, tightening a constraint cannot help and it might hurt.

8. **T F** For a max model, a Lagrange multiplier has the same interpretation as the shadow price that appears on the Solver output for LP models, although in general it is not constant over an RHS interval.

9. **T F** A quadratic programming model is always a special type of concave programming model.

10. **T F** An NLP is always either a concave or a convex programming model.

11. **T F** The constraint set defined by the following inequalities is convex.
$9x + 4y \leq 36$
$4x + 12y \leq 20$

12. **T F** In practice, to find a local max of a function of several variables, one first finds all stationary points. One then applies second-order tests to these points.

13. **T F** Although nonlinear programs are more difficult than LPs, in terms of finding an optimal solution it is nevertheless true that a corner-searching technique can be applied.

14. **T F** One problem in NLP is distinguishing between local and global solutions.

Multiple Choice

(In the questions below $f'(x)$ and $f''(x)$ denote the first and second derivatives of a function of a single variable, x, and x^* is a stationary point.)

15. Suppose that f is a function of a single variable. The condition $f''(x^*) > 0$
   a. is a necessary condition for a local min
   b. is a sufficient condition for a local min
   c. is a sufficient condition for a local max
   d. none of the above

16. Suppose that f is a function of a single variable. The condition $f'(x^*) = 0$ is
   a. a necessary condition for x^* to be a local max
   b. a necessary condition for x^* to be a local min
   c. a necessary condition for x^* to be a global min
   d. all of the above

17. In nonlinear models differential calculus is needed
   a. to avoid multiple (local) solutions
   b. to express optimality conditions

c. both a and b

d. neither a nor b

18. A point x^* with the property that $f'(x^*) = 0$ and $f''(x^*) > 0$ (where f is a function of a single variable) satisfies the sufficient conditions for x^* to be

a. a local max

b. a local min

c. neither a nor b

19. Which of the following is true of a concave function?

a. One can attempt to find a global maximizer by using a hill-climbing optimizer such as Solver.

b. Any local maximizer is also a global maximizer.

c. Both a and b above.

20. Which of the following is true?

a. For a general NLP, optimality conditions are directly used in solving NLP problems. That is, optimizers like Solver exist to directly solve these conditions, and this produces an NLP solution.

b. For a general NLP, optimality conditions are indirectly used in solving NLP problems. That is, optimizers like Solver exist to directly attack the NLP, employing, for example, a hill-climbing approach. The optimality conditions provide a termination criterion for such algorithms.

c. Optimality conditions are only of theoretic interest.

21. For concave programming models

a. the second-order conditions are more useful

b. any local optimum is a global optimum as well

c. both the constraint set and the objective function must be concave

22. Convexity

a. is a description that applies both to sets of points and to functions

b. is an important mathematical property used to guarantee that local solutions are also global

c. is useful in unconstrained as well as constrained optimization

d. all of the above

23. Which of the following is *not* generally true of a Lagrange multiplier?

a. It has an economic interpretation similar to that of shadow price.

b. It is the rate of change of OV as the RHS of a constraint is increased.

c. It is valid (i.e., constant) over an RHS range.

24. Which of the following is *not* true?

a. Even when global solutions cannot be guaranteed, optimization can still be a useful tool in decision making.

b. In LP, we need never worry about local solutions (i.e., every local solution is also global).

c. Since we can only guarantee that local solutions are global when the appropriate convexity (or concavity) properties exist, these are the only types of NLP problems that yield useful information.

25. Which is true of corner point solutions in NLP?

a. It makes no difference what objective function we have, the optimal solution will always be at a corner point.

b. We have to worry about corner points only if the objective function is linear.

c. In general, the optimum may not be at a corner point.

Answers

1.	T	8.	T	14.	T	20.	b
2.	F	9.	F	15.	d	21.	b
3.	F	10.	F	16.	d	22.	d
4.	T	11.	T	17.	b	23.	c
5.	F	12.	F	18.	b	24.	c
6.	F	13.	F	19.	c	25.	c
7.	T						

Self-Review Exercises Quadratic Programming

True-False

1. **T F** A quadratic programming model may have quadratic constraint functions.

2. **T F** Maximizing or minimizing any nonlinear objective function subject to a set of linear equality and inequality constraints, as well as possible nonnegativity conditions on the values of the decision variables, is a quadratic programming model.

3. **T F** Any LP model could be solved with a QP optimizer.

4. **T F** It is not possible to characterize extreme points of the feasible region of a QP.

5. **T** F The optimal solution to a QP model need not be a corner solution.

6. **T** F The optimal solution to a QP model must include at least as many positive variables as there are constraints.

7. **T** F Loosening a constraint in a QP either will not change or will improve the OV.

8. **T** F In a Max model the rate of improvement of OV is always the negative of the Lagrange multiplier.

9. **T** F The slope of the tangent to the graph of the function $OV(R)$ at the point $(\hat{R}, OV(\hat{R}))$ is the rate of change in the function $OV(R)$ at $R = \hat{R}$.

10. **T** F Changing a coefficient of a term in the objective function of a QP always changes the optimal solution.

11. **T** F The variance of the return from a portfolio is a linear function of the amount invested in each stock in the portfolio.

12. **T** F If there are three stocks in the portfolio, the feasible region will lie on a plane.

13. **T** F The portfolio model includes a lower bound on the expected return. In general this constraint need not be binding.

Multiple Choice

14. The definition of a QP model does not include
    a. quadratic constraint functions
    b. linear equality constraints
    c. nonlinear terms in the objective function

15. In a QP model in n variables, $(x_i, \ldots, x_n)$, the objective function may not include terms of the form
    a. x_j^2
    b. $x_i x_j$
    c. $x_i^2 x_j$
    d. $9x_i$

16. An LP is a special case of a QP because
    a. the LP feasible region is a special case of a QP feasible region
    b. the LP constraint functions are a special case of the QP constraint functions
    c. any nonnegativity conditions are special to an LP
    d. the LP objective function is a special case of the QP objective function

17. The optimal solution to a QP model with n constraints may not have
    a. negative values for some decision variables
    b. more than n positive decision variables
    c. fewer than n positive decision variables
    d. zero values for some decision variables

18. The optimal solution to a QP model
    a. must lie on a corner of the feasible set
    b. cannot be on a corner of the feasible set
    c. is always nondegenerate
    d. none of the above

19. In the optimal solution for a QP model, slack variables
    a. have no meaning
    b. have the same meaning as in an LP model
    c. have a different meaning than in an LP model
    d. are unrestricted in sign

20. Solver can be used to solve
    a. general nonlinear programming models
    b. QPs
    c. LPs
    d. all of the above

21. Loosening a constraint in a variance-minimizing portfolio model
    a. must increase the Lagrangian multiplier on that constraint
    b. must decrease the Lagrangian multiplier on that constraint
    c. may change the sign of the Lagrangian multiplier on that constraint
    d. cannot increase the objective function

Answers

1. F	7. T	12. T	17. a
2. F	8. F	13. T	18. d
3. T	9. T	14. a	19. b
4. F	10. F	15. c	20. d
5. T	11. F	16. d	21. d
6. F			

True-False

1. **T F** The opportunity cost segment of inventory holding cost is determined by factors such as breakage, pilferage, and insurance.

2. **T F** In inventory models, demand is always greater than or equal to sales.

3. **T F** In the EOQ model the annual ordering cost is directly proportional to the order quantity.

4. **T F** In the EOQ model the annual holding and ordering cost is reasonably insensitive to errors in estimating the cost parameters.

5. **T F** In the production lot size model, since production is at a steady rate, no setup cost is included in the model.

Multiple Choice

6. The following are some of the reasons inventory is held:
   a. protect against uncertainty in demand
   b. lower production costs
   c. store labor
   d. all of the above

7. Important considerations in deciding *when* and *how much* to order include all factors except
   a. the lead time
   b. the proportion of the holding cost that is due to the opportunity cost
   c. the possibility of quantity discounts
   d. the extent to which future demand is known

8. In the EOQ model
   a. each shipment arrives in a batch
   b. demand is known and occurs at a constant rate
   c. all demand must be satisfied
   d. all of the above

9. In the EOQ model if the price of the item increases and all other parameters remain the same, the optimal order quantity will typically
   a. increase
   b. decrease
   c. stay the same

10. In the EOQ model the optimal number of orders per year
    a. increases directly with
    b. increases as the square root of
    c. decreases directly with
    d. does not change with
    the annual rate of demand.

11. Consider an EOQ model with a quantity discount where a smaller per unit price applies to all units if B or more units are purchased. If Q_D^* minimizes AHO assuming the smaller price, and Q_R^* minimizes AHO assuming the regular price, and $Q_D^* > B$, the optimal order quantity is always
    a. Q_D^*
    b. either Q_R^* or B, depending on which yields the smaller annual total cost
    c. Q_R^*
    d. B

12. In the production lot size model, increasing the rate of production
    a. increases
    b. does not influence
    c. decreases
    the optimal number of orders to place each year.

Answers

1.	F	4.	T	7.	b	10.	b
2.	T	5.	F	8.	d	11.	a
3.	F	6.	d	9.	b	12.	a

Nonlinear Programming Problems

8-1. (a) Use Solver to maximize the function $f(x) = -8x^2 - 14x - 32$.
   (b) Use Solver to maximize this function over the interval $1 \le x \le 10$.
   (c) Can you tell whether this function is concave or convex?

8-2. (a) Use Solver to maximize the function $f(x) = -x^2 + 4x + 6$.
   (b) Use Solver to maximize this function over the interval $3 \le x \le 12$.
   (c) Can you tell whether this function is concave or convex?

8-3. Lenard Crumb, manager of Crumb Baking Services, is considering the offer of a distributor who sells an instant croissant mix. The total cost of x pounds of the mix is given by

$$\text{total cost} = x^3 - 50x^2 + 750x$$

What quantity of this mix will minimize *total cost per pound?*

8-4. Use Solver to minimize

$$f(x, y) = x^2 + 2xy + 2y^2 - 8x - 12y + 6.$$

Use the Data table and Chart Wizard to plot $f(x,y)$.

•• **8-5.** Hoot Spa imports coconut oil from his home town in Jamaica. He uses this oil to produce two kinds of tanning creme: Sear and Char. The price per kilogram at which he will be able to sell these products depends on how much of each he produces. In particular, if Hoot produces x_1 kilograms of Sear and x_2 kilograms of Char, he will be able to sell all he produces at the following prices (in dollars):

$$\text{price per kilogram of Sear} = 120 - x_1$$

and

$$\text{price per kilogram of Char} = 150 - 2x_2$$

The cost of manufacturing x_1 kilograms of Sear and x_2 kilograms of Char is

$$\text{cost of manufacturing the two cremes} = 1.2x_1 + 16.8x_2 + 1.3x_1x_2$$

Assuming that he can sell all he produces, Hoot wishes to determine how many kilograms of each creme he should schedule for production so as to maximize his profit.

8-6. We want to build a solid cylinder of volume 2π. If we would like to minimize the surface area of the cylinder (including both ends), what should be its radius and height? HINT: volume $= \pi r^2 h$, surface area $= 2\pi rh + 2\pi r^2$

•• **8-7.** *Linear Regression Analysis.* In the linear regression model, historical data points (x_i, y_i), $i = 1, \ldots, n$, are given. The linear model is an estimating equation (also called the regression line) $y = ax + b$, where a and b are chosen so as to minimize the sum of squared deviations

$$S(a, b) = \sum_{i=1}^{n} [y_i - (ax_i + b)]^2$$

(a) Use this approach to determine the estimating equation for the following data:

x	8	6	12
y	6	14	-18

(b) Use the same approach to determine the estimating equation for the following data:

x	10	17.4	20.1	12.6	14.9
y	25	10	5	20	15

8-8. (a) Solve the following problem:

$$\text{Min } 2x_1^2 + 3x_2^2 + x_1 - 9x_2 + 16$$
$$\text{s.t. } x_1 + x_2 = 5$$

(b) Use the Sensitivity Report to estimate the change in OV if the RHS of the constraint were to increase from 5 to 8 and compare that estimate to the actual result for that change.

8-9. (a) Solve the following problem:

$$\text{Max } - 3x_1^2 + 42x_1 - 3x_2^2 + 48x_2 - 339$$
$$\text{s.t. } 4x_1 + 6x_2 = 24$$

(b) Use the Sensitivity Report to estimate the change in OV if the RHS of the constraint were to increase from 24 to 28 and compare that estimate to the actual result for that change.

•• **8-10.** Ure industries gets a productivity of

$$f(x, y) = 2x^2y + 3xy^2 + 2y^3$$

from x units of labor and y units of capital. If labor costs \$50 per unit and capital costs \$100 per unit, how many units of labor and capital should Ure use, given that its budget is \$150,000?

(a) Formulate the Solver model and optimize from an initial point of $x = 0$ and $y = 1$.

(b) Optimize as in (a) but from a starting point of $x = 1,000,000$ and $y = 1,000,000$.

(c) Explain the two answers above.

8-11. Show that the solution found in the "optimal marketing expenditures" example (Section 8.5) is actually a global (as opposed to local) optimum.

•• **8-12.** Show that the optimum solution to Problem 8-10 satisfies

$$\frac{\text{Marginal productivity of labor}}{\text{Marginal productivity of capital}} = \frac{\text{Unit price of labor}}{\text{Unit price of capital}}$$

HINT: Remove the budget constraint and substitute constraints on x and y with each being less than or equal to their optimal values in Problem 8-10.

•• **8-13.** ••Solve Example 2, assuming $s_i = 1/2$ for $i = 1, 2, 3$, $p_1 = 2$, $p_2 = 2.8$, $p_3 = 4$, and budget $B = 250$. What is the Lagrange multiplier for the budget constraint?

••• **8-14.** Does the following set of constraints form a convex set? Why?

$$\begin{aligned} x + y &\leq 20 \\ -2x + y &\geq 10 \\ x^2 + 2x + 1 &\leq 100 \\ -x^4 - 2x^2 + 60 &\geq 36 \end{aligned}$$

•• **8-15.** *A Pooling Problem. Two* chemical products, X and Y, are made by blending three chemical inputs, A, B, and C. The inputs are contaminated by sulfur, and the outputs must meet restrictions on sulfur content. The three inputs are shipped mixed together in two tank cars. A is shipped in car 1, C is shipped in car 2, and B is shipped in car 1 and/or car 2. No more than 100 units of X and 200 units of Y may be sold. Using the data in the following table below, formulate a profit-maximizing nonlinear program and optimize it using Solver.

CHEMICAL	COST PER UNIT ($)	SULFUR CONTENT (%)
A	6	3
B	16	1
C	10	2
	Sales Price per Unit	
X	9	no more than 2.5
Y	15	no more than 1.5

8-16. Suppose in the Gulf Coast Oil model of Section 8.5 the octane number from Source i varies from month to month. Introduce a new variable, $OCTS1$, the octane number of Source 1, and replace all references to the octane number of Source 1 in the model with this variable. Add a constraint to the Solver model that sets $OCTS1$ equal to 93 and then optimize the NLP. Using the Sensitivity Report, *estimate* what would happen to the optimal profit if the octane number increased to 94, to 96, and to 98, then actually change the octane number to 94, then 96, and last to 98 and re-optimize each time, comparing the actual result with your estimate. Note that what we are really doing is a sensitivity analysis on a constraint coefficient.

8-17. *Economic Substitutes.* Suppose in the Astro and Cosmo model of Section 8.5 that Astros and Cosmos are economic substitutes. This means that an increase in the price of one causes an increase in demand for the other. More specifically, suppose that the new demand equations are

$$A = 1000 - 4.7PA + PC$$
$$C = 1000 + 2PA - 6.2PC$$

Reformulate the model, and optimize it using Solver. Interpret the Sensitivity Report.

Quadratic Programming Problems

•• **8-18.** "If *at least one* of the stocks in the portfolio has an expected return greater than or equal to the required return on the entire portfolio, then this formulation will never be infeasible." Under what conditions will this statement be true?

••8-19. Consider the portfolio model solved in Section 8.11. The current solution to this model is (AT&T = 0.53, GM = 0.3564, USS = 0. 1135). Is this point an extreme point of the feasible region? Why or why not?

8-20. Consider the portfolio model solved in Section 8.11. Assume you are considering adding the stock of the IMCRZY corporation to your portfolio selection model. This stock has a *negative* expected return. Under what conditions might the model select stock from IMCRZY to be in the portfolio?

8-21. Consider the portfolio model solved in Section 8.11. What is the allowable decrease on the constraint that limits the investment of GM stock to 75% of the portfolio?

8-22. As with pure LP analysis, there is a Sensitivity Report associated with QP. Why does this QP Sensitivity Report not include allowable increases and decreases on the RHS of constraints?

8-23. Consider the portfolio model solved in Section 8.11. Assume your objective is to maximize return subject to the constraint that the variability of the portfolio cannot exceed V. Rewrite the symbolic model with this modification.

8-24. Refer to Problem 8-23. Set $V = 0.0205$. If there are no alternative optima in the original model, what is the maximum expected return in your reformulated model? Explain.

••8-25. Stocks x, y, and z have expected returns of 7%, 6%, and 10%, respectively, and the following variance-covariance matrix:

	x	y	z
x	.01		
y	.001	.04	
z	.001	− .04	.08

    (a) Determine the fraction of the portfolio to hold in each stock so as to minimize the variance of the portfolio subject to a minimum expected return on the portfolio of 8%.

    (b) Can the variance of the portfolio be smaller than the variance of any individual stock? Explain.

    (c) Use the Lagrange multiplier information to estimate what would happen to the variance of the optimal portfolio if the minimum expected return were raised to 9%. Compare your estimate with the actual by resolving the model.

Inventory Problems

8-26. The demand for general books at the University Bookstore occurs at a constant rate of 18,000 books per year. The manager satisfies this demand without backlogging. He calculates the optimal order quantity based on ordering costs of $30 and an annual holding cost of $3 per book. Assume 250 days per year. What are the values for Q^*, N^*, and $AHO(Q^*)$?

8-27. A local hardware store sells 364,000 pounds of nails a year. It currently orders 14,000 pounds of nails every 2 weeks at a price of $0.50 per pound. Assume that
    1. Demand occurs at a constant rate.
    2. The cost of placing an order is $50 regardless of the size of the order.
    3. The annual cost of holding inventory is 12% of the value of the average inventory level.
    4. These factors do not change over time.
        (a) What is the average inventory level?
        (b) What is the annual holding cost?
        (c) What is the annual ordering cost?
        (d) What is the annual holding and ordering cost?
        (e) What is the annual total cost?
        (f) Would it be cheaper for the owner to order in lots larger than 14,000 (and less frequently) or smaller lots (and more frequently)?

8-28. The campus ice cream store sells 180 quarts of vanilla ice cream each month. The store currently restocks its inventory at the beginning of each month. The wholesale price of ice cream is $3 per quart. Assume that

1. Demand occurs at a constant rate.
2. The annual cost of holding inventory is 25% of the value of the average inventory level.
3. Last year the annual total cost was $7627.50.
4. These factors do not change over time.
    (a) Compute average inventory level.
    (b) Compute annual holding cost.
    (c) Compute the ordering cost.
    (d) Use Data Table 1 to graph annual holding costs, annual ordering costs, and AHO as a function of order quantity.
    (e) At what point is the AHO minimized? How much can the ice cream store save annually if it uses the optimal order quantity?

8-29. A young entrepreneur sells pencils at a constant rate of 25 per day. Each pencil costs $0.05. If ordering costs are $5 and inventory holding costs are 20% of the cost of the average inventory, what are the optimal order quantity and the optimal number of orders that should be placed each year?

••8-30. A credit card company has an annual income of $100,000,000. If the cost of sending out a billing statement is $30,000 and the prevailing interest rate is 6%, how often should the company send out bills?

••8-31. Specific Electric (SE) is a giant manufacturer of electrical appliances in the United States. It uses electric motors that it purchases from another firm at a constant rate. Total purchase costs during the year are $2,400,000. Ordering costs are $100, and annual inventory holding costs are 20% of the cost of the average inventory.
    (a) What is the dollar value of the optimal order quantity?
    (b) How many times a year should SE order?
    (c) What is the optimal cycle time in years and in days if there are 250 working days per year?
    HINT: If P is the cost per unit to Specific Electric and Q^* is the optimal quantity, PQ^* is the dollar value of the optimal order quantity.

8-32. If, in Problem 8-28, the ordering cost doubles, what is the change in the optimal order quantity?

••8-33. Strumm and Howell (S and H) is a local record store that specializes in country music. The store has been quite successful in recent years, with retail sales of $400,000 per year. Sales occur at a constant rate during the year. S and H buys its records from a major recording company. The retail sales price equals 5/3 times the cost to S and H. The ordering cost for each shipment of orders is $75, independent of the size of the order. Annual inventory holding costs are 10% of the cost of the average inventory level.
    (a) What is the dollar value of the optimal order quantity?
    (b) How often should S and H order each year?
    (c) What is the optimal cycle time in years?
    HINT: If P is the cost per unit to S and H and Q^* is the optimal order quantity, PQ^* is the dollar value of the optimal order quantity.

8-34. If, in Problem 8-28, the wholesaler offers to sell ice cream at $2.43 a quart when bought in a quantity of at least 1000 quarts, what is the campus ice cream store's optimal strategy?

••8-35. The Waukon, Iowa, outlet of Cheep Chicks orders baby chickens from the firm's central incubator in Des Moines. Twenty-two-and-one-half dozen chicks are demanded each day of the 360-day year. It costs $40 to process an order independent of the number of chicks ordered and $80 to hold a dozen chicks in inventory for a year. Assume that Cheep calculates inventory holding costs on the basis of the average inventory level.
    (a) What is the optimal order quantity?
    (b) How many orders should be placed each year?
    (c) What is the optimal cycle time in years? In working days?

8-36. The Napa Wine Company, the nation's largest distributor of California wine products, has a constant demand of 192 cases per month for its most popular product, Wino Delux. Its ordering cost is $100, annual holding costs are 25% of the average inventory, and the product costs $200 per case. Currently, it does not backlog demand and follows the optimal ordering policy. Allowing for vacations and religious holidays, there are 200 days per year. Under the current policy (no backlogging), find Q^*, N^*, and AHO(Q^*).

••8-37. Bed Bug, a local manufacturer of orthopedic mattresses, currently satisfies its constant production requirements of 500 coiled springs per day by using an EOQ model based on an ordering cost of $90, a product cost of $1 per spring, and an inventory holding cost of 15% of the cost of average inventory. Springy Steel, its supplier, has recently offered a 0.5% discount if Bed Bug orders in quantities of at least 20,000 springs, or a 0.7% discount if it orders quarterly. Assume 240 workdays per year.

(a) Find Q^* and the annual total cost under the current cost assumptions.

(b) What is the annual total cost for each of the discount alternatives?

(c) What should Bed Bug do?

8-38. If, in Problem 8-28, the holding cost % doubles, what is the change in the optimal order quantity?

8-39. XXX Distillery, a major producer of arthritis and nerve medicine in the Southeast, produces its stock in batches. In order to begin each run, the company owners must select a suitable location and assemble the equipment. The cost of this operation is $900. Production yields 60 gallons of product each day, each of which costs $0.025 per day to hold in inventory. Demand is constant at 1125 gallons per month. Assume 12 months, 300 days per year, and 25 days per month.

(a) Find Q^*, N^*, and the cycle time for the optimal production lot size.

(b) Find the maximum inventory and the length (in days) of each production run for the optimal production lot size.

(c) Find DHS(Q^*).

8-40. Because of the importance of business confidentiality, XXX Distillery in Problem 8-39 decides to make three production runs per year.

(a) Find the production order quantity, Q, cycle time (in days), length of production run, and maximum inventory level.

(b) Find DHS for the policy in part (a).

•••8-41. Consider Problem 8-39.

(a) Suppose that XXX Distillery purchased rather than produced its product and that the cost of placing an order is $900. Find Q^* and AHO(Q^*).

(b) How does AHO(Q^*) in part (a) compare with DHS(Q^*) when there is a production rate of 60 gallons per day? Explain this relationship.

(c) Use a Data Table to plot the DHS($Q^*[p]$) as a function of the daily production rate, p.

(d) Due to the economies of scale, unit production costs decrease as p increases. The exact relationship is $C(p) = 30/p$, where $C(p)$ is the unit production cost when the daily production rate is p. Find the minimum value of the sum of DHS and daily production costs for $p = 45$ and $p = 60$.

•••8-42. Due to technical obsolescence of its equipment, XXX Distillery (Problem 8-39) stops producing and functions only as a marketing organization. It now purchases its product from another producer. XXX must buy at least 1000 gallons per order to qualify for a quantity discount. What is the smallest discount per gallon that would persuade XXX to order 1000 gallons? Assume that now $P = \$5$, $C_h = \$2.50$, and $C_O = \$200$.

Case Study   Just-in-Time

Just-in-time! Although the just-in-time (JIT) concept is very young, perhaps 10 to 15 years old in this country, it is so widespread in American manufacturing and service that it is almost a cliché. Perhaps this is because the idea is so simple and so appealing. In short, the JIT strategy is to have "the right product at the right place at the right time." It implies that in manufacturing or service, each stage of the process produces exactly the amount that is required for the next step in the process. This notion holds true for all steps within the system. Suppose, for example, that in our plant all products pass through a drilling operation and then a milling operation. With JIT, the drill produces only what the mill will need next. It also holds for the

last step—that is, the system produces only what the customer desires.

Implementation of a JIT system typically includes emphasis on the following aspects of the production process:

1. Reduction of setup times and cost. Here the idea is to make it cost-effective to produce in very small lot sizes. The ideal is a lot size of one.

2. Emphasis on preventive maintenance. This is important because the manufacturing process must always be ready to go when you need it if you hope to be just-in-time.

3. Continuous process improvement to guarantee good quality. If you are going to make just the right number of units, you must be sure that they are of good quality—you cannot select the good items out of a larger lot with this approach. A continuous improvement process is typically based on a high level of employee involvement and empowerment.
4. Reduction of lead times through effective use of information technology and close relationships with vendors.

In many publications, JIT is placed at one end of a continuum with EOQ at the other. The EOQ model is portrayed as being old, out-of-touch, and possibly responsible for many of the problems faced by manufacturing firms in the United States. We would like to suggest an alternative interpretation. Is it possible that the concepts that form the basis for the EOQ model are consistent with the JIT philosophy, and that the problem has been in interpretation and implementation? Let's examine that possibility.

Questions

1. What is the effect of reducing setup cost on lot size in the EOQ model? Is the effect the same in a JIT system?
2. What is the role of quality and preventive maintenance in the EOQ model? Why?
3. Do you sense a difference in philosophy between the EOQ and the JIT approaches? In particular, what aspects of the production problem is it assumed we can influence in the two approaches?
4. Do you think that there are any general lessons to be learned in regard to modeling from the movement from EOQ to JIT?

| Case Study | Internal Revenue Service (1994–1995)[1] |

Al Swanson was worried. He was looking at the costs and results of the audit program conducted by the Internal Revenue Service (IRS) in fiscal year 1992.[2] Mr. Swanson, an analyst in the Planning and Analysis Division of the IRS, had just been appointed head of an inter-departmental committee to plan and review procedures for auditing individual income tax returns for 1995. The committee included members of the Planning and Analysis Division, which had broad responsibilities for improving IRS functioning, and the audit Division, which had the specific responsibility of ensuring taxpayer compliance with existing tax laws. The formation of this committee was part of a sweeping review of IRS functioning, and its recommendations would have a direct impact on the budget-allocations made by Congress.

What made Mr. Swanson's task all the more important was the development of the IRS' Business Master Plan (BMP), released on April 1, 1994, for Fiscal years 1995–2001. The Business Master Plan would replace the existing Strategic Business Plan and the Annual Servicewide Operating Plan. The genesis of the BMP was partly due to the Government

Performance and Results Act. This act requires government agencies to develop annual plans to support their strategic direction, cover all budgeted activities, provide annual performance goals and indicators, describe what is required to achieve the stated performance goals, and establish accountability throughout the process. It was hoped that the IRS, through the BMP, would be better able to present its case to the Office of Management and Budget (OMB), which helps shape the administration's budget proposals.

IRS Mission

Mr. Swanson brooded over the IRS mission statement:

> The purpose of the Internal Revenue Service is to collect the proper amount of tax revenue at the least cost; serve the public by continually improving the quality of our products and services; and perform in a manner warranting the IRS Business Vision.
>
> Our Business Vision is to administer a tax system for our customers that:
> - Provides simple, easy-to-understand forms; simple filing procedures; alternative filing methods to suit individual needs; and optional ways to interact with the IRS to obtain forms, ask procedural questions, or resolve account-related issues, to maximize the likelihood that everyone files and pays correctly;

---

[1]This case was prepared by Krishnan Anand and Haim Mendelson of the Stanford Business School. It is intended to serve as a basis for class discussion rather than to illustrate either effective or ineffective handling of an administrative situation.

[2]In each fiscal year, the IRS collects and processes taxes for the *previous* year. Most available data are compiled on a fiscal year basis, and this case follows this convention. Sometimes we use the tax year for pedagogic reasons. All such cases will be explicitly stated. In all other cases, years are stated as *fiscal* years.

- Ensures access by telephone at times convenient for taxpayers and quick, accurate responses to written correspondence;
- Allows taxpayers to discuss problems or issues with employees who treat them courteously and professionally, act in an ethical manner, and have immediate access to account information and the authority to resolve problems;
- Provides employees the ability to resolve taxpayers' issues in a timely and accurate manner, with systems and processes designed for that purpose;
- Provides privacy and confidentiality of tax return information and ensures security of data and systems; and
- Provides diverse taxpayers with the ability to interact with employees or systems in ways that meet their needs.

What Mr. Swanson knew to be of great concern to the IRS was the real or perceived erosion in their effectiveness in four key areas: (a) providing information to taxpayers; (b) collecting additional taxes; (c) making refunds when appropriate; and (d) monitoring tax compliance. While improving effectiveness in the first three tasks was to be accomplished partly by investments in people and computing power (to be discussed below) and partly through improved procedures, monitoring tax compliance was more difficult. The impact of increasing the budget for auditing would be less visible and harder to evaluate, and any such proposal would have to compete with other more visible programs. Thus, the three major problems facing Mr. Swanson's committee were *(i)* to develop reasonable guidelines and performance measures for the Auditing Division; *(ii)* to make forecasts of additional taxes and penalties collected as a function of the budget allocation, to select an auditing budget to request from the OMB, and to justify that request; and *(iii)* to optimize the use of the budget eventually approved by Congress for monitoring tax compliance. Most urgent was the need to make a strong case to the OMB for an increase in the budget and to optimally use the allotted budget. While the increase in resources allocated to the IRS was not commensurate with the increase in workload over time, what Mr. Swanson wanted to investigate was whether the resources were being used optimally.

To be sure, the erosion in IRS effectiveness in certain areas reflected an overwhelming increase in workload. Since the late 1980s, the annual number of returns filed had increased significantly, largely as a result of population growth, economic expansion and added reporting requirements. In addition, the organization had not kept pace with the kinds of productivity advancements that private industry had capitalized on for years.

While competition had forced the private sector to be ever-mindful of the potential for technology to improve the bottom line, the IRS had been doing business in much the same way for the last 40 years. As a result, shocking anachronisms abounded. Most of the tax processing, for instance, was done manually, with returns being passed factory-style down an assembly line known in the IRS as the "pipeline."

Historically, Congress and agency officials had addressed the agency's compliance problems Washington-style—by throwing money at them. Since 1982, the IRS operating budget had nearly tripled while its workforce had grown from less than 83,000 in 1982 to a peak of about 117,000 in 1992. Although the Service was collecting record amounts, its operational productivity, in terms of the cost of collections, had plummeted. As of 1992, the IRS was spending nearly 40 percent more to collect $100 than it did in 1982 (see Table 1).

The IRS budget had grown from $4.4 billion in fiscal year 1987 to around $7 billion now, representing a real growth of 3.7 percent per annum. About one-third of this growth had gone to the $23 billion project known as Tax Systems Modernization (TSM)—a program to update its antiquated computer systems. Over the same period, the IRS workload had grown about 10 percent. Thus, under the existing organizational structure and technology base, the IRS would need to add 2,000 more employees every year just to keep up with increases in workload, officials estimate. That, however, was not what management envisioned for the IRS of the future. On the contrary, it expected to eliminate some 17,000 positions over the next decade and cut hundreds of millions of dollars from labor-intensive operations such as the "pipeline."

TABLE 1 Internal Revenue Service Collections. Costs. and Employees (1986–1992)

FISCAL YEAR	OPERATING COSTS ($ MILLIONS)	COLLECTIONS ($ MILLIONS)	COST OF COLLECTING $100	NUMBER OF EMPLOYEES
1982	2,626	632,241	0.42	82,857
1986	3,842	782,252	0.49	95,880
1987	4,366	886,291	0.49	102,188
1988	5,069	935,107	0.54	114,873
1989	5,199	1,013,322	0.51	114,758
1990	5,440	1,056,366	0.52	111,858
1991	6,098	1,086,851	0.56	115,628
1992	6,536	1,120,800	0.58	116,673

Data include all collections (including income, employment, excise, gift, and estate taxes).

Mr. Swanson knew that very soon, the Cincinnati center, a sprawling low-rise building occupying a full city block on the Kentucky side of the Ohio River, would become the test site for a huge conglomeration of imaging equipment known as the Service Center Recognition/Image Processing System, or SCRIPS. A computer system costing nearly $90 million, SCRIPS was expected to pay for itself by increasing the accuracy and speed with which return information was entered into IRS computers and by reducing the center's heavy reliance on manual keyboarding of return information—number by number, line by line. The system was already in operation on a test basis, and it would pave the way for a more sophisticated $4 billion imaging package known as the Document Processing System (DPS), which was expected to be online by 2000. DPS would be able to capture tax data from nearly any document allowed for use by the IRS, eliminating much of the need for transcribers, who for years have formed the backbone of the tax processing system.

Streamlining tax processing was a wrenching aspect of the tax agency's decade-long TSM project. But the hope, as Mr. Swanson well knew, was that TSM's real breakthroughs would not be merely technological or limited to document-processing centers like Cincinnati. Sweeping changes in management and organizational structure throughout the agency were envisioned, that would redefine how, and how well, the IRS did its job.

High Stakes

There was far more riding on TSM than one agency's performance. As stated in an IRS publication,

> The purpose of the Nation's internal revenue tax system is to guarantee the fiscal soundness of the policies and programs of the United States Government.

Thus, when the IRS collects less than the full amount of tax due, this results in either less money for other public programs or more federal borrowing. The agency estimated that it had undercollected approximately $120 billion in income taxes in just the previous year. In addition, increasing the effectiveness of tax collections is a much less painful way for lawmakers to increase revenue than raising taxes. (Undercollection, by allowing people to get away with underpaying taxes, also encourages underreporting in succeeding years. Thus, it also has a serious long-term impact on collections.)

The IRS Business Master Plan for fiscal 1995–2001 was further broken down into specific goals for the first three years of the plan, viz., fiscal years 1995–1997. The primary objective of the IRS Master Plan for 1995–1997 was improving compliance. A strong and effective auditing and tax monitoring program would increase revenues directly through additional tax collections, and it would also have an indirect but significant impact on the extent of future voluntary compliance.

Mr. Swanson sighed, and took yet another look at the data he had on IRS performance over the past couple of years, especially the numbers relating to the audit function (see Table 2).

With over 100,000 employees and nearly 30,000 in just the examination (audit) function, the IRS has many of the strengths and weaknesses of large bureaucratic organizations. Even for personnel costs within the examination function, there are significant *fixed* costs, i.e., costs incurred by the agency independent of the level of examination activity or audit coverage. About 25%–30% of the personnel costs for the examination function were actually fixed, whereas the rest (slightly less than 75%) varied with the level of audit coverage.

On the collection side, there are substantial differences between individual and corporate tax returns. In terms of the relative importance of the two, Mr. Swanson observed that individual income taxes form the lion's share of total IRS receipts (Table 8.9). Total individual receipts had consistently been well over four times total corporate receipts for many years. Improving the functioning of the tax collection and compliance monitoring functions for individuals was therefore crucial to IRS plans for the future. In fact, individual income taxes had constituted at least 8% of the Gross Domestic Product (GDP) for the past 20 years.[3] Corporate income taxes had hovered at 1–2% of GDP during that period. Due to the magnitude of the individual income tax receipts, small changes in collections have a significant impact on the federal deficit. Thus, Mr. Swanson decided to further prioritize and focus his analysis for 1995 on individual income tax returns only, which will also be the focus of the rest of this case.

---

[3]The year 1976 was the one exception, when individual income taxes fell to 7.8% of GDP.

TABLE 2 Internal Revenue Service Costs and Personnel Employed (1991–1992)

		1991	1992
COSTS:	All Activities	6,098	6,536
($ millions)	Examination Function only	1,532	1,605
	Examination Function—Personnel Compensation	1,297	1,378
PERSONNEL COUNTS:	Service-Wide	117,017	117,945
	Examination Function	28,592	28,393

The table breaks down service-wide figures into those applicable to the examination (audit) function. (All costs in millions of dollars. Personnel numbers are annual averages.)

TABLE 3 Individual and Corporate Income Taxes (1986–1994)			
FISCAL YEAR	INDIVIDUAL INCOME TAX RETURNS (MILLIONS)	INCOME TAX RECEIPTS ($ MILLIONS) Individual	Corporate
1986	102.4	348,959	63,143
1987	103.5	392,557	83,926
1988	107.0	401,181	94,508
1989	110.3	445,690	103,291
1990	112.5	466,884	93,507
1991	113.8	467,827	98,086
1992	115.0	475,964	100,270
1993	114.2	509,680	117,520
1994	114.5*	549,901*	130,719*
1995	—	595,048*	140,437*
1996	—	627,652*	145,790*
1997	—	664,062*	149,822*
1998	—	701,620*	152,492*
1999	—	745,120*	157,152*

*IRS estimates.
Breakdown of income taxes from corporate and individual sources, number of individual returns filed over 1986–1994, and tax receipt estimates for 1994–1999. All estimates are from the IRS Management Information System for Top Level Executives.

Individual returns are typically far less complex than corporate returns and, therefore, their auditing costs are much lower. In the past, 56% of the total variable auditing costs had been incurred for auditing individual returns, and 44% for auditing corporate returns.

Mr. Swanson then looked at the numbers pertaining to his more immediate problem: the Additional Taxes Recommended (ATR) for collection on the basis of audits of individual filings. These had fluctuated considerably between 1986 and 1992, but did not exhibit a systematic trend (Table 8.10). However, considering that the number of individual *filings* had been rising more or less steadily during that period (see Table 8.9), Mr. Swanson was worried that the lack of a corresponding increase in the number of audits could signal weaknesses in the tax compliance and monitoring program of the IRS.

Audit Procedure: Individual Returns

For auditing purposes, income tax returns were first classified according to the type of return (e.g., individual versus corporate), then the subtypes (e.g., the types of forms filed) and finally according to the dollar amount of adjusted gross income before deductions. For individual returns,[4] this resulted in ten audit classes. To simplify his analysis, Mr. Swanson decided to

[4]The regular or "long" form for individuals is known as 1040. In certain cases, to simplify work both for tax payers and the IRS, a simplified form known as 1040A is allowed (form 1040EZ is a further simplified version). When an individual earns income from businesses or professions, he or she is required to attach a form known as Schedule C to the 1040 Form. Individuals with income from farming file a form known as Schedule F instead of Schedule C. Of course, some individuals may have both business and farming incomes, and so will need to file both Schedule C and Schedule F in addition to Form 1040.

categorize the individual returns into three classes based on the types of forms used: 1040A (including also 1040EZ), 1040 without schedules C/F and 1040 with schedule C or schedule F (or both). The primary result of this simplification would be that income effects within classes were ignored. However, there was considerable homogeneity *within* each such class regarding the complexity of the returns (and hence, the costs of processing and auditing returns), the types of problems observed in the filed returns, etc.

For each audit class, **audit coverage** is defined as the percentage of all returns in that class filed during a given year that are actually audited. The returns in each audit class are assigned a number known as "DIF," based on rank-ordering, prior to implementing audit coverage decisions. Starting about 1970, the DIF ranking is performed by a computer program that scores each individual return in terms of its anticipated capacity to generate additional taxes, if audited. Implementing audit coverage decisions requires auditing returns in each separate class in the rank ordering determined by the program until the desired percentage coverage for the class has been achieved. This procedure is repeated separately for each audit class. The IRS uses the term **ATR** for the "Additional Tax Recommended" as the result of an audit. The ATR may be negative (corresponding to a tax refund), zero (no change) or positive. Most cases result in a positive ATR. The audit may also result in interest charges and fines that are included in the ATR figure.

The actual audits are performed by revenue agents and tax auditors or through service centers. The most complex tax returns (with correspondingly the maximum expected additional taxes) are audited by revenue agents, who are experts on the staff of the Audit Division. Other returns are audited by IRS staff called tax auditors. Revenue agents and tax auditors conduct most of their examinations through face-to-face contacts with taxpayers and/or their representatives in the 63 district offices of the IRS. Some audits of noncomplex individual returns are handled through the mail by tax examiners in 10 service centers.

In addition to their role in determining IRS audit performance, audit coverage figures for each audit class, which are publicly released, have the role of signaling to the public the seriousness with which the Government views the underreporting of taxes. In view of this, the IRS has internal **policy constraints** on the **minimum audit coverage** it must attain for each audit class. These minimum coverages are specified both to fulfill the signaling role of the audit coverages and to ensure "fairness" to all constituencies. As seen in Tables 4 and 5, the total ATR for the 1992 audit program amounted to over 6 billion dollars, and a higher audit coverage would probably yield more revenue (even after accounting for auditing costs). However, the IRS did not audit more than around 1% of all filed returns primarily due to its budget constraints, determined by the Congressional budget allocation (Table 5 gives the 1992 audit coverages broken down by class). Even taking the budget allocation as given, the effectiveness of the audit plan *across* the different audit classes needed to be examined. Mr. Swanson's first priority was to analyze the optimal audit cov-

erages for each class for the coming year, subject to minimum audit coverage constraints, for different Congressional budget allocation scenarios. He also wanted to evaluate how accurate the less formal (and more intuitive) methods for determining audit coverages (used so far by the IRS) were, compared to the theoretical optimum.

Planning for 1995

Mr. Swanson's first priority was planning for 1995, that is deciding on how best the auditing function could work towards achieving the objectives of the Business Master Plan. The two (not necessarily incompatible) objectives of the BMP of direct relevance to the auditing function are *(i)* maximizing revenues, and *(ii)* improving voluntary compliance, with spending limited by the Congressional budget allocation. For any budget, the auditing arm had to decide on allocations among the different audit classes. Ideally, what Mr. Swanson wanted was to develop a methodology that would take different possible budgets as inputs, and calculate as its outputs the optimal audit coverages for each class as well as estimates of the additional taxes generated, while satisfying the budget and policy constraints. To do this, he needed more data.

He first looked at estimates of the number of individual returns filed for each audit class for tax year 1993 (these were the returns that would be subject to the forthcoming audits).

TABLE 4 Additional Taxes and Penalties for Individuals (1986–1992)

FISCAL YEAR	NUMBER OF AUDITS	ADDITIONAL NET TAX IN MILLIONS OF 1992 DOLLARS		
		Schedules C/F[a]	Other Individual	Total
1986	1,110,941	1,460	4,388	5,848
1987	1,109,212	1,685	4,228	5,913
1988	1,058,544	1,389	3,953	5,342
1989	982,456	1,218	3,007	4,225
1990	883,293	1,540	3,393	4,933
1991	1,099,505	1,872	4,793	6,665
1992	1,039,355	1,586	4,455	6,041

[a]**Schedule C** (Form 1040) is filed by self-employed individuals. **Schedule F** (Form 1040) is filed by individuals reporting profit or loss from farming.
Additional Taxes and penalties Recommended (ATR) by the auditing function of the IRS for individual tax returns, 1986–1992. Figures are in millions of 1992 dollars. "Schedule C/F" represents the total ATR for individuals that were self-employed or had income from farming (and, consequently, filed at least one of schedules C *or* F with their 1040 tax forms). "Other Individual" provides the ATR for all other individuals (1040 with no schedules, or the "short" forms 1040A and 1040EZ).

TABLE 5 1992 Auditing Record (Aggregated for Analysis)

TYPE OF RETURN	RETURNS FILED	RETURNS EXAMINED	AUDIT COVERAGE	ATR ($ MILLIONS)
1) 1040A[a]	43,430,500	300,480	0.69%	781
2) 1040 without Schedules C/F	62,977,400	575,493	0.91%	3,674
3) 1040 with Schedule C or F	7,421,300	163,382	2.20%	1,586
Overall	**113,829,200**	**1,039,355**	**0.91%**	**6,041**

[a]Including 1040EZ.
Breakdown of audit performance for the three primary audit classes, 1992. The total number of returns filed, the number of returns examined and the consequent audit coverage are shown for each class.

Since most of the returns for tax year 1993 had already been filed, he was confident that these numbers were reliable, and recorded them as Table 6.

When any single return is audited, the result may be no change or even a decrease in the tax due. The percentage of no-changes typically varies from 10% to 20%, depending on the audit class as well as the auditor. However, the majority of audits in all audit classes result in an additional tax being recommended. Since returns are ranked for auditing based on their ATR potential—the higher the DIF score, the greater the likelihood that an audit would result in an increase in the taxpayer's tax liability—those returns chosen for an audit are more likely to yield a positive ATR.

In planning the audit program for these tax returns, Mr. Swanson considered the relationship between audit coverage and the expected additional tax recommended (ATR) resulting from an audit a key part of his analysis. The expected ATR realizable from auditing each additional return tends to decline as percentage audit coverage increases. This decline, which had been validated by the IRS's data, occurs in each separate audit class because of the rank-ordering of returns that results from the DIF ranking procedure described above.

Earlier IRS studies have confirmed that, after an appropriate normalization for the number of returns filed, the general shape of the relationship between audit coverage and ATR is consistent across the different audit classes, and hence it can be represented by similar mathematical functions. Only the *parameters* of the relationships differ from class to class, reflecting the different levels of compliance behavior associated with each class. In addition, extended multi-year statistical analyses had shown that *within* each audit class, the relationship was generally stable over time in terms of both its *shape* and its *numerical parameters* after adjusting for differences in the number of returns filed over time.

The data required for this analysis were obtained through the Tax Compliance and Monitoring Program (TCMP) of the IRS. Briefly, under TCMP, random samples of tax returns filed for each year were drawn (over all classes of returns) and these samples were audited in detail. This helped the IRS in getting a thorough understanding of the extent of tax compliance by the public. The fact that the samples drawn by the TCMP program were *random* meant that the statistical properties of the sampled returns would mirror those of the entire population. For his own analysis, Mr. Swanson acquired a sample of returns within each class (1040A, 1040 without Schedules C/F and 1040 with Schedule C or Schedule F) from the TCMP results.

Mr. Swanson simplified the data made available from the TCMP to suit his objectives (for example, he eliminated addresses and other contact information from the data). This left him with a relational database consisting of three primary tables, whose structures are given below.

(i) TAX RETURN Table:

Tax Return	Social Security Number	Income	Audit Class	DIF

The *Audit Class* is one of the three audit categories: '1' for 1040A/1040EZ, '2' for 1040 without Schedule C/F, and '3' for 1040 with Schedule C or Schedule F. The *DIF* for each return is the score assigned in the preliminary computerized ranking of all returns: the higher the score, the greater the audit potential. The *Social Security Number* is the nine-character taxpayer I.D.

(ii) AUDITOR Table:

Auditor	ID	Auditor Name	Hourly Cost

The *Auditor ID* is a five-digit code used to identify an IRS auditor. Different auditors may be paid different wages based on seniority, prior experience, etc., and the *Hourly Cost* is the effective hourly cost of the auditor.

(iii) AUDIT Table:

Audit	Social Security Number	Auditor ID	ATR	Hours

TABLE 6 Estimated Number of Returns Filed for Tax Year 1993		
	TYPE OF RETURN	RETURNS FILED (TAX YEAR 1993)
1)	1040A[a]	43,619,000
2)	1040 without Schedules	63,315,200
3)	1040 with Schedule C or F	7,609,900
	Total	**114,544,100**

[a]Including 1040EZ.
Number of individual tax returns filed for Tax Year 1993 by type of return.

This table provides the key information on audit results: the additional taxes and penalties recommended *(ATR)* and the *Hours* spent on each audit, which could be used to derive costs. The *Social Security Number* is the identifying key, and the *Auditor ID* uniquely identifies an auditor from the **Auditor** table.

The first step in Mr. Swanson's analysis was to identify the relationship between audit coverage and expected ATR. This meant *(i)* identifying the underlying mathematical function relating audit coverage to the ensuing expected ATR, and *(ii)* estimating the parameters of this function for each audit class. First and foremost was the question of what function to estimate.

For this analysis, assume that there are N tax returns from an audit class that are candidates for being audited. The most "promising" tax return in the class has the highest DIF value and should be audited first. Continuing this process, the tax returns in the class should be ranked from the highest DIF to the lowest DIF and audited in that order. Each additional audit in the class is expected to generate additional ATR. Mr. Swanson defined the **Cumulative ATR *(n)* function** for each class as the expected total ATR from auditing the first n returns in that class in the ranked set of N returns. As n ranges from 1 to N, there is a general tendency for Cumulative ATR *(n)* values to rise, but at a decreasing rate, since ever-smaller values of incremental ATR are being accumulated. The last column of Table 8.11 shows values of the Cumulative ATR *(n)* function. For example, 0.69% of the 43.4305 million $(=N)$ 1040A Forms were audited, giving rise to $n = 300,480$ (0.69% times 43.4305 million), and the Treasury therefore re-

alized a Cumulative ATR of 781 million dollars in the 1040A audit class.

The cumulative ATR *(n)* function is very sensitive to the number of returns available, N. Thus, Mr. Swanson considered it important to use a function that was normalized for N. He decided to estimate the **Normalized Cumulative ATR *(n)* function,** obtained by dividing the Cumulative ATR *(n)* by the number of returns available in the class, N. He would then examine the relationship between the percent audit coverage and the Normalized Cumulative ATR, which should be stable for each audit class.

The Normalized Cumulative ATR function has a shape similar to that shown in Exhibit 1. Since returns are audited in descending order of their DIF scores, early audits would yield high ATR and later audits would yield progressively less ATR. The cumulative function would thus rise steeply at first and then more moderately.

The estimation of these functions was not trivial. For each audit class, Mr. Swanson asked for a random sample of $N = 2,000$ tax returns that participated in the TCMP program (totalling 6,000 returns across the three classes). These returns were then ranked by decreasing DIF within each audit class. To simplify matters, Mr. Swanson decided to analyze only the audit coverage range between $p = 0$ and 10%.[5] Thus, he asked the MIS personnel to provide him only the returns with the top 10% DIF values from each audit class sample. This resulted

---

[5]Mr. Swanson considered it unlikely that the audit coverage in any class would exceed 10%, and did not want the behavior for high levels of coverage to affect his results.

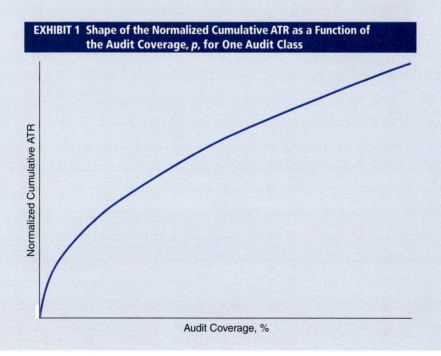

EXHIBIT 1 **Shape of the Normalized Cumulative ATR as a Function of the Audit Coverage, *p*, for One Audit Class**

in a subsample of 600 returns, consisting of the top 200 returns from each audit class.[6] Using regression analysis, Mr. Swanson proceeded with the estimation of the three Normalized Cumulative ATR functions (one for each audit class). As indicated earlier, the mathematical form of the function should be the same across classes, with only the parameter values changing.

---

[6]Recall that the returns in each class are ranked by declining DIF values from number 1 to number $N = 2,000$. Thus, Mr. Swanson received the data for returns 1–200 from each of these three ranked samples.

Mr. Swanson turned next to the estimation of the auditing costs. The auditing cost varies primarily with the complexity of the return. Thus, there are substantial cost differentials among the three audit classes. However, there was no identifiable systematic variation of the auditing costs within the three classes. He needed to estimate the auditing cost per return in each class.

Mr. Swanson reviewed all the materials he had on the problem. He decided that the tables he had put together, in addition to the TCMP data, were adequate for him to proceed to the next stage of analysis, which would be the derivation of the optimal audit coverages, and the associated total ATR values, for each audit class for fiscal 1995.

References

John Mulvey, "An Asset-Liability Investment System," *Interfaces,* 24, no. 3 (1994), 22–33.

Yosi Ben-Dov, Lakhbir Hayre, and Vincent Pica, "Mortgage Valuation Models at Prudential Securities," *Interfaces,* 22, no. 1 (1992), 55–71.

Multi-Objective Decision Making and Heuristics

CHAPTER OUTLINE

9.1 Introduction

9.2 Facility Scheduling (Sequencing Computer Jobs)

9.3 Scheduling with Limited Resources (Workload Smoothing)

9.4 Multiple Objectives

9.5 Analytic Hierarchy Process

9.6 Notes on Implementation

KEY TERMS

SELF-REVIEW EXERCISES

PROBLEMS

CASE STUDY: Sleepmore Mattress Manufacturing: Plant Consolidation

REFERENCES

APPLICATION CAPSULE   Facilities Planning at the University of Missouri

In the academic environment, the thrust for excellence in teaching, research, and extension service presents peculiar challenges for the facilities planner who must try to allocate limited resources to achieve the optimal trade-off among the often conflicting university objectives. The department of engineering management at the University of Missouri–Rolla benefited from a major expansion of its physical facilities in 1987. This included 5072 square feet of floor space to be developed into a computer integrated manufacturing (CIM) laboratory for teaching, research, and extension. The facility was intended to stimulate interest in teaching and research in advance manufacturing systems and was expected to evolve into a center for technical excellence for industry in the state.

The university saw the new CIM lab facility as a campus-wide resource to be used by all departments in the school of engineering and by various research centers within the university. This resulted in contentious debate and discussion concerning the best facility layout for the new lab. A task force was appointed to resolve the conflict. After identifying alternative layout proposals, 15 sections were identified to be located in the CIM lab (e.g., physical simulation area, Autocad, robot system, and so forth). The ideal area for each section was estimated. The sum of the ideal requirements was 6035 sq ft, nearly a 1000 more than was available.

The team had to find some systematic way to allocate actual space available to the desired sections in a manner consistent with the overall mission of the university. Five goals were established (e.g., develop new courses relying on the lab, heighten industry awareness of CIM concepts, and so on.) and analytic hierarchy process (AHP) was used to determine how to prioritize the goals. A questionnaire was administered to the team to elicit relative priorities. The preliminary analysis of the responses revealed several inconsistencies in the subjective pairwise comparison of attributes. The respondents had an opportunity to review and adjust their responses, which resulted in greater consistency in the subjective comparisons.

Once the priorities were established, a linear goal programming model was used to determine the allocation of space to each of the 15 areas. Nine of the 15 obtained space allocation factors less than 1.0, which suggested a reduction in the ideal areas originally allocated. Four areas were reduced significantly. The committee used the space allocation as a guide to developing the initial layout of the lab. Sensitivity analysis was also used to determine the effect of altering the priorities and the model was found to be fairly robust in response to priority rankings.

AHP was found to be an effective methodology to obtain group consensus in a highly political environment in a timely manner for a fairly complex institutional planning problem. Because this systematic planning methodology was adopted, the school of engineering readily accepted the department's proposals for the layout of the CIM lab and acknowledged that future lab development should be entrusted to the engineering management department. The CIM lab has handsomely fulfilled its teaching, research, and extension objectives. (See Benjamin et al.)

9.1   **INTRODUCTION**

From time to time a manager's model may be so complex that the mathematical model constructed to attack it cannot be solved with the traditional algorithms available to the analyst. This situation may occur because

1. The model, "correctly formulated," may be too large, too nonlinear, or logically too complex (requiring, for example, the use of many 0–1 variables in the formulation).

2. It is felt that the imposition of simplifying assumptions or approximations, which might make the model more tractable, would destroy too much of the important real-world structure of the model (i.e., would carry the model too far from reality to be useful).

Here is a real dilemma. The model at hand is too complex to solve. At the same time we are unwilling to simplify it in any ameliorative way. What does one do in this seemingly hopeless situation?

In part to answer this question, the field of heuristic programming has developed. In the discussion above, when we employed the phrase "the model is too complex to *solve*," we were using the word *solve* in a rigorous mathematical sense. We meant that the mathematical model was so complicated that, although a rigorous solution exists (e.g., an optimal solution in an optimization model), it is too difficult, too time-consuming, perhaps even impossible to discover with existing know-how and technology. In such a case a *heuristic algorithm* might be employed.

A **heuristic algorithm** is one that efficiently provides good approximate solutions to a given model. Often (but by no means always) in employing such an algorithm one may be able to measure precisely the "goodness" of the approximation. For example, in the optimization context, with some heuristic algorithms one can make a statement like "Upon termination you can be sure of being within _____ % of optimality." Or, "Under certain assumptions the heuristic answer will be optimal _____ % of the time." An important aspect of a heuristic algorithm is that it never gives a "bad" solution. It is more important always to have a fairly good solution than to have the best solution sometimes and a bad solution once in a while.

The term **heuristic** is also frequently encountered. A **heuristic** is an intuitively appealing rule of thumb for dealing with some aspect of a model. A collection of heuristics, or heuristic algorithms, is referred to as a **heuristic program.** Some computer codes to solve linear programs (like Excel's Solver), for example, employ heuristics in the initial phase of the simplex method to attempt to quickly find an initial corner. Heuristics are employed to get a quick start with the transportation algorithm, and so on.

As you can infer from the definitions above, you no doubt use heuristics frequently in everyday problem solving. You go to the bank, and to minimize your time waiting, you stand in the shortest line. Although this is by no means guaranteed to be optimal, it is a rule of thumb that often works quite well. In checking through customs you may prefer the bench occupied by a smiling officer, although he is certainly not guaranteed to be more lenient than others. The list goes on.

In the context of mathematical programming, heuristics are often employed in conjunction with, or as a special case of, more general or more rigorous problem-solving strategies. The important point to remember is that a heuristic procedure or algorithm is intuitively appealing but can only guarantee its results, if at all, in a statistical manner or within certain margins of uncertainty. It is employed mainly for efficiency—namely, to produce quickly what are hopefully good, if not optimal, results.

Generally speaking, from the viewpoint of a manager, a heuristic procedure may certainly be as acceptable as, and possibly (in terms of cost) even preferable to, a "more exact" algorithm that produces an optimal solution. The dominant considerations should be the amount of insight and guidance that the model can provide and the overall net benefit as measured by the difference "savings due to the model less cost of producing the model and its solution."

In the first part of this chapter we discuss several examples of heuristic algorithms as applied to large *combinatorial optimization* models. The term **combinatorial optimization** means there are only a finite number of feasible alternatives, and if all of these are enumerated, the optimal one can be found. The problem is that in practice this finite number often amounts to millions or even billions of possibilities, and hence even on high-speed computers complete enumeration is out of the question. Although such models can often be formulated as integer programs with 0–1 variables, they are often so large that even the IP formulation is prohibitively expensive to bring to optimality with the usual branch-and-bound or partial enumeration approach.

Following the examples in the first part of the chapter, we then look at models for which the objective is to achieve acceptable levels of certain "goals." For example, consider a model with multiple but conflicting objectives. The president of a firm wants high profits but also wants to maintain low prices in order to keep from losing clients. An executive with a fixed budget wants to invest in R&D to provide long-term benefits to the firm, but also wants to purchase raw materials to make a product that generates shorter-term profits. Such examples of multiple but conflicting objectives are typical in business applications. *Goal programming* deals with such models. The topic is closely related to heuristic programming, for in a sense goal programming itself could be thought of as a heuristic approach to dealing with multiple objectives.

Next, we will look at a hot new area called analytic hierarchy process (AHP), which is a tool to help managers choose between many different decision alternatives when there are multiple criteria that are used to score the alternatives. Numerous examples can be thought of that fit this general modeling area; for example, choosing a new computer or software package, selecting a university to attend or which job offer to accept. AHP brings good discipline to this decision methodology.

9.2 FACILITY SCHEDULING (SEQUENCING COMPUTER JOBS)

SEQUENCE-DEPENDENT SETUP TIME

Consider a single production facility through which numerous jobs must be processed— for example, a computer, a drill press, or an ice cream machine. Typically, the facility may have to shut down after processing one job in order to set up for the next. Such "downtime" is termed **setup**, or *changeover,* time. The length of the setup time may depend on the next job to be processed and the job just completed. A sequence of similar jobs (making French vanilla ice cream after New York vanilla) would be interrupted by less setup time (cleaning out the machine) than a sequence of dissimilar jobs (French vanilla after Dutch chocolate). A typical managerial problem would be to *sequence the jobs in such a way as to minimize total setup time.* This is a typical problem for a company such as Monsanto Chemical, which makes chemicals in common vats or transports them by tank cars. It makes a difference in which order the chemicals are produced or transported, as to the cost of changeover.

You can easily see that from the combinatorial point of view this can be a very large model. If there are only three jobs to be processed, say jobs A, B, and C, then any of the three could be taken first, with either of the remaining two second and the third determined (i.e., the single remaining job). The possible sequences can be displayed as a tree with each branch representing one sequence. The six possibilities are shown in Figure 9.1. In general, with n jobs, there are $n! = n(n - 1)(n - 2) \ldots 1$ possible combinations or sequences

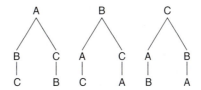

FIGURE 9.1

Tree Showing Six Possible Sequences for Three Jobs A, B, C

(*n!* is the mathematical term *n factorial*). Only ten jobs produces $10! = 3,628,800$ different sequences. You can see that this number of possible sequences *(n!)* increases rapidly with the size of *n*.

Obviously, one way to think about solving the minimization problem above is by complete enumeration. That is, generate each of the *n!* possible sequences of jobs and compute the total setup time required for each sequence. Then pick the sequence associated with the smallest total time. Although this algorithm would provide a true optimum, it is not practical even for modest values of *n* because of the large number of sequences that would have to be enumerated. If there were 20 jobs, and a computer could calculate 3,000,000 combinations each second (3 MIPS in computer language), it would take over 25,000 years to determine the optimal answer by listing every possible combination.

HEURISTIC SOLUTIONS

Heuristic rules, although they will not guarantee an optimal solution, are often applied to this model, for they will usually lead quite quickly to a satisfactory solution.

As an example, consider a computer operator who has three rather long batch jobs to be run on Monday afternoon. The computer is currently idle. For each of these jobs there is a setup time (searching for input tapes, hanging tapes, setting up the disk drive units and other auxiliary equipment) as specified in Figure 9.2. Since there are only $3! = 3 \cdot 2 = 6$ possible sequences, they can all be enumerated. The results appear in Table 9.1. As you can see, the optimal (minimum total setup time) sequence is $0 \rightarrow A \rightarrow C \rightarrow B$.

A Greedy Heuristic Let us now see how a heuristic rule might be applied to this model. The rule we shall illustrate is called the **next best rule,** sometimes called a **greedy algorithm.** The rule goes as follows:

1. At step 1 (e.g., in selecting the first job), perform the task with least initial setup time.
2. At each subsequent step, select the task with least setup time, based on the current state.

Let us now apply this rule to the data in Figure 9.2. The task with the least initial setup time is B. Hence, the first step is $0 \rightarrow B$. According to the greedy algorithm, given that we have just completed B, the task to be selected is C, since the setup for $B \rightarrow C$ is less than for $B \rightarrow A$. Thus, we have $0 \rightarrow B \rightarrow C$, and we can then finish only with A. Thus, we obtain

$$\text{greedy heuristic: } 0 \rightarrow B \rightarrow C \rightarrow A$$

$$\text{total setup time} = 21 + 46 + 46 = 113$$

Notice that this is far from optimal. In fact, in this example, the greedy heuristic, although intuitively appealing, provides the worst possible policy for our model. Although it is true that in general, for sequential decision models, the greedy algorithm does *not* lead to an optimal solution, there are in fact a few special models for which it does. (See, for example,

From job \ To job	A	B	C
0	27	21	32
A		35	22
B	49		46
C	46	12	

FIGURE 9.2

Setup Times in Minutes

	A	B	C
0	0	9	10
A		23	0
B	22		24
C	19	0	

FIGURE 9.3

Transformed Data

TABLE 9.1 Results of Complete Enumeration

SEQUENCE	SETUP TIME	TOTAL (MIN)
$0 \rightarrow A \rightarrow B \rightarrow C$	27 + 35 + 46	108
$0 \rightarrow A \rightarrow C \rightarrow B$	27 + 22 + 12	61
$0 \rightarrow B \rightarrow C \rightarrow A$	21 + 46 + 46	113
$0 \rightarrow B \rightarrow A \rightarrow C$	21 + 49 + 22	92
$0 \rightarrow C \rightarrow A \rightarrow B$	32 + 46 + 35	113
$0 \rightarrow C \rightarrow B \rightarrow A$	32 + 12 + 49	93

the problem of finding a minimal spanning tree in Chapter 6.) However, the rule is extremely easy to apply, and studies on this type of model have shown that *statistically,* for the above type of sequencing model, the rule is not bad. For example, one article [see Gavett] showed that the heuristic will often produce better results than could be obtained by a purely random selection of tasks.

A Better Heuristic The same article shows that the following modified heuristic gives even better results:

1. Transform the original data in Figure 9.2 by subtracting the minimum setup time in each column from all other entries in that column. This process produces the data in Figure 9.3.

2. Apply the greedy algorithm to this set of transformed data. Doing this, we obtain

Best first step	$0 \rightarrow A$
Best second step	$A \rightarrow C$
Third step	$C \rightarrow B$

and thus the modified heuristic produces the sequence $0 \rightarrow A \rightarrow C \rightarrow B$, which was already shown to be optimal for this model.

Although this modified heuristic will not always give the optimal solution, it is easy to implement, and in practice, for large models, it often produces quite good results.

9.3   SCHEDULING WITH LIMITED RESOURCES (WORKLOAD SMOOTHING)

Imagine a sequence of activities to be scheduled in order to complete a project. Basic models such as PERT and CPM, discussed in Chapter 14, will schedule the activities in such a way as to minimize total project completion time subject to the constraint that some activities cannot start until others have been completed. The resources (money, labor, machinery, and so on) needed to complete the individual activities are often considered to be available in any quantities required by any particular schedule. In reality, however, such resources may be limited, in which case resource availability becomes another constraint.

A SIMPLE EXAMPLE

As a simple example, consider the scheduling model shown in Figure 9.4 and Table 9.2. Figure 9.4 shows **precedence relationships** among the various activities. That is, it shows which activities must be completed before others can begin. For example, activity VIII cannot begin until VII is completed, and VII cannot begin until I is completed. Table 9.2

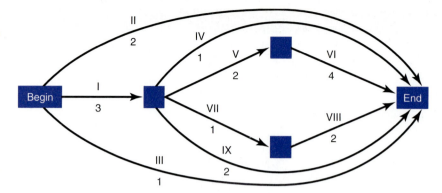

FIGURE 9.4

Precedence Relationships

TABLE 9.2 Requirements for Each Activity		
ACTIVITY	TIME REQUIRED TO COMPLETE (WEEKS)	NO. OF PEOPLE (PER WEEK) REQUIRED TO COMPLETE
I	3	6
II	2	3
III	1	3
IV	1	3
V	2	6
VI	4	5
VII	1	3
VIII	2	4
IX	2	3

shows the duration of each activity (in weeks) and the resources required (number of people) to complete each activity.

Ignoring the "Number of People Required" for now, this problem is simple, and thus the earliest possible completion time can be easily computed. It is nine weeks.[1] Figure 9.5 shows a proposed activity schedule that will achieve this overall completion time. Thus, Figure 9.5 respects the precedence relationships of Figure 9.4, and at the same time shows when each activity should start and how long (in weeks) it will take. In this proposed schedule, each activity starts as early as possible. You can see that I, II, and III start immediately (at the beginning of week 1). Activities IV, V, VII, and IX start at the beginning of week 4. Activity VI starts at the beginning of week 6, and activity VIII starts at the beginning of week 5.

Now consider the number of people per week required to implement the proposed schedule. The personnel data in Table 9.2 can be combined with the schedule in Figure 9.5 to produce the **personnel loading chart** shown in Figure 9.6. As you can see, the proposed schedule makes an erratic utilization of personnel, the requirements fluctuating between the extremes of 15 people in week 4 and only five in weeks 7, 8, and 9. It may be to management's advantage to have a schedule that employs resources more smoothly. Heuristic programs are often applied to accomplish such an objective.

---

[1]If you have studied PERT, you can see that activities I, V, and VI form the *critical* path (see Section 14.3).

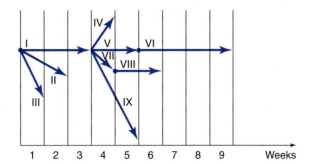

FIGURE 9.5

Proposed Schedule
of Activities

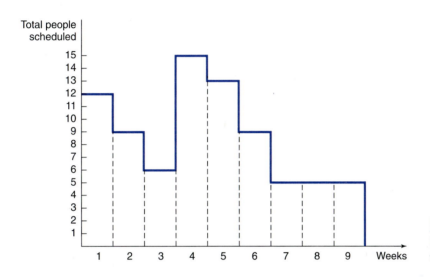

FIGURE 9.6

Personnel Loading Chart for
the Proposed Schedule

WORKLOAD SMOOTHING HEURISTIC

In order to discuss one such heuristic, let us define, for each activity, its **slack.**

> Slack is the maximum amount of time an activity can be delayed without delaying over-
> all project completion.

Note in Figure 9.5 that if the completion time of activity V were delayed, then activity VI
could not start at the beginning of week 6 and the project could not be completed by the end
of the ninth week. Thus activity V has no slack. In contrast, the completion of activity VIII
could be delayed by three weeks without delaying the completion of the project. Activity
VIII thus has a slack of three weeks.

   Now, using this concept, the following heuristic is given to help "reduce the peaks"
and "raise the valleys" in order to provide a smoother workload across time:

1. Determine the maximum required resources in the proposed schedule, say m workers/
week.
2. In each week, impose a new upper limit of $m - 1$ for resource utilization (remember
we're trying to reduce the peaks one step at a time), and, if possible, revise the proposed
schedule to satisfy this constraint. The revision is systematically performed as follows:
   a. Beginning with the earliest week violating the constraint, consider the activities
   contributing to the overload, and move forward the one with *most* slack as little as possible until it contributes to no overloading, but without delaying the completion of the

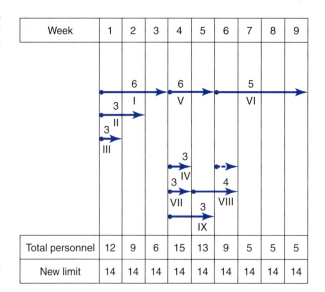

Week	1	2	3	4	5	6	7	8	9
Total personnel	12	9	6	15	13	9	5	5	5
New limit	14	14	14	14	14	14	14	14	14

FIGURE 9.7

First Proposal

entire project (which means that activities with zero slack may not be moved). If there are ties, move forward the activity that contributes *least* to the overload (i.e., requires the fewest people).

b. The heuristic terminates when the current overload cannot be decreased.

To apply this heuristic, let us portray the proposed plan as in Figure 9.7. In this figure, the activity label (e.g., I, II, and so on) appears *below* each arrow. *Above* each arrow is the number of people required each week. For example, the 6 above activity I implies that six people are required for each of the three weeks needed to complete activity I. Thus, you can read down the appropriate columns to obtain total personnel utilization in a given week. For example, since week 2 is intersected by activities I and II, the entry in the Total personnel row, under the week 2 column, is 9. Similarly, the distance from the head of each unfollowed arrow at the end of a series of jobs to the end of week 9 indicates the slack for such an arrow. Thus, activity IV has five weeks of slack, while activity VIII has three weeks of slack, and so on. For activity VII, which is a followed arrow, we compute the slack by noting that VII is followed only by VIII. Since the slack on VIII is three weeks, slack on activity VII must also be three weeks. Also notice that activities I, V, and VI have zero slack since they cannot be moved forward at all without increasing the overall completion time of nine weeks. In applying the foregoing heuristic we move forward only activities with positive slack, and hence activities I, V, and VI are not considered.

Applying the Heuristic Given these observations, we may now employ the heuristic. For the first proposal (see Figure 9.7), the maximum required resource is 15 in period 4. Thus, according to step 2, we impose a new upper limit of 14 in each week. This limit is violated only in week 4. The "movable" activities contributing to the overload are IV, VII, and IX (since V need not be considered). Of these, the one with most slack is IV. Moving IV forward 1 period reduces the utilization in week 4 by 3 units to 12 people, but creates a utilization of 3 additional units in week 5, giving a total of 16 in week 5, which overloads week 5 (i.e., violates the imposed upper limit of 14). Hence, it must be moved farther forward. You can see that by moving activity IV forward a total of 2 weeks (into week 6 as illustrated in Figure 9.7) no upper limit will be violated. This gives the second proposal, as shown in Figure 9.8.

In this figure the upper limit of 13 must be reduced to 12. The only overload is caused by VIII and IX in week 5. Activity IX has the most slack, and it must be advanced 3 weeks to begin in week 7, as shown. This gives the third proposal presented in Figure 9.9. Here the upper limit of 12 must be reduced to 11. There are violations in weeks 1 and 6. According to the algorithm, we first move III forward 2 weeks and then IV forward 1 week. Continuing with the heuristic, we obtain the fourth and fifth proposals shown in Figures 9.10 and 9.11.

Week	1	2	3	4	5	6	7	8	9
Total personnel	12	9	6	12	13	12	5	5	5
New limit	12	12	12	12	12	12	12	12	12

FIGURE 9.8

Second Proposal

Week	1	2	3	4	5	6	7	8	9
Total personnel	12	9	6	9	10	12	8	8	5
New limit	11	11	11	11	11	11	11	11	11

FIGURE 9.9

Third Proposal

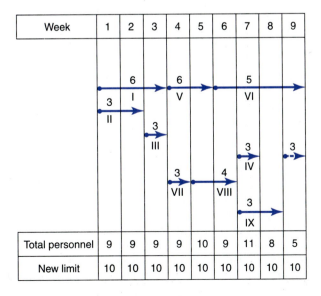

Week	1	2	3	4	5	6	7	8	9
Total personnel	9	9	9	9	10	9	11	8	5
New limit	10	10	10	10	10	10	10	10	10

FIGURE 9.10

Fourth Proposal

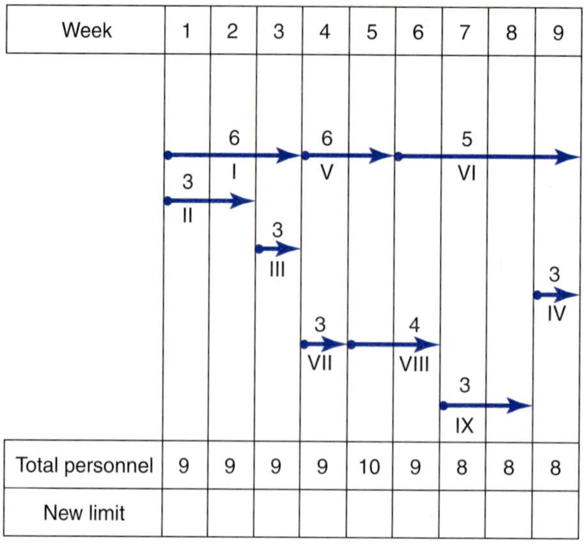

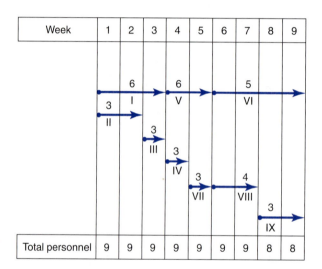

FIGURE 9.11

Fifth Proposal

FIGURE 9.12

Optimal Minimax Schedule

Heuristic Terminates The algorithm is unable to improve beyond the fifth proposal. To see this, note that the overload on week 5 can be reduced only by moving forward activity VIII. However, advancing VIII by 1, 2, or 3 weeks would increase the total personnel in weeks 7 and 8, or 8 and 9, to 12. Step 2b of the heuristic *is* thus satisfied, and hence this schedule is the heuristic solution. This final schedule has smoothed the utilization considerably from that shown in Figure 9.6, for the maximum utilization is now 10 (in week 5), and the minimum is 8.

For this model one might define an optimal solution to be a schedule that *minimizes the maximum utilization of* personnel. An optimal schedule, according to this *minimax* criterion, is shown in Figure 9.12. For this schedule the maximum utilization is 9. Although the heuristic algorithm did not lead to optimality (in this minimax sense—and it must be admitted that the schedule in Figure 9.12 is smoother than that in Figure 9.11), our heuristic approach did quite well. In large models (i.e., with many activities) it would not be possible to easily generate the optimal minimax schedule. It is for this reason that a heuristic is often employed to smooth requirements.

This section and the preceding one have given only a very brief introduction to the important topic of heuristic algorithms. Another example, assigning facilities to different locations within the building (sometimes called the "layout" model), is discussed in Problems 9-2, 9-3, and 9-4 at the end of this chapter.

9.4   MULTIPLE OBJECTIVES

In many applications, the planner has more than one objective. These different objectives may all be of equal importance or, at the very least, it may be difficult for the planner to compare the importance of one objective with that of another. The presence of multiple objectives is frequently referred to as the problem of "combining apples and oranges." Consider, for example, the corporate planner whose long-range goals are to (1) maximize discounted profits, (2) maximize market share at the end of the planning period, and (3) maximize existing physical capital at the end of the planning period. These goals are not commensurate, which means that they cannot be *directly* combined or compared. It is also clear that the goals are *conflicting*. That is, there are trade-offs in the sense that sacrificing the requirements on any one goal will tend to produce greater returns on the others. For example, spending fewer dollars on marketing is apt to reduce market share and thus prevent the firm from meeting its second goal. However, these dollars can be spent on new machinery in an effort to increase physical capital and satisfy the third goal.

The treatment of multiple objectives is a young but important area in application. At this time the analytic methods for handling models with multiple objectives have not been applied as often in practice as some of the other models, such as linear programming, forecasting, inventory control, and Monte Carlo simulation. However, the concepts involved are important, and some leaders in the management science community feel that they will become more important in the near future. The models have been found to be especially useful on problems in the public sector.

Several approaches to multiple objective models (also called multi-criteria decision making) have been developed. They are: use of multi-attribute utility theory, search for Pareto

---

APPLICATION CAPSULE   **The Taxman Cometh: Peoria Fine-Tunes Its Tax System with the Help of Goal Programming**

Designing an equitable tax system that provides sufficient revenue to sustain government programs without excessively burdening any single group of taxpayers is an extremely difficult (and unappreciated) task. The loss of revenue sources as residents and businesses flee the city for the suburbs has further complicated the problem for urban tax planners. Historically, property taxes have been the major source of city revenues, as they are for Peoria, Illinois. But reliance on this source has been diminished by a shrinking property base and a simmering taxpayer revolt. Higher property taxes tend to encourage the emigration of more-mobile, high-income households from the city, thus *decreasing* tax revenue in a vicious cycle.

Planners have therefore been forced to place greater reliance on other forms of taxation, including sales taxes. Sales taxes tend to place a proportionally greater burden on lower-income families. However, they also have certain advantages over property taxes:

1. They are less likely to prompt business migration from the city or discourage the start of new ventures.
2. They shift part of the tax burden to noncity residents who benefit from public services.
3. Because sales taxes are paid continually in small amounts, their burden is generally perceived to be less (or at least is felt less acutely) than that of taxes requiring lump-sum payments.

The city manager of Peoria enlisted the help of university consultants to explore ways of improving the city's tax structure. A multi-objective linear programming (MOLP) model was formulated to provide a better understanding of the alternatives available and the trade-offs involved in various plans. The model had four variables (the tax rates on property, general sales, durable goods, and gas) and several objectives, including

- Reducing property taxes
- Minimizing the tax burden on low-income households
- Minimizing the flight of businesses and shoppers to the suburbs to escape high sales taxes

It was essential to find ways of achieving these objectives without diminishing tax revenues or increasing the tax burden on the city's middle- and high-income families. Constraints were formulated to embody these requirements and others, such as limiting the general sales tax to between 1% and 3% and eliminating the food and drug tax previously in effect.

The solution produced 12 efficient tax plans for the city to consider. The best of these achieved a substantial decrease in the property tax rate, the lost revenue being made up by a gas tax of $0.033/gallon and an increase in the sales tax from 1% to 2%. (See Chrisman et al.)

optimal solutions via multi-criteria linear programming, analytic hierarchy process (AHP), and goal programming. Our discussion is limited to the last two: AHP and goal programming. AHP was developed by Thomas Saaty [see Saaty] and is a relatively new approach to help managers choose between many decision alternatives on the basis of multiple criteria. Goal programming (GP) was a concept introduced by A. Charnes and W. W. Cooper [see Charnes and Cooper] which in some ways can be thought of as a heuristic approach to the multiple-objectives model. GP is a powerful approach that builds on the development of linear programming presented in Chapters 3 through 5. Both areas are now experiencing considerable interest and development and are potentially important topics for future managers.

GOAL PROGRAMMING

Goal programming is generally applied to linear models; it is an extension of LP that enables the planner to come as close as possible to satisfying various goals and constraints. It allows the decision maker, at least in a heuristic sense, to incorporate his or her preference system in dealing with multiple conflicting goals. It is sometimes considered to be an attempt to put into a mathematical programming context the concept of *satisficing*. This term was coined by Herbert Simon, a Nobel Prize winner in economics, to communicate the idea that individuals often do not seek optimal solutions, but rather, they seek solutions that are "good enough" or "close enough"; or in other words, the desire to maximize several objectives simultaneously to at least satisfactory levels. We shall illustrate the method of goal programming with several examples.

Suppose that we have an educational program design model with decision variables x_1 and x_2, where x_1 is the hours of classroom work and x_2 is the hours of laboratory work. Assume that we have the following constraint on total program hours:

$$x_1 + x_2 \leq 100 \qquad \text{(total program hours)}$$

Two Kinds of Constraints In the goal programming approach there are two kinds of constraints: (1) *system constraints* (so-called hard constraints) that cannot be violated and (2) *goal constraints* (so-called soft constraints) that may be violated if necessary. The above constraint on total program hours is an example of a system constraint.

Now, in the program we are designing, suppose that each hour of classroom work involves 12 minutes of small-group experience and 19 minutes of individual problem solving, whereas each hour of laboratory work involves 29 minutes of small-group experience and 11 minutes of individual problem solving. Note that the total program time is at most 6000 minutes (100 hr * 60 min/hr). The designers have the following two *goals:* Each student should spend as close as possible to one fourth of the maximum program time working in small groups and one third of the time on problem solving. These conditions are

$$12x_1 + 29x_2 \cong 1500 \qquad \text{(small-group experience)}$$
$$19x_1 + 11x_2 \cong 2000 \qquad \text{(individual problem solving)}$$

where the symbol $\cong$ means that the left-hand side is desired to be "as close as possible" to the RHS. If it were possible to find a policy that exactly satisfies the small-group and problem-solving goals (i.e., exactly achieves both right-hand sides), without violating the system constraint on total program hours, then this policy would solve the model. A simple geometric analysis will show that no such policy exists. Clearly then, in order to satisfy the system constraint, at least one of the two goals will be violated.

To implement the goal programming approach, the small-group experience condition is rewritten as the goal constraint

$$12x_1 + 29x_2 + u_1 - v_1 = 1500 \ (u_1 \geq 0, v_1 \geq 0)$$

where $u_1 =$ the amount by which total small-group experience falls short of 1500

$v_1 =$ the amount by which total small-group experience exceeds 1500

Deviation Variables The variables u_1 and v_1 are called **deviation variables,** since they measure the amount by which the value produced by the solution deviates from the goal.

We note that by definition we want either u_1 or v_1 (or both) to be zero because it is impossible to simultaneously exceed and fall short of 1500. In order to make $12x_1 + 29x_2$ as close as possible to 1500, it suffices to make the sum $u_1 + v_1$ small.

In a similar way, the individual problem-solving condition is written as the goal constraint

$$19x_1 + 11x_2 + u_2 - v_2 = 2000 \ (u_2 \geq 0, v_2 \geq 0)$$

and in this case we want the sum of the two deviation variables $u_2 + v_2$ to be small. Our complete (illustrative) model is now written as follows:

$$
\begin{aligned}
\text{Min } u_1 \quad & + v_1 + u_2 + v_2 \\
\text{s.t.} \quad\quad x_1 + \ \ x_2 \quad\quad\quad\quad\quad & \leq 100 \quad \text{(total program hours)} \\
12x_1 + 29x_2 + u_1 - v_1 \quad & = 1500 \quad \text{(small-group experience)} \\
19x_1 + 11x_2 + u_2 - v_2 \quad & = 2000 \quad \text{(problem solving)} \\
x_1, x_2, u_1, v_1, u_2, v_2 & \geq 0
\end{aligned}
$$

Note: Both u_1 and v_1 can't be > 0.

This is an ordinary LP model and can now be easily solved in Excel. The optimal decision variables will satisfy the system constraint (total program hours). Also, it turns out that the Solver (for technical reasons that we shall not dwell on) will guarantee that either u_1 or v_1 (or both) will be zero, and thus these variables automatically satisfy this desired condition. The same statement holds for u_2 and v_2 and in general for any pair of deviation variables.

Note that the objective function is the sum of the deviation variables. This choice of an objective function indicates that we have no preference among the various deviations from the stated goals. For example, any of the following three decisions is acceptable: (1) a decision that overachieves the group experience goal by five minutes and hits the problem-solving goal exactly, (2) a decision that hits the group experience goal exactly and underachieves the problem-solving goal by five minutes, and (3) a decision that underachieves each goal by 2.5 minutes. In other words, we have no preference among the three solutions:

(1)	$u_1 = 0$	(2)	$u_1 = 0$	(3)	$u_1 = 2.5$
	$v_1 = 5$		$v_1 = 0$		$v_1 = 0$
	$u_2 = 0$		$u_2 = 5$		$u_2 = 2.5$
	$v_2 = 0$		$v_2 = 0$		$v_2 = 0$

We must have no preference because each of these three decisions yields the same value (i.e., 5) for the objective function.

Weighting the Deviation Variables Such a lack of preference for one solution over another certainly would not hold for all goal programming models. Differences in units alone could produce a preference among the deviation variables. Suppose, for example, that the individual problem-solving constraint had been written in hours; that is,

$$\frac{19}{60} x_1 + \frac{11}{60} x_2 + u_2 - v_2 = \frac{2000}{60}$$

It is hard to believe that the program designers would not prefer a one-minute excess of small-group experience $(v_1 = 1)$ to a 1-hour shortfall of individual problem solving $(u_2 = 1)$.

One way of expressing a preference among the various goals is to assign different coefficients to the deviation variables in the objective function. In the program-planning example one might select

$$\text{Min } 10u_1 + 2v_1 + 20u_2 + v_2$$

as the objective function. Since v_2 (overachievement of problem solving) has the smallest coefficient, the program designers would rather have v_2 positive than any of the other deviation variables (positive v_2 is penalized the least). Indeed, with this objective function it is better to be nine minutes over the problem-solving goal than to underachieve by one minute the small-group-experience goal. To see this, note that for any solution in which $u_1 \geq 1$, decreasing u_1 by 1 and increasing v_2 by 9 would yield a smaller value for the objective function.

Goal Interval Constraints Another type of goal constraint is called a **goal interval constraint.** Such a constraint restricts the goal to a range or *interval* rather than a specific numerical value. Suppose, for example, that in the previous illustration the designers were indifferent among programs for which

$$1800 \leq [\text{minutes of individual problem solving}] \leq 2100$$
$$\text{i.e., } 1800 \leq 19x_1 + 11x_2 \leq 2100$$

In this situation the interval goal is captured with two goal constraints:

$$19x_1 + 11x_2 - v_1 \leq 2100 \qquad (v_1 \geq 0)$$
$$19x_1 + 11x_2 + u_1 \geq 1800 \qquad (u_1 \geq 0)$$

When the terms u_1 and v_1 are included in the objective function, the LP code will attempt to minimize them. We note that when, at optimality, $u_1^* = 0$ and $v_1^* = 0$ (their minimum possible values), the total minutes of problem solving ($19x_1 + 11x_2$) fall within the desired range (i.e., $1800 \leq 19x_1 + 11x_2 \leq 2100$). Otherwise it will turn out that, at optimality, one of the two variables will be positive and the other 0, which means that only one side of the two-sided inequality can be satisfied.

Summary of the Use of Goal Constraints It may be useful at this point to summarize the various ways in which goal constraints can be formulated and employed. Each goal constraint consists of a left-hand side, say $g_i(x_1, \ldots, x_n)$, and a right-hand side, b_i. Goal constraints are written by using nonnegative deviation variables u_i, v_i. At optimality at least one of the pair u_i, v_i will always be zero. The variable u_i represents *underachievement;* v_i represents *overachievement.* Whenever u_i is used it is *added* to $g_i(x_1, \ldots, x_n)$. Whenever v_i is used it is *subtracted* from $g_i(x_1, \ldots, x_n)$. Only deviation variables (or a subset of deviation variables) appear in the objective function, and the objective is always to minimize. The decision variables $x_i, i = 1, \ldots, n$ do not appear in the objective. We have discussed four types of goals:

1. ***Target.*** Make $g_i(x_1, \ldots, x_n)$ as close as possible to b_i. To do this, we write the goal constraint as

$$g_i(x_1, \ldots, x_n) + u_i - v_i = b_i \qquad (u_i \geq 0, v_i \geq 0)$$

and in the objective we minimize $u_i + v_i$. At optimality, at least one of the variables u_i, v_i will be zero.

2. ***Minimize Underachievement.*** To do this, we can write

$$g_i(x_1, \ldots, x_n) + u_i - v_i = b_i \qquad (u_i \geq 0, v_i \geq 0)$$

and in the objective we minimize u_i, the underachievement. Since v_i does not appear in the objective function, and it is only in this constraint, hence the constraint can be equivalently written as

$$g_i(x_1, \ldots, x_n) + u_i \geq b_i \qquad (u_i \geq 0)$$

If the optimal u_i is positive, this constraint will be active, for otherwise u_i^* could be made smaller. This result is also clear from the equality form of the constraint. That is, if $u_i^* > 0$ then, since v_i^* must equal zero, it must be true that $g_i(x_1, \ldots, x_n) + u_i^* = b_i$.

3. ***Minimize Overachievement.*** To do this, we can write

$$g_i(x_1, \ldots, x_n) + u_i - v_i = b_i \qquad (u_i \geq 0, v_i \geq 0)$$

and in the objective we minimize v_i, the overachievement. Since in this case u_i does not appear in the objective function, the constraint can be equivalently written as

$$g_i(x_1, \ldots, x_n) - v_i \leq b_i \qquad (v_i \geq 0)$$

If the optimal v_i is positive, this constraint will be active. The argument is analogous to that in item 2 above.

4. Goal Interval Constraint. In this instance, the goal is to come as close as possible to satisfying

$$a_i \leq g_i(x_1, \ldots, x_n) \leq b_i$$

In order to write this as a goal, we first "stretch out" the interval by writing

$$a_i - u_i \leq g_i(x_1, \ldots, x_n) \leq b_i + v_i \qquad (u_i \geq 0, v_i \geq 0)$$

which is equivalent to the two constraints

$$\left. \begin{array}{l} g_i(x_i, \ldots, x_n) + u_i \geq a_i \\ g_i(x_i, \ldots, x_n) - v_i \leq b_i \end{array} \right\} \leftrightarrow \left\{ \begin{array}{ll} g_i(x_i, \ldots, x_n) + u_i - \hat{v}_i = a_i & (u_i \geq 0, \hat{v}_i \geq 0) \\ g_i(x_i, \ldots, x_n) + \hat{u}_i - v_i = b_i & (\hat{u}_i \geq 0, v_i \geq 0) \end{array} \right.$$

In the case of a goal interval constraint we minimize $u_i + v_i$ in the objective function. The variables $\hat{v}_i$ and $\hat{u}_i$ are merely surplus and slack, respectively (not deviation variables). As usual, at optimality, at least one of the deviation variables u_i, v_i will be 0. In dealing with two constraints representing a goal interval, the constraint with the nonzero deviation variable (if there is one) will be active.

In general, goal constraints are most often expressed in the appropriate equality form using deviation variables, surplus, and slack as required. The equivalent inequality forms that we have displayed will allow us, for models in two decision variables, to obtain some geometric insight into the solution procedure.

ABSOLUTE PRIORITIES

In some cases managers do not wish to express their preferences among various goals in terms of weighted deviation variables, for the process of assigning weights may seem too arbitrary or subjective. In such cases it may be more acceptable to state preferences in terms of **absolute priorities** (as opposed to weights) to a set of goals. This approach, which requires that goals be satisfied in a specific order, is illustrated in the following example. With weightings, the goal programming model is solved just once. With priorities, the goal programming model is solved in stages as a sequence of models.

Swenson's Media Selection Model: A Minicase Tom Swenson, a senior partner at J. R. Swenson, his father's advertising agency, has just completed an agreement with a pharmaceutical manufacturer to mount a radio and television campaign to introduce a new product, Mylonal. The total expenditures for the campaign are not to exceed $120,000. The client is interested in reaching several audiences with this campaign. To determine how well a particular campaign meets this client's needs, the agency estimates the impact of the advertisements on the audiences of interest. The impact is measured in *rated exposures*, a term that means "people reached per month." Radio and television, the two media the agency is considering using, are not equally effective in reaching all audiences. Data relevant to the Mylonal campaign are shown in Table 9.3.

After lengthy discussions with the client, Tom accepts the following goals for this campaign. Tom feels that the order in which he has listed his goals reflects the absolute priority among them.

TABLE 9.3 Exposures per $1000 Expenditure		
	TV	**RADIO**
Total	14,000	6000
Upper Income	1200	1200

1. He hopes total exposures will be at least 840,000.

2. In order to maintain effective contact with the leading radio station, he hopes to spend no more than $90,000 on TV advertising.

3. He feels that the campaign should achieve at least 168,000 upper-income exposures.

4. Finally, if all other goals are satisfied, he would like to come as close as possible to maximizing the total number of exposures. He notes that if he spends all of the $120,000 on TV advertising he would obtain 1,680,000 exposures (120*14,000), and this is the maximum obtainable.

This is clearly a model with a number of constraints. It is not quite a typical mathematical programming model, however, since Tom has a number of objectives. Nevertheless, he feels that a mathematical programming approach will help him understand and solve the model. He thus proceeds in the typical manner. To model the problem, he introduces the notation

$$x_1 = \text{dollars spent on TV} \quad \text{(in thousands)}$$
$$x_2 = \text{dollars spent on radio} \quad \text{(in thousands)}$$

Since his highest-priority goal is total exposures, he feels that a reasonable way to model the problem is to use total exposures as the objective function and to treat the other goals as constraints.

An Infeasible Model The formulation and spreadsheet solution of this model ("Base Case" of SWENSON.XLS) are shown in Figure 9.13. Each constraint and the objective function are labeled to indicate the purpose they serve. The Solver Results dialog box tells Tom that the model is infeasible. Clearly, since it is infeasible, there is no way to satisfy simultaneously the three goals (total expenditures, TV expenditure, and upper-income exposures) that Tom has stated as constraints. Since there are only two decision variables in this model, the graphical approach can be used to investigate Tom's initial

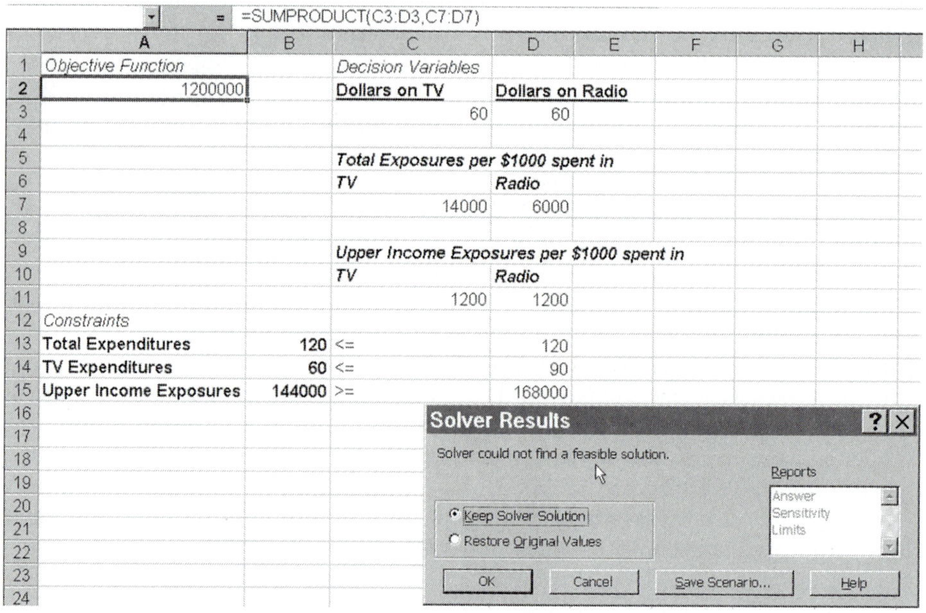

Cell	Formula	Copy To
A2	= SUMPRODUCT(C3:D3,C7:D7)	—
B13	= SUM(C3:D3)	—
B14	= C3	—
B15	= SUMPRODUCT(C3:D3,C11:D11)	—

FIGURE 9.13

Maximizing Total Exposures

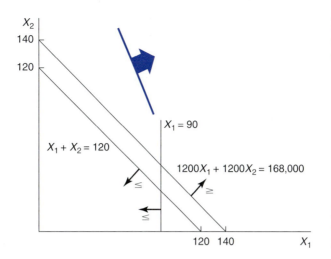

FIGURE 9.14

Maximizing Total Exposures:
A Graphical Approach

formulations. The analysis in Figure 9.14 clearly shows that there are no points that satisfy both the first (total expenditures) and the third (upper-income exposures) constraints. At this point, Tom could attempt to approach the model somewhat differently. He might change one or more of his goals, or perhaps the objective function, and start again. In general, however, this is not a satisfactory systematic approach. In models with many decision variables and several conflicting goals, restructuring the model to create a new model that has a feasible solution could prove to be difficult. More important, in this restructuring process, the essence of the real model could be lost.

Recall that Tom is not indifferent about the various goals; indeed, he has stated an absolute priority among them. Goal programming with absolute priorities is designed to handle exactly the type of decision process Tom Swenson wants. It is a sequential process in which goals are added one at a time (in the order of decreasing priority) to an LP model.

Swenson's Goal Programming Model In order to set up his model as a goal program, Tom notes that the first goal, if violated, will be underachieved. The second goal, if violated, will be overachieved, and so on. Employing this reasoning, he restates his goals, in descending priority, as

1. Minimize the underachievement of 840,000 total exposures (i.e., Min u_1, subject to the condition $14{,}000\,x_1 + 6000x_2 + u_1 \geq 840{,}000; u_1 \geq 0$).

2. Minimize expenditures in excess of $90,000 on TV (i.e., Min v_2, subject to the condition $x_1 - v_2 \leq 90; v_2 \geq 0$).

3. Minimize underachievement of 168,000 upper-income exposures (i.e., Min u_3, subject to the condition $1200x_1 + 1200x_2 + u_3 \geq 168{,}000; u_3 \geq 0$).

4. Minimize underachievement of 1,680,000 total exposures—the maximum possible (i.e., Min u_4, where $14{,}000x_1 + 6000x_2 + u_4 \geq 1{,}680{,}000; u_4 \geq 0$).

Note that Tom's priorities are now clearly stated in terms of either minimizing underachievement (i.e., minimizing a u_i) or minimizing overachievement (i.e., minimizing a v_i). His goals, as stated above, have been expressed as inequalities in accord with our previous discussion. This method will facilitate a graphical analysis.

Given that he has correctly formulated his priorities, Tom must distinguish between (1) *system constraints* (all constraints that may not be violated) and (2) *goal constraints*. In his model, the only system constraint is that total expenditures will be no greater than $120,000. Thus (since the units of x_1 and x_2 are thousands), we have

$$x_1 + x_2 \leq 120 \qquad \textbf{(S)}$$

In goal programming notation, Tom's model can now be expressed as follows in Figure 9.15:

$$\text{Min } P_1 u_1 + P_2 v_2 + P_3 u_3 + P_4 u_4$$

$$
\begin{array}{rrcll}
\text{s.t.} \quad & x_1 + x_2 & \leq & 120 & \text{(S)}\\
& 14{,}000 x_1 + 6000 x_2 + u_1 & \geq & 840{,}000 & \text{(1)}\\
& x_1 \quad\quad\quad - v_2 & \leq & 90 & \text{(2)}\\
& 1200 x_1 + 1200 x_2 + u_3 & \geq & 168{,}000 & \text{(3)}\\
& 14{,}000 x_1 + 6000 x_2 + u_4 & \geq & 1{,}680{,}000 & \text{(4)}\\
& x_1, x_2, u_1, v_2, u_3, u_4 & \geq & 0 &
\end{array}
$$

FIGURE 9.15

Goal Program Formulation

Note that the objective function consists only of deviation variables and is of the *Min* form. As already stated, all goal programming formulations are minimization models, as the objective is to come as close as possible to the goals. The terms serve merely to indicate priorities, with P_1 denoting highest priority, and so on. What the problem statement above means precisely is

1. Find the set of decision variables that satisfies the system constraint (S) and that also gives the Min possible value to u_1 subject to constraint (1) and $x_1, x_2, u_1 \geq 0$. Call this set of decisions FR I (i.e., "feasible region I"). Considering *only the highest goal,* all of the points in FR I are "optimal" (i.e., the best that Tom can do) and (again considering only the highest goal) he is indifferent as to which of these points he selects.
2. Find the subset of points in FR I that gives the Min possible value to v_2, subject to constraint (2) and $v_2 \geq 0$. Call this subset FR II. Considering only the ordinal ranking of the two highest-priority goals, all of the points in FR II are "optimal," and in terms of these two highest-priority goals Tom is indifferent as to which of these points he selects.
3. Let FR III be the subset of points in FR II that minimize u_3, subject to constraint (3) and $u_3 \geq 0$.
4. FR IV is the subset of points in FR III that minimize u_4, subject to constraint (4) and $u_4 \geq 0$. Any point in FR IV is an optimal solution to Tom's overall model.

Graphical Analysis and Spreadsheet Implementation of the Solution Procedure
Since Tom's marketing model has only two decision variables, the solution method above can be accomplished with graphical analysis. In all real-world models, the spreadsheet with its Solver tool would be used. In the next section we show how this can be done using LP.

1. In Figure 9.16, both the spreadsheet output (new sheet called "First Goal" in the same SWENSON.XLS) and the geometry reveal that the Min of u_1 s.t. (S), (1), and $x_1, x_2, u_1 \geq 0$ is $u_1^* = 0$. Although Solver returns optimal values for x_1^* and x_2^*, these values are not of interest. The important information is that $u_1^* = 0$, which tells us that the first goal can be completely attained. Alternative optima for the current model are provided by all values of (x_1, x_2) that satisfy the conditions

$$
\text{FR I} \begin{cases} x_1 + x_2 \leq 120 \\ 14{,}000 x_1 + 6000 x_2 \geq 840{,}000 \\ x_1, x_2 \geq 0 \end{cases}
$$

At any such point Tom's first goal is attained ($u_1^* = 0$) so that, in terms of only the first goal, these decisions are equally preferable. Thus FR I is the shaded area *ABC* in Figure 9.16.

The line labeled (1) represents goal 1. The arrow marked $u_1 = 0$ indicates that at all points to the right of line (1) goal 1 is achieved.
2. In the spreadsheet formulation in Figure 9.17 (new sheet called "Goal 2"), we have entered the constraints defining FR I (constraints in cells B10:D11), together with the new goal constraint (2) (shown in cells B12:D12), and we see that

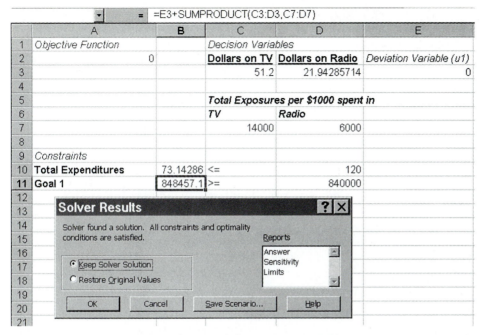

Cell	Formula	Copy To
A2	= E3	—
B10	= SUM(C3:D3)	—
B11	= E3+SUMPRODUCT(C3:D3,C7:D7)	—

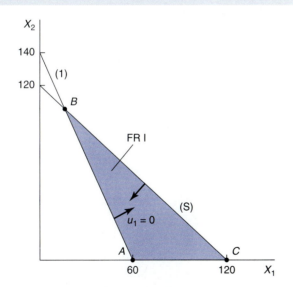

FIGURE 9.16

First Goal

$$\text{Min } v_2$$
$$\text{s.t.} \quad x \text{ in FR I, goal (2), and } v_2 \geq 0$$

is $v_2^* = 0$. Thus, FR II is defined by

$$\text{FR II} \begin{cases} x_1 + x_2 \leq 120 \\ 14{,}000x_1 + 6000x_2 \geq 840{,}000 \\ x_1 \leq 90 \\ x_1, x_2 \geq 0 \end{cases}$$

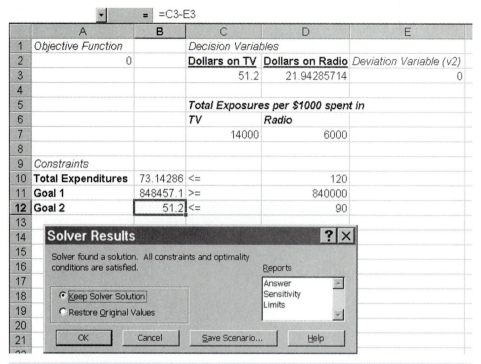

	A	B	C	D	E
			=	=C3-E3	
1	Objective Function		Decision Variables		
2		0	Dollars on TV	Dollars on Radio	Deviation Variable (v2)
3			51.2	21.94285714	0
4					
5			Total Exposures per $1000 spent in		
6			TV	Radio	
7			14000	6000	
8					
9	Constraints				
10	Total Expenditures	73.14286	<=	120	
11	Goal 1	848457.1	>=	840000	
12	Goal 2	51.2	<=	90	

Solver Results

Solver found a solution. All constraints and optimality
conditions are satisfied.

Reports

Answer
Sensitivity
Limits

◉ Keep Solver Solution

○ Restore Original Values

| OK | Cancel | Save Scenario... | Help |

Cell	Formula	Copy To
A2	= E3	—
B10	= SUM(C3:D3)	—
B11	= SUMPRODUCT(C3:D3,C7:D7)	—
B12	= C3–E3	—

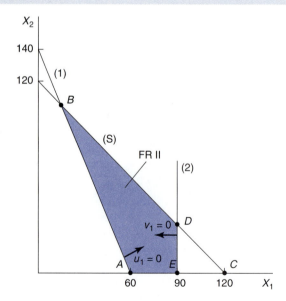

FIGURE 9.17

Goal 2

which is the shaded area *ABDE,* clearly a subset of FR I. As expected, the size of the feasible region has become smaller.

Continuing in this way, Figure 9.18 (new sheet called "Goal 3") shows that FR III is the line segment *BD.* In this case $u_3^* = 24{,}000$. Although the first two goals were completely attained (since $u_1^* = v_2^* = 0$), the third goal cannot be completely attained because $u_3^* > 0$. At this stage, Tom is indifferent about any decision satisfying

	B16	▼	=	=E3+SUMPRODUCT(C3:D3,C11:D11)		

	A	B	C	D	E	F
1	Objective Function		Decision Variables			
2	24000		**Dollars on TV**	**Dollars on Radio**	Deviation Variable (u3)	
3			81.429	38.571	24000	
4						
5			Total Exposures per $1000 spent in			
6			TV	Radio		
7			14000	6000		
8						
9			Upper Income Exposures per $1000 spent in			
10			TV	Radio		
11			1200	1200		
12	Constraints					
13	**Total Expenditures**	120	<=	120		
14	**Goal 1**	1371429	>=	840000		
15	**Goal 2**	81.42857	<=	90		
16	**Goal 3**	168000	>=	168000		

Cell	Formula	Copy To
A2	= E3	—
B13	= SUM(C3:D3)	—
B14	= SUMPRODUCT(C3:D3,C7:D7)	—
B15	= C3	—
B16	= E3+SUMPRODUCT(C3:D3,C11:D11)	—

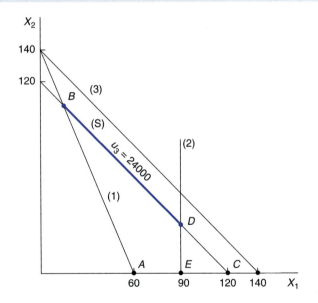

FIGURE 9.18

Goal 3

$$\text{FR III} \begin{cases} x_1 + x_2 \le 120 \\ 14{,}000x_1 + 6000x_2 \ge 840{,}000 \\ x_1 \le 90 \\ 1200x_1 + 1200x_2 \ge 168{,}000 - 24{,}000 = 144{,}000 \end{cases}$$

which defines the line segment BD.

Finally, Figure 9.19 (new sheet called "Optimal"), shows the optimal solution at point D. Recall that the fourth goal is to minimize underachievement of the maximum possible number of exposures, which is 1,680,000. Thus, we wish to minimize the underachievement u_4 where

B17		▼	=	=E3+SUMPRODUCT(C3:D3,C7:D7)		

	A	B	C	D	E	F
1	*Objective Function*		*Decision Variables*			
2	240000		**Dollars on TV**	**Dollars on Radio**	*Deviation Variable (u4)*	
3			90.000	30.000	240000	
4						
5			*Total Exposures per $1000 spent in*			
6			*TV*	*Radio*		
7			14000	6000		
8						
9			*Upper Income Exposures per $1000 spent in*			
10			*TV*	*Radio*		
11			1200	1200		
12	*Constraints*					
13	**Total Expenditures**	120	<=	120		
14	**Goal 1**	1440000	>=	840000		
15	**Goal 2**	90	<=	90		
16	**Goal 3**	144000	>=	144000		
17	**Goal 4**	1680000	>=	1680000		
18						

Cell	Formula	Copy To
A2	= E3	—
B13	= SUM(C3:D3)	—
B14	= SUMPRODUCT(C3:D3,C7:D7)	—
B15	= C3	—
B16	= SUMPRODUCT(C3:D3,C11:D11)	—
B17	= E3+SUMPRODUCT(C3:D3,C7:D7)	—

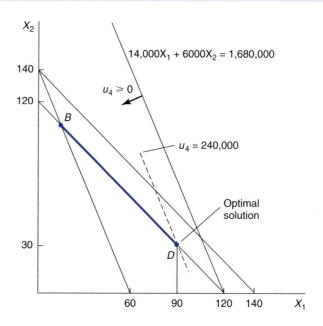

FIGURE 9.19

Optimal Solution

$$14{,}000x_1 + 6000x_2 + u_4 \geq 1{,}680{,}000$$

In Figure 9.19 we find the unique optimum $x_1^* = 90$ and $x_2^* = 30$; that is, Tom should spend $90,000 on TV advertising and $30,000 on radio advertising. This fact is verified in the geometric analysis, where it is clear that point D ($x_1 = 90$, $x_2 = 30$) is closer to the line that describes goal 4 ($14{,}000x_1 + 6000x_2 = 1{,}680{,}000$) than any other point in FR III (i.e., than any other point on the segment *BD*). We also note that $u_4^* = 240{,}000$. Thus, Tom achieves only $1{,}680{,}000 - 240{,}000 = 1{,}440{,}000$ exposures.

We see, then, that goal programming with absolute priorities allows a manager (like Tom) to solve a model in which there is no solution that achieves all the goals, but where he is willing to specify an absolute ranking among the goals and successively restrict his attention to those points that come as close as possible to each goal.

COMBINING WEIGHTS AND ABSOLUTE PRIORITIES

It is possible to combine, to some extent, the concepts of weighted and absolute priority goals. To illustrate this fact, we return to Tom Swenson's advertising model.

In reviewing the results of the absolute priority study, Tom and his client begin to discuss the importance of the older members of the Mylonal market. In particular, they focus on the number of exposures to individuals 50 years old or older. Again, they see that radio and TV are not equally effective in generating exposures in this segment of the population. The exposures per $1000 of advertising are as follows in Table 9.4:

TABLE 9.4		
EXPOSURE GROUP	**TV**	**RADIO**
50 and over	3000	8000

If there were no other considerations, Tom would like as many 50-and-over exposures as possible. Since radio yields such exposures at a higher rate than TV ($8000 > 3000$), Tom sees that the maximum possible number of 50-and-over exposures would be achieved by allocating all of the $120,000 available to radio. Thus, the maximum number of 50-and-over exposures is $960{,}000$ ($= 120 \times 8000$). Tom and his client would like to come as close as possible to this goal (minimize underachievement) once the first three goals are satisfied. Recall, however, that they also want to come as close as possible to the goal of $1{,}680{,}000$ total exposures (minimize underachievement) once the first three goals are satisfied. To resolve this conflict of goals, they decide to use a weighted sum of the deviation variables as the objective in the final phase of the absolute priorities approach. It is their judgment that underachievement in the fifth goal ($960{,}000$ exposures to the 50-and-over group) is three times as serious as underachievement in the fourth goal ($1{,}680{,}000$ total exposures). The formulation, its solution (a new sheet called "Weighted" in the same SWENSON.XLS), and graphical analysis are presented in Figure 9.20.

From the spreadsheet we see that the optimal solution to this model is point *B* (x_1^* $= 15$, $x_2^* = 105$). Recall that when the objective function was to minimize u_4, the optimal decision was point *D* ($x_1^* = 90$, $x_2^* = 30$). Thus, in the graphical analysis, we see that the new objective function has moved the optimal solution from one end of FR III to the other. There is no obvious graphical way to find the optimal solution to this model; that is, there is not an obvious objective function contour to push in a downhill direction that takes us to the point $x_1 = 15$, $x_2 = 105$. It is, however, intuitively appealing to see that the optimal solution is as close as possible to the more heavily weighted goal. We could perform a sensitivity analysis on the weights in the objective function to see when the solution changes to point *B* from point *D*.

This completes the analysis of Tom Swenson's advertising campaign model. The general sequential LP procedure described above for goal programming with absolute priorities holds for any model in which the system constraints and the goal constraints are formulated with linear functions. For each new model a single constraint is added to the previous model, and the objective function is modified slightly. Generally speaking, a fairly large number of decision variables can be involved. The example with two variables was useful because it made it possible to present, along with the spreadsheet results, geometric interpretations, which add insight to the solution technique.

	A2	▼		=	=3*F3+E3		

	A	B	C	D	E	F
1	Objective Function		Decision Variables			
2	1065000		**Dollars on TV**	**Dollars on Radio**	Deviation Variable (u4)	Deviation Variable (u5)
3			15.000	105.000	840000	75000
4						
5			Total Exposures per $1000 spent in			
6			TV	Radio		
7			14000	6000		
8						
9			Upper Income Exposures per $1000 spent in			
10			TV	Radio		
11			1200	1200		
12			Senior Exposures per $1000 spent in			
13			TV	Radio		
14			3000	8000		
15	Constraints					
16	Total Expenditures	120	<=	120		
17	Goal 1	840000	>=	840000		
18	Goal 2	15	<=	90		
19	Goal 3	144000	>=	144000		
20	Goal 4	1680000	>=	1680000		
21	Goal 5	960000	>=	960000		

Cell	Formula	Copy To
A2	= 3*F3+E3	—
B16	= SUM(C3:D3)	—
B17	= SUMPRODUCT(C3:D3,C7:D7)	—
B18	= C3	—
B19	= SUMPRODUCT(C3:D3,C11:D11)	—
B20	= E3+SUMPRODUCT(C3:D3,C7:D7)	—
B21	= F3+SUMPRODUCT(C3:D3,C14:D14)	—

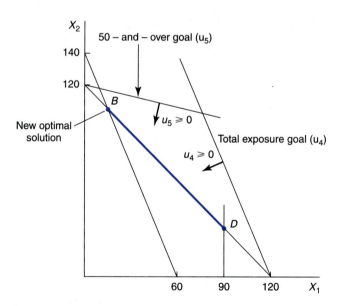

FIGURE 9.20

Weighting the Final Step

The foregoing model is useful in indicating how conflicting and noncommensurate goals (i.e., apples and oranges) can be simultaneously considered by means of goal programming. Thus, it gives some insight into why goal programming is a promising and increasingly useful tool in analyzing public policy questions.

9.5 ANALYTIC HIERARCHY PROCESS

This section deals with the real-world topic of making a decision when there are multiple objectives or criteria to consider. There are numerous examples where these kinds of decisions are made every day. Consider the following:

- Choosing which employment offer to accept from among several offers
- Picking which computer to buy (or which automobile, etc.)
- Deciding which new product to launch first
- Selecting a site for a new restaurant, hotel, manufacturing facility, and so on
- Selecting which university to attend
- Identifying the best business or engineering school in the country
- Rating the best cities to live in
- Choosing a new information system for your company that does payroll, accounting, and so forth (or choosing any new software package from competing vendors)
- Selecting what combination of taxes (property, sales, gas, etc.) to levy on the citizens of a locale.

For example, when you go to buy a car, you might consider numerous factors, not the least of which include the price, its safety, the engine size, fuel economy, and so forth. Each of the examples identified previously likewise would have numerous factors to consider in making these complex decisions.

A simple way to attack such a decision would be to assign weights to each of the criterion that were to be considered in making the decision. Then rank each decision alternative on a scale from 1 (worst) to 10 (best). Finally, you would multiply the weights times the rankings for each criterion and sum them up. The alternative with the highest score would be the most preferred. Let's consider an example.

Your boss has asked you to help her buy the next computer for the office. You have to choose between three computers: (1) Model A that runs a Pentium chip at 166 MHz, (2) Model B that runs a 486 DX chip at 133 MHz, and (3) Model C that runs a PowerPC chip at 200 MHz. The criterion that are important to you and your boss are price, speed, hard-disk size, and warranty/support. You decide that price should get 50% of the total weight in making the decision, speed 15%, hard-disk size 20%, and warranty/support 15%. Next you rank each of the three models on these four criteria. You rank them on a scale from 1–10 (as described earlier) as shown in the following spreadsheet (COMPUTER.XLS) in Figure 9.21.

As can be seen, Model B comes out with the highest weighted score (7.05) and thus would be your recommendation to your boss. This approach is quite simplistic and there are difficulties in setting the ranking scales on such different criterion.

EB		= =SUMPRODUCT($C$4:$C$7,E4:E7)				
	A	B	C	D	E	F	G
1							
2						Alternatives' Rankings	
3		Criterion	Weights		Model A	Model B	Model C
4		Price	50%		5	8	3
5		Speed	15%		7	5	9
6		Hard-Disk	20%		9	4	10
7		Warranty	15%		7	10	7
8			100%		6.4	7.05	5.9
9							

Cell	Formula	Copy To
C8	= SUM (C4:C7)	—
E8	= SUMPRODUCT ($C$4:$C$7, E4:E7)	F8:G8

FIGURE 9.21

Multi-Attribute Decision
Model for Buying a Computer

Analytic hierarchy process (AHP) also uses a weighted average approach idea, but it uses a method for assigning ratings (or rankings) and weights that is considered more reliable and consistent than the simple method described above. AHP is based on pairwise comparisons between the decision alternatives on each of the criterion. Then a similar set of comparisons are made to determine the relative importance of each criterion and thus produces the weights. The basic procedure is as follows:

1. Develop the ratings for each decision alternative for each criterion by
   - developing a pairwise comparison matrix for each criterion
   - normalizing the resulting matrix
   - averaging the values in each row to get the corresponding rating
   - calculating and checking the consistency ratio
2. Develop the weights for the criteria by
   - developing a pairwise comparison matrix for each criterion
   - normalizing the resulting matrix
   - averaging the values in each row to get the appropriate weights
   - calculating and checking the consistency ratio
3. Calculate the weighted average rating for each decision alternative. Choose the one with the highest score.

We will demonstrate this procedure on a new example. Sleepwell Hotels is looking for some help in selecting the "best" revenue management software package from among several vendors. Mark James is the director of revenue management for this chain of hotels and has been given the task of selecting the software package. He has identified three vendors whose software seems to meet their basic needs—Revenue Technology Corporation (RTC), PRAISE Strategic Solutions (PSS), and El Cheapo (EC). The criteria that he thinks are important in making this decision are (1) the total cost of the installed system, (2) the follow-up service provided over the coming year, (3) the sophistication of the underlying math engines, and (4) the amount of customization for Sleepwell. The first step in the AHP procedure is to make pairwise comparisons between the vendors for each criterion. The scale that is used in making these comparisons is a standard one and is described as follows:

Rating	Description
1	Equally preferred
3	Moderately preferred
5	Strongly preferred
7	Very strongly preferred
9	Extremely strongly preferred

Values of 2, 4, 6, or 8 may also be assigned and represent preferences halfway between the integers on either side (e.g., a 2 is between a 1 and a 3—somewhere between equally preferred and moderately preferred).

Mark starts with the first criterion (total cost) and generates the following data in his spreadsheet (sheet "Total Cost" in SLEEPWLL.XLS shown in Figure 9.22). The table is read as follows: The vendor in the row is being compared to the vendor in the column. If the vendor in the row is preferred to the vendor in the column, then a number from 1 to 9 (from the AHP table) is assigned to the cell at the intersection of the row and column. If, however, the vendor in the column is preferred to the vendor in the row, then 1 divided by (a number from 1 to 9) is assigned to the cell at the intersection of the row and column. Obviously since vendor 1 (RTC) is equally preferred to vendor 1, then a "1" is assigned to that row/column and in fact, all along the diagonal. Vendor 1 is moderately to strongly preferred to vendor 2 on the

B6		=	=1/D4	
	A	B	C	D
1				
2				
3		RTC	PSS	EC
4	RTC	1	4	0.5
5	PSS	0.25	1	0.142857
6	EC	2	7	1

Cell	Formula	Copy To
B5	= 1/C4	—
B6	= 1/D4	—
C6	= 1/D5	—

FIGURE 9.22

Pairwise Comparison on
Total Cost

B12		=	=B4/B$8		
	A	B	C	D	E
1					
2					
3		RTC	PSS	EC	
4	RTC	1	4	0.5	
5	PSS	0.25	1	0.142857	
6	EC	2	7	1	
7					
8	Sum	3.25	12	1.642857	
9					
10	NORMALIZED				
11		RTC	PSS	EC	Average
12	RTC	0.308	0.333	0.304	0.315
13	PSS	0.077	0.083	0.087	0.082
14	EC	0.615	0.583	0.609	0.602

Cell	Formula	Copy To
B8	= SUM(B4:B6)	C8:D8
B12	= B4/B$8	B12:D14
E12	= AVERAGE(B12:D12)	E13:E14

FIGURE 9.23

Normalized Matrix for
Total Cost

Total Cost basis and so a "4" is assigned in the first row, second column (cell C4). Vendor 3 (EC) is equally to moderately preferred to Vendor 1 (RTC) and so a "½" is assigned in row 1, column 3 (cell D4). Mark has set up his spreadsheet so that once that entries above and to the right of the diagonal are entered (cells C4, D4, and D5), it automatically calculates the reciprocal preferences. For example, since vendor 1 compared to vendor 2 was assigned a "4," then the comparison of vendor 2 to vendor 1 gets a "¼" automatically (cell B5).

Once all the relevant pairwise comparisons have been made, the matrix needs to be normalized. This is done by totaling the numbers in each column. Each entry in the column is then divided by the column sum to yield its normalized score. Mark has now done this in his spreadsheet and it is shown in cells B12:D14 of Figure 9.23. His next step is to calculate the average score of each vendor for the "Total Cost" criterion. These values are shown in column E of Figure 9.23. Mark sees that EC has the highest average score on this factor.

Once the normalized matrix is finished, he must calculate the consistency ratio and check its value. The purpose for doing this is to make sure Mark was consistent in the preference ratings he expressed in the original table. For example, if Mark expressed strong preference for vendor 1 over vendor 2 on the Total Cost criterion, and moderate preference for vendor 2 over vendor 3, then it would be inconsistent to express equal preference between vendors 1 and 3 or worse to express a preference for vendor 3 over vendor 1. There are three steps in order to arrive at the consistency ratio:

1. Calculate the consistency measure for each vendor.
2. Calculate the consistency index (CI).
3. Calculate the consistency ratio (CI/RI where RI is a random index).

To calculate the consistency measure we can take advantage of Excel's matrix multiplication function = MMULT(). As Mark shows us in Figure 9.24 that for vendor 1 (RTC) you multiply the average rating for each vendor (cells E12:E14) times the scores in the first row (cells B4:D4) one-at-a-time, sum these products up and divide this sum by the average rating for the first vendor (cell E12). A similar calculation is done for the second and third vendors. Ideally the consistency measures would be equal to the number of decision alternatives in the example (in our case, we have three vendors). To calculate the consistency index (CI), Mark takes the average consistency measure of the three vendors, subtracts the number of alternatives (n), and divides the whole quantity by $n - 1$. This is shown in cell F16 of Figure 9.24 and Mark sees that his CI has a value of 0.001. The final step to find the consistency ratio (CR) is to divide the CI by a random index (RI) that is provided by AHP and shown below:

n	Random Index
2	0.00
3	0.58
4	0.90
5	1.12
6	1.24
7	1.32
8	1.41
9	1.45
10	1.51

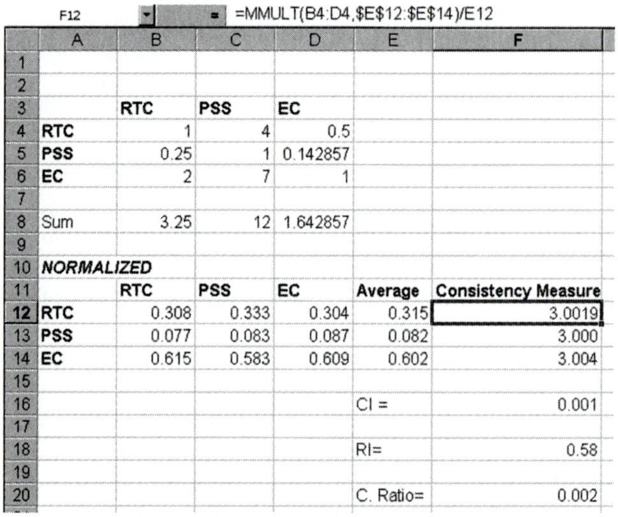

F12　　　=MMULT(B4:D4,$E$12:$E$14)/E12

	A	B	C	D	E	F
1						
2						
3		RTC	PSS	EC		
4	RTC	1	4	0.5		
5	PSS	0.25	1	0.142857		
6	EC	2	7	1		
7						
8	Sum	3.25	12	1.642857		
9						
10	NORMALIZED					
11		RTC	PSS	EC	Average	Consistency Measure
12	RTC	0.308	0.333	0.304	0.315	3.0019
13	PSS	0.077	0.083	0.087	0.082	3.000
14	EC	0.615	0.583	0.609	0.602	3.004
15						
16					CI =	0.001
17						
18					RI=	0.58
19						
20					C. Ratio=	0.002

Cell	Formula	Copy To
F12	= MMULT(B4:D4,$E$12:$E$14)/E12	F13:F14
F16	= (AVERAGE(F12:F14)-3)/2	—
F20	= F16/F18	—

FIGURE 9.24

Consistency Ratio for Total Cost

This consistency ratio is shown in cell F20 of Figure 9.24 and in Mark's example it equals 0.002.

For a perfectly consistent manager, the consistency measures will equal n and therefore, the CIs will be equal to zero and so will the consistency ratio. If this ratio is very large (Saaty suggests > 0.10), then the manager is not consistent enough and the best thing to do is go back and revise the comparisons (in most cases, you'll have a made a simple mistake and this calculation will alert you to that fact).

Mark must now do the same thing for the other three criteria. He can easily do this by copying the "Total Cost" sheet into three other sheets ("Service," "Sophistication," "Custom") and then simply changing the pairwise comparisons. The results of this are shown in Figures 9.25 to 9.27. Mark notes that in all three cases, the CR values range from 0.0 to 0.047, which means he's being consistent. He also notes that PSS is the winner on the Service criterion, RTC and PSS are tied for the best in terms of Sophistication, and PSS is considered the best on Customization.

All of this work concludes the first step in the procedure. The next step (2) in the procedure is to use similar pairwise comparisons to determine the appropriate weights for each of the criteria. The process is the same in that we make comparisons, except that now we make the comparisons between the criterion not the vendors as we did in step 1. Mark does this in a new sheet called "Weights" (in the same workbook) and it's shown in Figure 9.28.

F20   = =F16/F18

	A	B	C	D	E	F	G
1							
2							
3		RTC	PSS	EC			
4	RTC	1	0.5	6			
5	PSS	2	1	8			
6	EC	0.166667	0.125	1			
7							
8	Sum	3.166667	1.625	15			
9							
10	NORMALIZED						
11		RTC	PSS	EC	Average	Consistency Measure	
12	RTC	0.316	0.308	0.400	0.341	3.0200	
13	PSS	0.632	0.615	0.533	0.593	3.0315	
14	EC	0.053	0.077	0.067	0.065	3.0034	
15							
16					CI =	0.009	
17							
18					RI=	0.58	
19							
20					C. Ratio=	0.016	

FIGURE 9.25

Consistency Ratio for Service

F16   = =(AVERAGE(F12:F14) - 3)/2

	A	B	C	D	E	F	G
1							
2							
3		RTC	PSS	EC			
4	RTC	1	1	5			
5	PSS	1	1	5			
6	EC	0.2	0.2	1			
7							
8	Sum	2.2	2.2	11			
9							
10	NORMALIZED						
11		RTC	PSS	EC	Average	Consistency Measure	
12	RTC	0.455	0.455	0.455	0.455	3.0000	
13	PSS	0.455	0.455	0.455	0.455	3.000	
14	EC	0.091	0.091	0.091	0.091	3.000	
15							
16					CI =	0.000	
17							
18					RI=	0.58	
19							
20					C. Ratio=	0.000	

FIGURE 9.26

Consistency Ratio for Sophistication

	C8	▼	=	=SUM(C4:C6)			
	A	B	C	D	E	F	G
1							
2							
3		RTC	PSS	EC			
4	RTC	1	0.25	3			
5	PSS	4	1	6			
6	EC	0.333333	0.166667	1			
7							
8	Sum	5.333333	1.416667	10			
9							
10	NORMALIZED						
11		RTC	PSS	EC	Average	Consistency Measure	
12	RTC	0.188	0.176	0.300	0.221	3.0399	
13	PSS	0.750	0.706	0.600	0.685	3.1094	
14	EC	0.063	0.118	0.100	0.093	3.0131	
15							
16					CI =	0.027	
17							
18					RI=	0.58	
19							
20					C. Ratio=	0.047	

FIGURE 9.27

Consistency Ratio
for Customization

	G16	▼	=	=(AVERAGE(G12:G15) - 4)/3				
	A	B	C	D	E	F	G	H
1								
2								
3		Cost	Service	Sophistication	Customization			
4	Cost	1	6	0.5	3			
5	Service	0.166667	1	0.125	0.333333333			
6	Sophistication	2	8	1	5			
7	Customization	0.333333	3	0.2	1			
8	Sum	3.500	18.000	1.825	9.333			
9								
10	NORMALIZED							
11		Cost	Service	Sophistication	Customization	Average	Consistency Measure	
12	Cost	0.286	0.333	0.274	0.321	0.304	4.0713	
13	Service	0.048	0.056	0.068	0.036	0.052	4.0108	
14	Sophistication	0.571	0.444	0.548	0.536	0.525	4.0869	
15	Customization	0.095	0.167	0.110	0.107	0.120	4.0229	
16						CI =	0.016	
17								
18						RI=	0.9	
19								
20						C. Ratio=	0.018	

Cell	Formula	Copy To
B5	= 1/C4	—
B6	= 1/D4	—
B7	= 1/E4	—
C6	= 1/D5	—
C7	= 1/E5	—
D7	= 1/E6	—
B8	= SUM(B4:B7)	C8:E8
B12	= B4/B$8	B12:E15
F12	= AVERAGE(B12:E12)	F13:F15
G12	= MMULT(B4:E4,$F$12:$F$15)/F12	G13:G15
G16	= AVERAGE(G12:G15)/3	—
G20	= G16/G18	—

FIGURE 9.28

Consistency Ratio for
Weights on Criterion

Mark sees that Sophistication of the math algorithms gets the most weight (52.5% in cell F14), followed by Cost (30.4% in cell F12) based on the pairwise comparisons. Again, he's pleased that his consistency measures are close to 4 and therefore that his CI and CR are close to zero.

	B3		=	=Weights!F12	

	A	B	C	D	E
1			*Alternatives' Ratings*		
2	*Criteria*	*Weights*	RTC	PSS	EC
3	**Cost**	0.304	0.315	0.082	0.602
4	**Service**	0.052	0.341	0.593	0.065
5	**Sophistication**	0.525	0.455	0.455	0.091
6	**Customization**	0.120	0.221	0.685	0.093
7					
8	*Wtd Ratings*		0.378	0.376	0.245

Cell	Formula	Copy To
B3	= WEIGHTS!F12	B4:B6
C3	= TOTAL COST!E12	—
D3	= TOTAL COST!E13	—
E3	= TOTAL COST!E14	—
C4	= SERVICE!E12	—
D4	= SERVICE!E13	—
E4	= SERVICE!E14	—
C5	= SOPHISTICATION!E12	—
D5	= SOPHISTICATION!E13	—
E5	= SOPHISTICATION!E14	—
C6	= CUSTOM!E12	—
D6	= CUSTOM!E13	—
E6	= CUSTOM!E14	—
C8	= SUMPRODUCT($B$3:$B$6,C3:C6)	D8:E8

FIGURE 9.29

Weighted Average AHP Ratings Using AHP Weights

The final step is to calculate the weighted average ratings of each decision alternative and use the results to decide from which vendor to purchase the new software package. This last step is just like the simple example we gave at the beginning of this section, and Mark pulls the results from all his other worksheets in order to make this calculation (see the "Comparison" sheet in the same SLEEPWLL.XLS). This is shown in Figure 9.29. From these results, Mark sees that RTC (.378 in cell C8) barely edges out PSS (.376 in cell D8) for the new software contract, while EC remains a distant third.

9.6   **NOTES ON IMPLEMENTATION**

As is true of most types of quantitative models, heuristic approaches are typically implemented with the spreadsheet or some other computer program. One difference, in practice, between using heuristic procedures and using more formal models such as linear or quadratic programming, is that in the latter case the computer software already exists. In the heuristic case, however, the application is often *ad hoc,* which implies that the software must be constructed. A typical application of heuristics is, as stated earlier, the area of large combinatorial models, for which obtaining a solution either by enumeration or by applying a formal mathematical or integer programming model would be prohibitively expensive. In all applications of heuristics there is an implicit managerial judgment that "acceptability" rather than "optimality" is an appropriate way of thinking. In other words, it is felt that "good solutions" as opposed to "optimal solutions" can be useful and satisfactory. *This philosophy is particularly well suited to models that are rather vague in their statement, such as high-level models with surrogate objectives or for which there may be numerous con-*

flicting criteria of interest and for which, consequently there is not a clear, definitive single-objective function.

In practice, the use of heuristics is in some cases closely linked to the field of *artificial intelligence,* where the computer is programmed with heuristic techniques to prove theorems, play chess, and even write poems.

Perhaps the most common use of heuristics in management science has been, to date, in models of assembly-line balancing, job-shop scheduling, and resource allocation in project management. However, recently there has been an increase in the scope of applications to such areas as media selection in marketing, political districting, scheduling of university classes, or positioning urban systems.

In the implementation of all heuristic models, managerial interaction and feedback must play perhaps an even greater role than in the case of more formal modeling, for in the heuristic case the manager must assess not only the model but, implicitly, the heuristic algorithm as well. This assessment is necessary because, *for the same model, different heuristics will lead to different "solutions."*

This close interaction between the model and the decision maker is also manifest in goal programming when the decision maker must assign priorities to various goals, such as in the form of ordinal ranking (i.e., *absolute priorities*). Goal programming is an intuitively appealing, and in this sense a "heuristic," approach to models with multiple objectives. In goal programming with absolute priorities, the manager must consider carefully the relative importance or utility of his or her goals. Depending on the spreadsheet model output, the decision maker may wish to change priorities, or even the number of goals, and rerun the spreadsheet model. In other words, just as with LP, sensitivity analysis becomes an important aspect of implementation. Since goal programming is still more or less in its infancy, the field is developing, from a theoretical point of view, at a rapid rate, and it seems clear that this development will prompt greater use of the technique, especially as sensitivity analysis becomes better understood.

In practice, computer programs do exist for solving large scale goal programs in the batch processing mode, but typically these are not part of the standard program libraries. For models of modest size, the interactive mode is ideally suited to the sequential technique described in this chapter.

Key Terms

Heuristic Algorithm.   An algorithm that efficiently provides good approximate solutions to a given model, often with estimates as to the goodness of the approximation.

Heuristic.   An intuitively appealing rule of thumb for dealing with some aspect of a model.

Heuristic Program.   A collection of heuristics and/or heuristic algorithms.

Combinatorial Optimization.   An optimization model with a finite number of feasible alternatives.

Setup Time.   Time required before an activity can begin.

Greedy Algorithm.   An algorithm that says that the maximum improvement should be made at each step of a sequential process.

Next Best Rule.   Same as the greedy algorithm.

Precedence Relationships.   Means that certain activities must be completed before others may begin.

Personnel Loading Chart.   A bar chart showing the total number of people required per week in order to carry out a given schedule of activities.

Slack.   In the project scheduling context this refers to the maximum amount of time any given activity can be delayed without delaying completion of the overall project.

Goal Programming.   Seeks allowable decisions that come as close as possible to achieving specified goals.

Deviation Variables.   Variables used in goal programming to measure the extent to which a specified goal is violated.

Goal Interval Constraint. A constraint for which goals are specified by an interval of indifference, rather than by a specific numerical value.

Absolute Priority. A form of goal programming in which goals must be satisfied in a specific order.

Analytic Hierarchy Process (AHP). A procedure that uses pairwise comparisons to make decisions among competing alternatives when there are multiple criteria that are considered important.

Self-Review Exercises

True-False

1. **T   F** Heuristic algorithms are guaranteed to be within a specified percentage of optimality at termination.

2. **T   F** The optimal solution to a combinatorial optimization model can, in principle, be found by complete enumeration.

3. **T   F** An alternative heuristic in the model of scheduling with limited resources is to move forward that activity that contributes most to the overload (i.e., utilizes the largest number of people).

4. **T   F** Goal programming is the only quantitative technique designed for use on models with multiple objectives.

5. **T   F** Each step in goal programming with absolute priorities introduces a new goal and eliminates from further consideration all current candidates that do not satisfy this new goal as well as possible.

6. **T   F** Consider the goal constraint $12x_1 + 3x_2 + u_1 - v_1 = 100$. Suppose that, because of other constraints in the

model, the goal cannot be achieved. If u_1 is positive, the goal is overachieved.

7. **T   F** One way to state priorities among goals is to place weights on deviation variables.

8. **T   F** Consider the goal interval constraint $180 \le 4x_1 + 12x_2 \le 250$. A correct goal formulation is

$$4x_1 + 12x_2 - v_1 \le 250$$
$$4x_1 + 12x_2 - u_1 \ge 180$$

9. **T   F** If a goal interval constraint cannot be achieved (exactly satisfied), then one deviation variable will be positive, and the constraint in which that variable appears will be active.

10. **T   F** In goal programming a system constraint is not permitted to be violated.

11. **T   F** A goal programming model cannot be infeasible.

Multiple Choice

12. If changeover time of n jobs on a single machine is sequence-dependent, the problem of minimizing total setup time requires the inspection of
    a. n sequences
    b. 1 sequence
    c. $n!$ sequences
    d. $\binom{n}{2}$ sequences

13. The intuitively appealing notion that motivates a *greedy* algorithm is
    a. get as close as you can to the optimal solution
    b. do the best you can at the current step
    c. minimize the number of steps required
    d. none of the above

14. In the facility scheduling model, subtracting the minimum setup time in a column from the other entries in that column
    a. is a heuristic based on the notion that it is relative costs that matter
    b. is guaranteed to yield an optimal solution if the greedy algorithm is applied
    c. makes the greedy algorithm not useful
    d. all of the above

15. If a goal programming model includes the constraint $g_1(x_1, \ldots, x_n) + u_1 - v_1 = b_1$ and the term $6u_1 + 2v_1$ in the objective function, the decision maker

    a. prefers $g_1(x_1, \ldots, x_n)$ to be larger than, rather than smaller than, b_1
    b. prefers $g_1(x_1, \ldots, x_n)$ to be smaller than, rather than larger than, b_1
    c. is indifferent as to whether $g_1(x_1, \ldots, x_n)$ is larger than or smaller than b_1

16. Models with multiple objectives
    a. are difficult because it is often true that improving one objective will hurt another
    b. are difficult because the objectives may be in non-commensurate units (i.e., the problem of "combining apples and oranges")
    c. can sometimes be treated with the goal programming approach
    d. all of the above

Questions 17, 18, 19 apply to the following problem:

1. $g_1(x_1, x_2) \le b_1$ is a system constraint
2. minimizing underachievement of $g_2(x_1, x_2) = b_2$ is top priority
3. minimizing overachievement of $g_3(x_1, x_2) = b_3$ is next in priority

17. The first step of the solution procedure is
    a. Min u_2, s.t. $g_1(x_1, x_2) \le b_1$; $g_2 - u_2 = b_2$; $x_1, x_2, u_2 \ge 0$

b. Min u_2, s.t. $g_1(x_1, x_2) \leq b_1$; $g_2 + u_2 \geq b_2$; $x_1, x_2, u_2 \geq 0$

c. Min u_2, s.t. $g_1(x_1, x_2) \leq b_1$; $g_2 - u_2 \leq b_2$; $x_1, x_2, u_2 \geq 0$

18. Let FR I denote the points (x_1, x_2) obtained in the first step of the solution procedure. The second step is

a. Min $u_3 + v_3$, s.t. (x_1, x_2) in FR I and $g_3(x_1, x_2) + u_3 - v_3 = b_3$

b. Min u_3, s.t. (x_1, x_2) in FR I and $g_3(x_1, x_2) + u_3 \leq b_3$

c. Min v_3, s.t. (x_1, x_2) in FR I and $g_3(x_1, x_2) - v_3 \leq b_3$

19. In this model

a. at least one goal will be achieved

b. if the first goal is not achieved, the second goal will not be achieved

c. none of the above

20. Consider a goal program with the constraint

$$g_1(x_1, \ldots, x_n) - v_1 \leq b_1, v_1 \geq 0$$

with v_1 in the objective function. Then

a. the goal is to minimize overachievement

b. if $v_1^* > 0$ then the constraint will be active

c. neither of the above

d. both a and b

Answers

1. F	**6.** F	**11.** F	**16.** d
2. T	**7.** T	**12.** c	**17.** b
3. T	**8.** F	**13.** b	**18.** c
4. F	**9.** T	**14.** a	**19.** c
5. T	**10.** T	**15.** a	**20.** d

Problems

9-1. For the minimax scheduling model, find an alternative optimal solution to the one given in Figure 9.12.

Problems 9-2, 9-3, and 9-4 refer to the following example of the so-called *facilities layout model*:

Solomon Gemorah, high-priced management consultant, has been hired to redo the layout of a small bank. There are four key departments to be taken into consideration: (1) Trusts, (2) Estates, (3) Accounting, (4) Savings. These four departments must be assigned to four locations. The distances between locations are given in the table on the left below. Thus the distance from location 2 to location 4 is 1 unit, from 4 to 1 is 1 unit, and so on. A measure of the two-way "daily flows" between the four key departments is shown in the accompanying table on the right below.

TABLE 9.5 Distances Between Locations

	LOCATION			
LOCATION	1	2	3	4
1	0	2	3	1
2	2	0	3	1
3	3	3	0	2
4	1	1	2	0

TABLE 9.6 Flows Between Departments

	DEPARTMENT			
DEPT.	1	2	3	4
1	0	15	20	16
2	15	0	13	9
3	20	13	0	19
4	16	9	19	0

The problem is to assign the four departments to the four locations (one department per location) in such a way as to minimize the sum of the distance-weighted daily flows. For example, if we make the assignment of departments to locations as follows: $1 \rightarrow 1, 2 \rightarrow 2, 3 \rightarrow 3, 4 \rightarrow 4$, then the objective value will be

weighted two-way cost between facilities 1 and 2 = distance $\times$ flow = 2(15) = 30

weighted two-way cost between facilities 1 and 3 = distance $\times$ flow = 3(20) = 60

weighted two-way cost between facilities 1 and 4 = distance $\times$ flow = 1(16) = 16 weighted two-way cost between facilities 2 and 3 = distance × flow = 3(13) =   39

weighted two-way cost between facilities 2 and 4 = distance × flow = 1(9) =   9

weighted two-way cost between facilities 3 and 4 = distance × flow = 2(19) =   38

total cost =   192

9-2. Suppose Solomon assigned department 1 to location 4, department 2 to location 3, department 3 to location 2, and department 4 to location 1.

    (a) What would be the distance between departments?

    (b) What would be the total cost of Solomon's assignments?

    (c) What is the total number of possible assignments of facilities to locations that Solomon would consider if he were to attack the model by complete enumeration?

    (d) For the general model of assigning n facilities to n locations, what is the total possible number of assignments?

9-3. Suppose that department 1 is assigned to location 1. Draw a tree, analogous to Figure 9.1, showing the remaining possible assignments of departments 2, 3, and 4 to locations 2, 3, and 4.

••9-4. Still referring to Solomon and his layout model,

    (a) How many different pairs of departments can be selected from four departments?

    (b) Start from the answer to part (a) of Problem 9-2 to improve the assignment by employing the following Best Pairwise Exchange Heuristic,[2] as described below. How much have you improved your objective function?

    Step 1: Find the potential improvement in the objective function associated with each pairwise exchange of departments. For example, if departments 1 and 2 are exchanged, the new assignment will be $1 \rightarrow 3$, $2 \rightarrow 4$, $3 \rightarrow 2$, and $4 \rightarrow 1$. That is, the location of departments 1 and 2 are changed, but departments 3 and 4 remain unchanged.

    Step 2: Make the pairwise exchange that results in the largest improvement. Then repeat the procedure until no pairwise exchange will improve the value of the objective function.

9-5. Sam Hull is a marketing manager for a pharmaceutical company. He must assign five detail people to five hospitals. The expected sales are shown in the following table.

    (a) Use a greedy heuristic to assign each detail person to each hospital so that total expected sales are maximized.

    (b) Use the modified heuristic in Section 9.2 (i.e., after transforming the data by subtracting the maximum sales in each column from all other entries in that column, then use the greedy heuristic) to arrive at a new solution. How much better does this heuristic perform than the one used in part (a)?

TABLE 9.7

DETAIL PERSON	HOSPITAL				
	A	B	C	D	E
1	25	18	23	22	16
2	20	21	18	15	12
3	23	19	20	21	20
4	30	26	25	22	20
5	28	22	23	20	18

••9-6. Three jobs—J1, J2 and, J3—are to be machined on a lathe. The cost of setting up for a job depends on the setup for the previous job. The cost for changeovers is given in the accompanying table. Currently the lathe is not set up for any job.

    (a) Use the greedy heuristic to schedule the jobs. The objective is to minimize the total setup cost.

    (b) Use the modified heuristic in Section 9.2 to schedule the jobs.

    (c) Does the modified heuristic always produce a better result than the greedy one?

---

[2]Many heuristics have been proposed in the literature for attacking the facilities assignment model. In one study [see Mojena et. al.] involving 12 facilities, it is reported that achieving a true optimum with a branch-and-bound algorithm required two hours on a high-speed computer. In seven seconds the Best Pairwise Exchange Heuristic produced a proposal that was, in terms of associated objective values, within 3% of the optimum.

TABLE 9.8

	J1	J2	J3
No Setup	$50	$35	$39
J1	—	$30	$34
J2	$41	—	$30
J3	$35	$25	—

••9-7. Erma McZeal is in charge of quality control for the city of Chicago's water supply. There are currently three test stations located in Lake Michigan. Letting (x_1, x_2) denote coordinates in miles, the three existing locations are placed as follows:

$$\text{station 1: } x_1 = 2, x_2 = 10$$
$$\text{station 2: } x_1 = 6, x_2 = 6$$
$$\text{station 3: } x_1 = 1, x_2 = 3$$

Erma's job is to locate a new station in such a way as to minimize the total distance of the new station from the three existing stations. Assume that, because of existing channel marker locations, distance is measured rectangularly. In other words, if the new station is located at $(x_1 = 3, x_2 = 4)$, then it is a distance of $|3 - 2| + |4 - 10|$, or 7 $(= 1 + 6)$ units, from station 1; and so on. Let (x_1, x_2) denote the coordinates of the new station. Formulate a goal programming model to solve Erma's problem.

••9-8. Figure 9.30 is the precedence diagram for the activities in a project. The time and the personnel required for each activity are given in the following table. Use the workload smoothing heuristic to generate a schedule for this project.

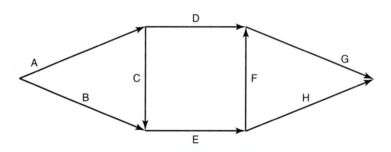

FIGURE 9.30

TABLE 9.9

ACTIVITY	TIME REQUIRED	PERSONNEL
A	1	4
B	2	5
C	1	3
D	2	2
E	2	7
F	1	7
G	1	5
H	1	4

9-9. **Product Mix.** A firm produces two products. Each one must be processed through two machines, each of which has available 240 minutes of capacity per day. Each unit of product 1 requires 20 minutes on machine 1 and 12 minutes on machine 2. Each unit of product 2 requires 12 minutes on machine 1 and 20 minutes on machine 2. In determining the daily product mix, management would like to achieve the following goals:

1. Joint total production of 12 units
2. Production of 9 units of product 2
3. Production of 10 units of product 1

Suppose that management wishes to minimize the underachievement of each of these goals and that predetermined priority weights w_1, w_2, and w_3 are to be assigned to the three goals, respectively. Formulate this as a goal programming model.

•• **9-10.** T & C Furniture Company (TCFC) manufactures tables and chairs. Write the goal constraints for the following objectives (let the variables T and C represent the number of tables and chairs, respectively, produced in a period):

    (a) A table takes 10 hours to make and a chair 5 hours. The total number of work hours available per period is 3200. Though idle time and overtime are acceptable, TCFC would like the total number of work hours to be as close to 3200 as possible.

    (b) A table uses one side of wood and a chair half a side; 300 sides of wood are available for a period and no more can be bought. TCFC would like to use as much of this wood as possible in one period.

    (c) TCFC makes tables to order and is committed to providing 200 tables in a period. Extra tables, if produced, have to be held in inventory, and the company would like to minimize the number of tables held in inventory.

    (d) The demand for chairs is uncertain, but is estimated to be between 200 and 250. The company would like to produce chairs as close to this range as possible.

9-11. Consider the goal programming model

$$\text{Min } P_1 v_1 + P_2 v_2 + P_3 u_3 + P_4(u_4 + v_4)$$

$$\begin{aligned}
\text{s.t.} \qquad x_2 + u_1 - v_1 &= 100 \\
x_1 + x_2 + u_2 - v_2 &= 80 \\
x_2 + u_3 &= 40 \\
x_1 + 2x_2 + u_4 - v_4 &= 160 \\
x_1, x_2, u_1, u_2, u_3, u_4, v_1, v_2, v_3, v_4 &\geq 0
\end{aligned}$$

    (a) Use the graphical method to solve the model.

    (b) Interpret the third goal $x_2 + u_3 = 40$.

    (c) Replace $x_2 + u_3 = 40$ with $x_2 + u_3 \geq 40$. What is the new interpretation?

    (d) Use the graphical method to solve the model with the replacement prescribed in (c).

9-12. Consider the goal programming model

$$\text{Min } P_1 v_1 + P_2 v_2 + P_3 v_3 + P_4(u_4 + v_4)$$

$$\begin{aligned}
\text{s.t.} \qquad x_2 + u_1 - v_1 &= 100 \\
x_1 + x_2 + u_2 - v_2 &= 80 \\
x_1 - v_3 &= 40 \\
x_1 + 2x_2 + u_4 - v_4 &= 160 \\
x_1, x_2, u_1, u_2, u_3, u_4, v_1, v_2, v_3, v_4 &\geq 0
\end{aligned}$$

    (a) Use the graphical method to solve the model.

    (b) Interpret the third goal $x_1 - v_3 = 40$.

    (c) Replace $x_1 - v_3 = 40$ with $x_1 - v_3 \leq 40$. What is the new interpretation?

    (d) Use the graphical method to solve the model with the replacement prescribed in (c).

9-13. Consider the following goal program:

$$\text{Min } P_1 u_2 + P_2 v_1 + P_3 u_3$$

$$\begin{aligned}
\text{s.t.} \quad x_1 + x_2 + u_1 - v_1 &= 80 \\
x_1 + u_2 - v_2 &= 100 \\
x_2 + u_3 &\geq 45 \\
x_1, x_2, u_1, v_1, u_2, v_2, u_3 &\geq 0
\end{aligned}$$

    (a) Solve by the graphical method.

    (b) Is the first-priority goal achieved?

    (c) What about the second and third?

    Note: In case of underachievement or overachievement, state actual numerical amounts of the violations.

•• **9-14.** Al transportation company operates warehouses and distributes goods to retail outlets. Al has warehouses at five different locations and has four retail customers. The transportation costs per unit, the demands, and the costs of operating the warehouses are given in the following table. All warehouses have unlimited capacity. Al would like to decide which warehouses should be operated and which should be closed. The greedy open heuristic for doing this consists of opening the warehouse that saves the most money and continuing to do this as long as money can be saved.
  (a)   Use the greedy open heuristic to solve this model. Which warehouses are opened?
  (b)   How much money is saved?

TABLE 9.10

WAREHOUSE	RETAILER				FIXED COST OF OPERATING WAREHOUSE
	A	B	C	D	
1	5	4	1	6	31
2	9	7	3	5	35
3	8	1	7	4	20
4	4	3	6	2	29
5	6	3	5	2	38
Demand	10	15	6	5	

9-15. There are six jobs to be processed on two machines (cutting and grinding). Each job must go through the cutting machine before being processed on the grinding machine. Assume that the sequence in which jobs are processed is the same on both machines.

   The accompanying table shows the time (in hours) required to finish a job on each machine. The objective is to schedule the jobs so that the time required to finish all jobs is minimized.
  (a)   How many alternatives should you compare for complete enumeration?
  (b)   What is the time required to finish all jobs if the jobs are processed in the ascending order of the total processing time?
  Note: A figure like Figure 9.7 may be helpful. In this application keep all tasks assigned to machine 1 in one row and those assigned to machine 2 in a second row.

TABLE 9.11

MACHINE	TIME REQUIRED FOR JOB (HOURS)					
	A	B	C	D	E	F
Cutting	3	4	2	1	5	3
Grinding	2	5	2	1	3	4
Total	5	9	4	2	8	7

•• **9-16.** Given the job-scheduling exercise in Problem 9-15, can you see any improvement when you apply the following heuristic method?
  Step 1: List the jobs along with their processing times on the cutting and grinding machines.
  Step 2: Find the job with the smallest processing time. If the smallest time is on the cutting machine, schedule the job as early as possible; if it is on the grinding machine, schedule it as late as possible. Break ties arbitrarily.
  Step 3: Eliminate the job from the list.
  Step 4: Repeat steps 2 and 3 until all jobs have been scheduled.

•• **9-17.** The city of Chicago is considering two projects. Each unit of Project A costs $400, generates 20 jobs, and returns $200 at the end of the year. Each unit of Project B costs $600, generates 40 jobs, and returns $200. The city planner would like to achieve the following goals:

1. Keep total expenditure at or below $2400.
2. Generate at least 120 jobs.
3. Maximize return at end of year.

Suppose that the three goals are in order of descending absolute priority.

(a) Use graphical analysis to find the optimal number of units to engage in each project.

(b) Are the goals achieved? If not, what are the underachievements?

(c) What are the net expenditure and the number of jobs generated?

••9-18. Another heuristic for solving Problem 9-14 is called the greedy close. In this case we start with all warehouses open and close the one which saves the most money. We continue to do this until we cannot close a warehouse without losing money.

(a) Solve Problem 9-14 using the greedy close heuristic.

(b) Is this solution better or worse than that in Problem 9-14?

••9-19. Use AHP to help Marlene Wyatt pick her first job out of college. She has three offers of employment (one in Bakersfield, California; one in Fresno, California; and one in Oildale, California) and has determined that there are three criteria (salary, stability of job, quality of town) that are important to her. See JOB.XLS on your student disk, which contains the following data shown in Figure 9.31.

	B6	=	=1/D4	
	A	B	C	D
1				
2				
3		Bakersfield	Fresno	Oildale
4	Bakersfield	1	4	0.5
5	Fresno	0.25	1	7
6	Oildale	2	0.14285714	1
7				

FIGURE 9.31

(a) What are the average ratings for the "Salary" criterion?

(b) Is Marlene consistent? How might you change the comparisons so that she is consistent?

(c) What are the average weights for each of the criterion?

(d) Which job would you recommend that Marlene take?

••9-20. Use AHP to help Mick Mott pick the university that he ought to attend for graduate school. He has two schools that have offered him scholarships (Harvard and Stanford) and has determined that there are four criteria (scholarship amount, prestige, cost to live there, quality of town) that are important to him. See COLLEGE.XLS on your student disk with the following data shown in Figure 9.32.

	A	B	C
1	⊕		
2			
3		Harvard	Stanford
4	Harvard	1	2
5	Stanford	0.5	1

FIGURE 9.32

(a) What are the average ratings for the "Prestige" criterion?

(b) What are the average weights for each of the criterion?

(c) Which university would you recommend that Mick attend in the fall?

••9-21. Use AHP to help Charles Shumway pick his brand new automobile. He has narrowed it down to three choices (Buick Regal, Toyota Camry, and Honda Accord) and has determined that there are three criteria (price, *Consumer Reports*'rating on reliability, speed/performance) that are important to him. See CAR.XLS on your student disk with the following data shown in Figure 9.33.

	A	B	C	D	E
1					
2					
3		Regal	Camry	Accord	
4	Regal	1	0.33333333	0.2	
5	Camry	3	1	0.5	
6	Accord	5	2	1	
7					

FIGURE 9.33

(a) What are the average ratings for the "Speed" criterion?

(b) What are the average weights for each of the criterion?

(c) Is Charles consistent with his weights?

(d) Which car would you recommend that Charles buy?

●●●**9-22.** Suppose that you have been hired by the city council of Peoria, Illinois (recall the second Application Capsule) to help them meet their overall tax goals. They have three goals (listed in order of descending priority):

1. Limit the tax burden on Lower Income (LI) people to $1.75 billion.

2. Keep the property tax rate under 1%.

3. Minimize the "flight to the suburbs" by keeping the tax burden on Middle Income (MI) people less than $2.5 billion and keeping the tax burden on High Income (HI) people to less than $1.25 billion.

4. Try to eliminate the food and drug sales tax if possible.

The city currently levies five types of taxes: (a) property taxes (where p is the tax rate), (b) sales tax on general items except food and drugs and durable goods (where s is the general sales tax rate), (c) sales tax on food and drugs (f is the sales tax rate on food and drugs), (d) sales tax on durable goods (d is the sales tax rate on durable goods), and (e) gasoline tax (g is the gasoline tax rate).

Relevant information on the revenue generated by a 1% tax is provided in Figure 9.34 (and in the workbook PEORIA.XLS) for each type of tax by category of income people (e.g., LI, MI, or HI).

	A	B	C	D	E	F	G	H	I	J
1			<---Type of Tax--->							
2	INCOME LEVEL	Property	Sales	Food&Drug	Durable	Gasoline				
3	Low (LI)	400	300	200	50	120				
4	Middle (MI)	1500	450	125	30	80		Table indicates the millions of		
5	High (HI)	1200	150	80	15	60		dollars raised by a 1% tax		

FIGURE 9.34

Assume that 10% of the LI people will move out of the city into the suburbs if their tax burden exceeds $1.75 billion, 20% of the MI people will move out of the city into the suburbs if their tax burden exceeds $2.5 billion, and 30% of the HI people will move out of the city into the suburbs if their tax burden exceeds $1.25 billion. You must work within the following "hard" constraints:

• The sales tax rate must be between 1% and 3%, as indicated in the Application Capsule.

• The total revenue raised must exceed the current level of $6.0 billion.

• The tax burden on the HI people can't exceed $1.5 billion.

• The tax burden on the MI people can't exceed $3.0 billion.

(a) Use goal programming to formulate this model.

(b) Which goals can you meet?

(c) What about the ones you can't?

W. Carl Lerhos, special assistant to the president of Sleepmore Mattress Manufacturing, had been asked to study the proposed consolidation of plants in three different locations. The company had just added several new facilities as a result of the acquisition of a competitor; some were in markets currently served by existing facilities. The president knew the dollar savings would be fairly easy to calculate for each location, but the qualitative factors and the trade-offs among them were more difficult to judge. This was the area in which he wanted Carl to spend most of his time.

The major objectives in evaluating a consolidation plan for the sites were to maximize manufacturing benefits, maximize sales benefits, and maximize direct financial benefits. These objectives would be composed of exploiting 13 attributes (see Exhibit 1). After spending some time looking at each attribute individually, Carl and the other officers of Sleepmore ranked them in order of most important to least important. They also added the best and worst possible outcomes for each attribute (see Exhibit 2).

Measurements

In each case, the attributes were assigned a number from 0 to 10, with 10 being the best possible outcome mentioned in Exhibit 2. Each location was in a different region, and each of the three locations involved a decision between two alternatives

—consolidate the plants there or keep them separate. The plants produced different product lines. Exhibits 3 to 5 give brief descriptions and scores of the three potential consolidation opportunities. Only the "consolidate" alternatives are scored; in other words, each "keep separate" alternative has a default score of 5 for each attribute. Therefore, the attributes are really scored *relative* to the current situation, in which the plants are separate.

---

[1]This case is to be used as the basis for class discussion rather than to illustrate either the effective or ineffective handling of an administrative situation. ©1990, Darden Graduate Business School Foundation. Preview Darden case abstracts on the World Wide Web at www.darden.virginia.edu/dems.

EXHIBIT 1 Hierarchy of Objectives

I. Maximize Manufacturing Benefits
   a. Labor
   b. Management effectiveness
      1. Talent availability
      2. Plant size
   c. Operability
      1. Product-line complexity
      2. Training
      3. Production stability
   d. Facilities
      1. Layout
      2. Location
      3. Space availability

II. Minimize Sales Benefits
   a. Maximize service
   b. Maximize quality

III. Maximize Direct Financial Benefits
   a. Minimize initial cost
   b. Maximize ongoing benefit

EXHIBIT 2 Thirteen Attributes Selected for Evaluation of Consolidation

RANK	ATTRIBUTE	WORST OUTCOME	BEST OUTCOME
1	Labor	Create hostile union	Eliminate hostile union
2	Quality	Drastically worsen quality	Strongly improve quality
3	Service	Lose business	Increase business
4	Annual savings	Lose $1 million/yr	Save $1 million/yr
5	Initial cost	Cost $5 million	Save $5 million
6	Management talent	Severely worsen management	Strongly improve management
7	Plant size (sales)	Create $35 million plant	Create $15 million plant
8	Plant location	Move from rural area to city	Move from city to rural area
9	Product-line complexity	Increased to full product line	Reduce product line
10	Space availability	Need a new facility (100,000 sq ft)	Save an expansion of 100,000 sq ft
11	Production stability	Increase demand variability	Decrease variability
12	Training	Train all new labor	Small layoff—no new training
13	Plant layout	Create poor layout	Eliminate poor layout

ATTRIBUTE	PLANT 1A	PLANT 1B	SCORE FOR COMBINING
Labor	Poor	Excellent	9; large improvement
Quality	Poor	Good	9
Service	Poor	Good	8
Annual savings	High overhead	Efficient; merger saves $1MM/yr	—
Initial cost	Save $1MM if plant merged	N/A	—
Management talent	Poor	Excellent	9
Plant size (sales)	$3 million	$27 million	—
Plant location	Large city	Rural area	10
Product-line complexity	2 major product lines	2 separate lines	0; very complex
Space availability	N/A	Has extra space; needs 0 new sq ft	—
Production stability	Small demand/high uncertainty	Large demand/low uncertainty	7; reduce variation
Training	N/A	Extra labor available	7.5
Plant layout	Congested plant	Well laid out	7.5

EXHIBIT 4 Consolidation Evaluated at Site 2: Put Plant 2B into Plant 2A

ATTRIBUTE	PLANT 2A	PLANT 2B	SCORE FOR COMBINING
Labor	Average	Poor	6
Quality	Average	Average	5
Service	Average	Good	7
Annual savings	Undercapacity; merger saves $500K	Undercapacity	—
Initial cost	N/A	Save $1MM if merge plant	—
Management talent	Average	Good	6
Plant size (sales)	$5 million	$10 million	—
Plant location	Industrial park	Large city	6
Product-line complexity	2 major product lines	2 different lines	0; very complex
Space availability	Need to add 50K sq ft if merge	No room	—
Production stability	Small demand/high uncertainty	Countercyclical demand	9; reduce variation
Training	Underutilized labor	Underutilized labor	9; small layoff
Plant layout	Excellent	Poor	9

EXHIBIT 5 Consolidation Evaluated at Site 3: Put Plant 3B into Plant 3A

ATTRIBUTE	PLANT 3A	PLANT 3B	SCORE FOR COMBINING
Labor	Below average	Good	3; may lose Plant 3A labor
Quality	Average	Average	5
Service	Average	Good	6
Annual savings	Undercapacity; merger saves $200K/yr	Efficient	—
Initial cost	N/A	Save $2MM if merge	—
Management talent	Average	Below average	6
Plant size (sales)	$9 million	$18 million	—
Plant location	Large city	Suburb	4
Product-line complexity	2 major product lines	2 different lines	0; very complex
Space availability	Need to add 30K sq ft if merge	No room	—
Production stability	Small demand/high uncertainty	Uncertain demand	6; demand not countercyclical
Training	Underutilized labor	N/A	3; some labor quits
Plant layout	Good	Cramped	7

The scores Carl assigned were based on subjective assessments after talking with the managers and visiting the sites.

Weights

After Carl had scored each attribute on his scale of 0–10, he faced the more difficult task of deciding how important one attribute was compared with another. The quantitative attributes would be fairly easy to weigh. He knew that the company's discount rate (15%), along with its planning horizon (10 years), might help in this regard, but he was not quite sure how.

He had heard the president say, "The smaller a plant, the easier it is to manage. If we could improve from a $35 million plant size to a $15 million plant, the gain would be equivalent to a savings from the status quo of $1 million a year in operating costs." Carl made a quick mental calculation that suggested the weight for plant size would be one-half the weight for annual savings—he'd have to check it later though.

The mattress-manufacturing industry required a lot of space. If a consolidation required a new plant or a significant addition, the hassle of moving, as well as hidden expenses, would be additional negative factors. The cost would be $25/sq ft for each additional sq ft of space.

To help him in assigning weights to the other, more qualitative attributes, Carl pulled out his notes from a meeting attended by the president, the vice-president of operations, and the vice-president of human resources. At this meeting, held at the time of the acquisition, the list shown in Exhibit 2 had been generated and the relative importance of each attribute had been discussed.

The vice-president of human resources had said, "Labor is the most important, because the quality of labor determines the major aspects of plant performance (like quality, profitability, and so on). Experience has shown that a good labor force can overcome many obstacles, but a poor labor force leads to trouble. In fact, I think labor is twice as important as the average of all 13 attributes." Carl wondered about the context for this statement. He verified that the vice-president had the ranges of Exhibit 2 in mind: improving labor relations from "create hostile union" to "eliminate hostile union" was twice as valuable as improving the average attribute from worst to best.

The vice-president of operations agreed with the comment about labor and said, "I think quality and service, although slightly less important than labor, are two other attributes that deserve more weight than average."

There seemed to be a consensus that management was the next most important qualitative attribute because, like labor, management would determine the fate of the plant. Unlike labor, however, management could be rather easily changed. Overall, this attribute was considered "average" in terms of importance.

The president then argued for consideration of plant location: "Plant location is as important as plant size. Our data show that plants in more congested areas (cities) tend to be less profitable than plants in rural areas."

The vice-president of operations said, "Because Sleepmore produces a different product line in different plants, consolidations could drastically increase complexity and reduce long-term efficiency. I move that product-line complexity be considered the next most important qualitative attribute, albeit its importance is about two-thirds the importance of management talent, in my opinion."

The remaining three attributes—stability, training, and layout—were agreed to have individual effects that were relatively small, but their combined effect was considered about twice that of product-line complexity.

The hardest task was to evaluate the trade-offs that management would be willing to make between quantitative and qualitative factors. In this regard, the president had expressed difficulty to Carl in choosing between a situation with initial cost savings of $7 million and a situation where a hostile union was eliminated.

Decision

Carl had to figure out an effective way to combine all this information about both quantitative and qualitative factors to make decisions whether to consolidate at *each* of the three sites. He wondered how sensitive his decisions would be to the weights he assigned each attribute.

References

Colin Benjamin, Ike Ehie, and Yildirim Omurtag, "Planning Facilities at the University of Missouri–Rolla," *Interfaces,* 22, no. 4 (1992), 95–105.

Abraham Charnes and William Cooper, *Management Models and Industrial Applications of Linear Programming* (New York: John Wiley, 1961).

James Chrisman, Timothy Fry, Gary Reeves, Holly Lewis, and Robert Weinstein, "A Multiobjective Linear Programming Methodology for Public Sector Tax Planning," *Interfaces* 19, no. 5 (1989), 13–30.

William Gavett, "Three Heuristic Rules for Sequencing Jobs to a Single Production Facility," *Management Science,* vol. 11 (1965), B166–B176.

Richard Mojena, Thomas Vollmann, and Yoshihiro Okamoto, "On Predicting Computational Time of a Branch-and-Bound Algorithm for the Assignment of Facilities," *Decision Sciences,* 7, no. 4 (1976), 856–867.

Thomas Saaty, *The Analytic Hierarchy Process* (New York: McGraw-Hill, 1988).

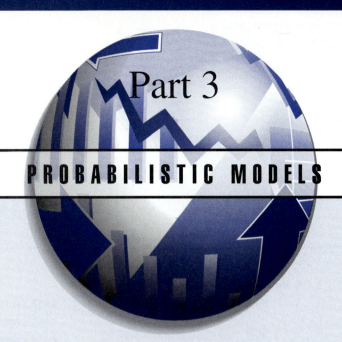

Part 3

PROBABILISTIC MODELS

We all know the saying: Only two things are sure, death and taxes. Although it can be taken as a complaint about governments, this remark also expresses a rather fundamental view of nature and human enterprise. It suggests that most earthly phenomena include some element of uncertainty and unpredictability. The biblical Book of Ecclesiastes makes the same observation about human endeavors: "Time and chance happeneth to them all."

We respond to this fact of life in various ways. In some situations we choose to ignore the uncertainty; in others we attempt to deal with it explicitly. We have spent the last nine chapters ignoring uncertainty. In the next five chapters we confront situations in which the level of uncertainty is too great to ignore, and we as managers must take this into account. There are many examples: The entire insurance industry is one. Others include investments in stocks, bonds, and real estate, as well as any business in which a product is created in anticipation of demand.

This part of the book is devoted to clarifying our way of thinking about uncertainty and developing methods for dealing with it in decision models. Our goal is to help you frame problems in which uncertainty plays a major role in a consistent and useful manner and to provide you with some helpful problem-solving techniques. The focus remains the same: We consider situations in which management has the opportunity to choose between several alternatives. But now the problem is complicated by the fact that we are not sure what the payoff will be for each of the alternatives.

Probability is the branch of mathematics that provides the foundation for the analysis in this part of the book. The language of probability is part of our everyday experience: Weather forecasts say that the *chance* of rain is 30%, *odds* on sporting events are quoted in the newspapers, and the government worries about the *probable* effects of the proposed tax law. Closer examination, however, often reveals considerable confusion about what such terms and statements really mean. To understand these chapters you will have to start with (or develop) an understanding of some concepts related to probability. Appendix A in the back of the book contains a brief introduction to the crucial concepts. The material in this appendix should provide an adequate background to enable you to master the material in this part of the text.

Probability is a difficult topic for many students. You may not find it hard to read these chapters and do the assignments; what is hard is making probability a part of your personal approach to problem solving. This will occur only when you come to think naturally about a *distribution* of profits or waiting times or demands and when you have convenient tools to use on real problems. Here again, computing plays an important role—especially in simulation. It is possible to simulate interesting problems using spreadsheets, and especially easy with the spreadsheet add-ins, Crystal Ball and @RISK. These tools are discussed in the simulation chapter of this part. We strongly encourage you to use this software and do the simulation exercises, which will greatly enhance the ultimate value of your study. The decision analysis and queuing chapters also introduce some nifty spreadsheet accessories to help you implement these tools successfully.

The following chapters are contained in this part:

Chapter 10 Decision Analysis

Chapter 11 Monte Carlo Simulation

Chapter 12 Queuing

Chapter 13 Forecasting

Chapter 14 Project Management: PERT and CPM

CHAPTER OUTLINE

10.1 Introduction

10.2 Three Classes of Decision Models

10.3 The Expected Value of Perfect Information: Newsboy Model Under Risk

10.4 Utilities and Decisions Under Risk

10.5 A Mid-Chapter Summary

10.6 Decision Trees: Marketing Home and Garden Tractors

10.7 Sensitivity Analysis

10.8 Decision Trees: Incorporating New Information

10.9 Sequential Decisions: To Test or Not to Test

10.10 Management and Decision Theory

10.11 Notes on Implementation

10.12 Summary

KEY TERMS

SELF-REVIEW EXERCISES

PROBLEMS

CASE STUDY: Johnson's Metal

CASE STUDY: To Drill or Not to Drill

CASE STUDY: Shumway, Horch, and Sager (A)

APPENDIX 10.1
    Conditional Probability and Bayes' Theorem

REFERENCES

APPLICATION CAPSULE   **Testing Student Athletes for Drug Use**

The athletic governing board of Santa Clara University had to decide whether to recommend implementing a drug-testing program for its intercollegiate athletes. The techniques of decision analysis were applied to the proposed drug-testing program. A simple decision model that treats the question of whether or not to test a single individual for the presence of drugs was developed.

The developer of the model believed that the most important aspect of this question was the consequence of testing errors. Another important issue was the benefits of identification of a drug user compared with the costs of errors (false accusations of usage and nonidentification of users). The basic decision tree has two main alternatives—"test" or "don't test." If no testing is performed, then the outcome of that decision is a lottery (random event) on whether the individual uses drugs or doesn't. The probability of these events is determined by the fraction of the student population that uses drugs. If the individual doesn't use drugs, there is no cost, but if he or she does there is a cost of having an unidentified user.

If the "test" alternative is chosen, the test would be administered and the results would be determined by the appropriate lab. The results could either be "+" or "−." If the result is "+" the de-

cision maker must decide whether to "act" or "not act." Generally, it was assumed that the decision maker will act if a "+" test is obtained. The consequence of acting is a lottery on the true state of drug usage by the individual. The probability that an individual is a drug user conditioned upon a "+" test result is known as a posterior probability and is determined by Bayes' Theorem and is not equal to 1.0. Interestingly enough, if the test is 95% reliable and approximately 5% of the student population are drug users, then there is only a 50% chance that the test will correctly predict whether the individual who tested positive is actually a drug user (i.e., it is no more predictive than tossing a coin)!

Next, the costs must be determined for each possible outcome. The accurate identification of a drug user was assigned a cost of 0. Falsely accusing a nonuser was given a cost of C_1, doing nothing with a drug user was assigned a cost of C_2, and finally the cost of invading the privacy of a nonuser by forcing him to take a drug test was given the cost of C_3. Based on these costs, conditions were developed under which the expected cost of testing was lower than that of not testing (meaning it would be the rational decision to test). The main condition related the posterior probability discussed earlier to a ratio of the three costs. If it were believed that the ratio of costs of the errors were one-tenth, then the posterior probability would have to be larger than 90%.

At the final board meeting where the issue was discussed and voted on, the athletic director reviewed the memo containing the decision analysis. The main discussion centered on evaluating the parameters of the decision model (e.g., the probabilities and costs). The board concluded that the incidence of drug use on campus was so low and the cost of false accusation so high that drug testing was not the correct decision. They thus voted unanimously not to recommend implementation of the testing program (See Feinstein).

10.1   INTRODUCTION

Decision analysis provides a framework for analyzing a wide variety of management models. The framework establishes (1) a system of classifying decision models based on the amount of information about the model that is available and (2) a decision criterion; that is, a measure of the "goodness" of a decision for each type of model.

In the first part of this chapter we will present the decision theory framework and relate it to models previously discussed. The second half of the chapter is devoted to decision trees. Decision trees apply decision theory concepts to sequential decisions that include uncertain events. They are a pragmatic and practical aid to managerial decision making.

In general terms, decision theory treats decisions against nature. This phrase refers to a situation where the result (return) from an individual decision depends on the action of another player (nature), over which you have no control. For example, if the decision is whether or not to carry an umbrella, the return (get wet or not) depends on the state of nature that ensues. It is important to note that in this model the returns accrue only to the decision maker. Nature does not care what the outcome is. This condition distinguishes decision theory from game theory. In *game theory* both players have an economic interest in the outcome.

In decision theory models, the fundamental piece of data is a **payoff table** like Table 10.1. The alternative decisions are listed along the side of the table, and the possible states of nature are listed across the top. The entries in the body of the table are the payoffs for all possible combinations of decisions and states of nature. The decision process proceeds as follows:

1. You, the decision maker, select one of the alternative decisions $d_1, \ldots, d_n$. Suppose that you select d_1.

2. After your decision is made, a state of nature occurs that is beyond your control. Suppose that state 2 occurs.

3. The return you receive can now be determined from the payoff table. Since you made decision d_1 and state of nature 2 occurred, the return is r_{12}.

Again, the decision is made first, then one of the states of nature occurs. Once the decision has been made, it can't be changed after the state of nature occurs. In general terms

---

TABLE 10.1 Payoff Table

DECISION	STATE OF NATURE			
	1	2	...	m
d_1	r_{11}	r_{12}	...	r_{1m}
d_2	r_{21}	r_{22}	...	r_{2m}
⋮	⋮	⋮	⋮	⋮
d_n	r_{n1}	r_{n2}	...	r_{nm}

the question is, Which of the decisions should we select? We would like as large a return as possible; that is, the largest possible value of r_{ij}, where i represents the decision made and j the state of nature that occurs. It is obvious that the decision we should select will depend on our belief concerning what nature will do, that is, which state of nature will occur. If we believe state 1 will occur, we select the decision associated with the largest number in column 1. If we believe the state of nature is more likely to be state 2, we choose the decision corresponding to the largest payoff in column 2, and so on.

In the following section we will consider different assumptions about nature's behavior. Each assumption leads to a different *criterion* for selecting the "best" decision, and hence to a different procedure.

10.2 THREE CLASSES OF DECISION MODELS

This section deals with three classes of decision models against nature. Each class is defined by an assumption about nature's behavior. The three classes are decisions under certainty, decisions under risk, and decisions under uncertainty. Of the three, we are most likely to encounter decisions under risk, but the other two classes are presented for completeness.

DECISIONS UNDER CERTAINTY

A **decision under certainty** is one in which you know which state of nature will occur. Alternatively, you can think of it as a case with a single state of nature. Suppose, for example, that in the morning you are deciding whether to take your umbrella to work and you know *for sure* that it will be raining when you leave work in the afternoon. In the payoff table for this model, Table 10.2, $7 is the cost of having your suit cleaned if you get caught in the rain. It enters the table with a minus sign since it is a table of returns and a cost is a negative return. Obviously, the optimal decision is to take the umbrella.

All linear programming models, integer programming models, nonlinear programming models, and other deterministic models such as the EOQ model can be thought of as decisions against nature in which there is only one state of nature. This is so because we are sure (within the context of the model) what return we will get for each decision we make. For a concrete example, consider the PROTRAC E and F model of Chapter 3:

$$\text{Max } 5000E + 4000F$$
$$\text{s.t.} \quad 10E + 15F \leq 150$$
$$20E + 10F \leq 160$$
$$30E + 10F \geq 135$$
$$E - 3F \leq 0$$
$$E + F \geq 5$$
$$E, F \geq 0$$

Table 10.3 presents this model in the form of a payoff table. In this table, a return of $-\infty$ is assigned to any infeasible decision. For example, since $E = 0$, $F = 0$ violates the third and fifth constraints, the associated return is defined to be $-\infty$. For any feasible pair (E, F) the return is defined to be the objective function value—namely, $5000E + 4000F$. For this model we know exactly what return we get for each decision (each choice of the

TABLE 10.2 Umbrella Example Payoff Table	
	RAIN
Take Umbrella	0
Do Not	−7.00

TABLE 10.3 Payoff Table for the PROTRAC *E* and *F* Model

DECISION	STATE OF NATURE
$E = 0, F = 0$	$-\infty$
$E = 5; F = 4$	41,000
⋮	⋮
$E = 6, F = 3.5$	44,000
⋮	⋮

pair *E, F*). We can thus list all returns in one column and think of it as representing one state of nature that we are sure will occur.

Conceptually, it is easy to solve a model with one state of nature. You simply select the decision that yields the highest return. In practice, as opposed to "in concept," finding such a decision may be another story. Since *E* and *F* can take on an infinite number of values, there will be an infinite number of rows for this model (see Table 10.3). Even in this simple model, enumerating the alternatives and selecting the best of them are not possible. Additional mathematical analysis (in this case, the Solver algorithm of Excel) is needed to find the optimal decision.

DECISIONS UNDER RISK

A lack of certainty about future events is a characteristic of many, if not most, management decision models. Consider how the decisions of the financial vice-president of an insurance company would change if she could know exactly what changes were to occur in the bond market. Imagine the relief of the head buyer for Maxwell House if he could know exactly how large next year's crop of coffee beans would be.

It thus seems clear that numerous decision models are characterized by a lack of certainty. It is also clear that those who deal effectively with these models, through either skill or luck, are often handsomely rewarded for their accomplishments. In the first book of the Old Testament, Joseph is promoted from slave to assistant Pharaoh of Egypt by accurately forecasting 7 years of feast and 7 years of famine.[1]

In quantitative modeling, the lack of certainty can be dealt with in various ways. For example, in a linear programming model, some of the data may be an estimate of a future value. In the above PROTRAC *E* and *F* model, next month's capacity (availability of hours) in department A (the right-hand side of the first constraint) may depend on factors that will occur next week, but the production plans, let us say, must be spelled out today. As previously described in Chapter 5 (LP sensitivity analysis), management might deal with this lack of certainty by estimating the capacity as 150 and then performing sensitivity analysis.

Definition of Risk Decision theory provides alternative approaches to models with less than complete certainty. One such approach is called **decisions under risk.** In this context, the term *risk* has a restrictive and well-defined meaning. When we speak of decisions under risk, we are referring to a class of decision models for which there is more than one state of nature and for which we make the assumption that *the decision maker can arrive at a probability estimate for the occurrence for each of the various states of nature.* Suppose, for example, that there are $m > 1$ states of nature, and let p_j be the probability estimate that state j will occur. Generally we will estimate the probability of state j occurring (p_j) using historical frequencies, meaning we'll look back over history and record what percentage of time that state j actually occurred out of our entire pool of observations. For example, if in the last

---

[1] As well as being an accurate forecaster, by virtue of his skill in successfully interpreting Pharaoh's dreams, Joseph has been called the first psychoanalyst. Less well known is the fact that Joseph was also the first management scientist. In anticipation of the famine, he advised Pharaoh to build storage facilities to hold inventories of grain. When it was all over and the famine had been survived, Joseph was asked how he had come to acquire such wisdom and knowledge. "Lean-year programming" was his reply.

1000 days, we find that it rained on 200 of those days, then we'll estimate the future probability of rain on a given day as 0.20 (= 200/1000). When this historical data is not available or the manager feels that it is not relevant to the future, the manager must make subjective estimates of these probabilities. This latter approach will be covered in Section 10.10.

Recall that the expected value of any random variable is the weighted average of all possible values of the random variable, where the weights are the probabilities of the values occurring. Since different returns are associated with different states of nature, the expected return associated with decision i is the sum, over all possible states j, of terms of the form: (return in state j when decision is i) times (the probability of state j), or $r_{ij} p_j$. We can then use the following equation to calculate ER_i, the expected return if we make decision i:

$$ER_i = \sum_{j=1}^{m} r_{ij} \cdot p_j = r_{i1}p_1 + r_{i2}p_2 + \cdots + r_{im}p_m \qquad (10.1)$$

For this type of model, *management should then make the decision that maximizes the expected return.*[2] In other words, $i*$ is the optimal decision where

$$ER_{i*} = \text{maximum over all } i \text{ of } ER_i$$

The Newsboy Model An example of such a model is the following newsboy model. (Similar models are treated in Chapter 11.) A newsboy can buy the *Wall Street Journal* newspapers for 40 cents each and sell them for 75 cents. However, he must buy the papers before he knows how many he can actually sell. If he buys more papers than he can sell, he simply disposes of the excess at no additional cost. If he does not buy enough papers, he loses potential sales now and possibly in the future (disgruntled customers may no longer buy their papers from him). Suppose, for the moment, that this loss of *future* sales is captured by a cost of lost goodwill of 50 cents per unsatisfied customer. For illustrative purposes and ease of computation, also suppose that the demand distribution he faces is

$$P_0 = \text{Prob}\{\text{demand} = 0\} = 0.1$$
$$P_1 = \text{Prob}\{\text{demand} = 1\} = 0.3$$
$$P_2 = \text{Prob}\{\text{demand} = 2\} = 0.4$$
$$P_3 = \text{Prob}\{\text{demand} = 3\} = 0.2$$

In this model, each of the four different values for demand is a different state of nature, and the number of papers ordered is the decision. The returns, or payoffs, for this model are shown in Table 10.4.

The entries in this table represent the net cash flow associated with each combination of number ordered and number demanded, less the cost of lost goodwill when the number ordered is not sufficient to meet the number demanded. These entries are calculated with the expression

payoff = 75 (number of papers sold) − 40 (number of papers ordered)

− 50 (unmet demand)

TABLE 10.4 Payoff Table for the Newsboy Model

	STATE OF NATURE (DEMAND)			
DECISION	0	1	2	3
0	0	−50	−100	−150
1	−40	35	−15	−65
2	−80	−5	70	20
3	−120	−45	30	105

---

[2]It will be shown that this is equivalent to another criterion: *minimizing* expected regret.

where 75 cents is the selling price per paper, 40 cents is the cost of buying a paper, and 50 cents is the cost of disappointing a customer (cost of lost goodwill). It is important to note that in this model, sales and demand need not be identical. Indeed, sales is the minimum of the two quantities (number ordered, number demanded). For example, when no papers are ordered, then clearly none can be sold, no matter how many are demanded, and the unmet demand will equal the demand. Thus, for all entries in the first row, the above expression for the payoff gives $75(0) - 40(0) - 50(\text{demand}) = -50(\text{demand})$. If 1 paper is ordered and none are demanded, then none are sold, the unmet demand is 0, and the payoff is $75(0) - 40(1) - 50(0) = -40$, which is the first entry in row 2. However, if 1 paper is ordered and 1 or more are demanded, then exactly 1 will be sold, the unmet demand will be 1 less than the demand, and the payoff becomes $75(1) - 40(1) - 50(\text{demand} - 1) = 85 - 50(\text{demand})$. Can you verify that the remaining values in the body of Table 10.4 are correct? Also think about why the possible decisions of ordering 4 or more papers were ignored.

Once all the data are assembled in Table 10.4, the process of finding the optimal decision is strictly mechanical. You use equation (10.1) to evaluate the expected return for each decision (ER_i for $i = 0, 1, 2, 3$) and pick the largest. We will first demonstrate this process by hand and then we'll show how to do it in a spreadsheet. For example, if you order two papers,

$$ER_2 = -80(0.1) - 5(0.3) + 70(0.4) + 20(0.2) = 22.5$$

The first term is the return if we order 2 papers and 0 are demanded multiplied by the probability that 0 are demanded. The second term is the return if we order 2 papers and 1 is demanded (see Table 10.4) multiplied by the probability that 1 paper is demanded. The other terms are similarly defined. The expected returns for all of the other possible decisions are calculated as follows:

$$ER_0 = 0(0.1) - 50(0.3) - 100(0.4) - 150(0.2) = -85$$
$$ER_1 = -40(0.1) + 35(0.3) - 15(0.4) - 65(0.2) = -12.5$$
$$ER_3 = -120(0.1) - 45(0.3) + 30(0.4) + 105(0.2) = 7.5$$

Since ER_2 is the largest of these four values, the optimal decision is to order 2 papers.

Another way to compare the decisions is to look at a graph of their risk profiles. The **risk profile** shows all the possible outcomes with their associated probabilities for a given decision and gives the manager an idea of the range of outcomes possible. Some managers find this more helpful than simply looking at one number (e.g., expected return) that summarizes all the available information (probabilities and potential outcomes). The risk profiles for the four decisions that the newsboy faces are shown in Figure 10.1.

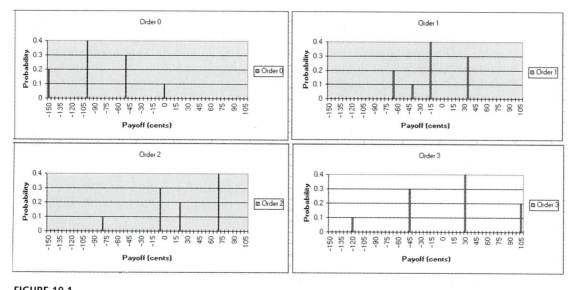

FIGURE 10.1

Risk Profiles of Four Newsboy Decisions

B7	▼	=$B$1*MIN($A7,B$6)-$B$2*$A7-$B$3*MAX(B$6-$A7,0)						
	A	B	C	D	E	F	G	H	I
1	Selling Price	75							
2	Purchase Cost	40							
3	Goodwill Cost	50							
4									
5				States of Nature					
6	Decision		0	1	2	3	Expected Return		
7		0	0	-50	-100	-150	-85		
8		1	-40	35	-15	-65	-12.5		
9		2	-80	-5	70	20	22.5		
10		3	-120	-45	30	105	7.5		
11									
12	Probabilities		0.1	0.3	0.4	0.2			
13									
14									
15							✥		
16									
17									
18									
19									

Cell	Formula	Copy To
B7	= $B$1*MIN($A7,B$6)–$B$2*$A7–$B$3*MAX(B$6–$A7,0)	B7:E10
F7	= SUMPRODUCT (B7:E7,$B$12:$E$12)	F8:F10

FIGURE 10.2

Newsboy Spreadsheet

We can see that all four of the possible outcomes for "Order 0" are less than or equal to zero. Seventy-five percent of the outcomes for "Order 1" are nonpositive, and 50% of the outcomes for "Order 2" and "Order 3" are nonpositive. We can also see that Order 2 has a high probability (40%) of generating the second highest payoff of all (70 cents). Of course, all of this information is available in the original payoff table, but sometimes it helps to see the data in a graph.

The Cost of Lost Goodwill: A Spreadsheet Sensitivity Analysis This decision is based on a cost, the cost of lost goodwill, whose value is much less certain than the other two parameters, the selling price and the purchase cost. What would happen to the optimal decision if the cost of lost goodwill were different? To answer this question we will perform a sensitivity analysis on the value of the cost of lost goodwill.

One possible way to do this would be to assume a different value for the cost of lost goodwill, recalculate the payoff matrix, recompute the expected returns, and see what happens to the optimal decision. This would be tiresome to do by hand, but is ideally suited to be done in Excel. Figure 10.2 shows the spreadsheet (NEWSBOY.XLS) for calculating the payoff matrix and expected returns.

The known prices and costs are entered with their labels in cells A1:B3. The payoff for any given combination of decision/state of nature is shown in the equation line of Figure 10.2 and is calculated as follows:

The first term calculates the revenue from sales: the Selling Price ($B$1) times the number sold (the smaller of the number ordered and the number demanded, = MIN($A7,B$6)). The second term subtracts the cost of the papers purchased: the Purchase Cost ($B$2) times the number of papers purchased ($A7). The final term subtracts the lost goodwill: the Goodwill Cost ($B$3) times the unmet demand (the larger of the demand minus the quantity ordered or 0, = MAX(B$6–$A7,0)).

This formula in cell B7 has been constructed carefully using Excel's relative and absolute cell referencing so that it can be copied to obtain all the other formulas in the payoff matrix. The expected return column (column F) can be generated by using the SUMPRODUCT formula. For example, in cell F7, we enter =SUMPRODUCT(B7:E7,$B$12:$E$12),

	A	B	C	D	E
15		-85	-12.5	22.5	7.5
16	0				
17	5				
18	10				
19	15				
20	20				
21	25				
22	30				
23	35				
24	40				
25	45				
26	50				
27	55				
28	60				
29	65				
30	70				
31	75				
32	80				
33	85				
34	90				
35	95				
36	100				

Table

Row input cell: [ ] OK

Column input cell: $B$3 Cancel

FIGURE 10.3

Data Table Setup for Newsboy Model

which is just the sum of the products of the probability of receiving a given payoff times the respective payoff.

Using the Data Table command, a table of expected returns can easily be generated for a range of Goodwill Costs. We've done this in a new spreadsheet "Sensitivity to Goodwill" in the same NEWSBOY.XLS. The Data Table will show the expected returns for the different order quantities for values of the Goodwill Cost between 0 and 150 in five-cent increments. In order to do this yourself, follow these steps:

1. Copy the entire "Base Case" spreadsheet over to the new spreadsheet "Sensitivity to Goodwill."

2. Enter the initial value (0) for the Goodwill costs we're going to investigate in cell A16.

3. Click back on cell A16, then click on the Edit menu, then Fill, then Series.

4. Click on "Series in Columns," enter a step value of 5 and a stop value of 150. Click on OK.

5. In cell B15 we want to enter the cell formula that gives us the expected return when we order 0 papers (=F7). In cells C15:E15 we want to do a similar thing so that the Data Table will give us the expected returns for ordering 1, 2, and 3 papers (i.e., enter =F8, =F9, =F10, respectively, in these cells).

6. Click on the Data menu, then Table. Enter the column input cell as $B$3 as shown in Figure 10.3. We're telling Excel to put the values found in column A into cell B3 (one-at-a-time) and then report back to us in columns B, C, D, and E the values it calculated in cells F7:F10.

After the Data Table does its calculations, we want to present a graph of the results to help us sort out this sea of numbers. To do this we use Excel's Graph Wizard as follows:

1. Highlight the range of data we want to graph (A16:E46).

2. Click on the Graph Wizard icon in Excel (which automatically walks us through several steps); drag and place it anywhere in the spreadsheet where you want the graph to be situated.

3. In the first step, you choose the kind of graph you want. Click on "Line" then click on the Chart sub-type you want (the default one [fourth] is fine) and then click on "Next>."

4. Now the Wizard shows us a sample of what the graph will look like. We only need to make one modification here. Click on the "Series" tab and then indicate that the

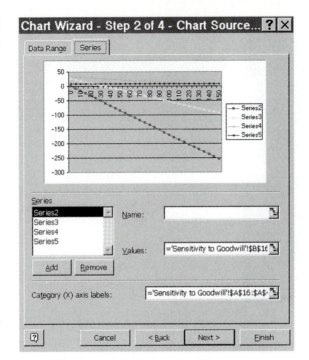

FIGURE 10.4

Chart Wizard for
Newsboy Model

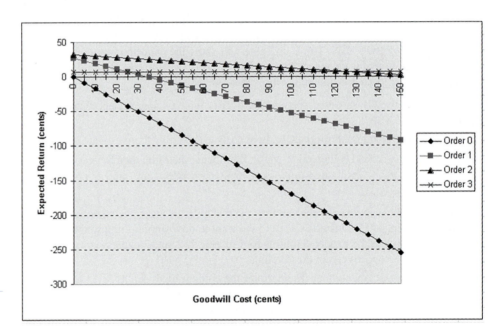

FIGURE 10.5

Graph of Sensitivity Analysis
for Goodwill Cost

"Category (X) axis labels" are found in A16:A46, as shown in Figure 10.4. Then we re-move Series 1 from the display since it now serves as our *X*-axis label. Click on "Next>."

5. Next we have the option to enter titles for the graph or labels for the axes. We enter the appropriate values and then click on "Next>."

6. Lastly, we indicate that we want the chart placed as an object in our current worksheet (which is the default choice) and click on "Finish."

7. A graph like that shown in Figure 10.5 is displayed. (We have altered the four series legends from a generic "Series 1, Series 2, Series 3, Series 4" to "Order 0, Order 1, Order 2, Order 3" by using some of the advanced features in Excel.)

Notice that as the Goodwill Cost increases, the expected returns either decrease (when 0, 1, or 2 papers are ordered) or remain constant (when 3 papers are ordered). For Goodwill Costs less than 125 cents, the optimal decision is to order 2 papers. For a Goodwill Cost of 125 cents, alternative optima exist: order 2 or 3 papers. For a Goodwill Cost greater than 125 cents, the optimal decision is to order 3 papers. Thus, it is not necessary to know the Goodwill Cost precisely, just whether it is greater than or less than 125 cents. These results are reminiscent of the sensitivity analysis of a cost coefficient in a linear programming model where the optimal solution did not change for values of the coefficient in a given range. With this example, we have now illustrated the most important class of decision models (decisions under risk) and the associated decision criterion (maximize the expected return).

DECISIONS UNDER UNCERTAINTY (OPTIONAL)

In **decisions under uncertainty** we again have more than one possible state of nature, but now the decision maker is unwilling or unable to specify the probabilities that the various states of nature will occur. There is a long-standing debate as to whether such a situation should exist; that is, should the decision maker always be willing to at least subjectively specify the probabilities even when he or she does not know very much (anything) about what state of nature is apt to occur? Although it is hard to imagine an actual business decision being made under such a cloud, we'll leave this debate to the philosophers and turn to the various approaches suggested for this class of models for those who are interested. Notice that we have indicated that this section is optional for those who consider "Decisions Under Risk" to be the most relevant topic. For such readers, please skip ahead to Section 10.3.

Laplace Criterion   The Laplace criterion approach interprets the condition of "uncertainty" as equivalent to assuming that all states of nature are equally likely. This is the point of view: "If I know nothing, then anything is equally likely." For example, in the newsboy model, assuming all states are equally likely means that since there are four states, each state occurs with probability 0.25. Using these probabilities converts the model to a decision under risk, and one could then compute the expected return. You can easily verify that, using these probabilities, expected return would again be maximized by the decision to order 2 papers. When using the Laplace criterion, since each state has equal probability, all you need to do to find the best decision is to add up all the payoffs for each decision and choose the decision with the largest sum (which will also have the largest average payoff).

Although in some situations this "equally likely" approach may produce acceptable results, in other settings it would be inappropriate. For example, consider your friend from Turkmenistan, about to watch the football game between Ohio State and Michigan in a year in which one team is experiencing a bad season and the other is thus heavily favored in the betting. Although your friend knows nothing about football and has no knowledge about the probability of either team winning, these probabilities clearly exist and are *not* equal. In other words, even though one has "no knowledge," there may be underlying probabilities on the various states of nature, and these probabilities may in no way be consistent with the "equal likelihood" assumption. With this realization, there may be contexts in which you would not wish to use the criterion of expected return based on the equal-likelihood assumption (i.e., the Laplace criterion).

For such cases, there are three different criteria that can be used to make decisions under uncertainty: *maximin, maximax,* and *minimax regret.* All of these criteria can be used without specifying probabilities. The discussion will be illustrated with the newsboy model. Look at the earlier payoff table for a moment and think of what criterion you might use to make a decision. By this we mean, think of a rule that you could describe to a friend. It has to be a general rule so that your friend could apply it to any payoff table and come up with a decision. Remember, you are willing to make no assumptions about the probabilities on states of nature. Now consider the following criteria.

Maximin Criterion   The **maximin criterion** is an extremely conservative, or perhaps pessimistic, approach to making decisions. It evaluates each decision by the worst thing that

TABLE 10.5 Newsboy Minimum Return Table

DECISION	MINIMUM RETURN
0	−150
1	−65
2	−80
3	−120

TABLE 10.6 Payoff Table: Maximin Counter Example

DECISION	STATE OF NATURE								
	1	2	3	4	5	6	7	8	9
1	100	100	2	100	100	100	100	100	100
2	3	3	3	3	3	3	3	3	3

can happen if you make that decision. In this case, then, it evaluates each decision by the *minimum* possible return associated with the decision. In the newsboy example the minimum possible return if 3 papers are ordered is −120; thus, this value is assigned to the decision "order 3 papers." Similarly, we can associate with each other decision the minimum value in its row. Following this rule enables the decision maker to prepare a table as shown in Table 10.5. The decision that yields the maximum value of the minimum returns (hence, maximin) is then selected. In this case, the newsboy should order 1 paper.

Maximin is often used in situations where the planner feels he or she cannot afford to be wrong. (Defense planning might be an example, as would investing your life savings.) The planner chooses a decision that does as well as possible in the worst possible (most pessimistic) case.

It is, however, easy to create examples in which most people would not accept the decision selected with the maximin criterion. Consider, for example, the payoff table in Table 10.6. Most people would prefer decision 1. It is much better than decision 2 for all states of nature except state 3, and then it is only slightly worse. Nevertheless, the maximin criterion would select decision 2. If you are among those who strongly prefer decision 1 in this example, you must then ask yourself the following question: "If the maximin criterion provides an answer that I don't like in this simple example, would I be willing to use it on more complicated and important models?" There is no correct answer to this question. The answer depends on the taste of the decision maker, but you begin to see why we don't stress the decision rules of this section as heavily as the maximize expected value rule of the "Decisions Under Risk" section.

Maximax Criterion The **maximax criterion** is as optimistic as maximin is pessimistic. It evaluates each decision by the best thing that can happen if you make that decision. In this case, then, it evaluates each decision by the maximum possible return associated with that decision. In particular, refer again to the payoff table for the newsboy model (Table 10.4). If the newsboy ordered 2 papers, the best possible outcome would be a return of 70. This value is thus assigned to the decision "order 2 papers." In other words, for each decision we identify the maximum value in that row. Using this rule, the manager prepares a table as shown in Table 10.7.

TABLE 10.7 Newsboy Maximum Return Table

DECISION	MAXIMUM RETURN
0	0
1	35
2	70
3	105

TABLE 10.8 Payoff Table: Maximax Counter Example

DECISION	STATE OF NATURE								
	1	2	3	4	5	6	7	8	9
1	100	100	100	100	100	100	100	100	100
2	3	3	101	3	3	3	3	3	3

The decision that yields the maximum of these maximum returns (hence, maximax) is then selected. In this case, then, the newsboy should order 3 papers. A point of caution is in order: Don't confuse the decision with the state of nature that produces the optimal payoff. The optimal *decision* under the maximax criterion is to "order 3 papers," not to "order 3 papers and have 3 customers."

The maximax criterion is subject to the same type of criticism as maximin; that is, it is easy to create examples where using the maximax criterion leads to a decision that most people find unacceptable. Consider the payoff table presented in Table 10.8, for example. Most people prefer decision 1 since it is much better than decision 2 for every state of nature except state 3, and then it is only slightly worse. The maximax criterion, however, selects decision 2.

Regret and Minimax Regret **Regret** introduces a new concept for measuring the desirability of an outcome; that is, it is a new way to create the payoff table. Some personnel managers believe that college graduates tend to choose between several first-job choices using the minimax regret criterion. They imagine themselves in the various jobs and decide which one would give them the least regret of being there.

So far, all the decision criteria have been used on a payoff table of dollar returns as measured by net cash flows. In particular, each entry in Table 10.4 shows the net cash flow for the newsboy for every combination of decision (number of papers ordered) and state of nature (number of papers demanded). Table 10.9 shows the regret for each combination of decision and state of nature. It is derived from Table 10.4 by

1. Finding the maximum entry in each column of Table 10.4 (e.g., 70 is the largest entry in the third State of Nature column (i.e., the column under State of Nature "2")).

2. Calculating the new entry by subtracting the current entry from the maximum in its column. Thus, the new entry in the second row, third column is

$$70 - (-15) = 85 \text{ (new entry second row, third column)}$$

In each column, these new entries, called regret, indicate how much better we can do. In other words, "regret" is synonymous with the "opportunity cost" of not making the best decision for a given state of nature. It follows that the manager would like to make a decision that minimizes regret, but (same old story) she does not know which state of nature

TABLE 10.9 Regret Table for the Newsboy Model				
	STATE OF NATURE			
DECISION	**0**	**1**	**2**	**3**
0	0	85	170	255
1	40	0	(85)	170
2	80	40	0	85
3	120	80	40	0

TABLE 10.10 Newsboy Maximum Regret Table	
DECISION	**MAXIMUM REGRET**
0	255
1	170
2	85
3	120

will occur. If she knew a probability distribution on the state of nature, she could minimize the expected regret. (In the next section, we will see that this is equivalent to maximizing expected net cash flow.) If she does not know the probability, the typical suggestion is to use the conservative *minimax criterion;* that is, to select that decision that does the best in the worst case (the decision that has the smallest maximum regret).

For example, consider the regret table for the newsboy model shown in Table 10.9. If 1 paper is ordered, the maximum regret of 170 occurs if 3 papers are demanded. The value 170 is thus associated with the decision, "order 1 paper." In other words, the maximum value in each row is associated with the decision in that row. Following this rule produces Table 10.10.

The manager then selects the decision that minimizes the maximum regret. In this case, the minimax regret criterion implies that the newsboy should order 2 papers. Our newsboy example illustrates that, when making decisions without using probabilities, the three criteria—maximin cash flow, maximax cash flow, and minimax regret—can lead to different "optimal" decisions.

10.3 THE EXPECTED VALUE OF PERFECT INFORMATION: NEWSBOY MODEL UNDER RISK

Let us return to the newsboy model under risk (i.e., with the probability distribution on demand shown in row 12 of Figure 10.2). Recall that, in this case, the optimal policy was to order 2 papers and that the expected return was 22.5. It is useful to think about this model in a very stylized fashion in order to introduce the concept of the expected value of perfect information. In particular, let us assume that the sequence of events in the newsboy's day (the "current sequence of events") proceeds as follows:

1. A genie, by drawing from the demand distribution for papers, determines the number of papers that will be demanded.

2. The newsboy, not knowing what demand had been drawn, but knowing the distribution of demand, orders his papers.

3. The demand is then revealed to the newsboy and he achieves an *actual* (as opposed to expected) return determined by his order-size decision and the demand.

Now consider a new scenario. The newsboy has an opportunity to make a deal with the genie. Under the new deal the sequence of events proceeds as follows:

1. The newsboy pays the genie a fee.
2. The genie determines the demand as above. It is important to stress that the genie can't make a certain demand come true; he simply has perfect knowledge of what will happen and is willing to sell that knowledge or information.
3. The genie tells the newsboy what the demand will be.
4. The newsboy orders his papers.
5. The newsboy achieves the return determined by the demand and the number of papers he ordered.

The question is, What is the largest fee the newsboy should be willing to pay in step 1? This fee is called the **expected value of perfect information.** In general terms,

$$\text{fee} = (\text{expected return with new deal}) - (\text{expected return with current sequence of events [no deal]})$$

With the new deal the newsboy, in step 4, will always order the number of papers that will give him the maximum return for the state of nature that will occur. However, the payment in step 1 must be made *before* he learns what the demand will be. Referring to Table 10.4 we see that if 0 papers will be demanded, he will order 0 papers and enjoy the maximum return of 0. Since the genie is drawing from the distribution of demand, there is a probability of 0.1 that what the newsboy will learn from the genie is that demand will in fact be 0. Similarly, he will learn with a probability of 0.3 that 1 paper will be demanded. If this occurs, he will order 1 paper and enjoy the maximum return of 35. Following this reasoning, his expected return under the new deal is

$$\text{ER(new)} = 0\,(0.1) + 35\,(0.3) + 70\,(0.4) + 105\,(0.2) = 59.5$$

This concept could be easily implemented in Excel using the $=\text{MAX}()$ function on the returns for each state of nature. We have already seen that in the absence of perfect information his optimal decision (order 2 papers) gives an expected return of 22.5. Thus, we can calculate the expected value of perfect information (EVPI) as follows:

$$\text{EVPI} = 59.5 - 22.5 = 37.0 \text{ cents}$$

This is the maximum amount our vendor should be willing to pay in step 1 for the deal with the genie. Although the story we have used to develop the concept is far-fetched, the expected value of perfect information (EVPI) has important practical significance. It is an upper bound on the amount that you should be willing to pay to improve your knowledge about what state of nature will occur. Literally millions of dollars are spent on various market research projects and other testing devices (geological tests, quality control experiments, and so on) to determine what state of nature will occur in a wide variety of applications. The expected value of perfect information indicates the expected amount to be gained from any such endeavor and thus places an upper bound on the amount that should be spent in gathering such information.

10.4   UTILITIES AND DECISIONS UNDER RISK

Utility is an alternative way of measuring the attractiveness of the result of a decision. In other words, it is an alternative way of finding the values to fill in a payoff table. Up to now we have used net dollar return (net cash flow) and regret as two measures of the "goodness" of a particular combination of a decision and state of nature.

Utility suggests another type of measure. Our treatment of this topic includes two main sections:

TABLE 10.11 Payoff Table (Net Cash Flows)

DECISION	STATE OF NATURE	
	White Ball	Black Ball
Play	−10,000	1,000,000
Do Not Play	0	0

1. A rationale for utility (i.e., why using net cash flow can lead to unacceptable decisions)
2. Creating and using a utility function

THE RATIONALE FOR UTILITY

In the preceding section we saw that the maximin and maximax decision criteria could lead to unacceptable decisions in simple illustrative models. We now point out that the criterion of maximizing expected net cash flow in a decision under risk can also produce unacceptable results. For example, consider an urn that contains 99 white balls and 1 black ball. You are offered a chance to play a game in which a ball will be drawn from this urn. Each ball is equally likely to be drawn. If a white ball is drawn, you must pay $10,000. If the black ball is drawn, you receive $1,000,000. You must decide whether to play. The payoff table based on net cash flow is shown in Table 10.11.

We now use the information in this table, together with the facts that the probabilities of a white and a black ball are, respectively, 0.99 and 0.01, to calculate the expected return for each decision (play or do not play) in the usual way.

$$ER(\text{play}) = -10,000\,(0.99) + 1,000,000\,(0.01)$$
$$= -9900 + 10,000 = 100$$

$$ER(\text{do not play}) = 0\,(0.99) + 0\,(0.01) = 0$$

Since ER(play) > ER(do not play), we should play if we apply the criterion of maximizing the expected net cash flow.

Now step back and ask yourself if you would decide to play this game. Remember that the probability is 0.99 that you will lose $10,000. Many people simply find this large "downside risk" to be unacceptable; that is, they are unwilling to accept the decision based on the criterion of maximizing the expected net cash flow. Thus, once again we see a simple example that shows a need to take care in selecting an appropriate criterion. This is all the more true in dealing with complicated real-world models. Another example from the real world where most people don't follow the criterion of maximizing expected returns is when they choose whether or not to purchase auto insurance. Suppose you own a new sports car and can choose to purchase collision insurance or not. The insurance costs you a yearly premium for a certain deductible. In essence, you are choosing between buying insurance or taking a gamble (that you won't have a collision). Most people choose to purchase the insurance even though you can be sure that the premium you pay to the insurance company is greater than the expected cost of damage from a collision (i.e., the insurance company makes a profit).

Fortunately, it is not necessary to reject the concept of maximizing expected returns. To adapt the expected return criterion to general decisions under risk it is only necessary to recognize that net dollar returns do not always accurately reflect the "attractiveness" of the possible outcomes from our decisions. To show what this means, ask yourself if you would be willing to win or lose 10 cents depending on the flip of a fair coin. (Most people would say yes.) How about winning or losing $10,000, depending on a flip of the same coin? (Here most people would say no.) What is the difference? A 10-cent gain seems to balance a 10-cent loss. Why does a $10,000 gain not balance a $10,000 loss? The answer is that in the latter situation most people are **risk-averse,** which means they would feel that the loss of $10,000 is more painful than the benefit obtained from a $10,000 gain.

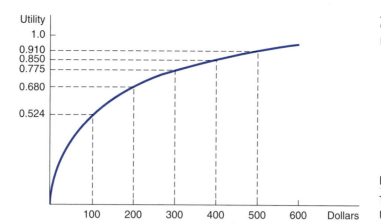

FIGURE 10.6

Typical Risk-Averse
Utility Function

Decision analysis deals with this behavior by introducing a function that measures the "attractiveness" of money. This function is called a *utility function,* where for the sake of this discussion the word *utility* can be thought of as a measure of "satisfaction." A typical risk-averse function is shown in Figure 10.6. Two characteristics of this function are worth noting:

1. It is nondecreasing, since more money is always at least as attractive as less money.

2. It is concave. An equivalent statement is that the marginal utility of money is nonincreasing. To illustrate this phenomenon, let us examine Figure 10.6.

First suppose that you have $100 and someone gives you an additional $100. Note that your utility increases by

$$U(200) - U(100) = 0.680 - 0.524 = 0.156$$

Now suppose that you start with $400, and someone gives you an additional $100. Now your utility increases by

$$U(500) - U(400) = 0.910 - 0.850 = 0.060$$

In other words, 100 additional dollars is less attractive to you if you have $400 on hand than it is if you start with $100. Another way of describing this phenomenon is that at any point, the gain of a specified number of dollars increases utility less than the loss of the same number of dollars decreases utility. For example, using the utility function in Figure 10.6, we have already calculated that the gain in utility of going from $400 to $500 is 0.060. The loss in utility of going from $400 to $300, however, is $U(400) - U(300) = 0.850 - 0.775 = 0.075$, which is greater. Another way to think about it is that for most people receiving $1,000,000 would be tremendously exciting, but receiving $2,000,000 would not be twice as exciting. Similarly, finding $100 would be a nice windfall, but the difference between receiving $1,000,000 and $1,000,100 is negligible. Thus we see that the same increment has a decreasing utility for most people, or to get the same utility, each increment must be larger.

Figure 10.7 shows two other general types of utility functions. The first is a **risk-seeking** (convex) function, where a gain of a specified amount of dollars increases the utility more than a loss of the same amount of dollars decreases the utility. For example, if you start with $200 and increase your holding by $100 to $300, your utility increases by

$$U(300) - U(200) = 0.590 - 0.260 = 0.330$$

whereas if you start with $200 and decrease your holding by $100 to $100, your utility decreases by

$$U(200) - U(100) = 0.260 - 0.075 = 0.185$$

Thus, with a risk-seeking utility function an increase of $100 increases your utility more than a decrease of $100 decreases it. As we have seen, exactly the opposite statement holds for a risk-averse (concave) function like the one shown in Figure 10.6.

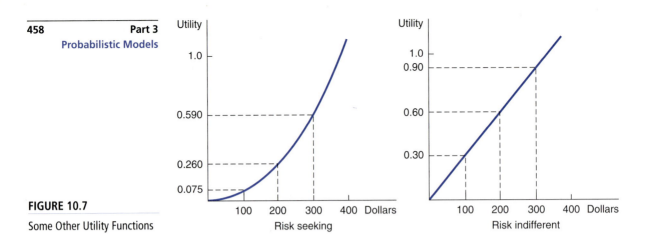

FIGURE 10.7

Some Other Utility Functions

For the **risk-indifferent** function shown on the right of Figure 10.7, a gain or a loss of a specified dollar amount produces a change of the same magnitude in your utility.

CREATING AND USING A UTILITY FUNCTION

We will discuss two methods for creating the utility function. The first is a more accurate, yet tedious process, while the second method is faster because it assumes a predetermined shape. The first method of creating a utility function, like the one shown in Figure 10.6, requires the manager, in our case the newsboy, to make a series of choices between a sure return and a lottery. In more formal language, the manager is called on to create an **equivalent lottery.** This, however, is the second step. Let us start at the beginning.

The newsboy can arbitrarily select the endpoints of his utility function. It is a convenient convention to set the utility of the smallest net dollar return equal to 0 and the utility of the largest net return equal to 1. Since in the newsboy example the smallest return is -150, and the largest is $+105$, he sets $U(-150) = 0$ and $U(105) = 1$. These two values play a fundamental role in finding the utility of any quantity of money between -150 and 105. It is perhaps easiest to proceed by example.

Assume that the decision maker starts with $U(-150) = 0$ and $U(105) = 1$ and wants to find the utility of 10 (i.e., $U[10]$). He proceeds by selecting a probability p such that he is indifferent between the following two alternatives:

1. Receive a payment of 10 for sure.
2. Participate in a lottery in which he receives a payment of 105 with probability p or a payment of -150 with probability $1 - p$.

Clearly if $p = 1$, the decision maker prefers alternative 2, since he prefers a payment of 105 to a payment of 10. Equally clear, if $p = 0$, he prefers alternative 1, since he prefers a payment of 10 to a loss of 150 (i.e., a payment of -150). It follows that somewhere between 0 and 1 there is a value for p such that the decision maker is indifferent between the two alternatives. This value will vary from person to person depending on how attractive the various alternatives are to them. We can call this value of p the utility for 10. For example, suppose that the manager chooses p to be 0.6. Then the expected value of the lottery is $0.6(105) + 0.4(-150) = 3$. In other words, he is expressing indifference between a sure payment of 10 and a gamble with a smaller expected value, 3. This means he is seeking risk, because he requires a sure payment larger than the expected return to compensate him for the loss of the possibility of making more than the expected return.

Now suppose he had chosen $p = 0.8$, the expected value of the lottery would have been $0.8(105) + 0.2(-150) = 54.0$. This means he is averse to risk, because he requires an expected value larger than the sure payment to compensate for the riskiness of the lottery. In some sense, the larger the value of p he chooses, the more risk-averse he is, because he requires a larger expected value of the lottery to compensate his for its riskiness. By solving the equation

$$p(105) + (1 - p)(-150) = 10$$
$$255p - 150 = 10$$
$$p = \frac{160}{255} = 0.6275$$

we find the value of p for which the expected value of the lottery is equal to the sure payment of 10. If the manager chooses a value of p greater than 0.6275, he is averse to risk; equal to 0.6275, indifferent to risk; and less than 0.6275, seeking risk. By repeating this same procedure for all other possible dollar returns from the newsboy example, we could completely assess the entire utility function. This is obviously a lot of work and one may wonder how many managers have the skill in probability theory and patience to do this exercise consistently and correctly. Another concern of decision analysts who work with corporations to aid in determining utility functions is that they have to be very careful that the manager uses the corporation's view of money rather than his own personal values. Individuals tend either to be afraid to risk a few thousand dollars or to get blasé about millions of dollars. Thus, there is a distinct difference between corporate utility and personal utility. Furthermore, we have not *proved* that using the probability p to define an equivalent lottery is a meaningful way to construct a utility function. An understandable discussion of why this approach works would carry us far beyond the scope of this text. We must be content to stop with the how and leave the why to other advanced courses.

Due to all the challenges mentioned above, the second, more popular way to assess utility functions is to use an exponential utility function. This function has a predetermined shape (i.e., it's concave → risk averse) and requires the assessment of only one parameter. It has been used to analyze financial investment decisions and other business applications. The function has the following form:

$$U(x) = 1 - e^{-x/r}$$

where x is the dollar amount that we're going to convert to utility. As can be seen the only parameter to assess is r, which is a constant that measures the degree of risk aversion. That is, the *larger* the value of r, the *less* risk-averse the company or person is (i.e., the more risk he or she is willing to take). Likewise, the *smaller* the value of r, the *more* risk-averse the company or person is.

There are many ways to determine the value of r. Two of the easiest are shown below. First, we must determine the dollar amount r such that the manager is indifferent between the following two choices:

1. A 50-50 gamble where the payoffs are a gain of r dollars or a loss of $r/2$ dollars
2. A payoff of zero

Let's suppose our newsboy is indifferent between a bet where he wins $100 or loses $50 with equal probability and not betting at all, then his r is $100.

The second way to determine r comes from empirical evidence gathered by a famous decision analyst, Ron Howard. Dr. Howard has consulted with many corporations and he has found some very valuable rules of thumb (see Howard) that relate a company's net income, equity, and net sales to the degree of risk aversion, r. For example, he found that r is approximately equal to 124% of net income, 15.7% of equity, and 6.4% of net sales. In other words, a large company with net income of $1 billion, would have an r of 1.24 billion, whereas a smaller company with net sales of $5 million would have an r of 320,000. Of course, these are only guidelines, but they can be very helpful and certainly indicate the trend for larger companies to have larger r values and less aversion to risk.

Now let's return to our newsboy example and assess his utility function. Because he owns a very small business, he opts for using the predetermined exponential utility function approach and he uses the 50-50 gamble approach we discussed to determine his r value ($100). He wants to enter the utility function in a new spreadsheet called "Utility" in the same workbook (NEWS-BOY.XLS), and assess the utility of all the dollar payoffs. Using this new exponential utility function to make decisions when the probabilities of the states of nature are known is a straightforward process. To be specific, the newsboy creates a new payoff table where the entries are

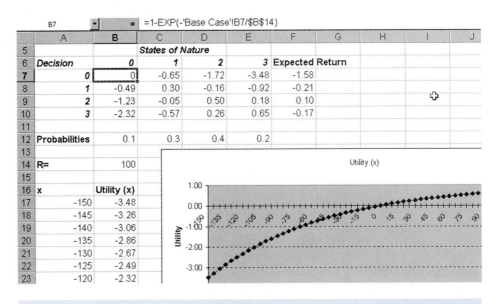

| | | | =1-EXP(-'Base Case'!B7/$B$14) |

FIGURE 10.8

Newsboy Utility Spreadsheet

Cell	Formula	Copy To
B7	$= 1 - EXP(-\text{'Base Case'}!B7/\$B\$14)$	B7:E10
F7	$= SUMPRODUCT(B7:E7,\$B\$12:\$E\$12)$	F8:F10

the utility of the net cash flow associated with each combination of a decision and a state of nature (i.e., he substitutes the utility of the net cash flow for that cash flow). For example, row 3 (Order 2), column 3 (Demand is 2) in Table 10.4 shows a net cash flow of 70. His spreadsheet (presented in Figure 10.8) translates this into a utility of about 0.50, which becomes the new entry in row 3, column 3. The newsboy now proceeds as before; that is, he calculates the expected utility for each decision. This is shown in column F of Figure 10.8. Finally he desires to graph his utility function to see its shape, which is also shown in Figure 10.8.

To create this spreadsheet, the newsboy does the following:

1. Create a new spreadsheet called "Utility" in the same workbook (NEWSBOY.XLS).

2. Copy cells A5:F12 of the "Base Case" spreadsheet into the new spreadsheet, change the formula in cell B7 to $= 1 - \exp(-\text{'Base Case'}!B7/\$B\$14)$ and then copy it to B7:E10.

3. Enter an initial value of -150 in cell A17.

4. Click back on cell A17 and click on Edit, Fill, and then Series.

5. Click on "Series in Columns" and enter a step value of 5 and a stop value of 105. Click on OK.

6. Enter the formula (shown in the equation line of Figure 10.8 to convert dollars to utility) into cell B17 and copy it down to B68.

7. Use the Chart Wizard with the data in A17:B68 to create a graph of the utility function like that shown in the lower right of Figure 10.8.

We see in column F of Figure 10.8 that, on the basis of the criterion of maximizing the expected utility, the newsboy would order 2 papers (it has the highest expected utility of 0.10). Referring to the discussion of decisions under risk in Section 10.2, we see that if the newsboy based his decision on maximizing the expected net cash flow, he would also order 2 papers. It is not always true, however, that the decision that has the largest expected cash flow will also have the largest expected utility. The fact that this phenomenon occurred in this particular example does not imply that it will occur in general. Let's consider a real-world example where expected utility and expected return do not generate the same decision.

G4   =SUMPRODUCT(E4:F4,$E$6:$F$6)

	A	B	C	D	E	F	G	H
1	Annual Premium	$ 1,000			States of Nature			
2	Deductible	$ 250		Decision	Collision	No Collision	Expected Return	
3				Buy	$ 1,250	$ 1,000	1001.25	
4				Don't	$50,000	0.00	250.00	
5	Prob. of Collision	0.50%						
6	Amount of Damage	$50,000		Probabilities	0.50%	99.50%		
7								

Cell	Formula	Copy To
E3	= B2+B1	—
F3	= B1	—
E4	= B6	—
F4	= 0	—
G3	= SUMPRODUCT(E3:F3,$E$6:$F$6)	G4
E6	= B5	—
F6	= 1−B5	—

FIGURE 10.9

Auto Insurance Spreadsheet

F12   =1-EXP(F3/$F$8)

	A	B	C	D	E	F	G	H
1	Annual Premium	$ 1,000		Payoffs	States of Nature			
2	Deductible	$ 250		Decision	Collision	No Collision	Expected Return	
3				Buy	$ 1,250	$ 1,000	1001.25	
4				Don't	$50,000	0.00	250.00	
5	Prob. of Collision	0.50%						
6	Amount of Damage	$50,000		Probabilities	0.50%	99.50%		
7								
8					r =	10000		
9								
10				Utilities	States of Nature			
11				Decision	Collision	No Collision	Expected Return	
12				Buy	-0.13	-0.11	-0.11	
13				Don't	-147.41	0.00	-0.74	

Cell	Formula	Copy To
E12	= 1−EXP(E3/$F$8)	E12:F13
G12	= SUMPRODUCT(E12:F12,$E$6:$F$6)	G13

FIGURE 10.10

Auto Insurance
Utility Spreadsheet

Consider the following auto insurance example. Carol Lane is 10 years out of Stanford's Graduate School of Business and has just bought a beautiful new Lexus. She calls her insurance company and determines that the annual premium for collision insurance would be $1000 with a $250 deductible. There is only a 0.5% chance she will cause a collision in the next year, in which case she can expect about $50,000 worth of damage. Since she owns the Lexus outright (i.e., no loan), she is not required to buy the collision insurance. Should she buy the insurance or not? Carol has modeled this situation in the spreadsheet (AUTOINSU.XLS) shown in Figure 10.9.

On a "maximize expected return" basis, Carol sees that it would be less expensive for her, on average, to not buy the insurance ($250 versus $1001.25). However, she knows the decision can't be that easy and feels somewhat uncomfortable. She remembers the concept of utility from her days at business school. She decides that she is risk-averse, and estimates her r value to be $10,000 (using the first method [50–50 gamble] taught in this section). She creates a new spreadsheet called "Utility" in the same workbook to incorporate her utility as shown in Figure 10.10.

On this basis, she sees that the decision "Buy insurance" maximizes expected utility (-0.11 versus -0.74) because of the severe negative utility incurred in the situation created by the combination of the decision that she doesn't buy insurance with the state of nature that she has a collision. Based on her expected utility analysis, Carol feels that it is worth buying the insurance (and paying the extra $751 per year on average) to have the peace of mind that she won't have to take $50,000 out of her savings on the off-chance that she causes a collision.

10.5 A MID-CHAPTER SUMMARY

The preceding three sections provided the theoretical foundation on which the rest of the chapter is based. The ensuing sections are devoted to procedures that play an important role in solving real-world models. It is useful to summarize what we have achieved before moving ahead.

Section 10.2 provided a general framework for a class of models identified as decisions against nature. In this framework, the model can be described by a payoff table in which the returns to the decision maker depend on the decision selected and the state of nature that subsequently occurs. Three specific cases were identified:

1. *Decisions under certainty:* The decision maker knows exactly what state of nature will occur. The "only" problem is to select the best decision. Deterministic models such as linear programming, integer programming, nonlinear programming, and the EOQ inventory model fall into this category.

2. *Decisions under risk:* A probability distribution is specified on the states of nature. The decision maker may use the following criteria to select a "best decision":

    a. Maximize expected return as measured by net dollar return

    b. Minimize expected regret (opportunity cost)

    c. Maximize expected return as measured by utility

We saw that criteria a and b always lead to the same decision. Most management decision models fall into this category of decisions under risk.

3. *Decisions under uncertainty:* Here it is assumed that the decision maker has *no* knowledge about which state of nature will occur. The decision maker might apply the Laplace criterion; that is, assign equal probabilities to the various states of nature and then choose a decision that maximizes expected return. Alternatively, the decision maker may attack the model without using probabilities. In this case, we discussed three different criteria for making a "best decision":

    a. Maximize minimum net dollar return

    b. Maximize maximum net dollar return

    c. Minimize maximum regret

Each of these criteria will, in general, lead to different decisions and can produce decisions that many managers feel uncomfortable with.

Section 10.3 was devoted to the concept of the expected value of perfect information (EVPI). This entity plays an important role by establishing an upper bound on the amount you should pay to gain new information about what state of nature will occur.

Finally, in Section 10.4 we discussed utility as an alternative measure of the attractiveness of each combination of a decision and a state of nature. The desire to use a utility function is motivated by the fact that in some cases, for example, because of the magnitudes of the potential losses, the decision that maximizes the expected net dollar return is not the decision that you would want to select. A couple of methods were described for assessing the utility function.

The remaining sections in this chapter will deal with extensions of the most common model (decisions under risk). They consider decision trees, a technique of significant practical importance, via the use of a spreadsheet add-in called TreePlan and introduce two important concepts: the use of new information in decision making and the analysis of sequential decision models. Because of the sequential nature of these new, more complex models, the decision or payoff tables of previous sections will no longer work.

10.6 DECISION TREES: MARKETING HOME AND GARDEN TRACTORS

A **decision tree** is a graphical device for analyzing decisions under risk; that is, models in which the decisions and the probabilities on the states of nature are specified. More precisely, decision trees were created to use on models in which there is a sequence of decisions, each of which could lead to one of several uncertain outcomes. For example, a concessionaire typically has to decide how much to bid for each of several possible locations at the state fair. The result of this decision is not certain, since it depends on what the competitors decide to bid. Once the location is known, the concessionaire must decide how much food to stock. The result of this decision in terms of profits is also not certain since it depends on customer demand.

Our discussion of decision trees is organized in the following manner: In this section we introduce the basic ideas and introduce you to a spreadsheet add-in, TreePlan, that draws decision trees in a spreadsheet. This software package was developed by Michael Middleton and is made available as shareware. Check out his website at http://www.treeplan.com. (If you like the software and plan to use it beyond this class, you are expected to pay a nominal registration fee. Details are available in TreePlan's online help.) Section 10.7 examines the sensitivity of the optimal decision to the assessed values of the probabilities. Section 10.8 shows how Bayes' Theorem is used to incorporate new information into the process, and Section 10.9 considers a sequential decision model. The entire discussion is motivated by the following production and marketing model faced by the management of PROTRAC.

ALTERNATE MARKETING AND PRODUCTION STRATEGIES

The design and product-testing phase has just been completed for PROTRAC's new line of home and garden tractors. Top management is attempting to decide on the appropriate marketing and production strategy to use for this product. Three major alternatives are being considered. Each alternative is identified with a single word.

1. *Aggressive (A):* This strategy represents a major commitment of the firm to this product line. A major capital expenditure would be made for a new and efficient production facility. Large inventories would be built up to guarantee prompt delivery of all models. A major marketing campaign involving nationwide sponsorship of television commercials and dealer discounts would be initiated.

2. *Basic (B):* In this plan, production of E-4 (the small crawler tractor) would be moved from Joliet to Moline. This move would phase out the trouble-plagued department for adjustable pelican and excavator production. At the same time, the E-4 line in Joliet would be modified to produce the new home and garden product. Inventories would be held for only the most popular items. Headquarters would make funds available to support local or regional advertising efforts, but no national advertising campaign would be mounted.

3. *Cautious (C):* In this plan, excess capacity on several existing E-4 lines would be used to produce the new products. A minimum of new tooling would be developed. Production would be geared to satisfy demand, and advertising would be at the discretion of the local dealer.

Management decides to categorize the condition of the market (i.e., the level of demand) as either strong (S) or weak (W). In reality, the demand is characterized by a continuum of possible outcomes. For this introductory example, we will limit it to two possible states (Strong and Weak) for simplicity. For discussion of the issue on how to deal with infinite states of nature, see Section 10.11. The spreadsheet shown in Figure 10.11 (PROTRACDT.XLS) presents the payoff table and management's best estimate of the probability of a strong or a weak market. The payoffs in the body are the net profits measured in millions of dollars. They were generated by carefully calculating the sales, revenues, and costs associated with each decision/state of nature combination. It is interesting to note that a cautious (C) decision yields a higher profit with a weak market than it does with a strong market. If there is a strong market and PROTRAC is cautious, not only will the

D6	▼	=	=SUMPRODUCT(B6:C6,$B$1:$C$1)				

	A	B	C	D	E	F	G	H
1	Probabilities	0.45	0.55					
2								
3		States of Nature						
4	DECISION	Strong (S)	Weak (W)	Expected Return				
5	Aggresive (A)	30	-8	9.1				
6	Basic (B)	20	7	12.85				
7	Cautious (C)	5	15	10.5				
8								

FIGURE 10.11

PROTRAC's Basic
Marketing Spreadsheet

Cell	Formula	Copy To
D5	= SUMPRODUCT (B5:C5, $B$1:$C$1)	D6:D7

competition capture the small tractor market, but as a result of the carryover effect of these sales, the competition will seriously cut into PROTRAC's current market position for accessories and other home products.

We are dealing here with what we have termed decisions under risk and we will calculate the expected return for each decision and select the best one (just as we did in Section 10.2), except that here we'll start off in a spreadsheet and skip the "by hand" approach. The formula for the expected return is shown in the equation bar of Figure 10.11 as well as the resulting expected payoffs for each of the three decisions in column D. The optimal decision if you are risk-indifferent is to select (B), the basic production and marketing strategy, which yields the highest expected payoff of $12.85 million.

CREATING A DECISION TREE

This marketing model can also be represented by a decision tree we will demonstrate below. In our exposition of decision trees, a **square node** (decision node in TreePlan) will represent a point at which a decision must be made, and each line leading from a square will represent a possible decision. The **circular nodes** (event node in TreePlan) will represent situations when the outcome is not certain. Each line leading from a circle represents a possible outcome. The term **branches** will be employed for the lines emanating from the nodes, whether square or circular. The steps to create the decision tree for the PROTRAC model in TreePlan are as follows:

1. Place the cursor in cell A10 and click on Tools, then TreePlan. (If TreePlan is not a choice in your menu, you'll need to add it. To do so, Click on Tools, then Add-Ins. Click on the Browse option and find TREEPLAN.XLA on your computer [either your hard drive or network]. Double click on the TREEPLAN.XLA once you find it and it should then be available on your Tools menu.) *Note:* Version 1.61 is used here.

2. Click on "New Tree" and it will draw a default tree with 2 decision nodes.

3. Because PROTRAC needs 3 decision nodes, we click on the decision node (cell B14 in our case) and hit Ctrl-t. This brings up TreePlan's context-sensitive menu.

4. Click on "Add branch" (if it's not the default choice), then click OK.

5. Label the 3 branches as Aggressive, Basic, and Cautious (in cells D11, D16, D21).

6. Because we want to replace the terminal node with a random event node, click on the terminal node (cell F12) as shown in Figure 10.12, then hit Ctrl-t to bring up the menu.

7. Click on "Change to event node," indicate that we want 2 branches, then click OK.

8. TreePlan draws the resulting tree as shown in Figure 10.13. Notice that it enters default probabilities of 0.5 for each of the 2 random events, as well as default names (Events 4 and 5).

9. We change the labels from the generic "Event 4" and "Event 5" to "Strong" and "Weak" markets respectively.

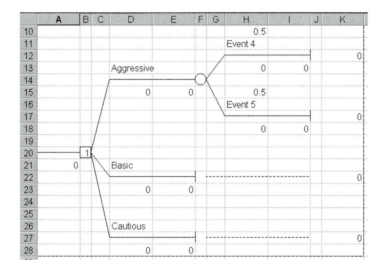

FIGURE 10.12

Adding an Event Node to the
Decision Tree for the Home
and Garden Tractor Model

FIGURE 10.13

Partially Completed Decision
Tree for the Home and
Garden Tractor Decision Tree

Note: We want to repeat this process (steps 6–9) for the other 2 terminal nodes. Fortunately, TreePlan has a Copy feature we can take advantage of (shown in steps 10–12 below).

10. To copy a node (or any subtree), click on the cell you wish to copy (cell F14) and hit Ctrl-t.

11. Click on "copy subtree," then click on OK.

12. Click on the cell where you want to copy the node (cell F22), hit Ctrl-t, click on "Paste subtree," and click on OK.

13. We do the same thing (steps 10–12) for the last terminal node (cell F27 in Figure 10.13).

14. Because the tree is starting to get pretty big, we change the zoom feature to 75% and we see all the branches of the tree as shown in Figure 10.14.

Note we still need to add the endpoints or terminal values and the probabilities, but we're making good progress. For the home and garden tractor model, the decision tree in Figure 10.14 shows the initial node in cell B24. Since it is square, a decision must be made. Thus, management must choose one of the strategies: Aggressive (A), Basic (B), or Cautious (C). Depending on which decision is selected, a new position will be attained on the tree. For example, selecting strategy A leads us from cell B24 to cell F14.

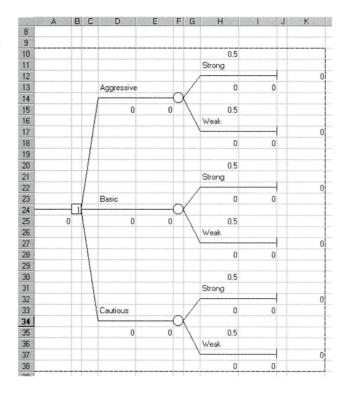

FIGURE 10.14

All Branches of the Decision Tree for the Home and Garden Tractor Model

Since this new node is a circle, the next branch that will occur is not known with certainty. If the market condition turns out to be strong, cell J12 is attained. If, instead, the market proves to be weak, cell J17 is attained. Since they represent the end of the decision process, cells such as J12 and J17 are referred to as **terminal positions.** Also, since the nodes in cells F14, F24, and F34 are not followed by other nodes, they are called **terminal nodes.**

APPENDING THE PROBABILITIES AND TERMINAL VALUES
The decision tree presented in Figure 10.14 provides an efficient way for management to visualize the interactions between decisions and less-than-certain events. However, if management wishes to use the decision tree to select an optimal decision, some additional information must be appended to the diagram. In particular, one must assign the return associated with each terminal position. This is called the **terminal value.** One must also assign a probability to each branch emanating from each circular node. For the basic model this is a relatively simple task, and can be done as follows:

1. Change the default probabilities in cells H10 and H15 from 0.5 and 0.5 to the formulas =B1 (containing the value 0.45) and =C1 (containing the value 0.55), respectively. Do the same for cells H20, H25, H30, and H35. (Note that if you mistakenly enter probabilities that don't add to exactly 1.0, the expected value of the event node [cell to the left] will return a value of "#NA," which is a hint for you to go back and check your probabilities.)
2. Change the terminal values for each branch from their default values of zero. For example, in cell H13 (representing the combination of the Aggressive decision, with the state of nature "Strong market") enter the formula =B5 (representing the return of $30 million in Figure 10.11). Likewise in cell H18 (representing the combination of the Aggressive decision, with the state of nature "Weak market") enter the formula =C5 (for the return of −8). Enter the similar formulas =B6, =C6, =B7, =C7 (for the values of $20, $7, $5, and $15) in cells H23, H28, H33, and H38, respectively.

These steps yield the decision tree presented in Figure 10.15.

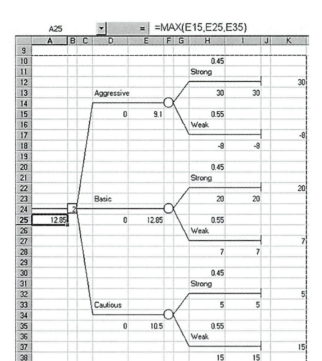

FIGURE 10.15

Complete Decision Tree for Home and Garden Tractor Model

FOLDING BACK

Using a decision tree to find the optimal decision is called solving the tree. TreePlan does this for us automatically. To solve a decision tree one works backward (i.e., right to left) or, in the jargon of the trade, by **folding back** the tree. First, the terminal branches are *folded back* by calculating an expected value for each terminal node. For example, consider the event node in cell F14. The calculation to obtain the expected value for this node is

$$\text{expected terminal value} = 30(0.45) + (-8)(0.55) = 9.10$$

In other words, the expected value to be obtained if one arrives at cell F14 is 9.10. Now the branches emanating from that particular node are folded back (i.e., eliminated) and the expected value of 9.10 is assigned to the node, as shown in cell E15 of Figure 10.15. Performing the same calculations for nodes in cells F24 and F34 yields their expected values as shown in cells E25 and E35 of Figure 10.15. Note that the expected terminal values on all three of these nodes are identical to the expected returns computed earlier in this section (see Figure 10.11) for decisions A, B, and C, respectively. Management now faces the simple problem of choosing the alternative that yields the highest expected terminal value. In this case, as we have seen earlier, the "optimal" choice is the Basic strategy (alternative B), and this is indicated by TreePlan in cell B24 with the "2," meaning choose the second branch or the Basic strategy.

More complex trees can be analyzed by TreePlan by following the same procedures. At each circle the software determines the sum of the expected values of each branch that emanates from it, while at each square it chooses the "best" branch (maximum value), going from right to left.

The above discussion provides a simple illustration of how the basic model can be analyzed with a decision tree. In Sections 10.8 and 10.9 you will see the use of decision trees in more complex scenarios. However, this introductory discussion illustrates an important point: *For the basic model a decision tree simply provides another, more graphic, way of viewing the same model.* Exactly the same information is utilized, and the same calculations are made whether one uses the steps described in Section 10.2 or a decision tree to solve the model.

In recent years, the wholesale electric power market in the Southeastern United States has become very active. Florida's population and power needs have grown faster than the state's power generation capacity. At the same time, the availability of surplus power in neighboring states, like Georgia, has grown with large nuclear and coal-fired plants coming on line. The result is substantial power flows from Georgia and nearby states (Alabama, South Carolina) into Florida.

Oglethorpe Power Corporation (OPC) is a generation and transmission cooperative that provides wholesale power. It provides approximately 20% of the power in the state of Georgia. Late in 1990, OPC management learned that Florida Power Corporation (FPC) wanted to expand its connections to Georgia with another 500 kilovolt line capable of transmitting over 1000 MW. The key question facing OPC was whether to add this additional transmission capacity and if so, in what form. They had three choices on the decision of whether to add the line: (1) go it alone, (2) do it as a joint venture with Georgia Power, or (3) not do it. Depending on how OPC structured the investment and operated the line, the investment could be $100 million or more and the annual savings could be $20 million or more. The investment would be one of OPC's biggest and the annual savings were on the order of several percent of its annual budget.

OPC managers realized it was an extremely important decision and so formal decision analysis techniques were used.

Decision analysis had become quite popular in the electric power industry in the United States because of the active encouragement provided by the Electric Power Research Institute. As the issue was studied, OPC realized there were actually three decisions, not just one as they had originally thought. It must decide whether to build the transmission line, whether to upgrade the associated transmission facilities, and the nature of the control over the new facilities.

There were five major uncertainties—the cost of building the new facilities, the demand for power in Florida, the competitive situation, OPC's market share, and the spot price for electricity. The uncertainties combined with the decisions to create nearly 8000 branches of the decision tree. The challenge was to come up with the optimal decision which maximized expected savings. After performing some sensitivity analysis, OPC decided it should learn more about one of the uncertain factors—the competitive situation—before making a major commitment regarding the transmission line.

After doing so, the recommendation that came out of the model was that OPC should begin negotiations independently with FPC, leading to either going it alone or not doing the line. Interestingly enough, the policy that had appeared to be the leading idea going in (joint venture with Georgia Power), came out as the least attractive decision (See Borison).

10.7 SENSITIVITY ANALYSIS

EXPECTED RETURN AS A FUNCTION OF THE PROBABILITY FOR A STRONG MARKET

Before proceeding to the next main topic, a model in which new information becomes available concerning the likelihood of the uncertain events, it will be useful to consider again the expected return associated with each of the decisions in our previous example. We have already noted that to calculate the expected return of strategy A, one uses the relationship

$$ER(A) = (30)P(S) + (-8)P(W)$$

where $P(S)$ is the probability of a strong market and $P(W)$ is the probability of a weak market. We also know that

$$P(S) + P(W) = 1, \text{ or } P(W) = 1 - P(S)$$

Thus

$$ER(A) = 30P(S) - 8[1 - P(S)] = -8 + 38P(S)$$

This expected return, then, is a linear function of the probability that the market response is strong. A similar function can be found for alternatives B and C since

$$ER(B) = 20P(S) + 7[1 - P(S)] = 7 + 13P(S)$$

and

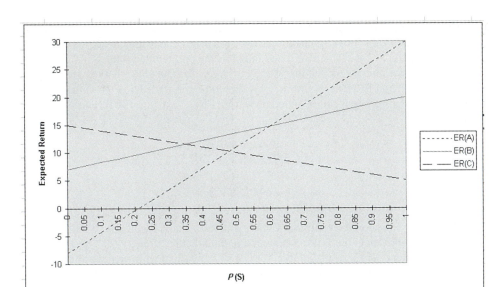

FIGURE 10.16

Expected Return as a
Function of $P(S)$

$$ER(C) = 5P(S) + 15[1 - P(S)] = 15 - 10P(S)$$

Plotting each of these three functions on the same set of axes is easily accomplished in Excel by using the Data Table command. To do this, we simply:

1. Copy A1:D7 from the "Base Case" spreadsheet into a new spreadsheet called "Exp. Return vs. $P(S)$." Change the entry in cell C1 from 0.55 to a formula ($=1-B1$). This makes it more general and allows us to do a one-way Data Table.

2. In cell A10, we enter an initial value of 0.

3. Click back on A10, then Edit, Fill, and Series.

4. Click on "Series in Columns" and enter a step value of 0.05 and a stop value of 1.0. Click on OK.

5. In cells B9:D9 we enter the quantities [ER(A), ER(B), and ER(C)] we want to track for each value of $P(S)$ that we've entered in column A. These formulas are $=D5$, $=D6$, and $=D7$, respectively.

6. Highlight the area A9:D30, and click on Data, then Table.

7. Enter the Column input cell as B1 and click on OK.

8. Excel automatically calculates the expected returns from the three different strategies for $P(S)$ values between 0 and 1.

9. Use the Graph Wizard to produce a chart as shown in Figure 10.16.

Let's look at Figure 10.16 more closely. The vertical axis is expected return and the horizontal axis is $P(S)$, the probability that the market is strong. Note that when $P(S) = 0$, then ER(A) = -8. To see that this makes sense, recall that when $P(S) = 0$, we are sure that the market will be weak; Figure 10.11 shows that if the market is weak and we make decision A, the return is -8. A similar argument shows that ER(A) should be 30 when $P(S) = 1$ since in this case we are sure that the market is strong. The fact that a straight line connects these two points follows from the fact that

$$ER(A) = -8 + 38P(S)$$

which is a linear function of $P(S)$. Since the criterion for making a decision is to select the decision with the highest expected return, Figure 10.16 shows which decision is optimal for any particular value of $P(S)$. For example, if as in Figure 10.11, the value of $P(S)$ is 0.45, then Figure 10.16 shows that ER(B) > ER(C) > ER(A). Hence, as we have already computed, for this value of $P(S)$ the optimal decision is B. On the other hand, if $P(S) = 0.8$, we see that ER(A) > ER(B) > ER(C) and thus A is the optimal decision.

In more general terms we see that if $P(S)$ is larger than the value of $P(S)$ at which the graphs of ER(A) and ER(B) cross, strategy A should be selected. The $P(S)$ value at which strategy A becomes optimal can be found by setting ER(A) equal to ER(B) and solving for $P(S)$; that is

$$ER(A) = ER(B)$$
$$-8 + 38P(S) = 7 + 13P(S)$$
$$25P(S) = 15$$
$$P(S) = 0.6$$

In a similar way, it is easily determined that the graphs of ER(C) and ER(B) cross when $P(S) = 0.348$. (You should try this calculation yourself.) Thus, Figure 10.16 indicates that PROTRAC should select the Basic production and marketing strategy (i.e., decision B) if $P(S)$ is larger than 0.348 and smaller than 0.6. This is consistent with what we already computed under the assumption that $P(S) = 0.45$. However, the analysis of Figure 10.16 provides considerably more information than we had previously. It is now clear, for example, that the optimal decision in this case is not very sensitive to the precision of our estimate for $P(S)$. The same strategy, B, remains optimal for an increase or decrease of more than 0.10 in the previously estimated probability of 0.45.

Similarly, it could also be important to consider how sensitive the decision is to the estimates of the cash flow returns. For example, suppose that the return of the Aggressive strategy is greater than $30 million when the market is strong. We could do a similar analysis to find out how sensitive our decision is to the estimate of a return of $30 million when the market is strong.

Although a diagram such as Figure 10.16 can be used only when there are two possible states of nature, it provides a useful pedagogical device for illustrating the sensitivity of the optimal solution to the estimates of the probabilities and returns. For higher dimensions, generalizations of this approach exist, but such a discussion would go beyond the introductory level of this chapter.

10.8   DECISION TREES: INCORPORATING NEW INFORMATION

A MARKET RESEARCH STUDY FOR HOME AND GARDEN TRACTORS

The management of PROTRAC's domestic tractor division was just on the verge of recommending the basic (B) marketing and production strategy when the board of directors insisted that a market research study had to be performed first. Only after such a study would the board be willing to approve the selection of a marketing and production strategy. As a result of the board's decision, management consulted the corporate marketing research group at PROTRAC headquarters. It was agreed that this group would perform a market research study and would report within a month on whether the study was encouraging (E) or discouraging (D). Thus, within a month the new-product planners would have this additional information. This new information should obviously be taken into account before making a decision on the marketing and production strategy.

Management could treat the new information informally; that is, once the test results were available, management's estimate of $P(S)$, the probability that the market would be strong, could be updated. If the study turned out to be encouraging (E) presumably management would want to increase the estimate of $P(S)$ from 0.45 to 0.50, 0.60, or maybe more. If the study results were discouraging (D), then $P(S)$ should be decreased. The question is: How should the updating be accomplished? There is a formal way to do this, based on the concept of *conditional probability*. The mathematics of why this approach works is detailed in Appendix 10.1. Here we will take a tabular approach that is suited to implementation in a spreadsheet program.

The marketing research group has agreed to report within a month whether, according to their study, the test is encouraging (E) or discouraging (D). We would certainly hope their report would be perfectly reliable—that is, if their report is encouraging, then the market is absolutely guaranteed to be strong and if their report is discouraging, then the market is definitely going to be weak. This would amount to their report always revealing the true state of nature. We will see, however, that marketing's report may be useful even if it is not perfectly reliable. This raises the issues of how to quantify "reliability." We will use conditional probabilities.

Conditional Probability Suppose that A and B are two events. An informal definition of the **conditional probability,** $P(A|B)$, is the probability that the event A occurs *given* that the event B occurs. For example, $P(E|S)$ would be the conditional probability that marketing gives an encouraging report *given* that the market is in fact going to turn out to be strong. If marketing were perfectly reliable, this conditional probability would be 1; that is, they would always give an encouraging report when the market is in fact strong. However, marketing's track record is not perfect. In the past when the market has in fact been strong, they have issued an encouraging report only 60% of the time. Thus, $P(E|S) = 0.6$. Since marketing always issues an encouraging or discouraging report, the value of $P(D|S)$ must be $1 - 0.6$, or 0.4; that is, they issued a discouraging report 40% of the time when in fact the market was strong.

What happens when the market is in fact weak? Marketing is somewhat better at predicting weak markets, but is still not perfect: $P(D|W) = 0.7$. That is, in the past when the market has in fact been weak, marketing has issued a discouraging report 70% of the time. Of course, $P(E|W) = 0.3$.

Calculating the Posterior Probabilities Suppose that marketing has come back with an encouraging report. What is the probability that the market is in fact strong? It is the conditional probability $P(S|E)$. Note that this probability is in general *not* the same as $P(E|S)$. We will see that it depends on the reliabilities and the initial estimates of the probabilities of a strong or weak market. These initial estimates are called **prior probabilities,** while conditional probabilities such as $P(S|E)$ are called **posterior probabilities.** The domestic tractor division has already estimated the prior probabilities (given initially in Figure 10.11) as $P(S) = 0.45$ and $P(W) = 0.55$.

The key to obtaining the posterior probabilities is Bayes' Theorem. We will use a tabular spreadsheet approach that is justified by the argument given in Appendix 10.1. This process has been carried out in a new spreadsheet called "Probabilities" of the same workbook (PROTRACDT.XLS) and is shown in Figure 10.17.[3] The procedure is as follows:

1. Enter the given Reliabilities (conditional probabilities) as a table (A1:C4). *Note:* the conditional probability, $P(A|B)$, is found at the intersection of row A and column B. Also notice that the column sums must be 1, while the row sums may be either greater than, less than, or equal to 1.

2. Generate a new table by multiplying each column of the reliability table by the corresponding prior probability. For example, multiply each entry in the Strong column of Figure 10.17 by $P(\text{Strong})$. This table is a table of the *joint probabilities* (see Appendix 10.1).

---

[3]Note that the posterior probability table in Figure 10.17 is read differently from the reliability table. For example, the probability in row D and column W of the posterior probability table is $P\{W|D\}$, whereas the probability in row D and column W of the reliability table is $P\{D|W\}$. In general, the probability $P\{A|B\}$ in the posterior probability table is found at the intersection of *column* A and *row* B. This convention is employed to simplify the copying of formulas in the spreadsheet that is used to generate the posterior probability table. If the convention for the reliability table also had to be observed in the posterior probability table, then the first *column* of the table would be the first *row* of the table in step 2 divided by its row sum, the second column of the table would be the second row of the table in step 2 divided by *its* row sum, and so on. These operations would be difficult to perform in one step with most spreadsheet programs.

	A	B	C	D	E	F	G	H
	B19	▾	=	=B12/$D12				
1		RELIABILITIES						
2		Strong	Weak					
3	Encouraging	0.6	0.3					
4	Discouraging	0.4	0.7	<--Probability of D given W, p (D|W)				
5								
6		PRIOR PROBABLITIES						
7		Strong	Weak					
8		0.45	0.55					
9								
10		JOINT & MARGINAL PROBABLITIES						
11		Strong	Weak					
12	Encouraging	0.27	0.165	0.435				
13	Discouraging	0.18	0.385	0.565	<--Probability of D, p (D)			
14		0.45	0.55					
15					Probability of D and W, p(D & W)			
16								
17		POSTERIOR PROBABLITIES						
18		Strong	Weak					
19	Encouraging	0.621	0.379					
20	Discouraging	0.319	0.681	<--Probability of W given D, p (W|D)				
21								

Cell	Formula	Copy To
C8	$=1 - B8$	—
B12	$= B3*B\$8$	B12:C13
D12	$= SUM (B12:C12)$	D13
B14	$= SUM (B12:B13)$	C14
B19	$= B12/\$D12$	B19:C20

FIGURE 10.17

Calculation of
Posterior Probabilities

3. For each row of this new table, compute the sum of the entries. In the example at hand this gives the *marginal probabilities, P*(E) and *P*(D) in cells D12 and D13.

4. Generate the "Posterior Probabilities" table by dividing each entry in a row of the joint probability table by its row sum (e.g., B12 would be divided by D12).

In this spreadsheet the tables labeled Reliabilities and Prior Probabilities are given and the tables labeled Joint & Marginal Probabilities and Posterior Probabilities are calculated according to the four-step procedure above. The spreadsheet makes it easy to calculate the sensitivity of the posterior probabilities to the reliabilities and the prior probabilities. For example, the Data Table command can be used to generate all posterior probabilities of a strong market ($P[S|E]$ and $P[S|D]$) for values of the prior probability $P(S)$ between 0 and 1 in increments of 0.1. The results are shown in Figure 10.18. The steps to do this in Excel are:

1. In cell I3, we enter an initial value of 0.

2. Click back on I3, then click on Edit, Fill, and then Series.

3. Click on "Series in Columns" and enter a step value of 0.1 and a stop value of 1.0. Click on OK.

4. In cells J2:K2 we enter the formulas for the quantities we want to track ($P[S|E]$ and $P[S|D]$) for each of the values for $P(S)$ that we've entered in column I. These formulas are =B19 and =B20, respectively.

5. Highlight the area I2:K13, and click on Data, then Table.

6. Enter the Column input cell as B8 and click on OK.

7. Excel automatically calculates the two conditional probabilities for values of $P(S)$ between 0 and 1.

	J	K
⊕	*P(S|E)*	*P(S|D)*
Prior, P(S)	0.621	0.319
0	0	0
0.1	0.182	0.060
0.2	0.333	0.125
0.3	0.462	0.197
0.4	0.571	0.276
0.5	0.667	0.364
0.6	0.750	0.462
0.7	0.824	0.571
0.8	0.889	0.696
0.9	0.947	0.837
1	1	1

FIGURE 10.18

Sensitivity of
Posterior Probabilities to
Prior Probabilities

Note that as the prior probability of a strong market increases, so does the posterior probability of a strong market given either an encouraging or a discouraging test result. Note too that the posterior probability of a strong market is greater than the prior probability given an encouraging test result, but the posterior probability is less than the prior, given a discouraging test result (except when $P(S) = 0$ or 1, in which case the prior and posterior probabilities are equal).

INCORPORATING POSTERIOR PROBABILITIES IN THE DECISION TREE

We now represent management's model with the decision tree presented in Figure 10.19. The first node (I) corresponds to performing the marketing research. The node is circular because the outcome is not certain. There are two possible results. The test is either encouraging (E) or discouraging (D); $P(E)$ and $P(D)$ represent the probabilities of those two outcomes and were shown in cells D12 and D13 of Figure 10.17 previously.

If the test is encouraging, we proceed to node II, which is square because a decision must be made. Management must decide to select one of the three marketing strategies (A or B or C). Suppose that management selects A. We are then led to node IV, another situation with two possible outcomes, namely whether the market is strong (S) or weak (W). If it turns out to be strong, PROTRAC will enjoy a net return of 30, which is the terminal value on the branch.

It is important to note that the tree is created in the chronological order in which information becomes available and decisions are required; that is,

1. Result of marketing research survey (Encouraging or Discouraging)
2. Make decision on which marketing strategy to pursue (Aggressive, Basic, or Cautious)
3. Market condition (Strong or Weak)

In order to solve this tree we must fill in the values for $P(S|E)$, $P(W|E)$, $P(S|D)$, $P(W|D)$, $P(E)$, and $P(D)$. The first four probabilities are found in the table labeled Posterior Probabilities in Figure 10.17 (cells B19:C20). For example, the probability $P(W|E)$ is found in *column* W and *row* E of the table (again, note that this is the opposite of the convention used to read the Reliabilities table but is more convenient for the spreadsheet representation). So, for example, $P(W|E) = 0.379$.

Thus, the event of an encouraging test result and the use of Bayes' Theorem allow us to update the prior value of $P(S)$, namely 0.45, to a higher value, $P(S|E) = 0.621$. Similar calculations yield $P(S|D) = 0.319$, and $P(W|D) = 0.681$. These probabilities are attached to the decision tree. TreePlan then automatically folds back the tree to solve our decision model. To do this in TreePlan we basically follow the same steps as before.

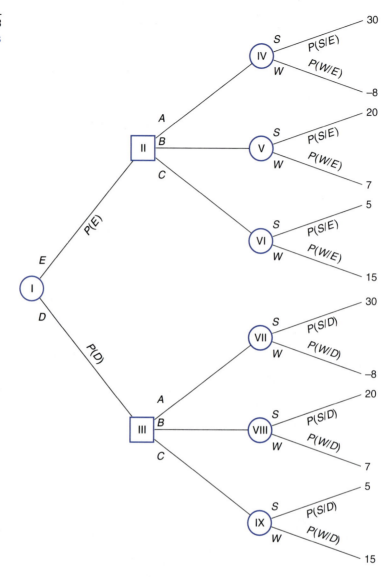

FIGURE 10.19

Decision Tree with
Test Results

The results are shown in Figures 10.20 and 10.21 (upper and lower half of the tree). Highlights are given below:

1. Hit Ctrl-t to bring up the menu and select "New Tree." (*Note:* TreePlan can't have more than 1 tree in a spreadsheet so we created a new spreadsheet called "PROTDT2.XLS" for this new model.)

2. Click on the default decision node, and hit Ctrl-t. Select "Change to event" and click OK.

3. At the terminal node, hit Ctrl-t and select "Change to decision" with 3 branches. Click OK.

4. Repeat step 3 for the other terminal node.

5. Click on the new terminal node at the top of the tree, hit Ctrl-t, and select "Change to event" with 2 branches. Click OK.

6. Copy the node created in step 5 to the other 2 terminal values nearest it (use TreePlan's Copy subtree and Paste subtree commands, not Excel's normal Copy and Paste features).

7. Once we get the upper half of the tree done (Node II and everything to the right in Figure 10.19), we can then copy it and paste it on Node III effectively.

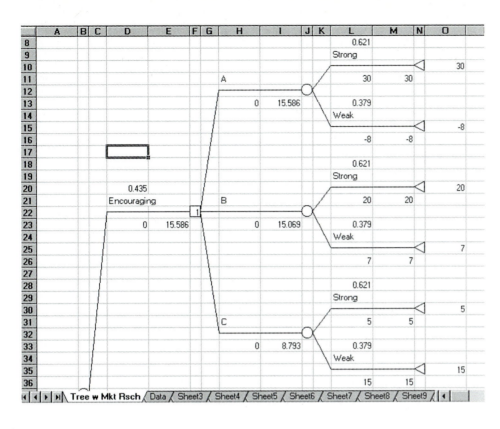

FIGURE 10.20

Upper Half of Decision Tree
with New Information

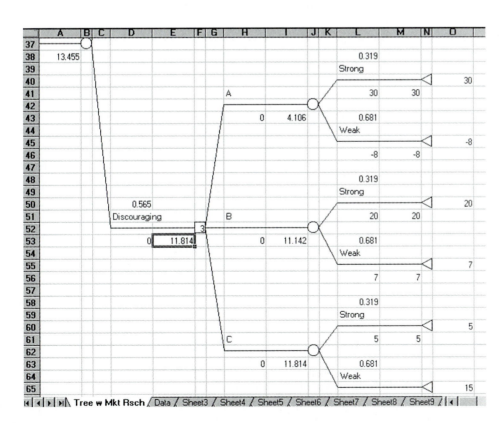

FIGURE 10.21

Lower Half of Decision Tree
with New Information

These figures can be used to determine the optimal decisions. We see that if the test is encouraging, E (see Figure 10.20), we arrive at cell F22. Then to maximize the expected return, we should take action A (TreePlan indicates this with a "1" in cell F22, meaning take the first branch); that is, follow the Aggressive production and marketing strategy. Similarly, if the test result is discouraging, D (see Figure 10.21), we should take action C. Why? Because 11.81 is the largest possible expected return when the test is discouraging.

THE EXPECTED VALUE OF SAMPLE INFORMATION

Suppose that we use the optimal decisions determined above to fold back the decision tree (shown in Figures 10.20 and 10.21) one more step. Cell B37 (of Figure 10.21) shows us the expected return at the initial event node is

$$ER = 15.586(0.435) + 11.814(0.565) = 13.455$$

This value is the expected return of performing the market test and making optimal decisions after determining the results.

In Section 10.6 we saw that if the market test is not performed, the optimal decision is to select B, the basic strategy, and that this decision has an expected return of 12.85. Clearly, then, performing the market test increases PROTRAC's expected return by $0.61 million (=$13.46 million − $12.85 million). Even though the market test is not perfectly reliable, it still has some value ($0.61 million, to be precise). Appropriately enough, this quantity is called the **expected value of sample information (EVSI)**. In general terms

$$EVSI = \begin{pmatrix} \text{maximum possible} \\ \text{expected return} \\ \text{with sample} \\ \text{information} \end{pmatrix} - \begin{pmatrix} \text{maximum possible} \\ \text{expected return} \\ \text{without sample} \\ \text{information} \end{pmatrix}$$

The EVSI is an upper bound of how much one would be willing to pay for this particular sample information.

Let us now calculate the expected value of *perfect* information. Recall from Section 10.3 that this is the amount that management would be willing to pay for perfect information. The payoff table was originally presented in Figure 10.11. If it were sure that the market would be strong, management would pick decision A and enjoy a return of 30. Similarly, if it were sure that the market would be weak, management would pick decision C and enjoy a return of 15. How much would management pay for perfect information? Since perfect information will reveal a strong market with probability 0.45, and a weak market with probability 0.55, we see that

$$EVPI = (30)(0.45) + (15)(0.55) - 12.85 = 8.90 \tag{10.2}$$

Equation (10.2) tells us that perfect information will bring us an expected increase of $8.90 million over the previous expected return. This is the maximum possible increase in the expected return that can be obtained from new information. The expected value of sample information (EVSI) is the increase in the expected return that was obtained with the information produced by the market test. Since EVPI = 8.9 and EVSI = 0.61, we see that the market test is not very effective. If it were, the value for EVSI would be much closer to EVPI. In other words, as the probabilities of correct sample information increase, EVSI approaches EVPI. In fact, when $P(E|S) = 1.00$ and $P(D|W) = 1.00$, then EVSI=EVPI.

10.9   SEQUENTIAL DECISIONS: TO TEST OR NOT TO TEST

In the preceding section, we assumed that the board of directors had decided to have a market research study done. We then considered the question of how the management of PROTRAC's domestic tractor division should use the information generated by the study to update the decision model. Let us step back for a moment. It seems clear that the decision to have a market study done is in essence no different from the decision to adopt one marketing and production strategy or another. Management must carefully weigh the cost of performing the study against the gain that might result from having the information that the study would produce. Suppose that the market test will cost $500,000 (or $0.5 million). It is also clear that the decision on whether to have a market research test is not an isolated decision. If the test is given, management must still select one of the marketing and production strategies. Thus, the value of performing the test depends in part on how PROTRAC uses the information generated by the test. In other words, the value of an initial decision depends on a *sequence* of decisions and uncertain events that will follow the initial decision. This is called a **sequential decision model.**

ANALYZING SEQUENTIAL DECISIONS

This is an extremely common type of management model and is actually the kind of situation that decision trees are designed to handle. It is in situations where there are a number of interrelated decisions and events with more than one possible outcome that the ability to display the model graphically is especially useful.

Figures 10.22 and 10.23 show the test or no-test tree. In terms of structure and the probabilities, you see that the upper (test) branch is the tree from Figures 10.20 and 10.21 with

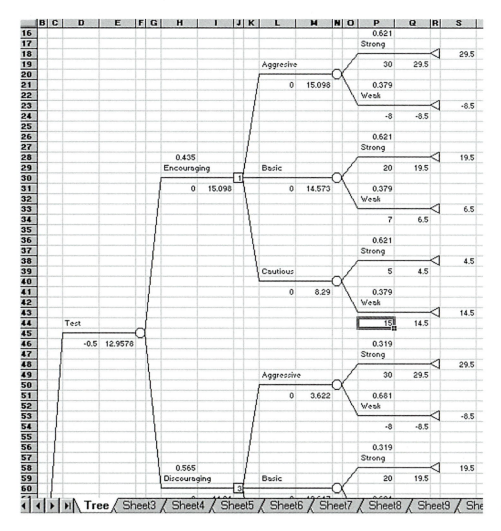

FIGURE 10.22

Upper Half of Decision Tree with New Information

slightly modified terminal values to account for the market test cost and the lower (no-test) branch is the tree from Figure 10.15. To do this in TreePlan we basically follow the same steps as before. We created a new spreadsheet called "PROTDT3.XLS" for this new decision model. Highlights are given below:

1. Hit Ctrl-t to bring up the menu and select "New Tree."

2. At the first terminal node (cell F45 in Figure 10.22), hit Ctrl-t and select "Change to event" with 2 branches. Click OK.

3. Click on the new terminal node at the top of the tree (cell J30 in Figure 10.22), hit Ctrl-t, and select "Change to decision" with 3 branches. Click OK.

4. Copy the node created in step 3 to the other terminal node (cell J60 in Figure 10.22) nearest it. (Use TreePlan's Copy subtree and Paste subtree commands, not Excel's normal Copy and Paste features.)

5. To finish the upper half of the tree, click on the new terminal node at the top of the tree (cell N20 in Figure 10.22), hit Ctrl-t, and select "Change to event" with 2 branches. Click OK.

6. Copy the node created in step 5 to the other five terminal nodes nearest it (cells N30, N40, N50, N60, N70). This completes the upper half of the tree.

7. You can then copy the decision node with its 3 branches followed by event nodes of 2 branches (cell J30 or J60) to the node (cell F90 in Figure 10.23) at the bottom half of the tree.

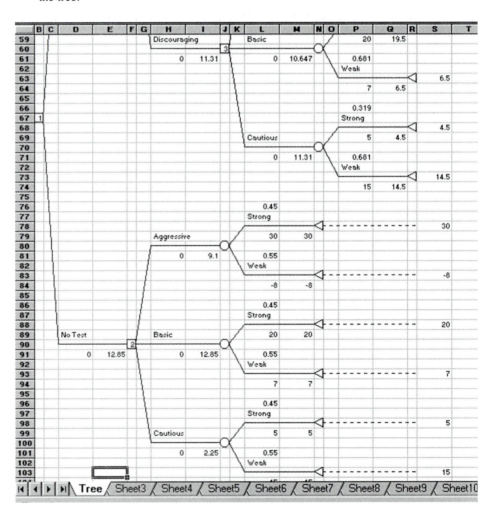

FIGURE 10.23

Lower Half of Decision Tree with New Information

The terminal values merit some discussion. They are determined in a two-step process:

1. Assign the appropriate cash flow to each decision and uncertain event. In this model we have assumed that the market test costs $500,000. Since all costs and returns are measured in millions, a figure of -0.5 is placed by the test branch (cell D46 of Figure 10.22) and a figure of 0 is placed by the no-test branch (cell D91 of Figure 10.23). Similarly, a figure of 30 is placed on the upper branch (cell P19 in Figure 10.22) since this is the profit if PROTRAC selects A and the market is strong.

2. TreePlan determines a particular terminal value by adding the cash flows on all branches between the first node and the terminal position. For example, the number 29.5 on the uppermost terminal position (cell S18 in Figure 10.22) comes from adding the costs on the path Test-Encouraging-Aggressive-Strong (i.e., returns of $-0.5 + 0 + 0 + 30 = 29.5$).

Again, TreePlan solves this tree by folding it back. It folds back a circular (event) node by calculating the expected returns. It folds back a square (decision) node by selecting the decision that yields the highest expected return.

The *optimal strategy* is a complete plan for the entire tree. It specifies what action to take no matter which of the uncertain events occurs. To determine the optimal strategy for the test or no-test tree, we refer to Figures 10.22 and 10.23. At the first decision node (test or no-test), we see that since $12.96 > 12.85$, PROTRAC should conduct the market test. If the result of the test is encouraging (E), then an Aggressive campaign (A) is the best decision since it yields the largest expected return (15.098). Similarly, if the result of the test is discouraging (D), then a Cautious campaign (C) is the best decision (with expected return of 11.31).

THE IMPACT OF UTILITIES

It is simple to incorporate utilities into a decision tree. Suppose that the utilities of all possible payoffs are given in Table 10.12 and were calculated in a manner similar to that shown in Section 10.4.

TABLE 10.12 Utilities of Payoffs	
PAYOFF	**UTILITY**
-8.5	0.300
-8	0.320
4.5	0.695
5	0.709
6.5	0.748
7	0.760
14.5	0.910
15	0.914
19.5	0.941
20	0.943
29.5	0.962
30	0.963

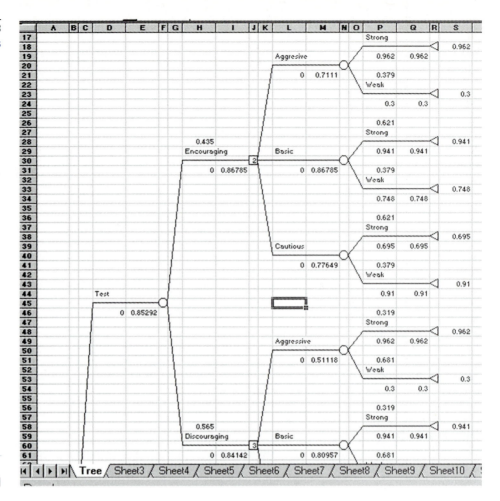

FIGURE 10.24

Upper Half of Test or No-Test
Tree with Utilities Incorporated

A graph of utility versus payoff would show that PROTRAC is risk-averse. For example, the additional utility of increasing the payoff from 20 to 30 is only 0.020 (= 0.963 − 0.943), while the additional utility of increasing the payoff from 5 to 15 is 0.205 (= 0.914 − 0.709).

To incorporate the utilities into the decision tree, all you need to do is replace the payoffs in Figures 10.22 and 10.23 with their utilities and fold back the tree as before. This is done in a new spreadsheet (PROTDT4.XLS) and is shown in Figures 10.24 and 10.25.

It turns out that with these utilities the optimal decision is still to test. However, if the test is encouraging, alternative B is now chosen rather than A because it has a higher expected utility (0.868 versus 0.711). Even though A's maximum payoff ($29.5) is larger than B's ($19.5), B's minimum payoff is larger than A's ($6.5 versus −$8.5). The combination of PROTRAC's utility function and the given posterior probabilities now causes the expected utility of B to be higher than that of A.

OTHER FEATURES OF TREEPLAN

If you click on the feature labeled "Options", you get the following dialog box (see Figure 10.26), which demonstrates two additional features of TreePlan. First note that TreePlan has a built-in exponential utility function. To activate it, click on the "Use Exponential Utility Function," and TreePlan will automatically assume a risk-averse utility

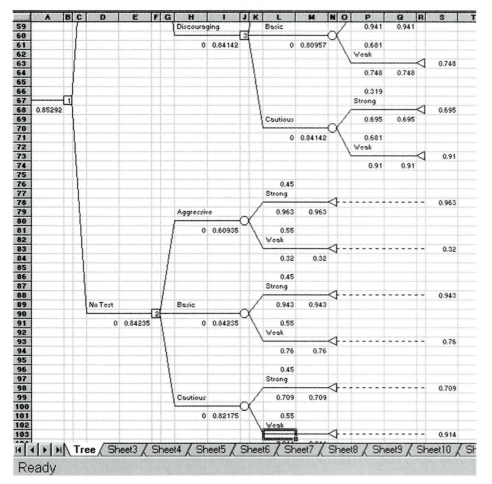

FIGURE 10.25

Lower Half of Test or No-Test Tree with Utilities Incorporated

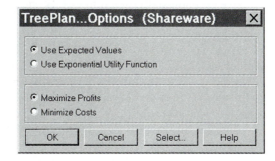

FIGURE 10.26

TreePlan Options Dialog Box

function and calculate the utilities for the given cash flows already on the tree. The second feature is that TreePlan defaults to a "Maximize Profits" approach to folding back the tree (i.e., at a decision node it picks the branch with the *largest* payoff). If you want to do a cost-minimization model, you must change this to "Minimize Costs" so that it picks the branch with the *smallest* payoff at the decision nodes. It's also worth mentioning that TreePlan has online help available to those who need it.

J4   = =SUMPRODUCT(L4:M4,N4:O4)

	F	G	H	I	J	K	L	M	N	O
1	Test Branch	0.853		Best			#'s for Exp. Utility Calculations			
2		Encouraging Report			0.868	Exp. Utility	P(S|E)	P(W|E)	Utility if S	Utility if W
3			0.435	Aggressive		0.711	0.621	0.379	0.962	0.3
4				Basic		0.868	0.621	0.379	0.941	0.748
5				Cautious		0.777	0.621	0.379	0.695	0.91
6				Best						
7		Discouraging Report			0.842	Exp. Utility	P(S|D)	P(W|D)	Utility if S	Utility if W
8			0.565	Aggressive		0.511	0.319	0.681	0.962	0.3
9				Basic		0.809	0.319	0.681	0.941	0.748
10				Cautious		0.842	0.319	0.681	0.695	0.91
11				Best						
12	No Test Branch				0.842	Exp. Utility	P(S)	P(W)	Utility if S	Utility if W
13		Aggressive				0.609	0.45	0.55	0.963	0.32
14		Basic				0.842	0.45	0.55	0.943	0.76
15		Cautious				0.822	0.45	0.55	0.709	0.914
16										
17										
18										
19	Decision:	Test								
20	Maximum Utility	0.853								

Cell	Formula	Copy To
G1	= G3*I2+G8*I7	—
I2	= MAX(J3:J5)	I7, I12
G3	= D12	—
J3	= SUMPRODUCT(L3:M3, N3:O3)	J4:J5, J8:J10, J13:J15
L3	= B$19	L3:M5
G8	= D13	—
L8	= B$20	L8:M10
L13	= B$8	L13:M15
G19	= IF(G20=G1,"Test","NoTest")	—
G20	= MAX(G1,I12)	—

FIGURE 10.27

Spreadsheet Representation of Test/No-Test Decision Tree

SENSITIVITY OF THE OPTIMAL DECISION TO PRIOR PROBABILITIES

Whether cash returns or utilities are used in the decision tree, it is important to see how sensitive the optimal decision is to various parameter values. For example, how sensitive is the optimal decision to the initial estimate of a strong market, the prior probability $P(S)$? The spreadsheet shown in Figure 10.27 (PROTDT5.XLS) reproduces the graphical analysis shown in Figures 10.24 and 10.25. The first step was to copy the "Probabilities" worksheet of PROTRACDT.XLS (see Figure 10.17) over into cells A1:E20 (not shown). The rest of the spreadsheet is shown in Figure 10.27. The main advantage of the spreadsheet formulation is the ease with which various parameters can be changed and the tree effectively recalculated.

The graph of Figure 10.28 was generated by varying the value of $P(S)$ between 0 and 1 in increments of 0.01. This is done easily in Excel using the Data Table feature as follows:

1. In Cell A24, we enter an initial value of 0.

2. Click back on A24, then click on Edit, Fill, and then Series.

3. Click on "Series in Columns" and enter a step value of 0.01 and a stop value of 1.0. Click on OK.

4. In cells B23:C23 we enter the formulas for the quantities we want to track (Exp. Utility[Test] and Exp. Utility[NoTest]) for each of the values for $P(S)$ that we've entered in column A. These formulas are =G1, and =I12, respectively.

5. Highlight the area A23:C124, and click on Data, then Table.

6. Enter the Column input cell as B8 and click on OK.

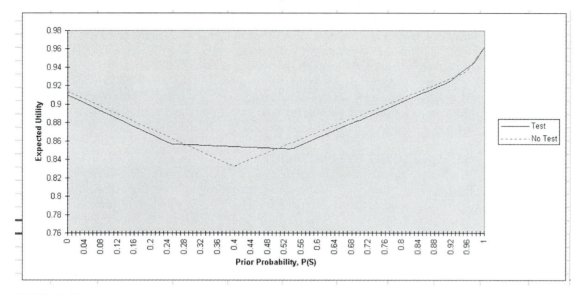

FIGURE 10.28

Expected Utility of Test and No-Test

7. Excel automatically calculates the two expected utilities for values of $P(S)$ between 0 and 1.

The solid line in Figure 10.28 represents the expected utility of the Test decision, while the dotted line represents the expected utility of the No-Test decision. Whenever the two curves cross, the optimal decision changes. Since the curves cross four times (although it is hard to see the last time because the curves are so close together), the optimal decision changes four times: No-Test, Test, No-Test, Test, No-Test. Test is the optimal decision for values of $P(S)$ between (approximately) 0.29 and 0.50 and between 0.94 and 0.96. No-Test is optimal for the values of $P(S)$ between 0 and 0.29, between 0.5 and 0.94, and between 0.96 and 1.

10.10 MANAGEMENT AND DECISION THEORY

A typical management decision has the following characteristics:

1. It is made once and only once (e.g., should I buy 100 shares of Intel stock today or not?).
2. The return depends on an uncertain event that will occur in the future (e.g., the price of Intel stock will go up or down), and we have no historical information about this future event.

We know about related events that may tell us something about the likelihood of the various outcomes (e.g., the behavior of the price of Intel stock last week or the last 52 weeks). But we cannot perform an experiment to provide a good, reliable estimate of the relevant probabilities (e.g., we cannot perform an experiment that tells us about the price of Intel stock next week.)

What does the material in this chapter contribute to our understanding of how to attack this model? In brief, this chapter recommends the following conceptual framework:

1. For each decision, determine the utility of each possible outcome.
2. Determine the probability of each possible outcome.
3. Calculate the expected utility of each decision.
4. Select the decision with the largest expected utility.

Once the first two steps have been completed, the next two steps are easy, at least conceptually. But how can you *know* the probabilities and the utilities?

The answer is that there are no values to *know*. These are not entities, the "true" value of which can be revealed by experimentation or further analysis. Indeed, these two quantities, *probabilities* and *utilities,* are *subjective* and represent the *best judgment and taste of the manager.* Certainly the manager's evaluation of these two quantities can be influenced by study, but there is no opportunity for direct experimentation with the underlying phenomena, as there would be, for example, in physical or biological science.

There is, nevertheless, some structure to cling to in this sea of subjectivity. The structure is provided by a logical device called an *equivalent lottery.* This concept gives one a *consistent framework* for quantifying both probabilities and utilities. We saw in Section 10.4 how a manager can use an equivalent lottery to create a utility function.

ASSESSING SUBJECTIVE PROBABILITIES

The manager can use this approach to assess a subjective probability. Suppose, for example, that on this date you wish to assess the probability that Colin Powell will be the Republican candidate for president in 2000. The first step is to think of two games. In game 1 you receive $100 if Powell is the candidate and $0 if he is not. In game 2 you receive $100 with probability p and $0 with probability $1 - p$. You now adjust the value of p until you are indifferent between the two games. The resulting value of p is *your* subjective probability that Powell will be the Republican candidate in 2000. It is clear that your assessment of Powell's chances may be different from that of Colin Powell's assessment or anyone else's for that matter.

We have argued that the equivalent lottery allows one to quantify both subjective probability and utility. We now stress again that the values obtained through this process are personal and a matter of judgment, and thus by definition they will vary from person to person. Certainly, then, two individuals, each of whom is facing the same decision and using the recommended approach, may arrive at different decisions. And why not? The recommended approach allows the manager to incorporate personal knowledge (and experience), and surely there is no reason to believe that everyone will "know" the same things at the moment of decision.

However, a cynic might ask, "Why bother with all this machinery?" If judgment and taste play such an important role in these assessments, isn't it better to use judgment in a holistic approach and simply select the alternative that intuitively seems best? What do we gain from assessing probability and utility separately? The reply is that separating the two assessments makes it possible for a manager to concentrate attention on each of these entities (probability and utility), one at a time. The problem with a simple intuitive approach is that we humans have a hard time thinking about more than one thing at a time. While thinking about payoffs, it is hard to be thinking at the same time about likelihoods and then to combine them in one's head. In other words, the simple, intuitive approach makes it too easy to put heavy emphasis on a particularly awful outcome (or a particularly attractive outcome) and not enough weight on the fact that this outcome may be extremely unlikely. As an example, look at the number of people who won't fly in an airplane, but will drive in a car, even though the probability of being killed in an auto accident is vastly higher than that of dying in a plane crash. (Presumably, they are influenced by the thought that they *might* survive an auto accident, whereas they would be unlikely to live through a plane crash.) *Separating the assessments of probabilities and utilities forces a manager to give appropriate and separate consideration to each before combining the two to determine the final decision.*

The revolution in personal computing and the explosion in software that has accompanied it have had an impact on decision analysis. A decade ago, general-purpose decision analysis programs from commercial software suppliers were not widely available. Some companies created programs for their own purposes, but these were not available to the general public. We have demonstrated in this chapter the use of a very popular spreadsheet add-in, TreePlan, and also point out that there are other spreadsheet add-in packages available (PrecisionTree by Palisade), as well as stand-alone software packages (DPL by Applied Decision Analysis, DATA, Arborist, Riskcalc, and Supertree). Many of these packages also include the ability to draw influence diagrams, which help the manager to bring structure to all the variables involved in the model by identifying which variables influence the others.

10.11   NOTES ON IMPLEMENTATION

Ralph Keeney, a leading scholar in the field (see Keeney and Raiffa; Keeney [B]), defines decision analysis as "a formalization of common sense for decision models which are too complex for informal use of common sense." Decision analysis, which is based on axioms originally stated by John von Neumann and Oskar Morgenstern, involves assigning probabilities and utilities to possible outcomes and maximizing expected utility. This approach is applied to highly complex models that are typically sequential in nature. It can be thought of as having four parts: (1) structuring the model, (2) assessing the probability of the possible outcomes, (3) determining the utility of the possible outcomes, and (4) evaluating alternatives and selecting a strategy.

Much of the material in this chapter concerns item (4), the technical process of evaluating alternatives and selecting a strategy. This is appropriate since this is the conceptual heart of decision analysis. In practice, however, this is the easy part of the model. A significantly greater proportion of effort is spent on the other three areas. Structuring the model, which involves generating alternatives and specifying objectives in numerically measurable terms, is a particularly unstructured task. In some of the real-world applications, objectives have been quantified in the areas of environmental impact, public health and safety, and so on.

ROLE OF PERSONAL JUDGMENT

It is important to understand that decision analysis does *not* provide a completely objective analysis of complicated models. Many aspects of a decision analysis require personal judgment—whether it be structuring the model, assessing probabilities, or assigning utilities. In many important complex models there simply are not enough empirical data to provide a basis for complete analysis. Nevertheless, experience has shown that the framework provided by decision analysis has been useful. Indeed, there are many qualitative and nonobjective factors involved in all decision making, but the important role of decision analysis is to make it consistent, not just "objective" and devoid of any subjective judgments. There is room for subjectivity, but it should not depend on how you "feel" at the moment.

In the early 1960s decision analysis began to be successfully applied to a number of models in the private sector. These included models of gas and oil exploration as well as capital investment. Although developments have continued on private-sector models, two other general modeling areas have witnessed a wide variety of applications of decision analysis. In the health-care field, decision analysis has been applied to such diverse models as the evaluation of new drugs, the analysis of treatment strategies for diseases, and the selection of medical technology for a particular facility. The second modeling area concerns applications in the government. In particular, decision analysis has been applied to everything from the seeding of hurricanes, to the negotiation of international oil tanker standards, to the choice between coal and nuclear technology for large scale power plants (Keeney-A).

One final note: We can see that the decision trees can get rather large and cumbersome as the number of decision alternatives or random states of nature multiply (≥ 3 to 5 decisions or random outcomes per node). In decision models where the number becomes too large, we may have to make simplifying assumptions about the possible outcomes or limit the number of decision alternatives we will evaluate if we wish to press ahead with decision analysis. For example, consider the random outcome of a lawsuit or random demand for a product (one can easily see that there is a continuous range of possible outcomes [i.e., an infinite number]) and that it would be nigh impossible to model this as a decision tree in an explicit sense. There are two main options to handle such a situation: (1) approximate the continuous outcomes with a Pearson-Tukey approach (3 branches [representing the 0.05 fractile, the 0.5 fractile, and the 0.95 fractile with "optimal" weights of 0.185, 0.63, and 0.185, respectively] are used to approximate the infinite number of possibilities), or (2) use the technique of Monte Carlo simulation which is introduced in Chapter 11 and is designed to handle probability distributions of a continuous nature.

10.12   SUMMARY

The first part of this chapter dealt with the fundamentals of decision theory. A summary of that material was provided in Section 10.5.

The following four sections of the chapter expounded on the role of decision trees in facilitating the decision process. A decision tree is a graphical device for attacking models in which a sequence of decisions must be made, and these decisions are interspersed with events that have several possible outcomes. It is typically true that square nodes are used to represent decisions and circular nodes are used to represent events. The branches emanating from a square node are the possible decisions, and the branches emanating from a circular node are the possible outcomes. When a decision tree has been completed, a path from the start of the tree to a terminal node represents a specific sequence of decisions and uncertain events. The complete tree represents all possible such sequences.

Solving a decision tree is a sequential process that starts at the terminal nodes and proceeds back to the start of the tree in a process that is described as "folding back." The process includes two steps: The branches emanating from a circular node are folded back by assigning to the node the expected value of the chance events; branches emanating from a decision node are folded back by selecting the alternative with the maximum expected return and assigning this value to the decision node. This "folding back" has been greatly automated through the use of such spreadsheet add-ins as TreePlan. The solution of a decision tree yields an optimal strategy; that is, it specifies what sequence of actions should be taken for any of the possible sequences of chance events.

Bayes' Theorem plays an important role in the construction of decision trees, because this is the device that makes it possible to incorporate new information into the decision process in a formal way. Bayes' Theorem is based on the concept of conditional probability, and thus some time is devoted to that general topic.

The expected value of sample information is a measure of the value of incorporating sample information into a decision with uncertainty. The expected value of perfect information is an upper bound on the expected value of sample information.

Key Terms

Payoff Table.   A table showing the returns for each possible state of nature-decision combination in a decision against nature.

Decision Under Certainty.   A decision against nature in which the state of nature is known with certainty.

Decision Under Risk.   A decision against nature in which a probability distribution on the states of nature is known.

Risk Profile.   For a given decision, the profile shows all the possible outcomes with their associated probabilities, usually in a graphical format.

Decision Under Uncertainty.   A decision against nature with no knowledge about the likelihood of the various states of nature.

Maximin Criterion.   A conservative decision criterion of maximizing the minimum return.

Maximax Criterion.   An optimistic decision criterion of maximizing the maximum return.

Regret.   A measure of how much better the decision maker could have done had he or she known the state of nature (the opportunity cost of not making the best decision for a given state of nature).

Expected Value Of Perfect Information (EVPI).   An upper bound on the value of new information.

Utility.   In this chapter, a measure of the "attractiveness" of an outcome to an individual.

Risk-Averse.   A preference to avoid downside risks, precisely reflected in a concave utility function.

Risk-Seeking.   A preference for upside returns, precisely reflected in a convex utility function.

Risk-Indifferent.   Reflected by a linear utility function.

Equivalent Lottery.   A device for creating a utility function.

Decision Tree.   A graphical device for analyzing decisions under risk.

Square Node.   A point at which a decision must be made in decision tree diagrams.

Circular Node.   Indicates a nondeterministic event on a decision tree.

Branches. The lines emanating from the nodes in a decision tree.

Terminal Position. The end of a branch emanating from a terminal node.

Terminal Node. A node in a decision tree that is not succeeded by other nodes.

Terminal Value. The net return associated with a terminal position.

Folding Back. The process of solving a decision tree by working backward.

Conditional Probability. The probability of an event (say, B) given that another event (say, A) occurs; denoted $P(B|A)$ and defined $P(B|A) = P(B \text{ and } A)/P(A)$.

Prior Probabilities. The originally assessed values for probabilities.

Posterior Probabilities. An updated probability. The updating combines the prior probabilities and new information using Bayes' Theorem.

Expected Value of Sample Information (EVSI). The difference between the maximum possible expected returns with and without sample information.

Sequential Decision Model. A model in which the value of an initial decision depends on subsequent decisions and uncertain events.

Self-Review Exercises

True-False

1. **T F** Decision trees involve sequences of decisions and random outcomes.

2. **T F** In decision theory, returns are dependent on the actions of an indifferent adversary termed "nature."

3. **T F** One underlying aspect of decision theory is that, regardless of what we assume about nature, in terms of whether we know probabilities of various random states, we are led to the same criterion for selecting a "best decision."

4. **T F** Many deterministic optimization models can be thought of as decision making under certainty, where there is only one state of nature and one selects a decision that maximizes returns.

5. **T F** One way to deal with decision making in the "uncertainty" context is to treat all states of nature as equally likely and maximize expected return.

6. **T F** The computation of the value of perfect information is based on the concept that all randomness has been eliminated.

7. **T F** Maximizing expected net dollar return always yields the same optimal policy as minimizing expected regret.

8. **T F** A risk-averse utility function is convex.

9. **T F** Decision trees are solved by folding forward.

10. **T F** Bayes' Theorem provides a formula for how one can use new information to update a prior probability assessment.

Multiple Choice

11. Decision theory is concerned with
    a. the amount of information that is available
    b. criteria for measuring the "goodness" of a decision
    c. selecting optimal decisions in sequential models
    d. all of the above

12. Concerning decision making under risk, which of the following is not true?
    a. We assume that the decision maker knows the probability with which each state of nature will occur.
    b. We use the criterion of maximizing return.
    c. We use the criterion of maximizing expected return.
    d. We use the criterion of minimizing expected regret.

13. Which of the following criteria does *not* apply to decision making under uncertainty?
    a. maximin return
    b. maximax return
    c. minimax regret
    d. maximize expected return

14. Maximin return, maximax return, and minimax regret are criteria that
    a. lead to the same optimal decision
    b. can be used without probabilities
    c. both a and b

15. The expected value of perfect information (EVPI)
    a. places two-sided bounds (upper and lower) on how much should be spent in gathering information
    b. can be determined without using probabilities
    c. refers to the utility of additional information
    d. equals the expected regret of the optimal decision under risk

16. The concept of utility is a way to
    a. measure the attractiveness of money
    b. take into account aversion to risk
    c. take into account inclination to take risk
    d. both a and b
    e. a, b, and c

17. Which of the following does not apply to a decision tree?
    a. A square node is a point at which a decision must be made.
    b. A circular node represents an encounter with uncertainty.
    c. One chooses a sequence of decisions that has the greatest probability of success.
    d. One attempts to maximize expected return.

18. The expected value of perfect information (EVPI)
    a. shows the cost necessary to produce perfect information about the future
    b. shows the maximum possible increase in expected return with sample information
    c. shows the expected increase in information required to select the optimal decision
    d. all of the above

19. When computing the expected value of perfect information (EVPI), it is important that the payment is made
    a. in advance of receiving the information
    b. after receiving the information
    c. in an irrevocable way
    d. both a and c

20. When decisions are made sequentially in time
    a. decision trees cannot be employed
    b. Bayes' Theorem must be used
    c. the terminal value at the end of each sequence of branches is the net of the cash flows on that sequence
    d. the terminal value at the end of each sequence of branches is an expected net cash flow

Answers

1.	T	6.	F	11.	d	16.	e
2.	T	7.	T	12.	b	17.	c
3.	F	8.	F	13.	d	18.	b
4.	T	9.	F	14.	b	19.	d
5.	T	10.	T	15.	d	20.	c

Problems

10-1. Consider the payoff table in Table 10.13, in which the entries are net dollar returns. Assume that this is a decision with no knowledge about the states of nature.
    (a) What is the optimal decision if the Laplace criterion is used?
    (b) What is the optimal decision if the maximin criterion is used?
    (c) What is the optimal decision if the maximax criterion is used?
    (d) Create the payoff table in which the entries are regret.
    (e) What is the optimal decision if the criterion of minimax regret is used?

TABLE 10.13

DECISION	STATE OF NATURE			
	1	2	3	4
1	35	22	25	12
2	27	25	20	18
3	22	25	25	28
4	20	25	28	33

10-2. Consider the payoff table in Table 10.14, in which the entries are net dollar returns. Assume that this is a decision with no knowledge about the states of nature.
    (a) What is the optimal decision if the Laplace criterion is used?
    (b) What is the optimal decision if the maximin criterion is used?
    (c) What is the optimal solution if the maximax criterion is used?
    (d) Create the payoff table in which the entries are regret.
    (e) What is the optimal decision if the criterion of minimax regret is used?

TABLE 10.14

DECISION	STATE OF NATURE		
	1	2	3
1	5	7	8
2	6	6	6
3	3	9	1

10-3. Consider the payoff table in Table 10.13. Assume that the following probabilities are specified for the states of nature:

$$P(1) = 0.1, P(2) = 0.4, P(3) = 0.3, P(4) = 0.2$$

(a) Find the decision that maximizes the expected net dollar return.
(b) Find the decision that minimizes the expected regret.
(c) Comment on the relationship between the answers to parts (a) and (b).

•• **10-4.** Consider the payoff table in Table 10.14. Assume that the probabilities of the states of nature are as follows:

$$P(1) = 0.3, P(2) = 0.6, P(3) = 0.1$$

(a) Find the decision that maximizes the expected net dollar return.
(b) Find the decision that minimizes the expected regret.
(c) Suppose that $P(1)$ and $P(2)$ are not known, but $P(3)$ is estimated to be 0.1. Plot expected net dollar return versus $P(2)$ for the three decisions in the same graph, and find the range for $P(2)$ for which each decision is optimal.
(d) Plot expected regret versus $P(2)$ for the three decisions in the same graph, and find the range for $P(2)$ for which each decision is optimal.
(e) What did you find in the above two answers?

10-5. Phil Johnson of Johnson's Printing in Chicago must decide to either accept a contract for a government printing job or fly to Los Angeles to bid on a brochure. Capacity constraints prohibit him from doing both jobs, and he must decide on the government contract before the bidding process starts. He estimates the payoff table in terms of net dollar return as shown in Table 10.15.

TABLE 10.15

DECISION	STATE OF NATURE	
	Do Not Get Brochure Job, NJ	Get Brochure Job, J
Accept Government Contract, G	1000	1000
Accept Brochure Job, B	−1000	4000

(a) What is the optimal decision based on the maximin criterion?
(b) If the probability that he gets the brochure job is ⅓, which decision will maximize his expected net dollar return?
(c) Let $P(J)$ be the probability that he gets the brochure job. Plot the expected return for each decision as a function of $P(J)$ on the same axis.
(d) What is the smallest value of $P(J)$ for which Phil Johnson should decide to go to LA if he wishes to maximize his expected net dollar return?
(e) What is the optimal decision if minimax regret is the decision criterion?

TABLE 10.16

DECISION	STATE OF NATURE			
	Cold	Cool	Warm	Hot
Small	0	1000	2000	3000
Medium	−1000	0	3000	6000
Large	−3000	−1000	4000	8000

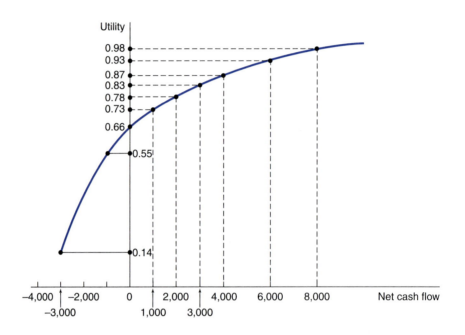

FIGURE 10.29

Utility Function

(f) What is the optimal decision if minimize expected regret is the decision criterion and $P(J) = 1/3$?

(g) Assume that the purchasing agent for the brochure job has already decided who will receive the bid but Phil doesn't know the result. If Phil believes that $P(J) = 1/3$, what is the maximum amount that Phil should pay to have this information?

(h) What would you call the quantity calculated in part (g)?

•• **10-6.** A souvenir vendor discovers that sales in July depend heavily on the weather. Products must be ordered in January. The wholesaler offers small, medium, and large variety packs at special prices, and the vendor must decide to buy one of them. The payoff table in terms of net dollar return is shown in Table 10.16. The utility function for money is presented in Figure 10.29. If the vendor believes that each state of nature is equally likely

(a) Which decision maximizes the expected net dollar return?

(b) Which decision maximizes the expected utility?

(c) Explain the relationship between the answers to parts (a) and (b).

•• **10-7.** Phil Johnson of Johnson's Printing (see Problem 10-5) has decided to use the utility function shown in Figure 10.29 to determine if he should bid on the brochure job.

(a) What is the optimal decision if the decision criterion is to maximize the expected net dollar return and the probability of getting the brochure job is 1/3? What is the expected net dollar return of the optimal decision?

(b) Would you expect the decision to change if the decision criterion is to maximize the expected utility? Discuss.

(c) What is the expected utility of the optimal decision?

(d) What is the utility of the expected dollar return from submitting a bid for the brochure?

(e) What is the expected utility of submitting a bid for the brochure?

(f) Are the answers to parts (d) and (e) the same? Should they be?

•• **10-8.** Assign a utility of 0 to a net cash flow of $-\$20,000$ and a utility of 1 to a net cash flow of $50,000. Create your own utility function by the following steps:

(a) Find equivalent lotteries for net cash flows of $0 and $20,000.

(b) Plot the four points on your utility function, and connect them with straight lines.

(c) On the basis of this utility function, are you risk-averse, risk-seeking, risk-indifferent, or none of the above?

••• **10-9.** Assume you are risk-averse and have assigned the following two endpoints on your utility function:

$$U(-30) = 0$$
$$U(70) = 1$$

(a) What is a lower bound on $U(30)$?

Suppose that you are indifferent between a sure payment of 30 and a lottery with a probability of 0.7 of winning 70 and a probability of 0.3 of losing 30.

(b) What is a lower bound on your utility for a sure payment of 50?

(c) What is the smallest upper bound of your utility for a sure payment of 10?

HINT: Recall that a utility function is nondecreasing and, if the decision maker is risk-averse, it is concave.

••• **10-10.** Assume that you have assigned the following two endpoints on your utility function:

$$U(-30) = 0$$
$$U(70) = 1$$

Suppose that you are indifferent between a sure payment of 30 and a lottery with a probability of 0.3 of winning 70 and a probability of 0.7 of losing 30. Furthermore, you feel that a sure payment of 10 is equivalent to a gamble with a probability of 0.9 of losing 30 and a probability of 0.1 of winning 30.

(a) How can you describe your utility function? Are you a "risk-taker"?

(b) What are upper and lower bounds on $U(50)$?

(c) What are upper and lower bounds on $U(25)$?

•• **10-11.** The customer service manager for PROTRAC is responsible for expediting late orders. To do the job effectively, when an order is late the manager must determine if the lateness is caused by an ordering error or a delivery error. If an order is late, one or the other of these two types of errors must have occurred. Because of the way in which this system is designed, both errors cannot occur on the same order. From experience, the manager knows that an ordering error will cause 8 out of 20 deliveries to be late, whereas a delivery error will cause 8 out of 10 deliveries to be late. Historically, out of 1000 orders, 30 ordering errors and 10 delivery errors have occurred. Assume that an order is late. If the customer service manager wishes to look first for the type of error that has the largest probability of occurring, should it be an ordering error or a delivery error?

••• **10-12.** The Scrub Professional Cleaning Service receives preliminary sales contracts from two sources: (1) its own agents and (2) building managers. Historically, ¼ of the contracts have come from Scrub agents and ¾ from building managers. Unfortunately, not all preliminary contracts result in actual sales contracts. Actually, only ⅜ of those preliminary contracts received from building managers result in a sale, whereas ⅞ of those received from Scrub agents result in a sale. The net return to Scrub from a sale is $1000. The cost of processing and following up on a preliminary contract that does not result in a sale is $150.

(a) What is the probability that a preliminary contract leads to a sale? What is the expected return associated with a preliminary sales contract?

(b) Which party, agents or building managers, contributes more to the expected return? Scrub keeps all of its sales filed by the source of reference: that is, it maintains one file for sales resulting from preliminary contracts submitted by Scrub agents and another for sales resulting from preliminary contracts submitted by building managers. Scrub knows that John Jones holds one of its sales contracts, and it wishes to have more information about him.

(c) Which file should it search first to have the higher probability of finding his name?

••• **10-13.** Clyde's Coal Company sells coal by the ½-ton, 1-ton, or 2-ton load. The probability is 0.20 that an order is from town A, 0.30 from town B, and 0.50 from town C. The relative frequency of the number of orders of each size from each town is shown in Table 10.17.

TABLE 10.17 Relative Frequencies of Number of Orders for Each Town

TOWN	LOAD SIZE (TONS)		
	½	1	2
A	0.50	0.00	0.50
B	0.00	0.50	0.50
C	0.25	0.75	0.00

(a) What is the probability that an order will be for ½ ton?

(b) If an order is for ½ ton, what is the probability that it came from town A?

(c) Clyde makes a different amount of profit on each type of load of coal in each city. The profit figures are shown in Table 10.18. Find the expected profit per load for Clyde.

TABLE 10.18 Profit in Dollars per Load

TOWN	LOAD SIZE (TONS)		
	½	1	2
A	100	190	370
B	90	200	360
C	70	130	270

10-14. Walter's Dog and Pony Show is scheduled to appear in Cedar Rapids on July 10. The profits obtained are heavily dependent on the weather. In particular, if the weather is rainy, the show loses $15,000, and if sunny the show makes a profit of $10,000. (We assume that all days are either rainy or sunny.) Walter can decide to cancel the show, but if he does he forfeits a $1000 deposit he put down when he accepted the date. The historical record shows that on July 10 it rained ¼ of the time in the last 100 years.

(a) What decision should Walter make to maximize his expected net dollar return?

(b) What is the expected value of perfect information?

10-15. Consider the model faced by Walter in Problem 10-14. Walter has the option to purchase a forecast from Victor's Weather Wonder. Victor's accuracy varies. On those occasions when it has rained, he has been correct (i.e., he predicted rain) 90% of the time. On the other hand, when it has been sunny, he has been right (i.e., he predicted sun) only 80% of the time.

(a) If Walter had the forecast, what strategy should he follow to maximize his expected net dollar return?

(b) How much should Walter be willing to pay for the forecast?

10-16. A gambler has an opportunity to play the following two-stage game. At stage 1 he pays $5 and draws a ball at random from an urn containing 5 white and 5 red balls. The balls are identical except for color. The player may now quit or move on to play stage 2 at the cost of an additional $10. In stage 2, if a white ball was drawn in stage 1, the player draws a ball at random from a white urn that contains 2 blue and 8 green balls. If a red ball was drawn in stage 1, the player draws a ball at random from a red urn that contains 6 blue and 4 green balls. If in stage 2 the player draws a blue ball, the house pays him $35. If he draws a green ball, the house pays him $0. Use a decision tree to determine the optimal strategy for the gambler.

10-17. A certain retail firm places applicants for credit into two categories, bad risks and good risks. Statistics indicate that 10% of the population would be classified as a bad risk by the firm's standards. The firm uses a credit-scoring device to decide whether credit should be granted to an applicant. Experience suggests that if a good risk applies, the person will get credit 90% of the time. If a bad risk applies, credit will be granted 20% of the time. Management believes that it is reasonable to assume that the persons who apply for credit are selected at random from the population. What is the probability that a person granted credit will be a bad risk? (Use Bayes' Theorem.)

10-18. Three workers produce a certain part at the same rate. Larry averages 3 defective parts per hundred while Moe and Curly average 6 and 9 defectives per hundred, respectively.
   (a) How many defective parts do you expect out of 1000 produced?
   (b) What is the probability that a defective part selected at random was produced by Curly?

10-19. Johnson's Metal (JM), a small manufacturer of metal parts, is attempting to decide whether to enter the competition to be a supplier of transmission housings for PROTRAC. In order to compete, the firm must design a test fixture for the production process and produce 10 housings that PROTRAC will test. The cost of development, that is, designing and building the fixture and the test housings, is $50,000. If JM gets the order, an event estimated as occurring with probability 0.4, it will be possible to sell 10,000 items to PROTRAC for $50 each. If JM does not get the order, the development cost is essentially lost. In order to produce the housings, JM may either use its current machines or purchase a new forge. Tooling with the current machines will cost $40,000 and the per-unit production cost is $20. However, if JM uses its current machines, it runs the risk of incurring overtime costs. The relationship between overtime costs and the status of JM's other business is presented in Table 10.19. The new forge costs $260,000, including tooling costs for the transmission housings. However, with the new forge, JM would certainly not incur any overtime costs, and the production cost will be only $10 per unit. Use a decision tree to determine the optimal set of actions for JM.

TABLE 10.19 Cost and Probability Data for Johnson's Metal Model

OTHER BUSINESS	PROBABILITY	OVERTIME COST TO JM
Heavy	0.2	$200,000
Normal	0.7	100,000
Light	0.1	0

••10-20. It is January 1 and Justin Case, chief counsel for Chemgoo, is faced with a difficult challenge. It seems that the firm has two related lawsuits for patent infringement. For each suit, the firm has the option of going to trial or settling out of court. The trial date for one of the suits, which we will cleverly identify as suit 1, is scheduled for July 15 and the second (suit 2, of course) is scheduled for January 8, next year. Preparation costs for either trial are estimated at $10,000. However, if the firm prepares for both trials, the preparation costs of the second trial will be only $6000. These costs can be avoided by settling out of court. If the firm wins suit 1, it pays no penalty. If it loses, it pays a $200,000 penalty. Lawyers for the firm assess the probability of winning suit 1 as 0.5. The firm has the option to settle out of court for $100,000. Suit 2 can be settled out of court for a cost of $60,000. Otherwise, a trial will result in one of three possible outcomes: (1) The suit is declared invalid and the firm pays no penalty; (2) the suit is found valid but with no infringement, and the firm pays a penalty of $50,000; or (3) the suit is found valid with infringement, and the firm pays a penalty of $90,000. The likelihood of these outcomes depends in general on the result of suit 1. The judge will certainly view suit 1 as an important precedent. The lawyers' assessment of the probability of the three possible outcomes of suit 2 under three sets of possible conditions (relating to suit 1) are presented in Table 10.20.

TABLE 10.20

OUTCOMES	NO INFORMATION CONCERNING SUIT 1[a]	FIRM WINS SUIT 1	FIRM LOSES SUIT 1
Invalid	0.3	0.7	0.1
Valid, No infringement	0.3	0.2	0.5
Valid, Infringement	0.4	0.1	0.4

[a]That is, suit 1 is settled out of court.

(a)   Represent the firm's model with a decision tree.

(b)   Solve the decision tree, and find the optimal strategy for the firm.

(c)   What is the expected loss that the firm will incur if it follows the optimal strategy?

(d)   What decisions would be made if the firm treated each suit independently, ignoring any interactions between the two? What is the expected savings from the decision analysis of this scenario?

HINT: Since all the figures are costs, you may find it easier to work with the cost figures and minimize the expected cost.

10-21.   Jenny Lind is a writer of romance novels. A movie company and a TV network both want exclusive rights to one of her most popular works. If she signs with the network she will receive a single lump sum, but if she signs with the movie company the amount she will receive depends on the market response to the movie. Jenny's payoffs are summarized in Table 10.21.

TABLE 10.21

DECISION	STATE OF NATURE		
	Small Box Office	Medium Box Office	Large Box Office
Sign with Movie Company	$200,000	$1,000,000	$3,000,000
Sign with TV Network	900,000	900,000	900,000

If the probability estimates for the states of nature are $P(\text{Small}) = 0.3$, $P(\text{Medium}) = 0.6$, $P(\text{Large}) = 0.1$, to whom should Jenny sell the rights? What is the most Jenny should be willing to pay to learn what the size of the box office would be before she decides with whom to sign?

10-22.   Kelly Construction wants to get in on the boom of student condominium construction. The company must decide whether to purchase enough land to build a 100-, 200-, or 300-unit condominium complex. Many other complexes are currently under construction, so Kelly is unsure how strong demand for its complex will be. If the company is conservative and builds only a few units, it loses potential profits if the demand turns out to be high. On the other hand, many unsold units would also be costly to Kelly. Table 10.22 has been prepared, based on three levels of demand.

TABLE 10.22

DECISION	DEMAND		
	Low	Medium	High
Build 50	$400,000	$400,000	$400,000
Build 100	100,000	800,000	800,000
Build 150	−200,000	500,000	1,200,000

(a)   What is the optimal decision if the maximin criterion is used?

(b)   What is the optimal decision if the maximax criterion is used?

(c)   What is the optimal decision if the criterion of minimax regret is used?

(d)   If $P(\text{Low}) = 0.3$, $P(\text{Medium}) = 0.5$, and $P(\text{High}) = 0.2$, which decision will maximize the expected net dollar return?

(e)   What is the expected value of perfect information?

10-23.   Marple Manufacturing is planning the introduction of a new product. The cost to set up to manufacture one of the product's components is very high, so Marple is considering purchasing that component rather than manufacturing it. Once set up to manufacture the component, however, Marple's variable cost per unit would be low in comparison to the purchase price of the component. Marple's materials manager has calculated the net profit in thousands of dollars for three different levels of demand in Table 10.23. The states of nature have probabilities $P(\text{Low}) = 0.4$, $P(\text{Medium}) = 0.3$, and $P(\text{High}) = 0.3$. Draw a decision tree and use it to decide whether Marple should make or buy the component.

TABLE 10.23

DECISION	DEMAND		
	Low	Medium	High
Make Component	11	32	53
Buy Component	15	30	45

10-24. Chuck drives to a consulting job in Palo Alto on Wednesdays. He returns to San Jose the same day right at the evening rush hour. If he takes Route 280 home he has observed that his travel time is highly variable from one week to the next, but if he takes El Camino his travel time is relatively constant. On the basis of his experience, Chuck has set up the pay-off table shown in Table 10.24, which gives his travel time in minutes.

    (a) Chuck estimates that about 90% of the time the traffic will be light. Which route should he take to minimize his expected travel time?

    (b) Chuck's wife Boots gets very worried if he is even a little late in coming home. Which route would you recommend he take now? Explain.

TABLE 10.24

DECISION	STATE OF NATURE	
	Light Traffic	Heavy Traffic
Take 280	25	55
Take El Camino	35	40

10-25. A small hospital in rural Albemarle County buys blood each month from a distant blood bank. A certain rare blood type must be restocked each month because its shelf life is only one month long. If the order is placed one month in advance, the cost to the hospital is $10 per unit. If the demand for the rare blood type during the month exceeds the supply, it must be special-ordered at a cost of $100 per unit. The demand for the past 3 years is shown in Table 10.25.

    (a) Develop a payoff table for the hospital.

    (b) How many units should the hospital order each month?

TABLE 10.25

DEMAND	FREQUENCY
0	24 months
1	8
2	4
Total	36 months

10-26. Lawrence Roberts, head of purchasing at Marple Manufacturing, must decide from which vendor to buy a particular component. Vendor A will supply the components in lots of 1000 for $10 a unit while Vendor B will charge only $9.50 a unit. However, 20% of the time Vendor B's lots will contain 10% defectives and 80% of the time they will contain 1% defectives, while Vendor A's lots will contain 1% defectives 99% of the time and 3% defectives 1% of the time. The cost of a defective to Marple Manufacturing is $100 due to the high cost of scrapping or reworking the assemblies containing defective components.

    (a) Draw a decision tree for this model.

    (b) Using the criterion of expected cost, from which vendor should Lawrence purchase the component?

10-27. Rick O'Shea is an independent trucker operating out of Tucson. He has the option of either hauling a shipment to Denver or hauling a different shipment to Salt Lake. If he chooses the shipment to Denver, he has a 90% chance of finding there a return shipment to Tucson. If he does not find a return shipment he will return to Tucson empty. If he chooses the shipment to Salt Lake, he has a 50% chance of finding a return shipment to Tucson. His payoffs are shown in Table 10.26.

TABLE 10.26

	RETURN SHIPMENT	NO RETURN
Salt Lake	$4000	$3500
Denver	3850	3350

(a) Draw the decision tree for this model.
(b) Using the criterion of expected net dollar return, to which city should Rick go?

•• 10-28. Jenny Lind's payoff table (Problem 10-21) is given in Table 10.27.

TABLE 10.27

	STATE OF NATURE		
DECISION	Small Box Office	Medium Box Office	Large Box Office
Sign with Movie Company	$200,000	$1,000,000	$3,000,000
Sign with TV Network	900,000	900,000	900,000
Probability	0.3	0.6	0.1

She may hire a market research firm to conduct a survey at a cost of $100,000. The result of the survey would be either a favorable (F) or unfavorable (U) public response to the movie. The firm's ability to assess the market as measured by conditional probabilities is

$$P(F|Small) = .3 \qquad P(U|Small) = .7$$
$$P(F|Medium) = .6 \qquad P(U|Medium) = .4$$
$$P(F|Large) = .8 \qquad P(U|Large) = .2$$

(a) Draw the decision tree for this model.
(b) Should Jenny have the survey conducted? How should she use the results of the survey?
(c) What is the EVSI? What is the most Jenny should be willing to pay for the survey?

••• 10-29. Kelly Construction (Problem 10-22) wants to reduce the uncertainty about the number of units it should build. It has decided to conduct a survey which will result in one of three measures of demand: M_1, weak; M_2, moderate; M_3, strong. The payoff table is shown in Table 10.28. The reliabilities are given in Table 10.29.

TABLE 10.28

	DEMAND		
DECISION	Low, D_1	Medium, D_2	High, D_3
Build 100, B_1	$500,000	$500,000	$500,000
Build 200, B_2	0	1,000,000	1,000,000
Build 300, B_3	−700,000	400,000	1,500,000
Probability	0.3	0.5	0.2

TABLE 10.29

	$P(M_j|D_i)$		
	D_1	D_2	D_3
M_1	.7	.3	.1
M_2	.2	.4	.3
M_3	.1	.3	.6

(a) Draw the decision tree for this model.

(b) What is Kelly's optimal strategy?

(c) What is the EVSI? Compare it with the EVPI by computing the ratio EVSI/EVPI and noting that the most this ratio could be is 1.

•••10-30. The payoff table for the hospital in Albemarle County (Problem 10-25) is given in Table 10.30.

TABLE 10.30

	DEMAND		
ORDER QUANTITY	0, D_1	1, D_2	2, D_3
0, Q_1	0	100	200
1, Q_2	10	10	110
2, Q_3	20	20	20
Probability	$\frac{2}{3}$	$\frac{2}{9}$	$\frac{1}{9}$

The hospital administrator has decided to check the scheduled surgeries each month to see if there will be any operations requiring the rare blood type. He may find that there are no scheduled surgeries (S_1), one scheduled surgery (S_2), or two scheduled surgeries (S_3), requiring the rare blood type. The conditional probabilities are given in Table 10.31.

TABLE 10.31

	$P(S_j|D_i)$		
	D_1	D_2	D_3
S_1	.95	.05	.02
S_2	.04	.8	.08
S_3	.01	.15	.9

(a) Draw the decision tree for this model.

(b) What is the EVSI?

(c) How much can the administrator expect to save each month by checking the surgery schedule?

Case Study   Johnson's Metal

Shirley Johnson, president of Johnson's Metal (JM), is facing the decision presented in Problem 10-19, but a new element has entered the picture. Shirley has the opportunity to hire Compal, a consulting firm that does what it calls "competitive analysis." In particular, in this situation Compal offers to do a detailed study of the other firms that will compete to supply transmission housings to PROTRAC. After the analy-sis, Compal will report to JM that conditions for JM to get the contract are either encouraging or discouraging.

Compal states that, if conditions are encouraging, then JM will get the PROTRAC contract with probability equal to 0.5. On the other hand, Compal states that, if conditions are discouraging, the probability that JM will get the PROTRAC contract is only 0.35. At this time Compal states that the probability of encouraging and discouraging conditions are equally likely. Compal charges $1000 for its services.

Shirley asks Linus Drawer, her assistant, to determine if JM should hire Compal. Indeed she asks Linus to determine the optimal strategy.

Linus prepares the decision tree for the model and by working back through it, determines that the optimal strategy is

1. Hire Compal to do the study
2. If conditions are encouraging
   a. Build the test fixture
   b. If JM gets the order, use current tools
3. If conditions are discouraging
   a. Build the test fixture
   b. If JM gets the order, use current tools

He makes an appointment to discuss the results with Shirley. The meeting proceeds as follows:

Shirley: Linus! I see the decision tree and I'm duly impressed, but the result doesn't make any sense. Why should I pay Compal $1000 if we take the same action no matter what it says?

Linus: Surely, Shirley, you don't mean that the analysis did not make a difference. I understand that your statement holds now

that the analysis is complete, but how would you have known what strategy to follow without the decision tree?

Shirley: Linus! You missed my point! No matter what costs or probabilities are involved, I say that we should build the test fixture, and then use the current tools if we get the order. This simply has to be a better strategy than to hire Compal and then do the same thing no matter what it says.

Linus: I understand, but I know I've done the decision tree right, so I don't know what to tell you.

Shirley: I don't have the time or interest to check the details of your analysis. All I know is that I want to make a decision about Compal tomorrow morning and I want to have an answer that makes sense. Your job is to provide me with that answer.

Questions

1. Is Shirley right; that is, is it impossible for Linus' strategy to be optimal?
2. Is Linus right; that is, is his analysis correct given the data at his disposal?
3. Assume Linus' role; that is, it is now your job to provide Shirley with an answer that makes sense.

Case Study   To Drill or Not to Drill

Terri Underhill has recently been assigned to the economic analysis section of Global Oil. Prescot Oil has just offered to buy the Burns Flat lease from Global for $15,000 and Terri has been assigned the task of preparing Global's response. The Burns Flat lease gives Global the right to explore for oil under 320 acres of land in western Oklahoma. Terri must recommend either to sell the lease or to drill.

If Global drills, the results are uncertain. On the basis of drilling records in western Oklahoma and current market prices, Terri prepares a table showing the possible outcomes, the probability of each outcome, and the net return to Global (Table 10.32).

Terri, however, knows that she does not have to make the decision simply on the basis of historical records. DRI, Drilling Resource, Inc., will perform a test for $6000 to determine the

underground formation of the Burns Flat terrain. The test will indicate which of three categories (plate, varied, or ridge) best describes the underground structure. The conditional probabilities of the possible outcomes vary with the underground structure. Table 10.33 shows the results of the last 50 tests.

If the test is taken, the opportunity to sell the lease is forfeited. The market for oil leases understands that a decision to sell after the test has been performed indicates that drilling does not appear to be profitable.

Questions

1. On the basis of these data, should Global drill or sell the lease?
2. What is the most that Global should pay in advance to know what the outcome of drilling would be?
3. Use a decision tree to determine the optimal strategy for Global.
4. What is the expected return associated with the optimal policy?
5. What is the maximum *additional* amount that Global should be willing to pay DRI for the test?

TABLE 10.32

POSSIBLE OUTCOMES	PROBABILITY	NET RETURN
Dry Well	0.2	−100,000
Gas Well	0.4	40,000
Oil and Gas	0.3	90,000
Oil Well	0.1	200,000

TABLE 10.33

TEST RESULT/OUTCOME	PLATE	VARIED	RIDGE	TOTAL
Dry	8	2	0	10
Gas	2	16	2	20
Gas and Oil	0	14	1	15
Oil	0	0	5	5
	10	32	8	50

Case Study — Shumway, Horch, and Sager (A)[4]

Claire Christensen was involved in a new project in her second year with the management consulting firm of Shumway, Horch, and Sager (SHS). It appeared to be another situation in which she was expected to jump quickly out of the blocks with the project and make some clever money-saving recommendation, then find the follow-on project to produce next month's billable days.

The client was an organization of magazine publishers that had become aware of the large amounts of money being wasted printing copies that were not sold. Industry practice had been always to print and deliver to newsstands more magazines than would be needed. The practice ensured that every customer requesting a copy at the newsstand could have one, thereby keeping numbers high for both newsstand circulation and advertising revenues. It also produced a phenomenal number of unsold copies. SHS was hired to look into this practice and make some recommendations for improved procedures.

Another related issue was the establishment of a rate base. This was the amount of copies that *Good Housekeeping* guaranteed selling each month and was used to determine the advertising rates. If they did not meet the base value, they would refund an amount proportional to the shortage. If they exceeded the base, they were not able to go back and collect more advertising revenues.

Christensen thought saving money on production would be assured, provided she could find a way to forecast each issue's sales. She started on this task by picking the magazine *Good Housekeeping* and probing whether she could forecast January 1988 sales using previous data. She had obtained data on total circulation over the past 9 years (July 1979–June 1988) from the Publisher's Statement to the Audit Bureau of Circulation (see SHSA.XLS). Without looking at this information, she tucked away the last 6 months of data to use later to test her methods of forecasting. The first 8 ½ years of data (through December 1987) are shown in Table 10.34. She was aware that about 10 million copies of this magazine were generally printed.

[4]This case is to be used as the basis for class discussion rather than to illustrate either the effective or ineffective handling of an administrative situation. ©1990, Darden Graduate Business School Foundation.

Christensen pondered how time patterns in past sales might help her predict the sales of a future issue. (See Exhibit 1 for a graph of the circulation data.) *Good Housekeeping* was not a magazine that she read, but she had seen it while waiting for the dentist, and her aunt had it in her house. She knew that the December issue greatly increased newsstand sales because of its holiday recipes and gift-giving ideas. The January issue always seemed to be low, because people evidently felt like they had overspent and overeaten during the holidays and were trying to cut back. Changes in the interests of purchasers and in the content of the magazine, were also important forces that could gradually move the sales up or down over time.

Once Christensen had the best forecast, the next question was whether to produce the forecast amount or a higher or lower amount. Unsold magazines were generally worthless when the next issue hit the newsstand. She knew this particular magazine sold for $1.95 at the newsstand, but she only had an estimate of the variable costs to produce the magazine ($.70) and the price to the wholesaler ($1.20) and the price from the wholesaler to the newsstand operator ($1.50). There was no risk to the retailer or the wholesaler, because they could return for full price any magazines not sold.

Just as Christensen was going to dive into the calculations, a representative from *Good Housekeeping* called and said they had just been given the opportunity to raise their advertising rate base from its current level of 4.78 million copies. The representative said they had already planned to use a new value effective August 1, but now he wanted to know if they should raise it one month early. The rate base was used as follows:

Advertising revenue equaled $1*the rate base, but there was a contingent penalty. If circulation was less than the rate base, they must make up the advertising in an amount equal to $1.25 in value for every impression they were off.

The new rate base talked about was 5.1 million and again the decision rested upon a forecast of circulation. Christensen knew that she would quickly have to find the best method of forecasting based on the 8.5 years of data she had, then test the

TABLE 10.34 *Good Housekeeping* Circulation Figures (July 1979–December 1987)

DATE	OBS.#	CIRCULATION	DATE	OBS.#	CIRCULATION
Jul 79	1	5264165	Jan 84	55	5198585
	2	5313127		56	5501741
	3	5117969		57	5329592
	4	5098771		58	5322838
	5	5187708		59	5178815
	6	5645295		60	5247590
Jan 80	7	5023173	Jul 84	61	5194827
	8	5333352		62	5118408
	9	5224234		63	5291564
	10	5079207		64	5047946
	11	5167277		65	5105056
	12	5006445		66	5448542
Jul 80	13	5150974	Jan 85	67	5023818
	14	5180346		68	5099829
	15	5223467		69	5253739
	16	5153303		70	5138210
	17	5247109		71	5251664
	18	5789798		72	5450869
Jan 81	19	5350502	Jul 85	73	5022522
	20	5371371		74	5206132
	21	5327700		75	5042725
	22	5269993		76	5096277
	23	5240438		77	5067717
	24	5273266		78	5508198
Jul 81	25	5439920	Jan 86	79	5133963
	26	5378584		80	5180897
	27	5329516		81	5161222
	28	5292129		82	5174238
	29	5378127		83	5047775
	30	5736465		84	5152063
Jan 82	31	5073651	Jul 86	85	5001222
	32	5553245		86	5232314
	33	5439363		87	5235207
	34	5363948		88	5009584
	35	5367404		89	5352370
	36	5316957		90	5498755
Jul 82	37	5412745	Jan 87	91	5159840
	38	5387779		92	5274075
	39	5439224		93	5179002
	40	5341392		94	5269295
	41	5396853		95	5005048
	42	5961612		96	5166569
Jan 83	43	5335737	Jul 87	97	5068848
	44	5618540		98	5007388
	45	5604606		99	5265191
	46	5343116		100	5046595
	47	5294990		101	5300978
	48	5327995		102	5526153
	49	5177176			
Jul 83	50	5290109			
	51	5449099			
	52	5344570			
	53	5334053			
	54	5763516			

EXHIBIT 1 Graph of *Good Housekeeping* Total Sales over Time

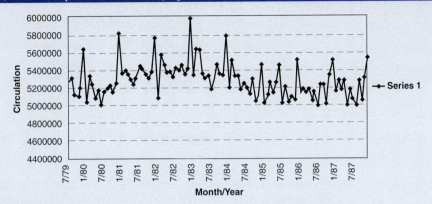

method on the 6 months of data she had held out (see Table 10.35), and then hopefully apply the same method for July 1988.

Questions

1. Assume that the distribution of demand (circulation) for July 1988 is as follows:

Circulation	Probability
4857K	0.2
4932K	0.2
4983K	0.2
5034K	0.2
5109K	0.2

Should Claire recommend to raise the rate base one month early? Why?

2. Assume that the forecast of demand for January 1988 is a normal distribution with mean of 5,082,329 and standard deviation of 98,324. How many copies of the magazine should be printed?

TABLE 10.35 Hold-out Data

OBS.#	CIRCULATION
103	5012276
104	5056537
105	5061844
106	5005226
107	5000500
108	5030805

APPENDIX 10.1   CONDITIONAL PROBABILITY AND BAYES' THEOREM

While dice and urns filled with balls do not seem to be very relevant to managerial decision making, they do make it easy to assign probabilities, and so we will use them (as statisticians are fond of doing) to explain conditional probability and Bayes' Theorem. Suppose that we draw a ball from an urn according to the following two-stage process (shown in Figure 10.30):

1. A fair die is thrown.

2. The value of the die is used to determine which of three urns we draw the ball from.

Each urn contains 100 balls, but with a different number of white (*W*) and black (*B*) balls. Urn 1, with 28 white and 72 black balls, is chosen if a 1 is thrown. Urn 2, with 40 white and 60 black balls, is chosen if a 2 or 3 is thrown. Urn 3, with 92 white and 8 black balls, is chosen if a 4, 5, or 6 is thrown.

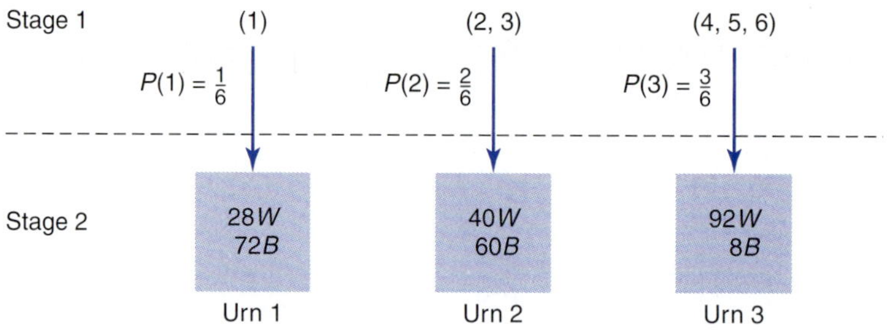

Stage 1   (1)   (2, 3)   (4, 5, 6)

$P(1) = \frac{1}{6}$ $P(2) = \frac{2}{6}$ $P(3) = \frac{3}{6}$

Stage 2

28W 72B	40W 60B	92W 8B
Urn 1	Urn 2	Urn 3

FIGURE 10.30

Two-Stage Process

Since we are throwing a fair die, the probability that Urn 1 is selected is 1/6; that is, $P(1) = 1/6$. Similarly, if we throw a 2 or 3, we will draw a ball from Urn 2. This implies that $P(2) = 2/6$. Finally, if a 4, 5, or 6 is thrown, we will draw a ball from Urn 3, and thus $P(3) = 3/6$ (see Figure 10.30). If this seems unduly abstract, it may be helpful in the following discussion to think of the different urns as representing three different states of nature corresponding to three different levels of market demand, 1 being the smallest level and 3 the largest. Think of the two ball colors as two possible results of a marketing test to assess the true state of nature, White (*W*) being an encouraging test result and Black (*B*) being a discouraging test result.

Conditional Probabilities The notation $P(W|1)$ signifies a *conditional probability*. The vertical line is read "given." Thus, $P(W|1)$ is read "the probability of *W*, given 1." It means the probability of drawing a white ball (*W*) assuming that the drawing is made from Urn 1 (or the probability of an encouraging test result given that the market strength is the smallest, 1). Recall that once an urn is selected, a ball is chosen at random, which means that each ball in the urn is equally likely to be drawn. Looking at Figure 10.30, we see that

$$P(W|1) = 0.28 \quad \text{and} \quad P(B|1) = 0.72$$
$$P(W|2) = 0.40 \quad \text{and} \quad P(B|2) = 0.60$$
$$P(W|3) = 0.92 \quad \text{and} \quad P(B|3) = 0.08$$

In the marketing-test example these probabilities are not known precisely. They would have to be estimated from past marketing tests for other products and the assumption would have to be made that the results would be valid for this product. For example, the same values for $P(W|1)$ and $P(B|1)$ would be obtained if in 100 past tests it turned out that the market was weak, in 28 the test was encouraging, and in 72 the test was discouraging.

In the marketing-test example we would also be interested in conditional probabilities such as $P(1|B)$, for this would be the probability that the market strength is 1 given that the market test was discouraging. In the die-and-urn example, this is the probability that the ball was drawn from Urn 1, given that we know it is black. To clarify this, assume that a friend goes through the two-stage process in the next room, after which he comes in and reports that the ball is black. He then asks, "What is the probability that it came from Urn 1?"

Before answering that question, suppose that he had asked, "What is the probability that the ball I drew came from Urn 1?" *without* telling you the color of the ball. In this case all you know is that he would have drawn from Urn 1 if he had thrown a 1 with his fair die. Thus, the *unconditional probability* that the ball came from Urn 1 is $P(1) = 1/6$. In the marketing example, this corresponds to asking what the probability of a strength 1 market is before performing the marketing test.

Now that you know the ball is black and that Urn 1 has the highest percentage of black balls, your intuition probably suggests that the probability of Urn 1 has increased. If so, your intuition is correct. We will now use conditional probabilities to lend some precision to that intuitive feeling.

Joint Probability In order to calculate $P(1|B)$, we use the following relation, which is developed in courses dealing with probability and statistics. Let X and Y denote *any* two random events. Then

$$P(X \text{ and } Y) = P(X|Y)P(Y) \tag{A.1}$$

$$P(X \text{ and } Y) = P(Y \text{ and } X) \tag{A.2}$$

$$P(Y \text{ and } X) = P(Y|X)P(X) \tag{A.3}$$

$$P(Y|X) = \frac{P(X|Y)P(Y)}{P(X)} \tag{A.4}$$

The first equation says that *joint probability* of *both* X and Y occurring is equal to the conditional probability of X occurring given that Y occurs times the *marginal probability* that Y occurs. The second equation says that the probability of X and Y occurring is the same as Y and X occurring. The third equation is simply another way of stating the first equation, since X and Y represent any two events. The last equation is implied by the first three and gives a means for finding a given conditional probability if the "reverse" conditional probability is known.

To apply these general results to the case at hand, let $Y = 1$ and $X = B$. Then (A.4) allows us to write immediately that

$$P(1|B) = \frac{P(B|1)P(1)}{P(B)} \tag{A.5}$$

We know $P(B|1)$ and $P(1)$ but what is $P(B)$? To find out, we use a common trick in probability theory. The event B occurs (i.e., a black ball is drawn) if and only if a ball is drawn from Urn 1 and it is black or a ball is drawn from Urn 2 and it is black or a ball is drawn from Urn 3 and it is black. Thus

$$P(B) = P(1 \text{ and } B) + P(2 \text{ and } B) + P(3 \text{ and } B)$$
$$= P(B \text{ and } 1) + P(B \text{ and } 2) + P(B \text{ and } 3)$$
$$= P(B|1)P(1) + P(B|2)P(2) + P(B|3)P(3) \tag{A.6}$$

Bayes' Theorem and the Calculation of Posterior Probabilities If we substitute this expression for $P(B)$ in (A.5) we get an example of the application of *Bayes' Theorem.*

$$P(1|B) = \frac{P(B|1)P(1)}{P(B|1)P(1) + P(B|2)P(2) + P(B|3)P(3)} \tag{A.7}$$

Since all terms on the right-hand side of (A.7) are known, Bayes' Theorem provides a way to compute $P(1|B)$.

$$P(1|B) = \frac{{}^{72}\!/_{100} * {}^{1}\!/_{6}}{{}^{72}\!/_{100} * {}^{1}\!/_{6} + {}^{60}\!/_{100} * {}^{2}\!/_{6} + {}^{8}\!/_{100} * {}^{3}\!/_{6}} = \frac{1}{3} \tag{A.8}$$

Recall that the unconditional probability (i.e., with no additional information) that the ball was drawn from Urn 1 is 1/6. Once we are told that the ball is black, the probability that it came from Urn 1 increases. In this particular case it doubles. In terms of the market-test example, based on the information at hand before the test, the probability of a strength 1 market (weakest market) is 1/6. After performing the test and getting a discouraging result (B), the probability increases to 1/3.

We would also like to compute $P(1|W)$ and the other conditional probabilities. We could do it by formulas similar to (A.7) but instead we will present a tabular approach that is easy to implement in a spreadsheet program. Tables 10.36 and 10.37 contain the initially known probabilities—what in the marketing-test example might be called *reliabilities,* because they are related to how reliable the test is—and the *prior probabilities* of the states of nature. The joint probabilities in Table 10.38 are calculated from those tables by multiplying each column i of Table 10.36 by the prior probability found in the corresponding

TABLE 10.36 Reliabilities

TEST RESULT	STATE OF NATURE		
	1	2	3
B	$P(B|1) = .72$	$P(B|2) = .60$	$P(B|3) = .08$
W	$P(W|1) = .28$	$P(W|2) = .40$	$P(W|3) = .92$
Column Sums	1	1	1

TABLE 10.37 Prior Probabilities

STATE OF NATURE			
1	2	3	ROW SUM
$P(1) = 1/6$	$P(2) = 2/6$	$P(3) = 3/6$	1

TABLE 10.38 Joint and Marginal Probabilities

TEST RESULT	STATE OF NATURE			ROW SUMS
	1	2	3	
B	$P(B \text{ and } 1) = .12$	$P(B \text{ and } 2) = .20$	$P(B \text{ and } 3) = .04$	$P(B) = .36$
W	$P(W \text{ and } 1) = .0467$	$P(W \text{ and } 2) = .1333$	$P(W \text{ and } 3) = .46$	$P(W) = .64$
Column Sums	$P(1) = .1667$	$P(2) = .3333$	$P(3) = .50$	1

TABLE 10.39 Posterior Probabilities

TEST RESULT	STATE OF NATURE			ROW SUMS
	1	2	3	
B	$P(1|B) = .333$	$P(2|B) = .556$	$P(3|B) = .111$	1
W	$P(1|W) = .073$	$P(2|W) = .208$	$P(3|W) = .719$	1

TABLE 10.40 Data on 300 Market Tests

TEST RESULT	STATE OF NATURE			ROW SUMS
	1	2	3	
B	72	60	8	140
W	28	40	92	160
Column Sums	100	100	100	300

column *i* of Table 10.37. The row and column sums of Table 10.38 give the *marginal probabilities.* The *posterior probabilities of* Table 10.39 are calculated from Table 10.38 by dividing the joint probabilities in each row by the row sum.

   We conclude with a final point that some find confusing. If in the market-test example the reliabilities are estimated from past data, why can't we use the same data to estimate the posterior probabilities? For example, suppose we have the data shown in Table 10.40 on 300 past market tests classified according to marketing's test report and the state of nature that actually occured.

We estimated $P(B|1)$ as 72/100. Why can't we estimate $P(1|B)$ as 72/140?

First note that this does in fact give us a different answer; 72/140 = 0.514 is not the same as 0.333 calculated in (A.8). The reason is that we have implicitly used a different set of prior probabilities. If we set $P(1) = 100/300$, $P(2) = 100/300$, and $P(3) = 100/300$ and apply Bayes' Theorem, we will then get $P(1|B) = 0.514$, because we have set the prior probabilities to reflect the historical frequency of states 1, 2, and 3. If we believe the prior probabilities should be different from the historical frequencies, then we will get a different answer. As an extreme example, suppose we have information that leads us to believe very strongly that the market demand for the product must be very strong; that is, $P(3) = 1.0$. Then applying Bayes' Theorem gives $P(1|B) = 0$, $P(2|B) = 0$, and $P(3|B) = 1.0$; even a discouraging test report will not alter our prior probabilities. *The point is that the posterior probabilities depend on the prior probabilities, and the prior probabilities may differ from the historical frequencies.*

References

Adam Borison, "Oglethorpe Power Corporation Decides about Investing in a Major Transmission System," *Interfaces,* 25, no. 2 (1995), 25–36.

Robert Clemen, *Making Hard Decisions: An Introduction to Decision Analysis* (Boston: PWS-KENT Publishing Company, 1991).

Charles Feinstein, "Deciding Whether to Test Student Athletes for Drug Use," *Interfaces,* 20, no. 3 (1990), 80–87.

Ron Howard, "Heathens, Heretics, and Cults: The Religious Spectrum of Decision Aiding," *Interfaces,* 22, no. 6 (1992), 15–27.

Ralph Keeney (A), "Decision Analysis: An Overview," *Operations Research,* 30, no. 5 (1982), 803–838.

Ralph Keeney (B), *Value-Focused Thinking* (Cambridge, MA: Harvard University Press, 1992).

Ralph Keeney and Howard Raiffa, *Decisions with Multiple Objectives: Preferences and Value Tradeoffs* (New York: Wiley, 1976).

Monte Carlo Simulation

CHAPTER OUTLINE

11.1 Introduction

11.2 Generating Random Variables

11.3 Simulating with a Spreadsheet

11.4 Simulating with Spreadsheet Add-ins

11.5 An Inventory Control Example: Foslins Housewares

11.6 Simulation of Foslins' Model with a More Realistic Demand Assumption

11.7 Midwest Express: Airline Overbooking Model

11.8 Capacity Balancing

11.9 Notes on Implementation

11.10 Summary

KEY TERMS

SELF-REVIEW EXERCISES

PROBLEMS

CASE STUDY: CyberLab (A)

CASE STUDY: Sprigg Lane (A)

REFERENCES

APPLICATION CAPSULE   **AT&T's Call Processing Simulator**

In the mid and late 1970s, there were some technology changes which made it much easier to use 1-800 phone number services for marketing purposes. It became the way America shops—it has become the front door for about $200 billion in sales. This has given rise to the call center industry. An inbound call center consists of: telecommunications lines carrying telephone calls to a specific location, switching machines to sort and allocate calls, and agents who receive the calls. The primary purpose of the inbound center would be to receive calls for catalog purchases or for airline or hotel reservations, to handle customer service questions, and so forth. There are also outbound call centers like those used for telemarketing.

The call center concept has evolved into an $8 billion service industry linking customers, businesses, and a long-distance carrier, like AT&T. In 1993, roughly 350,000 businesses employ 6.5 million people in call center environments. These centers have enjoyed 20% annual growth rates through the 1990s and are forecasted to continue double digit growth through 2000. Several factors have contributed to this trend: less discretionary time for consumer shopping, more single-head-of-household and dual-income families, increased cost of face-to-face selling, and deregulation of the telecommunications industry. A recent legislative change, called 800 portability, allows businesses to keep their same 800 number

even if they switch long-distance carriers. This has greatly increased the competition in this field.

The costs of labor and communications associated with these call centers have increased and businesses are attempting to improve their call centers' ability to serve their callers. Therefore AT&T introduced a simulation model to study various operating scenarios for their existing as well as potential clients. Many factors must be considered by such a model, such as staffing, the length of the calls, the number of 800 lines, the hours of operation, and busy signals. Another reality that must be modeled is the behavior of the caller. If a caller is put on hold, some will immediately hang up, others will wait for a short period of time, and others will wait a very long time for an agent to get to them. For those that abandon the call, some will try to call again, while others will take their business to a competitor. The initial simulation model AT&T developed was for a major airlines reservation center. Because of its great success, AT&T decided to develop a standard simulation model, based on a PC, that could be used as a sales-support tool.

A specific example of a success story concerns Northwest Airlines, who implemented the recommended results of such a simulation study to increase by 20% the number of calls answered, with 20% fewer agent hours and 27% less overtime, with the bottom-line result being a 5% increase in booked revenue for the airline. Over 2000 simulation studies were done in 1992, with the cumulative effect that AT&T increased or regained more than $1 billion out of the $8 billion in the 800-network market. In addition, the business customers involved in implementing these studies increased their annual profits by more than $750 million (Brigandi, et al.)

11.1   INTRODUCTION

Many people believe that "experience is the best teacher." Unfortunately, it is often too costly (in time or money) to obtain real experience. This dilemma provides a primary motivation for the use of simulation: to find a quick, inexpensive way to acquire the knowledge that is usually gained through experience.

> The basic idea of simulation is to build an experimental device, or **simulator,** that will "act like" (simulate) the system of interest in certain important aspects in a quick, cost-effective manner.

The goal is to create an environment in which information about possible alternative actions can be obtained through experimentation. The use of simulation is fundamental to many applied experiments; for example,

- Testing of medicine on laboratory animals. Here the animal responses *simulate* human responses.
- Driving automobiles on test tracks. Here the test track *simulates* the environment the auto will face.
- Testing wing designs for airplanes in wind tunnels. The wind tunnel *simulates* flight conditions.
- Training airline pilots in actual cabins with *simulated* out-of-the-window displays under *simulated* conditions.

In the context of quantitative analysis, simulation has come to mean experimentation based on a mathematical model. Although simulation and optimization (e.g., by means of LP) both use quantitative models, they are based on very different concepts. The fundamental difference lies in the role of decision variables in the two approaches.

> Simulation versus optimization
>
> - In an optimization model the values of the decision variables are *outputs*. That is, the model provides a set of values for the decision variables that maximizes (or minimizes) the value of the objective function.
> - In a **simulation model** the values of the decision variables are *inputs*. The model evaluates the objective function for a particular set of values.

To see what this means, consider the following example. Suppose that a supermarket wants to decide how to assign checkout personnel (checkers and baggers) during the weekend. The goal is to minimize labor cost, subject to the restrictions imposed by the labor contract and the constraint that customers should not have to wait too long.

If we had an optimization model, we would need to supply the model parameters. Perhaps these would be quantities such as the arrival rate of customers, the distribution of time it takes to check out a customer with and without the use of a bagger, and so on. When the model was solved, the answer would include the best way to assign personnel, the corresponding value of the objective function (the total cost), and an indication as to whether there was slack in any of the constraints. We have seen this approach many times in the mathematical programming sections of this text.

In a simulation model, the inputs would include the parameters we described above (customer arrival rates and the like), an expression for the objective function (total costs), and *a possible assignment of personnel.* The model would produce a specific set of results showing how well the solution performed by various measures, such as total cost, customer waiting time, staff utilization, and so on. In general, the model measures the *quality* of the suggested solution as well as how much variability there might be in the various performance measures due to randomness in the inputs. Simulation allows for a lot of experimentation and interaction with the modeler, but it will not necessarily optimize the goal of interest. The simulator is usually a much cheaper and faster way to experiment with many factors of interest.

WHEN SHOULD SIMULATION BE USED?

From this brief description, it seems as if no one would ever want to use a simulation model. Why not use a model that always yields the best answer, that is, an optimization model? Indeed, in the past simulation was often seen as the technique of last resort, to be used only when analytical methods failed. It is true that if an analytical model is available, exact results can be obtained quickly, and often an optimizing procedure can be used to determine the optimal results. However, simulation today is one of the most frequently used tools of quantitative analysis. Why are simulation models so popular?

1. First, analytical models may be difficult or impossible to obtain, depending on complicating factors. What a complicating factor is depends on the specific model. Complicating factors for capital budgeting models include random demand. Complicating factors for queuing models are nonexponential random variables, while complicating factors for inventory models are multiple stocking points or locations.

2. Analytical models typically predict only average or "steady-state" (long-run) behavior. In real-world models, however, it is often important to understand the possible variability in the performance measures, or how the performance measures vary in the short run.

3. Simulation can be performed with a great variety of software, from spreadsheets alone (Excel, Lotus) to spreadsheet add-ins (Crystal Ball, @Risk) to general computer programming languages (PASCAL, C++) to special-purpose simulation languages (SIMAN). As simulation models can now be created and run on a PC or a workstation, the level of computing and mathematical skill required to design and run a useful simulator has been substantially reduced. It is now quite reasonable to build and use a simulator even when it is clear that an analytic (optimization) model could be constructed with more time and effort.

The ability of simulation models to deal with complexity, capture the variability of performance measures, and reproduce short-run behavior make simulation a powerful tool.

SIMULATION AND RANDOM VARIABLES

Simulation models are often used to analyze a *decision under risk*—that is, a model in which the behavior of one or more factors is not known with certainty. There are many examples: demand for a product during the next month, the return on an investment, the number of trucks that will arrive to be unloaded tomorrow between 8:00 and 9:00 A.M., and so on. In such cases the factor that is not known with certainty is thought of as a **random variable.** The behavior of a random variable is described by a **probability distribution.** (Perhaps at this point we should remind you that we assume some knowledge of probability theory in this section of the book. The basic information you will need, including the definition of a probability distribution and some examples, is contained in Appendix A.) This

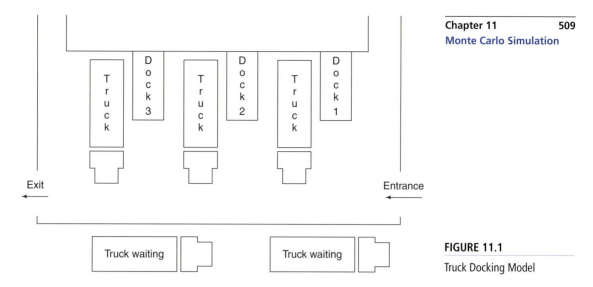

Exit

Entrance

Truck waiting

Truck waiting

FIGURE 11.1

Truck Docking Model

type of simulation is sometimes called a **Monte Carlo method,** after the roulette wheels in Monte Carlo, which can be seen as devices for generating uncertain or random events. Let us look at several examples of this approach.

Design of Docking Facilities A typical model is illustrated in Figure 11.1. Here trucks, perhaps of various sizes carrying different types of loads, arrive at a warehouse to be unloaded. The uncertainties are when a truck will arrive, what kind and size of load it will be carrying, and how long it will take to unload. In modeling these uncertainties, each uncertain quantity would be a random variable characterized by a probability distribution.

Here planners must address a variety of design questions:

- How many docks should be built?
- What type and quantity of material-handling equipment are required?
- How many workers are required over what periods of time?

The design of the unloading dock will affect its cost of construction and operation. This cost can be reduced by building fewer docks, buying less material-handling equipment, and hiring fewer personnel. However, these options will increase the amount of time it takes to unload the trucks and the amount of time a truck has to wait before unloading begins. Management must balance the cost of acquiring and using the various resources against the cost of having trucks wait to be unloaded.

A similar model of designing docking facilities for oil tankers is important to the oil companies because of the high cost of having a supertanker full of oil waiting for an open dock. Such models are in the formal domain of "queuing models" (waiting lines), described in Chapter 12. To be solved by the methods of that chapter, however, queuing models must meet certain strict assumptions. If the arrival and service times can be described by the *exponential distribution,* then the analytical results of Chapter 12 may be used to predict waiting times and other characteristics of the system. (The exponential distribution is discussed later in this chapter, as well as in Appendix A.) If, however, this distribution is not a good fit, or if there are other complexities in the model that don't fit the standard assumptions, then it may be difficult or impossible to obtain analytic results. Then simulation would have to be used.

Determination of Inventory Control Policies Simulation can be and is used to study a variety of models in the general area of inventory control. One such model is illustrated in Figure 11.2. In this system, the factory produces goods that are sent to the warehouses to satisfy customer demand. Assume that daily demand at each warehouse is a random variable.

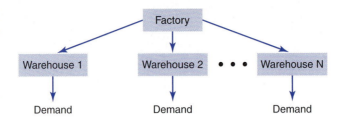

FIGURE 11.2

Distribution System

Shipping times from the factory to a warehouse may also be random. Here, some of the operational questions are:

- When should a warehouse reorder from the factory and how much?
- How much stock should the factory maintain to satisfy the orders of the warehouses?

The main costs here are the cost of holding inventory, the cost of shipping goods from the factory to the warehouses, and the cost of not being able to satisfy customer demand at a warehouse. Because the demands at the warehouses are uncertain, unless a warehouse maintains an unreasonably high inventory, there will be times when it will not be able to meet all customer demand. An alternative to high inventories would be to have frequent shipments to the warehouses from the factory. This would keep inventory at the warehouse low, but now the shipping cost would be high. As in the inventory models with known demand, management's objective is to find a stocking and ordering policy that keeps the total of holding plus shipping cost low while meeting a desired fraction of the customers' demands at the warehouses. Another way simulation might be used in the inventory area is to see what the "worst case" might be in terms of stockouts and to develop a policy that will cover the company 99% of the time.

This model is in the domain of inventory theory. Most analytic results in inventory theory are for a single item stocked at a single location. Multi-item, multi-location models like the one above are much more difficult to analyze, and so are often attacked with simulation. This chapter will discuss how to perform simulation either using the spreadsheet alone or using the two most popular spreadsheet add-ins (Crystal Ball and @Risk).

To gain a fuller understanding of the nature of simulation we will next discuss how to generate the random variables (e.g., demand) and then develop a Monte Carlo simulation of a capital budgeting model. After seeing what is involved in performing this basic simulation, we will analyze by simulation the Foslins Housewares model. In Foslins, we will be able to compare the simulation approach and the analytic approach. Finally, we'll study an airline overbooking model as found in a typical service industry setting, and then a capacity balancing model as found in a typical manufacturing setting.

11.2   GENERATING RANDOM VARIABLES

In our simulation of the upcoming models, it will be necessary to generate values for random variables. In this section we will explore how to *draw a random sample* from a given probability distribution, which we take to be synonymous with generating a random variable. There are two broad categories of random variables: discrete and continuous. Discrete random variables can assume only certain, specific values (e.g., integers), and continuous random variables may take on any fractional value (an infinite number of possible outcomes).

The topic of generating random variables is dealt with at several levels. The first level shows how to use a spreadsheet to generate observations from an arbitrary discrete distribution. This is sufficient to obtain the basic view of how a simulator with random elements operates. The following section on a generalized method shows how to generate random variables from any continuous distribution. It uses the exponential and normal distributions to motivate the presentation. Finally, the method is demonstrated when using spreadsheet add-ins.

General Motors of Canada has committed over $2 billion to automating its production facilities. An example of this approach is the GM assembly plant in Oshawa, Ontario. The plant is designed to produce hundreds of cars per shift, using over 600 industrial robots to perform various welding, loading, and assembly tasks. In addition, 1200 automatic guided vehicles (AGVs) will be used to transport cars and parts through various phases of assembly.

AGVs can handle a wide variety of loads, following a path selected by the user. They are controlled by a microprocessor and receive commands through a network of antennae and receivers embedded in the floor. The use of AGVs instead of the familiar conveyer belt has enabled GM to break the assembly line into small work groups, each with the ability to control its own work speed.

The implementation of such an automated, integrated assembly system is very complex. Each component must be tested first in isolation and then as part of an integrated working unit. Any changes in such a unit tend to be costly and time-consuming. It is therefore crucial to have a fast and inexpensive way of evaluating different work configurations. Simulation provides such a tool.

GM performed a simulation study to analyze one important section of the plant—the AGV body-framing system. The basic layout of this section has 100 work stations, each capable of independent operation. Only three of the 28 work stations devoted to actual processing are operated by humans. AGVs are used to deliver heavy parts to machines at each station. The finished product is a fully welded, framed auto body lacking only doors, hood, front fenders, and trunk lid.

The computer simulation investigated such questions as

- What is the system's maximum production rate? Could a reliable throughput of 525 cars/shift be achieved?
- Where could "parking" spots for idle AGVs most effectively be located to avoid bottlenecks?
- What is the sensitivity of the system to increased equipment failure or faster machine cycle time?
- How many AGVs are needed to make production quotas?

This last question was of particular importance—too few carriers starve the system, while too many choke it. Moreover, at $50,000 each, AGVs are a major cost element.

Thirteen configurations of the framing line were modeled, with the number of AGVs ranging from 54 to 79. Each configuration was simulated in 20 separate runs of an 8.5 hour shift (including breaks and lunch). The runs took only 15–20 minutes each on a PC. The study found that the maximum throughput of 630 cars was obtained using 74 AGVs. However, if the aim was simply to achieve the target figure of 525 cars, this could be realized at least 99% of the time using only 42 to 44 AGVs.

The simulation model also investigated the sensitivity of the production system to an increase in the failure rate of the three most important work stations and to changes in the cycle time of the automated processes. Neither factor was found to have a very marked effect on throughput, indicating that the system was both fairly stable and robust.

This study, which required few resources, provided valuable information to help management with an important capital budgeting decision (See Bookbinder et al).

It is easy to think of a physical device that could be used to generate the demand in a given model. The game spinner shown in Figure 11.3 would work well for the upcoming omelet pan example and is equally likely to point to any point on the circumference of the circle. Therefore, the chance that the spinner lands in a sector that comprises 30% of the circumference (or, equivalently, 30% of the area) is 30%. If the areas of the sectors are made to correspond to the probabilities of different demands, the spinner can be used to simulate demand. In this omelet pan example, there is a 10% chance that demand will be 8 pans, a 20% chance that demand will be 9 pans, a 30% chance that demand will be 10 x 100 pans, a 20% chance that demand will be 11 pans, a 10% chance that demand will be 12 pans, and a 10% chance that demand will be 13 pans. For example, if the spinner stops in the sector shown in Figure 11.3, a demand of 9 would be generated. To simulate another **trial,** or pass through the simulator, we would simply spin again.

USING A RANDOM NUMBER GENERATOR IN A SPREADSHEET

While the spinner is easy to understand, this method has an obvious defect if thousands of trials are necessary or if the process is to be performed on a computer. For this reason *random number generators (RNG)* have been developed in spreadsheets.

To generate demand for a given model, we first need to assign a range of random numbers to each possible demand. This assignment is arbitrary to a degree. The only

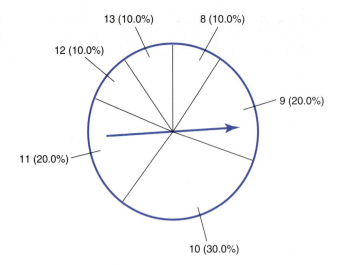

FIGURE 11.3

Game Spinner for Omelet
Pan Demand

Random Number	Demand
0.0-0.09999	8
0.1-0.29999	9
0.3-0.59999	10
0.6-0.79999	11
0.8-0.89999	12
0.9-0.99999	13

FIGURE 11.4

Associating Random
Numbers with Demands

requirement for a correct assignment is that the proportion of total numbers assigned to a demand must equal the probability of that demand. We will assign pieces of the interval from 0 to 1 to demands from the omelet pan example. One possible assignment is shown in Figure 11.4. Note that in this example, 10% (.90–.9999) of the entire interval (0–.9999) is assigned to a demand of 13. The probability of drawing a random number in the range .90–.9999 is 1 out of 10, or 0.1, which is exactly the same as the probability that the demand is 13 x 100.

Clearly, this is not the only possible correct assignment. We could assign a demand of 13 to *any* interval of length of 10%—for example, 0.1–0.19999 or 0.45–0.5499—since the probability of drawing a value in either one of these 10% intervals is also 0.1.

A GENERALIZED METHOD

The method we have just demonstrated is useful for generating discrete random variables. Many models, however, involve *continuous* random variables, which require a modification of the discrete RNG approach. Fortunately, there is a general method that can be used to generate both discrete and continuous random variables. We will develop this method and illustrate it with several examples.

To generate a discrete random variable with the RAND() function in a spreadsheet, we needed two things: (1) the ability to generate discrete uniform random variables and (2) the distribution of the discrete random variable to be generated. Similarly, to generate continuous random variables, we will need (1) the ability to generate continuous uniform random variables on the interval 0 to 1 and (2) the distribution (in the form of the *cumulative distribution function*) of the random variable to be generated.

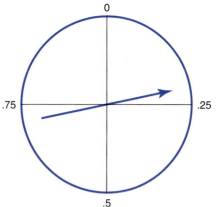

FIGURE 11.5

Game Spinner for Uniform
Random Variables

Continuous Uniform Random Variables In what follows, it is important to distinguish between the uniform random variable on the interval 0 to 1, U, and a specific realization of that random variable, u. One way to generate a continuous uniform random variable would be to use a version of the game spinner introduced earlier. Figure 11.5 shows a game spinner that, conceptually at least, can be used to generate values of U. Every point on the circumference of the circle corresponds to a number between 0 and 1. For example, when the pointer is in the 3 o'clock position, it is pointing to the number 0.25.

While this device is useful for gaining an intuitive understanding of the uniform random variable, it is even more limiting in practice than the spinner for the omelet pan model, in that it requires us to be able to read the exact point at which the pointer is pointing. (For example, imagine trying to discern whether the number indicated is 0.500000 or 0.499999.) We have seen, however, that in practice we do not need to be dependent on such "analog" devices as game spinners. With the use of RAND() in the spreadsheet, we can approximate U to any number of decimal places we choose.

The Cumulative Distribution Function The second key to generating a continuous random variable is the random variable's **cumulative distribution function** (CDF). Consider a random variable, D, the demand in our omelet pan example model. The CDF for D, which we will designate $F(x)$, is then defined as the probability that D takes on a value less than or equal to x—that is, $F(x) = \text{Prob}\{D \leq x\}$. Recall that if we know the probability distribution for D, as we did in the omelet pan model, we can easily find the CDF. Indeed, the CDF for key values of D is as follows:

X	8	9	10	11	12	13
F(x)	0.1	0.3	0.6	0.8	0.9	1.0

We will show how to use the general approach to generate observations of the random variable D. You will see that it is as easy as the approach based on the probability distribution, but certainly no easier. So why adopt this general approach? The answer is a technical one. With a continuous random variable, the probability that any *specific* value occurs is, strictly speaking, 0. Thus you cannot use an approach based on the probability distribution. Indeed, continuous random variables do not have probability distributions; the density function and the CDF are the two functions used to define a continuous random variable.

A graph of the CDF is shown in Figure 11.6. To generate a demand using the graph, draw a particular value u of the random variable and locate this value on the vertical axis of the graph. From this value on the vertical axis draw a line horizontally across to the plot of the CDF, and then down vertically to the horizontal axis to obtain the value of the demand, d. For example, when $u = 0.5$, the demand is 10 (see Figure 11.6).

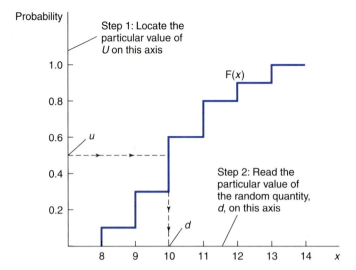

FIGURE 11.6

CDF of Omelet Pan Demand

Values for RAND()	=INT(8+5*RAND())
0 <= RAND() < 0.2	8
0.2 <= RAND() < 0.4	9
0.4 <= RAND() < 0.6	10
0.6 <= RAND() < 0.8	11
0.8 <= RAND() < 1.0	12

FIGURE 11.7

Using RAND() to Generate Discrete Demands

Why does this procedure work? It works because the probability of generating a particular demand is the probability of that demand occurring. For example, we want the probability of generating a demand of 10 to be 0.3. A demand of 10 will be generated when u lies between 0.3 and 0.6 on the vertical axis of Figure 11.6. But since U is a uniform random variable, this probability is just the length of the interval, $0.6 - 0.3 = 0.3$. Similarly, we want the probability of generating a demand of 11 to be 0.2. A demand of 11 will be generated when the value of u lies between 0.6 and 0.8, which happens with a probability of $0.8 - 0.6 = 0.2$, and so on. (You might wonder what happens if u is exactly 0.6. Should a demand of 10 or 11 be generated? The answer is that it doesn't really matter, as the probability of generating a value of u *exactly* equal to 0.6 is 0. One convention is to take the larger value. This works except when u is 1 when the larger value is not defined. In that case, just take the demand to be 13.)

The technique we have just illustrated with the omelet pan model can be applied back to any general discrete distribution. Now, let's suppose we want to model a **discrete uniform distribution** of demand where the values of 8 through 12 all have the same probability of occurring (uniform, because each value is equally likely). Recall that the spreadsheet has a function, =RAND(), that returns a random number between 0 and 1, all values being equally likely. RAND() is an example of a **continuous uniform distribution.** The question then is: Can we use a continuous, uniform distribution to generate a discrete, uniform distribution? We note that 5*RAND() will result in the creation of a continuous random number between 0 and 5, so that 8 + 5*RAND() will produce a continuous number between 8 and 13 (i.e., up to 12.99999 . . .). If we then make use of the INT function in Excel, which returns the integer part of the number, we can generate a discrete, uniform distribution of the integers between 8 and 12 with the formula: INT(8 + 5*RAND()). Figure 11.7 shows what the value of the formula would be for different values of RAND().

Since the intervals are all of equal length (1/5), RAND() is equally likely to fall into any one of them, and thus the formula is equally likely to yield any one of the five integer

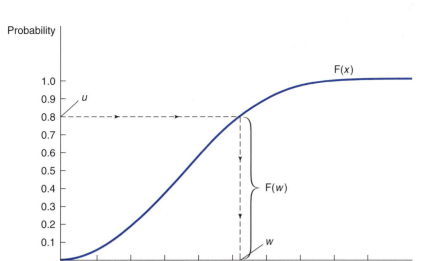

FIGURE 11.8

Generating Random
Quantities

values. In general, if we want a discrete, uniform distribution of integer values between x and y, we can use the formula:

$$INT(x + (y - x + 1)*RAND())$$

Later, in Section 11.7, we will show how to generate a binomial random variable (which is also discrete). We shall now see how the general method can be used to generate any continuous random variable, with specific illustrations for the exponential and normal distributions.

THE GENERAL METHOD APPLIED TO CONTINUOUS DISTRIBUTIONS

The two-step process for generating a continuous random variable W is illustrated in Figure 11.8. As before, the crucial element in the graph is the cumulative distribution function of W, $F(x) = \text{Prob}\{W \leq x\}$. The figure shows a typical function of this type, namely, one that goes from 0 to 1, is nondecreasing, and is *continuous* (that is, unlike the CDF for a discrete distribution, there are no jumps in the curve). Exactly as before, the process starts by drawing a particular value u of the random variable U and locating this value on the vertical axis (0.8 in Figure 11.8). You then read horizontally across to the plot of the distribution function and then vertically down to the horizontal axis to obtain the value of the random quantity (approximately 5.1 in Figure 11.8). We should stress that Figure 11.8 motivates the *concept* underlying the technique of generating an arbitrary continuous random variable. In practice, the process is typically performed in the computer with either an analytic or tabular representation of a graph like Figure 11.8. We illustrate both procedures below.

The graphical procedure illustrated above is equivalent to an algebraic procedure. That procedure is to solve the equation

$$u = F(w) = \text{Prob}\{W \leq w\}$$

for w. This can be seen from Figure 11.8 where the vertical distance on the vertical axis is u and is equal to the vertical distance from w on the horizontal axis to the plot of the CDF. When the CDF has a simple enough analytic expression, it is possible to solve for w in terms of u.

Generating from the Exponential Distribution An important distribution for which this is the case is the **exponential distribution.** As we will see in Section 12.2, the exponential distribution is often used to model the time between arrivals in a queuing model. Its CDF is given by

$$F(w) = \text{Prob}\{W \leq w\} = 1 - e^{-\lambda w}$$

where $1/\lambda$ equals the mean of the exponential random variable, W. Therefore we want to solve the following equation for w:

$$u = 1 - e^{-\lambda w} \tag{11.1}$$

The solution is

$$w = -1/\lambda \ln(1 - u) \tag{11.2}$$

For example, suppose we want to draw a sample from the exponential distribution with mean equal to 20 using this equation and a random number generator. We would

1. Generate a continuous, uniform random number with RAND(). For example, suppose that we obtain the number 0.75.

2. We then take the natural logarithm of $1 - 0.75 = 0.25$, which is -1.386, and multiply by -20. The observation from the exponential distribution is $(-20)(-1.386) = 27.72$.

To summarize, we would simply put the expression $= -20 * \text{LN}(1 - \text{RAND}())$ in a cell in the spreadsheet and it would generate exponentially distributed random numbers with a mean of 20.

Generating from the Normal Distribution The **normal distribution** plays an important role in many simulation and analytic models. In simulation, we often assume that random quantities are normally distributed. To illustrate, we look ahead to Marie Ford and Foslins' omelet pan model (see Section 11.6). We will find Marie making the assumption that a normal distribution with a mean of 1000 and a standard deviation of 100 described the demand that would occur.

To use simulation to estimate the expected cost of a given order size, Marie would have to draw a random demand from a normal distribution with a mean (μ) of 1000 and a standard deviation (σ) of 100 for each iteration. It turns out that if Z is a unit normal random variable (a normal with a mean of 0 and a standard deviation 1), then $\mu + Z\sigma$ is a normal random variable with mean μ and standard deviation σ. So the problem reduces to drawing from a unit normal distribution. The difficulty here is that the CDF of the unit normal is complicated enough that it is not possible to get an analytical expression for z in terms of u. Fortunately, Excel has a built-in function that can do this for us.

So, to generate a normal random variable with mean of 1000 and standard deviation of 100 in Excel, Marie will use this simple formula: =NORMINV(RAND(),1000,100). Excel will automatically return a normally distributed random number with mean of 1000 and standard deviation of 100.

GENERATING RANDOM VARIABLES USING ADD-INS

The topic of generating random variables is now dealt with for both Crystal Ball and @Risk. These two software packages have different approaches. In Crystal Ball, for each cell in the spreadsheet that represents a random variable, we must go through the "Define Assumption" menu, select from a gallery of distributions, and indicate what the appropriate distribution's parameters are. In @Risk, we must actually place a formula for the random number generator (RNG) in each cell of the spreadsheet that represents a random variable. Both add-in packages offer us a number of features not available in Excel. First, add-in packages offer us numerous random distributions that are not directly available in a spreadsheet (e.g., Poisson, Binomial, Lognormal, etc.). Second, they offer easy commands to set up and run many more iterations (no limit in Crystal Ball; up to 32,767 in @Risk) than we could in Excel. Finally, they automatically gather statistical and graphical summaries of our results.

To enter the information for a particular RNG in Crystal Ball, menus are used. These menus are illustrated with examples in Sections 11.4, 11.5, 11.6, and 11.8. Table 11.1 provides the @Risk format (demonstrated in Section 11.7) for some of the most common RNGs you'll use for your simulation modeling.

TABLE 11.1

DISTRIBUTION	@RISK FORMULA	DESCRIPTION OF RNG
Binomial	=RiskBinomial (n, p)	Returns the number of "successes" in a sample of n trials, where p is the probability of success for an individual trial.
Chi-square	=RiskChisq(λ)	Returns a value from the chi-square distribution with mean λ. Useful when summing normally distributed random variables.
Cumulative	=RiskCumul$(a, b, \{x_1, x_2,..., x_n\}, \{p_1, p_2,..., p_n\})$	Returns a value from a general distribution where a is the minimum, b is the maximum, and p_i represents the probability that a value of x_i or less will be drawn from the distribution.
Discrete (General)	=RiskDiscrete $(\{x_1, x_2,..., x_n\}, \{p_1, p_2,..., p_n\})$	Returns one of the n values from x_1 to x_n. The probabilities p_i represent the chance that x_i will be returned by the RNG.
Discrete (Uniform)	=RiskDuniform $(\{x_1, x_2,..., x_n\})$	Returns one of the n values from x_1 to x_n with equal probability.
Exponential	=RiskExp(β)	Returns value from exponential distribution with mean β. Useful for queuing models (time between arrivals).
Lognormal	=RiskLognorm(μ, σ)	Returns a value from the lognormal distribution with mean μ and standard deviation σ. Useful for such quantities as the sizes of oil fields or bank accounts.
Normal	=RiskNormal(μ, σ)	Returns a value from the normal distribution with mean μ and standard deviation σ. Useful for such quantities as the distribution of heights or weights or test scores.
Poisson	=RiskPoisson(λ)	Returns a value from the Poisson distribution with mean λ. Useful for describing the number of events that happen in a given time interval.
Triangular	=RiskTriang(a, b, c)	Returns a value from the triangular distribution with parameters (a = minimum, b = most likely, c = maximum). Useful when not much is known about the shape of the distribution other than the aforementioned parameters.
Uniform (Continuous)	=RiskUniform(a, b)	Returns a value from the uniform distribution with parameters (a = minimum, b = maximum). Useful when only the range of uncertainty is known and each value is equally likely to occur.

@Risk also offers truncated distributions for a few of the above distributions (e.g., Exponential, Lognormal, Normal). To use Table 11.1, let's suppose that you want to generate random demand in @Risk from the following distribution: 10% chance of 8 sales, 20% chance of 9 sales, 30% chance of 10 sales, 20% chance of 11 sales, 10% chance of 12 sales, and a 10% chance of 13 sales. All you need to do is type =RiskDiscrete({8,9,10,11,12,13}, {0.1,0.2,0.3,0.2,0.1,0.1}) into the cell of the spreadsheet that represents demand.

For a graph of the general shapes of these distributions, look ahead to the Crystal Ball gallery of distributions shown in Figure 11.17. You'll notice that some of the distributions listed in the preceding table are available directly in Crystal Ball (e.g., Poisson, Normal, Continuous Uniform), whereas others must be entered via the "Custom" distribution (e.g., Discrete, Cumulative), and some are not available at all (e.g., Chi-square).

The next two sections address the issue of actually doing a simulation in a spreadsheet depending on what software you have available. If you don't have any simulation add-in software available, proceed to Section 11.3, which will teach you the basics of doing a simulation with just the spreadsheet tools found in Excel, then skip Section 11.4. Otherwise (meaning you do have an add-in package available), skip Section 11.3 and go directly to Section 11.4.

11.3   SIMULATING WITH A SPREADSHEET

Most simulations are performed in a spreadsheet, because the number of calculations required soon overwhelms human capability. Simulations can be performed with spreadsheets alone (without the help of special add-in software), as this section will demonstrate. In this section we present a capital budgeting example to show the use of a spreadsheet for simulation and to establish some important facts about the output from a spreadsheet simulation.

A CAPITAL BUDGETING EXAMPLE:
ADDING A NEW PRODUCT TO PROTRAC'S LINE

June Wilson is the manager of new-product development and is considering the financial implications of a possible addition to PROTRAC's heavy equipment line. Startup costs for the proposed model G-9s (which include purchase of some new equipment, training of personnel, and so on) are estimated at $150,000. The new product would be sold at a price of $35,000 per unit. Fixed costs are estimated to run at $15,000 per year, while variable costs should be about 75% of revenues each year. Tax depreciation[1] on the new equipment would be $10,000 per year over the expected 4-year product life of the G-9. The salvage value of the equipment at the end of the 4 years is uncertain, so June conservatively estimates it to be zero. PROTRAC's cost of capital is 10%, and its tax rate is 34%.

The most uncertain aspect of the proposal is the demand for the new product. If June knew the demand, she could easily calculate the *net present value* (NPV) of the proposal using a spreadsheet program. For example, if June assumes that the demand for G-9s is 10 units for each of the next 4 years, the spreadsheet in Figure 11.9 (WILSON.XLS) shows that the NPV would be $12,455.60.

THE MODEL WITH RANDOM DEMAND

However, it is unlikely that the demand will be exactly the same every year. June feels it would be more realistic to model the demand each year not as a common constant value, but as a sequence of random variables. This model of demand is appropriate when there is a constant base level of demand that is subject to random fluctuations from year to year. When the base level demand is 10 units, actual demands for the next 4 years might turn out to be 12, 9, 8, and 10, because of the random factors affecting demand.

Sampling Demand with a Spreadsheet June decides to generate random demands for the 4 years to see what effect the variability of the demands has on the NPV. She assumes initially that demand in a year will be either 8, 9, 10, 11, or 12 units with each value being equally likely to occur. This is an example of a discrete, uniform distribution. Using her new knowledge from Section 11.2, she devises the formula =INT(8+5*RAND()) to sample from the discrete uniform distribution on the five integers 8, 9, 10, 11, 12. Since the value of RAND() will change every time the spreadsheet is recalculated, June can easily perform **multiple trials**—that is, draw a new sample of demands simply by pressing the recalculation key for her spreadsheet (F9 usually). After doing this a few times, she is surprised to find that on some trials she obtains a negative NPV.

Figure 11.10 shows that the NPV corresponding to a random sequence of demands is $2,515.71, about 80% less than the NPV if demand were constant at 10 per year. If June were to hit the F9 key, she would get a different sample of demands, and hence thus possibly a different NPV. Because the demands can vary from sample to sample, the NPV can also vary. Put more technically, the demands are random variables, so the NPV is also a random variable.

---

[1] Depreciation is first subtracted to determine before-tax profit and then added back to determine net cash flow.

	B19		=NPV($D$3,C17:F17)+B17								
	A	B	C	D	E	F	G	H	I	J	
1	Assumptions										
2	Startup Costs	$ 150,000	Variable Costs		75%	of Revenue					
3	Selling Price	$ 35,000	Cost of Capital	10%							
4	Fixed Costs	$ 15,000	Tax Rate	34%							
5	Depreciation/Yr	$ 10,000									
6			Demand/Yr	10.0	units						
7											
8		Year 0	1	2	3	4					
9	Demand		10.0	10.0	10.0	10.0					
10	Revenue		350,000	350,000	350,000	350,000					
11	Fixed Cost		15,000	15,000	15,000	15,000					
12	Variable Cost		262,500	262,500	262,500	262,500					
13	Depreciation		10,000	10,000	10,000	10,000					
14	Profit before Tax		62,500	62,500	62,500	62,500					
15	Tax		21,250	21,250	21,250	21,250					
16	Profit after Tax		41,250	41,250	41,250	41,250					
17	Net Cash Flow	(150,000)	51,250	51,250	51,250	51,250					
18											
19	Net Present Value	$12,455.60									
20											
21											
22											

Initial / Random Demand / NPV Distribution / 100 Iterations / Sheet4 / Sheet5 / Sheet6 /

Cell	Formula	Copy To
C10	=C9*$B$3	D10:F10
C11	=$B$4	D11:F11
C12	=C10*$D$2	D12:F12
C13	=$B$5	D13:F13
C14	=C10−SUM(C11:C13)	D14:F14
C15	=$D$4*C14	D15:F15
C16	=C14−C15	D16:F16
B17	=−$B$2	—
C17	=C16+C13	D17:F17
B19	=NPV($D$3,C17:F17)+B17	—

FIGURE 11.9

Wilson's Initial Spreadsheet

	C9		=INT(8+5*RAND())								
	A	B	C	D	E	F	G	H	I	J	K
1	Assumptions										
2	Startup Costs	$ 150,000	Variable Costs		75%	of Revenue					
3	Selling Price	$ 35,000	Cost of Capital	10%							
4	Fixed Costs	$ 15,000	Tax Rate	34%							
5	Depreciation/Yr	$ 10,000									
6			Demand/Yr	10.0	units						
7											
8		Year 0	1	2	3	4					
9	Demand		10.0	8.0	9.0	11.0					
10	Revenue		350,000	280,000	315,000	385,000					
11	Fixed Cost		15,000	15,000	15,000	15,000					
12	Variable Cost		262,500	210,000	236,250	288,750					
13	Depreciation		10,000	10,000	10,000	10,000					
14	Profit before Tax		62,500	45,000	53,750	71,250					
15	Tax		21,250	15,300	18,275	24,225					
16	Profit after Tax		41,250	29,700	35,475	47,025					
17	Net Cash Flow	(150,000)	51,250	39,700	45,475	57,025					
18											
19	Net Present Value	$2,515.71									
20											
21											
22											

Initial / Random Demand / NPV Distribution / 100 Iterations / Sheet4 / Sheet5 / Sheet6 /

Cell	Formula	Copy to
C9	=INT(8+5*RAND())	D9:F9

FIGURE 11.10

Wilson's Spreadsheet with Randomly Selected Demands

EVALUATING THE PROPOSAL

June realizes that she needs to build a simulation model to help her answer two questions about the NPV distribution: (1) What is the *mean* or **expected value** of the NPV? and (2) What is the probability that the NPV assumes a negative value? The larger the mean NPV and—perhaps even more important—the less likely it is that the NPV is negative, the more attractive the proposal to add the G-9 to PROTRAC's product line.

So, the next step is to run the simulation automatically a number of times and capture the resulting NPV in a separate spreadsheet. This can be done rather easily with the spreadsheet's Data Table command as follows:

1. Click the Insert menu.
2. Select Worksheet.
3. Double click on the tab at the bottom with the name of the spreadsheet (usually some default name like "Sheet3") and rename the spreadsheet "100 Iterations."
4. Type the starting value (1) in cell A2 and hit Enter.
5. Click back on cell A2.
6. Click the Edit menu, choose Fill, then Series.
7. Select the Series in Columns option and enter a stop value of 100.
8. Click OK.

Excel will automatically fill in the column below the selected cell (A2) with values increasing by 1 (the step value) until it reaches the stop value of 100. In order to track the NPV, we enter the following formula in cell B2 of the new spreadsheet: =Random Demand!B19. We also enter labels in cells A1 and B1 for clarity. We now use the Data Table command. This is done as follows:

1. Select the range A2:B101.
2. Click the Data menu, then Table.
3. In the Table dialog box, enter cell C1 for the Column input cell.
4. Click OK.

Excel then substitutes each value in the range A2 to A101 into cell C1 (which has no real effect), recalculates the spreadsheet, and stores the resulting NPV in the adjacent cells in column B. After doing this, you should have a list of values in column B representing 100 possible values for the NPV, similar to those shown in Figure 11.11. The numbers you generate will not match those shown in Figure 11.11. Remember the procedure shown here generates a random sample of 100 trials from an infinite number of possible outcomes. Hopefully, the overall characteristics of your sample should be similar to the ones shown here.

In order to focus on these 100 observations, let's turn the formulas into values by following a simple procedure:

1. Select the range B2:B101.
2. Click on the Edit menu, then Copy.
3. Click on the Edit menu again, then Paste Special.
4. Select the Values option, then click OK.

In order to get a summary of our 100 iterations, we can use Excel's built-in data analysis tool. (If the Data Analysis option is not on your Tools menu, select the Add-ins option from the Tools menu, then select the Analysis ToolPak option.) This tool generates numerous descriptive statistics (e.g., mean, standard deviation, minimum, maximum, etc.) automatically. To use it, simply do the following:

1. Click the Tools menu, then Data Analysis.
2. Click Descriptive Statistics, and complete the dialog box as shown in Figure 11.12.
3. Click OK.

	B3	▼	{=TABLE(,C1)}				
	A	B	C	D	E	F	G
1	Simulation #	NPV					
2	1	$10,633.29					
3	2	$ 8,116.76					
4	3	$ 13,327.32					
5	4	$ (3,251.01)		✛			
6	5	$ 23,772.10					
7	6	$ 7,122.77					
8	7	$ 3,344.03					
9	8	$ 16,711.61					
10	9	$ 6,688.89					
11	10	$ 16,751.06					
12	11	$ 12,850.04					
13	12	$ 29,889.86					
14	13	$ 39,873.15					
15	14	$ 16,439.45					
16	15	$ 21,689.45					
17	16	$ (643.76)					
18	17	$ 10,333.52					

FIGURE 11.11

Wilson's Simulation Results

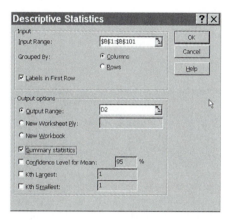

FIGURE 11.12

Descriptive Statistics
Dialog Box

Based on this limited sample, the results are shown in Figure 11.13 and indicate that the estimated mean NPV is $12,100.37 and the standard deviation is a rather large $12,351.69.

Downside Risk and Upside Risk June also wants to know what's the best possible outcome as well as the worst possible. In this sample, we can see from Figure 11.13 that the largest NPV was $39,955.98 and the smallest was −$11,100.37. This gives her a better idea about the range of possible NPVs that could occur.

Distribution of Outcomes Although the data in Figure 11.13 offer more insight than just the base case NPV, there are other factors we should consider. How likely are these extreme outcomes (best case, worst case) to occur? In order to answer this question, we need to know something about the shape of the distribution of the NPV. Fortunately, Excel also has some built-in features to help us. To generate a histogram (a graphical distribution of the NPVs) as well as a numerical frequency table, just follow these steps:

1. Click on the Tools menu, then Data Analysis.
2. Choose Histogram and complete its dialog box as shown in Figure 11.14.
3. Click OK.

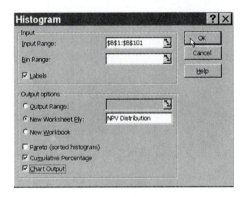

	E21	▼		=$E$4-1.96*$E$8/SQRT($E$16)					
	A	B	C	D	E	F	G	H	I
1	Simulation #	NPV							
2	1	$10,633.29			NPV				
3	2	$ 8,116.76							
4	3	$ 13,327.32		Mean	12100.37122				
5	4	$ (3,251.01)		Standard Error	1235.168989				
6	5	$ 23,772.10		Median	10483.40277				
7	6	$ 7,122.77		Mode	16751.05867				
8	7	$ 3,344.03		Standard Deviation	12351.68989				
9	8	$ 16,711.61		Sample Variance	152564243.2				
10	9	$ 6,688.89		Kurtosis	-0.471723205				
11	10	$ 16,751.06		Skewness	0.35637559				
12	11	$ 12,850.04		Range	51056.34861				
13	12	$ 29,889.86		Minimum	-11100.36883				
14	13	$ 39,873.15		Maximum	39955.97978				
15	14	$ 16,439.45		Sum	1210037.122				
16	15	$ 21,689.45		Count	100				
17	16	$ (643.76)		Confidence Level(95.0%)	2450.843684				
18	17	$ 10,333.52							
19	18	$ 5,071.68							
20	19	$ 12,104.55		**95% Confidence Interval**					
21	20	$ 1,139.11		**Lower Bound**	$ 9,679.44				
22	21	$ 21,567.17		**Upper Bound**	$ 14,521.30				

|◄ ◄ ► ►|\ Initial / Random Demand \ **100 Iterations** / NPV Distribution / Sheet4 / Sheet5 / Sheet6 /|◄ |

FIGURE 11.13

Descriptive Statistics
Summary

Cell	Formula
E21	=$E$4−1.96*$E$8/SQRT($E$16)
E22	=$E$4+1.96*$E$8/SQRT($E$16)

FIGURE 11.14

Histogram Dialog Box

In this case, we saved the results in a separate spreadsheet called "NPV Distribution". It is shown in Figure 11.15. The Frequency column shown in column B indicates the number of our 100 trials that fell into the bins defined by Excel in column A. For example, 1 observation was less than or equal to ($11,100.37). Ten observations were greater than ($5,994.73) and less than or equal to ($889.10). The greatest number of observations (16) fell in the interval of being greater than $9,322.17 and less than or equal to $14,427.81. The histogram shown on the right of Figure 11.15 gives a visual representation of the possible outcomes for the NPV. It has somewhat of a bell shape to it.

The Cumulative % column shown (column C) indicates that more than 15% of the NPV observations were negative (less than 0). This data can be helpful in answering other questions June or her chief financial officer might come up with.

How Reliable Is the Simulation? June now has the answers to her two questions about the NPV distribution: (1) What is the *mean* value of the NPV? (A: $12,100), and (2) What is the probability that the NPV assumes a negative value? (A: > 15%). We now ask some questions: How much confidence do we have in the answers June came up with? Would we have more confidence if we ran more trials?

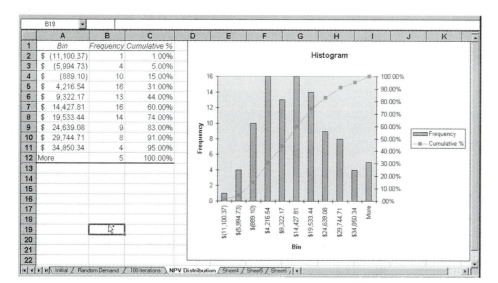

	A	B	C
1	*Bin*	*Frequency*	*Cumulative %*
2	$ (11,100.37)	1	1.00%
3	$ (5,994.73)	4	5.00%
4	$ (889.10)	10	15.00%
5	$ 4,216.54	16	31.00%
6	$ 9,322.17	13	44.00%
7	$ 14,427.81	16	60.00%
8	$ 19,533.44	14	74.00%
9	$ 24,639.08	9	83.00%
10	$ 29,744.71	8	91.00%
11	$ 34,850.34	4	95.00%
12	More	5	100.00%

FIGURE 11.15

Histogram and
Frequency Table

Certainly, it is intuitive that the more trials we run, the more confidence we ought to have in our answers. But how much confidence can we have in the 100 iterations we actually sampled? From the world of statistics, we remember that we can construct confidence intervals based on the results we obtained. For example, we can have 95% confidence that the true mean NPV is contained in an interval of ± 1.96 standard deviations about the estimated mean. In this case, the standard deviation of the mean is the reported standard deviation divided by the square root of the number of trials. This 95% confidence interval for the mean was calculated by June and reported in Figure 11.13 as ($9679.44; $14,521.30). Said another way, we can have 95% confidence that the true mean NPV is somewhere between $9679 and $14,521, with our current best guess that it is $12,100.

We must be careful *not* to fall in the "expected value" trap! Many students believe that the true mean NPV can always be calculated by setting all the random values to their means (set all the demands to 10 in this example). This is what June had in her initial spreadsheet (see Figure 11.9), but there is no guarantee that the NPV obtained in this manner will also be the true simulated mean. Although it may seem logical, there are some potential weaknesses in this reasoning. First of all, the way in which the demand values are used to calculate yearly cash flows and then turned into a single NPV number (or any other performance measure) could be highly nonlinear. There are other subtleties that will not be mentioned here, but be forewarned: Don't fall into the "expected value" trap!

There are cases where this "intuitive" reasoning will work, but not always. A simple example from one of life's common experiences ought to convince you that the NPV (or any other bottom-line performance measure) at the expected value of the random variables is not necessarily the same as the expected NPV. Consider a waiting line at the grocery store. Suppose the expected time to serve a customer is 0.9 minutes and the average time between customer arrivals is 1 minute. Looking at the situation using the expected values, you would predict the average waiting time to be 0 minutes (because customers are served faster than they arrive), but we all know that the *average* waiting time is greater than 0 minutes even though we sometimes get lucky and don't have to wait.

In summary, June needs more than 100 trials if she wants more accurate answers to her questions. What have we learned?

1. Increasing the number of trials is apt to give a better estimate of the expected return, but even with a large number of trials there can be some difference between the simulated *average* and the true expected return. Note that the true expected NPV in June's example turns out to be $12,455; the average NPV with 100 samples was $12,100 (a 2.85% error).

2. Simulations can provide useful information on the distribution of results. Even with a small sample of 100 trials there was an indication (a probability of greater than 0.15) that this project might yield a negative NPV. This is valuable information and something that could not have been determined with simply the base case analysis, or even Upside/Downside Risk analysis.

3. Simulation results are sensitive to assumptions affecting the input parameters. The next section shows that if June changes her assumptions about the distribution of demand (to a **Poisson distribution** with the same mean of 10), there is a significant impact on the probability of a negative NPV (it increases from about .15 to about .27).

Perhaps the most important impact of the simulation is on the decision-making process. If June had not performed any simulation analysis, she would have given an enthusiastic recommendation to proceed with the proposed addition to the heavy equipment line based on the mean NPV. However, after performing the simulation, she feels the project is too risky to recommend. While this is a qualitative judgment on her part, she can support it with the quantitative results of the simulation model. As we have noted before, models do not relieve managers from the responsibility of making decisions, but they do supply additional information for making those decisions well informed.

11.4　SIMULATING WITH SPREADSHEET ADD-INS

Spreadsheet add-ins, such as Crystal Ball and @RISK, make the task of simulation much easier than doing it alone in a spreadsheet. In particular, these programs greatly simplify the processes of generating random variables and assembling the statistical results. As we will see, both add-ins also greatly facilitate the capture and display of the output of the simulation. In this section we present a capital budgeting example to show how to use Crystal Ball [student version 4.0c] for simulation and to establish some important facts about the output from a spreadsheet simulation. In other sections and their examples, we will continue to demonstrate the use of Crystal Ball, which is distributed free with this textbook in a student version. We will also briefly demonstrate @Risk [version 3.5e] in Section 11.7.

Simulation in a spreadsheet without the help of add-in packages can be time-consuming and tedious (to put it kindly) even for simple models. For more complicated models, more complicated distributions, or greater number of iterations, these characteristics are exacerbated. Fortunately, computers can be easily programmed to generate random quantities from any specific distribution in large quantities, both rapidly and accurately. As we have seen, the add-in packages have a number of different preprogrammed functions that will produce random variables automatically. For all of these reasons, almost all spreadsheet simulations are performed with the help of add-in packages.

A CAPITAL BUDGETING EXAMPLE: ADDING A NEW PRODUCT TO PROTRAC'S LINE

June Wilson is the manager of new-product development and is considering the financial implications of a possible addition to PROTRAC's heavy equipment line. Startup costs for the proposed model G-9s (which include purchase of some new equipment, training of personnel, and so on) are estimated at $150,000. The new product would be sold at a price of $35,000 per unit. Fixed costs are estimated to run at $15,000 per year, while variable costs should be about 75% of revenues each year. Tax depreciation[2] on the new equipment would be $10,000 per year over the expected 4-year product life of the G-9. The salvage value of the equipment at the end of the 4 years is uncertain, so June conservatively estimates it to be zero. PROTRAC's cost of capital is 10%, and its tax rate is 34%.

The most uncertain aspect of the proposal is the demand for the new product. If June knew the demand, she could easily calculate the *net present value* (NPV) of the proposal using a spreadsheet program. For example, if June assumes that the demand for G-9s is 10

---

[2]Depreciation is first subtracted to determine before-tax profit and then added back to determine net cash flow.

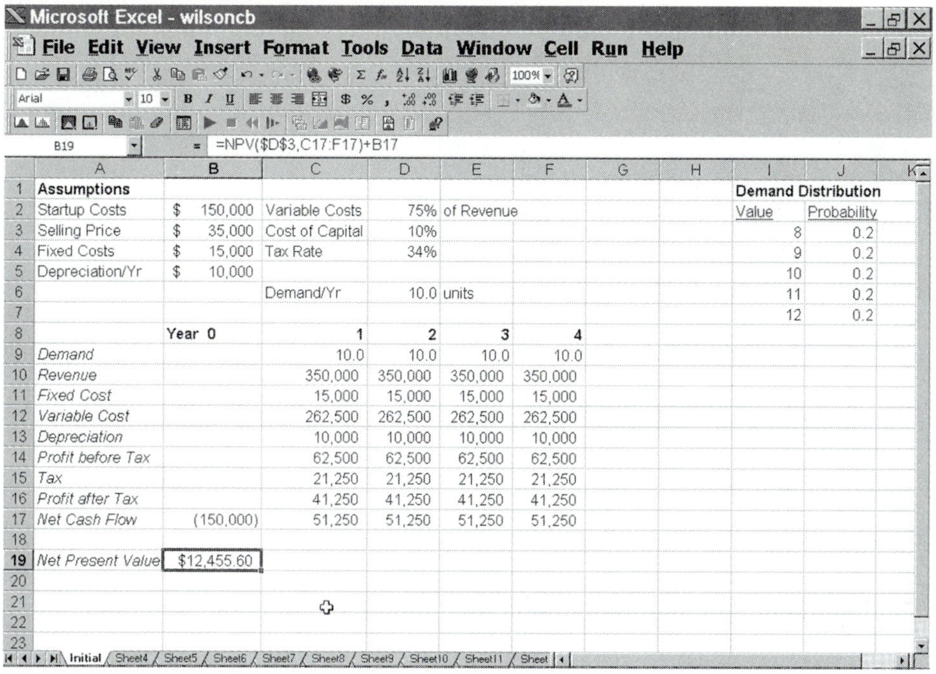

	A	B	C	D	E	F	G	H	I	J
1	Assumptions								Demand Distribution	
2	Startup Costs	$ 150,000	Variable Costs	75%	of Revenue				Value	Probability
3	Selling Price	$ 35,000	Cost of Capital	10%					8	0.2
4	Fixed Costs	$ 15,000	Tax Rate	34%					9	0.2
5	Depreciation/Yr	$ 10,000							10	0.2
6			Demand/Yr	10.0	units				11	0.2
7									12	0.2
8		Year 0	1	2	3	4				
9	Demand		10.0	10.0	10.0	10.0				
10	Revenue		350,000	350,000	350,000	350,000				
11	Fixed Cost		15,000	15,000	15,000	15,000				
12	Variable Cost		262,500	262,500	262,500	262,500				
13	Depreciation		10,000	10,000	10,000	10,000				
14	Profit before Tax		62,500	62,500	62,500	62,500				
15	Tax		21,250	21,250	21,250	21,250				
16	Profit after Tax		41,250	41,250	41,250	41,250				
17	Net Cash Flow	(150,000)	51,250	51,250	51,250	51,250				
18										
19	Net Present Value	$12,455.60								

Cell	Formula	Copy To
C9	=$D$6	—
C10	=C9*$B$3	D10:F10
C11	=$B$4	D11:F11
C12	=C10*$D$2	D12:F12
C13	=$B$5	D13:F13
C14	=C10−SUM(C11:C13)	D14:F14
C15	=C14*$D$4	D15:F15
C16	=C14−C15	D16:F16
B17	=−B2	—
C17	=C16+C13	D17:F17
B19	=NPV($D$3,C17:F17)+B17	—

FIGURE 11.16

Wilson's Initial Spreadsheet

units for each of the next 4 years, the spreadsheet in Figure 11.16 (WILSNCB1.XLS) shows that the NPV would be $12,455.60.

THE MODEL WITH RANDOM DEMAND

However, it is unlikely that the demand will be exactly the same every year. June feels it would be more realistic to model the demand each year not as a common constant value, but as a sequence of random variables. This model of demand is appropriate when there is a constant base level of demand that is subject to random fluctuations from year to year. When the base level demand is 10 units, actual demands for the next 4 years might turn out to be 12, 9, 8, and 10, because of the random factors affecting demand.

Sampling Demand with a Spreadsheet June decides to generate random demands for the 4 years to see what effect the variability of the demands has on the NPV. She assumes initially that demand in a year will be either 8, 9, 10, 11, or 12 units with each value being equally likely to occur. This is an example of a discrete, uniform distribution. To "generate a random demand" for this probability distribution in Crystal Ball, June has to enter this discrete distribution in a two-column format for Crystal Ball to be able to use it. This is

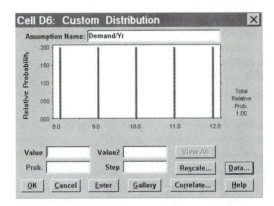

FIGURE 11.17

Crystal Ball
Distribution Gallery

FIGURE 11.18

PROTRAC's Custom Random
Number Generator

shown in columns I and J of Figure 11.16. To accomplish entering all this probability distribution information into Crystal Ball, June does the following:

1. Click on cell D6, which is the cell where Crystal Ball will generate random values for demand.
2. Click on the first Crystal Ball icon (Define Assumption).
3. Click on the "Custom" distribution from the resulting Distribution Gallery as shown in Figure 11.17, then click on OK (or alternatively you could have double clicked on the "Custom" distribution).
4. Click on the "Data" button and enter the cell range where you entered the information on this discrete distribution (I3:J7); then click on OK.
5. Crystal Ball shows the distribution back to you as you have entered it (see Figure 11.18).

To get Crystal Ball to draw a new random sample of demands, you simply click on the twelfth icon (Single Step), which is shown in Figure 11.19. After June does this a few times, she is surprised to find that on some trials she obtains a negative NPV. Figure 11.19 shows that the NPV corresponding to a random sequence of demands is $1,604.55, about 87% less than the NPV if demand were constant at 10 per year. If June were to hit the Single Step icon again, she would get a different sample of demands, and hence thus possibly a different NPV. Because the demands can vary from sample to sample, the NPV can also vary. Put more technically, the demands are random variables, so the NPV is also a random variable.

EVALUATING THE PROPOSAL

June realizes that she needs to build a simulation model to help her answer two questions about the NPV distribution: (1) What is the *mean* or **expected value** of the NPV? and

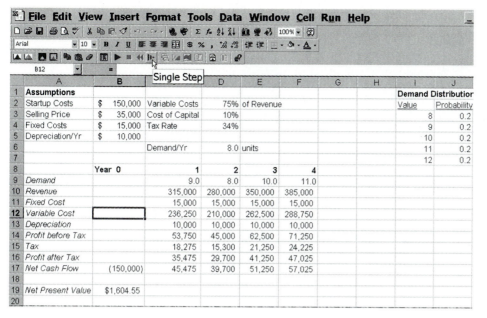

File Edit View Insert Format Tools Data Window Cell Run Help

B12

Single Step

	A	B	C	D	E	F	G	H	I	J
1	Assumptions								Demand Distribution	
2	Startup Costs	$ 150,000	Variable Costs	75%	of Revenue				Value	Probability
3	Selling Price	$ 35,000	Cost of Capital	10%					8	0.2
4	Fixed Costs	$ 15,000	Tax Rate	34%					9	0.2
5	Depreciation/Yr	$ 10,000							10	0.2
6			Demand/Yr	8.0	units				11	0.2
7									12	0.2
8		Year 0	1	2	3	4				
9	Demand		9.0	8.0	10.0	11.0				
10	Revenue		315,000	280,000	350,000	385,000				
11	Fixed Cost		15,000	15,000	15,000	15,000				
12	Variable Cost		236,250	210,000	262,500	288,750				
13	Depreciation		10,000	10,000	10,000	10,000				
14	Profit before Tax		53,750	45,000	62,500	71,250				
15	Tax		18,275	15,300	21,250	24,225				
16	Profit after Tax		35,475	29,700	41,250	47,025				
17	Net Cash Flow	(150,000)	45,475	39,700	51,250	57,025				
18										
19	Net Present Value	$1,604.55								
20										

FIGURE 11.19

Wilson's Spreadsheet with Randomly Selected Demands

Cell B19: Define Forecast

Forecast Name: Net Present Value

Units:

Forecast Window Size: ○ Small ● Large

☑ Display Window Automatically ○ While Running

● When Stopped (faster)

OK   Cancel   Set Default   Help

FIGURE 11.20

Crystal Ball "Define Forecast" Dialog Box

(2) What is the probability that the NPV assumes a negative value? The larger the mean NPV and—perhaps even more important—the less likely it is that the NPV is negative, the more attractive the proposal to add the G-9 to PROTRAC's product line.

So, the next step is to run the simulation automatically a number of times and capture the resulting NPV. This can be done much more easily with Crystal Ball than the spreadsheet alone. After setting up the base case model as we have done, and entering the RNGs in the appropriate cells (C9:F9), all we have to do is:

1. Click on cell B19 (the NPV cell).

2. Click on the second Crystal Ball icon (Define Forecast), which brings up a dialog box.

3. Change the Window size to "Large" and change the Display to "When Stopped (faster)" in the dialog box as shown in Figure 11.20. Also click on "Set Default" if you want this to be the default choice in the future.

4. Click on OK.

5. Click on the eighth icon (Run Preferences) and change the "Maximum Number of Trials" to 500 as shown in Figure 11.21.

6. Click on OK.

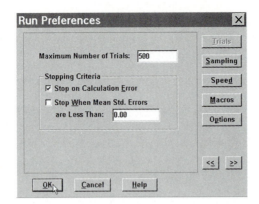

FIGURE 11.21

Crystal Ball "Run Preferences" Dialog Box

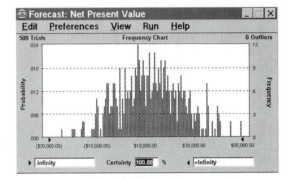

FIGURE 11.22

PROTRAC's Simulation Histogram of NPV

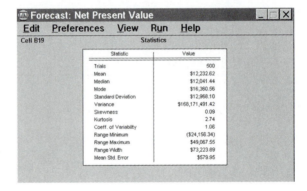

FIGURE 11.23

PROTRAC's Simulation Statistics

7. Click on the ninth icon (Start Simulation) and after Crystal Ball has run the 500 iterations, it tells you that "Maximum number of trials reached." After clicking on OK, it automatically produces the histogram shown in Figure 11.22.

8. To look at the statistics from the simulation, click on View, then Statistics, and Crystal Ball displays a table as shown in Figure 11.23.

Notice how much faster and easier it is to run 500 iterations in Crystal Ball as opposed to 20 or 100 with the spreadsheet alone (if you covered Section 11.3), and it doesn't take up 500 rows in the spreadsheet. After doing this, you should have results similar to those shown in Fig 11.23 (representing 500 outcomes of the NPV). The numbers you generate will not exactly match those shown in Figure 11.23. Remember the procedure shown here generates a random sample of 500 trials from an infinite number of possible outcomes. Hopefully, the overall characteristics of your sample should be similar to the ones shown here. Based on this sample, the results indicate that the estimated mean NPV is $12,232.62

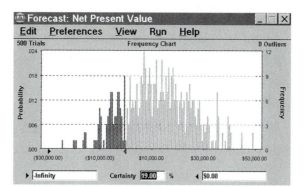

FIGURE 11.24

Wilson's Crystal Ball
Percentiles

and the standard deviation is a rather large $12,968.10. Note this is much closer to the true mean NPV than we would generally get with the limited number of trials we would run with the spreadsheet alone.

Downside Risk and Upside Risk   June also wants to know what's the best possible outcome as well as the worst possible. In this same display, we can see in Figure 11.23 that the largest NPV was $49,067.55 and the smallest was −$24,156.34. This gives her a better idea about the range of possible NPVs that could occur (almost $75,000).

Distribution of Outcomes   Although this information offers more insight than just the base case NPV, there are other factors we should consider. How likely are these extreme outcomes (best case, worst case) to occur? In order to answer this question, we need to know something about the shape of the distribution of the NPV. Fortunately, Crystal Ball has some built-in features to help us. We already generated a histogram (a graphical distribution of the NPVs) in Figure 11.22, and it gives us a visual representation of the possible outcomes for the NPV. It has a definite bell shape to it. One of the nice features of Crystal Ball is that it has already tabulated a tremendous amount of statistical and graphical information. Some of the information is automatically displayed; other pieces of information we must ask for. As an example of some information we have to ask for, suppose we want to determine the exact probability that the NPV will be nonpositive (≤ 0). We can simply enter 0 in the "◀" cell shown in the lower right corner of Figure 11.24 (meaning all values to the left of 0) and hit enter, and Crystal Ball will automatically return the percentage number in the corresponding percentile cell labeled "Certainty _____ %." In this case it returns 19.0%, meaning that 19.0% of the observed NPV values were less than or equal to 0. In like manner we could find out what percentage fell below or was above any arbitrary dollar amount. Also, by clicking on "View, Percentiles," Crystal Ball automatically displays the 10th, 20th, 30th, . . . , 90th percentiles of the NPV distribution. We notice that this is more precise information than we could get from Excel's Histogram feature or its Descriptive Statistics feature (which was shown in Section 11.3). This data can be helpful in answering other questions June or her chief financial officer might come up with.

How Reliable Is the Simulation?   June now has the answers to her two questions about the NPV distribution: (1) What is the *mean* value of the NPV? (A: $12,232.62), and (2) What is the probability that the NPV assumes a negative value? (A: 19.0%). We now ask some questions: How much confidence do we have in the answers June came up with? Would we have more confidence if we ran more trials?

Certainly, it is intuitive that the more trials we run, the more confidence we ought to have in our answers. But how much confidence can we have in the 500 iterations we actually sampled? From the world of statistics, we remember that we can construct confidence intervals based on the results we obtained. For example, we can have 95% confidence

	B9	▼	=	=B3-1.96*B4/SQRT(B5)	
	A		B	C	D
1	Crystal Ball Results				
2					
3	Mean		$12,232.62		
4	Std Dev		$12,968.10		
5	# Iterations		500		
6					
7	95% Confidence Interval				
8	Upper Limit		$13,369.32		
9	Lower Limit		$11,095.92		
10					

Cell	Formula
B8	=B3+1.96*B4/SQRT(B5)
B9	=B3−1.96*B4/SQRT(B5)

FIGURE 11.25

Wilson's Confidence Interval for the Mean Value of the NPV

that the true mean NPV is contained in an interval of ± 1.96 standard deviations about the estimated mean. In this case, the standard deviation of the mean is the reported standard deviation of the sample divided by the square root of the number of trials. This 95% confidence interval for the mean was calculated by June and is reported in Figure 11.25 as ($11,095.92; $13,369.32). Said another way, we can have 95% confidence that the true mean NPV is somewhere between $11,096 and $13,369, with our current best guess that it is $12,232.62. Notice that this interval is tighter than the one we would generally develop with a spreadsheet alone where a smaller number of iterations would generally be used. The spreadsheet WILSCB1C.XLS (found on the CD distributed with this book) contains all of this completed information if you did not create it as you read along.

We must be careful *not* to fall in the "expected value" trap! Many students believe that the true mean NPV can always be calculated by setting all the random values to their means (set all the demands to 10 in this example). This is what June had in her initial spreadsheet (see Figure 11.16), but there is no guarantee that the NPV obtained in this manner will always be the true simulated mean. Although it may seem logical, there are some potential weaknesses in this reasoning. First of all, the way in which the random demand values are used to calculate yearly cash flows and then turned into a single NPV number (or any other performance measure) could be highly nonlinear. There are other subtleties that will not be mentioned here, but be forewarned: Don't fall into the "expected value" trap!

There are cases, like this model, where this "intuitive" reasoning works, but not always. A simple example from one of life's common experiences ought to convince you that the NPV (or any other bottom-line performance measure) at the expected value of the random variables is not necessarily the same as the expected NPV. Consider a waiting line at the grocery store. Suppose the expected time to serve a customer is 0.9 minutes and the average time between customer arrivals is 1 minute. Looking at the situation using the expected values, you would predict the average waiting time to be 0 minutes (because customers are served faster than they arrive), but we all know that the *average* waiting time will turn out to be greater than 0 minutes even though we sometimes get lucky and don't have to wait.

OTHER DISTRIBUTIONS OF DEMAND

June is concerned about the estimates of demand that she used in the previous simulation. In that model she assumed that the mean demand in each period would be 10 units, and then allowed for random variation in demand around that mean (between 8 and 12 units). She is quite confident that the mean demand will indeed remain essentially the same in each of the next four years, but she is not at all sure that it will necessarily be 10. If the

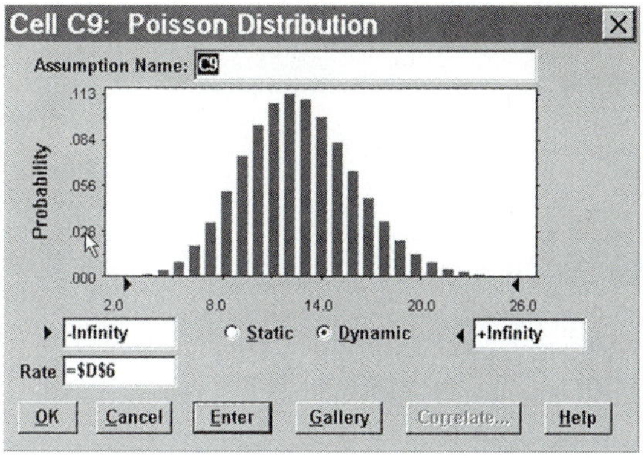

FIGURE 11.26

Wilson's Modified
Distribution Dialog Box

economy is slow, it might be 8; if the federal bridge repair program is approved by Congress, it might be 13. After some thought, June decides that the mean demand could be anywhere between 6 and 14 units a year, with all values in between being equally likely. To express this uncertainty she decides to model the mean demand as a continuous, uniform distribution between 6 and 14.

She would also like to explore the impact of different demand distributions on the NPV. She has read in a probability and statistics text that when mean demand is relatively small, a distribution called the **Poisson distribution** is often a good fit. The Poisson is a *one-parameter* distribution, because specifying only one parameter, the mean value of the random variable, completely determines it. The Poisson is also a discrete distribution, since a Poisson random variable can take on only nonnegative integer values. June will put this new information in a new spreadsheet called WILSNCB2.XLS. To sample from a Poisson distribution with a mean of 10, June has only to call up Crystal Ball's Distribution Gallery and indicate that she wants a Poisson distribution with a mean of 10. To sample from a continuous, uniform distribution between 6 and 14, she has to call up Crystal Ball's Distribution Gallery and indicate that she wants a uniform distribution with a "min" value of 6 and a "max" value of 14. The only changes June has to make in her spreadsheet then are the following: indicate to Crystal Ball that the cell D6 will have the uniform distribution discussed above and that cells C9 through F9 will have a poisson distribution with a mean value driven by the value in cell D6. To do this last step in Crystal Ball, we click on cell C9, then click on "Define Assumption" to bring up the Crystal Ball distribution gallery dialog box and enter the information as shown in Figure 11.26 (make sure you change to the "Dynamic" button). To get the same information from cell C9 to cells D9:F9, we can use Crystal Ball's "Copy Data" and "Paste Data" features (the fifth and sixth icons) to save us time, or we can just enter all the same information as we did for cell C9 into cells D9, E9, and F9 on an individual basis.

June decides to sample 1000 times from the distribution of the NPV and base her estimates on the 1000 values she obtains. She simply tells Crystal Ball to perform 1000 iterations in the "Run Preferences" dialog box and to capture the NPV in cell B19 for each of the iterations (using the "Define Forecast" icon). She must also tell Crystal Ball to "Reset Simulation" (eleventh icon) so that it clears the results from the simulation run previously. After the 1000 iterations are completed, June can view a histogram of the results. The histogram is shown in Figure 11.27, and the related statistics reveal that the average NPV over the 1000 iterations is $9,816.11 and that there is a large probability of a negative NPV (27.5%). The mean NPV is lower than it was with the previous distribution, and the probability of a negative outcome has increased significantly (19% to 27.5%).

The graph gives a qualitative impression of the distribution, but more detailed information can be obtained. Some of the other simulation statistics June could view are: the largest value observed, $44,729; and the smallest value observed, −$19,817 (a range of approximately $65,000). This completed model is found on the CD as WILSCB2C.XLS.

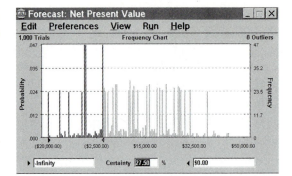

FIGURE 11.27

Wilson's NPV Histogram
Using a Modified Distribution

We have now seen three evaluations of June's G-9 capital budgeting problem: (1) a deterministic model (Figure 11.16), (2) a simulation with 500 trials but restricted assumptions about demand (Figure 11.19), and (3) a simulation with 1000 trials (Figure 11.27), based on what June feels is a more realistic representation of demand. What have we learned?

1. Increasing the number of trials is apt to give a better estimate of the expected return, but even with a large number of trials there can sometimes be a difference between the simulated *average* and the true expected return.

2. Simulations can provide useful information on the distribution of results. With the sample of 500 trials and restricted assumptions about demand, there was an indication (a probability of 0.19) that this project might yield a negative NPV. This is valuable information and something that could not have been determined with simply the base case analysis, or even Upside/Downside Risk analysis.

3. Simulation results are sensitive to assumptions affecting the input parameters. We saw that if June changes her assumptions about the distribution of demand (from a discrete, uniform distribution to a Poisson distribution with the same mean of 10), there is a significant impact on the probability of a negative NPV (it increases from about 19% to about 27.5%).

Perhaps the most important impact of the simulation is on the decision-making process. If June had not performed any simulation analysis, she would have given an enthusiastic recommendation to proceed with the proposed addition to the heavy equipment line based on the mean NPV. However, after performing either of the simulations, she feels the project is too risky to recommend. While this is a qualitative judgment on her part, she can support it with the quantitative results of the simulation model. As we have noted before, models do not relieve managers from the responsibility of making decisions, but they do supply additional information for making those decisions well informed.

**11.5   AN INVENTORY CONTROL EXAMPLE:
        FOSLINS HOUSEWARES**

June Wilson's capital budgeting model provided an example of the use of simulation in a "yes or no" situation: June had to decide whether or not to accept the project. There are other situations, however, in which the question is, "How much of this should we do?" Simulation can be used for models of this type as well. However, there are some new concerns (or perhaps variations of old concerns) to consider when using simulation in this way. This section uses an inventory control model to provide another illustration of simulation. It will also serve to motivate a discussion of the proper interpretation of results.

Chapter 11   533

Monte Carlo Simulation

THE OMELET PAN PROMOTION: HOW MANY PANS TO ORDER?

Marie Ford is the chief buyer for housewares at Foslins, one of Denver's leading retailers. The chief buyer's role is important in a retail organization like Foslins. Marie is responsible for designing the overall retailing strategy and operating procedures for her area. She also supervises a group of buyers who make specific purchase decisions.

Certain sections of the housewares department have just suffered their second consecutive bad year. Competing shops, such as Box and Barrel, which specialize in imported cooking and dining articles, have made serious inroads into Foslins' once secure position. The gourmet cooking, glassware, stainless flatware, and contemporary dishes sections of Foslins are not generating enough revenue to justify the amount of floor space currently committed to them.

Marie plans to meet this challenge head-on. She has reorganized the sections that are in trouble to create a store within a store. To achieve the same ambiance as her competitors, she has adopted display techniques that feature natural wood and modern lighting. She has essentially created a specialty shop, like her competitors, within the housewares department. With these changes, plus the store's reputation for quality and service, she feels that Foslins can effectively compete.

To introduce the new facility at Foslins, Marie decides to make the month of October "International Dining Month." This promotion will feature a sale on five special articles, each from a different country. These articles will be especially made for Foslins and include a copper omelet pan from France, a set of 12 long-stem wine glasses from Spain, and so on. Each of the items has been selected by a buyer on Marie's staff. The design and price are agreed on. The items have to be ordered at least 6 months in advance, and they will not become part of Foslins' regular product line. Any items left at the end of October will be sold to a discount chain at a reduced price. In addition, Foslins has adopted the policy that if it runs out of the special sale items, a more expensive item from its regular line of merchandise will be substituted at the sale price. It is all part of the "once-in-a-lifetime" promotion.

In the case of the omelet pans, Foslins will buy the special pans for $22 and will sell them for $35. Any pans left at the end of the sale will be sold to Clampton's Discount Chain for $15 each. If Foslins runs out of the special pans, it will substitute one of its regular copper omelet pans and sell it for the sale price of $35. Regular pans, which normally sell for $65, cost $32 each.

Marie's problem is that she must decide how many of the special pans to order without knowing in advance what the demand for them will be. For example, suppose she ordered 1000 pans and the demand turned out to be 1100 pans. Then she would have to buy 100 pans ($1100 - 1000$) at $32 per pan after buying 1000 pans at $22 per pan and would sell all 1100 pans at $35 per pan. Thus her net profit would be

$$\$35(1100) - \$32(100) - \$22(1000) = \$13,300$$

In general, let y = number of pans ordered and D = demand. Then for $D > y$,

$$\text{Profit} = 35D - 32(D - y) - 22y = 3D + 10y$$

If, on the other hand, she ordered 1000 pans and demand turned out only to be 200 pans, then she would sell 200 pans at $35 and 800 pans ($1000 - 200$) at $15 to Clampton's. Her net profit would be

$$\$35(200) + \$15(800) - \$22(1000) = -\$3000$$

In general, for $D < y$,

$$\text{Profit} = 35D + 15(y - D) - 22y = 20D - 7y$$

(You can see that for $D = y$, the two formulas become identical.)

Note that Marie's calculations assume that using regular pans to satisfy promotional demand will *not* create any unsatisfied regular demand. Because of the location of her regular pan supplier, the supply is large enough that this complication need not be considered.

Marie has modeled this in Excel as FOSLNCB1.XLS and it is shown in Figure 11.28. The spreadsheet assumes that Marie decides to order 11 omelet pans (i.e., $y = 11$). The random demand turns out to be 8 (i.e., $D = 8$), and the order quantity is greater than the demand ($y > D$). This means we have 3 extra pans leftover. Thus the profit of this single simulated promotion is $\$35(8) + \$15(3) - \$22(11) = \$83$.

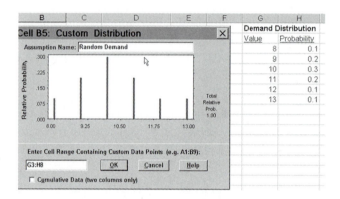

FIGURE 11.28

Foslins' Base Case

Cell	Formula
B7	=MAX(0,B3−B5)
B9	=MAX(0,B5−B3)
B11	=IF(B3≥B5,E3*B5+E4*B7−E5*B3,E3*B5−E8*B9−E5*B3)

FIGURE 11.29

Foslins' Random
Demand Generator

PROFIT VERSUS ORDER QUANTITY

Marie is naturally interested in determining how the number of pans she orders affects her expected profit on the promotion and the likelihood of the promotion losing money. We will see how to attack this question with simulation, beginning with a simple illustrative example. Later, in Section 11.6, we will treat the more realistic assumption of a *normal demand distribution* ($\mu = 1000$, $\sigma = 100$). Let us now assume that demand has the following probability distribution.

$$\text{Prob \{demand} = 8\} = 0.1$$
$$\text{Prob \{demand} = 9\} = 0.2$$
$$\text{Prob \{demand} = 10\} = 0.3$$
$$\text{Prob \{demand} = 11\} = 0.2$$
$$\text{Prob \{demand} = 12\} = 0.1$$
$$\text{Prob \{demand} = 13\} = 0.1$$

These demands have been chosen artificially small in order to simplify the example. To generate random demand for this probability distribution in Crystal Ball, Marie has to enter this discrete distribution in a two-column format for Crystal Ball, as shown in the previous section. This is shown in columns G and H of Figure 11.29.

To accomplish entering all this probability distribution information into Crystal Ball, Marie does the following:

1. Click on cell B5 which is the cell where Crystal Ball will generate random values for demand.

2. Click on the first Crystal Ball icon (Define Assumption).

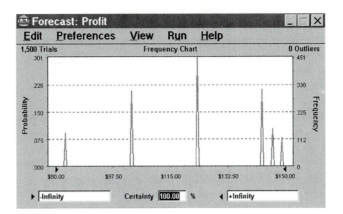

FIGURE 11.30

Foslins' Simulation Histogram of Profit

3. Click on the "Custom" distribution from the resulting Distribution Gallery (shown previously in Figure 11.17); then click on OK (or alternatively you could have double clicked on the "Custom" distribution).

4. Click on the "Data" button and enter the cell range where you entered the information on this discrete distribution (G3:H8 as shown in Figure 11.29); then click on OK.

5. Crystal Ball shows the distribution back to you as you have entered it (see Figure 11.29).

We are now prepared to use simulation to calculate the average profit. To do so, we must generate a number of trials, setting $y = 11$ and generating a new demand on each trial. The profit that results on any given trial depends, of course, on the value of demand that was generated on that particular trial. The *average profit* over all trials, then, is an estimate of the expected profit. Again, this can be done easily with Crystal Ball as follows:

1. Click on cell B11 (the Profit cell).

2. Click on the second Crystal Ball icon (Define Forecast), which brings up a dialog box.

3. Change the Window size to "Large" and change the Display to "When Stopped (faster)" in the dialog box if this is not already your default setting (shown previously in Figure 11.20). Also click on "Set Default" if you want this to be the default choice in the future.

4. Click on OK.

5. Click on the eighth icon (Run Preferences) and change the "Maximum Number of Trials" to 500 (shown previously in Figure 11.21).

6. Click on OK.

7. Click on the ninth icon (Start Simulation) and after Crystal Ball has run the 500 iterations, it tells you that "Maximum number of trials reached." After clicking on OK, it automatically produces the histogram shown in Figure 11.30.

8. To look at the statistics from the simulation, click on View, then Statistics, and Crystal Ball displays a table as shown in Figure 11.31.

The numbers you generate will not exactly match those shown in Figure 11.31. Remember the procedure shown here generates a random sample of 500 trials from an infinite number of possible outcomes. Hopefully, the overall characteristics of your sample should be similar to the ones shown here. According to Figure 11.31, the average profit for the 500 trials

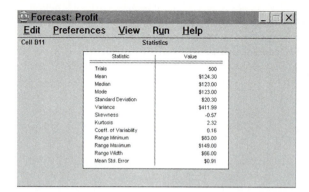

FIGURE 11.31

Foslins' Simulation Statistics

is \$124.30. Thus, based on these 500 trials, Marie's best estimate of the expected profit of ordering 11 pans is \$124.30. The completed spreadsheet is found on the CD as FOSLCB1C.XLS.

Marie can use the same approach to calculate the average profit associated with any order quantity. She need only place a different order size in cell B3 of the "Base Case" spreadsheet and rerun the simulation.

But note that since the demand is random, the average profit will also be random. This means that if Marie ran another set of 500 trials with the same order size of 11 pans, the simulator could generate a different series of demands and thus would most likely obtain a different average profit.

Expected Value Versus Order Quantity   With this simple example, Marie can easily calculate the true *expected* profit associated with any order quantity as opposed to relying on her estimate of profit from 500 trials (this is often not the case for more realistic examples and is only done here for pedagogical reasons). This can be done by using the spreadsheet shown in Figure 11.28 to calculate the profit resulting from each of the six possible demand levels (8, 9, . . . , 13). All Marie does is place the six different possible demand values in cell B5 (one at a time) and note what profit is produced. Each of these profit values is then multiplied by the probability of that demand occurring (e.g., the profit produced when demand = 10 is multiplied by 0.3, the probability that demand will in fact be 10). Finally, the resulting terms are added. The calculation is shown in Table 11.2.

Simulated Versus Expected Profits   Assuming that risk is not a factor, Marie would like to select the order quantity that yields the largest expected profit. To do so, she would calculate the expected profit for all the possible order quantities (8, 9, 10, . . . , 13), just as she did for an order quantity of 11, and select the order quantity that yields the largest profit. If she were to use simulation, she would use the same procedure that she used to determine the *average profit* with an order quantity of 11 for the other possible order quantities (8, 9, 10, 12, 13) and then select that order quantity that yielded the largest average profit.

It is no surprise that for any particular order quantity, the average profit generated by the spreadsheet simulator does not equal the true expected profit, as we have already seen that different runs will produce different values for the average profit. The implication of this fact on the process of making a decision is interesting. The computed expected profits and simulated average profits for order sizes of 9, 10, 11, and 12 pans are shown in Table 11.3.

We have only shown the work behind the simulated and true expected profit for ordering 11 pans. We leave it as an exercise for the student to verify the other entries in the table (see Problems 11-9 through 11-11).

TABLE 11.2 Expected Profit When Ordering 11 Pans				
(A) ORDER QUANTITY	(B) DEMAND	(C) PROFIT	(D) PROBABILITY OF DEMAND	(E) COLUMN (C) * (D)
11	8	$ 83	.10	8.3
11	9	$103	.20	20.6
11	10	$123	.30	36.9
11	11	$143	.20	28.6
11	12	$146	.10	14.6
11	13	$149	.10	14.9
			Expected Profit =	*$123.9*

TABLE 11.3		
NUMBER ORDERED	TRUE EXPECTED PROFIT	SIMULATED AVERAGE PROFIT (500 TRIALS)
9	$119.2	$118.88
10	**$124.1**	$124.18
11	$123.9	**$124.30**
12	$120.3	$118.81

Here we see that if Marie were to base her decision on the simulated average profit for this particular set of trials, the profit-maximizing decision would be to order 11 pans. To maximize the true expected profit, however, she should order 10 pans. This is, of course, a deliberately oversimplified example, but it is an excellent illustration of the fact that *simulation, in general, is not guaranteed to achieve optimality.*

In Marie's case, the decision to order 11 pans rather than 10 is not critical, for it reduces her true expected profit by less than 0.2%. In some instances, however, simulation can lead to results that are farther from the optimal. Marie may therefore wonder whether there is anything she can do to improve the accuracy of her simulation. Can she increase the likelihood that a simulation will in fact produce an optimal decision?

Although the nature of simulation makes it impossible to *guarantee* that an optimal decision will be identified, there is a very simple way to increase the likelihood of this outcome: *increase the number of trials.* The greater the number of trials, the more reliable the results of the simulation tend to be—just as the more often you toss a coin, the more closely the proportion of heads is likely to approach 50%. This fact leads to the following important observation:

Suppose that, in a decision under risk, management would like to make the decision that minimizes expected cost or maximizes expected profit. With simulation, the decision may be wrongly identified if care is not taken to simulate a sufficient number of trials.

We should reemphasize that in a real problem you would not *both* calculate the true expected profit and use simulation to calculate an average profit. Simulation is used when it is computationally impractical or even not possible to calculate the expected profit associated with the alternative decisions, or when it is important to assess the variability of the performance measure for various solutions. This simple example serves to illustrate relationships between simulation and analytic models.

RECAPITULATION

Let us summarize and comment on several aspects of what we have seen so far:

1. A spreadsheet simulator takes parameters and decisions as inputs and yields a performance measure (or measures) as output.

2. Each iteration of the spreadsheet simulator (for the same parameters and decisions) will generally yield a different value for the performance measure.

3. In Marie's model the performance measure (for an order of size 100) was taken to be profit. The 500 trials taken together combine to produce another measure of the goodness of the particular order size: *average profit.*

Note that even more information is available. If we wanted to know how often a shortage occurred (demand exceeded the quantity ordered), we would need to click on cell B9, add it as a "Forecast" cell, and rerun the simulation. Figure 11.32 shows that a shortage occurred in 95 of the 500 trials (19%). This is additional data with which to assess the "goodness" of ordering 11 pans, and it shows how, with simulation, numerous "performance measures" can be produced.

Yet another important property of simulation is illustrated by a previous figure (see Figure 11.31). The 500 trials have produced a distribution of profit: It varies from $83 to $149, with a mean of $124.30. We also previously generated the histogram shown in Figure 11.30. This provides some indication as to the **variability** associated with the policy being evaluated (ordering 11 pans). Indicators of variability are important products of simulation studies. *Management usually seeks policies for which the potential outcome is highly predictable, which means low variability.*

4. Increasing the number of iterations of the spreadsheet simulator (for the same parameters and decisions) will usually improve the accuracy of the estimate of the expected value of the performance measure. In other words, if Marie had used 1000 or 5000 trials in her simulation, the average profit for each order quantity would almost certainly be closer to the corresponding true expected profit.

5. In a simulation we can never be sure that we have found the optimal decision, although we can use our confidence interval knowledge from statistics to make sure we have performed enough trials that we have 95% or 99% confidence. This lack of 100% confidence is because a simulation can provide only an estimate of the expected effectiveness and not the exact value when randomness is present.

6. Management must assess four main factors in a simulation study:

    a. Does the model capture the essence of the real problem? (See Section 11.9 for further discussion of this point.)

    b. Are the influence of the starting and ending conditions of the simulation properly accounted for? (See Section 11.8 for a specific example.)

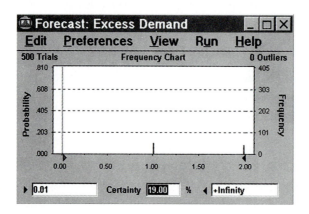

FIGURE 11.32

Foslins' Shortage Results

c. Have enough trials been performed for each decision so that the average value of the measure (or measures) of performance is a good indication of the true expected value?

d. Have enough decisions (and the right decisions) been evaluated so that we can believe that the best answer found is "close enough" to the optimum?

11.6 SIMULATION OF FOSLINS' MODEL WITH A MORE REALISTIC DEMAND ASSUMPTION

Although we have already analyzed the Foslins Houseware model in Section 11.5, recall that we had assumed a simplified demand distribution when a more realistic model of demand is the normal distribution with a mean of 1000 and a standard deviation of 100. In this section we will use a normal distribution of demand, perform 1000 trials (the maximum allowed by the student version of Crystal Ball), and determine the optimal order quantity.

In the development of this example we will practice how to generate a normal random variable with a specific mean and standard deviation. We will also see how variability in a simulation can be reduced, allowing a better estimate of the difference in profit between two decisions. In addition, the example provides an opportunity for examining the distinction between average profit and true expected profit, as well as a further illustration of what is meant by the distribution of profits for a specific order quantity.

THE FOSLINS' SPREADSHEET: SIMULATING DEMAND MORE REALISTICALLY

Recall our spreadsheet (FOSLNCB1.XLS) from Figure 11.28. To modify the model, we will start with a new spreadsheet (FOSLNCB2.XLS) and then change the quantity ordered to 1020 and notify Crystal Ball that we want to change the random distribution of demand from a customized one (discrete, general) to the normal distribution with a mean value of 1000 and a standard deviation of 100, as shown in Figure 11.33. (*Note:* To do this in Excel alone, all you have to do is type the following in cell B5: NORMINV (RAND(),1000,100), or you can replace the 1000 and 100 with appropriate cell references.)

To simulate 1000 trials, we follow the same procedure we did before in Section 11.5, where we ran 500 trials by modifying the Run Preferences dialog box to indicate the larger number of iterations. The other change we make is to indicate that we wish to use the same 1000 random values for demand in each of the upcoming simulations (for the different order quantities we'll compare). This is known as setting the seed value. The procedure to do this is as follows:

1. Click on "Sampling" in the Run Preferences dialog box.
2. Place a check mark in the box that says "Use Same Sequence of Random Numbers."
3. Enter an "Initial Seed Value" of 422 (or any number you like), as shown in Figure 11.34.
4. Click on OK.

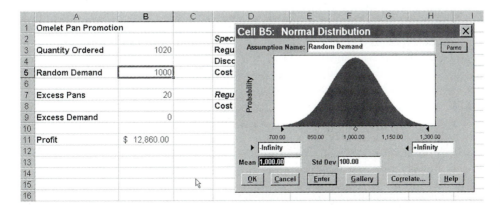

FIGURE 11.33

Foslins' Spreadsheet Assuming Normal Demand

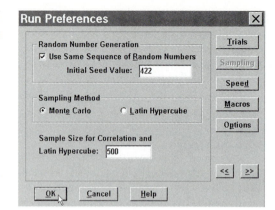

FIGURE 11.34

Foslins' New "Run
Preferences" Dialog Box

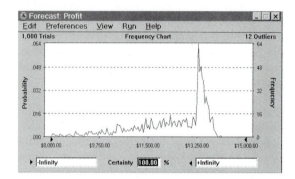

FIGURE 11.35

Foslins' Histogram of Profits
when Ordering 1020 Pans

It is important that the demands not change, because we want to compare the average profit for *different* order quantities but the *same* set of random demands. Then profit will differ only because of different order quantities and not because a different set of demand values had been sampled.

This process of decreasing variability in simulation results is called *variance reduction,* and it is an important technique in reducing the amount of computation necessary to obtain valid simulation results. Indeed, the ability to use the *same* set of random variables to evaluate competing alternatives is a unique experimental advantage of simulation. All branches of science attempt to reduce exogenous variability in their experiments. For example, agronomists plant different varieties of corn in the same field to insure that weather and soil conditions do not vary. With simulation, using the same sequence of random variables provides us with complete control of the random elements.

THE EFFECT OF ORDER QUANTITY

Figure 11.35 shows a histogram of the profit values generated for the 1000 iterations under the assumption of ordering 1020 pans. The average profit of $12,270.44 is shown in Figure 11.36, along with some other statistics. By entering different order quantities in cell B3 of the spreadsheet and rerunning the simulation, we could get an idea of how the average profit varies for a range of order quantities and a *given* set of demands. To reset the simulation:

1. Place a new order quantity in cell B3.

2. Click on the eleventh icon (Reset Simulation) and click OK in response to the question asked.

3. Click on the seventh icon (Start Simulation). This simulation could take a few minutes, depending on the speed of your computer.

Forecast: Profit
Edit Preferences View Run Help
Cell B11 Statistics

Statistic	Value
Trials	1,000
Mean	$12,270.44
Median	$12,762.54
Mode	---
Standard Deviation	$1,452.80
Variance	$2,110,628.46
Skewness	-1.32
Kurtosis	4.72
Coeff. of Variability	0.12
Range Minimum	$4,357.15
Range Maximum	$14,071.30
Range Width	$9,714.15
Mean Std. Error	$45.94

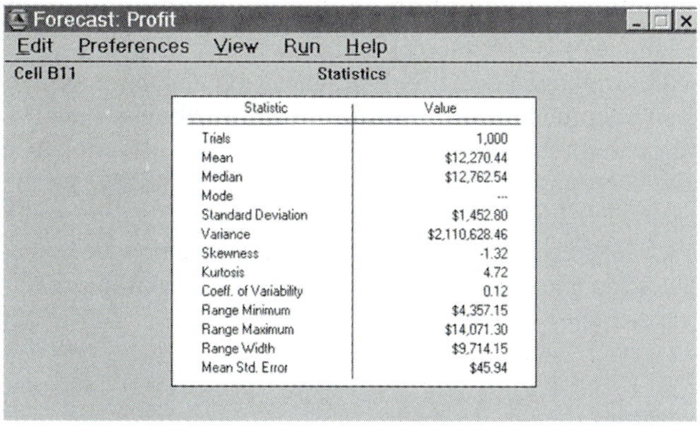

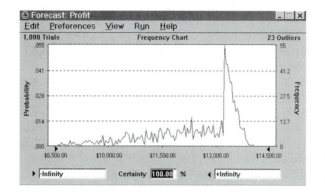

FIGURE 11.36

Foslins' Statistical Output when Ordering 1020 Pans

FIGURE 11.37

Foslins' Histogram of Profit for Ordering 1017 Pans

To search for the optimal order quantity is an iterative process. After running the simulation at an order quantity of 1020, Marie next can check order quantities of 1010 and 1030. After running 1000 iterations at each new order quantity, Marie finds that the expected profits are $12,268.95 and $12,264.60, respectively. Since the expected profit for the order quantity of 1020 is best so far, Marie next decides to check the order quantities on either side (e.g., 1015 and 1025). She finds that the expected profits are $12,270.70 and $12,268.34. At this point, an order quantity of 1015 seems to give the highest expected profit so she checks some order quantities on either side (e.g., 1013 and 1017) of the best order quantity so far (i.e., 1015). Marie finds that the expected profits are $12,270.29 and $12,270.77, respectively. The order quantity of 1017 now seems to give the highest expected profit. Just to make sure, though, Marie reruns the simulation and tries the order quantities of 1016 and 1018. She finds that their expected profits are $12,270.76 and $12,270.71, respectively, and is now fairly confident that an order quantity of 1017 really is the best decision, albeit only by a few cents. The completed spreadsheet is found on the CD as FOSLCB2C.XLS.

As a result of this iterative process, Marie has found that while the order quantity of 1017 pans maximizes the *average* profit *for the given set of 1000 demands,* it may not maximize the true *expected* profit. As we have said before, it is nearly impossible to guarantee that the optimal solution will be found using simulation. But remember, an optimal solution is a theoretical as opposed to a real-world concept. At best, an optimal solution represents a "good decision" for the real-world problem. In this case, the average profit for order quantities between 1015 and 1018 only varied by a couple of pennies, and so even if we didn't get the exact optimal order quantity, we are certainly confident that we are "close enough."

The Probability Distribution of Profit We may, however, want to know more about the solution suggested by simulation (ordering 1017 pans). For example, how much variability can we expect around the average profit of $12,270.77? Could we make much more or much less than the average? Could this decision *lose* money? The definitive answer to these questions is given in the form of the probability distribution (or histogram) of profit as shown in Figure 11.37.

Figure 11.37 shows the distribution of profit for an order quantity of 1017 based on a sample of 1000 trials. This gives a nice visual picture of the range of risk that Foslins will be taking in ordering 1017 pans, and may have more impact on Marie and her boss than just numbers and averages. The distribution appears to have somewhat of a bell shape to it, with a long left tail. The peaked distribution to the right of the expected value ($12,271) means that there is a definite probability that the profit will exceed the mean profit. The long tail to the left of the expected profit means that there is some chance of obtaining a result several thousand dollars below the expected profit. There is very little chance, however, of losing money on this promotion: In 1000 trials, no profit was less than $4370.

11.7　MIDWEST EXPRESS: AIRLINE OVERBOOKING MODEL

Most of the models we have discussed in this chapter so far have been from the manufacturing side of the economy (PROTRAC and Foslins). Now that well over half of the United States' Gross Domestic Product is from the service sector, the chapter would not be complete without an example from the sector. The travel and hospitality industry is a huge, multi-billion-dollar industry. Many of the different industries (e.g., airlines, hotels, rental cars, cruise lines, etc.) within that broad group practice a set of quantitative tools called revenue management. The airlines were the first ones to pioneer the use of these tools, with American Airlines generally considered to be the leader. For example, American Airlines started the practice of auctioning off the value of a seat on a given flight when more customers showed up than it had seats available. This was a very innovative way to deal with the potential problem that exists when airlines overbook their flights. American Airlines estimates that overbooking alone adds over $200 million per year to its bottom line (see Smith et. al.). Other areas besides overbooking that are practiced in the revenue management area include forecasting, seat allocation among the various fare classes, and control of the entire network of flight legs.

This example will focus on a very successful, regional carrier (Midwest Express Airlines). Midwest Express is headquartered in Milwaukee, Wisconsin, and was started by the large consumer products company Kimberly Clark, which has large operations in nearby Appleton, Wisconsin. Laura Sorensen is the manager of revenue management. She has been reviewing the historical data on the percentage of no-shows for many of Midwest Express' flights. She is particularly interested in Flight 227 from Milwaukee to San Francisco. She has found that the average no-show rate on this flight is 15%. The aircraft (MD88) has a capacity of 112 seats in a single cabin. There is no First Class/Coach cabin distinction at Midwest Express. All service is considered to be premium service. You would believe that if you could smell the chocolate chip cookies baking as you fly along.

The question Laura wants to answer is to what level should she overbook the aircraft. Demand is strong on this primarily business route. The average fare charged on this flight is $400. If Laura accepts only 112 reservations on this flight, it is almost certain to go out with empty seats because of the no-shows that represent an opportunity cost for Midwest Express as it could have filled each seat with another customer and made an additional $400. On the other hand, if she accepts more reservations than seats, she runs the risk that even after accounting for the no-shows, more customers will show up than she has seats available. The normal procedure in the event that a customer must be denied boarding is to put the "extra" customers on the next available flight, provide them some compensation toward a flight in the future and possibly a voucher for a free meal and a hotel. This is all done to mitigate the potential ill will of the "bumped" customer. Laura figures this compensation usually costs Midwest Express around $600 on average.

To solve this challenging model, Laura built the spreadsheet shown in Figure 11.38 (MIDWSTRK.XLS). We will demonstrate the use of @Risk with this example.

In cell B12, we have modeled a binomial random variable using @Risk. For each of the reservations that Midwest Express chooses to accept, the model randomly generates the

	B18		=	=B12*B5-B14*B6

	A	B	C
1	Flight 227 Overbooking Model		
2			
3	Seats Available	112	
4			
5	Avg. Fare/Seat	$ 400.00	
6	Cost of Bumping	$ 600.00	
7	No-show probability	15%	
8			
9	Decision:		
10	Reservations to Accept	112	
11			
12	Number that Board	95	
13			
14	Number Denied Boarding	0	
15			
16	Number Empty Seats	17	
17			
18	Profit	$ 38,000.00	
19			

Cell	Formula
B10	=RiskSimtable ({112,114,116,118,120, . . . , 144,146})
B12	=RiskBinomial (B10,1−B7)
B14	=MAX (0,B12−B3)
B16	=MAX (0,B3−B12)
B18	=B12*B5−B14*B6

FIGURE 11.38

Midwest Overbooking Model

number who actually show up. Some simple calculations are then done to determine either the number of empty seats (cell B16) or the number of customers who are denied boarding (cell B14). This is essentially what Laura is trading off. The more reservations she accepts, the less likely she is to have empty seats, but she increases the likelihood that she'll have to deny boarding to a customer. She seeks to find the optimal overbooking level that maximizes her profit. This profit formula (cell B18) is shown in Excel's equation line of Figure 11.38 and takes the number of show-ups times the average fare and subtracts the costs of denied boarding (number of customers who are denied boarding times the cost of bumping a passenger). The model assumes that the fares are fully refundable due to the heavy percentage of business travelers on this route. That is, if a customer doesn't show up, she doesn't have to pay.

Since the value returned by @Risk will change every time the spreadsheet is recalculated, Laura can easily perform multiple trials—that is, draw a new sample of demands simply by pressing the recalculation key for her spreadsheet (F9 key usually). After doing this a few times, she is surprised to find that on some trials she obtains a profit that is several thousand dollars less than her base case. In order to see this with @Risk, you must make sure that @Risk's display is set to "Monte Carlo," as opposed to "Expected Value," in order to see the different random values returned for each iteration. To turn on this feature, simply:

1. Click on the third @Risk icon (simulation settings), then on the second tab (Sampling).
2. Indicate in the "Standard Recalc" section that you want Monte Carlo (not Expected Value), as shown in Figure 11.39.

The next step is to use simulation to help Laura determine the optimal overbooking level. She knows that if she accepts only 112 reservations, she'll never have to worry about angry customers due to denied boarding, but she'll also lose a lot of potential profit in the form of empty seats. She decides to look over the range of 112 to 146 reservations (in increments of 2) and see which value maximizes Midwest Express' profit. This ability to check numerous decisions in one grand simulation is a strength of @Risk. All Laura needs to do is:

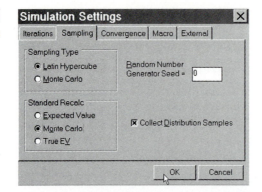

FIGURE 11.39

@Risk's Monte Carlo
Display Feature

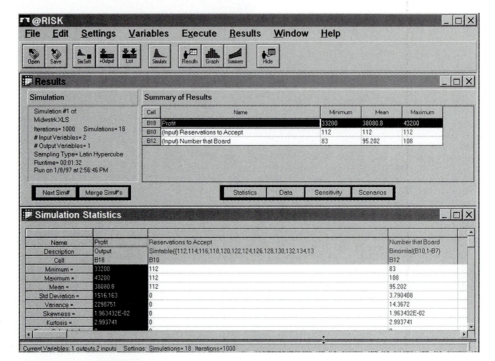

FIGURE 11.40

@Risk Initial
Simulation Display

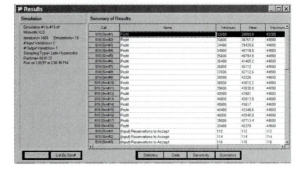

FIGURE 11.41

@Risk Display of
All 18 Simulations

1. Enter =RiskSimtable({112, 114, 116, . . . , 142, 144, 146}) in cell B10.
2. Click on third @Risk icon (Simulation Settings), then the "Iterations" tab and indicate that there are 18 simulations of 1000 iterations each.
3. Click on cell B19 and then click on the fourth @Risk icon (Add Output Cell).

@Risk automatically displays the results of these 18 simulations as shown in Figure 11.40. It's much more helpful to click on the "Merge Sim#'s" button as shown in Figure 11.40 and get the display as shown in Figure 11.41.

A comment is in order on the convergence monitoring feature of @Risk. This is a very helpful feature that indicates to us when we have performed enough iterations that the output cells (performance measures) are not changing appreciably. A "frowning" face indicates we haven't done enough, whereas a "smiling" face indicates the results seem to have converged and we probably have done enough iterations. If you want to turn this feature off in order to speed up the simulation, simply click on the third icon (Simulation Settings) and then on the "Convergence" tab. Finally, click on the box that says "monitor convergence?" so that the "X" disappears.

Looking at this @Risk output, Laura sees that if she accepted only 112 reservations (the plane's capacity), her average profit would be $38,080 (shown as Sim#1). As she increases the number of reservations accepted, the average profit climbs slowly for a while. For example, Sim#4 (accept 118 reservations) generates an average profit of $40,118.8. She finds that a value of 134 reservations (Sim #12) maximizes the average profit at $43,901, a 15.3% improvement in profit! This would represent overbooking the plane by 22 reservations, or 19.6% of its capacity. Beyond 134 reservations, the average profit starts to decline as the cost of denied boarding starts to outweigh the opportunity cost of an empty seat. Laura feels confident in her newfound answer of 134 reservations.

If we enlarge the bottom half of the statistical output shown in Figure 11.40, we can see the different fractiles of the NPV distribution (e.g., 10th, 20th, . . ., 90th). We will explore an extension of this model in Problem 11-22 by allowing for random demand. In this model, Laura has assumed that whatever number of reservations she makes available would actually be requested by customers. In reality, there is a probability distribution that describes this demand and in fact, demand may on occasion fall short of the overbooking level Laura chooses.

APPLICATION CAPSULE   **Checks and Balances: An Ohio Bank Uses Simulation to Streamline Its Operations**

In 1984, BancOhio National Bank had 266 branches statewide. Checks were consolidated at 31 of these branches for encoding and then sent on to Columbus or Cleveland for computer processing, sorting, and preparation for clearance. Realizing that improvements in the efficiency of these activities would reduce costs and improve throughput, management sought to address the following questions:

- How many encoding sites were actually needed to serve the branch network, and at which branches should they be located?
- Which branches should each site serve?
- What resources and costs should be considered in evaluating the alternatives?

To help find answers, BancOhio engaged a consulting company that had developed a simulation package called CHECKSIM. This program generates efficient routes for the messengers who pick up checks at branches and deliver them to the processing centers. The simulation output reports the check volume delivered to the processing center by time of day, thus providing the information needed to make staffing decisions. Since the model can simulate only one processing center at a time, the following procedure was used.

- First, planners would select a particular scenario—that is, a set of branches to function as processing centers.
- Next, a number of plausible schemes for assigning the branches to be served by each center were evaluated with the simulator.
- Finally, once the most economical assignment scheme for each scenario had been determined, the costs of the different scenarios were compared, using the program's interface with Lotus 1-2-3.

In all, management evaluated five different scenarios, involving 31, 22, 16, 12, and 7 processing centers. The two best scenarios were found to be those with 22 and 7 centers. The 22-center scenario had the lower transportation costs. However, the 7-center scenario made more effective use of facilities, resulting in lower encoding costs. Consequently, it was nearly $288,000 per year less expensive.

These results prompted management to consider the possible advantages of consolidating additional functions at the proposed processing centers. Thus the project was expanded to incorporate operations management, returns, customer inquiries, and MICR cash balancing in the same centers. The result was an additional saving in indirect operating costs of $1.38 million per year. (See Davis et al.)

FIGURE 11.42

Michaelson's Work Cell

Raw Material   WS1   WIP   WS2

11.8 CAPACITY BALANCING

Simulation is a powerful tool for gaining insights into the planning and operation of a manufacturing facility. In this section, we explore the assertion that capacity should be "balanced" throughout a manufacturing plant. We will see that variation in processing times can lead to unexpected results. This example is enlightening in several ways: (1) It shows how to use a spreadsheet to model a multiperiod problem in which results from one period are carried into the next. In this model, as in many real situations, inventory is carried from period to period. (2) It provides a graphic lesson on the risk of drawing conclusions based on relatively short simulation runs. (3) It provides useful intuitive insights into the consequences of balancing production rates in a serial manufacturing operation.

MODELING A WORK CELL

Paul Michaelson, an industrial engineer at PROTRAC, is trying to determine the appropriate capacity to install in the small work cell shown in Figure 11.42. This cell takes a raw material, processes it at the first work station (WS1), holds it in a temporary storage area if the second work station (WS2) is busy, and then processes it at WS2. The completed part is used on one of PROTRAC's assembly lines at the rate of 3 per hour. Consider how expensive it would be actually to set up a factory to implement and test the work cell for several days, compared to the cost of a spreadsheet simulation!

Paul has several goals in designing this work cell. He wants to meet the demand for this part on the assembly line, to keep work in process (WIP) between the two work stations down, and (in order to keep costs down) to minimize the capacity of the work stations subject to achieving the first two goals. He decides to do a simulation to help him make his capacity decisions.

SIMULATING BALANCED CAPACITY

Since the assembly area needs the part at a rate of 3 per hour, Paul initially decides to set the capacity of both work stations at 3 per hour. That is, the capacities of WS1 and WS2 are *balanced.* However, because of processing time variability, a work station might be able to process anywhere from 1 to 5 units in an hour. Suppose that during any given hour period, a work station will have the capability of processing 1, 2, 3, 4, or 5 units with equal probability (discrete, uniform distribution). Then the *average* output of that work station will be 3 units per hour *provided it always has something on which to work.* Paul assumes that sufficient raw material will always be available to WS1 so that it will never be *starved.* However, because the processing times are variable at WS1, there may be times when WS2 is idled for lack of material.

The Initial Conditions Figure 11.43 is a picture of the spreadsheet (MICHCB1.XLS) representing the first 16 simulated hours of operation of the work cell. The *initial conditions* at the beginning of the first hour of the simulation are no work in process (WIP), and WS1 and WS2 are idle. Next, Paul needs to enter discrete, uniform RNGs in cell C10 (WS1 Output) and cell D10 (Potential WS2 Output) to produce one of 5 possible values (1, 2 . . . , 5) with equal probability. This is done by typing in the data in a nice tabular format for Crystal Ball. Paul entered the following values in cells C1:D6 for WS1 and WS2 (not shown):

F10	▼	=	=B10+C10-E10

	A	B	C	D	E	F	G
8				Potential	Actual		
9	Hour	Initial WIP	WS1 Output	WS2 Output	WS2 Output	Final WIP	Avg WIP
10	1	0	3	3	0	3	3
11	2	3	3	3	3	3	3.00
12	3	3	3	3	3	3	3.00
13	4	3	3	3	3	3	3.00
14	5	3	3	3	3	3	3.00
15	6	3	3	3	3	3	3.00
16	7	3	3	3	3	3	3.00
17	8	3	3	3	3	3	3.00
18	9	3	3	3	3	3	3.00
19	10	3	3	3	3	3	3.00
20	11	3	3	3	3	3	3.00
21	12	3	3	3	3	3	3.00
22	13	3	3	3	3	3	3.00
23	14	3	3	3	3	3	3.00
24	15	3	3	3	3	3	3.00
25	16	3	3	3	3	3	3.00

Cell	Formula	Copy To
E10	=MIN(B10,D10)	E11:E25
F10	=B10+C10−E10	F11:F25
G10	=AVERAGE($F$10:F10)	G11:G25
B11	=F10	B12:B25

FIGURE 11.43

Michaelson's Spreadsheet

OUTPUT RATE	PROBABILITY
1	0.2
2	0.2
3	0.2
4	0.2
5	0.2

Cell E10 (Actual WS2 Output) has the formula = MIN(B10,D10). For example, if the actual output of WS2 during the second hour is 1, even though there were 5 units available to work on, it would be because the random variable drawn to represent the potential WS2 Output turned out to be only 1 unit during that hour. The Final WIP (cell F10) is calculated by adding the Initial WIP (cell B10) to the WS1 Output (cell C10) and subtracting Actual WS2 Output (cell E10). The Initial WIP for a subsequent hour is simply the Final WIP for the previous hour. Average WIP at the end of any given hour is defined to be the average of the Final WIP values for all the hours observed to that point. In order to enter the discrete, uniform RNGs for WS1 Output and Potential WS2 Output in Crystal Ball, Paul must do the following:

1. Click on cell C10, which is the first cell where Crystal Ball will generate random values for the output rate. NOTE: Because the student version of Crystal Ball limits the number of Assumption cells to 6 and the number of Forecast cells to 6, we have a potential problem with this model (which has 32 Assumption cells and up to 16 Forecast cells). To get around this restriction, we will use a trick on the Assumption cells (see step #2) and limit the number of Forecast cells to 6 of the 16 hours we could possibly track.

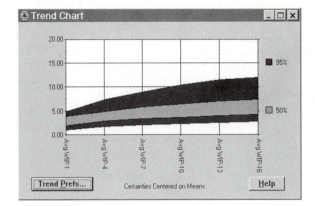

FIGURE 11.44

Michaelson's Trend Chart of
Average WIP

2. Enter = CB.Custom($C$2:$D$6) in the cell. This effectively does the same thing as:

   a. Click on the first Crystal Ball icon (Define Assumption).

   b. Click on the "Custom" distribution from the Distribution Gallery; then click on OK.

   c. Click on the "Data" button and enter the cell range where you entered the information on this discrete distribution ($C$2:$D$6), then click on OK.

   but it allows us to bypass the limitation of 6 Assumption cells.

3. Crystal Ball shows the shape of the distribution you have entered. Click on OK.

4. With the cursor still on cell C10, click on Excel's "Copy" icon.

5. Highlight the range C10:D25 and then click on Excel's "Paste" icon. This copies the exact same uniform, discrete distribution to all 32 of these cells.

6. Ideally, we'd like to highlight all 16 cells that track Avg. WIP at the end of each hour (G10:G25), but since we are limited to 6 by the student version, we will limit ourselves to choosing cells G10, G13, G16, G19, G22, and G25.

7. After clicking on each cell mentioned in step 6, click on the second Crystal Ball icon (Define Forecast) which brings up a dialog box.

8. Change the Window size to "Large" and change the Display to "When Stopped (faster)" in the dialog box if this is not already the default (as shown previously). You may also modify the name to reflect which hour of the 16 it represents. Click on OK.

9. Repeat step 8 for each of the 6 Forecast cells that Crystal Ball automatically prompts you with (or alternatively, you can use the Copy/Paste feature with the Forecast cells to avoid doing this 6 times).

10. Click on the eighth icon (Run Preferences) and change the "Maximum Number of Trials" to 1000.

11. Click on OK.

12. Click on the ninth icon (Start Simulation) and after Crystal Ball has run the 1000 iterations, it automatically produces an individual histogram for each of the 6 forecast cells.

13. If you find this too cluttered, click on Run, then "Open Trend Chart," and you'll get a neater summary like that shown in Figure 11.44.

Here, Crystal Ball plots for us the distribution of Average WIP over the first 16 hours by using the six selected hours that we indicated. The centermost light-colored band indicates the mean value for average WIP $\pm$ 25% (or a 50% confidence interval); and the next darker band is a similar 95% confidence interval. We can see from this that Average WIP seems to be growing slightly over these first 16 hours and certainly the distribution is widening over time. The completed spreadsheet is found on the CD as MICHCB1C.XLS.

Beyond the Initial Conditions Paul realizes that running the simulation for only 16 hours can be very misleading, so he copies the formulas down for another 184 hours (in a new

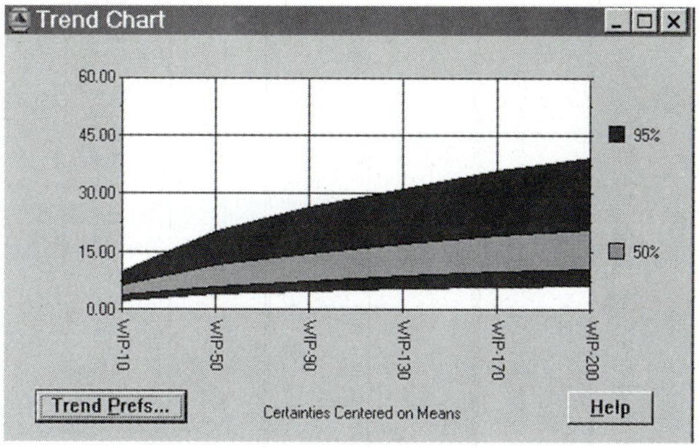

FIGURE 11.45

Average Work in Process,
Balanced Capacity

spreadsheet called MICHCB2.XLS). He reruns Crystal Ball using the same basic steps as the 16-hour simulation. Paul is quite surprised when he graphs Average WIP versus time for the first 200 hours of operation (see Figure 11.45). He knows that the initial condition of 0 WIP should lead to low values of Average WIP initially. He expects to see average WIP grow, but then to level off around some *steady-state* value. What he did not expect was the continued growth of average WIP. It appears that the longer the cell is in operation, the greater the amount of WIP that accumulates. This is somewhat counterintuitive, since it appears that with both work stations operating at an average rate of 3 units per hour there should be no tendency for WIP to grow. The completed spreadsheet is found on the CD as MICHCB2C.XLS.

A simple queuing model, however, predicts this unexpected growth. As we shall see in Chapter 12, when the average arrival rate to a queue is equal to the average service rate, the number of customers in the queue will grow without bound. Here in this model, "customers" are parts leaving WS1, and the queue is the temporary storage area before WS2. Because raw material is readily available, the output rate of WS1, and hence the average arrival rate to the queue, is 3 units per hour. The average service rate, the rate at which WS2 can process WIP, is also 3 units per hour. Thus, the average arrival rate and average service rate are equal when the capacities of the two work stations are balanced. Hence the continued growth of Average WIP.

SIMULATING UNBALANCED CAPACITY

On the basis of these considerations, Paul decides to add capacity to WS2 so that its average production rate is now 3.5 units per hour (using a discrete, uniform distribution between 2 and 5 units). He models this in a new spreadsheet called "Unbal. 200 Hrs" (in MICHCB3.XLS). First he copies the entire MICHCB2.XLS spreadsheet into the new one and then he adds the distribution of the potential Workstation 2 Output in cells G1:H5 as follows:

OUTPUT RATE	PROBABILITY
2	0.25
3	0.25
4	0.25
5	0.25

He then has to change the formulas in cells D10:D209 to be: =CB.Custom($G$2:$H$5). He selects six forecast cells, spread evenly across the 200 hours and then runs 1000 iterations. The new graph of average WIP over time (Figure 11.46) now shows a much lower average WIP. His results suggest that there is no long-term growth in the Average WIP, with the steady-state value lying somewhere between 5 and 7 units.

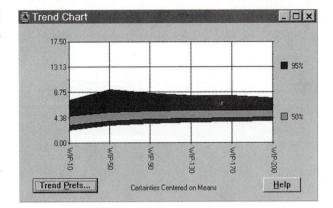

FIGURE 11.46

Average Work in Process,
Unbalanced Capacity

Paul's final conclusion is that the capacity of the two work stations should not be balanced (equal output rates). If WIP is to be kept to reasonable levels, then the downstream work station (WS2) should have a somewhat greater capacity. If Paul had simulated fewer than 200 hours of operation, he would have been seriously misled about the long-term behavior of WIP in the balanced design. By running the simulation for a longer period of time, the effect of the initial conditions was overcome, and the true long-term behavior could be discerned. A general observation about simulation can be drawn from this example:

> Simulation results are useful only when care is taken in the experimental design to eliminate extraneous effects such as starting or ending conditions. Simulations that are too short may give very misleading results.

11.9   NOTES ON IMPLEMENTATION

Simulation is a powerful and flexible analytic tool that can be used to study a wide variety of management models. It is generally used in cases where a good analytic model either does not exist or is too complicated to solve. Simulation can also demonstrate the effects of variability and initial conditions, as well as the length of time needed to reach steady state. This description encompasses a large segment of real-world models and, as a result, surveys of the use of management science techniques typically put simulation at or near the top. However, there are a number of important factors for management to consider before making a commitment to a simulation study.

Simulation Versus Analytic Models As stated above, simulation is frequently used when no convenient analytic model is available. With an analytic model the laws of mathematics can be used, often to obtain optimal decisions and sometimes sensitivity data (provided, of course, that the analysis is not so complex as to be prohibitive). In a simulation with random events, by contrast, optimality is not guaranteed, and it may be difficult to obtain even an approximately optimal solution. Often a number of iterations are required just to get a good estimate of the "goodness" of a particular decision. However, simulation models can provide information that analytic models find it difficult or impossible to supply, such as the impact of variability, behavior before steady state is reached, and so on.

Designing a Spreadsheet Simulator The acronym KISS for "Keep It Simple, Stupid" is popular among professionals in the decision modeling area of business. The idea applies with special force to simulation. A common and often fatal error in devising simulation models is making them too complicated. This may be an overreaction to the freedom gained by moving from analytic models to simulation models. Analytic models are often quite restrictive in their assumptions. Once we depart from linear functions or very simplistic assumptions, the mathematics gets harder by an order of magnitude. The result is that many of the popular analytic models have limited applicability. Simulation can be much more permissive. Since we are typically just generating an observation from a function (rather than solving a set of equations), linear functions do not facilitate the analysis in simulation as much as they do in analytic models.

Whatever the motivation, there is typically a strong urge to include many factors in a simulation model. For example, it may not seem difficult to add a customer return feature to an inventory control model. In essence, all that is required is some additional modeling in the spreadsheet to generate this feature and incorporate it into the model. "There is no theoretical barrier, so why not do it?" This impression can be seriously wrong.

Large, complicated simulations incorporating a large number of "lifelike" features are at first blush appealing to management. However, they suffer from at least two serious problems:

1. They are often expensive to model and document.

2. Complex simulation models often produce so much data that the results are difficult to interpret.

Lean, abstract models that capture the essence of the real problem and set encumbering details aside are as important to successful simulation models as they are to good analytic models. Casual observation suggests that more simulation modeling projects have died from too grand an original conception than from any other disease.

Simulation Add-in Software The importance and widespread use of simulation has led to the creation of special simulation add-in software. Two guidelines that are useful in all quantitative studies are especially important in simulation studies:

Documentation. Insist on good documentation. A new manager should be able to understand the input required, the assumptions of the model, and the meaning of the output with a reasonable amount of effort. This requires clear documentation. Too often the usefulness of a simulation model effectively ends with the tenure of the originator. The only reasonable cure for this problem is good documentation. It is difficult to overemphasize the importance of this guideline.

Group Dynamics. All quantitative modeling efforts require intensive interaction and communication between modeler and end user. This is particularly true of simulation projects. The end user must understand how to enter decisions and parameters and how to analyze output. The firsthand knowledge of the user is essential in making sure that the simulation captures the essence of the real problem. Also, the fact that the user has an intimate knowledge of the real problem can be an important part of the search for good solutions.

Good documentation and group dynamics are closely interrelated and are an important part of managing any project based on quantitative modeling and analysis.

11.10 SUMMARY

Section 11.1 pointed out that the use of experimentation to evaluate alternatives is an important part of applied science and that spreadsheet-based simulation is the most common experimental approach to management decision models. It also discussed the use of simulation on decisions under risk; that is, on models in which the behavior of one or more factors can be represented by a probability distribution.

Random numbers are at the basis of the technique of simulating random events. Section 11.2 presented the procedure used to generate random variables from several different probability distributions, both in Crystal Ball and @Risk. Both discrete and continuous distributions were presented.

Section 11.3 introduced an example that dealt with capital budgeting, which involved an unpredictable element (demand). It was shown how some basic simulation could be carried out using the spreadsheet by itself. Section 11.4 was a replay of Section 11.3 with the added benefit of being able to use simulation add-in software (Crystal Ball).

Section 11.5 introduced an example dealing with inventory control, which also involved the unpredictable element of demand. All of these models were used to illustrate how random events are incorporated into a simulation model. The examples showed that simulation results will not necessarily lead to the same decision that would be derived if one could use the analytic criterion of maximizing the expected profit. By its very nature the output from a simulation with random components is random. Generally, using a large number of trials will make the simulated average profit closer to the theoretic expected profit. The examples also demonstrated how multiple measures of effectiveness can be produced and, more important, how simulation with multiple trials provides an indication of the variability with a given decision or policy.

Section 11.6 returned to the inventory model discussed in Section 11.5 to show how a much more realistic distribution of demand (i.e., normal) can be modeled. The topic of variance reduction was also addressed.

Section 11.7 turned to the service sector of the economy for an example from the airline industry. The example looked at determining the optimal overbooking level for a very successful airline, Midwest Express. A new discrete probability distribution (binomial) was introduced.

Section 11.8 turned back to an example from manufacturing to explore the question of whether balancing the production capacity of all work stations necessarily leads to an optimal result. The example illustrated the importance of designing a simulation so as to eliminate extraneous effects such as those associated with starting or ending conditions.

The final section was devoted to the topic of implementation. The discussion took a general management point of view and considered such topics as designing a simulation, good documentation, and group dynamics.

Key Terms

Simulator.   An experimental device that in important respects acts like a system of interest.

Simulation Model.   A series of logical and mathematical operations that provides a measure of effectiveness for a particular set of values of the parameters and decisions.

Random Variable.   An entity that will take on a numerical value; the likelihood of it assuming any particular value is given by a probability function.

Probability Distribution.   A means of specifying the likelihood of an uncertain quantity.

Monte Carlo Method.   A type of simulation that uses probability distributions to determine whether random events occur.

Trial.   A single run of a simulation model (i.e., a single pass through the simulator).

Cumulative Distribution Function.   The probability that a random variable takes on a value less than or equal to a specified number.

Discrete Uniform Distribution.   A probability distribution that assigns equal probability to each member of a finite set of consecutive integers.

Continuous Uniform Distribution.   A probability distribution that assigns equal likelihood to each member of an interval of real numbers. (See Appendix A for the mathematical form of this function)

Exponential Distribution.   A probability distribution typically used to describe the time between arrivals at a queuing system. (See Appendix A for the mathematical form of this function)

Normal Distribution.   A probability distribution that is a good model for many phenomena that occur in nature and business, such as fluctuating prices and demands; also, the distribution of the sample mean calculated for any random variable. (See Appendix A for details)

Multiple Trials.   Multiple passes through the simulator, each pass using the same values for decisions and parameters, but a different series of random numbers and hence possibly different outcomes for random events.

Expected Value.   A statistical concept referring to the average, or mean, of some random quantity with a specified probability distribution.

Poisson Distribution.   A probability distribution often used to describe the number of arrivals to a queuing system during a specified interval of time. (See Appendix A for the mathematical form of this function)

Variability.   In simulation, a reference to the amount of fluctuation in performance measures as numerous trials are performed.

True-False

1. **T F** The basic concept of simulation is to build an experimental device that will "act like" the system of interest in important respects.

2. **T F** A deterministic model (one with no random elements) can be used as a simulation model.

3. **T F** If a simulation includes random elements, two successive trials with the same parameter values will produce the same value for the performance measure.

4. **T F** In a simulation with random elements it is impossible to guarantee that the decision that maximizes expected profit has been selected.

5. **T F** In real-world problems, it is common practice to compare the expected cost associated with a decision with the average cost for that decision produced by a simulation.

6. **T F** In a simulation with several distinct random outcomes, a correct association of random numbers and events implies that each random number must represent one of the outcomes.

7. **T F** With small sample sizes the results of a simulation can be very sensitive to the initial conditions.

8. **T F** Simulation is sometimes described as a last resort technique since it is generally not employed until analytic approaches have been examined and rejected.

9. **T F** A common error in designing a simulation is to use such restrictive assumptions that the model fails to capture the essence of the problem.

10. **T F** Adding additional factors in a simulation model is sure to increase the simulation cost but may also improve the quality of the solution.

Multiple Choice

11. In a typical simulation model, input provided by the manager includes
    a. values for the parameters
    b. values for the decision variables
    c. a value for the performance measure
    d. all of the above
    e. both a and b

12. An advantage of simulation, as opposed to optimization, is that
    a. often multiple measures of goodness can be examined
    b. some appreciation for the variability of outcomes of interest can be obtained
    c. more complex scenarios can be studied
    d. all of the above

13. Consider a simulator with random elements that uses profit as a measure of effectiveness. For a specified assignment of parameter values
    a. the average profit over a number of trials is used as an estimate of the expected profit associated with a decision
    b. the average profit is always closer to the expected profit as the number of trials increases
    c. the average profit over 10 trials is always the same
    d. none of the above

14. A random number refers to
    a. an observation from a set of numbers (say, the real numbers from 0–1), each of which is equally likely
    b. an observation selected at random from a normal distribution
    c. an observation selected at random from any distribution provided by the manager
    d. none of the above

15. The random number 0.63 has been selected. The corresponding observation, v, from a *normal* distribution is determined by the relationship:
    a. v is "the probability that the normally distributed quantity is ≤ 0.63"
    b. v is the number such that "the probability that the normally distributed quantity is $\leq v$" equals 0.63
    c. v is the number such that "the probability that the normally distributed quantity equals v" is 0.63
    d. none of the above

16. Analytic results are sometimes used before a simulation study
    a. to identify "good values" of the system parameters
    b. to determine the optimal decision
    c. to identify "good values" of the decision variables for the specific choices of system parameters
    d. all of the above

17. To reduce the effect of initial conditions in a simulation study, one can
    a. vary the values of the system parameters
    b. increase the number of alternative decisions studied
    c. increase the sample size and ignore data from a number of the first runs for each set of parameters and decisions
    d. all of the above

18. If both an analytic model and a simulation model could be used to study a problem including random events, the analytic model is often preferred because
    a. the simulator generally requires a number of runs just to get a good estimate of the objective value (such as expected cost) for a particular decision
    b. the analytic model may produce an optimal decision

c. the simulation study may require evaluating a large number of possible decisions

d. all of the above

19. Large complicated simulation models suffer from the following problem(s):

a. average costs are not well defined

b. it is difficult to create the appropriate random events

c. they may be expensive to model

d. all of the above

20. In performing a simulation it is advisable to

a. use the results of earlier decisions to suggest the next decision to try

b. use the same number of trials for each decision

c. simulate all possible decisions

d. none of the above

Answers

1.	T	**6.**	F	**11.**	e	**16.**	c
2.	T	**7.**	T	**12.**	d	**17.**	c
3.	F	**8.**	T	**13.**	a	**18.**	d
4.	T	**9.**	F	**14.**	a	**19.**	c
5.	F	**10.**	T	**15.**	b	**20.**	a

Problems

In the following problems you will be asked to perform a number of iterations. Remember that due to the nature of random numbers, your answers may vary slightly from those given in Appendix D.

11-1. Cite examples of the use of simulation (in the broad sense) by the military.

11-2. Cite examples of the use of simulation (in the broad sense) in professional sports.

•• **11-3.** Consider the following model with LP formulation:

$$\text{Max } 20A + 30C$$

s.t.

$$A \le 70$$
$$C \le 50$$
$$A + 2C \le 120$$
$$A, C \ge 0$$

a. Construct a flowchart showing how to approach this problem as a simulation.

b. Use the flowchart to evaluate the two potential solutions: ($A = 40, C = 30$) and ($A = 50, C = 30$).

11-4. Given in the following table are 50 weeks of historical car sales at Sally's Solar Car Co.

NUMBER OF SALES/WEEK	NUMBER OF WEEKS
0	2
1	5
2	12
3	16
4	8
5	7

a. What probability distribution would you assign to demand so that the probability of a particular demand in the simulation is equal to the relative frequency of that demand over the last 50 weeks?

b. Simulate 120 weeks of demand if using a spreadsheet add-in (do 12 weeks if using Excel alone).

•• **11-5.** Comment on the following statement: The simplex algorithm is a type of simulation, since it has to evaluate a number of alternative solutions en route to finding the optimal solution.

•• **11-6.** Jerry Tate is responsible for the maintenance of a fleet of vehicles used by the power company in constructing and repairing electric transmission lines. Jerry is especially concerned with the cost projections for replacing a large derrick on these vehicles. He would like to simulate the number of derrick failures each year over the next 20 years. Jerry has looked at the last 10 years of data and compiled the following table:

NUMBER OF DERRICK FAILURES	NUMBER OF YEARS
0	4
1	3
2	1
3	1
4	1

He decides to simulate the 20-year period. Conduct the simulation for Jerry. How common is it for the total number of failures during three consecutive years to exceed 3?

11-7. PROTRAC has a cash management problem. In this model PROTRAC's cash balance is determined each morning. The change in the cash balance from one morning to the next is a random variable. In particular, it increases by $10,000 with probability 0.3, decreases by $10,000 with probability 0.2, and remains the same with probability 0.5. What probability distribution would you assign to these events so as to accurately reflect the correct probability in a simulation?

•• **11-8.** Consider the following brand-switching model. In this model probabilities are used to describe the behavior of a customer buying beer. Three particular beers (A, B, and C) are incorporated in the model. Customer behavior is summarized in the accompanying table. Thus, we see in the first row that a customer who buys beer A in week 1 will buy the same beer in week 2 with probability 0.90, will buy beer B with probability 0.06, and will buy beer C with probability 0.04. A similar interpretation holds for the other rows. Consider a customer who buys beer A in week 1. Assume that you wish to simulate his behavior for the next 10 weeks. We know that in week 2 he would buy beers A, B, and C with probabilities 0.90, 0.06, and 0.04. If in week 2 he bought beer B, he would buy beers A, B, and C with probability 0.12, 0.78, and 0.10, respectively. Define the random events you would need to model and the appropriate random number generators for these events so as to accurately reflect the correct probabilities.

TABLE 11.4			
	PROBABILITY OF PURCHASE IN WEEK $i + 1$		
BEER PURCHASED IN WEEK i	A	B	C
A	0.90	0.06	0.04
B	0.12	0.78	0.10
C	0.09	0.07	0.84

11-9. In the example model in Section 11.5, we calculated the true expected profit and simulated average profit using 500 trials assuming that we ordered 11 omelet pans. Verify the same two performance measures (true expected profit, simulated average profit using 500 trials) under the assumption of ordering 9 pans.

11-10. In the example model in Section 11.5, we calculated the true expected profit and simulated average profit using 500 trials assuming that we ordered 11 omelet pans. Verify the same two performance measures (true expected profit, simulated average profit using 500 trials) under the assumption of ordering 10 pans.

11-11. In the example model in Section 11.5, we calculated the true expected profit and simulated average profit using 500 trials assuming that we ordered 11 omelet pans. Verify the same two performance measures (true expected profit, simulated average profit using 500 trials) under the assumption of ordering 12 pans.

•• **11-12.** The probability mass function of the Poisson distribution is given by

$$p = (x; \lambda) = \frac{\lambda^x}{x!} e^{-\lambda}, x = 0, 1, \ldots$$

Let $\lambda = 2$, and calculate the probability you observe x, for $x = 0, 1, \ldots, 5$.

•• **11-13.** Simulate a sample of 50 periods for the omelet pan model described in Section 11.5 (do 10 periods if using Excel alone). Assume that you have 10 pans on hand at the beginning of each period. Develop the proper probability distribution for the demand given in Section 11.5.

    a. Calculate the average profit per period.

    b. Record the number of stockouts (count a stockout as occurring when demand > 10).

•• **11-14.** The weekly demand for milk for the last 50 weeks at the All-Ways-Open convenient market is shown in the following table.

    a. Assign the proper probability distribution to demands so that the probability of a particular demand in the simulation is equal to the relative frequency of that demand over the last 50 weeks.

    b. The store orders 42 cases every week. What are the average shortage and average excess inventory for 100 simulated weeks? (*Hint:* Simulate 10 weeks if using Excel alone.)

    c. What are the expected shortage and the expected excess inventory?

TABLE 11.5

SALES (CASES)	NUMBER OF WEEKS
40	4
41	10
42	12
43	9
44	8
45	7
Total	50

•• **11-15.** The number of disk brake jobs performed by the service department of the Green Cab Company during each of the last 30 weeks is shown in the following table.

    a. Assign the proper probability distribution to the number of brake jobs performed so that the probability of a particular number of jobs in the simulation is equal to the relative frequency of that number of jobs over the last 30 weeks.

    b. Simulate 100 weeks of demand (10 weeks if using Excel alone). What is the simulated average number of brake jobs/week?

TABLE 11.6

NUMBER OF BRAKE JOBS	NUMBER OF WEEKS
5	3
6	8
7	9
8	6
9	4
Total	30

•• **11-16.** STECO currently carries inventory for stainless steel sheets in two nearby cities, Los Gatos (L) and Alameda (A). Weekly demands (in trucks) and the probabilities for each city are shown in the accompanying table. Assume that the demands are independent.

TABLE 11.7

DEMAND	PROBABILITY L	PROBABILITY A
1	0.2	
2	0.3	
3	0.3	0.1
4	0.1	0.1
5	0.1	0.3
6		0.3
7		0.2

Los Gatos starts each week with 4 trucks of inventory on hand. Alameda starts each week with 6 trucks of inventory on hand.

a. Simulate 500 weeks of demand at Los Gatos (20 weeks if using Excel alone), and record the number of stockouts.

b. Simulate 500 weeks of demand at Alameda (20 weeks if using Excel alone), and record the number of stockouts.

Suppose that STECO centralized its stainless steel sheet inventory and satisfied all demand from Los Gatos and Alameda out of one new warehouse (call it LA).

c. If LA started each week with 10 trucks of inventory on hand, would you expect the number of stockouts to increase, decrease, or remain the same as compared with when L and A operated independently? Why?

d. Use the same random sequence of demands you used in parts (a) and (b) to simulate 500 weeks of operation for the new warehouse, LA (do 20 weeks if using Excel alone). Record the number of stockouts. Does this result agree with your answer to part (c)?

•• **11-17.** The time between arrivals at the drive-up window of the Slippery Savings and Loan is shown in the following table. All customers form a single line and are served in the order of arrival. Assume that it takes exactly 8 minutes to serve each customer. Also assume that no one is being served or waiting to be served when the first customer arrives. Simulate the arrival of 800 customers (80 if using Excel alone), and record the number of customers who have to wait.

TABLE 11.8

TIME BETWEEN ARRIVALS (MIN)	PROBABILITY
5	0.25
10	0.50
15	0.25

•• **11-18.** The Homeburg Volunteer Fire Department makes an annual door-to-door solicitation for funds. There are 3000 households to solicit. The department asks households to be supporters (a $10 donation) or patrons (a $25 donation). An analysis of data from previous years indicates that

1. No one is home at 15% of the homes visited. If no one is home, the home is not revisited, and thus no donation is obtained. When someone is home, 80% of the time a woman answers the door and 20% of the time a man answers the door.

2. Of the women, 40% make a contribution; 70% of them are supporters, and 30% are patrons.

3. Of the men, 70% make a contribution; 25% of them are supporters, and 75% are patrons.

a. What is the expected value of money received from the annual solicitation?

b. Make a flowchart for this process. The output should be the contribution that occurs from calling on a house.

c. Use the flowchart in part (b) to simulate 200 visits (20 visits if using Excel alone), and record the total contribution from these 200 visits. What is your estimate of the return from the annual solicitation based on this simulation?

d. Simulate 1000 visits (100 visits if using Excel alone) to answer the same question as in part (c).

••• **11-19.** Laura Lene owns a flower stand near the new, beautiful Denver International Airport. She buys her flowers from a wholesaler at $0.25 per flower and sells them for $0.50 per flower. Laura wonders what is the optimal number of flowers to order each day. Based on looking at her past 3 years of history, she has found that demand can be approximated by a normal distribution with a mean of 100 and a standard deviation of 20. When she ends the day with more flowers than customers, she can sell all the leftovers for $0.05 per flower. Conversely, when she has more customers than flowers, she estimates that there is some lost goodwill in addition to the lost profit on the potential sale of $0.25. Laura estimates lost goodwill costs her the next two sales opportunities (i.e., dissatisfied customers will go to the competitor the next 2 times they want to buy flowers, but will then try Laura again).

a. Use a spreadsheet simulation model with 1000 iterations (100 iterations if using Excel alone) to determine the optimal number of flowers to order each day. Use the INT function in Excel to truncate the normal random variable values to an integer value.

b. Construct a 95% confidence interval for the expected profit from the optimal ordering decision.

••• **11-20.** Not wanting to leave your beloved alma mater, you have come up with a scheme to stay around for 5 more years: You have decided to bid on the fast-food concession rights at the football stadium. You feel sure that a bid of $30,000 will win the concession, which gives you the right to sell food at football games for the next 5 years. You estimate that annual operating costs will be 40% of sales and annual sales will average $50,000. Your Uncle Ned has agreed to lend you the $30,000 to make your bid. You will pay him $7700 at the end of each year. Your tax rate is 28%.

a. Use a spreadsheet model to answer the following question. What is your average annual after-tax profit? Assume that the yearly payments of $7700 are tax deductible.

b. You realize that sales will probably vary from year to year. Suppose that sales can vary plus or minus 40% from the average of $50,000. You are concerned about the minimum after-tax profit you can earn in a year. You can survive if it is at least $7000. Model annual sales for the 5 years as 5 continuous uniform random variables. Based on a sample of 4000 five-year periods (400 periods if using Excel alone), estimate the probability that over any five-year period the minimum after-tax profit for a year will be at least $7000. Will you bid for the concession?

••• **11-21.** You are the manager of Tex Electronics and are planning a promotion on a discontinued model of 27" color TVs. The promotion will last 10 days, at the end of which any sets that you ordered but have not sold will be sold to another retailer for $250 each. You must order the sets from the manufacturer before you know what the demand during the promotion will be. Your cost is $350 per set and you will sell them for $600. You estimate that on 20% of the days you will sell 2 sets, 30% of the days you will sell 1 set, and 50% of the days you will sell no sets.

a. What is the expected demand during the promotion? Should you necessarily order the expected demand?

b. Estimate the optimal number of TVs to order. Simulate order quantities of 7, 8, 9, 10, and 11. In the 10 cells containing the daily demands, use a discrete, general probability distribution. Have one cell that contains the total net profit for the promotion. Based on 1000 trials (100 trials if using Excel alone), what order quantity maximizes the average net profit? What is the simulated average net profit?

••• **11-22.** In the Midwest Express airline overbooking example in Section 11.7, it was assumed that the demand would materialize for whatever number of reservations Laura Sorensen chose to make available. In this model, we will make the model more realistic, by allowing the demand to be random according to the following discrete, general distribution:

Demand:	100	105	110	115	120	125	130	135	140	145
Probability:	0.03	0.05	0.08	0.12	0.18	0.20	0.12	0.10	0.08	0.05

Modify the MIDWSTRK.XLS file on your student data diskette to accommodate this new assumption.

a. A priori, would you expect the optimal overbooking level to change with this new assumption?

b. What is the new optimal overbooking level? What's the expected profit associated with this level?

••• **11-23.** Les Izmore, the CFO of Exxaco Oil, has a difficult problem. He wants to submit a bid for an offshore oil tract near the north shore of Alaska. Although the exact value of the tract is unknown, United States' geologists report that they expect it to be $20 million. However, there is some uncertainty in their estimates and the standard deviation is $3 million. Assume a normal distribution for the value of the tract. Les knows that his competitor, Texon, will also submit a bid for this attractive site. Both companies will contract their own individual studies on the value of the tract. Assume that the estimates obtained from these studies will have measurement errors that are normal with a mean of $0 and a standard deviation of $2 million. Modify either the EXXACOCB.XLS (if you want to use Crystal Ball) or EXXACORK.XLS (if you prefer @Risk) file on your student data diskette to answer the following:

a. How many iterations should Les perform to be confident in his answer?

b. How much should Les bid in order to maximize Exxaco's expected profit? What's the expected profit associated with this bid?

CyberLab was a new venture in the field of lab robotics. The company had a patent pending on the CyberLab system and had just finished construction of a small manufacturing facility in New Milford, Connecticut. It also had operational prototypes for all its products, but now needed a capital infusion to develop a major manufacturing facility and to provide working capital for expanded operations. CyberLab had offered 30% equity in the firm to the Precision Instrument Corporation (PRICO) in exchange for $1 million in capital and an agreement whereby PRICO would market CyberLab products through its existing international distribution system. PRICO was a major manufacturer of laboratory equipment. Some aspects of the CyberLab proposal were attractive to James Campbell, President of PRICO, but others were downright frightening. A significant new market could be harvested by his company, or the million dollar investment could vanish down a rat hole. Mr. Campbell needed to understand the financial soundness of PRICO's opportunity.

The Inception of CyberLab

CyberLab started in 1985 as a result of the frustration of Dr. H. Meltzer, a biochemist working at the New York Psychiatric Institute. Dr. Meltzer was preparing and testing human enzymes[1] in bioassays.[2] Preparing samples was taking an inordinate amount of time and expense; human enzymes were extremely expensive, and manual sample preparation tended to waste enzyme. Dr. Meltzer was looking for an automated system that could prepare his samples, but none existed with the accuracy and reliability he needed for his tests. When he outlined his needs to his son, Walter Meltzer thought a system could be developed and the project began.

Two years later, the CyberLab system prototype was complete. Walter had designed the prototype with the idea that, eventually, all the components that needed machining could be subcontracted, and the remaining parts could be purchased from readily available sources.

Laboratory Robotics

Francis Zenie, president of a major lab-robot developer and manufacturer (Zymark Corporation), summed up the need for laboratory automation: "You've got 10 or 20 years of advancements in instrumental data measurements and data reduction,

but our interviews revealed that people are still preparing samples like they did in the Dark Ages." Zymark personnel spent six months interviewing laboratory chemists and chemical-industry personnel by asking "What is your biggest problem?" The most common answer: sample preparation prior to analysis. Zymark correctly identified a need for new technology and introduced the first laboratory robot in 1982.

Laboratory technicians worked in the 2-D environment: *d*ull and *d*emanding. Preparing lab samples was tedious and required a high level of concentration. Humans could work as quickly as robots, but robots could maintain their work pace indefinitely (excluding maintenance and downtime) and were not prone to errors such as mixing up samples. The advantage of robotics lay in the increased output, enhanced consistency of preparations, and lower labor costs. Most robots currently on the market operated on a work-station principle, with the station arranged in a circle about an arm fixed in the center. The arm moved the sample to the stations for various preparations and tests. The CyberLab 800, however, worked in three dimensions and the arm was controlled by a computer such as the IBM PC. Programming involved numerous commands to control each movement. Starting and stopping the arm in the same place was the critical factor. It allowed the arm to "find" the sample and move it to the next station. Programming was essentially specific to each application and therefore took time to implement and verify.

CyberLab Products

The CyberLab 800 System was a robot, although it certainly did not have the futuristic appearance of the more publicized of its kind (see Exhibit 1). Simply put, the CyberLab 800 was a liquid transfer or pipetting device. It was capable of performing any repetitive laboratory liquid-preparation procedure currently done by hand. The system consisted of three separate components and a computer to execute the functions. A brief description of each component follows.

CyberLab 800. A pipette transport device that worked in three dimensions using eight independent probes (or channels) for transferring liquid into or out of the test tubes. The probes could accommodate four sizes of disposable pipette tips. (The disposable nature was essential to prevent sample contamination.) The "800" had a shaker table that mixed the samples right in the test tubes. The system also allowed hot or cold water to flow around the test tubes, controlling the temperature and thus the reactions taking place. The "800" was extremely accurate; it operated within an accuracy range of 1% with volumes as low as 10 microliters (a microliter is one millionth of a liter).

CyberPump 300. A precision syringe pump with three channels. Each channel was simply an individual syringe siphon pump that delivered the liquid to the pipetting system (CyberLab 800). A typical setup for the system had 2 of these "300" units.

CyberPump 200. This pump also delivered liquid to the "800" system. It differed from the "300" in that it only had two channels and was a reversible pump. The primary advantage of this pump over the "300" was its ability to move large volumes at

[1]Enzymes are complex protein substances that are essential to life. They act as catalysts in promoting reactions at cell temperatures without undergoing destruction in the process.

[2]A bioassay is the determination of the relative effective strength of a new substance by comparing its effect on a test organism with that of a standard substance.

This case is to be used as the basis for class discussion rather than to illustrate either the effective or ineffective handling of an administrative situation. © 1988, Darden Graduate Business School Foundation. Preview Darden case abstracts on the World Wide Web at: www.darden.virginia.edu/dems.

a faster rate with no loss in accuracy. The reversible feature allowed samples that were complete to be drawn out of the test tubes and transferred to other analytical equipment for further testing.

At the end of the summer of 1987, one complete CyberLab system was at work in the New York Psychiatric Institute. Dr. Meltzer used federal grant money to pay for the machine. It replaced two lab technicians who were doing sample preparation, saving over $70,000 the first year. Dr. Meltzer's review of the new system's performance showed that less enzyme was being wasted and that the samples being prepared were more accurate.

News of the system spread within the psychiatric community, as well as without, because of the system's accuracy, associated savings in wasted material, and relatively low cost. By the end of July 1988, CyberLab had sold 4 units, and had interested buyers for 25 more.

Competition in the Laboratory Robotics Industry

An estimated 18,000 sites in the United States could use the CyberLab system. In addition, Zymark had indicated that the worldwide market was around 30,000 to 50,000 units. At the end of the second quarter of 1988, only 3,050 of those potential sites had lab robots installed. Zymark, the first entrant in the lab robot industry in 1982, had 42% of the installations to date. Two other competitors, Cetus and Micromedic, entered in 1983 and had 15% and 17% of installations, respectively. Cetus was acquired in 1986 by Perkin-Elmer, a large corporation in the analytical instruments field with $1.3 billion in sales for fiscal year 1987. Three more players entered in 1985, one of which was Beckman Instruments, a subsidiary of SmithKline Beckman, a very large corporation in the health-care and life-sciences industry with $4.3 billion in sales in fiscal year 1987. In 1987, Hewlett-Packard and Dynatech entered the market. See Exhibit 2 for a more complete description of the major competitors.

In spite of the eight other companies manufacturing lab robots, CyberLab believed its presence was needed because none of the existing players offered a machine similar to the "800" system for a similar cost. A CyberLab system cost $32,470 and would replace one chemist (average salary of $41,800 in 1987). Thus CyberLab had a payback of 0.78 years.

The Current Negotiations

In order to obtain necessary financing, Tom Friedlander, CEO of CyberLab, had approached Dean Witter and Salomon Brothers, but with no luck. He then hired a full-time consultant from a large venture capital firm to help him find the money. This consultant had interested one of the venture capital firm's partners (PRICO) in the CyberLab proposal. The terms of the possible deal were about to be negotiated between PRICO and CyberLab. CyberLab had offered 30% of its equity and the rights to market CyberLab products through PRICO's international distribution system in exchange for $1 million in capital. Under this agreement, PRICO would become the sole purchaser and marketer of the CyberLab systems. CyberLab would manufacture the machines and sell them at a prearranged transfer price to PRICO. Exhibit 3 shows the spreadsheet (CYBER.XLS), developed by CyberLab to evaluate its manufacturing-only venture under this agreement. *Note:* The assumptions used for both Exhibits 3 and 4 are shown in Exhibit 5.

The current proposal required PRICO to analyze the project as a package containing both the marketing opportunity and the equity investment. Based on the relevant costs and margins, was taking on the marketing and receiving 30% equity worth $1,000,000, or was a higher equity percentage and/or higher margin (i.e., lower transfer price) necessary to make the deal attractive?

On the marketing issue, PRICO would provide its established name, sales force, and advertising in exchange for a 23% margin. The company had been in the laboratory-equipment business for over 50 years and currently had 100 sales and service offices in the United States and 220 such offices in 60 countries throughout the world. It certainly seemed reasonable to Mr. Campbell that if the patent was worth the $700,000 he was effectively paying CyberLab upfront, then his company's marketing clout was worth at least the $262,258 he had calculated as the net present value (NPV) of the marketing agreement (see Exhibit 4).

In dollar terms, PRICO would actually incur initial expenses of $150,000, for a one-time seminar and new brochures to train all the salesmen on the new product, as well as ongoing expenses of $51,000 the first year and approximately $60,000 per year for the second and third years for advertising. Additional expenses included a commission of $600 per CyberLab system sold.

Another possible expense was the sales force. Frank Adams, the vice president of sales, argued there was an "opportunity" cost associated with using the sales force. He estimated the new product would take about 1% of each salesperson's schedule the first year and 1.5% for years two and three. The total sales expense the previous year for PRICO was $12 million, which made the opportunity cost equal $120,000 (.01 * 12,000,000). Because the average salary for one salesman was $24,000 a year in addition to expenses of $36,000 a year, this "cost" was the equivalent of two full-time sales people the first year and three in years two and three.

PRICO would not actually have to hire any new salespeople, but adding CyberLab products would take away some of the sales force's time spent on existing products. In a "typical" sales call to a lab director, part of the time was spent ordering routine supplies (beakers, cylinders, test tubes, pipettes, etc.), while the remainder was spent talking about new and existing nonroutine products. Mr. Campbell did not believe that there would not be any significant erosion of the standard-supply selling; Mr. Adams and his staff concurred. Even if there were some erosion, it would probably be made up by the increase in disposable pipette tips sales that would certainly accompany sales of the CyberLab system. Because PRICO would not have to pay any money out of pocket, Vince Pauli, the financial analyst for new ventures at PRICO, had argued that the sales force's time should not be included as an expense in the analysis.

The projected cash flows from PRICO's perspective, for the marketing aspect only is shown in Exhibit 4. (*Note:* This exhibit includes the opportunity cost for the sales force's time in the "sales expense" line.) The lab-instrument manufacturing industry average for return on sales (based on profit before tax) was 5.1%. Other major corporations in this industry had values for return on equity of 12 to 13%. Overall, for the million dollar investment, PRICO would get 30% of the value of CyberLab or $342,327 (.3*$1,141,090) plus the value of the marketing agreement, $262,258 for a net of −$395,415.

Mr. Campbell thought he had some negotiating room, even though CyberLab had made it clear that it wanted both the marketing arrangement and an investment. Mr. Friedlander had just called to say that he had received an offer from a privately held company, Sperling Equipment Co., to buy a fixed number of units per year for the first three years and market them in exchange for a 30% discount from retail price. This raised the question whether PRICO would want to do the marketing alone on a non-exclusive basis without the 30% equity interest if CyberLab would let them.

This was an interesting question, but the immediate task was to evaluate the offer on the table. Is the marketing/investment opportunity attractive? If it is worth pursuing, should Campbell counter offer a higher equity position in exchange for the $1 million capital infusion? Or should they just back away from the whole idea?

Questions

1. Using the information on the uncertain quantities given in the Addendum that follows, how would you use simulation to evaluate the investment/marketing opportunity from PRICO's point of view?
2. Conduct five trials evaluating the opportunity.
3. Suppose you had available the results of many trials (think about how many you need). How could you use these results to decide whether PRICO should take this opportunity?
4. How could you use simulation to evaluate counteroffers you may wish to carry into negotiation with CyberLab?

CyberLab Addendum

The following information is provided for the major uncertainties for each variable including the range of possible values along with their appropriate probabilities.

Lab-Robot Market Growth

Lab robots were highly suited for any area that required repetitive testing and sample preparation on a large scale. These areas included such biotechnology industries as pharmaceuticals, agricultural products, genetic engineering, and medical technology, in addition to the research and development division of almost any company. The biotechnology market anticipated sales of $1.2 billion in 1988 and was expecting to grow to $25 billion by 2000, which would represent 28.8% annual growth. R&D expenditures were forecast by Predicasts to grow at 7% to 9% annually in the near future. Lab and analytical equipment sales were forecast to grow from $1.65 billion in 1985 to $2.35 billion in 1990—an annual growth rate of 7.3%. In the past two years, sales had grown 5% and 9%. Experts believed that the future annual growth would be as likely to fall between 6% and 8% as it would to fall outside that range, but growth rates as high as 10% and as low as 0 were possible over several years. The rates generally centered around 7%. Retention of the 20% R&D tax credit would provide continued investment incentives.

Market Size for Current Year

Based on Zymark's actual 1987 sales of $15 million and the cost of its systems of $50,000 to $70,000, Zymark sold approximately 250 units (15,000,000/$60,000) in 1987. When Cyberlab combined this estimate with Zymark's estimated 42% share of installations to date, the result was an estimate of the annual market of 595 units (250/0.42).

A high-side estimate of the market was made using Zymark's average cost as $50,000 and assuming that its market share had dropped to about 35% in 1987 from the 42% share of total installations from 1982 to 1987. This approach gave an estimated market size of 809 units. Similarly, a low-side estimate was calculated of 510 units, using an average cost of $70,000 and assuming that current-year market share equaled cumulative market share.

CyberLab Market Share

Walter Meltzer estimated that first-year market share could be as low as 0 if the product completely bombed and as high as 7%, with a median value of 5%. In his mind, market share was equally likely to be between 4% and 6% as it was to be outside this range. In the second and successive years, he figured CyberLab would grab an extra 2.5% of the market over the first-year share.

Cost of Materials and Labor

Meltzer, the CyberLab-system inventor, had kept track of how long it took him to machine the 80 parts he bought and then machined, as well as what it cost to buy the other 75 parts he used unchanged in creating the system. To estimate the total cost, he added up the cost of the 75 purchased parts and his estimate of the labor and material cost for the 80 machined parts. The labor portion of the machined parts' cost was calculated by multiplying the time he took by the labor rate charged by local machine shops in New England ($100/hour). His conservative estimate of the total cost came out to be $8,651.

Both the time to do the machining and the rate charged for machined parts could vary significantly from previous estimates. Therefore, because Meltzer was very conservative when assigning the overall costs, he estimated they could vary as high as 5% above his estimate or as low as 9% below his estimate.

Tax Rate

A 35% tax rate was used as an estimate (the top federal rate was 33%; the top Connecticut rate 7%), but if the company did not do well, the tax rate would be much lower. Another factor that could change the tax rate was the fickle nature of the Congress and the President.

Of all these variables that had been estimated, the three that were believed to have the most impact on the bottom line were the following:

The first quantity was CyberLab's *first-year market share*. It could be as low as 0% and as high as 7% with it being equally likely to be greater than or less than 5%. For a graph of the cumulative probability distribution function, see Exhibit 6.

The next quantity was the *cost of materials and direct labor for the system*. The total cost could vary as much as 9% below the engineer's prediction of $8,651 to 5% above the prediction and that any percentage in this interval was possible. The following risk table was developed.

Cost Variance (Percent)	Probability of Value or Less
−9	0
−5	0.25
−2	0.50
0	0.75
+5	1.0

The last quantity was *total market growth.* The fastest the lab-robot market would grow was 10% and the slowest it would grow was 0%. It was equally likely in his mind that the actual growth would be greater than or less than 7%. He also felt that there was a 50% chance that the growth would be between 6 and 8% with the other 50% representing growth rates outside this range.

EXHIBIT 1

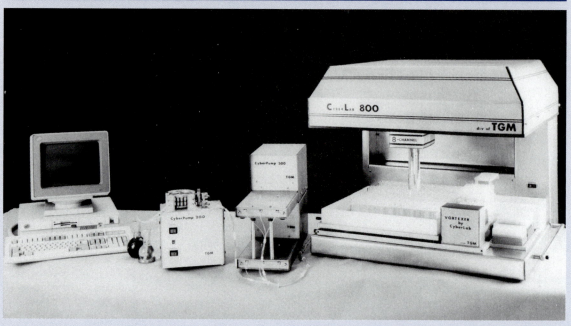

EXHIBIT 2

Company Name	Yrs in Bsns	# Instld to Date	% Instld to Date	Genl Description of Company	Sales of Company ($MM)	Sales of Lab Instr Div ($MM)	Competing Product Description
Zymark	6	1000	42	First one to market, privately held	15	15	Slow, cost 50K to 70K
Micromedic	5	400	17	Subsidiary of ICN Biomedicals, govt contract, Intl sales	43	17	Only dilutes & dispenses, cost 5K
Perkin-Elmer/Cetus	5	350	15	Design and mfg of hi-tech analytic equip. Intl sales	1334	416	No computer, robot arm, Cost 50K
Tecan	3	300	13	Subsidiary of Swiss corp, been in US 4 yrs	?	??	Limited use & warranty, cost 20K
Beckman	2.5	175	7	Technology intensive hlth care/life science company, Intl sales	4329	693	Moves smpl to probe, cost 26K
Hamilton	3	100	4	Been in lab equip bsns 30 years, Intl sales	25	25	One probe w/ 5 steel tip, cost 20K
HP/Genenchem	1	50	2	Established force in computers, starting in scientific equip	8090	405	Slow w/ genl purpose, only works w/ HP cmpt, cost 40–55K
Dynatech	1	4	0.2	Plan to go national	305	13	Cost 6K

Sources: Annual reports, S&P OTC reports, *Million Dollar Directory*

EXHIBIT 3

| | C37 | | =C33-C36 | | | |

	A	B	C	D	E	F	G
26	CYBERLAB'S PRO FORMA INCOME STATEMENT: MANUFACTURING ONLY						
27							
28	YEAR		1	2	3		
29	Selling Price/Unit		$25,000	$25,000	$25,000		
30	Matrl & Labor/Unit		$8,651	$8,651	$8,651		
31	Units Sold		29	47	51		
32							
33	Sales Revenue		$725,000	$1,175,000	$1,275,000		
34	Material, Dir Labor		250,879	406,597	441,201		
35	Overhead		138,000	196,430	207,641		
36	Cost Of Goods Sold		$388,879	$603,027	$648,842		
37	Gross Margin		$336,121	$571,973	$626,158		
38	Selling, Gen & Admin		$258,044	$343,047	$344,908		
39	Depreciation		16,000	9,600	5,760		
40	Profit before tax		$62,077	$219,326	$275,490		
41	Taxes		$24,831	$87,730	$110,196		
42	Profit after tax		$37,246	$131,596	$165,294		
43							
44	RETURN ON SALES		5.14%	11.20%	12.96%		
45	EQUITY AT		$1,000,000	$1,037,246	$1,168,842		
46	BEGINNING OF YEAR						
47	RETURN ON EQUITY		3.72%	12.69%	14.14%		
48							
49	YEAR		1	2	3	TERM VALUE	
50	PAT		37,246	131,596	165,294		
51	DEP'N ADD-BACK		16,000	9,600	5,760		
52	CHANGE IN WORK CAP		(47,176)	(58,841)	(72,912)		
53	CASH FLOW FR. OPNS		6,070	82,355	98,142	1,635,700	
54							
55	NPV		$1,141,090				
56	IRR		16.99%				
57							

EXHIBIT 4

	H	I	J	K	L	M
			CYBERLAB (A)			
		PRICO'S PRO FORMA INCOME STATEMENT: MARKETING ONLY				
YEAR		1	2	3		
Selling price/unit		$32,470	$32,470	$32,470		
Transfer price/unit		$25,000	$25,000	$25,000		
Margin/unit		$7,470	$7,470	$7,470		
PRICO Margin (%)		23.0%	23.0%	23.0%		
Units Sold		29	47	51		
Sales Revenue		$941,630	$1,526,090	$1,655,970		
Cost Of Goods Sold		725,000	1,175,000	1,275,000		
Gross Margin		$216,630	$351,090	$380,970		
Advertising		$51,000	$60,000	$60,000		
Sales expense		$137,400	$208,200	$210,600		
Total Sell.,Gen.& Admin		$188,400	$268,200	$270,600		
Profit before tax		$28,230	$82,890	$110,370		
Taxes		$11,292	$33,156	$44,148		
Profit after tax		$16,938	$49,734	$66,222		
RETURN ON SALES		1.80%	3.26%	4.00%		
RETURN ON INVESTMENT		11.29%	33.16%	44.15%		
YEAR		1	2	3	TERM VALUE	
PAT		16,938	49,734	66,222		
DEP'N ADD-BACK		0	0	0		
CASH FLOW		16,938	49,734	66,222	509,400	
NPV		$262,258				
IRR		51.07%				

EXHIBIT 5

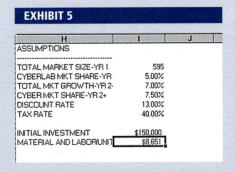

	H	I	J
	ASSUMPTIONS		
	TOTAL MARKET SIZE-YR 1	595	
	CYBERLAB MKT SHARE-YR	5.00%	
	TOTAL MKT GROWTH-YR 2-	7.00%	
	CYBER MKT SHARE-YR 2+	7.50%	
	DISCOUNT RATE	13.00%	
	TAX RATE	40.00%	
	INITIAL INVESTMENT	$150,000	
	MATERIAL AND LABOR/UNIT	$8,651	

EXHIBIT 6

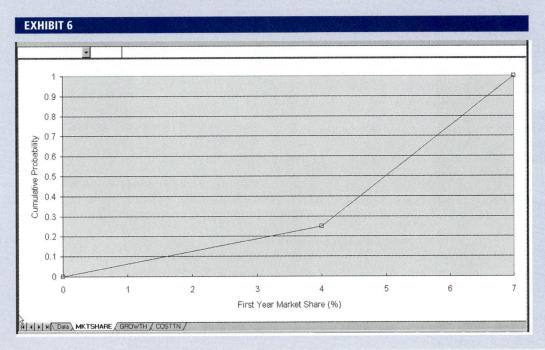

Cumulative Probability vs. First Year Market Share (%)

Data / MKTSHARE / GROWTH / COSTTN

563

May 19, 1988, was a beautiful day in Charlottesville, Virginia. Tom Dingledine could see some cows grazing the pasture on the rolling hillside outside his window. He was grateful for the bucolic setting, which was made possible by his doing well with the projects he managed, one of which now required some concentration. Tom was the president of Sprigg Lane Natural Resources, a subsidiary of the Sprigg Lane Investment Corporation (SLIC). The decision at hand was whether to invest in the Bailey Prospect natural gas opportunity.

The Company

Sprigg Lane was a privately held investment corporation founded in 1961. It had become a diversified corporation composed of two major groups. The first was devoted to manufacturing high-quality home furnishings. Its masthead company was Virginia Metalcrafters, which produced hand-crafted brass giftware. Other companies in the group included an outdoor lantern company in Maine and an antique reproduction furniture company in Maryland. With the establishment of National Legal Research Group in 1970, another major group—The Research Group—was started. Since then four other research companies had been added in the fields of consumer product marketing, computer software, tax research, and investment financial analysis.

The group's recent formation of Sprigg Lane Development Corporation, which was involved in the purchase and development of real estate, brought the total number of company subsidiaries to nine. SLIC sales for 1987 approximated $30 million and it employed over 525 people.

Drilling and Developing a Well[1]

The most common drilling rig in operation in 1988 was the rotary rig composed of five major components—the drill string and bit, the fluid-circulating system, the hoisting system, the power plant, and the blowout-prevention system. To facilitate the drilling process, generally a fluid known as drilling mud (composed of water and special chemicals) was circulated around the hole being drilled. In some cases, such as the Bailey Prospect, air was used as the "drilling mud." The major purpose of the drilling mud was to lubricate the drill bit and to carry to the surface the cuttings that could otherwise remain in the hole and clog it.

After the well was drilled, and if gas were found, the well had to be completed and prepared for production. A metal pipe of 8.625 inches diameter called casing was generally inserted about 1300 feet into the ground. Then a pipe of 4 1/2 inches di-

ameter called production casing was inserted into the cased hole all the way down through the production zone (about 5400 feet) and cemented. After the cement set, the production casing was perforated so that gas could flow to the surface through it.

The cost to drill an "average" well in Doddridge County, West Virginia, location of the Bailey Prospect, was $160,000. There was some uncertainty, however, in the cost from well to well because of such factors as differing depths of wells and different types of terrain that had to be drilled. Experts in the local area said that there was a 95% chance that the cost for any given well would be within $5400 of the average cost, assuming a normal distribution.

SLIC's Entry into Natural Gas

In January 1987, Tom, who had been working as the CFO of a private oil and gas exploration and development company, met the president of SLIC and joined the company to find some investment opportunities for it. Tom became convinced that the company could enjoy higher potential returns (30–40% after tax) from natural resource exploration than from other investment opportunities, including real estate, which were yielding 15–20%. Although natural resource exploration was clearly riskier, Tom felt the risk could be managed by drilling only sites that were surrounded on three to four sides by existing wells. Through further research, he found two other factors that helped reduce the risk: First, contracts with the pipeline distributors typically locked in the natural gas selling prices for four years, and second, well operating expenses were covered by contracts that allowed increases only every three years, with the increase capped at 15% per three-year period. Tom thought that the annual increase in the total well cost would be equivalent to one-half the rate of inflation.

The president of SLIC was so impressed with Tom's presentation on the entire subject that he offered him the job as president of a new division to be called Sprigg Lane Natural Resources (SLNR). Tom took the offer, and in his first year on the job (1987), SLNR had drilled four wells. It had not been difficult operationally to drill the four wells, but it had been challenging to find enough high-quality investment opportunities. Tom considered wells to be "good" if they met all the following criteria: (1) payback of initial cash investment in 42 months or less, (2) at least 25% internal rate of return (IRR) on an after-tax basis, and (3) at least 15% IRR on a pretax basis.

In the first five months of production, one of the wells had already paid back 52% of its initial investment—well ahead of its target 28-month payout. The other wells were also doing well, and all of them were at least on schedule for meeting their targeted return on investment. Even though things had gone favorably for Tom so far, he knew the pressure was still on him to make good decisions because SLNR was planning to drill 20 more wells in 1988.

Investment Strategy

SLNR acted as the managing general partner in the gas drilling ventures it formed, which gave it full responsibility for

[1]U.S. Department of Energy, *The Oil and Gas Drilling Industry,* 1981, pp. 13–16.

choosing sites and managing the well if gas were found. SLNR gathered information from the state of West Virginia and from other companies drilling in the vicinity of a well (if they were willing to engage in "information trading"). Tom would then put together a package of 10 wells that he considered good investments based on all the information he had gathered. The total initial investment for a typical package would be around $1.6 million. SLNR would retain about 25% ownership and sell the rest to several other general partners.

As managing general partner, SLNR was responsible for hiring a general contractor who would actually hire a firm to do the drilling, and SLNR's geologist, Brad Thomas, would determine whether there really was enough gas to make it worth completing a well. If the decision was to go ahead, the general contractor would also be in charge of the day-to-day operations of a well. SLNR had entered into a joint venture with Excel Energy of Bridgeport, West Virginia, in which they agreed that Excel would act as the general contractor for all the wells on which SLNR acted as managing general partner.

The first-year production level varied significantly from well to well. Tom found the uncertainty could be described with a lognormal probability distribution with a mean of 33 million cubic feet and a standard deviation of 4.93 million cubic feet.

The Bailey Prospect

Exhibit 1 is a copy of the spreadsheet (SPRIGG.XLS) Tom had developed to analyze one well, called the Bailey Prospect, as a potential member of the package of 10 wells he was currently putting together (years 13–25 are not shown). As Tom thought about the realization of this one well, he knew the Bailey Prospect was surrounded by producing wells from the target gas-producing formation. It was virtually certain, therefore, that SLNR would hit the formation and decide to complete the well, but there was a 10% chance that either an operational failure would cause zero production or that the gas formation would be depleted because of the surrounding wells, resulting in essentially zero production. In either of these cases, the pre-tax loss would be $160,000. In the more likely case, there would be gas produced and Tom would then find out how much the well would produce in the first and subsequent years. He would also learn what the BTU content (see Exhibit 2 for an explanation of the more commonly used abbreviations and terms in the well-drilling business) was for the gas, which would affect the total revenue generated by the well.

Revenues and Expenses. The spreadsheet was basically an income statement over the well's life. The price per mcf was calculated by multiplying the contracted price per MMBTU times the BTU content divided by 1000. The production in mcf was then estimated for the first year and calculated for each succeeding year based on the percentage decline values given in the assumptions. The gross revenue was just the product of the price per mcf times the mcf of gas produced in a given year. Out of the gross revenue came a 15.23% royalty payment to the owner of the mineral rights, leaving net revenue. Several expenses were deducted from net revenue to arrive at the profit before tax:

1. Monthly operating costs of $300 were paid to Excel Energy in addition to a budgeted amount of $3000 for other operating expenses that might occur on an annual basis. These costs were increased annually by the well-expense inflation factor.

2. Local taxes of 4.5% times the gross revenue were paid to the county and a severance tax (see Exhibit 2) of 3.4% times the gross revenue was paid to the state of West Virginia.

3. Depreciation expense for year 0 equaled the intangible drilling cost, which was 72.5% of the total well cost. The remainder of the initial drilling cost was depreciated on a straight-line basis over seven years.

To compute profit after tax, the following equations applied:

Profit after tax = Profit before tax − Depletion − State Income Tax − Federal Income Tax

Where: Depletion = minimum of .5 * (Profit before tax) *or* .15 * (Net revenue)

State Income Tax = State tax rate * (Profit before tax − Depletion) − 1/2 * (Severance tax)

Federal Income Tax = Federal tax rate * (Profit before tax − Depletion − State income tax) − Section 29 credit

Section 29 of the Federal tax code had been passed by Congress in 1978 in order to stimulate drilling for a particular kind of natural gas that was especially difficult to extract from the ground, namely, that found in rock called devonian shale, which composed the Bailey Prospect. This rock consists of many very small pockets where the gas resides until it is ferreted out. It provided, in 1988, a tax credit of $0.76 per decatherm. This tax credit rate was increased each year with inflation, but its future value was in the hands of Congress and thus far from certain.

Initial Results and Investment Considerations. To find the net present value (NPV), Tom added back the depreciation and depletion to the profit after tax to come up with the yearly cash flows. These flows were then discounted at the company's hurdle rate of 15% for projects of this risk (see Exhibit 3 for a listing of rates of return for investments of varying maturities and degrees of risk) to calculate the NPV through any given year of the well's life. His pro forma analysis indicated the project had an IRR of 41.1% and an NPV of $110,263.

Tom was feeling good about the Bailey Prospect, even though he knew he had made many assumptions. He'd used 1155 BTU/FT^3 to estimate the heat content of the gas because it was the expected (mean) value, when in reality he knew it could be as low as 1055 or as high as 1250, with the most likely value (mode) being 1160. He also guessed that inflation, as measured by the Gross National Product (GNP) Deflator (a measure similar to the Consumer Price Index or CPI), would average 3.5% over the 25-year project life, but he thought he ought to check a couple of forecasts and look at the historical trends. See Exhibit 4 for both forecasts of GNP Deflator values as well as historical GNP Deflator values and historical natural gas prices. Tom's idea was to use the GNP Deflator to forecast natural gas prices after the four-year contract expired and to increase the value of the natural gas tax credit on an annual basis.

Further Questions and Uncertainties. When Tom showed the results to Henry Ostberg, a potential partner, Henry was impressed with the "expected" scenario but asked, "What is the downside on an investment such as this?" Tom had done his homework and produced Exhibits 5 and 6 together (again years 13–25 are not shown). Exhibit 5 showed the results if there was not enough gas to develop. Exhibit 6 showed what would happen if there was enough gas, but all other uncertain quantities were set at their 1 chance in 100 worst levels. Henry was somewhat disturbed by what he saw but said, "Hey, Tom, we're businessmen. We're here to take risks; that's how we make money. What we really want to know is the likelihood of this sort of outcome."

Tom realized he had not thought enough about the probabilities associated with potential risks that a project of this kind involved. He also put his mind to work thinking about whether he had considered all the things he had seen that could change significantly from one project to another. The only additional uncertainty he generated was the yearly production decline, which could vary significantly for a given well. He had used what he considered the expected values in this case, but now he realized he ought to multiply each one by some uncertain quantity, with a most likely value of 1.0, a low of 0.5, and a high of 1.75, to allow for the kind of fluctuation he had seen.

Tom wondered what would be the most effective way to incorporate all six of the uncertainties (total well cost, whether the well produced gas or not, first-year production of gas, the BTU content, rate of production decline, and the average inflation over the next 25 years) into his investment analysis. He remembered doing "what if" tables with Lotus back in business school, but he had never heard of a six-way table. As he skimmed back through his quantitative methods book, he saw a chapter on Monte Carlo simulation and read enough to be convinced that this method was ideally suited to his current situation.

When Tom told Henry about this new method of evaluation he was contemplating, his partner laughed and said, "Come on, Tom, it can't be that hard. What you're talking about sounds like something they'd teach brand-new MBAs. You and I have been doing this type of investing for years. Can't we just figure it out on the back of an envelope?" When Tom tried to estimate the probability of his worst-case scenario, it came out to .00000001%—not very likely! There was no way he was going to waste any more time trying to figure out the expected NPV by hand based on all the uncertainties, regardless of how intuitive his friend thought it should be. Consequently, Tom thought a little more about how Monte Carlo simulation would work with this decision.

In his current method of evaluating projects, he had used the three criteria mentioned earlier (<42-month payback of initial cash investment, >15% IRR on pretax basis, and >25% IRR on after-tax basis). He could see that calculating the average IRR after several Monte Carlo trials wouldn't be very meaningful, especially since there was a 10% chance that you would spend $160K on a pretax basis and get no return! It would be impossible to find an IRR on that particular scenario. He did feel he could calculate an average NPV after several trials and even find out how many years it would take until the NPV became positive. As he settled into his chair to finish reading the chapter, which looked vaguely familiar, he looked up briefly at the verdant hillside and wondered for a moment what resources were under the hill.

Questions

1. Based on the base case scenario and the two alternative downside possibilities, is this investment economically attractive?
2. What benefit can Monte Carlo simulation add to Tom's understanding of the economic benefits of the Bailey Prospect?
3. Incorporate uncertainties into the spreadsheet using @Risk or Crystal Ball. What do the Monte Carlo results reveal? What is the probability that the NPV will be greater than zero? Should Tom invest?

EXHIBIT 1 Sprigg Lane (A) Bailey Prospect Base Case Spreadsheet

WELL

ASSUMPTIONS		ENVIRONMENT		***RESULTS***	
TOTAL WELL COST	$160,000	FEDERAL TAX RATE	34.00%	EQUITY PAYOUT (AFTER-TAX) =	23.26 MONTHS
INTANGIBLE COST(%OFTOTAL)	72.50%	STATE TAX RATE	9.75%	INTERNAL RATE OF RETURN (CF AFTER-TAX) =	41.07%
		SEVERANCE TAX RATE	3.40%	INTERNAL RATE OF RETURN (PBT) =	16.65%
MONTHLY OPERATING COSTS	$300	COUNTY TAX RATE	4.50%		
ANNUAL LEASE EXPENSE	$3,000	SECTION 29 TAX CREDIT($/M	$0.7600		
INFL TION FACTOR-WELL EXPENSE	1.75%	% QUALIFIED	100.00%	NET PRESENT VALUE (CFAT) @ 15%	$110,263
PRODUCTION DATA:		GNP DEFLATOR	3.50%	CUMULATIVE CASH FLOW AFTER-TAX	$432,235
ENOUGH(0=NO,1=YES)?	1				
1st YEAR Mcf	33,000	ROYALTIES	15.2344%		
PRODUCTION DECLINE AFTER…		GAS PRICE DATA			
YEAR 1 =	22.50%				
YEAR 2 =	17.50%	CURRENTPRICE($/MMBTU)	$1.90		
YEAR 3-5 =	12.50%	BTUCONTENT(BTU/FT3)	1,155		
YEAR 6-14 =	10.00%	1ST YEAR OF			
YEAR 15-24 =	5.00%	PRICE INCREASE	5		

YEAR	0	1	2	3	4	5	6	7	8	9	10	11
INITIAL INVESTMENT	($160,000)											
PRICE PER MCF		2.19	2.19	2.19	2.19	2.27	2.35	2.43	2.52	2.61	2.70	2.79
PRODUCTION(MCF)		33,000	25,575	21,099	18,462	16,154	14,135	12,721	11,449	10,304	9,274	8,347
GROSS REVENUE		$72,419	$56,124	$46,303	$40,515	$36,691	$33,228	$30,952	$28,832	$26,857	$25,017	$23,304
LESS:ROYALTIES		11,033	8,550	7,054	6,172	5,590	5,062	4,715	4,392	4,092	3,811	3,550
NET REVENUE		$61,386	$47,574	$39,249	$34,343	$31,101	$28,166	$26,237	$24,440	$22,766	$21,206	$19,753
OPERATING EXPENSES		6,600	6,716	6,833	6,953	7,074	7,198	7,324	7,452	7,583	7,715	7,850
SEVERANCE & COUNTY TAX		5,721	4,434	3,658	3,201	2,899	2,625	2,445	2,278	2,122	1,976	1,841
DEPRECIATION	116,000	6,286	6,286	6,286	6,286	6,286	6,286	6,286				
PROFIT BEFORE TAX	($116,000)	$42,779	$30,139	$22,472	$17,904	$14,843	$12,057	$10,182	$14,710	$13,061	$11,514	$10,062
DEPLETION		9,208	7,136	5,887	5,151	4,665	4,225	3,936	3,666	3,415	3,181	2,963
STATE INC. TAX	(11,310)	2,042	1,289	830	555	369	199	83	587	484	387	296
FEDERAL INC. TAX	(35,595)	(18,247)	(15,853)	(14,484)	(13,821)	(12,937)	(12,141)	(11,631)	(9,231)	(8,796)	(8,393)	(8,022)
PROFIT AFTER TAX	($69,095)	$49,777	$37,567	$30,238	$26,018	$22,746	$19,775	$17,795	$19,688	$17,958	$16,339	$14,825
AFTER TAX CASH FLOW	($113,095)	$65,270	$50,989	$42,411	$37,455	$33,697	$30,285	$28,016	$23,354	$21,373	$19,520	$17,788
CUMUL. AFT TAX CASH FLOW	($113,095)	($47,825)	$3,164	$45,575	$83,030	$116,727	$147,013	$175,029	$198,383	$219,756	$239,276	$257,064
NPV THROUGH YEAR N	($113,095)	($56,339)	($17,784)	$10,102	$31,518	$48,271	$61,364	$71,896	$79,531	$85,606	$90,432	$94,255

EXHIBIT 2 Sprigg Lane (A) Explanation of Commonly Used Terms

BTU	British Thermal Unit—amount of heat required to raise the temperature of 1 pound of water by 1° Fahrenheit.
MMBTU	1 million BTUs.
Decatherm	1 MMBTU.
FT^3	1 cubic foot.
mcf	1000 cubic feet.
Intangible well costs	Any expense for something which could not be used again (e.g., fees to the drilling crew, cement costs). A purchase of metal pipe, on the other hand, would represent a tangible cost.
Severance	Sales tax to state on gas or oil withdrawn and sold.
Depletion	Generally the concept is similar to depreciation. It compensated the company for the money spent to acquire the right to drill. Generally accepted accounting principles recognized only cost depletion, which amortized the cost on a unit of production basis (e.g., # of mcf produced this year divided by the total mcf in the ground times the cost). The IRS, however, allowed the company to calculate depletion under the more favorable of two methods. One of these being cost depletion, the other is called percentage depletion. The latter was in the spreadsheet and was almost always more favorable.

EXHIBIT 3 Sprigg Lane (A) Interest Rates and Yields

		TREASURIES						MOODY'S[a]	
		BILLS	NOTES AND BONDS						
		1-Yr	3-Yr	5-Yr	7-Yr	10-Yr	30-Yr	Aaa	Baa
1985		7.81	9.64	10.12	10.5	10.62	10.79	11.37	12.72
1986		6.08	7.06	7.30	7.54	7.68	7.78	9.02	10.39
1987		6.33	7.68	7.94	8.23	8.39	8.59	9.38	10.58
1988	Jan	6.52	7.87	8.18	8.48	8.67	8.83	9.88	11.07
	Feb	6.21	7.38	7.71	8.02	8.21	8.43	9.40	10.62
	Mar	6.28	7.50	7.83	8.19	8.37	8.63	9.39	10.57
	May 18	7.34	8.23	8.66	8.90	9.20	9.30	10.22	11.45

[a]Based on yields to maturity on selected long-term corporate bonds.
Sources: *Federal Reserve Bulletin*, June 1988, and *Wall Street Journal*, May 19, 1988.

EXHIBIT 4 Sprigg Lane (A) Historical and Forecast Data

HISTORICAL NATURAL GAS PRICES

Year	Wellhead Price ($/MCF)	Year	Wellhead Price($/MCF)
1987	1.78	1975	0.44
1986	1.94	1974	0.30
1985	2.51	1973	0.22
1984	2.66	1972	0.19
1983	2.59	1971	0.18
1982	2.46	1970	0.17
1981	1.98	1969	0.17
1980	1.59	1968	0.16
1979	1.18	1967	0.16
1978	0.91	1966	0.16
1977	0.79	1965	0.16
1976	0.58	1964	0.15

ALL YEARS: MEAN=$0.976 STD DEV=$0.922
LAST 8 YEARS: MEAN=$2.189 STD DEV=$0.412

Source: *Basic Petroleum Data Book*, January 1988, Section VI, Table 2.

PERCENTAGE CHANGE FROM PREVIOUS PERIOD IN GNP DEFLATOR

Year	% Chg	Year	% Chg
1987	3.0	1969	5.6
1986	2.6	1968	5.0
1985	3.2	1967	2.6
1984	3.7	1966	3.6
1983	3.9	1965	2.7
1982	6.4	1964	1.5
1981	9.7	1963	1.6
1980	9.0	1962	2.2
1979	8.9	1961	1.0
1978	7.3	1960	1.6
1977	6.7	1959	2.4
1976	6.4	1958	2.1
1975	9.8	1957	3.6
1974	9.1	1956	3.4
1973	6.5	1955	3.2
1972	4.7	1954	1.6
1971	5.7	1953	1.6
1970	5.5		

LAST 16 YEARS: ARITHMETIC MEAN=6.31%, STD DEV=2.45%
LAST 25 YEARS: ARITHMETIC MEAN=5.39%, STD DEV=2.51%
LAST 35 YEARS: ARITHMETIC MEAN=4.5%, STD DEV=2.59%
25 YEAR MOVING AVERAGE: MEAN=4.91%, STD DEV=0.46%

Source: *Economic Report of the President*, 1988, p. 253

FORECASTS FOR PERCENTAGE CHANGE IN GNP DEFLATOR

	1988	1989	1990	AVG 1988–90
Data Resources[a]	3.1	3.8	4.5	3.8
Wharton[b]	3.8	4.5	4.5	4.3
UCLA[c]	2.7	2.8	3.9	3.1

[a]*Data Resources Inc.*, November 1987, p. 99.
[b]*Wharton Econometrics*, September 1987, p. 9.7–9.8.
[c]*UCLA National Business Forecast*, December 1987, p. 47.

EXHIBIT 5 SPrigg Lane (A) Spreadsheet with No Gas Produced

	****ASSUMPTIONS****		ENVIRONMENT				****RESULTS****					
TOTAL WELL COST	$160,000		FEDERAL TAX RATE	34.00%			EQUITY PAYOUT (AFTER-TAX) =	#DIV/0!				MONTHS
INTANGIBLE COST(%OFTOTAL)	72.50%		STATE TAX RATE	9.75%								
			SEVERANCE TAX RATE	3.40%			INTERNAL RATE OF RETURN (CF AFTER-TAX) =	#NUM!				
MONTHLY OPERATING COSTS	$300		COUNTY TAX RATE	4.50%			INTERNAL RATE OF RETURN (PBT) =	#NUM!				
ANNUAL LEASE EXPENSE	$3,000		SECTION 29 TAX CREDIT($/MI	$0.7600								
INFLTION FACTOR-WELL EXPENSE	1.75%		% QUALIFIED	100.00%			NET PRESENT VALUE (CFAT) @ 15%	($95,304)				
PRODUCTION DATA			GNP DEFLATOR	3.50%			CUMULATIVE CASH FLOW AFTER-TAX	($95,304)				
ENOUGH(0=NO,1=YES)?	0											
1st YEAR Mcf	33,000		ROYALTIES	15.2344%								
PRODUCTION DECLINE AFTER...			GAS PRICE DATA									
YEAR 1 =	22.50%		CURRENTPRICE($/MMBTU)	$1.90								
YEAR 2 =	17.50%		BTUCONTENT(BTU/FT3)	1,155								
YEAR 3-5 =	12.50%		1ST YEAR OF									
YEAR 6-14 =	10.00%		PRICE INCREASE	5								
YEAR 15-24 =	5.00%											

	0	1	2	3	4	5	6	7	8	9	10	11
YEAR	0	1	2	3	4	5	6	7	8	9	10	11
INITIAL INVESTMENT	($160,000)											
PRICE PER MCF		2.19	2.19	2.19	2.19	2.27	2.35	2.43	2.52	2.61	2.70	2.79
PRODUCTION(MCF)		0	0	0	0	0	0	0	0	0	0	0
GROSS REVENUE		$0	$0	$0	$0	$0	$0	$0	$0	$0	$0	$0
LESS: ROYALTIES		0	0	0	0	0	0	0	0	0	0	0
NET REVENUE		$0	$0	$0	$0	$0	$0	$0	$0	$0	$0	$0
OPERATING EXPENSES		0	0	0	0	0	0	0	0	0	0	0
SEVERANCE & COUNTY TAX		0	0	0	0	0	0	0	0	0	0	0
DEPRECIATION	160,000											
PROFIT BEFORE TAX	($160,000)	$0	$0	$0	$0	$0	$0	$0	$0	$0	$0	$0
DEPLETION		0	0	0	0	0	0	0	0	0	0	0
STATE INC. TAX	(15,600)	0	0	0	0	0	0	0	0	0	0	0
FEDERAL INC. TAX	(49,096)	0	0	0	0	0	0	0	0	0	0	0
PROFIT AFTER TAX	($95,304)	$0	$0	$0	$0	$0	$0	$0	$0	$0	$0	$0
AFTER TAX CASH FLOW	($95,304)	$0	$0	$0	$0	$0	$0	$0	$0	$0	$0	$0
CUMUL. AFT TAX CASH FLOW	($95,304)	($95,304)	($95,304)	($95,304)	($95,304)	($95,304)	($95,304)	($95,304)	($95,304)	($95,304)	($95,304)	($95,304)
NPV THROUGH YEAR N	($95,304)	($95,304)	($95,304)	($95,304)	($95,304)	($95,304)	($95,304)	($95,304)	($95,304)	($95,304)	($95,304)	($95,304)

EXHIBIT 6 Sprigg Lane (A) Spreadsheet with Gas Found but All Other Uncertainties Set at 1 Chance in 100 Worst Level

****ASSUMPTIONS**** — WELL

TOTAL WELL COST	$166,237
INTANGIBLE COST(%OFTOTAL)	72.50%
MONTHLY OPERATING COSTS	$300
ANNUAL LEASE EXPENSE	$3,000
INFLTION FACTOR-WELL EXPENSE	1.34%
PRODUCTION DATA	
ENOUGH(0=NO,1=YES)?	1
1st YEAR Mcf	24,000
PRODUCTION DECLINE AFTER….	
YEAR 1 =	37.20%
YEAR 2 =	28.93%
YEAR 3-5 =	20.67%
YEAR 6-14 =	16.53%
YEAR 15-24 =	8.27%

ENVIRONMENT

FEDERAL TAX RATE	34.00%
STATE TAX RATE	9.75%
SEVERANCE TAX RATE	3.40%
COUNTY TAX RATE	4.50%
SECTION 29 TAX CREDIT($/MI	$0.7600
% QUALIFIED	100.00%
GNP DEFLATOR	2.67%
ROYALTIES	15.2344%
GAS PRICE DATA	
CURRENTPRICE($/MMBTU)	$1.90
BTUCONTENT(BTU/FT3)	1,060
1ST YEAR OF PRICE INCREASE	5

****RESULTS****

EQUITY PAYOUT (AFTER-TAX)=	65.09 MONTHS
INTERNAL RATE OF RETURN(CF AFTER-TAX) =	#NUM!
INTERNAL RATE OF RETURN(PBT) =	#DIV/0!
NET PRESENT VALUE (CFAT) @ 15%	($30,202)
CUMULATIVE CASH FLOW AFTER-TAX	($18,138)

Yearly Projection

YEAR	0	1	2	3	4	5	6	7	8	9	10	11
INITIAL INVESTMENT	($166,237)											
PRICE PER MCF		2.01	2.01	2.01	2.01	2.07	2.12	2.18	2.24	2.30	2.36	2.42
PRODUCTION(MCF)		24,000	15,072	10,712	8,498	6,741	5,348	4,464	3,726	3,110	2,596	2,167
GROSS REVENUE		$48,336	$30,355	$21,573	$17,114	$13,939	$11,353	$9,723	$8,338	$7,146	$6,124	$5,248
LESS: ROYALTIES		7,364	4,624	3,287	2,607	2,124	1,730	1,482	1,270	1,089	933	799
NET REVENUE		$40,972	$25,731	$18,287	$14,507	$11,816	$9,624	$8,247	$7,068	$6,057	$5,191	$4,448
OPERATING EXPENSES		6,600	6,688	6,778	6,868	6,960	7,053	7,147	7,243	7,340	7,438	7,537
SEVERANCE & COUNTY TAX		3,819	2,398	1,704	1,352	1,101	897	769	659	565	484	415
DEPRECIATION	120,522	6,531	6,531	6,531	6,531	6,531	6,531	6,531				
PROFIT BEFORE TAX	($120,522)	$24,023	$10,114	$3,274	($244)	($2,776)	($4,857)	($6,199)	($834)	($1,847)	($2,731)	($3,503)
DEPLETION		6,146	3,860	1,637	(122)	(1,388)	(2,429)	(3,100)	(417)	(924)	(1,365)	(1,752)
STATE INC. TAX	(11,751)	921	94	(207)	(303)	(372)	(430)	(468)	(182)	(212)	(237)	(260)
FEDERAL INC. TAX	(36,982)	(13,569)	(10,372)	(8,469)	(7,347)	(6,380)	(5,594)	(5,107)	(3,689)	(3,335)	(3,035)	(2,779)
PROFIT AFTER TAX	($71,789)	$30,525	$16,532	$10,313	$7,528	$5,364	$3,596	$2,475	$3,455	$2,623	$1,906	$1,287
AFTER TAX CASH FLOW	($117,504)	$43,202	$26,922	$18,481	$13,937	$10,506	$7,698	$5,906	$3,038	$1,700	$541	($464)
CUMUL. AFT TAX CASH FLOW	($117,504)	($74,302)	($47,380)	($28,899)	($14,962)	($4,456)	$3,242	$9,148	$12,186	$13,886	$14,427	$13,962
NPV THROUGH YEAR N	($117,504)	($79,937)	($59,580)	($47,428)	($39,460)	($34,236)	($30,908)	($28,688)	($27,695)	($27,212)	($27,078)	($27,178)

References

Anthony Brigandi, Dennis Dargon, Michael Sheehan, and Thomas Spencer, "AT&T's Call Processing Simulator (CAPS) Operational Design for Inbound Call Centers," *Interfaces,* 24, no. 1 (1994), 6–28.

James Bookbinder and Terrence Kotwa, "Modeling an AGV Automobile Body-Framing System," *Interfaces,* 17, no. 6 (1987), 41–50.

Samuel Davis, George Kleindorfer, Gary Kochenberger, Edward Reutzel, and Emmitt Brown, "Strategic Planning for Bank Operations with Multiple Check-Processing Locations," *Interfaces,* 16, no. 6 (1986), 1–12.

Barry Smith, John Leimkuhler, and Ross Darrow, "Yield Management at American Airlines," *Interfaces,* 22, no. 1 (1992), 8–31.

CHAPTER OUTLINE

12.1 Introduction

12.2 The Basic Model

12.3 A Taxonomy of Queuing Models

12.4 Little's Flow Equation and Related Results

12.5 The $M/G/1$ Queue

12.6 Model 1: An $M/M/s$ Queue (Hematology Lab)

12.7 Economic Analysis of Queuing Systems

12.8 Model 2: A Finite Queue (WATS Lines)

12.9 Model 3: The Repairperson Model

12.10 Transient Versus Steady-State Results: Order Promising

12.11 The Role of the Exponential Distribution

12.12 Queue Discipline

12.13 Notes on Implementation

12.14 Summary

KEY TERMS

SELF-REVIEW EXERCISES

PROBLEMS

CASE STUDY: How Many Operators?

REFERENCES

APPLICATION CAPSULE | **Shortening the New York City Police Department's Arrest-to-Arraignment Time**

In 1988, New York City (NYC)'s arrestees were in custody waiting to be arraigned for an average of 44 hours, occasionally for more than 72 hours. Moreover, they were held in crowded, noisy conditions that were emotionally stressful, unhealthy, and often physically dangerous. In March 1990, the *New York Times* ran a front-page story on a woman who spent 45 hours in pre-arraignment detention in the Bronx with the headline "Trapped in the Terror of New York's Holding Pens." Arrestees were being denied a speedy court appearance and the lengthy delays greatly diminished the efficiency of the justice system. That same year, the NY Supreme Court ruled that the city was to attempt to arraign within 24 hours or release the prisoner.

Under these circumstances, NYC undertook the single most ambitious management science project to date in its history with the goal of reducing the arrest-to-arraignment (ATA) time. There were basically four different boroughs (Manhattan, Bronx, Brooklyn, and Queens), each with its own idiosyncratic way of doing things. The basic process included the following basic steps, which comprise a large queuing system: arrest by an officer of NYPD; taken to precinct where prisoner is searched, fingerprinted, and detained while an arrest report is completed; taken to central booking where fingerprints are faxed to state capital for identifica-

tion and report of criminal history; the arresting officer fills out more paperwork including the sworn complaint with the assistant district attorney; and the arrestee is lodged to await arraignment.

In 1988, in these four boroughs alone, over 325,000 arrests were made for which the defendants could be detained awaiting arraignment (i.e., more serious crimes). Unlike many other jurisdictions in the United States, in NYC felonies predominate, many of them involving violence or illicit drugs. Thus, an arrestee might find himself in the same holding cell with violent repeat offenders or defendants in drug episodes.

The project team mounted an extensive two-year effort. While the lengthy delays in ATA time were the key factor to study, the high costs associated with the current ATA process were an additional item of study. One of the contributors to these high costs was that arresting officers were spending an average of more than eight hours from the time they departed central booking until they swore out the complaint. Much of this time was overtime and the task itself only required 30 minutes! They were waiting in line for 7½ hours!

The whole process was modeled as a series of stages. Some of the stages were modeled as single-server queues, others as multiple-server queues, and some were even more complex. The statistical distributions and their corresponding parameters for each stage had to be determined. The overall model could then look at various different what-if scenarios involving combinations of workloads and arrest processing policies. The model generated several types of output including average overall ATA time and average times for completing individual stages of the process. The cost of each of the scenarios could also be generated by a companion spreadsheet model. NYC could then choose between several different alternatives, each with its own cost and performance measure.

In May 1990, Mayor David Dinkins released the findings of this project at a press conference with his strong endorsement of its rec-ommended changes. The model saved the city over $10 million per year in police overtime costs alone. The city has reduced the average ATA time delay from 44 hours to about 24 hours citywide. Arrestees gain the right to a speedier trial and are no longer "warehoused" under horrible conditions for longer than absolutely necessary. The city has also greatly reduced its costs for prisoner supervision and transportation by about $11 million per year. One final recommendation was the elimination of a single arraignment courtroom. This resulted in additional savings of $9.5 million for the city and state (see Larson et. al.).

12.1 INTRODUCTION

Queuing models are everywhere. This fact is obvious even to the most casual observer. Airplanes "queue up" in holding patterns, waiting for a runway so they can land, and then they line up again to take off. People line up for tickets, to buy groceries, and, if they happen to live in England, for almost everything else. Jobs line up for machines, orders line up to be filled, and so on. As you can probably tell, *queue* is the British term for any type of line for waiting. The Danish engineer A. K. Erlang is credited with founding queuing theory by studying telephone switchboards in Copenhagen for the Danish Telephone Company. He developed many of the queuing results used today. One of the greatest uses of queuing theory in the United States is for analyzing automobile traffic flow—studying how many lanes to have, how to regulate the traffic lights, and so forth—in order to maximize the flow of traffic.

Monte Jackson might not subscribe to the notion that all of life is a queue, but as administrative director of St. Luke's Hospital in Philadelphia, he must deal with a number of situations that can be described as queuing models. Briefly, a **queuing model** is one in which you have a sequence of items (such as people) arriving at a facility for service, as shown in Figure 12.1. At this moment, Monte is concerned about three particular "queuing models."

Model 1: St. Luke's Hematology Lab St. Luke's treats a large number of patients on an outpatient basis; that is, there are many patients who come to the hospital to see the staff doctors for diagnosis and treatment but who are not admitted to the hospital. Outpatients plus those admitted to the 600-bed hospital produce a large flow of new patients each day. Most new patients must visit the hematology laboratory as part of the diagnostic process. Each such patient has to be seen by a technician. The system works like this: After seeing a doctor, the patient arrives at the laboratory and checks in with a clerk. Patients are assigned on a first-come, first-served basis to test rooms as they become available. The technician assigned to that room performs the tests ordered by the doctor. When the testing is complete, the patient goes on to the next step in the process (perhaps X-ray), and the technician sees a new patient.

Monte must decide how many technicians to hire. Superficially, at least, the trade-off is obvious. More technicians means more expense for the hospital, but quicker service for the patients.

FIGURE 12.1

General Queuing Models

Arrivals

00000 ⟶ Service facility ⟶

TABLE 12.1 Some Queuing Models		
PROBLEM	ARRIVALS	SERVICE FACILITY
1	Patients	Technicians
2	Telephone Calls	Switchboard
3	Broken Equipment	Repairpeople

Model 2: Buying WATS Lines As part of its remodeling process, St. Luke's is designing a new communications system. Monte must decide how many WATS lines the hospital should buy. WATS (Wide Area Telephone Service) is an acronym for a special flat-rate, long-distance service offered by some phone companies. When all the phone lines allocated to WATS are in use, the person dialing out will get a busy signal, indicating that the call can't be completed. Monte knows that when people pick up the phone, they want to get through without having to try several times. How many lines he needs to achieve that result at a reasonable cost is not so clear.

Model 3: Hiring Repairpeople St. Luke's hires repairpeople to maintain 20 individual pieces of electronic equipment. The equipment includes measuring devices such as the electrocardiogram machine, small dedicated computers like the one used for lung analysis, and equipment such as the CAT scanner. If a piece of equipment fails and all the repairpeople are occupied, it must wait to be repaired. Monte must decide how many repairpeople to hire. He must balance their cost against the cost of having broken equipment.

As Table 12.1 indicates, all three of these models fit the general description of a queuing model. Monte will resolve these models by using a combination of analytic and simulation models. However, before we reach the level of sophistication required to deal with Monte's specific models, it is necessary for us to spend some time with the basic queuing model. In the process we will learn some terminology, and we will see the type of analytic results that are available.

12.2   THE BASIC MODEL

Consider the Xerox machine located in the fourth-floor secretarial service suite. Assume that users arrive at the machine and form a single line. Each arrival in turn uses the machine to perform a specific task. These tasks vary from obtaining a copy of a 1-page letter to producing 100 copies of a 25-page report. This system is called a single-server (or single-**channel**) queue. Questions about this or any other queuing system center on four quantities:

1. The number of people in the system: the number of people currently being served, as well as those waiting for service.
2. The number of people in the queue: the number of people waiting for service.
3. The waiting time in the system: the interval between when an individual enters the system and when he or she leaves the system. Note that this interval includes the service time.
4. The waiting time in the queue: the time between entering the system and the beginning of service.

ASSUMPTIONS OF THE BASIC MODEL

1. *Arrival Process.* Each arrival will be called a "job." Since the time between arrivals (the **interarrival time**) is not known with certainty, we will need to specify a probability distribution for it. In the basic model a particular distribution, called the *exponential distribution* (sometimes called the *negative exponential distribution*), is used. This distribution plays a central role in many queuing models. It provides a reasonable representation

of the arrival process in a number of situations, and its so-called **lack of memory** property makes it possible to obtain analytic results. The exponential distribution is *not* symmetric, a fact that bothers people who think that an "average" must have as many values above the mean as below it. For example, if customers arrive, on the average, every 5 minutes according to an exponential distribution, then approximately ⅔ of them will have interarrival times less than 5 minutes, and only about ⅓ of them longer than 5 minutes (but some of those may be very long and thus "skew" the average). The exponential distribution describes many services (bank tellers, postal clerks). About ⅔ of the service times will be below the mean time (a lot of short, quick transactions) and ⅓ of the service times will be above the mean (someone with the cash receipts from his or her business, or a person mailing a package overseas).

The words *Poisson input* are also used to describe the arrival process when the time between arrivals has an exponential distribution. This is because of the relationship between the exponential distribution and the Poisson distribution. In particular, if the interarrival time has an exponential distribution, the number of arrivals in a specified length of time (say, three hours) has a Poisson distribution.

The exponential distribution and its relationship to the Poisson is discussed in some detail in Section 12.11. At this point, it is only necessary to understand that the exponential distribution is completely specified by one parameter. This parameter, called λ, is the *mean arrival rate;* that is, how many jobs arrive (on the average) during a specific period of time. In a moment we will consider an example in which $\lambda = 0.05$ jobs per minute. This implies that *on the average* ⁵⁄₁₀₀ of a job arrives every minute. It is probably more natural to think in terms of a longer time interval. An equivalent statement is that *on the average* one job arrives every 20 minutes. Using more technical terms, we say that *the mean interarrival time is* 20 minutes. Mean interarrival time is the average time between two arrivals. Thus, for the exponential distribution

$$\text{average time between jobs} = \text{mean interarrival time} = \frac{1}{\lambda} \qquad (12.1)$$

Thus, if $\lambda = 0.05$,

$$\text{mean interarrival time} = \frac{1}{\lambda} = \frac{1}{0.05} = 20$$

2. *Service Process.* In the basic model, the time that it takes to complete a job (the **service time**) is also treated with the exponential distribution. The parameter for this exponential distribution is called μ. It represents the *mean service rate* in jobs per minute. In other words, μT is the number of jobs that would be served (on the average) during a period of T minutes if the machine were busy during that time. In the upcoming example we will assume that $\mu = 0.10$. This implies that on the average 0.10 of a job is completed each minute. An equivalent statement is that on the average one job is completed every 10 minutes. The *mean, or average, service time* (the average time to complete a job) is $1/\mu$. When μ, the mean service rate, is 0.10, the average service time is 10 since $1/\mu = 1/0.10 = 10$.

3. *Queue Size.* There is no limit on the number of jobs that can wait in the queue. The queue is said to be infinite.

4. *Queue Discipline.* Jobs are served on a first-come, first-served basis; that is, in the same order as they arrive at the queue.

5. *Time Horizon.* The system operates as described continuously over an infinite horizon.

6. *Source Population.* There is an infinite population available to arrive.

Consider these assumptions in the context of the Xerox model. Suppose that the average arrival time between jobs is 20 minutes. As we have seen, the fact that the interarrival time has an exponential distribution means that $1/\lambda = 20$, and thus $\lambda = 0.05$, or that the jobs arrive at the rate of 0.05 job per minute. Similarly, if the average time to complete a job is 10 minutes, we know that $1/\mu = 10$, and thus $\mu = 0.10$, or that jobs are completed at the rate of 0.10 job per minute when the machine is operating.

TABLE 12.2 Operating Characteristics for the Basic Model		
CHARACTERISTIC	SYMBOL	FORMULA
Utilization	—	$\dfrac{\lambda}{\mu}$
Expected Number in System	L	$\dfrac{\lambda}{\mu - \lambda}$
Expected Number in Queue	L_q	$\dfrac{\lambda^2}{\mu(\mu - \lambda)}$
Expected Waiting Time (Includes Service Time)	W	$\dfrac{1}{\mu - \lambda}$
Expected Time in Queue	W_q	$\dfrac{\lambda}{\mu(\mu - \lambda)}$
Probability That the System is Empty	P_0	$1 - \dfrac{\lambda}{\mu}$

CHARACTERISTICS OF THE BASIC MODEL

The values of these two parameters (together with the assumptions) are all that is needed to calculate several important **operating characteristics** of the basic model. The necessary formulas are presented in Table 12.2. WARNING! *The formulas in Table 12.2 hold only if* $\lambda < \mu$. If this condition does not hold (i.e., if $\lambda \geq \mu$), the number of people in the queue will grow without limit.

Consider, for example, a specific case where $\lambda = 0.25$ and $\mu = 0.10$. Remember that $1/\lambda$ is the average interarrival time. Thus, since $1/\lambda = 1/0.25 = 4$, on the average a job arrives every 4 minutes. Similarly, $1/\mu$ is the average time it takes to complete a job. Since $1/\mu = 1/0.10 = 10$, on the average it takes 10 minutes to complete a job. It seems clear that in this case the service operation will get further behind (the queue will grow longer) as time goes by.

Now return to the Xerox model, in which $\lambda < \mu$ and the formulas in Table 12.2 hold. Spreadsheets are ideal for crunching the numerical results from such formulas. We will use an Excel spreadsheet (Q.XLS) that was originally developed by Professor David Ashley and that already has these formulas entered. When you first open the spreadsheet you see the introductory page as shown in Figure 12.2 (note that there are four different worksheets [MMs, MG1, finiteQ, finitePopulation] to be used as indicated by the tabs at the bottom of the spreadsheet).

Plugging the numerical values from the Xerox model, $\lambda = 0.05$ and $\mu = 0.10$, into the appropriate cells (E2 and E3) of the appropriate worksheet ("MMs" in this example) yields the results presented in Figure 12.3. We also have to tell it that we have only one server (i.e., one copy machine) and that our time unit is minutes.

Steady-State Results These numbers require some interpretation. *L,* for example, is the expected number of people in the system (those being served plus those waiting) after the queue has reached *steady state.* In this sentence, **steady state** means that the probability that you will observe a certain number of people (say, 2) in the system does not depend on the time at which you count them. If a steady state has been achieved, the probability that there are two people using and/or waiting for the Xerox machine should be the same at 2:30 P.M. and at 4:00 P.M.

The other characteristics presented in Figure 12.3 have a similar interpretation. Thus, in a steady state, (1) the system is empty with a probability of one half (cell F7 shows that $P_0 = 0.5$); (2) on the average there is 0.5 person in the queue (cell F8 shows that $L_q = 0.5$); (3) on the average an arrival must wait 10 minutes before starting to use the machine (cell F10 shows that $W_q = 10$); and (4) on the average an arrival will spend

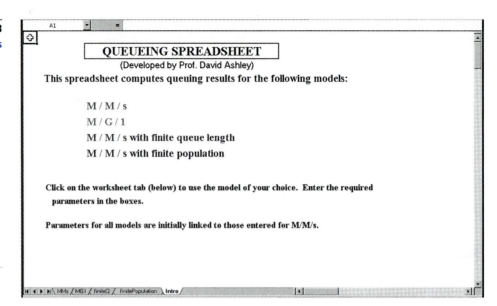

FIGURE 12.2

Introductory Page of
Queuing Workbook

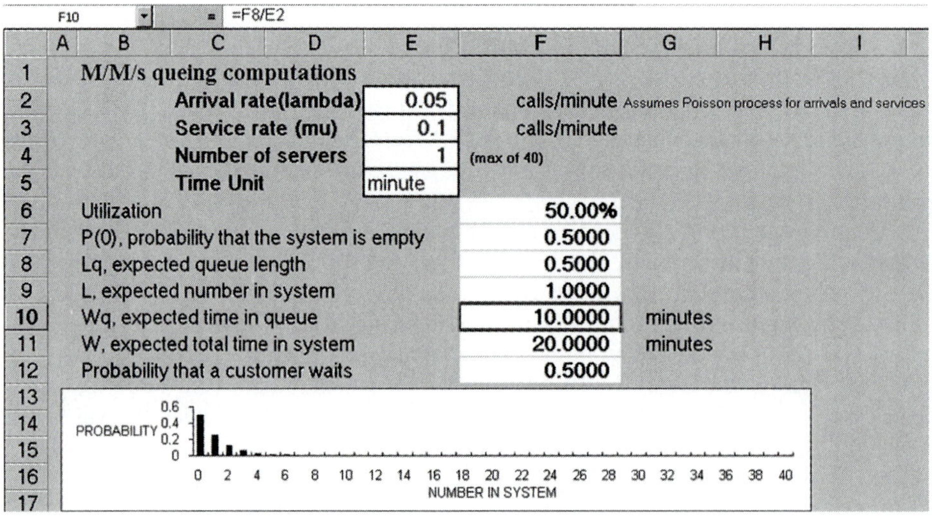

FIGURE 12.3

Evaluating the Operating
Characteristics of the
Basic Model

20 minutes in the system (cell F11 shows that $W = 20$). Remember that these values are averages and, as such, may have the same characteristics as the exponential distribution ($\frac{2}{3}$ of observations below mean, $\frac{1}{3}$ above). Thus, $\frac{2}{3}$ of the customers will spend less than 10 minutes in line, while $\frac{1}{3}$ will spend more than 10 minutes in line.

Using the Results These results hold for the basic model and the particular values for the parameters ($\lambda = 0.05$ and $\mu = 0.10$). They provide information that is useful to management in analyzing this service facility. Suppose, for example, that management makes the following calculations: Since $\lambda = 0.05$, on the average $\frac{5}{100}$ of a job arrives each minute. During each 8-hour day there are $8 \times 60 = 480$ minutes. Thus, during each day there is on the average a total of

$$(0.05)(480) = 24$$

arrivals. From the calculations in Figure 12.3 we know that on the average each person spends 20 minutes in the system ($W = 20$). Thus, a total of (24 arrivals per day) (20 minutes per arrival) = 480 minutes, or 8 hours, is spent at this facility. Management might well feel that this is too long. A variety of steps might be taken:

1. A new machine might be purchased with a smaller mean service time.

2. Another machine might be purchased and both machines used to satisfy the demand. This would change the system to a two-server queue.

3. Some personnel might be sent to a different and less busy copying facility. This would change the arrival process.

Management might select one of these alternatives, or perhaps some other option. But in any case, management must balance the cost of providing service against the cost of waiting. The results in Figure 12.3 and similar results for other systems would be a central part of the analysis. These ideas will be developed in more detail in the context of Monte Jackson's models.

12.3   A TAXONOMY OF QUEUING MODELS

There are many possible queuing models. For example, if the interarrival time in the basic model had been given a different distribution (not the exponential) we would have had a different model, in the sense that the previous formulas for L, L_q, and so on, would no longer hold. To facilitate communication among those working on queuing models, D. G. Kendall proposed a taxonomy based on the following notation:

$$A/B/s$$

where
$A =$ arrival distribution
$B =$ service distribution
$s =$ number of servers

APPLICATION CAPSULE — **Merging Traffic: A Queuing Simulation Helps Eliminate a Costly Bottleneck**

The Westinghouse Hanford Company in Richland, Washington, is a secured work facility: All vehicles and passengers are checked at a guard station before being allowed onto the premises. This security checkpoint created enormous traffic backups during shift changes, when the volume of entering vehicles was greatest. The result was a severe hazard for the workforce and a major loss of productivity for the company as personnel were detained in long lines. An in-house engineering group was therefore asked to study the problem and make recommendations for changes.

The study group found that each workday morning an average of 7 buses and 283 cars and vans arrived at the plant. Upon approaching the entrance gate, the vehicles formed one line to pass through the checkpoint, which was normally manned by two guards during rush periods. The line extended past the available queue space (which could accommodate only 40 cars) and spilled out onto the adjacent highway, causing a major safety problem. Because of the long line, drivers of other vehicles often elected to continue down the highway to a second gate. This option meant additional time and distance for the employees, as well as an unknown wait at the other gate.

The standard analytical queuing model predicted—correctly—that because the service rate at the checkpoint was equal to the arrival rate, the queue would continue to grow without limit as long as

cars kept arriving. This, however, merely confirmed what had already been observed. A simulation was therefore developed. The model was run to reproduce the current situation and then to try out alternatives.

- The first alternative scenario increased the number of guards to three while keeping the single lane of traffic. This approach reduced the maximum queue length from 45.5 to 28, but increased costs.

- The second scenario had vehicles forming two lines, with a security guard assigned to each line. When a bus arrived, it was routed around the two vehicle lines and serviced immediately by one guard while the other guard temporarily worked both lines. This solution produced a maximum queue length of 14 vehicles and a waiting time of only about 12 minutes, compared to over 30 minutes for the existing configuration.

The second scenario appeared to be a good solution involving no additional cost. When it was implemented on a trial basis, the queue length was indeed drastically reduced. The biggest surprise was that the number of vehicles using the gate rose from 285 to 345. Obviously vehicles that had been regularly bypassing the main gate had started using it again. Thanks to the shorter queues, the new system easily handled the increased traffic load (Landauer and Becker 1989).

Different letters are used to designate certain distributions. Placed in the A or the B position, they indicate the arrival or the service distribution, respectively. The following conventions are in general use:

$$M = \text{exponential distribution}$$
$$D = \text{deterministic number}$$
$$G = \text{any (a general) distribution of service times}$$
$$GI = \text{any (a general) distribution of arrival times}$$

We can see, for example, that the Xerox model is an $M/M/1$ model; that is, a single-server queue with exponential interarrival and service times.

12.4   LITTLE'S FLOW EQUATION AND RELATED RESULTS

It can be proven that in a steady-state queuing process

$$L = \lambda W \qquad (12.2)$$

This result states that L, the expected number of people in the system, equals λ, the arrival rate, times W, the expected waiting time. To perform a quick numerical check, see if the numbers derived for the Xerox model (Figure 12.3) satisfy (12.2). The calculation is shown in (12.3).

$$L = 1.0 = 0.05 \times 20 = \lambda W \qquad (12.3)$$

To understand the intuitive foundation for this result, consider the diagram in Figure 12.4. In Scene 1 our hero arrives and joins the queue. In Scene 2 he has just completed service. Assume the system is in steady state. Since in this case the average number of people in the system is independent of time, let us measure this quantity when our hero completes being served. At this time, the number of people in the system is precisely the total number who arrived after he did (i.e., the individuals who arrived during his waiting time). Therefore, if W is his waiting time and people arrive at a rate of λ, we would expect L, the average number in the system, to equal λW.

Equation (12.2) is often called Little's flow equation. Note that it applies to any steady-state queuing process and is thus applicable to a wide variety of models. The proof used to establish (12.2) also shows that

$$L_q = \lambda W_q \qquad (12.4)$$

A numerical check for the Xerox model shows that

$$L_q = 0.5 = 0.05 \times 10 = \lambda W_q$$

which again agrees with the result in Figure 12.3.

One must take some care in applying this result in more complicated cases. It is essential that λ represents the rate at which arrivals *join* the queue. This may be different from the rate at which people actually "arrive." Consider, for example, a queue with an upper

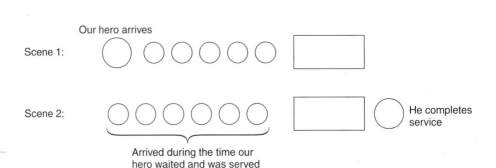

FIGURE 12.4

Little's Flow Equation

limit on the number of items that can wait in the queue (called a **finite queue**). A modern phone system that will hold a certain number of calls (say, 10) in a queue until a service representative becomes available provides a good example of such a queue. In such a system a person who calls and finds the system full simply receives a busy signal—in other words, is sent away. He or she does not join the queue. This is called a **balk.** Thus, if $\lambda = 0.25$ (the arrival rate) and the mean time between calls is 4 minutes, this is *not* the rate at which people *join.* Thus, the relationship $L = 0.25W$ will not hold for this system. Similarly, a customer may tire of waiting in line (or being on hold) and leave without being served. This is called **reneging.** Here again, $L = 0.25W$ will not hold for this system.

Another important general result depends on the observation that

expected waiting time = expected waiting time in queue + expected service time

For the basic model we have already made use of the fact that

$$\text{expected service time} = \frac{1}{\mu}$$

Putting the general result in symbols yields

$$W = W_q + \frac{1}{\mu}$$

For the Xerox model we have

$$W = 20 = 10 + \frac{1}{0.10} = W_q + \frac{1}{\mu} \tag{12.5}$$

Not only does this hold for the basic model, but the general result (equation [12.5]) holds for any queuing model in which a steady state occurs.

Equations (12.2), (12.4), and (12.5) make it possible to compute the four operating characteristics L, L_q, W, and W_q once one of them is known. To illustrate this fact, let us start the Xerox model all over again. We begin as last time using the second formula in Table 12.2 to calculate L:

$$L = \frac{\lambda}{\mu - \lambda} = \frac{0.05}{0.10 - 0.05} = 1$$

Now rather than using the other formulas in Table 12.2 that are specifically for the basic model, we will use the two general results that we have just presented. First, from Little's flow equation (12.2) we know that

$$L = \lambda W$$

Thus, knowing $L = 1$ and $\lambda = 0.05$, we obtain $W = L/\lambda = 20$. Then, turning to (12.5), we see that

$$W = W_q + \frac{1}{\mu}$$

$$W_q = W - \frac{1}{\mu} = 20 - \frac{1}{0.10} = 10$$

Finally, (12.4) shows that

$$L_q = \lambda W_q = 0.05 \times 10 = 0.5$$

This alternative method of obtaining numerical results will turn out to be most useful when analyzing more complicated systems than the basic model.

12.5 THE *M/G/1* QUEUE

While the exponential distribution accurately describes the arrival process in many situations, it may not fit the service process very well. Fortunately, there is a generalization of the basic model that permits the distribution of the service time to be arbitrary. It is not even necessary to know the service time distribution, only its mean, $1/\mu$, and its variance, σ^2. The operating characteristics for the generalized model are given in Table 12.3.

TABLE 12.3 Operating Characteristics for the Generalized Model

CHARACTERISTIC SYMBOL		FORMULA
Utilization	—	$\dfrac{\lambda}{\mu}$
Expected Number in System	L	$L_q + \dfrac{\lambda}{\mu}$
Expected Number in Queue	L_q	$\dfrac{\lambda^2\sigma^2 + (\lambda/\mu)^2}{2(1 - \lambda/\mu)}$
Expected Waiting Time	W	$W_q + \dfrac{1}{\mu}$
Expected Time in Queue	W_q	$\dfrac{L_q}{\lambda}$
Probability That the System is Empty	P_0	$1 - \dfrac{\lambda}{\mu}$

Note that we have made use of the results of Section 12.4 in obtaining all the operating characteristics except for L_q. As a check on the validity of these formulas, suppose that the arbitrary service time distribution is exponential. The variance of an exponential distribution is $(1/\mu)^2$ if the mean is $1/\mu$. Therefore,

$$L_q = \frac{\lambda^2(1/\mu)^2 + (\lambda/\mu)^2}{2(1 - \lambda/\mu)} = \frac{\lambda^2}{\mu(\mu - \lambda)}$$

which is the same result as in the basic model.

As σ^2 increases, L, L_q, W, and W_q all increase. This means that the consistency of a server may be as important as the speed of the server. Suppose you must hire a secretary, and you have to select one of two candidates. Secretary 1 is very consistent, typing any document in exactly 15 minutes. Secretary 2 is somewhat faster, with an average of 14 minutes per document, but with times varying according to the exponential distribution. The average workload in the office is three documents per hour, with interarrival times varying according to the exponential distribution. Which secretary will give you shorter average turnaround times on documents? This can be easily solved with the "MG1" and "MMs" worksheets of SECRETRY.XLS shown in Figures 12.5 and 12.6.

Since Secretary 1 types every document in exactly 15 minutes, σ^2 is equal to 0. The values of the other parameters are $\lambda = 3$ per hour (or 0.05 per minute) and $\mu = 1/15$ per minute. These values are entered in the input parameters section of the "MMs" spreadsheet (cells E3:E6), which automatically incorporates the appropriate values into the "MG1" worksheet. The results are shown in Figure 12.5.

We could also verify this manually by using the formulas shown in Table 12.3.

$$L_q = \frac{(0.05)^2(0) + [0.05/(1/15)]^2}{2[1 - 0.05/(1/15)]} = 9/8$$

$$W_q = (9/8)/0.05 = 45/2 = 22.5 \text{ minutes}$$

$$W = 45/2 + 15 = 37.5 \text{ minutes average turnaround time}$$

Again, using the spreadsheet model for Secretary 2, we enter the parameters as $\lambda = 0.05$, $\mu = 1/14$ per minute, and $\sigma = 14$ minutes. The results are shown in Figure 12.6.

We could also use either the basic model (Table 12.2) or the generalized model (Table 12.3) to verify the spreadsheet answer for Secretary 2. Using the generalized model, we get

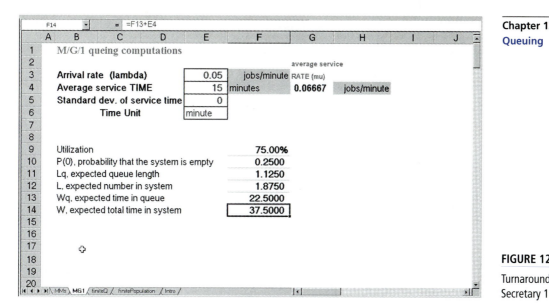

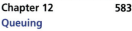

FIGURE 12.5

Turnaround Time for
Secretary 1

FIGURE 12.6

Turnaround Time for
Secretary 2

$$L_q = \frac{(0.05)^2(14)^2 + [0.05/(1/14)]^2}{2[1 - 0.05/(1/14)]} = 49/30 = 1.633 \text{ minutes}$$

$$W_q = (49/30)/0.05 = 98/3 = 32.67 \text{ minutes}$$

$$W = 98/3 + 14 = 46.67 \text{ minutes average turnaround time}$$

Even though Secretary 2 is "faster," her average turnaround times are longer because of the high variability of her service times.

12.6   MODEL 1: AN *M/M/s* QUEUE (HEMATOLOGY LAB)

Recall that as we started this chapter, our stated goal was to attack three particular models at St. Luke's Hospital with queuing models. In the preceding sections we have laid the groundwork for this process. We have introduced, defined, and illustrated the characteristics of the systems that we will consider (e.g., expected number in queue, expected waiting

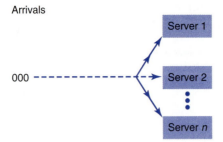

FIGURE 12.7

Multiserver Queue

time, etc.) as well as developed a spreadsheet that can automatically calculate such characteristics. We have also made some general results such as Little's flow equation available for use in future analysis. We are now in a position to turn our attention to Monte Jackson's models.

The system described in Model 1 of Section 12.1, the blood-testing model, is illustrated in Figure 12.7. Note that each patient joins a common queue and, on arriving at the head of the line, enters the first examining room that becomes available. This type of system must not be confused with a system in which a queue forms in front of each server, as in the typical grocery store.

Assume that the interarrival time is given by an exponential distribution with parameter $\lambda = 0.20$ per minute. This implies that a new patient arrives every 5 minutes on the average, since

$$\text{mean interarrival time} = \frac{1}{\lambda} = \frac{1}{0.20} = 5$$

Also, assume that each server is identical and that each service time is given by an exponential distribution with parameter $\mu = 0.125$ per minute. This implies that the mean service time is 8 minutes, since

$$\text{mean service time for an individual server} = \frac{1}{\mu} = \frac{1}{0.125} = 8$$

Note that if there were only one server, the queue would grow without limit, since $\lambda > \mu$ ($0.20 > 0.125$). For a multiserver queue, however, a steady state will exist as long as $\lambda < s\mu$, where s is the number of servers. For example, if we have two servers, we will achieve a steady state because $0.20 < 0.25$ ($= 2* 0.125$).

The Key Equations As before, we want to find values L, L_q, W, and W_q. However, since this is a multiserver queue (not a single-server queue as in the Xerox model), we must use different formulas. To evaluate these formulas it is convenient to start with the expression for P_0, the probability that the system is empty. For this model

$$P_0 = \frac{1}{\displaystyle\sum_{n=0}^{s-1} \frac{(\lambda/\mu)^n}{n!} + \frac{(\lambda/\mu)^s}{s!}\left(\frac{1}{1-(\lambda/s\mu)}\right)} \tag{12.6}$$

and L_q, the expected number of people in the queue, is expressed as

$$L_q = P_0\left[\frac{(\lambda/\mu)^{s+1}}{(s-1)!(s-\lambda/\mu)^2}\right] \tag{12.7}$$

Equations (12.6) and (12.7) and the general results in (12.2), (12.4), and (12.5) make it possible to calculate values for W_q, W, and L for any specified parameter values (μ and λ) and any number of servers (value of s). Again, these new formulas are already entered in the "MMs" worksheet of our queuing template in our workbook (HEMATLGY.XLS).

Example Calculations Assume, for example, that Monte decided to hire two technicians. Then, since $s = 2$, $\lambda = 0.20$, and $\mu = 0.125$, we can put these values into the "MMs" worksheet of HEMATLGY.XLS and get the following results shown in Figure 12.8.

F8 | = =F7*(L1^(E4+1))/((Q3/E4)*(E4-L1)^2)

	A	B	C	D	E	F	G	H	I
1		M/M/s queuing computations							
2			Arrival rate (lambda)		0.2	people/minute Assumes Poisson process for arrivals and services			
3			Service rate (mu)		0.125	people/minute			
4			Number of servers		2	(max of 40)			
5			Time Unit		minute				
6		Utilization				80.00%			
7		P(0), probability that the system is empty				0.1111			
8		Lq, expected queue length				2.8444			
9		L, expected number in system				4.4444			
10		Wq, expected time in queue				14.2222	minutes		
11		W, expected total time in system				22.2222	minutes		
12		Probability that a customer waits				0.7111			

FIGURE 12.8

Results for Hematology Lab with 2 Servers

F9 | = =F8+F6*E4

	A	B	C	D	E	F	G	H	I
1		M/M/s queuing computations							
2			Arrival rate (lambda)		0.2	people/minute Assumes Poisson process for arrivals and services			
3			Service rate (mu)		0.125	people/minute			
4			Number of servers		3	(max of 40)			
5			Time Unit		minute				
6		Utilization				53.33%			
7		P(0), probability that the system is empty				0.1872			
8		Lq, expected queue length				0.3129			
9		L, expected number in system				1.9129			
10		Wq, expected time in queue				1.5646	minutes		
11		W, expected total time in system				9.5646	minutes		
12		Probability that a customer waits				0.2738			

FIGURE 12.9

Results for Hematology Lab with 3 Servers

We see that the utilization $(\lambda/s\mu) = 0.8$ (cell F6) and the probability that the system is empty is 0.11 (cell F7). These two values can be used in equation (12.7) to find $L_q = 2.84$ (cell F8). That is, the expected number of people in the queue is somewhat less than 3. Using equation (12.4), $L_q = \lambda W_q$, we see that, on the average, a patient waits for 14.22 minutes (cell F10) before entering an examining room.

Lastly, the template uses the general observation that

expected waiting time = expected waiting time in queue + expected service time

to calculate that the expected waiting time $(W) = 22.22$ minutes (cell F11). On the average, then, a patient spends 22.22 minutes in the hematology area, waiting for a technician and having tests.

Monte now wants to check what happens if he adds a third or fourth technician (server). These results are shown in Figures 12.9 and 12.10, respectively.

There is a dramatic shortening of waiting time (W_q) with a third server (down to 1.57 minutes), but at the cost of having an extra server. Adding a fourth server doesn't make such a dramatic difference, as it reduces waiting time in the queue to 0.30 minutes. Another factor to take into account is how busy the servers would be in each scenario. We see in Figures 12.8 to 12.10 that the utilization drops from 80% to 53.3% to 40%. The more servers added, the higher the percentage of idle time for the technicians, which could lead to boredom and sloppy work.

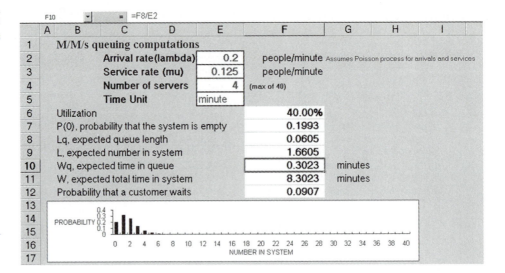

F10   =F8/E2

	A	B	C	D	E	F	G	H	I
1	M/M/s queuing computations								
2		Arrival rate(lambda)			0.2	people/minute Assumes Poisson process for arrivals and services			
3		Service rate (mu)			0.125	people/minute			
4		Number of servers			4	(max of 40)			
5		Time Unit			minute				
6	Utilization					40.00%			
7	P(0), probability that the system is empty					0.1993			
8	Lq, expected queue length					0.0605			
9	L, expected number in system					1.6605			
10	Wq, expected time in queue					0.3023	minutes		
11	W, expected total time in system					8.3023	minutes		
12	Probability that a customer waits					0.0907			

FIGURE 12.10

Results for Hematology Lab with 4 Servers

These calculations provide lots of information to help Monte make his decision. With one technician, since $\lambda > \mu$, the system is unstable and the queue will steadily grow. This could be considered irresponsible. With two technicians, the average waiting time in the queue is less than 15 minutes. By current hospital standards, this is a small and acceptable value. Obviously by adding more servers, Monte can reduce the average waiting time but at significant expense to St. Luke's. If, in some cases the queue gets uncomfortably long with two servers (remember that W_q is an expected value, and the actual time in the queue will vary), the supervisors of the hematology laboratory can temporarily move one of the blood analysts to a technician's position. Monte thus feels comfortable with the idea of hiring two full-time technicians without performing a detailed cost analysis.

We note that this example model is identical to the models that are faced by fast-food franchise managers: how many people to put on a shift to keep the average customer wait below a certain value. McDonalds reportedly figures it will lose a customer if the total wait is more than five minutes.

12.7   ECONOMIC ANALYSIS OF QUEUING SYSTEMS

Monte selected the number of lab technicians to hire by looking at the operating characteristics and using his judgment. This is not an unusual approach in queuing models and is especially common in the not-for-profit sector. Monte realizes that he is balancing the cost of hiring more technicians against the costs he incurs by forcing the patients to wait. The cost of hiring additional technicians is fairly clear. The waiting cost is not.

Monte first notes that the cost to the patient is irrelevant to his decision, except as it affects the patient's willingness to use the hospital. It really does not matter who is waiting—a consultant who charges $250 per hour for his services or an unemployed person with no opportunity cost—unless the waiting time persuades the patient to use another health facility. This observation explains why certain monopolies like government agencies and utilities can be so casual about your waiting time. There is no place else to go!

Besides the possible effect on demand, the hematology lab could cost the hospital money if it reduced the output of the hospital. Suppose, for example, that the outpatient clinics could process 50 new patients each day, but that the hematology lab could handle only 10 patients. (This is clearly an extreme example to establish a point.) In this case, the hospital would be wasting a valuable resource, the doctors and other staff in the clinics, because of a bottleneck in the hematology lab. However, having stated this, it still is not easy to assess an explicit cost of a patient waiting.

Cost Parameters If you are willing and able to estimate certain costs, you can build expected cost models of queuing systems. Consider, for example, the hematology lab model (in general terms any multiserver queue with exponential interarrival and service times), and suppose the manager is willing to specify two costs:

C_s = cost per hour of having a server available

C_w = cost per hour of having a person wait in the system (a very "fuzzy" or qualitative cost)

With these it is possible to calculate the total costs associated with the decision to use any particular number of servers. Let us start by calculating the total cost of hiring 2 servers for an 8-hour day. There are two components:

$$\text{server cost} = (C_s)(2)(8)$$

where C_s is the cost per hour for one server, 2 is the number of servers, and 8 is the number of hours each server works, and

$$\text{waiting cost} = (C_w)(L_2)(8)$$

where L_2 is the number of people in the queue when there are 2 servers. This second calculation may not be as obvious, but the rationale is the same as for the server cost. If there are, on the average, L_2 people waiting when the system has 2 servers, then L_2 times 8 is the average number of waiting "hours" per day. Hence, $(C_w)(L_2)(8)$ is the average waiting cost for the 8-hour day.

If we wanted to calculate the total cost of using 4 servers for a 6-hour day, we would take

$$(C_s)(4)(6) + (C_w)(L_4)(6)$$

or

$$[(C_s)(4) + (C_w)(L_4)]6$$

The term in square brackets, $[(C_s)(4) + (C_w)(L_4)]$, then, is the total cost per hour of using 4 servers.

The Total Cost per Hour We now define

$$TC(s) = \text{total cost per hour of using } s \text{ servers}$$

and we see that

$$TC(s) = (C_s)(s) + (C_w)(L_s)$$

Our goal is to choose s, the number of servers, to minimize this function. We can see that as s increases, the waiting cost will decrease and the server cost will increase. The idea is to find that value of s that minimizes the sum of these two costs.

Figure 12.11 shows the worksheet Monte created called "Econ. Analysis" in his HEMATLGY.XLS workbook to determine the optimal value of s. Unfortunately it is not possible to derive a formula that gives the optimal value of s. (This is in contrast to the EOQ model, where we can find the optimal order quantity, Q^*, with the equation $Q^* = \sqrt{2DC_0/C_h}$, as in Chapter 8.)

In this example, let's put a relatively large cost on waiting and see if the decision changes from Monte's original decision of choosing two servers. We establish C_s = \$50/server/hour and C_w = \$100/customer/hour (see cells B1 and B2), and then we can calculate the server cost and waiting cost for 2, 3, and 4 servers. We'll assume we want to compare the cost over an 8-hour shift (cell E1), and we must enter in cells B6:B8 the values for L (expected number in system) for each value of s we want to explore (obtained from Figures 12.8 to 12.10). We can see that 3 servers minimizes the Total Cost at \$2730 (cell E7).

Next Monte creates a data table to determine the sensitivity of this decision to the "fuzzy" cost, C_w. He decides he wants to explore values for C_w from 0 to \$180. The steps for Monte to do this in his spreadsheet are:

1. Enter the initial value of 0 in cell A11.

2. Click back on cell A11, then choose Edit, Fill, and then "Series."

C7   =$B$1*A7*$E$1

	A	B	C	D	E
1	Cost of server/hour	$ 50.00		# hrs in shift	8
2	Cost of waiting/hour	$ 100.00			
3					
4					
5	Number of servers	Avg. # in queue	Server Cost	Waiting Cost	Total Cost
6	2	4.444	800	3555.2	$4,355.20
7	3	1.913	1200	1530.4	$2,730.40
8	4	1.66	1600	1328	$2,928.00
9					
10	Cost of waiting/hr	4355.2	2730.4	2928	
11	0	$ 800.00	$ 1,200.00	$ 1,600.00	
12	20	$ 1,511.04	$ 1,506.08	$ 1,865.60	
13	40	$ 2,222.08	$ 1,812.16	$ 2,131.20	
14	60	$ 2,933.12	$ 2,118.24	$ 2,396.80	
15	80	$ 3,644.16	$ 2,424.32	$ 2,662.40	
16	100	$ 4,355.20	$ 2,730.40	$ 2,928.00	
17	120	$ 5,066.24	$ 3,036.48	$ 3,193.60	
18	140	$ 5,777.28	$ 3,342.56	$ 3,459.20	
19	160	$ 6,488.32	$ 3,648.64	$ 3,724.80	
20	180	$ 7,199.36	$ 3,954.72	$ 3,990.40	

FIGURE 12.11

Economic Analysis for
Hematology Lab with
2, 3, or 4 Servers

Cell	Formula	Copy To
C6	=$B$1*A6*$E$1	C7:C8
D6	=$B$2*B6*$E$1	D7:D8
E6	=SUM(C6:D6)	E7:E8

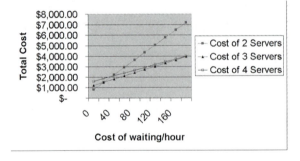

FIGURE 12.12

Graph of Sensitivity Analysis
on Cost of Waiting for
Hematology Lab

3. Click on "Series in Columns," enter a step value of 20 and a terminal value of 180. Click on OK.

4. Enter the formulas for the quantities we want to track (total cost with 2 servers, total cost with 3 servers, total cost with 4 servers) in cells B10:D10. These formulas are =E6, =E7, and =E8, respectively.

5. Highlight the range A10:D20, and click on Data, then "Table."

6. Enter the Column Input Cell as B2. Click on OK.

7. Excel automatically fills in the table as shown in cells A10:D20 of Figure 12.11.

Finally, Monte wants to graph the results of this sensitivity analysis to look for patterns and trends. To do this, he highlighted the range A11:D20, clicked on the Chart Wizard, and then followed the steps to generate the graph shown in Figure 12.12.

We can see that 2 servers is optimal for $C_w = 0$, while 3 servers is optimal from $C_w = \$20$ up to $\$180$. It does look as though 4 servers will become the optimal decision for values of $C_w \geq \$200$.

Let us complete our examination of the hematology lab model with these observations: We have seen how to find values for L, L_q, W, and W_q. These values were then used to select the appropriate number of technicians (servers). This decision might be made on intuitive grounds or on the basis of an explicit economic analysis. Sensitivity analysis is also important to perform, especially on harder-to-quantify parameters like C_w. We now move on to Monte's second model.

12.8 MODEL 2: A FINITE QUEUE (WATS LINES)

Do not be misled by the title of this section. It is devoted to Model 2, Monte's attempt to select the appropriate number of WATS lines for St. Luke's. Fortunately, in this case he can expect help from the telephone company. It has a great deal of expertise in such matters, since queuing models have found extensive use in the field of telephone traffic engineering. The problem of how many lines are needed by a switchboard was typically attacked by using the *M/G/s* model, "with blocked customers cleared." You already know that this model is a multichannel queue with *s* servers (*s* lines), exponential interarrival times for the calls, and a general distribution for the service time, which in this case is the length of each call. The phrase "blocked customers cleared" is queuing jargon. It means that *when an arrival finds all of the servers occupied (all of the lines busy), he or she does not get in a queue but simply leaves.* This phrase clearly describes the behavior of the traditional telephone switchboard. More sophisticated systems now provide for queuing of a finite number of customers, in some cases even providing the lucky customer the opportunity to enjoy a Muzak version of Elton John's "Can You Feel the Love Tonight?" or the "Macarena."

Probability of *j* Busy Servers The problem of selecting the appropriate number of lines (servers) is attacked by computing the steady-state probability that exactly *j* lines will be busy. This, in turn, will be used to calculate the steady-state probability that all *s* lines are busy. Clearly, if you have *s* lines and they are all busy, the next caller will not be able to place a call.

The steady-state probability that there are exactly *j* busy servers given that *s* lines (servers) are available is given by the expression

$$P_j = \frac{(\lambda/\mu)^j/j!}{\sum_{k=0}^{s}(\lambda/\mu)^k/k!} \tag{12.8}$$

where λ = arrival rate (the rate at which calls arrive)

$\dfrac{1}{\mu}$ = mean service time (the average length of a conversation)

s = number of servers (lines)

The expression is called the *truncated Poisson distribution* or the *Erlang loss distribution*. It is noteworthy that although we are considering a general service-time distribution, the value P_j defined by (12.8) depends only on the mean of this distribution.

Consider a system in which $\lambda = 1$ (calls arrive at the rate of 1 per minute) and $1/\mu = 10$ (the average length of a conversation is 10 minutes). Here $\lambda/\mu = 10$. Suppose that we have five lines in the system ($s = 5$) and want to find the steady-state probability that exactly two are busy ($j = 2$). From (12.8) we see that

$$P_2 = \frac{(\lambda/\mu)^2/2!}{\sum_{k=0}^{5}(\lambda/\mu)^k/k!}$$

$$= \frac{(10)^2/2 \cdot 1}{1 + 10^1/1 + 10^2/(2 \cdot 1) + 10^3/(3 \cdot 2 \cdot 1) + 10^4/(4 \cdot 3 \cdot 2 \cdot 1) + 10^5/(5 \cdot 4 \cdot 3 \cdot 2 \cdot 1)}$$

$$= \frac{50}{1 + 10 + 50 + 166.67 + 416.67 + 833.33}$$

$$= \frac{50}{1477.67} = 0.034$$

In other words, on the average, two lines would be busy 3.4% of the time. An alternative way of obtaining P_j that is easy to implement in a spreadsheet (because of its sequential formulation) is as follows:

$$P_i = P_{i-1}(\lambda/\mu)/i$$

So for example, once we know P_2, we can calculate P_3 as:

$$P_3 = P_2(10)/3$$
$$= (0.034)(10)/3$$
$$= 0.1133$$

Likewise, P_4 is found as

$$P_4 = P_3(10)/4$$
$$= (0.1133)(10)/4$$
$$= 0.2833$$

Each successive P_{i-1} is multiplied by (λ/μ) and divided by i to achieve the new P_i.

The more interesting question is: "What is the probability that all of the lines are busy?" since in this case a potential caller would not be able to place a call on the WATS lines. To find the answer to this question, we simply set $j = s$ (in our example $s = 5$) and we obtain

$$P_5 = P_4(10)/5$$
$$= (0.2833)(10)/5$$
$$= 0.564$$

or on the average the system is totally occupied 56.4% of the time.

Again, it is easy enough to implement all these formulas in a spreadsheet. The probability that the system is totally occupied (all servers are busy) is calculated in a new worksheet called "finiteQ" in the workbook WATS.XLS. We can see that the probability that a customer balks with 5 servers is much more easily calculated in a spreadsheet, as shown in Figure 12.13. Of course, we get the same value (0.564 in cell F13). We can then build a data table to determine this value for several different values of s. Figure 12.14 shows such a data table that Monte built for examining the possibility of between 0 and 10 phone lines.

The steps for Monte to do this in the spreadsheet are:

1. Enter the initial value of 0 in cell A23.
2. Click back on cell A23, then choose Edit, Fill, and then "Series."
3. Click on "Series in Columns," enter a step value of 1 and a terminal value of 10. Click on OK.
4. Enter the formulas for the quantity we want to track (probability that a customer balks) in cell C22. The formula is =F13.
5. Highlight the range B22:C33, and click on Data, then "Table."
6. Enter the Column Input Cell as E4. Click on OK.

Excel automatically fills in the table as shown in Figure 12.14. Next we can create column D that calculates the marginal improvement in this probability as we add servers. This is also shown in Figure 12.14. Here it is clear that the marginal effect of adding more servers decreases. For example, adding a second line when there was one in service decreases the probability of the system being busy by 0.089, whereas adding the tenth line when there were already nine in service decreases this probability by 0.059.

Average Number of Busy Servers Another interesting and useful quantity in the design of phone installations is the average number of busy lines. This quantity is called the *carried load* in queuing jargon. If we define $\bar{N}$ as the average number of busy servers, then

F13   ▾   ▪ =VLOOKUP(Q5,U10:V52,2)

	A	B	C	D	E	F	G	H
1			M/M/s with Finite Queue					
2			Arrival rate		1			
3			Service rate		0.1			
4			Number of servers		5	(max of 40)		
5			Maximum queue length		0	(max of 40 combined)		
6			Utilization			87.21%		
7			P(0), probability that the system is empty			0.0007		
8			Lq, expected queue length			0.0000		
9			L, expected number in system			4.3605		
10			Wq, expected time in queue			0.0000		
11			W, expected total time in system			10.0000		
12			Probability that a customer waits			0.0000		
13			Probability that a customer balks			0.5640		

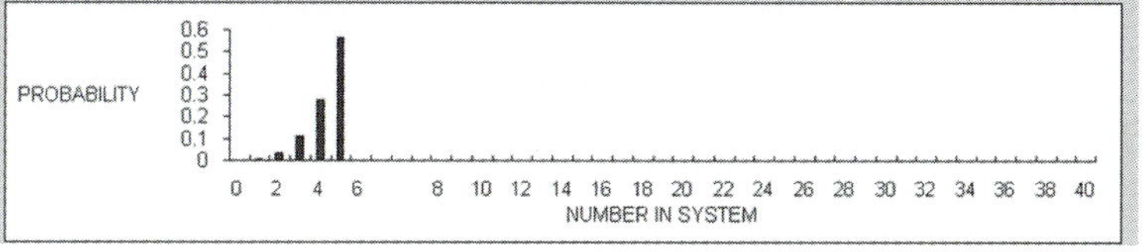

PROBABILITY — bar chart, NUMBER IN SYSTEM (0 to 40)

FIGURE 12.13

Finite Queue Spreadsheet Calculation of Probability that Customer Balks

D24   ▾   ▪ =C23-C24

	A	B	C	D	E
21			Prob. That All Busy		
22		s	0.563952177	Decrease in Prob.	
23		0	1		
24		1	0.909	0.091	
25		2	0.820	0.089	
26		3	0.732	0.088	
27		4	0.647	0.085	
28		5	0.564	0.083	
29		6	0.485	0.079	
30		7	0.409	0.075	
31		8	0.338	0.071	
32		9	0.273	0.065	
33		10	0.215	0.059	

FIGURE 12.14

Data Table for Probability that Customer Balks for Different Values of s

$$\bar{N} = (\frac{\lambda}{\mu})[1 - \text{Prob. That a Customer Will Balk}] \qquad (12.9)$$

Assume now that in Monte's model with WATS lines for St. Luke's, $\lambda = 1$ and $1/\mu = 10$. Thus, if he purchases 10 lines, we see in Figure 12.14 that the probability that all 10 are busy = 0.215 (cell C33). It follows from (12.9) that

$$\bar{N} = 10(1 - 0.215) = 7.85$$

In other words, the entire system will be busy with probability 0.215 or about one fifth of the time and, on the average, almost 8 lines will be busy. After $\bar{N}$ has been calculated, the server utilization can be calculated by dividing $\bar{N}$ by s (the number of servers). Thus, for the situation at St. Luke's, the server utilization is 7.85/10 = 78.5%, which means that each server (on average) is busy 78.5% of the time and idle 21.5% of the time.

Monte feels that ten lines is a reasonable compromise. There does not seem to be a great deal of excess capacity, but, on the other hand, the probability of finding the system busy is in a region (70 to 80%) that he feels is appropriate for the hospital. If he is uncomfortable with this solution, based on a subjective balancing of the number of lines and the probability of finding the system busy, and is willing to specify a cost for each time a caller finds the system busy, he can select the number of lines to minimize the expected cost per hour. He would proceed in the same manner as in the *M/M/s* system of Sections 12.6 and 12.7.

12.9   MODEL 3: THE REPAIRPERSON MODEL

In this model Monte must decide how many repairpersons to hire to maintain 20 pieces of electronic equipment. Repairpersons deal with machines on a first-come (perhaps first-failed is more accurate), first-served basis.

A single repairperson treats each broken machine. You can thus think of the failed machines as forming a queue in front of multiple servers (the repairpersons).

This is another *M/M/s* model, but it differs in a fundamental way from the *M/M/s* system (the blood-testing model) considered in Section 12.6. In this model there is a limited number of items (20) that can join the queue, whereas in the hematology lab model an unlimited number could potentially join the queue.

A queuing model, like the repairperson model, in which only a finite number of "people" are eligible to join the queue is said to have a *finite* **calling population.** Models with an unlimited number of possible participants are said to have an *infinite calling population.*

Consider the model with 20 machines and 2 repairpersons. Assume that when a machine is running, the time between breakdowns has an exponential distribution with parameter $\lambda = 0.25$ per hour; that is, the average time between breakdowns is $1/\lambda = 4$ hours. Similarly, assume that the time it takes to repair a machine has an exponential distribution and that the mean repair time is 0.50 hour (i.e., $1/\mu = 0.50$). This model is an *M/M/2* model with a maximum of 18 items in the queue (20 including the 2 in service) and a finite calling population. In this case the general equations for the steady-state probability that there are n jobs in the system is a function of λ, μ, s (the number of repairpersons), and N (the number of machines). In particular,

$$P_n = \frac{N!}{n!(N-n)!}(\lambda/\mu)^n P_0 \text{ for } 0 \leq n \leq s$$

$$P_n = \frac{N!}{(N-n)!s!s^{n-s}}(\lambda/\mu)^n P_0 \text{ for } s < n \leq N \tag{12.10}$$

We also know that

$$\sum_{n=0}^{N} P_n = 1 \tag{12.11}$$

We thus have $N + 1$ linear equations (N from equation [12.10] and 1 from equation [12.11]) in the $N + 1$ variables of interest ($P_0, P_1, \ldots, P_n$). This makes it possible (if painful) to calculate values of P_n for any particular model. One can see that each model becomes a bit more complex than the previous one, and that the formulas of P_n become more complex.

There are, however, no simple expressions (even by these standards) for the expected number of jobs (broken machines) in the system or for waiting. If the values for P_n are computed, then it is (truly) a simple task to find a numerical value for the expected number in the system. You must just calculate

$$\text{expected number in system} = L = \sum_{n=0}^{N} nP_n$$

If God had intended humans to perform this kind of calculation by hand, He would not have let spreadsheets be invented. Figure 12.15 shows the setup of the "finitePopulation" worksheet in the REPAIR.XLS workbook that can be used to compute values of P_n, the expected number in the system, and the expected number waiting, for a variety of different systems. As shown, the user enters the typical system parameters (λ, μ, and s) in the "MMs" worksheet, then clicks on the new worksheet "finitePopulation" and adds the size of the finite population (cell E5), and the spreadsheet does the rest. In this case, "the rest" consists of numerically evaluating the equations for P_n and using the results to find the expected number in the system. There is one "trick" with this kind of model, when you enter the value for the arrival rate (λ) in the "MMs" worksheet, you actually need to enter N*λ, or the entire population's arrival rate.

As you see in Figure 12.15, for this system, L_q, the average number of machines waiting for service, is 3.348 (cell F8) and W, the expected time in the system, is 1.405 hours (cell F11).

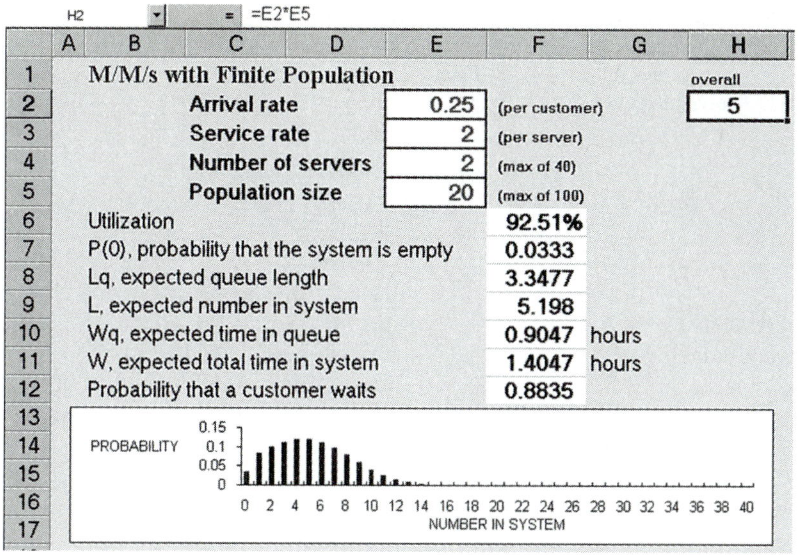

H2   = =E2*E5

	A	B	C	D	E	F	G	H
1	M/M/s with Finite Population							overall
2		Arrival rate			0.25	(per customer)		5
3		Service rate			2	(per server)		
4		Number of servers			2	(max of 40)		
5		Population size			20	(max of 100)		
6	Utilization					92.51%		
7	P(0), probability that the system is empty					0.0333		
8	Lq, expected queue length					3.3477		
9	L, expected number in system					5.198		
10	Wq, expected time in queue					0.9047	hours	
11	W, expected total time in system					1.4047	hours	
12	Probability that a customer waits					0.8835		
13								

PROBABILITY — NUMBER IN SYSTEM (histogram, 0 to 40)

FIGURE 12.15

Finite Population Spreadsheet for the Repairperson Model

The utilization is high at 92.5% and we see from the histogram that there's a 3.3% chance that the system is empty, an increasing probability of there being one machine (8.3%), and the probabilities keep growing for increasing numbers of machines until it reaches a maximum at 4 and 5 machines (they're tied at 11.8%). Then the probabilities decline for machines beyond five.

12.10 TRANSIENT VERSUS STEADY-STATE RESULTS: ORDER PROMISING

It is not always the case that we are interested in steady-state results, or that an analytical model is available to predict the behavior of the queuing system of interest. In this section we will consider a situation in which we are interested in the *transient* behavior of the system and must use simulation to obtain the desired answers.

Manufacturing processes can be viewed as complex queuing systems. Probably the most frequently used management science tool in manufacturing is queuing systems simulation. Larry Lujack, a production planner at PROTRAC and a recent graduate of the University of Chicago's Graduate Business School, is wondering if what he learned about queuing models in his last semester of school could help him decide when to *promise* a new customer order. The order is for 20 units of an item that requires sequential processing at two work stations. The average time to process a unit at each work station is 4 hours. Each work station is available for 8 hours every working day.

By considering when the last of the 20 units will be completed, Larry initially estimates that it will take 10.5 days to process the order. The last unit must wait at Work Station 1 for the first 19 units to be completed, then it must be processed at Work Station 1 and then at Work Station 2. Assuming that it does not have to wait when it gets to Work Station 2, Larry calculates as follows:

$$(19 \text{ units} \times 4 \text{ hours/unit} + 4 \text{ hours} + 4 \text{ hours}) \div 8 \text{ hours/day} = 10.5 \text{ days}$$

However, this analysis is somewhat simplistic. It ignores the variability of the processing times and the possibility of queuing at Work Station 2. Larry feels that the exponential distribution is an appropriate distribution for processing times because the 4-hour figure was arrived at by averaging many processing times that were less than 4 hours with a few processing times that were significantly longer than 4 hours (see Section 12.11). These few long processing times were due to equipment failures at a work station while processing a unit.

D8		=	=MAX(C8,E7)			

	A	B	C	D	E	F	G
1	**Average time at WS1**	4	hours		# hrs/day	8	
2	**Average time at WS2**	4	hours		Finish time	10.5	days
3							
4							
5			**Work station 1**		**Work station 2**		
6	**Unit #**	*Start*	*Stop*	*Start*	*Stop*		
7	1	0	4	4	8		
8	2	4	8	8	12		
9	3	8	12	12	16		
10	4	12	16	16	20		
11	5	16	20	20	24		
12	6	20	24	24	28		
13	7	24	28	28	32		
14	8	28	32	32	36		
15	9	32	36	36	40		
16	10	36	40	40	44		
17	11	40	44	44	48		
18	12	44	48	48	52		
19	13	48	52	52	56		
20	14	52	56	56	60		
21	15	56	60	60	64		
22	16	60	64	64	68		
23	17	64	68	68	72		
24	18	68	72	72	76		
25	19	72	76	76	80		
26	20	76	80	80	84		

Cell	Formula	Copy To
C7	= $B$1 + B7	C8:C26
D7	=C7	—
E7	=D7+$B$2	E8:E26
B8	=C7	B9:B26
D8	=MAX(C8, E7)	D9:D26
F2	= E26/F1	—

FIGURE 12.16

Order Promising Spreadsheet

Next Larry checks to see whether the assumptions of the basic queuing model are met. The output from Work Station 1 are the arrivals to Work Station 2, and the time between arrivals is exponential because the processing time at Work Station 1 is exponential. The service time at Work Station 2 is exponential because it is the same as the processing time. The units are processed on a first-come, first-served basis at Work Station 2, and there is sufficient buffer capacity between the work stations so that the queue size is for all practical purposes infinite. However, the assumption of an infinite time horizon is not met. Larry is interested only in the behavior of the system until "customer" 20 ends its processing.

Larry decides to apply the basic model anyway and use it as an approximation. He approximates the time it takes to process 20 units as follows. First, he estimates that the last unit in the batch of 20 will leave Work Station 1 after $20 \times 4 = 80$ hours. Then this unit will wait in the queue in front of Work Station 2. Finally, it will complete processing at Work Station 2, at which time all 20 units will have been completed. The total time that the last unit spends at Work Station 2 is W. Thus, Larry's estimate is $20 \times 4 + W$. In the basic model, W is given by the formula $1/(\mu - \lambda)$. Larry now realizes his dilemma: μ and λ are equal (1 unit per 4 hours) and the formula is valid only when μ is *greater* than λ.

Larry decides to set up a spreadsheet (ORDER.XLS) to simulate the flow of the 20 units through the 2 work stations. His spreadsheet is shown in Figure 12.16. Larry assumes that raw material is always available at Work Station 1 (WS1) so that the next unit at Work Station 1 can start as soon as the current unit is finished. This means that for Work Station 1 the start time of a unit is the stop time of the previous unit. For example, the formula in

@RISK

File   Edit   Settings   Variables   Execute   Results   Window   Help

Open Save SimSett +Output List   Simulate Results Graph Summary   Hide

Results

Simulation

Simulation #1 of:
order
Iterations= 1000   Simulations= 1
# Input Variables= 40
# Output Variables= 1
Sampling Type= Latin Hypercube
Runtime= 00:00:21
Run on 1/30/97 at 8:46:14 AM

Summary of Results

Cell	Name	Minimum	Mean	Maximum
F2	Finish time	6.628769	12.51541	21.12836
C7	(Input) Stop	2.539721E-04	3.998022	29.93898
E7	(Input) Stop	2.116696E-03	4.000389	29.72219
C8	(Input) Stop	1.332514E-03	3.997909	29.33873
E8	(Input) Stop	3.429307E-04	3.995966	28.89822
C9	(Input) Stop	3.31145E-03	4.003757	33.47185
E9	(Input) Stop	2.170549E-03	3.998415	29.61019

Statistics   Data   Sensitivity   Scenarios

Simulation Statistics

Name	Finish time	Stop	Stop	Stop	Stop	Stop	Stop	Stop	Sto
Description	Output	Expon($B$1)	Expon($B$2)	Expon($B$1)	Expon($B$2)	Expon($B$1)	Expon($B$2)	Expon($B$1)	Exp
Cell	F2	C7	E7	C8	E8	C9	E9	C10	E1
Scenario #1 =	>75%								
Scenario #2 =	<25%								
Scenario #3 =	>90%								
Target #1 (Value)=	18.2796859741211								
Target #1 (Perc%)=	99%								
Target #2 (Value)=									
Target #2 (Perc%)=									

FIGURE 12.17

Statistical Output for Order Completion Model

cell B8 of the spreadsheet is =C7. The start time of a unit at Work Station 2 is either the stop time of that unit on Work Station 1 or the stop time of the previous unit on Work Station 2, whichever is larger. So, for example, the formula in cell D8 is =MAX(C8,E7). The stop time of a unit is just the start time plus the processing time. The finish time in days is shown in cell F2 and is calculated by dividing the stop time at Work Station 2 of the last unit by the number of hours/day (8 in cell F1). The spreadsheet calculates this time to be 10.5 days *if* every unit takes exactly 4 hours at every work station.

To analyze the impact of processing time variability, Larry replaces the constant processing time of 4 at WS1 in his spreadsheet with the appropriate random distribution [in Crystal Ball, he chooses the exponential distribution from the gallery; in @RISK, he enters =Risk Expon($B$1), which samples from an exponential distribution with a mean of 4. This makes the finish time a random variable. Larry would like to know the 99th *percentile* of this random variable (the number that 99% of the time the random variable will be less than or equal to). He could then promise the order in that number of days and be 99% sure that it would actually be completed on time.

Using Crystal Ball or @RISK, it is a simple matter to find any percentile of any random variable in the spreadsheet. Figure 12.17 shows the 99th percentile for cell F2 (the finish time in days) based on 1000 iterations (1000 sets of 40 random processing times— 20 for Work Station 1, 20 for Work Station 2). First, note that the expected finish time ("Mean" for cell F2 in Figure 12.17) is 12.52 days, 2 days longer than Larry's initial calculation. The extra 2 days is the average queuing delay caused by the variability of the processing times. If Larry wants to be 99% sure of having the order completed by the time he promises, he should set the due date to be 18.28 days ("Target #1(Value)=" in Figure 12.17) after the material becomes available at Work Station 1.

The queuing that takes place at Work Station 2 has increased the *lead time* (time from the start of the order to its completion) by nearly 8 days (18.28 less 10.5) over what it would be if there were no variability in the processing times. Figure 12.18 shows the histogram of the finish time, and we can see that the time can vary from 6.5 days up to 21 days.

Even though the basic model was not applicable in this case, it helped Larry to think about the model and to understand this answer from his spreadsheet simulation. Problem 12-29 explores a slightly different situation in which the basic model can be used to estimate the average finish time and the 99th percentile.

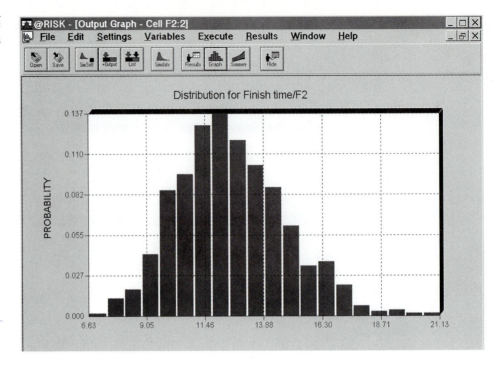

FIGURE 12.18

Histogram of Finish Times for Order Completion Model

12.11   THE ROLE OF THE EXPONENTIAL DISTRIBUTION

There is an enormous body of literature concerning queuing systems, and it is virtually impossible for a manager to be aware of all the results. There are, however, some general considerations that are useful in helping a manager think about the use of queuing models. One such consideration is the role of the exponential distribution in analytic queuing models.

There are essentially no analytic results for queuing situations that do not involve the exponential distribution either as the distribution of interarrival times or service times or both. This fact makes it important for a manager to recognize the set of circumstances in which it is reasonable to assume that an exponential distribution will occur. The following three properties of the exponential distribution help to identify it:

1. *Lack of memory:* In an arrival process this property implies that the probability that an arrival will occur in the next few minutes is not influenced by when the last arrival occurred; that is, the system has no memory of what has just happened. This situation arises when (1) there are many individuals who could potentially arrive at the system, (2) each person decides to arrive independently of the other individuals, and (3) each individual selects his or her time of arrival completely at random. It is easy to see why the assumption of exponential arrivals fits the telephone system so well.

2. *Small service times:* With an exponential distribution, small values of the service time are common. This can be seen in Figure 12.19. This figure shows the graph of the probability that the service time S is less than or equal to t (Prob $\{S \leq t\}$) if the mean service time is 10; that is, $\mu = 0.1$ and $l/\mu = 10$. Note that the graph rises rapidly and then slowly approaches the value 1.0. This indicates a high probability of having a short service time. For example, when $t = 10$, the probability that $S \leq t$ is 0.632. In other words, more than 63% of the service times are smaller than the average service time. This compares to a normal distribution where only 50% of the service times are smaller than the average. The practical implication of this fact is that an exponential distribution can best be used to model the distribution of service times in a system in which a large proportion of "jobs" take a very short time and only a few "jobs" run for a long time.

It is said that engineers think that the whole world is exponentially distributed, while social scientists think that the whole world is normally distributed. A quick and dirty way to check what kind of distribution you have is to see if the average of the data is close to its

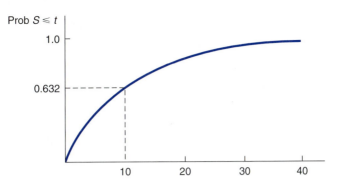

Prob $S \leq t$

1.0

0.632

10   20   30   40

FIGURE 12.19

A High Probability of Short Service Times

standard deviation. If it is, then most likely the numbers are exponentially distributed. If it is 1/3 or less of the mean, it is probably normally distributed.

3. Relation to the Poisson distribution: While introducing the basic model (Section 12.2) we noted the relationship between the exponential and Poisson distributions. In particular, if the time between arrivals has an exponential distribution with parameter λ, then in a specified period of time (say, T) the number of arrivals will have a Poisson distribution with parameter λT. Then, if X is the number of arrivals during the time T, the probability that X equals a specific number (say, n) is given by the equation

$$\text{Prob}\{X = n\} = \frac{e^{-\lambda T}(\lambda T)^n}{n!}$$

This equation holds for any nonnegative integer value of n (i.e., $n = 0, 1, 2,$ and so on).

The relationship between the exponential and the Poisson distributions plays an important role in the theoretical development of queuing theory. It also has an important practical implication. By comparing the number of jobs that arrive for service during a specific period of time with the number that the Poisson distribution suggests, the manager is able to see if his or her choices of a model and parameter values for the arrival process are reasonable.

12.12   QUEUE DISCIPLINE

In the previous sections we specified the arrival distribution, the service distribution, and the number of servers to define a queuing system. Queue discipline is still another characteristic that must be specified in order to define a queuing system. In all of the models that we have considered so far, we have assumed that arrivals were served on a first-come, first-served basis (often called FIFO, for "first-in, first-out"). This is certainly an appropriate assumption for telephone systems and for many systems where people are the arrivals. This is not necessarily the case for other systems, however. In an elevator the last person in is often the first out (LIFO). And in the repairperson model, there is really no reason to fix the machines in the same order as they break down. If a certain machine can be returned to production in 5 minutes, it seems like a good idea to do it first, rather than making it wait until a 1-hour job on a machine that broke down earlier is completed.

Adding the possibility of selecting a good queue discipline makes the queuing models more complicated. Models of this sort are often referred to as scheduling models, and there is an extensive literature that deals with them, which is left to more advanced courses.

12.13   NOTES ON IMPLEMENTATION

The models discussed in this chapter are useful representatives of only a small portion of the broad expanse of queuing models. The results presented here in general require that either the time between arrivals, the service time, or both have an exponential distribution. They are important because they yield tight analytic results and because, in many circumstances, it is reasonable to assume that the arrival process is a Poisson process. In particular, we have noted that a large (essentially infinite) calling population in which individual members of the population decide at random to arrive at service facilities generates an exponential distribution for the time between arrivals. It is not surprising, then, that the analytic models are often used on systems with this type of arrival mechanism. Communication networks (especially the telephone system) and traffic control systems are two important examples of such systems.

Discrete event dynamic simulation (DEDS) is a popular approach for studying queuing models that do not fit the analytic mold. Indeed, current programs such as Arena (by Systems Modeling), Extend, and Alpha/SIM have been created to facilitate the simulation process.

12.14   SUMMARY

This chapter provided an introduction to the subject of queuing. It pointed out that many interesting models can be cast in the arrival/service mode of a queuing model.

Section 12.2 was devoted to the basic model, a single-channel queue with exponential interarrival times and service times. Four system characteristics—expected number in system, L; expected number in queue, L_q; expected waiting time, W; and expected time in queue, W_q—were defined. Formulas were presented for these characteristics as a function of the parameters of the arrival and service processes. A numerical example was presented.

Section 12.3 briefly introduced a system of notation for describing queuing systems. Little's flow equation, $L = \lambda W$, was presented in Section 12.4. This equation plus the general fact that

$$W = W_q + \text{expected service time}$$

were offered as alternative means for computing queue characteristics.

Section 12.5 generalized the basic model to allow for an arbitrary service time distribution. Section 12.6 considered a multiserver queue. Some new formulas were presented. These formulas were combined with results from Section 12.4 to compute numerical results in an Excel spreadsheet for a staffing model in a hematology lab. Section 12.7 was devoted to an economic analysis of the staffing model in the hematology lab.

Sections 12.8 and 12.9 continued the consideration of multiserver queues. Section 12.8 was devoted to an $M/G/s$ system, in which customers who arrive and find all the servers occupied do not wait, but simply leave. This model is particularly useful in the design of telephone systems. A specific example of this type was presented.

Section 12.9 considered the repairperson model, an $M/M/s$ system with a finite calling population. It also illustrates the use of spreadsheets in obtaining numerical results for a particular model.

Section 12.10 showed how a spreadsheet simulation can be used to explore the transient rather than the steady-state behavior of a system.

Section 12.11 described the importance of the exponential distribution in the analytic analysis of queuing systems. It also presented two characteristics of the exponential distribution: the lack of memory property and the high probability of small values.

Section 12.12 briefly considered the topic of queue discipline.

Key Terms

Queuing Model. A model that involves waiting in line.

Channel. A synonym for *server* in queuing jargon (e.g., a single-channel queue is a queue with a single server).

Arrival Process. That part of a queuing model that determines the arrival pattern.

Interarrival Time. The amount of time between two consecutive arrivals at a service facility. Typically a random quantity.

Lack of Memory. A characteristic of the exponential distribution that makes it possible to derive analytic results for many queuing models.

Service Process. That part of a queuing model that determines the service time for each item.

Service Time.   The amount of time that it takes an item to pass through the service facility. Typically a random quantity.

Queue Size.   The limit on the number of items that are permitted to wait in line for service.

Queue Discipline.   The rule used by the service facility to determine which items to serve. First-come, first-served is a typical example.

Operating Characteristics.   Quantities such as the expected number in queue that describe the operation of the queuing system.

Steady State.   A condition in which the probability of viewing a certain situation (e.g., an empty queue) does not depend on the time at which you look.

Finite Queue.   A queue with an upper limit on the number of items that can wait in the queue.

Balk.   A balk occurs when a customer arrives at a finite queue that is fully occupied.

Reneging.   Reneging occurs when a customer leaves a system without being served.

Calling Population.   The number of items that might call on the system for service: thus, a factor in determining the arrival process.

Self-Review Exercises

True-False

1.   **T   F** The number of people in the system means the number waiting in line.

2.   **T   F** The waiting time includes the service time.

3.   **T   F** The exponential distribution is a two-parameter distribution that is defined by a mean and a standard deviation.

4.   **T   F** The mean interarrival time is the reciprocal of the mean arrival rate, and the mean service time is the reciprocal of the mean service rate.

5.   **T   F** The basic model is $M/M/1$.

6.   **T   F** As the number of servers increases, the cost of waiting generally increases.

7.   **T   F** The assumption that the mean service rate is less than the mean arrival rate is enough to eliminate the formation of infinitely long queues.

8.   **T   F** Little's flow equation states a directly proportional relationship between expected waiting time and expected number of people in the system.

9.   **T   F** The notation $G/M/2$ means the service distribution is general, the arrival distribution is exponential, and there are two parallel servers.

Multiple Choice

10.   Which of the following does not apply to the basic model?
  a.   exponentially distributed arrivals
  b.   exponentially distributed service times
  c.   finite time horizon
  d.   unlimited queue size
  e.   the discipline is first-come, first-served

11.   A major goal of queuing is to
  a.   minimize the cost of providing service
  b.   provide models that help the manager to trade off the cost of service
  c.   maximize expected return
  d.   optimize system characteristics

12.   Characteristics of queues such as "expected number in the system"
  a.   are relevant after the queue has reached a steady state
  b.   are probabilistic statements
  c.   depend on the specific model
  d.   all of the above

13.   In Little's flow equation, which of the following is *not* true?
  a. λ is the constant of proportionality between expected number in the queue and expected time in the queue.

  b. λ is the constant of proportionality between expected number in the system and expected time in the system.
  c. λ is the arrival rate, including those arrivals who choose not to join the system.

14.   The most difficult aspect of performing a formal economic analysis of queuing systems is
  a.   estimating the service cost
  b.   estimating the waiting cost
  c.   estimating use

15.   In a multiserver system with blocked customers cleared, which one of the following does not apply?
  a.   When all servers are busy, new arrivals leave.
  b.   Interesting characteristics are the probability that all servers are busy and the average number of busy servers.
  c.   One would never do an expected-cost-per-hour analysis.

16.   For the exponential distribution, which of the following is *not* a characteristic?
  a.   lack of memory
  b.   typically yields service times greater than the mean
  c.   a single parameter

Problems

12-1. Barges arrive at the La Crosse lock on the Mississippi River at an average rate of one every 2 hours. If the interarrival time has an exponential distribution,
  (a) What is the value of λ?
  (b) What is the mean interarrival time?
  (c) What is the mean arrival rate?

12-2. Cars arrive at Joe's Service Station for an oil change every 15 minutes, and the interarrival time has an exponential distribution. The service station is capable of serving up to 48 cars during an 8-hour period with no idle time. Assume that the service time is also a random variable with an exponential distribution. Estimate:
  (a) The value of λ.
  (b) The mean arrival rate.
  (c) The value of μ.
  (d) The mean service time.
  (e) The mean service rate.

12-3. An immigration agent at Heathrow Airport in London could on the average process 120 entrants during her 8 hours on duty if she were busy all of the time. If the time to process each entrant is a random variable with an exponential distribution,
  (a) What is the value of μ?
  (b) What is the mean service time?
  (c) What is the mean service rate?

12-4. For the data in Problem 12-2, determine:
  (a) The expected number of cars in the system.
  (b) The expected number of cars in the queue.
  (c) The expected waiting time.
  (d) The expected time in the queue.
  (e) The probability that the system is empty.

12-5. Consider the immigration officer mentioned in Problem 12-3. Assume that the basic model is a reasonable approximation of her operation. Recall that if she were busy all the time she could process 120 entrants during her 8-hour shift. If on the average an entrant arrives at her station once every 6 minutes, find:
  (a) The expected number in the system.
  (b) The expected number in the queue.
  (c) The expected waiting time.
  (d) The expected time in the queue.
  (e) The probability that the system is empty.

•• **12-6.** Consider the La Crosse lock mentioned in Problem 12-1. Assume that the basic model is a reasonable approximation of its operation. The new estimate of the mean interarrival time for the coming season is 60 minutes for barges, and on the average it takes 30 minutes to move a barge through the lock. Find:
  (a) The expected number in the system.
  (b) The expected number in the queue.
  (c) The expected waiting time.
  (d) The expected time in the queue.
  (e) The probability that the system is empty.
  (f) The longest average service time for which the expected waiting time is less than 45 minutes.

12-7. Consider a single-channel queue. Assume that the basic model is a reasonable approximation of its operation. Comment on the following scheme to estimate λ:
1. Let N equal the number of arrivals between 8:00 A.M. and 4:00 P.M.
2. Set $\lambda = 8/N$.

•• **12-8.** Consider the basic model. Let $\lambda = 5$, and plot the expected number in the system for $\mu = 6, 7, \ldots, 15$.

•• **12-9.** Consider the basic model. Let $\mu = 10$, and plot the probability that the system is empty for $\lambda = 0, 1, \ldots, 10$.

12-10. Use the answers to Problem 12-6 to show that Little's law holds.

•• **12-11.** Use Little's flow equation and the fact that $L = \lambda/(\mu - \lambda)$ in the basic model to derive the expression for W.

•• **12-12.** Use Little's flow equation, the expression for the mean service time, and the fact that $L = \lambda/(\mu - \lambda)$ in the basic model to derive the expression for W_q.

12-13. At the Homeburg Savings and Loan, customers who wish to buy certificates of deposit form a single line and are served on a first-come, first-served basis by a specific bank officer. Service time is normally distributed with a mean of 5 minutes and a standard deviation of 1 minute. Customers arrive at the rate of one every 8 minutes. A time study shows that customers spend an average of 11.833 minutes in the system (i.e., waiting and being served). What is the average number of people in the system?

12-14. A doctor spends, on average, 20 minutes with her patients. If the expected waiting time is half an hour, what is the expected time in the queue?

••• **12-15.** Assume that it is stated in Problem 12-14 that patients arrive at the rate of seven per hour. Comment on this problem.

12-16. Solve (a) through (e) of Problem 12-6 using the generalized model for the case in which the variance of the service time distribution is equal to its mean.

12-17. The Homeburg Savings and Loan uses three tellers on Saturdays. The interarrival time and the service time for customers each has an exponential distribution. Customers arrive at the rate of 20 per hour, and the mean service time is 6 minutes. Customers form a single queue and are served by the first available teller. Under steady-state conditions, find:
(a) The probability that no customers are waiting or being served.
(b) The expected number of people in the queue.
(c) The expected waiting time in the queue.
(d) The expected waiting time.
(e) The expected number of people in the system.

••• **12-18.** The Darden Business School reserves ten high-speed Ethernet connections to the Internet for faculty use. If a faculty member attempts to log on and all the connections are occupied, he is told the server is busy and must try again at a later time. To estimate the system characteristics, the director of information technology wants to know the steady-state values of the characteristics assuming a finite calling population of 100 and an infinite queue. (This is an approximation because faculty who are turned away must try again.) Each faculty member wants to browse the World Wide Web once every 8 hours on average, and the interarrival time is exponentially distributed. Faculty spend an average of 30 minutes surfing the Web once they're connected, exponentially distributed. Find:
(a) The probability that all ports are open.
(b) The expected number of people in the queue.
(c) The expected waiting time in the queue.
(d) The expected waiting time.
(e) The expected number in the system.

12-19. Describe a $M/D/3$ queuing system in words.

12-20. For Problem 12-18, estimate the probability that all connections are busy using the spreadsheet template ("finiteQ") shown in the chapter. (Assume an $M/G/s$ model with blocked customers cleared, an infinite calling population, and an arrival rate 100 times that for a single faculty member.)

••• **12-21.** STECO has 100 sales representatives in the United States. They call orders into a central office where an office worker using the central inventory control system confirms product availability, price, and delivery date. The representative calls directly from the customer's office before signing a contract. Calls are held in a queue and served by the first available office worker on a first-come, first-served basis. Calls arrive at the rate of 40 per hour, and the mean service time is 6 minutes. Management estimates that it costs $20 per hour to have a sales representative call in and order, and $12 per hour to employ an office worker. Model this situation as an *M/M/s* queue with an infinite calling population, and calculate the expected total cost per hour if STECO hires five office workers.

•• **12-22.** Find the expected total cost for the system in Problem 12-21 if STECO hires six office workers.

•• **12-23.** Use the solutions to Problems 12-21 and 12-22 to determine the value for the ratio C_s/C_w for which STECO is indifferent between having five or six office workers.

••• **12-24.** In a particular manufacturing cell, one repairman has to maintain four machines. For the machines, the time between breakdowns is exponentially distributed with an average of four hours. On the average, it takes half an hour to fix a machine.

(a) Find the probabilities that there are 0, 1, 2, 3, or 4 machines under repair.

(b) Find the average number of machines under repair.

•• **12-25.** A telephone exchange has seven lines. Calls arrive at the rate of two per minute, and the interarrival time has an exponential distribution. Conversations have a normal distribution with a mean of 5 minutes and a standard deviation of 1 minute. When all seven lines are occupied, the caller simply receives a busy signal.

(a) What is the probability that exactly three lines are busy?

(b) What is the probability that the system is totally occupied?

(c) What is the average number of busy servers?

•• **12-26.** A market research group has three interviewers located in adjacent booths in a suburban shopping mall. A contact person meets people walking in the mall and asks them if they are willing to be interviewed. They estimate that customers willing to agree to the interview arrive at the rate of 15 per hour, and the interarrival time has an exponential distribution. On the average the interview takes 15 minutes. If all booths are occupied, a person who has agreed to be interviewed will not wait and simply goes about his or her business.

(a) Comment on the following statement: Since $\lambda > \mu s$, this system will grow without bound.

(b) Calculate the probability that exactly one interviewer is occupied.

(c) Find the probability that all three interviewers are occupied.

(d) Find the average number of busy interviewers.

12-27. Consider again the La Crosse lock mentioned in Problems 12-1 and 12-6. Suppose that the mean interarrival time is 60 minutes and that on the average it takes 30 minutes to move a barge through the lock, but that the standard deviation of this service time is 3 minutes. Re-answer (a) through (e) of Problem 12-6. How did your answers change and why?

12-28. Repair requests are handled by a handyman at an apartment complex on a first-come, first-served basis. Requests arrive at the rate of 1 per hour on average. The time it takes the handyman to make a repair is normally distributed with a mean of 30 minutes and a standard deviation of 15 minutes. How long on the average is the time between when a repair request is made and the repair is completed?

•• **12-29.** Larry Lujack is unhappy with the long lead times he is having to quote to customers (see Section 12.10). He feels that PROTRAC is going to start losing business to competitors who can quote shorter lead times. Larry initially assumed that processing times were exponentially distributed. After taking a closer look at the data, he discovers that 90% of the time it takes 3 hours to process a unit on either Work Station (WS) 1 or 2 and 10% of the time it takes 13 hours on either WS1 or WS2. Thus the average time is .9 * 3 + .1 * 13 = 4.0 hours. After talking with the production supervisor of these stations he learns that the high time is due to equipment failure when processing a unit. Invariably, it takes 10 hours to repair the equipment once a failure occurs. Larry has heard that preventive maintenance can reduce the chance of equipment failure and wonders what the value would be of decreasing the chance of failure from 10% to 1%.

(a) Use Crystal Ball or @RISK to find the average time to complete 20 units and the 99th percentile of the time if at each work station there is a 10% chance of equipment failure while processing a unit. How do your answers compare to those of Section 12.10, where the processing times were exponentially distributed?

(b) Now assume that at each work station there is a 1% chance of equipment failure while processing a unit. What is the value of preventive maintenance if it reduces equipment failures to this level?

••• **12-30.** Suppose Larry Lujack has another order to promise (see Section 12.10). This order is also for 20 units, but the average processing time is 6 hours per unit at Work Station 1 and 4 hours per unit at Work Station 2.

    (a) Using the basic model, estimate the average time needed to complete the order.

    (b) Assuming that processing times are exponentially distributed, use a spreadsheet simulation to compute the average time. How does it compare with your answer to part (a)?

    (c) When both arrival and service times are exponentially distributed, then in the basic model waiting plus processing time is also exponentially distributed. Use this fact to estimate without simulation the 99th percentile of the time to complete all 20 units.

    (d) Use Crystal Ball or @RISK to find the 99th percentile of the time it takes to complete all 20 units. Compare with your answer to part (c).

    (e) Suppose that the times were reversed; that is, that processing took an average of 4 hours per unit at Work Station 1 and 6 hours per unit at Work Station 2. Can you use the basic model to estimate the mean and 99% fractile? Why or why not? Use simulation and compare with your answers to parts (b) and (d).

Case Study   How Many Operators?

L. L. Bean realizes the importance of people to its success. The emphasis on training and employee relations tells us that L. L. Bean understands a basic fact of management: People play the major role in determining how well most systems operate. It is obvious that a concern for people in an organization is reflected in the way individuals are treated on a day-to-day basis. It may not be quite as obvious that this same concern plays a fundamental role in designing business systems.

Mail order is the heart of L. L. Bean's business. This business is based on orders received over the phone. Bean's lines are open 24 hours a day, 365 days a year. They have an average rate of 78,000 calls per day. A moment's reflection suggests that these calls do not arrive at a uniform rate. There clearly are seasonal effects, as well as variability during each day. To meet its need for phone operators, Bean offers three types of work arrangements: full time, permanent part time, and temporary. This strategy allows for great flexibility in adjusting the number of operators on duty at any moment. It also provides flexibility for employees, who can structure an arrangement that fits with other demands on their time.

However, the nagging question remains: "How many operators does Bean need, and when?" It seems clear that the company wants to balance customer service against staffing expense. Its approach is to consider each of the 168 hours in a week as a period to be staffed. For each hour, the system is modeled as an *M/M/s* queue—that is, a multiserver queue with exponential arrival and service times and *s* servers (operators). The arrival rate and service rate are estimated from historical data. Cost balancing is done in an intuitive manner: A service standard that management believes is appropriate is the basis of the design. In particular, the Bean system is designed so that no more than 15% of calls wait more than twenty seconds before reaching an operator.

Let's look at a simplified version of this model. Suppose there is a single phone line that answers those who call on the 1-800 phone number in the period of 1 A.M.–5 A.M. (clearly a dramatically slow time). The company has gathered some data on this line (Exhibit 1).

We see that the first call arrives at 0.45 minutes and it takes 3.66 minutes to process the order for a total amount of $51.40. When the next caller phones at 0.945 minutes, the operator is still servicing the first caller, and so he or she gets a busy signal. The spreadsheet (BEAN.XLS) has data for the first 100 phone calls.

Questions

1. Analyze the data to determine what the average length of a call is. What is the average interarrival time? What is the average order amount?

2. Plot a histogram of this data and decide whether you think an exponential distribution is the right one to use for the arrival rate. For the service rate? (HINT: Crystal Ball has a built-in feature to fit data like this to the best distribution.)

3. What percentage of the time is the operator busy?

4. What percentage of the calls are lost due to the busy signal?

The current model gives a busy signal if someone else is being helped, but L. L. Bean could certainly add more lines and place the customers on hold until its only operator were able to get to them. After these extra lines were full, additional callers would then get the busy signal. Assume the fixed cost of each extra line is $35 per month and that the average completed call on the 1-800 number costs the company an additional $2 on average per call. L. L. Bean wonders how to analyze the trade-off if it added the ability for callers to be placed on hold. Assume the profit margin is 45% on all orders placed.

More Questions

5. Use the "finiteQ" template to analyze the increased number of calls that could be handled if L. L. Bean added 1, 2, 3, 4, or 5 extra lines. What extra revenue and profit would each of these scenarios generate?

6. Is the extra profit worth the increased cost? What is the optimal number of lines to add?

EXHIBIT 1 Phone Order Data

E5 = =IF(C5=0,B5+D5,E4)

	A	B	C	D	E	F
1		Arrival		Length of Call		
2	Customer #	(minutes)	Busy?	(minutes)	End Service	Order Amt
3	1	0.452	0	3.660	4.112	$ 51.40
4	2	0.945	1	NA	4.112	NA
5	3	7.553	0	2.086	9.639	$ 58.12
6	4	10.803	0	1.217	12.020	$ 55.86
7	5	12.217	0	1.914	14.131	$ 37.81
8	6	16.426	0	0.319	16.745	$ 61.82
9	7	18.136	0	1.012	19.148	$ 43.44
10	8	25.242	0	6.883	32.125	$ 49.15
11	9	27.753	1	NA	32.125	NA
12	10	30.159	1	NA	32.125	NA
13	11	31.395	1	NA	32.125	NA
14	12	32.042	1	NA	32.125	NA
15	13	32.380	0	0.049	32.429	$ 37.75
16	14	36.803	0	2.165	38.968	$ 56.18
17	15	36.911	1	NA	38.968	NA
18	16	40.864	0	2.434	43.299	$ 63.83
19	17	45.586	0	5.860	51.445	$ 59.18
20	18	46.211	1	NA	51.445	NA

References

Edwin Landauer and Linda Becker, "Reducing Waiting Time at Security Checkpoints," *Interfaces,* 19, no. 5 (1989), 57–70.

Richard Larson, Michael Cahn, and Martin Shell, "Improving the New York City Arrest-to-Arraignment System," *Interfaces,* 23, no. 1 (1993), 76–96.

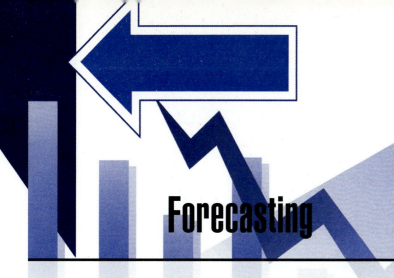

Forecasting

CHAPTER OUTLINE

13.1 Introduction

13.2 Quantitative Forecasting

13.3 Causal Forecasting Models

13.4 Time-Series Forecasting Models

13.5 The Role of Historical Data: Divide and Conquer

13.6 Qualitative Forecasting

13.7 Notes on Implementation

KEY TERMS

SELF-REVIEW EXERCISES

PROBLEMS

CASE STUDY: Bank of Laramie

CASE STUDY: Shumway, Horch, and Sager (B)

CASE STUDY: Marriott Room Forecasting

REFERENCES

APPLICATION CAPSULE   Forecasting Improvement at L. L. Bean

L. L. Bean is a widely known retailer of high-quality outdoor goods and apparel. The majority of its sales are generated through telephone orders via 800-service, which was introduced in 1986. Ten percent of its $870 million in 1993 sales was derived through store transactions, 18% was ordered through the mail, leaving the bulk (72%) from orders taken at the company's call center.

Calls to L. L. Bean's call center fit into two major classifications, telemarketing (TM) and telephone inquiry (TI), each with its own 800-number. TM calls are primarily the order-placing calls that generate the vast majority of the company's sales. TI callers are mainly customers who ask about the status of their orders, report problems about orders, and so on. The volume of calls and average duration of each call are quite different for these two classes. Annual call volumes for TM are many times higher than those of TI, but the average length is much less. TI agents are responsible for customer inquiries in a variety of areas and thus require special training. Thus it is important to accurately forecast the incoming call volumes for TI and TM separately to properly schedule these two distinct server groups.

The real focus of these forecasts is on the third week ahead. Once the forecast is made, the schedulers can make up a weekly schedule for their workers and give them two weeks' advance notice. Inaccurate forecasts are very costly to L. L. Bean because they result in a mismatch of supply and demand. Understaffing of TM agents increases opportunity costs due to diminished revenues from lost orders (a percentage of customers who don't get through im-

mediately, abandon the call, and never call back). Understaffing of TI agents decreases overall customer satisfaction and erodes customer loyalty. In both cases, understaffing leads to excessive queue times, which causes telephone-connect charges to increase dramatically. On the other hand, overstaffing of either group of agents incurs the obvious penalty of excessive direct labor costs for the underutilized pool of agents on duty.

The staff-scheduling decisions would be quite routine if it were not for the erratic nature and extreme seasonality of L. L. Bean's business. For example, the three-week period before Christmas can make or break the year, as nearly 20% of the annual calls come during this short period. L. L. Bean will typically double the number of agents and quadruple the number of phone lines during this period. After this period, there is, of course, the exact opposite problem, the build-down process. In addition, there is a strong day-of-week pattern throughout the year in both types of calls, with the volume in the week the highest on Monday and monotonically decreasing down to the low on Sunday.

Other factors that must be considered by the forecasting model is the effect of catalog mailings or "drops." These are generally done so that the bulk of the catalogs arrive around Tuesday, which disrupts the normal pattern of calls tremendously. Many eager customers order immediately, which creates a surge of new calls around the time of the "drop." The new forecasting model that was developed had much greater forecast accuracy than L. L. Bean's previous approach and was able to produce a mean absolute percentage error of 7.4% for the TM group and 11.4% for the TI group on five years of historical data. So far, on future three-week ahead forecasts, the new forecasting model has had about the same accuracy as that demonstrated on the historical data. The increased precision afforded by these models is estimated to translate into $300,000 annual savings for L. L. Bean through more efficient scheduling (See Andrews et. al.)

13.1 INTRODUCTION

The date is June 15, 1941. Joachim von Ribbentrop, Hitler's special envoy, is meeting in Venice with Count Ciano, the Italian foreign minister, whereupon von Ribbentrop says: "My dear Ciano, I cannot tell you anything as yet because every decision is locked in the impenetrable bosom of the Führer. However, one thing is certain: If we attack, the Russia of Stalin will be erased from the map within eight weeks" (see Bullock). Nine days later, Nazi Germany launched operation Barbarossa and declared war on Russia. With this decision, a chain of events that led to the end of the Third Reich had been set in motion, and the course of history was dramatically changed.

Although few decisions are this significant, it is clearly true that many of the most important decisions made by individuals and organizations crucially depend on an assessment of the future. Predictions or forecasts with greater accuracy than that achieved by the German General Staff are thus fervidly hoped for and in some cases diligently worked for. There are a few "wise" sayings that illustrate the promise and frustration of forecasting:

"It is difficult to forecast, especially in regards to the future."

"It isn't difficult to forecast, just to forecast correctly."

"Numbers, if tortured enough, will confess to just about anything!"

Economic forecasting considered by itself is an important activity. Government policies and business decisions are based on forecasts of the GDP, the level of unemployment, the demand for refrigerators, and so on. Among the major insurance companies, one is hard-pressed to find an investment department that does not have a contract with some expert or firm to obtain economic forecasts on a regular basis. Billions of dollars of investments in mortgages and bonds are influenced by these forecasts. Over 2000 people show up each year at the Annual Forecast Luncheon sponsored by the University of Chicago to hear the views of three economists on the economic outlook. The data are overwhelming. Forecasting is playing an increasingly important role in the modern firm.

Not only is forecasting increasingly important, but quantitative models are playing an increasingly important role in the forecasting function. There is clearly a steady increase in the use of quantitative forecasting models at many levels in industry and government. A conspicuous example is the widespread use of inventory control programs that include a forecasting subroutine. Another example is the reliance of several industries (airlines, hotels, rental cars, cruise lines) in the services sector of the economy on accurate forecasts of demand as inputs to their sophisticated mathematical optimizers used for revenue management (e.g., How much to overbook? How many units should be made available at different discount levels?). For economic entities such as the GDP or exchange rates, many firms now rely on econometric models for their forecasts. These models, which consist of a system of statistically estimated equations, have had a significant impact on the decision processes in both industry and government.

There are numerous ways to classify forecasting models and the terminology varies with the classification. For example, one can refer to "long-range," "medium-range," and "short-range" models. There are "regression" models, "extrapolation" models, and "conditional" or "precedent-based" models, as well as "nearest-neighbor" models. The major distinction we employ will be between *quantitative* and *qualitative forecasting techniques.*

13.2 QUANTITATIVE FORECASTING

Quantitative forecasting models possess two important and attractive features:

1. They are expressed in mathematical notation. Thus, they establish an unambiguous record of how the forecast is made. This provides an excellent vehicle for clear communication about the forecast among those who are concerned. Furthermore, they provide an opportunity for systematic modification and improvement of the forecasting technique. In a quantitative model coefficients can be modified and/or terms added until the model yields good results. (This assumes that the relationship expressed in the model is basically sound.)

2. With the use of spreadsheets and computers, quantitative models can be based on an amazing quantity of data. For example, a major oil company was considering a reorganization and expansion of its domestic marketing facilities (gasoline stations). Everyone understood that this was a pivotal decision for the firm. The size of the proposed capital investment alone, not to mention the possible influences on the revenue from gasoline sales, dictated that this decision be made by the board of directors. In order to evaluate the alternative expansion strategies, the board needed forecasts of the demand for gasoline in each of the marketing regions (more than 100 regions were involved) for each of the next 15 years. Each of these 1500 estimates was based on a combination of several factors, including the population and the level of new construction in each region. Without the use of computers and quantitative models, a study involving this level of detail would generally be impossible. In a similar way inventory control systems that require forecasts that are updated on a monthly basis for literally thousands of items could not be constructed without quantitative models and computers.

The technical literature related to quantitative forecasting models is enormous, and a high level of technical, mainly statistical, sophistication is required to understand the intricacies of the models in certain areas. In the following two sections we summarize some of the important characteristics and the applicability of such models. We shall distinguish two categories based on the underlying approach. These are *causal models* and *time-series models*.

13.3 CAUSAL FORECASTING MODELS

In a **causal forecasting** model, the forecast for the quantity of interest "rides piggyback" on another quantity or set of quantities. In other words, our knowledge of the value of one variable (or perhaps several variables) enables us to forecast the value of another variable. In more precise terms, let y denote the true value for some variable of interest, and let $\hat{y}$ denote a predicted or forecast value for that variable. Then, in a causal model,

$$\hat{y} = f(x_1, x_2 \ldots, x_n)$$

where f is a forecasting rule, or function, and $x_1, x_2, \ldots, x_n$ is a set of variables.

In this representation the x variables are often called *independent variables,* whereas $\hat{y}$ is the *dependent* or *response variable.* The notion is that we know the independent variables and use them in the forecasting model to forecast the dependent variable.

Consider the following examples:

1. If y is the demand for baby food, then x might be the number of children between seven and 24 months old.

2. If y is the demand for plumbing fixtures, then x_1 and x_2 might be the number of housing starts and the number of existing houses, respectively.

3. If y is the traffic volume on a proposed expressway, x_1 and x_2 might be the traffic volume on each of two nearby existing highways.

4. If y is the yield of usable material per pound of ingredients from a proposed chemical plant, then x might be the same quantity produced by a small-scale experimental plant.

For a causal model to be useful, either the independent variables must be known in advance or it must be possible to forecast them more easily than $\hat{y}$, the dependent variable. For example, knowing a functional relationship between the pounds of sauerkraut and the number of bratwurst sold in Milwaukee in the same year may be interesting to sociologists, but unless sauerkraut usage can be easily predicted, the relationship is of little value for anyone in the bratwurst forecasting business. More generally, companies often find by looking at past performance that their monthly sales are directly related to the monthly GDP, and thus figure that a good forecast could be made using next month's GDP figure. The only problem is that this quantity is not known, or it may just be a forecast and thus not a truly independent variable.

To use a causal forecasting model, then, requires two conditions:

1. There must be a relationship between values of the independent and dependent variables such that the former provides information about the latter.

2. The values for the independent variables must be known and available to the forecaster at the time the forecast must be made.

Before we proceed, let's reemphasize what we mean by point 1. Simply because there is a mathematical relationship does not guarantee that there is really cause and effect. Since the Super Bowl began in 1967, almost every time an NFC team wins, the stock market's Standard & Poor 500 indicator increases for that year. When an AFC team wins, the market usually goes down. In 30 years this rule has worked 90% of the time (27 out of 30)! If you really believed there was a significant relationship between these two variables (which team wins the Super Bowl and subsequent stock market performance that year), then in 1997 you would have put as much savings (or you might even have borrowed some money) as you could into the stock market because the Green Bay Packers (NFC) beat the New England Patriots (AFC) early in that year.

One commonly used approach in creating a causal forecasting model is called **curve fitting.**

CURVE FITTING: AN OIL COMPANY EXPANSION

The fundamental ideas of curve fitting are easily illustrated by a model in which one independent variable is used to predict the value of the dependent variable. As a specific example, consider an oil company that is planning to expand its network of modern self-service gasoline stations. It plans to use traffic flow (measured in the average number of cars per hour) to forecast sales (measured in average dollar sales per hour).

The firm has had five stations in operation for more than a year and has used historical data to calculate the averages shown in Figure 13.1 (OILCOMP.XLS). These data are plotted in Figure 13.2. Such a plot is often called a **scatter diagram.** In order to create this diagram (or chart) in Excel, we must do the following:

1. Highlight the range of data (B2:C6); then click on the Chart Wizard.

2. In the first step, indicate that you want the *XY* (Scatter) type of chart (the fifth choice), then indicate you want the first subtype of scatter chart you can choose (only the data points, no lines connecting).

3. In the second step, click on "Next>" because all of Excel's default choices are fine.

4. In the third step, enter the *X*-axis label as "Cars/hour" and the *Y*-axis label as "Sales/hour ($)"; then click on "Next>".

	A	B	C
1	Station	Cars per Hour	Sales per Hour
2	1	150	$ 220.00
3	2	55	$ 75.00
4	3	220	$ 250.00
5	4	130	$ 145.00
6	5	95	$ 200.00

FIGURE 13.1

Sales and Traffic Data

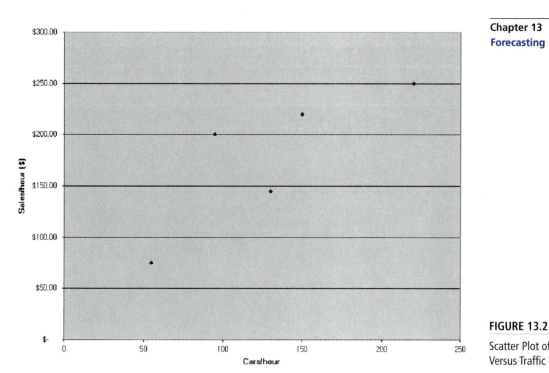

FIGURE 13.2

Scatter Plot of Sales
Versus Traffic

5. In the final step, click on "As new sheet" to place the chart in a separate worksheet called "Chart1"; then click on "Finish."

We now wish to use these data to construct a function that will enable us to forecast the sales at any proposed location by measuring the traffic flow at that location and plugging its value into the function we construct. In particular, suppose that the traffic flow at a proposed location in Buffalo Grove is 183 cars per hour. How might we use the data in Figure 13.2 to forecast the sales at this location?

Least Squares Fits The **method of least squares** is a formal procedure for curve fitting. It is a two-step process.

1. Select a specific functional form (e.g., a straight line or a quadratic curve).
2. Within the set of functions specified in step 1, choose the specific function that minimizes the sum of the squared deviations between the data points and the function values.

To demonstrate this process, consider the sales-traffic flow example. In step 1, assume that we select a straight line; that is, we restrict our attention to functions of the form $y = a + bx$. Step 2 is illustrated in Figure 13.3. Here values for a and b were chosen (we'll show how to do this in Excel momentarily), the appropriate line $y = a + bx$ was drawn, and the deviations between observed points and the function are indicated. For example,

$$d_1 = y_1 - [a + bx_1] = 220 - [a + 150b]$$

where y_1 = actual (observed) sales/hr at location 1 (i.e., 220)
x_1 = actual (observed) traffic flow at location 1 (i.e., 150)
a = intercept (on the vertical axis) for function in Figure 13.3
b = slope for the function in Figure 13.3

The value d_1^2 is one measure of how close the value of the function $[a + bx_1]$ is to the observed value, y_1; that is, it indicates how well the function fits at this one point.

We want the function to fit well at all points. One measure of how well it fits overall is the sum of the squared deviations, which is $\sum_{i=1}^{5} d_i^2$. Let us now consider a general model with

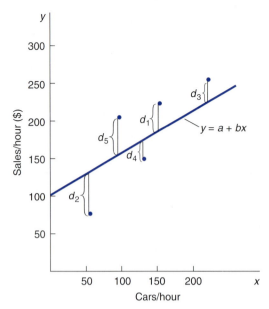

FIGURE 13.3

Method of Least Squares

n as opposed to 5 observations. Then, since each $d_i = y_i - (a + bx_i)$, the sum of the squared deviations can be written as

$$\sum_{i=1}^{n} (y_i - [a + bx_i])^2 \tag{13.1}$$

Using the method of least squares, we select a and b so as to minimize the sum shown in equation (13.1). The rules of calculus can be used to determine the values of a and b that minimize this sum. Over a century ago, mathematicians could not determine the straight line that minimized the absolute deviation or error $| y_i - \hat{y}_i |$, but they could use calculus to determine the line that minimized the squared error $(y_i - \hat{y}_i)^2$. Thus, forecasting has been inundated with "least squares" formulas and rationalizations as to why "squared" errors should be minimized. Today, with the advent of spreadsheets, we are able to use other error measures (e.g., Mean Absolute Deviation [MAD] and Mean Absolute Percentage Error [MAPE]) because spreadsheets combined with the Solver algorithm can now minimize the sums of absolute errors or percentage errors as well. These two, newer error measures will be used and demonstrated extensively in Section 13.4.

To continue with the development of the traditional least squares approach, the procedure is to take the partial derivative of the sum in equation (13.1) with respect to a and set the resulting expression equal to zero. This yields one equation. A second equation is derived by following the same procedure with b. The equations that result from this procedure are

$$\sum_{i=1}^{n} -2(y_i - [a + bx_i]) = 0 \quad \text{and} \quad \sum_{i=1}^{n} -2x_i(y_i - [a + bx_i]) = 0$$

Recall that the values for x_i and y_i are the observations, and our goal is to find the values of a and b that satisfy these two equations. The solution can be shown to be

$$b = \frac{\sum_{i=1}^{n} x_i y_i - \frac{1}{n} \sum_{i=1}^{n} x_i \sum_{i=1}^{n} y_i}{\sum_{i=1}^{n} x_i^2 - \frac{1}{n} \left(\sum_{i=1}^{n} x_i\right)^2}$$

$$a = \frac{1}{n} \sum_{i=1}^{n} y_i - b \frac{1}{n} \sum_{i=1}^{n} x_i \tag{13.2}$$

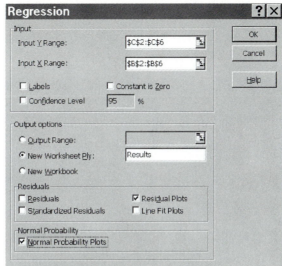

FIGURE 13.4

Excel's Regression Tool
Dialog Box

	A	B	C	D	E	F	G	H	I
1	SUMMARY OUTPUT								
2									
3	*Regression Statistics*								
4	Multiple R	0.8330373							
5	R Square	0.6939511							
6	Adjusted R Square	0.5919348							
7	Standard Error	44.176596							
8	Observations	5							
9									
10	ANOVA								
11		*df*	*SS*	*MS*	*F*	*Significance F*			
12	Regression	1	13275.28502	13275.29	6.802356	0.079813424			
13	Residual	3	5854.714984	1951.572					
14	Total	4	19130						
15									
16		*Coefficients*	*Standard Error*	*t Stat*	*P-value*	*Lower 95%*	*Upper 95%*	*Lower 95.0%*	*Upper 95.0%*
17	Intercept	57.104235	50.38799691	1.13329	0.339471	-103.2530105	217.46148	-103.25301	217.4614796
18	X Variable 1	0.9299674	0.356564467	2.608133	0.079813	-0.204780908	2.06471576	-0.2047809	2.064715761

FIGURE 13.5

Results of Regression

The next step is to determine the values for $\sum x_i$, $\sum x_i^2$, $\sum y_i$, $\sum x_i y_i$. Note that these quantities depend only on the data we have observed and that we can find them with simple arithmetic operations. Of course, Excel is highly capable of doing this for us and in fact has some predefined functions that will do this automatically. To do this, we simply,

1. Click on Tools, then "Data Analysis." (If you don't see this as a choice on the submenu, you will need to click on "Add-ins" and then select "Analysis ToolPak.")

2. Choose "Regression" and it brings up the dialog box shown in Figure 13.4. Enter the *Y*-range as $C$2:$C$6 and the *X*-range as $B$2:$B$6.

3. Indicate that we want the results reported to us in a separate spreadsheet entitled "Results."

4. Click on OK.

The results that are automatically calculated and reported by Excel are shown in Figure 13.5.

There is a wealth of information that is reported to us, but the parameters of immediate interest to us are contained in cells B17:B18. We note that the "Intercept" (*a*) and "X Variable 1" value (*b*) are reported as:

$$b = 0.92997$$
$$a = 57.104$$

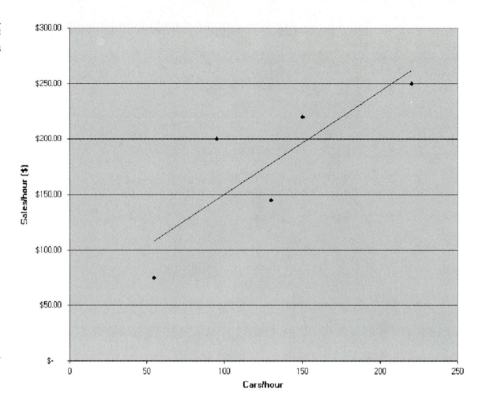

FIGURE 13.6

Least Squares Linear
Trend Line

To add the resulting least squares line we must follow these steps:

1. Click on the worksheet with our original scatter plot (Chart 1).
2. Click on the data series so that they're highlighted.
3. Click on the Chart menu, followed by "Add Trendline."
4. In responding to the type of trendline we want, click on OK (because the linear trend is the default choice).
5. Click on OK.

The result is shown in Figure 13.6 as a solid line.

Let's explore what some of the other information reported in the regression's "Summary Output" means. The "R Square" value reported in cell B5 of Figure 13.5 is given as 69.4%. This is a "goodness of fit" measure, like the sum of squared deviations. This number represents the R^2 statistic discussed in introductory statistics classes. It ranges in value from 0 to 1 and gives us an idea of how much of the total variation in Y from its mean is explained by the new line we've drawn. Put another way, statisticians like to talk about the three different sums of errors (Total Sum of Squares [TSS], Error Sum of Squares [ESS], and Regression Sum of Squares [RSS]). The basic relationship between them is:

$$TSS = ESS + RSS$$

and they are defined as follows:

$$TSS = \sum_{i=1}^{n}(Y_i - \bar{Y})^2$$

$$ESS = \sum_{i=1}^{n}(Y_i - \hat{Y}_i)^2$$

$$RSS = \sum_{i=1}^{n}(\hat{Y}_i - \bar{Y})^2 \qquad \textbf{(13.3)}$$

The ESS is the quantity that we tried to minimize with the Regression tool. Essentially, the sum of squared errors that is left after regression has done its job (ESS) is the amount of variation that can't be explained by the regression. The RSS quantity is effectively the amount of the original, total variation (TSS) that we could remove by using our newfound regression line. Another way, R^2 is defined is:

$$R^2 = \frac{RSS}{TSS}$$

If we could come up with a perfect fitting regression line (ESS = 0), we note that RSS = TSS and the R^2 = 1.0 (its maximum value). In our case, R^2 = .694, meaning we can explain approximately 70% of the variation in the Y values by using our one explanatory variable (X), cars per hour.

Now let's get back to our original task—should we build a station at Buffalo Grove where the traffic is 183 cars/hour? Our best guess at what the corresponding sales volume would be is found by placing this X value into our new regression equation:

$$\text{Sales/hour} = 57.104 + 0.92997 * (183 \text{ cars/hour})$$

This gives us a forecasted sales/hour of $227.29. How confident are we in our forecast? It would be nice to be able to state a 95% confidence interval around our best guess. The information we need to do that is also contained in Excel's summary output. In cell B7, Excel reports that the standard error (S_e) is 44.18. This quantity represents the amount of scatter in the actual data around our regression line and is very similar in concept to the ESS. In fact, its formula is

$$S_e = \sqrt{\frac{\sum_{i=1}^{n}(Y_i - \hat{Y}_i)^2}{n - k - 1}} \qquad (13.4)$$

where n is the number of data points (five in our example), and k is the number of independent variables (one in our example). We can see that equation (13.4) is equivalent to

$$= \sqrt{\frac{ESS}{n - k - 1}}$$

Once we have this S_e value, we can take advantage of a rough thumb rule that is based on the normal distribution and states that we can have 68% confidence the actual value of sales/hour would be within $\pm 1\, S_e$ of our predicted value ($227.29). Likewise we have 95% confidence that the actual value of sales/hour would be within $\pm 2\, S_e$ of our predicted value ($227.29), meaning our 95% confidence interval would be

$$[227.29 - 2(44.18); 227.29 + 2(44.18)] \text{ or } [\$138.93; \$315.65]$$

To be more precise on these confidence intervals requires that we calculate S_p (the standard prediction error), which is always larger than S_e but is more complicated to derive and beyond our scope of an introductory coverage. The intuition to remember here is that when we're trying to predict Y based on values of X that are near $\bar{X}$ then S_p is very close to S_e. The farther away the X values get from $\bar{X}$, the larger the difference between S_p and S_e.

Another value of interest in the Summary report is the t-statistic for the X variable and its associated values (cells D18:G18). The t-statistic is given in cell D18 as 2.61. The P-value in cell E18 is 0.0798. We desire to have the P-value less than 0.05. This would represent that we have at least 95% confidence that the slope parameter (b) is statistically significantly different than zero (a zero slope would be a flat line and indicate no relationship between Y and X). In fact, Excel provides the 95% confidence interval for its estimate of b. In our case, we have 95% confidence the true value for b is between -0.205 and 2.064 (cells F18 and G18) and thus we can't exclude the possibility that the true value of b might be zero.

Lastly, the F-significance reported in cell F12 is identical to the P-value for the t-statistic (0.0798) and will always be so if there is only a single independent variable. In the case of more than one X variable, the F-significance tests the hypothesis that all the X variable parameters as a group are statistically significantly different than zero.

One final note as you move into multiple regression models: As you add other X variables, the R^2 statistic will always increase, meaning the RSS has increased. But in order to keep from overmassaging the data, you should keep an eye on the Adjusted R^2 statistic (cell B6) as the more reliable indicator of the true goodness of fit because it compensates for the reduction in the ESS due to the addition of more independent variables. Thus it may report a decreased adjusted R^2 value even though R^2 has increased, unless the improvement in RSS is more than compensated for by the addition of the new independent variables.

We should point out that we could have obtained the same parameter values for a and b by using the Solver algorithm (set our objective function as the sum of the squared deviations, let the decision variables be a and b and then turn the Solver loose in trying to minimize our nonlinear objective function).

Note that our forecast also "predicts" earning \$57.10 (the value for a) when no cars arrive (i.e., cars/hour = 0). At this point it might be well to establish limits on the range over which we feel that the forecast is valid (e.g., from 30 to 250 cars) or seek a logical explanation. Many service stations have convenience foods and also do a walk-in business. Thus "a" might represent the amount of walk-in business (which would be constant regardless of how much car traffic there is).

Fitting a Quadratic Function The example above has shown how to make *linear fits* for the case of one independent variable. But the method of least squares can be used with any number of independent variables and with any functional form. As an illustration, suppose that we wish to fit a quadratic function of the form

$$y = a_0 + a_1 x + a_2 x^2$$

to our previous data with the method of least squares. Our goal, then, is to select a_0, a_1, and a_2 in order to minimize the sum of squared deviations, which is now

$$\sum_{i=1}^{5} (y_i - [a_0 + a_1 x_i + a_2 x_i^2])^2 \tag{13.5}$$

We proceed by setting the partial derivatives with respect to a_0, a_1, and a_2 equal to zero. This gives the equations

$$5a_0 + \left(\sum x_i\right) a_1 + \left(\sum x_i^2\right) a_2 = \sum y_i$$

$$\left(\sum x_i\right) a_0 + \left(\sum x_i^2\right) a_1 + \left(\sum x_i^3\right) a_2 = \sum x_i y_i$$

$$\left(\sum x_i^2\right) a_0 + \left(\sum x_i^3\right) a_1 + \left(\sum x_i^4\right) a_2 = \sum x_i^2 y_i \tag{13.6}$$

This is a simple set of three linear equations in three unknowns. Thus, the general name for this least squares curve fitting is "Linear Regression." The term *linear* comes not from a straight line being fit, but from the fact that simultaneous linear equations are being solved.

Finding the numerical values of the coefficients is a straightforward task in a spreadsheet. This time instead of using the "Regression" tool in Excel, we will demonstrate the use of the Solver algorithm. We use the new spreadsheet called "Quadratic" in the same OILCOMP.XLS workbook that is shown in Figure 13.7.

The steps to find the optimal values for the parameters (a_0, a_1, and a_2) are indicated below:

1. Click on the Tools menu, and then "Solver."

2. Complete the Solver Parameters dialog box, as shown in Figure 13.8. Click on "Solve." We are basically setting up an unconstrained, nonlinear optimization model, where the three parameters (cells B2:B4) are our decision variables (changing cells) and our objective function is to minimize the sum of squared errors (cell F13).

D7	▼	=	=$B$2+$B$3*B7+$B$4*B7^2		

	A	B	C	D	E	F
1	Parameters					
2	a0 =	0				
3	a1 =	0				
4	a2 =	0				
5				Forecast		
6	Station	Cars per Hour	Sales per Hour	Sales/Hour	Error	Squared Error
7	1	150	$ 220.00	0	220.00	48,400
8	2	55	$ 75.00	0	75.00	5,625
9	3	220	$ 250.00	0	250.00	62,500
10	4	130	$ 145.00	0	145.00	21,025
11	5	95	$ 200.00	0	200.00	40,000
12						
13					SUM=	177,550

Cell	Formula	Copy To
D7	$= \$B\$2+\$B\$3*B7+\$B\$4 \times B7 \wedge 2$	D8:D11
E7	$= C7-D7$	E8:E11
F7	$= E7 \wedge 2$	F8:F11
F13	$= SUM(F7:F11)$	—

FIGURE 13.7

Quadratic Trend Spreadsheet

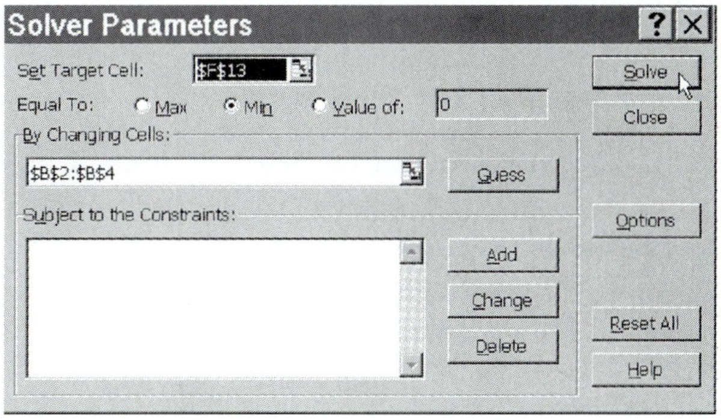

Solver Parameters ? ✕

Set Target Cell: $F$13

Equal To: ○ Max ● Min ○ Value of: 0

By Changing Cells:

$B$2:$B$4   Guess

Subject to the Constraints:

Add
Change
Delete

Solve
Close
Options
Reset All
Help

FIGURE 13.8

Solver Dialog Box for Quadratic Trend

3. When Solver returns its dialog box showing that it has found a solution, click on OK and you see the results shown in Figure 13.9.

We see the optimal parameters are:

$$a_0 = -13.586$$
$$a_1 = 2.147$$
$$a_2 = -0.0044$$

which yields a sum of squared errors of 4954. *Note:* Excel has a built-in function to help us calculate this quantity directly (i.e., we could do it without columns E and F) known as =sumxmy2 (range 1, range 2) and it is shown in cell F15 of Figure 13.9. The function takes the values in the second range and subtracts them from the values in the first range (one at a time), squares the difference, and sums these squared differences up for all the values in the range. To plot the original data and this quadratic function, we use the Chart Wizard with the following steps:

1. Highlight the original range of data (B7:C11) in the "Quadratic" spreadsheet, then click on the Chart Wizard.

2. In the first step, indicate that you want the *XY* (Scatter) type of chart (the fifth choice), then indicate that you want the first subtype of scatter chart you can choose (only the data points, no lines connecting).

| F15 | ▼ | = | =SUMXMY2(C7:C11,D7:D11) |

	A	B	C	D	E	F
1	**Parameters**					
2	*a0* =	-13.58618463				
3	*a1* =	2.146774483				
4	*a2* =	-0.004381271				
5				**Forecast**		
6	**Station**	**Cars per Hour**	**Sales per Hour**	**Sales/Hour**	**Error**	**Squared Error**
7	1	150	$ 220.00	209.8513819	10.15	103
8	2	55	$ 75.00	91.23306603	(16.23)	264
9	3	220	$ 250.00	246.6506672	3.35	11
10	4	130	$ 145.00	191.451012	(46.45)	2,158
11	5	95	$ 200.00	150.8164171	49.18	2,419
12						
13					**SUM=**	4,954
14						
15				(Nifty formula)	**SSE =**	4954.4
16						

Cell	Formula		Copy To
D7	= \$B\$2+\$B\$3*B7+\$B\$4+B7^2		D8:D11
E7	= C7−D7		E8:E11
F7	= E7^2		F8:F11
F13	= SUM(F7:F11)		—
F15	= SUMXMY2(C7:C11,D7:D11)		—

FIGURE 13.9

Results for Optimal
Quadratic Parameters

3. In the second step, click on "Next>" because all of Excel's default choices are fine.

4. In the third step, enter the *X*-axis label as "Cars/hour" and the *Y*-axis label as "Sales/hour($)"; then click on "Next>."

5. In the final step, click on "As new sheet" to place the chart in a separate worksheet called "Chart2"; then click on "Finish."

6. Click on the data series in Chart2 so that they're highlighted.

7. Click on the Chart menu, followed by "Add Trendline."

8. In responding to the type of trendline we want, click on "Polynomial" of order 2.

9. Click on OK and you get the graph shown in Figure 13.10.

To do this same thing with the "Regression" tool, you must first create a column for a second independent variable, $X_2 = X_1^2$, and then regress Y (Sales/hr) on both X_1 (Cars/hr) and X_2 ([Cars/hr]^2)]. We leave this as an exercise for the student (see Problem 13-23).

Comparing the Linear and Quadratic Fits In the method of least squares, we have selected the sum of the squared deviations as our measure of "goodness of fit." We can thus compare the linear and the quadratic fit with this criterion. In order to make this comparison, we have to go back and use the linear regression "Results" spreadsheet and make the corresponding calculation in the original "Data" spreadsheet. This work is shown in Figure 13.11.

We see that the sum of the squared deviations for the quadratic function is indeed smaller than that for the linear function (i.e., 4954 < 5854.7). Indeed, the quadratic gives us roughly a 15% decrease in the sum of squared deviations. The general result has to hold in this direction; that is, the quadratic function must always fit better than the linear function. A linear function is, after all, a special type of a quadratic function (one in which $a_2 = 0$). It follows then that the best quadratic function must be at least as good as the best linear function.

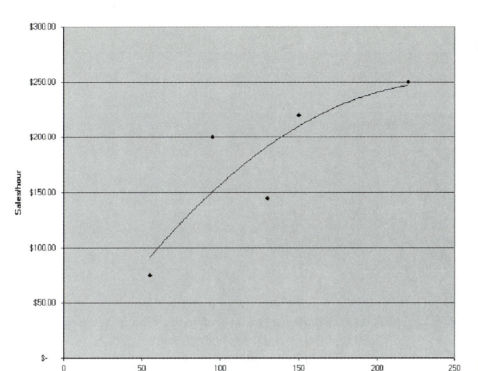

FIGURE 13.10

Quadratic Least Squares
Function Fit to Data

D2		=	=Results!$B$17+Results!$B$18*B2		
	A	B	C	D	E	F
1	Station	Cars per Hour	Sales per Hour	Forecast Sales per Hour	Error	Squared Error
2	1	150	$ 220.00	196.60	23.40	547.59
3	2	55	$ 75.00	108.25	(33.25)	1,105.72
4	3	220	$ 250.00	261.70	(11.70)	136.82
5	4	130	$ 145.00	178.00	(33.00)	1,089.00
6	5	95	$ 200.00	145.45	54.55	2,975.58
7						
8					SUM=	5,854.71

Cell	Formula	Copy To
D2	= Results!$B$17+Results!$B$18*B2	D3:D6
E2	= C2−D2	E3:E6
F2	= E2^2	F3:F6
F8	= SUM(F2:F6)	—

FIGURE 13.11

Sum of Squared Errors
Calculation for Linear
Regression Results

WHICH CURVE TO FIT?

If a quadratic function is at least as good as a linear function, why not choose an even more general form, such as a cubic or a quartic, thereby getting an even better fit? In principle the method can be applied to any specified functional form. In practice, functions of the form (again using only a single independent variable for illustrative purposes)

$$y = a_0 + a_1x + a_2x^2 + \ldots + a_nx^n$$

are often suggested. Such a function is called a **polynomial of degree *n*,** and it represents a broad and flexible class of functions (for $n = 2$ we have a quadratic, $n = 3$ a cubic, $n = 4$ a quartic, etc.). One can obtain an amazing variety of curves with polynomials, and thus they are popular among curve fitters. One must, however, proceed with caution when fitting data with a polynomial function. Under quite general conditions it is possible, for example, to find a $(k − 1)$-degree polynomial that will perfectly fit k data points. To be more

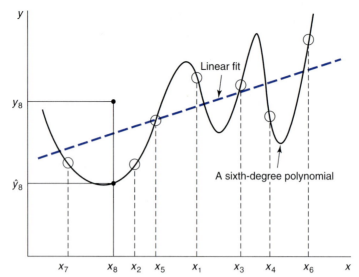

FIGURE 13.12

A Sixth-Degree Polynomial
Produces a Perfect Fit

specific, suppose that we have on hand seven historical observations, denoted (x_i, y_i), $i = 1, 2, \ldots, 7$. It is possible to find a sixth-degree polynomial

$$y = a_0 + a_1 x + a_2 x^2 + \ldots + a_6 x^6$$

that exactly passes through each of these seven data points (see Figure 13.12).

This perfect fit (giving zero for the sum of squared deviations), however, is deceptive, for it does not imply as much as you may think about the predictive value of the model for use in future forecasting. For example, refer again to Figure 13.12. When the independent variable (at some future time) assumes the value x_8, the true value of y might be given by y_8, whereas the predicted value is $\hat{y}_8$. Despite the previous perfect fit, the forecast is very inaccurate. In this situation a linear fit (i.e., a first-degree polynomial) such as the one indicated in Figure 13.12 might well provide more realistic forecasts, although by the criterion of least squares it does not "fit" the historical data nearly as well as the sixth-degree polynomial. Also, note that the polynomial fit has hazardous extrapolation properties. That is, the polynomial "blows up" at its extremes; x values only slightly larger than x_6 produce very large predicted y's. Looking at Figure 13.12, you can understand why high-order polynomial fits are referred to as "wild."

One way of finding which fit is truly "better" is to use a different standard of comparison, the "mean squared error" or MSE—which is the sum of squared errors/(number of points − number of parameters). For our linear fit, the number of parameters estimated is 2 (a, b), so MSE = 5854/(5 − 2) = 1951.3; and for the quadratic fit, the MSE = 4954/(5 − 3) = 2477.0. Thus, the MSE gets worse in this case, even though the total sum of squares will always be less or the same for a higher-order fit. (*Note:* This is similar to how the adjusted R^2 statistic works.) We still have to be somewhat careful even with this new standard of comparison, because when there is a perfect fit, both the total sum of squares and MSE will be 0.00. Because of this, most prepackaged forecasting programs will fit only up through a cubic polynomial, since higher degrees simply don't reflect the general trend of actual data.

What Is a Good Fit?　The intent of the paragraphs above is to suggest that a model that has given a good fit to historical data may provide a terrible fit to future data. That is, a good historical fit may have poor predictive power. So what is a good fit?

The answer to this question involves considerations both philosophic and technical. It depends, first, on whether one has some idea about the underlying real-world process that relates the y's and the x's. To be an effective forecasting device, the forecasting function must to some extent capture important features of that process. The more one knows, the better one can do. To go very far into this topic, one must employ a level of statistics that would extend well beyond this introductory coverage. For our purposes it suffices to state that knowledge of the underlying process is typically phrased in statistical language. For example, linear curve fitting, in the statistical context, is called **linear regression.** If the statistical assumptions about the linear regression model are precisely satisfied (e.g., errors are normally distributed around the regression line), then in a precise and well-defined sense statisticians can prove that the linear fit is the "best possible fit."

But in a real sense, this begs the question. In the real world one can never be completely certain about the underlying process. It is never "served to us on a silver platter." One only has some (and often not enough) historical data to observe. The question then becomes: How much confidence can we have that the underlying process is one that satisfies a particular set of statistical assumptions? Fortunately, quantitative measures do exist. Statistical analysis, at least for simple classes of models like linear regression, can reveal how well the historical data do indeed satisfy those assumptions.

And what if they do not? One tries a different model. Let us regress (digress) for a moment to recall some of the philosophy involved with the use of optimization models (which is exactly what least squares fitting is—an unconstrained nonlinear optimization). There is an underlying real-world problem. The model is a selective representation of that problem. How good is that model, or representation? One usually does not have precise measures, and many paragraphs in this text have been devoted to the role of managerial judgment and sensitivity analysis in establishing a model's credibility. Ideally, to test the goodness of a model, one would like to have considerable experience with its use. If, in repeated use, we observe that the model performs well, then our confidence is high.[1] However, what confidence can we have at the outset, without experience?

Validating Models One benchmark, which brings us close to the current context, is to ask the question: Suppose the model had been used to make past decisions; how well would the firm have fared? This approach "creates" experience by *simulating* the past. This is often referred to as **validation** of the model. One way to use this approach, in the forecasting context, is called "divide and conquer" and is discussed in Section 13.5. Typically, one uses only a portion of the historical data to create the model—for example, to fit a polynomial of a specified degree. One can then use the remaining data to see how well the model would have performed. This procedure is specified in some detail in Section 13.5. At present, it suffices to conclude by stressing that in curve fitting the question of "goodness of fit" is both philosophic and technical, and you do not want to lose sight of either issue.

SUMMARY

A causal forecasting model uses one or more independent variables to forecast the value of a dependent or response variable. The model is often created by fitting a curve to an existing set of data and then using this curve to determine the response associated with new values of the independent variable(s). The method of least squares is a particularly useful method of fitting a curve. We illustrated the general concept of this method and considered the specific problems of fitting a straight line, a quadratic function, and higher-order polynomials to a set of data. For simplicity, all of our illustrations involved a single independent variable but the same techniques apply to models with many variables.

These few examples of causal forecasting models demonstrate that even in simple models the required calculations are tedious. The wide availability of spreadsheets has reduced the problem of performing the necessary calculations so that it is insignificant. The important questions are: What model, if any, can do a reliable job of forecasting, and are the data required for such a model available and reliable?

---

[1] No matter how much observation seems to substantiate the model, we can never conclude that the model is "true." Recall the high degree of "substantiation" of the flat earth model. "If you leave port and sail westward you will eventually fall off the earth and never be seen again."

We have discussed both philosophic and technical issues that the "curve fitting" manager must address. Comments on the role of causal models in managerial decision making are reserved for Section 13.7. We now turn our attention to time-series analysis.

13.4   TIME-SERIES FORECASTING MODELS

Another class of quantitative forecasting techniques comprises the so-called **time-series forecasting** models. These models produce forecasts by *extrapolating the historical behavior of the values of a particular single variable of interest.* For example, one may be interested in the sales for a particular item, or a fluctuation of a particular market price with time. Time-series models use a technique to *extrapolate* the historical behavior into the future. Figuratively, the series is being lifted into the future "by its own bootstraps." Time-series data are historical data in chronological order, with only one value per time period. Thus, the data for the service station from the previous section are *not* time-series data and cannot be analyzed using the techniques in this section.

EXTRAPOLATING HISTORICAL BEHAVIOR

In order to provide several examples of bootstrap methods, let us suppose that we have on hand from the *Wall Street Journal* the daily closing prices of a March cocoa futures contract for the past 12 days, including today, and that from this past stream of data we wish to predict tomorrow's closing price. Several possibilities come to mind:

1. If it is felt that all historical values are important, and that all have equal predictive power, we might take the *average* of the past 12 values as our best forecast for tomorrow.

2. If it is felt that today's value (the 12th) is far and away the most important, this value might be our best prediction for tomorrow.

3. It may be felt that in the current "fast-trending market" the first six values are too antiquated, but the most recent six are important and each has equal predictive power. We might then take the average of the most recent six values as our best estimate for tomorrow.

4. It may be felt that *all* past values contain useful information, but today's (the 12th observation) is the most important of all, and, in succession, the 11th, 10th, 9th, and so on, observations have decreasing importance. In this case we might take a *weighted average* of all 12 observations, with increasing weights assigned to each value in the order 1 through 12 and with the 12 weights summing to 1.

5. We might actually plot the 12 values as a function of time and then draw a linear "trend line" that lies close to these values. This line might then be used to predict tomorrow's value.

Let us now suppose that tomorrow's actual closing price is observed and consider our forecast for the day after tomorrow, using the 13 available historical values. Methods 1 and 2 can be applied in a straightforward manner. Now consider method 3. In this case we might take tomorrow's actual observed price, together with today's and the previous four prices, to obtain a new 6-day average. This technique is called *a simple 6-period moving average,* and it will be discussed in more detail in the following sections.

Let us now refer to method 4. In this instance, since we employ all past values, we would be using 13 rather than 12 values, with new weights assigned to these values. An important class of techniques called *exponential smoothing models* operate in this fashion. These models will also be explored in the ensuing discussion.

Finally, we shall explore in more detail the technique mentioned in item 5. This provides another illustration of forecasting by a *curve fitting method.*

We mention at this point that whenever we have values for a particular (single) variable of interest, which can be plotted against time, these values are often termed a *time-series,* and any method used to analyze and extrapolate such a series into the future falls within the general category of *time-series analysis.* This is currently a very active area of research in statistics and management science. We will be able to barely scratch the surface in terms of formal development. Nevertheless, some of the important concepts, from the manager's viewpoint, will be developed. In this section, we will use the error measures of

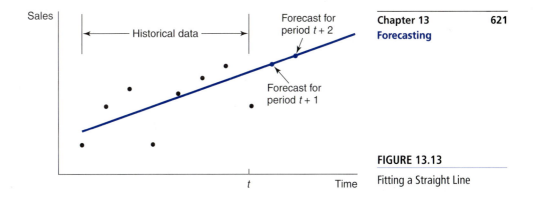

FIGURE 13.13

Fitting a Straight Line

MAD (mean absolute deviation) and MAPE (mean absolute percentage error) instead of mean squared error (MSE), which was used extensively in Section 13.3.

CURVE FITTING

We have already considered curve fitting in the discussion of causal models. The main difference in the time-series context is that the independent variable is time. The historical observations of the dependent variable are plotted against time, and a curve is then fitted to these data. The curve is then extended into the future to yield a forecast. In this context, extending the curve simply means evaluating the derived function for larger values of t, the time. This procedure is illustrated for a straight line in Figure 13.13.

The use of time as an independent variable has more serious implications than altering a few formulas, and a manager should understand the important difference between a causal model using curve fitting and a time-series model using curve fitting. One of the assumptions with curve fitting is that all the data are equally important (weighted). This method produces a very stable forecast that is fairly insensitive to slight changes in the data.

The mathematical techniques for fitting the curves are identical, but the rationale, or philosophy, behind the two models is basically quite different. To understand this difference, think of the values of y, the variable of interest, as being produced by a particular underlying process or system. The causal model assumes that as the underlying system changes to produce different values of y, it will also produce corresponding differences in the independent variables and thus, by knowing the independent variables, a good forecast of y can be deduced. The time-series model assumes that the system that produces y is essentially *stationary* (or *stable*) and will continue to act in the future as it has in the past. Future patterns in the movement of y will closely resemble past patterns. This means that time is a surrogate for many factors that may be difficult to measure but that seem to vary in a consistent and systematic manner with time. If the system that produces y significantly changes (e.g., because of changes in environment, technology, or government policy), then the assumption of a *stationary process* is invalid and consequently a forecast based on time as an independent variable is apt to be badly in error.

Just as for causal models, it is, of course, possible to use other than linear functions to extrapolate a series of observations (i.e., to forecast the future). As you might imagine, one alternative that is often suggested in practice is to assume that y is a higher-order polynomial in t, that is,

$$y_t = b_0 + b_1 t + b_2 t^2 + \ldots + b_k t^k$$

As before, appropriate values for the parameters $b_0, b_1, \ldots, b_k$ must be mathematically derived from the values of previous observations. The higher-order polynomial, however, suffers from the pitfalls described earlier. That is, perfect (or at least extremely good) historical fits with little or no predictive power may be obtained.

MOVING AVERAGES: FORECASTING STECO's STRUT SALES

The assumption behind models of this type is that the average performance over the recent past is a good forecast of the future. The fact that only the most recent data are being used to forecast the future, and perhaps the weighting of the most recent data most heavily, produces a forecast that is much more *responsive* than a curve-fitting model. This new type of model will be sensitive to increases or decreases in sales, or other changes in the data. It is perhaps surprising that these "naive" models are extremely important in applications. Many of the world's major airlines need to generate forecasts of demand to come by fare class in order to feed these forecasts into sophisticated revenue management optimization engines. A great number of the airlines use a particular type of moving average called exponentially weighted moving averages. In addition, almost all inventory control packages include a forecasting subroutine based on this same type of moving average (exponentially weighted moving averages). On the basis of a criterion such as "frequency of use," the method of moving averages is surely an important forecasting procedure.

One person who is deeply concerned about the use of simple forecasting models is Victor Kowalski, the new vice-president of operations of STECO. His introduction to inventory control models is discussed in Chapter 8. Since he is responsible for the inventory of thousands of items, simple (i.e., inexpensive) forecasting models are important to him. In order to become familiar with the various models, he decides to "try out" different models on some historical data. In particular he decides to use last year's monthly sales data for stainless steel struts to learn about the different models and to see how well they would have worked if STECO had been using the models last year. He is performing what is called a *validation* study.

The forecasting models are presented, of course, in symbols. Victor feels that it would be useful to use a common notation throughout his investigation. He thus decides to let

$$y_{t-1} = observed \ sales \ \text{of struts in month } t - 1$$
$$\hat{y}_t = forecast \ \text{of sales for struts in period } t$$

He is interested in forecasting the sales one month ahead; that is, he will take the known historical values $y_1, \ldots, y_{t-1}$ (demand in months 1 through $t - 1$) and use this information to produce $\hat{y}_t$ the forecast for demand in month t. In other words, he will take the actual past sales, up through May, for example, and use them to forecast the sales in June; then he will use the sales through June to forecast sales in July, and so on. This process produces a sequence of $\hat{y}_t$ values. By comparing these values with the observed y_t values, one obtains an indication of how the forecasting model would have worked had it actually been in use last year.

Simple *n*-Period Moving Average

The simplest model in the moving average category is the **simple *n*-period moving average.** In this model the average of a fixed number (say, n) of the most recent observations is used as an estimate of the next value of y. For example, if n equals 4, then after we have observed the value of y in period 15, our estimate for period 16 would be

$$\hat{y}_{16} = \frac{y_{15} + y_{14} + y_{13} + y_{12}}{4}$$

In general,

$$\hat{y}_{t+1} = \frac{1}{n}(y_t + y_{t-1} + \ldots + y_{t-n+1})$$

The application of a 3-period and a 4-period moving average to STECO's strut sales data is shown in Table 13.1.

We see that the 3-month moving average forecast for sales in April is the average of January, February, and March sales, $(20 + 24 + 27)/3$, or 23.67. *Ex post* (i.e., after the forecast) actual sales in April were 31. Thus in this case the sales forecast differed from actual sales by $31 - 23.67$, or 7.33.

Comparing the actual sales to the forecast sales using the data in Table 13.1 suggests that neither forecasting method seems particularly accurate. It is, however, use-

TABLE 13.1 Three- and Four-Month Simple Moving Averages

MONTH	ACTUAL SALES ($000s)	THREE-MONTH SIMPLE MOVING AVERAGE FORECAST	FOUR-MONTH SIMPLE MOVING AVERAGE FORECAST
Jan.	20		
Feb.	24		
Mar.	27		
Apr.	31	(20 + 24 + 27)/3 = 23.67	
May	37	(24 + 27 + 31)/3 = 27.33	(20 + 24 + 27 + 31)/4 = 25.50
June	47	(27 + 31 + 37)/3 = 31.67	(24 + 27 + 31 + 37)/4 = 29.75
July	53	(31 + 37 + 47)/3 = 38.33	(27 + 31 + 37 + 47)/4 = 35.50
Aug.	62	(37 + 47 + 53)/3 = 45.67	(31 + 37 + 47 + 53)/4 = 42.00
Sept.	54	(47 + 53 + 62)/3 = 54.00	(37 + 47 + 53 + 62)/4 = 49.75
Oct.	36	(53 + 62 + 54)/3 = 56.33	(47 + 53 + 62 + 54)/4 = 54.00
Nov.	32	(62 + 54 + 36)/3 = 50.67	(53 + 62 + 54 + 36)/4 = 51.25
Dec.	29	(54 + 36 + 32)/3 = 40.67	(62 + 54 + 36 + 32)/4 = 46.00

ful to replace this *qualitative impression* with some *quantitative measure* of how well the two methods performed. The measures of comparison we'll use in this section are the mean absolute deviation (MAD) and the mean absolute percentage error (MAPE), where

$$MAD = \frac{\sum_{\text{all forecasts}} |\text{actual sales} - \text{forecast sales}|}{\text{number of forecasts}}$$

$$MAPE = \frac{\sum_{\text{all forecasts}} \frac{|\text{actual sales} - \text{forecast sales}|}{\text{actual sales}} * 100\%}{\text{number of forecasts}} \tag{13.7}$$

The MAD is calculated for the 3-month (beginning with April) and 4-month (beginning with May) moving average forecast in a new spreadsheet (STRUT.XLS), which is shown in Figure 13.14. Since the 3-month moving average yields a MAD of 12.67 (cell D16), whereas the 4-month moving average yields a MAD of 15.59 (cell F16), it seems (at least historically) that including more historical data harms rather than helps the forecasting accuracy.

A simple moving average will always lag behind rising data and stay above declining data. Thus, if there are broad rises and falls, simple moving averages will not perform well. They are best suited to data with small erratic ups and downs, providing some stability in the face of the random perturbations.

The simple moving average has two shortcomings, one philosophical and the other operational. The *philosophical* problem centers on the fact that in calculating a forecast (say, $\hat{y}_8$), the most recent observation (y_7) receives no more weight or importance than an older observation such as y_5. This is because each of the last n observations is assigned the weight $1/n$. This procedure of assigning equal weights stands in opposition to one's intuition that in many instances the more recent data should tell us more than the older data about the future. Indeed, the analysis in Figure 13.14 suggests that better predictions for strut sales are based on the most recent data.

	C5	▼	=	=AVERAGE(B2:B4)	

	A	B	C	D	E	F
1	Month	Actual Sales (000)	3month MA Fcst	Absolute Error	4month MA Fcst	Absolute Error
2	January	20				
3	February	24				
4	March	27				
5	April	31	23.67	7.33		
6	May	37	27.33	9.67	25.50	11.50
7	June	47	31.67	15.33	29.75	17.25
8	July	53	38.33	14.67	35.50	17.50
9	August	62	45.67	16.33	42.00	20.00
10	September	54	54.00	0.00	49.75	4.25
11	October	36	56.33	20.33	54.00	18.00
12	November	32	50.67	18.67	51.25	19.25
13	December	29	40.67	11.67	46.00	17.00
14						
15			Sum =	114.00	Sum =	124.75
16			MAD =	12.67	MAD =	15.59

Cell	Formula	Copy To
C5	=AVERAGE(B2:B4)	C6:C13
D5	=ABS(B5-C5)	D6:D13
E6	=AVERAGE(B2:B5)	E7:E13
F6	=ABS(B6-E6)	F7:F13
D15	=SUM(D5:D13)	F15
D16	=AVERAGE(D5:D13)	F16

FIGURE 13.14

Mean Absolute Deviation Comparison for Three- and Four-Month Moving Average Forecasts

The second shortcoming, which is *operational,* is that if *n* observations are to be included in the moving average, then $(n - 1)$ pieces of past data must be brought forward to be combined with the current (the *n*th) observation. All this data must be stored in some way, in order to calculate the forecast. This is not a serious problem when a small number of forecasts is involved. The situation is quite different for the firm that needs to forecast the demand for thousands of individual products on an item-by-item basis. If, for example, STECO is using 8-period moving averages to forecast demand for 5000 small parts, then for each item 7 pieces of old data must be stored for each forecast, in addition to the most recent observation. This implies that a total of 40,000 pieces of data must be stored. Another example where the number of forecasts is huge comes from the airline industry. Consider an airline with a large number of flights departing per day (like United Airlines or Continental). Suppose it has 2000 flights departing every day and it tracks all flights for 300 days in advance. This means it has 600,000 flights to track and forecast on an ongoing basis. In both these cases, storage requirements, as well as computing time, may become important factors in designing a forecasting and/or inventory control system.

Weighted *n*-Period Moving Average The notion that recent data are more important than old data can be implemented with a **weighted *n*-period moving average.** This generalizes the notion of a simple *n*-period moving average, where, as we have seen, each weight is $1/n$. In this more general form, taking $n = 3$ as a specific example, we would set

$$\hat{y}_7 = \alpha_0 y_6 + \alpha_1 y_5 + \alpha_2 y_4$$

where the α's (which are called weights) are nonnegative numbers that are chosen so that smaller weights are assigned to more ancient data and all the weights sum to 1. There are, of course, innumerable ways of selecting a set of α's to satisfy these criteria. For example, if the weighted average is to include the last three observations (a weighted 3-period moving average), one might set

$$\hat{y}_7 = \frac{3}{6} y_6 + \frac{2}{6} y_5 + \frac{1}{6} y_4$$

F5 | =SUMPRODUCT($B$1:$B$3,E2:E4)

	A	B	C	D	E	F	G
1	alpha2 =	0.167		Month	Actual Sales (000)	3month WMA Fcst	Absolute Error
2	alpha1 =	0.333		January	20		
3	alpha0 =	0.500		February	24		
4	SUM OF WTS=	1.00		March	27		
5				April	31	24.83	6.17
6				May	37	28.50	8.50
7				June	47	33.33	13.67
8				July	53	41.00	12.00
9				August	62	48.33	13.67
10				September	54	56.50	2.50
11				October	36	56.50	20.50
12				November	32	46.33	14.33
13				December	29	37.00	8.00
14							
15						Sum =	99.33
16						MAD =	11.04

Cell	Formula	Copy To
B4	=SUM(B1:B3)	—
F5	=SUMPRODUCT($B$1:$B$3, E2:E4)	F6:F13
G5	=ABS(E5-F5)	G6:G13
G15	=SUM(G5:G13)	—
G16	=AVERAGE(G5:G13)	—

FIGURE 13.15

Initial Three-Month Weighted Moving Average

Alternatively, one could define

$$\hat{y}_7 = \frac{5}{10} y_6 + \frac{3}{10} y_5 + \frac{2}{10} y_4$$

In both these expressions we have decreasing weights that sum to 1. In practice, the proper choice of weights could easily be left to the Solver algorithm.

To get some idea about its performance, Victor applies the 3-month weighted moving average with initial weights 3/6, 2/6, 1/6 to the historical stainless strut data. The forecasts and the MAD are developed by Victor in a new sheet "WMA" in the same workbook (STRUT.XLS) and are shown in Figure 13.15. Comparing the new MAD Victor obtained of 11.04 (cell G16) to the MAD of the 3-month simple moving average (12.67) and the 4-month simple moving average (15.59) confirms the suggestion that recent sales results are a better indicator of future sales than are older data.

Of course, if we let the Solver choose the optimal weights for us, we can do even better than our initial guess at the weights. To let Solver choose the weights that minimize the MAD, we do the following:

1. Click on Tools, then "Solver".
2. Set the Target cell to G16 and tell Solver we want to minimize it.
3. Indicate that the changing cells are B1:B3.
4. Add the constraints that (a) B4 = 1.0, (b) B1:B3 $\geq$ 0, (c) B1:B3 $\leq$ 1, (d) B1 $\leq$ B2, and (e) B2 $\leq$ B3 .
5. Click on Solve and you get the results shown in Figure 13.16.

Here we see that the optimal weighting is to place all the weight on the most recent observation, which yields a MAD of 7.56 (a 31.5% reduction in error from our initial guess). This continues to confirm our idea that we should give more weight to the most recent observation (to the extreme in this example).

Although the weighted moving average places more weight on more recent data, it does not solve the operational problems of data storage, since $(n - 1)$ pieces of historical sales data must still be stored. We now turn to a weighting scheme that cleverly addresses this problem.

F5   ▼   = =SUMPRODUCT($B$1:$B$3,E2:E4)

	A	B	C	D	E	F	G
1	alpha2 =	0.000		Month	Actual Sales (000)	3month WMA Fcst	Absolute Error
2	alpha1 =	0.000		January	20		
3	alpha0 =	1.000		February	24		
4	SUM OF WTS=	1.00		March	27		
5				April	31	27.00	4.00
6				May	37	31.00	6.00
7				June	47	37.00	10.00
8				July	53	47.00	6.00
9				August	62	53.00	9.00
10				September	54	62.00	8.00
11				October	36	54.00	18.00
12				November	32	36.00	4.00
13				December	29	32.00	3.00
14							
15						Sum =	68.00
16						MAD =	7.56

FIGURE 13.16

Optimal Three-Month
Weighted Moving Average

EXPONENTIAL SMOOTHING: THE BASIC MODEL

We saw that, in using a weighted moving average, there are many different ways to assign decreasing weights that sum to 1. One way is called **exponential smoothing,** which is a shortened name for an *exponentially weighted moving average.* This is a scheme that weights recent data more heavily than past data, with weights summing to 1, but it avoids the operational problem just discussed. In this model, for any $t \geq 1$ the forecast for period $t + 1$, denoted $\hat{y}_{t+1}$, is a weighted sum (with weights summing to 1) of the actual *observed sales in period t* (i.e., y_t) and *the forecast for period* t (which was $\hat{y}_t$). In other words,

$$\boxed{\text{Forecast for } t + 1} \quad \boxed{\text{Observed in } t} \quad \boxed{\text{Forecast for } t}$$
$$\hat{y}_{t+1} = \alpha y_t + (1 - \alpha)\hat{y}_t \quad \textbf{(13.8)}$$

where α is a user-specified constant such that $0 \leq \alpha \leq 1$. The value assigned to α determines how much weight is placed on the most recent observation in calculating the forecast for the next period. Note in equation (13.8) that if α is assigned a value close to 1, almost all the weight is placed on the actual demand in period t.

Exponential smoothing has important computational advantages. To compute $\hat{y}_{t+1}$, only $\hat{y}_t$, need be stored (together with the value of α). As soon as the actual y_t is observed, we compute $\hat{y}_{t+1} = \alpha y_t + (1 - \alpha)\hat{y}_t$. If STECO wanted to forecast demand for 5000 small parts, in each period, then 10,001 items would have to be stored (the 5000 $\hat{y}_t$ values, the 5000 y_t values, and the value of α), as opposed to the previously computed 40,000 items needed to implement an 8-period moving average. Depending on the behavior of the data, it might be necessary to store a different value of α for each item, but even then much less storage would be required than if using moving averages. The thing that is nice about exponential smoothing is that by saving α and the last forecast, all the previous forecasts are being stored *implicitly.*

In order to obtain more insight into the exponential smoothing model, let us note that when $t = 1$ the expression used to define $\hat{y}_2$ is

$$\hat{y}_2 = \alpha y_1 + (1 - \alpha)\hat{y}_1$$

In this expression $\hat{y}_1$ is an "initial guess" at the value for y in period 1, and y_1 is the observed value in period 1. To get the exponential smoothing forecast going, we need to provide this "initial guess." Several options are available to us: (1) First and most commonly, we let $\hat{y}_1 = y_1$ (i.e., we assume a "perfect" forecast to get the process rolling, but we don't count this error of zero in our calculation of the MAD). Other choices include (2) looking ahead at all the available data and letting $\hat{y}_1 = \bar{y}$ (average of all available data), or (3) letting $\hat{y}_1 = $ the average of just the first couple of months. We will choose the first approach.

At this point Victor decides to use the spreadsheet "EXPSMTH" in the same workbook (STRUT.XLS) to apply exponential smoothing to the stainless steel strut data. Figure 13.17 shows actual sales and estimated sales for 12 months using an initial value for $\alpha = 0.5$.

	F3		▾		=	=$B$1*E2+(1-$B$1)*F2	

	A	B	C	D	E	F	G
1	alpha =	0.500		Month	Actual Sales (000)	Fcst Sales	Absolute Error
2				January	20	20.00	
3				February	24	20.00	4.00
4				March	27	22.00	5.00
5				April	31	24.50	6.50
6				May	37	27.75	9.25
7				June	47	32.38	14.63
8				July	53	39.69	13.31
9				August	62	46.34	15.66
10				September	54	54.17	0.17
11				October	36	54.09	18.09
12				November	32	45.04	13.04
13				December	29	38.52	9.52
14							
15						Sum =	109.17
16						MAD =	9.92

Cell	Formula	Copy To
F3	=$B$1*E2 + (1−$B$1)*F2	F4:F13
G3	=ABS(E3−F3)	G4:G13
G15	=SUM(G3:G13)	—
G16	=AVERAGE(G3:G13)	—

FIGURE 13.17

Exponential Smoothing Forecast, Initial $\alpha = 0.5$

He has also calculated the MAD for February through December. Indeed, the exponential smoothing model with $\alpha = 0.5$ yields a smaller MAD (9.92 in cell G16) than the moving average models (see Figure 13.14) or our initial guess at a weighted moving average model (see Figure 13.15).

Victor knows he can find a better model by using the Solver to select the optimal value of α (one that minimizes the MAD), but he is pleased with the initial results. The MAD is smaller than what he obtained with several previous models, and the calculations are simple. From a computational viewpoint it is reasonable to consider exponential smoothing as an affordable way to forecast the sales of the many products STECO holds in inventory.

Although the results obtained from the exponential smoothing model are impressive, it is clear that the particular numerical values (column F of Figure 13.17) depend on the values selected for the smoothing constant α and the "initial guess" $\hat{y}_1$. In order to find the optimal value of α, we just set up a nonlinear optimization model using Excel's Solver tool. Of course, if we let the Solver choose the optimal α for us, we can do even better than our initial guess of $\alpha = 0.5$. To let Solver choose the α that minimizes the MAD, we do the following:

1. Click on Tools, then "Solver."
2. Set the Target cell to G16 and tell Solver we want to minimize it.
3. Indicate that the changing cell is B1.
4. Add the constraints that (a) B1 $\geq$ 0 and (b) B1 $\leq$ 1.
5. Click on Solve and you get the results shown in Figure 13.18.

Again, as with the weighted moving average approach, we see that because of the linear trend (up, then down) in the data, that the more weight we can put on the most recent observation, the better the forecast. So, not surprisingly, the optimal $\alpha = 1.0$, and this forecasting approach gives Victor a MAD of 6.82 (cell G16), which is the best performance he has seen so far.

Because of the importance of the basic exponential smoothing model, it is worth exploring in more detail how it works and when it can be successfully applied to real models.

	G8		▼	=	=ABS(E8-F8)	
	A	B	C	D	E	F	G
1	alpha =	1.000		Month	Actual Sales (000)	Fcst Sales	Absolute Error
2				January	20	20.00	
3				February	24	20.00	4.00
4				March	27	24.00	3.00
5				April	31	27.00	4.00
6				May	37	31.00	6.00
7				June	47	37.00	10.00
8				July	53	47.00	6.00
9				August	62	53.00	9.00
10				September	54	62.00	8.00
11				October	36	54.00	18.00
12				November	32	36.00	4.00
13				December	29	32.00	3.00
14							
15						Sum =	75.00
16						MAD =	6.82

FIGURE 13.18

Exponential Smoothing
Forecast, Optimal α

We will now examine some of its properties. To begin, note that if $t \geq 2$ it is possible to substitute $t - 1$ for t in (13.8) to obtain

$$\hat{y}_t = \alpha y_{t-1} + (1 - \alpha)\hat{y}_{t-1}$$

Substituting this relationship for $\hat{y}_t$ back into the original expression for $\hat{y}_{t+1}$ (i.e., into [13.8]) yields for $t \geq 2$,

$$\hat{y}_{t+1} = \alpha y_t + \alpha(1 - \alpha)y_{t-1} + (1 - \alpha)^2 \hat{y}_{t-1}$$

By successively performing similar substitutions, one is led to the following general expression for $\hat{y}_{t+1}$:

$$\hat{y}_{t+1} = \alpha y_t + \alpha(1 - \alpha)y_{t-1} + \alpha(1 - \alpha)^2 y_{t-2} + \ldots$$
$$+ \alpha(1 - \alpha)^{t-1} y_1 + (1 - \alpha)^t \hat{y}_1 \quad \textbf{(13.9)}$$

For example,

$$\hat{y}_4 = \alpha y_3 + \alpha(1 - \alpha)y_2 + \alpha(1 - \alpha)^2 y_1 + (1 - \alpha)^3 \hat{y}_1$$

Since usually $0 < \alpha < 1$, it follows that $0 < 1 - \alpha < 1$. Thus,

$$\alpha > \alpha(1 - \alpha) > \alpha (1 - \alpha)^2$$

In other words, in the previous example y_3, the most recent observation, receives more weight than y_2, which receives more weight than y_1. This illustrates the general property of an exponential smoothing model—that *the coefficients of the y's decrease as the data become older.* It can also be shown that *the sum of all of the coefficients (including the coefficient of $\hat{y}_1$) is 1*; that is in the case of $\hat{y}_4$, for example,

$$\alpha + \alpha(1 - \alpha) + \alpha(1 - \alpha)^2 + (1 - \alpha)^3 = 1$$

We have thus seen in equation (13.9) that the general value $\hat{y}_{t+1}$ is a weighted sum of *all previous observations* (including the last observed value, y_t). Moreover, the weights sum to 1 and are decreasing as historical observations get older. The last term in the sum, namely $\hat{y}_1$, is not a historical observation. Recall that it was a "guess" at y_1. We can now observe that as t increases, the influence of $\hat{y}_1$ on $\hat{y}_{t+1}$ decreases and in time becomes negligible. To see this, note that the coefficient of $\hat{y}_1$ in (13.9) is $(1 - \alpha)^t$. Thus, the weight assigned to $\hat{y}_1$ decreases exponentially with t. Even if α is small (which makes $[1 - \alpha]$ nearly 1), the value of $(1 - \alpha)^t$ decreases rapidly. For example, if $\alpha = 0.1$ and $t = 20$, then $(1 - \alpha)^t = 0.12$. If $\alpha = 0.1$ and $t = 40$, then $(1 - \alpha)^t = 0.015$. Thus, as soon as enough data have been observed, the value of $\hat{y}_{t+1}$ will be quite insensitive to the choice for $\hat{y}_1$.

Obviously, the value of α, which is a parameter input by the manager, affects the performance of the model. As you can see explicitly in (13.8), it is the weight given to the data value (y_t) most recently observed. This implies that the larger the value of α, the more

VARIABLE	COEFFICIENT	$\alpha = 0.1$	$\alpha = 0.3$	$\alpha = 0.5$
y_t	α	0.1	0.3	0.5
y_{t-1}	$\alpha(1 - \alpha)$	0.09	0.21	0.25
y_{t-2}	$\alpha(1 - \alpha)^2$	0.081	0.147	0.125
y_{t-3}	$\alpha(1 - \alpha)^3$	0.07290	0.10290	0.0625
y_{t-4}	$\alpha(1 - \alpha)^4$	0.06561	0.07203	0.03125
y_{t-5}	$\alpha(1 - \alpha)^5$	0.05905	0.05042	0.01563
y_{t-6}	$\alpha(1 - \alpha)^6$	0.05314	0.03530	0.00781
y_{t-7}	$\alpha(1 - \alpha)^7$	0.04783	0.02471	0.00391
y_{t-8}	$\alpha(1 - \alpha)^8$	0.04305	0.01729	0.00195
y_{t-9}	$\alpha(1 - \alpha)^9$	0.03874	0.01211	0.00098
y_{t-10}	$\alpha(1 - \alpha)^{10}$	0.03487	0.00847	0.00049
Sum of the Weights		0.68619	0.98023	0.99610

TABLE 13.2 Weights for Different Values of α

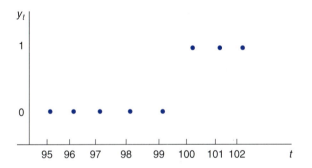

FIGURE 13.19

System Change when $t = 100$

strongly the model will react to the last observation (we call this a *responsive* forecast). This, as we will see, may or may not be desirable. When $\alpha \approx 0.0$, this means almost complete trust in the last forecast and almost completely ignoring the most recent observation (i.e., last data point). This would be an extremely *stable* forecast. Table 13.2 shows values for the weights (in equation [13.9]) when $\alpha = 0.1$, 0.3, and 0.5. You can see that for the larger values of α (e.g., $\alpha = 0.5$) more relative weight is assigned to the more recent observations, and the influence of older data is more rapidly diminished.

To illustrate further the effect of choosing various values for α (i.e., putting more or less weight on recent observations), we consider three specific cases.

Case 1 (Response to a Sudden Change) Suppose that at a certain point in time the underlying system experiences a rapid and radical change. How does the choice of α influence the way in which the exponential smoothing model will react? As an illustrative example consider an extreme case in which

$$y_t = 0 \text{ for } t = 1, 2, \ldots, 99$$
$$y_t = 1 \text{ for } t = 100, 101, \ldots$$

This situation is illustrated in Figure 13.19. Note that in this case if $\hat{y}_1 = 0$, then $\hat{y}_{100} = 0$ for any value of α, since we are taking the weighted sum of a series of zeros.

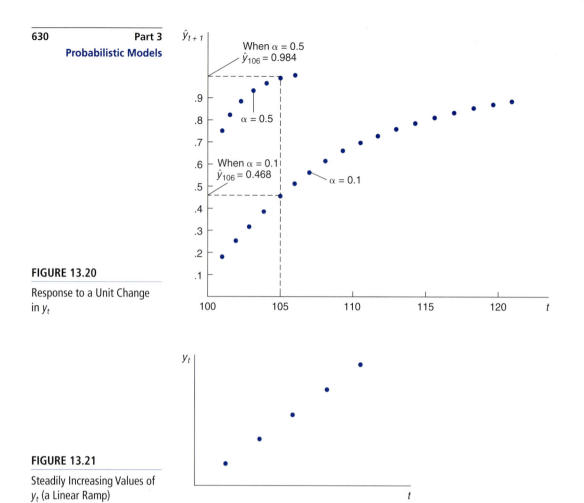

FIGURE 13.20

Response to a Unit Change in y_t

FIGURE 13.21

Steadily Increasing Values of y_t (a Linear Ramp)

Thus, at time 99 our best estimate of y_{100} is 0, whereas the actual value will be 1. At time 100 we will first see that the system has changed. The question is: How quickly will the forecasting system respond as time passes and the information that the system has changed becomes available?

To answer this question, we plot $\hat{y}_{t+1}$ for $\alpha = 0.5$ and $\alpha = 0.1$ in Figure 13.20. Note that when $\alpha = 0.5$, $\hat{y}_{106} = 0.984$; thus at time 105 our estimate of y_{106} would be 0.984, whereas the true value will turn out to be 1. When $\alpha = 0.1$ our estimate of y_{106} is only 0.468.

We see then that a forecasting system with $\alpha = 0.5$ responds much more quickly to changes in the data than does a forecasting system with $\alpha = 0.1$. The manager would thus prefer a relatively large α if the system is characterized by a low level of random behavior, but is subject to occasional enduring shocks. (Case 1 is an extreme example of this situation.)

However, suppose that the data are characterized by large random errors but a stable mean. Then if α is large, a large random error in y_t will throw the forecast value, $\hat{y}_{t+1}$, way off. Hence, for this type of process a smaller value of α would be preferred.

Case 2 (Response to a Steady Change) As opposed to the rapid and radical change investigated in Case 1, suppose now that a system experiences a *steady* change in the value of *y*. An example of a steady growth pattern is illustrated in Figure 13.21. This example is called a *linear ramp*. Again the questions are: How will the exponential smoothing model respond, and how will this response be affected by the choice of α?

In this case, recall that

$$\hat{y}_{t+1} = \alpha y_t + \alpha(1 - \alpha)y_{t-1} + \dots$$

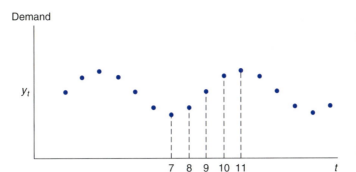

Demand

y_t

7 8 9 10 11 t

FIGURE 13.22

Seasonal Pattern in y_t

Since all previous y's ($y_1, \ldots, y_{t-1}$) are smaller than y_t, and since the weights sum to 1, it can be shown that, for any α between 0 and 1, $\hat{y}_{t+1} < y_t$. Also, since y_{t+1} is greater than y_t, we see that $\hat{y}_{t+1} < y_t < y_{t+1}$. Thus our forecast will *always* be too small. Finally, since smaller values of α put more weight on older data, the smaller the value of α, the worse the forecast becomes. But even with α very close to 1 the forecast is not very good if the ramp is steep. The moral for managers is that exponential smoothing (or indeed any weighted moving average), without an appropriate modification, is not a good forecasting tool in a rapidly growing market or a declining market. The model can be adjusted to include the trend and this is called Holt's model (or exponential smoothing with trend), and the method will be shown in more detail later in this section.

In reality, the observation that Victor made with the struts in our previous example (i.e., both weighted moving average and exponential smoothing placed ALL the weight on the most recent observation) is a good clue to you as a manager that there is an obvious trend in the data and that you should consider a different forecasting model.

Case 3 (Response to a Seasonal Change) Suppose that a system experiences a regular *seasonal pattern* in y (such as would be the case if y represents, for example, the demand in the city of Denver for swimming suits). How then will the exponential smoothing model respond, and how will this response be affected by the choice of α? Consider, for example, the seasonal pattern illustrated in Figure 13.22, and suppose it is desired to extrapolate *several periods forward*. For example, suppose we wish to forecast demand in periods 8 through 11 based only on data through period 7. Then

$$\hat{y}_8 = \alpha y_7 + (1 - \alpha)\hat{y}_7$$

Now to obtain $\hat{y}_9$, since we have data only through period 7, we assume that $y_8 = \hat{y}_8$. Then

$$\hat{y}_9 = \alpha y_8 + (1 - \alpha)\hat{y}_8 = \alpha \hat{y}_8 + (1 - \alpha)\hat{y} = \hat{y}_8$$

Similarly, it can be shown that $\hat{y}_{11} = \hat{y}_{10} = \hat{y}_9 = \hat{y}_8$. In other words, $\hat{y}_8$ is the best estimate of all future demands.

Now let us see how good these predictions are. We know that

$$\hat{y}_{t+1} = \alpha y_t + \alpha(1 - \alpha)y_{t-1} + \alpha(1 - \alpha)^2 y_{t-2} + \ldots$$

Suppose that a small value of α is chosen. By referring to Table 13.2 we see that when α is small (say, 0.1) the coefficients for the most recent terms change relatively slowly (i.e., they are nearly equal to each other). Thus, $\hat{y}_{t+1}$ will resemble a simple moving average of a number of terms. In this case the future predictions (e.g., $\hat{y}_{11}$) will all be somewhere near the average of the past observations. The forecast thus essentially ignores the seasonal pattern. If a large value of α is chosen, $\hat{y}_{11}$, which equals $\hat{y}_8$, will be close in value to y_7, which is obviously not good. In other words, the model fares poorly in this case regardless of the choice of α.

The exponential smoothing model $\hat{y}_{t+1} = \alpha y_t + (1 - \alpha)\hat{y}_t$ is intended for situations in which the behavior of the variable of interest is essentially stable, in the sense that deviations over time have nothing to do with *time,* per se, but are caused by *random effects* that do not follow a regular pattern. This is what we have termed the *stationarity* assumption. Not surprisingly, then, the model has various shortcomings when it is used in situations (such as a linear ramp or swimming suit demand) that do not fit this prescription. Although this statement may be true, it is not very constructive. What approach should a manager take when the exponential smoothing model as described above is not appropriate? In the case of a seasonal pattern, a naive approach would be to use the exponential smoothing model on "appropriate" past data. For example, the airlines or hotels, which exhibit strong day-of-week seasonality, could take a smoothed average of demand on previous Mondays to forecast demand on upcoming Mondays. Another business with monthly seasonality might take a smoothed average of sales in previous Junes to forecast sales this June. This latter approach has two problems. First, it ignores a great deal of useful information. Certainly sales from last Tuesday to Sunday in the airline or hotel example (or July through this May in the other example) should provide at least a limited amount of information about the likely level of sales this Monday (or June). Second, if the cycle is very long, say a year, this approach means that very old data must be used to get a reasonable sample size. The above assumption, that the system or process producing the variable of interest is essentially *stationary* over time, becomes more tenuous when the span of time covered by the data becomes quite large.

If the manager is convinced that there is either a trend (Shumway, Horch, and Sager (B) Case) or a seasonal effect (Marriott Room Forecasting Case) in the variable being predicted, a better approach is to develop forecasting models that incorporate these features. When there is a discernible pattern of seasonality (which can be seen fairly easily by graphing the data in Excel) there are methods, using simple moving averages, to determine a seasonality factor. Using this factor, the data can be "deseasonalized," some forecasting method used on the deseasonalized data, and the forecast can then be "reseasonalized." This approach will be shown after the trend model in the next section.

HOLT'S MODEL (EXPONENTIAL SMOOTHING WITH TREND)

As discussed above, simple exponential smoothing models don't perform very well on models that have obvious up or down trend in the data (and no seasonality). To correct this, Holt developed the following model:

$$\hat{y}_{t+k} = L_t + kT_t$$

where:

$$L_t = \alpha y_t + (1 - \alpha)(L_{t-1} + T_{t-1}) \qquad \textbf{(13.10)}$$
$$T_t = \beta(L_t - L_{t-1}) + (1 - \beta)T_{t-1}$$

Holt's model allows us to forecast up to k time periods ahead. In this model, we now have two smoothing parameters, α and β, both of which must be between 0 and 1. The L_t term indicates the long-term level or base value for the time-series data. The T_t term indicates the expected increase or decrease per period (i.e., the trend).

Let's demonstrate how to make this model work with a new example. Amy Luford is an analyst with a large brokerage firm on Wall Street. She has been looking at the quarterly earnings of Startup Airlines and is expected to make a forecast of next quarter's earnings. She has the following data and graph available to her in a spreadsheet (STARTUP.XLS) as shown in Figure 13.23.

Amy can see that the data has obvious trend to it, as she would expect for a successful new business venture. She wants to apply Holt's trend model to the data to generate her forecast of earnings per share (EPS) for the thirteenth quarter. This forecasting approach is demonstrated in her spreadsheet "Holt" in the same workbook (STARTUP.XLS) and is shown in Figure 13.24. She needs initial values for both L and T. She has several choices: (1) let L_1 = actual EPS for quarter 1 and $T_1 = 0$, (2) let L_1 = average EPS for all 12 quarters and T_1 = average trend for all 12 quarters, and many other variations in between. Amy chooses the first option.

With initial guesses for $\alpha = 0.5$ and $\beta = 0.5$, she sees that the mean absolute percentage error (MAPE) is 43.3% (cell F18). Although this is fairly high, Amy tries putting in a

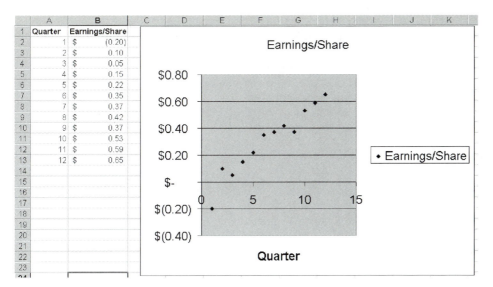

FIGURE 13.23

Startup Airlines Earnings
per Share

	D6	= =$B$2*(C6-C5)+(1-$B$2)*D5

	A	B	C	D	E	F	G
1	alpha =	0.50					
2	beta =	0.50					
3							
4	Quarter	Earnings/Share	Level Term	Trend Term	Fcst EPS	Abs. % Error	
5	1	$ (0.20)	$ (0.20)	0	NA	NA	
6	2	$ 0.10	$ (0.05)	0.075	$ (0.20)	300.0%	
7	3	$ 0.05	$ 0.04	0.081	$ 0.03	50.0%	
8	4	$ 0.15	$ 0.13	0.089	$ 0.12	20.8%	
9	5	$ 0.22	$ 0.22	0.088	$ 0.22	1.6%	
10	6	$ 0.35	$ 0.33	0.098	$ 0.31	11.5%	
11	7	$ 0.37	$ 0.40	0.084	$ 0.43	15.7%	
12	8	$ 0.42	$ 0.45	0.068	$ 0.48	14.9%	
13	9	$ 0.37	$ 0.44	0.031	$ 0.52	40.4%	
14	10	$ 0.53	$ 0.50	0.044	$ 0.48	10.3%	
15	11	$ 0.59	$ 0.57	0.055	$ 0.55	7.3%	
16	12	$ 0.65	$ 0.64	0.062	$ 0.62	4.1%	
17					$ 0.70		
18						43.3% = MAPE	

Cell	Formula	Copy To
C5	=B5	—
C6	=$B$1*B6 + (1-$B$1)*(C5+D5)	C7:C16
D6	=$B$2* (C6-C5)+(1-$B$2)*D5	D7:D16
E6	=SUM(C5:D5)	E7:E17
F6	=ABS(B6-E6)/B6	F7:F16
F18	=AVERAGE(F6:F16)	—

FIGURE 13.24

Exponential Smoothing with
Trend Model for
Startup Airlines

β of zero (as if there were no trend and she was back to simple exponential smoothing to see if she's gaining anything by this new model), and she sees in Figure 13.25 that the MAPE is much worse at 78.1% (see Figure 13.25).

Finally, she decides to use Solver to help her find the optimal values for α and β because she knows Solver can do better than her initial guesses of 0.5. To let Solver choose the α and β that minimize the MAPE, she does the following:

1. Click on Tools, then "Solver."
2. Set the Target cell to F18 and tell Solver we want to minimize it.

C6 = =$B$1*B6+(1-$B$1)*(C5+D5)

	A	B	C	D	E	F	G
1	alpha =	0.50					
2	beta =	0.00					
3							
4	Quarter	Earnings/Share	Level Term	Trend Term	Fcst EPS	Abs. % Error	
5	1	$ (0.20)	$ (0.20)	0	NA	NA	
6	2	$ 0.10	$ (0.05)	0.000	$ (0.20)	300.0%	
7	3	$ 0.05	$ -	0.000	$ (0.05)	200.0%	
8	4	$ 0.15	$ 0.08	0.000	$ -	100.0%	
9	5	$ 0.22	$ 0.15	0.000	$ 0.08	65.9%	
10	6	$ 0.35	$ 0.25	0.000	$ 0.15	57.9%	
11	7	$ 0.37	$ 0.31	0.000	$ 0.25	32.8%	
12	8	$ 0.42	$ 0.36	0.000	$ 0.31	26.3%	
13	9	$ 0.37	$ 0.37	0.000	$ 0.36	1.4%	
14	10	$ 0.53	$ 0.45	0.000	$ 0.37	30.7%	
15	11	$ 0.59	$ 0.52	0.000	$ 0.45	24.0%	
16	12	$ 0.65	$ 0.58	0.000	$ 0.52	20.1%	
17					$ 0.58		
18						78.1%	= MAPE

FIGURE 13.25

Spreadsheet Model for Startup Airlines with No Trend

F6 = =ABS(B6-E6)/B6

	A	B	C	D	E	F	G
1	alpha =	0.59					
2	beta =	0.42					
3							
4	Quarter	Earnings/Share	Level Term	Trend Term	Fcst EPS	Abs. % Error	
5	1	$ (0.20)	$ (0.20)	0	NA	NA	
6	2	$ 0.10	$ (0.02)	0.074	$ (0.20)	300.0%	
7	3	$ 0.05	$ 0.05	0.074	$ 0.05	0.0%	
8	4	$ 0.15	$ 0.14	0.080	$ 0.12	17.4%	
9	5	$ 0.22	$ 0.22	0.080	$ 0.22	0.2%	
10	6	$ 0.35	$ 0.33	0.093	$ 0.30	14.2%	
11	7	$ 0.37	$ 0.39	0.080	$ 0.42	14.1%	
12	8	$ 0.42	$ 0.44	0.067	$ 0.47	12.2%	
13	9	$ 0.37	$ 0.43	0.033	$ 0.51	37.4%	
14	10	$ 0.53	$ 0.50	0.050	$ 0.46	13.2%	
15	11	$ 0.59	$ 0.57	0.060	$ 0.55	6.5%	
16	12	$ 0.65	$ 0.64	0.064	$ 0.63	2.5%	
17					$ 0.71		
18						38.0%	= MAPE

FIGURE 13.26

Optimal Exponential Smoothing with Trend Spreadsheet Model for Startup Airlines

3. Indicate that the changing cells are B1:B2.

4. Add the constraints that (a) B1:B2 ≥ 0, and (b) B1:B2 ≤ 1.

5. Click on Solve to get the results shown in Figure 13.26.

Amy sees that the $\alpha^* = 0.59$ and $\beta^* = 0.42$ and the MAPE has been lowered to 38%, which is nearly a 12.5% improvement over the MAPE with her initial guesses of $\alpha = 0.5$ and $\beta = 0.5$.

The other forecasting approach Amy could have tried where she could see that there was obvious trend in her data (and therefore that simple exponential smoothing and weighted moving averages would not be effective) would be to do a linear regression on the data with time being the independent variable. We'll leave this as an exercise for the student (see Problem 13-19).

SEASONALITY

When making forecasts using data from a time series, one can often take advantage of seasonality. **Seasonality** comprises movements up and down in a pattern of constant length that repeats itself.

For example, if you were looking at monthly data on sales of ice cream, you would ex-

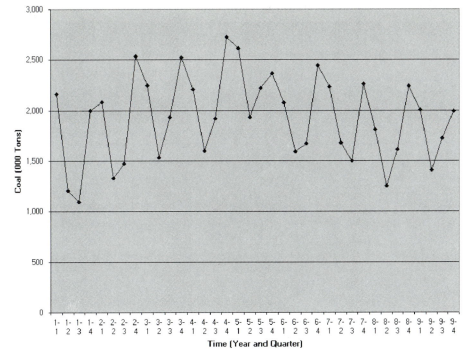

FIGURE 13.27

Coal Receipts over a
Nine-Year Period

pect to see higher sales in the warmer months (June to August in the Northern Hemisphere) than in the winter months, year after year. The seasonal pattern would be 12 months long. If we used weekly data, the seasonal pattern would repeat every 52 periods. The number of time periods in a seasonal pattern depends on how often the observations are collected.

In another example we may be looking at daily data on the number of guests staying overnight at a downtown business hotel. Our intuition might tell us that we expect high numbers on Monday, Tuesday, and Wednesday nights, low numbers on Friday and Saturday, and medium numbers on Thursday and Sunday. So our pattern would be as follows, starting with Sunday: Medium, High, High, High, Medium, Low, Low. The pattern would repeat itself every seven days.

The approach for treating such seasonal patterns consists of four steps: (1) Look at the original data that exhibit a seasonal pattern. From examining the data and from our own judgment, we hypothesize an *m*-period seasonal pattern. (2) Using the numerical approach described in the next section, we deseasonalize the data. (3) Using the best forecasting method available, we make a forecast in deseasonalized terms. (4) We reseasonalize the forecast to account for the seasonal pattern.

We will illustrate these concepts with data on U.S. coal receipts by the commercial/residential sectors over a nine-year period (measured in thousands of tons) [see Quarterly Coal Reports]. Frank Keetch is the manager of Gillette Coal Mine and he is trying to make a forecast of demand in the upcoming two quarters. He has entered the following data for the entire industry in a spreadsheet (COAL.XLS) and it is graphed in Figure 13.27. Intuition tells Frank to expect higher than average coal receipts in the first and fourth quarters (winter effects) and lower than average in the second and third quarters (spring/summer effects).

Deseasonalizing The procedure to deseasonalize data is quite simply to average out all variations that occur within one season. Thus for quarterly data an average of four periods is used to eliminate within-year seasonality. In order to deseasonalize a whole time series, the first step is to calculate a series of *m*-period moving averages, where *m* is the length of the seasonal pattern. In order to calculate this four-period moving average, he has to add two columns (C and D) to his Excel spreadsheet, which is shown in Figure 13.28.

	A	B	C	D	E	F	G
6	Time	Coal	4 Period	Centered	Ratio of Coal Receipts to	Seasonal	Deseason
7	Year-Qtr	Receipts	Moving Average	Moving Average	Centered Moving Average	Indices	Data
8	1-1	2,159	-----	-----	-----	1.108	1,948.
9	1-2	1,203	-----	-----	-----	0.784	1,535.
10	1-3	1,094	1,613	1,603	0.682	0.860	1,272.
11	1-4	1,996	1,594	1,610	1.240	1.234	1,617.
12	2-1	2,081	1,626	1,674	1.244	1.108	1,877.
13	2-2	1,332	1,721	1,788	0.745	0.784	1,700.
14	2-3	1,476	1,856	1,877	0.787	0.860	1,716.
15	2-4	2,533	1,898	1,923	1.317	1.234	2,053.
16	3-1	2,249	1,948	2,005	1.122	1.108	2,029.
17	3-2	1,533	2,063	2,061	0.744	0.784	1,956.
18	3-3	1,935	2,060	2,055	0.942	0.860	2,250.
19	3-4	2,523	2,050	2,058	1.226	1.234	2,045.
20	4-1	2,208	2,066	2,064	1.070	1.108	1,992.
21	4-2	1,597	2,061	2,087	0.765	0.784	2,038.
22	4-3	1,917	2,112	2,163	0.886	0.860	2,229.
23	4-4	2,726	2,213	2,255	1.209	1.234	2,209.
24	5-1	2,612	2,297	2,335	1.119	1.108	2,356.
25	5-2	1,931	2,373	2,328	0.830	0.784	2,464.
26	5-3	2,223	2,282	2,215	1.004	0.860	2,585.
27	5-4	2,363	2,148	2,105	1.123	1.234	1,915.
28	6-1	2,074	2,062	1,994	1.040	1.108	1,871.
29	6-2	1,589	1,925	1,935	0.821	0.784	2,028.
30	6-3	1,673	1,945	1,964	0.852	0.860	1,945.
31	6-4	2,443	1,984	1,995	1.225	1.234	1,980.
32	7-1	2,?21	2,006	1,984	1.124	1.108	2,013.

Data Chart / CMA / DeseasChart \ Data /

Cell	Formula	Copy To
C10	=AVERAGE(B8:B11)	C11:C42
D10	=AVERAGE(C10:C11)	D11:D41
E10	=B10/D10	E11:E41
F8	=$E$1	F12, F16, F20, F24, F28, F32, F36, F40
F9	=$E$2	F13, F17, F21, F25, F29, F33, F37, F41
F10	=$E$3	F14, F18, F22, F26, F30, F34, F38, F42
F11	=$E$4	F15, F19, F23, F27, F31, F35, F39, F43

FIGURE 13.28

Spreadsheet
to Deseasonalize the Data

Column C of Figure 13.28 shows a four-period moving average of the data in column B. The first number is the average of the first four periods,

$$(2159 + 1203 + 1094 + 1996)/4 = 1613$$

The second number is the average of the next four periods, and so on.

Frank really would like to center the moving average in the middle of the data from which it was calculated. *If m is odd,* the first moving average (average of points 1 to m) is easily centered on the $(m + 1)/2$ point (e.g., suppose you have daily data where $m = 7$, the first seven-period moving average is centered on the $(7 + 1)/2$ or fourth point). This process rolls forward to find the average of the second through $(m + 1)$st point, which is centered on the $(m + 3)/2$ point, and so forth.

If m is even, as it is in Frank's situation, the task is a little more complicated, using an additional step to get the moving averages centered. Since the average of the first four points should really be centered at the midpoint between the second and third data point, and the average of periods two through five should be centered halfway between periods three and four, the value to be centered at period three can be approximated by taking the average of the first two averages. Thus the first number in the *centered moving average* column (column D) is

$$(1613 + 1594)/2 = 1603$$

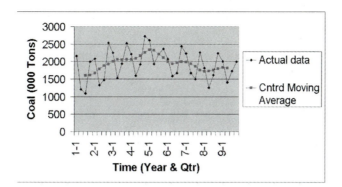

FIGURE 13.29

Graph of Data and Its Centered Moving Average

	E	F	G	H	I	J	K	L	M	N	O
1	1.108	1st	-----	1.244	1.122	1.070	1.119	1.040	1.124	1.052	1.096
2	0.784	2nd	-----	0.745	0.744	0.765	0.830	0.821	0.863	0.724	0.776
3	0.860	3rd	0.682	0.787	0.942	0.886	1.004	0.852	0.806	0.920	-----
4	1.234	4th	1.240	1.317	1.226	1.209	1.123	1.225	1.284	1.246	-----

Cell	Formula	Copy To
E1	=AVERAGE(H1:O1)	E2
E3	=AVERAGE(G3:N3)	E4

FIGURE 13.30

Ratios by Quarter and Their Averages

A graph of the original data along with their centered moving averages is shown in Figure 13.29. Notice that as Frank expected, coal receipts are above the centered moving average in the first and fourth quarters, and below average in the second and third quarters. Notice that the moving average has much less volatility than the original series; again, the averaging process eliminates the quarter-to-quarter movement.

The third step is to divide the actual data at a given point in the series by the *centered* moving average corresponding to the same point. This calculation cannot be done for all possible points, since at the beginning and end of the series we are unable to compute a centered moving average. These ratios represent the degree to which a particular observation is below (as in the .682 for period three shown in cell E10 of Figure 13.28) or above (as in the 1.24 for period four shown in cell E11) the typical level. Note that these ratios for the third quarter tend to be below 1.0 and the ratios for the fourth quarter tend to be above 1.0. These ratios form the basis for developing a "seasonal index."

To develop the seasonal index, we first group the ratios according by quarter (columns G through O), as shown in Figure 13.30. We then average all of the ratios to moving averages quarter by quarter (column E). For example, all the ratios for the first quarter average 1.108. This is a seasonal index for the first quarter, and Frank concludes that the first quarter produces coal receipts that are on average about 110.8% relative to the average of all quarters.

These seasonal indices represent what that particular season's data look like on average compared to the average of the entire series. A seasonal index greater than 1 means that season is higher than the average for the year; likewise an index less than 1 means that season is lower than the average for the year.

The last step of deseasonalization is to take the actual data and divide it by the appropriate seasonal index. This is shown in columns F and G of Figure 13.31. The deseasonalized data are graphed in Figure 13.32.

Frank notices that the deseasonalized data seem to "jump around" a lot less than the original data.

	G8	▼	=	=B8/F8	

	C	D	E	F	G
6	4 Period	Centered	Ratio of Coal Receipts to	Seasonal	Deseasonalized
7	Moving Average	Moving Average	Centered Moving Average	Indices	Data
8	-----	-----	-----	1.108	1,948.1
9	-----	-----	-----	0.784	1,535.4
10	1,613	1,603	0.682	0.860	1,272.3
11	1,594	1,610	1.240	1.234	1,617.8
12	1,626	1,674	1.244	1.108	1,877.8
13	1,721	1,788	0.745	0.784	1,700.0
14	1,856	1,877	0.787	0.860	1,716.6
15	1,898	1,923	1.317	1.234	2,053.1
16	1,948	2,005	1.122	1.108	2,029.3
17	2,063	2,061	0.744	0.784	1,956.5
18	2,060	2,055	0.942	0.860	2,250.4
19	2,050	2,058	1.226	1.234	2,045.0
20	2,066	2,064	1.070	1.108	1,992.3
21	2,061	2,087	0.765	0.784	2,038.2
22	2,112	2,163	0.886	0.860	2,229.5
23	2,213	2,255	1.209	1.234	2,209.5
24	2,297	2,335	1.119	1.108	2,356.9
25	2,373	2,328	0.830	0.784	2,464.5
26	2,282	2,215	1.004	0.860	2,585.3
27	2,148	2,105	1.123	1.234	1,915.3
28	2,062	1,994	1.040	1.108	1,871.4
29	1,925	1,935	0.821	0.784	2,028.0
30	1,945	1,964	0.852	0.860	1,945.7
31	1,984	1,995	1.225	1.234	1,980.1
32	2,006	1,984	1.124	1.108	2,013.1
33	1,963	1,940	0.863	0.784	2,137.8
34	1,917	1,864	0.806	0.860	1,748.0
35	1,812	1,759	1.284	1.234	1,831.0
36	1,706	1,720	1.052	1.108	1,632.3
37	1,734	1,731	0.724	0.784	1,600.5
38	1,729	1,753	0.920	0.860	1,875.9
39	1,777	1,796	1.246	1.234	1,814.0
40	1,815	1,829	1.096	1.108	1,808.3

FIGURE 13.31

Calculation
of Deseasonalized Values

Cell	Formula	Copy To
G8	=B8/F8	G9:G43

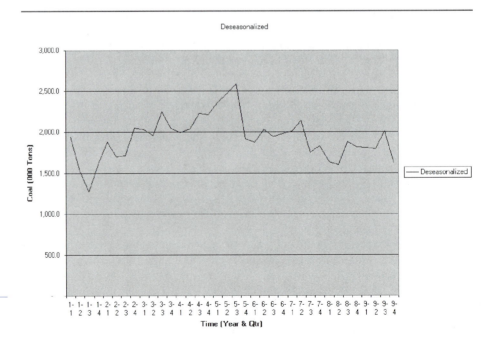

FIGURE 13.32

Graph
of Deseasonalized Data

	Time	Coal	4 Period	Centered	Ratio of Coal Receipts to	Seasonal	Deseasonalized			alpha =
	Year-Qtr	Receipts	Moving Average	Moving Average	Centered Moving Average	Indices	Data	Forecast		0.653
8	1-1	2,159	-----	-----	-----	1.108	1,948.1	1,948.1		
9	1-2	1,203	-----	-----	-----	0.784	1,535.4	1,948.1		MSE =
10	1-3	1,094	1,613	1,603	0.682	0.860	1,272.3	1,678.5		47,920
11	1-4	1,996	1,594	1,610	1.240	1.234	1,617.8	1,413.1		
12	2-1	2,081	1,626	1,674	1.244	1.108	1,877.8	1,546.8		
13	2-2	1,332	1,721	1,788	0.745	0.784	1,700.0	1,763.0		
14	2-3	1,476	1,856	1,877	0.787	0.860	1,716.6	1,721.9		
15	2-4	2,533	1,898	1,923	1.317	1.234	2,053.1	1,718.4		
16	3-1	2,249	1,948	2,005	1.122	1.108	2,029.3	1,937.1		
17	3-2	1,533	2,063	2,061	0.744	0.784	1,956.5	1,997.4		
18	3-3	1,935	2,060	2,055	0.942	0.860	2,250.4	1,970.7		
19	3-4	2,523	2,050	2,058	1.226	1.234	2,045.0	2,153.4		
20	4-1	2,208	2,056	2,064	1.070	1.108	1,992.3	2,082.6		
21	4-2	1,597	2,061	2,087	0.765	0.784	2,038.2	2,023.6		
22	4-3	1,917	2,112	2,163	0.886	0.860	2,229.5	2,033.2		
23	4-4	2,726	2,213	2,255	1.209	1.234	2,209.5	2,161.4		
24	5-1	2,612	2,297	2,335	1.119	1.108	2,356.9	2,192.8		
25	5-2	1,931	2,373	2,328	0.830	0.784	2,464.5	2,300.0		
26	5-3	2,223	2,282	2,215	1.004	0.860	2,585.3	2,407.5		
27	5-4	2,363	2,148	2,105	1.123	1.234	1,915.3	2,523.7		
28	6-1	2,074	2,062	1,994	1.040	1.108	1,871.4	2,126.2		
29	6-2	1,589	1,925	1,935	0.821	0.784	2,028.0	1,959.7		
30	6-3	1,673	1,945	1,964	0.852	0.860	1,945.7	2,004.4		
31	6-4	2,443	1,984	1,995	1.225	1.234	1,980.1	1,966.0		
32	7-1	2,231	2,006	1,984	1.124	1.108	2,013.1	1,975.2		
33	7-2	1,675	1,963	1,940	0.863	0.784	2,137.8	2,000.0		
34	7-3	1,503	1,917	1,864	0.806	0.860	1,748.0	2,090.0		
35	7-4	2,259	1,812	1,759	1.284	1.234	1,831.0	1,866.5		
36	8-1	1,809	1,706	1,720	1.052	1.108	1,632.3	1,843.3		
37	8-2	1,254	1,734	1,731	0.724	0.784	1,600.5	1,705.5		
38	8-3	1,613	1,729	1,753	0.920	0.860	1,875.9	1,636.9		
39	8-4	2,238	1,777	1,796	1.246	1.234	1,814.0	1,793.0		
40	9-1	2,004	1,815	1,829	1.096	1.108	1,808.3	1,806.7		

Cell	Formula	Copy To
H8	=G8	—
H9	=$J$7*G8+(1−$J$7)*H8	H10:H44
J10	=SUMXMY2(G9:G43,H9:H43)/COUNT(G9:G43)	—

FIGURE 13.33

Spreadsheet for Exponential Smoothing Forecast of Deseasonalized Data

Forecasting Once the data have been deseasonalized, a deseasonalized forecast can be made. This should be based on an appropriate methodology that accounts for the pattern in the deseasonalized data (e.g., if there is trend in the data, use a trend-based model). In this example, Frank chooses to forecast coal receipts for the first quarter of the tenth year by simple exponential smoothing. Using this forecasting method, it turns out that the optimal smoothing constant is $\alpha^* = .653$, which yields an MSE of 47,920 (see Figure 13.33). Frank determines that the deseasonalized forecast would be 1726 thousand tons for the first quarter of next year (cell H44). This would also be the deseasonalized forecast amount for the second quarter given the data we currently have.

Reseasonalizing The last step in the process is for Frank to reseasonalize the forecast of 1726. The way to do this is to *multiply* 1726 by the seasonal index for the first quarter (1.108) to obtain a value of 1912. A seasonalized forecast for the second quarter would be 1726 times its seasonal index (0.784), giving a value of 1353. These values would represent Frank's point forecasts for the coming two quarters.

THE RANDOM WALK

The moving average and exponential smoothing techniques discussed above are examples of what are called time-series models. Recently, much more sophisticated methods for time-series analysis have become available. These methods, based primarily on developments by G. E. P. Box and G. M. Jenkins (see Box and Jenkins), have already had an important impact on the practice of forecasting, and indeed the Box-Jenkins approach is incorporated in several computer-based forecasting packages.

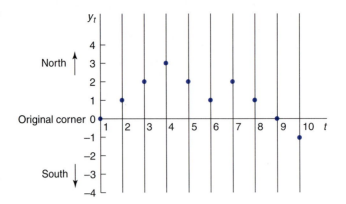

FIGURE 13.34

Classic Random Walk

These time-series forecasting techniques are based on the assumption that the true values of the variable of interest, y_t, are generated by a stochastic (i.e., probabilistic) model. Introducing enough of the theory of probability to enable us to discuss these models in any generality seems inappropriate, but one special and very important (and very simple) process, called a **random walk**, serves as a nice illustration of a stochastic model. Here the variable y_t is assumed to be produced by the relationship

$$y_t = y_{t-1} + \epsilon$$

where the value of ϵ is determined by a random event. To illustrate this process even more explicitly, let us consider a man standing at a street corner on a north-south street. He flips a fair coin. If it lands with a head showing (H), he walks one block north. If it lands with a tail showing (T), he walks one block south. When he arrives at the next corner (whichever one it turns out to be), he repeats the process. This is the classic example of a random walk. To put this example in the form of the model, label the original corner zero. We shall call this the value of the first observation, y_1. Starting at this point, label successive corners going north $+1$, $+2$, ... Also starting at the original corner label successive corners going south -1, -2, . . . (see Figure 13.34). These labels that describe the location of our random walker are the y_t's.

In the model, $y_t = y_{t-1} + \epsilon$, where (assuming a fair coin) $\epsilon = 1$ with probability 1/2 and $\epsilon = -1$ with probability 1/2. If our walker observes the sequence H, H, H, T, T, H, T, T, T, he will follow the path shown in Figure 13.34.

Forecasts Based on Conditional Expected Value Suppose that after our special agent has flipped the coin nine times (i.e., he has moved nine times, and we have [starting with corner 0] ten observations of corners), we would like to forecast where he will be after another move. This is the typical forecasting problem in the time-series context. That is, we have observed $y_1, y_2, \ldots, y_{10}$ and we need a good forecast $\hat{y}_{11}$ of the forthcoming value y_{11}. In this case, according to a reasonable criterion, the best value for $\hat{y}_{11}$ is the *conditional expected value* of the random quantity y_{11}. In other words, the best forecast is the expected value of y_{11} given that we know $y_1, y_2, \ldots, y_{10}$. From the model we know that y_{11} will equal $(y_{10} + 1)$ with a probability equal to ½ and y_{11} will equal $(y_{10} - 1)$ with a probability equal to ½. Thus, $E(y_{11} \mid y_1, \ldots, y_{10})$, the conditional expected value of y_{11} given $y_1, y_2, \ldots, y_{10}$, is calculated as follows:

$$E(y_{11} \mid y_1, \ldots, y_{10}) = (y_{10} + 1)\, ½ + (y_{10} - 1)½ = y_{10}$$

Thus we see that for this model the data $y_1, \ldots, y_9$ are irrelevant, and *the best forecast of the random walker's position one move from now is his current position.* It is interesting to observe that the best forecast of the next observation y_{12} given $y_1, \ldots, y_{10}$ (the original set) is also y_{10}. Indeed, the best forecast for any future value of y_t, given this particular model, is its current value.

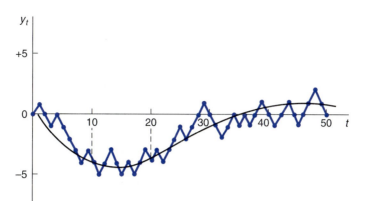

FIGURE 13.35

Time-Series Data

Seeing What Isn't There This example is not as silly as it may seem at first glance. Indeed, there is a great deal of evidence that supports the idea that stock prices and foreign currency exchange rates behave like a random walk and that the best forecast of a future stock price or of an exchange rate (e.g., yen/$) is its current value. Not surprisingly, this conclusion is not warmly accepted by research directors and technical chartists who make their living forecasting stock prices or exchange rates. One reason for the resistance to the random walk hypothesis is the almost universal human tendency when looking at a set of data to observe certain patterns or regularities, no matter how the data are produced. Consider the time-series data plotted in Figure 13.35. It does not seem unreasonable to believe that the data are following a sinusoidal pattern as suggested by the smooth curve in the figure. In spite of this impression, the data were in fact generated by the random walk model presented earlier in this section. This illustrates the tendency to see patterns where there are none. In Figure 13.35, any attempt to predict future values by extrapolating the sinusoidal pattern would have no more validity than flipping a coin.

In concluding this section we should stress that it is *not* a general conclusion of time-series analysis that the best estimate of the future is the present (i.e., that $\hat{y}_{t+1} = y_t$). This result holds for the particular random walk model presented above. The result depends crucially on the assumption that the expected or mean value of ϵ, the random component, is zero. If the probability that ϵ equals 1 had been 0.6 and the probability that ϵ equals -1 had been 0.4, the best forecast of y_{t+1} would not have been y_t. To find this forecast one would have had to find the new value for $E(y_{t+1} \mid y_1, \ldots y_t)$. Such a model is called a *random walk with a drift.*

13.5   THE ROLE OF HISTORICAL DATA: DIVIDE AND CONQUER

Historical data play a critical role in the construction and testing of forecasting models. One hopes that a rationale precedes the construction of a quantitative forecasting model. There may be theoretical reasons for believing that a relationship exists between some independent variables and the dependent variable to be forecast and thus that a causal model is appropriate. Alternatively, one may take the time-series view that the "behavior of the past" is a good indication of the future. In either case, however, if a quantitative model is to be used, the parameters of the model must be selected. For example:

1. In a causal model using a linear forecasting function, $y = a + bx$, the values of a and b must be specified.

2. In a time-series model using a weighted n-period moving average, $\hat{y}_{t+1} = \alpha_0 y_t + \alpha_1 y_{t-1} + \ldots + \alpha_{n-1} y_{t-n+1}$, the number of terms, n, and the values for the weights, $\alpha_0, \alpha_1, \ldots, \alpha_{n-1}$, must be specified.

3. In a time-series model using exponential smoothing, $\hat{y}_{t+1} = \alpha y_t + (1 - \alpha)\hat{y}_t$, the value of α must be specified.

In any of these models, in order to specify the parameter values, one typically must make use of historical data. A useful guide in seeking to use such data effectively is to "divide and conquer." More directly, this means that it is often a useful practice to use part of the data to estimate the parameters and the rest of the data to test the model. With real data, it is also important to "clean" the data—that is, examine them for irregularities, missing information, or special circumstances, and adjust them accordingly.

For example, suppose that a firm has weekly sales data on a particular product for the last two years (104 observations) and plans to use an exponential smoothing model to forecast sales for this product. The firm might use the following procedure:

1. Pick a particular value of α, and compare the values of $\hat{y}_{t+1}$ to y_{t+1} for $t = 25$ to 75. The first 24 values are not compared, so as to negate any initial or "startup" effect; that is, to nullify the influence of the initial guess, $\hat{y}_1$. The manager would continue to select different values of α until the model produces a satisfactory fit during the period $t = 25$ to 75.

2. Test the model derived in step 1 on the remaining 29 pieces of data. That is, using the best value of α from step 1, compare the values of $\hat{y}_{t+1}$ to y_{t+1} for $t = 76$ to 104.

If the model does a good job of forecasting values for the last part of the historical data, there is some reason to believe that it will also do a good job with the future. On the other hand, if by using the data from weeks 1 through 75, the model cannot perform well in predicting the demand in weeks 76 through 104, the prospects for predicting the future with the same model seem dubious. In this case, another forecasting technique might be applied.

The same type of divide-and-conquer strategy can be used with any of the forecasting techniques we have presented. This approach amounts to *simulating* the model's performance on past data. It is a popular method of testing models. It should be stressed, however, that this procedure represents what is termed a *null test*. If the model fails on historical data, the model probably is not appropriate. If the model succeeds on historical data, *one cannot be sure that it will work in the future*. Who knows, the underlying system that is producing the observations may change. It is this type of sobering experience that causes certain forecasters to be less certain.

13.6   QUALITATIVE FORECASTING

EXPERT JUDGMENT

Many important forecasts are not based on formal models. This point seems obvious in the realm of world affairs—matters of war and peace, so to speak. Perhaps more surprisingly it is also often true in economic matters. For example, during the high-interest-rate period of 1980 and 1981, the most influential forecasters of interest rates were not two competing econometric models run by teams of econometricians. Rather, they were Henry Kaufman of Salomon Brothers and Albert Wojnilower of First Boston, the so-called Doctors Doom and Gloom of the interest-rate world. These gentlemen combined relevant factors such as the money supply and unemployment, as well as results from quantitative models, in their own intuitive way (their own "internal" models) and produced forecasts that had widespread credibility and impact on the financial community.

The moral for managers is that qualitative forecasts can well be an important source of information. Managers must consider a wide variety of sources of data before coming to a decision. Expert opinion should not be ignored. A sobering and useful measure of all forecasts—quantitative and qualitative—is a record of past performance. Good performance in the past is a sensible type of null test. An excellent track record does not promise good results in the future. A poor record, however, hardly creates enthusiasm for high achievement in the future. Managers should thus listen to experts cautiously and hold them to a standard of performance. This same type of standard should be applied by individuals to the thousands of managers of stock and bond mutual funds. Every quarter the *Wall Street Journal* publishes the ranking of the different mutual funds' performance for the previous

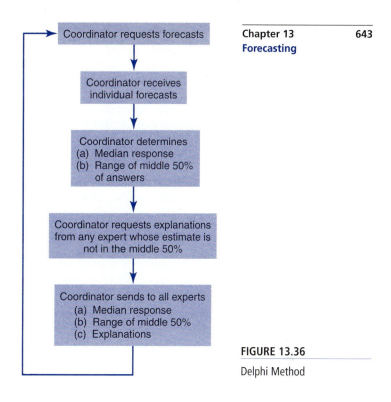

FIGURE 13.36

Delphi Method

quarter, year, and five-year period. Wise investors check the track record of the different funds although it is not a guarantee of future performance.

There is, however, more to qualitative forecasting than selecting "the right" expert. Techniques exist to elicit and combine forecasts from various groups of experts, and we now turn our attention to these techniques.

THE DELPHI METHOD AND CONSENSUS PANEL

The **Delphi Method** confronts the problem of obtaining a combined forecast from a group of experts. One approach is to bring the experts together in a room and let them discuss the event until a consensus emerges. Not surprisingly, this group is called a **consensus panel.** This approach suffers because of the group dynamics of such an exercise. One strong individual can have an enormous effect on the forecast because of his or her personality, reputation, or debating skills. Accurate analysis may be pushed into a secondary position.

The Delphi Method was developed by the Rand Corporation to retain the strength of a joint forecast, while removing the effects of group dynamics. The method uses a coordinator and a set of experts. No expert knows who else is in the group. All communication is through the coordinator. The process is illustrated in Figure 13.36.

After three or four passes through this process, a consensus forecast typically emerges. The forecast may be near the original median, but if a forecast that is an outlier in round 1 is supported by strong analysis, the extreme forecast in round 1 may be the group forecast after three or four rounds.

GRASS ROOTS FORECASTING AND MARKET RESEARCH

Other qualitative techniques focus primarily on forecasting demand for a product or group of products. They are based on the concept of asking either those who are close to the eventual consumer, such as salespeople, or consumers themselves, about a product or their purchasing plans.

Consulting Salesmen In **grass roots forecasting,** salespeople are asked to forecast demand in their districts. In the simplest situations, these forecasts are added together to get a total demand forecast. In more sophisticated systems individual forecasts or the total may be adjusted on the basis of the historical correlation between the salesperson's forecasts and the actual sales. Such a procedure makes it possible to adjust for an actual occurrence of the stereotyped salesperson's optimism.

Grass roots forecasts have the advantage of bringing a great deal of detailed knowledge to bear on the forecasting problem. The individual salesperson who is keenly aware of the situation in his or her district should be able to provide better forecasts than more aggregate models. There are, however, several problems:

1. *High cost:* The time salespeople spend forecasting is not spent selling. Some view this opportunity cost of grass roots forecasting as its major disadvantage.

2. *Potential conflict of interest:* Sales forecasts may well turn into marketing goals that can affect a salesperson's compensation in an important way. Such considerations exert a downward bias in individual forecasts.

3. *Product schizophrenia (i.e., stereotyped salesperson's optimism):* It is important for salespeople to be enthusiastic about their product and its potential uses. It is not clear that this enthusiasm is consistent with a cold-eyed appraisal of its market potential.

In summary, grass roots forecasting may not fit well with other organization objectives and thus may not be effective in an overall sense.

Consulting Consumers   **Market research** is a large and important topic in its own right. It includes a variety of techniques, from consumer panels through consumer surveys and on to test marketing. The goal is to make predictions about the size and structure of the market for specific goods and/or services. These predictions (forecasts) are usually based on small samples and are qualitative in the sense that the original data typically consist of subjective evaluations of consumers. A large menu of quantitative techniques exists to aid in determining how to gather the data and how to analyze them.

Market research is an important activity in most consumer product firms. It also plays an increasingly important role in the political and electoral process.

13.7   NOTES ON IMPLEMENTATION

Whether in the private or public sector, the need to deal with the future is an implicit or explicit part of every management action and decision. Because of this, managing the forecasting activity is a critical part of a manager's responsibility. A manager must decide what resources to devote to a particular forecast and what approach to use to obtain it.

The question of "what resources" hinges on two issues:

1. The importance of the forecast, or more precisely, the importance of the decision awaiting the forecast and its sensitivity to the forecast.

2. The quality of the forecast as a function of the resources devoted to it.

In other words, how much does it matter, and how much does it cost? These are the same questions that management must ask and answer about many of the services it purchases.

In actual applications, the selection of the appropriate forecasting method for a particular situation depends on a variety of factors. Some of the features that distinguish one situation from the next are

1. The importance of the decision.

2. The availability of relevant data.

3. The time horizon for the forecast.

4. The cost of preparing the forecast.

5. The time until the forecast is needed.

6. The number of times such a forecast will be needed.

7. The stability of the environment.

The importance of the decision probably plays the strongest role in determining what forecasting method to use. Curiously, *qualitative approaches* (as opposed to *quantitative*) dominate the stage at the extremes of important and not very important forecasts. On the low end of the importance scale, think of the many decisions a supermarket manager makes on what are typically implicit forecasts: what specials to offer, what to display at the ends of the aisles, how many baggers to employ. In such cases, forecasts are simply business judgments. The potential return is not high enough to justify the expenditure of resources required for formal and extensive model development.

On the high end, the decisions are *too important* (and perhaps too complex) to be left entirely to formal quantitative models. The future of the company, to say nothing of the chief executive, may hinge on a good forecast and the ensuing decision. *Quantitative models may certainly provide important input. In fact, the higher the planning level, the more you can be sure that forecasting models will be employed at least to some extent.* But for very important decisions, the final forecast will be based on the judgment of the executive and his or her colleagues.

The extent to which a quantitative model is employed as an input to this judgment will depend, in the final analysis, on management's assessment of the model's validity. A consensus panel (a management committee) is often the chosen vehicle for achieving the final forecast. For example, what forecasts do you think persuaded Henry Ford IV to reject Lee Iacocca's plan to move Ford into small, energy-efficient cars in the late 1970s? Also, what forecasts led Panasonic to introduce a tape-based system while RCA introduced a disk-based system for the TV player market? And what about the Cuban missile crisis? The Bay of Pigs? Clearly, management's personal view of the future played an important role.

APPLICATION CAPSULE   **Yes, Virginia . . . : An Economic Forecasting Model Helps Keep an Unemployment Insurance Trust Fund in the Black**

Unemployment insurance operates on the same risk-sharing philosophy as any other insurance policy: funds are collected from a large population to help pay unexpected costs for a small percentage of that population. The obvious question is, How much must a state collect from whom in order to provide for the payments dictated by its unemployment legislation? This question can be answered only by making forecasts of future cash inflows and outflows.

The Commonwealth of Virginia has created the unemployment insurance econometric forecasting model (UIEFM) to help answer this question. The model has two main sections: a projection model and a financial forecasting model. The projection model uses regression analysis to forecast cash *outflows* as a function of fundamental economic factors, including:

1. Rates of unemployment
2. Rates of increase in wage levels
3. Changes in the insured labor force and payrolls
4. Minimum and maximum amounts of weekly benefits

The financial forecast program is concerned with two issues:

1. The impact of the projected cash flow on the taxing mechanism of the UI system, that is, on the cash *inflow* to the system
2. The level of funds in the UI trust after ten years

The financial forecast program is quite complex because the Virginia unemployment tax law includes three taxing alternatives. Virginia employers are taxed on the basis of their previous unemployment experience. The idea is that those employers who add to the ranks of the unemployed should pay a larger proportion of unemployment expenditure. In addition, each employer pays a "pool" tax to help cover expenses not covered by the experience tax. Finally, a third tax is assessed when the UI trust fund falls below the 50% solvency level defined in the unemployment act. Indeed, a large part of the motivation for the UIEFM model came from the dramatic decline in the Unemployment Insurance Trust Fund between 1975 and 1980.

An important contribution of the forecasting model was to alert planners to the possibility of a surplus. The model predicted that under favorable economic conditions the funds in the unemployment trust could exceed the expectations of those who passed the original unemployment insurance act. As a result, several policies to deal with this situation were devised. The model was then used to evaluate their potential impact, helping legislators to choose the most effective proposals. More generally, the commissioner of the Virginia Employment Commission has stated that "the preponderance of legislation in Virginia is underpinned by simulations and analysis from the model" (see Lackman et al.).

Quantitative models play a major role in producing directly usable forecasts in situations that are deemed to be of "midlevel importance." This is especially true in short-range (up to one month) and medium-range (one month to two years) scenarios. Time-series analyses are especially popular for repetitive forecasts of midlevel importance in a relatively stable environment. The use of exponential smoothing to forecast the demand for mature products is a prototype of this type of application.

Causal models actively compete with various experts for forecasting various economic phenomena in the midlevel-medium range. Situations in which a forecast will be repeated quite often, and where much relevant data are available, are prime targets for quantitative models, and in such cases many successful models have been constructed. As our earlier discussion of interest rates forecasts indicated, there is ample room in this market for the "expert" with a good record of performance. In commercial practice one finds that many management consulting groups, as well as specialized firms, provide forecasting "packages" for use in a variety of midlevel scenarios.

As a final comment, we can make the following observations about the use of forecasting in decision making within the public sector: Just as in private industry, it is often the case that the higher the level of the planning function, the more one sees the use of forecasting models employed as inputs. In such high-level situations there is a high premium on expertise, and forecasting is, in one sense, a formal extension of expert judgment. Think of the Council of Economic Advisors, the Chairman of the Federal Reserve Board, or the Director of the Central Intelligence Agency. You can be sure that forecasts are of importance in these contexts, and you can be sure that there is within these environments a continued updating and, one hopes, improvement of forecasting techniques. As always, the extent to which the results of existing models are employed is a function of the executive's overall assessment of the model itself.

Key Terms

Causal Forecasting.   The forecast for the quantity of interest is determined as a function of other variables.

Curve Fitting.   Selecting a "curve" that passes close to the data points in a scatter diagram.

Scatter Diagram.   A plot of the response variable against a single independent variable.

Method of Least Squares.   A procedure for fitting a curve to a set of data. It minimizes the sum of the squared deviations of the data from the curve.

Polynomial of Degree n.   A function of the form $y = a_0 + a_1x + a_2x^2 + \ldots + a_nx^n$. Often used as the curve in a least-squares fit.

Linear Regression.   A statistical technique used to estimate the parameters of a polynomial in such a way that the polynomial "best" represents a set of data. Also sometimes used to describe the problem of fitting a linear function to a set of data.

Validation.   The process of using a model on past data to assess its credibility.

Time-Series Forecasting.   A variable of interest is plotted against time and extrapolated into the future using one of several techniques.

Simple n-Period Moving Average.   Average of last n periods is used as the forecast of future values; $(n-1)$ pieces of data must be stored.

Weighted n-Period Moving Average.   A weighted sum, with decreasing weights, of the last n observations is used as a forecast. The sum of the weights equals 1; $(n-1)$ pieces of data must be stored.

Exponential Smoothing.   A weighted sum, with decreasing weights of *all* past observations, the sum of the weights equals 1; only one piece of information need be stored.

Holt's Model.   A variation of simple exponential smoothing that accounts for either up or down trend in the data.

Seasonality. Movements up and down in a pattern of constant length that repeats itself in a time-series set of data.

Random Walk. A stochastic process in which the variable at time t equals the variable at time $(t-1)$ plus a random element.

Delphi Method. A method of achieving a consensus among experts while eliminating factors of group dynamics.

Consensus Panel. An assembled group of experts that produces an agreed-upon forecast.

Grass Roots Forecasting. Soliciting forecasts from individuals "close to" and thus presumably knowledgeable about the entity being forecast.

Market Research. A type of grass roots forecasting that is based on getting information directly from consumers.

Self-Review Exercises

True-False

1. **T F** Minimizing total deviations (i.e., $\sum_{i=1}^{n} d_i$) is a reasonable way to define a "good fit."

2. **T F** Least squares fits can be used for a variety of curves in addition to straight lines.

3. **T F** Regression analysis can be used to prove that the method of least squares produces the best possible fit for any specific real model.

4. **T F** The method of least squares is used in causal models as well as in time-series models.

5. **T F** In a weighted three-period moving-average forecast, the weights can be assigned in many different ways.

6. **T F** Exponential smoothing automatically assigns weights that decrease in value as the data get older.

7. **T F** Average squared error is one way to compare various forecasting techniques.

8. **T F** *Validation* refers to the process of determining a model's credibility by simulating its performance on past data.

9. **T F** A "random walk" is a stochastic model.

10. **T F** At higher levels of management, qualitative forecasting models become more important.

Multiple Choice

11. Linear regression (with one independent variable)
    a. requires the estimation of three parameters
    b. is a special case of polynomial least squares
    c. is a quick and dirty method
    d. uses total deviation as a measure of good fit

12. An operational problem with a simple k-period moving average is that
    a. it assigns equal weight to each piece of past data
    b. it assigns equal weight to each of the last k observations
    c. it requires storage of $k-1$ pieces of data
    d. none of the above

13. A large value of α puts more weight on
    a. recent
    b. older
    data in an exponential smoothing model.

14. If the data being observed can be best thought of as being generated by random deviations about a stationary mean, a
    a. large
    b. small
    value of α is preferable in an exponential smoothing model.

15. A divide-and-conquer strategy means
    a. Divide the modeling procedure into two parts:
       (1) Use all the data to estimate parameter values, and (2) use the parameter values from part (1) to see how well the model works.
    b. Divide the data into two parts: (1) Estimate the parameters of the model on the first part. (2) See how well the model works on the second part.
    c. Compare two models on the same database.
    d. None of the above.

16. The Delphi Method
    a. relies on the power of written arguments
    b. requires resolution of differences via face-to-face debate
    c. is mainly used as an alternative to exponential smoothing
    d. none of the above

17. Conflict of interest can be a serious problem in
    a. the Delphi Method
    b. asking salespeople
    c. market research based on consumer data
    d. none of the above

Answers

Problems

•• **13-1.** Consider the data set shown (contained in 13-1.XLS):

x	100	70	30	40	80	60	50	20	10	90
y	57	40	35	33	56	46	45	26	26	53

    (a) Plot a scatter diagram of these data.
    (b) Fit a straight line to the data using the method of least squares.
    (c) Use the function derived in part (b) to forecast a value for y when $x = 120$.

•• **13-2.** Consider the following set of data where x is the independent and y the dependent variable (contained in 13-2.XLS):

x	30	25	20	15	10	5
y	15	20	30	35	45	60

    (a) Plot the scatter diagram for these data.
    (b) Fit a straight line to the data by the method of least squares.

•• **13-3.** Consider the following set of data (contained in 13-3.XLS):

x	1	2	3	4	5	6	7
y	2.00	1.50	4.50	4.00	5.50	4.50	6.00

    (a) Plot a scatter diagram of the data.
    (b) Fit a straight line to the data by the method of least squares. Plot the line on the scatter diagram.
    (c) Fit a quadratic function to the data by the method of least squares. Plot the curve on the scatter diagram.

•• **13-4.** Fit a quadratic function to the data in Problem 13-2 by the method of least squares.

•• **13-5.** Compare the goodness of fit on the data in Problem 13-3 for the least squares linear function and the least squares quadratic function by calculating the sum of the squared deviations.

•• **13-6.** Compare the goodness of fit on the data in Problem 13-2 for the least squares linear function and the least squares quadratic function (derived in Problem 13-4) by calculating the sum of the squared deviations. Is the answer for 13-4 always better than that for 13-2?

•• **13-7.** Further investigation reveals that the x variable in Problem 13-1 is simply 10 times the time at which an observation was recorded, and the y variable is demand. For example, a demand of 57 occurred at time 10; a demand of 26 occurred at times 1 and 2.
    (a) Plot actual demand against time.
    (b) Use a simple four-period moving average to forecast demand at time 11.
    (c) By inspecting the data, would you expect this to be a good model or not? Why?

•• **13-8.** Consider the following data set (contained in 13-8.XLS):

TIME	1	2	3	4	5	6	7	8	9	10	11	12
DEMAND	10	14	19	26	31	35	39	44	51	55	61	54

    (a) Plot this time-series. Connect the points with a straight line.
    (b) Use a simple four-period moving average to forecast the demand for periods 5–13.
    (c) Find the mean absolute deviation.
    (d) Does this seem like a reasonable forecasting device in view of the data?

•• **13-9.** Consider the data in Problem 13-7.

    (a) Use a four-period weighted moving average with the weights 4/10, 3/10, 2/10, and 1/10 to forecast demand for time 11. Heavier weights should apply to more recent observations.

    (b) Do you prefer this approach to the simple four-period model suggested in Problem 13-7? Why?

    (c) Now find the optimal weights using the Solver. How much have you reduced your error measure compared to (a)?

•• **13-10.** Consider the data in Problem 13-8.

    (a) Use a four-period weighted moving average with the weights 0.1, 0.2, 0.3, and 0.4 to forecast demand for time periods 5–13. Heavier weights should apply to more recent observations.

    (b) Find the mean absolute deviation.

    (c) Do you prefer this approach to the simple four-period model suggested in Problem 13-8? Why?

    (d) Now find the optimal weights using the Solver. How much have you reduced your error measure compared to the method of (a)?

•• **13-11.** Consider the time-series data in Problem 13-7.

    (a) Let $\hat{y}_1 = 22$ and $\alpha = 0.4$. Use an exponential smoothing model to forecast demand in period 11.

    (b) If you were to use an exponential smoothing model to forecast this time-series, would you prefer a larger (≥ 0.4) or smaller value for α? Why?

    (c) Find the optimal value for α using Solver by minimizing the mean absolute percentage error.

•• **13-12.** Consider the time-series data in Problem 13-8.

    (a) Assume that $\hat{y}_1 = 8$ and $\alpha = 0.3$. Use an exponential smoothing model to forecast demand in periods 2–13.

    (b) Find the mean absolute percentage error.

    (c) Repeat the analysis using $\alpha = 0.5$.

    (d) If you were to use an exponential smoothing model to forecast this time-series, would you prefer $\alpha = 0.3$, a larger (≥ 0.3), or smaller, value of α? Why?

    (e) What is the optimal value for α? How much does it reduce the MAPE from part (a)?

•• **13-13.** The president of Quacker Mills wants a subjective evaluation of the market potential of a new nacho-flavored breakfast cereal from a group consisting of (1) the vice-president of marketing, (2) the marketing manager of the western region, (3) ten district sales managers from the western region. Discuss the advantages and disadvantages of a consensus panel and the Delphi Method for obtaining this evaluation.

•• **13-14.** Given that y_t is produced by the relationship $y_t = y_{t-1} + \epsilon$ where ϵ is a random number with mean zero and $y_1 = 1$, $y_2 = 2$, $y_3 = 1.5$, $y_4 = 0.8$, $y_5 = 1$, what is your best forecast of y_6?

•• **13-15.** Given your current knowledge of the situation, would you recommend a causal or a time-series model to forecast next month's demand for Kellogg's Rice Crispies? Why?

•• **13-16.** If $\alpha = 0.3$, in calculating $\hat{y}_5$, what is the weight on

    (a) $\hat{y}_1$

    (b) y_1

    (c) y_4

••• **13-17.** In some cases it is possible to obtain better forecasts by using a trend-adjusted forecast.

    (a) Use the Holt trend model with $\hat{y}_1 = 22$ to forecast the sequence of demands in Problem 13-7.

    (b) Use the MSE error measure to compare the simple exponential smoothing model (Problem 13-11) with the trend-adjusted model from part (a) on forecasting demand.

••• **13-18.** In some cases it is possible to obtain better forecasts by using a trend-adjusted forecast.

    (a) Use the Holt trend model with $\hat{y}_1 = 8$ to forecast the sequence of demands in Problem 13-8.

    (b) As in Problem 13-17, compare the above result with the result from Problem 13-12 (simple exponential smoothing).

•• **13-19.** In Section 13.4 we presented the Holt trend model for forecasting the earnings of Startup Airlines by Amy Luford. Use the same data to

    (a) Develop a trend model using linear regression with time as the independent variable.

    (b) How does its forecasting performance compare with the Holt trend model?

•• **13-20.** Discuss the merit of the measure "mean squared error." In comparing two forecasting methods, is the one with a smaller average squared error *always* superior?

•• **13-21.** If a company experiences an exponential sales growth, how would you alter the sales forecasting model to account for this?

•• **13-22.** The spreadsheet AUTO.XLS contains data from *Business Week* on auto sales by month for 43 months.

    (a) Deseasonalize the data.

    (b) Find the best forecasting method for the deseasonalized data.

    (c) What is your forecast for period 44?

    (d) How much confidence do you have in your forecast?

•• **13-23.** Using the OILCOMP.XLS data, use the "Regression" tool of Excel to fit a quadratic function curve to the data. HINT: You must first create a column for a second independent variable, $X_2 = X_1^2$, and then regress Y (Sales/hr) on both X_1 (Cars/hr) and X_2 ([Cars/hr] ^2).

    (a) How do the results compare to those found in the chapter by using the Solver?

    (b) Which technique seems easier?

    (c) Which error measures can you use to compare these two approaches?

Case Study   The Bank of Laramie

Jim Cowan was reviewing the staffing needs for the Proof Department. He was the president of the Bank of Laramie and one of his first priorities was to evaluate a staffing and scheduling problem.

Company Background

The Bank of Laramie conducted retail and corporate banking activities and provided a full line of trust services to its customers. It provided its customers a full line of corporate banking services, including cash management, and money market services. It had total assets of $19 million and net income of $300 thousand.

Proof Department

The Proof Department was the heart of the bank's check-clearing operations. The department received and processed checks and other documents to clear them in the shortest possible time in order to save on float, which averaged $450 thousand a day. The department was charged with the responsibility for sorting checks, proving the accuracy of deposits, distributing checks, and listing transactions arising from the daily operations of the bank.

The physical facility consisted of a room with two proof machines and several tables. The department operated from 8:00 A.M. to 5:30 P.M. on Monday through Friday. Despite the practice by other banks of handling check processing almost entirely at night, the Bank of Laramie believed it was important to give its employees a normal workday.

The volume of items processed in the Proof Department had increased significantly in the last two years, from 780 thousand/year to 1.6 million/year. The scheduling problem in the department was magnified because of the uneven nature of the volume. Exhibit 1 contains *deseasonalized* weekly proof volumes going back to the beginning of the prior year. This

volume pattern led management to use a part-time staff to cover peak loads. Currently, one full-time and two part-time proof operators were working at the bank. Each operator had an average processing rate of 700 items per hour.

Forecasting

The first thing Mr. Cowan had to do was forecast demand for next week, week 67, and then he would need to work out a schedule for the number of full- and part-time staff to meet the predicted demand. A couple of simple forecasting methods appealed to him—namely, using the previous week's actual demand for the next week's forecast or just using the weekly average over the past 66 weeks. He wondered how accurate these simple methods were, however, and whether or not there was a better way.

He would use his forecast to determine how many hours of additional part-time workers to schedule for the next week. His base schedule was enough to do 15,000 checks; he could add as many additional part-time hours as he wished to the schedule. (*Note:* The base schedule includes the number of checks that could be processed by one full-time and two part-time workers along with their other duties.) If he scheduled either full- or part-time hours, he had to pay for them even if the workers completed the check processing early. On the other hand, if the volume of checks was so high that the checks couldn't be processed in the hours he scheduled for the week, he would need to pay overtime wages (which were 50% above regular wages) in order to complete the work for the week. There was no requirement to finish the checks in a given day during the day, but all the checks for the week had to be done by Friday afternoon.

His first task was to get a handle on the forecasting problem; then he could easily use it to find the number of part-time hours to schedule.

EXHIBIT 1 The Bank of Laramie Deseasonalized Weekly Proof Volumes

WEEK	VOLUME (000)	WEEK	VOLUME (000)
1	23.4	34	31.1
2	26.4	35	31.0
3	28.7	36	29.6
4	26.5	37	31.5
5	28.6	38	31.3
6	29.4	39	31.1
7	29.9	40	34.9
8	29.3	41	32.3
9	32.2	42	35.6
10	28.7	43	33.8
11	27.8	44	31.3
12	31.1	45	31.2
13	32.7	46	30.4
14	32.5	47	31.1
15	28.9	48	32.7
16	31.8	49	34.8
17	32.8	50	34.5
18	32.7	51	36.0
19	31.7	52	28.3
20	32.5	53	27.8
21	32.7	54	30.4
22	30.9	55	28.4
23	30.5	56	29.3
24	31.3	57	28.9
25	30.1	58	33.5
26	32.4	59	32.6
27	28.5	60	32.0
28	29.9	61	30.6
29	31.7	62	31.9
30	30.7	63	31.3
31	31.6	64	31.6
32	32.1	65	31.1
33	30.1	66	32.0

Questions

1. Look at the following five procedures for forecasting the weekly workload requirements of the Proof Department suggested below:

   Method 1: This simple forecasting scheme uses the previous week's volume to forecast each succeeding week's volume (e.g., the forecast for week 10 would be 32.2, the volume for week 9).

   Method 2: This approach uses the average volume over all the previous weeks as the forecast. Thus, the forecast for week 23 would be 30.05 (the average over the first 22 weeks). To forecast week 67, weeks 1 through 66 would be averaged together.

   Method 3: This method is exponential smoothing with alpha = 0.5. Use the spreadsheet (BANK.XLS) that already has the data from Exhibit 1 entered and the exponential smoothing forecast calculated for an alpha of 0.5.

   (Notice that this forecasting method requires an initial average to get things started. The spreadsheet used 23.4 as this average; in essence taking a "best-case" approach by assuming the first average was perfect.)

   Method 4: This method takes a moving average approach. The number of periods in the moving average is up to you. Try several different values to come up with the best forecasting method you can.

   Method 5: This method is called linear regression. It basically fits a straight line through the data, looking for the overall trend.

2. Which of the forecasting methods presented would you recommend to forecast weekly volumes? Adjust the smoothing constant if needed to improve method 3.

3. How many part-time hours should Mr. Cowan schedule for next week? HINT: Think about the costs of over- and underscheduling the number of hours.

Christensen started to look at the circulation data of some of the other monthly magazines represented by the client organization. The first set of data was for *Working Woman* (found in the "WkgWom" sheet of SHSB.XLS and shown in Exhibit 1), which was targeted at women who were in management careers in business. Contents included sections devoted to entrepreneurs, business news, economic trends, technology, politics, career fields, social and behavioral sciences, fashion, and health. It was sold almost entirely through subscriptions, as evidenced by the latest figures reported to the Audit Bureau of Circulation (823.6K subscriptions out of 887.8K total circulation).

[1]This case is to be used as the basis for class discussion rather than to illustrate either the effective or ineffective handling of an administrative situation. © 1990 by the Darden Graduate Business School Foundation. Preview Darden case abstracts on the World Wide Web at www.darden.virginia.edu/demso.

The next graph represented circulation data for *Country Living* (found in the "CtryLiving" sheet of SHSB.XLS and shown in Exhibit 2), a journal that focused on both the practical concerns and the intangible rewards of living on the land. It was sold to people who had a place in the country, whether that was a working farm, a gentleman's country place, or a weekend retreat.

The third set of data was for *Health* (found in the "Hlth" sheet of SHSB.XLS and shown in Exhibit 3), which was a lifestyle magazine edited for women who were trying to look and feel better. The magazine provided information on fitness, beauty, nutrition, medicine, psychology, and fashions for the active woman.

A fourth graph was for *Better Homes and Gardens* (found in the "BH&G" sheet of SHSB.XLS and shown in Exhibit 4), which competed with *Good Housekeeping* and was published

EXHIBIT 1 Graph of *Working Woman* Circulation

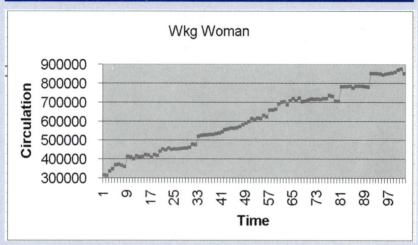

EXHIBIT 2 Graph of *Country Living* Circulation

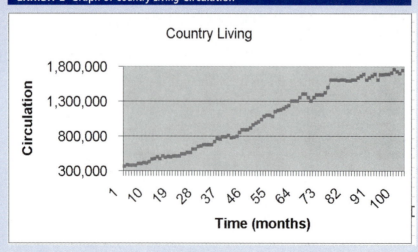

for husbands and wives who had serious interests in home and family as the focal points of their lives. It covered these home-and-family subjects in depth: food and appliances, building and handyman, decorating, family money management, gardening, travel, health, cars in your family, home and family entertainment, new-product information, and shopping. The magazine's circulation appeared to be experiencing increased volatility over time. Was this the beginning of a new pattern?

The last magazine was *True Story* (found in the "TrueStry" sheet of SHSB.XLS and shown in Exhibit 5). It was edited for young women and featured story editorials as well as recipes and food features, beauty and health articles, and home

management and personal advice. This journal's circulation appeared to have a definite downward trend over the past nine years. Was the cause a general declining interest in the subject matter, or was this a cycle that would correct itself in the future (like the sine wave Christensen had studied in trigonometry)?

Question

1. What's the best forecasting method for each of the five magazines? Use the concept of "Divide and Conquer" to really test your different forecast methods.

EXHIBIT 3 Graph of *Health* Circulation

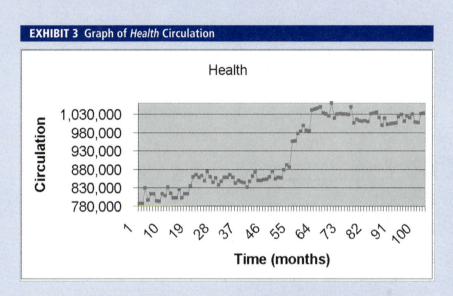

EXHIBIT 4 Graph of *Better Homes & Gardens* Circulation

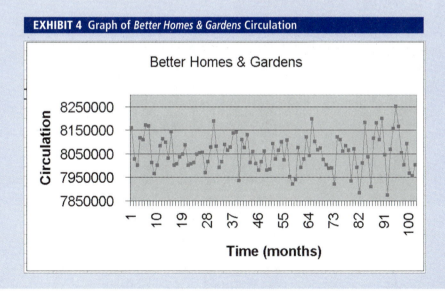

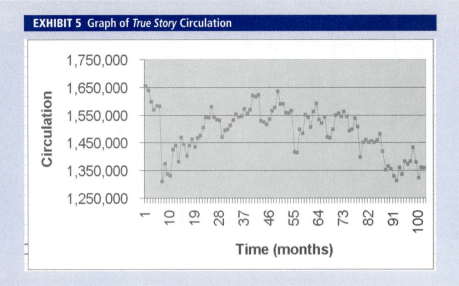

EXHIBIT 5 Graph of *True Story* Circulation

Marriott Room Forecasting[1]

"A hotel room is a perishable good. If it is vacant for one night, the revenue is lost forever." Linda Snow was commenting on the issue of capacity utilization in the hotel business. "On the other hand, the customer is king with us. We go to great pains to avoid telling a customer with a reservation at the front desk that we don't have a room for him in the hotel."

As Reservation Manager of one of Marriott's hotels, Linda faced this trade-off constantly. To complicate the matter, customers often booked reservations and then failed to show, or cancelled reservations just before their expected arrival. In addition, some guests stayed over in the hotel extra days beyond their original reservation and others checked out early. A key aspect of dealing with the capacity-management problem was having a good forecast of how many rooms would be needed on any future date. It was Linda's responsibility to prepare a forecast on Tuesday afternoon of the number of rooms that would be occupied each day of the next week (Saturday through Friday). This forecast was used by almost every department within the hotel for a variety of purposes; now she needed the forecast for a decision in her own department.

Hamilton Hotel

The Hamilton Hotel was a large downtown business hotel with 1877 rooms and abundant meeting space for groups and conventions. It had been built and was operated by Marriott Hotels, a company that operated more than 180 hotels and resorts world-

wide and was expanding rapidly into other lodging-market segments. Management of The Hamilton reported regularly to Marriott Corporation on occupancy and revenue performance.

Hotel managers were rewarded for their ability to meet targets for occupancy and revenue. Linda could not remember a time when the targets went down, but she had seen them go up in the two years since she took the job as reservation manager. The hotel managers were continuously comparing forecasts of performance against these targets. In addition to overseeing the reservations office with eight reservationists, Linda prepared the week-ahead forecast and presented it on Tuesday afternoon to other department managers in the hotel. The forecast was used to schedule, for example, daily work assignments for housekeeping personnel, the clerks at the front desk, restaurant personnel, and others. It also played a role in purchasing, revenue, and cost planning.

Overbooking

At the moment, however, Linda needed her forecast to know how to treat an opportunity that was developing for next Saturday. It was Tuesday, August 18, and Linda's forecasts were due by midafternoon for Saturday, August 22 through Friday, August 28. Although 1839 rooms were reserved already for Saturday, Linda had just received a request from a tour company for as many as 60 more rooms for that night. The tour company would take any number of rooms less than 60 that Linda would provide, but no more than 60. Normally Linda would be ecstatic about such a request: selling out the house for a business hotel on a Saturday would be a real coup. The request, in its entirety, put reservations above the capacity of the hotel, however. True, a reservation on the books Tuesday was

[1]This case is to be used as the basis for class discussion rather than to illustrate either the effective or ineffective handling of an administrative situation. © 1989 by the Darden Graduate Business School Foundation. Preview Darden case abstracts on the World Wide Web at: www.darden.virginia.edu/dems.

not the same as a "head in the bed" on Saturday, especially when weekend nights produced a lot of "no-show" reservations. "Chances are good we still wouldn't have a full house on Saturday," Linda thought out loud. "But if everybody came and someone was denied a room due to overbooking, I would certainly hear about it, and maybe Bill Marriott would also!"

Linda considered the trade-off between a vacant room and denying a customer a room. The contribution margin from a room was about $90, since the low variable costs arose primarily from cleaning the room and check-in/check-out. On the other side, if a guest with a reservation was denied a room at The Hamilton, the front desk would find a comparable room somewhere in the city, transport the guest there, and provide some gratuity, such as a fruit basket, in consideration for the inconvenience. If the customer were a Marquis cardholder (a frequent guest staying more than 45 nights a year in the hotel), he or she would receive $200 cash plus the next two stays at Marriott free. Linda wasn't sure how to put a cost figure on a

denied room; in her judgment, it should be valued, goodwill and all, at about twice the contribution figure.

Forecasting

Linda focused on getting a good forecast for Saturday, August 22, and making a decision on whether to accept the additional reservations for that day. She had historical data on demand for rooms in the hotel; Exhibit 1 shows demand for the first three weeks for dates starting with Saturday, May 23. (Ten additional weeks [weeks 4–13] are contained in MARRIOTT.XLS and thus Saturday, August 22, was the beginning of week 14 in this database.) "Demand" figures (column C) included the number of turned-down requests for a reservation on a night when the hotel had stopped taking reservations because of capacity plus the number of rooms actually occupied that night. Also included in Exhibit 1 is the number of rooms booked (column D) as of the Tuesday morning of the *week prior* to each date. (Note that this Tuesday precedes a date by a number of days that

EXHIBIT 1 Historical Demand and Bookings Data

	E5	▼	=	=C5/D5		
	A	B	C	D	E	F	G

1	DOW index: 1=Saturday, 2=Sunday, 3=Monday, 4=Tuesday, 5=Wedn¢

	Week	DOW indicator	Demand	Tuesday Bookings	Pickup Ratio	DOW Index
5	1	1	1470	1512	0.972	0.865
6		2	870	864	1.007	0.914
7		3	986	827	1.192	0.977
8		4	1247	952	1.310	1.024
9		5	1109	740	1.499	1.072
10		6	1197	908	1.318	1.108
11		7	1500	1311	1.144	1.041
12	2	1	1854	2034	0.912	0.865
13		2	1489	1584	0.940	0.914
14		3	1792	1682	1.065	0.977
15		4	1708	1684	1.014	1.024
16		5	1787	1600	1.117	1.072
17		6	1314	1077	1.220	1.108
18		7	1136	956	1.188	1.041
19	3	1	1537	1455	1.056	0.865
20		2	1132	1001	1.131	0.914
21		3	1368	1131	1.210	0.977
22		4	1488	1151	1.293	1.024
23		5	1392	942	1.478	1.072

Cell	Formula	Copy To
E5	=C5/D5	E6:E91

depends on the date's day of week. It is four days ahead of a Saturday date, seven days ahead of a Tuesday, ten days ahead of a Friday. Also note that on a Tuesday morning, actual demand is known for Monday night, but not for Tuesday night.)

Linda had calculated pickup ratios for each date where actual demand was known in Exhibit 1 (column E). Between a Tuesday one week ahead and any date, new reservations were added, reservations were canceled, some reservations were extended to more nights, some were shortened, and some resulted in no-shows. The net effect was a final demand that might be larger than Tuesday bookings (a pickup ratio greater than 1.0) or smaller than Tuesday bookings (a pickup ratio less than 1.0). Linda looked at her forecasting task as one of predicting the pickup ratio. With a good forecast of pickup ratio, she could simply multiply by Tuesday bookings to obtain a forecast of demand.

From her earliest experience in a hotel, Linda was aware that the day of the week (DOW) made a lot of difference in demand for rooms; her recent experience in reservations suggested that it was key in forecasting pickup ratios. Downtown business hotels like hers tended to be busiest in the middle of the workweek (Tuesday, Wednesday, Thursday) and light on the weekends. Using the data in her spreadsheet, she had calculated a DOW index for the pickup ratio during each day of the week, which is shown in column F of Exhibit 1. Thus, for

example, the average pickup ratio for Saturday is about 86.5% of the average pickup ratio for all days of the week. Her plan was to adjust the data for this DOW effect by dividing each pickup ratio by this factor. This adjustment would take out the DOW effect, and put the pickup ratios on the same footing. Then she could use the stream of adjusted pickup ratios to forecast Saturday's adjusted pickup ratio. To do this, she needed to think about how to level out the peaks and valleys of demand, which she knew from experience couldn't be forecasted. Once she had this forecast of adjusted pickup ratio, then she could multiply it by the Saturday DOW index to get back to an unadjusted pickup ratio. "Let's get on with it," she said to herself. "I need to get an answer back on that request for 60 reservations."

Questions

1. Verify the Day-of-Week indices in column F of Exhibit 1.
2. What forecasting procedure would you recommend for making the Tuesday afternoon forecast for each day's demand for the following Saturday through Friday?
3. What is your forecast for Saturday, August 22? What will you do about the current request for up to 60 rooms for Saturday?

References

Bruce Andrews and Shawn Cunningham, "L. L. Bean Improves Call-Center Forecasting," *Interfaces,* 25, no. 6 (1995), 1–13.

George E. P. Box, and Gwilym M. Jenkins, *Time Series Analysis, Forecasting and Control* (San Francisco: Holden-Day, Inc., 1970).

Alan L. C. Bullock, *Hitler: A Study in Tyranny* (New York: Harper & Row, 1962).

Conway Lackman and Alex Valz, "Risk Funding of Unemployment Insurance: An Econometric Approach," *Interfaces,* 18, no. 2 (1988), 64–71.

Quarterly Coal Reports published by the Department of Energy, Energy Information Administration.

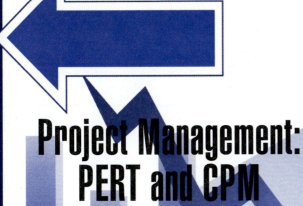

Project Management: PERT and CPM

CHAPTER OUTLINE

14.1 Introduction

14.2 A Typical Project: The Global Oil Credit Card Operation

14.3 The Critical Path—Meeting the Board's Deadline

14.4 Variability in Activity Times

14.5 A Mid-Chapter Summary: PERT

14.6 CPM and Time-Cost Trade-offs

14.7 Project Cost Management: PERT/Cost

14.8 Notes on Implementation

14.9 Summary

KEY TERMS

SELF-REVIEW EXERCISES

PROBLEMS

REFERENCES

APPLICATION CAPSULE

When Is the Synchronized Swimming, por favor? Management Science Goes to the Barcelona Olympics

As host for the 1992 summer Olympic games, the city of Barcelona was faced with an extremely complex logistical problem: scheduling more than 2000 events in a 15-day period. The problem was not only very large but included a great many different types of constraints, some of them not ordinarily encountered in the scheduling of more familiar projects.

First were the precedence relationships—for example, qualifying rounds obviously had to take place before quarterfinals, semifinals, and finals. Then, there was the need to spread out the events, in both time and space. One concern was to avoid traffic jams that might result if two or more popular events were scheduled in nearby facilities at the same time. But even when different venues were involved, it was desirable to schedule the most attractive events at different times, to allow the largest possible audience for the greatest number of events. The requirements of live TV coverage of different events for different time zones also had to be considered. For instance, interest in soccer matches would be high in Europe, Africa, and South America, but not in North America. Finally, there were constraints on the available equipment (such as TV cameras) and personnel (for example, security).

This complex problem provided an interesting challenge for two professors at the Universitat Politecnica de Catalunya in Barcelona. It soon became evident that no single existing program was adequate for the task. They therefore developed a collection of interactive algorithms to supplement the more conventional project management software, along with a set of graphical aids to help compare different schedule characteristics.

It was found useful first to create a calendar (assigning competitions to days), and then to refine the precise timetable of events on each day. This approach allowed rough schedules to be generated quickly. It also proved useful to work with time divisions both larger and smaller than an "event."

- The modelers discovered that each sport had its own rhythm and that it helped to think in terms of blocks of days that fit that rhythm. A particular sport, for example, might be best served by scheduling three consecutive days of preliminary competition, a day off, and then the finals.

- Equally helpful was the concept of a "unit"—a part of an event having intrinsic interest as a spectacle. Thus the end of the marathon, for example, was treated as a unit.

The objective function for the scheduling process incorporated several criteria, each of which was evaluated on a numerical scale. Among these were continuity (the number of days between the first and last activity for a particular event) and temporal profile (a measure of how well the schedule distributed the activities throughout the two-week period, compared to an ideal distribution).

The TV scheduling problem could be formulated as a binary integer programming model, but solving it would have required an impractical amount of computer time. Instead, a simpler greedy algorithm, designed for the situation, proved useful in developing timetables tailored to the needs of specific audiences.

A key feature of the resulting system, called SUCCESS92, is its speed and flexibility. In the event of weather problems, an alternative schedule can be quickly devised. SUCCESS92 has been received with great enthusiasm by the organizers of the games (see Andreu et al.).

14.1 INTRODUCTION

The task of managing major projects is an ancient and honorable art. In about 2600 B.C., the Egyptians built the Great Pyramid for King Khufu. The Greek historian Herodotus claimed that 400,000 men worked for 20 years to build this structure. Although these figures are now in doubt, there is no question about the enormity of the project. The Book of Genesis reports that the Tower of Babel was not completed because God made it impossible for the builders to communicate. This project is especially important, since it establishes a historical precedent for the ever-popular practice of citing divine intervention as a rationale for failure.[1]

Modern projects ranging from building a suburban shopping center to putting a man on the moon are amazingly large, complex, and costly. Completing such projects on time and within the budget is not an easy task. In particular, we shall see that the complicated problems of scheduling such projects are often structured by the interdependence of activities. Typically, certain of the activities may not be initiated before others have been completed. In dealing with projects possibly involving thousands of such dependency relations, it is no wonder that managers seek effective methods of analysis. Some of the key questions to be answered in this chapter are

1. What is the expected project completion date?
2. What is the potential "variability" in this date?
3. What are the scheduled start and completion dates for each specific activity?
4. What activities are *critical* in the sense that they must be completed exactly as scheduled in order to meet the target for overall project completion?
5. How long can *noncritical* activities be delayed before a delay in the overall completion date is incurred?
6. How might resources be concentrated most effectively on activities in order to speed up project completion?
7. What controls can be exercised on the flows of expenditures for the various activities throughout the duration of the project in order that the overall budget can be adhered to?

PERT and **CPM,** acronyms for Program Evaluation Review Technique and Critical Path Method, respectively, will provide answers to these questions. Each of these approaches to scheduling represents a project as a network, and hence the material in this chapter can be viewed as an extension of the deterministic networks discussed in Chapter 6. When a project involves uncertain elements, the representation of the project requires a stochastic network, which introduces an additional level of complexity not present in Chapter 6.

PERT was developed in the late 1950s by the Navy Special Projects Office in cooperation with the management consulting firm of Booz, Allen, and Hamilton. The technique

---

[1]The *Chicago Tribune* (August 5, 1977) noted the following comment concerning the blackout in New York in July of that year: "Con Ed called the disaster an act of God."

received substantial favorable publicity for its use in the engineering and development program of the Polaris missile, a complicated project that had 250 prime contractors and over 9000 subcontractors. Since that time, it has been widely adopted in other branches of government and in industry and has been applied to such diverse projects as construction of factories, buildings, and highways, research management, product development, the installation of new computer systems, and so on. Today, many firms and government agencies require all contractors to use PERT.

CPM was developed in 1957 by J. E. Kelly of Remington Rand and M. R. Walker of Du Pont. It differs from PERT primarily in the details of how time and cost are treated. Indeed, in actual implementation, the distinctions between PERT and CPM have become blurred as firms have integrated the best features of both systems into their own efforts to manage projects effectively. The implementation of PERT and CPM had an immediate impact on scheduling projects because it allowed the practice of "management by exception." Although there might be 10,000 activities in the course of a project, perhaps only 150 of them would be "critical" and need to be watched closely. To put an American on the moon during the days of the Apollo project, North American Aviation used PERT to bring its part of the project in six weeks early. There were over 32,000 events and hundreds of thousands of activities, but only a few hundred needed constant monitoring.

In keeping with our philosophy throughout the text, we approach the topic of project management on two levels. First, the essential techniques will be developed in an easily grasped illustrative example. Second, the use of the spreadsheet will be illustrated to indicate how one would handle the techniques in a large scale, real-world application.

14.2 A TYPICAL PROJECT: THE GLOBAL OIL CREDIT CARD OPERATION

No one would claim that it is like building the Great Pyramid, but the impending move of the credit card operation to Des Moines, Iowa, from the home office in Dallas is an important project for Rebecca Goldstein and Global Oil. The board of directors of Global has set a firm deadline of 22 weeks for the move to be accomplished. Becky is a manager in the Operations Analysis Group. She is in charge of planning the move, seeing that everything comes off according to plan, and making sure that the deadline is met.

The move is difficult to coordinate because it involves many different divisions within the company. Real estate must select one of three available office sites. Personnel has to determine which employees from Dallas will move, how many new employees to hire, and who will train them. The systems group and the treasurer's office must organize and implement the operating procedures and the financial arrangements for the new operation. The architects will have to design the interior space and oversee needed structural improvements. Each of the sites that Global is considering is an existing building with the appropriate amount of open space. However, office partitions, computer facilities, furnishings, and so on, must all be provided.

A second complicating factor is that there is an interdependence of activities. In other words, some parts of the project cannot be started until other parts are completed. Consider two obvious examples: Global cannot construct the interior of an office before it has been designed. Neither can it hire new employees until it has determined its personnel requirements.

THE ACTIVITY LIST

Becky knows that PERT and CPM are specifically designed for projects of this sort, and she wastes no time in getting started. The first step in the process is to define the activities in the project and to establish the proper precedence relationships. This is an important first step since errors or omissions at this stage can lead to a disastrously inaccurate schedule. Table 14.1 shows the first **activity list** that Becky prepares for the move (the columns labeled "Time" and "Resources" are indications of things to come). This is the *most important*

TABLE 14.1 First Activity List

ACTIVITY	DESCRIPTION	IMMEDIATE PREDECESSORS	TIME	RESOURCES
A	Select Office Site	—		
B	Create Organizational and Financial Plan	—		
C	Determine Personnel Requirements	B		
D	Design Facility	A, C		
E	Construct Interior	D		
F	Select Personnel to Move	C		
G	Hire New Employees	F		
H	Move Records, Key Personnel, etc.	F		
I	Make Financial Arrangements with Institutions in Des Moines	B		
J	Train New Personnel	H, E, G		

part of any PERT or CPM project and usually is done with several people involved, so that no important activities are missed. This must be a group effort—not done in isolation.

Conceptually, Table 14.1 is straightforward. Each activity is placed on a separate line, and its **immediate predecessors** are recorded on the same line. The immediate predecessors of an activity are those activities that must be completed prior to the start of the activity in question. For example, in Table 14.1 we see that Global cannot start activity C, determine personnel requirements, until activity B, create the organizational and financial plan, is completed. Similarly, activity G, hire new employees, cannot begin until activity F, select the Global personnel that will move from Texas to Iowa, is completed. This activity, F, in turn, cannot start until activity C, determine personnel requirements, is completed.

The activity list with immediate predecessors and the yet-to-be-obtained time estimates will provide the essential ingredients to answer the first five questions at the start of this chapter. We shall shortly see how PERT and CPM are used to produce these answers. In practice, however, another graphical approach, the Gantt chart, also is used commonly to attack such problems. We thus make a slight detour to consider this precursor of the network approaches (PERT and CPM) before returning to the main thrust of the chapter.

THE GANTT CHART

The Gantt chart was developed by Henry L. Gantt in 1918 and remains a popular tool in production and project scheduling. Its simplicity and clear graphical display have established it as a useful device for simple scheduling problems. The Gantt chart for Becky's problem is shown in Figure 14.1. Each activity is listed on the vertical axis. The horizontal axis is time, and the anticipated as well as actual duration of each activity is represented by a bar of the appropriate length. The chart also indicates *the earliest possible starting time* for each activity. For example, activity C cannot start before time 5 since, according to Table 14.1, activity B must be completed before activity C can begin. As each activity (or part thereof) is completed, the appropriate bar is shaded. At any point in time, then, it is clear which activities are on schedule and which are not. The Gantt chart in Figure 14.1 shows that as of week 13 activities D, E, and H are behind schedule, while G has actually been completed (because it is all shaded) and hence is ahead of schedule.

This simple example shows how the Gantt chart is mainly used as a record-keeping device for following the progression in time of the subtasks of a project. As Figure 14.1 shows, we can see which individual tasks are on or behind schedule. It seems important to note at

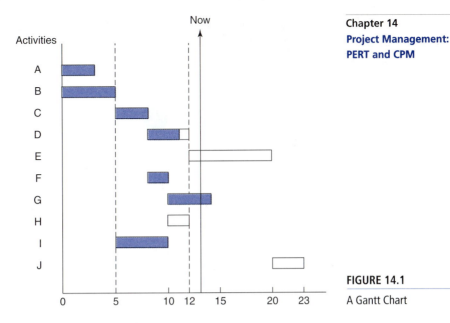

FIGURE 14.1

A Gantt Chart

this point that in the Gantt chart context the phrase "on schedule" means "it has been completed no later than the earliest possible completion time." Thus Figure 14.1 shows that D and H could have been completed, at the earliest, by week 12. Since they are not completed by week 13 they are, in this sense, behind schedule. As we shall see, this is too simple a concept for whether an activity is on schedule. The appropriate point of view should be whether *the overall project* is being delayed in terms of a target completion date. The Gantt chart fails to reveal some of the important information needed to attack this question. For example, the Gantt chart fails to reveal which activities are *immediate predecessors* of other activities. In Figure 14.1 it may appear that F and I are immediate predecessors of G since G can start at 10 and F and I can each finish at 10. In fact, however, Table 14.1 tells us that only F is an immediate predecessor of G. A delay in I would *not* affect the potential starting time of G, or for that matter of any other activity. It is this type of "immediate predecessor" information that must be used to deduce the impact on completion time for the overall project. This latter type of information is of obvious importance to the manager. The overall weakness of Gantt charts is reflected by their uselessness in making such inferences. We shall now see that the network representation contains the immediate predecessor information that we need.

THE NETWORK DIAGRAM

In a PERT **network diagram** each activity is represented by an arrow that is called a **branch** or an **arc.** The beginning and end of each activity is indicated by a circle that is called a **node.** The term **event** is also used in connection with the nodes. An event represents the completion of the activities that lead into a node. Referring to the activity list in Table 14.1, we see that "select office site" is termed activity A. When this **activity** is completed, the *event* "office site selected" occurs.

Constructing the Network Diagram Figure 14.2 shows a network diagram for activities A through C. We emphasize at the outset that the numbers assigned to the nodes are arbitrary. They are simply used to identify events and do not imply anything about precedence relationships. Indeed, we shall renumber the node that terminates activity C several times as we develop the network diagram for this project, but *correct precedence relationships will always be preserved.* In the network diagram each activity must start at the node in which its immediate predecessors ended. For example, in Figure 14.2, activity C starts at node ③ because its immediate predecessor, activity B, ended there. We see, however, that complications arise as we attempt to add activity D to the network diagram. Both A and C

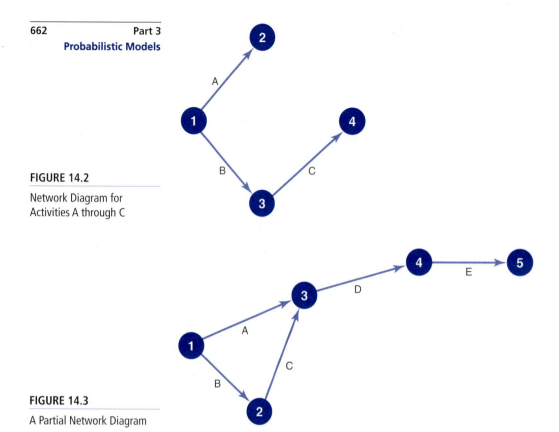

FIGURE 14.2

Network Diagram for
Activities A through C

FIGURE 14.3

A Partial Network Diagram

are immediate predecessors to D, and since we want to show any activity such as D only once in our diagram, nodes ② and ④ in Figure 14.2 must be combined, and D should start from this new node. This is shown in Figure 14.3. Node ③ now represents the event that both activities A and C have been completed. Note that activity E, which has only D as an immediate predecessor, can be added with no difficulty. However, as we attempt to add activity F, a new problem arises. Since F has C as an immediate predecessor, it would emanate from node ③ (of Figure 14.3). We see, however, that this would imply that F also has A as an immediate predecessor, which is incorrect.

The Use of Dummy Activities This diagramming dilemma is solved by introducing a **dummy activity,** which is represented by a dashed line in the network diagram in Figure 14.4. This dummy activity is fictitious in the sense that it requires no time or resources. It merely provides a pedagogical device that enables us to draw a network representation that correctly maintains the appropriate precedence relationships. Thus, Figure 14.4 indicates that activity D can begin only after both activities A and C have been completed. Similarly, activity F can occur only after activity C is completed.

We can generalize the procedure of adding a dummy activity as follows. Suppose that we wish to add an activity A to the network starting at node N, but not all of the activities that enter node N are immediate predecessors of the activity. Create a new node M with a dummy activity running from node M to node N. Take those activities that are currently entering node N and that are immediate predecessors of activity A and reroute them to enter node M. Now make activity A start at node M. (Dummy activities can be avoided altogether if, instead of associating activities with arcs (commonly known as activity on the arc [AOA]), we associate them with nodes. An example of this activity on the node (AON) approach is presented in the box that follows.)

Figure 14.5 shows the network diagram for the first activity list as presented in Table 14.1. We note that activities G and H both start at node ⑥ and terminate at node ⑦. This does not present a problem in portraying the appropriate precedence relationships, since

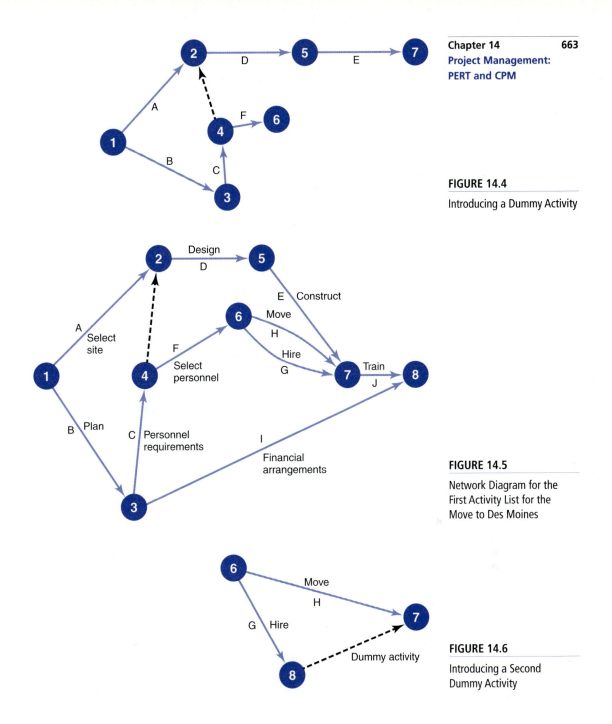

FIGURE 14.4

Introducing a Dummy Activity

FIGURE 14.5

Network Diagram for the
First Activity List for the
Move to Des Moines

FIGURE 14.6

Introducing a Second
Dummy Activity

only activity J starts at node ⑦. This might, however create a problem for certain software packages used to solve PERT and CPM problems. In some of these programs, each activity is identified by the number of its *starting and ending* node. If such a program is to be used, the representation of G and H in Figure 14.5 would lead the computer to regard them as the same activity. This would be incorrect, since in fact activities G and H are not the same. A dummy activity can be used to cure this condition. Figure 14.6 illustrates the procedure. Since the dummy activity requires no time, the correct time and precedent relationships are maintained. This new representation has been introduced into Figure 14.7. Many software packages do not require that these dummy activities be input. Thus, for our purposes, they serve mainly the pedagogical goal of correctly portraying the precedence relations (i.e., as used in Figure 14.4).

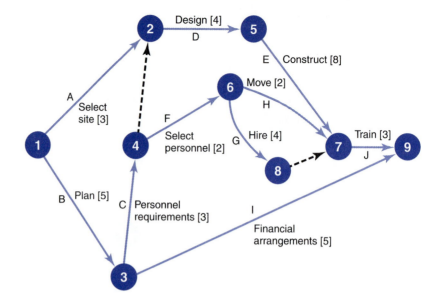

FIGURE 14.7

Network Diagram with
Expected Activity Times

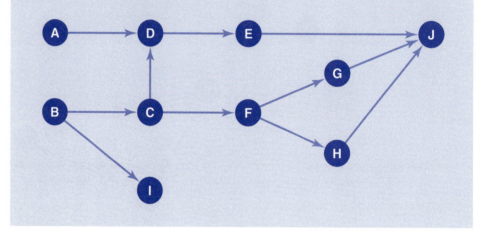

An Activity-on-Nodes Example

In the activity-on-nodes approach to representing a project as a network, the activities are associated with the nodes of the network while the arcs of the network display the precedence relationships. The Global Oil network in Figure 14.5 would be represented as shown below. For example, activity J has activities E, G, and H as immediate predecessors because there are arcs entering J from the nodes labeled E, G, and H. Note that there is no special difficulty in making A and C immediate predecessors of D, and C (but not A) an immediate predecessor of F.

14.3   THE CRITICAL PATH—MEETING THE BOARD'S DEADLINE

The activity list and an appropriate network diagram are useful devices for representing the precedence relationships among the activities in a project. Recall that the board has set a firm goal of 22 weeks for the overall project to be completed. Before Becky can tell if she can meet this goal, she will have to incorporate time estimates into the process.

The PERT-CPM procedure requires management to produce an estimate of the expected time it will take to complete each activity on the activity list. Let us assume that Becky has worked with the appropriate departments at Global to arrive at the expected time

TABLE 14.2 First Activity List with Expected Activity Times in Weeks

ACTIVITY	DESCRIPTION	IMMEDIATE PREDECESSORS	EXPECTED ACTIVITY TIME (WKS)	RESOURCES
A	Select Office Site	—	3	
B	Create Organizational and Financial Plan	—	5	
C	Determine Personnel Requirements	B	3	
D	Design Facility	A, C	4	
E	Construct Interior	D	8	
F	Select Personnel to Move	C	2	
G	Hire New Employees	F	4	
H	Move Records, Key Personnel, etc.	F	2	
I	Make Financial Arrangements with Institutions in Des Moines	B	5	
J	Train New Personnel	H, E, G	3	

estimates (in weeks) shown in Table 14.2. (In Section 14.4 we shall discuss in more detail the way in which these time estimates were produced.) Figure 14.7 shows the network diagram with the expected activity times appended in brackets.

THE CRITICAL PATH CALCULATION
From Table 14.2 you can see (by adding up the separate expected activity times) that the total working time required to complete all the individual activities would be 39 weeks. However, the total calendar time required to complete the entire project can clearly be less than 39 weeks, for many activities can be performed simultaneously. For example, Figure 14.7 shows that activities A and B can be initiated at the same time. Activity A takes 3 weeks and B takes 5 weeks. If management arranges to begin both activities at the same time (at calendar time 0), both will be completed by calendar time = 5. To obtain a prediction of the minimum calendar time required for overall project duration, we must find what is referred to as a *critical path* in the network.

A **path** can be defined as a sequence of connected activities that leads from the starting node ① to the completion node ⑨. For example, the sequence of activities B–I, requiring 10 weeks to complete, is a path. So is the sequence B-C-D-E-J, requiring 23 weeks to complete. You can identify several other paths in Figure 14.7. To complete the project, the activities *on all paths* must be completed. In this sense we might say that "all paths must be traversed." Thus, we have just seen that our project will take *at least* 23 weeks to complete, for the path B-C-D-E-J must be traversed. However, numerous other paths must also be traversed, and some of these may require even more time. Our task will be to analyze the total amount of calendar time required for all paths to be traversed. Thus, we wish to determine the *longest path* from start to finish. This path, called the **critical path,** will determine the overall project duration, because no other path will be longer. If activities on the longest path are delayed, then, since these activities must be completed, the entire project will be delayed. For this reason the activities on the critical path are called the **critical activities** of the project. It is this subset of activities that must be kept on schedule.

This is the opposite problem from the one in Section 6.8 (the shortest-route problem). Here, the longest route from beginning (start) to end (finish) is needed. We can either change this PERT problem to a shortest-route model and use the algorithm in Section 6.8 or change the algorithm to fit the problem. It is easier in this case to change the algorithm.

Earliest Start and Earliest Finish Times Another difference between the shortest-route problem and this longest route (critical path) is that the interest is not just in the longest path in the network, but in the earliest and latest times each activity can be started and not affect the current solution. Thus, what is needed is *sensitivity analysis* of each activity and, therefore, finding the earliest and latest start times (and finish times) for each activity. We now specify the steps employed in finding a critical path. Fundamental in this process will be the **earliest start time** for each activity. To illustrate this idea, consider activity D, "design facility." Now assume that the project starts at time zero and ask yourself: "What is the earliest time at which activity D can start?" Clearly, it cannot start until activity A is complete. It thus cannot start before time = 3. However, it also cannot start before the dummy activity (that requires 0 time) is complete. Since the dummy cannot start until B and C are complete (a total of 8 weeks), we see that D cannot start until 8 weeks have passed. In this calculation, it is crucial to note that activities A and B both start at time 0. After 3 weeks A is complete, but B still requires another 2 weeks. After a total of 5 weeks, B is complete and C can start. After another 3 weeks, a total of 8 from the start, C is completed. Thus, after 8 weeks, both A and C are complete and D can start. In other words,

$$\text{earliest start time for activity D} = 8 \text{ weeks}$$

Another important concept is **earliest finish time** for each activity. If we let

$$ES = \text{earliest start time for a given activity}$$
$$EF = \text{earliest finish time for a given activity}$$
$$t = \text{expected activity time for a given activity}$$

then, for a given activity, the relation between earliest start time and earliest finish time is

$$EF = ES + t$$

For example, we have just shown that for activity D we have ES = 8. Thus, for activity D,

$$EF = ES + t$$
$$= 8 + 4 = 12$$

We now recall that each activity begins at a node. We know that a given activity leaving a node cannot be started until *all* activities leading into that node have been finished. This observation leads to the following rule.

> ***Earliest Start Time Rule:*** The ES time for an activity leaving a particular node is the ***largest*** of the EF times for all activities entering the node.

Let us apply this rule to nodes ①, ②, ③, and ④ of Becky's network, Figure 14.7. The result is shown in Figure 14.8. We write in brackets the earliest start and earliest finish times for each activity next to the letter of the activity, as shown in Figure 14.8. Note that the earliest start time rule applied to activity D says that ES for activity D is equal to the larger value of the EF times for the two precedent activities C (via the dummy) and A. Thus, the ES for D is the larger of the two values [8, 3], which is 8.

Continuing to each node in a **forward pass** through the entire network, the values [ES, EF] are then computed for each activity. The result is shown in Figure 14.9. Note that the earliest finish time for J is 23 weeks. This means that the earliest completion time for the entire project is 23 weeks. This answers the first of the questions itemized in Section 14.1: "What is the expected project completion date?"

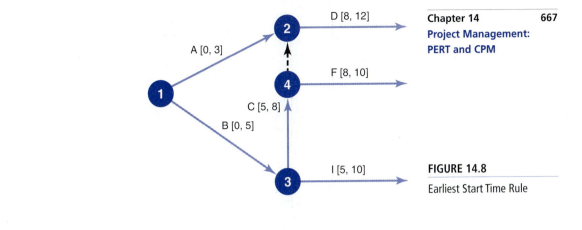

FIGURE 14.8

Earliest Start Time Rule

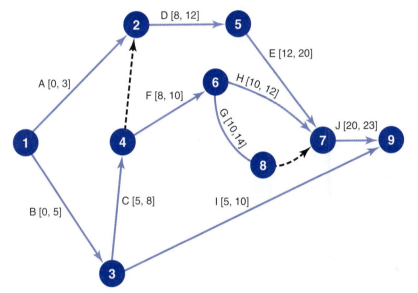

FIGURE 14.9

Global Oil Network with
Earliest Start and Earliest
Finish Times Shown

Latest Start and Latest Finish Times In order to identify possible start and completion dates, the activities on the critical path, and how long noncritical activities may be delayed without affecting the overall completion date (answering the third, fourth, and fifth questions of Section 14.1), we now proceed with a **backward pass** calculation. The idea is that since we now have a target completion date (23 weeks from the start of the project), we can work backward from this date, determining the *latest* date each activity can finish without delaying the entire project. The backward pass begins at the completion node, node ⑨. we then trace back through the network computing what is termed a **latest start time** and **latest finish time** for each activity. In symbols,

LS = latest start time for a particular activity

LF = latest finish time for a particular activity

The relation between these quantities is

$$LS = LF - t$$

For activity J we define the latest finish time to be the same as its earliest finish time, which is 23. Hence, for activity J,

$$LS = LF - t = 23 - 3 = 20$$

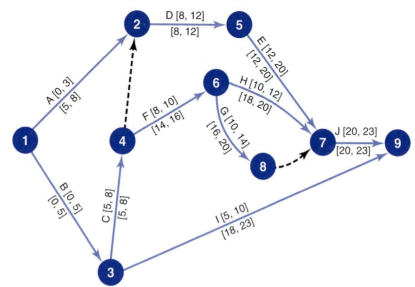

FIGURE 14.10

Global Oil Network with
LS and LF Times Shown
Below Activities

Since the latest start time for activity J is 20, the latest activities E, H, and G can finish is 20. Thus, the latest E can start is $20 - 8 = 12$, the latest H can start is $20 - 2 = 18$, and the latest G can start is $20 - 4 = 16$. To determine the latest finish time for activity F is a little more complicated. We apply the following general rule:

> **Latest Finish Time Rule:** The LF time for an activity entering a particular node is the **smallest** of the LS times for all activities leaving that node.

Thus, for activity F, which enters node ⑥, we apply the rule to see that LF = 16, because the latest start times for the activities leaving node ⑥ (activities H and G) are 18 and 16. The complete network with LS and LF entries is shown in Figure 14.10. These entries appear on the arc for each activity in brackets, directly under the ES and EF times.

Slack and the Critical Path Based on Figure 14.10, the next step of the algorithm is to identify another important value, the amount of slack, or free time, associated with each activity. **Slack** is the amount of time an activity can be delayed without affecting the completion date for the overall project. *Slack* is the same concept covered in LP and is the extra time that could be spent on that path without affecting the length of the critical path. An easy and important mathematical check is that every activity on the critical path should have the same slack, namely 0. For each activity, the slack value is computed as

$$\text{slack} = \text{LS} - \text{ES} = \text{LF} - \text{EF}$$

For example, the slack for activity G is given by

$$\begin{aligned}
\text{slack for G} &= \text{LS for G} - \text{ES for G} \\
&= 16 - 10 \\
&= 6
\end{aligned}$$

and the same value is given by

$$\text{LF for G} - \text{EF for G} = 20 - 14 = 6$$

This means that activity G could be delayed up to 6 weeks beyond its earliest start time without delaying the overall project. On the other hand, the slack associated with activity C is

$$\text{slack for C} = \text{LS for C} - \text{ES for C}$$
$$= 5 - 5$$
$$= 0$$

Thus, activity C has no slack and must begin as scheduled at week 5. *Since this activity cannot be delayed without affecting the entire project, it is a critical activity and is on the critical path.*

PERT critical paths can also have alternative optimal solutions (again, just as in LP). If activity F took 8 weeks, then the path B-C-F-G-J would also be a critical path.

> The critical path activities are those with zero slack.

Spreadsheet Approach for the Network The spreadsheet solution (GLOBAL.XLS) of this problem is most easily done with an activity-on-the-node approach (shown in the figure on page 664) and is shown in Figure 14.11. The Earliest Finish column (E) is the Activity Time column (C) plus the Earliest Start column (D). Similarly, the Latest Start column (F) is the Latest Finish column (G) minus the Activity Time column (C). The Slack column (H) could either be the Latest Start column (F) minus the Earliest Start column (D) or equivalently the Latest Finish column (G) minus the Earliest Finish column (E). The formula for the minimum project length in cell E15 is =MAX(E2:E12), the largest Earliest Finish time.

The cumbersome part of creating the spreadsheet is entering the information that is conveyed by the network diagram. For example, since the Latest Finish time of activity F is the smallest of the Latest Start times of activities G, H, and K, the formula in cell G7 is =MIN(F8,F9,F12) as shown in Figure 14.11. Since the Earliest Start time of activity D is the largest of the Earliest Finish times of activities A and C, the formula in cell D5 is =MAX(E2,E4). Note that the word "Yes" is printed in the "Critical?" column for those activities with zero slack. Thus, we can see from this spreadsheet output that the critical path for Becky's project is B-C-D-E-J. The minimum overall completion time is 23 weeks, which is the sum of the times on the critical path, as well as the earliest finish time for the last activity (J). Figure 14.11 also provides the answers to questions 3, 4, and 5 raised in Section 14.1. In other words, we have, up to this point, answered the following questions from that section.

1. What is the expected project completion date?

   Answer: 23 weeks.

3. What are the scheduled start and completion dates for each specific activity?

   Answer: An activity may be scheduled to start at any date between "earliest start" and "latest start." The scheduled completion date will be "start date + expected activity time." For example, activity G can be scheduled to start anywhere between time = 10 and time = 16. As shown in Table 14.2, the expected activity time is 4 weeks. Hence, the scheduled completion date will be "start date + 4."

4. What activities are *critical* in the sense that they must be completed exactly as scheduled in order to meet the target for overall project completion?

   Answer: The activities on the critical path: namely, B, C, D, E, J.

5. How long can *noncritical* activities be delayed before a delay in overall completion date is incurred?

   Answer: Any activity may be started as late as the "latest start" date without delaying the overall project completion.

	D11	▼	=	=MAX(E6,E8,E9)					
	A	B	C	D	E	F	G	H	I
1	Activity	Description	Time	EST	EFT	LST	LFT	Slack	Critical?
2	A	Select site	3	0	3	5	8	5	No
3	B	Create plan	5	0	5	0	5	0	Yes
4	C	Personnel Reqmts	3	5	8	5	8	0	Yes
5	D	Design Facility	4	8	12	8	12	0	Yes
6	E	Construct	8	12	20	12	20	0	Yes
7	F	Select Personnel	2	8	10	14	16	6	No
8	G	Hire New	4	10	14	16	20	6	No
9	H	Move Records	2	10	12	18	20	8	No
10	I	Make Financial	5	5	10	18	23	13	No
11	J	Train	3	20	23	20	23	0	Yes
12									
13		Minimum Project Length			23				

Cell	Formula	Copy To
D4	=MAX(E3)	—
D5	=MAX(E2,E4)	—
D6	=MAX(E5)	—
D7	=MAX(E4)	—
D8	=MAX(E7)	—
D9	=MAX(E7)	—
D10	=MAX(E3)	—
D11	=MAX(E6,E8,E9)	—
E2	=D2+C2	E3:E11
F2	=G2−C2	F3:F11
G2	=MIN(F5)	—
G3	=MIN(F4,F10)	—
G4	=MIN(F5,F7)	—
G5	=MIN(F6)	—
G6	=MIN(F11)	—
G7	=MIN(F8,F9)	—
G8	=MIN(F11)	—
G9	=MIN(F11)	—
G10	=E13	—
G11	=E13	—
H2	=F2−D2	H3:H11
I2	=IF(H2=0,"Yes","No")	I3:I11
E13	=MAX(E2:E11)	—

FIGURE 14.11

Spreadsheet Scheduling Summary for Global Oil

Three questions, namely 2, 6, and 7, remain to be answered. But first, before proceeding further, let us take an overview of what we have learned. It is clear from the critical path analysis that Becky has a problem. The board of directors wants the credit card operation to start operating in Des Moines in 22 weeks, and with the current plan 23 weeks are required. Obviously, something must change if this goal is to be met.

WAYS OF REDUCING PROJECT DURATION

There are two basic approaches to reducing the time required to complete a project:

1. *A strategic analysis:* Here the analyst asks: "Does this project have to be done the way it is currently diagrammed?" In particular, "Do all of the activities on the critical path have to be done in the specified order?" Can we make arrangements to accomplish some of these activities in a different way not on the critical path?

2. *A tactical approach:* In this approach the analyst assumes that the current diagram is appropriate and works at reducing the time of certain activities on the critical path by

devoting more resources to them. The current expected times assume a certain allocation of resources. For example, the 8 weeks for construction (activity E) assumes a regular 8-hour workday. The contractor can complete the job more rapidly by working overtime, but at increased costs.

The tactical approach will get us into consideration of CPM models, to be discussed in Section 14.6. For now, let us deal with the so-called strategic questions.

A Strategic Analysis Becky starts with a strategic analysis, since she is anxious to keep the cost of the move as low as possible. This is analogous to "What if?" analysis done with spreadsheets. After some study she suddenly realizes that the current network assumes that activity J, the training of new employees, must be carried out in the new building (after E is complete), and after records and key personnel have been moved (after H is complete). After reconsidering, she believes that these requirements can be changed. First of all, J can be accomplished independently of H. The previous specification that H should be an immediate predecessor of J was simply incorrect. Moreover, she believes that she can secure an alternative training facility by arranging to use surplus classroom space in Des Moines at a minimal cost. She can then have the new employees trained and ready to start the moment that construction ends. On the other hand, she has to add another activity to the activity list: Secure a training facility (to be denoted as activity K). Although she feels that such a rearrangement may be helpful, it is possible that in this redefined network she may have created a new critical path with a still unsatisfactory minimum time (i.e., one greater than 22 weeks).

Spreadsheet Output for the Redefined Network Figure 14.12 shows the redefined activity list in the form of the activity-on-the-arc (AOA) diagram. Note that the dummy activities are given a normal duration (expected activity time) of 0. Some of the entries (Crash duration, Normal cost, and Crash cost) do not have to be specified for this particular analysis. Becky has to do only a limited amount of modifying the input data from her previous definition of the network. Thus, she must add activity K and change the ending node numbers for activities E, G, and H. Figure 14.13 shows the network diagram for the redefined project in the activity-on-the-node (AON) diagram.

Becky then enters the information into the spreadsheet ("Redefined" worksheet in the same GLOBAL.XLS) to solve the problem, and the results shown in Figure 14.14 are produced. Here we see that the redefined project can be completed in 20 weeks (the sum of the times on the critical path), so the board's deadline can be met. It is also apparent that the activity "train" (J) is no longer on the critical path. In spite of the fact that 3 weeks is needed to secure a training facility, activity J has a slack of 3 weeks. The spreadsheet solution

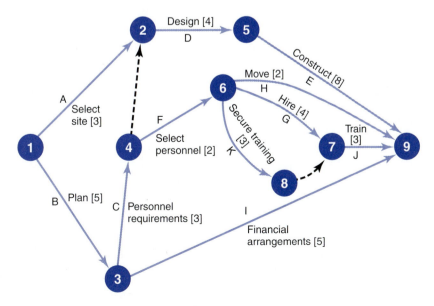

FIGURE 14.12

AOA Network Diagram for the Redefined Activity List

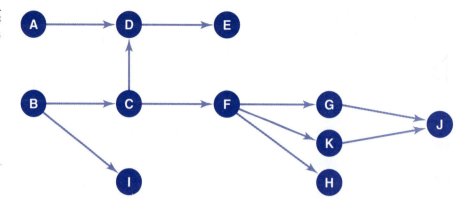

FIGURE 14.13

AON Network Diagram for the Redefined Project

	G7	▼	=	=MIN(F8,F9,F12)				
	A	B	C	D	E	F	G	H	I
1	Activity	Description	Time	EST	EFT	LST	LFT	Slack	Critical?
2	A	Select site	3	0	3	5	8	5	No
3	B	Create plan	5	0	5	0	5	0	Yes
4	C	Personnel Reqmts	3	5	8	5	8	0	Yes
5	D	Design Facility	4	8	12	8	12	0	Yes
6	E	Construct	8	12	20	12	20	0	Yes
7	F	Select Personnel	2	8	10	11	13	3	No
8	G	Hire New	4	10	14	13	17	3	No
9	H	Move Records	2	10	12	18	20	8	No
10	I	Make Financial	5	5	10	15	20	10	No
11	J	Train	3	14	17	17	20	3	No
12	K	Secure Training	3	10	13	14	17	4	No
13									
14		Minimum Project Length			20				

Cell	Formula	Copy To
D4	=MAX(E3)	—
D5	=MAX(E2,E4)	—
D6	=MAX(E5)	—
D7	=MAX(E4)	—
D8	=MAX(E4)	—
D9	=MAX(E7)	—
D10	=MAX(E3)	—
D11	=MAX(E8,E12)	—
D12	=MAX(E7)	—
E2	=D2+C2	E3:E12
F2	=G2−C2	F3:F12
G2	=MIN(F5)	—
G3	=MIN(F4,F10)	—
G4	=MIN(F5,F7)	—
G5	=MIN(F6)	—
G6	=E14	—
G7	=MIN(F8,F9,F12)	—
G8	=MIN(F11)	—
G9	=E14	—
G10	=E14	—
G11	=E14	—
G12	=MIN(F11)	—
H2	=F2−D2	H3:H12
I2	=IF(H2=0,"Yes","No")	I3:I12
E14	=MAX(E2:E12)	—

FIGURE 14.14

Spreadsheet Solution for the Redefined Project

shows that the critical path for the redefined project is B-C-D-E. (Recall that "Yes" in the "Critical?" column indicates that an activity is on the critical path.)

14.4   VARIABILITY IN ACTIVITY TIMES

Let us now consider the second question raised in the introduction: "What is the potential variability in the expected project completion date?" So far, we have been acting as though the activity times and the derived values for ES, LS, EF, and LF were all deterministic. This may not be strictly correct, for in reality the activity times are often not known in advance with certainty. In view of this fact, PERT employs a special formula for estimating activity times. We shall now present the details, and in so doing it will be seen that the PERT approach can also be used to calculate the probability that the project will be completed by any particular time.

ESTIMATING THE EXPECTED ACTIVITY TIME

The PERT system of estimating activity times requires someone who understands the activity in question well enough to produce three estimates of the activity time:

1. **Optimistic time** (denoted by a): the minimum time. Everything has to go perfectly to achieve this time.

2. **Most probable time** (denoted by m): the most likely time. The time required under normal circumstances.

3. **Pessimistic time** (denoted by b): the maximum time. One version of Murphy's Law is that if something can go wrong, it will. The pessimistic time is the time required when Murphy's Law is in effect.

Consider, for example, activity E, construct the interior. Becky and the general contractor carefully examine each phase of the construction project and arrive at the following estimates:

$$a = 4$$
$$m = 7$$
$$b = 16$$

The relatively large value for b is caused by the possibility of a delay in the delivery of the air-conditioning unit for the computer. If this unit is delayed, the entire activity is delayed. Moreover, in this case, since E is on the critical path, a delay in this activity will delay overall project completion.

In the original development of the PERT approach (during the late 1950s), the procedure for estimating the expected value of the activity times was motivated by the assumption that the activity time was a random variable with a particular probability distribution. This distribution (the **beta distribution**) has a minimum and maximum value, unlike the normal distribution, which has an infinite range of values. It also is capable of assuming a wide variety of shapes, again unlike the normal, which is always symmetrical about its most likely value. A typical beta distribution is shown in Figure 14.15. The expected value of a beta distribution is approximately $(a + 4m + b)/6$; thus the formula used to estimate the expected activity time is

$$\text{estimate of expected activity time} = \frac{a + 4m + b}{6} \qquad \textbf{(14.1)}$$

Note that the estimate is a weighted average of the values of $a, m,$ and $b,$ where the weights (1/6, 4/6, 1/6) sum to 1. This means that the estimate will always lie between a and b. Thus for activity E,

$$\text{estimate of expected activity time} = \frac{4 + 4(7) + 16}{6} = 8$$

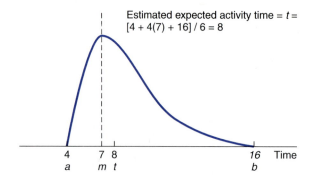

FIGURE 14.15

Unimodal Beta Distribution

TABLE 14.3 Time Estimates						
ACTIVITY	a	m	b	$(a + 4m + b)/6$ (EXPECTED VALUE)	$(b - a)/6$ (STD. DEV.)	$[(b - a)/6]^2$ (VARIANCE)
A	1	3	5	3	2/3	4/9
B	3	4.5	9	5	1	1
C	2	3	4	3	1/3	1/9
D	2	4	6	4	2/3	4/9
E	4	7	16	8	2	4
F	1	1.5	5	2	2/3	4/9
G	2.5	3.5	7.5	4	5/6	25/36
H	1	2	3	2	1/3	1/9
I	4	5	6	5	1/3	1/9
J	1.5	3	4.5	3	1/2	1/4
K	1	3	5	3	2/3	4/9

By working with the appropriate individuals in Global Oil, Becky used (14.1) to estimate each of the expected activity times that were presented in Table 14.2 and subsequently used in the critical path analysis.

Estimating the Standard Deviation of an Activity Time The standard deviation of an activity time is estimated by assuming that there are six standard deviations between the optimistic and pessimistic times:

$$\text{estimate of the standard deviation of activity time} = \frac{b - a}{6} \qquad \textbf{(14.2)}$$

Thus, for activity E,

$$\text{estimate of standard deviation} = \frac{16 - 4}{6} = 2$$

Table 14.3 shows the three estimates *(a, m, b)*, the expected activity times, the standard deviation of the activity times, and the *variance* of the activity times for the redefined activity list. The variance is simply the square of the standard deviation. It is useful to record the variance of each activity since these values will be used in making statements about the probability of completing the overall project by a specific date.

In an application, it is of course possible to use any procedure that seems appropriate to estimate the expected value and standard deviation of the activity time. Indeed, in some circumstances data may be available and various statistical procedures can be used to estimate these parameters of the model.

PROBABILITY OF COMPLETING THE PROJECT ON TIME

The fact that activity times are random variables implies that the completion time for the project is also a random variable. That is, there is potential variability in the overall completion time. Even though the redefined project has an *expected* completion time of 20 weeks, there is no guarantee that it will actually be completed within 20 weeks. If *by chance* various activities take longer than their expected time, the project might not be completed within the desired 22-week schedule. In general, it would be useful to know the probability that the project will be completed within a specified time. In particular, Becky would like to know the probability that the move will be completed within 22 weeks.

The analysis proceeds as follows:

1. Let T equal the total time that will be taken by the activities on the critical path.
2. Find the probability that the value of T will turn out to be less than or equal to any specified value of interest. In particular, for Becky's project we would find Prob$\{T \le 22\}$. A good approximation for this probability is easily found if two assumptions hold.

    a. *The activity times are independent random variables.* This is a valid assumption for most PERT networks and seems reasonable for Becky's problem. There is no reason to believe that the time to construct the interior should depend on the design time, and so on.

    b. *The random variable* T *has an approximately normal distribution.* This assumption relies on the *central limit theorem,* which in broad terms states that the sum of independent random variables is approximately normally distributed.

Now recalling that our goal is to find Prob$\{T \le 22\}$, where T is the time along the critical path, we will want to convert T to a standard normal random variable and use Table A.0 in Appendix A to find Prob$\{T \le 22\}$. The first step in this process is to find the standard deviation of T. To do this we need the variance of T. When the activity times are independent, we know that the variance of the total time along the critical path equals the sum of the variances of the activity times on the critical path. Thus, for Becky's problem

$$\text{var } T = \begin{pmatrix} \text{variance for} \\ \text{activity B} \end{pmatrix} + \begin{pmatrix} \text{variance for} \\ \text{activity C} \end{pmatrix} + \begin{pmatrix} \text{variance for} \\ \text{activity D} \end{pmatrix} + \begin{pmatrix} \text{variance for} \\ \text{activity E} \end{pmatrix}$$

Using the numerical values in Table 14.3 yields

$$\text{var } T = 1 + \frac{1}{9} + \frac{4}{9} + 4 = \frac{50}{9}$$

Finally,

$$\text{std. dev. } T = \sqrt{(\text{var } T)} = \sqrt{\frac{50}{9}} = 2.357$$

We now proceed to convert T to a standard normal random variable, Z, in the usual way: $Z = \frac{T - \mu}{\sigma}$. Recalling that 20 weeks is the mean (i.e., the expected completion time), we have

$$\text{Prob}\{T \le 22\} = \text{Prob}\left\{\frac{T - 20}{2.357} \le \frac{22 - 20}{2.357}\right\}$$

$$= \text{Prob}\{Z \le 0.8485\}$$

If we consult Table A.0 at the end of the text for the area under a normal curve from the left-hand tail to a point that is 0.8485 standard deviations above the mean, we find that the answer is about 0.80. Thus, there is about an 80% chance that the critical path will be completed in less than 22 weeks.

This analysis shows how to shed light on the second of the questions asked in the introduction. In particular, it shows how to find the probability that the *critical path* will be finished by *any* given time. It illustrates the importance of considering the variability in individual activity times when considering overall project completion times. The analysis for Becky's problem indicates that, using expected time as our "real-world forecast," the expected project duration will be 20 weeks and, if so, it will be completed 2 weeks ahead of the desired date. The analysis of uncertainty above sheds additional light on this estimate. It shows a significant probability (i.e., $0.2 = 1 - 0.8$) that *the critical path* will not be completed by the desired completion date. The implication is that there is *at least* a probability of 0.2 that the overall project may not be completed by the desired date. The modifier "at least" has been employed because of the following complicating factor: Because of randomness, some other path, estimated as being noncritical, may in reality take longer to complete than the purported critical path.

As an example of how this uncertainty can work in the business/educational world, San Diego State University and Georgia Tech contracted with some construction firms to build parking towers. The construction firms gave them two bids: one if PERT charts were used and a lower bid if PERT charts were *not* used. In the latter bids, the firms would not promise when the structures would be done so that if workers were needed on another project (which did have deadlines), they could be taken off the universities' projects for several days or weeks and used elsewhere. In exchange for this uncertainty, the educational institutions got cheaper construction rates for helping the contractors with their personnel balancing.

TESTING THE ASSUMPTIONS WITH SPREADSHEET SIMULATION

For small projects, it is not too cumbersome to use a spreadsheet program to do a critical path analysis as we have shown previously with Figures 14.11 and 14.14. Once the basic relationships have been entered, it is very easy to alter the activity times and see what effect this has on the minimum project length and the activities on the critical path. By making the activity times random with Crystal Ball and recalculating the spreadsheet (using its "Single Step" feature), one can get a feel for the variability of both the project length and the critical path. Figure 14.16 shows one example ("Random" worksheet in the same GLOBAL.XLS). Note that all activity times are between their pessimistic *(a)* and optimistic *(b)* times, but that the critical path is different, in this case B-C-F-G-J. This result demonstrates that the path with the longest *expected* length (B-C-D-E) may not turn out to be the critical path. This fact implies that the expected project length may be greater than the value calculated by the PERT analysis.[2]

FIGURE 14.16

Simulated Activity Times for Global Oil

	A	B	C	D	E	F	G	H	I
1									
2	Activity	Description	Time	EST	EFT	LST	LFT	Slack	Critical?
3	A	Select site	4	0	4	4	7	4	No
4	B	Create plan	3	0	3	0	3	0	Yes
5	C	Personnel Reqmts	2	3	6	3	6	0	Yes
6	D	Design Facility	3	6	9	7	11	2	No
7	E	Construct	6	9	15	11	17	2	No
8	F	Select Personnel	3	6	9	6	9	0	Yes
9	G	Hire New	5	9	13	9	13	0	Yes
10	H	Move Records	2	9	11	14	17	6	No
11	I	Make Financial	4	3	8	12	17	9	No
12	J	Train	4	13	17	13	17	0	Yes
13	K	Secure Training	2	9	11	11	13	3	No
14									
15		Minimum Project Length			17				
16									

[2] The key result needed to show this is that the expected value of the maximum of two random variables is greater than or equal to the maximum of the expected values: $E[\max(X, Y)] \geq \max(E[X], E[Y])$.

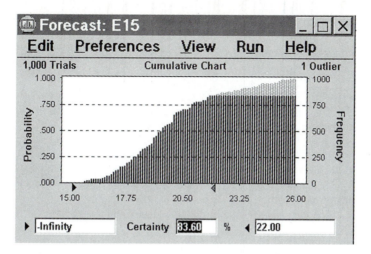

FIGURE 14.17

Distribution of Project Length

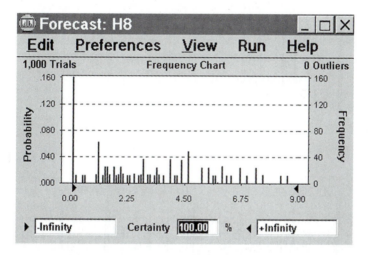

FIGURE 14.18

Distribution of Slack for
Activity F

To estimate the true expected project length, we should recalculate the spreadsheet many times and average the minimum project lengths obtained on each recalculation. The Crystal Ball add-in makes this easy to do. Since Crystal Ball includes the beta distribution in its Distribution Gallery, and the PERT analysis of activity times was based on the beta distribution, we indicate that the values in column C should be drawn from the appropriate beta distributions. Figure 14.17 shows the distribution of minimum project length calculated by Crystal Ball based on a sample of 1000 iterations. The estimated average project length is in fact smaller than what was calculated by the PERT analysis, but only slightly so (19.76 versus 20.0). Crystal Ball also makes it easy to calculate the probability that the project length is less than or equal to any given target value. Figure 14.17 shows that for a target value of 22 weeks, that the probability is 83.6%, slightly higher than the 80% calculated by the PERT analysis. In this case, at least, it seems that PERT's simplifying assumptions are justified.

Crystal Ball also makes it easy to generate histograms like the one shown in Figure 14.18. This is a histogram of the slack for activity F. While the *expected* slack is close to the PERT analysis value of 3 weeks, the histogram shows that there is considerable variation around this average value. Note particularly that there is a spike of probability for slacks close to zero. If the slack is zero, then F is on the critical path. If the slack is close to zero, then the schedule for F can slip very little without delaying the entire project. This means that activity F *may* turn out to be a critical activity. This is an insight that the PERT analysis, with its large slack of 3 weeks for activity F, might obscure.

14.5 A MID-CHAPTER SUMMARY: PERT

Using the PERT approach the analyst must provide the following inputs:

1. A list of the activities that make up the project.
2. The immediate predecessors for each activity.
3. The expected value for each activity time [using $t = (a + 4m + b)/6$].
4. The standard deviation for each activity time [using std. dev. $t = (b - a)/6$].

The PERT estimation procedure uses pessimistic, most likely, and optimistic estimates of the activity time to obtain the expected value and the standard deviation for each activity. The standard deviation is required only if the analyst wishes to make probability statements about completing the project by a certain date.

The analysis uses the inputs listed above to

1. Calculate the critical path;
2. Calculate the minimum expected time in which the project can be completed;
3. Show slack values for each activity, together with the latest expected time that any activity can start (or finish) without delaying the project; and
4. Calculate the probability that the current critical path will be completed by a specified date if estimates of the standard deviation are provided.

If the project cannot (or is unlikely to) be completed by a desired date, the project must be redefined either by

1. Strategic analysis, in which the project network is modified by introducing new activities or changing the relationships between existing activities, or
2. Tactical analysis, in which activity times are changed by the application of additional resources.

Finally, we can observe that PERT is not only a planning system. You can now see that it can also be used to monitor the progress of a project. Management can compare the actual activity times as they occur with those that were used in the planning process. If, for example, activity B took 6 or 7 weeks, rather than the 5 weeks used in the network diagram, Becky would know that the project is behind schedule. This would give her the opportunity to arrange to assign more resources to some other activity on the critical path in an effort to shorten that activity and meet the desired overall due date.

Identification of the critical path and prompt reporting give management a powerful tool to deal with the difficult problem of bringing a complicated project in on schedule.

14.6 CPM AND TIME-COST TRADE-OFFS

As we have just seen, PERT provides a useful approach to the analysis of scheduling problems in the face of *uncertainty about activity times.* Such uncertainty will often occur in new or unique projects where there is little previous time and cost experience to draw upon. In other types of projects there may be considerable historical data with which one may make good estimates of time and resource requirements. In such cases it may be of interest to deal more explicitly with costs in the sense of analyzing possibilities to shift resources in order to reduce completion time. The concept that there is a trade-off between the time that it takes to complete an activity and the cost of the resources devoted to that activity is the basis of a model that was originally part of the CPM method.

The model assumes that cost is a linear function of time. Consider, for example, Figure 14.19. This figure illustrates that management has the opportunity to aim at an activity time anywhere between a minimum value and a maximum value. The choice of an activity time implies an activity cost as specified by the diagram.

Given the availability of such a time-cost trade-off function for each activity in the project, management has the opportunity to select each activity time (within limits) and incur

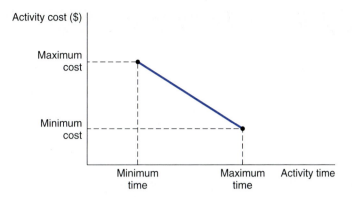

FIGURE 14.19

Time-Cost Trade-off Function

ACTIVITY	IMMEDIATE PREDECESSOR	NORMAL TIME (HR)
DIP (Design Information Processor)	—	32
WIP (Write Information Processor)	DIP	40
DAP (Design Analysis Package)	—	50
WAP (Write Analysis Package)	DAP	24
INT (Introduce System)	WIP, WAP	120

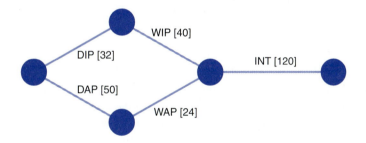

FIGURE 14.20

Activity List and Network Diagram for the Financial Analysis Project

the associated cost. Clearly, the choice of individual activity times affects the project completion time. The question becomes: "What activity times should be selected to yield the desired project completion time at minimum cost?" The CPM approach to answering this question will be presented in the context of the creation of a financial analysis package by the Operations Analysis Group at Global.

A FINANCIAL ANALYSIS PROJECT FOR RETAIL MARKETING

In addition to the move to Des Moines, Becky is responsible for a new financial analysis package that will be used in the retail marketing section of Global. The program is used in evaluating potential outlets (gas stations) in terms of location and other characteristics. The systems design is complete. The computer programming must still be done, and the package must be introduced to the retail marketing section.

Figure 14.20 shows the activity list and network diagram for this project. The time shown is termed the **normal time.** This corresponds to the maximum time shown in Figure 14.19. Recall that we are here assuming that activity times can be estimated with good accuracy, and hence "normal time" is a known quantity. From Figure 14.20 it is clear that the longest path through the network is DAP-WAP-INT, and hence this is the critical path. The earliest completion time for the project is 194 hours.

TABLE 14.4 Time-Cost Data for the Financial Analysis Project

ACTIVITY	(1) NORMAL TIME	(2) NORMAL COST ($)	(3) CRASH TIME	(4) CRASH COST ($)	(5) MAXIMUM CRASH HOURS	(6) COST PER CRASH HOUR ($)
DIP	32	640	20	800	12	13.33
WIP	40	480	30	720	10	24.00
DAP	50	1000	30	1200	20	10.00
WAP	24	288	15	360	9	8.00
INT	120	4800	70	5600	50	16.00
TOTAL		$7208				

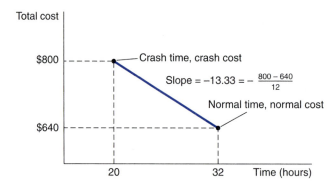

FIGURE 14.21

Time-Cost Trade-off Function for DIP

Required Activity Data The CPM system is based on four pieces of input data for each activity:

1. **Normal time:** the maximum time for the activity.
2. **Normal cost:** the cost required to achieve the normal time.
3. **Crash time:** the minimum time for the activity.
4. **Crash cost:** the cost required to achieve the crash time.

These data for the financial analysis project are presented in the first four columns of Table 14.4. The fifth column shows the maximum crash hours, defined by

$$\text{Max crash hours} = \text{normal time} - \text{crash time}$$

Figure 14.21 shows how these data are used to create the time-cost trade-off function for activity DIP, design the information processor.

Note that, according to Table 14.4, using all normal times leads to a total project cost of $7208. Also note that the last column in Table 14.4 shows how much it costs per hour (as computed in Figure 14.21) to reduce each activity time to less than its normal time. In CPM jargon, the process of reducing an activity time is called **crashing.** For example, management could choose to have DIP completed in 31 hours, rather than the normal 32 hours, for a marginal cost of $13.33. The normal time of 32 hours costs $640, and a time of 31 hours would therefore cost 640 + 13.33 = $653.33.

CRASHING THE PROJECT

We have noted that, using only the normal time for each activity, the earliest completion time for this project is 194 hours (along the critical path DAP-WAP-INT). Management is now in a position to determine the minimum-cost method of reducing this time to specified

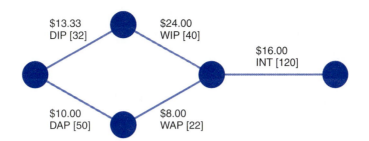

FIGURE 14.22

Marginal Costs of Crashing
the Financial Analysis Project

levels. To reduce the project time to 193, Becky would crash an activity on the critical path by 1 hour. Since it costs less per hour to crash WAP than either of the other two activities on the critical path ($8 < $10 and $8 < $16), Becky would first crash WAP by 1 hour. This decision yields a project time of 193 hours, a critical path of DAP-WAP-INT, and a total project cost of $7216 (= $7208 + $8). If Becky wants to achieve a time of 192 hours, exactly the same analysis would apply, and she would crash WAP by another hour and incur a marginal cost of $8.

If Becky has crashed WAP by 2 hours to achieve a project time of 192 hours and still wants to crash the project by another hour (to achieve 191), the analysis becomes more complicated. Figure 14.22 shows the situation. The dollar figure in the diagram is the marginal cost of crashing. Note that there are now two critical paths, DIP-WIP-INT and DAP-WAP-INT, and that both require 192 hours. Crashing one of the four activities (DIP, WIP, DAP, or WAP) by 1 hour would bring one path down to 191 hours, but would still leave the project time at 192, since there would still be a critical path of 192 hours. A time of 191 could be obtained only by crashing activities on both paths. If Becky crashed DIP and WAP by 1 hour each it would reduce both paths to 191 hours, and it would cost her $13.33 + $8.00 = $21.33. Alternatively, INT could be crashed by 1 hour for a cost of $16.00. Can you see that there are other alternatives to consider?

Although it is possible to do this sort of marginal cost analysis in any CPM network, it is clear that it would be difficult and tedious to carry it out in a complicated network. This consideration leads us to an LP formulation of the problem.

A LINEAR PROGRAMMING MODEL

The problem of obtaining a specific project time at minimum cost can be formulated as a linear programming problem. Figure 14.23 shows the spreadsheet formulation and solution of the financial analysis problem (GLOBFIN.XLS) with a limit of 184 hours on the project time. To understand this formulation, let

$$CWIP = \text{hours crashed on activity WIP}$$

$$ESWIP = \text{earliest start time for activity WIP}$$

$$EFINT = \text{earliest finish time for activity INT}$$

The other decision variables follow this same pattern. From these definitions it follows that

1. The objective function is the total cost of crashing the network. This is the appropriate objective. The cost of completing the project on normal time is already determined. You can think of management's problem as deciding how much (and where) to crash to obtain the desired earliest finish time at minimum additional cost.

2. The constraints in cells B9:D12 establish limits for the earliest start time for activities WIP, WAP, and INT. For example, rewriting the first constraint (ESWIP), whose formula is in B9:D9, yields

$$ESWIP \geq 32 - CDIP$$

We note that since 32 is the normal time for DIP and CDIP is the amount that DIP is crashed, the right-hand side is the time that activity DIP will take after it has been crashed. Thus, this constraint states that the earliest start time for WIP must be $\geq$ the modified activity time for

B11		= =I2+C2-G2							
A	B	C	D	E	F	G	H	I	J
1	CDIP	CWIP	CDAP	CWAP	CINT	ESWIP	ESWAP	ESINT	EFINT
2 Amount	0	0	0	2	8	32	50	72	184
3 Per unitCost	$ 13.33	$ 24.00	$ 10.00	$ 8.00	$ 16.00				
4 Max Crash Time	12	10	20	9	50				
5									
6 Total Cost	144								
7									
8 Constraints									
9 Early Start WIP	32	>=		32					
10 Early Start WAP	50	>=		50					
11 Early Start INT(WIP)	40	>=		40					
12 Early Start INT(WAP)	24	>=		24					
13 Defn of EFINT	120	=		120					
14 Early Finish INT Goal	184	<=		184					
15									

Cell	Formula	Copy To
B6	=SUMPRODUCT(B2:F2,B3:F3)	—
B9	=B2+G2	—
B10	=H2+D2	—
B11	=I2+C2−G2	—
B12	=I2+E2−H2	—
B13	=J2+F2−I2	—
B14	=J2	—

FIGURE 14.23

LP Solution of the Financial Analysis Problem

DIP. Since DIP is *the only* predecessor for WIP, we know that the earliest start time for WIP is exactly this modified activity time of DIP. You will thus expect to see

$$\text{ESWIP} = 32 - \text{CDIP}$$

A $\geq$ constraint is used rather than an $=$ constraint because, in general, there could be several paths leading into a node, and the earliest start time of an activity leaving that node is determined by the entering path that takes the longest time. This is illustrated by the two constraints for ESINT. Rewriting these constraints yields

$$\text{cells B11:D11} \rightarrow \text{ESINT} \geq 40 - \text{CWIP} + \text{ESWIP}$$

$$\text{cells B12:D12} \rightarrow \text{ESINT} \geq 24 - \text{CWAP} + \text{ESWAP}$$

The first constraint states that INT cannot start until WIP is complete, and the second makes a similar statement for WAP. It will often be the case that only one of these will be active in an optimal solution.

3. Cells B13:D13 contain the definition of earliest finish time for activity INT:

$$\text{EFINT} = \text{ESINT} \underbrace{+\ 120 - \text{CINT}}_{\substack{\text{activity time for} \\ \text{INT after crashing}}}$$

4. The last constraint (cells B14:D14) sets an upper limit on the project time we want to achieve. This constraint depends on the fact that the finish time for activity INT determines the finish time for the overall project. In general, a similar constraint would be required for each activity leading into the terminal mode. Here we have only one such activity, INT.

5. Finally we need to add some constraints directly in the Solver Dialog box that limit the amount of crashing on each activity. The limit is given originally by column 5 in Table 14.4, "Maximum Crash Hours." For the Solver, we simply indicate that B2:F2 < = B4:F4.

The solution in Figure 14.23 shows that WAP should be crashed by 2 hours and INT by 8 hours to achieve a minimum cost reduction of 10 hours in the project completion time (i.e., the optimal value of EFINT is 184, and this is the project completion time). As usual with LP output, however, this is only a small part of the information available. For example, Figure 14.24 shows us that it will cost $16 to crash the network for 1 additional hour

Microsoft Excel 8.0 Sensitivity Report
Worksheet: [globfin.xls]184 hrs
Report Created: 3/14/97 10:08:10 AM

Chapter 14   683
Project Management:
PERT and CPM

Adjustable Cells

Cell	Name	Final Value	Reduced Cost	Objective Coefficient	Allowable Increase	Allowable Decrease
$B$2	Amount CDIP	0	5.33	13.33	1E+30	5.33
$C$2	Amount CWIP	0	16	24	1E+30	16
$D$2	Amount CDAP	0	2	10	1E+30	2
$E$2	Amount CWAP	2	0	8	2	5.33
$F$2	Amount CINT	8	0	16	5.33	8
$G$2	Amount ESWIP	32	0	0	5.33	8
$H$2	Amount ESWAP	50	0	0	2	8
$I$2	Amount ESINT	72	0	0	5.33	8
$J$2	Amount EFINT	184	0	0	16	1E+30

Constraints

Cell	Name	Final Value	Shadow Price	Constraint R.H. Side	Allowable Increase	Allowable Decrease
$B$9	Early Start WIP CDIP	32	8	32	2	7
$B$10	Early Start WAP CDIP	50	8	50	7	2
$B$11	Early Start INT(WIP) CDIP	40	8	40	2	7
$B$12	Early Start INT(WAP) CDIP	24	8	24	7	2
$B$13	Defn of EFINT CDIP	120	16	120	42	8
$B$14	Early Finish INT Goal CDIP	184	-16	184	8	42

FIGURE 14.24

Sensitivity Report for the Financial Analysis Problem

(shadow price on "Early Finish INT Goal"). The right-hand-side ranges show that this rate of $16 per hour holds for a decrease of another 42 hours. In this simple problem you can see that this next 42 hours of crashing (beyond the first 10) should be done on INT. In general this type of LP sensitivity information can provide useful guidance to management in the attempt to control the progress of large projects.

In concluding this section, we recall the sixth of the questions raised in Section 14.1: "How might resources most effectively be concentrated on activities in order to speed up project completion?" In this section we have seen that in a context where time and costs are suitably defined, as in the CPM model, *project crashing* allows management to answer this question.

We now proceed to discuss the final question raised in Section 14.1: "What controls can be exercised on the flows of expenditures for the various activities throughout the duration of the project in order that the overall budget can be adhered to?"

14.7   PROJECT COST MANAGEMENT: PERT/COST

The desirability of a project typically depends on its total costs and revenues. (Discounting to account for the time value of money may be necessary to express costs and/or returns in current dollars if the project is of long duration.) Once a project has been selected, effective cost management includes two important functions: planning and control.

PLANNING COSTS FOR THE CREDIT CARD PROJECT: THE PERT/COST SYSTEM

Large projects can strongly influence the financial situation within a firm. The need to pay for the various activities creates a demand on both the firm's overall budget and the daily cash flow. Obviously, the times at which activities are scheduled determine when

On February 27, 1991, President Bush stated, "We said the aggression would not stand, and the aggression did not stand!" The armed conflict in the Kuwaiti Theater of Operations ended in one of the most resounding military victories in history. How was project management instrumental in the successful execution of the military operation and particularly in those fateful 100 hours of the ground war?

General Schwarzkopf directed that the logistics community keep a 60-day supply of material on hand. This included medical supplies, diesel fuel, motor gasoline, and so forth. Looking at medical supplies alone, the best initial estimate was 26,352 short tons. Then the figure was modified based on the specifics of operations in Kuwait. For example, the amount of saline solution for rehydration of personnel was greater than that required in Europe (due to the arid climate). Also, there were insufficient refrigeration units on hand to properly store whole blood. U.S. ground forces were projected to use 1,600,000 gallons of diesel fuel and 180,000 gallons of motor gasoline per day, but when the forces went on the offensive those figures would double. The combat units usually carry only one to two days' worth of supplies, and thus rely heavily on a steady source of new supplies. The combat unit is specifically designed for mobility and survivability on the battlefield, not for storing extraneous amounts of supplies.

One of the most successful results was a resupply technique that cut the resupply time for a heavy brigade in half (from six hours to three hours), and allowed both the supply unit and supported combat unit to be moving during resupply activities. Minimizing the resupply time has three major benefits. First, it increases security. While the vehicles are congregated for resupply, they are more subject to detection by the enemy. Second, the supply vehicles can make more round trips in the same amount of time. Third, the tactical commander has greater flexibility in planning because less time is taken up by resupply activities.

A famous saying in the U.S. forces is "tacticians win battles, but logistics win wars." All in all, the successful implementation of the numerous details of such a complex project as Desert Storm is a large part of what made the victory so decisive (see Staats).

---

budget demands occur. This is a good example of how management science models can be hooked together. First, a PERT network model is made of the Global Oil move, then perhaps an LP model is used to crash to an acceptable time frame, and finally a spreadsheet financial model can be made to aid in financial planning. Thus, the output of each model becomes the input for the next, and so it is crucial to constantly check the model results for accuracy.

It is important for a firm to be able to anticipate budget demands in order to be able to handle them economically and effectively. The **PERT/Cost** system is specifically designed to help management anticipate such demands in a clear and consistent manner. PERT/Cost is essentially an alternative approach to cost accounting. Typically, cost accounting systems are organized on a cost center basis (e.g., by departments). The PERT/Cost system is organized on a project basis, where the basic elements of control are the activities.

In order to apply the PERT/Cost system to the project of moving the credit card operation to Des Moines, Becky must now complete Table 14.2 by filling in the final column, titled "Resources." This is an estimated or "expected" total cost of completing each activity. These expected activity costs, together with the expected activity times, the earliest start time, and the latest start time, are presented in Table 14.5 for the redefined credit card project. The earliest start and latest start data are taken from the spreadsheet solution, Figure 14.14.

The goal of the PERT/Cost system is to construct a graph of budget demands over time. This requires knowledge of how funds will be spent throughout the life of an activity. For example, the demands on the budget are different if the $32,000 for activity E, construct the interior, is due at the beginning of the 8-week activity time or at the end of it. PERT/Cost makes the assumption that expenditures occur uniformly throughout the life of the activity; that is, for E a budget demand of $4000 occurs during each of the 8 weeks. Table 14.6 shows the budget demands by time if all activities start at their *earliest start time*. This table is constructed by assigning a row to each activity and recording the budget demands for that activity in the appropriate column (week) as determined by the earliest start time. In forming this table, "earliest start" times are interpreted as referring to the end of the appropriate week. Thus activity B starts at time 0 (the end of week 0 = beginning of week 1) and requires 5 weeks to complete. This means that activity C, as shown in Table 14.6, cannot start until the end of week 5. It lasts 3 weeks and makes a budget demand of $600 per week. This information is summarized in the third row of Table 14.6.

TABLE 14.5 Resource Requirements for the Redesigned Project

ACTIVITY	EXPECTED TIME	EARLIEST START	LATEST START	TOTAL RESOURCES REQUIRED ($)
A	3	0	5	2,100
B	5	0	0	5,000
C	3	5	5	1,800
D	4	8	8	4,800
E	8	12	12	32,000
F	2	8	11	1,000
G	4	10	13	2,800
H	2	10	18	7,000
I	5	5	15	4,000
J	3	14	17	30,000
K	3	10	14	1,500
Total				$92,000

The total weekly cost is determined by adding down a column, that is, by adding the budget demands during the week from all the activities. For example, the budget demand during the thirteenth week is $5200, the sum of $4000 from E, $700 from G, and $500 from K.

The cumulative project cost is found by cumulating the weekly costs from the beginning of the project. For example, note that the weekly cost is $1700 for each of the first 3 weeks. The total project cost after 3 weeks is therefore $5100. The total cost at the end of the project (week 20) must, of course, be the total cost for the entire project.

Table 14.7 creates the profile of budget demands over time if each activity starts at its *latest start time.*

The information from Tables 14.6 and 14.7 is combined in Figure 14.25. The upper line is a plot of the earliest start time costs from Table 14.6, and the lower line is a plot of the latest start time costs from Table 14.7. The shaded area between the lines shows the area of feasible cumulative budgets for total project costs if the project is completed on time. The fact that the actual budget demands must fall within the envelope created by the earliest start time and the latest start time makes it easy for management to anticipate its cumulative expenditures. For example, Becky can see that by the end of week 12 Global Oil will have to have spent between $14,200 and $28,100.

We have progressed step by step through the budget calculations for the PERT/Cost planning system because this is a useful exercise from the pedagogical point of view. In practice these calculations are typically done on a computer. Figure 14.26 shows a computer output that corresponds to Tables 14.6 and 14.7.

CONTROLLING PROJECT COSTS

The concept behind any control system is to compare the *actual performance* with *planned performance* and to take remedial action if it is necessary. The thermostat in your house is a control system that operates continuously in time by comparing the actual temperature with the desired temperature and turning the furnace (air conditioner) off or on as necessary.

The PERT/Cost system compares actual costs or budgeted project costs at regular intervals so that management has an early indication if the project is not proceeding according to plan. Management is then in a position to take appropriate action.

TABLE 14.6 Budget Demands: Earliest Start Time

	COST PER WEEK ($)																			
ACTIVITY	1	2	3	4	5	6	7	8	9	10	11	12	13	14	15	16	17	18	19	20
A	700	700	700																	
B	1,000	1,000	1,000	1,000	1,000															
C						600	600	600												
D									1,200	1,200	1,200	1,200								
E													4,000	4,000	4,000	4,000	4,000	4,000	4,000	4,000
F									500	500										
G											700	700	700	700						
H											3,500	3,500								
I						800	800	800	800	800										
J															10,000	10,000	10,000			
K											500	500	500							
Weekly Cost	1,700	1,700	1,700	1,000	1,000	1,400	1,400	1,400	2,500	2,500	5,900	5,900	5,200	4,700	14,000	14,000	14,000	4,000	4,000	4,000
Cumulative Project Cost	1,700	3,400	5,100	6,100	7,100	8,500	9,900	11,300	13,800	16,300	22,200	28,100	33,500	38,000	52,000	66,000	80,000	84,000	88,000	92,000

TABLE 14.7 Budget Demands: Latest Start Time

	COST PER WEEK ($)																			
ACTIVITY	1	2	3	4	5	6	7	8	9	10	11	12	13	14	15	16	17	18	19	20
A						700	700	700												
B	1,000	1,000	1,000	1,000																
C					1,000	600	600	600												
D									1,200	1,200	1,200									
E												1,200	4,000	4,000	4,000	4,000	4,000	4,000	4,000	4,000
F												500	500							
G														700	700	700	700			
H																			3,500	3,500
I																800	800	800	800	800
J																		10,000	10,000	10,000
K															500	500	500			
Weekly Cost	1,000	1,000	1,000	1,000	1,000	1,300	1,300	1,300	1,200	1,200	1,200	1,700	4,500	4,700	5,200	6,000	6,000	14,800	18,300	18,300
Cumulative Project Cost	1,000	2,000	3,000	4,000	5,000	6,300	7,600	8,900	10,100	11,300	12,500	14,200	18,700	23,400	28,600	34,600	40,600	55,400	73,700	92,000

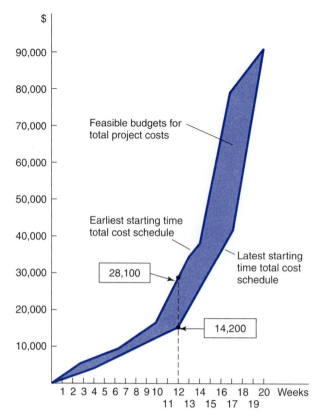

FIGURE 14.25

Cumulative Budget Demands
Versus Time

RESOURCE USAGE PROFILE ACCORDING TO EARLIEST START TIME			
Time Interval		Resource Usage	
From End of Week	To End of Week	Weekly	Cumulative
0.00→	3.00	1700.00	5100.00
3.00→	5.00	1000.00	7100.00
5.00→	8.00	1400.00	11300.00
8.00→	10.00	2500.00	16300.00
10.00→	12.00	5900.00	28100.00
12.00→	13.00	5200.00	33300.00
13.00→	14.00	4700.00	38000.00
14.00→	17.00	14000.00	80000.00
17.00→	20.00	4000.00	92000.00

RESOURCE USAGE PROFILE ACCORDING TO LATEST START TIME			
Time Interval		Resource Usage	
From End of Week	To End of Week	Weekly	Cumulative
0.00→	5.00	1000.00	5000.00
5.00→	8.00	1300.00	8900.00
8.00→	11.00	1200.00	12500.00
11.00→	12.00	1700.00	14200.00
12.00→	13.00	4500.00	18700.00
13.00→	14.00	4700.00	23400.00
14.00→	15.00	5200.00	28600.00
15.00→	17.00	6000.00	40600.00
17.00→	18.00	14800.00	55400.00
18.00→	20.00	18300.00	92000.00

FIGURE 14.26

Computer Analysis of
Budget Demands

	(1)	(2)	(3) [(1)/100] × (2)	(4)	(5) (4)−(3)
ACTIVITY	PERCENT COMPLETE	BUDGET ($)	BUDGETED COST TO DATE ($)	ACTUAL COST TO DATE ($)	COST OVERRUN TO DATE ($)
A	100	2,100	2,100	2,300	200
B	100	5,000	5,000	4,900	(100)
C	100	1,800	1,800	1,800	0
D	75	4,800	3,600	4,600	1,000
E	0	32,000	0	0	0
F	100	1,000	1,000	1,200	200
G	25	2,800	700	1,400	700
H	50	7,000	3,500	5,400	1,900
I	20	4,000	800	500	(300)
J	0	30,000	0	0	0
K	0	1,500	0	0	0
Total		92,000	18,500	22,100	3,600

TABLE 14.8 Project Costs After 11 Weeks

The PERT/Cost Control Report Table 14.8 is a PERT/Cost *control report* prepared 11 weeks after the start of the redefined project to move the credit card operation to Des Moines. The labels on the columns indicate how the report is prepared. Column (4), the actual cost, and column (3), the budgeted cost, provide the basic information used in the control function. The actual cost, column (4), is self-explanatory. *The budgeted cost, column (3), is calculated on the assumption that the percentage of budget used up by an activity is the same as the percentage of that activity that is completed.* Thus, when an activity is 50% complete, its budgeted cost is 50% of the entire budget (column [2]) for that activity. Note that if an activity is completed, the entry in column (1) is 100, and this means the entry in column (3) will be the same as the entry in column (2).

Consider, for example, activity A, "select office site." We see from column (1) of Table 14.8 that this activity, by the end of week 11, is 100% complete. Thus, its budgeted cost, column (3), is equal to its entire budget (column [2]) of $2100. Since its actual cost is $2300, there is a cost overrun of $200. This number is recorded in the last column. A similar interpretation applies to activity I, "make financial arrangements." It is 20% complete and has a budget of $4000; thus, its budgeted cost is $800 ($800 = 0.20 × $4000). Since only $500 has been spent, there is a budget surplus of $300. The parentheses in the last column indicate a budget surplus.

In this situation, since activities A and F are already completed, their cost overruns cannot be corrected. However, activities D, G, and H, none of which are yet complete, are showing significant overruns to date, and these activities should be promptly reviewed. This type of periodic managerial intervention is often required to keep the total project cost within the budget.

Potential Implementation Problems Although PERT/Cost can provide an effective control procedure, it is well to be aware of potential implementation problems. For example, the required recording of data can involve significant clerical effort, especially when many projects with many activities are under way. Moreover, some costs, such as overhead, may be common to several activities. The allocation of such common costs can be problematic.

Finally, as we mentioned at the beginning of Section 14.7, the PERT/Cost system differs in organization from typical cost accounting systems. The typical departmental cost center orientation needs to be substantially revised to handle the PERT/Cost activity-oriented system. Such redesign may be politically as well as materially expensive.

14.8 NOTES ON IMPLEMENTATION

Some 40 years after its inception, the critical path concept is an important part of current practice. Almost any time you have a large project with a number of interrelated activities, you will find a network-based planning and reporting system being used. Over time, the distinctions between PERT and CPM have become blurred. Firms have developed their own internal computer-based models incorporating those features of the original PERT and CPM systems that are important to their specific activity. EDS (Electronic Data Systems) has been using AutoCAD (an automatic drafting program) to draw PERT charts for clients for several years now. Managers find that this visual aid helps them and their clients to keep projects on track, to spot possible problems early on, and acts as a good communication device. The charts are printed across several pages, making a large "banner" that can be posted in the office.

It is common to think of using critical path methods on large one-of-a-kind projects (e.g., the U.S. space shuttle). However, the methods can and do apply to activities that occur at quite regular intervals. A good example of such an activity is the major overhaul of the dragline in a particular coal mining operation. This maintenance must be performed on a fairly regular schedule and is of major importance because when the dragline is not operating, the mine is not operating. The firm can and does use the network diagram for the previous overhaul in planning for an upcoming overhaul. The network plays an important role in assuring that all those involved understand the various steps and their interrelationship, as well as ensuring that all the requisite parts and materials are available when they are needed. Given the turnover in personnel, and human frailties, the network serves as a convenient way to capture past experience. The activities associated with the overhaul vary from time to time, so the chart must be reworked, but the previous version generally provides a good starting point.

For our example firm, estimating time variability is not an important part of creating its PERT-CPM network. Indeed, it relies on a single best estimate rather than the three that are part of the PERT approach. The crucial element in developing an economical plan for the overhaul is the availability of various skilled workers (electricians, pipefitters, and so on). Each time an overhaul is to be performed, the tasks vary somewhat, and thus the demand for workers varies from year to year. In addition, the supply of available workers within the firm varies from time to time depending on the level of other activities. The planning operation typically involves running the model under a variety of assumptions. Alternatives might include regular employees working regular time, regular employees doubling up (i.e., working two shifts), bringing in outside workers, and so on. Such calculations can make it clear, for example, that it pays to spend $20,000 in overtime for electricians if it puts the mine back in operation a day earlier.

The computer has had a major impact on the use of CPM and PERT. Large construction projects may require 1000 or more nodes. In the 1960s it was not unusual to find the network diagram for such a project spread out over three walls of a room that was dedicated to that purpose for the duration of the project. Major changes in the plan were a major pain in their own right, and communication among the multiple contractors was cumbersome. The computer has changed all of that. The analysis is now done on a computer. There is a whole host of microcomputer software (e.g., Harvard Project Manager, InstaPlan, MacProject II, Microsoft's Project for Windows) that will aid in project management, combining PERT and CPM with budget information and control. It is quite a simple matter to use the software to draw the boxes (actually combining activities and events) and then to connect them by pointing to the activities that precede each other. The program does the rest (determining the critical path, earliest and latest starting and finishing times). Multiple runs spanning the life of the project are the order of the day. In the early phases it is important to ensure that orders for major components are placed early enough. Complicated systems (i.e., generators, furnaces, and so on) may have a delivery time of several years. Regular updating based on supplier reports enables management to see when it is necessary to expedite an order. New information is fed into the model, and the program is rerun on a weekly basis. Obviously, the information obtained from such runs influences the allocation of resources. It may even affect the design of the project. If a cost control report more or less like the one shown in Table 14.8 indicates serious cost overruns early enough, later parts of the project may be redesigned. For example, one firm reported reworking a heating plant design based on one boiler rather than two after the cost of excavation and driving piles ran far ahead of budget. This change enabled the firm to bring the project in on time *and* within budget.

14.9   SUMMARY

This chapter dealt with the role of PERT and CPM in project management. The fundamental concept is to represent a project as a network. Section 14.2 showed how to use an activity list to construct a network diagram for a project, where the activity list identifies each activity in the project and its immediate predecessors. Section 14.3 showed how the network diagram and the expected activity times are used to determine the critical path, which is a longest path through the network. In the process, the terms *earliest start time, earliest finish time, latest start time, latest finish time,* and *slack* were defined.

Section 14.4 introduced the notion of variability in activity times. It dealt with two main topics: the PERT system of estimating times and the probability that all the activities on the critical path will be completed by a specified date. The PERT system of estimating time is based on the assumption that activity time has a beta distribution. It uses an optimistic, a most probable, and a pessimistic time estimate to derive the expected activity time and the standard deviation of the activity time.

Management would like to know the probability that the project under consideration will be completed by a specific date. If one assumes that activity times are independent and that the sum of the activity times on the critical path has a normal distribution, it is a straightforward exercise to calculate *the probability that the critical path will be completed by a specified date.* This is not the probability that the project will ultimately be completed by the specified date, for the effect of randomness could turn a supposedly noncritical path into a critical one. However, this does give an upper estimate for the probability that the overall project will be completed by a specific date.

Section 14.6 presented the CPM framework for analyzing the problem of time-cost trade-offs. The amount of time that an activity takes is determined by the level of resources devoted to that activity. The model in this section employs the notion of project crashing. The model is intended to help management select a completion time for each activity so as to achieve a specified completion date for the overall project at minimum cost. The basic input for the model is a set of functions, one for each activity. Each function portrays the activity cost as a linear function of activity time within specified limits on the time. These data are then used either in a marginal cost analysis or in a linear programming model to select the best activity times.

Section 14.7 considered project cost management via the PERT/Cost system. It dealt with both a cost planning and a cost control model. The planning model produces a graph of the feasible budget demands as a function of time. This graph is constructed from the resource usage profiles based on the earliest start time and the latest start time.

The project cost control model is a system of comparing actual costs with budgeted costs. The budgeted cost model uses the assumption that for partially completed activities, the budgeted cost is equal to the budget for the completed activity multiplied by the proportion of the activity that has been completed. The model allows management to recognize cost overruns on various activities before they are completed.

Key Terms

PERT.   An acronym for Program Evaluation Review Technique, a method for scheduling and controlling projects.

CPM.   An acronym for Critical Path Method, a method for scheduling and controlling projects.

Activity List.   A list of jobs in a project with their immediate predecessors, expected times, and resources required.

Immediate Predecessors.   Those activities that must be completed immediately prior to the start of the activity in question.

Network Diagram.   A graphical method of representing a project with nodes and arcs.

Branch.   A line in a PERT network indicating an activity (in AOA) or precedence (in AON). Also called an *arc*.

Node.   A circle in a PERT network indicating the completion of certain activities and the initiation of others (in AOA) or the activity itself (in AON).

Event.   The completion of all activities leading into a node in a PERT network using AOA.

Activity.   A job that must be completed as part of a project.

Dummy Activity.   An imaginary activity that requires no time and is used to maintain the appropriate precedence relationships in a PERT network diagram using AOA.

Path.   A sequence of activities leading from the starting node to the completion node of a network.

Critical Path.   A sequence of activities that determines the longest path through the network that yields the minimum time in which an entire project can be completed.

Critical Activities.   The activities on the critical path.

Earliest Start Time.   In a PERT network, the earliest moment at which an activity can start.

Earliest Finish Time.   In a PERT network, the earliest moment at which an activity can be completed.

Forward Pass.   The process of moving along a network from beginning to end, computing the earliest start time and earliest finish time for each activity.

Backward Pass.   The process of moving backward along a network from end to beginning, computing the latest finish time and then the latest start time for each activity.

Latest Start Time.   In a PERT network, the latest moment at which an activity can start without delaying completion of the overall project.

Latest Finish Time.   The latest time at which an activity can be completed without delaying the completion of the overall project.

Slack.   The time that an activity can be delayed beyond its earliest start time without delaying the completion of the overall project.

Optimistic Time.   The time required to complete an activity if everything goes perfectly.

Most Probable Time.   The time required to complete an activity under normal circumstances.

Pessimistic Time.   The time required to complete an activity under the most unfavorable conditions.

Beta Distribution.   A probability distribution used to model the activity times in PERT.

Normal Time.   In CPM, the maximum time for completion of an activity, corresponding to minimal resource usage.

Normal Cost.   The cost required to achieve the normal time.

Crash Time.   In CPM, the minimum possible time for completion of an activity, corresponding to maximal resource concentration.

Crash Cost.   The cost required to achieve the crash time.

Crashing.   A term in the CPM method describing the process of reducing the time required to complete an activity.

PERT/Cost. A system for determining the feasible patterns of cash flow during a project.

True-False

1. **T F** In a PERT network diagram using AOA, each activity is represented by a circle called a node.

2. **T F** The term *event* is used to refer to nodes in a PERT network using AOA.

3. **T F** A dummy activity is required in a correct network representation of the following activity list.

ACTIVITY	IMMEDIATE PREDECESSORS
1	—
2	—
3	1
4	2, 3
5	2
6	5

4. **T F** The earliest finish time for an activity depends on the earliest finish time for the project.

5. **T F** The latest finish time for an activity depends on the earliest finish time for the project.

6. **T F** All activities on the critical path have their latest finish time equal to their earliest start time.

7. **T F** A strategic analysis of a PERT network concentrates on the allocation of resources to reduce the time on the critical path.

8. **T F** The probability of completing the project by time *T* is equal to the probability of completing the critical path by time *T*.

9. **T F** The standard deviation of an activity time is estimated as $(b - a)/6$, where b is the pessimistic and a is the optimistic time.

10. **T F** The CPM approach to time-cost trade-offs assumes that cost is a linear function of time.

11. **T F** The LP formulation of the network crashing problem minimizes the total cost of crashing subject to an upper bound on project duration.

12. **T F** In the PERT/Cost model the earliest starting time total cost schedule always is less than or equal to the latest starting time total cost schedule.

13. **T F** Time variabilities leading to a longer-than-expected total time for the critical path will always extend the project completion date.

14. **T F** If a noncritical activity is delayed more than its slack time, all other factors remaining unchanged, then the project completion date will be extended.

15. **T F** Gantt charts provide useful immediate predecessor information.

Multiple Choice

16. Of all paths through the network, the critical path
    a. has the maximum expected time
    b. has the minimum expected time
    c. has the maximum actual time
    d. has the minimum actual time

17. The earliest start time (ES) for an activity leaving node C (in the AOA approach)
    a. is the Max of the earliest finish times for all activities entering node C
    b. equals the earliest finish time for the same activity minus its expected activity time
    c. depends on all paths leading from the start through node C
    d. all of the above

18. The latest finish time (LF) for an activity entering node H (in the AOA approach)
    a. equals the Max of the latest start times for all activities leaving node H
    b. depends on the latest finish time for the project
    c. equals the latest start time minus the activity time for the same activity
    d. none of the above

19. The slack for activity G
    a. equals LF for G − LS for G
    b. equals EF for G − ES for G
    c. equals LS for G − ES for G
    d. none of the above

20. Estimating expected activity times in a PERT network
    a. makes use of three estimates
    b. puts the greatest weight on the most likely time estimate
    c. is motivated by the beta distribution
    d. all of the above

21. The calculation of the probability that the critical path will be completed by time *T*
    a. assumes that activity times are statistically independent
    b. assumes that total time of the critical path has approximately a beta distribution
    c. requires knowledge of the standard deviation for all activities in the network
    d. all of the above

22. In the CPM time-cost trade-off function
   a. the cost at normal time is 0
   b. within the range of feasible times, the activity cost increases linearly as time increases
   c. cost decreases linearly as time increases
   d. none of the above

23. The marginal cost of crashing a network could change when
   a. the activity being crashed reaches its crash time
   b. the activity being crashed reaches a point where another path is also critical
   c. both a and b

24. Fundamental ideas in the LP network crashing models are
   a. activity time equals normal time + crash time
   b. earliest start time for an activity leaving a node equals the Max of the earliest finish times for activities leaving that node
   c. earliest finish time equals latest finish time minus activity time
   d. none of the above

25. The PERT/Cost model assumes that
   a. each activity achieves its optimistic time
   b. the costs are uniformly distributed over the life of the activity
   c. activity times are statistically independent
   d. none of the above

26. The PERT/Cost control report
   a. requires a budget for each activity
   b. requires a report on the percentage of completion of each activity
   c. calculates cost overruns
   d. all of the above

Answers

1.	F	8.	F	15.	F	21.	a
2.	T	9.	T	16.	a	22.	c
3.	T	10.	T	17.	d	23.	c
4.	F	11.	T	18.	b	24.	d
5.	T	12.	F	19.	c	25.	b
6.	F	13.	T	20.	d	26.	d
7.	F	14.	T				

Problems

•• 14-1. The Build-Rite Construction Company has identified 10 activities that take place in building a house. They are
   1. Walls and Ceiling (erect the wall frames and ceiling joists).
   2. Foundation (pour the foundation slab).
   3. Roof Timbers (put up the roof timbers).
   4. Roof Sheathing (install roof sheathing over the timbers).
   5. Electrical Wiring (install the electrical wiring).
   6. Roof Shingles (shingle the roof).
   7. Exterior Siding (put on the exterior siding).
   8. Windows (install the window units).
   9. Paint (paint the interior and exterior).
   10. Inside Wall Board (hang the inside wall board).
   In addition, the following customs are typically observed:
   1. Wiring is done from the interior side of the wall, while the window unit is mounted after the wall frame has been erected.
   2. Inside wall board and exterior siding are installed over the window unit.
   3. Painting is not begun until the house is watertight.
      (a) Make a list showing each activity and its immediate predecessors.

14-2. Quacker Mills hires engineering undergraduates and moves them through six management experiences (activities) to prepare them to be plant managers. There are three disciplines and two positions (starting and advanced) in each discipline. These six activities are shown in the following table. Further, a person who has not been a production line engineer cannot be department head, nor can someone who has not been a foreperson be a product line scheduler.

Make an activity list showing each activity and its immediate predecessors.

TABLE 14.9

	DISCIPLINE		
	Plant Engineering	Line Supervision	Production Planning
Starting	Production Line Engineer 1	Foreperson 2	Assistant Product Line Scheduler 3
Advanced	Plant Engineer 4	Department Head 5	Product Line Scheduler 6

14-3. Construct the network diagram using activity-on-the-arc for the house construction system used by Build-Rite Construction Company in Problem 14-1.

14-4. Construct a CPM network diagram (AON) of the activities given in the following table.

TABLE 14.10

ACTIVITY	IMMEDIATE PREDECESSORS
1	—
2	—
3	2
4	1, 3
5	2
6	1, 5
7	1, 5
8	2
9	4, 6
10	6
11	7, 8
12	9, 10, 11

14-5. Build-Rite has estimated the times given in the accompanying table as necessary to complete each of the tasks involved in building a house. For each activity, give the
   (a) Earliest start time
   (b) Earliest finish time
   (c) Latest start time
   (d) Latest finish time
   (e) Slack
In addition, identify the critical path.

TABLE 14.11

ACTIVITY NUMBER	ACTIVITY	IMMEDIATE PREDECESSORS	EXPECTED TIME (DAYS)
1	Walls and Ceiling	2	5
2	Foundation	—	3
3	Roof Timbers	1	2
4	Roof Sheathing	3	3
5	Electrical Wiring	1	4
6	Roof Shingles	4	8
7	Exterior Siding	8	5
8	Windows	1	2
9	Paint	6, 7, 10	2
10	Inside Wall Board	8, 5	3

•• **14-6.** As a project manager, you are faced with the activity network and estimated activity times shown in Figure 14.27. For each activity, give the
  (a) Earliest start time
  (b) Earliest finish time
  (c) Latest start time
  (d) Latest finish time
  (e) Slack
  In addition, identify the critical path.

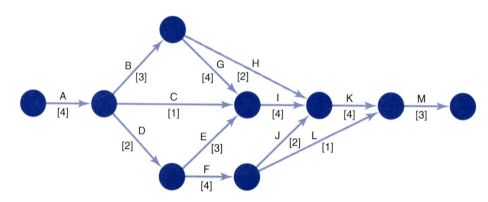

FIGURE 14.27

•• **14-7.** You are called in as a production consultant. The plant currently uses a PERT-CPM approach to a production run described by the activity network of Figure 14.28. Based on your evaluation, however, the immediate predecessors of each activity are shown in the following table.

ACTIVITY	IMMEDIATE PREDECESSORS
A	—
B	—
C	A
D	B
E	B
F	C
G	D
H	E
I	G
J	E
K	H
L	F
M	L, I, K, J

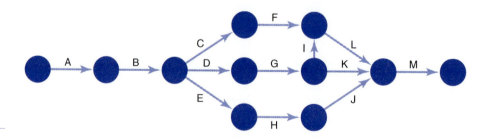

FIGURE 14.28

  (a) Draw the revised activity network.
  (b) Compute earliest and latest start and finish times for the revised network based on the assumption that each activity takes 1 hour longer than its alphabetic predecessor (i.e., A = 1 hour, B = 2 hours, etc.).
  (c) Find the slack of each activity. Identify the critical path.
  (d) How much less time does the production run take under this revised activity network than it did with the original network?

•••14-8. Consider the network and activity times shown in Figure 14.29. You would like to reduce the minimum time to complete the project. Suppose that you can reduce an activity time as much as you like as long as you increase some other activity or activities by the same amount. For example, you can reduce G by 1 hour if you increase C and D by 1/2 hour each. Assume that activity times of zero are permissible.

   (a) Find the current critical path and the minimum time required to complete the project.
   (b) Reallocate times to achieve the minimum possible time to complete the project. Note that in this network, the total of all activity times must equal the current total of 20 hours.

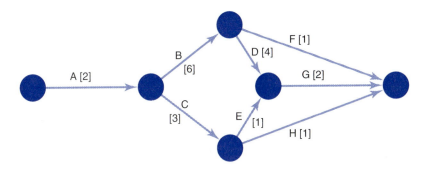

FIGURE 14.29

14-9. On the basis of company history, Build-Rite's management has determined that the optimistic, most probable, and pessimistic times for each activity are shown in the following table. Compute the expected activity time and the standard deviation for each activity.

ACTIVITY NUMBER	ACTIVITY	OPTIMISTIC TIME (DAYS) a	MOST PROBABLE TIME (DAYS) m	PESSIMISTIC TIME (DAYS) b
1	Walls and Ceiling	3	5	7
2	Foundation	2	3	4
3	Roof Timbers	1	2	3
4	Roof Sheathing	1	2	9
5	Electrical Wiring	4	4	4
6	Roof Shingles	4	8	12
7	Exterior Siding	1	3	17
8	Windows	1	2	3
9	Paint	2	2	2
10	Inside Wall Board	2	3	4

••14-10. On the basis of the activity network shown in Figure 14.30 and the associated activity times given in the accompanying table, compute the expected value and the standard deviation for each activity time.

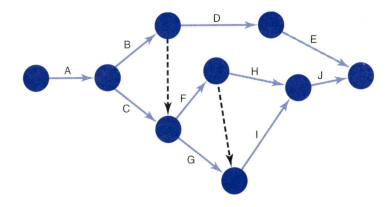

FIGURE 14.30

(a) Find the earliest start times, earliest finish times, latest start times, latest finish times, and slack for each activity.

(b) Specify the critical path.

ACTIVITY	OPTIMISTIC	MOST PROBABLE	PESSIMISTIC
A	2	3	4
B	2	4	6
C	1	2	3
D	1	3	5
E	2	3	4
F	1	4	7
G	2	2	2
H	2	5	8
I	1	3	5
J	2	3	4

•• **14-11.** Assume that activity times in Build-Rite's activity network (see Problems 14-1, 14-5, and 14-9) are independent of each other and that the sum of any combination of activity times is normally distributed.

(a) What is the probability that all the activities on the current critical path will be completed within 12 days?

(b) Within 25 days?

(c) Is this the same as the probability that a house will be completed in 25 days? Comment.

14-12. For the network in Problem 14-10, answer the following questions:

(a) Under the usual assumptions, find the probability that the activities on the critical path will be completed within 20 weeks.

(b) How many weeks should be allowed to give a 95% probability of completing the critical path on time?

•• **14-13.** Build-Rite's engineers have calculated the cost of completing each activity in both normal time and crash time, where the values for normal time and crash time, respectively, correspond to the estimates of expected time and optimistic time from the table in Problem 14-9. Their results are given in the following table.

(a) Specify the normal time, normal cost, crash time, crash cost, maximum crash days, and cost per crash day for each activity. Assume linear cost relationships.

(b) Compute the expected cost of the project (based on normal time).

(c) Suppose that the company has to reduce the completion time by 7 days. How much would this reduction cost?

(d) How much would it cost to reduce the completion time by 11 days?

NUMBER	ACTIVITY	NORMAL COST ($)	CRASH COST ($)
1	Walls and Ceiling	50	72
2	Foundation	20	30
3	Roof Timbers	15	30
4	Roof Sheathing	8	20
5	Electrical Wiring	30	30
6	Roof Shingles	13	21
7	Exterior Siding	45	65
8	Windows	45	52
9	Paint	40	40
10	Inside Wall Board	22	34

••• **14-14.** Consider the activity network in Problem 14-10. The following are estimates of costs for completion in crash time and normal time, where the times correspond to the optimistic and expected time, respectively.

ACTIVITY	CRASH COST ($)	NORMAL COST ($)
A	20	12
B	50	40
C	40	30
D	20	14
E	60	45
F	35	20
G	30	30
H	25	10
I	30	15
J	12	10

   (a) Prepare a table showing the normal time, normal cost, crash time, crash cost, maximum crash weeks, and cost per crash week for each activity.

   (b) What would be the minimum cost of the project if it were to be completed in

      (i) 19 weeks?

      (ii) 18 weeks?

      (iii) 17 weeks?

   (c) Formulate a linear programming model that will assess the additional cost of reducing the completion time to 9 weeks. What is the best way to accomplish the reduction? What's the additional cost?

•••**14-15.** Refer to Problems 14-3 and 14-13 and formulate a linear programming model that would allow Build-Rite to assess the cost of crashing its activity network by x hours.

•••**14-16.** Consider the activity network and normal activity times shown in Figure 14.31, as well as the data in the following table.

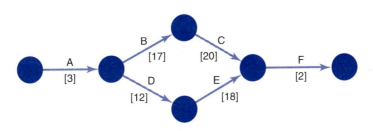

FIGURE 14.31

ACTIVITY	COST/CRASH UNIT ($)	MAX CRASH UNITS
A	10	2
B	20	8
C	5	5
D	5	5
E	15	2
F	—	0

   (a) Find the critical path and the minimum time required to complete the project.

   (b) Prepare a table showing which activities to crash as project length decreases.

••**14-17.** Use the normal costs from Problem 14-13 and the time data from Problem 14-5 to construct early-start and late-start cost tables and the graph of cumulative expenditures versus time for Build-Rite.

••**14-18.** The resources required for the activities in Problem 14-6 are given in the accompanying table. Construct early-start and late-start cost tables, and graph cumulative budget demands versus time, for both schedules.

ACTIVITY	TOTAL RESOURCES REQUIRED ($)
A	2,800
B	3,000
C	900
D	3,000
E	6,000
F	12,000
G	3,200
H	3,200
I	7,200
J	7,000
K	2,400
L	2,000
M	4,500

••**14-19.** Build-Rite's record of historical expenditures at the end of day 15 is as follows:

TABLE 14.12

ACTIVITY NUMBER	ACTIVITY	COST INCURRED TO DATE ($)
2	Foundation	22
1	Walls and Ceiling	46
3	Roof Timber	15
4	Roof Sheathing	10
6	Roof Shingles	4.50
5	Electrical Wiring	20
8	Windows	22.50
10	Inside Wall Board	20
7	Exterior Siding	40
9	Paint	0

Evaluate the current project costs based on the assumptions that budgeted costs are the normal costs given in Problem 14-13, that the time required is as given in Problem 14-5 and that either
(a) All activities begin on the earliest possible date, or
(b) All activities begin on the latest possible start date.
In both cases, assume that budgeted cost is equal to the budget for the completed activity multiplied by the proportion of the activity that is complete.

14-20. Review the data for Problem 14-18. Prepare an analysis of the cost of the project to date if the figures in the following table represent the status as of the end of the eight unit of time. Assume that the budgeted cost is equal to the budget for the completed activity multiplied by the proportion of the activity that is complete.

TABLE 14.13

ACTIVITY	% COMPLETE	COST TO DATE ($)
A	100	2700
B	100	3200
C	100	900
D	100	3500
E	50	2000
F	70	8000
G	20	700
H	50	1700
I	0	0
J	0	1000
K	0	0
L	0	500
M	0	0

•••14-21. This is a more complex version of Problem 14-8. As the production supervisor for the Hurricane Fan Company, you have used PERT-CPM techniques to schedule your production runs. Your current activity network and activity times are shown in Figure 14.32. A production consultant has pointed out that, due to the similarity in job skills needed for each activity, resources are perfectly transferable between activities (i.e., the time required to do an activity can be reduced by any amount by increasing the time required for another job by the same amount). If the consultant is correct, how much can the time needed for each production run be reduced?

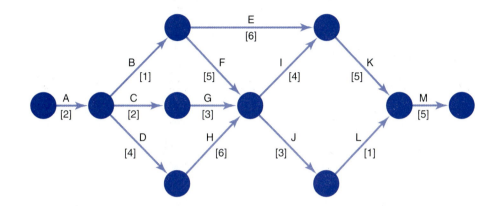

FIGURE 14.32

•••14-22. This problem is a further examination of the PERT assumptions. Consider a project with five activities and the precedence relationships given in the accompanying table. The Range column indicates the possible range of days it might take to complete an activity.

(a) Suppose that any time within the range is equally likely (i.e., a uniform distribution). Use the standard PERT analysis and compute the expected project length. Also calculate the probability that the project will be completed in the expected project length + 5 days. Use the fact that if the range is a to b then the mean time is $\dfrac{(a + b)}{2}$ and the variance of the time is $\dfrac{(b - a)^2}{12}$.

TABLE 14.14

ACTIVITY	PREDECESSORS	RANGE
A	none	20 to 60
B	none	25 to 29
C	A	20 to 60
D	B	25 to 29
E	D	25 to 29

(b) Now set up a spreadsheet to simulate the project (using Crystal Ball or @Risk if available). Simulate 100 trials and compute the mean project length. Is it larger or smaller than your previous answer? Why?

(c) What is the probability that the project will be completed before the expected time for part (a) + 5 days. Is it larger or smaller than your previous answer? Why?

•••14-23. This problem is the same as Problem 14-22, but now assume that the activity times are normally distributed with the following means and standard deviations:

TABLE 14.15

ACTIVITY	MEAN	STANDARD DEVIATION
A	40	11.5
B	27	1.15
C	40	11.5
D	27	1.15
E	27	1.15

(a) Use the standard PERT analysis and compute the expected project length. Also calculate the probability that the project will be completed in the expected project length + 5 days. Is your answer the same as in part (a) of Problem 14-22? Why?

(b) Now set up a spreadsheet to simulate the project (using Crystal Ball or @Risk, if available). Simulate 100 trials and compute the mean project length. Is it larger or smaller than your previous answer? Why?

(c) What is the probability that the project will be completed before the expected time from part (a) + 5 days. Is it larger or smaller than your previous answer? Why?

(d) How sensitive is the simulation analysis to the form of the activity time distribution (uniform in Problem 14-22, normal in Problem 14-23)?

References

Rafael Andreu and Albert Corominas, "SUC-CESS92: A DSS for Scheduling the Olympic Games," *Interfaces,* 19, no. 5 (1989), 1–12.

Richard Staats, "Desert Storm: A Re-examination of the Ground War in the Persian Gulf, and the Key Role Played by OR," *OR/MS Today* (December 1991), 42–56.

Basic Concepts in Probability

▌ ▊ INTRODUCTION

Probability is the branch of mathematics that is used to model the uncertainty that occurs in nature, in science, and in business. Biologists use probability to model genetic evolution, physicists use probability to model the behavior of electrons in atoms, and economists use probability to model the behavior of stock prices. Texts such as this often use simple gambling games to motivate instruction in probability. For example, we can use probability to model the outcome of a roll of a pair of dice. The fundamental purpose of probability theory is to enable us to use what we know about simple uncertain events to calculate the probability of more complicated uncertain events. Thus, we can use our model of the probability of specific outcomes of rolling a pair of dice to calculate the probability of winning at the game of craps.

RANDOM VARIABLES

It is impossible to talk about probability without talking about random variables. Unfortunately, it is difficult to talk about random variables in a precise manner without getting into more abstract detail than this brief appendix allows or that is really required for this text. For our purposes, think of a random variable as an uncertain event that takes on a numerical value—for example, the face showing after the role of a die, the number of swimsuits sold by Spiegel during July, the price of Intel stock at the end of next week, the number of snowy days in Nome, Alaska, in 2003, and so on.

TYPES OF PROBABILITIES

There are two basic types of probability models: discrete and continuous. The difference between them is not important in terms of the concepts used in management science. However, each type requires the use of a different branch of mathematics. Arithmetic is really all we need to handle discrete probabilities, but integral and differential calculus must be used for continuous random variables.

⬤ **II**   **DISCRETE PROBABILITIES**

A. THE PROBABILITY MASS FUNCTION (PMF)

Discrete probabilities are defined with the probability mass function, $f(x)$. Specifically, $f(x)$ is the probability that the random variable of interest takes on the value x. Consider the following examples.

Example 1: A Discrete Uniform Distribution. Suppose that we continue with the example of the roll of a die, and assume that each face of the die is equally likely to appear. Then

$$f(x) = 1/6 \quad (x=1, 2, 3, 4, 5, 6)$$
$$= 0 \quad \text{(otherwise)}$$

The pmf for this distribution is shown in Figure A.1(a).

Example 2: An Arbitrary Discrete Distribution. Assume that an urn contains five balls that are identical except for the numbers written on them. Two balls have a 23 on them and the other three have 37 written on them. Assume that a ball is chosen at random, that is, each ball is equally likely to be chosen. Then

$$f(x) = 2/5 \quad (x=23)$$
$$= 3/5 \quad (x=37)$$
$$= 0 \quad \text{(otherwise)}$$

We note that $f(x) \geq 0$ and that $\Sigma f(x) = 1$. These two conditions must hold for any pmf.

Example 3: The Binomial Distribution. This distribution is used to model the results of a series of independent trials when, at each trial, a specific event either occurs or does not occur. (See Section V-B, pg. A-11, for a definition of independence.) We encounter the binomial distribution in Chapter 11 where it is used to determine the probability of a customer with a reservation showing up for a flight departure in an airline's revenue management system. This distribution has two parameters: n, the number of trials, and p, the probability that the event occurs at each trial. It follows that $(1-p)$ is the probability that the event does not occur. (The standard example is flipping a coin; the event is the occurrence of a head, and it is assumed that $p = 0.5$). The binomial distribution then is used to calculate the probability that the event occurs x times in n trials—for example, that there are seven heads in ten tosses of a coin. The pmf for the binomial distribution is

$$f(x) = \binom{n}{x} p^x (1-p)^{n-x} \quad (x=0, 1, \cdots, n)$$
$$= 0 \quad \text{(otherwise)}$$

Here the symbol $\binom{n}{x}$ is the number of ways that one can select x items out of n. It is calculated as follows:

$$\binom{n}{x} = \frac{n!}{x! \, (n-x)!} = \frac{(n) \, (n-1) \cdots (1)}{[(x) \, (x-1) \cdots (1)] \, [(n-x) \, (n-x-1) \cdots (1)]}$$

For example, we see that the probability of seven heads in ten tosses of a coin, where the probability of a head at a single toss is 0.5 (i.e., $p = 0.5$), is

$$f(7) = \frac{(10) \, (9) \, (8)}{(3) \, (2) \, (1)} (0.5^7) \, (0.5^3) = 0.117$$

Example 4: The Poisson Distribution. This distribution is often used to model the number of arrivals in a specific time interval in a queuing system (Chapter 12). The pmf is

$$f(x) = \frac{e^{-M} M^x}{x!} \quad (x = 0, 1, 2, \cdots)$$
$$= 0 \quad \text{(otherwise)}$$

where M is a parameter supplied by the manager.

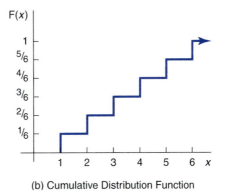

(a) Probability Mass Function

FIGURE A.1 (a)

(b) Cumulative Distribution Function

FIGURE A.1 (b)

B. THE CUMULATIVE DISTRIBUTION FUNCTION (CDF)

The cumulative distribution function $F(x)$ is the probability that the random variable takes on a value less than or equal to x. Since the probability mass function, $f(x)$, is the probability that the random variable takes on the value x, it follows that

$$F(x) = \sum_{j=-\infty}^{x} f(j)$$

Example 1 (continued): Discrete Uniform Distribution. If the random variable is the value showing on the throw of a fair die, then

$$
\begin{aligned}
F(x) &= 0 & (x < 1) \\
&= 1/6 & (1 \le x < 2) \\
&= 2/6 & (2 \le x < 3) \\
&= 3/6 & (3 \le x < 4) \\
&= 4/6 & (4 \le x < 5) \\
&= 5/6 & (5 \le x < 6) \\
&= 1 & (6 \le x)
\end{aligned}
$$

The CDF for this distribution is shown in Figure A.1(b).

Example 2 (continued): Arbitrary Discrete Distribution.

$$
\begin{aligned}
F(x) &= 0 & (x < 23) \\
&= 2/5 & (23 \le x < 37) \\
&= 1 & (37 \le x)
\end{aligned}
$$

III   CONTINUOUS PROBABILITIES

A. THE PROBABILITY DENSITY FUNCTION

Continuous probabilities are defined by the probability density function (pdf). If $f(x)$ is the pdf for a random variable, then we know that $f(x) \ge 0$ for all x, and

$$\int_{-\infty}^{\infty} f(x)dx = 1$$

This is the continuous analog of the fact that the pmf for a discrete random variable is always greater than or equal to 0 and must sum to 1.

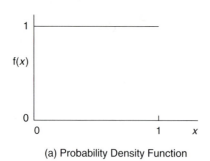

(a) Probability Density Function

FIGURE A.2 (a)

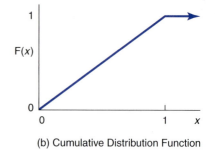

(b) Cumulative Distribution Function

FIGURE A.2 (b)

B. THE CUMULATIVE DISTRIBUTION FUNCTION

The cumulative distribution function retains its definition for both continuous and discrete random variables—that is, $F(x)$ is the probability that the random variable takes on a value less than or equal to x. For continuous random variables, the relationship between the probability density function (pdf) and the cumulative distribution function (CDF) is as follows

$$F(x) = \int_{-\infty}^{x} f(r)dr$$

Here we integrate the density function from $-\infty$ to x to determine the probability that the random variable is less than or equal to x. With discrete probabilities the concept is the same, but we sum the probability mass function rather than integrating the probability density function.

C. IMPORTANT EXAMPLES

Here we describe three distributions that play an important role in this text and in applied business problems.

Example 5: The Continuous Uniform Distribution. The uniform distribution on the interval 0 to 1 plays a crucial role in simulation, in that it is used to generate random variables (see Chapter 11).

$$
\begin{aligned}
f(x) &= 0 & (x < 0) \\
&= 1 & (0 \le x \le 1) \\
&= 0 & (1 < x)
\end{aligned}
$$

Then by definition

$$
\begin{aligned}
F(x) &= \int_{-\infty}^{x} f(r)dr \\
&= 0 & (x < 0) \\
&= x & (0 \le x \le 1) \\
&= 1 & (1 \le x)
\end{aligned}
$$

Figure A.2(a) and (b) show the pdf and the CDF for the continuous uniform distribution.

Example 6: The Exponential Distribution. The exponential distribution is used to describe the interarrival time between events in most queuing systems (Chapter 12). It is a one-parameter distribution. The parameter is typically denoted by λ. The pdf takes the form

$$
\begin{aligned}
f(x) &= 0 & (x < 0) \\
&= \lambda e^{-\lambda x} & (0 \le x)
\end{aligned}
$$

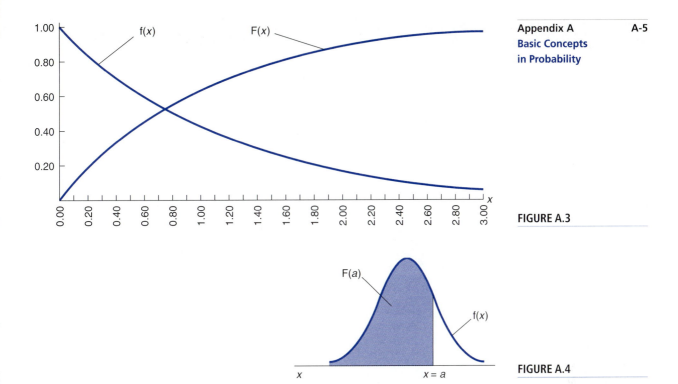

FIGURE A.3

FIGURE A.4

Using the definition for the CDF we see that

$$F(x) = 0 \qquad\qquad (x < 0)$$
$$= 1 - e^{-\lambda x} \quad (0 \le x)$$

Figure A.3 shows the pdf and the CDF for an exponential distribution with parameter $\lambda = 1$.

Example 7: The Normal Distribution. The normal distribution plays a fundamental role in probability and statistics. In this text, it occurs in a number of places—for example, it is used to represent uncertain demand in Chapter 11, as well as the probability that a project will be completed by a specific time in Chapter 14.

   The normal is a two-parameter distribution. The parameters are μ, the mean, and σ, the standard deviation, which is required to be greater than 0. There is, of course, a mathematical expression for the density function of a normal pdf, but we will not show it here since we never make direct use of this expression. The pdf of the normal distribution is not integrable in closed form—that is,

$$\int_{-\infty}^{x} f(r)dr$$

cannot be written as a combination of elementary functions of x, when $f(r)$ is a normal distribution. Tables such as Table A.0 are used to evaluate $F(x)$, the CDF, for the normal distribution (represented graphically in Figure A.4). The next section is devoted to using Table A.0 to determine values for normal probabilities.

D. USING THE NORMAL TABLE
The Standard Normal Distribution Table A.0 can be used to find values for the CDF, $F(x)$, of a normal distribution with mean μ and standard deviation σ. (See Section IV, pg. A7, for a definition of μ and σ.) Actually, the table provides values for $F(x)$ for a normal distribution with $\mu = 0$ and $\sigma = 1$. (In a moment we will show how this table can be used to find values for the CDF of any normal distribution.) The values in the body of Table A.0

TABLE A.0 Areas for the Standard Normal Distribution

ENTRIES IN THE TABLE GIVE THE AREA UNDER THE CURVE BETWEEN THE MEAN AND Z STANDARD DEVIATIONS ABOVE THE MEAN. FOR EXAMPLE, FOR $Z = 1.25$ THE AREA UNDER THE CURVE BETWEEN THE MEAN AND Z IS 0.3944.

z	0.00	0.01	0.02	0.03	0.04	0.05	0.06	0.07	0.08	0.09
0.0	0.0000	0.0040	0.0080	0.0120	0.0160	0.0199	0.0239	0.0279	0.0319	0.0359
0.1	0.0398	0.0438	0.0478	0.0517	0.0557	0.0596	0.0636	0.0675	0.0714	0.0753
0.2	0.0793	0.0832	0.0871	0.0910	0.0948	0.0987	0.1026	0.1064	0.1103	0.1141
0.3	0.1179	0.1217	0.1255	0.1293	0.1331	0.1368	0.1406	0.1443	0.1480	0.1517
0.4	0.1554	0.1591	0.1628	0.1664	0.1700	0.1736	0.1772	0.1808	0.1844	0.1879
0.5	0.1915	0.1950	0.1985	0.2019	0.2054	0.2088	0.2123	0.2157	0.2190	0.2224
0.6	0.2257	0.2291	0.2324	0.2357	0.2389	0.2422	0.2454	0.2486	0.2518	0.2549
0.7	0.2580	0.2612	0.2642	0.2673	0.2704	0.2734	0.2764	0.2794	0.2823	0.2852
0.8	0.2881	0.2910	0.2939	0.2967	0.2995	0.3023	0.3051	0.3078	0.3106	0.3133
0.9	0.3159	0.3186	0.3212	0.3238	0.3264	0.3289	0.3315	0.3340	0.3365	0.3389
1.0	0.3413	0.3438	0.3461	0.3485	0.3508	0.3531	0.3554	0.3577	0.3599	0.3621
1.1	0.3643	0.3665	0.3686	0.3708	0.3729	0.3749	0.3770	0.3790	0.3810	0.3830
1.2	0.3849	0.3869	0.3888	0.3907	0.3925	0.3944	0.3962	0.3980	0.3997	0.4015
1.3	0.4032	0.4049	0.4066	0.4082	0.4099	0.4115	0.4131	0.4147	0.4162	0.4177
1.4	0.4192	0.4207	0.4222	0.4236	0.4251	0.4265	0.4279	0.4292	0.4306	0.4319
1.5	0.4332	0.4345	0.4357	0.4370	0.4382	0.4394	0.4406	0.4418	0.4429	0.4441
1.6	0.4452	0.4463	0.4474	0.4484	0.4495	0.4505	0.4515	0.4525	0.4535	0.4545
1.7	0.4554	0.4564	0.4573	0.4582	0.4591	0.4599	0.4608	0.4616	0.4625	0.4633
1.8	0.4641	0.4649	0.4656	0.4664	0.4671	0.4678	0.4686	0.4693	0.4699	0.4706
1.9	0.4713	0.4719	0.4726	0.4732	0.4738	0.4744	0.4750	0.4756	0.4761	0.4767
2.0	0.4772	0.4778	0.4783	0.4788	0.4793	0.4798	0.4803	0.4808	0.4812	0.4817
2.1	0.4821	0.4826	0.4830	0.4834	0.4838	0.4842	0.4846	0.4850	0.4854	0.4857
2.2	0.4861	0.4864	0.4868	0.4871	0.4875	0.4878	0.4881	0.4884	0.4887	0.4890
2.3	0.4893	0.4896	0.4898	0.4901	0.4904	0.4906	0.4909	0.4911	0.4913	0.4916
2.4	0.4918	0.4920	0.4922	0.4925	0.4927	0.4929	0.4931	0.4932	0.4934	0.4936
2.5	0.4938	0.4940	0.4941	0.4943	0.4945	0.4946	0.4948	0.4949	0.4951	0.4952
2.6	0.4953	0.4955	0.4956	0.4957	0.4959	0.4960	0.4961	0.4962	0.4963	0.4964
2.7	0.4965	0.4966	0.4967	0.4968	0.4969	0.4970	0.4971	0.4972	0.4973	0.4974
2.8	0.4974	0.4975	0.4976	0.4977	0.4977	0.4978	0.4979	0.4979	0.4980	0.4981
2.9	0.4981	0.4982	0.4982	0.4983	0.4984	0.4984	0.4985	0.4985	0.4986	0.4986
3.0	0.4986	0.4987	0.4987	0.4988	0.4988	0.4989	0.4989	0.4989	0.4990	0.4990

Reprinted with permission from Richard I. Levin and Charles A. Kirkpatrick, *Quantitative Approaches to Management, 3rd Edition,* McGraw-Hill, Inc., New York, NY, 1975.

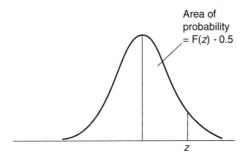

Area of
probability
= F(z) - 0.5

z

FIGURE A.5

are the probability that a standard normal random variable (SNRV) takes on a value between the mean, 0, and the value of z shown in the row and column headings. Thus by looking in the row 0.4 and the column 0.05, we discover that a SNRV takes on a value between
0 and 0.45 with probability 0.1736.

Using this table and the fact that an SNRV is symmetrical about the mean allows us to
find the probability that an SNRV falls into any range of numbers. Here are some examples
(referring to the accompanying figure may provide some visual help in understanding the
calculations).

$$\text{Prob}\{\text{SNRV} \leq 0.45\} = 0.5 + 0.1736 = 0.6736$$
$$\text{Prob}\{\text{SNRV} > 0.45\} = 1.0 - 0.6736 = 0.3264$$
$$\text{Prob}\{\text{SNRV} \leq -0.45\} = 0.5 - 0.1736 = 0.3264$$

You have probably observed that there are many different ways to calculate these results. For
example, we knew that Prob$\{\text{SNRV} \leq -0.45\} = 0.3264$ from the facts that Prob$\{\text{SNRV} > 0.45\} = 0.3264$ and that the normal distribution is symmetrical about the mean.

Any Normal Random Variable   Let NRV be a normal random variable with mean μ and
standard deviation σ. To find the probability that this random variable falls into a range of
values, we make use of this fundamental relationship.

$$\text{Prob}\{\text{NRV} \leq x\} = \text{Prob}\{\text{SNRV} \leq (x - \mu)/\sigma\}$$

Here is an example. Suppose that NRV has $\mu = 50$ and $\sigma = 100$ and we want to find the
probability that NRV ≤ 95. We proceed as follows:

$$\text{Prob}\{\text{NRV} \leq 95\} = \text{Prob}\{\text{SNRV} \leq (95-50)/100\}$$
$$= \text{Prob}\{\text{SNRV} \leq 0.45\} = 0.6736.$$

This procedure becomes second nature with a little practice.

IV   EXPECTED VALUES

The expected cost or profit is often the objective in decisions under uncertainty—that is, in
decision problems in which the payoff from a decision is a random variable. We first introduce the expected value of a random variable and then turn to the expected value of a function of a random variable.

A. EXPECTED VALUE OF A RANDOM VARIABLE
The expected value of a random variable—say, X—is typically written E(X). It is called the
mean of the random variable, typically denoted with the Greek letter μ. We will define E(X)
for both discrete and continuous random variables.

Discrete Random Variables   For a discrete random variable where f(x) is the probability
mass function,

$$E(X) = \mu = \sum_{-\infty}^{\infty} x f(x)$$

Here are some examples.

Example 1 (continued): Discrete Uniform Distribution.

$$E(X) = 1\left(\frac{1}{6}\right) + 2\left(\frac{1}{6}\right) + 3\left(\frac{1}{6}\right) + 4\left(\frac{1}{6}\right) + 5\left(\frac{1}{6}\right) + 6\left(\frac{1}{6}\right) = 3.5$$

It is interesting to note that the expected value of a random variable does not have to be one of the values that the random variable can assume. For example, a die cannot take on the value 3.5. A physical interpretation is that the expected value is the center of gravity of the probability mass function. That is, if you think of the probabilities in a pmf as weights and place a fulcrum under the expected value, the pmf will balance. The expected value has a second intuitive interpretation. Think of a series of independent observations of a random variable. If you calculate the average of the values, you expect it to be close to the expected value.

Example 2 (continued): Arbitrary Discrete Distribution.

$$E(X) = 23\left(\frac{2}{5}\right) + 37\left(\frac{3}{5}\right) = 31.4$$

Example 3 (continued): Binomial Distribution. Here we state without providing a proof that for a binomial random variable, X, with parameters n and p,

$$E(X) = np$$

This result is intuitively appealing. If we flip a fair coin ten times, on the average we would expect to observe five heads.

Example 4 (continued): Poisson Distribution. The expected value of the Poisson distribution is M. The variance is M as well. These results are easily derived, but the derivations are not central to our purpose.

Continuous Random Variables The definition of the expected value of a continuous random variable is essentially the same as for the discrete case. Here, however, we must use the pdf and integration, that is

$$E(X) = \int_{-\infty}^{\infty} x\, f(x)\, dx$$

Example 5 (continued): Continuous Uniform Distribution.

$$E(X) = \int_{0}^{1} x \cdot 1 \cdot dx = \left.\frac{x^2}{2}\right|_{0}^{1} = \frac{1}{2}$$

It is easy to see that $\frac{1}{2}$ is the center of gravity for the density function shown in Figure A.2(a).

Example 6 (continued): Exponential Distribution.

$$E(X) = \int_{0}^{\infty} x\lambda e^{-\lambda x} dx = 1/\lambda$$

This integration requires a technique called integration by parts, and the details have been omitted.

B. EXPECTED VALUE OF A FUNCTION OF A RANDOM VARIABLE

The General Concept Let $G(x)$ be any function defined on x. Then for a discrete random variable X with pmf $f(x)$, the expected value of $G(x)$, $E[G(X)]$, is defined as follows:

$$E[G(X)] = \sum_{x=-\infty}^{\infty} G(x)f(x)$$

A similar definition using integrals holds for continuous random variables.

We have two main reasons for being interested in the expected value of functions of random variables. One is to define the variance of a random variable and the other is to define expected costs or profits. These topics are discussed in the following sections.

Variance and Standard Deviation of a Random Variable The variance is a measure of dispersion of the distribution of a random variable. It is typically denoted as σ^2 and is defined as follows:

$$\text{Var}(X) = \sigma^2 = E[(X-E(X))^2] = \sum_{-\infty}^{\infty}(x-E(X))^2 f(x)$$

The variance plays an important role in statistics. It is the most popular measure of dispersion of the distribution of a random variable, and it is one of the two parameters of the normal distribution (see Example 7 on p. A-5). To develop a feeling for the interpretation of variance as a measure of dispersion, consider two random variables X and Y. Let $f_X(x)$ be the pmf for X and $f_Y(y)$ be the pmf for Y. Let

$$f_X(x) = \frac{1}{2} \qquad (x = 4, 6)$$
$$= 0 \qquad (\text{otherwise})$$

and

$$f_Y(y) = \frac{1}{2} \qquad (y = 1, 9)$$
$$= 0 \qquad (\text{otherwise})$$

Note that both random variables have an expected value of five. You should be able to verify that $\text{Var}(X) = \sigma^2 = 1$ and $\text{Var}(Y) = \sigma^2 = 16$. The intuitive notion is that a random variable that has a greater probability of being further from the mean will have a larger variance. That notion is consistent with this example.

The standard deviation, typically denoted by σ, is simply the square root of the variance, that is,

$$\text{Standard Deviation of } X = (\text{Variance of } X)^{\frac{1}{2}}$$

or

$$\sigma = (\sigma^2)^{\frac{1}{2}}$$

C. EXPECTED RETURN

In most business applications, management is interested in the returns (or costs) associated with the occurrence of a random event.

Discrete Random Variables To calculate the expected return, we let $R(x)$ be the return if the random variable x occurs and use the standard definition for the expected value of a function of a random variable.

$$E[R(X)] = \sum_{x=-\infty}^{\infty} R(x)f(x)$$

Example 1 (continued): Discrete Uniform Distribution. A gambler offers to pay you $10 times the value of the face of the die that is showing if a 3, 4, 5, or 6 occurs and nothing if a 1 or 2 occurs. What is the expected value of this game?

x	R(x)	f(x)	R(x)f(x)
1	0	⅙	0
2	0	⅙	0
3	30	⅙	5
4	40	⅙	6⅔
5	50	⅙	8⅓
6	60	⅙	10

Expected Value $= \Sigma R(x)f(x) = 30$

Continuous Random Variables The concept of finding the expected value of the function R(X) remains the same as in the discrete case. As usual, in the continuous case we must use integration and the pdf.

Example 5 (continued): Continuous Uniform Distribution. We will observe a random variable from a continuous uniform distribution on the interval 0 to 1. A gambler offers to pay 0 if the value is between 0 and 0.2 and \$10 times the value of the random variable if the value is greater than 0.2 and less than or equal to 1. It follows that

$$R(x) = 0 \qquad\qquad (x \le 0.2)$$
$$= 10x \qquad (0.2 < x \le 1)$$

Then

$$E[R(x)] = \int_0^{.2} 0\cdot 1 \cdot dx + \int_{.2}^1 10x\cdot 1 \cdot dx = 10\left. \left(\frac{x^2}{2}\right)\right|_{0.2}^1$$

$$= 4.8$$

Ⅴ **MULTIVARIATE DISTRIBUTIONS**

This section introduces the mathematics and the concepts that are used when there is more than one random variable under consideration. Such situations are common in practice. In a PERT network (Chapter 14), the time required to complete a path in a project is equal to the sum of the times required to complete each activity on that path. Similarly, the return from a portfolio of stocks (Chapter 8) is equal to the sum of the returns of the individual stocks held in the portfolio.

Multivariate random variables are introduced in Appendix 10.1 in the discussion of Bayes' Theorem, although the term multivariate is not mentioned there. It will be useful to refer to that discussion in what follows.

A. JOINT DISTRIBUTIONS
Discrete Random Variables It is useful to introduce some new notation in the discussion of multivariate random variables. Let

$f_{X,Y}(x, y)$ = the probability that the random variable X takes on the value x *and* the random variable Y takes on the value y.

Then $f_{X,Y}(x, y)$ is the *joint* probability mass function for the random variables X and Y. The word "and" is important in this definition. It indicates that both events (x, y) must happen.

The following game is introduced in Appendix 10.1.

1. A fair die is thrown.

2. The value of the die is used to determine from which of three urns we will draw a ball. Assume that each of the balls in a given urn is equally likely to be drawn.

The details are summarized in the following table.

DIE	URN	CONTENTS OF URN
1	1	28 White and 72 Black Balls
2 or 3	2	40 White and 60 Black Balls
4 or 5 or 6	3	92 White and 8 Black Balls

This game can now be used to illustrate a joint pmf. Let X be the value of the urn chosen; $Y = 1$ if a white ball is selected and $Y = 2$ if a black ball is selected. The values for $f_{X,Y}(x,y)$ are presented below.

X	$Y = 1$	$Y = 2$
1	$(1/6)(28/100) = .0467$	$(1/6)(72/100) = .12$
2	$(2/6)(40/100) = .1333$	$(2/6)(60/100) = .20$
3	$(3/6)(92/100) = .4600$	$(3/6)(8/100) = .04$

These values were derived from the definition of conditional probability:

$$f_{X,Y}(x,y) = f_X(x)f_{Y|X}(y|x)$$

A discussion of this relationship can be found in Appendix 10.1.

Continuous Random Variables Multivariate distributions also exist for continuous random variables. Indeed, the equation that defines the relationship between joint and conditional probabilities is used to define joint probability density functions and conditional probability density functions.

B. INDEPENDENT RANDOM VARIABLES
Two random variables, X and Y, are independent if

$$f_{X,Y}(x,y) = f_X(x)\, f_Y(y)$$

Since in general

$$f_{X,Y}(x,y) = f_{X|Y}(x|y)\, f_Y(y)$$

we see that X and Y are independent if

$$f_{X|Y}(x|y) = f_x(x)$$

The last equation says that knowing that the random variable Y takes on the value y tells us nothing about the probability that X will take on the value x. In other words, X and Y are independent.

C. EXPECTATION AND VARIANCE OF SUMS
The Expected Value of $X + Y$. It is always true (whether X and Y are independent or not) that

$$E(X + Y) = E(X) + E(Y)$$

The Variance of $X + Y$ The variance of $(X + Y)$ is defined as follows:

$$\text{Var}(X + Y) = \text{Var}(X) + \text{Var}(Y) + 2\text{Cov}(X, Y)$$

or

$$\sigma^2_{(X+Y)} = \sigma^2_X + \sigma^2_Y + 2\sigma_{XY}$$

The Covariance of _X_ and _Y_ In the previous expression, $\text{Cov}(X,Y)$ is the covariance of X and Y. It is denoted by σ_{XY} and is itself defined as follows:

$$\text{Cov}(X,Y) = \sigma_{XY} = E([X-E(X)][Y-E(Y)])$$

The covariance of X and Y is an indication of how X and Y relate to each other, but it is difficult to have an intuitive feeling for what a particular value of the covariance means. The correlation coefficient is better suited to convey this. Note, however, that when X and Y are independent random variables $\sigma_{XY} = 0$.

The Correlation Coefficient of _X_ and _Y_ The correlation coefficient of X and Y is typically denoted as ρ_{XY} and is defined as follows

$$\rho_{XY} = \frac{\text{Cov}(X,Y)}{[\text{StdDev}(X)]\,[\text{StdDev}(Y)]} = \frac{\sigma_{XY}}{\sigma_X \sigma_Y}$$

The correlation coefficient can take on values from -1 to 1. A large positive value suggests that X and Y tend to move together—that is, when X is large then Y is apt to be large as well. Negative values suggest that X and Y move in opposite directions—that is, when X is large Y is apt to be small. If $\sigma_{XY} = 0$, X and Y are said to be uncorrelated.

The Expectation and Variance for the Sum of Several Random Variables Let

$$Z = \sum_{i=1}^{N} X_i$$

That is, Z is the sum of N random variables $X_1, X_2, \ldots, X_N$. Then

$$E(Z) = \sum_{i=1}^{N} E(X_i)$$

In words, the expected value of a sum equals the sum of the expected values.

$$\text{Var}(Z) = \sum_{i=1}^{N} \text{Var}(X_i) + 2 \sum_{i=1}^{N-1} \sum_{j>i}^{N} \text{Cov}(X_i, X_j)$$

In words, the variance of the sum is equal to the sum of the variances plus two times the sum of the covariances of all possible pairs of random variables.

Excel Features Useful for Modeling

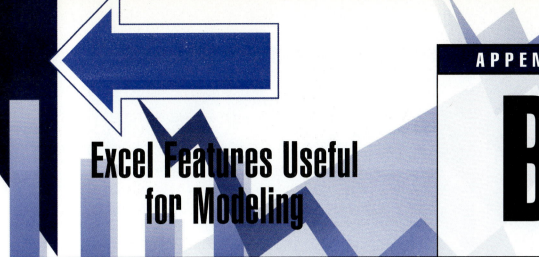

This is a summary of the features of Excel useful for modeling. It is set up in a format with tasks listed in the margin along with the steps for completing those tasks on the right-hand side. If you see an unfamiliar task listed, or would like a quick review, simply follow the directions. More complete summaries of a topic are given in Excel's online Help.

Where listed, "Win" means Windows Excel as implemented on Windows-compatible computers and "Mac" means Macintosh Excel as implemented on Apple-compatible computers. Other than for minor differences in appearance, dialogs, and operating system interactions, both versions of Excel are nearly identical. One exception is in the keyboard shortcuts. Both use two-key (and on occasion three-key) shortcut combinations, denoted here by "name_of_first_key" + "name_of_second_key." In many cases, a Win keyboard shortcut involving the "Ctrl" key, such as "Ctrl+z", is effected on Mac by substituting the Command key, that is, the "⌘" key, such as "⌘+z". Figure B.1 shows the typical layout of an Excel window. Its major components are labeled for future reference.

CONFIGURING THE WORKSHEET

Each of the features in Figure B.2(a) can be controlled when the "Options..." item is selected from the Tools menu, and the View tab in Figure B.2(b) is chosen. If a box is checked, the item will appear on the screen display of the worksheet. (To control the *printer* output

Tools Options View...

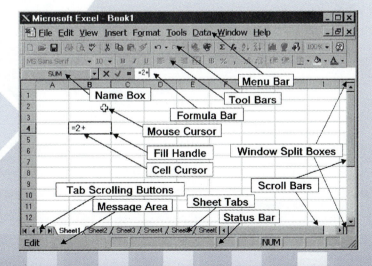

FIGURE B.1

Excel Window Organization

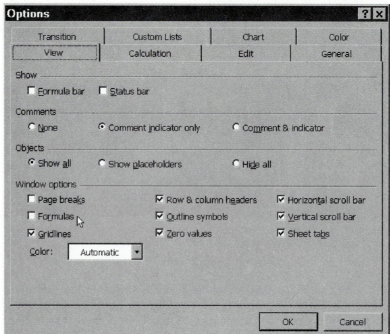

FIGURE B.2(a)

Options

FIGURE B.2(b)

Options View

for similar features, such as grid lines, use Excel's Page Setup options.) Default selections are shown in the figure. Checking the Formulas box, under the cursor in Figure B.2(b), will replace all worksheet cell contents by their formulas, where applicable.

Tools Options General...

Each of the features in Figure B.3 can be controlled when the "Options..." item is selected from the Tools menu, and the General tab is chosen. It is suggested that you use defaults similar to those shown in the figure.

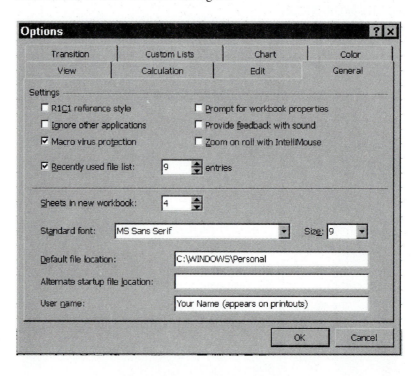

FIGURE B.3

Options General

For Mac, it is suggested that you turn "on" Command Underline, as shown in Figure B.4. It is useful for keyboard shortcuts.

Each of the features in Figure B.5 can be controlled when the Transition tab is chosen. It is suggested that you set Alternate Menu Key to the "/" character, allowing you to press "/" followed by the underlined letters in menu selection items as a fast shortcut to menuing. The suggested Save Excel file type assures backward compatibility at the cost of larger file sizes and the loss of some Excel 97 features. Unchecking the "Transition navigation keys" option produces a more predictable application of Excel's keyboard shortcuts and is recommended.

Each of the features in Figure B.6 can be controlled when the Edit tab is chosen. It is suggested that you check the "Edit directly in cell" option to allow editing cell entries without going to the Formula Bar—just double click at the point you wish to begin editing in the cell. Unchecking "Move selection after Enter" allows multiple "What if?" projections for a single model input cell without cursoring.

Each of the features in Figure B.7 can be controlled when the Calculation tab is chosen. If you create large Data Tables or very large worksheet models, selecting "Automatic except Tables" or "Manual," respectively, will improve response times when editing worksheets. In either case, Excel will signal whenever the worksheet needs to have its tables or formulas recomputed, i.e., recalculated, by displaying "Calculate" in the Message Bar, as shown in Figure B.8.

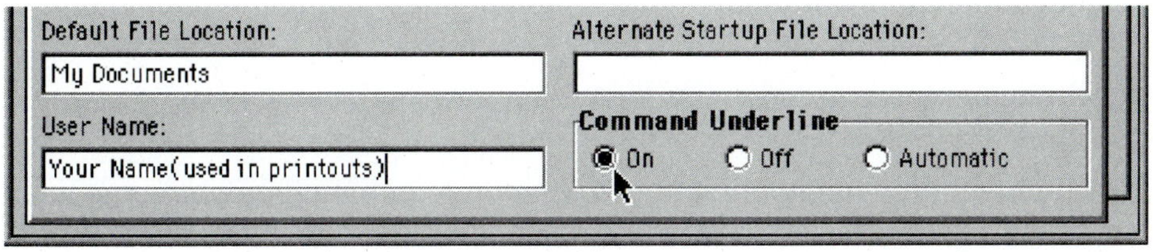

Tools Options Transition...

Tools Options Edit...

Tools Options Calculation...

FIGURE B.4

Command Underline "On"
for Macintosh

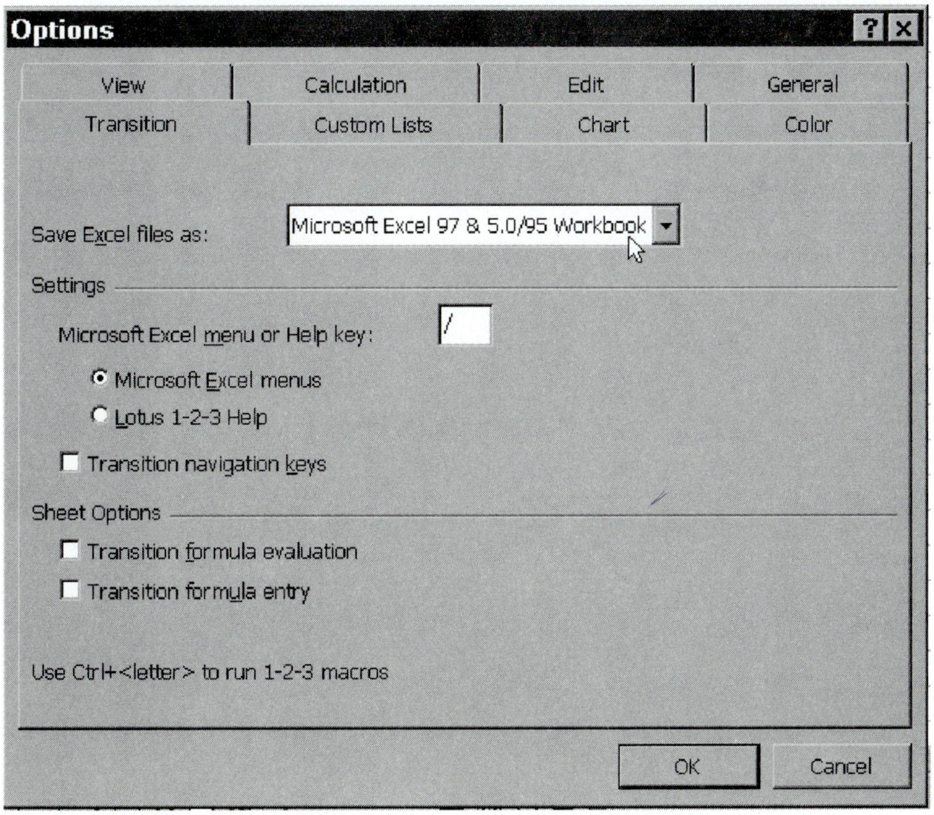

FIGURE B.5

Options Transition

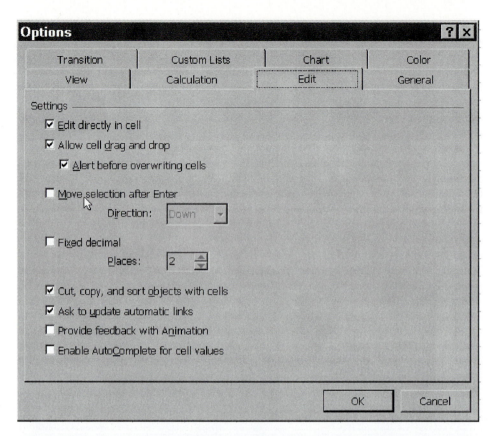

FIGURE B.6

Options Edit

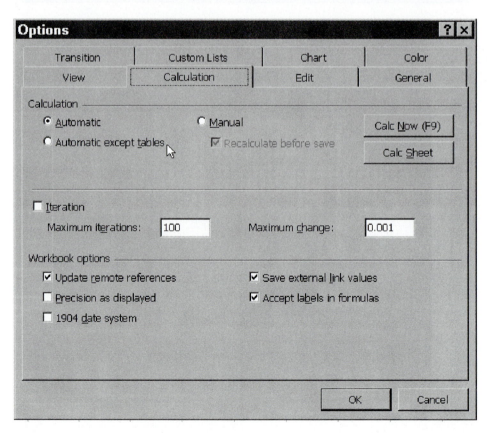

FIGURE B.7

Options Calculation

When necessary, the worksheet can be recalculated manually by pressing the F9 key (Win or Mac), or the Ctrl+= (Win or Mac) or ⌘+= (Mac) key combination.

MANIPULATING WINDOWS AND WORKSHEETS

A worksheet may be split into two panes by positioning the mouse cursor over one of the Window Split boxes until it changes shape ╬ and then dragging it into the window. Repeating this for the other Window Split Box produces another two panes, as shown in Figure B.9. Additional Scroll Bars appear to allow independent scrolling of rows and columns across panes. Positioning the mouse cursor over a pane bar until it changes to ╬ and double clicking removes the pane. *Note:* The Split item in the Window menu is equivalent to using the Window Split boxes.

Multiple Panes

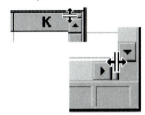

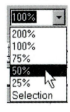

FIGURE B.9

Multiple Window Panes

The Freeze Panes item in the Window menu is similar to the use of panes in Figure B.9. In this case, however, the panes above and to the left of the cell cursor are not scrollable. This feature is often used to lock column-headings and row-stub entries into place while scrolling over large worksheet models. Place the cell cursor in the upper left cell of the area to remain unfrozen (scrollable), and select Freeze Panes from the Window menu. Rows 1 and 2 and column A will be frozen, for the example shown in Figure B.10.

Freezing Panes

The Zoom tool may be used to increase or decrease the displayed size of a worksheet. Selecting small percentages displays more cells of the worksheet in the window. Selecting a range of cells and choosing the Selection item in the list will adjust the magnification to have the selected cells exactly fill the screen. Selecting "100%" returns the worksheet display to normal.

Zooming Worksheets

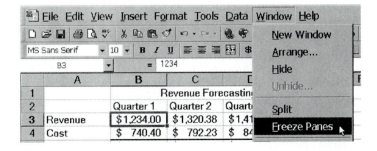

FIGURE B.10

Freezing Panes

Selecting the New Window item from the Window menu, as shown in Figure B.11a, opens a second window to the active workbook, which may be moved and scrolled independently of the first window. However, both are windows showing the contents of the *same* underlying workbook. Selecting the Arrange item from the Window menu, also shown in Figure B.11b, and clicking the Tiled option in the Arrange Windows dialog will divide the screen into equal-sized areas holding each window, as shown in Figure B.12.

Multiple Windows

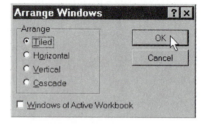

FIGURE B.11(a)

Creating a New Window

FIGURE B.11(b)

Arranging Windows

Multiple windows to a workbook offers additional flexibility, for example, displaying other worksheets in the same workbook. In addition, each window can be split into panes, yielding a wide variety of viewing options for large worksheet models. In the example in Figure B.12, both the worksheet and its formulas are displayed by setting the right-hand window to display worksheet formulas.

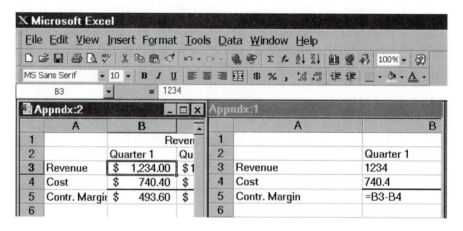

FIGURE B.12

Two Tiled Windows

Hiding Windows

Windows may be hidden temporarily to get them out of the way by selecting the Hide item in the Window menu. The Unhide item in the same menu reverses this operation to bring the window back.

Hiding Worksheets

Similar to hiding windows, worksheets within a workbook may be hidden for convenience. Selecting the "Sheet   Hide" item in the Format menu will hide the active worksheet. The adjacent Unhide item in the same menu reverses this operation. (See Figure B.13.)

Renaming Worksheets

Selecting "Sheet   Rename" in the Format menu (or double clicking the worksheet name tab) allows editing the worksheet default name, see Figure B.14.

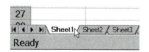

SELECTING CELLS

To select one row or column of cells, click the row or column heading, as shown in Figure B.15. To select multiple contiguous rows or columns, click-drag across row or column headings, as shown in Figure B.16. To select the entire worksheet, click the blank box in the upper-left corner of the worksheet grid, as shown in Figure B.17. To select a range of cells, click-drag across the range of cells, as shown in Figure B.18, or

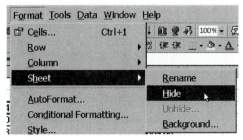

FIGURE B.13

Hiding the Active Worksheet

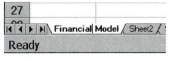

FIGURE B.14

Renaming a Worksheet

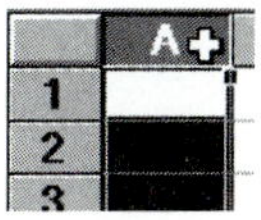

FIGURE B.15

One Row or Column

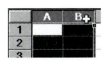

FIGURE B.16

Multiple Contiguous Rows or Columns

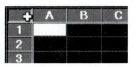

FIGURE B.17

Entire Worksheet

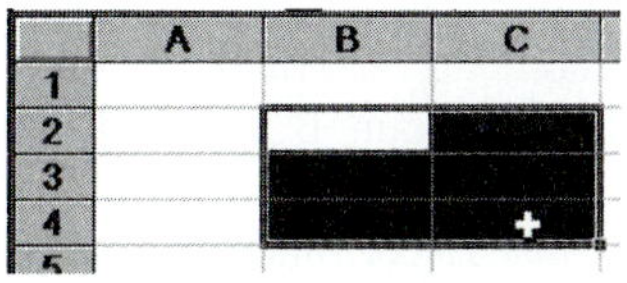

FIGURE B.18

A Range of Cells

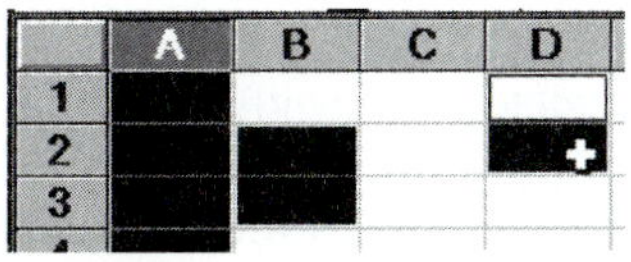

FIGURE B.19

Discontiguous Selections

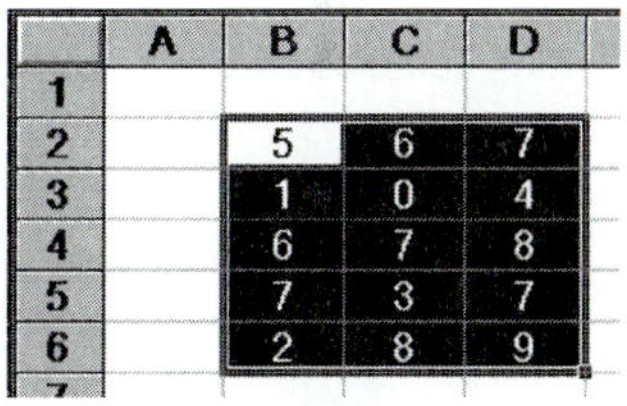

FIGURE B.20

Selecting a Rectangular Range

1. Select the first cell,
2. Hold down SHIFT key or depress F8 key to turn Extend mode on,
3. Press the arrow keys to extend selection, and
4. Release SHIFT key or depress F8 key to turn Extend mode off.

To select discontiguous cells, rows, or columns, click-drag across the first set of cells, rows, or columns. Then, while holding down the Ctrl key (Win) or Command key (Mac), use the mouse to drag across the next set of cells, rows, or columns, and so forth (see Figure B.19).

Alternatively,

1. Select the first cell or range of cells,
2. Press SHIFT+F8 to turn Add mode on,
3. Select first cell of next selection,
4. Depress F8 key to turn Extend mode on,
5. Repeat steps 2, 3, and 4 above for each new selection, and
6. Depress F8 key to turn Add mode off.

To select a rectangular range, select any cell within the rectangular range of nonempty cells, as shown in Figure B.20. Press Ctrl+SHIFT+8. (Use the "8" key on the main keyboard, not the keypad.)

To move cell cursor to the edge of a range, select the first cell within the range, press Ctrl+ARROW (Win or Mac), or press Command+ARROW (Mac), where "AR-ROW" is a keyboard arrow key in the desired direction (left, right, up, or down). (The Transition Navigation Keys setting under Options should be "off" for all arrow keys to work.)

To select cells from cell cursor to the edge of a range, select the first cell within the range, press Ctrl+SHIFT+ARROW (Win or Mac), or press Command+SHIFT+ARROW (Mac), where "ARROW" is a keyboard arrow key in the desired direction (left, right, up, or down). (The Transition Navigation Keys setting under Options should be "off.") Repeating the command for the opposite arrow key direction will reverse the previous direction, depending on the ARROW key pressed. Then, pressing SHIFT+ARROW will augment the selection in the ARROW direction. With cell cursor starting on cell B2, Ctrl+SHIFT+↓ was pressed for the example in Figure B.21. If SHIFT+← were then pressed, the selection would extend to include A2:B4.

	A	B	C	
1	5	6	7	
2	1	0	4	
3	6	7	8	
4	7	3	7	
5				

FIGURE B.21

Extending Selections

EDITING CELLS

Editing Cell Contents

Editing of a cell's formula or content is evoked by selecting the cell, clicking in the Formula Bar and deleting (delete or backspace key) or inserting characters (by typing). Depress the ENTER key (or click the ✓ tool) to finish editing the cell, or depress the ESC key (or click the ✕ tool) to abort editing the cell, returning it to its previous contents. Alternatively, double click on the cell to edit directly within the cell itself, as shown in Figure B.22 (available only if enabled by Options Edit setting; see Figure B.6).

Click the *fx* tool during formula entry to insert a predefined Excel function via the Function Wizard, which is described later.

Clicking the Name Box will insert the last function used (in the example in Figure B.23, the IF() function will be inserted); clicking the Name Box drop-down arrow will present a list of recently used functions for insertion into the formula.

F	G	H
	Year 1	Year 2
Revenue	$ 1,234	=1.23*G2

FIGURE B.22

Editing Cells

IF		✕ ✓ =	=B3*(1+C1)

	A	B	C
1		Growth Rate	7%
2		Quarter 1	Quarter 2
3	Revenue	$ 1,234.00	3*(1+C1)

FIGURE B.23

Formula Editing

As shown in Figure B.24, clicking the = tool opens the cell for formula editing and displays the Formula Result bar. When it is showing, the Formula Result bar displays the value of the formula as you enter it, as shown in Figure B.25.

IF		✕ ✓ =	=B3*(1+C1)
?	Formula result = $	1,320.38	OK	Cancel

	B	C		
2	Quarter 1	Quarter 2	Quarter 3	Quarter 4
3 Revenue	$ 1,234.00	3*(1+C1)	$1,412.81	$1,511.70

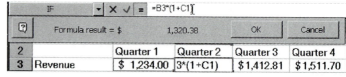

FIGURE B.24

Edit Formula Tool

FIGURE B.25

Formula Result Bar

In formulas, absolute references for cells are designated by dollar signs ($) before the row number and/or before the column letter. For example, $E$5 is an absolute reference. When included in a formula that is being copied or cut, it will always address the same E5 cell, no matter where the formula is pasted. Absolute references can be applied to just the row or just the column. For instance, E$5 will always refer to row 5, no matter where it is pasted. Likewise, $E5 will always refer to column E, no matter where it is pasted. This is useful when using the Fill Down and Fill Right commands. The $ characters may be typed directly into formulas when typing cell references, or you can highlight the cell address(es) in the formula and press the F4 key (Win) or the Command+t key combination (Mac) to automatically insert the $ characters.

In formulas, relative references occur when no $ character(s) are used in a cell address appearing in a formula, causing Excel to remember the cell reference relative to the cell in which the formula or reference is contained. Using a formula with relative references and copying it (via a Fill command or Copy and Paste), causes Excel to update those references to be relative to the new location. For example, if the formula in cell G10 is =F10+G9 and that formula is copied to cell G11, the formula in G11 becomes =F11+G10 because relative references are maintained when copying.

On the Edit menu, or via Ctrl-x (Win) or Command+x (Mac), or via the ✂ tool, the cut command allows you to remove the contents and formatting from a cell or selected range of cells or remove text from the Formula Bar to the Clipboard, usually in preparation for pasting elsewhere.

On the Edit menu, or via Ctrl-c (Win) or Command+c (Mac), or via the ▤ tool, the copy command allows you to copy the contents and formatting of a cell or selected range of cells or copy text from the Formula Bar to the Clipboard, usually in preparation for pasting elsewhere.

On the Edit menu, or via Ctrl-v (Win) or Command+v (Mac), or via the ▤ tool, the Paste command places a selection from the Clipboard starting at the active cell overwriting any existing cell contents and formatting or inserts Clipboard text if the insertion point is active in the Formula Bar.

If you position the cursor over the border of a selection and then click-drag, the selection will be moved to the new location, as if cut and pasted, as shown in Figure B.26. If you hold down SHIFT and click-drag, it will be inserted to the new location. If you hold down Ctrl (Win) or Command (Mac) and click-drag, the selection will be copied and pasted.

Copy Picture is used to insert Excel items as a "picture" into other applications. Select the graphic object or range of cells you wish to copy as a picture object. Hold down the SHIFT key and select Copy Picture from the Edit menu. A dialog box will appear for selecting Copy Picture options (See Figure B.27(a) and (b)).

Absolute Cell References

Relative Cell References

Cut

Copy

Paste

Moving/Copying a Range of Cells

Copy Picture

	B	C	D	E
1	Growth Rate	7%		
2	Quarter 1	Quarter 2	Quarter 3	D1:E1
3	$ 1,234.00	$1,320.38	$1,412.81	$1,311.70

FIGURE B.26

Moving or Copying Selected Cells

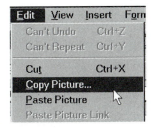

FIGURE B.27(a)

Copy Picture

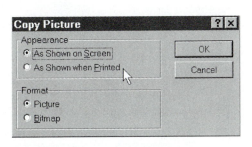

FIGURE B.27(b)

Copy Picture Options

The "As Shown on Screen" option copies the picture just as it appears on the screen, including grid lines if present, to another worksheet or to another application via the Clipboard. The default Picture "metafile" format requires less memory but may not print fonts properly on printers lacking scaleable fonts if the object is rescaled. The optional Bitmap format requires more memory and has lower resolution, but will print properly on any printer if the object is rescaled.

The "As Shown when Printed" option copies the picture to another worksheet, or to another application via the Clipboard as it would appear when printed. Grid lines, and row and column headings will also be copied if they are so designated to print in the worksheet's Page Setup options.

Undoing or Redoing a Command

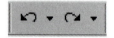

Most Excel commands may be undone or reapplied to another selection by clicking one of the two tools shown, respectively. Shortcut keys are Ctrl+z (undo) and Ctrl+y (redo) for Win and Command+z (undo) and Command+y (redo) for Mac. Recent versions of Excel support multiple levels of undo or redo commands; the list of commands is presented by the drop-down button arrows.

Shortcut Menus

A menu of popular commands is presented when the right mouse button is clicked (Win) or the Command+Option+mouse_button (Mac) is clicked. Depending upon where the mouse cursor is pointing (cell, object, chart, toolbar, row or column heading, etc.), one of several shortcut menus is displayed. Figure B.28 shows two examples, one giving cell commands and one giving column commands.

FILLING CELLS

Fill Left/Right/Up/Down

On the Edit menu, Fill is useful for copying formulas and other cell contents to cells adjacent and to the left/right/up/down of the source cell(s). (See Figure B.29.) Type the first entry, select the range of cells to fill, including the first entry, and choose Fill Left/Right/Up/Down from the Edit menu to fill out the rest of the selected cells.

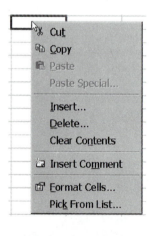
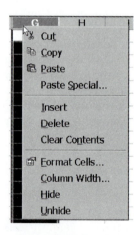

FIGURE B.28

Shortcut Menus

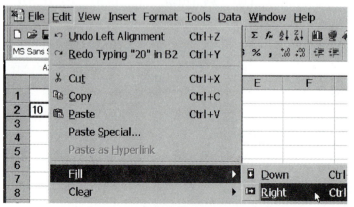

FIGURE B.29

Filling Cells

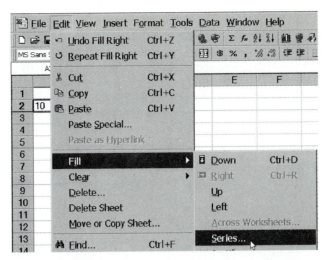

FIGURE B.30(a)

Fill Series

FIGURE B.30(b)

Fill Series Options

Fill Series

Useful for copying a progression of values from the source cell, this command fills in a row or column of numbers or dates in a specified order, as shown in Figure B.30(a). Select the cell where the series will start, then choose "Fill   Series. . ." from the Edit menu.

Specify whether the series should progress in a row or in a column; the type of series: linear, growth, or date, and if a date, then the date unit. Specify the "Step value" and the "Stop value," and click OK. Alternatively, highlight the range of cells to be filled with the series first, omit the Stop value in the dialog box, and click OK. (Most of the common Series fills can be more easily handled by the AutoFill shortcut, described next.) The example in Figure B.30(b) creates a column of values starting at 10, incrementing each row entry by 15 and stopping at 75.

Select one or more cells containing a partial series of data. Move the cursor over the Fill Handle in the lower right of the selection until it changes to a cross hair, as shown in Figure B.31(a).

AutoFill

FIGURE B.31(a)

AutoFill

Then (in this example) click-drag to the right to Fill Right (overwriting the old contents of any cells dragged over). If you have selected a recognizable number series or common series of text entries, Excel will "AutoFill" the balance of the series, as shown in Figure B.31(b).

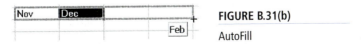

FIGURE B.31(b)

AutoFill

To defeat AutoFill and simply copy the cells, depress Ctrl while click-dragging. If you depress SHIFT while click-dragging, new empty cells will be inserted instead of overwriting existing cells. Also, as shown in Figure B.31(c), if you drag the Fill Handle inside the range of a selection and release, the grayed cells will be cleared.

AutoFill can be applied to entire rows or columns. (If you select a row or column, the Fill Handle moves to the first cell.)

The table below shows examples of AutoFill operations on selected cells.

Data Selected	Series Created
1, 2	3, 4, 5, 6, ...
1, 3	5, 7, 9, 11, ...
100, 95	90, 85, ...
Mon	Tues, Wed, Thu, ...
Qtr2	Qtr3, Qtr4, Qtr1, Qtr2, ...
1st Period	2nd Period, 3rd Period, ...
text1, textA	text2, textA, text3, textA, ...
Jan-98, Apr-98	Jul-98, Oct-98, Jan-99, ...
1, 3, 4	5.66, 7.16, 8.66, ... (best-fit linear trend)

FORMATTING CELLS

Row Height

Move the cursor over the line separating the row headings slowly until it changes to a crossbar, ✛ (Figure B.32). When it has changed, double click to AutoFit height (see AutoFit section), or click-drag the line to the desired new row height.

To define the row height of a range of several rows, select the row headings, and drag one of the row separator lines. All selected rows will take the same height. Alternatively, you can define the row height (of a row or range of selected rows) by selecting "Row Height..." from the Format menu (Figure B.32) and typing the number of the desired height (in "points" of font measure). Typing a "0" for the height is the same as selecting the "Row   Hide" item. (Selecting "Row   Unhide" reverses this latter operation.)

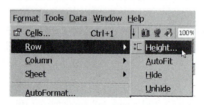

FIGURE B.32

Setting Row Height

Column Width

Move the cursor over the line separating the column headings slowly until it changes to a crossbar, ✛ (Figure B.33). When it has changed, double click to AutoFit (see AutoFit section that follows), or click-drag the line to the desired new column width.

To define the column width of a range of several columns, select the column headings, and drag one of the column separator lines. All selected columns will take the same width. Alternatively, you can define the column width (of a column or range of selected columns) by selecting "Column   Width..." from the Format menu (see Figure B.33) and typing the number of the desired width (in number of characters). Typing a "0" for the width is the same as selecting the "Column   Hide" item. (Selecting "Column   Unhide" reverses this latter operation.)

Column AutoFit Width
(Row Autofit Height)

Move the cursor over the line separating the column headings until it changes to a crossbar (Figure B.33). When it has changed, double click to automatically size the column to the width of the widest cell contents in that column. Or select cells of interest in a column and choose the "Column   AutoFit Selection" item from the Format menu to widen the column to the width of the widest selected cell's contents. (These operations described for columns work similarly for changing the height of rows.)

Formatting Numeric Cells

Select a cell, row, or column, or select a range of cells, rows, or columns, and if applicable, click one of the tools in Figure B.34 for popular numeric format styles. The right

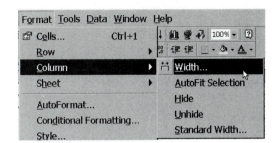

two tools in Figure B.34 increase or decrease the decimal precision displayed for numbers. (Excel's internal precision of the numbers is never altered by formatting.)

FIGURE B.34

Formatting Numeric Cells

Changing Cell Fonts

Select a cell, row, or column, or select a range of cells, rows, or columns, and click one of the tools in Figure B.35 to Bold, Italicize, or Underline cell contents or select a font/size item from the appropriate list.

FIGURE B.35

Changing Cell Fonts

Cell Alignment

Select a cell, row, or column, or select a range of cells, rows, or columns, and click on one of the tools in Figure B.36 that defines alignment.

FIGURE B.36

Cell Alignment Tools

The rightmost tool, also shown in Figure B.37, merges selected cells and centers the leftmost cell contents in the merged cells, useful for report labeling. Merge and Center also works across rows. *Note:* The Format Cells command, described later, must be used to remove the Merge and Center operation.

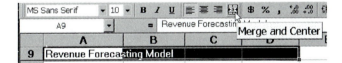

FIGURE B.37

Merge and Center Across Cells

Cell Borders

Select a cell, row, or column, or select a range of cells, rows, or columns, and click on one of the tools in the Border Drop-down Pallet shown in Figure B.38 that defines common border styles. The last border tool selected will become the tool's default.

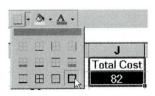

FIGURE B.38

Cell Borders

Detailed Cell Formatting

Figure B.39(a) shows more complete cell formatting options than are available from the Toolbar. Select a cell, row, or column, or select a range of cells, rows, or columns, and choose "Cells..." from the Format menu or press Ctrl+1 (Win) or Command+1 (Mac). Click on each of the desired format tab(s) in the dialog, and select the format option within the dialog.

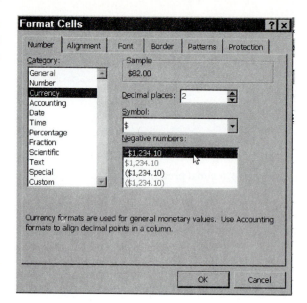

FIGURE B.39(a)

Detailed Cell
Formatting Options

Report formatting and model management are improved if long labels are *not* split across cells. For long labels use the Alignment tab dialog to "Wrap text" each label within its cell, and optionally, center the labels horizontally and vertically, as shown in the first example in Figure B.39(b). *Note:* You can override the Wrap text break point and force manual break(s) in the text to be inserted by pressing Alt+ENTER (Win) or Option+Command+RETURN (Mac) at other place(s) in the label, as shown in the second example in Figure B.39(b).

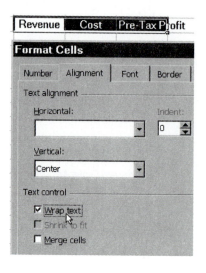

FIGURE B.39(b)

Wrapping Labels

Cells may also be wrapped and/or merged in the vertical direction, a trick that often results in more compact models, as illustrated in Figure B.40.

Custom Cell Formats

A variety of custom formats can be specified, as given in the example of fractional dollar formatting in Figure B.41. The Sample value in the dialog indicates how the selected cell(s) will appear. Fields separated by ";" characters apply to positive; negative; and zero values, respectively. A custom format of ";;;" will display none of a cell's contents. Excel also supports conditional expressions enclosed in "[]" to select alternative formats. Also, Conditional Formatting (in the Format menu) can be selected to alter the appearance of cells depending on values in them. Refer to Excel's Help for examples of the many formatting options available.

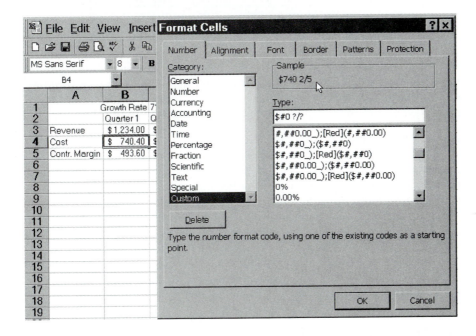

FIGURE B.40

Vertically Wrapped and
Merged Cells

FIGURE B.41

Custom Formatting

Cell Dressing

Character strings enclosed on quotations may be inserted before or after any field in a custom format, as shown in Figure B.42. Called a "cell dressing," these characters will be displayed along with the other formatting information for the cell. Cell dressings and conditional formats can be used for data validation, as indicated in the examples below. The first column gives the cell input and the second column shows how it will be displayed.

Cell Input	Custom Format: $0.00;"Enter a Positive Number";"-"0"-"
123	$123.00
-123	Enter a Positive Number
0	-0-

Cell Input	Custom Format: [>1000]"Too Big "0.00;[<100]0.00" Too Small";0.00
1002	Too Big 1002.00
-10	-10.00 Too Small
333	333.00

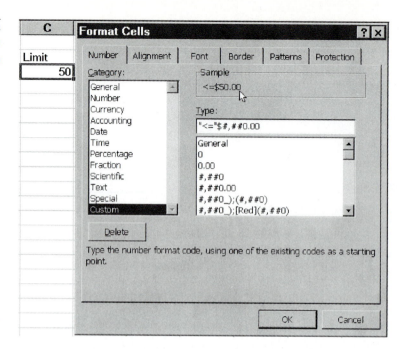

FIGURE B.42

Cell Dressing

Format Painter

Select a cell with the desired format, click the Format Painter tool and drag over a range of cells to apply the selected cell's format. To apply the cell's format in many different locations, double click the Format Painter tool. (When finished, cancel by clicking the tool again.)

ARRAYS OF CELLS

Definition

An array is simply a range of adjacent cells on an Excel worksheet. The notation for an array includes the top left corner cell followed by a colon (:) followed by the address of the bottom right corner cell. For example, "A1:B3" denotes an array that is two columns wide and three rows long. This array begins at cell A1, includes cells A2, A3, B1, B2, and ends with cell B3. Many Excel functions will accept arrays, that is, cell ranges, as input arguments provided that the final calculation produces a single value for the cell, such as "=SUM(A1:B3)", which adds up the contents of the six cells in the given range.

The SUMPRODUCT Function

The SUMPRODUCT function multiplies corresponding cells in the given (equal-sized) arrays and returns the sum of those products, hence the name SUMPRODUCT. (See Figure B.43.) The formula is entered into the cell in the form

$$=SUMPRODUCT(array\_1,array\_2,...)$$

where array_1, and array_2 are the arrays whose corresponding cells you want to multiply together and then add up the results. The array arguments must have the same dimensions; that is, the same number of rows and columns for each array (otherwise, SUMPRODUCT returns the "#VALUE!" error). For example, in Figure B.43, "P1, P2, P3" is the price paid for each of three items and "Q1, Q2, Q3" is the corresponding quantity of each item purchased. Total Cost is the sum of the corresponding three "price times quantity" calculations, that is, 3*2 + 4*7 + 8*6. Especially for larger arrays, using the ranges of the cells in the SUMPRODUCT function is more efficient than writing a single long formula containing the intermediate calculations. *Important:* SUMPRODUCT treats array member cells that are not numeric as if they contained zeros.

F2	▼		=SUMPRODUCT(B2:D2,B4:D4)				
	A	**B**	**C**	**D**	**E**	**F**	**G**
1		P1	P2	P3		Total Cost	
2		3	4	8		82	
3		Q1	Q2	Q3			
4		2	7	6			

FIGURE B.43

SUMPRODUCT Function

The VLOOKUP function (the HLOOKUP function is similar) is used to map a given value into another value according to the definition given in an array of cells comprising a table. The VLOOKUP function has the following syntax:

VLOOKUP(lookup_value,table_array,col_index_num,range_lookup)

where "lookup_value" is the input value, "table_array" is the table of data, "col_index_num" is the column number to return output values from, and if present, a "range_lookup" value of FALSE means the lookup must be an exact match.

The data in Figure B.44 represent automobile insurance rates for big city drivers and small town drivers as a function of the driver's age. The range B3:D7 is range-named "Table" in the example.

	B	C	D
2	Age	City	Town
3	16	$714	$630
4	18	$630	$588
5	21	$441	$420
6	25	$420	$420
7	60	$462	$462

FIGURE B.44

VLOOKUP Example

Note: If not specified, "range_lookup" defaults to TRUE; that is, an exact match is not required. In this default case the values in the first column, B, must be in ascending order.

VLOOKUP(16,Table,3) equals 630; that is, a 16-year-old driver living in a small town pays $630 for auto insurance.

VLOOKUP(23,TABLE,2) equals 441; that is, a 23-year-old driver living in a big city pays $441 for auto insurance. (Any lookup_value between 21 and 24.99999 will return $441 in this example.)

VLOOKUP(65,Table,3) equals 462. (Any lookup_value equal to or greater than 60 will return $462 in this example.)

VLOOKUP(15,Table,2) equals #NA, because 15 is less than the smallest value in column B.

VLOOKUP(23,Table,2,FALSE) equals #NA because "range_lookup" of FALSE requires an exact Age match.

As indicated in the examples above, a formula may accept a range of cells, that is, an array, as input to calculations. Unfortunately, it is easy to defeat this simple idea of using arrays of cell references in constructing formulas. For example, suppose that instead of using "=SUM(A1:B3)" to add up the six cell values, you wish to compute their "sum of squares"; that is, you wish to square the contents of each of the six cells first and then add up those squared values. The obvious formula "=SUM(A1:B3^2)" does not work—Excel returns a "#VALUE!" error—because the intermediate squaring operation (...^2) does not accept an array argument. Excel will accept such constructions if you declare the cell's formula to be an "array formula." Array formulas generalize the notion of submitting arrays of cells as inputs to formula computations.

A formula is designated as an array formula by holding down the Ctrl+SHIFT keys while pressing the ENTER key to complete your formula entry. Excel signals the presence of an array formula by placing curly brackets on either side of the formula. In the example above, the sum of the squares of the array can be correctly calculated by means of an array formula "{=SUM(A1:B3^2)}".

Remember: To create an array formula, you *must* hold down the Ctrl+SHIFT keys while pressing the ENTER key when finishing formula entry *and* after each time you edit the formula. Do *not* type the curly brackets yourself.

In addition to allowing arrays of cells as formula inputs, array formulas are also used to compute an array of formula results; that is, an array of results to be stored into a range of target cells. Although giving the same result as if a regular formula were copied to all the cells in the target range, array formulas require less memory, calculate faster, and are easier to use and maintain, especially for large models.

To use array formulas for producing arrays of results, (1) select the range of target array cells, each of which will receive one of the computed array result values; (2) create the first cell's formula by typing and/or click-dragging, as usual; and (3) hold down the Ctrl+SHIFT keys while pressing the ENTER key to complete formula entry. Excel will apply the formula to all the selected target cells, using appropriate values for any input cell ranges in the formula, if given. For example, target cell range B5:E5 was selected in Figure B.45, and a single subtraction formula was typed using the indicated input cell ranges as arguments.

FIGURE B.45

Array Formula Example

	A	B	C	D	E
	IF		X ✓ = =B3:E3-B4:E4		
	A	**B**	**C**	**D**	**E**
3	Revenue	$ 1,234.00	$1,320.38	$1,412.81	$1,511.70
4	Cost	$ 740.40	$ 792.23	$ 847.68	$ 907.02
5	Contr. Margin	=B3:E3-B4:E4			

Formula entry was completed by holding down the Ctrl+SHIFT keys while pressing the ENTER key, which causes Excel to evaluate the formula for each selected target cell in the output range B5:C5, as shown in Figure B.46. *Remember:* To use array formulas, you must hold down Ctrl+SHIFT while pressing the ENTER key each time you edit that array formula in the future; otherwise, it will revert to a regular formula (or yield an error message). Also, you cannot edit the formula for any subset of the cells in an array result; editing is allowed only for the whole array result.

FIGURE B.46

Completed Array
Formula Example

	A	B	C	D	E
	D5		= {=B3:E3-B4:E4}		
	A	**B**	**C**	**D**	**E**
3	Revenue	$ 1,234.00	$1,320.38	$1,412.81	$1,511.70
4	Cost	$ 740.40	$ 792.23	$ 847.68	$ 907.02
5	Contr. Margin	$ 493.60	$ 528.15	$ 565.12	$ 604.68

An Array Formula Example

Suppose you want to subtract each cell in the rightmost column in Figure B.47 from each cell in the bottom row, a requirement for several network optimization models covered in Chapter 6.

FIGURE B.47

An Array Example

				10
				15
				35
				40
22	24	39	42	

The common approach uses the Transpose option in the Paste Special dialog from the Edit menu to copy the rightmost column as a new pasted row and then perform the subtraction for the cells in the two rows. Array formulas can do this in one operation. First, highlight the result cells, B19:E19 and then create the formula in the first cell, B19, as shown in Figure B.48.

FIGURE B.48

Another Array
Formula Example

	B	C	D	E	F
14					10
15					15
16					35
17					40
18	22	24	39	42	
19	=B18:E18-TRANSPOSE(F14:F17)				

Complete the formula by holding down Ctrl+SHIFT while pressing the ENTER key to produce the array result for all selected cells, as shown in Figure B.49.

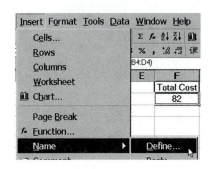

FIGURE B.49

Completed Array
Formula Example

NAMING CELLS

Select the cell or cell range you wish to name, and choose "Name   Define..." from the
Insert menu, as shown in Figure B.50.

FIGURE B.50

Naming a Cell or Cell Range

Excel will guess at the desired name if there is a nearby cell containing text labels. No
spaces (or special characters) are allowed in names, and so, an underline character is often
used instead of a space, such as in "Total_Cost" in Figure B.51. Click the Add button to add
the name to the list of names already defined. Note that names are global to a workbook;
that is, each defined name has its worksheet name pre-pended to the cell reference(s) so that
a name in one worksheet can be referenced by a cell formula in another worksheet.

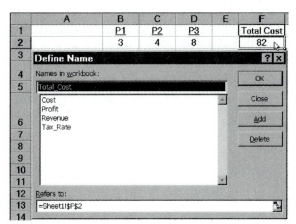

FIGURE B.51

"Total_Cost" Refers to
Cell F2 on Sheet1

Alternatively, to define a name, select the cell(s), and type the name directly into the
Name Box (Figure B.52).

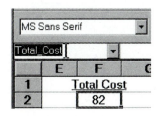

FIGURE B.52

The Name Box

If column (or row) label(s) are already available in adjacent cell(s), cell naming can be done directly by selecting the cells and choosing "Name → Create..." from the Insert menu. (See Figure B.53.)

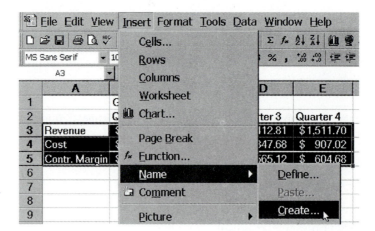

Confirm or override Excel's guess as to the location of the label(s) as shown in Figure B.54. Excel will replace spaces by underlines and drop special characters in creating the names. Note that all names for all sheets in a given workbook will be listed in the Define Name dialog.

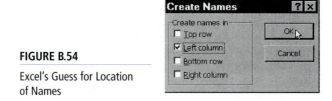

FIGURE B.54

Excel's Guess for Location
of Names

Using names will make your formulas easier to understand and helps document a model (Figure B.55). To use a previously defined name in a formula, you may type it directly, or select the name from the Name Box to ensure that the name is defined and spelled correctly.

FIGURE B.55

Using Names in Formulas

For documentation, a list of all defined names and their cell references may be pasted into the worksheet (Figure B.56).

FIGURE B.56

Paste List of Names

First, choose a cell in a empty region of the worksheet, select the "Name → Paste..." item from the Insert menu, and click the Paste List button in the Paste Name dialog (Figure B.57).

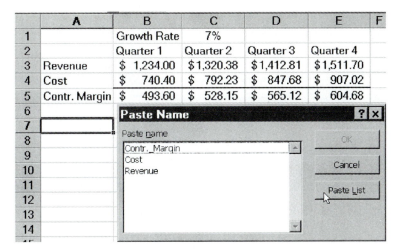

FIGURE B.57

Paste Name Dialog Box

A list of all the defined names in the workbook is pasted into the active sheet. Each name has the name of the worksheet it refers to pre-pended to the defined range to avoid ambiguity (Figure B.58).

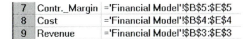

FIGURE B.58

Pasted List of Defined Names

WIZARDS

Detailed documentation of Excel's many built-in functions is given by clicking the Paste Function tool (Figure B.59). Click the Help button for additional documentation on any selected function.

Function Wizard

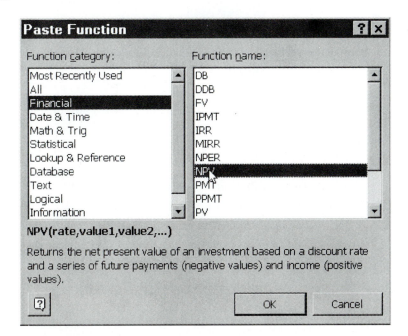

FIGURE B.59

Excel's Built-In Functions

Clicking OK pastes the desired function into the formula bar and opens the Formula Result bar, as shown in Figure B.60. The arguments are listed (the required arguments are boldfaced), and sample values or cell ranges may be inserted into the dialog in order to build up the formula and see the calculated result.

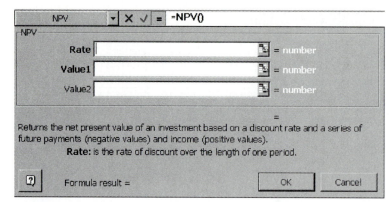

FIGURE B.60

Formula Result Bar for
NPV Function

Chart Wizard

Excel's charting is best done by the Chart Wizard, as shown in Figure B.61: (1) Select the range of data cells to chart, (2) click the Chart Wizard tool , and (3) follow the steps for the four Chart Wizard dialogs. Where present, click the Help button for additional detailed documentation for any dialog.

Charting via the Chart Wizard is facilitated if the first column contains the "X-axis" data (when each data series is a column) or if the first row contains the "X-axis" data (when each data series is a row). Although work-arounds exist, it is generally easier to rearrange the data to place the "X-axis" data at the beginning of the data array before clicking the Chart Wizard.

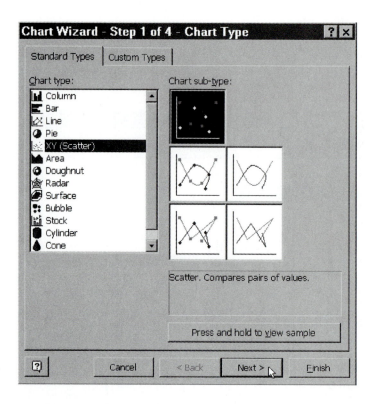

FIGURE B.61

Standard Chart Types

Important: The "*XY* (Scatter)" in Figure B.61 is the *only* chart type that plots the X-axis data scaled according to their values. All other chart types plot the X-axis data as if they were categorical data; that is, the X-axis data are equally spaced regardless of its values. This is illustrated in Figure B.62 for a "Line" chart on the left and an *XY* (Scatter) chart of the same data on the right.

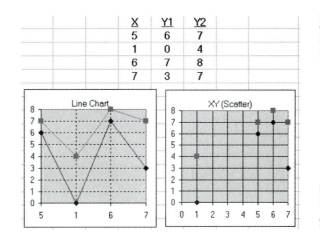

FIGURE B.62

"Line" Chart and
Scatter Chart

Pasting data from another application, such as Word, into Excel often yields a single column of text, of little use if the text contains data. To parse or "break out" the data into separate Excel columns, select the text cells down the (single) column and select the "Text to Columns" item from the Data menu (Figure B.63).

Text to Columns Wizard

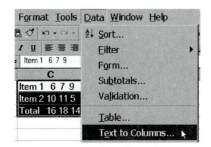

FIGURE B.63

Text to Columns Wizard

Select one of the parsing options in step 1 of the "Text to Columns..." Wizard, as shown in Figure B.64. (If available, the preferred format for the original data is "Delimited," using, for example, comma or tab separators. Otherwise, the "Fixed width" option will allow most of the parsing to be done correctly.)

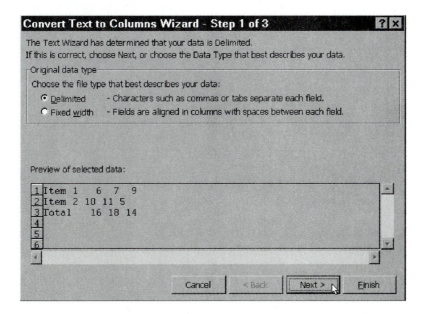

FIGURE B.64

"Text to Columns..." Wizard
Step 1

Complete step 2 in Figure B.65, as appropriate, and select data type options in step 3 (not shown).

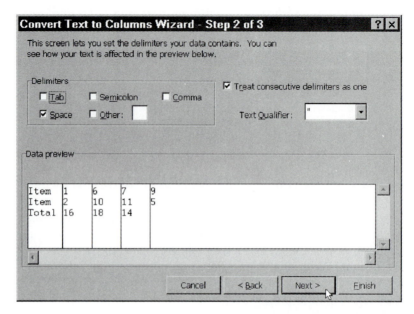

FIGURE B.65

"Text to Columns..." Wizard
Step 2

The completed breakout of text to columns is shown in Figure B.66. The results may need some manual fix-up if the source text was not of fixed width or separated by delimiters.

FIGURE B.66

Breakout of Data
into Columns

	C	D	E	F
Item 1	6	7	9	
Item 2	10	11	5	
Total	16	18	14	

OTHER USEFUL COMMANDS

Sorting Rows

The two tools in Figure B.67(a) sort rows of the worksheet. If a range of cells is selected first, then the sort is done on the leftmost column in the selected range. If no range of cells is selected, then the rectangular block of contiguous nonempty cells surrounding the cell cursor is automatically selected, and the sort is performed for all the rows along the column containing the active cell. Since it is easy to get confused, a more step-by-step dialog is offered by selecting the "Sort..." item from the Data menu (Figure B.67b).

FIGURE B.67(a) AND (b)

Sorting Rows

AutoSum Tool

Placing the cell cursor at the bottom of a column of nonempty cells or to the right of a row of nonempty cells and clicking the AutoSum tool will insert the formula "=SUM()" with Excel's guess of the intended range of cells to sum highlighted (Figure B.68). If the guess is wrong, drag over the correct range before pressing the ENTER key.

FIGURE B.68

AutoSum Guess

	A	B	C
1	5	6	7
2	1	0	4
3	6	7	8
4	7	3	7
5		=SUM(B1:B4)	

Cell entries of a range of cells or a worksheet may be checked for spelling by clicking the Spelling tool or selecting "Spelling..." from the Tools menu (Figure B.69).

FIGURE B.69

Spelling Command

To display and print formulas, it is recommended you select the "Move or Copy Sheet..." item from the Edit menu, as shown in Figure B.70, to make a complete copy of your (final, debugged) worksheet model as another worksheet in your workbook (Figure B.71).

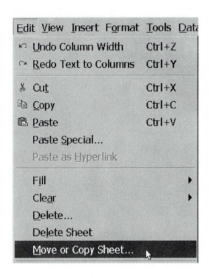

FIGURE B.70

"Move or Copy Sheet..."

This allows independent adjustments of fonts, column widths, and so on, for the formulas that usually need to be formatted differently from that of the model's worksheet.

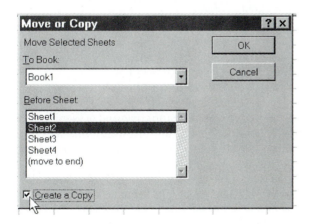

FIGURE B.71

Copying a Worksheet

Switch to that copied sheet by clicking its tab. Double click its tab to change its default name to be more meaningful, such as "Sheet1 Formulas" shown in Figure B.72.

Select the "Options   Display..." item from the Tools menu and click the Formulas item in the View tab dialog. Next, adjust the column widths for best printing appearance, using the "Column   Autofit Selection" from the Format menu, described previously. Then adjust all formats for best appearance.

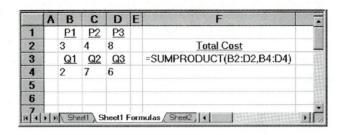

FIGURE B.72

Worksheet Formulas

Important: If you change your original worksheet model in the future, you must recopy the worksheet model—this time by copying the changed cells and pasting them to this sheet—to document any changed formulas or data.

Auditing Formulas

Selecting cell(s) containing formula(s) and choosing one of the Auditing items from the Tools menu, as shown in Figure B.73, produces a visual representation of formula cell references that is useful for documentation and debugging.

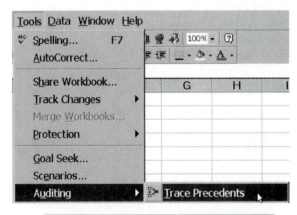

FIGURE B.73

Auditing Formulas

Paste from Excel to Word

When used with a Copy command from Excel, the Paste command in Word will insert the cell contents into a spreadsheet-like Table in Word. While in a Word Table, the cell contents can be edited as separate entities. If Paste is used following a Copy as Picture command, the selection will appear as a graphic object that has limited editing options once it has been pasted, but is easy to crop or rescale.

Paste Special

This command shown in Figure B.74 is used to alter the default assumptions in a normal Paste command to paste just the formulas, just the values, just the formats, and the like. You can also add the copied formula or value(s) to the entries in the paste area, subtract them, and so forth, by clicking an Operation option. For example, to multiply the data in E4:G4 by 150, place the 150 in a cell and copy it. Select the cells E4:G4 and choose the Paste Special item from the Edit menu.

Click the Multiply Operation in the Paste Special dialog shown in Figure B.75 and click OK. The target data items will be multiplied by the copied constant, as shown in Figure B.76.

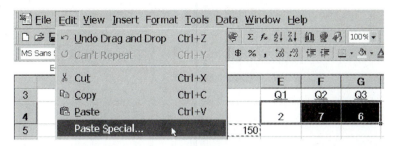

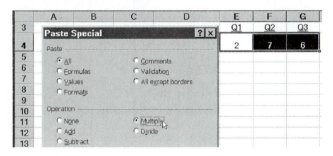

FIGURE B.74

Paste Special Example

FIGURE B.75

Multiply by Copied Cell

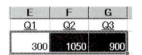

FIGURE B.76

Completed Paste
Special Example

Copying a range of cells, selecting Paste Special, and checking the Transpose box pastes columns as rows and vice versa up to Excel's maximum of 256 columns. Clicking the Paste Link button pastes a pointer to the selected (source) cells into another location as a "hot" (updateable) link to the source cells (Figure B.77).

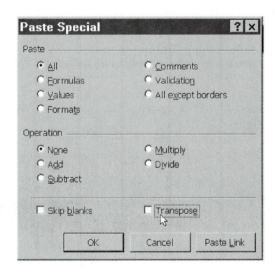

FIGURE B.77

Paste Special Dialog

Paste from Word to Excel

If you select Paste Special after cutting/copying an object from Microsoft Word or similar application, the Paste Special dialog box will change to reflect the object on the Clipboard (Figure B.78). Paste Link maintains a "hot" link to the source document. A Document Object maintains a Microsoft OLE link to allow future editing of it in the originating application. Picture (or Bitmap) copies the item as a graphic object. Normally, you would select Text, which will paste selected characters into cell(s).

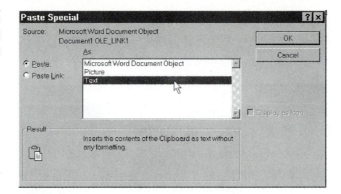

FIGURE B.78

Pasting from Word to Excel

Drawing Toolbar

The drawing tools are useful for documenting a worksheet model. The drawing tools are contained in a Drawing Toolbar. To evoke it, click the Drawing tool or select the Drawing item from the View menu, as shown in Figure B.79. The Drawing toolbar may be moved around by clicking its leftmost end and click-dragging it.

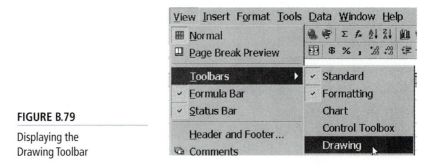

FIGURE B.79

Displaying the Drawing Toolbar

The floating Text Box object and the arrow tools on the Drawing Toolbar can be used to annotate a model's result, or to present critical formulas (by copying the Formula Bar characters to the text box), as shown in Figure B.80. Other drawing tools in the Drawing Toolbar may be used for more stylish effects and callouts.

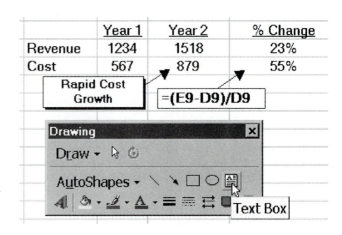

FIGURE B.80

Floating Text Box Option on Drawing Toolbar

Excel has several ways to offer help. The first is the Office Assistant. (Note: holding the cursor over any tool icon and pausing for a few seconds causes Excel to display a short description of the tool, as shown in Figure B.81).

FIGURE B.81

Getting Help

Clicking the Office Assistant tool opens a dialog that allows a search of the Help system for a topic word, the display of a Tip, and the setting of Office Assistant options to indicate for which types of actions the Office Assistant should pop up to offer help (Figure B.82).

FIGURE B.82

Office Assistant

Clicking the "What's This?" item on the Help menu changes the cursor to show a question mark (Figure B.83).

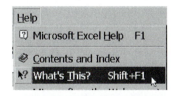

FIGURE B.83

What's This? Item

The next item you click will evoke the Excel Help system, displaying the help topic pertinent to the item you just clicked. This is a fast way to get more information on a menu item or tool.

The complete Excel Help system is available under the Help menu (Win) or under the ⑦ menu (Mac). It is also evoked by the F1 key (Win or Mac). In addition to an index of all help topics, selecting the Office Assistant, typing a phrase, and clicking the Search button allows a keyword search. The example in Figure B.84 shows the result of searching for the NPV function. In addition to the documentation, examples and other very useful guidelines are offered by Excel's Help system when specific Help topics are displayed.

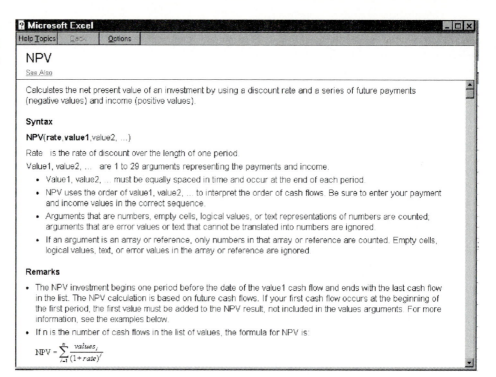

FIGURE B.84

Result of Searching for the
NPV Function

Add-Ins

Excel supports extensions to its default functionality in the form of "Add-In" files that are managed by selecting "Add-Ins" from the Tools menu as shown in Figure B.85. Useful Add-Ins to enable are the Analysis ToolPak, which contains many financial and statistical data analysis functions; Lookup Wizard, which helps form VLOOKUP formulas; AutoSave to periodically back up your workbook; and Solver, a required add-in for optimizing worksheet models.

Note: Availability of the files listed in the Add-In dialog is installation dependent. For example, the Solver Add-In file is *not* installed during normal software installation of Excel via Microsoft's "Setup" procedure unless specifically selected as part of a Custom setup. If Solver is not present in the Tools menu nor the Add-In dialog, rerun Setup from your original Microsoft software disks or CD-ROM to custom install Solver.

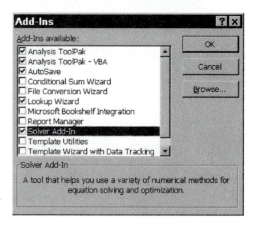

FIGURE B.85

Add-Ins Dialog

FIGURE B.86

Common Excel Add-Ins

Appndx:2

	A	B	C	D	E	F	G	H	I	J
1		Growth Rate	7%		Cost Rate	60%				
2			Quarter 1	Quarter 2	Quarter 3	Quarter 4				
3	Revenue	$ 1,234.00	$ 1,320.38	$ 1,412.81	$ 1,511.70				
4	Cost	$ 740.40	$ 792.23	$ 847.68	$ 907.02				
5	Contr. Marg	$ 493.60	$ 528.15	$ 565.12	$ 604.68				

Sheet1 / Sheet2 / Sheet3 / Sheet4 /

Appndx:1

	A	B	C	D	E
1		Growth Rate	0.07	Cost Rate	0.6
2		Quarter 1	Quarter 2	Quarter 3	Quarter 4
3	Revenue	1234	=B3*(1+$C$1)	=C3*(1+$C$1)	=D3*(1+$C$1)
4	Cost	=$E$1*B3	=$E$1*C3	=$E$1*D3	=$E$1*E3
5	Contr. Margin	=B3-B4	=C3-C4	=D3-D4	=E3-E4

	A	B	C
9		Revenue	Cont. Mar.
10	Growth Rate	$ 1,511.70	$ 604.68
11		5.0%	
12		5.5%	
13		6.0%	
14		6.5%	
15		7.0%	
16		7.5%	
17		8.0%	
18		8.5%	
19		9.0%	
20		9.5%	

FIGURES B.87(a) Example Model for Data Table **and (b)** Data Table Layout for One Input

If the Add-In files were installed into your version of Excel, enabling, for example, the Analysis ToolPak, AutoSave, and Solver, then these extensions will be added to Excel's functionality. This can be verified by the appearance of their menu items on the Tools menu, as shown in Figure B.86.

A one input data table, called a Data Table 1, is a range of cells that shows the results of one or more formulas when substituting different values of a single parameter. In the example in Figure B.87(a) and (b), we want to tabulate different Quarter 4 Revenues and Contribution Margins for the model given a set of Growth Rate parameter values. Cells B10:C10 contain the formulas "=E3" and "=E5", respectively. Data Table 1 will substitute each of the growth rates in column A into cell C1—the input cell—and tabulate the resulting model output values into the corresponding cells below the formulas in cells B10:C10.

Data Table (One-Input)

To set up a one-input data table as shown in Figure B.87(b), enter the formulas that refer to the model output cells in the row above and one cell to the right of the column of parameter values (B10:C10 in this example). Select the range of cells containing the reference formulas and the parameter values to substitute (in this case, A10:C20), and choose "Table..." from the Data menu shown in Figure B.88.

FIGURE B.88

Data Table 1 Setup

Since the parameter values to be substituted are in a column, enter the reference to the input cell in the "Column input cell" dialog box, leaving the "Row input cell" blank (Figure B.89). Click OK.

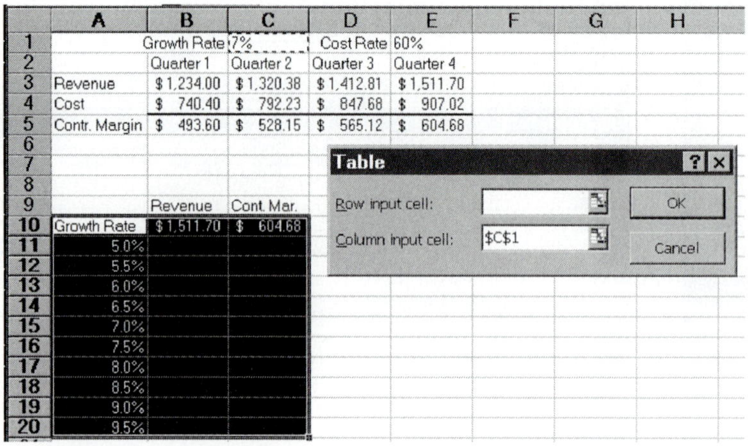

FIGURE B.89

Input Cell Specification for One Input Data Table

The final table should look as shown in Figure B.90.

	Revenue	Cont. Mar.
Growth Rate	$ 1,511.70	$ 604.68
5.0%	$ 1,428.51	$ 571.40
5.5%	$ 1,449.01	$ 579.61
6.0%	$ 1,469.71	$ 587.89
6.5%	$ 1,490.61	$ 596.24
7.0%	$ 1,511.70	$ 604.68
7.5%	$ 1,532.99	$ 613.20
8.0%	$ 1,554.48	$ 621.79
8.5%	$ 1,576.17	$ 630.47
9.0%	$ 1,598.07	$ 639.23
9.5%	$ 1,620.16	$ 648.06

FIGURE B.90

Final Data Table

If the growth rate parameter values were originally presented in a row instead of in a column, then the C1 reference would be specified in the "Row input cell" in Figure B.89. This is illustrated in an example in Section 2.3. *Note:* Filling in cell references for both "Row input cell" and "Column input cell" in the dialog in Figure B.89 is used only for the two input data table case, called a Data Table 2. It is described in Section 2.4.

Solver Tips and Messages

Listed below are the four types of model analyses that Solver can perform. Constrained optimization is the most general; the others are special cases of constrained optimization. Solver can apply each of the four types of analyses to either linear or nonlinear formulations.

1. Find a Feasible Solution: No Cell Address Is Given in Solver's Set Target Cell Box. If the cell address in the Set Target Cell box is empty, Solver will stop when it finds a feasible solution to the model; that is, a set of values for the Changing Cells that satisfies all the constraints. If all the constraints are linear functions of the Changing Cells, setting Assume Linear Model in the Solver Options dialog will speed up the feasible solution process.

2. Find a Goal: No Cell Address Given in Solver's Set Target Cell Box and Only Equality Constraints, or a Target Value for the Cell in the Set Target Cell Box and No Constraints. This formulation is called a goal-seeking model. Solver handles two varieties of goal seeking: (a) traditional goal seeking (solve to find a target value given no constraints) and (b) solve to find those Changing Cell values that simultaneously satisfy a system of constraints given no target value. Variety (a) is identical in concept to Excel's Goal Seeking command except the search method uses a different procedure. For variety (b), Solver finds the solution to the system of equations represented by the constraint cells with the Changing Cells as unknowns. (Solver can also solve a system of equations and inequalities, that is, constraints having lower- or upper-bounds. In this case, Solver finds a feasible solution, as in 1 above.) If all the constraints are linear functions of the Changing Cells, setting Assume Linear Model in the Solver Options dialog will speed up the solution process.

3. Find an Unconstrained Optimum: Maximization or Minimization of a Model with No Constraints. This is often called an "unconstrained optimization" model and makes sense only if the objective function is a nonlinear function of the Changing Cells—optimization of a linear objective function without constraints will always produce an unbounded answer. Solver will solve for a point along the objective function's curvature where the objective function cell reaches a maximum or minimum. If the (nonlinear) objective function has multiple maxima or minima, Solver will find one of them (a local optimum), which may not be the global optimum. The particular local optimum found by Solver is dependent upon the initial values of the Changing Cells. In the case of a nonlinear model with multiple optima, repeatedly re-solving the model via some systematic search strategy with differing initial values of the Changing Cells is the only way to discover the global optimum. For large models (many Changing Cells) exhaustive search may not be a practical strategy. Thus, there is always the risk that the global optima will not be found for a nonlinear model.

4. Find a Constrained Optimum: Maximization or Minimization of a Model with Constraints. The most general and perhaps most common type of model involves both constraints and an objective function cell to be maximized or minimized—a "constrained optimization" model. If the objective function cell and all the constraints are linear functions of the Changing Cells, it is a linear optimization or linear programming model, and it can be optimized faster, more reliably, and with more detailed sensitivity information by setting Assume Linear Model in the Solver Options dialog. Otherwise, it's a nonlinear optimization model.

In the case of a nonlinear optimization model, Solver will solve for a point along the objective function's curvature where the optimum cell reaches a maximum or minimum subject to satisfying the constraints. If the nonlinear objective function has multiple maxima or minima that satisfy the constraints, Solver will find one of them (a local optimum), which may not be the global optimum. The particular local optimum found by Solver that satisfies the constraints is dependent upon the initial values of the Changing Cells. In the case of a nonlinear model with multiple optima, repeatedly re-solving the model via some systematic search strategy with differing initial values of the Changing Cells is the only way to discover the global optimum. For large models (many Changing Cells) exhaustive search is rarely a practical strategy. Thus, there is always the risk that the global optima satisfying the constraints will not be found for a nonlinear model.

COMMON SOLVER MODELING PROBLEMS

Solver is a very sophisticated program performing complicated calculations on the model contained in an Excel worksheet. As a result, there are numerous opportunities for mistakes or other difficulties to arise in model formulation, Solver dialog settings, Solver optimization procedures, and interpretation of Solver results. Moreover, mistakes or solution difficulties do *not* always result in Solver error messages, a trap that frequently ensnares the unwary modeler. Even when Solver error messages do occur, their resolution is often not straightforward. Therefore, an ounce of prevention as given in the modeling "hygiene" list below will often avoid many frustrating hours attempting to resolve Solver difficulties once they occur.

1. Many difficulties in optimization modeling with spreadsheets are not related to Solver but to incorrect formulations. Developing the symbolic model on paper first will help resolve any inconsistencies. Often, writing down the symbolic model and making the Excel worksheet version mirror that model leads to a worksheet model structure that is clean and easy to work with, ultimately taking less total time to debug.

2. The second most common difficulty is inconsistent constraints that produce an over-constrained model with no feasible solution. Double-check the direction of all inequality constraints ("<=" was used when you meant to use ">="). Try to avoid equality constraints unless dictated by the managerial situation being modeled or unless they are a definitional connection among variables, for example, "Profit = Revenue − Cost."

3. For linear models, a common oversight is forgetting the nonnegativity constraints on the Changing Cells when the logic of the situation requires them.

4. Poorly scaled models cause an insidious difficulty because often no messages are produced to suggest this problem, or worse yet, the Solver error messages that are produced may be entirely spurious. Linear and especially nonlinear model optimizations by Solver are very sensitive to the scaling of numbers in the model. Avoid units of measure in models that produce numbers whose differences span more than about 6 or 7 orders of magnitude. For example, a model computing Interest Expense by multiplying an Interest Rate of 12% by a Loan Balance of $60,500,000 spans more than 8 orders of magnitude (10^8) between the Interest Rate and Loan Balance data. This will lead to cumulating roundoff and/or truncation errors as Solver optimizes the model that may result in wrong Changing Cell solutions or bogus error messages. Re-scaling the model's data to reduce the spread is easy and loses no generality nor accuracy in results. For the example above, re-scaling the Loan Balance (and all related worksheet quantities) to be measured in millions of dollars and entering a $60.5 in the Loan Balance cell reduces the span to 2 orders of magnitude. For versions of Excel prior to Excel 97, the Use Automatic Scaling item in Solver Options is *inoperative* if Assume Linear Model is also checked; it works only for nonlinear models. For this reason alone, you are advised to upgrade older versions of Excel to Excel 97. Even for nonlinear models, do not depend upon the automatic scaling feature. For some nonlinear models the internal re-scaling generated by Use Automatic Scaling may not be enough to avoid this problem in unusual circumstances.

5. Finally, the use of an Excel "IF()" function or related functions that introduce discontinuities in worksheet cell(s) will very likely invalidate responsible use of Solver if the objective function cell formula or any constraint formulas depend directly or indirectly upon the cell(s) containing those functions. Not only does the IF() function void linearity, but it likely introduces discontinuities into the feasible region or the set of possible objective function values. This in turn affects the partial derivative estimates computed internally by Solver that guide it toward optimality. Neither Solver nor any known optimization procedure can be guaranteed to handle such discontinuities reliably for all models. Therefore, inclusion of *any* Excel function, such as IF(), into the worksheet model that produces a discontinuity in the graph of its output values for valid ranges of Changing Cells vitiates any use of Solver. If the situation being modeled requires use of the IF() function, consider an integer programming formulation (See Chapter 7).

USEFUL TIPS TO REMEMBER

- For nonlinear models, the Changing Cell values kept from a previous Solver run, if any, become the initial Changing Cell values used if Solver is rerun; that is, if it is feasible, Solver starts from where a previous Solver run left off. In contrast, for linear models (Assume Linear Model checked in Solver Options) the initial values of Changing Cells are ignored even if they produce a feasible solution; Solver uses a separate procedure to find a starting feasible set of values for the Changing Cells that overwrites any initial Changing Cell values.

- Because arithmetic precision of calculations is finite, constraints cannot always be satisfied exactly. The Precision value in Solver Options is used to assess whether a constraint is adequately satisfied. For properly scaled linear models (Assume Linear Model set in Solver Options) there is little reason to alter the Precision value in Solver Options. In any event, do not increase the Precision value in Solver Options to be a value larger than .001, i.e., 1E-3, nor smaller than .00000001, i.e., 1E-8.

- Although acceptable to Solver, it is poor modeling practice to put formulas as the right-hand-side entry of the Solver Add Constraint dialog or the Solver Change Constraint dialog. Always put references to spreadsheet cells in constraint Solver dialogs. Also, referencing RHS cells that contain formulas may cause interpretation problems in Sensitivity Reports if the objective function or the Changing Cell values are influenced by those formulas during optimization.

- Integer or binary constraints may only be defined directly on decision variables (Changing Cells). Also, do not type the words "integer" nor "binary" in the Solver Constraint dialog. Select "int" or "bin" from the drop down list instead.

- Solver optimization of a model having integer constraints is computationally very intensive, and hence convergence is slow. To speed up solution time Solver uses a Tolerance value (set in Solver Options) permitting a "slightly" less than optimal objective function value. For example, the default setting of Tolerance = 5% means that an approximate solution with objective function value within 5% of the true optimum while satisfying the constraints is acceptable (e.g., because estimation errors in model coefficients make higher precision solutions of questionable additional managerial value). Overriding this default by setting Tolerance = 0% forces Solver to continue optimizing the model until an optimal integer solution is found. For large models, this continuation might increase solution times by 10 fold or 100 fold or much more. *Note:* Tolerance is used by Solver only for models with integer constraints. See Section 7.6 for additional details on Tolerance and its use in Solver's branch-and-bound method. Remember: The default Tolerance value guarantees a solution that is within 5% of the optimum for integer models.

The following tips are for more obscure situations that can safely be ignored by most Solver users. They reflect rarely encountered Solver difficulties and are included for completeness.

- Do not use any defined Range Names that begin with "Solver" in your model's workbook.

- Do not run more than one instance of Excel at a time on your computer if you plan to run any Add-Ins like Solver during each instance. (DLL conflicts may otherwise occur.)

- Using the Save Model feature in Solver Options to save multiple model formulations for a worksheet is an infrequently needed option. However, if used, do not Save Model to any other workbook or worksheet. Save Model only to empty cells in the active worksheet containing the original Excel model formulation to be optimized.

- For nonlinear models, changing the Derivatives method in Solver Options away from the "Forward" default to the "Central" alternative may produce incorrect Sensitivity Report numbers in unusual circumstances.

- Do not record macros involving Solver optimization, if the version of Excel for your country does not use the "." as a decimal point separator in numbers.

- Do not attempt to optimize a model if the worksheet or workbook containing it is protected.

- Do not invoke Solver while in Group Edit or Data Entry mode in Excel.

- Do not reference the Changing Cells in the Solver Parameters dialog to other than the active worksheet containing your model.

- Do not attempt to specify more than 16 discontiguous array ranges for decision variables within Solver's Changing Cells dialog box.

- Some versions of Excel will not accept dialog box entries, Solver included, if the total string length of the input exceeds 255 characters. This can happen with long range names and many discontiguous arrays specified in Changing Cells dialog.

SOLVER OPTIONS

Detailed information on Solver Options settings is given in Section 7.6 for integer optimization and at the end of Section 8.5 for nonlinear optimization. Discussion of Convergence settings is given below under Interpreting Solver Messages.

For linear optimization, there is rarely any reason to alter any of Solver's Options settings. However, maximum accuracy occurs for Precision of 1E-6 and use of the Central Differencing search option. For experimental purposes, checking the Show Iteration Results in Solver Options causes Solver to pause after visiting each extreme (corner) point solution. In this way the path taken by Solver's Simplex method during the solution process can be followed.

INTERPRETING SOLVER MESSAGES

There are many combinations of model formulations and Solver analyses to understand, each with its own set of potential difficulties and message possibilities. In addition to the four types of analyses applied to linear or nonlinear model formulations discussed above, the model formulations may include noninteger constraints or integer constraints or a mix of the two. Moreover, for nonlinear models, the source of nonlinearity may be in the objective function (with linear constraints), the constraints (with linear objective function), or both. This leads to 32 different formulation-analysis combinations that need to be understood (four analysis techniques applied to each of linear and three varieties of nonlinear models, each of which in turn may or may not have integer constraints), a daunting task given the dozen or so possible Solver completion messages for each such combination. We will cover only the most common Solver messages.

When Solver stops, the worksheet receives the Changing Cell results of the last Solver calculation, and Excel recalculates the worksheet to update any other cell formulas they affect. A Solver Results dialog appears with a message indicating the condition that caused the Solver optimization to terminate. The appearance of the Solver Results dialog itself does *not* mean that the optimal solution has been found by Solver; it means only that Solver has terminated its optimization procedure. Solver must terminate with one of its "successful completion" messages before it can be concluded that an optimum *may* have been found. To repeat: Completion alone of the Solver optimization process does *not* mean that the optimal solution has been found, and even if Solver terminates with one of its successful completion messages, it does not *necessarily* mean that the optimal solution has been found. For example, a linear model may have "alternative optima" only one of which will be found by Solver, or Solver may successfully terminate its optimization of a nonlinear model at a local optimum instead of the global optimum.

The Solver Results dialog that appears after Solver terminates its optimization displays a completion message. Clicking OK will keep the final Changing Cell values found by Solver; clicking Cancel will restore their previous cell contents before the Solver run. Listed below are the most common Solver messages and their meanings. For simplicity, the message documentation will be limited to the case of constrained model optimization (model analysis 4 above).

SUCCESSFUL COMPLETION MESSAGES
Solver found a solution. All constraints and optimality conditions are satisfied.
This is the most desirable Solver completion message. It means that all constraints are satisfied to within the Solver Option's Precision setting, and an optimum (maximum or minimum) value has been found for the objective function cell in the Set Target Cell box. (For an integer model it means that an optimum value within the Tolerance setting percentage of the true optimum has been found; see below.)

For a linear model (Assume Linear Model in Solver Options is checked), this message means that Solver has unambiguously found an optimal solution. It is possible that there are other solutions with the same objective function value, that is, "alternative optimal" solutions. In this case, mathematically, there are an infinite number of alternative optimal solutions (each with different values of the Changing Cells), all of which produce the same optimal objective function cell value and satisfy the constraints. The infinite set of alternative optimal solutions will involve linear combinations of a finite set of extreme (corner) point alternative optimal solutions, and Solver has discovered one of the set of extreme point optimal solutions satisfying the constraints.

If the solution is nondegenerate and the model is linear, a zero Allowable Increase or Decrease entry for the Objective Coefficient range portion of the Solver Sensitivity Report signals existence of alternative optimal solutions. Other than this, no information is given in Solver reports as to the Changing Cell values of any other alternative extreme point optimal solutions, and a repeated search strategy of rerunning Solver with slightly differing Objective Coefficient values is required to identify the other (extreme point) alternative optima.

For a nonlinear model (Assume Linear Model is not checked), this completion message means that Solver has found a *locally* optimal solution. There may be other sets of values for the Changing Cells that yield the same (alternative optima) or better (other local optima) values for the objective function cell. In general, there is no way to know by looking at Solver reports if the solution is a local or a global optimum nor if there are alternative optima. Repeatedly re-solving the model via some systematic search strategy that utilizes new values of initial Changing Cell values is the only way to discover any other optima, and ultimately, the global optimum. However, for large models (many Changing Cells), a thorough search over the space of all possible initial Changing Cell values is analogous to exhaustive enumeration of the model, an impractical strategy. Thus, there is always the risk that the global optimum (or global optima in the case of alternative optimal solutions) satisfying the constraints will not be discovered. The more numerous and complex the nonlinear relationships are in the model, the more likely the global optimum (optima) will be missed. (See Section 8.6 for an extended discussion.)

Even if a nonlinear model's set of feasible objective function values is known mathematically to be unimodal (i.e., having only one—necessarily global—optimum), the closeness of Solver's successful-completion solution to the true solution is influenced by the Solver Options settings (for example, the Precision value); the shape of the model's nonlinear objective function and/or nonlinear constraints (having discontinuities introduced by Excel IF( ) statements, or very sharp peak(s) to name two); the initial values of the Changing Cells; the model's rate of convergence toward the optimum; and the internal arithmetic accuracy of the computer used.

For integer linear models (any model with at least one integer constraint) with Tolerance = X% (set in Solver Options—default is 5%), Solver has found a solution satisfying the constraints whose objective function value is *within* X% of the true optimal objective value. In particular, if Tolerance = 0% and a linear integer model was optimized (at least one integer constraint and Assume Linear Model set in Solver Options), Solver has found the true integer optimal solution. If the Tolerance = X% and a nonlinear integer model was optimized, Solver has found a locally optimal integer solution within X% of a true locally optimal integer solution.

Solver has converged to the current solution. All constraints are satisfied.
This message should appear only for nonlinear models (Assume Linear Model is not checked). Otherwise, review the model for unintended nonlinear relationships or poorly scaled data.

Solver has stopped because the objective function cell is changing very slowly for the last few iterations or trial solutions. That is, the value in the objective function cell named in Set Target Cell (or if the solution is not yet feasible, the sum of the constraint violations) is changing at a rate below a convergence rate tolerance cutoff for the last N trial solutions. (Prior to Excel 97, the values for N and the convergence rate tolerance cutoff are fixed at unpublished values within Excel Solver software and were *not* alterable; that is, no Solver Options settings could affect them. Indirect evidence suggests that the convergence tolerance was about .00001 and N was approximately 5. In Excel 97 the Convergence box in Solver Options allows the convergence rate to be changed, but not the value of N which is fixed at 5. In Excel 97 reducing Convergence from its default of .0001 to .00001 may help to allow a model producing this message to continue to find an optimal solution.)

This completion message means that an optimal solution *may* have been found, but it is also possible that Solver is making very slow progress toward an optimal solution, or that the precision setting (Precision in the Solver Options dialog) is too low, or that the initial values for the Changing Cells were initialized too far from the optimal solution. More precisely, Solver stops if the absolute value of the relative change in the objective function is less than the convergence rate for the last N iterations. *Note:* A poorly scaled nonlinear model is more likely to trigger this stopping condition, even if Use Automatic Scaling in the Options dialog is checked. Although the "6 or 7 orders of magnitude" scaling rule for linear models is usually sufficient scaling for most nonlinear models as well, in unusual cases no more than about 4 or 5 orders of magnitude may be necessary to avoid this condition.

If you believe your (nonlinear) model is well formulated and scaled and that Solver has stopped prematurely, accept the final results (i.e., check the "Keep Solver solution" option in the Solver Results dialog) and then immediately rerun Solver. Keeping the Solver results will initialize the model's Changing Cells to the final Solver values from the prior run, which then become the starting values for the new run. That buys you another N iteration to see if the convergence rate will improve or if Solver will ultimately (and slowly) converge to a solution yielding the desirable successful completion message above. Many Solver reruns may be required to get past the slow-convergence plateau, if at all. If this strategy fails, try initializing the model to a completely different set of initial Changing Cell values, ones that are far removed from the region of slow convergence. The nonlinear model may converge more quickly to a (local) optimum if Solver starts toward it from a different direction. Alternatively, in Excel 97 try decreasing the Convergence value in the Solver Options dialog.

UNSUCCESSFUL COMPLETION MESSAGES

Solver cannot improve the current solution. All constraints are satisfied. This rarely occurring message should appear only for nonlinear models (Assume Linear Model is not checked in Solver Options). It means that although an optimal solution has not been found, Solver cannot find a better set of Changing Cell values than the values being displayed. One possible cause is the model is degenerate, and Solver is cycling internally due to technical difficulties with Solver's nonlinear optimization algorithm. If this message occurs, check to see if some of the model's constraints are redundant, and therefore, can be removed from the model without affecting the optimal solution. If present, removing redundant constraints will very likely reduce or remove the degeneracy and eliminate the internal cycling. Otherwise, there are few options available other than switching to another optimization software package whose algorithms might be more immune to this rarely occurring technical difficulty.

Solver could not find a feasible solution. Solver was unable to find a set of Changing Cell values that simultaneously satisfy all the constraints to within the Solver Options Precision setting. This frequently occurring message is usually triggered when the constraints of the model are inconsistent, producing an "overconstrained" model. The most likely culprits are too many equality constraints or mistakenly choosing the wrong direction for one or more inequality constraints. Examine the worksheet for a possible mistake in the constraint formulas or the choice of constraints.

Also check that the model is properly scaled.

For nonlinear models (Assume Linear Model unchecked in Solver Options), it may be that Solver could not find a feasible solution after searching in the neighborhood of the initial Changing Cell values. Try initializing the Changing Cells to completely different values and rerun Solver. Better yet, initialize the model's Changing Cells to a feasible solution that is known to be near the optimal solution, based upon similar model results or prior knowledge, if possible.

The Excel 97 version of Solver is prone to generating this message even if the model is correct and is displaying a feasible solution or even the optimal solution. If the displayed solution is feasible try one or both of (a) immediately re-optimizing the model a second time or (b) reducing the Precision parameter in Solver Options and re-optimizing. In the case of an integer program if neither of the previous two options works, try decreasing the Tolerance parameter in Solver Options to 1% or even 0% and re-optimizing the model.

Solver encountered an error value in a target or constraint cell. One or more of the model's formulas yielded an Excel error value, such as "#DIV/0!" or "#NUM!", on the latest Solver recalculation. Solver cannot find new trial solutions under these conditions. Find the cell containing the error and modify its formula to avoid generating such errors, thereby producing an appropriate numeric value. Also, consider adding constraints to force Solver to stay away from troublesome regions. For example, if a nonlinear model has cell A7 unconstrained, and the model has a formula in some other cell containing "LOG(A7)", then Solver may investigate model behavior using values of A7<=0 for which the LOG() function is undefined. Adding a constraint, such as A7>=0.0001 or A7>=.02 or the like, may be required to force Solver to avoid visiting the error generating region(s).

This message will also appear if an invalid Range Name is present in the Solver Parameters dialog.

Solver stopped at user's request. You interrupted the solution process by pressing the ESC key (Windows) or Command+. (Mac) or chose Cancel in the dialog box when the Show Iterations Results was set in Solver Options.

The problem is too large for Solver to handle. There are too many Changing Cells or constraints in the model. (Similar "Too many adjustable cells" or "Too many constraints" messages are produced by the checks made by Solver within the Solver Parameters dialog.) Microsoft Excel Solver limits the number of decision variables (Changing Cells) for linear and nonlinear models to no more than 200.

For linear models (Assume Linear Model checked in Solver Options), there is no limit on the number of constraints provided there is sufficient computer memory for Solver. However, a linear model with more constraints than decision variables (Changing Cells) is either overconstrained or has redundant constraints. The former reflects model logic errors and may produce the "Solver could not find a feasible solution" message. Other than increasing solution times, the latter is usually harmless but may cause difficulty in unusual circumstances (See discussion under "Solver cannot improve the current solution . . .").

For nonlinear models the limit is 100 constraints plus up to 100 constant RHS upper-bound constraints plus up to 100 constant RHS lower-bound constraints directly on the Changing Cells plus up to 200 integer constraints on the decision variables, if any.

The limits above are relaxed for enhanced versions of the Solver Add-In commercially available from its original developer, Frontline Systems (http://www.frontsys.com/).

The conditions for Assume Linear Model are not satisfied. The Assume Linear Model was checked in Solver Options, and Solver computed its trial points using linear extrapolation to arrive at the solution shown, but the final worksheet recalculation yields values for the constraints and/or the objective function cell (Set Target Cell) that do not agree with the linear extrapolation. Review the model logic to verify the source of the nonlinearity and correct. Or commit to a nonlinear model and abandon linear optimization; that is, uncheck the Assume Linear Model option in Solver Options.

If reviewing the model logic verifies it to be linear, then consider if poor scaling of numbers in the model caused the (spurious) message. Versions of Excel prior to Excel 97 are more susceptible to this message. Upgrading to Excel 97 will often eliminate this difficulty, if re-scaling the model's data is not sufficient.

If you are sure your model is linear and are using Excel 97, try one or both of (a) immediately re-optimizing the model a second time or (b) reducing the Precision parameter in Solver Options and re-optimizing the model. In the case of an integer linear program if neither of the previous two options works, try decreasing the Tolerance parameter in Solver Options to 1% or even 0% and re-optimizing the model.

The maximum time or iteration limit was reached. The maximum amount of time allowed for the solution process or the maximum number of iterations (set with the Max Time and Iterations boxes in Solver Options) has been reached without finding a satisfactory solution. Increasing the maximum number of iterations or time may be warranted for very large models, but examine the current solution values for insights into possible modeling problems first.

The Set Target Cell values do not converge. The objective function cell (Set Target Cell) is increasing (or decreasing) without bound, even though all the constraints are satisfied. The current worksheet values probably indicate how the solution is diverging. The most likely cause is omitted constraints in the model. Check the formal model for over-looked constraints or other logic errors that invalidate one or more constraints (e.g. wrong direction of an inequality, etc.).

For a nonlinear model, the objective function formula may have been incorrectly specified.

Problem to solve not specified. Needed Solver information was omitted from the Solver Parameters dialog, such as no Changing Cells given, or missing Set Target Cell coupled with no given constraints.

Solver: An unexpected internal error occurred, or available memory was exhausted. Please verify that your model is correctly entered and all cells contain numeric values. This is a "catch all" error message for difficulties not otherwise identified by Solver. A common cause of this message is that a cell range previously valid in the Solver Parameters dialog has been invalidated by subsequent deletion of some of the referenced rows or columns in the worksheet. This is more likely to occur if range names were originally used in the Solver Parameters dialog, producing a "#Ref!" error string within the dialog box for the now-undefined references to deleted columns/rows. If so, manually edit out the "#Ref!" error string and re-specify the cell range or valid Range Name. In versions prior to Excel 97 a side effect of this "#Ref!" error is that some Solver Parameter dialog buttons may replay this message if clicked, thereby making it impossible to remove or edit out the error string that causes the error message, a frustrating dilemma. The following incantation should work in this case:

1. Dismiss the Solver Parameters dialog.
2. Select the Name Define item from Excel's Insert menu.
3. Enter the string solver_num into the Names in Workbook field.
4. Enter a 0 into the "Refers to" field, and click OK.
5. Evoke Solver, and edit the Solver Parameters fields as usual.

If you are a Windows 95 user and suspect memory was exhausted, save your workbook, quit Excel, close unnecessary applications and windows, and restart Excel to free up so-called USER and GDI memory. If you are a Macintosh user and suspect memory was exhausted, save your workbook, quit Excel, close unnecessary applications and windows, expand the Excel application's Preferred memory size via the Command-i procedure and restart Excel.

Index

Absolute priorities, in goal programming, 411–19
  combining weights and, 419–20
Active constraints, 141–43, 159–61
Activity list, 659
Activity times
  expected, estimation of, 673–75
  variability in, 673–77
Add-ins
  generating random variables using, 516–18
  software, 551
  spreadsheet, simulating with, 524–32
Aggregation data, 17–18
Airline overbooking model, 542–45
All-integer linear programs, 290
Allowable RHS range, 184
Alternative optima, 145
Alternative optimal solutions, objective function coefficients and, 186–88
American Airlines, crew pairing at, 288
American League, 232
Analog models, 9, 10
Analytic hierarchy process (AHP), 408, 421–27
  basic procedure, 422
Annual holding and ordering cost (AHO), 368
Application capsules
  American League assignment model, 232
  asset and liability management, 328
  AT&T call processing simulator, 506–7
  AT&T Capital Corporation (AT&T CC), 2–3
  AT&T mixed integer program, 302
  automatic guided vehicles (AGVs), 511
  Barcelona Olympics, 657–58
  Coast Guard tender operations, 28–29
  crew-pairing at American Airlines, 288
  diet model, 152
  drug testing of student athletes, 442–43
  economic forecasting model, 645
  expansion of power transmission capacity, 468
  facilities planning at U. of Missouri, 397
  fleet assignment at Delta Air Lines, 66
  forecasting at L.L. Bean, 605–6

Peoria tax system, 407
Persian Gulf War project management, 684
portfolio structuring, 357
product planning at Chinese plant, 173
shortening arrest-to-arraignment time, 573–74
simulations
  AT&T call processing, 506–7
  automatic guided vehicles (AGV's), 511
  queuing merging traffic, 579
  streamlining banking operations, 545
United States Air Force (USAF), 130
Wellborn Cabinet, Inc., 190
Arc, 240
  in network diagram, 661
Arrival process, 575–76
Ashley, David, 577
Assignment models, 226, 232–39
  maximization models, 237–39
  solving, by complete enumeration, 233–35
  for unequal supply and demand, 236–37
Astro/Cosmo problem, 100–101, 338–39
AT&T, 506–7
AT&T Capital Corporation, 2–3
Auto insurance, 461-62

Backlogging, 365
  costs, 365
Backward pass, 667
Balk, 581
BancOhio National Bank, 545
Bank of Laramie, 650–51
Barcelona Olympics, 657–58
Bayes' Theorem
  calculation of posterior probabilities and, 471–73, 503–5
  conditional probability and, 501–3
Beta distribution, 673
Biglow Toy Company, 285–87
Binary (0-1) integer linear programs, 290–91
Binary variables
  capital budgeting and, 296–98
  logical conditions and, 298–300
  LP relaxation and, 296–97

Binding constraint, 79
Binomial distribution, A8
Black box models, 13
Blending problems
  Crawler Tread, 97–100
  gruel blending, 101
Bottleneck, elimination of, 579
Branch-and-bound algorithm, ILP example of, 304–13
  branching, 305–10
  LP relaxation, 304–5
  summary, 310–13
Branches, 240, 464
  in PERT network diagram, 661
Break-even model, 103
Bumles, Inc., 266–68, 283–85

Calling population, 592
Capacitated transshipment model, 239–42
Capacity balancing, 546–50
Capital budgeting, spreadsheet simulation example, 518–32
Cases
  Red Brand Canners (RBC), 215–16
  Oak Products, Inc., 52–56
  PROTRAC, 78–80
  Rosa Raisins (RR), 45–52
  Simon Pie Company, 29–38
  Xertech Copy, Inc., 38–45
Cash flow matching, 326–27
Causal forecasting models, 607–20
  curve fitting, 608–19
  method of least squares, 609–14
  quadratic functions, 614–16
Certainty, decision analysis under, 444–45, 462
Channel, in queuing model, 575
Charnes, A., 408
Churchman, C. West, 15
Circular nodes, 464
Coast Guard tender operations, modeling, 28–29
Combinatorial optimization, 399
Commonwealth of Virginia, 645
Complete enumeration, solving assignment models by, 233–35
Computers, 3

Concave functions, 331, 348–49
Concave programs, 347–50
Conditional probability, 470, 471
  Bayes' Theorem and, 501–3
Consensus panel, 643
Consequence variables, 13
Constrained optimization models, 56, 67, 69
Constraint function, 71
Constraints
  active, 141–43
  adding, effect of, 135–36
  adding/deleting, 161–62
  conversion to equality, 174–75
  defined, 56
  important, 159–61
  inactive, 141–43
  inequality, 71
    tightening/loosening, 157–58
  in linear programming, 68–69
  lot size, 299
  plotting, 134–35
  redundant, 158–59
  upper/lower bound, 201–4
Constraint set, 146
Continuous distributions, general method
  applied to, 515–16
Continuous probabilities, A1, A3–7
Continuous uniform distribution, 514, A4, A8
Continuous uniform random variables, 513
Contours, plotting, 132–33
Convex functions, 348–49
Convex programs, 347–50
Convex set of points, 347
Cooper, W.W., 408
Corners, optimal, 145
Corner solutions, Solver equality
  constraint form, 177–78
Correlation coefficient, A12
Costs
  lost goodwill, 448–51
  sunk, 76–77
  variable, 76
Covariance, 35, A12
CPM (Critical Path Method), 658–59
  activity list, 659–60
  backward pass, 667
  earliest start/finish times, 666
  forward pass, 666
  GANTT chart, 660–61
  latest start/finish times, 667–68
  network diagram, 661–63
  path calculation, 665–73
  reducing project duration, 670–73
  slack and, 668–69
  time–cost trade-offs and, 678–83
    financial analysis for retail
      marketing, 679–80
    linear programming model, 681–83
    project crashing, 680–81
Crash cost, 680
Crashing, 680–81
Crash time, 680
Crawler Tread, 97–100, 216–19
  Solver sensitivity analysis, 189–97

Critical activities, 665
Critical path, 665
Crystal Ball, 516–18
Cumulative distribution function (CDF),
  A3, 512–15
  examples, A4–5
Currency trading, application of modeling
  to, 126–29
Curve fitting
  causal models, 607–20
  time-series models, 621
CyberLab, 559–63

Dalian Dyestuff plant, 173
Dantzig, George, 171
Data
  aggregation, 17–18
  forms and sources, 17
  modeling with, 14, 15–17
  refinement, 18
Data tables, 39–41, 46, 48–49
Debugging symbolic LP model, 81
Decision analysis, 442–86
  application capsules, 442, 468
  case studies
    "To Drill or Not to Drill", 498–99
    Johnson's Metal, 497–98
    Shumway, Horch, and Sager (SHS),
      499–501
  decision trees. See Decision trees
  expected value of perfect information,
    454–55
  implementation of, 485
  introduction, 443–44
  management and decision theory, 483–84
  personal judgment and, 485
  under risk, 445–51, 462
  sensitivity analysis, 468–70
  sequential decisions. See Sequential
    decisions
  under uncertainty, 444–45, 451–54, 462
  utilities/decisions under risk, 455–62
Decision models, 11
Decision support use of models, 3
Decision theory, management and, 483–84
  assessing subjective probabilities, 484
Decision trees, 463–67
  appending probabilities and terminal
    values, 466
  creating, 464–65
  folding back, 467
  incorporating new information in,
    470–76
    expected value of sample
      information, 476
    market research study for
      home/garden tractors, 470–76
    posterior probabilities, 471–76
  sensitivity analysis, 468–70
Decision values, in spreadsheets, 79
Decision variables, 72
Degeneracy
  Solver and, 178
  in transportation models, 230

Delphi Method, 643
Delta Air Lines, fleet assignment at, 66
Demand
  inventory control and, 365–66
  for new product, 518, 524–25
  sampling, 518–20
Dependent decisions, in ILP, 298–99
Deseasonalizing, 635–39
Destinations, in transportation models, 227
Deterministic models, 1
  importance of, 19
Deviation variables, goal programming and,
  408–10
Diet model, 152
Discrete probabilities, A2–3
Discrete uniform distribution, 514, A2–3, A8
Distributions
  continuous uniform, 513, 514, A4, A8
  discrete uniform, 514, A2–3, A8
  exponential, 515–16, A4–5, A8
  joint, A10–12
  multivariate, A10–12
  normal, 516, A5–7
  of outcomes, 521–22
  Poisson, 531, A2, A8
  probability, 508
Docking facilities, simulation of, 509
Downhill direction, 146–47
Downside risk, 521, 529
Dummy
  activities, network diagrams and,
    662–64
  origins, in transportation models, 231
Dynamic models, 258–70
  examples, 266–70
    Bumles, Inc., 266–68
    Winston-Salem Development
      Corporation, 268–70

Earliest finish time, in CPM, 666
Earliest start time, in CPM, 666
Economic order quantity (EOQ) model,
  366–71
  annual holding and ordering cost, 368
  assumptions of, 367
  EOQ formula, 369–70
  just-in-time (JIT) system, 388–89
  production lot size model, 375–78
  quantity discounts, 371–74
  sensitivity analysis, 370–71
Efficient frontier, 364
Endogenous variables, 13
Enumeration, complete, 233–34, 295
Environment, model building and, 12
Equality-constrained NLPs, 334–35
Equality constraint, 99
Equality constraint form, in Solver
  Sensitivity Report, 174–78
  optimal values of slack, 175–77
  positive variables, 177–78
  surplus variables, 175–77
Equivalent lottery, 458, 484
Erlang, A.K., 574
Erlang loss distribution, 589

Events, nodes and, 661
Excel spreadsheets/modeling, 29–59. *See also* Solver
  arrays of cells, B16–21
  editing cells, B8–10
  filling cells, B10–12
  formatting cells, B12–16
  selecting cells, B6–8
  useful commands/tools, B24–32
  Windows organization, B1
  Windows/worksheets manipulation, B5–6
  Wizards, B21–24
  worksheet configuration, B1–5
Exogenous variables, 12–13
Expectation and variance of sums, A11–12
Expected return
  as function of $P(S)$, 468–70
  of portfolio, 358
  random variables and, A9–10
Expected values
  of function of random variable, A8–9
  of NPV, 520
  of perfect information, 454–55
  of random variable, A7–8
  of sample information (EVSI), 476
Expert judgment, in forecasting, 642–43
Exponential distribution, 515–16, A4–5
  in queuing models, 575, 596–97
Exponential smoothing, 626–32
Exposure units, 255
Extreme points, 144–45

Feasible decisions, 73
Feasible regions, 137–38
  nonlinear models, 332
Feasible solutions, 137–38
Finite queue, 581, 589–91
First-order optimality conditions, 330
Fixed charge model, 300–304
Fixed costs, 76–77
Flow balance equation, 241
Flying Tiger Line, 313
Folding back, 467
Forecasting, 605–606
  application capsules, 605, 645
  case studies
    Bank of Laramie, 650–51
    Marriott Hotels, 654–56
    Shumway, Horch, and Sager, 652–53
  causal models, 607–20
    curve fitting, 608–19
    method of least squares, 609–14
    quadratic functions, 614–16
  historical data and, 641–42
  implementation of, 644–45
  introduction, 606
  qualitative, 642–44
  quantitative, 607
  time-series models, 620–41
    curve fitting, 621
    exponential smoothing, 626–32
    extrapolating historical behavior, 620–21

Holt's model, 632–34
  moving averages, 621–26
  random walk, 640–41
  seasonality, 634–39
Foreign exchange markets, application of modeling to, 126–29
Formulation, in model building, 12–14
Forward pass, in CPM, 666
Foslins Housewares, 532–38, 539–42

Game theory, 443
Gantt, Henry L., 660
General Motors of Canada, 511
Geometric representations. *See* Linear programming
Global Oil, 498–99
Goal constraints, 408
Goal interval constraints, 410–11
Goal programming, 408–20
  absolute priorities and, 411–19
  combining weights and absolute priorities, 419–20
  constraints in, 408
    goal interval, 410–11
  deviation variables in, 408–9
    weighting, 409–10
  graphical analysis and spreadsheet implementation of solution procedure, 414–19
Goal Seek, 41–45
Goodwill costs, 448–51
Graphical sensitivity analysis, 151–53
Graphical solution method, 133–41
Grass roots forecasting, 643–44
Greedy algorithm, 400
GRG (generalized reduced gradient), 347
Gulf Coast Oil, 339–44

Hanshin Expressway, 246
HASTUS system, 225–26
Heuristic algorithm, 398
Heuristic program, 398
Heuristics, 398–407
  application capsule, 397
  case study
    plant consolidation, 437–39
  facility scheduling, 399–401
  implementation of, 427–28
  introduction, 398–99
  next-best rule, 400
  precedence relationships and, 401
  scheduling with limited resources, 401–7
  workload smoothing, 403–7
Holding costs of inventories, 364–65
Holt's forecasting model, 632–34
Hunt-Wesson Foods, 313–14

Immediate predecessors of an activity, 660
Important constraints, 159–61
Inactive constraints, 141–43, 159–61
Inconsistency, 150
Independent random variables, A11
Inequalities, plotting, 131–32

Inequality constraints, 71
  NLP models with, 338–46
  tightening/loosening, 157–58
Infeasibility, 150
Infeasible models, 150–51
  goal programming and, 412–13
Influence diagrams, 30
Initial guess, in using Solver, 344–46
Inputs, 12–13
Integer linear programming (ILP)
  binary (0-1) integer linear programs, 290–91
  binary variables, 295–300
    capital budgeting, 296–98
    dependent decisions, 298–99
    k of m constraints, 299–300
    logical conditions, 298–300
    lot size constraints, 299
    LP relaxation, 296–97
    optimal ILP solution, 297–98
  branch-and-bound algorithm, 304–13
  case studies
    assigning sales representatives, 322–23
    cash flow matching, 326–27
    municipal bond underwriting, 324–25
  fixed charge model, 300–304
  graphical interpretations, 291–95
    LP relaxation, 292–94
    optimizing ILP model, 291–92
    rounded solutions, 294
  implementation of, 313–14
  importance of, 289–90
  LP *vs.*, 290
  model types, 290–91
  sensitivity in, 312–13
  summary, 314–15
Integer optimal solutions, 244
Integrality conditions, 75
Interarrival time, in queuing model, 575
Internal Revenue Service (IRS), 389–96
Integer-valued solutions, 231
Intuition, quantitative models and, 7
Inventories, defined, 364
Inventory control, 364–71. *See also* Economic order quantity (EOQ) model
  costs associated with, 364–65
  simulation, 509–10, 532–38
Inventory models
  dynamic, 259–61
  examples, 371–78
Isocost lines, 132
Isoprofit lines, 132
Isoquants, 132

Johnson's Metal, 497–98
Joint distributions, A10–12
Joint probabilities, 471, 503
Just-in-time (JIT) system, 388–89

Kaufman, Henry, 642
Keeney, Ralph, 485
Kelly, J.E., 659

Kelly-Springfield Tire Company, 313
Kendall, D.G., 579
Kiwi Computer, 221–24

Lack of memory property, 576, 596
Lady Lynn Cosmetics, 322–23
Lagrange multipliers, 333
   economic interpretation of, 339
Laplace Criterion, 451
Latest finish time, in CPM, 667–68
Latest start time, in CPM, 667–68
Least-squares fits, 609–17
Linear fits, quadratic fits compared to, 616
Linear programming (LP), 18–19. *See also*
      Integer linear programming (ILP);
      Quadratic programming (QP)
   application capsules
      Dalian Dyestuff plant, 173
      diet model, 152
      Hanshin Expressway, 246
      HASTUS system, 225–26
      United States Air Force (USAF),
        130
      Wellborn Cabinet, Inc., 190
   applications
      assignment model, 226, 232–39
      dynamic models, 258–70
      financial/production planning,
        251–54
      media selection model, 226, 254–58
      network models, 239–51
      transportation model, 226–32
   cases
      Biglow Toy Company, 285–87
      Bumles, Inc., 283–85
      Crawler Tread, 216–19
      currency trading, 126–29
      Kiwi Computer, 221–24
      Red Brand Canners (RBC), 123–25,
        215–16
      Saw Mill River Feed and Grain
        Company, 220–21
      Trans World Oil Company, 281–83
   compared with QP, 352, 353
   costs in, 76–78
   evaluating decisions, 72–74
   examples
      Astro and Cosmo, 100–101
      blending problem, 101
      constrained break-even analysis,
        103–4
      Crawler Tread, 97–100
      PROTRAC, 69–75, 78–80
      scheduling problem, 101–3
   formulating models, 68–75, 104–6
      constraints in, 68–69
      guidelines on, 75–76
   geometric representations/graphical
      analysis, 130–64
      active constraints, 141–43
      adding constraints, effect of, 135–36
      extreme points, 144–45
      feasible region, 137–38
      finding optimal solution, 140–41

      graphical sensitivity analysis, 151–53
      graphical solution method, 133–41
      inactive constraints, 141–43
      inequality constraints,
        tightening/loosening, 157–58
      infeasible models, 150–51
      max model and, 146
      min model and, 146–48
      objective function coefficients,
        changes in, 153–54
      plotting constraints, 134–35
      plotting contours, 132–33
      plotting inequalities, 131–32
      plotting objective function, 138–40
      redundant constraints, 158–59
      right-hand sides, changes in, 155–57
      unbounded models, 149–50
   ILP *vs.*, 290
   integrality condition in, 75
   interpreting Solver Sensitivity Report,
   95–97, 173–224
      for Crawler Tread, 189–97
      equality constraint form, 174–78
      objective function coefficient
        sensitivity, 186–88
      of PROTRAC model, 179–86
      reduced cost, 188–89
      RHS sensitivity, shadow price and,
        181–86
      solution output synopsis, 198
   introduction, 67–68
   modeling rules, 82–84
   NLP compared with, 332–34
   objective function, 69
   optimization and, 57
   project management and, 681–83
   simplex method, 171–72
   slack in, 79–80
   spreadsheet model, 78–80
   symbolic model, 74–78
      spreadsheet representation of, 78–80
Linear regression, 609–14, 619
Little's flow equation, 580–81
L.L. Bean, 603–4, 605–6
Local *vs.* global solutions, LP-NLP
   comparison, 334
Longer Boats Yacht Company, 103–4
Loosening an inequality constraint, 157–58
Lot size
   constraints, 299
   economic order quantity (EOQ) model
      and, 375–78
Lower-bound constraints, 201–4
LP relaxation, 291, 292–93
   branch-and-bound algorithm and, 304–5

Management
   decision making by, 3–5
   decision theory and, 483–84
   models and, 6
Marginal probabilities, 472
Market research, grass roots forecasting
   and, 643–44
Marriott Hotels, 654–56

Marshall's, 239
Maximal-flow model, 248–49
Maximax criterion, 452–53
Maximin criterion, 451–52
Maximum profit line, 140
Max model, graphical solution method for,
   146
Max transportation models, solving, 231
Media selection models, 226, 254–58,
   411–20
Middleton, Michael, 463
Midwest Express Airlines, 542–45
Minimax regret, 453–54
Min model, graphical method applied to,
   146–48
Mixed integer linear programs (MILPs),
   290
   Steco warehouse location, 301–4
Modeling
   with data, 14, 15–16
   process, 3–5
Models
   building, 12–14
   decision support use of, 3
   deterministic, 1, 18–19
   in firm, roles played by, 5
   managers and, 6
   philosophy and, 6–7
   probabilistic, 19
   types, 9–11
Monte Carlo simulation. *See* Simulation
Morgenstern, Oskar, 485
Most probable time, 673
Moving averages, in forecasting, 621–26
Multiperiod inventory models, 259, 261–66
Multiple objectives, 407–20
   goal programming, 408–11
Multiple optima, 145
Multivariate distributions, A10–12
Municipal bond underwriting, 324–25

Net present value (NPV), 518
Network diagrams, 240
   activity-on-nodes example, 664
   project management and, 661–63
Network models, 226, 239–51
   application capsules
      Hanshin Expressway, 246
      Marshall's, 239
   capacitated transshipment model,
   239–42
      efficient solution procedures, 244
      general formulation, 242–44
      LP formulation, 240–41
      network terminology, 240
      properties of LP, 241–42
   implementation of, 249–51
   maximal-flow model, 248–49
   shortest-route model, 244–48
Neumann, John von, 485
Newsboy model, 446–51
   under risk, 454–55
New York City Police Department, 573–74
Next best rule, 400

Node-arc incidence matrix, 241
Nodes, 240
    in PERT network diagram, 661
    square, 464
Noncorner optima, 332, 333
Nondegeneracy/nondegenerate solution,
    Solver and, 178
Nonlinear optimization
    with constraints, 331–35
        graphical solution, 332
    introduction, 329
    unconstrained in two or more decision
        variables, 330–31
Nonlinear programs
    case studies
        Internal Revenue Service
            (1994–1995), 389–96
        just-in-time (JIT) system, 388–89
    with constraints, 331–35
    equality constrained models, 334-35
    implementation of, 378
    with inequality constraints, 338–46
    LP compared with, 332–34
    optimality in, 339–44
    that can be solved, 347–50
    that we try to solve, 350–52
    using Solver for, 335–36
Nonnegative quadrant, 134
Non-negativity conditions, 72
Normal cost, 680
Normal distribution, 516, 675, A5–7
Normal table, for CDF, A5–7
Normal time, 679

Oak Products, Inc., 52–56, 67
Objective coefficient ranges, 186
    meaning of, 187–88
Objective function coefficients
    changes in, 153–54
    sensitivity of, 186–88
Objective functions, 13, 69
    extreme points and, 144–45
    optimizing, 73
    plotting, 138–39
Objective value, 74
Oglethorpe Power Corporation (OPC), 468
Operating characteristics of basic queuing
    model, 577
Opportunity costs, 365
Optimal decisions, 73
Optimality, 7
    in NLPs, 339–40
Optimal objective value, 141
Optimal order quantity, in inventory control,
    367
Optimal production plan, 70
Optimal product mix, 70
Optimal solutions, 7, 73
    extreme points and, 144–45
    finding, 140–41, 147–48
    Min model and, 147–48
    unique, 140
Optimal values (OV)
    LP relaxation and, 292

in quadratic programming, 356–58
    of slack, 175–77
Optimistic time, 673
Optimization models, 55–56
    costs in, 76–78
Optimizing direction, 139
Ordering costs of inventories, 364, 365
Order quantity
    effect of, 540–42
    profit *vs.,* 534–38
Origins, in transportation models, 227
Outputs, 12, 13

Pacific Financial Asset Management
    Company, 328
Parameters, 13, 153
Parametric analysis, 153
Path, defined, 665
Payoff table, 443
Penalty costs, 365
Peoria tax system, 407
Perfect information, expected value of,
    454–55
Performance measures, 13
Persian Gulf War, project management in,
    684
Personal judgment, in decision analysis, 485
Personnel loading chart, 402
PERT (Program Evaluation Review
    Technique), 658–59
    activity list, 659
    cost management (PERT/Cost system),
        683–90
        controlling project costs, 685–90
    implementation of, 690–91
    network diagram in, 661
    variability in activity time, 673–77
        estimating expected activity time,
            673–74
        probability of completing project on
            time, 675–76
        testing assumptions with spreadsheet
            simulation, 676–77
Pessimistic time, 673
Philosophy, models and, 6–7
Physical models, 9, 10
Plotting
    constraints, 134–35
    contours, 132–33
    inequalities, 131–32
    objective functions, 138–40
Poisson distribution, 531, 589, 594, 597,
    A2–A8
Polynomial of degree *n,* 617
Pooling model, 339
Portfolio analysis/selection, 357–64
    model formulation, 358–60
    with three assets, 360–64
    with two assets, 358–60
Positive variables, Solver equality constraint
    form and, 177–78
Posterior probabilities, Bayes' Theorem and,
    471–73, 503–5
Postoptimality analysis, 152

Precedence relationships, 401
Prior probabilities, 471
    sensitivity of optimal decision to,
        482–83
Probabilistic models, 19
Probability density function, A3
Probability distribution, 508
Probability (-ies)
    conditional, 470, 471
    continuous, A3–7
    discrete, A2–3
    joint, 471
    marginal, 472
    posterior, 471–73
    prior, 471
    random variables and, A–1
    revised, based on new information,
        471–73
    subjective, 484
    types, A1–7
Probability mass function (PMF), A2
Production lot size model, 375–78
Production model, 52–54
Product mix problem, example of, 100–101
Profit
    order quantity *vs.,* 534–38
    probability distribution of, 541–42
Project management, 657–702
    activity list and, 659–60
    application capsules, 657–58, 684
    example of typical project, 659–63
    GANTT chart, 660–61
    implementation of, 690–91
    introduction, 658–59
    network diagrams and, 661–64
PROTRAC
    data in model building, 15–17
    financial/production planning,
        251–54
    graphical solution method, 133–41
    linear programming, 69–75, 159
    media selection model, 255–58
    Solver for optimizing, 86–95
    Solver sensitivity analysis of, 179–89
    spreadsheet model, 78–80
    transportation model, 226–30
Prudential Securities, 357

Quadratic fits, linear fits compared to, 616
Quadratic functions, 352
    in forecasting, 614–16
Quadratic programming (QP)
    compared with LP, 352, 353
    geometric interpretation of, 354–58
        optimal value of objective function,
            356–58
        tracing optimal solution, 355–56
    geometric representation, 352–53
    problems, Solver solution of, 353–54
Qualitative forecasting, 642–44
Quantitative forecasting, 607
Quantitative modeling, 3
Quantitative models, 9–11
Quantity discounts, 371–74

Queue
  discipline, 576, 597
  size, 576
Queuing models, 573–98
  application capsules, 573–74, 579
  basic model, 575–79
  case study, 603–4
  defined, 574
  economic analysis of, 586–89
  exponential distribution in, 596–97
  finite, 589–91
  implementation of, 597–98
  introduction, 574–75
  Little's flow equation, 580–81
  M/G/1 queue, 581–83
  M/M/s queue, 583–86
  queue discipline, 576, 597
  repair person model, 592–93
  taxonomy of, 579–80
  transient *vs.* steady-state results, 593–95

Random number generators (RNGs), 511
Random variables
  continuous, 513
  expected return, A9–10
  expected value of, A7–8
  expected value of function of, A8–9
  generating, 510–18
    cumulative distribution function,
      512, 513–15
    from exponential distribution,
      515–516
    generalized method, 512–15
    general method applied to
      continuous distributions, 515–16
    from normal distribution, 516
    using add-ins, 516–18
  independent, A11–12
  probability and, A–1
  simulation and, 508–10
Random walk, 639–41
Rated exposures, 411
Realism, models and, 6
Red Brand Canners, 215–16
Reduced cost, in Solver Sensitivity Report,
  188–89
Reduced gradients, 338
Redundant constraints, 158–59
Regret, 453–54
Reneging, 581
Reseasonalizing, 639
Right-hand side (RHS), 71
  allowable range, 184
  changes in, 155–57
  sensitivity, shadow price and, 181–86
  Solver and, 96–97
Risk
  decision analysis under, 445–51, 462
    utilities and, 455–62
  defined, 445–46
  downside, 521, 529
  profile, 447
  upside, 521, 529
@Risk, 516–18

Risk-averse function, 456–57
Risk-indifferent function, 458
Risk profiles, 447
Risk-seeking function, 457
Rosa Raisins (RR), 45–52
Rounded solution, 289, 294

Saaty, Thomas, 408
Sample information, expected value of, 476
Sampling demand, with spreadsheet,
  518–20
Santa Clara University, drug testing
  program for athletes at, 442–43
Satisficing concept, 408
Savage, Sam, 3
Saw Mill River Feed and Grain Company,
  220–21
Scatter diagram, 608
Scheduling problem, 101–3
Seasonality, in forecasting, 634–39
Second-order optimality conditions, 330
Sensitivity analysis, 49–52
  geometric interpretation of, in quadratic
    programming, 354–58
    optimal value of objective function,
      356–58
    tracing optimal solution, 355–56
  graphical, 151–62
  ILP solutions and, 312–13
  with Solver, 173–204
Sequence-dependent setup time, 399–400
Sequential decision model, 477
Sequential decisions, 476–83
  analyzing, 477–79
  impact of utilities, 479–80
  sensitivity of optimal decision to prior
    probabilities, 482–83
  TreePlan features, 480–81
Service process, 576
Service time, 576
Setup time, 399
Shadow price, 333
  interpretation, 204
  RHS sensitivity and, 181–86
Shortest-route model, 244–48
Shumway, Horch, and Sager (SHS),
  499–501, 652–54
Simon, Herbert, 408
Simon Pie Company, 29–38
Simple *n*-period moving average, 622–24
Simple upper and lower bounds, 201–4
Simplex method, 85, 171–72
Simulation, 506–72
  airline overbooking model, 542–45
  analytic models *vs.*, 550
  application capsules, 506–7, 511, 545
  capacity balancing, 546–50
  case studies
    CyberLab, 559–63
    Sprigg Lane, 564–71
  implementation of, 550–51
  introduction, 507–10
  inventory control examples, 509–10,
    532–38, 539–42

Monte Carlo, 509
  random variables and, 508–18
  with spreadsheet, 518–24
    demand for new product, 518,
      524–30
    evaluating proposal, 520–24
    sampling demand, 518–20
  with spreadsheet add-ins, 524–30
    demand distributions, 530–32
    demand for new product, 524–25
    evaluating proposal, 526–30
    random demand and, 525–26
  when to use, 508
Simulator, spreadsheet, 507
  designing, 550–51
Slack, 79–80, 143
  critical path and, 668–69
  optimal values of, 175–77
  workload smoothing heuristic and, 403
Sleepmore Mattress Manufacturing, 437–39
SLP (successive linear programming), 347
Smith, Frederick W., 3
Société de la Communauté Urbaine de
  Montreal (S.T.C.U.M.), 225–26
Software add-ins, 551
Solutions
  alternative optimal, 186–88
  corner, 177–78
  feasible, 137–38
  integer optimal, 244
  inter-valued, 231
  Min model and, 147–48
  optimal
    extreme points and, 144–45
    finding, 140–41, 147–48
  rounded, 289
  unique, 140
Solver, 69, 80, 81, 85–87
  application package, 57
  common modeling problems, C2–3
  initial guess in, 344–46
  interpreting messages, C5
  interpreting Sensitivity Reports of,
    173–224
    Crawler Tread sensitivity analysis,
      189–97
    equality constraint form, 174–78
    PROTRAC sensitivity analysis,
      179–89
  model analyses performed by, C1–2
  NLP models and, 335–36
  optimizing PROTRAC model with,
    87–95
  options, C4
  overview, 84–85
  QP problems and, 353–54
  recommendations for LP models, 95–97
  successful completion messages, C5–7
  terminology, 86
  tips/messages, C1–9
  unsuccessful completion messages,
    C7–9
Spreadsheets
  application capsule, 28–29

lost goodwill analysis, 448–51
modeling with
    examples, 29–56, 78–80
    LP model and, 80–82
    rules for LP, 82–84
optimizing, 80
random number generators in, 511–12
simulating with
    demand for new product, 518, 524–30
    evaluating proposal, 520–24
    PERT and, 676–77
    sampling demand, 518–20
simulating with add-ins
    demand distribution, 530–32
    demand for new product, 524–25
    evaluating proposal, 526–30
    random demand and, 525–26
Spreadsheet simulator, 507
    designing, 550–51
Spreadsheet software, 3
Sprigg Lane, 564–71
SQP (successive quadratic programming), 347
Square nodes, 464
Standard deviation, 359
    of an activity time, estimating, 674–75
Static models, 258
Stationary points, 330
Steady-state results
    in queuing model, 577–78
    transient *vs.*, 593–95
Steady-state value, 549
Steco, 300–302
    inventory control, 365–66, 370–78
Stigler, George, 171–72
Stockout costs of inventories, 364, 365
Stockouts, 365
Subjective probabilities, assessing, 484
Sunk costs, 76–77
Supply and demand, assignment problem
    and, 231

Surplus, 143
Surplus variables, 175–77
Symbolic construction, model building and, 14
Symbolic models, 9–11
    LP, 74–78
        debugging, 81
        spreadsheet representation of, 78–80
System constraints, goal programming and, 408

Terminal
    nodes, 466
    positions, 466
    values, 466
Termination criterion, 331
Tightening an inequality constraint, 157–58
Time–cost trade-offs
    linear programming model, 681–83
    project crashing, 680–81
Time–cost trade-offs, CPM and, 678–83
    financial analysis for retail marketing, 679–80
Transportation models, 226–32
    degeneracy in, 230
    variations on, 230–32
Trans World Oil Company, 281–83
Trials
    multiple, 537
    simulation, 511

Unbalanced capacity, simulating, 549–50
Unbounded constraint set, 150
Unbounded models, 149–50
Uncertainty, decision analysis under, 451–54, 462
Unconstrained optimization, in two or more
    decision variables, 330–31
Unique optimal solution, 140
United States Air Force (USAF), 130

University of Missouri, facilities planning
    at, 397
Uphill direction, 139
Upper-bound constraints, 201–4
Upside risk, 521
Urban Development Planning Commission, 248–49
Utilities
    decisions under risk and, 455–62
    impact of, decision trees and, 479–80
    rationale for, 456–58
Utility functions, 456–58
    creating/using, 458
    risk-averse, 456
    risk-indifferent, 458
    risk-seeking, 457

Validation of models, 619
Variability, 538
Variable costs, 76
Variables
    consequence, 13
    endogenous, 13
    exogenous, 12–13
Variance, 358
Variance reduction, 540

Walker, M.R., 659
Weighted *n*-period moving average, 624–25
Wellborn Cabinet, Inc., 190
Westinghouse Hanford Company, 579
"What if" projection, 36–37
What's Best (application package), 57
Winston-Salem Development Corporation, 268–70
Wojnilower, Albert, 642
Workload smoothing heuristic, 403–7

Xertech Copy, Inc., 38–45

LICENSE AGREEMENT AND LIMITED WARRANTY

READ THE FOLLOWING TERMS AND CONDITIONS CAREFULLY BEFORE OPENING THIS DISK PACKAGE. THIS LEGAL DOCUMENT IS AN AGREEMENT BETWEEN YOU AND PRENTICE-HALL, INC. (THE COMPANY). BY OPENING THIS SEALED DISK PACKAGE, YOU ARE AGREEING TO THE TERMS AND CONDITIONS OF THIS AGREEMENT. IF YOU DO NOT AGREE WITH THESE TERMS AND CONDITIONS, DO NOT OPEN THE DISK PACKAGE. PROMPTLY RETURN THE UNOPENED DISK PACKAGE AND ALL ACCOMPANYING ITEMS TO THE PLACE YOU OBTAINED THEM. THESE TERMS APPLY TO ALL LICENSED SOFTWARE ON THE DISK EXCEPT THAT THE TERMS FOR USE OF ANY SHAREWARE OR FREEWARE ON THE DISKETTES ARE AS SET FORTH IN THE ELECTRONIC LICENSE LOCATED ON THE DISK.

GRANT OF LICENSE:

In consideration of your payment of the license fee, which is part of the price you paid for this product, and your agreement to abide by the terms and conditions of this Agreement, the Company grants to you a nonexclusive right to use and display the copy of the enclosed data disk (hereinafter the SOFTWARE). The Company reserves all rights not expressly granted to you under this Agreement.

OWNERSHIP OF SOFTWARE:

You own only the magnetic or physical media (the enclosed disks) on which the SOFTWARE is recorded or fixed, but the Company retains all the rights, title, and ownership to the SOFTWARE recorded on the original disk copy(ies) and all subsequent copies of the SOFTWARE, regardless of the form or media on which the original or other copies may exist. This license is not a sale of the original SOFTWARE or any copy to you.

RESTRICTIONS ON USE AND TRANSFER:

This SOFTWARE and the accompanying printed materials and user manual (the Documentation) are the subject of copyright and is licensed to you only. You may not sell or license copies of the DATA DISK or the documentation to others and you may not transfer or distribute it, except to instructors and students in your school who are users of the Company textbook that accompanies this SOFTWARE, You may not reverse engineer, disassemble, decompile, modify, adapt, translate or create derivative works based on the SOFTWARE or the Documentation without the prior written consent of the Company. You may be held legally responsible for any copying or copyright infringement which is caused or encouraged by your failure to abide by the terms of these restrictions.

TERMINATION:

This license is effective until terminated. This license will terminate automatically without notice from the Company and become null and void if you fail to comply with any provisions or limitations of this license. Upon termination, you shall destroy the Documentation and all copies of the SOFTWARE. All provisions of this Agreement as to warranties, limitation of liability, remedies or damages, and our ownership rights shall survive termination.

MISCELLANEOUS:

THIS AGREEMENT SHALL BE CONSTRUED IN ACCORDANCE WITH THE LAWS OF THE UNITED STATES OF AMERICA AND THE STATE OF NEW YORK, APPLICABLE TO CONTRACTS MADE IN NEW YORK, AND SHALL BENEFIT THE COMPANY, ITS AFFILIATES AND ASSIGNEES.

LIMITED WARRANTY AND DISCLAIMER OF WARRANTY:

The Company warrants that the SOFTWARE, when properly used in accordance with the Documentation, will operate in substantial conformity with the description of the SOFTWARE set forth in the Documentation. The Company does not warrant that the SOFTWARE will meet your requirements or that the operation of the SOFTWARE will be uninterrupted or error-free. The Company warrants that the media on which the SOFTWARE is delivered shall be free from defects in materials and workmanship under normal use for a period of thirty (30) days from the date of your purchase. Your only remedy and the Company's only obligation under these limited warranties return of the warranted item for replacement of the item. Any replacement of SOFTWARE or media under the warranties shall not extend the original warranty period. The limited warranty set forth above shall not apply to any SOFTWARE which the Company determines in good faith has been subject to misuse, neglect, improper installation, repair, alteration, or damage by you. EXCEPT FOR THE EXPRESSED WARRANTIES SET FORTH ABOVE, THE COMPANY DISCLAIMS ALL WARRANTIES, EXPRESS OR IMPLIED, INCLUDING WITHOUT LIMITATION, THE IMPLIED WARRANTIES OF MERCHANTABILITY AND FITNESS FOR A PARTICU-LAR PURPOSE. EXCEPT FOR THE EXPRESS WARRANTY SET FORTH ABOVE, THE COMPANY DOES NOT WARRANT, GUARANTEE, OR MAKE ANY REPRESENTATION REGARDING THE USE OR THE RESULTS OF THE USE OF THE SOFTWARE IN TERMS OF ITS CORRECT-NESS, ACCURACY, RELIABILITY, CURRENTNESS, OR OTHERWISE. IN NO EVENT, SHALL THE COMPANY OR ITS EMPLOYEES, AGENTS, SUPPLIERS, OR CONTRACTORS BE LIABLE FOR ANY INCIDENTAL, INDIRECT, SPECIAL, OR CONSEQUENTIAL DAMAGES ARISING OUT OF OR IN CONNECTION WITH THE LICENSE GRANTED UNDER THIS AGREEMENT, OR FOR LOSS OF USE, LOSS OF DATA, LOSS OF INCOME OR PROFIT, OR OTHER LOSSES, SUSTAINED AS A RESULT OF INJURY TO ANY PERSON, OR LOSS OF OR DAMAGE TO PROPERTY, OR CLAIMS OF THIRD PARTIES, EVEN IF THE COMPANY OR AN AUTHORIZED REPRESENTATIVE OF THE COMPANY HAS BEEN ADVISED OF THE POSSIBILITY OF SUCH DAMAGES.

SOME JURISDICTIONS DO NOT ALLOW THE LIMITATION OF IMPLIED WARRANTIES OR LIABILITY FOR INCIDENTAL, INDIRECT, SPECIAL, OR CONSEQUENTIAL DAMAGES, SO THE ABOVE LIMITATIONS MAY NOT ALWAYS APPLY. THE WARRANTIES IN THIS AGREEMENT GIVE YOU SPECIFIC LEGAL RIGHTS AND YOU MAY ALSO HAVE OTHER RIGHTS WHICH VARY IN ACCORDANCE WITH LOCAL LAW.

ACKNOWLEDGMENT

YOU ACKNOWLEDGE THAT YOU HAVE READ THIS AGREEMENT, UNDERSTAND IT, AND AGREE TO BE BOUND BY ITS TERMS AND CONDITIONS. YOU ALSO AGREE THAT THIS AGREEMENT IS THE COMPLETE AND EXCLUSIVE STATEMENT OF THE AGREEMENT BETWEEN YOU AND THE COMPANY AND SUPERSEDES ALL PROPOSALS OR PRIOR AGREEMENTS, ORAL, OR WRITTEN, AND ANY OTHER COMMUNICATIONS BETWEEN YOU AND THE COMPANY OR ANY REPRESENTATIVE OF THE COMPANY RELATING TO THE SUBJECT MATTER OF THIS AGREEMENT.

Should you have any questions concerning this agreement or if you wish to contact the Company for any reason, please contact customer service at 1-800-922-0579.